MIDDLE EAST
PATTERNS

SIXTH EDITION

SIXTH EDITION

MIDDLE EAST
PATTERNS

Places, Peoples, and Politics

COLBERT C. HELD
Baylor University

JOHN THOMAS CUMMINGS
Former USAID Economist

Cartography by John V. Cotter

WESTVIEW
PRESS
A Member of the Perseus Books Group

Copyright © 2016 by Westview Press

Published by Westview Press,
A Member of the Perseus Books Group

All photos are by author Held unless otherwise attributed.

Find us on the World Wide Web at www.westviewpress.com.

Every effort has been made to secure required permissions for all text, images, maps, and other art reprinted in this volume.

Westview Press books are available at special discounts for bulk purchases in the United States by corporations, institutions, and other organizations. For more information, please contact the Special Markets Department at the Perseus Books Group, 2300 Chestnut Street, Suite 200, Philadelphia, PA 19103, or call (800) 810-4145, ext. 5000, or e-mail special.markets@perseusbooks.com.

Library of Congress Cataloging-in-Publication Data

Held, Colbert C.
Middle East patterns : places, people, and politics / Colbert C. Held, Baylor University and John Thomas Cummings, former USAID economist. — Six edition.
    pages   cm
Includes bibliographical references and index.
ISBN 978-0-8133-4877-3 (pbk.) — ISBN 978-0-8133-4878-0 (e-book) 1. Middle East. 2. Middle East—Geography. 3. Middle East—Social conditions. 4. Middle East—Politics and government. I. Cummings, John Thomas. II. Title.
DS44.H418 2013
915.6—dc23   2013016715

ISBN 978-0-8133-5020-2 (economy edition)

To
Mildred McDonald Held,
with love and with gratitude from both authors and their families
for her support through the years during the Middle East perils and
pleasures and during realization of the several editions of this book

Contents

PART ONE

PHYSICAL AND CULTURAL GEOGRAPHY

1 Tricontinental Junction: An Introduction   3

2 The Face of the Earth   13

3 Patterns of Time: Historical-Geographical Foundations   57

PART TWO

REGIONAL GEOGRAPHY

Maps, Illustrations, and Tables

Figures

Tables

Graphs

Preface and Acknowledgments to the Sixth Edition

Publication of the first of the six editions of *Middle East Patterns* twenty-five years ago filled a critical need in its field, since so much had been happening in the region and the latest book on the subject had appeared nearly twenty years earlier. Serving as a reference book for specialists and a textbook for college students, *Middle East Patterns* in its successive editions and in its comprehensive coverage has long been the standard book in the field.

This sixth edition has been extensively rewritten to include the dramatic developments in the Arab world across North Africa and in the heart of the Middle East since late 2010 that have been termed the "Arab Spring." As with all previous editions, it completely updates not only the hundreds of data in the sixteen tables but also all figures and facts discussed in the text. In addition, social aspects of the area that have recently become more significant—the changing situations women and children face, for example—are given due attention.

In an effort to make the volume more useful and readable for students, we have added a brief paragraph of "Key Points" at the beginning of each chapter and, in Part Two, at the beginning of each country section. Along with the introductory summary for each country, the essential facts provide a helpful entry into the specific section. Also newly added are more frequent subsection headings, and the more pointed topic sentences should assist the reader in following the subject lines. As complex events in the region continue to unfold, a major addition is a website (**www.middleeastpatterns.com**) for use by all readers and lecturers to gain access to greater detail, additional topics, the latest major developments, and a detailed bibliography.

Although we focus primarily on spatial patterns, we interweave economic, historical, and ethnographic elements of the regional mosaic. The book is therefore useful for courses not only in the geography of the Middle East but also in economics, political science, history, regional studies, security studies, and anthropology. Like past editions, it reflects the topical and regional duality of the discipline of geography: nine chapters in Part One cover the Middle East from a topical or systematic perspective (biophysical, historical, ethnographic, economic, and geopolitical), and twelve chapters in Part Two cover the area from a regional viewpoint, country by country. It should be noted that in this edition, the former Chapter 8 has been split in two, and the coverage of states of the Gulf and southern Arabian Peninsula has been rearranged, requiring an extra chapter in Part Two. Many discussions in Part One cover to some extent the "broader" or "extended" Middle East, comprising North Africa, the Trans-Caucasus republics, the Central Asian "stans," and Afghanistan and Pakistan on the eastern periphery.

Together, we two authors have served nearly fifty years in official positions in nine Middle East countries, with fieldwork and intensive travel in all the other countries of the region. Dr. Held began his diplomatic career in Beirut in 1957, and Dr. Cummings taught in Baghdad in 1965, so we have had the opportunity to experience intimately the emergence of this intriguing area from an underdeveloped corner of the world to become a dynamic and diverse region that regularly dominates political and financial headlines.

Dr. Held had nearly fifty years of diplomatic assignments and academic fieldwork in the Middle East, along with teaching and research about the region. During his years in the Foreign Service with the Department of State beginning in 1957, he was not only assigned to Lebanon, Saudi Arabia, and Iran, but also to successive extended temporary duty in all Middle East countries. He authored the first four editions of *Middle East Patterns*, always with major assistance from his wife, Mildred, and other family members; Dr. Cummings joined as coauthor for the fifth edition. And now for the sixth edition, although Dr. Held continued, at age ninety-five, to work on several aspects of the manuscript and artwork, Dr. Cummings has done almost all of the text revising.

Dr. Cummings spent two years teaching in Baghdad in the mid-1960s and, after pursuing graduate study in economics, taught many university courses and undertook research related to economic development in the Middle East, authoring or coauthoring four books and numerous journal articles on related subjects. Leaving academia for the region, he then spent more than twenty-seven years, mostly with the US Department of the Treasury, the US Agency for International Development (USAID), the UK Department for International Development, and the World Bank in Riyadh, Addis Ababa, Nicosia, Cairo, Baghdad, Kabul, Jerusalem, and Damascus. He has also traveled extensively in every country in the region.

As coauthors, we also have the advantage that Dr. Cummings's wife, Dr. Held's younger daughter, Joanne, has a master's degree in geography and has spent much of her life in the Middle East. She is a Foreign Service Officer in the Department of State, and maintaining family tradition she has specialized in the region, having served most recently in Syria and Yemen. Her experiential and practical advice on this edition has been especially valuable.

Every edition of *Middle East Patterns* has involved a great range of assistance and support by more people and agencies than we can possibly thank individually; however, invaluable help from some individuals must be acknowledged. Dr. Held's Foreign Service colleagues have provided major assistance: Ambassadors Charles Cecil, April Glaspie, Nathaniel Howell, Andrew Killgore, David Newton; and Foreign Service Officers Thomas Carolan, Philip Griffin, Clay Nettles, and Douglas Silliman.

Over the years, Dr. Held's fieldwork has been greatly facilitated by nongovernmental organizations (NGOs) and other agencies, including oil companies, in virtually every Middle East country, especially Crescent Petroleum Co. of Sharjah and its president, Hamid Jafar; Saudi Arabian Oil Co. (Saudi Aramco), which provided numerous briefings and arranged visits to many of its facilities through the years, and supplied photographs through Arthur Clark and Sarah Miller of Aramco Services; and Bahrain Petroleum Co.

(Bapco), Petroleum Development Oman (PDO), Dubai Petroleum Co. (Dupetco), and Amoco Egypt. Dr. James Mandaville, formerly with Aramco, generously vetted chapters and consulted on plant geography.

Dr. Cummings wishes to acknowledge the generous amounts of time he was given by many people in the preparation of this edition, including Ambassador Robert Ford, Consul General Justin Siberell, Steve Bondy, Lisa Carle, Bill Cavness, Steve Conlon, Jack Doutrich, Joey Hood, Ludovic Hood, Neil Hop, Dan Joyce, Allen Keiswetter, Brian Kelley, Barbara Leaf, Jesse Levinson, Walter Parrs, and Linda Specht, all of the Department of State, Brett Hansen of the US Agency for International Development, and Rev. Bill Schwartz of Doha, Qatar. He also wishes to thank his son Donny Cummings for contributing his considerable computer skills at critical junctures, as well as son Liam and friends Rick and Molly, without whom the last two editions would not have happened.

Baylor University student assistant Tiffany Clark updated hundreds of statistics in revising the sixteen tables and in preparing new graphs and charts. Westview editors and technicians through the years have patiently led Dr. Held and now both authors through the intricacies of book preparation and publishing, with Anthony "Toby" Wahl and Carolyn Sobczak the latest talented and supportive editors, and to them we extend warm thanks. And once again, as in the fifth edition, we extend profound appreciation to Annette Wenda for her superb copyediting.

Middle East Patterns is something of a family enterprise, with both of our wives, Mildred McDonald Held and Joanne Held Cummings, and the other Held daughter, Melinda Brunger, contributing substantively to the book in many ways. Melinda, with legal expertise in the energy industry, edited and in some cases drafted sections of earlier editions. Melinda's son, Christopher Brunger, served as a valuable research assistant, especially for preparing the country statistical summaries.

Notwithstanding all the deeply appreciated contributions and support from others, we joint authors assume complete responsibility for every aspect of Middle East Patterns. We invite readers to bring to our attention any errors and oversights, and we welcome all comments and suggestions.

CCH
JTC
May 2013

A Note on Transliteration

For transliteration of place-names from Arabic, Hebrew, and Greek, we have generally followed the recommendations of the US Board on Geographic Names (BGN), except that we elected to omit diacritical marks on transliterations from those three languages. We retained diacritics in Turkish words (except we do not dot the capital "I"; thus "Istanbul"), since Turkish uses a basically Roman alphabet in which diacritics are an integral part of the written language. Indicating the ain and the hamza in Arabic words merely confuses the general reader who knows no Arabic and adds little of essence for readers who do. We have deliberately accepted inconsistency in using conventional forms and spellings for certain names—Cairo (rather than al-Qahirah), Damascus (al-Dimashq), Yemen (al-Yaman), Bab el-Mandeb (Bab al-Mandab), Dubai (Dubayyah), Medina (al-Madinah), Doha (al-Dawhah), Bekaa (Biqa), and others. We have also dropped the definite article (al) in many names (Aqabah, Riyadh, Qatif), and where we have retained it we have used it only in the basic form, not in the form modified by "sun letters" (Sharm al-Shaykh, not Sharm ash-Shaykh; Jabal al-Ruwaq, not Jabal ar-Ruwaq). Occasionally, we have deliberately been inconsistent in using the standard BGN transliteration in general discussion and then following the spelling employed in proper names, as in "amirates" and "United Arab Emirates" and in "Zayid" and "Shaykh Zayed Road." We have also retained certain spellings that have become ingrained through use by oil companies.

Some names create certain problems. For example, the Gulf is called the Persian Gulf by Iran and many other countries and the Arabian Gulf by Arab states and some other countries. Many names in former Palestine—and the use of the name Palestine itself—imply particular biases: West Bank versus Samaria and Judea, Gulf of Aqabah versus Gulf of Elat, al-Quds or Jerusalem versus Yerushalayyem, and others. Jordan's disengagement from the West Bank in July–August 1988 has rendered even the applicability of the term "West Bank" a question mark. Revolutionary Iran changed many place-names because they connoted the Pahlavi royal family: for example, Bandar-e Pahlavi is now Bandar-e Anzali, Rezaiyeh is Urumiyeh (conventional: Urmia), and Bandar-e Shahpur is Bandar-e Khomeyni. We have used the new names that have been publicly announced.

CCH
JTC

PART ONE

PHYSICAL AND CULTURAL GEOGRAPHY

1

Tricontinental Junction
An Introduction

KEY POINTS: Middle East has always been of great significance if only because of location in the hub of the World Island—Eurasia and Africa. Trade and travel routes have crossed region since earliest human migrations. Cradle of civilization, especially in Fertile Crescent. Rich history, ancient and mediaeval. Birthplace of three great monotheistic religions. Many ethnolinguistic-religious groups, with Arabs dominant in center and Turks and Persians across North. Home of Islam, which still dominates religion and culture. Holds half of world's petroleum reserves, hence of crucial world significance. Some debate over what constitutes Middle East, but this volume uses traditional grouping. Focus of political and ideological ferment, especially in Arab Spring in 2011–2013, as well as of intractable Arab-Israel conflict. Region in headlines but background poorly understood.

MIDDLE EAST PREVIEW

Located at the tricontinental hub of Europe, Asia, and Africa, the Middle East is unique both historically and geopolitically. It is the cradle of civilization, birthplace of the three great monotheistic religions, crossroads of movement and trade, base of extensive empires, resource area for half of the world's petroleum, home to more than 350 million people in sixteen countries, source and concentration of political and ideological ferment, and locus of intractable and explosive conflicts since World War II. Major developments in the region resonate worldwide, as did the disturbances associated with the 2011–2012 "Arab Spring," and no country can disregard them.

War and Conflict. The Middle East has featured prominently in the news almost daily through more than six decades of warfare: six major Arab-Israeli wars plus several more limited conflicts; the almost uninterrupted cycle of violence involving Arabs and Israelis; the First and Second Intifadahs of the Palestinians; internecine fighting in Lebanon in 1958 (ended by landing of US forces) and from 1975 to 1991 (involving US forces on two occasions); Turkey's invasion and partial occupation of Cyprus beginning in 1974; Iraq's war with Iran in the 1980s, its invasion of and consequent expulsion from Kuwait in 1990–1991, the international sanctions imposed on it afterward, and its occupation by the US-led coalition from 2003 onward; US operations in Afghanistan after September

11, 2001; military operations involving Kurds in the four countries of the region in which they historically dwell; civil wars and insurgencies in Yemen in the 1960s, 1986, 1994, and again in the new century; the sanctions on and explicit threat of military action against an allegedly nuclear-arming Iran; and civil war in Syria beginning in 2011, spilling over into Lebanon.

Beyond open fighting, there has been an ongoing Arab-Israeli "Peace Process" dating to Henry Kissinger's "Shuttle Diplomacy" in the mid-1970s, hostage taking in Lebanon in the 1970s and 1980s, the overthrow of the shah and the American Embassy hostage crisis in Tehran in 1979–1980, terrorist attacks in most of the countries in the region, Cold War crises ranging from Iran and Turkey in the 1940s to peripheral Afghanistan in the 1980s, varying levels of civil disturbance and strife associated with the Arab Spring since 2011, and dozens of other headline-worthy events.

More News, Less Understanding?　During the past two decades, reporting on the Middle East has become more extensive, and in many cases more nuanced. But the media are limited in their ability to offer in-depth, objective analyses of the region's complex underlying patterns of regions, peoples, cultures, politics, and aspirations. More significantly, for various domestic reasons—political, religious, economic, historical, and others—the media frequently fail to balance their coverage with viewpoints across the multiplicity of countries, ethnic and religious groups, economic factors, and regional sources of information. As a result, many Americans have perceived the Muslim Middle East, and particularly the Arab Middle East, in negative terms since the late 1940s, reinforcing prejudices and stereotypes that have roots going as far back as the Crusades. Especially after the attacks of September 11, 2001, ("9/11") on the New York World Trade Center and the Pentagon,

American antagonisms increased almost exponentially, with little or no distinction made between the violent objectives of extremist groups such as al-Qaida, on the one hand, and the goals of the many peaceful cultural and political elements in the region, on the other. Although it is still too early for a full appraisal of the thinking and planning behind the US policies that led to the unexpected reactions of the various elements of Iraqi society after the 2003 invasion, it is obvious that future policy making must be grounded in a much better understanding and recognition of the region's ethnic, cultural, religious, and geopolitical complexity. These, in turn, are all grounded in the fundamental geographic and economic factors that are analyzed in this study.

Why This Book?　For much of the world, including both industrialized and developing countries, the unfolding of economic and political events is closely tied to the resources found in the Middle East and to the factors that affect the availability and movement of those resources. These factors derive from the histories, traditions, aspirations, value systems, problems of development and change, regional and international linkages, and agendas of the peoples and states of the region. The collapse of the Soviet Union, the consequent realignment of transnational relationships in Eurasia, the events following 9/11, the escalating global demand for hydrocarbon fuels and by-products—all these have led to the Middle East's becoming the geopolitical focus not just of the West but of the rest of the world as well.

In view of the foregoing, it is the aim of this book to examine the natural and cultural patterns of the Middle East and their influence on political and economic developments; to analyze and interpret the more significant national, regional, and global relations; and thus to afford a greater knowledge of and deeper insights into this crucial region.

Why All These Numbers, and More? A note to the reader: this book contains a considerable amount of detailed information—numbers, dates, names of ancient cities, empires, battles, and long-dead leaders—and the book's associated website has even more. The authors have included this material not to burden the reader with immense amounts of trivia, but in order to try to paint a broad picture of this complex region and its even more complex history and development.

The reader needs always to keep in mind that detailed statistics can be useful tools, but that retention of them is not an end in itself. In other words, the authors warn the reader, "Do not lose the forest for the trees (or, perhaps more appropriately, the underbrush)."

Map 1.1 The Middle East as tricontinental hub, centrally located at the heart of the World-Island.

World-Island

Because of its tricontinental location (Map 1.1) and its central position in the "World-Island" (see Chap. 8), the region has historically been a global crossroads, as reflected in the title of the late Professor George B. Cressey's 1960 study of Middle East geography. Despite the multifaceted character that has evolved from its crossroads role, the region is often perceived in highly particularistic terms—of petroleum or terrorism or Islamic resurgence or Israeli security or regime change or other single issues—thus obscuring its breadth and complexity. Short-term, simplistic perceptions are also misleading; for example, they imply that the Middle East has become important only recently or that it is typified by the oil crisis of 1973, or the Iranian Revolution of 1979, or the situation in Iraq after 1991 or 2003, or the turmoil accompanying the Arab Spring, or rich oil shaykhs in desert principalities, or fanatical suicide bombers. In fact, the region blends a diverse geography, rich historical traditions, and complex cultural, national, and religious groupings to produce dynamic patterns that evolve and change over time. The text and illustrations in this book depict some of these complexities and contrasts (Figs. 1.1 and 1.2).

Lands and Seas.   One significance of the location of the Middle East derives from its irregular shape. Seas penetrate deeply into the land and alternate with peninsulas and land bridges around the Syrian-Mesopotamian core. The Red, Mediterranean, Black, and Caspian Seas, plus the Persian/Arabian Gulf, have facilitated maritime movements of the peoples of the area for more than five thousand years, provided access to the region, and, conversely, served as natural insulation between regional cultural groups.

Cradle of Civilization

Evidence of the earliest known humans has been found in eastern Africa, and the migration of their descendants to the rest of the world clearly traversed the Middle East. Thus, this region has had human inhabitants for scores of millennia, and it seems to have produced the earliest integrated civilizations, agricultural villages and developed towns, and religious-political systems. Although very old human skeletons and tools have been found in other areas, it is the Middle East that is commonly known as the "cradle of civilization." As will be discussed in Chapter 3, these civilizations evolved in the Fertile

Figure 1.1 Barren, wind-rippled dunes in Saudi Arabia's Rub al-Khali (Empty Quarter).

Figure 1.2 Village surrounded by green fields of corn (maize) and well-forested slopes in Turkey's Pontic Mountains, an area of moderately heavy precipitation just south of the Black Sea.

Crescent, an arc of fertile land that extends along the Levant and around the Syrian Desert to the Gulf and particularly through the Mesopotamian Basin, the depression occupied by the Tigris and Euphrates Rivers (see Map 3.1). From this geographical core, the ideas, techniques, and implements of the Fertile Crescent diffused to other similar environments—westward to the Nile Valley in Egypt, eastward to the Indus Valley in present-day Pakistan, and beyond, mixing with advanced civilizations in those areas.

Writing, Science, Mathematics. More than five thousand years ago, the seminal culture hearth of Mesopotamia produced what is generally held to be the earliest known writing,[1] along with high levels of science and mathematics. The Middle East thus became a matrix for later Western and Oriental civilizations. The cultural complex that spread outward from the Mesopotamian core also gave rise to successive confrontations among expanding ancient empires. The high level of civilization achieved by successive empires suggests a capacity for adaptation that is still evident in the region. Several power foci, which will be discussed in Chapter 3, emerged through the centuries and have persisted for more than forty-five hundred years to the present.

Religious Societies

In addition to clashes among successive empires, the Middle East gave rise to the three major monotheistic religions: Judaism, Christianity, and Islam. Each is rooted in earlier religions, yet each is distinctive and each became global in extent. Their respective origins within the region provide one measure of the cultural richness and unique significance of the Middle East.

Just as Christianity gave rise to a general civilization referred to as Christendom, so Islam engendered the Islamic civilization. The cradle of both the religion of Islam and the corollary culture of Islam, the Middle East remains the heartland of the Islamic culture realm. The original core area of this culture—Mecca and Medina in western Saudi Arabia—is the goal of the annual Muslim *hajj*, or pilgrimage, and is a religious focus for most Muslims, who pray daily facing Mecca.

Islamic civilization is the most pervasive unifying factor in the Middle East, and the correlation between religion and culture, on the one hand, and geographical area and environment, on the other, is a major element in any study of the region. This civilization of the Middle East region served two influential roles during medieval times. During the so-called Dark Ages in Europe, while the Byzantine Empire engaged in political and theological disputes, the Islamic Middle East was translating and interpreting classical writings—literary, philosophical, and scientific—thus preserving the classical heritage, much of which might otherwise have been lost. Also, contemporaneously, the Middle East served as a remarkable commercial crossroads, maintaining contacts with potent East Asian civilizations, partly through Muslim missionaries, and later linking those civilizations with a revived Mediterranean area and Renaissance Europe.

Twenty-First-Century Importance

Aside from the region's historical importance, five contemporary facets dominate global perceptions of the Middle East: unequaled petroleum resources, the ongoing Arab-Israeli conflict and related cycles of violence and war, terrorism, rivalries among leaders and states, and extremism among zealous Muslims, Jews, and Christians. This study will treat each of these five, but introductory mentions of oil and the cycles of warfare are appropriate at this point.

Most of the Middle East's petroleum—close to half of the world's known reserves[2]—is found in a broad depression extending southeastward from near Elazığ, Turkey, along the axis of the Gulf, to the Arabian Sea coast of Oman. Of the 75.7 million barrels of daily global petroleum production in 2012, 24 million barrels, or about 31.7 percent, originated in this region (see Chap. 6 for more details). On the other hand, the oil producers depend heavily upon imports of goods and technical and managerial expertise from industrialized countries. Interdependence has increased as the industrialized countries seek stable energy supplies—as the oil crisis of 2008 demonstrated—and as the oil-producing countries continue to require Western technology for development.

The Arab-Israeli wars in 1948–1949, 1956, 1967, 1973, 1982, and 2006, the First and Second Intifadahs, and the Israeli attacks on Hamas in Gaza in 2008–2009 and 2012 resulted in thousands of casualties and the diversion of billions of dollars needed on all sides for development. The oil boycott in 1973, periodic outbreaks of fighting in the Levant, and nearly continuous international efforts to broker a peace process all attest to the destabilizing effects of the Arab-Israeli conflict. Farther east, the internecine Gulf wars of 1980–1988, 1990–1991, 2003, and after resulted in many more casualties and damage to infrastructure than earlier battles in the Levant.

THE MIDDLE EAST: DEFINITION AND DELIMITATION

Definition

What exactly is the proper designation of the Middle East, and what does the root term mean? Terms used historically have almost all been Eurocentric in origin—"the East," "the Orient," "the Outremer," "the Levant," "the Near East," "the Middle East."[3] All indicate an area across the sea and east of those European countries whose political and economic empires increasingly dominated the world from the fifteenth century on into the mid-twentieth century. During the sixteenth century, Ottoman Empire realms became

known as the "Near East" in contrast to the "Far East" of East and Southeast Asia; not until World War II and after was "Near East" generally supplanted by "Middle East." Even so, "Near East" survives in some usages, including the designation of the US Department of State bureau responsible for the general area, the Bureau of Near Eastern Affairs.

Delimitation

Scholars universally accept that the Fertile Crescent is the nucleus of the Middle East, and they widely consider the core region to comprise the general area from Northeast Africa to South Asia. Here we will follow the broad consensus that the region extends from the western border of Egypt to the eastern border of Iran and from the Black Sea to the Arabian Sea (see Map 1.2). Because the peripheral regions of our sixteen-state core affect and interact with the core, this study also includes some consideration of the broader region.

Our core area could well have also embraced states such as Libya and the Sudan on the basis of their location and close links to states that have been included. Other states like Afghanistan or even Somalia also have links with our sixteen-state Middle East through ongoing political and military events. Still others like the Central Asian "stans" and the Trans-Caucasus nations with similarly hydrocarbon-dominated economies interact with our core region.

The Maghrib and the Mashriq.   The importance of both the historical and the contemporary interconnections between the Middle East and North Africa demands recognition. From the Atlantic to the Nile, the lands of North Africa have for millennia maintained relations with the Middle East heartland. The ties strengthened profoundly after the seventh-century Muslim conquest of North Africa, and although later European colonial-

Map 1.2 Map delineating Middle East boundaries as defined for this book. The map shows only international boundaries, country names, capital cities, and seas. The radius of the circle is 1,250 mi/ 2,012 km. Note central location of Baghdad.

ism disturbed the relations, ties have been re-newed to varying degrees in recent years.

The western extension is considered to comprise the five North African states of Morocco, Algeria, Tunisia, Libya, and Sudan, all also Arab and Muslim. The area of north-western Africa is referred to as the Maghrib (or Maghreb, "west"), and, less commonly, the Arab lands east of Libya are termed the Mashriq ("east"). (Technical and unusual terms are explained in the Glossary following Chapter 21.) Many scholars and observers maintain that the links between the two areas create an Arab unit, a Greater Middle East, a Middle East/North Africa (MENA) unit. Chapter 8 includes a brief discussion of the "Broader Middle East" concept in a general context.

Despite religious and historical links, North Africa and the Middle East proper have differing historical influences, interests, and agendas. The Mashriq has had more intimate relations with Turks and Persians. Lands west of the Nile have had their own regional influences and, unlike the Mashriq, were subject to direct European colonization in the nineteenth century. Especially since World War II, the Arab states of the Mashriq have increasingly interacted with one another, despite periodic divisive influences. Israel on the west, Iran on the east, and Turkey on the north—all non-Arab—are of greater concern to the Middle East than to North Africa. It is for these reasons that this study focuses on the sixteen-state core Middle East (plus Palestine) delimited above.

In the following chapters, it will be shown that, despite obvious diversity, there is a basic geographic, historic, political, and economic unity across the core region—a unity that lessens in the periphery.

REGIONAL UNITY OF EMPIRES

Interwoven historical-political-geographical developments have, over many centuries, exercised integrating influences on the region. For four thousand years, up to the end of World War I, the Middle East experienced varying degrees of control by a series of great empires centered in several of the power cores, or foci, in the region. The empires echo many familiar names: Babylonian, Hittite, Egyptian, Assyrian, Chaldean, Persian, Seleucid, Ptolemaic, Roman, Byzantine, Parthian, Sassanian, Umayyad, Abbasid, and Ottoman. A score of other, smaller, empires are less familiar: Aramaean, Phoenician, Sabaean, Nabataean, Fatimid, and others.

Power Foci.   Except for the Roman Empire, governed originally from outside the Middle East, the major empires centered in four focal points of power: Mesopotamia, Asia Minor, the Nile Valley, and the Iranian Plateau, with the Syrian realm a possible fifth. Each of the

power foci has functioned two or three times as an imperial power center over the millennia, and at one time or another each major part of the Middle East has controlled most or much of the rest of the region. Conversely, almost every part of the Middle East has been controlled by each of the other major parts. During periods of close political unity, an interchange of ideas, mores, goods, and people among areas added to a unifying cultural identity. These power foci and additional minor cores are a major theme of this book and will be analyzed in both their historical and their geopolitical contexts (see Chaps. 3 and 8).

AIMS AND CONCEPTS: AT A GLANCE

In recognition of the reciprocal relationships between geography and history, this book integrates historical highlights with a geographical analysis of patterns, particularly cultural patterns, as the title of the work indicates. These cultural patterns are especially influenced by time, so that process becomes an essential element in the several analyses. Biophysical patterns—the patterns of fundamental natural elements—generally change more slowly than cultural ones, but they, too, yield to noteworthy processes. We therefore examine the interaction of people and biophysical phenomena, not only in the context of their spatial relations but also in the context of their historical processes over time.

Further, geography emphasizes the complementary character of the patterns of human activity and natural elements, revealing the discipline's dual character—cultural and physical. Human or cultural elements include both people (their number, distribution, ethnic types, and other group characteristics, including their sense of identity) and their great variety of works (settlements, agriculture and related facilities, transportation routes and facilities, industries, and other cultural features). Major biophysical

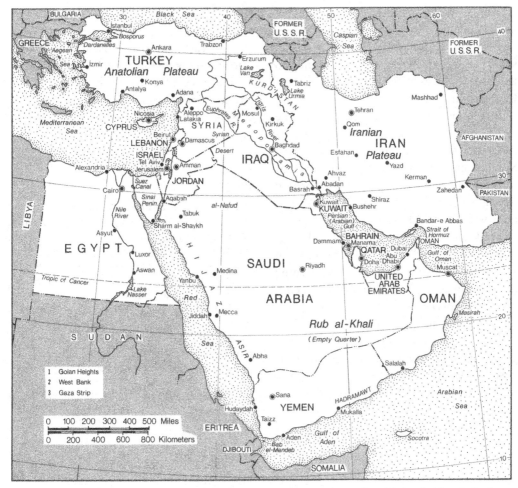

Map 1.3   Reference map showing most of the names frequently used in this book. Note latitudes and interpenetration of land and water.

or natural elements include landforms, water resources, climate, soils, vegetation, animal life, mineral resources, and economic characteristics.

Following a survey of patterns of the biophysical elements of the Middle East in Chapter 2 from both a systematic and a regional perspective, Chapter 3 reviews the historical foundations. Chapters 4 through 9 examine the area from a broad systematic or topical perspective, examining thematic patterns, both natural and cultural. Chapters 10 through 21 shift perspective and focus on in-

dividual countries of the Middle East. In this regional approach, the overall Middle East region is subdivided into meaningful segments (subregions or minor regions) that are examined both as individual units and as interrelated parts of the whole. For the purposes of this book, the main regional unit of analysis is the sovereign nation, or state (Map 1.3). Therefore, this book studies the Middle East not only as a whole, in terms of elements or topics, but also as seventeen states/regions (including Palestine). Within each country, the component "landscapes" or third-order regions (that is, sub-subregions) are identified and numbered on particular country maps. Two summary tables in Chapter 8 suggest some major characteristics of each country in the extended areas of North Africa, the Trans-Caucasus, and Central Asia.

Perceptions of environment vary from one cultural group to another and change over time. For example, to the Bedouin of eastern Saudi Arabia during the early twentieth century, their habitat was a typical desert area in which they, as nomadic pastoralists, could migrate with their flocks in search of pasturage. By contrast, petroleum geologists and engineers after the mid-1930s, concentrating on subsurface features, perceived that same desert as an area of vast potential petroleum resources. This book incorporates such varying environmental perceptions.

In summary, this book is a broadly geographical study of the Middle East that focuses on spatial relations among peoples, human activities, biophysical elements, and economic measures and resources—their overall configuration and also microlevel interactions. In the process, analysis of the region reveals both variations and similarities, and synthesis reveals its unity and diversity, with an overall focus on those factors that produce the remarkable panorama of interacting patterns in the contemporary Middle East.

NOTES

1. Early writing consisted of hundreds of different signs that alone or in combination stood for words. Alphabetic writing came later; an interesting recent find attributes the first alphabet not to an elite group of scribes or officials but to Canaanites working in the southern Sinai turquoise and copper mines. See *Haaretz,* May 25, 2012.

2. The region's share of global reserves has been adjusted downward recently as the extensive tar sands of Canada and Venezuela have technologically and economically feasible sources of petro products, and global reserve figures have been adjusted upward as a result.

3. French *Outremer* = overseas. *Levant*, from Latin = the rising.

2

The Face of the Earth

KEY POINTS: Physical environment of fundamental significance in any region: landforms (coasts, uplands, plains), water bodies (seas, lakes, rivers), climate (temperature, precipitation, pressure belts, winds and storms), soils, vegetation (or lack of it), and animals all form a natural domain with which human activity interacts. Each affects all the others. The long human drama unfolds on this reactive stage. Many natural features of historical—including scriptural—importance and familiarity: Tigris, Euphrates, Jordan, Nile Rivers; Galilee, Dead Sea; Sinai Peninsula; Samarian Hills. Many specific names and data may be overwhelming, but they afford relative basis for understanding desert and steppe, steppe and Mediterranean climate, foehn and monsoon winds.

AN OVERVIEW

A basic tenet of geography is that physical features on the earth's surface and their related bioclimatic elements reciprocally interact with patterns of population, peoples, and human activities. Although the physical environment should not be said to determine the human condition, it must nevertheless be understood to influence, sometimes powerfully, many aspects of human activities. Such influence can readily be seen to affect Middle East societies' modes of living, urban development, transportation, access to irrigation water, share of energy resources, and level of economic development. Furthermore, each environmental factor interacts with every other factor: precipitation affects vegetation, elevation affects temperature, type of bedrock affects soils, and so on. We hardly need to be reminded of the impact on human lives of earthquakes, volcanic eruptions, tsunamis, hurricanes, sandstorms, tornadoes, floods, mudslides, and other phenomena that show that the environment is not simply a passive stage on which the human drama is enacted.

A basic appreciation of the Middle East physical environment and its influences is essential for an understanding of the regional culture, history, economy, and political development. From such a viewpoint, this chapter focuses on the basic physical environmental aspects of the Middle East—landforms, climate, soils, and natural vegetation. Chapters 3–9—that is, the remainder of Part One—consider history, peoples, and the range of human activities. Major influences of these factors on the peripheral areas of North

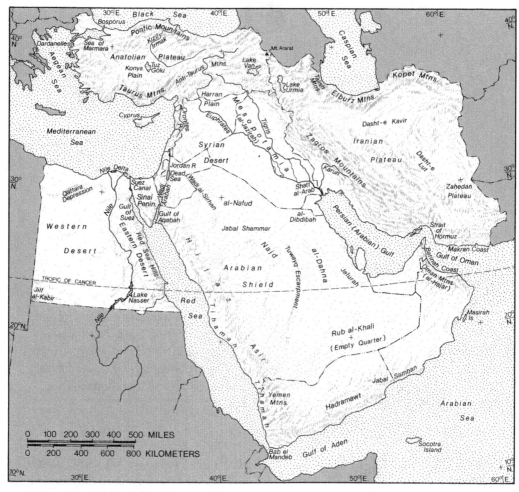

Map 2.1 Major geomorphic (landform) features of the Middle East.

Africa and Central Asia mentioned in Chapter 1 will be briefly considered, with additional in-depth information on the *Middle East Patterns* website (**www.middleeastpatterns .com**). Since the related factors of geomorphology (landforms) and climate have the greatest effects on cultural and economic patterns, those two factors are examined first.

FORMS OF THE LAND

General Patterns

Lands. Map 2.1 and Figure 2.1 show that land and sea areas alternate like broad spokes around the Middle East hub, with four land areas forming great promontories into the seas and, conversely, five seas penetrating deeply into the land. In the northwest, Asia Minor, embracing the Anatolian Plateau, serves as a peninsular bridge to southeastern Europe. Clockwise southeastward from eastern Anatolia, the Iranian Plateau extends into Asia proper; then there is the massive rectangular Arabian Peninsula, which split from Africa along the axis of the Red Sea, beyond which Egypt occupies the square northeastern corner of the continent of Africa. Finally, in the center, the regional hub consists of the Fertile Crescent area, which constitutes the zone between the northern (Anatolian-

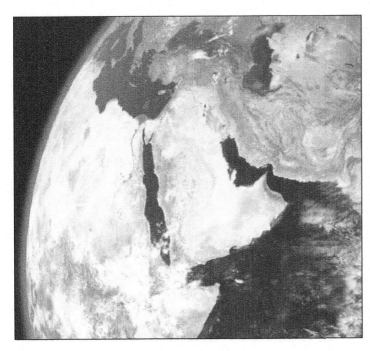

Figure 2.1
Image from space of the Eastern Hemisphere, enlarged to emphasize the Middle East. (Photograph courtesy of the National Aeronautics and Space Administration)

Iranian) and southern (Egyptian-Arabian) belts of the region.

Seas. The largest of the five water bodies reaching into Middle East lands, the deep Mediterranean Sea on the west washes the shores of seven of the core Middle East states[1] as well as the four Arab Maghrib countries of North Africa. The Black Sea, to the north of Asia Minor, lies between Turkey and the other five littoral states and overflows to the Mediterranean through the fabled and picturesque straits of the Bosporus and Dardanelles. The Caspian Sea to the northeast is in fact an inland salt lake with no outlet to the sea and with its surface well below sea level. The Persian/Arabian Gulf—or usually just "the Gulf"—occupies the drowned, downbuckled tectonic trough between Arabia and Iran. The Red Sea, with its two extensions to the north, the Gulfs of Suez and Aqabah, and the related Gulf of Aden to the south, floods the great rift (linear split) that separates the Arabian Peninsula from Africa

(Fig. 2.2) and connects with the Mediterranean through the artificial Suez Canal.

Penetration of seas into the land has several major consequences. Physically, the seas—the Mediterranean especially—intersperse sources of moisture in areas that would be far more desertic without them. In addition, deep penetration of the seas creates a great deal more coastline, which in turn increases the opportunities for human contacts with the outside world. The seaways provide, as they have for millennia, major routes for trade and movement of peoples.

Plates and Faults. As elsewhere on earth, major landform provinces and features of the Middle East generally originated because of the tectonic shifting of large segments of the earth's outermost crust over millions of years. These crustal segments, or "plates," in the lithosphere jostle one another periodically and in so doing profoundly affect one another's adjacent edges. According to the theory of plate tectonics,[2] at least four, and

Figure 2.2 Image from space looking northeast across the Sinai Peninsula, with the Gulf of Suez on the west (lower edge of figure) and the Gulf of Aqabah on the east. The great Levant Rift System extends from lower right to upper left and cradles the Dead Sea and Sea of Galilee. The Suez Canal is left center, and the Mediterranean Sea is in the upper left corner. Dark, rugged, ancient basement rocks are exposed in the southern Sinai and along the eastern coast of the Gulf of Aqabah. (Photograph courtesy of the National Aeronautics and Space Administration)

perhaps six or more, plates have collided or been pulled apart to create the present landform pattern of the Middle East (Map 2.2; see also Fig. 2.1). Local tectonic movements, erosion by water or wind, and combined wind erosion and deposition are some typical factors. For example, some of the extensive sand deserts of Arabia are reshaped deposits of sand blown in from appreciable distances, sometimes over hundreds of miles, constantly changing form.

Wind and Water.   Elsewhere are broad plains areas of "desert pavement," where the surface is blanketed with a layer of pebbles left behind after finer particles have been blown away by persistent winds, forming a layer of armor for the underlying sand particles in a delicate ecological balance. Unfortunately, that equilibrium has been severely upset in extensive Middle East desert areas by modern development and activity.

Running water, now relatively limited in the vast arid realms that dominate the region, has profoundly altered some of the desert landforms. Many were shaped by streams that developed in earlier geological ages when rainfall was greater and streams were much larger, with proportionately greater erosive power. Weathering and erosion of rock in arid areas produce a greater angularity and sharpness of outline, even on the small scale shown in weathered lava known as *hamadah* (Fig. 2.3). In more humid areas,

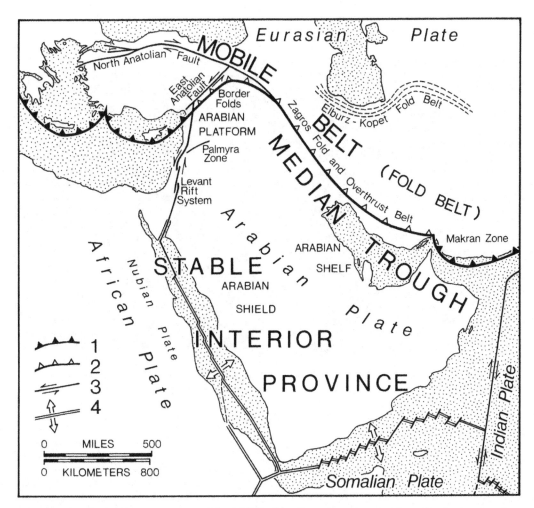

Map 2.2 Generalized tectonic map of the Middle East. Note the concentration of tectonic zones in eastern Anatolia. Symbols: 1 = collision zone involving subduction of sea floor along arcurate plate contacts; 2 = collision zone involving continental overthrusting (western Iran); 3 = horizontal displacement along transform faults (arrows indicate left-lateral or right-lateral); 4 = seafloor spreading, the pulling apart of the ocean's crust.

such as northern Turkey, the silhouettes are more rounded.

Quakes and Volcanoes. Usually the result of tectonic plate shifts, significant seismic activity and especially volcanism are widespread in the region. The map of earthquakes (Map 2.3) both indicates zones of actively colliding plates and also illustrates the especially high incidence of seismic events in Anatolia, Iran,

and Cyprus. Tectonic plate activity and folding become even more intensive in the junction area of Afghanistan, Iran, and Pakistan, as is clear from space imagery. Colliding plates, separating plates, and some shearing plates generate outpourings of lava either explosively from volcanoes or quietly through vents and fissures. Anatolia has numerous classic volcanic cones, including Mount Ararat, and large areas of southwestern Syria,

Figure 2.3 Rock-strewn steppe landscape in southwestern Syria—one type of *hamadah*. A thin lava flow has broken down to produce this type of surface. Angularity is typical of weathering in a dry climate area.

Figure 2.4 The extensive volcanic fields of the Western Arabian Shield include al-Wahbah explosion crater (*above center*) and scores of cinder cones, such as the one shown here.

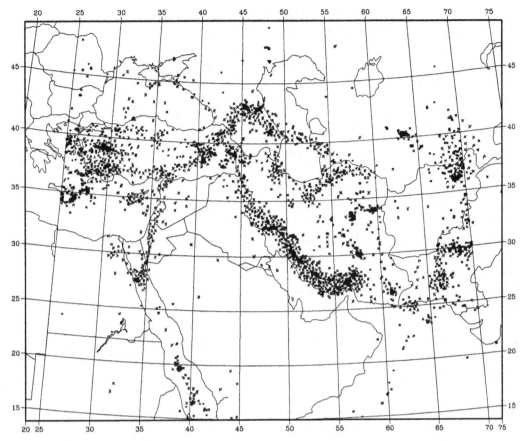

Map 2.3 Major Middle East earthquakes, 1966–2009 (magnitude of more than 4.5 and depth less than 31 mi/50 km). Note the concentration of seismicity along the Zagros Fold and Overthrust Belt and in western and eastern Anatolian Turkey. Compare with Map 2.2. Boundaries as shown on NEIC compilation. (Updated from USGS website on earlier map by special courtesy of the National Earthquake Information Center, US Geological Survey)

central Jordan, western Yemen, and especially western Saudi Arabia are buried under extensive lava flows (Fig. 2.4).

Stable Interior Province

On a broad scale, the landform patterns of the Middle East may be grouped into three general structural and landform provinces: the Stable Interior Province, the Mobile Belt, and, intermediate between the two, the Median Trough (see Map 2.2). This threefold division serves as a basis for a survey of major Middle Eastern landforms that will, in turn,

aid in understanding the region's cultural patterns. Maps 2.1 and 2.2 show most of the features mentioned below, but reference to a more detailed map is recommended for the study of this chapter.[3]

Nubian-Arabian Shield.   The Stable Interior Province lies in the southwesterly 60 percent of the Middle East proper, its nucleus an extensive area of ancient metamorphic basement rock constituting the Nubian-Arabian Shield. Planed down over millions of years, the shield is primarily a plateau in character but displays many remarkable volcanic features (see Fig. 2.4) as well as scores of faults and mountain ridges along ancient sutures. A prominent uptilt has created mountains on either side of the Red Sea rift.

The shield's ancient basement rocks, most 560–890 million years old or more by radiometric dating, have split open along the Red Sea axis of seafloor spreading and are exposed along both uptilted coasts of this slowly widening rift. After it was well developed, the shield was depressed except to the southwest, and the flanks were covered by thousands of feet of sedimentary rocks, principally limestones. The oldest strata deposited on sea floors more than 500 million years ago, these sedimentaries now outcrop in and underlie the great arc of territory sweeping from northern Egypt through the Fertile Crescent countries and around the eastern and southeastern flanks of the Arabian Peninsula. Some of these sedimentaries contain huge oil reservoirs.

Arabian Peninsula.   In the east, a narrow coastal plain, Tihamah, extends virtually the full length of the Arabian Peninsula's Red Sea coast and is backed by a formidable mountain range. This linear barrier, the Hijaz Mountains, averages 7,000 ft/2,135 m and forms the uptilted western edge of the Arabian Shield. Back of the Hijaz, the ancient basement rocks of the shield extend in a semicircle, convex eastward, to the heart of the Arabian Peninsula. There, uplift bowed up the shield into the Central Arabian Arch, greatly increasing erosion to cause an eastward retreat of the edge of the older sedimentary cover that formerly blanketed much of western Arabia millions of years ago.

The opening of the Red Sea rift through rifting and seafloor spreading, plus faulting in the shield, induced extrusion of several extensive flows of basaltic lava—one as large as 7,720 mi^2/20,000 km^2 (see Fig. 2.4). Successive older lava series reach thousands of feet in thickness in the peninsula's southwestern

corner and constitute the rugged mountains that give the High Yemen its character (shown in Chaps. 4 and 18).

To the north, northeast, and southeast of central Arabia, the basement is depressed and is buried under layers of sedimentary rock, the Arabian Shelf. These have a vital significance in the world economy, since around and under the Gulf they contain the world's greatest known oil resources.

Sand, wind, aridity, and open space have combined to create three large and several small sand deserts in the Arabian Peninsula. In the south center lies the Rub al-Khali (Empty Quarter), the world's largest single contiguous sand dune area (see Fig. 1.1). In the north is the Nafud (or the Great Nafud), one-fifth the size of the Rub al-Khali. Extending in a great arc from the Nafud to the Rub al-Khali through eastern Arabia is a belt of red sand known as the Dahna.

At the southeastern corner of the Arabian Peninsula are the rugged and curious Oman Mountains (or Jabal al-Hajar), with elevations typically around 5,000 ft/1,525 m but peaking at 10,000 ft/3,048 m. They are a product of collision between the Arabian Plate and the Iranian subplate but are a case of the unusual process of obduction (the reverse of subduction). At their northern end, the Oman Mountains culminate in the dramatic Musandam Peninsula, aptly referred to as the Horn of Arabia.[4]

Egyptian Deserts.   Between the Red Sea and the Nile Valley, Egypt's Eastern Desert culminates in the Red Sea Hills, a moderately rugged and barren mountain mass of dominantly basement rocks. These ancient crystalline rocks are part of the Nubian Shield, corresponding to the Arabian Shield east of the Red Sea. Unlike the exposed Red Sea Hills rocks, relatively thin sedimentary strata blanket the Western Desert section of the shield to the south, with thicker and younger strata to the north. Depressions cradle five oases,

Figure 2.5 The Jordan River meandering across its floodplain (*al-Zor*), flowing sluggishly from upper right (from the Sea of Galilee, just out of the picture) to lower left. The higher terrace, wider on the left bank (right side of picture), is *al-Ghor*.

examined in Chapter 19, and the profound Qattara Depression in the north descends 436 ft/133 m below sea level. The Nile River separates the two major deserts, and its great delta lies in a former embayment of the Mediterranean coast.

Central Areas. In the heart of the Middle East, the same general sedimentary sequence continues from the eastern Arabian Peninsula to the basement rocks in the Fertile Crescent and Syrian Desert areas. The strata are more level in the central area, and vast expanses show level to undulating surfaces of Cretaceous limestones.

Jordan Valley and Related Features. A major geomorphic feature of the western Fertile Crescent is the Levant Rift System, a great

trench that extends from the northwestern end of the Red Sea up the Gulf of Aqabah and along the axis of the Wadi al-Arabah, Dead Sea, Jordan Valley, and Bekaa of Lebanon to the Ghab Depression in northwestern Syria (Fig. 2.5; see also Fig. 2.2). This feature is primarily a transform fault, similar to the San Andreas Fault in California, that resulted chiefly from counterclockwise rotation of the Arabian Plate away from the African Plate. The bottom of the trench is below sea level from well south of the Dead Sea to north of the Sea of Galilee, with the steadily shrinking Dead Sea the lowest point on the globe (see the "Middle East Lakes" section later in this chapter).

The Great Rift. The first of the rift system's three main segments comprises the trench and related features extending from the Gulf of Aqabah north to and including the Huleh Basin. A second segment, the most seismically active of the three, begins at the southern border of Lebanon, where the Levant Rift bends to the northeast into the Bekaa valley. At the northern border of Lebanon, the third segment of the fault zone turns north again and finally disappears just beyond the Ghab Depression in northwestern Syria (pictured in Fig. 5.4).

Mobile Belt

The Mobile Belt (or Fold Belt) is an extremely complex continuous band of folded, faulted, and compressed mountains extending from western to eastern Anatolia and then southeastward across Iran and eastward into the Pamirs and Himalayas (see Fig. 2.1).

Asia Minor (Anatolia).   South of and generally parallel to the Black Sea coast, the Pontic Mountains (5,000–13,000 ft/1,524–3,962 m) stretch virtually the full length of Turkey. For much of their extent, they lie north of the great North Anatolian Transform Fault (see Map 2.2), where periodic slippage produces devastating earthquakes including the disastrous impact south of Istanbul in August 1999 (see Chap. 20).

Rimming the southern side of Asia Minor are the Taurus Mountains (7,000–9,000 ft/ 2,135–2,745 m), whose complexity reflects the severity of the compression that formed them (see Map 2.2).

At its southwestern end, the East Anatolian Transform Fault links with both the northern end of the Levant Rift System and the eastern end of the Cyprus Subduction Zone. At its northeastern end, it intersects the North Anatolian Fault. The proximity of these several seismic belts results in frequent and severe earthquakes (see Map 2.3), such as the three catastrophic quakes in the Erzincan area in 1938, 1983, and 1992. Volcanic vents in the East Anatolian Accretionary Complex (Fig. 2.6) have also opened and are now

marked by massive volcanoes (Mount Ararat near the Turkish-Iranian border reaches 16,948 ft/5,166 m), crater lakes, cinder cones, and lava flows. Mineralization along these various plate contacts gives Turkey, and also Iran, more nonfuel mineral wealth than any other countries in the Middle East. In between this East Anatolian system and the western mountains is the exceedingly complicated central Anatolian intermontane plateau, with its lowest part an almost flat-floored basin occupied by the shallow Tuz Gölü (Turkish: Salt Lake).

Aegean Zone.   More than 600 mi/965 km to the west, the Aegean coastal zone of extreme western Anatolia is an area of block mountains, alternating uplifted and downdropped masses (horsts and grabens). These structures have produced a series of rugged east-west promontories and deeply indented bays on the Aegean coast, which beckoned Ionian Greeks to settle in the sixth century BCE. In the northwest, a large foundered block flooded to form the Sea of Marmara, which links the Aegean and Black Seas through flooded valleys to its southwest and northeast.

Cyprus.   About 55 mi/88 km off the Mediterranean coast of Turkey, the island of Cyprus probably resulted from the same plate collision that produced the Taurus range. An exposed granitic intrusion forms the core of the highly mineralized mountain mass of the Troodos (6,407 ft/1,953 m), in southern Cyprus, and an uplifted linear limestone reef produced the narrow Kyrenia range (3,360 ft/1,025 m) along the northern coast. Between the two lies Cyprus's breadbasket, the sediment-filled basin of the Mesaoria.

Iranian Plateau and Ranges.   Complex folding in the Mobile Belt extends farther eastward and southeastward from Anatolia into the Iranian mountain and intermontane plateau regions. From the junction of Turkey,

Figure 2.6 Eastern Anatolian Mountains west of Lake Van—rugged, snow covered, cloud shrouded, and geologically very complex. Heavy precipitation makes this mountain area a major hydrographic center, spawning such major rivers as the Tigris and Euphrates.

Iran, and Iraq to the Arabian Sea, compression and subduction between the Arabian Plate and the Iranian subplate have crumpled, faulted, and thrust-faulted mostly sedimentary rocks along the longest and most prominent fold belt in the Middle East, the Zagros Mountains (10,000–14,000 ft/3,000–4,300 m) (Fig. 2.7; note caption). In the southern Zagros, scores of salt plugs have been pushed to or near the surface, creating stratigraphic structures that in many instances have entrapped large quantities of petroleum and natural gas. Farther southeast, the Makran range, behind Iran's coast on the Gulf of Oman, is the result of recent uplift of oceanic crust and exhibits forms that are distinctly different from the Zagros geomorphology and related to the Oman Mountains across the Gulf.

High linear ridges compressed between the rigid core blocks of Iran and the Russian Platform of the Eurasian Plate extend across northern Iran. The Elburz Mountains south of the Caspian Sea and the series of ridges in the Kopet Mountains along the Iran-Turkmenistan border reach elevations of 12,000–15,000 ft/3,660–4,575 m. As in eastern Turkey, plate collision in the Elburz belt squeezed lava out of volcanic vents, with the towering cone of Mount Damavand (18,600 ft/5,669 m) the highest point in the entire Middle East. Scattered volcanoes—including Iran's only recently active vent—appear along the eastern Iranian border near Afghanistan and Pakistan, and complex fold mountains around the Zahedan Plateau enclose the third side of the triangular Iranian Plateau. As in central Anatolia, the lowest part of Iran's

Figure 2.7 Denuded pitching anticline in typical structures of the Folded Zagros Mountains of western Iran. In such subsurface folds are found the great petroleum reservoirs of the area. Compare with Figure 9.4, which shows salt domes that also form oil-reservoir structures.

inner basin contains ephemeral salt lakes (playas), known in Iran as *kavirs*. Compressional highland chains extend still farther eastward into Central Asia, increasing in complexity and elevations to become the globe's mightiest mountain masses—the Hindu Kush, Tien Shan, and Himalayas, with the Pamir Knot tying them together.

Median Trough

The Mesopotamian-Gulf trough, one of the most conspicuous geomorphic features of the Middle East, forms the northeastern edge of the Stable Interior Province along the median axis between the Arabian Plate and the Iranian subplate. It is also the world's greatest petroleum province, a zone of downbuckling and subsidence on the flanks of the Arabian Shield. The sea invades the southeastern half of the structural trough from the Indian Ocean through the Strait of Hormuz. One of the world's most strategic chokepoints, the strait is physically as well as economically and strategically significant, and this area will be discussed in detail in later sections.

MIDDLE EAST WATERS

Seas and Gulfs

Even after the sea basins of the Middle East settled into their present contours, even slight crustal adjustments and climatic variations caused major modifications. Especially during the Pleistocene glacial period, when millions of cubic meters of ocean water were frozen into ice sheets, the sea fell to more than 395 ft/120 m below its current level. During those same periods of glacial maxima, the Middle East enjoyed pluvial periods of appreciably greater precipitation that charged the regional aquifers and induced environmental conditions more favorable for human cultural development during the long Paleolithic period. During glacial retreats, eustatic (sea-level) changes from water freed from glacial ice sheets, brought seas 180–195 ft/55–60 m higher than at present, giving a total differential of more than 590 ft/180 m over the 1.3 million years of the glacial Pleistocene.

The great drop in sea level during glacial maxima left the straits of the region as dry sills between basins—the Strait of Gibraltar, connecting the Mediterranean and the Atlantic; the Bosporus and Dardanelles, connecting the Mediterranean and the Black Sea; and the Strait of Hormuz, connecting the Gulf and the Indian Ocean. Without inflowing water, these three inland basins gradually became extensive deep desert basins. The residual salt in these basins still affects the chemical composition of rocks, water, and soil in the region. When the interglacial thaw induced a rise in sea level, the mounting water crested the formerly dry straits and roared in thunderous cascades to refill the desert basins.

Red Sea and Gulf of Aden. The Red Sea occupies an elongated, escarpment-bounded depression 1,220 mi/1,965 km long and 155–280 mi/250–450 km wide. Tectonically, it is a northward extension of the great African Continental Rift extending from Mozambique in the south, through the Levant Rift, to Turkey in the north. The rifting mentioned earlier opened the Red Sea in two phases several million years ago, and it is still continuing along the sea's entire length. A narrow inner axial trough within the sea's main trough south of 21° N Lat is about 6,500 ft/2,000 m deep, formed by seafloor spreading processes during the past 4 million years. North of 25°, the inner axial trough is lacking, and the floor has an irregular, faulted surface. Between the shores and the center axis, a narrow continental shelf extends along both coasts.

Seafloor spreading conveys molten lava into the bottom of the trench, which heats the seawater above it and stimulates the formation of hot brines and the development of sludge with high concentrations of zinc, copper, silver, gold, and other metals. Saudi Arabia and Sudan formed a Red Sea Commission in 1975 to consider exploitation of the metals, which, although not commercially feasible at present, may well be a major future source for the metals.

Rifting along both branches of the Red Sea at the northern end (see Fig. 2.2) is of two different types and ages. With great depths, exceeding 5,900 ft/1,800 m, the Gulf of Aqabah is a pull-apart zone associated with the Levant Rift and is morphogenetically related to the Dead Sea, the Sea of Galilee, and the Huleh Basin. The much shallower Gulf of Suez, at only about 150 ft/45 m, is a much older structure that split from the Red Sea Hills to the west and subsided over a long period.

At the southern end of the Red Sea, the Gulf of Aden opened by seafloor spreading along a rift at right angles to the Red Sea; it has proceeded further to become an example of a young ocean basin. It exhibits well-defined continental margins, small ocean basins, an oceanic crust floor, an active midocean ridge (Sheba Ridge), and a spreading center characterized by a rift valley and transverse fracture zones. This triple junction of the rifts (see Map 2.2) creates a magnificent laboratory for observing the mechanics and processes of active seafloor spreading, especially in and around Djibouti and the Danakil region of Ethiopia.

Persian/Arabian Gulf.   Lying in a tectonically downfolded basin of Late Pliocene to Pleistocene age, the shallow Gulf (Arabic: al-Khalij) is a marginal sea that exhibits striking contrasts with the Red Sea and the Gulf of Aden. Although it reaches depths of more than 330 ft/100 m near the Strait of Hormuz, its average depth is only 115 ft/35 m. It covers approximately 87,000 mi²/226,000 km² and is about 620 mi/1,000 km long and 125–185 mi/201–300 km wide. Since the floor slope and depth are greater on the Iranian side, the basin has a marked bathymetric asymmetry across its axis, reflecting the downfolding between the Arabian Plate and Iranian subplate. The generally level low coastal area of the Arabian Shelf's eastern half slopes gently under the shallow Gulf waters and is fringed with offshore sand islands and sand spits. One such sand spit is Ras Tanura, the location of three large oil installations on the Saudi coast (see Fig. 6.4).

Huge petroleum accumulations are exploited in a broad, shallow area of the Gulf 33–66 ft/10–20 m deep, studded with numerous shoals and salt-dome islands, lying to the east of the anticlinal Qatar Peninsula. Formerly the world's greatest natural-pearl fishing area, the Great Pearl Bank Barrier extends eastward, and the concave southern coast of the Gulf is covered by low, evaporitic, supratidal flats (*sabkhahs*) that reach widths of more than 6 mi/10 km along the coast of the United Arab Emirates (UAE). On the east, in contrast, the Iranian coast rises steeply to the folded ridges of the Zagros Foreland.

The Gulf varies widely in temperature and salinity because of its considerable supply of fresh water, shallowness, and limited connection with the ocean. In summer, the surface waters are warm and evaporation is high, and water temperature is about 68°F/20°C even in winter. Salinity varies from 7 percent (twice that of average seawater) in protected Arabian lagoons to less than 3.7 percent near the Strait of Hormuz. Tidal ranges in the western Gulf are moderate, with average maximums of about 8 ft/2.5 m.

Oil and Pollution.   With more than a score of major oil-export terminals in operation in the Gulf virtually around the clock, and with forty to fifty large tankers sailing up or down the Gulf daily, pollution of the waters and beaches has long been a grave concern around the littoral. Despite efforts by governments, oil companies, and shippers, as many as a quarter of a million barrels of oil pollute the Gulf annually. The rapidly growing population around the littoral discards many tons of waste into the water daily. A major pollution crisis occurred in January 1991, when Iraqi forces retreating from Kuwait engaged in ecoterrorism by dumping several million barrels of crude oil (the amount can only be estimated) into the Gulf off the coast of the amirate. This largest oil spill in history spread south to the Qatar coast within sixty days, killing countless fauna as well as fouling flora and beaches and posing a threat to desalination plant intakes. The crisis was a global wake-up call to the potential catastrophe posed by current oil technologies, reinforced by the massive Deepwater Horizon oil spill in the Gulf of Mexico in 2010.

Mediterranean Sea. Of complex origin, the Mediterranean is partially a western remnant of the pre-Miocene Tethys Sea and partially a collapsed structure along the collision zone between the African and Eurasian Plates. Since its re-creation with the most recent melting of the Pleistocene ice, it has been virtually enclosed (its name is from the Latin "in the middle of the land"), connecting with the global oceans only through the narrow Strait of Gibraltar. An artificial link with the Red Sea opened with construction of the Suez Canal in 1869. The Mediterranean's greatest depth (15,072 ft/4,594 m) is west of Crete, and a basin off the Levant coast is 4,787 ft/1,459 m. Mediterranean coasts descend sharply under the fringing waters, and except for the Nile sediments borne seaward by currents in the southeast, few Mediterranean ports face the major dredging problems that plague virtually all Gulf ports.

The extensive, deep Mediterranean waters profoundly affect the climate of much of the Middle East and North Africa, with the elongated basin channeling weather-maker low-pressure systems. Ships of many nations have traversed the sea for thousands of years, linking North Africa with Europe and the Levant. The interrelations among Mediterranean littoral peoples produced a "Mediterranean" subrace, diet, agriculture, music, and history. Fishing in this virtually inland sea has supplied a crucial element in the diet of the littoral peoples for millennia.

Black Sea. The Black Sea (also known as the Euxine Sea, the ancient Pontus Euxinus) is relatively shallow near the Danube Delta in the northwest but has depths exceeding 7,000 ft/2,135 m across much of its southern extent. The northern slopes of Turkey's Pontic Mountains plunge steeply into the Black Sea, giving deepwater access to Turkey's many northern ports. Receiving several smaller rivers in the south, the Black Sea's plentiful freshwater inflow from rivers in the north and south limits its salinity. Virtually tideless, it overflows freely

through the Bosporus into the Sea of Marmara and thence through the Dardanelles into the Aegean. The six Black Sea littoral states have recognized key common interests and environmental threats. Pollution and other issues have demanded growing attention since the Black Sea, like the Gulf and the Caspian Sea, has become a major factor in the burgeoning oil industry of the region: pipelines to the north and south of, and even under, the Black Sea are already in operation, and more are in the planning stage (see Chaps. 6 and 20 for more details).

Caspian Sea. Unlike the other seas, the inland Caspian has no present outlet, and its surface averages about 92 ft/28 m below sea level. With most of the fluviatile inflow coming from the Volga at the northern end, the level of the Caspian slowly dropped until the late 1970s, as Russia increasingly utilized Volga water for irrigation. The trend reversed in 1977, and by 1995 the Caspian had peaked by rising 8 ft/2.4 m: since then, there have been small slow oscillations in the level. Most vessels on the Caspian are fishing boats seeking the famous Caspian sturgeon, the source of valuable Russian and Iranian caviar.

As in the Persian/Arabian Gulf area, huge accumulations of petroleum and natural gas formed in structures around and under the seabed created by Caspian Basin tectonics. Some of the world's earliest major oil production came from the still-active Baku field on the Azerbaijan coast; however, before 1991, the Soviet Union's negligence in protecting the environment caused the entire Caspian Basin to become frighteningly polluted.[5]

The focus of the very considerable geopolitical significance of the Caspian shifted after 1991 from a bilateral rivalry between the Soviet Union and Iran to more complex multilateral relationships among Russia, Iran, and three former Soviet republics. The three newly independent littorals—Azerbaijan, Kazakhstan, and Turkmenistan—are now major players in the Great Oil Game of the Caspian Basin. One problem has been defining the complicated median lines that specify what areas of the seabed fall to the respective littorals for offshore oil drilling. Increasingly booming after the mid-1990s, the oil industry of the Caspian Basin–Central Asian states is noted in Chapter 6.

Rivers Great and Small

The major river systems in the southwestern and north-central sectors of the Middle East rise in external upstream areas with significant water surpluses. Structural conditions in some of the more humid sectors interrupt drainage lines to divert a considerable percentage of the interior runoff into closed basins. Although limited both qualitatively and quantitatively, the major river systems have played dramatic roles in the long history of the region.

The two largest stream systems in the core Middle East are the Nile in the southwest and the Tigris-Euphrates in the center, with all three rivers rising in distant, wetter, highlands before crossing hundreds of miles of desert in their lower reaches. Along with the Jordan, these historic flows have had renewed roles in current events, particularly in Israel/Palestine, Egypt, and Iraq. Escalating disputes over transboundary waters are among the potentially serious confrontations that governments in the region face in the twenty-first century (see Chap. 8, "Regional Conflicts"). The interests of downstream consuming countries (Sudan and Egypt, Syria and Iraq) have long been in competition with those of the better-watered countries controlling the sources of the three major rivers.

Conflicting Riparian Rights.   In the Middle East, as elsewhere in the world, states face political and economic, as well as geographic, barriers to collaboration over water resources. Upstream Turkey is stronger both militarily and economically than either of the downstream consumers of Euphrates and Tigris waters, although a larger part of the river basin lies in Iraq and Syria, which have historically relied on the rivers for most of their agricultural production. Downstream Egypt's investments in hydraulic infrastructure, on the other hand, lead it to demand that the share of the Nile's waters reaching its border is not reduced by the newer development of hydroelectric and irrigation facilities in the poorer upstream countries of eastern Africa.

Different Rationalizations.   Turkey's argument is based on sovereign rights to the water falling on its territory; Egypt's relies on historic productive use. Although considerable negotiations stretching over decades have tried to resolve such conflicts, an internationally agreed-upon adjudication system for the resolution of these disputes is still lacking. The fresh waters of the Nile, Euphrates, and Tigris and the seawaters of the Gulf are shared by many countries that vary in size, strength, and reliance on the waters in question.

Seasonal Flow.   With the major exception of the Nile, virtually all Middle East rivers have a maximum runoff in late spring and a minimum flow in early fall. Most are fed by runoff from snowmelt, which comes later than the actual precipitation maximum, November through February; their minimum flow after the hot, dry summer is supplied primarily by springs and other groundwater discharge. The Nile regime is precisely the reverse, as it floods in late summer and early fall, following the heavy summer monsoon rains in the Ethiopian highlands, and is at its minimum in the spring.[6]

Tigris and Euphrates Rivers.   The fabled Tigris (Arabic: Dijlah; Turkish: Dicle) and Euphrates (Arabic: al-Furat; Turkish: Firat) Rivers enter the Gulf through a common 100-mi/160-km channel, the Shatt al-Arab, but each is otherwise a separate stream. Both rise in the snowy eastern Anatolian highlands, the hydrographic center of Turkey, with their headwaters only a few miles from each other (see Map 2.1). Additional tributaries augment their flow, but both lose water through evaporation and diversion for irrigation as they cross arid land. With diminished flow, they lose carrying capacity, drop some of their loads of silt, and continue to build up a common vast deltaic plain, with each channel also building natural levees.[7]

The longer of the two and with the greater drainage basin, the Euphrates begins in eastern Turkey and ends at its junction with the Tigris at the head of the Shatt al-Arab. More than 1,700 mi/2,700 km long, it drains a basin of 171,430 mi^2/444,000 km^2. About 28 percent of its basin is in Turkey, 17 percent in Syria, 40 percent in Iraq, and 15 percent in Saudi Arabia. However, more than 90 percent of the actual water flow is from runoff in Turkey, and no tributaries enter it in Iraq. Mean annual flow at Hit, in central Iraq, was formerly 31,820 mn m^3 (million cubic meters) per year; however, damming of the Euphrates at four places in Turkey and at al-Thawrah (formerly Tabaqah) in Syria greatly diminished the river's mean flow after the mid-1990s. The consequent political disputes are considered in Chapters 8, 10, and 14.

Draining an area of more than 43,110 mi^2/111,655 km^2 above Samarra, the Tigris, unlike the Euphrates, receives significant contributions from tributaries in Iraq. Bringing snowmelt and rainwater from the high Zagros in northeastern Iraq, all the tributaries enter along the left bank. Although shorter than the Euphrates, the Tigris (1,150 mi/1,850 km) formerly carried an average 42,230 mn m^3 of water per year, 25 percent more than the Euphrates, and since the Turkish and Syrian diversions of the Euphrates, the difference is even greater. To compensate for the dwindling lower Euphrates, water can be diverted north of Baghdad by the Samarra barrage from the Tigris to the Euphrates by way of Lake Tharthar, a flood-control facility occupying a depression between the two rivers. The lower Tigris is subject to sudden flooding, especially when the Zab rivers flood simultaneously, but flood-control measures have done much to alleviate the impact of floods. Unlike the Nile, neither river is satisfactory for regular navigation.

A Common Delta. The enormous load of silt carried by the Tigris (about 40 mn m^3 annually past Baghdad), and formerly by the Euphrates (whose silt now largely settles in Turkish and Syrian reservoirs and in flood-control basins between Ramadi and Karbala in Iraq), has built a huge delta beyond Hit on the Euphrates and beyond Samarra on the Tigris. The much more rapidly advancing combined fan and delta of the Karun River has, however, in effect dammed the outlet of the Tigris-Euphrates system into the Gulf, causing the Tigris-Euphrates streams to slow down and drop their silt load prior to overflowing the barrier. The silting process created over thousands of years a maze of marshes and channels northwest of Basrah, many of which were drained by Saddam Husayn for political reasons (see Chap. 14 for map of drainage and pictures of Marsh Arabs).

Nile River. With a length of 4,240 mi/6,825 km, the Nile is the world's longest river. Its drainage basin of 1.15 mn mi^2/2.98 mn km^2 is almost one-tenth the land area of Africa, although the Amazon, Mississippi/Missouri, and Congo Rivers have still larger watersheds. Seen anywhere along its lower course, the Nile, with an average annual flow at Aswan of 2,951.2 bn ft^3/83.6 bn m^3 per year, is an amazingly large stream to have traversed the full distance of the eastern Sahara. Completion of the Aswan High Dam in 1971 greatly altered the river's millennia-long regime and seasonal rhythm, and today's Nile is quite different from that famed in history.

The Nile's longest tributary, the White Nile, rises in the lake district of East Africa and carries a relatively uniform overflow northward from Lake Victoria and into the Sudd, the world's largest freshwater swamp, in South Sudan. The river flows northward and crosses progressively more desertic terrain to join the Blue Nile at Khartoum. It is the White Nile that gives the Nile its steady flow.

The Blue Nile is fed by heavy summer monsoon rains on the high Ethiopian Plateau and therefore has a different regime from the more uniform White Nile. Prior to the two Aswan dams, the historically famous annual Nile flood in Egypt was fueled by the summer Blue Nile floods, supplying about 80 percent of the river's water. From Khartoum, the Nile flows over a series of five cataracts (a sixth is now drowned under Lake Nasser). Debouching into the Mediterranean 1,680 mi/2,705 km below the Atbara confluence, the Nile has for millennia dropped a great silt load to build up the extensive delta that is an integral part of the country. However, the Aswan High Dam has changed the river regime, and the Nile no longer adds significant silt to its delta. Over the past 150 years, several barrages and major dams have been constructed to regulate the Nile flow, with the climactic structure the Aswan High Dam. Major political problems concerning the Nile are discussed in Chapter 8.

Fold Belt Rivers. Of the perennial streams in Asia Minor and the western Iranian highlands, only a limited number carry noteworthy volume. Clockwise, they include the Büyük Menderes in southwestern Anatolia; Gediz, debouching just north of Izmir; Sakarya, draining the highlands between Ankara and Istanbul and reaching the Black Sea west of Zonguldak; Kızıl, or Kızılırmak (Turkish *ırmak* = river); the ancient Halys, with its basin covering much of north-central Anatolia; and Yeşil, debouching across its delta east of Samsun. Most of these rivers have been dammed for power generation.

Continuing clockwise, farther east the Aras forms the Turkish-Armenian and Iranian-Azerbaijan borders and empties into the Caspian Sea over the combined Kura-Aras delta south of Baku. In Iran, the Qezel Owzan-Safid drains a considerable area between Tehran and Tabriz and then cuts through a steep-sided gorge in the western Elburz (where it has been dammed) to empty into the southwestern Caspian over an appreciable delta; the Zayandeh, or Zayandeh Rud (Persian *rud* = river), is important for its irrigation of a considerable area around Esfahan before losing itself in a sump southeast of the city; and the Karun carries the largest volume of all Iranian rivers across a huge delta built jointly with its tributary, the Dez, and the nearby Karkheh. In Turkey, the two parallel Ceyhan and Seyhan Rivers drain into the northeastern corner of the Mediterranean across the extensive Çukurova (Turkish *ova* = plain), the combined deltaic plain built by the two rivers.

Three Levant Rivers. Three modest rivers in the Levant have economic and political importance (see Chap. 8) far beyond their physical dimensions. The Jordan River (al-Urdunn), with religious significance as well, has several headwaters draining southeastern Lebanon, southwestern Syria, and northern Israel; its major tributary, the Yarmuk, enters on the left (east) bank just south of the Sea of Galilee. The Zarqa enters from the plateau south of the Yarmuk. With a low gradient and meandering slowly along the flat rift valley floor, the Jordan has cut through old lakebed deposits laid down in the late Pleistocene pluvial periods, when the ancestral Dead Sea's water level was as much as 655 ft/200 m higher than now (see Fig. 2.5). Increased diversion of the Jordan and its tributary waters for irrigation purposes by Israel and Jordan utilizes most of the river's water before it reaches the Dead Sea, and both the Jordan River and the Dead Sea are shrinking, leading to serious environmental and economic concerns.

The two other Levant rivers of note, both fed by springs, arise within a few hundred meters of each other near Baalbak in the northern Bekaa of Lebanon and then flow in opposite directions. The Litani, the ancient Leontes, flows southward and below the Qirawn Dam enters a rapidly deepening and colorful gorge before turning westward to the Mediterranean. Its course lies entirely within Lebanon, but Israeli water planners have long sought to divert Litani water and increase irrigation supplies for Israel. The historic Orontes River (Arabic: Asi) flows northward along the bend in the Levant Rift into Syria and continues through Homs and Hamah, enters the reclaimed Ghab Marshes at the north end of the rift valley, and debouches into the Mediterranean after flowing through Antakya (Antioch) in Turkey.

Middle East Lakes

Few natural freshwater lakes occur in the Middle East outside the Tigris and Euphrates valleys. Large dams constructed on several major rivers during recent decades have impounded impressive freshwater reservoirs that are noted elsewhere. However, five lakes of the Middle East—only one with fresh water—are noteworthy here and are discussed in more detail in country chapters.

Sea of Galilee. The two most familiar lakes in the region lie in the Jordan Trench. Although not large, the Sea of Galilee in Israel (also called Lake Tiberias and Lake Kinneret) has both religious-historical significance and crucial contemporary economic and political importance. Covering an average of only 64 mi^2/165 km^2, the lake's surface varies between 685 and 710 ft/209 and 214 m below sea level, and its maximum depth is 138 ft/ 42 m. The lake occupies one of the enlarged basins in the Levant Rift System (see Fig. 2.2) and, fed mainly by and drained by the Jordan River, is now regulated as the control basin for Israel's national water system. Its gener-

ally fresh water is locally briny owing to underwater salt springs, especially near Tiberias on its west coast. Access by Syria to the northeast shore of the lake remains an issue of sharp debate in the evolution of the borders of Israel.

Dead Sea. Farther south in the Levant Rift lies the Middle East's most famous salt lake, the Dead Sea. The lowest water body on earth, its surface by 2011 had dropped to some 1,388 ft/423 m below sea level,[8] and its maximum depth was an additional 1,237 ft/ 377 m lower. Like other inland lakes with no outlet, the Dead Sea has become increasingly saline because of the evaporation from its surface—roughly 96.8 mn ft^3/2.74 mn m^3 per day—and because of the addition of salt from surrounding springs. Its water shows the highest salinity of all the world's water bodies, 35 percent, ten times that of average seawater. As a result, fish cannot survive in the water (hence its name), and the buoyancy is so great that people cannot sink in its waters.

Dissolved salts are present in such quantities that they are precipitated naturally or in evaporation pans, so that they are "mined" on a large scale in Israel and Jordan. This evaporation and a steadily diminishing inflow of water from the Jordan River in the north—the lake's main supply of fresh water—owing to an increasing use of the river basin's water for irrigation, mean that the lake's surface is steadily dropping. The surface fell some 89 ft/27 m from 1960 through the early 2010s, and over the past two decades, the rate of decrease has averaged about a meter a year. A resort on the Israeli side, originally established at the water's edge, was a mile from the receding shoreline by 2008. The southern basin has now shrunk to a small pond and is now only a few inches deep,[9] but it is of major economic significance since Jordanian and Israeli facilities for recovering valuable minerals through evaporation are located on its shores (see Chaps. 12 and 13).

Numerous large saltwater lakes occupy closed tectonic basins in northwestern Iran and on the Anatolian Plateau. The two largest are Lake Van and Lake Urmia, the two lying on either side of the Turkish-Iranian boundary. Nestled in the rugged eastern Anatolian highlands, Lake Van, whose water is bitter because of several salts, is 82 ft/25 m deep, has a surface elevation of 5,400 ft/1,646 m, and covers 1,434 mi²/3,714 km². Lake Urmia is shallower, not more than 66 ft/20 m deep, and very salty; it expands in size by one-third with the spring runoff to cover 2,317 mi²/6,000 km².

The structurally and topographically complex southwestern part of Anatolia cradles a dozen salt lakes between Denizli on the west and Konya on the east. In northwestern Anatolia, lakes also occupy inland extensions of grabens both east and south of the Sea of Marmara. Tuz Gölü is a shallow evaporation pan in the central Anatolian sump that expands and contracts markedly according to seasonal precipitation.

Groundwater

In addition to surface water, underground water is of vital significance in the Middle East and has been for thousands of years. Some groundwater comes to the surface in natural springs—artesian springs (*ayns* in the Arab lands), or contact springs—or emerges from caverns formed in limestone. Other water is tapped by hand-dug wells, familiar from biblical and Quranic accounts, many 50–100 ft/15–30 m deep. Some wells in desert areas, especially those sunk by nomads, may be only a few feet deep, dug into the sand and gravel of a broad wadi or an alluvial fan.

Especially in Iran, but also in other Middle Eastern areas, water in alluvial fans is tapped by a remarkable *qanat* system (also called *foggara, falaj, karez*), underground tunnels with spaced access wells reaching the surface (see Chap. 5 and an aerial view, Fig. 21.3). Thus, oases in the desert may be supplied by river water (Nile, Tigris, Euphrates), natural springs (in Egypt's Western Desert and in Saudi Arabia's Hofuf and Qatif oases), or dug wells (many in Iran and Saudi Arabia's Najd).

A Nonrenewable Resource. Rapidly growing populations, greatly increased supplies of capital, and more intense exploitation of the environment in the Middle East focused modern regional and national attention on water resources in general by the 1970s. Vast areas have no dependable surface runoff, but modern hydrogeological studies have discovered that some places have surprisingly large underground water supplies—for example, the great alluvial fans in the UAE. Especially after oil developments, technology has been applied to the search for and exploitation of underground water, with the result that previously unexpected supplies are being pumped by electric or internal combustion engines from deep wells. Much of this water, usually in the deeper aquifers, is nonrenewable fossil water that was accumulated thousands of years ago, especially during the pluvial periods of the Pleistocene. Other aquifers receive short-term recharge, even in areas receiving only minimal precipitation. Modern technology, in the form of ever-deeper wells and (subsidized) powerful pumps, permitted such an overuse of these limited water supplies that critical shortages have developed, and without sizable investments in desalination facilities, current living conditions in some Middle East countries will become unsustainable within two or three decades.

In the central Arabian Peninsula, outcropping sedimentary strata of the Arabian Shelf contain aquifers that are recharged by the low annual rainfall in Najd and then carry the water at increasing depths underground very slowly eastward toward the Gulf coast. Some of this water emerges in artesian springs in Hofuf, Qatif, and Bahrain, as well as from the Gulf bottom near Bahrain; some is pumped from wells drilled in the recharge area itself.

Enormous amounts of fossil water in the Cretaceous Wasia and Biyadh aquifers are being heavily exploited, although recently in decreasing amounts, in central Saudi Arabia. About four-fifths of this nonrenewable resource has been depleted by the early 2010s.[10] In the Western Desert of Egypt, the widespread Nubian sandstone, which overlies the Nubian Shield, also contains huge amounts of fossil water that is being increasingly exploited. Some of this water emerges in the five oases of the area. Groundwater also plays a vital role in the water supplies of Mount Lebanon, western Jordan, the coastal plain of Israel, and, indeed, every country of the Middle East, as will be discussed in later chapters.

Thus, the significance of the patterns of physical features goes far beyond that of the landforms as such. Great importance attaches to the features' influence on and interaction with other patterns, cultural and biophysical. Topography has always influenced and will always influence where people cultivate their fields, build their settlements, align their transportation routes, construct their ports, fight their battles, and conduct their other activities. Similarly, landforms have interacted with climate, soils, and vegetation to create the infinitely varied natural environment. Above all, the utilization of water has been and is the single most critical aspect of the human experience in the Middle East. Economic and political aspects of the water problem are discussed further in Chapter 8.

Along with geomorphology, climate and its major effects play an important part in Middle East culture and regional developments.

THE SKIES AND THE WINDS: CLIMATE

Climate in its interaction with other biophysical elements has as much direct and indirect impact on people and their activities as any geographic factor. It affects the preferred places for human habitation, the clothes people wear, the design of their houses, the vigor of their outdoor labor, the need for energy to cool or heat their homes, where their various crops grow best, and many of their daily activities. Temperature, precipitation, and winds, for example, influence other natural elements in the landscape—vegetation especially but also soils, landforms, and animal life. In turn, temperature and precipitation types and amounts are influenced by elevation and mountain barriers.

Factors of Middle East Climate

Climate is the long-term average of day-to-day weather conditions and may be thought of as "statistical weather." Six basic factors control climates everywhere: latitude, seasonal pressure belts, passing pressure systems, land-water relationships, ocean currents, and landforms.[11] All of these except ocean currents, which are not of major importance in this area, are examined below in their Middle East context.

Latitude. The latitudinal location of a place has two critical direct influences that in turn exercise major indirect influences. First, it determines at what angle the rays of the sun strike the earth and thus the amount of insolation, or solar radiation, a place receives; and second, as the vertical rays of the sun shift latitudinally with the seasons, belts of atmospheric pressure and winds shift accordingly. Located between 13° and 42° N Lat, the Middle East lies in the lower to middle latitudes. The 35th parallel may be used as a rough dividing line between the more humid northern areas of the Middle East and the more arid southern three-fourths, with the Levant coast and other highland areas forming exceptions to this division.

Seasonal Pressure Belts. Atmospheric pressure, whether in a belt or in a cell, influences whether air is descending or rising and determines the strength, direction, duration, and other characteristics of winds in a given area.

Figure 2.8 Giant sand dunes in vast dune field of al-Liwa in southwestern Abu Dhabi, UAE, indicating the extreme desert conditions of the lower Gulf region. Although surficially useless even for nomadic herding, the area has subsurface structures that contain huge petroleum and natural gas reservoirs.

In general, two main pressure belts affect Middle East weather conditions.

First, most of the arid southern zone of the Middle East south of the 35th parallel lies much of the year under a subtropical high-pressure belt, a discontinuous east-west zone in which descending dry air heats adiabatically (by compression) and desiccates. The belt itself is marked by calms; however, once the subsiding air reaches the surface, it pours outward both northward and southward. The airflow toward the pole joins the belt of the westerlies, and the flow toward the equator veers counterclockwise to become the northeast trade winds. The dry high pressure and the dry northeast trades produce a desert belt that extends from the Atlantic Ocean eastward across North Africa, including the great Sahara (Arabic *sahra* = desert), then across Arabia and Iran to merge with the interior midlatitude deserts of Central Asia (Fig. 2.8; see also Fig. 2.1).

Second, the more humid areas north of 35°, extending from the Aegean and Mediterranean to northern Iran, are primarily a zone of transition between pressure belts and generally have a typical Mediterranean climate. In this climate type, conditions alternate between hot, dry summers and cool or cold, relatively moist, winters. In summer, this zone lies under dry continental trade winds or descending hot, dry air, a seasonal extension of the full desert conditions farther south. In winter, this same zone lies under a belt of stormy westerlies and passing atmospheric depressions that migrates southward during the low-sun season.

Monsoons. An added contrast between winter and summer conditions in the southernmost Middle East results from the seasonal reversal of the great Asian pressure systems and the monsoons (Arabic *mawsim*

= seasons). Extending across the extreme southern Arabian Peninsula, the Intertropical Convergence Zone (ITCZ) breeds critical late-spring and early-fall precipitation in Asir and Yemen in the southwestern part of the peninsula and in Dhufar in southern Oman in the southeast. More discussion is given to this phenomenon in the "Precipitation" section below.

Passing Pressure Systems. Passing low-pressure systems—depressions, or "lows"—are the winter weather makers for the northern and central parts of the Middle East. Cyclonic depressions periodically move from west to east, following several regular tracks across the northern third of the Middle East.

These precipitation producers pass near Cyprus and continue across Lebanon, Syria, and Iraq into Iran, although one track goes north of Asia Minor through the Black Sea. Less frequently, low-pressure systems cross Israel and Jordan and veer southeastward into the Arabian Peninsula. In most of the region, these weather makers bring the winter precipitation that is characteristic of the Mediterranean climate.

Land-Water Relationships. The land-water patterns in the region are major influences on climatic conditions in the region. Since the sea is the ultimate source of all moisture, the presence of water bodies, especially on the windward side, increases the potential for precipitation and humidity. Large bodies of water also moderate the temperature of the air above them, warming onshore winds in winter and cooling them in summer in a heat exchange. This phenomenon influences the coastal rims of all five Middle East seas, but it especially affects the more northern areas, along the Black Sea and Caspian coasts and along the eastern Mediterranean shores.

Landforms. Topography influences every aspect of climate. Highlands such as the Anatolian Plateau divert passing storms to the north or south, influencing the storm tracks and other climatic elements. Highland areas enjoy temperatures lower than those of adjacent plains, and many favored mountain areas in the Middle East become bustling resort centers during the hot summers, like those in Lebanon.

Highlands may also produce orographic (mountain-induced) precipitation from moisture-laden winds. Mount Lebanon is a classic example: Moist westerly winds from the Mediterranean hit the windward slopes of the north-south mountain range behind Tripoli, Beirut, and Sidon. As they move upslope, they rapidly cool adiabatically at 5.5°F/3.1°C for each 1,000 ft/305 m, reach cloud stage and then dew point as they lose capacity to hold moisture, and precipitate rain at middle elevations and snow on the upper slopes (Fig. 2.9). Similar orographic influences operate on the windward slopes north and south of Mount Lebanon, as well as in the Anatolian, Zagros, Elburz, and Yemen Mountains. Areas on the leeward side of mountain chains, by contrast, tend to be drier, or even arid in the rain shadow.

Elements of Middle East Climate

The climate factors just reviewed combine to produce various climate characteristics, such as temperature, winds, precipitation, humidity, and evaporation, which in turn produce certain climate types in specific areas: deserts, steppes, and humid temperate zones. Temperature and precipitation patterns are shown in two maps (2.4 and 2.5), and data for those same elements at selected stations are listed in Table 2.1. The table also gives elevation, latitude and longitude, and climate type for each of the stations; the distributional patterns of the climate types are given in Map 2.6.

Temperature. The hallmarks of Middle East climate are without question heat and aridity. Thus, temperature is the premier element in

Figure 2.9 Dahr al-Baydar, pass in central Mount Lebanon, with its typical heavy winter snow cover. Moist winds blowing off the Mediterranean ascend the steep west-facing slopes and, during January to March, drop several feet of snow at upper elevations. Apple orchards are on the terraces in the foreground. Jabal Baruk is in the distance, with one of the remaining groves of Cedars of Lebanon.

this survey of the regional climate. Markedly high temperatures prevail more than half of the year in most of the lowland areas of the Middle East, especially interior areas or those subject to airflow from the interior (Map 2.4A). Although July and August are the hottest months, the period from April through October is warm to hot in most of the region. Afternoon temperatures of 100°F/38°C are registered in the middle Nile Valley and in the interior of Arabia by early March, and such temperatures may continue well into November. Daily averages of more than 90°F/32°C for the hottest months are common for extensive areas of Iraq (95°F/35°C for July in Baghdad), Iran, and especially the Arabian Peninsula. The cloudless summer skies, typical of desert and Mediterranean climate conditions, add to elevated daytime temperatures. However, in data for desert stations, the averages mask the extremes of temperature.

Beating the Heat.   Before air-conditioning became common in the region, many older homes in the region included an underground room (in Iraq, a *sirdab*) where the family sought relief from the heat. In the hotter areas, especially along the humid coasts, summer nights bring little respite from the heat of day, either because of a small diurnal range of temperature (difference between day and night), because of high humidity, or both. Many village families and city dwellers slept on the typical flat roof of the home to escape the interior heat, and many still commonly do so in lower-income households. By contrast, at considerable elevations or in open deserts, summer nights can be cool or even chilly (Map 2.4B). The temperature of

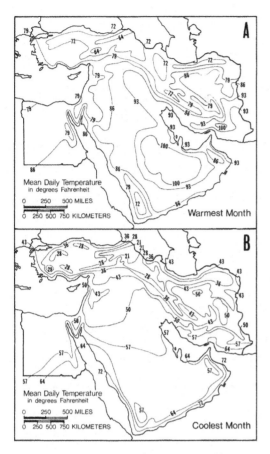

Mean Daily Temperature
in degrees Fahrenheit

0   250   500 MILES

0 250 500 750 KILOMETERS

Warmest Month

Mean Daily Temperature
in degrees Fahrenheit

0   250   500 MILES

0 250 500 750 KILOMETERS

Coolest Month

Map 2.4 Temperatures for warmest and coolest months.

25°F/14°C cooler than that at Dhahran, near sea level in Saudi Arabia.

The degree of contrast between summer and winter temperatures depends primarily on latitude, interior location, and elevation. Samsun, on Turkey's northern coast, and Ankara, 115 mi/185 km inland, have the same August mean temperature, but Samsun's January mean is 12°F/7°C higher than Ankara's because of the warming effect of the Black Sea. The uplands of Anatolia and Iran, with higher elevations and more northerly and continental influences, register the coldest winters of the Middle East. These cold conditions are reflected in the data for Erzurum in eastern Anatolia and for Tabriz in northwestern Iran (Table 2.1).

Climate Change. Some predictive models have indicated that climate change will affect the Middle East by increasing extremes, and the drought conditions of recent years may become even more common throughout the eastern Mediterranean. Rising sea levels could negatively impact areas like the Nile Delta and locations around the Gulf. More discussion of this subject can be found in Chapter 4 ("Patterns: Climate Change").

some interior locations is moderated by elevation, allowing the day's heat to radiate back into the cloudless sky and dry air at night, dropping the predawn minimum temperatures as much as 35–40°F/20–22°C.

Several resorts in the mountains behind Beirut and in similar climate areas in the mountains of Syria, Turkey, and Iran offer temperature relief, especially in the evenings, and have become prosperous summer resorts not only for local lowlanders but also for visitors from the Gulf states, Saudi Arabia, and elsewhere. Cities on the Anatolian and Iranian Plateaus combine characteristics of dry highland summers, and thus clear nights, with the effects of a more northerly latitude. For example, the highest mean at Ankara is

Precipitation. The crucial importance of temperature in the Middle East is matched by the significance of precipitation, shown clearly by the correlation between the pattern of heavier precipitation, or its runoff, and concentrations of population (compare Map 2.5 and maps of population in Chap. 4). Water plays a vital role even in those regions of the world in which it is plentiful, but its role in the Middle East, where water supplies are marginal in so much of the region, is critical. Water is life.

Little Rain. High seasonal temperatures in much of the region typically accompany low precipitation, making "dryness" the key word for the climate in most of this region. At the

TABLE 2.1 Selected Middle East Temperatures and Precipitation (°C and mm)

CLIMATE STATION		JAN	FEB	MAR	APR	MAY	JNE	JLY	AUG	SPT	OCT	NOV	DEC	ANNUAL
Istanbul, Turkey 40°58'N/29°05'E	40 m Csa	6 94	6 71	8 58	12 43	17 30	21 23	23 18	23 15	21 28	16 54	11 89	8 102	14°C 625 mm
Izmir, Turkey 38°26'N/27°10'E	25 m Csa	9 141	9 100	11 72	15 43	20 39	25 8	28 3	27 3	23 11	18 41	14 93	10 141	17°C 695 mm
Ankara, Turkey 30°57'N/32°53'E	894 m Csa	0 37	1 36	5 36	11 37	16 49	20 30	23 14	23 9	18 17	13 24	7 30	2 43	12°C 362 mm
Rize, Turkey 41°02'N/40°30'E	4 m Cfa	7 259	7 215	8 187	11 97	16 97	20 131	22 150	23 211	20 270	16 299	12 278	9 246	14°C 2440 mm
Erzurum, Turkey 39°55'N/41°16'E	1863 m Dfb	-11 25	-9 28	-3 35	5 54	10 73	14 54	18 28	18 18	13 25	7 48	0 35	-7 22	5°C 445 mm
Anzali, Iran 37°28'N/49°28'E	-15 m Cfa	8 133	8 125	9 111	13 75	19 56	22 57	26 45	25 131	23 298	18 326	14 227	10 173	16°C 1757 mm
Tabriz, Iran 38°08'N/46°15'E	1362 m BSh	-3 28	-1 28	5 61	12 61	17 46	22 20	27 3	26 5	22 10	15 36	7 25	1 33	13°C 356 mm
Esfahan, Iran 32°37'N/51°40'E	1598 m BWh	4 19	6 16	10 18	16 16	20 8	25 1	28 5	26 1	23 0	16 3	9 19	4 20	16°C 126 mm
Tehran, Iran 35°37'N/51°40'E	1519 m BSh	2 43	5 38	10 38	17 33	22 15	28 3	31 3	29 3	26 3	19 10	12 25	6 30	17°C 244 mm
Zahedan, Iran 29°28'N/60°53'E	1370 m BWh	6 30	12 24	15 14	19 16	23 7	27 0	28 0	26 0	22 0	18 0	12 13	7 9	18°C 113 mm
Nicosia, Cyprus 35°09'N/33°17'E	217 m Csa	11 74	11 43	12 37	17 17	21 21	26 9	28 1	28 2	25 7	21 21	16 32	12 75	19°C 339 mm
Aleppo, Syria 36°11'N/37°13'E	392 m Csa	6 63	7 46	10 36	16 35	21 14	25 4	28 0	29 2	24 0	19 18	12 27	8 74	17°C 319 mm
Damascus, Syria 33°29'N/36°14'E	729 m Csa	8 38	9 33	12 23	17 13	21 5	25 0	27 0	28 0	24 0	21 10	14 25	9 43	18°C 190 mm
Dayr al-Zawr, Syria 35°20'N/40°09'E	203 m BSh	8 35	10 33	13 32	19 20	24 7	30 2	32 0	32 0	28 0	21 3	14 12	8 33	20°C 177 mm
Beirut, Lebanon 33°47'N/35°29'E	16 m Csa	14 113	14 80	15 77	18 26	21 10	24 1	26 0	27 0	26 7	23 20	19 78	16 105	20°C 517 mm
Bhamdun, Lebanon 33°46'N/35°39'E	1130 m Csa	7 302	7 262	9 194	13 95	17 40	20 1	22 1	22 1	19 3	17 54	13 132	9 239	15°C 1324 mm
Jerusalem 31°47'N/35°13'E	810 m Csa	9 128	10 106	12 85	16 17	20 4	22 0	23 0	24 0	22 1	20 8	15 61	11 76	17°C 486 mm

Station	Elev.	Köppen													Annual
Elat, Israel 29°33'N/34°57'E	11 m	BWh	16	18	20	24	29	32	34	34	31	27	22	17	25°C
			2	5	5	3	0	0	0	0	0	0	2	9	26 mm
Amman, Jordan 31°57'N/35°57'E	771 m	Csa	8	9	12	16	21	24	26	26	23	21	15	10	18°C
			68	59	44	13	5	0	0	0	1	4	31	48	273 mm
Mosul, Iraq 36°19'N/43°09'E	222 m	Csa	6	9	12	17	24	30	33	34	30	20	13	8	20°C
			70	67	65	55	20	1	0	0	0	7	43	62	390 mm
Baghdad, Iraq 33°20'N/44°24'E	34 m	BWh	10	12	16	22	28	33	34	35	31	25	17	11	23°C
			25	25	29	16	7	0	0	0	0	3	22	26	153 mm
Basrah, Iraq 30°34'N/47°47'E	2 m	BWh	12	14	18	24	29	32	33	34	31	26	19	14	24°C
			26	17	25	22	7	0	0	0	0	1	28	38	164 mm
Kuwait, Kuwait 29°20'N/47°57'E	11 m	BWh	14	16	20	26	31	35	37	37	33	27	21	15	26°C
			15	7	8	11	3	0	0	0	0	0	25	41	110 mm
Hayil, Saudi Arabia 27°31'N/41°44'E	914 m	BWh	12	13	17	20	25	29	31	30	28	23	19	12	22°C
			9	8	6	11	7	0	0	0	0	11	22	3	77 mm
Dhahran, Saudi Ar 26°16'N/50°10'E	25 m	BWh	17	17	22	27	32	35	37	36	34	29	24	18	27°C
			26	15	12	2	3	0	0	0	0	0	4	24	86 mm
Riyadh, Saudi Arab 24°42'N/46°43'E	609 m	BWh	14	17	21	27	32	34	36	36	33	28	22	17	26°C
			13	10	30	30	13	0	0	0	0	0	5	10	111 mm
Jiddah, Saudi Arab 21°30'N/39°12'E	12 m	BWh	23	23	24	27	30	31	31	32	30	29	27	26	28°C
			17	2	13	11	13	1	1	0	0	0	6	12	77 mm
Sharjah, UAE 25°21'N/55°23'E	2 m	BWh	18	18	22	25	28	30	31	33	34	28	24	20	26°C
			34	13	9	18	1	0	0	2	0	0	18	21	116 mm
Muscat, Oman 22°37'N/58°35'E	5 m	BWh	22	22	25	30	34	36	34	32	32	30	26	23	29°C
			28	13	10	10	1	3	1	1	3	3	10	18	99 mm
Aden, Yemen 12°50'N/45°02'E	3 m	BWh	26	26	27	29	31	33	32	32	29	31	27	26	29°C
			7	3	6	0	1	0	2	7	1	3	3	6	39 mm
Sana, Yemen 15°23'N/44°11'E	2350 m	BWh	17	18	20	21	22	24	23	24	19	20	17	16	20°C
			0	4	21	46	46	20	102	20	9	3	0	0	251 mm
Alexandria, Egypt 31°12'N/29°57'E	7 m	BSh	15	15	17	19	21	24	26	27	26	24	21	17	21°C
			44	25	11	3	1	0	0	1	0	7	30	48	172 mm
Cairo, Egypt 30°08'N/31°34'E	74 m	BWh	14	15	18	21	25	28	29	29	26	24	20	16	22°C
			5	5	3	3	0	0	0	0	0	0	3	5	24 mm
Luxor, Egypt 25°40'N/32°42'E	89 m	BWh	14	16	20	25	30	32	32	32	30	27	21	16	25°C
			0	0	0	0	0	0	0	0	0	0	0	0	0 mm

Table includes station latitude and longitude, elevation in meters, and Koeppen classification. See text for explanation of Koeppen symbols. *Original source:* Willy Rudloff, *World Climates* (Stuttgart: Wissenschaftliche Verlagsgesellschaft mbH, 1981) (except Bhamdun and Hayil) (used with permission). Twelve stations updated from National Climatic Data Center: www.ncdc.noaa.gov/oa/ncdc.html.

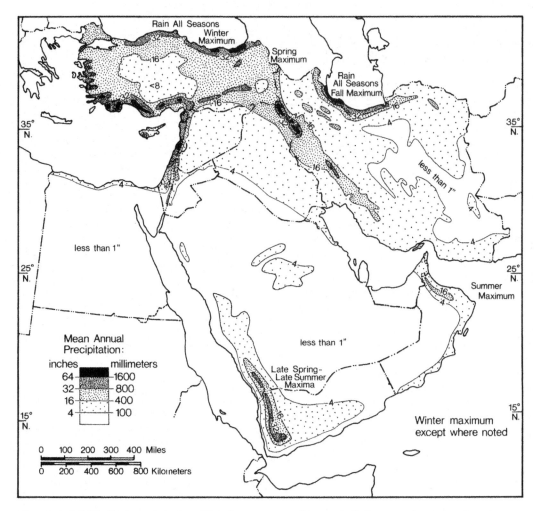

Map 2.5 Middle East precipitation. Note heavy orographic precipitation on mountains rimming Asia Minor and on other mountain ranges—Elburz, Zagros, Lebanon, Asir, and Oman.

extreme, the Rub al-Khali in the interior of the southern half of the Arabian Peninsula may see no rainfall for several successive years.

Vast arid areas of the Middle East and of the peripheral areas of the Sahara and Central Asian deserts receive only 1–5 in/25–125 mm of precipitation annually (Map 2.5). This zone of aridity lies too far south to benefit from the west-east passage of rain-bearing depressions in winter and too far north to receive monsoon rain from the ITCZ in summer. The quarter of the Middle East generally north of the 35th parallel is, however, influ-

enced by the westerlies and receives 15–40 in/380–1,015 mm of precipitation. Obviously, a rather sharp contrast exists in rainfall amounts, and thus in vegetation and agriculture, between the northern one-fourth and the southern half of the region.

Except in the southern Arabian Peninsula and in limited areas in the north, by far most of the Middle East's precipitation falls during the months October–April, which is typical of the Mediterranean climate (cf. Beirut, Jerusalem, and Mosul in Table 2.1). Annual totals generally increase with increasing latitude, elevation, and western exposure.

The limited precipitation at desert stations varies greatly from year to year, and by its very nature desert rainfall tends to be sporadic. In December 2003, an area southwest of the Dead Sea received its normal total annual rainfall amount in a single one-hour downpour. The sudden rains penetrate quickly into the porous ground in a sand desert area to produce a sudden growth of grass and flowers, which soon attract Bedouin herdsmen with their camels, sheep, or goats. In less absorptive sand areas, and with little vegetation to absorb the rain, the runoff quickly concentrates into the local wadis—dry drainage channels—and causes flash floods.

More Rain.   The mountains in the southwestern corner of Turkey demonstrate the orographic influence of west-facing slopes, receiving more than 60 in/1,525 mm of winter precipitation. The mountains of northern Lebanon receive a similar amount, much of it as heavy snows supporting several ski resorts. Atmospheric depressions reaching the southeastern corner of the Black Sea rise up mountain slopes and yield more than 90 in/2,285 mm at Rize, probably the highest total precipitation in the Middle East. Inland, 25–40 in/635–1,015 mm of precipitation, much of it as snow, falls on the upper ridges of the Zagros Mountains and the higher slopes of the eastern Anatolian Mountains. The spring and summer snowmelt in the eastern Anatolian hydrographic center supplies the runoff for the Tigris and Euphrates Rivers and other streams rising in these highlands.

Snow falls every winter in the uplands of the Middle East north of about 35° N Lat. Once or twice in most winters, it also falls as far south as the Jerusalem hill country and the Jordanian highlands. The Mesopotamian deserts receive occasional snowfalls, and it has snowed in Riyadh and—in 1987, for the first time in memory or records—even in the Buraymi Oasis on the United Arab Emirates–Oman border.

The seasonal reversal of monsoon winds gives the southern fringe of the Arabian Peninsula a distinctive climate regime, especially regarding precipitation. The rugged Yemen Mountains and their extension into the Asir of Saudi Arabia intercept moisture-laden southwest monsoon winds between April and September, producing 20–40 in/500–1,000 mm of orographic rain on west-facing slopes. These monsoon rains come twice a year: first, during the migration of the convergence belt northward in late April–early May, and then again during its shift southward in August (see Sana, Table 2.1). This relatively abundant rainfall earned the area its ancient designation Arabia Felix (Fortunate Arabia). The coastal area of Dhufar in southern Oman also has an unusual regime, with the lingering of the ITCZ during the summer months creating a local cool, cloudy, misty summer that attracts thousands of visitors seeking relief from the heat of the Muscat area and elsewhere. The Oman Mountains similarly receive light rain from these summer conditions.

Winds.   Wind is both a factor and an element in climate. As it transfers large amounts of air from one place to another, wind influences temperature, humidity and precipitation, evaporation, and bodily responses in both people and animals. Higher-velocity winds create or reduce sand dunes by shifting large amounts of sand; also, by using sand and other rock particles as tools, they are major agents in desert erosion. On Middle East waterways, mariners have depended upon the steady winds for centuries. The influence of wind on precipitation is of particular significance.

The ITCZ equatorial low-pressure belt, displaced northward and intensified in its May–August persistence over the Indian subcontinent, controls winds over the entire Middle East for more than four months during the summer. So strong are these southwest

Figure 2.10 Persian wind towers (*badgirs*), center, in a historic preservation area of Dubai City, surrounded by modern structures. With air-conditioning now virtually universal in this cheap energy region, only a few preserved *badgirs* remain of the thousands formerly common around the Gulf.

monsoon winds that they pull the surface waters away from the south shore of the Arabian Peninsula, causing an upwelling of cool water from the deeps next to the coast and enhancing fishing conditions. Middle East sailors have followed the summer winds eastward to the Indian subcontinent for millennia.

Well to the north of the low-pressure belt, air circulation pulls in the northeast trade winds toward the ITCZ. Blowing on clear, cloudless summer days, these strong northerly winds in the Aegean and the Mediterranean are useful to sailors when moderate, but hazardous when their velocity is higher.

Using the Wind. These prevailing winds continue over the low relief of Egypt as normal northeast trade winds and blow steadily through the Nile Valley for most of the year. They are of great value to Egypt, since they fill the sails of river craft sailing upstream against the current, which then furl their sails and drift downstream for the return trip. On the other side of the Arabian Peninsula, blowing down the Mesopotamian trough and the Gulf basin, is the early summer *shamal* (Arabic for "north"). This dry wind blows at 25–30 mph/40–50 kph in June and early July, bringing frequent dust storms from Mesopotamia before moderating to 15–20 mph/25–32 kph in late summer. At higher velocities, the *shamal* poses hazards to small sailing dhows and even to huge oil tankers loading at Gulf terminals. Wind-borne dust is common in all seasons, primarily in the most barren desert areas, which have a minimal vegetative cover to hold the loose surface particles. Seasonal winds, temperatures, and precipitation are often significant factors in military planning in the region.

Humidity. Humidity in the Middle East has three main characteristics. First, generally low humidity characterizes deserts and higher elevations. The low humidity in Egypt has preserved human and animal mummies and delicate inlaid wood for more than four thousand years. In interior deserts, relative humidity for the three summer months can average between 12 and 18 percent, falling to 5 percent and occasionally even to an extreme 3 percent. Accompanied by high temperatures and brisk winds, as is usual, such low humidity parches the skin and scorches vegetation.

Second, humidity along the coasts, even in arid areas, tends to be quite high in summer, causing an uncomfortable combination of heat and humidity. Cities on the Levant coast of the Mediterranean, on the Caspian and Red Sea coasts, and all around the Gulf are very humid during August and early September, with average readings of 70–75 percent. Third, humidity is moderate and exercises no remarkable effects in much of Asia Minor, which has percentages within a moderate range.

Evaporation. Evaporation plays a key role in determining aridity but is difficult to measure precisely. If the mean annual water loss exceeds the mean annual precipitation, conditions tend toward aridity. Measurements of evaporation in the central Arabian Peninsula show rates ranging from thirty-five to one hundred times the local mean annual rainfall. Actual evaporation in al-Sulayyil, in the southern Najd, for example, averages 207 in/ 5,250 mm annually,[12] more than one hundred times the mean annual rainfall. Similar conditions exist in southern Egypt—where evaporation from Lake Nasser is a major problem—and southern Iran. However, other influences—season of precipitation, temperature, soil conditions—can be of major importance and can affect the ecology. Other factors being equal, natural vegetation is indicative of aridity and, indirectly, of evaporation.

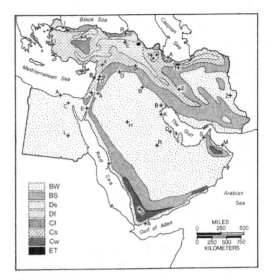

Map 2.6 Climate types according to modified Koeppen system. BW = desert; BS = steppe. Initials indicate climate stations listed in Table 2.1. See text for explanation of other symbols.

OTHER ENVIRONMENTAL ASPECTS

Soils and Their Ecological Relationships

Elements of the environment exert complex reciprocal effects, and their interactions with human activities constitute a fundamental dynamic in the geographic system. It follows that a change in any one element in the ecosystem generates a change in the system as a whole.

A soil is the product of several environmental factors: parent material, climate, vegetation, fauna (especially humans), relief, and time. Comparing this chapter's maps reveals a pattern among the factors that influence the general character of soils in the Middle East. For example, predominant aridity and heat are two of the strongest general influences on the soils of the vast area from Morocco to Pakistan, excluding Asia Minor and the Levant. Limited vegetation cover in this same general area, also largely a consequence of aridity, deprives soils of humus. Extensive rock outcroppings, as well as loose sand, also profoundly affect soil characteristics. Mountain soils are especially influenced by relief, specifically the slope on which they develop. Proper management is important for all soils, and one characteristic that is amenable to management is soil salinity, a serious problem especially in southern Mesopotamia but also in most desert areas where crops are irrigated on poorly drained land.

Deserts: No True Soils.   Large desert areas are totally lacking in true soils—widespread expanses of sand and virtually bare rock are obvious examples. The surface materials in much of the region have not developed a mature soil "profile," a cross section that reveals identifying horizons (the vertical sequence of colors and textures that differentiate soils). Lack of a mature soil profile results from several ecological conditions, including extreme aridity. In arid areas, there is no soil water to move downward and leach chemicals and other materials into the lower horizons of the soil profile.

With little or no organic matter on the surface or in the upper horizon of soils, especially those of desert areas, soils of light color predominate in the region. Light color likewise prevails in soils that have an accumulation of salt near the surface. In moderate amounts, both salt and gypsum reduce soil productivity, and in large quantities they render soils unfit for cultivation.

Thus, agriculture in desert areas is limited not only directly by aridity but also indirectly by the effects of aridity on soil development. There are, nevertheless, exceptionally productive soils in certain desert areas—in numerous oases, the Nile Valley and Delta, and the floodplains of the Tigris and Euphrates Rivers, for example (Map 2.7).

Mature Soils.   The coastal plains, plateaus, and rolling lands of the northern and northwestern areas of the Middle East boast soils that have reached mature development be-cause of humid, temperate conditions. In Asia Minor, western Iran, and the Fertile Crescent, where annual precipitation exceeds 10 in/255 mm and averages perhaps 25 in/635 mm, there are extensive areas of well-developed and productive soils. These regions exhibit greater varieties of soil groups as well as greater variations within the groups.

Middle East Soil Patterns

The systematic classification and nomenclature of soils—soil taxonomy—has presented problems ever since the burgeoning of soil science. Rather than introducing technical detail that is confusing to the nonspecialist, the following discussion utilizes a simpler and more familiar taxonomy based on the traditional ecological-genetic concept.

Barren Sands and Rock, Other Nonsoils. Generally speaking, the area of barren land and desert soils in the Middle East lies south of the 35th parallel—that is, southward from the 10-in/250-mm rainfall line (see Map 2.5). Approximately half of the area extending from western Egypt across the Arabian Peninsula and the Syrian Desert to eastern Iran is so barren that it lacks either true soil or appreciable vegetation cover on its virtually bare rock or its gravel, loose sand, and dune sand (see Figs. 1.1 and 2.11). Prominent sand areas include western Egypt and, on the Arabian Peninsula, the Great Nafud in the north and the enormous Rub al-Khali in the south, with the arc of Dahna sands connecting the two. Huge gravel plains lacking true soils extend across the north of the Arabian Peninsula and appear in extensive tracts in the eastern third of the peninsula.

Large areas of Lithosols (rock soils) extend along the east side of the Levant Rift System–Red Sea rift on the basaltic lava outpourings. A particularly common type of landscape in this area is the *hamadah,* typically an extensive plain with barren rock or a surface cover of stones (see Fig. 2.3). Actual soil development

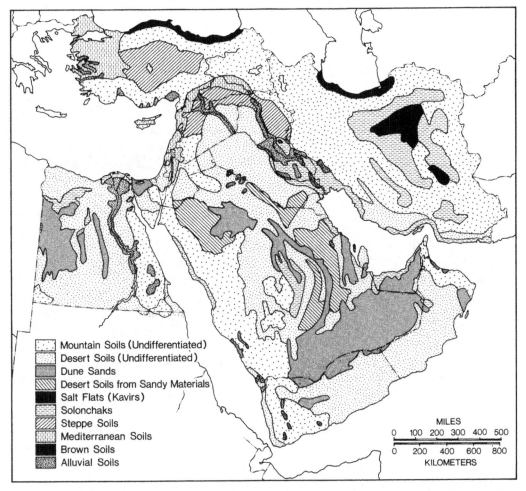

Legend:
- Mountain Soils (Undifferentiated)
- Desert Soils (Undifferentiated)
- Dune Sands
- Desert Soils from Sandy Materials
- Salt Flats (Kavirs)
- Solonchaks
- Steppe Soils
- Mediterranean Soils
- Brown Soils
- Alluvial Soils

MILES
0 100 200 300 400 500

0 200 400 600 800
KILOMETERS

Map 2.7 Middle East soils. (Adapted from several sources, especially United Nations Educational, Scientific, and Cultural Organization [UNESCO], "Soil Map of the World")

is limited, and vegetal cover is generally lacking. Even larger areas of Lithosols extend over the limestones of eastern Syria and Jordan, of Iraq west of the Euphrates, and along the axis of the north-south escarpments in central Arabia. Soils of the Lithosol group are also intermixed with varied Mountain soils in all the mountainous areas and are grouped with Undifferentiated Mountain soils on Map 2.7.

True Soils in the Desert. The other half of the desert areas referred to above contains true soils with developed profiles and vegetation cover. Some profiles are weakly devel-

oped, and some of the vegetation is thin and scattered, but the landscape is less barren than the desert areas of Egypt, the Nafud, and the Rub al-Khali.

Desert soils are light gray or light brownish gray, are low in organic matter, and closely overlie calcareous (calcium-containing) material, typically limestone. They normally support scattered shrubby desert plants but can be quite productive when irrigated. The Red Desert soils are similar and tend to develop in the hotter parts of the deserts. Sierozems are more widely scattered but are found in two large areas: on the

Figure 2.11 Vegetation and soils, eastern Arabia. These *adher* and *rimth* bushes grow on compact, sandy soils southwest of Dhahran. Animal tracks indicate grazing of the vegetation by desert animals.

floor of the great central basin of Turkey around Tuz Gölü and in much of northern Syria, where they support scattered short grass and brush as well as desert shrubs.

Solonchak soils are especially found in large interior undrained basins and low-lying areas: the Dasht-e Lut and the even saltier Dasht-e Kavir (Salt Desert) on the Iranian Plateau, the Qattara Depression in northwestern Egypt, southern Mesopotamia back from the river floodplains, in the tidal flats (*sabkhahs*) along low coastlines on both sides of the Arabian Peninsula, and over the inland coastal plain of the Gulf (Fig. 2.12; see also Map 2.7). Because of either interior drainage or periodic tides, all these areas have high saltwater tables that supply salty water to the surface; evaporation of this water forms the typical salt crust of Solonchaks. Most Solonchaks are useless for agriculture, but some can be made reasonably productive by artificially flushing the salt with fresh water and then ap-

plying proper fertilization. One area of special interest suffering seriously from salt accumulation in otherwise irrigable and cultivable soils is southern Iraq.

Alluvial Soils. Alluvial soils—or, more properly, soils on alluvium as a parent material—are among the most intensively cultivated and productive in the world, certainly in the Middle East. They include the limited but rich soils of the Nile Valley and Delta, floodplains of the Tigris and Euphrates Rivers, valleys of west-central Iran, and small scattered oases and larger wadi bottoms of the Arabian Peninsula. They possess young profiles, are usually of good texture and tillability, and display most of the other characteristics of an ideal agricultural soil. Most fortunately, water for irrigating the soils is typically nearby.

Soils of Humid Areas. Except for the irrigated alluvial soils, most of the cultivated and

Figure 2.12 Sabkhat Matti, a typical *sabkhah* (tidal salt flat). With a white crust of silty salt, such flats are inviting to vehicles and aircraft, but using them can be risky, especially after a rain. The soil on the *sabkhah* is a Solonchak, as the salt crust suggests.

agriculturally productive soils of the Middle East are in Asia Minor, the Fertile Crescent proper, and western Iran. On the inner, less humid side of the curve of the Fertile Crescent, there is an irregular belt of grassland soils that have developed in a zone receiving 6–10 in/150–250 mm of annual precipitation. Such soils vary from well developed and deep to poorly developed and thin on hillsides. Most are calcareous, especially since many overlie the widespread limestones of Jordan, Syria, southeastern Turkey, and Iraq, where they receive sufficient precipitation to permit grain farming without irrigation.

In a major portion of the Mediterranean climate areas, a particular group of soils develops because of the regime of cool, wet winters and hot, dry summers. Usually called Mediterranean soils (as on Map 2.7), they are reddish-brown because of their iron content, and are referred to as *terra rossa* (red earth). This soil contrasts dramatically with the white limestone hills of southern Turkey and the Levant.

Although badly eroded on limestone slopes in many areas, *terra rossa* has been productive for thousands of years throughout the Mediterranean Basin, influencing the pattern and character of human activity.

Most of the remaining soil pattern is a complex one, forming a mosaic of soils of Anatolia, northwestern Iran, and the mountains behind the eastern Mediterranean coast. These soil associations produce a great variety of foods, fodder, and industrial crops, including timber forests and tree crops of nuts and fruits, on moderate slopes in the better climate areas.

Vegetation

As a product of interacting influences on landscape, the natural vegetation of an area is often an effective indicator of the general character of the local ecosystem. Like the region's topography and soils, Middle East vegetation has undergone natural changes during recent geological times. Certain plants are survivals

Figure 2.13 Cultivated Reddish-Chestnut steppe soils in the western Fertile Crescent south of Aleppo, Syria. This is productive wheat country. Archaeological excavations in the foreground are of ancient Ebla.

from earlier periods; other plants from those periods have completely disappeared, from either natural or human causes, and their former presence is indicated only by seeds, spores, fruits, or leaves in old lakebeds or in archaeological mounds (tells).

Human activities, including agriculture, have especially altered vegetation as well as other aspects of the environment in the millennia since the Agricultural Revolution. Unfortunately, the human impact on natural vegetation in the Middle East has been one of destruction as well as change. People have cleared forests not only to gain land for agricultural purposes but also in search of timber and fuel. Cedars of Lebanon and other trees of the Levant and Anatolia supplied timbers for ships of several ancient peoples, from the Phoenicians and Egyptians to the Ottomans. Wood has also been used in the Middle East for making charcoal, long used in heating and cooking and in lime and pottery kilns. Not only trees but also grasses, shrubs, and

other low vegetation have been degraded or destroyed because of human activity and because of overgrazing by sheep and goats.

Middle East Vegetation Patterns

Varied vegetation types extend from the dense high forests inland from the Black Sea and Caspian coasts to the scattered desert shrub of the Arabian Peninsula and the barren, salty *kavirs* of the interior Iranian Plateau (Map 2.8). Notwithstanding extensive forests in several northern mountain areas, the vegetal formations occupying the greatest expanses of the region are annual grasses and broadleaf annuals and shrubs of the steppes and deserts. Rather specialized scrub forms known as maquis and garigue are typical of the Mediterranean areas with their cool, wet winters and hot, rainless summers (Fig. 2.14).

The phytogeographical (*phyto* = plant) patterns examined here are primarily the plant associations, inferred from existing

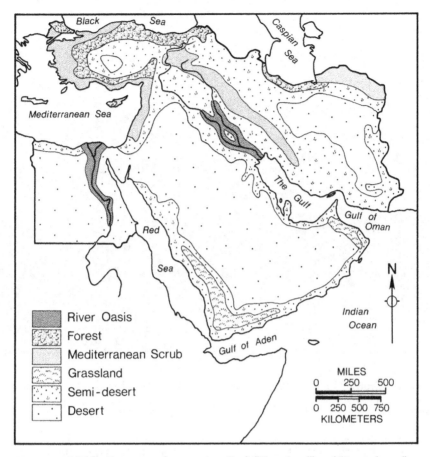

Map 2.8 Middle East natural vegetation. Both "Grassland" and "Semi-desert" may be roughly equivalent to steppe.

vegetation in noncultivated areas, that would exist without human interference.[13]

Desert Shrubs. The true desert is the product of aridity, and its xerophytic (dry plant) vegetation gives the desert its true expression. This environment supplies plants with favorable warmth and light but then imposes unfavorable moisture conditions. Some plants tolerate drought, some resist it, and some avoid it. When water occasionally does become available, plants respond immediately and profusely.

Areas that are barren of vegetation generally match the areas of barren sands, rock, and salt surfaces on the soil map (Map 2.7), as well as the areas that receive less than 1 in/25 mm of annual rainfall. Even so, the Rub al-Khali has areas that have surprisingly well-developed vegetation. Deserts that are truly barren of vegetation are less common than is often supposed, and the typical desert exhibits at least a scattering of especially equipped dry bush or shrub (see Fig. 2.11).

Beginning with its small size—3–5 ft/ 1–1.5 m—and the wide spacing among individual plants to accommodate the limited supply of moisture, xerophytic vegetation has an impressive array of survival devices. With low shoot-to-root ratios, some shrubs have root systems that extend to depths of 30–50 ft/ 9–15 m. Their leaves are small, are often coated

Figure 2.14 Typical Mediterranean flora on south-facing slopes of the Taurus Mountains of southern Turkey. Growing in limestone-derived soil in this summer-dry climate, the taller vegetative association is maquis; the lower is garigue. The road at lower left fringes the Mediterranean shore.

against excess transpiration (moisture loss), and in some species curl or even drop during unusually dry periods. Tough stems resist drought, and the shrubs often have thorns for protection against grazing animals. Some of the lower bushes, 6–18 in/15–46 cm high, have woody or wiry stems and tiny leaves but a deep root system. By contrast, other desert plants, such as *Euphorbia,* store water in expandable succulent parts.

Other low vegetal forms (4–12 in/10–30 cm) sometimes constitute more than two-thirds of the typical desert plant community—some perennial, some annual, and a few both, depending upon their ecology. After an ephemeral life cycle of six to ten weeks, most lie dormant as seeds that burst into sprouts with the next rain, sometimes several years later. Demonstrating a very different survival mode, they "avoid" the dry season instead of trying to endure it.

Shrubs in extensive fields of eolian (wind-blown) sand may be passive sand dwellers or sand binders; the latter hold the sand around extensive root systems and thus build prominent phytogenic (plant-created) mounds or hillocks. Some salty soils support halophytic (salt plant) vegetation. Over much of the eastern Arabian Peninsula, a common salt-bush popularly called *rimth*—useful for fodder and dietary salt for camels and other animals—is usually associated with at least slightly salty groundwater in poorly drained areas (see Fig. 2.11). However, on the true *sabkhahs* along the eastern Arabian Peninsula coast and on the *kavirs* of interior Iran, with their salt crust and briny subsurface, not even the most salt-tolerant plants can survive (see Fig. 2.12).[14]

The acacia, one of the largest desert shrubs, grades into a modest tree—up to 20 ft/6 m—in moister soils. With its characteristic umbrella crown, it is a prominent and readily identifiable vegetative form in the silts, sands, and gravels in drainage channels or sheets from the central to the southern Arabian Peninsula. Often where no other shade is available from the broiling sun, the acacia offers welcome relief to animals and people.

Grasslands (Steppes). Like most other boundaries in nature, the change from desert to grassland is actually a zone of transition. As moisture increases away from the desert, the more xerophytic species increasingly yield to plants adapted to the greater precipitation and better-developed soils. More important, plant population density increases until the grasses form a virtually continuous vegetal cover.

The steppes constitute a discontinuous belt extending from the Sinai Peninsula northward through western Jordan and Syria, across southeastern Turkey and northern Syria, in an arc around northern Iraq, and along the Zagros piedmont. Some of the region's most extensive steppes are in central Anatolia and smaller areas in scattered locations in west-central Iran. (Steppe and semidesert are much the same in many areas.) With their short-grass vegetation, the steppe lands are thus the historically and agriculturally significant core of the Fertile Crescent.

Mediterranean Zone. Whereas desert and steppe plants are especially equipped to survive a drought that lasts even many years, Mediterranean floras survive the characteristic summer drought of two to six months and then take advantage of the winter rain. The typical denser flora appears as a low evergreen forest with scattered small trees and more closely spaced bushes and scrub. The height of the plants and the density of their growth increase from the dry side, where the vegetation zone is similar to the wooded steppe, to the more humid part of the habitat with its shorter summer drought, where the zone

grades into the full forest of the highlands across the northern sector of the Middle East (see Fig. 2.14). In between is the typical Mediterranean garigue (lower and more limited) and maquis (taller and better developed). Some plant geographers also distinguish a third category of Mediterranean vegetation, *batha,* a kind of subgarigue. Commonly found on steeper, uncultivated hillsides in the Levant and in western and southern Asia Minor, garigue is a last safeguard against soil erosion. Maquis, which is typical of more favorable habitats than is garigue, forms a woodland dominated by low sclerophyllous evergreen trees and shrubs up to about 12 ft/ 3.7 m in height. In better maquis stands are trees—oaks, pistachios, and pines, especially the widespread Aleppo pine. Culinary herbs, such as thyme, marjoram, and laurel, and flowering bushes, such as oleanders, are associated with both garigue and maquis.

Forests. Although few areas in the Middle East now have well-developed woodlands, historical evidence indicates that twenty-five hundred to three thousand years ago, forests clothed slopes that are now almost bare— forests such as the Cedars of Lebanon or the forests of Asia Minor. Current reforestation and afforestation programs in several Middle East states are demonstrating that many previously treeless habitats can, given proper care, produce impressive forests of selected species.

The most extensive high forests extend along the Pontic Mountains from Istanbul eastward to the Iranian border and include impressive stands of beech, mixed with areas of spruce (especially *Picea orientalis*) in the east. On the southern, inner, slopes of the Pontic Mountains, and especially in the western highlands, there are extensive areas of oak and pine. The great Euxinian Forest of northern Anatolia extends, with some discontinuity, into northern Iran to link up with the Hyrcanian or Caspian Forest in the Elburz Mountains. This humid forest facing the Caspian

Figure 2.15 Mediterranean forests in the Troodos Mountains of Cyprus: wild pine (*Pinus brutia*) and Troodos pine (*P. nigra*) clothe the upper slopes (*foreground*), with mixed maquis and garigue scrub forest on the slopes in the distance. Summer homes are scattered in the fragrant pine forests.

Sea is almost tropical in its luxuriance, with a rich variety of undergrowth as well as tall trees: linden, ash, oak, beech, elm, hornbeam, walnut, maple, and evergreens. Beech, dominant on the lower open slopes, is gradually replaced higher up, so that at 6,000–8,000 ft/ 1,830–2,440 m one finds the most magnificent trees in the Middle East—primarily oaks (*Quercus macranthera* and others) but also elm, ash, hornbeam, and maple.

In the higher elevations of the Zagros chains, there is a somewhat dry, deciduous forest in which oaks dominate. With smaller and more widely spaced trees, and with a limited number of species, this Zagrosian Forest differs appreciably from the humid Euxinian and Hyrcanian Forests.

Reforesting.   In the west, scattered woodlands survive in areas of former extensive forests in the Levant highlands—in Israel, Jor-dan, Lebanon, and Syria—and on the island of Cyprus (Fig. 2.15). Most of these forests are either small remnants of great expanses of trees in the past—the Cedars of Lebanon, for example—or woodlands planted in recent decades through government programs of reforestation or afforestation.

The endemic Aleppo pine, *P. halepensis*, is the tree most frequently planted in the regional forestry programs. Sometimes called the "umbrella pine," it has come to be identified with the Levant highlands. Efforts to regenerate forests of Cedars of Lebanon (*Cedrus libani*) have encountered many problems, especially slow growth. The broad-leaved tree most often used in plantation programs is a rapidly growing oak, *Q. ithaburensis*. In drier areas, the pistachio serves well in planted woodlands; in still more arid areas, the tamarisk is utilized. *Tamarix aphylla* is used in group plantings and *T. gallica* as windbreaks.

Animal Life

Historical Changes. The varied Middle East environments support a rich variety of fauna. Iran alone has approximately the same number of species of mammals as all of Europe west of the pre-1991 Soviet border. Unfortunately, to judge by early writings and the physical record, many larger species have become extinct in the Middle East. Still others have been reduced to a fraction of their former count, are nearing extinction, or now occupy only a remnant of their original range.

Appreciably different environmental conditions in the Middle East during the Tertiary period and the Pleistocene epoch supported animal groups unlike those of modern times. For example, although the ancestor of *Bos taurus,* wild and domesticated cattle, came from the Taurus Mountains of southern Anatolia, there is fossil evidence of *Bos* in the Rub al-Khali during pre-Pleistocene times. Some gazelle were numerous in the steppes and more vegetated deserts, and several species of deer grazed the wooded steppe and open forests. Wild sheep and goats kept to the heights. Lions, tigers, leopards, cheetahs, and other felines were formerly common in parts of the Fertile Crescent and Iran, and other carnivores, such as the wolf, fox, jackal, and hyena, roamed much of the same area.

All of these larger mammals have been decimated by nature and people, and the lion and tiger have virtually disappeared from the region. The crocodile disappeared about 1900, the ostrich in the early 1930s. The ruggedness of the north and the aridity of the south have given refuge to individual survivors and to small groups of gazelle, deer, mountain sheep and goats (including ibex), wild boar, and similar mammals, along with an occasional leopard, wolf, jackal, hyena, or fox. A considerable baboon population is found in the woodlands of Asir in southwestern Arabia. Hundreds of hamadryas baboons scurry through the brush among the granite knobs of the national park along the escarpment west of Abha; heedless of park visitors, they nimbly steal any food left unattended.

The gazelle population of the Syrian and Arabian deserts has declined precipitously, primarily as a result of hunting with rifles from vehicles. As endangered species, gazelle and oryx (a type of antelope) are now protected. In small numbers, oryx can survive in the arid Rub al-Khali by ingesting only moisture from the leaves they eat. During the 1990s, some governments in the eastern Arabian Peninsula initiated programs for the preservation, scientific breeding, and restoration of the gazelle and oryx populations. By 2004, the programs showed notable success; the Arabian oryx facility in Oman has been declared a World Heritage Site.

The numerous domesticated animals of the Middle East—including sheep, camels, goats, donkeys, and cattle—are of great economic significance and are discussed with land use in Chapter 5.

Some Common Types. The smaller mammals are much more numerous than the larger animals in both species and population and include hare, squirrel, hedgehog, honey badger, mongoose, and many species of rodents (jerboa, gerbil, hamster, field mouse, sand rat). The many species of reptiles include few harmful types, but there are a few vipers, cobras, and adders.

Lizards, represented by dozens of species, are common in all parts of the Middle East. One common lizard of the Arabian Desert is the burrowing *dabb,* or spiney-tailed lizard, a heavy-bodied herbivorous species that grows to 18–20 in/45–50 cm and is eaten by the Bedouin. The longer but slimmer *waral,* or desert monitor, is carnivorous and more aggressive; unlike the *dabb,* it is not considered edible. The small *tuhayhi,* an agamid lizard, seeks protection by vibrating its body and sinking into loose sand. The sand-swimming skink and other lizards also use submergence in sand as a temperature-regulating device, since lizards—and many other animals—must maintain body temperature within a fairly narrow range. Stinging scorpions are especially numerous in the more arid areas. Since they are nocturnal, they can generally be avoided by the exercise of reasonable care.

Birds. The Middle East has traditionally been rich in bird life and is estimated to have at least five hundred species. During spring and fall, the great eastern Mediterranean flyway is used by many flocks of migrating birds. The narrowness of the corridor affords an exceptional opportunity for bird observation but also adds to the vulnerability of the migrating birds to hunters. Marshes along the many coasts attract thousands of waterfowl, and many game birds are present, although now in reduced numbers. Among the common birds of prey are falcons, traditionally used by the Bedouin for hunting—a sport that has become increasingly popular in the Arabian Peninsula and the drier areas of the Fertile Crescent. Field birds are especially numerous along the Nile Valley, and cotes for pigeons and doves are a common sight around villages. Doves, which are rarely hunted, are seen everywhere outside the cities in Israel. A variety of songbirds frequent the forests of the Pontic Mountains of northern Turkey and the Elburz in Iran, and birds are often referred to in Persian literature.

Insects. Some insects in the region are major pests and dangers to health. Malaria-spreading mosquitoes remain a serious problem despite intensive pesticide programs. Flies (Diptera) are not only a widespread nuisance but also a serious health threat, since they spread eye diseases as well as gastrointestinal disorders. Incredibly, even in the open desert far from any settlement, clouds of persistent flies will descend on travelers who stop for a meal. There were formerly plagues of locusts, sometimes catastrophic, but concerted action has reduced the locust danger to a minimum; however, in 2003–2004, locusts swarmed in Northwest Africa, and small swarms descended on Egypt, Cyprus, Lebanon, and Israel.

Having surveyed the major aspects of the natural environment, this study turns next to the other side of the coin to examine human patterns.

NOTES

1. Including Palestine (Gaza).

2. The theory of plate tectonics has been a major focus of earth science since the late 1950s. Simplified presentations are given in most leading atlases, and evolving aspects are discussed periodically in many journals, such as *Scientific American.* See National Geographic Society 1983, 2004. No single work in English covers the geomorphology of the Middle East and the peripheral areas, but see Brown and Coleman 1972; US Geological Survey 1966–1967, 1975, and 1989; R. Said 1962; and the very technical Dixon and Robertson 1984. Vita-Finzi 1986 is scientific yet readable and uses many examples and illustrations from the Middle East and North Africa.

3. Two or three National Geographic Society maps are very useful, especially "Heart of the Middle East" (2002), with an excellent space-landscape image map on the reverse. Also useful is "Afghanistan, Pakistan, and the Middle East" (2003). Any good atlas would also be helpful.

4. The term "Horn of Arabia" was used for the first time of which the authors are aware by Erhard F. Gabriel in Gabriel 1988, 233.

5. See Cullen 1999, which includes a very useful National Geographic map supplement.

6. Although all of Ethiopia is north of the equator, its annual weather pattern is more like that of the Southern Hemisphere.

7. Both rivers are examined in detail in Kolars and Mitchell 1991. See also Rogers and Lydon 1994 (which has a good bibliography); Ventner 1998; Soffer 1999; and Biswas et al. 1997.

8. The variable water level of the Dead Sea is monitored by the Israel Marine Data Center (ISRAMAR); see http://isramar.ocean.org.il/isramar2009/DeadSea and the Watchers, http://thewatchers.adorraeli.com /2011/05/29/dead-sea-disappearing-day-by-day/.

9. Kreiger 1988 is a readable account of several aspects of the Dead Sea and includes a useful bibliography.

10. *National Geographic Daily News*, Dec. 17, 2012; see http://news.nationalgeographic.com/news/2012 /12/121217-saudi-arabia-water-grabs-ethiopia/.

11. Factors and elements of Middle East climate are examined in Taha et al. 1981 and Rudloff 1981. Interesting data are in the Arabian American Oil Company n.d. (ca. 1978), which is, unfortunately, hard to find. Detailed data for individual major regional stations are available from the National Climatic Data Center website, http://ncdc.noaa.gov /oa/climate/afghan/, with factors discussed in the respective country narratives. Additional climate maps and diagrams may be found in most good world atlases.

12. Mandaville 1990, quoting data from Saudi Arabia's Ministry of Agriculture and Water.

13. See Zohary 1962 and his many other studies. Hills 1966 has general coverage of vegetation in arid lands. The interrelationships between plants and soils are also examined in Hills. Two sheets of UNESCO's "Soil Map of the World" cover the Middle East: VII-1 and V-2. A major recent contribution to the study of the flora of eastern Arabia is Mandaville 1990.

14. Mandaville 1990, 16; Schulz and Whitney 1986; and Mandaville n.d.

3

Patterns of Time
Historical-Geographical Foundations

KEY POINTS: The Cradle of Civilization, Middle East has long history, rise and fall of many empires, great and small. Many archaeological tells. Fascinating and often at least vaguely familiar historical narratives. As in climate data, many names and dates, but significance is in the major empires and dates—for example, conquests of Alexander the Great in fourth century BCE, rise of Islam in seventh century CE, Ottoman conquest of Constantinople in 1453, establishment of modern Israel in 1948. Succession of empires yields pattern of a few cores or foci of persistent power, especially Nile Valley, Anatolian Plateau, and Iranian Plateau, lesser cores elsewhere in region.

PERSISTENCE OF PATTERNS

Succession of Landscapes

Evolving over thousands of years and over a wide range of physical and cultural environments, the region's cultural mosaic and political patterns are exceedingly complex. Chronologically successive cultures and empires have partially erased yet partially preserved preceding patterns, creating by this long development a marvelous geographical palimpsest. This sequential development, its traces in the modern Middle East, and its significant impact on contemporary human and political affairs are the themes of this chapter, which deals with the historical-political geography of the region.

Evidence of sequent occupance,[1] or the settlement and exploitation of the same region by successive cultures, dates from earliest times and characterizes many Middle Eastern landscapes. In the narrow coastal plain of southern Lebanon, for example, a modern oil pipeline extends along or over Ottoman Turkish buildings, medieval Muslim mosques, a Crusader castle, Byzantine mosaics, Roman tombs, ruins of the Phoenician port of Sidon, Bronze Age pottery shards, and Neolithic flints (Fig. 3.1). The wrinkled hand of the past has fashioned much of the landscape of the Middle East.

Even if ruins and artifacts from the distant past are not visible on the surface, they are often stratified in successively older layers beneath the surface. In the more favorable environments of the Middle East, few excavations fail to yield some kind of evidence of ancient human occupation or use of the land. The past is nearly always present.

Figure 3.1 Excavated ruins of Byblos, Lebanon, one of the most significant archaeological sites in the Middle East. Finds date from the Neolithic and include later Egyptian, Amorite, Phoenician, Persian, Roman, and Crusader ruins.

Heritage of Patterns

Prior to surveying the evolution of the regional palimpsest, we can gain appreciation of the significance of its long heritage by glancing at six selected topics as examples of that heritage. These examples underscore the relevance of even the distant past to present-day patterns and problems.

1. Religion.   Certain sites and towns settled in ancient times had religious motivations or gained religious importance for later groups. Many of the centers have retained their significance or achieved even greater emotional impact, so they attract hundreds of thousands of pilgrims—and, in some cases, secular tourists—annually, thereby maintaining major economic importance. For example, before the development of Saudi Arabia's oil

fields, pilgrims to Mecca and Medina provided the major basis for the kingdom's economy. Similarly, control of Jerusalem generated foreign exchange for the Ottoman Empire and successor governments. Religious sites often hold significance for multiple religious groups, leading to disputes over which historical "layer" is to be recognized, preserved, or excavated. Such controversies center on several sites in and around Jerusalem, especially the Haram al-Sharif, or Temple Mount. Muslim shrines such as those in Najaf and Karbala in Iraq, Qom and Mashhad in Iran, and Konya in Turkey are especially noteworthy.

2. Infrastructure.   Infrastructural features— basic facilities supporting other development, including irrigation systems, caravan routes, and hillside terracing to facilitate farming—

have evolved over centuries. Numerous ancient examples still survive, enhancing the value of particular areas and influencing relative levels of prosperity in the region. The middle and lower Tigris-Euphrates Valley, the Nile Valley and Delta, and the Jordan Valley, for example, have been developed over thousands of years into productive irrigated farming areas. Such development required enormous efforts by earlier peoples to achieve the clearing of dense vegetation, drainage, leveling, cultivation, irrigation by means of an elaborately engineered system of canals, and restoration after periodic flooding. Thus, modern economies rely on ancient infrastructures and on the cultural heritage of ancient technologies.

3. *Natural Resources.* Settlements and human activities have long correlated with patterns of natural resources, notably those of water, fertile soils, metallic ore deposits, and, more recently, oil. Such sites often show signs of a remarkable sequent occupance, with infrastructural elements from Roman aqueducts to modern pipelines. However, some ecological problems also persist. Increasingly serious are problems with salt-impregnated soils resulting from faulty irrigation of poorly drained areas or soil erosion caused by improperly cultivated slopes or by overgrazing. Stone tools found along former lakeshores in deserts of the Arabian Peninsula signal environmental deterioration. Meanwhile, new areas have become habitable, with oil providing an economic base and with new technologies, such as pumping and desalination, providing the necessary water. The long history of civilization in the region yields practical information about its patterns of natural resources and their evolution over time.

4. *Strategic Features.* The strategic significance of Middle East seas, straits, coastal plains, mountain passes, river valleys, and major trade and invasion routes was displayed in ancient times and persists into the twenty-first century. For example, the Strait of Hormuz and the Gulf are both still important strategically despite the development of sophisticated military aircraft and missiles that can easily cross over them.

5. *Culture and Art.* Virtually every contemporary city in the Middle East is on the site of an ancient town, and excavations for foundations of modern buildings commonly uncover pottery, statues, monuments, or other ancient remains. Logically enough, certain locational factors exercise a persistent attraction for human occupation and cross-country routes. Ruins of monuments and other structures, found by the thousands throughout the settled Middle East, have become tourist attractions in, and major revenue-producing assets for, many countries, while transportable artifacts, stone and clay inscriptions, documents on papyrus and vellum, and other antiquities are preserved in museums all over the world. Beyond their economic value, such items are valuable to researchers because they provide clues about the historical evolution of the area. Unfortunately, thousands of artifacts have been—and still are—illegally excavated and traded on the black market. Unauthorized removals from archaeological sites abound during periods of political chaos— for example, Lebanon in the 1980s, Iraq in the 2000s, and Syria in the 2010s. The looting of the Iraqi National Museum in 2003 was a cultural tragedy for the world.

6. *Political and Military Models and Conflict.* Sequent occupance over millennia has resulted in competing claims to the same lands and pressure on inhabited areas to accommodate high population growth, refugees, and new immigrants. The founding of the modern state of Israel, in which a Jewish population has largely displaced a Palestinian one, exemplifies this type of political and territorial

conflict. The war between Iran and Iraq in the 1980s echoed numerous territorial and religious rivalries of earlier periods along the same fracture zone, as has the contemporary Cyprus struggle. Thus, any analysis of modern conflicts and political antagonisms in the region must take cognizance of the roots of such strife in the area's historical-political geography. Although five former Middle East monarchies are now republics, six states are still monarchies (and another is a quasi-republican federation of seven monarchies), a heritage of a long history of kingdoms, empires, and principalities.

EARLY PATTERNS

Primitive Peoples, Pristine Environments

The more favorable Middle East environments attracted human habitation as early as the Paleolithic period, or Old Stone Age, contemporary with Pleistocene glaciation (about 1.6 million years ago to 12,000 BCE). Primitive Paleolithic human (or humanoid) groups were environmentally bound to sites that offered fresh water, easily gathered food, and natural shelters, especially caves. Particularly favorable sites were found in the western and eastern limbs of the Fertile Crescent (Map 3.1) and adjacent areas of the Anatolian Plateau.[2] The earliest known humanoid site in the region, dating from more than a million years ago, is in northern Saudi Arabia, near the village of Shuwayhitiyah. The study of this site in the mid-1980s introduced an entirely new concept of human migration into Asia from the area of hominid origin in East Africa. Stone tools from several of these extremely ancient sites in Arabia have now been found. Until the 1980s, the earliest site studied dated from 600,000 years ago at Ubaydiyah, on an ancient lakeshore in the Jordan Valley just south of the Sea of Galilee. Numerous Paleolithic sites more than 100,000 years old are scattered from the Nile Valley to the piedmont arc around Meso-

potamia and include one excavated in Sharjah in 2010. Evidence of human migration across the Sinai/Palestine land bridge 100,000 years ago has been found at two sites in the Galilee region (see Chapter 13).

Climatic changes that caused the northward retreat of the last ice sheets in Eurasia beginning about 15,000 years ago also modified the ecology of the Middle East. Open woodlands and grasslands soon characterized the Fertile Crescent, a contrast to the damp forests that invaded Eurasian areas uncovered by the melting and retreating glaciers. As one consequence, the Fertile Crescent population increased and developed, ushering in the Mesolithic period, or Middle Stone Age—sometimes called Epipaleolithic—which began in about 12,000 BCE.

Neolithic Revolution in a Special Environment

Ameliorating climatic conditions after 9000 BCE brought further steady improvements in the Fertile Crescent environment, which encouraged not only an increase in the number of Mesolithic peoples but also the growth and spread of wild plants and animals that made up their food supply. This favorable environment of grasslands with scattered trees became the native habitat of early forms of wheat and barley, varieties of which are still found in the northern Fertile Crescent. Wild varieties of both were widely harvested for many centuries; they were gradually domesticated and cultivated along with other major food plants, including vegetables and nut trees. At about the same time, animals that still dominate the farm scene were domesticated—sheep, goats, cattle, pigs, and dogs. Hence, in about 8000 BCE, in the arc from the Levant to the western Zagros, there occurred the Agricultural Revolution, or Agricultural Transformation, the most important single innovation in human history.

Thus, a particular environment, a special plant community, and an adaptive population

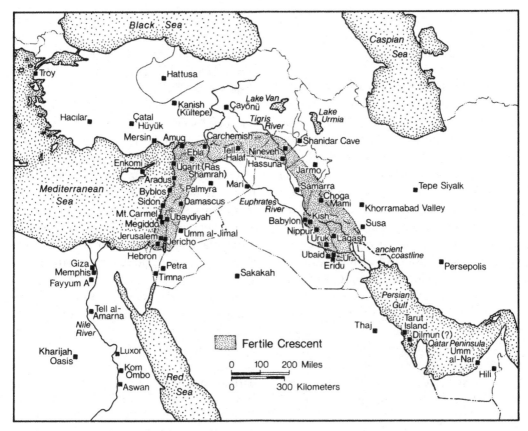

Map 3.1 Selected major ancient sites. The Fertile Crescent is often referred to in the text.

combined to initiate the Neolithic period, the New Stone Age. Heralded especially by the Agricultural Revolution, the Neolithic period also saw the systematic development of organized settlements. Such settlements were not feasible prior to the planned cultivation of plants and the domestication of animals, so that the agricultural and urban revolutions functioned reciprocally. Moreover, these stimulated, or at least were accompanied by, a further complex of cultural processes—political administration, organized religion, trade, and, finally, writing—in both Mesopotamia and Egypt.

The Archaeological Tell

Giving mute, fascinating, and vital testimony regarding Neolithic and later settlements is the archaeological mound, a common feature

of the Middle East landscape. Usually referred to by the Semitic word "tell,"[3] an archaeological mound marks an ancient site on which successive settlements were established on the debris of earlier ones. Typical tells contain layers of cultural remains accumulated over thousands of years, the height of the mound generally indicating the length of time the site was occupied. With characteristically flat tops and sharply sloping sides, tells are prime targets for archaeological excavations. Correlation of finds among tells reveals patterns of cultures and settlement, including economic and political relations, that existed more than five thousand years ago.

Many of the thousands of tells scattered over the Middle East are world renowned and attract scores of scholars and thousands of tourists annually. Familiar examples include

Troy in northwestern Asia Minor, Babylon in central Mesopotamia, and Jericho in the Jordan Valley (all shown on Map 3.1).

Agriculture, Cities, and Civilization

The human advance from food gathering to food producing in about 7000 BCE[4] and the consequent expansion of the food supply accompanied a great increase in population in more favorable areas. As well as providing a more balanced diet, agriculture also permitted the accumulation of a food surplus for nonproductive seasons and for famines, as well as for supporting a growing proportion of the population not involved in the production of food. In addition, farming permitted and encouraged experimentation, cooperative planning, and a concentration of people into villages, which resulted in a widening of social exchange, organization, and trade within and among settlements. Food-storage facilities, key evidence of early agriculture, and food-preservation techniques required group planning.

Irrigation Introduced.   About 5500 BCE, Fertile Crescent farmers took another giant step forward—minimizing their dependence on local rainfall: they extended, then gradually shifted, farming from the Zagros piedmonts above the Tigris-Euphrates Basin down to the Mesopotamian plain along the riverbanks. The new agriculture was irrigated cultivation, utilizing a system of canals to feed river water to the planted fields.

Along with the earlier rainfed farming advances, irrigated farming accompanied or had a "feedback" effect on key social developments in Mesopotamia: cooperative planning; organized engineering; expanded storage facilities for harvest surpluses; trade relations to exchange excess food for other items; cities to accommodate people, goods, and expanded activities, as well as to permit specialization of labor; defenses for the protection of food supplies, irrigation works, settlements, and temples; centralized administration to apportion water and to coordinate activities; and for inventories and trade, a system of writing, the basis for future law, literature, and long-distance communication.

Evidence of origins of agriculture in areas outside Mesopotamia is contradictory. Rather than having been borrowed from the Tigris-Euphrates Basin, systematic agriculture in the Nile Valley may have had independent beginnings. Certainly, farming—and, by necessity, irrigation—began very early in Egypt, as it did also in Southeast Asia. However, evidence for Mesopotamia as the source area for the diffusion of settled agriculture remains strong.

Other Advances.   Specific innovations developed as Mesopotamian irrigation agriculture evolved. With all dates BCE, the plow appeared in about 3000–4000; the wheel was well known in Mesopotamia by 3500, but apparently not in Egypt until 1700; and stamp and cylinder seals (possibly ancestors of writing) had appeared in some quantity by 3500. Impressive temples had been constructed in Uruk (Erech of the Old Testament, Warka in modern Iraq) by 3300; earliest evidences of writing also appeared about 3300, and cuneiform (wedge-shaped) writing on clay was common by 2400;[5] and a dozen major Sumerian cities, and many more villages, existed in Mesopotamia by 2700.

Excavations of early Mesopotamian cities reveal cultural achievements and urban developments that were remarkably advanced for their time (4000–3500 BCE). The ruins of Uruk, southeast of Baghdad (see Map 3.1), suggest a population of 50,000, and the outline of the walls extends for 5.6 mi/9 km. Impressive temples, some on stepped platforms, and terraced towers, or ziggurats, dominated several cities on the Mesopotamian plain, and the Hanging Gardens of Babylon and the Tower of Babel of the Old Testament were almost certainly ziggurats. Regrettably, many of the great Mesopotamian sites were dam-

Figure 3.2 Temple of Hatshepsut (Dayr al-Bahari), in ancient Thebes, Egypt. The temple (fifteenth century BCE) faces east toward the Nile and Karnak and Luxor on the east bank of the river. Behind the cliff, to the west, is the Valley of the Kings.

aged, some very badly, during the fighting and looting that began in 2003.

Early Regional Links. The building of terraced or stepped towers in Mesopotamia was generally contemporary with pyramid construction in Egypt, and the stepped design of the Pyramid of Zoser at Saqqara, the oldest known pyramid along the Nile, suggests that it was borrowed from the Mesopotamian ziggurat concept. Thus, evidence from five thousand years ago clearly shows remarkable interaction between peoples and environment in the Tigris-Euphrates Basin. Irrigation farming and urban development were twin manifestations of the evolving and expanding early culture.

Mud Brick and Stone. Another major factor in the human-environmental relationship was the availability of building materials for the growing number of structures erected in Mesopotamia. In the southern part of the basin, only the clays and silts laid down by the Tigris and Euphrates Rivers on their lower alluvial plain were directly available for building. Unshaped river mud (*tawf*) supplied the material for the earlier structures in the area, and it is still a common construction material for houses in villages of southern Iraq. Later structures were of sun-dried mud brick, and still later buildings were faced with fired brick. Southern Mesopotamian ziggurats, temples, and palaces of the third and second millennia BCE are therefore less well preserved than are the massive Egyptian temples and pyramids, which were constructed mostly of the limestone plentiful in the Nile Valley (Fig. 3.2). Similarly, Assyrian palaces in northern Mesopotamia, built of limestone from nearby quarries, have survived remarkably well.

HISTORICAL-POLITICAL EVOLUTION

The rise and expansion of Middle East empires after 4000 BCE display political-geographical pattern dynamics that are still relevant today. For this reason, the following condensed survey of the evolution of ancient and medieval patterns serves as a prelude to studying the modern region. Obviously, in this brief survey, only the more noteworthy developments can be considered; few of the extremely important migrations of peoples, especially those into the region, can be given the attention they merit.

Early Mesopotamian States

Sumer.   Middle East recorded history begins in the fourth millennium BCE in southern Mesopotamia with the Sumerians, whose origins are unknown and whose written language is unrelated to any other known language. Earliest records show them in control of the irrigation works and related settlements in ancient Sumer, remembered as Shinar in the biblical account found in Genesis 10 and 11. Functioning as city-states, the major cities of Sumer in the middle of the third millennium BCE were Eridu, Uruk, Ur (later Ur of the Chaldees, home of Abraham of both the Old Testament and the Quran), and others (shown on Map 3.2). The partially excavated ruins of these famous settlements of forty-five hundred to five thousand years ago now lie well away from any river, but the towns were originally established along the banks of the Euphrates, which later changed course. The Euphrates, with its slower, more manageable flow, offered advantages for the siting of cities and fields that the more rapidly flowing Tigris could not provide.

Akkad.   North of Sumer lived the Akkadians, the first of many Semitic groups to enter Mesopotamia. They probably came from the Arabian Peninsula, a source region for successive waves of Semites into the Fertile Crescent

Map 3.2 Mesopotamia and adjacent lands, showing earliest known states as well as earliest known cities—Uruk, Eridu, Ur, Lagash, and others. Dashed line indicates approximate limits of the Old Babylonian Empire.

for three thousand years. They overwhelmed the Sumerians in about 2335 BCE, unified the former city-states, and developed the first known empire. In the realm extending from the Zagros Mountains westward to the Mediterranean, their language became the lingua franca, or common language, of the civilized Middle East for centuries. After a short but productive period, the Akkadian heartland was overrun briefly in about 2200 BCE by the Gutians from the Zagros Mountains. This invasion was a precursor of many later conflicts between powers based in the adjacent strongholds of the Tigris-Euphrates Basin and, to the east, the Zagros Mountains–Iranian Plateau—the latest in the 1980s.

Reemerging as a culturally mixed people, the persistent Sumerians established a United

Sumer and Akkad with a capital at Ur. This empire reached its peak of brilliance in about 2000 BCE, developing a thriving trade with the Indus Valley peoples and establishing ports of call on the sea route to the Indus. Ruins of such ports have been found along the shores of the modern UAE and Oman and on islands in the Gulf, especially on Bahrain. There, excavations have uncovered well-preserved, impressive ruins of what is believed to have been the *Dilmun* referred to in Sumerian records.

Babylon. The first Babylonian Empire emerged soon after 2000 BCE and absorbed Sumer. It was created by another Semitic group, the Amorites (which means "westerners" in Amorite), who migrated into central Mesopotamia from the Syrian Desert in about 2000 BCE. From their power center in Babylon, they controlled all of Mesopotamia, and between 1792 and 1750 BCE they were ruled by one of the most famous kings in oriental history, Hammurabi (or Hammurapi) the Great. His famous legal code collected and systematized Sumerian and Akkadian laws from earlier centuries and brought a new sophistication to political administration and control. Babylonians developed advanced mathematical calculations that were used for more than a millennium; their sexagesimal system is still standard in our sixty-second minute, sixty-minute hour, and 360° circle. Babylon and Babylonia played important roles in Mesopotamia for more than two thousand years.[6]

Hittites and Hurrians. Other noteworthy power centers evolved and expanded in several parts of the region after 1700 BCE, demonstrating the persistence of imperial realms in certain environments. Mesopotamia lost its isolated self-sufficiency as peoples with new languages and new cultures entered Asia Minor, the Iranian Plateau, the Levant, and the Caucasus. These included the Indo-European Hittites, who controlled Asia Minor for more

than four hundred years from their stronghold of Hattusa (or Hattushash) in Anatolia. They destroyed Babylon during an incursion in the sixteenth century BCE but mysteriously withdrew following their triumph, after which the Indo-European Kassites, in another instance of a basin-mountain clash, emerged from the Zagros Mountains to rule the weakened Babylonian area for more than four centuries. Another group, the Hurrians (biblical Horites), spoke a language that was neither Semitic nor Indo-European and relied on an Indo-European warrior aristocracy and horse-drawn chariots to build the Kingdom of Mitanni in about 1500 BCE. Hurrian military power pushed the borders of Mitanni control westward to the Mediterranean and eastward to the Zagros.

However, of all the ancient Middle East civilizations and empires outside Mesopotamia, none could match the fabled culture of the Nile, the Pharaonic kingdoms of Upper and Lower Egypt.

Early Egypt

The steadily evolving Mesopotamian culture of the late Neolithic period and early Bronze Age diffused not only eastward to the Indus Valley and beyond but also westward to the Nile Valley. Ancient well-developed cultures already present there adapted Mesopotamian influences and made them distinctly "Egyptian." For example, the writing developed in Sumer as a practical method of recording inventories and trade transactions was a relatively simple technique that required only quick incisions with a reed stylus on damp clay, with both reed and clay widely available. The concept of writing was apparently borrowed by the Egyptians, who used their familiar materials, bronze chisel and stone, to carve elaborate hieroglyphics (lit., "sacred carving") for religious or royal inscriptions.[7]

Very Different River Valleys. Basic environmental differences between Mesopotamia and Egypt influenced other historical and cultural differences. Both rivers of Mesopotamia, the Tigris and the Euphrates, have irregular flow regimes, run in shallow beds, flood unpredictably (or did so especially before the hydraulic works of the twentieth century), shift courses, and generally lack a dependable rhythm. The Nile, in contrast, has eroded a wall-bounded valley in the rock desert, has a regular floodplain and flood time (late summer), seldom shifts course (except in the Delta), and follows a regular rhythm documented over centuries.

Although links between culture and environment can be overstated, certain correlations can be drawn for the early Nile civilization. Egyptian cultural stability followed the rhythm of the river and was influenced by the relative isolation enforced by the desert beyond the Nile Valley. The Nile's physical unity facilitated early political unity after a certain cultural level developed along the river (Map 3.3). Well before 3000 BCE, sailboats proceeded upstream, blown by the northeast trade winds, and drifted downstream, carried by the river's current. Only limited east-west traffic left the Nile Valley, since regular commercial movement over the deserts flanking the valley was hazardous.

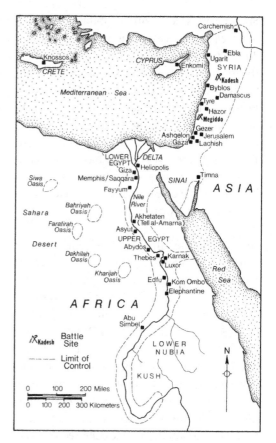

Map 3.3 Ancient Egypt and the Levant, showing major ancient sites. Dashed line shows approximate maximum limit of the new kingdom control.

Millennia of Continuity.   Also, a unified administration coordinated efforts to construct and maintain major canals, allocate water, protect riparian rights of access to the Nile, resurvey fields after the annual floods that deposited the fertile silt, and maintain a god-king leadership figure. The continuity and stability of the cosmos were dominant concepts among the ancient Egyptians; the fact that wood, cloth, and papyrus, even the desiccated remains of people and animals, were naturally preserved in their hot, dry climate may have influenced their perception of life as a benevolent rhythm.

The Egyptians constructed temples and tombs and other advanced architectural works

that are stunning even today. They created sophisticated jewelry, inlaid ornaments, vases, and sculpture. New discoveries during the 1990s and later have further enhanced the already fabulous corpus of well-preserved artifacts from tombs and temples. To obtain such materials as gold, ebony, cedar, and turquoise, the Egyptians carried on active trade, especially with peoples of the upper Nile, along the Red Sea, and in the eastern Mediterranean—including Minoans, Mycenaeans, Hittites, Canaanites, and others. Along with such trade, sustained Egyptian military and imperial activities in the Levant and elsewhere engendered a cross-fertilization of ideas and techniques. Enriched by these contacts, Egyptian culture in turn influenced Greek and Roman development, and thereby Western civilization.

Decline. Egyptian power declined after about 1090 BCE and succumbed to outside control as Libyans, Ethiopians, and Assyrians imposed their respective dynasties. The Persians then conquered Egypt in 525 BCE and, with only a brief interruption, held it for 200 years until they in turn were overcome by Alexander the Great in 332 BCE. Under Alexander's Hellenistic successors, the Greek-Macedonian Ptolemies, Egypt achieved independence again for 250 years, experiencing a cultural resurgence before passing to Roman control in 30 BCE. Although it enjoyed long periods of autonomy under successive hegemons, Egypt was not to achieve true sovereignty again for almost 2,000 years, until after World War II. But through all the centuries and conquerors, something essentially Egyptian survived.

Mesopotamia to the Roman Conquests

Assyrian Empire. Along with Babylonia, Assyria was one of the most persistent of Fertile Crescent imperial states. It emerged about 1350 BCE, centered in the upper Tigris Basin, and dominated the Middle East for 300 years after 935 BCE as the prototypical Oriental monarchy (Map 3.4A). The Assyrian Empire maintained control by means of its sternness, organization, efficiency, engineering, commerce, communications, and record keeping. During its eighth-century expansion, Assyria mastered the Levant, conquered the biblical kingdom of Israel, and in the latter case dispersed the population, a practice the Assyrians often followed with vanquished peoples. Assyria disappeared from history after being overwhelmed by Babylonians and Medes, who took Nineveh in 612 BCE.

Discoveries of superbly detailed bas-relief friezes and other finds in the ruins of Assyrian palace complexes at Khorsabad, Nimrud, and Nineveh in the early nineteenth century launched modern systematic archaeology. They also stimulated an appreciation of ancient Mesopotamian history as it emerged from the translation of some of the twenty-two thousand clay tablets found in the palace library at Nineveh.

Neo-Babylonian (Chaldean) Empire. With Assyria destroyed, Babylonia once again became the dominant power in Mesopotamia. This Neo-Babylonian Empire was led for almost a century by the Chaldeans, a Semitic people from the Syrian Desert, like the Semitic Amorites of the Old Babylonian Empire 1,400 years earlier. The great imperial capital, Babylon, was revitalized by the Chaldean king Nebuchadrezzar the Great (also known as Nebuchadnezzar), who reigned 604–562 BCE. Its Hanging Gardens (a ziggurat with planted terraces) were considered one of the Seven Wonders of the Ancient World, and the Ishtar Gate remains impressive even in ruins. The excavated extensive ruins of Nebuchadrezzar's palace were very impressive but were rather debased by unduly extensive reconstruction by the Iraqi government during the 1980s. Babylon's excavated ruins, although damaged during the fighting, looting, and subsequent occupation in 2003 and after, afford significant insight into the life of 2,000 to 4,000 years ago. The biblical account of the destruction of Jerusalem and other Judean cities by Nebuchadrezzar and of the deportation of the Judeans into Babylonian exile in 586 BCE provides an enduring record of this monarch and his empire.

Persian (Achaemenid) Empire. After its brilliant Chaldean revival, Babylonia fell to the Persian king Cyrus the Great in 539 BCE. Babylon itself, captured without a struggle, survived for another six centuries—Alexander the Great died there in 323 BCE—but by 100 CE it had been abandoned. The Chaldean Babylonian Empire was the last native Mesopotamian state of antiquity. The Tigris-Euphrates Basin

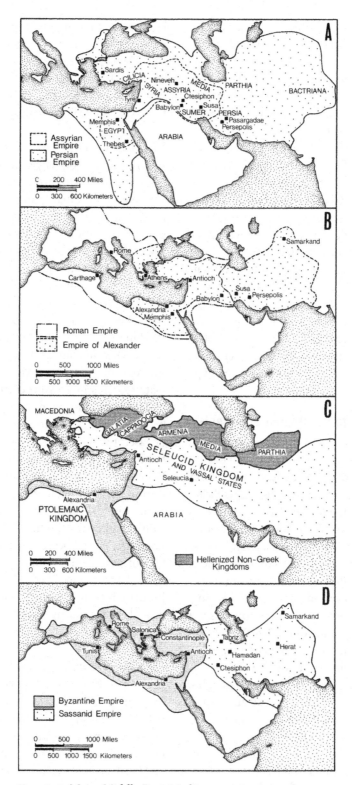

Map 3.4 Major Middle East–Mediterranean empires from before 1000 BCE to the rise of Islam.

Figure 3.3 Persepolis in modern Iran. The wonderfully detailed bas-reliefs on the staircase and platform of the Apadana (fifth century BCE), built by Darius the Great and his son Xerxes, depict representatives of subject peoples and reveal much about the social and political situation of the time.

was ruled by outsiders for the next 2,500 years, well into the twentieth century.

The Persians were an Indo-European tribe that swept down on Babylonia from their stronghold on the Iranian Plateau. The plateau had already disgorged the Gutians and the Indo-European Kassites and Medes, and from it later erupted other conquering Persian-related groups—the Parthians, Sassanians, and Safavids. Thus, the plateau has been the source area for Indo-European conquerors and immigrants into the Fertile Crescent as the Arabian Peninsula has been for Semitic invaders.

Having merged with the Medes, the Persians during the Achaemenid dynasty swiftly established an empire that was more extensive than any of its predecessors. Their territories reached from the Balkan Peninsula and Nile Valley on the west to the Indus Valley and Turanian Basin on the east (see Map 3.4A). Thus,

for the first time, one Middle East power center controlled all the other power centers, excepting only the barren and inaccessible Arabian Peninsula.

In addition, Persia profited from, inherited, and improved on Assyrian efficiency and on their communications, as was exemplified in the Persian Royal Road from Susa (in southwestern Iran) to Sardis (in western Asia Minor; see Map 3.4A). Some already established cities played more powerful roles, especially Susa, Ecbatana (modern Hamadan), and the legendary Persepolis (Fig. 3.3). The Persian Empire continued for more than 200 years until it was conquered by Alexander the Great between 334 and 326 BCE. Although Persia never regained the territorial dominion of Achaemenid times, Iranian peoples again controlled the plateau within a century after Alexander's death. They have demonstrated for 2,300 years that they are a culturally and politically significant power.

The Empire of Alexander.   Leaving his small Macedonian home base in northern Greece in 334 BCE, Alexander the Great had conquered the entire Persian Empire by 326 BCE and had established his eastern frontier beyond the Indus (see Map 3.4B). By far the largest state of its time, his realm included all of the area covered in this book except the Arabian Peninsula—some 2.0 mn mi²/5.2 mn km². Of the dozens of cities he founded, many still carry forms of his name—among them Alexandria (al-Iskandariyah), Egypt; Iskenderun, Turkey; and Qandahar, Afghanistan. He engendered cultural interchange, encouraged ethnic intermixing, and spread Hellenistic ideas and practices while expanding his own empire. His death in Babylon at age thirty-three left a power vacuum, and imperial lands were parceled out among Alexander's top generals. Ultimately, a threefold division emerged that, alongside revived Persian power, survived for 250 years.

Seleucid and Ptolemaic Empires.   With slightly shifting boundaries, the two most important Hellenistic states in the Middle East were the Seleucid and the Ptolemaic (see Map 3.4C), and ruins and other physical and cultural vestiges of these empires are still evident in scores of sites in Egypt and the Levant. Asia Minor fragmented into a complex mosaic of kingdoms. An Armenian state persisted for centuries and became the base for an Armenian national identity that still endures. The northeastern Iranian Plateau area embraced the Iranian Parthian kingdom, and a Hellenized Greco-Bactrian kingdom dominated lands farther east.

Hellenistic cultural influences continued into the Roman and Byzantine Empires in the Middle East, spanning a period of almost a millennium. Two Hellenistic cities in the Middle East are noteworthy: Antioch (now Antakya, Turkey), on the lower Orontes River, succeeded Seleucia on the Tigris as the capital of the Seleucid Empire and continued

a rich history up to today; and in the Ptolemaic kingdom, Alexandria, founded in 331 BCE by Alexander near one of the mouths of the Nile, became a brilliant center of Hellenism with a large Greek population. Its lighthouse (Pharos), built in about 300 BCE and more than 400 ft/122 m high, was one of the Seven Wonders of the Ancient World and aided navigation for some 1,600 years until brought down by successive earthquakes in the fourteenth century CE. The Ptolemaic Empire ended with Cleopatra's suicide in 30 BCE, when Egypt entered 673 years of control by the Roman and Byzantine Empires. The Seleucid Empire also collapsed before the advancing Romans, and Syria became a Roman province in 64 BCE.

Smaller Semitic Kingdoms.   Other noteworthy cultures contemporaneous with these extensive empires include those of the Hebrews, Canaanite-Phoenicians, and Aramaeans. The Hebrews, a Semitic tribe, appear to have emerged from the Arabian Desert, as did other Semites mentioned earlier. Legends of their early culture and migrations, typical of many tribal groups of the time, are recorded in the book of Genesis. These biblical narratives yield insights into both the Hebrew culture and also many of the attitudes of the time.[8] In Canaan, the Hebrews not only confronted the native Canaanites in the hill country, but were also long kept from the southern coast by other recent arrivals—the Sea Peoples, especially the Philistines, coming from the Aegean region. Archaeological discoveries have now shown that the Philistine civilization was not the uncouth culture traditionally associated with the term "philistine," but was, indeed, generally superior to that of their Israelite neighbors. It was from Philistia, land of the Philistines, that the later names Palestina (Latin), Falastina (Arabic), and Palestine were derived.

The biblical narrative indicates that a unified Israelite kingdom finally emerged (about

1020 BCE) and lasted less than a century, dividing in 922 BCE after the death of Solomon. The northern kingdom, Israel, lasted about 200 years and was conquered by the Assyrians in 722 BCE; some of its people scattered as the fabled ten lost tribes. Judah, the southern kingdom, with Jerusalem as its capital, survived Israel by 136 years but fell to Nebuchadrezzar in 586 BCE, when thousands of the Judean elite were deported to Babylon. Many returned to Judea after 50 years of Babylonian captivity, but others remained, forming a thriving Jewish colony in Mesopotamia that lasted 2,500 years. It may be noted that from 922 BCE until the twentieth century, the Palestine area was a sovereign state under a native administration in de jure control of a unified territory for only a few decades under the Hasmoneans (Maccabees), a reign that was ended by the Romans in 63 BCE. Most of the Jews of Palestine had dispersed, voluntarily or involuntarily, over the Mediterranean Basin and the Middle East by the middle of the second century CE.[9]

The "land of Canaan" comprised the general area of the western Syria–Palestine realm. Although the individualistic Canaanite city-states maintained active common cultural and economic ties, including an intermingling of some elements of their language and religion along with trade, they failed to unify politically or militarily. Thus, because they were vulnerable to invading Egyptians, Amorites, Israelites, Assyrians, and others, the more extended Canaanite civilization declined after about the eleventh century BCE.

The Canaanite cultural genius, however, long stimulated and diversified through interaction with the advanced Egyptian civilization, now became concentrated among the northern coastal groups, who became known as Phoenicians. These extraordinary innovators developed remarkable city-states around ports at Tyre, Sidon, Beirut, Byblos, Tripoli, and Aradus. Because they were crowded into an isolated narrow coastal plain with limited agricultural land, the Phoenicians turned to the sea, developing an aggressive maritime trade, which reached as far as the western Mediterranean, and founding colonies over a wide area. Their most powerful colony, Carthage, founded in about 800 BCE, challenged Rome itself for supremacy in the three Punic (Phoenician) Wars of the second and third centuries BCE. While conducting their wide-ranging trade, the Phoenicians simplified and carried with them the first true alphabet, derived from characters developed by Semitic peoples in the Levant. This alphabet was subsequently adapted by the Greeks, Etruscans, and Romans.[10]

The Aramaeans, who—like the neighboring Canaanites—were long indigenous, were inland traders who diffused their culture along with their Semitic language. The Aramaic tongue spread along land trading routes and became the lingua franca of commerce and diplomacy from Egypt to Mesopotamia. It was still spoken in Syria and Palestine at the time of Christ. According to Old Testament accounts, Damascus and other Aramaean city-states, the biblical Aram, were overcome by the Hebrew King David. However, they regained their independence and continued as Aramaean centers until conquered by the Assyrians in 732 BCE. The Aramaean culture gradually faded, but dialects of the Aramaic language continued into the present time in several church liturgies and are still spoken in northern Iraq and in villages north of Damascus.

Roman and Successor Empires

Roman. Although Hellenistic control over much of the Middle East originated from an outside area (Macedonia), Rome was the first power from outside the region to maintain hegemony over large areas of the region for a lengthy period. However, extensive as it was, Roman territorial control in the region never equaled that of the Persian and Hellenistic empires (see Map 3.4). Even so, Egypt and

Syria-Palestine felt the lingering Roman/Byzantine influence until the seventh century CE, and Asia Minor did so for several centuries longer.

Roman legions failed to venture beyond Mesopotamia. They contended with Iranian-based armies along the Euphrates and in Armenia but were never successful in sustained desert operations. To symbolize their military presence, however, they constructed lines of forts and boundary markers to form the *Limes Arabicus* (Arabian Boundary), similar to the *limes* constructed in central Europe. In northwestern Syria, well-preserved stretches of Roman roads still exist, a part of ancient infrastructure underlying the modern Middle East. Vestiges of their presence—roads, forts, theaters, temples, aqueducts, baths—are prominent features in the landscapes of Asia Minor, the Levant, Egypt, and across North Africa, partly because Roman construction in those areas was monumental and well engineered (Figs. 3.4 and 3.5). Some structures combine Hellenistic, Roman, and Byzantine construction from different periods, and these Greco-Roman ruins, from Istanbul in the northwest to Dura Europos on the upper Euphrates in the east, attract many visitors from around the world.

Parthian.   Although Alexander conquered the Persian Empire, the Iranian identity reasserted itself a century later through the Iranian Parthians. Emerging as a native kingdom in 248 BCE, the Parthian Kingdom became an empire within 75 years, extending over the Iranian Plateau and Mesopotamia. Observing the historic strategic value of the narrowest width of the middle Tigris-Euphrates interfluve, the Parthians established Ctesiphon as their capital across the Tigris from Seleucia—about 22 mi/35 km south of modern Baghdad.

Sassanian.   The Parthian Empire was overthrown in 226 CE and was succeeded by another Iranian empire, the Sassanian (or Sassanid). The powerful Sassanians expanded northeastward across the Oxus River (modern Amu Darya, between the contemporary republics of Turkmenistan and Uzbekistan) and eastward to the Indus, as well as across the Gulf into the Qatif area of Arabia and into Oman (see Map 3.4D). They maintained Ctesiphon as a capital (Fig. 3.6) and also inherited Rome and its Byzantine successor as a perennial territorial adversary in Syria-Mesopotamia. The Sassanian Empire collapsed entirely under the assault of invading Arab Muslims in the 630s and 640s.

Byzantine.   Although the Western Roman Empire and its formerly great capital declined after the fourth century CE, the eastern empire and its capital thrived. Founded by the first eastern emperor, Constantine, and named after its founder, Constantinople was earlier Byzantium and later Istanbul. Steadily orientalized, the eastern empire became less Latin and more Greek and after the fall of Rome in 476 was referred to as the Byzantine Empire. It gradually expanded to embrace, at its greatest extent in the mid- to late sixth century, the Italian and Balkan Peninsulas in Europe, Egypt and the southern Mediterranean coast in North Africa, and Asia Minor and the Levant in between. After holding these extensive lands for many centuries (see Map 3.4D), it gradually contracted, until the only remaining territory was an enfeebled Constantinople and its environs, which fell to the Ottomans in the watershed year of 1453. Allowing for expansions and contractions, it survived for 1,123 years, longer than any other empire in the Middle East.[11]

Having battled each other to a standstill for control of the Fertile Crescent, the mutually exhausted Byzantines and Sassanians suddenly faced a common Arab invader. The weakened Byzantines lost Egypt and the Levant in the 630s to the Muslim assault but were able to hold on to their Anatolian stronghold.

Figure 3.4 Famous Greco-Roman ruins: the dramatic amphitheater on a cliffside in Pergamum (modern Bergama, Turkey)

Figure 3.5 Another well-known Greco-Roman ruin: colonnaded street in the ruins of Jarash, north of Amman, a great Roman provincial city. Note the paved street, which has a well-engineered storm drain underneath.

Figure 3.6 Ruins of the great vaulted hall (*al-Madain*) in Ctesiphon, the Sassanian capital (Map 3-4D), on the left bank of the Tigris River southeast of Baghdad. The brick vault of the third century is one of the highest freestanding brick arches ever constructed. Note two figures standing right of lower center.

The Sassanians were forced to surrender not only Mesopotamia but also their entire Iranian Plateau power base, and both areas experienced profound and permanent transformation. The Middle East had entered a new era, that of Islam.

Islamic Empires

The Arab irruption into Mesopotamia and Syria-Palestine in 633 CE was another in the series of Semitic waves from interior Arabia extending back over 3,000 years. This particular invasion, however, was more purposeful, involved many more people and far more territory than had previous ones, and had incalculably greater ramifications. With it, the present cultural patterns of the region began to emerge.

Beginnings.   The founder of Islam, the Prophet Muhammad, had unified the Arabs of the Hijaz (western Arabia) and then of the entire Arabian Peninsula. This he achieved on three levels: a new religion (the adherents of which were called Muslims—see Chap. 4), a political organization (virtually a theocracy), and ethnic identity. Precepts for all three are found in the Muslim scriptures, the Quran. After Muhammad's death in 632, dedicated Muslims poured northward, under the first caliphs (successors to the Prophet), to spread the faith and to seize new lands for its flowering. Within a century, Muslim forces appeared before Tours in France, the high point of their westward spread, while other Muslims held Central Asia. At its maximum extent in the eighth century, the Arab Empire exceeded in size all previous Middle East empires (about 5 mn mi^2/13 mn km^2) and compared with the Roman Empire at its maximum (cf. Maps 3.4 and 3.5). The Muslim invasion marked the first Semitic conquest of the Iranian Plateau, although the conquerors imposed only the religion of Islam and their

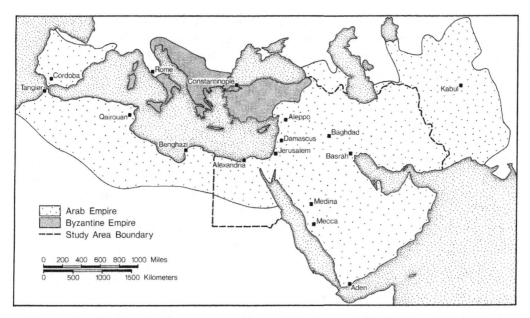

Map 3.5 Arab Empire at its maximum extent, late eighth century. Arabs never succeeded in conquering Asia Minor.

alphabet, not their Semitic language, Arab identity, or physical characteristics.

However, even more than the Roman Empire, the Arab Empire and its successor Muslim empires and kingdoms shifted capitals and cores, broke into parts, recombined in different patterns, and changed composition. But unified or fragmented, the region retained one enduring characteristic—Islam as religion and culture. The development of the Muslim religion and the Islamic state were two highly integrated aspects of the same phenomenon. These aspects not only still thrive but, having been remolded in the contemporary state system, have also become resurgent traditions,[12] as has been seen in the reawakening of the Arab Spring since 2011 (see Chap. 8).

Umayyads, Abbasids. With the founding of the Umayyad Empire in 661, power shifted from the Hijaz to Syria, with the new capital in Damascus. The character of the Muslim state altered accordingly, from a religion-centered theocracy to an empire imitative of

Byzantine and Persian courts. Under the Umayyad caliphs, the unified Muslim state reached its maximum extent in the middle of the eighth century.

In 750, the Abbasid dynasty seized control of the Arab Empire and the caliphate,[13] transferring the center from Damascus to Mesopotamia. After governing from several centers, the Abbasids built their new capital, Baghdad, on the narrowest segment of the Tigris-Euphrates interfluve, which had been occupied earlier by a succession of imperial capital cities. The next century brought the reign of Harun al-Rashid, the Abbasid caliph of *Arabian Nights* fame. During the same century, however, evidence of the decline of the Abbasids appeared as the court weakened and breakaway kingdoms rose, expanded, and were absorbed.[14]

Seljuks, Crusaders, and Mongols

Seljuks. Besides the breakaway states, several other kingdoms were established by invaders from outside the Middle East. Islamized Seljuk Turks from Central Asia moved into the Iranian Plateau and entered Baghdad in 1055 but kept the Abbasid caliphs as figureheads. From Mesopotamia they forced their way westward and, in the watershed battle of Manzikert north of Lake Van (1071), defeated Byzantine armies. They then carried Islam into inner Anatolia for the first time. Islam gradually expanded over all of Asia Minor, and it has remained entrenched there ever since. With the way open into Anatolia, the Seljuks established the Sultanate of Rum (Rum = Rome, that is, Europe) in 1077 and indirectly paved the way for the later expansion of the Turkish Ottoman Empire.

Crusaders. The second group of states established by outside invaders arose primarily in response to the Seljuk incursions and their threat to the Byzantines (see Fig. 10.2). After the Byzantines' defeat at Manzikert, and with Seljuk territorial control continuing to expand, the Byzantines petitioned for help from the Roman Catholic feudal states of western Europe. Successive waves of Christians—French, English, German, Italian, and other Europeans, all labeled "Franks" by the Middle East Muslims[15]—surged eastward in response to the Byzantine request. The human waves became known as the Crusades. The First Crusade began in 1096, capturing Jerusalem in 1099; succeeding ones started in 1147, 1189, 1202, 1218, and 1228, and there were others unconnected with the original purpose.

The First Crusade established several Crusader kingdoms that occupied a relatively small area along a coastal strip at the eastern end of the Mediterranean. After almost two centuries, Muslim resistance finally expelled the occupiers, with the last Crusader foothold on the mainland, Acre, falling in 1291.[16] Although the Crusades had only a modest impact on the Middle East at the time, the reverse effects were momentous, since they were a major stimulus for the European Renaissance. The movement became a major chapter in European medieval history, embel-

lished with adventure and romance, while on the other hand establishing hostility toward Muslims as the Western norm for centuries to come. Among Middle East Muslims, the rankling memories of these successive European invasions have recently become rekindled—especially among Palestinians, to whom even the word "crusades" is painful.[17] In the Levant, numerous ruined Crusader castles remain as romantic symbols of early European imperialism in the Middle East (as well as important tourism sites). Some castles, like other more ancient Middle East monuments, served military purposes intermittently into the twenty-first century because of their massive walls and strategic sites.[18]

Mongols. In the thirteenth century, invading horse-mounted Mongol and Tatar-Mongol archers made far-ranging territorial conquests in the Middle East to add to their vast empires in Asia. Generally short-lived, the conquests nevertheless yielded the Il-Khanid dynasty in Persia (1256–1349) through Genghis Khan's grandson Hulagu. Genghis Khan, Hulagu (who sacked Baghdad in 1258), and Tamerlane (Timur Leng, who took Baghdad in 1393) successively laid waste to extensive areas of the Middle East. So devastating was Hulagu's ravaging of Mesopotamia that the complex, centuries-old irrigation system and roads were not restored to their former efficiency until the twentieth century.

Ottoman Empire and Contemporaries

Like the Seljuks, the Ottomans were a Turkish tribe who converted to Islam in Central Asia and then migrated into the plateaus of Iran and Anatolia. Beginning in the early fourteenth century, the Ottomans steadily expanded from their small principality in northwestern Asia Minor until they controlled a vast area from the Danube to Yemen (see Map 8.3). The Ottoman Middle East holdings remained fairly constant from the early 1600s until World War I—with the notable exception of Egypt, which gradually disengaged itself. Like the Byzantines, whom they displaced, the Ottomans gained and lost territories, but they were remarkable for their political longevity: an unbroken dynasty held the sultanate for six hundred years. Chapters 8, 9, and 20 explain how the Ottoman Empire had a crucial impact on regional developments in the early twentieth century.

Persia Redux. Reviving Persian political organization once again, a kingdom under the Safavids emerged in the Iranian Plateau in 1500. With changes in dynasty in 1736 (Afshars), 1750 (Zands), 1794 (Qajars), and 1925 (Pahlavis), Persia steadily progressed— periodically contending with the Ottomans over Mesopotamia—as a monarchy until early 1979. It changed its official name from Persia to Iran in 1935 and to the Islamic Republic of Iran after the 1979 revolution.

Bipolar Region. Thus, from about 1500 until World War I, two major powers, each based in one of the two strongest power foci, contended with each other, primarily along the line of the Zagros piedmont: the Ottoman Empire, based in Anatolia, and the Persian Empire, based on the Iranian Plateau. Still occupying a third power focus, but with limits on its former greatness, Egypt gradually eased away from direct Ottoman control during the early nineteenth century but was under British protection by World War I. The isolated interior of the Arabian Peninsula largely escaped Ottoman control and remained tribally fragmented until the 1930s, when most of the peninsula was unified as Saudi Arabia.

The End of Empires

In the nineteenth and early twentieth centuries, imperial and would-be imperial powers from Europe returned to the Middle East. Anxious to protect the route to its rich Indian holdings, Britain established itself in Cyprus in 1878 after the opening of the Suez Canal,

annexing the island outright at the onset of World War I. After establishing a coaling station at Aden in the middle of the nineteenth century, Britain gradually expanded its dominance over the southern hinterland of modern Yemen (see Chaps. 16 and 17 for Britain's role in eastern Arabia). Following World War I, it assumed League of Nations mandate control over Transjordan, Palestine, and Iraq (see Chaps. 12, 13, and 14 for details).

France, which had annexed modern Algeria starting in 1830 and established protectorates over Tunisia and most of Morocco in 1881 and 1912, respectively, cited its long association with Levantine Christian groups to avail itself of post–World War I mandates over Syria and Lebanon (see Chaps. 10 and 11). Italy invaded Libya in 1911, and after World War I it hoped to receive a large chunk of southwestern Anatolia, possibly as a mandate; it had to be content with formally annexing the previously Ottoman-controlled and still Greek-inhabited Dodecanese Islands in the Aegean and Mediterranean.[19] Greece's attempts to annex Thrace and western Anatolia came to naught in a disastrous war with resurgent Turkey from 1919 to 1922.

Compared to earlier imperial presences, these nineteenth- and twentieth-century incursions proved relatively fleeting. Despite the mandatory powers' efforts to the contrary, especially by the French, the local inhabitants resisted attempts to turn their lands into colonies; starting with Iraq in 1932, the mandates were all terminated by 1948. The British lingered longer in Aden and eastern Arabia, but after India gained its independence in 1947, their presence there proved a luxury the country could no longer afford, and it was completely concluded by 1971.

SOME INFERENCES: POWER CORES

The foregoing review of the evolution of political-geographical patterns of the Middle East reveals several broad, persistent factors.

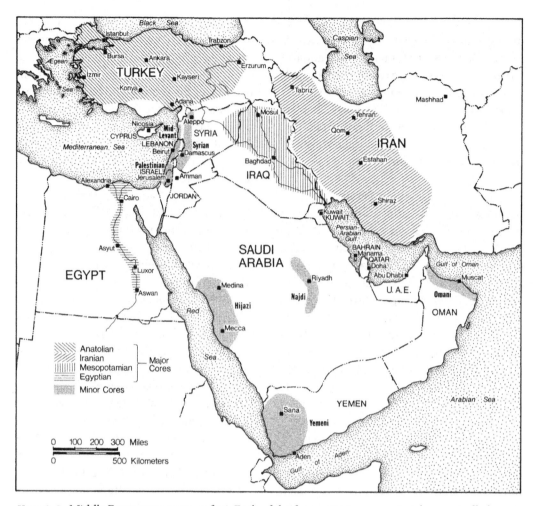

Map 3.6 Middle East power cores, or foci. Each of the four main power centers has controlled most of the Middle East at some time, but none has controlled all other cores simultaneously.

Significant lessons to be drawn from the review are relevant not only as a basis for the rest of this book, and thus for better understanding the Middle East, but also as parameters for formulating practical foreign policies in the region.

1. Four major power foci, or cores, and two minor ones have appeared and reappeared in the Middle East throughout history: the Anatolian Plateau (Asia Minor), Iranian Plateau, Tigris-Euphrates Basin (Mesopotamia), and Nile Valley are the four major cores, and the western Fertile Crescent and central and western Arabian Peninsula

are the two minor cores. Lesser centers of strength have been the Yemen and Oman areas (Map 3.6).[20]

2. The two most persistently powerful foci, and the two from which the most extensive geographical areas have usually been controlled, have been the two intermontane plateaus, Anatolia and Iran. These two mountain-rimmed centers now host two of the three most populous states—which are also among the most powerful states—in the Middle East: Turkey, Iran, and Egypt.

3. No one power has ever succeeded in conquering and occupying the entire core

Middle East as the region is defined in Chapter 1.[21] Regardless of the extent of the existing imperial power during any given period, some other part of the region maintained its independence.

4. The one area that has always been able to maintain its independence, or at least its separateness, from outside powers is the interior of the Arabian Peninsula (Najd). The peninsula was a center of imperial territorial control during the middle of the seventh century, but otherwise it has been relatively isolated, except as a source of migrants who appeared in Syria and Mesopotamia between 2500 BCE and 700 CE.

5. Although Mesopotamia was the earliest power focus and remained the main core for seventeen hundred years, it gradually weakened as a separate center and later functioned as a focus of power only when connected to the Iranian Plateau center. Under the sovereignty of Iraq, Mesopotamia demonstrated renewed potency for a brief period beginning in the 1980s.

6. The political-geographical history of the Middle East has, to a great extent, revolved around the cyclic interaction of the powers occupying Asia Minor and the Iranian Plateau. Each power often sought control of Mesopotamia, which was sometimes used as a springboard against the power on the other side of the basin.

7. Powers centered in the three northern foci have controlled the Nile Valley at various times, but never has the Nile Valley power controlled any one of the three major northern foci. Rather, sustained Egyptian control outside Egypt has been limited to the western limb of the Fertile Crescent (Syria-Palestine realm) plus some brief inroads into southeastern Anatolia by Egyptian forces in the 1830s.

Neither history nor geography can dictate the future. Changing technology, fervent ideologies, outside influences, or other developments might alter the relative significance of the several power foci in the Middle East. Since the 1950s, the emergence of Israel and the rise of the Middle East's petroleum age have unquestionably reorchestrated political, military, and economic interrelationships. Yet to consider historical and geographical factors in the region's role as mere academic curiosities is to misread vital lessons and to risk repetition of the mistakes of the past. The roles of the centers at the present time are revisited in Chapters 8 and 9, which examine contemporary Middle Eastern political-geographical development.

NOTES

1. Whittlesey 1929.

2. Remarkable archaeological discoveries in southeastern Anatolia during the late 1900s and early 2000s found new evidence of early civilization in several sites.

3. A *tell* is termed a *tepe* or *chega* in Persian, *hüyük* in Turkish, and *kom* in Egyptian usage.

4. The Wendorf team found evidence that indicated, through laboratory dating, much earlier cultivation in the Nile Valley. See Wendorf and Schild 1980.

5. See Schmandt-Bessarat 1978 and other articles by her. See also the readable but scholarly Redman 1978, with its attention to environmental factors; Robinson 1995, 8–13, 58–87; and *New York Times*, Apr. 6, 1999.

6. Among scores of accounts of Mesopotamian prehistory and early historical geography, many are in scarce technical journals. Available accounts are in Redman 1978; Saggs 1995; Burenhult 1994, 16–59; and Potts 1997.

7. German archaeologists claimed in late 1989 that some inscriptions found at Abydos gave radiocarbon dates of 3200–3400 BCE, thus predating Mesopotamian writing.

8. See Finkelstein and Silberman 2001, which examines recent discoveries and theories about ancient cultures in the Levant, especially with reference to biblical narratives.

9. Among myriad books and articles on ancient Israel, see Aharoni 1967; Baly 1957; and G. Smith 1935 for consideration of geographical factors. See also Finkelstein and Silberman 2001 and R. Friedman 1997. A readable history is Grant 1984.

10. For more recent treatment, see Gore 2004.

11. Among several excellent accounts of the Byzantines, see the standard Shaw 1976; Shaw and Shaw 1977; and Norwich 1997.

12. B. Lewis 1973.

13. At least theoretically, up until the 1920s, most Muslims held there could be only one true caliph or successor; there were, however, countless disagreements over who the true successor was and how he should be chosen.

14. Many good histories cover the Islamic Arab empires and later developments. The older classic is Brockelmann 1949. A useful later one is Hourani 1991.

15. The commonly used Arabic word *firinjiyah* for foreigner is believed by some to have been derived from Frank.

16. Regimes originating with the Crusaders held on in Rhodes and Cyprus until the islands fell to Ottoman Turks in 1522 and 1571, respectively.

17. As, for example, when George W. Bush began using the term in the wake of the 9/11 bombings: for example, "This crusade, this war on terrorism is going to take a while." Office of the Press Secretary, White House, Sept. 16, 2001.

18. The standard work on the Crusades is Runciman 1954.

19. The islands reverted to Greece in 1947 with Italy's defeat in World War II. However, the maritime boundaries of the Greek islands and Turkey remain unsettled to the present (see Chaps. 8 and 20).

20. Based on "Middle East Power Foci and Their Persistence," paper given by author Held, Apr. 15, 1991, to the Association of American Geographers in Miami.

21. Alexander was uninterested in Arabia and the same was true of the Persians, the Romans never conquered Persia, the early Arab empire lacked Anatolia, and the Ottomans neither moved their border east of Mesopotamia nor ever held much sway in central and southern Arabia.

The reader is advised to consult this book's associated website (**www.middleeastpatterns.com**) for time lines of both the historic empires and the modern states of the region.

4

Patterns of Peoples, Cultures, and Settlements

A Demographic Overview

KEY POINTS: Patterns are of interchanging relations: language often a key indicator of ethnicity (Arabic is the language of Arabs); religion often relates to ethnicity (Orthodox Coptic Christianity is typical of Copts of Egypt); religion often relates to language (Judaism uses Hebrew as a liturgical language). A few ethnic groups in region are of major significance (obviously Arabs, Turks, Iranians, Kurds, Jews, Azeris, Greeks). Settlement types vary with environments and with ethnicity. Former nomads and villagers are increasingly townsmen and urban. Many great cities—Cairo, Tehran, Istanbul, Riyadh. Former fishing villages are fine cities—Dubai, Abu Dhabi, Doha, Kuwait. Region is obviously vigorously developing and increasingly matching industrialized countries in urbanization and communications.

OVERVIEW

The exceedingly complex patterns of distribution of population and peoples in the Middle East are shaped by many interacting biophysical, cultural, and historical influences. Obviously highly correlated are the geographical patterns of population and precipitation and water supply; other factors have constantly been at work to shape unique patterns of peoples, languages, religions, and ethnic groups. Ethnic complexity, for example, often suggests that alternating mountains and valleys compartmentalize different groups of peoples or give refuge to weaker groups.

Statistical Difficulties. Enumerating populations has been difficult in most Middle East countries, and quantifying religions and linguistic groups has been even more of a problem because it often has confronted sensitive issues. Governments may attempt to obscure the number—and therefore the influence—of minority ethnic groups, such as Kurds in Turkey (and other countries overlapping "Kurdistan"), or expatriates in Saudi Arabia. Similarly, official enumerators may manipulate religious minority data—for example, Egypt with the Copts and Iran with Armenians, Zoroastrians, and Bahai. Therefore, figures vary widely, even in the best reports, and the following discussion and related tables represent a careful compromise among several authoritative sources. Data in the text are usually kept consistent with those in the tables and the country summaries, although more recent figures (for example, population data for some countries) are sometimes introduced.

Censuses in some Middle East countries have faced various problems: nomads are difficult to locate, technical difficulties can limit accuracy, definitions and terminology may not be universally accepted, and sensitivity may cause some results to be withheld for perceived security or political reasons. Although advanced in many ways, Lebanon, with its multiplicity of antagonistic religious communities and associated political factions, has not taken a census since 1932. Saudi Arabia conducted only basic demographic sampling until its 1974 partial census, and it was reticent about some data collected in subsequent efforts. Rapid growth in oil states like Kuwait, the United Arab Emirates, and Saudi Arabia often rendered statistics obsolete before they were published. The Iraqi invasion of Kuwait in August 1990 prompted the exodus of hundreds of thousands of the amirate's inhabitants, greatly altering its demographics. Qatar took its first census in 1986, and Oman in 1993. Even the statistics-conscious state of Israel experienced difficulty for several years in maintaining reliable data during the influx of immigrants from the Former Soviet Union (FSU) beginning in 1989. Although it has quietly manipulated emigration data, Israel has an excellent Central Bureau of Statistics. Bahrain, Cyprus, Egypt, and Turkey also regularly collect and publish good country statistics.

Middle East governments have made vast and admirable improvement since the 1960s and 1970s in gathering statistical data and making at least much of it available to the public. In view of the foregoing, however, it is obvious that accurate, extensive, intensive quantitative analyses of the region are impossible and that there is appreciable statistical unevenness across the Middle East.[1] In the extended region, statistics in North African reporting are reasonably reliable, while those in the Central Asian "stans" are still evolving,

especially in Afghanistan. Figures from Pakistan are quite good except for the northwestern tribal areas.

Enormous Population Growth. The core sixteen countries (plus Palestine) of the Middle East had an estimated 2012 population total of 385 million, about 5.5 percent of the estimated world population of 7.02 billion. This was almost five times the 1950 total of 79.7 million, prior to the explosive population growth accompanying the oil boom. During the more than sixty-year period after 1950, population increased by some twenty-two times in Kuwait and by an astonishing fifty times in the UAE, and the population in most of the other states—including in the countries of the extended region—increased at least three- or fourfold.

Arabs and Muslims. Two comparisons regarding Muslim and Arab populations may be noted. First, of approximately 1.57 billion Muslims in the world, about 26.7 percent are in the core Middle East and another 23.8 percent in the fifteen extended region states. Second, of the estimated 2012 total population of all twenty-two Arab League states (including Palestine) of 343.8 million,[2] 217.6 million are in the twelve Middle East member states (plus Palestine). For these and other geographical and historical reasons, the core Middle East constitutes the center of Islamic and Arab identity.[3] But it should always be kept in mind both that most Muslims are not Arabs and that not all Arabs are Muslims.

The following discussion of patterns of Middle Eastern peoples reveals the richness and complexity of the region's cultural patterns and gives insights into the human dynamics behind major trends and events in the area: the underlying political patterns, historical and contemporary conflicts, traditional group hostilities, changing cultural patterns, migrations of ethnic and religious groups, and irredentist claims. Although

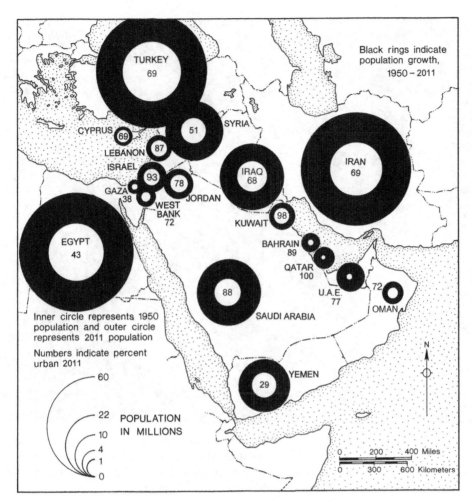

Map 4.1 Middle East population growth, 1950–2011. The dominance of the "big three"—Egypt, Iran, and Turkey—in population size is obvious. The thickness of the outer ring indicates population increase during the past half century.

these patterns have long demonstrated their critical impact on geopolitical interactions, their impact in Iraq has appeared in news headlines daily since 2003 as world attention suddenly began to focus on, for example, the patterns of Kurds, Sunnis, Shii, Turkmans, and others.

PATTERNS: POPULATION

Distribution

The distribution of population in the Middle East (see Maps 4.1 and 4.2, Fig. 4.1, and, later

in this chapter, Map 4.7 on urban population) is not only of great significance in itself; it also reflects where are found the more favorable environments and greater economic opportunities—twin magnets that attract people. The degree of urbanization (Map 4.7) reflects both the historical role of cities in the Middle East and the rapid urbanization after 1950. The region is notably more urbanized than may be assumed.

By 2012, about three hundred cities in the region had more than 100,000 people, and some thirty cities exceeded 1 million.[4] Cities

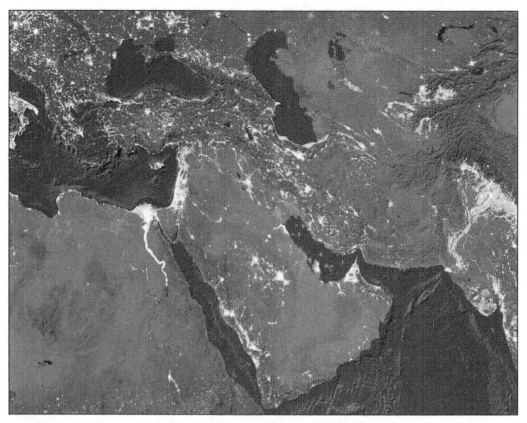

Figure 4.1 Image from space of the Middle East and adjacent areas at night. The concentrations of lights indicate concentrations of population (compare Maps 4.2 and 4.7). The gray spots show reddish natural gas flares, especially offshore facilities in the Gulf area. (Copyright 2004, National Geographic Society, Washington, DC, July 2004. Used with NGS permission)

with between 100,000 and 500,000 have become more numerous since the 1970s and are found in almost all Middle East countries and peripheral states. Nevertheless, despite the trend of increasing urbanization, a high proportion of the people of the extended region still live in villages.

Some of the scattered dots on Map 4.2 represent nomadic pastoralists, whose numbers in most countries can only be estimated. Their high mobility has made them historically difficult to count, but their numbers have been steadily decreasing. Several hundred thousand Bedouin of the Arabian Peninsula are known to have settled between 1960 and 2012, and the same is happening

with Bedouin elsewhere, partly because of official pressures and incentives. Rough estimates for the region are 600,000 Bedouin, 1.5 million other nomads, and 2.5 million who move their livestock between mountain and lowland pastures with the seasons—a lifestyle called "transhumance" or "vertical nomadism" (Fig. 4.2).

Largest to Smallest. Populations of the extended region's states vary greatly, as Table 4.1 and Graph 4.1 indicate for the sixteen core states. As is true anywhere, population variations can be traced to six major factors: quality of the geographical environment, range and quality of natural resources, effectiveness

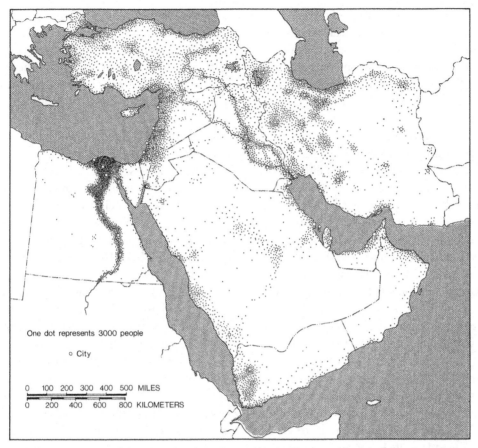

Map 4.2 Dot map of distribution of rural population. The proverbial density of population in the Nile Valley and Delta is clearly shown. Scattered smaller villages are underrepresented. Compare with Figure 4.1.

Figure 4.2
Bedouin in Saudi Arabia, watering their camels at wells in the broad Wadi Sahba, west of Harad, enjoy a joke with author Held.

of the national economy (and outside aid)—including food supply and health care—social and political pressures for or against population increase, incidental or planned (and even forced) immigration and emigration, and territorial size. In Part Two, these factors are explored for each country, but some quantitative comparisons can be made here.

In 2012, all three of the largest populations are clustered around 75 to 83 million—Egypt, Iran, and Turkey (see Graph 4.1); they are among the four geographically biggest countries and are also three of the four major power cores (see Map 3.6). Iraq has the fourth-largest population and is the fourth major power core. Slightly smaller, the fifth-largest population inhabits the geographically biggest state in the region—Saudi Arabia. Yemen and Syria, next in size, have moderately large populations for their partly rugged and partly arid environments. Israel's population growth has depended on periodically explosive immigration and capital transfers; similar growth has been experienced by the UAE, as expatriate labor has been attracted by the demands of its economy. Jordan, populated somewhat out of proportion to its scant natural resources, has also seen considerable immigration—of Palestinian refugees. Lebanon, on the other hand, has grown much more slowly, partly because of low birth rates by regional standards and partly because of emigration induced by years of civil strife. Oman has a relatively small population for its size because of extensive barren areas with small numbers of nomads. Kuwait, Qatar, Bahrain, and Cyprus are still smaller with prosperous populations; except for Cyprus, they are basically city-states.

Density

Along with the basic patterns of population distribution, those of population density—the number of persons per unit of area—are also significant. However, these figures for most regional countries are not comparable

to those for European countries, where few extensive areas are uninhabited. As the dots in Map 4.2 show, Middle Easterners congregate heavily in a few locales, and there are large extents that are uninhabited or have only a few nomads or widely scattered villages. Thus, aside from favored areas like Asia Minor and the Levant, concentrations are in "islands" of better environments.

Some small oases may be widely scattered, with only a few families occupying each, as in the Jiwa (Liwa) oases in western Abu Dhabi; by contrast, tens of millions may be crowded into a narrow, intensively cultivated valley, like that of the Nile. In both cases, only a small percentage of total state area is actually occupied. For example, Egypt's 83.7 million people have an overall density of 217.2 per mi^2/83.9 per km^2. However, population density based on the area actually inhabited and cultivated, about 3.5 percent of Egypt's total area, soars to more than 6,200 per mi^2/2,390 per km^2. The overall density on the small island of Bahrain is very high (4,440 per mi^2/1,710 per km^2), but it is two to three times higher in the areas actually occupied. The anomalous density in the Gaza Strip—more than 12,210 per mi^2/4,700 per km^2—reflects the appalling crowding of refugees in this artificial territory.

Rates of Birth, Death, and Increase

Statistics show a sharp decline over the twentieth century in crude death rates (deaths per 1,000 population) in developing countries. Better hygiene, health education, and healthcare facilities have lowered infant and maternal mortality and lengthened the average human life. Birthrates have not really increased overall (those for live births have, however), but death rates have decreased notably in many countries. The result has been a marked rise in population.

As shown in Table 4.1, the growth rates of the sixteen core countries, plus Palestine, show high population growth, due to high birthrates and immigration rates. Whereas the

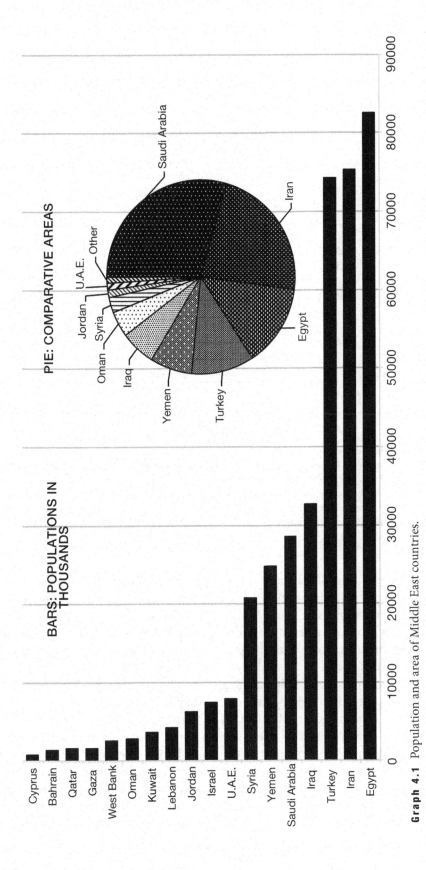

Graph 4.1 Population and area of Middle East countries.

TABLE 4.1 Area and Demography

Country	1 Area in sq. mi.	2 Area in sq. km.	3 Pop in 1000s	4 Density per sq. mi.	5 Density per sq. km.	6 % Pop. Urban	7 % Annual Growth
Bahrain	292	757	1,325	4537.7	1750.3	88.5	6.6
Cyprus[a]	3,572	9,251	1,118	313.0	120.9	68.8	1.7
Egypt	386,874	1,002,000	82,537	213.3	82.4	42.6	1.8
Iran	636,374	1,648,200	75,276	119.0	45.9	68.5	1.5
Iraq	167,618	434,128	32,665	194.9	75.2	67.9	3.0
Israel	8,357[b]	21,643	7,431[c]	889.2	343.3	91.6	1.7
Jordan[d]	34,277	88,778	6,180	180.3	69.6	78.3	2.2
Kuwait	6,880	17,818	3,650	530.5	204.8	98.3	3.4
Lebanon	4,036	10,452	4,143	1,026.5	396.4	86.6	1.5
Oman	119,500	309,500	2,810	23.5	9.1	71.5	2.4
Qatar	4,468	11,571	1,624	363.5	140.4	100.0	10.1
Saudi Arabia	830,000	2,149,690	24,780	29.9	11.5	87.7	2.4
Syria	71,498	185,180	20,766	290.4	140.4	100.0	10.1
Turkey	303,224	785,347	74,306	245.1	94.6	69.2	1.4
UAE	32,280	83,600	7,891	244.5	94.4	76.7	11.0
Yemen	203,891	528,076	24,800	121.6	47.0	28.6	3.6
Gaza	141	365	1,574	11,163.1	4,312.3	—	3.1
West Bank	2,183	5,655	2,551	1,168.6	451.1	71.6	2.4
TOTAL/AVG.	2,815,465	7,292,011	379,219	134.7	52.0	69.3	3.5
United Kingdom	93,851	243,073	62,675	667.8	257.8	89.5	0.7
Venezuela	353,841	916,445	29,437	83.2	32.1	87.2	1.6

Area includes internal waters. Population data are estimates for 2011. Percentage of population that is urban (Column 6) from most recent census. Percentage of annual growth rate (Column 7) is average for the period 2006–2011. [a]Data are for the entire island. [b]Excludes the West Bank and Gaza Strip. [c]Includes Golan Heights and East Jerusalem, and excludes Israelis in the West Bank. [d]Excludes the West Bank, formerly under Jordanian administration. The text sometimes uses more recent population data taken from the CIA *World Factbook 2012*. Data for the UK and Venezuela given for comparison. (*Source: Britannica World Data 2012* [used with permission])

crude birthrates of Syria, Oman, and Yemen all exceeded 40 per 1,000 population several years ago—similar to rates in many African countries—only Yemen's rate remained in that grouping into the 2010s.[5] Some countries, particularly Egypt, Turkey, and Iran, have emphasized government-supported family-planning programs, but some groups resist because traditional customs encourage large families. In Israel, where as a group Jews have one of the lowest birthrates in the region, the state encourages more Jewish births to offset the higher Arab birthrate—but aside from ultrareligious groups and some West Bank settlers, success has been limited.

Important Distinctions.   Birthrates vary both from country to country and, within countries, among groups and classes—for example, across religious and ethnic groups (sometimes equivalent to economic classes) in all Middle East countries. The rate is substantially lower among Coptic Christians than Muslims in Egypt, lower among Maronites than Shii in Lebanon, lower among secular Jews than ultra-Orthodox and Oriental Jews in Israel, and lower among Greeks than Turks in Cyprus. These differences can accentuate political antagonisms because they might lead to changes in the balance of power. Population pyramids (Graph 4.2) show the distribution of

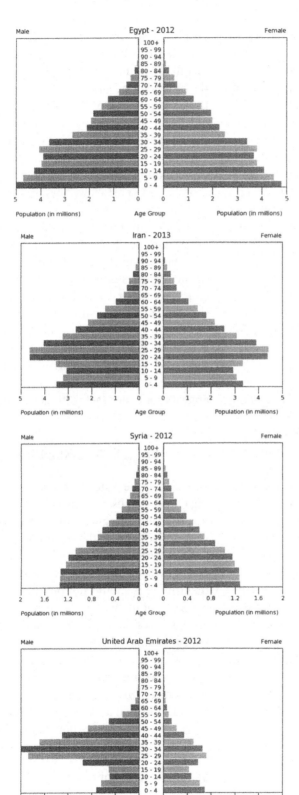

Graph 4.2
Contrasting population pyramids
of four Middle East countries.
(*Source:* US Census Bureau,
International Data Base)

age cohorts (see Glossary), varying in shape from country to country depending on factors like changes in birthrates and migration. For Egypt and Syria, the relative overall youth of the population is obvious (and probably a significant factor in the political upheavals in both countries since 2011). For Syria and especially Iran, declining birthrates have slowed population growth; under the shah, family planning was stressed, but the Islamic Republic at first reversed this policy before reinstating it (see Chap. 21). The UAE (like other Gulf states) has a large number of male expatriates of working age.

Migration

All three basic aspects of migration—immigration, emigration, and internal migration—play major roles in defining the contemporary pattern of peoples in the Middle East. For example, immigration into the region (by Jews and South Asians, for example) and migration within the region (by Palestinians, Jordanians, Egyptians, Jews, Lebanese, and Kurds) have dramatically increased some populations and profoundly altered the ethnic makeup of some states. The extraordinary influx of Jews into Israel from 1945 to 1951 and again after 1989 from the Former Soviet Union completely reconstituted the population, character, and political orientation of traditional Palestine.

Generally, emigration from the region has not been so large. However, since the middle of the twentieth century, hundreds of thousands have fled limited economic opportunities, conflict, and discrimination, going to the United States, Canada, Western Europe, and Australia—particularly Turks, Palestinian Arabs, Christian Lebanese, Syrians, Jordanians, Kurds, Israelis, Iranians, and, in the 2000s, Iraqis.

PATTERNS: PEOPLES

It is the cultural differentiation among peoples—variations in language, religion, customs and dress, values, and historical experiences—that creates separate group identities and nations. Thus, examination of the mosaic of peoples, or ethnic groups, is a major component of this analysis of the region. Cultural patterns are, in effect, shuffled three times—on the basis of language, religion, and ethnic groups. The first two, dominant culturally, deserve individual attention; those sections are followed by a survey of ethnic groups.

Two salient points about the patterns of peoples are worth noting at the outset: somewhat more than 40 percent of the population of the region is non-Arab (although twelve countries are Arab), and within its essential theological unity Islam carries ethnic and political imprints but has several sectarian variations. Thus, the region has great cultural diversity.[6] When the extended Middle East states are considered, even greater variety appears—a major factor hindering regional unity.

PATTERNS: LANGUAGES

Language is the principal criterion for defining ethnic groups, particularly if the distinction is an ethnolinguistic one. Thus, Map 4.3 summarizes one of the most revealing patterns in the cultural geography of the Middle East. The depiction of only six main linguistic groupings should not obscure the presence of about twenty-five other language groups in less accessible basins, valleys, and plateaus. Some of these languages appear on Map 4.3, but many others are covered in the listing of ethnic groups later in the chapter, and some of them are discussed in this section. The principal languages of the region are, in order of speaker populations, Arabic, Turkish, Farsi, Kurdish, Azeri, and Hebrew.

Semitic and Berber

The Semitic language group includes Arabic, the numerically predominant regional lan-

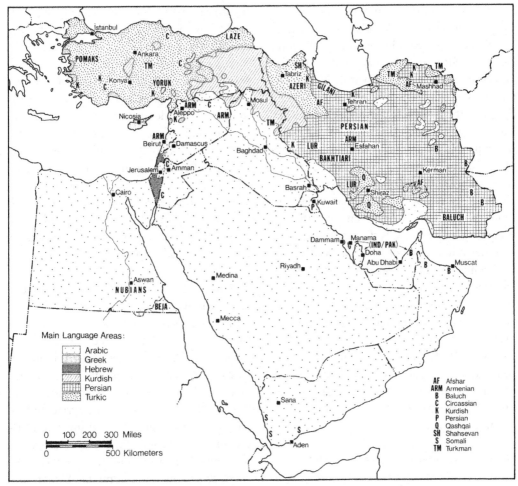

Map 4.3 Middle East languages, indicating ethnolinguistic groups. This pattern has been the basis for numerous political developments and regional conflicts. Note that the complexity of the pattern of languages is greatest in mountain areas, especially in Iran.

guage; Hebrew, spoken in Israel; and vestiges of Aramaic, formerly spoken widely throughout the Middle East going back more than twenty-five hundred years. The North African Berber and Coptic languages are grouped here with the Semitic languages, although they belong to different subfamilies.

Arabic. Arabic is the national language of twelve of the core countries of the region (plus Palestine)[7] and is spoken by more than half the total population of the core countries, about 215 million people. It is spoken by

about another 105 million North Africans and Sudanese. Three levels of usage prevail: (1) colloquial, informal spoken Arabic, varying across the region; (2) modern standard Arabic, or "newspaper Arabic," the more formal version used in the media; and (3) classical Arabic, the formal and highly conventionalized style based on the language of pre-Islamic poetry, the Quran, and writings from the first few Islamic centuries. Educated Arabs understand all three, but the uneducated have difficulty with the two more formal levels. In addition, there are four major dialects in the twelve Arab countries in the Mashriq: those of Egypt, Syria (western Arabic), Iraq (eastern Arabic), and the Arabian Peninsula. Significant differences of vocabulary and pronunciation exist among, and even within, these four. One major example is the pronunciation in Egypt of the Arabic "j" (*jiim*) as a hard "g." Thus, *jabal* (mountain) is pronounced *gabal* in Egypt: this creates problems transliterating place-names. Variants across North Africa (the Maghrib) are even further removed.

Speaking Arabic as a mother tongue is more the hallmark of being an Arab than is genetic history. Since it is the language of the Quran, the holy book of Islam, it has a mystical quality for many Arabs. It has additional emotional overtones as the language in which speeches and documents on Arab nationalism are prepared. In written form, it even plays a central role in art, since calligraphy is widely used in traditional decorative motifs in lieu of the sometimes proscribed human and animal forms; it is one of the highest Islamic fine arts. (See the excellent example in the opening pages of this book.)

Hebrew.   Compared with Arabic, Hebrew is the mother tongue in a relatively limited area for a comparatively small number of people, a little more than 5 million—not of all the Jews in the region or even of all Israeli Jews. An ancient language, it was the vernacular for more than one thousand years in the traditional Old Testament area of Israel. It ceased to be a working language centuries ago, but for Jewish communities it has remained the language of religion, much as Latin, Greek, and Syriac have been used in Christian liturgies. As a scriptural language, like Arabic for Muslims, it has a mystical quality for religious Jews. For the ultrareligious, it is so sacred that it is reserved only for rituals; some regard as near blasphemy its vernacular use and employ instead Yiddish or other languages. Many recent FSU emigrants have resisted adopting Hebrew, hold-

ing on to Russian. As a second language, it is spoken by many Arabs in both Israel proper and the Palestinian areas.

Hebrew was revived in the late nineteenth century under the stimulus of the Zionist movement—because a unifying language was needed as an added stimulus for Jewish immigrants to Palestine. Contemporary usage has required adaptation of old terms and the coinage of new ones; its evolution has been much influenced by other languages, both regional and international. Because Israeli scholarly and scientific writings would have only limited readership in Hebrew, English is commonly used in journals.

Aramaic.   Now primarily of historical interest, Aramaic served for more than fifteen hundred years as the lingua franca of the Fertile Crescent; it had replaced Hebrew as the language of Palestine well before the time of Christ and was, it is generally agreed, his language.[8] Like Latin to the West, Aramaic was used in Bible translations. The Syriac form of Aramaic is used in the scriptures and liturgies of several Oriental Christian churches— Maronite, Nestorian, and Chaldean—and by such sects as the Mandaeans and Samaritans. Modern dialects of it are also still spoken by many Assyrians in Iraq and by a number of Christians in a small mountainous area northwest of Damascus.

Berber.   A subfamily language in the Afro-Asiatic language family, Berber is spoken by more than 14 million North Africans, especially in Morocco and Algeria. In the core Middle East, only a few thousand Berbers live in oases in northwestern Egypt.

Coptic.   With a name derived from *Qibt*, a corruption of the Greek word *Aigyptos* (Egypt), Coptic was the latest form of the ancient Egyptian language. Greek influenced it during the Hellenistic period, but it was Egypt's vernacular until, over the centuries, it was gradually supplanted by Arabic after the Muslim conquest. The discovery that many Coptic words came directly from ancient Egyptian aided in the deciphering of hieroglyphics. By the sixteenth century, it was used primarily in the liturgy of the Coptic Christian church in Egypt; that remains the case today, although there has been a movement to revive the language since the late nineteenth century that has had some modest success.

Altaic Turkic Languages

The Altaic family includes a large number of languages spoken in the FSU and in China, as well as Magyar (Hungarian) and Finnish in Europe and more than a score of Turkic languages spoken in Central Asia, the Trans-Caucasus, and the Middle East.

Turkish. The best known of the Turkic languages, Turkish is spoken by the largest number of Turkic-language speakers. The national language of the Republic of Turkey, it was brought into the region by tribes migrating from Central Asia in the tenth to thirteenth centuries. As they adopted Islam and settled in Asia Minor, the language absorbed loanwords from Arabic and literary Persian.

Lacking a standard alphabet of its own, for eight to nine hundred years Turkish was rather inadequately written in Arabic script. In 1928, the Latin alphabet, with some borrowed diacritical marks, was officially adopted, and the language was "purified" of Arabic and Persian terms. In the region, it is spoken throughout the Republic of Turkey and by Turkish Cypriots in northern Cyprus; elsewhere, it is spoken by small scattered groups in the Fertile Crescent.

Azeri. Azeri (or Azerbaijani) is the second major Turkic language in the region, centered in northwestern Iran, adjacent areas in Iraq, and the Republic of Azerbaijan. Variations appear in the western Elburz and the southern Caspian littoral among the Afshar,

Shahsavan (now called Ilsavan), and Qajar groups. Like Turkish, Azeri entered with migrating tribes during the Abbasid era.

Other Turkic languages, spoken by several hundred thousand people each in Iran, Turkey, and Iraq, include Qashqai (spoken by tribes in the southern Zagros Mountains of Iran) and various Turkman dialects spoken by scattered peoples in the Anatolian-Iranian mountains and basins and in small areas in northeastern Iraq. Still others are the national tongues of peripheral "stan" states: Turkman in Turkmenistan and northern Afghanistan, Uzbek in Uzbekistan and northern Afghanistan, Kazakh in Kazakhstan, and Kyrgyz in Kyrgyzstan.

Indo-European Languages

The Indo-European languages of the region include more than a score of Indo-Iranian tongues, the main ones being Farsi (Persian), Kurdish, Baluchi, and Luri (with its related dialect of Bakhtiari). Armenian and Greek—in the Indo-European family—are spoken by several hundred thousand people each. Four other languages in this family, which are spoken by millions of people in the eastern areas of the peripheral states, are also discussed below.

Farsi (Persian). The primary Indo-Iranian language is Farsi, a name taken from the ancient Iranian province of Fars. After Arabic and Turkish, it is spoken by the third-largest language group in the region. The Persian languages were brought to the Iranian Plateau more than fifteen hundred years before Turkic languages were heard in the area. After the Muslim conquest of Iran in the seventh century, Persian, like Turkish, incorporated hundreds of Arabic loanwords, adopting a modified Arabic script.

It is the primary language of Iran, although nearly half of Iranians speak another mother tongue—including Azeri, Kurdish, Gilaki, Luri, Baluchi, and Arabic. However, as the official language and that used by the mass media, government, and educational institutions, Farsi is a second language for most minority groups. Persian literature has a rich history dating from the transcription into an ancient form of the language in the Zoroastrian scriptures, the *Avesta,* before 500 BCE. It has official status with many native speakers in Afghanistan and Tajikistan as well.

Kurdish.   The second most common Indo-Iranian language in the region, Kurdish is found across a geographical range extending from the streets of Beirut eastward to remote valleys in Afghanistan, though its main concentration of more than 30 million speakers is in the mountains of Kurdistan. It is grammatically and lexically distinct from Persian, and two major dialects may be distinguished.[9] The pattern of Kurdish speakers exploded into a major factor in Iraq after 2003. Reflecting the extension of Kurdistan into several hegemonies, Kurdish is written with the Arabic alphabet in Iraq and Syria, the adapted Arabic alphabet in Iran, and the Latin alphabet in Turkey.

Other Indo-Iranian Languages.   Baluchi is spoken in Baluchistan in southeastern and eastern Iran; even more speakers are in the adjacent areas of Pakistan and Afghanistan. It is also spoken by several thousand Baluch across the Gulf in the UAE and Oman. Luri, a dialect of Persian, is spoken by nomadic tribes in the central Zagros, both by the Lur themselves and also, in a slightly different dialect, by their Bakhtiari neighbors. Sometimes called "Caspian" languages, a half-dozen Indo-Iranian dialects, mixed with one or two Turkic tongues, are spoken along the southern Caspian coast and on the northern slopes of the Elburz Mountains. Indo-European languages—some spoken by as many as 50 million people—common in the peripheral countries include Tajik in Tajikistan, Pushtun (or Pashtu or Pakto) in Afghanistan and Pakistan, Punjabi (or Panjabi) in Pakistan, and Dari (closely related to, or perhaps more accurately, a dialect of Farsi) and Hazara in Afghanistan.

Armenian and Greek.   Armenian and Greek, two Indo-European languages, were formerly spoken over more extensive areas in the region than at present. Armenian was the dominant language for more than two thousand years in the area of historical Armenia—the highlands at the junction of Turkey, Iran, and the modern Republic of Armenia. However, Armenian speakers in the core Middle East are now found mainly in urban centers, such as Istanbul, Aleppo, Damascus, Beirut, Nicosia, Tehran, Cairo, Baghdad, and Jerusalem. The language is, of course, the national tongue of the adjacent Republic of Armenia.

Similarly, Greek was a major language in western Asia Minor two thousand years before Turks arrived in significant numbers, and it took root on numerous Mediterranean islands, including Cyprus. As the urban and intellectual language of the Levant for centuries after Alexander the Great, Greek was the original language for much of the New Testament, as well as for the Septuagint, the oldest surviving version of the Old Testament. However, only a few thousand Greek speakers remain in Asia Minor, the Levant, and Egypt; the main concentration is now in southern Cyprus.

PATTERNS: RELIGIONS

Complex Patterns of Religion

At first glance, the pattern of religions appears simple: Islam embraces more than 90 percent of the people of the core Middle East. This pattern, however, is complicated by the interwoven and disparate segments of Islam, by the basic divisions within Islam between Sunni and Shii, and by the splintering of Shii sects.

Divisions within Christianity, which developed in the region, are even more numerous. Differing theological interpretations resulted in major schisms, which were later only partly mended by the church in Rome, until more than a dozen sects claimed sole possession of Christian truth.

Several million Jews are now concentrated in Israel, where ethnic and sectarian subdivisions periodically dispute such issues as conversion and the proper observance of the Sabbath. Ancient or syncretic religions—Zoroastrian, Yazidi, Mandaean, Alawi/Alevi, Druze, and Bahai—constitute small but significant Middle Eastern minorities.

Religious divisions have long played, and now increasingly play, significant cultural-political-geographical roles in the Middle East. In recent decades, political instability and social violence have increasingly devolved from intensification of religious and ethnic consciousness. In turn, political polarization resulting from religious fervor has inflamed communal feelings and weakened national bonds. The increasing linkages between politics and religion have been a cause of growing apprehension since the 1970s, and especially after 9/11. This topic is explored in Chapters 8 and 9.

Roots of Modern Patterns. The pattern of religions has been strongly influenced by two historical factors in relatively modern times. First, when Muslims conquered the area from the Nile River to the Iranian Plateau in the seventh century, there were millions of Christians and Zoroastrians, scores of thousands of Jews, thousands of Mandaeans, and many other smaller groups. In general, the Muslim invaders proselytized these conquered peoples. However, the Quran taught that Jews and Christians were *ahl al-kitab* (people of the book), permitted to keep their religions and communities under certain conditions. Later, Mandaeans, Zoroastrians, and even Berbers were accepted as people of the book. Therefore, religious groups had a strong group identity linked with their courts, areas of residence, occupations, and usually language, as well as religion. This group identity

persists, and it continues to affect regional relationships and the internal politics of Middle East states.

In a second historical development, the concept of people of the book was codified in the Ottoman Empire into the *millet* system (from *millah*, "religion" or "religious community"), and *millets* further imprinted group consciousness on the non-Muslims of the Middle East. Religious affiliation assumed great cultural-political significance, and identity cards in Lebanon and Israel, for example, still indicate in some way the individual's religion.

Three Monotheistic World Religions

The Middle East is familiarly and significantly known as the birthplace of the world's three major monotheistic religions: the Abrahamic religions—Judaism, Christianity, and Islam (Map 4.4; Fig. 4.3), all of which worship the same God and trace their origins to the patriarch Abraham. Judaism and Christianity both arose in the hills between the Mediterranean coastal plain and the Jordan Valley, and Islam originated 700 mi/1,125 km to the southeast on the heights inland from the Red Sea. As Judaism borrowed from Mesopotamian and Canaanite traditions, so Christianity evolved from Judaic and other practices of the region, and Islam borrowed heavily from Judaism, Christianity, and local Hijazi customs. In the early twenty-first century, Muslims number about 345 million, more than 90 percent of the population of the region. Christianity is the second-largest religion, with some 18 to 22 million adherents, and Judaism third with approximately 6 million.

The following discussion focuses on spatial relations rather than historical evolution or theology. Islam is examined first and in somewhat more detail because of its greater geographical and quantitative importance in the region and because it is less well known or understood outside the Muslim world.

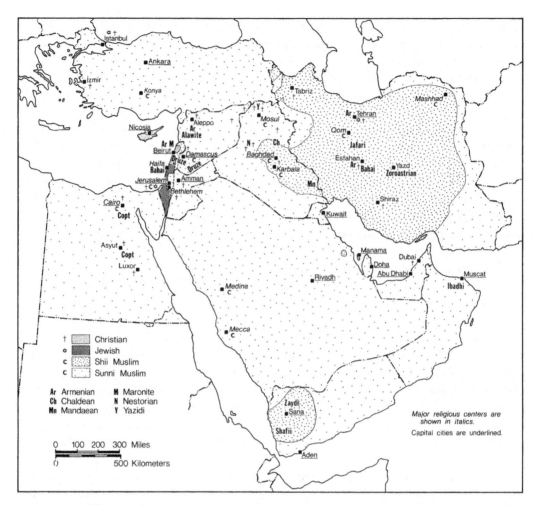

Map 4.4 Middle East religions. Note the overwhelming dominance of Islam and the extension of Shiism into southern Iraq.

Islam. The Arabic word "Islam" signifies submitting oneself to God's will, and a Muslim is "one who submits." The term "Muhammadan" is a misnomer, since it suggests a parallel with "Christian"—a worshiper of Christ—whereas Muslims do not worship Muhammad. Rather, they revere him and his teachings, and they consider him the Seal of the Prophets, that is, the last and greatest of the prophets, a line that had stretched from Adam, Noah, and Abraham to John the Baptist and Jesus.[10]

The origins of Islam are regional in character. Mecca, the Arabian town in which

Islam evolved, was an important caravan post between Yemen and Syria. Its importance was enhanced by the Well of Zamzam, since water was scarce along Tihamah, the barren Red Sea coastal plain followed by the caravans. It was also the site of an ancient shrine, the *Kaabah,* which contained an array of idols and housed the revered Black Stone (a meteorite). Rapid development in the sixth century stimulated intellectual exchange, as townspeople and Bedouin from the Hijaz mingled with the caravan travelers from Syria, Yemen, and elsewhere.

Figure 4.3
St. Sophia (Greek: Haghia Sophia; Turkish: Aya Sofya [Divine Wisdom]) in Istanbul. Originally built as a Byzantine church in the sixth century, it was converted into a mosque when Constantinople was captured by the Ottomans in 1453. Deconsecrated in 1934, it is now a museum and a major tourist attraction.

Muhammad. One Mecca merchant who was inspired by the ideas being discussed was Muhammad ibn Abdullah, a member of the Hashim clan of the Quraysh tribe.[11] While meditating in a nearby cave, he received what he later explained were dictations from the Angel Gabriel of the Holy Word of the one God (Arabic *Allah* = the God). Preaching his revelations, he denounced the Kaabah idols and thereby endangered Mecca's pilgrim trade. Harassed by local merchants, Muhammad and his followers—the original Muslims— emigrated to Yathrib, 210 mi/340 km north of Mecca. Yathrib later became known as al-Madinat al-Nabi (the City of the Prophet), or simply al-Madina (the City). The migration was in 622 CE, which became the first year of the Islamic calendar. Muslim years, comprising twelve lunar months (ten or eleven days shorter than Gregorian or solar years),[12] are designated as Anno Hegirae (AH), year of the Hegira (Arabic *hijrah* = flight).

The Quran. In Medina, the Prophet recited dictations from the Angel to his followers until his death in 632. These were assembled in 651 into the Muslim scriptures, the Quran (Koran), meaning "recitation"—the essential core of Islam. Accepted by Muslims as the exact Word of God linking God and believers, the Quran uses poetic language reflecting the Hijaz and village and Bedouin traditions, just as the Old and New Testaments refer to the desert traditions of Sinai and the Syro-Palestinian area.

Translation of the Quran from Arabic was long strongly discouraged, since that would mean altering the direct Word of God, and converts perforce had to learn the language in order to understand the scriptures. As Islam spread throughout the Middle East and North Africa to Spain and into Central Asia (Map 4.5), the Arabic language also spread, with crucial historical and political-geographical consequences.

The Muslim place of worship is the mosque (from Arabic *masjid,* "place of worship"). Each mosque has an exterior minaret and interior *mihrab,* which indicates where worshipers should direct their prayers— toward Mecca. Figure 4.4 pictures one type of mosque; styles are nearly unlimited. Over the

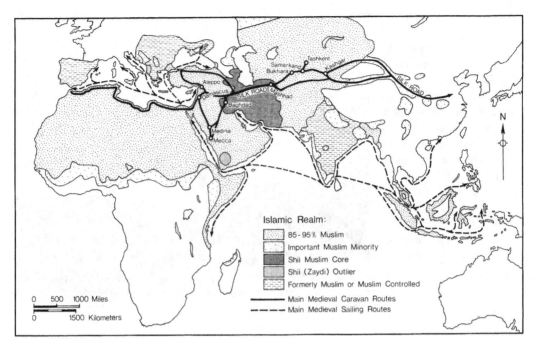

Map 4.5 Present extent of Islam, with major medieval caravan and sea routes that contributed to the spread and persistence of Islam.

centuries, thousands of shrines have been built all over the Islamic world; they are interesting and moving features in many otherwise barren landscapes (Fig. 4.5).

Pillars of Islam.   Although Islam, like all religions, has elaborated a complex and subtle body of theology, both its essential message and its practice are simple and straightforward, and that is one of the reasons for its rapidly growing numbers. Its one fundamental essential is that a convert express and believe the *shahadah,* or profession of faith: "There is no god but God; Muhammad is the messenger of God," a translation of the euphonious Arabic *La ilaha illa Allah; Muhammadun rasulu Allah.* The *shahadah* and four additional primary obligations constitute the five pillars of Islam, which have profoundly affected regional character in the Islamic world: *salah,* devotional worship or prayer five times a day facing toward the Kaabah, the House of God, in Mecca (Fig. 4.6); *zakah,*

religious tax (and *sadaqah,* voluntary almsgiving, additionally meritorious); *sawm,* fasting during the holy month of Ramadan, ninth in the year; and, for those who have the means, undertaking the *hajj,* the pilgrimage to Mecca.

Sharia.   The Quran underlies Sharia, the sacred law of Islam, which covers all aspects of the lives of Muslims—not only religious and private but also political and public, social and economic. Sharia still plays an important role in the legal systems of several Middle East countries—notably Saudi Arabia, Qatar, and Iran—and complements the more Westernized legal codes of countries such as Egypt, Syria, and Iraq. Resurgent Islamic fundamentalism, which has received so much attention since 9/11 and even more since the onset of the Arab Spring in 2011, has brought a renewed interest in Sharia, especially since it is at times in conflict with modern secular trends in the region.

Figure 4.4
Martyrs' Mosque, Baghdad. The unusual architectural style incorporates certain Persian influences from the East and Umayyad influences from the West.

Figure 4.5 Muslim shrine and tomb of Shaykh Ahmad bin Isa in the Wadi Hadramawt, eastern Yemen. A visit to the tomb is a poignant experience, and many such shrines are found throughout the Middle East.

Figure 4.6 Muslim members of the Jordanian Desert Patrol performing one of the five daily prayers, near Petra. (Tor Eigeland/Saudi Aramco World/SAWDIA)

Islam was for many centuries both religion and government, and when Sharia was compiled, it combined religious and civil matters. The caliph (Arabic *khalifah* = successor) thus led both the community of believers (the *ummah*) and the Islamic state. Although subsequent schisms placed severe strains on the unity of religion and state, resurgent fundamentalism—Islamism—has revived ferment for Islamized control in several states, from Morocco to Afghanistan and Pakistan.

Schisms and Conflicts.   The most momentous dispute within Islam occurred with the seventh-century division between Sunni and Shia.[13] It has led to wars, assassinations, civil conflict, and rancor throughout the Muslim world for more than thirteen hundred years and has major repercussions in the Middle East today.

Sunnis.   The Sunni—*ahl al-sunnah wa-l-jamaah*, "the people of custom and community"—consider themselves the original orthodox Muslims and have always been in the overwhelming majority. They believe that caliphs should be chosen by leaders of the *ummah* primarily to be secular leaders.

Shia.   The Shia—*shiat Ali*, "partisans (or supporters) of Ali"—separated beginning in 657, holding that only descendants of Muhammad, through his daughter Fatima and son-in-law Ali, were legitimate successors to the Prophet. To the Shia, these successors are divinely guided, sinless, infallible religious leaders (imams) with authority to interpret the Prophet's spiritual knowledge. The schism has accentuated political, social, and cultural divisions both historically and currently—perhaps as bitterly today as at any time in the past—in Iraq particularly, but also in Lebanon, Yemen, Saudi Arabia, and Bahrain, as well as in peripheral Pakistan (see Chaps. 8 and 9).

After the initial split, the Shia further divided over succession issues (Table 4.2):

1. The predominant group accepted Ali and eleven of his descendants as the true imams and became known as Twelvers (also *Ithna Asharis, Imamis,* and *Jafaris*). They are concentrated in Iran and Iraq, but at least some are found in every Middle East country.

2. A smaller group preferred a different seventh imam, Ismail, and became known as Seveners (also *Ismailis*). Some of them split off later into heterodox sects such as the Druze and the Alawi. They had political power between the tenth and thirteenth centuries. Early Ismaili dynasties ruled in Syria and Bahrain, and the Fatimids, named for Muhammad's daughter, achieved an Egyptian renaissance during the tenth to twelfth centuries. Ismaili "assassins" engaged in political sabotage and murder, primarily in northern Iran. Found today mainly in India, Syria, the Gulf area, and East Africa, contemporary Ismailis form three communities— the largest is headed by the Agha Khan.

3. A third group of Shia chose a different fifth imam, Zayd, and became known as Fivers (also *Zaydis*). They are concentrated in Yemen, where Zaydi secular imams held power until the overthrow of Imam Muhammad al-Badr in 1962. Yemeni Shii links originated in the support given Ali by Yemeni tribesmen settling in southern Mesopotamia after the Arab Muslim conquest of the area.

Ibadhis.   An isolated, little-known group of Muslims, the Ibadhis, live in Inner Oman, where they were banished from southern Iraq in the seventh century. They are descendants of the Kharijites (*khawarij* = those who went out), who assassinated Ali but differed with both Sunni and Shii beliefs regarding caliphal succession. They maintained their imamate in

Inner Oman and periodically fought for control of Muscat and all of Oman into the midtwentieth century. With Nazwa as their main center, they are now a conservative group integrated into Omani development.

Heterodox Sects.   Two offshoots mentioned above deserve attention; both have Ismaili roots. The Druze originated in Cairo in 1017 with followers of the Fatimid caliph al-Hakim. Although they called themselves *Muwahhidun* (Unitarists), outsiders called them Druze after the name of an early missionary. They won large numbers of converts among isolated mountain peoples in southern Lebanon and adjacent areas, and they are still concentrated in that region. They constitute an esoteric and nonproselytizing sect, and their present connections to the rest of Islam are tenuous at best.

The second offshoot sect, the Alawis (also known as *Nusayris* and sometimes *Ansariyahs*), are concentrated in northwestern Syria and nearby parts of Turkey. Although "Alawi" indicates "followers of Ali," the rituals of their esoteric religion include pre-Christian, Christian, and Sabian elements as well as Shii practices; ethnically nearly all Alawi are Arabs. Using neither mosques nor churches, Alawis conduct rites at shrines near revered tombs and sacred groves.

In Turkey, a sect somewhat similar and notably larger (with numerous differences in origin, beliefs, and practices) than the Alawi is that of the Alevi; Arabs, Turks, and Kurds are numbered among its estimated millions of adherents, and they often conceal their heterodoxy. Again, their connection with contemporary Islam is disputed.

Another sect with Islamic origins is the Ahmadiyya Community, which arose in the late nineteenth century in what is now Pakistan. For the most part, they are not considered to be Muslims by either Sunnis or Shia and are subject to persecution in their original base, Pakistan. There are very few who profess the faith openly in the region considered in

TABLE 4.2 Religions of the Middle East

Religion, Church, Sect (Including Alternate Names)	Main Center or Pat. Seat	Liturgical Language	Main Areas in Which Found in Mideast
— ISLAM —			
Sunni Islam (largest sect by far)	None (Mecca)	>Ar; Turk, Farsi	Most of Mideast
Shia Islam (second-largest sect by far)	None (Mecca, Karbala)	Farsi, Arabic	Iran, southern Iraq, South Lebanon
Imamis (Jafaris, "Twelvers," Ithna Ashari)	——	Farsi, Arabic	Iran, Iraq
Ismailis ("Seveners")	——	Arabic	Levant
Zaydis ("Fivers")	——	Arabic	Yemen
Alawis/Alevis (Alawites, Nusayris, Ansaris)	None	Arabic, Turkish	W Syria, Turkey
Druze (Muwahhidun ["Unitarians"])	None	Arabic	S Syr, C Leb, N Isr
Ibadhis	Nazwa, Oman	Arabic	Inner Oman, <Iran
— CHRISTIANITY —			
Churches with no outside affiliation			
Coptic Orthodox Church (COC, Alexandria)	Cairo	Coptic, Arabic	C and N Egypt
Armenian Orthodox Ch. (Arm. Georgian Church)	Antilyas, Leb	Armenian	C Middle East
Syrian Orth. Ch. (Jacobite Ch., W. Syr. Church)	Damascus	Syriac, Arabic	Syria, Iraq
Ethiopian Orthodox Church (Ethiopian Church)	Addis Ababa	Geez	Egypt
Church of the East (Nestorian Church, East Syrian Church, Assyrian Church)	Baghdad (official)	Syriac	Syria, Iraq
Churches affiliated with the Patriarchate of Constantinople			
Orthodox Patriarchate of Constantinople (Greek Orthodox Church of Const., the Great Church)	Istanbul	Greek	Levant
Greek Orth. Church of Antioch (Rum Orth., etc.)	Damascus	Arabic	Levant
Greek Orth. Church of Alexandria (Ch. of Alexandria)	Alexandria	Greek, Arabic	Egypt
Greek Orth. Church of Jerusalem (Ch. of Jerusalem)	Jerusalem	Arabic, Greek	Levant
Greek Orthodox (several other names)	(Several)	(Several)	Levant
Uniate Churches: Churches united with the Roman Catholic Church			
Coptic Catholic Church (Coptic Cath. Ch. of Alex.)	Cairo	Coptic, Arabic	Egypt
Maronite Church (Maronite Church of Antioch)	Bkirke, Leb	Syriac, Arabic	Central Lebanon
Syrian Catholic Ch. (Patriarchate of Antioch)	Beirut, Leb	Syriac, Arabic	Levant
Armenian Cath. Church (Arm. Cath. Ch. Cilicia)	Bzummar, Leb	Armenian	Levant
Chaldean Catholic Church (Chaldean Church)	Baghdad	Syriac, Arabic	Iraq
Melkite Church (Rum Catholic Church, Greek Catholic Church of Antioch)	Damascus	Arabic	Syria
Western Churches			
Roman Catholic Church	Rome	(Various)	Mideast
Protestant Churches (Presbyterians, Methodists, Baptists, Anglicans, several others)	——	English, others	Mideast
— JUDAISM —			
Orthodox Judaism	(Jerusalem)	Hebrew	Israel, <other ME
Hasidic Judaism [ultra-Orthodox Judaism]	(Jerusalem)	Hebrew	Israel
Samaritanism [offshoot of Judaism]	Nabulus, Holon	Aramaic	West Bank, Israel
— OTHERS —			
Yazidism (erroneously: "Devil Worship")	None	Kurdish, Ar	NW Iraq, NE Syria
Mandaeism (Sabianism, Mendaism)	None	Aramaic dial.	Baghdad, S Iraq
Bahaism	Haifa	(Several)	Iran, Levant
Zoroastrianism	None	Farsi	Central Iran

"Pat." = Patriarchal. "PA" = Palestinian Authority. Some liturgies use local languages (Arabic, Turkish, Farsi [Persian]) in addition to the traditional languages. Syriac is a form of Aramaic. Memberships vary widely, from more than 320 million Muslims to about 709 Samaritans. (*Sources:* Various, including Joseph 1983; *Britannica World Data 2012*; CIA *World Factbook; Background Notes 2009–11*; and authors' field research) this book except for a small number in Haifa, Israel.

Sufis. Before leaving this section, a brief word about another strand of Islam is in order. Sufism is not a separate sect; it is a form of mysticism with strong roots in Islam that adherents claim dates back to the time of the Prophet. The influence of this highly personal and meditative form of religion has waxed and waned over the centuries, and as in the past modern Sufis may come from either Sunni or Shii backgrounds. Many of its practices resemble those of Shiism—for example, reverence for the tombs of saints—and in recent years Sunni fundamentalists have targeted both Sufi shrines and adherents.

Salafis. Similarly, Salafis are not accurately described as a separate sect, nor is it really appropriate to use the term "fundamentalists" to describe them.[14] Because of the prominence of Salafis in the twenty-first century and especially since the onset of the Arab Spring, it is useful to consider them here briefly. Salafism includes a broad range of conservative Sunni movements that have in common high esteem for the practices, beliefs, and sayings of the earliest Muslims—the Companions of the Prophet Muhammad and the next generation or so of their disciples and followers (the *salaf*)—and an abhorrence of what its adherents see as additions to or modifications of the faith preached in the earliest days of Islam. Salafism is not identical with Wahabbism (the conservative interpretation of Islam identified with the ruling dynasty in Saudi Arabia); it opposes both Sufism and Shiism. Many Salafi scholars condemn terrorist groups that claim to be Salafist, but some Salafis are prone to declaring other Muslims as *takfir*—unbelievers—which then legitimates the use of deadly force against them or the governments dominated by them.

To briefly summarize some basic statistics, a comprehensive report on global Islam pub-

lished in 2009 makes the following points relevant to this study: these sixteen countries (plus Palestine) are home to about 22.6 percent of the world's 1.57 billion Muslims; the twenty-two members of the Arab League have about 20.3 percent; the vast majority of Muslims are neither Arab nor live in the Middle East; between 10 and 13 percent of Muslims worldwide and of Muslims in our core area are members of one of the Shii sects; and about 65 percent of all Shia live in the countries in this book.[15]

Christianity. Middle East Christianity today embraces more than a dozen sects centered on the spiritual and ethical teachings of Jesus of Nazareth, who is believed to have lived and taught in Palestine two thousand years ago.[16] In the Occidental world, calendar years have long been designated (with an inadvertent error of about four years) as *anno Domini* (AD), indicating years that have elapsed since the birth of Jesus. In this book, we use a more religiously neutral term—CE, Common (or, as some may prefer, Christian) Era.

Although other religions share the messianic concept, Christianity preaches, as a central belief, that Jesus was the long-awaited Messiah (Greek *Christos* = "the anointed") of Jewish prophecy. The early apostles and their followers compiled his teachings in the Gospels (good tidings) and added their own preachings and letters. Assembled, these writings form the New Testament (New Covenant), the main Christian scriptures—coupled with the Old Testament to constitute the Christian Bible. From its earliest years, Christianity incorporated influences from the region's several cultures—Jewish, Greek, Roman, and Aramaic.

By New Testament accounts, Jesus was acclaimed during his three-year ministry in Judea, Galilee, and nearby places. However, only a few of his followers, mainly converted Jews, remained faithful after his crucifixion by the Roman authorities. From the beginning,

Figure 4.7 The famous St. Katherine's Monastery, an Orthodox monastery of the sixth century, nestled at the foot of Mount Sinai (Jabal Musa) in the southern Sinai Peninsula.

Jews who followed Jesus were on uneasy terms with the Jewish religious establishment, and when in 66 CE these early Christians did not support the Jewish revolt, the break from their former compatriots became more overt, but a full separation took place over many years.

Even before this breach, the apostle-missionaries preached to the Gentiles (Greeks) in Asia Minor and Syria. Antioch was the first Christian center outside historic Palestine, soon followed by Edessa (modern Şanlıurfa), farther east. Suppressed for more than two hundred years by Roman authorities as inimical to the imperial religion, Christianity was officially permitted by the Edict of Milan (313), then personally accepted by Emperor Constantine after the imperial capital was moved from Rome to Constantinople in 330, and became the state religion of the empire in 380. A series of ecumenical (universal) councils, convened in or near the new capital, debated heresies and sought unity but often actually engendered fragmentation. Christianity was the dominant religion of the Middle East outside Iran and the Arabian Peninsula from the fourth to seventh centuries, but today it is a minority faith in an overwhelmingly Muslim area (Fig. 4.7).

Contemporary Christians. The approximately 18 to 22 million Christians in the Middle East are divided among more than a dozen Orthodox and Catholic sects; a small number are Protestants (see Table 4.2). Although exact figures are unknown, it is possible to estimate the number of Christians in the main groups. Copts, about 10 percent of Egypt's population, are the largest; most are Orthodox,[17] some are Catholics, and a few are Protestants. The second-largest group is found in Syria—about 2.5 million adherents of several Orthodox and Catholic sects. Third are the Christians of Lebanon—perhaps 1.6 million. The Maronites

(Catholics) are the most prominent, not only religiously but politically and economically as well. Before 2003, there were more than a million Iraqi Christians, most being Assyrians, divided into Catholic and Nestorian sects. However, the chaos and intercommunal violence of the past decade has seen the emigration of as much as half these communities; in 2012–2013, this phenomenon unfortunately seemed to be repeating itself in Syria. Fifth largest is the Greek Orthodox community of Cyprus—more than 850,000 who are nearly 100 percent of the population of the southern part of the island. Finally, Israel/Palestine, Turkey, Iran, and Jordan each have sizable Christian minorities: at least 400,000 in Israel/Palestine, about 350,000 in Jordan, and perhaps 250,000 in Iran and slightly fewer in Turkey. Essentially uncountable are the Christians among the expatriate populations in most Arab countries and in Israel.[18] Antagonisms among Christian sects persisted for centuries, but in the past fifty years or so, these have lessened considerably, both because of global ecumenism and the need of minorities to make common cause to preserve their rights.

Judaism. The oldest of the three great monotheistic religions, Judaism evolved over a period of more than fifteen hundred years, a development that is the theme of the Old Testament. It takes its name from Judah, the tribe of King David, from which the term "Jew" is also derived. The patriarch Jacob, whose religious name was Israel, is the eponymous ancestor of the *Bnai Yisrael,* or Children (lit. "Sons") of Israel.[19]

Judaism's roots lie in the traditions of a seminomadic Aramaean tribe personified in the patriarch Abraham. In the Old Testament narrative, the original group migrated from southern Mesopotamia, Ur of the Chaldees, up the Euphrates Valley to the Harran and then, traditionally around 1700 BCE, southwestward to the southern hills of Canaan. Abraham's grandson Jacob (Israel) migrated

to Egypt, where his descendants multiplied; later, perhaps in the thirteenth century BCE, they made their "Exodus" from Egypt to claim Canaan as their "promised land." In the biblical account, it was out of the tribal growth and development of the *Bnai Yisrael* during the Exodus that evolved the monotheistic religion that came to be known as Judaism. It revolved around the one God (Yahweh), the covenant between God and the people of Israel, the comprehensive law, and, for many Jews, the land.

Missionary activity among the Hebrews (referred to as Jews after the fifty-year Babylonian Exile) following the return of many exiles in 538 BCE reflected the belief in Israel's election by God to mediate divine blessings to all nations. By the time of Jesus, Judaism was winning many converts throughout the Roman Empire. However, after the Romans destroyed the temple in Jerusalem in 70 CE and dispersed many Palestinian Jews, proselytizing almost ceased. Particularism and separatism, as opposed to universalism, increasingly characterized Judaism, which then had a mostly token presence in its original territory for more than eighteen centuries.

Torah and Talmud. Different interpretations of the Torah (the Law, the Pentateuch, the first five books of the Old Testament) and the Talmud (a body of commentary and guidance) have led to various groupings within Judaism. In modern times, it embraces such groups as the ultra-Orthodox Hasidim ("those who are pious"), Orthodox, Conservative, Reform, and Reconstructionist Judaism. Neither Reform Judaism, which has sought to bring the faith into modern Western life, nor Conservative Judaism, which has taken a middle position, achieved any recognition in Israel until the 1970s; in the new century, non-Orthodox Judaism still has a second-class status because of the overwhelming preeminence and official status of the Orthodox establishment.[20] This is the cause of much bitterness on the part of the majority of American and other Jews in the diaspora who are not Orthodox. The debate is especially relevant to individuals converted to Judaism by more liberal (and even by some foreign Orthodox) rabbis and who emigrate to Israel where their conversions are not recognized.

Nevertheless, Judaism has not historically experienced the degree of institutionalized sectarian fragmentation suffered by Christianity and Islam. Reimplanted in its native locale in the mid-twentieth century, Judaism has become for many of its adherents a belief system that is quite different from its original theology. Surveys have shown that only a minority of Israeli Jews actually practice the religion, and distinctions must be drawn among Jews, practitioners of Judaism, Zionists, and Israelis. The cleavage between ultra-Orthodox and secular Jews in Israel is discussed in Chapter 13.

Surviving Sects.   Two ancient Jewish sects also have a presence in Israel. The Karaites differ from other Jews by holding that Moses did not receive any oral law at Mount Sinai; they therefore do not accept the Talmud as authoritative. They also use patrilineal, not matrilineal, descent to determine who is a Jew. Once quite numerous among both European and Middle East Jewry, there are now perhaps 40,000 Karaites in Israel.[21] A much older and smaller sect is the Samaritans, who trace their origins to the refusal of some Israelites to obey King David's command that all temple worship must be in Jerusalem. They once numbered in the millions but have shrunk now to a remnant of about 750, half in Israel, half on the West Bank near their historic shrine on Mount Gerizim outside Nablus.

Other Religions

Zoroastrianism.   Commonly and eponymously called after its traditional founder, Zoroaster (Greek form of Zarathustra), who is believed to have lived in the sixth century BCE, Zoroastrianism is also known as Mazdaism and Magianism. It was the established religion of the Achaemenid and Sassanian Empires. Essentially monotheistic in its worship of *Ahura Mazda* (Lord Wisdom), its characteristic dualism significantly influenced both Judaism and Christianity from the time of the biblical Babylonian Captivity in the sixth century BCE onward. Taught by magi as priests, it emphasizes the eternal cosmic contest between good and evil, falsehood and truth, darkness and light. Traditional practices include veneration of fire—the life energy—and exposure of the dead to vultures on "towers of silence" (*dakhmes* or *qala-e khamushan*) to avoid polluting either the earth or fire. Its scripture is the *Avesta,* supplemented by the commentary *Zend-Avesta.* Out of favor for some time after the seventh-century Muslim invasion of Iran, many eventually converted to Islam. Somewhat favored under the shah because of the identification of the religion with historic Iranian nationalism, they are now at a definite disadvantage in their homeland under the current fundamentalist government, although the religion continues to have official recognition. They survive primarily in the Yazd and Kerman areas of central Iran, numbering perhaps 25,000. Larger numbers of coreligionists include the Parsees in India and other diasporic communities.

Yazidism.   The primarily Kurdish Yazidis (or Yezidis), who are scattered across northern Syria and northern Iraq and in adjacent areas of Turkey and Iran, call themselves *Dawasin,* and are called *Dasnayis* by the Syrians; they are strictly self-segregated and endogamous. Their highly syncretic religion borrows heavily from Zoroastrianism, Judaism, Nestorian Christianity, and Islam; prominent in their beliefs is a repentant and pardoned Satan, the Peacock King. Their practice of "prudent propitiation" of the Peacock King has been mistakenly interpreted as devil worship.

Mandaeans. A small religious group concentrated in Iraq that has received renewed attention since 2003 is the Mandaeans (from Aramaic *manda*, "knowledge"), also called Sabians (baptizers) and (somewhat inappropriately) "John the Baptist Christians." Although Mandaeans are not Christians, John the Baptist is a central figure in this highly syncretic religion, which has Jewish, Iranian, Babylonian, Gnostic, and Christian elements. Their scriptures and liturgy are in Syriac. Because they have stressed the importance of regular absolutions, they lived near running water, mostly along the lower Tigris River. The Iraqi community, which perhaps numbered 60,000 before 2003, is now considerably smaller.

Bahai. A fairly new eclectic faith, Bahai, arose in Iran in the 1840s as an offshoot of Shii Islam. Mysticism spread rapidly after a Shii religious leader was acclaimed the *bab* (gate) between the worldly and the spiritual realms. Advocating a universalistic faith synthesizing Islam, Judaism, and Christianity, Bahai has spread widely in Europe and North America. Its world center is on Mount Carmel in Haifa, Israel, and its worldwide membership is more than 5 million. In the Middle East, the largest numbers are in Iran—perhaps as many as 300,000—where they have been persecuted as apostates since the Islamic revolution and where their situation has become increasingly dire in the new century.[22] There are small numbers in several other countries in the region in most of which they live under somewhat constricted situations.

PATTERNS: ETHNIC GROUPS

Aspects of language and religion patterns may now be merged in a survey of ethnic groups (Table 4.3), examining four major aggregates—Arabs, Turks, Persians, and Jews—briefly discussing related smaller groups associated with each. The relationship between primary group and associated groups may involve language, religion, cultural affinity, or geographical proximity, including shared nationality. For example, the Lur and the Bakhtiari are considered with Persians, since all three live in Iran, speak Indo-Iranian languages, and are Shii Muslims. Similarly, the Maronites and Druze are considered with Arabs, since both are associated with Lebanon and speak Arabic, even though the Maronites are Christians and the Druze are a heterodox offshoot of Shii Islam. Given cultural and historical complexities, the categories used are not always exclusive. The significance of minority ethnic groups in the region's various bodies politic is directly addressed in Chapter 8.[23]

Arabs and Related Groups

Arabs. Even with diverse traits and distribution over vast distances, the ethnic identity of the Arabs is one of the basic realities of the pattern of peoples in the region. Numbering about 192 million, not only are Arabs the overwhelmingly dominant ethnolinguistic group in the twelve Arab countries of our sixteen core states, but they also include at least 1 million nationals in three other countries—Israel, Turkey, and Iran—and are numerically negligible only in Cyprus. In the five Arab countries in North Africa plus Sudan, they number close to another 100 million.

All Arabs share two cultural elements, and most share a third. First, the Arabic language provides an element common to all, despite dialect variations. As the language of the Quran, it has deep religious and cultural significance for most Arabs. As mentioned earlier, the language is more a determinant of Arabness than DNA. Second, the centuries-long Islamic cultural heritage embodied in architecture, design, calligraphy, and art provides a common Arab history—Muslim and Christian, orthodox and heterodox, Bedouin

TABLE 4.3 Ethnic Groups of the Middle East (with Ethnolinguistic Groupings)

Ethnic Group (and Alt. Names)	Main Language	Main Religion	No., 1,000s	Main Areas/Comments
	— AFRO-ASIATIC: Semitic and Berber —			
ALAWI (Alawites, Nusayris)	Arabic	Alawi	3,050	W Syria, N Lebanon
ARABS	Arabic	Islam (>Sunni)	198,570	Mideast, N Africa
ASSYRIANS (Aissores)	Syriac, Arabic	Christn (Nest., Cath.)	? 1,000	NE Syria, N Iraq
BERBERS	Berber	Sunni Islam	1,650	NW Egypt (mils. to W)
CHALDEANS (Assyrians)	Syriac, Arabic	Christian	327	NE Syria, N Iraq
COPTS	Arabic	Christian (Coptic)	7,450	C and N Egypt
DRUZE (Muwahhidun)	Arabic	Druze	1,000	S Syr, C Leb, N Israel
JEWS (Yahudis)	Hebrew, Ar.	Judaism	6,000	Israel, Iran, Turkey
MANDAEANS (Sabians, Mendai)	Ar., Aramaic	Mandaean	25	Baghdad, S Iraq, Iran
MARONITES	Ar., French	Christian (Maronite)	985	NC and C Lebanon
SAMARITANS	Ar., Aram. di.	Samaritan	<1	709 in Nablus, Holon
	— URAL-ALTAIC: Turkic —			
AFSHAR (include several groups)	Azeri	Shii Islam	? 750	NW Iran, SC Iran
AZERIS (Azerbaijanis)	Azeri	Shii Islam	13,500	NW Iran
ILSAVAN/SHAHSAVAN (several)	Azeri	Shii Islam	? 410	NW Iran, other Iran
QAJARS (include several groups)	Azeri	Shii Islam	? 300	SE Caspian Coast
QASHQAI	Qashqai	Shii Islam	? 950	Iran: C Zagros Mts.
TATARS ("Tartars")	Tatar Turkic	Sunni Islam	? 5,350	E Turkey, N Iran
TURKMANS (Turcomans)	Turkman	Sunni Islam	2,300	N Iran, NE Iraq, Trky
TURKS	Turkish	Sunni Islam	62,000	Turkey; few scattered
YORUK	Turkish	Sunni Islam	? 1,500	W and SE Turkey
	— INDO-EUROPEAN: Indo-Iranian, Armenian, and Greek —			
ARMENIANS (Hai)	Armenian	Christian (>Arm Orth)	900	Leb, Syria, Iran, Trky
BAKHTIARI	Luri	Shii Islam	1,070	Iran: C Zagros Mts.
BALUCH (Baluchis)	Baluchi	Sunni Islam	2,485	SE Iran (& Pak & Afgh)
GILANI/GILAKI (incl. sev. grps.)	Gilaki	Shii Islam	? 3,250	SW Caspian Coast
GREEKS (Elleniki)	Greek	Christian (Orthodox)	753	Cyprus, Istanbul, Egypt
HAZARAS (Berberis)	Hazaragi	Shii Islam	? 300	E Iran; >in Afgh, Pak
KURDS	Kurdish	Sunni Islam	33,120	Iran, Iraq, Syria, Trky
LUR (include several groups)	Luri	Shii Islam	5,420	C Zagros Mts., E Iraq
MAZANDARANI (incl. sev. grps)	Mazandarani	Shii Islam	? 3,839	SW Caspian Coast
PERSIANS	Farsi (Persian)	Shii Islam	48,000	C & N Iran; <Iraq, UAE
PUSHTUN (Pukhtun, Pathans)	Pashto	Sunni Islam	560	E Iran (mils. to E)
YAZIDIS (Dasnayi, Asdais)	Kurdish	Yazidi	? 300	N Iraq, NW Syria
ZOROASTRIANS (Parsis, Gabres, Zardoshti)	Farsi (Persian)	Zoroastrian	? 160	SC Iran (Yazd), Tehran (also many in India)
	— CAUCASIC —			
CIRCASSIANS (Adyghe, Cherkes)	Circassian	>Sunni Islam	450	Trky, Syria, Jrdn, Israel
GEORGIANS	Georgian	>Sunni Islam	? 200	N Turkey, WC Iran
LAZE (Laz, Chan)	Laz, Turkish	Sunni Islam	? 100	SE Black Sea Coast
	— MISCELLANEOUS —			
BEJA	Beja	Sunni Islam	<20	<SE Egypt (>NE Sudan)
GYPSIES (Rom, many others)	Romany, etc.	Various	? 1,320	Scattered
NUBIANS	Nubian, Ar.	Sunni Islam	150	<S Egypt (>N Sudan)

Groups may overlap and are, therefore, not necessarily mutually exclusive (e.g., Druze and Alawis are Arabs). Some categories are basically religious groups that have also become ethnically differentiated (e.g., Copts). Some groups are closely related (e.g., Gilani/Gilaki and Mazandarani). Numbers can be only rough estimates in some cases and may not match data in other sections because of rounding. (*Sources: Britannica World Data 2012; CIA World Factbook 2012; Ethnologue 2009;* Weekes 1984; Department of State *Background Notes 2011–2012;* and the authors' field research) and city dweller, Syrian and Qatari, Moroccan and Egyptian. It underlies modern Arab political identity, relevant in many modern problems and conflicts (Chap. 8). Third, since more than 92 percent of Middle East Arabs are Muslim, Islam links the majority.[24]

Copts.   Coptic ethnic identity derives primarily from religion. About 10 percent of the population of Egypt, Copts are the largest non-Muslim ethnic group in the region, a remnant of the ancient Hamitic Egyptians who became Christians. Practicing endogamy and segregation from other Egyptians and from invaders, they preserved their Monophysite Christianity[25] as well as a sometimes disputed genetic physical kinship with early Egyptians and distinction from their fellow Muslim citizens. Their language survived as the vernacular until supplanted by Arabic one thousand years after the Islamic conquest. Outside the urban centers of Cairo and Alexandria, they are concentrated in Upper Egypt. Friction with the majority Muslims is discussed in Chapter 19.

Maronites.   Like the Copts, Maronites are differentiated primarily on the basis of religion. However, geographical isolation in the Lebanon Mountains encouraged independence and endogamy, producing cultural differentiation and substantial political autonomy. Arabic supplanted Syriac during the eighteenth century as a working language, and historic ties with the French culminating in the mandate years (1920–1943) promoted French as a second language. The determined separatism of the Maronites has been a compelling dynamic in Lebanese political-geographical events (see Chap. 11).

One group, accused of heresy in Syria in the tenth century, settled in the mountains around Qadisha Gorge with an already established Christian group. Their cooperation with the Crusader invaders alienated them from the Muslim population, and a small group of Maronites left with the retreating Crusaders to settle in Cyprus, where a community remains. The exact origins of their long adherence to the Church of Rome are in dispute, but the link has clearly existed since the twelfth century.[26] Many thousands began to emigrate in the late nineteenth century, and the civil conflicts of the last half of the twentieth century accelerated emigration again. As many as 1 million Maronites remain in the Levant, most in Lebanon, but a few are in Cyprus, Syria, and Israel.

Druze.   Druze identity also originated in religion, with cultural and physical differentiations developing over the centuries. Originating in Egypt, the Druze won adherents in the Mount Hermon area, where they are still centered. Additional contemporary concentrations are in the Shuf area in central Mount Lebanon and in the Jabal al-Druze (officially now Jabal al-Arab) of southern Syria. Worldwide, they number 1 million or so, with about 45 to 50 percent in Syria, 35 to 40 percent in Lebanon, and less than 10 percent in Israel. Recently there has been a growing Druze diaspora.

As heretics, the Druze were alienated from other Shii and even more from Sunnis; they clashed with Maronites as both groups migrated into central Mount Lebanon one thousand years ago. Rejected by their neighbors, they separated themselves through endogamy. Their fierce sense of independence and separatism gave them a military orientation, which they exhibited against opposing Crusaders, against Maronites in the 1840s–1850s and 1958, and in the 1975–1991 civil conflict in Lebanon.[27] Druze in Israel generally accepted the Jewish government in 1948–1949; they are the only Arabs permitted to serve in the Israeli Army. Even so, Druze-Israeli relations deteriorated after Israel's annexation of the Golan Heights in 1981 and the Israeli occupation of southern Lebanon in 1978–2000.

Alawi. The Alawi are also primarily distinguished by religion, and like the Maronites and Druze, they too have developed distinct cultural attributes through segregation and endogamy. They are concentrated in and around the Jabal al-Sahiliyah in northwestern Syria and constitute about 11 percent of the country's population.

The Alawi have preserved no ancient language and use Arabic. Although criticized by other Syrians for cooperating with French-mandate authorities, after World War II and independence they were trusted in the army and in government because of their minority status. A climax of the group's role came in 1969, when Syrian Air Force general Hafez al-Assad, an Alawi, seized power in Damascus. He held the presidency from 1971 until his death in June 2000, when he was succeeded by his Alawi son. Resentment of the role of the Alawi under the Assads has been a major factor in the spread of insurrection in Syria since 2011 (see Chap. 10). In religion, they are somewhat akin to the more numerous Alevi in Turkey (see Chap. 20);[28] however, the latter are not considered to be a distinct ethnic group.

Assyrians. Distinguished principally by their religion and, for many, their language, Assyrians preserve certain Nestorian and Jacobite traditions (though not necessarily theologies). They consider themselves to be ethnic descendants of ancient Mesopotamians. A Christological controversy in the fifth century cost them communion with the rest of Christendom; they remained outside and east of the Byzantine Empire. A considerable number retained their identity in Mesopotamia and remain there and in adjacent areas today; those in Iraq constitute the country's largest group of Christians.

One group of Assyrians separated from the Nestorian-descended church in 1551, reuniting with Rome in the uniate Chaldean Catholic Church—now the larger sect. The original Nestorian Assyrians have retained their ancient independence, but have rather recently split into two sects—the Assyrian Church of the East and the Ancient Church of the East. Along with related groups, they all have preserved a common ethnic identity, and have retained Syriac in their liturgies; however, the Chaldeans and certain Suryanis have increasingly adopted the local language in church and in the home—mostly Arabic but also, in adjacent areas, Turkish or Farsi. A large number of Nestorian Assyrians still use neo-Aramaic (or Syriac) as a vernacular.

With the sects well intermixed in much of their common area, Assyrians numbered as many as 1 million by some estimates before 2003. Many lived in Baghdad, but others continued to live in northern Iraq (especially in Kirkuk, Irbil, Mosul, and adjacent rural areas), eastern Syria, and northwestern Iran. They have periodically suffered persecution; thousands fled decimation in Iraq, notably after the 1933 massacre in the north. As a community, both Catholics and Nestorians have suffered particularly in the past decade, and as many as half may have left the country, while others have fled Baghdad for the relative calm of the Kurdish-ruled north. Assyrians in the West may now outnumber the core population by as much as four or five times.[29]

Nubians. Nubians lived in the area between Aswan, Egypt, and the Dongola region of Sudan for perhaps three thousand years before the construction of the Aswan High Dam. More African in appearance than the Egyptians farther north on the Nile, the Nubians converted to Christianity in the sixth century and resisted Islam until 1366. Nearly all speak the Nubian language, but most of them also speak Arabic. Of the total Nubian population in Egypt and the Sudan, about one-third live in Egypt and are Sunni Muslims. (See more about them in Chap. 19.)

Others. Smaller ethnic groups interrelate with the dominant Arab group because of geographical proximity. Some are differentiated by language, some by religion, and some by both.

The Beja are nomadic pastoralists migrating seasonally into southeastern Egypt from northeastern Sudan. The Berbers are a major ethnic group in North Africa, numbering more than 11 million from Egypt westward to the Atlantic. However, only a few thousand live in the Middle East as covered in this study, primarily in Egypt's long-isolated Siwa Oasis. The Romans called them *barbari* (barbarians)—hence their name. The Mandaeans, mentioned earlier, are a dwindling group in Iraq living in al-Amarah, Suq al-Shuyukh, and Baghdad. The Shabak are another small group in the "ethnic shatter zone" of northern Iraq. Originally Sufi mystics in the fourteenth and fifteenth centuries, they became secretive and heretical, practiced endogamy, and became a closed and isolated community.

The Sulaba (or Sulayb) are a nomadic people in the Arabian Peninsula who, in small groups, follow Bedouin tribes in their migrations and serve as tinkers, musicians, and entertainers for the Bedouin and villagers. They are not considered Arabs, and they are so ostracized that their origins and traditions are little known. Gypsies wander by the thousands in many parts of the Middle East as traditional migrants. Many claim to be Muslims, but others engage in varied religious practices. They probably originated in northwestern India and share linguistic roots with other Gypsies, speaking dialects of Romany, an Indic branch of Indo-Iranian, as well as, in many cases, local languages.

Turks and Related Groups

Turks. The second-largest ethnolinguistic group in the core Middle East (after the Arabs), ethnic Turks number some 60 million, somewhat more than one-third of the total number of Turkic-speaking peoples of the world. Generally, they speak Turkish as a primary language, are Muslims (90 percent

are Sunni), claim a Turkish heritage, and are patriotic about the Republic of Turkey. Culturally, they combined Persian, Arab, Byzantine, and Anatolian cultural elements with their former nomadic Central Asian culture. Turks, Tatars, and Turkmans are difficult to differentiate, in spite of distinctive characteristics, partly because of intermarriage and cultural assimilation.[30]

Four groups of Turks can be identified through cultural and geographical differences. First, the Anatolian Turks in Asia Minor are a thorough biological mixture of earlier Anatolian peoples. Second, the Rumelian Turks (from Rum, meaning "Roman," or European) are European Turks who remained in Europe after Ottoman days but later returned to Turkey. More than 400,000 were expelled from Greece in the 1920s with a similar number of Greeks forced from Turkey; many thousands more arrived later in Turkey from Bulgaria, Romania, and Yugoslavia. Also from Bulgaria came about 150,000 Pomaks—Bulgar converts to Islam when the Ottomans controlled the Balkans. Now highly Turkified, they live in western Anatolia. Third are descendants of Turks who stayed in various parts of the Middle East separated from the Ottoman Empire after World War I. They are steadily becoming Arabized. Fourth are some 200,000 Turkish Cypriots, descendants either of Turks who moved to the island after the Ottoman conquest in the sixteenth century or of Greek Cypriot converts to Islam. They have been joined by more than 50,000 Turks from the mainland since 1974, along with 35,000–40,000 Turkish troops.

Azeris. Azeris are the second-largest Turkic group and the fifth-largest ethnolinguistic group in the region. They live to the north and east of the more numerous Kurds; related groups—including the Ilsavan/Shahsavan, Afshar, and Qajars—live farther to the east. Some Azeris live in Turkey and Iraq—perhaps 1 million. They are the dominant group—some 11.5 million—in two provinces (East and West Azerbaijan) of northwestern Iran. Another 7.5 million live in the oil-rich Azerbaijan Republic. Like the Persians, and unlike most Turks, they are Shii Muslims. Tabriz is an Azeri center, although its population is ethnically complex.

Turkmans (also Turkmens or Turkomans). Despite having a similar Turkic language, Turkmans are distinct from Turks and Tatars. Most live in historic Turkistan—primarily in the Republic of Turkmenistan, north of Iran and east of the Caspian. Highly tribalized, their tribal names are commonly known as designations for their traditional hand-knotted rugs. One of the most widely scattered ethnic groups in the region, there are concentrations in central and eastern Anatolia, northeastern Iraq in the foothills near Mosul and Kirkuk, and across northern Iran, particularly in the northeastern mountains of Khorasan. They tend to live in mountainous areas and to preserve their nomadism for both economic and defensive reasons; however, as with most nomadic groups, the Turkmans are integrating into the sedentary economy. They are all Muslims, about two-thirds Sunni and one-third Shia.

Yoruk (or Yörük). The Yoruk are descendants of some of the earliest Turkish tribes to enter Asia Minor; as evidence, their Turkish language has been less influenced by Arabic and Persian than has the national Turkish language. Nominally Muslim, their Islam is unorthodox, with neither clergy nor mosques. The changes in Yoruk habitat and lifestyle are indicative of development in the region. Under the Ottomans, they were nomads in western Anatolia in the uplands between Konya and Bursa. Intensive government projects during the 1920s and 1930s to develop pastures and to improve agriculture interfered with their seasonal migrations, producing gradual sedentarization. But in the mid-

twentieth century, several thousand migrated to southeastern Turkey, where they resumed nomadic pastoralism, using trucks rather than camels. Rug knotting is a traditional skill.

Ilsavan/Shahsavan. The name Shahsavan (shah lovers) was impolitic after the 1979 overthrow of the monarchy, and so they became the Ilsavan (tribe lovers). They are a large nomadic group closely related to the Azeris and Afshars, traditionally sharing territory and migrations to some extent. Like those groups, the Ilsavan are Shia. They were given special tribal status in the seventeenth century because they were loyal to the shah, and they traditionally supported the ruling dynasty; however, they seem to have accepted the revolutionary government.

Qashqai. The Qashqai are descendants of Turkic tribes who left Central Asia in the eleventh century and moved into the Zagros Mountains in the fifteenth century. Like the great majority of Iranian ethnic groups, they are Shii. Their persistent nomadism, both horizontal and vertical (transhumance), is legendary. Herding large flocks of sheep, they make an arduous seasonal migration, over distances up to 350 mi/560 km, between summer and winter pastures. Incomes are supplemented by making knotted rugs, *kilims* (woven rugs), and bags in traditional patterns.[31]

Afshars. The Afshars are another Turkic group that probably moved from Turkistan onto the Iranian Plateau during the Middle Ages. Like the Ilsavan (with whom they at times migrate), they are sometimes considered a subdivision of the Azeris: all three speak related dialects, practice Shii Islam, and engage in nomadism. They are widely distributed in the northern Zagros Mountains, from north of Tabriz to Hamadan, and there are two other concentrations—in Iran in the mountains south of Kerman and in Turkey east of Kayseri.

Qajars. The Turkic-speaking Qajars are one of several interlocked ethnic groups in northwestern Iran and the southern Caspian littoral. Some related groups belong to the Turkic family and others to the Iranian-language family. The Qajars supplied a dynasty that ruled Persia from 1794 to 1925. Mostly settled farmers, with small groups of seasonal nomads, they form a small enclave among the more numerous Mazandarani along the southeastern Caspian coast.

Tatars. Sometimes incorrectly called "Tartars," the Tatars (archers) were named after (but not directly descended from) the Ta-Ta Mongols who invaded the region in the thirteenth century. Over time, they intermarried with Turks, resulting in a widespread Turko-Tatar group. Turks, Turkmans, Tatars, Turko-Tatars, and Mongols are often confused in historical writings. The Tatars north of the Black and Caspian Seas are far more numerous than those in the Middle East. Thousands emigrated from Russia to Turkey during the nineteenth century; they have since become assimilated. Tatars speak a Turkic Kipchak language rather than a Mongolic tongue, and virtually all are Muslim, most of them Sunni.

Turkish Groups in the Periphery. Millions of members of additional Turkic peoples have long inhabited the steppes and mountain valleys of Central Asia. Their homelands became independent republics after 1991. Some of the groups received particular attention after the global focus shifted to Afghanistan and its neighbors following the 9/11 attacks. Noteworthy are Uzbeks, Kirghiz, and Kazakhs.

Persians and Related Groups

Persians are the third-largest ethnolinguistic group after Arabs and Turks. Indo-Iranians entered the mountains and basins south and southwest of the Caspian during the second millennium BCE. One branch went south-eastward into the Indus Valley and eventually dominated the subcontinent; others halted in the rugged folds of the Zagros Mountains and settled in western Iran. Those south of the Caspian became the Medes (or Medians); those in the southern Zagros became Persians. They called themselves Aryans (nobles) and named their new homeland after themselves—Iran.

Persians. After a thousand years in the folds of the Zagros, the Persians emerged as a unified sedentary people in the sixth century BCE and built an unprecedented empire (see Chap. 3). Although later defeated by Alexander the Great and then overwhelmed by Arab Muslims in the seventh century, they repeatedly restored a power base on the intermontane Iranian Plateau. Since World War I, the Persians have become the leading ethnic group in Iran, filling most government, industrial, professional, and cultural positions. By the 1970s, most educated Persians spoke French or English in addition to Farsi, and many were educated in the United States or Europe; however, after the Islamic Revolution, the authorities have tried to discourage Westernization, forcing a return to Islamic fundamentalism.

More than 95 percent of Persians adhere to the Twelver (*Jafari*) sect of Shii Islam, for nationalistic as much as for theological reasons. A small but significant number are Zoroastrians and Bahai. Living throughout Iran, Persians are the majority of the population in many of the foothills, valleys, basins, and plateaus and predominate in the cities of Hamadan, Qom, Tehran, Shiraz, and Kerman.

In addition to the some 40 million Persians in Iran (about half the population), another million live on the west side of the Gulf, in the Qatif and al-Hasa oases in the Eastern Province of Saudi Arabia (where they are Arabized), and near the Shii shrines in Iraq. Wherever they live, they proudly differentiate themselves by their language, Shii religion, history, two thousand years of literature, and distinctive arts. The cleavage between Persians and Arabs along the Zagros piedmont has periodically erupted over the centuries, most recently in the bloody 1980–1988 Iran-Iraq War.[32]

Kurds. The fourth-largest ethnolinguistic group in the region, the Kurds occupy a historic mountain homeland—politically fragmented Kurdistan—at the junction of and comprising parts of Turkey, Iran, Iraq, and Syria (see Map 4.3). They not only predominate there but also mix with neighboring Azeris and Armenians, as well as with Turks, Turkmans, Arabs, Assyrians, and others. Both their total population and its distribution among the countries that share Kurdistan can only be estimated and are subject to controversy. Kurdish leaders claim much higher numbers than officials and scholars accept. Reasonable figures in 2012 suggest more than 30 million or so in the core of "Kurdistan"— 15 million in Turkey, 7 million in Iran, 7 million in Iraq, and perhaps 2 million in Syria—plus others in Armenia, Lebanon, central Anatolia, the central Zagros Mountains, and the Elburz and Kopet Mountains.

Language, heritage, culture, and a fierce sense of independence combine to define Kurdishness, along with physical attributes; many consider themselves descendants of the Medes, while others believe they were formerly part of the Lur. Most are Sunni Muslims, separating them from the Shii Persians, although some in Iran and Iraq are Shii. Retaining a tribal structure, they are settled farmers, herdsmen, and townsmen. Especially in their core mountain home area, they have historically resisted outside authority. Those in Iraq have notably battled for self-government, especially in 1974–1975, during the 1980s Iran-Iraq War, during and after the 1991 Gulf War, and after 2003. Similarly, Kurds in Turkey engaged in a decades-long fight for recognition in which 30,000 died during the 1980s and 1990s.

Both the historical and the contemporary plights of the Kurds became the focus of intensive media coverage after the Gulf War of 1990–1991, and again in the 2000s. Further details on the situation of the Kurds in the respective countries that share Kurdistan are given in Chapters 10, 14, 20, and 21, and the general Kurdish problem is discussed in Chapter 8.

Yazidis. The Yazidis have Kurdish ethnic roots (some in the group dispute this and claim distinct ethnicity) but are mainly distinguished by their heterodox religion. They are settled farmers concentrated in the Jabal Sinjar west of Mosul and in the hills northwest of Aleppo, with scattered groups in adjacent states. Yazidis do not interact with neighboring tribes; they practice endogamy and prohibit conversion into the group. Many who formerly lived in Turkey have emigrated to Europe.

Baluch. Like the Kurds, the Baluch (sometimes Baloch) are primarily Sunni, speak an Indo-Iranian language, and have a relatively isolated traditional homeland—Baluchistan— at the junction of three countries: Iran, Pakistan, and Afghanistan. However, it is arid, and they are much more nomadic or seminomadic than the Kurds, with only a few in impoverished villages. Tribal organization remains strong among them, but the tribes are not closely integrated. In their spare desert and mountain environment, they are the poorest and most neglected major group in Iran. Probably a mixture of Dravidians from India and Arab invaders, they are culturally more closely related to Pakistanis and the Pushtun of Afghanistan than to the Persians.

Emigrants from poverty, they crossed the Gulf of Oman to both Oman and the present UAE, where their round tents originally provided a contrast to the rectangular Arab tents. They serve in large numbers in the various military forces of the southeastern Arabian Peninsula. Since the 1990s, there has been a resurgence of Baluch separatist activity in both Pakistan and Iran.

Lur. Of uncertain origin, the Lur speak a dialect of Persian and are linguistically and culturally related to the Persians and the nearby Bakhtiari. They occupy Lorestan, a homeland in the central Zagros Mountains between Bakhtaran (Kermanshah) and Shiraz, and are racially mixed.

The basic social unit among the Lur is the tribe (*il*). Some nomadic tribes are summer migrants to the high mountains; other tribes have become sedentary or semisedentary, especially in the eastern valleys, and have adopted Persian (Farsi) as a second language. Tribal structure has gradually become less rigid as the power of the chiefs (*khans*) has been undermined by the central government. Most Lur are Shii but hold some beliefs that are inconsistent with Persian and Bakhtiari Shiism. Of the Lur who have spilled over into Iraq, a few roam the Zagros piedmont in the Mandali area east of Baghdad, while others work in towns along the Tigris. Estimates of their numbers vary widely.

Bakhtiari. Tribes in the *Il-e Bakhtiari* confederation relate geographically and culturally not only to the nearby Lur but also to the Turkic Qashqai. Like the latter, the Bakhtiari are tribally organized, disciplined, and still largely nomadic. Historically having a powerful role in Iranian politics, Bakhtiari leaders often held high government positions until the 1920s; the political influence of the *khans* was restricted by the central government after World War I. They had a long tradition of services in the Iranian army. Their ethnic dress evokes statues and bas-reliefs of Parthians of two thousand years ago. Like many Iranian tribes, they produce handmade rugs with distinctive designs.

Zoroastrians. Zoroastrians are probably the least physically mixed ethnic Persians in Iran,

comparable to the Copts in Egypt—so sharply distinguished by their religion that they constitute a distinct ethnic group like the Maronites or Druze in the Levant. By adhering to a definite geographical area, practicing endogamy, and exercising group determination, they have survived and preserved their identity despite persecution. There may be as many as 100,000 in Iran.[33] Many fled to western India after the Arab invasion in the seventh century where they became known as Parsees; concentrated in Bombay, they include some of the major industrialist families of southern Asia. There is also a diaspora in Europe and the United States.

Others. Another score of ethnic groups related to the Persians are found in pockets on the Iranian Plateau, further illustrating the complexity of the ethnic pattern in the eastern Middle East. Two are fairly large—numbering about 3 million each; neither are sharply differentiated from their neighbors, and both are farmers and fishermen along the Caspian shore. The Gilani live along the southwestern shore around Rasht; the Mazandarani are in the coastal lowlands and adjacent mountains to the southeast.

Jews and Samaritans

Jews. After a series of unsuccessful revolts against the Romans and the destruction of the Temple built by Herod, many Jews were deported from Palestine. In this second dispersion of the Jews (the first was to Babylon), the exiles joined the many sizable Jewish communities already established around the Mediterranean. For example, the community in Alexandria in Egypt thrived for more than twenty-two hundred years until after World War II; it was here that the Old Testament was translated into Greek—the famous Septuagint—in the third century BCE, for the use of non-Palestinian Jews and Gentiles attracted to Judaism but unfamiliar with Hebrew. For Muslims, Jews (like Christians) were *ahl al-kitab*—"people of the book"; under the Ottomans, they constituted a *millet,* and their minority rights were sufficiently protected that tens of thousands of Sephardic (Spanish) Jews fleeing the Inquisition in the sixteenth century settled in the Ottoman Empire. They thus became citizens of successor Arab states after 1918.

Ashkenazi (German) Jews from Europe migrated to the Middle East rather recently, from the late nineteenth century into the twentieth, especially in waves of immigration (*aliyah*) after World War II. After the establishment of Israel in 1948, most of the Jews in Middle East Arab countries emigrated, largely to Israel—an estimated 300,000 from Egypt, Lebanon, Syria, Iraq, and Yemen—by the early 1990s. Smaller proportions of the Turkish and Iranian Jewish communities have also emigrated.

Despite generally endogamous traditions, Jewish immigrants in Israel exhibited physical differences related to their countries of origin, plus a variety of linguistic, political-geographical (or national), and ideological backgrounds. Subethnic divisions emerged between Ashkenazis and Mizrahim (Oriental or Eastern Jews, including Sephardim). Sabras—native-born Israelis—form another subgroup. The continuing question "Who is a Jew?" and the distinctions among observant Jews, nonobservant (or nonpracticing) Jews, *Halakhic* Jews (strict adherents to religious law), assimilated Jews, and even Christian Jews complicate citizenship problems regarding the Law of Return. Of a world total of about 14.5 million Jews, about 6 million lived in Israel in 2012. About 35,000 more live in the rest of the Middle East (out of about 1 million pre–World War II), mainly in Iran and Turkey.

Samaritans.   The Samaritans, mentioned in the New Testament, are now a tiny but still very interesting group. They are descended from Israelites who remained in Samaria during the Babylonian Exile and, through intermarriage with other groups, emerged as a new people. They found themselves estranged from the much changed Jews who returned from Babylon, and the two groups remain theologically incompatible even today. Much more than decimated in battles with the Romans and Byzantines, they were almost extinct a century ago (155 members in 1908), and they still numbered only about 750 in 2012. About half of them today live near Nablus, north of Jerusalem, and the other half in Holton, near Tel Aviv.[34] The group scarcely reproduces itself but nevertheless maintains a long-standing strict policy of endogamy. There is some evidence that many Palestinians are descendants of Samaritans who converted to Christianity and Islam.[35]

Greeks, Armenians, and Others

Greeks.   Greek migrants have settled in different areas of the Middle East for millennia. They occupied the Aegean Sea fringe of Asia Minor beginning around 1000 BCE, reaching a population of some 2 million before World War I. Following the failure of a Greek military expedition against the new Turkish Republic in 1922, another in a centuries-long series of hostilities between Greeks and Turks, many fled or were expelled, while others were exchanged for Turks in Greece. Only a few thousand remain in Turkey—mostly in Istanbul. Greeks lived in Egypt and Syria-Palestine from the time of Alexander the Great; thousands left Egypt because of nationalist pressure during the 1950s and 1960s. Jerusalem has a small Greek colony, considerably Arabized. A religious presence remains in the form of historic Greek Orthodox Patriarchates in Istanbul, Alexandria, Antioch, and Jerusalem. More than 800,000 Greeks live in Cyprus, the largest concentration in the region today. They maintain their strong identity not only through the Greek language but also through close ties with Greece, with which many sought *enosis* (union) during the civil war of the 1950s (see Chap. 11).

Armenians. Armenians date back more than three thousand years, to about the time the Hittites disappeared from Anatolia. Prior to World War I, they were centered in the Lake Van area and surrounding eastern Anatolian mountains where the ancient kingdom of Armenia was located. It was the first state to adopt Christianity as its official religion.

Although Armenians were once an influential *millet* in the Ottoman Empire, relations between Armenians and Turks became hostile after 1878, and there were battles in 1895–1896, 1909, 1915–1917, and 1920–1921. In a confused, complex, and disputed series of circumstances (including Kurdish-Armenian-Turkish-Russian relations), hundreds of thousands of Armenians in central and eastern Asia Minor were persecuted, massacred, and deported; thousands more fled into adjacent lands for safety. A post–World War I Armenian republic, proposed by the Allies at the Paris Peace Conference, had a short-lived existence, but a sustained independent Armenia materialized in 1991 after the collapse of the Soviet Union.

Although the Armenians survived in their traditional homeland only under Ottoman and Russian overlords, they have maintained a strong, separate ethnic identity, language, and religion, partly through a tradition of endogamy there and in the considerable diaspora.[36] They center on the church (mostly Orthodox, some Catholics), school, newspaper, and businesses and have a cultural emphasis on education and achievement. In the core Middle East, they total about 900,000—in Syria (where they are more than 2 percent of the total population, found especially in Aleppo and Damascus and now very troubled by the current civil war), Lebanon, Jordan, Iran, Turkey, and Iraq. The independent Armenian Republic now has more than 3 million people, and thousands of Middle East Armenians have emigrated there as well as to the West since World War II.

Georgians. A Christian group nestled in the ethnically complex southern Caucasus Mountains, the Georgians kept to their historic homeland, although many were dispersed over Asia Minor and Iran from the seventeenth century on, when some became Muslims. Like Armenians and Azeris, the Georgians were briefly independent after World War I, but their state was incorporated into the USSR in the 1920s. Eventually a separate Soviet republic, it became independent again in 1991 with a population of nearly 5 million. Totaling perhaps 200,000 in the Middle East, small communities of Georgians live in Turkey and are being gradually assimilated.

Circassians. Half a million Circassians (or Adyghe) migrated into the region from the area northeast of the Black Sea when czarist Russia seized their homeland after the Congress of Berlin in 1878. A non-Semitic Islamic people, they were permitted by the Ottomans to settle along an axis from Damascus southward to Amman and beyond, as well as in Asia Minor and in the mountains of Kurdistan. They still live in these areas and have played modest roles in Syria, Jordan, and northern Israel. Prior to its destruction by the Israelis, Qunaytirah, in the Golan Heights, was a center of Circassian settlement. Many in the Syrian community of somewhere between 50,000 and 100,000 have shown interest in returning to their homeland since the outbreak of civil war in Syria.[37]

Chechens. Muslim Chechens migrated into the region from the northern Caucasus in the mid-nineteenth century, when 40,000 arrived in Turkey, where most have been assimilated. Later, other small groups of Chechens settled farther south in the Ottoman Empire; more than 2,000, sometimes called Shishanis, still live in west-central Jordan alongside their fellow Caucasians, the Circassians.

Laze.   Many Laze also left the southern Caucasus after 1878 following Russia's seizure of the area, settling across the border in northeastern Turkey. Traditionally seafarers and fishermen living on or near the Black Sea coast, where Rise is a Laze center, they often serve on Black Sea ships or in the Turkish navy. They speak their own language, Laz, which is akin to Georgian.

PATTERNS: HUMAN DEVELOPMENT— WOMEN, MEN, CHILDREN

Over the past two generations, there has been considerable improvement in the living standards of the people who inhabit the Middle East. Within the region, there were notable differences before the oil boom, and at the same time differences persist, but there have been significant changes in the intraregional and intergender patterns of these differences.

Measures of income across countries and across time, like gross domestic product (GDP), are commonly used despite the acknowledged limitations these indicators have. Using the purchasing-power parity adjustment is of some value, but there are some other tested statistics that we can consider in the quest to identify changes in the quality of the lives of Middle Easterners over the past generation.[38]

Since 1990, the UN Development Programme (UNDP) has published the Human Development Index, with components representing health, education, and income. The London-based Legatum Institute annually computes a more broadly defined measure of well-being, the Prosperity Index, which also includes several health and education indicators. To examine regional patterns here, we will look briefly at a number of parameters contained in these two sectors, noting gender differences as appropriate where data are available.[39]

Health

Women and Men: Living Longer.   Life expectancy at birth is the statistic most employed with regard to gains over time and patterns across countries as far as health is concerned.[40] From the early 1950s through 2012, there were major advances in this regard in all regional countries. The median male life expectancy some 60 years ago was 41.95 years, for females 44.00 years; more recently, for men it was 72.89 years and for women 77.15 years—gains of 73.8 percent and 75.3 percent, respectively. But there remain significant differences across countries—Yemen especially lags behind the rest of the region, and Israel, Jordan, and Cyprus are well out in front. Almost as significant as these gains is the fact that women in the Middle East now show the same pattern of living notably longer than men as do women in the developed world—a historical advantage of about 4.00 or more years. In the 1950s, the median difference between the genders in the region was only 2.10 years; by 2012, this advantage has risen to a median of 4.23 years.

Mothers.   Much of this increased advantage of women relative to men has to do with a reduction in maternal mortality, but the span of years for which data are available is unfortunately shorter. Still, the numbers are illustrative: in 1988, the median for the region was 200 deaths per 100,000 live births, and by about 2010 this figure had fallen to 24. But the extent of the recent range remains troubling—as low as 7 in Israel and Qatar and 10 in Cyprus, but still as high as 200 in Yemen.

Children.   Among the health measures that can show how the situation of children has changed is the mortality rate in the first five years of life. In 1960, the median rate was 233 per 1,000 births; by 2011, this had fallen to 11, a decline of 94.5 percent. In both years, there was a sizable spread across the region—in 1960, rates above 250 were seen in Egypt, Saudi Arabia, Oman, and Yemen; some narrowing has occurred, and in 2011 the rates ranged from 3 in Cyprus, 4 in Israel, and 7 in the UAE to 38 in Iraq and 77 in Yemen. The rate in Iraq soared in the late 1990s and early 2000s to more than 120 by some estimates, so some recent recovery is apparent.

In computing its annual Global Hunger Index (GHI), the International Food Policy Research Institute (IFPRI) uses under-five mortality and percentage of underweight children under five as inputs. For most of the region's developing economies for which comparative data over the past two decades are available, both the underweight measurement and the GHI show notable improvements; the median percentage of underweight children fell from 10.45 to 5.40 between 1990 and 2012. But in both cases, Yemen was a prominent outlier; despite some improvement, in 2012 about 39 percent of young Yemenis were underweight.[41]

Clean Water.   Improvements for children also are notable in the access to clean water and sanitation, as well as immunization rates. In the 1970s, in Iran, Iraq, Oman, and Yemen, less than 70 percent of the population had reliable access to clean drinking water, and in Egypt, Syria, and Turkey, the percentage was between 71 and 85 percent. By 2010, only Iraq and Yemen were still below 85 percent. In the 1970s, sanitation availability was less than 50 percent for Egyptians, Iraqis, Omanis, Saudis, Syrians, and Yemenis and only between 50 and 75 percent for the populations of Iran and Jordan. By the late 2000s, in all countries except Yemen and Iraq sanitation availability exceeded 90 percent.[42]

Immunization Gains.   Three basic immunizations—polio, diphtheria/tetanus, and measles—have seen much greater application in the past two decades. Around 1990, fewer than 75 percent of children had been immunized for polio in Yemen and Turkey, and for Qatar, Lebanon, Iraq, and Egypt the rate was only between 75 and 90 percent. By 2011, immunization improvements had raised rates across the region: the lowest rates were now between 80 and 90 percent in Yemen and Iraq, and eleven countries reported coverage above 95 percent. For diphtheria and tetanus, again these same six countries reported 1990 rates in the same ranges as for polio; by 2011, again the lowest rates (between 80 and 90 percent) were in Yemen and Iraq, and 12 countries had achieved 95 percent coverage or better. Measles immunization covered less than half of Lebanese and Yemeni children in 1990, while rates for Turkey, Qatar, Cyprus, and the United Arab Emirates were between 65 and 80 percent. By 2011, Yemen's rate was still lowest but had risen to 71 percent and Cyprus's to 87 percent, but thirteen countries reported coverage exceeding 95 percent.[43]

The pattern in these improvements for children's welfare is clear in almost every country—gains not only for those in the wealthy oil exporters in the Gulf, but also for those living in countries with more modest economies, like Egypt, Jordan, and Syria. The children in two outliers, however, still face considerable problems. Iraq's physical infrastructure and health system[44] were two of the biggest casualties of the accumulated effects of three decades of warfare, sanctions, and internal turmoil. However, Iraq does have considerable financial resources potentially available as the turmoil slows, as it has in the early 2010s, and there is good reason to expect that there will be notable improvements in the welfare of both its children and its adults. For Yemen, the situation is less optimistic; the country will need substantial external assistance for the foreseeable future to solidify the welfare gains that have occurred and to accelerate the process toward those levels enjoyed by its neighbors (see Chap. 18 for more details).

Health and Development.   Historically, as societies have become more socially developed and economically prosperous, the pattern that has prevailed elsewhere is what has been seen over the past two generations in the Middle East. Improvements in public health, cleaner water, proper sanitation, and more and better nutrition contribute to lower child mortality and thus to increased life expectancy. Basic care in pregnancy and at delivery further lowers maternal mortality, as do increases in female literacy, and contributes to women gaining what seems to be a genetic advantage over men in life expectancy.

But not every change is positive. Developing countries in recent decades have also experienced what can be categorized as "lifestyle changes" that have had negative effects on health. Nutrition may be more ample, but if it involves forsaking traditional foods for foreign imports, it may not be qualitatively better. People in urbanizing societies are more sedentary than rural agriculturists; less activity, more food, and empty calories lessen physical fitness, contribute to several noncontagious diseases, and erode some of the health gains already made.

For more information on the patterns related to health problems and to female genital mutilation, see the website associated with this book: www.middleeastpatterns.com.

Education

There are a number of available measures illustrating educational progress. Female adult literacy in the region in 1970 was generally low; in half the countries the rate was less than 20 percent, and the median rate for the region was only 30 percent. By the late 2000s, the median had risen to 81 percent—still quite low in Yemen (47 percent) but above 70 percent in all but two countries. Male rates have risen as well, with the median at 93 percent, while the gap between the female and male rates has been reduced, with a median difference at 11 percent. The percentage of girls among secondary school students has risen sharply even as total secondary enrollment has grown faster than population. In the late 1960s, a rate of 31.95 percent was the median; by 2005, this had climbed to 48.10 percent. In every country except Israel, the annual growth rate for girls in secondary education was higher than the growth of total enrollment. In thirteen countries (including Palestine), the percentage of girls from the relevant age cohorts attending secondary school in 2005 was greater than or about equal to the corresponding percentage of boys; in twelve countries, this percentage of girls in school exceeded 75 percent. Again, both Yemen and Iraq are the outliers, with the proportions of both girls and boys receiving secondary training well below the rest of the region. The figures for school life expectancy—that is, the number of years an entering student is expected to stay in school—are also revealing: in the seventeen countries, girls lead boys in seven, boys lead girls also in seven, and in three the figure is the same. For both boys and girls, the median is thirteen years.

Educational Quality.   How good the education Middle Eastern children are actually receiving is another question entirely. One bit of evidence can be seen in a poll taken by the Global Economic Forum in 2012 that included twelve of the region's countries. When asked how the respondents (mostly business executives) rated their own countries' educational systems, their answers, with a few exceptions, generally pointed to mediocrity—with a median score of 4.2 out of 7.0. However, there has been some improvement in this rating over the past few years; Qatar, Lebanon, and the UAE were highest, while Egypt and Yemen were rated quite low.[45]

All Together.   In summary, the pattern that emerges from considering these indicators is one of improved living standards over the past generation or so, with women and children being particular beneficiaries of health and educational advances. However, the cross-regional picture is mixed. Not surprisingly, the richest countries have uniformly registered impressive gains, but Jordan and, to a lesser extent, Syria and Lebanon have also seen considerable improvement (Syria's civil war is endangering its progress in the education sphere, as it is in so many other areas). Of the three largest countries, Turkey has probably gained the most over the past generation or so, followed by Iran; Egypt, on the other hand, while seeing gains in literacy and the degree of girls' education, has encountered problems in raising educational quality. War-plagued Iraq has a great deal of catching up to do following the restoration of relative peace, but it also has the oil income to do so. Yemen, on the other hand, will advance the welfare of its people only with considerable outside assistance.

PATTERNS: SETTLEMENTS

Variety of Patterns

The Middle East has a wide range of settlement types, forms, and functions within a great variety of environments, historical traditions, and state systems. The variety is greatly increased when peripheral North Africa and Central Asia are considered. In size, settlements range from hamlets of a dozen families to one of the largest cities in the world (Cairo). Villages by the scores of thousands dot the rural landscape, from European Turkey to the cultivated valleys of northeastern Iran (see Figs. 4.8, 4.9, and 4.10), and more than three hundred cities have passed the 100,000 population mark. In morphology, settlements have traditionally exhibited a wide variety of forms, from very compact to widely dispersed, depending on topography, water supply, and other influences.[46]

In intensively irrigated areas like the Nile Valley and Delta, settlements are compact to conserve valuable farmland (Chap. 19), whereas villages on Syrian and Iranian steppes are more dispersed (see Fig. 4.8). Settlements that were—or still are—walled exhibit the usual crowding of enclosed places, but expansion since World War II has tended to open the texture on the fringes, and newly established suburbs are more dispersed than settlements of earlier centuries (Map 4.6). The typical Middle East urban structure has certain characteristics traditionally designated as "Islamic" (see "Internal Structures of Cities" below).

The agricultural-settlement landscapes of the region differ markedly from those of humid western Europe and eastern North America. From house design and construction materials to street patterns and connecting roads, they express their regional context and are somewhat comparable to those in northern Mexico and the southwestern United States. The irregular fields around the agricultural villages on the Jordanian steppe contrast sharply with the geometric grid of the US Corn Belt, and the pattern of wheat and barley fields in the inner Fertile Crescent bears little resemblance to those in intensively irrigated Egypt. Similarly, Iranian agricultural villages and their surrounding fields, irrigated by *qanats,* contrast with villages perched on terraced slopes in Lebanon and Yemen (Fig. 4.11).

Five Types of Patterns

Five patterns have evolved: (1) the house and its elements (courtyard, storage facilities, garden—perhaps even its construction materials); (2) houses and other structures within the settlement; (3) distribution of settlements and their fields over the landscape; (4) interdependent relationships among the settlements (central places); and (5) links (roads and paths) between settlements. Although there is much more complexity since the 1950s, these fundamental categories are the same.

However managed, these five settlement patterns interact and are interrelated in a regional spatial system. Nomads or scattered peasants are interdependent with nearby villages and cities, villages with their central

Figure 4.8 One type of traditional agricultural village in the Middle East: mud village with open pattern in northwestern Iran, with dung patties for fuel in lower right of picture.

Figure 4.9 More compact traditional "cellular" mud village of Majmaah in the Sudayr area of Najd, central Saudi Arabia. Majmaah has been greatly modernized since this 1965 view.

Figure 4.10 Kurdish village in open steppe landscape of southeastern Turkey.

city, cities with their hinterland villages, and so on up and down the hierarchy. Since no one element is an isolate, each can be fully understood only in its regional context.[47]

Determinants of Patterns. Many factors influence patterns of distribution, density, and dispersion of human groupings and their structures. Water supply is always a basic consideration, but other ecological factors are also significant: topography, vegetation, climate, and soils. Cultural factors are often equally influential: traditions (including religion), aesthetics, transportation facilities, government support and other political aspects, regional function, defense, citizen action, and industrial relationships. Such considerations condition a settlement's size, shape, morphology, function, and position within the regional hierarchy of places. Moreover, as Middle East settlements have vividly demonstrated since World War II, the historical-technological context is a compelling factor.

Obviously, then, how people group themselves and their structures says much about how they manage the space in which they live. Countryside, village, and city are a spatial system, an ensemble of interacting subsystems combining in a dynamic whole. None is a discrete realm unto itself.

Overall Settlement Pattern

Population distribution has been examined above (see Map 4.2). Map 4.7 shows the main settlement concentrations in the Nile Valley and Delta, Asia Minor, western Iran, and the Levant, with secondary loci along the Tigris and Euphrates Rivers. Map 4.2 indicates the virtually uninhabited areas of the region, emphasizing the repelling influence of extreme aridity on permanent human settlement. Figure 4.1 dramatically portrays the pattern of settlements and the concentration of cities, not only in the core Middle East but also in Libya, the Trans-Caucasus, Central Asia, and the Indus Valley.

124

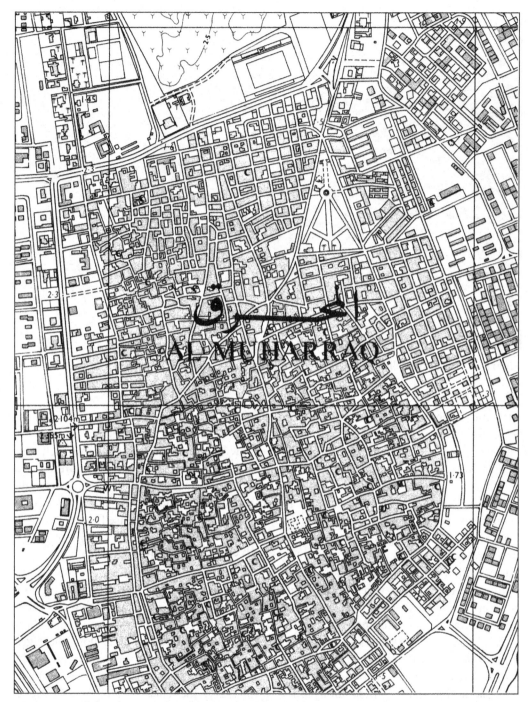

Map 4.6 Traditional street pattern, Muharraq, Bahrain. The core of Muharraq, like other Islamic cities, is unplanned, narrow, and winding. On the edges of the old core are planned, right-angle streets with larger blocks from the post-1960 period. The area shown is the same as that in Fig. 4.12. (Map courtesy of Survey Directorate, Bahrain)

Figure 4.11 Yemeni agricultural hamlet perched on mountain shoulder, surrounded by steep, terraced slopes of escarpment west of Sana. Well protected from surprise attack, settlements in these areas are small and close together, since farmers prefer not to have to walk very far to their fields in such rugged topography.

Until the mid-twentieth century, the overwhelming majority of Middle Easterners lived in villages. With the exception of nomads, whose mode of "settlement" is a special case, the isolated rural resident was rare, found only in some Asia Minor and northwestern Iran locales. Although cities had long been important in the region's socioeconomic pattern, they had declined in number, size, and importance after the sixteenth century. Modernization, especially in the newly wealthy oil states, reversed the rural-urban percentages, giving rise to rapid urbanization (see Maps 4.1 and 4.7 and Fig. 4.1).

Urbanization

By the late 1980s, about 50 percent of the population of the Middle East lived in cities; by the early 2010s, the overall percentage was about 62.5 percent (with a median percent-age across the seventeen countries of 72.5 percent[48]) in rapidly growing populations. The urban trend was primarily the result of internal migrations from the villages to the cities and, in the Gulf, of labor flow and immigration from areas such as India, Pakistan, Jordan, Yemen, and Southeast Asia.

Unusual circumstances have created extraordinary urban percentages in some areas. Petroleum development attracted concentrations in city-states on the western coastal fringe of the Gulf, which once supported only fishing hamlets on the coast and scattered nomads in the hinterland. Now almost the entire population here is technically urban. Kuwait City, for example, exploded from about 50,000 people in 1940 to 2.6 million in 2012. Similar urbanization has occurred in Bahrain, Qatar, and the UAE since the 1960s.

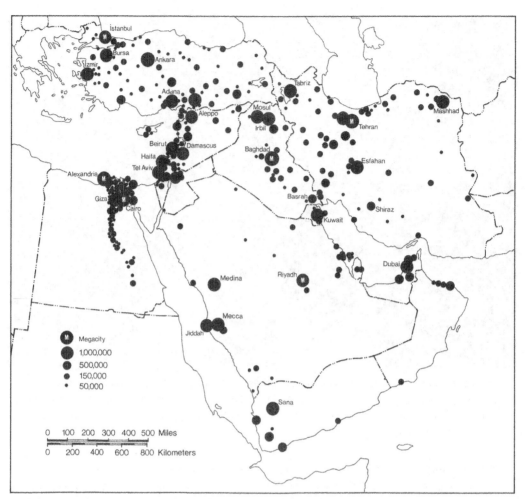

Map 4.7 Pattern of distribution of urban population. Note the concentration of cities in the northern half of the region, in the Levant, and especially in the Nile Valley and Delta. Istanbul, Ankara, Tehran, Baghdad, Alexandria, Cairo, and Riyadh are in the multimillion population category. From the most recent data available, primarily 2010–2012.

For different reasons, urbanization is also high in Israel, despite the existence of scores of small settlements. Even Egypt, the agricultural country par excellence, has 43 percent urbanization. Surplus workers from the villages have migrated into Cairo especially, swelling the population of the Greater Cairo region to more than 18 million. Alexandria and other cities have likewise expanded. In Iran, a similar inpouring of villagers into Greater Tehran has caused its population to surge to close to 11 million, with Mashhad about 2.5 million and Esfahan, Karaj, Tabriz, and Shiraz more than 1.5 million each. Saudi Arabia experienced remarkable urbanization during the 1970s and 1980s. Dammam and nearby fishing villages rocketed from a few hundred dwellers to a conurbation of more than 1 million population. In the interior, Greater Riyadh, a desert capital of 30,000 before World War II, exploded during the oil boom and was estimated to have more than 4.7 million inhabitants in 2012. The country as a whole, still envisioned by many foreigners as peopled mostly by desert-roaming nomads, is more than 80 percent urban.

Expatriates and Bedouin. Similarly, the urbanization that has characterized population movements in much of the world over a half century has resulted in permutations peculiar to the Middle East and some of the peripheral countries. Millions of expatriates swelled the populations of the Gulf cities—Kuwait, Jubail, Dammam, al-Khobar, Manama, Doha, Abu Dhabi, Dubai, Ahvaz, and Bandar-e Abbas—while hundreds of thousands of nomads have abandoned their lifestyle to become city dwellers. Sedentarization has been one of the major socioeconomic phenomena of the region for several decades. It has gone hand in hand with a reduction of nomad numbers to a level of near insignificance relative to total population. However, former nomads remarkably retain their tribal consciousness and relationships for many years after becoming urbanized.

Internal Structures of Cities

The internal morphological and structural patterns of settlements reflect interaction between urban development and historical-geographical influences. These include the street pattern, placement of central squares and other open areas, siting of religious and government structures, location and shape of the central market and commercial activities, and presence and character of ethnic concentrations. Identification and analysis of such characteristics aid understanding the initial role intended for a settlement in its regional system, as well as subsequent accretions to its functions, successive modifications of the urban morphology, and the interrelations between it and its neighbors.

For centuries, the traditional settlement, whether village or city, has had a highly irregular pattern of narrow streets. Before the twentieth century, house blocks, typically uneven in size, were "cellular," with an open

courtyard usual in each (Fig. 4.12; see also Fig. 4.9). Such an appearance identifies the older core of virtually every city and typifies villages that predate the nineteenth century. The fundamental compactness of settlements in hot arid areas minimized the length of water conduits and reduced heat from the direct sun. Streets were pathways among the houses; wheeled vehicles were rarely used when most towns evolved morphologically; the narrow lanes were sufficient for pedestrians and animals.

Urban Core Elements. Except in Israel, Cyprus, and parts of Lebanon, virtually every older town and city follows the traditional Islamic pattern of a core area comprising six elements: (1) a large Friday Mosque (*Masjid al-Jami*); (2) the city's principal educational facilities, the madrasah, typically conjoined to the mosque; (3) the main public water-based facilities—drinking fountains, latrines, and baths (*hammams*); (4) courts and other institutions of justice (*al-adl*) along with related administrative institutions, depending upon the city's role; (5) the citadel (*al-qalah*), often large and well fortified; and, (6) most extensive of all in area, the commercial district.

The last element—the characteristic Middle Eastern *suq* (Arabic), *bazaar* (Persian), or *çarsı* (Turkish)—may surround the other core elements or radiate along one main axis in an alignment conditioned by environmental factors. A major *suq* includes numerous craft shops in which artisans produce such items as copper- and brassware, leather goods, textiles, jewelry, and perhaps such specialty goods as inlaid woods. Inns (*caravanserais* and *khans*), used to house travelers and their animals, were included in or were adjacent to the *suq*. Offices for levying customs (*gumruk*), banking facilities—especially for currency exchange—and related financial offices were usually in the commercial core, and some still are. A quiet stroll through any of the traditional *suqs* or *bazaars* of Istanbul, Cairo, Aleppo, Damascus,

Figure 4.12 Traditional pattern of houses and streets in Muharraq, Bahrain, a small Islamic city. This aerial view from the mid-1960s looks southwest along the old causeway connecting Muharraq (*foreground*) with Manama, capital of Bahrain. Compare patterns in this photograph with the map of the area (Map 4.6).

Baghdad, Mosul, Tehran, or Esfahan becomes a brief education in local history, geographical relationships, economy, customs, and culture of the area.

Traditional Urban Quarters.   Although the system is declining, the city in the Middle East and the periphery has traditionally been divided into "quarters" (*harat, rayyat, mahallat, akhtat*). Many such quarters were closely knit and homogeneous communities in which people sought safety and protection among others of their own kind. Such group protection was the main or only recourse during many periods, and identity factors included religion, ethnicity, and village of origin. There were commonly quarters, among religions, for Christians, Jews, and Muslims; among Muslims, for Kurds, Turkmans, Per-

sians, and Turks; and among Arab Muslims, for Sunni, Shii, Druze, or migrants from specific villages.

The contemporary quarters in most older cities had their genesis during the tenth century, two or three hundred years after the entrenchment of Islam in most of the region. It was during this time that the concept of "clients" (*mawali*) and "people of the book" (*ahl al-kitab*) became firm. There were as many as thirty-seven quarters in medieval Cairo, forty in Jerusalem (but only nine major ones), fifty in Aleppo, and seventy in Damascus. Sectors for Europeans were long set aside in the Galatea section of Constantinople by both Byzantines and Ottomans. Similar European quarters evolved in other cities after 1900, especially in Beirut, Damascus, Cairo, Baghdad, Tehran, and major Gulf cities. Thus, the concept and pattern of quarters became deeply ingrained in the region. Even with the less sharp definition of boundaries, the expansion of cities on a vast scale, and the growing homogeneity of population in the various *mahallat,* the designation of quarters often continues as a tradition.

Modern Quarters. The expansion of diplomatic communities added to the "foreign" quarters and in some cases created predominantly *corps diplomatique* enclaves. When Saudi Arabia permitted the shift of embassies from Jiddah to Riyadh in the early 1980s, it set aside a spacious new area for a splendid exclusive diplomatic quarter, even assisting poorer countries to build there. The Omani government established a handsome diplomatic quarter in the new suburb of al-Khuwayr, west of Muscat, where both government ministries and embassies are concentrated.

Religious Considerations. In most cities in the region, each major quarter replicated the city core on a reduced scale. When most major Middle East cities evolved, a neighborhood mosque was required every few blocks so the *azan* (alternatively, *adhan*—the call to prayer), given by the *muazzin* from the minaret, could be heard by all. A hierarchy of mosques often developed, with the main mosque in a quarter becoming the hub for smaller versions of the institutions and facilities found in the city core. In addition to the mosque, facilities needed for a quarter's social life were a *suq,* including bakeries, greengrocers, spice and ghee merchants, and a public kitchen or restaurant; a *hammam;* and a *khan.* Spacing among mosques increased in the twentieth century as amplifiers and loudspeakers increased the distance over which the *muazzin* could be heard. Indeed, the *azan* and Quranic readings have increasingly been recorded, even televised.

In several Islamic cities, as in many cities in Christendom, the urban nucleus is a religious monument or shrine dedicated to a re-ligious leader or saint. The shrine attracts the usual array of ancillary facilities and institutions, particularly to service visitors. Mecca is the prime pilgrimage destination in Islam; it had an important shrine and served a significant commercial function prior to the time of Muhammad. Other major shrine cities are Medina, with the tomb of the Prophet Muhammad; Karbala and al-Najaf, just west of the Euphrates in Iraq, with the two main Shii shrines; Kadhimiya and Samarra in Iraq and Mashhad and Qom in Iran, all with important Shii tombs; and such multifunctional cities as Jerusalem, Damascus, Konya, and Istanbul with major sites attracting thousands of pilgrims annually.

Residential Characteristics. Significant as mosques and related elements may be, residences obviously occupy most of a city. Here the texture is finer and more uniform than in the grosser pattern of the core. Traditional houses, although not necessarily contemporary dwellings, in the Middle Eastern city are modest in size, with walls built to the edge of the property line, an open courtyard in the center or to one side, and different living quarters for males and females. The men of the family have more open quarters; women's quarters have shuttered windows and greater privacy. Typically, the house is one or two stories high, and the staircase to the second story, if any, is in the courtyard. A flat roof is often surrounded by a low parapet and is regularly—or was traditionally, before the advent of air-conditioning—used by the family as a sleeping area during the summer, which is also the dry season in most of the region. The overall pattern of such houses, built wall against wall in small blocks divided by narrow zigzagging streets, is one of cellular regularity (see Fig. 4.12).

These traditional characteristics have been appreciably modified as settlements have expanded and modernized virtually everywhere in the Middle East since 1950. New and old have come face-to-face. Although the traditional has yielded to modern technology, the heritage of the past in many cities, but not in all parts and not in all cities, is often still perceptible in both architecture and city planning. Villages especially retain the character of fortified compounds and protected sites (see Fig. 4.11).

Air-conditioning is now almost universal in the Gulf amirates and Saudi Arabia; here, the ancient tradition of sleeping on the roof during the summer has almost disappeared; it is still common in many other parts of the region, particularly in villages. Air-conditioning permits flexibility in house design, especially in window arrangement, and in many ways middle- and upper-middle-class residences in many cities would be acclaimed by Westerners of comparable income levels. Nevertheless, the construction of walls along property lines, the preference for courtyards, and limited yard or garden areas remain. The broad green lawns of an American suburb are impractical in the water-deficient region, although smaller ones are seen around many homes in well-watered Tehran and some mansions in Riyadh and in Jewish settlements in the Occupied Territories, for example.

Modern Sprawl.   A more striking departure from tradition is seen in urban street design. With very high automobile ownership per family in much of the region, especially in the Gulf, Cyprus, and Israel, new streets are generously wide. Cities like Kuwait, Doha, Riyadh, Dammam, and Dubai had ample areas of desert into which to expand, and planners took advantage of the space to provide broad boulevards and wide secondary and tertiary streets in new sections, in contrast to the traditional narrow lanes in older quarters. In Egypt, where population pressure, especially around Cairo, saw urbanization devouring scarce farmland at an alarming rate, new development in the valley from the 1980s on has been directed along an east-west axis—that is,

perpendicular to the Nile and out into the desert.

Commercial Quarters.   Blending traditional and modern also characterizes the commercial sections of many cities. The *suq* is too deeply ingrained in tradition and has served the purpose too well and too long to be discarded entirely for foreign mercantile fashions. The old vaulted aisles or palm frond–covered lanes lined with shops still exist in less affluent areas or in carefully preserved places. Centuries-old markets retain their distinct traditional mystique in Istanbul, Esfahan, Aleppo, Damascus, Sana, and Cairo, as well as in peripheral cities like Casablanca, Samarkand, Kabul, and Peshawar.

However, many old *suqs* have been supplanted in the most extensively modernized cities with attractive air-conditioned commercial centers. These combine the traditional *suq* with the shopping-mall concept—itself a twentieth-century adaptation of the *suq*. The range of goods traditionally offered for sale has also been enormously expanded, so that shops in Beirut, Riyadh, Doha, Abu Dhabi, Dubai, Tehran, and Ankara now also offer virtually every type of consumer goods: Japanese and Swiss watches, mobile telephones, laptops, iPods, Xboxes, and so on. Dubai has complemented its wide range of *suqs* with superluxury shops, catering to the very wealthy from the UAE and other Gulf states.

Urban areas planned and constructed since 1960 display a markedly different morphology from older sectors, and dramatic changes in structural and textural patterns designate the lines beyond which the new planning has been carried out (see Map 4.6). Such changes are obvious in Damascus, Jerusalem, Ankara, and Tehran; the urban morphology of the West is especially evident in Gulf cities from Kuwait (Fig. 4.13) to Dubai, but also in Istanbul, Cairo, Beirut, and Tel Aviv. High-rise office and apartment buildings, extensive suburbs, the coalescence of

Figure 4.13 Central Business District of Kuwait City, entirely developed since the late 1950s.

cities into conurbations, divided freeways (dual carriageways), and futuristic airports became commonplace in only two decades.

Urban Problems and Prospects

In many cities where expansion was extreme, whether in Ankara, Amman, Abu Dhabi, Beirut, Baghdad, or a score of other explosively growing metropolises, newcomers poured into the urban fringe and erected spontaneous (squatter) settlements faster than adequate housing could be planned and constructed. In much of the Gulf area, government oil funds were fortunately available for adequate public housing to replace the squatter huts, although construction initially lagged behind the influx of new population. Lacking oil income, Turkey, Lebanon, Jordan, and Egypt have found it difficult to fund housing in expanding areas. Jordan, Lebanon, Syria, and the Palestinian areas faced the special problem of having both unofficial and official Palestinian refugee camps spring up around

Jericho, Amman, Irbid, Sidon, Beirut, and Dara. Official camps were given basic support from the United Nations Relief and Works Agency (UNRWA). Improved refugee housing was financially and politically difficult to provide over more than six decades.

Israel. Israel is a special case in that foreign aid from both private and government sources supplied reasonably adequate amounts for housing—after some delay—the flood of immigrants in the late 1940s and the 1950s. Later *olim* (immigrants) were very well housed, and impressive homes were built—a large number in settlements in the occupied Palestinian territories—for many of the hundreds of thousands who arrived from the FSU during the 1990s. Principal funding came from controversial multibillion-dollar US-guaranteed loans in 1991–1992 and 2003. Housing issues came to the fore in the summer of 2011 with large-scale protests in Tel Aviv, Jerusalem, and other cities, especially by young people and the elderly who have found themselves facing rapidly rising rents as developers have concentrated on the market for luxury housing (see Chap. 13).

Turkey. Spontaneous settlements in Turkey, *gecekondus*, were first built when rural families began migrating into main urban centers—Istanbul, Izmir, Ankara—after World War II. They erected simple huts on the urban fringes, and under Turkish law a house built and roofed before the authorities prohibit further construction must be allowed to stand where and as built. Most of the huts were constructed between dusk and dawn to avoid observation, hence the name *gecekondu* (built overnight), and the government generally did not prohibit these self-built settlements.

Iraq. Under similar circumstances in Iraq, when villagers and Bedouin poured into Baghdad in search of employment and improved living standards during the 1950s, authorities were overwhelmed in their limited efforts to provide funding, planning, space, and quarters for thousands of migrants. The settlers themselves built the same type of mud huts that members of lower economic groups had built in Mesopotamia for thousands of years—solid mud walls, with palm fronds and reed mats forming a pitched roof. Spaced only a few feet apart and lacking basic amenities, these *sarifahs* multiplied into sprawling settlements until they were replaced by public housing as oil income increased. In the early 2010s, after more than two decades of war, sanctions, occupation, domestic turmoil, and population displacement, Iraq is facing a serious shortage of affordable housing. As many as 3 million units are needed in the near future, and despite rising oil revenues, adequate funding for the task has not been immediately available.[49]

Urban Planning. Despite the problems, town planning in the Middle East has been on a scale unprecedented in the region's history and impressive on a world scale. The reconstruction of war-devastated cities in Europe during the 1950s demanded extraordinary town-planning efforts, and expertise developed at that time was later applied to the unparalleled urban expansion in the Gulf area. Initially, urban planners had to be imported by most of the rapidly expanding Middle East countries, since their own experts were few in number and relatively inexperienced in such large-scale planning.

Most of the Gulf states turned to the British for expertise, since these countries had been under British tutelage prior to gaining independence in the 1960s and early 1970s. One consequence is that major Gulf cities bear the unmistakable stamp of British town-planning concepts—for example, the traffic "roundabout," known as a rotary or traffic circle in the United States, where it is rarely used. Local technicians were rapidly trained in town planning, and governments soon took over the enormous task of planning their own cities and villages. Some of the designs are striking, having been facilitated by the fact that cost was often no object.

Planning in Israel was unique in that a high degree of expertise developed among Jewish newcomers under the mandate; also, many planning experts emigrated to the Jewish state. As the new state grew, there was a highly coordinated and well-financed planning program at every level. The site of each settlement was carefully selected, whether on or near a razed Arab village, a restoration of a known or supposed biblical site, or completely new. Once the site was chosen, the internal design was drawn up and a selection of house types was supplied by the planners. This ensured balanced distribution of immigrants, efficient use of water, economic activity for the new inhabitants, and a systematic security pattern in the expanding state.[50] The category of settlement for a given site was also determined by the central planners—*kibbutz, moshav, nahal,* or multifunction town (see Chap. 13). Similar planning went into the scores of highly controversial "settlements" built in the Israeli-occupied West Bank and Gaza Strip.

Traffic.   Despite planning, virtually every Middle Eastern city—especially those with more than 500,000 inhabitants—has found itself faced with the same problems as similar cities elsewhere, particularly in developing countries. Traffic problems often top the list: increasing affluence may double or triple the number of vehicles crowding into the space allotted to them, which expands only slowly. Crowded streets; inexperienced drivers; lack of parking facilities and adequate traffic policing; narrow streets in the older sections, often the commercial core; problems with traffic lights; and, in some cities (Cairo, for example), admixtures of animals and carts—all combine to create traffic nightmares. Tehran, Beirut, Cairo, and Istanbul rank high on a world traveler's list of cities with the worst traffic. Cairo, Dubai, Istanbul, and Tehran now have metro networks that alleviate some of the surface chaos, and several more systems are at various stages of project implementation.

Utilities and Services.   Along with traffic, some big cities struggle with serious shortages of water, gas, electricity, sewerage facilities, telephones, and other utilities and services; urban populations are growing, while per capita water resources are declining. Increasing unpredictability of precipitation and stream flow due to climate change adds more stress to both rural and urban systems. Even cities in the more humid areas—Istanbul, Beirut, Haifa—suffer water shortages during long, dry summers because distribution systems are inadequate. Cairo, even with a plentiful source of water in the Nile, has the same problem. For many years, municipal water was supplied in Ankara for only brief periods two or three times a day. Jiddah has periodically gone waterless in the summer, but the in-

tense downpour in November 2009 generated floods that killed at least 120 and left thousands homeless after 3.55 in/90 mm fell in four hours. In Beirut, apartment houses, even in normal times, are, by design, supplied with water through such small pipes that it must be stored during the night in roof tanks, one for each apartment. Similarly, homes in Cyprus have prominent but essential water tanks on their roofs next to solar panels for hot water. Residents of Amman, capital of water-poor Jordan, store water when they receive scheduled deliveries.

Water Recycling.   Coastal cities in Israel recycle treated sewage to stretch the water supply, pumping it back into the aquifers under the coastal plain from which much of the supply is obtained. Continuous recycling without plentiful recharging by natural runoff in dry years affects the taste of drinking water in the Tel Aviv area and worries some Israeli planners, but the procedure is a conservational success—in 2004, 189 mn gal/0.71 mn m3 of treated wastewater were available daily. Occasional wet seasons, such as the winters of 1997–1998, 2002–2003, and 2009–2010, help counteract some of the problem, but Israel, like the entire eastern Mediterranean, experienced a very dry period after 2003.

Desalination.   Kuwait City is unique in having developed with virtually no natural surface or underground water. In earlier times, the small village on Kuwait Bay brought most of its fresh water in goatskins and other similar containers by boat from the Shatt al-Arab, south of Basrah. When oil revenues exploded, Kuwait took advantage of large supplies of fuel (and funds) to distill seawater. In the mid-1950s, a gallon of water delivered by tanker truck cost the same as a gallon of gasoline. As the population doubled and redoubled, Kuwait installed additional and more efficient distillation facilities, while exploiting newly discovered groundwater supplies. Desalination has been increasingly important in other Gulf cities and on the Red Sea coast since 1970. By the late 1990s, Saudi Arabia—which annually uses more than 900 percent of its total renewable water resources—had installed more than thirty large desalination plants, providing 70 percent of the drinking-water supply. Nearly forty more such plants were to be in operation in the region by the early 2010s.[51] In 2004, some 275 bn gal/1.033 bn m³ were produced through desalination and another 45 bn gal/0.133 bn m³ through wastewater treatment.

Water and Politics.   Governments in the region have struggled with their stewardship of water resources, balancing political expediency against optimal service provision and sustainable use. As water becomes increasingly scarce, especially in relation to the growing demands of demographic and lifestyle changes, competition among users will create challenges for still developing institutional processes. In countries relying on externally sourced rivers, desalination, and highly variable precipitation, patterns of unproductive water use and squandered public finances contribute to potential conflict.

Agriculture vs. Cities.   While the specific impacts of climate change are still being evaluated, the key points of agreement regarding the Middle East include reduced stream flow, less precipitation, and higher temperatures. Areas with lower precipitation already have high variability, and this uncertainty over water availability strains relations among resource users, like agriculture, industry, urban dwellers, and the basic needs of the environment.[52] At a bare minimum, one person requires 1 cubic meter—265 gallons—of drinking water per year; that same amount of water will produce only 1 kilogram of grain in arid-land irrigated agriculture.[53] The latter sector, which claims 80 to 90 percent of water in most countries of the region, will demand

even more with higher temperatures and lower soil moisture; cities, growing in size and prosperity, will cut into the resources available for rural areas. Competition between the enormous agricultural base in Egypt, with its still memorable land redistribution to smallholders, and the ponderous Cairo metropolis exemplifies the political quandary some countries in the region face.

The agricultural experience of millennia has enabled farmers in Egypt, Yemen, Iraq, and other areas to develop modifications of simple technologies, allying traditional social relations with relatively predictable arrivals of water. While limited technology imposed certain constraints, the development of new mechanisms to create and provide fresh water has posed problems for user communities over the social and political structures necessary to ensure just and efficient distribution. From an economic perspective, large hydraulic projects required the significant financing available only to national governments. In some cases, this permitted elite groups to "capture" water resources, restricting access and increasing costs for the rest of the population.

Water Quality.   Partly because of a failure to modernize, for either financial or technical reasons, and partly because of problems with distribution networks, many Middle East cities, and far more towns and villages, have water that cannot be safely relied upon for drinking. Since many residents nevertheless drink the water, intestinal parasitic diseases are endemic. Whereas Istanbul, Nicosia, Cairo, Damascus, Riyadh, and Tel Aviv supply residents with relatively safe potable water, Ankara, Beirut, Amman, and present-day Baghdad,[54] among other capitals, do not. Bottled water is preferred, or essential, in much of the region. People living in areas not served by a piped distribution system in good repair must either take water from a possibly polluted source or buy it from private tankers, costing the poor much more than the wealthy may be paying for city water. Besieged Gaza may not be so much a special case but a dismal harbinger of problems other cities will face in the future: from several sources in 2012 came estimates that as much as 95 percent of the water available to the heavily urbanized area is too polluted to drink safely. Degraded water quality is high on the list of reasons a recent UN report estimates that Gaza may be uninhabitable by 2020.[55]

Electricity. Nearly all Middle East cities have the capacity to supply reasonably reliable electrical power to their citizens. The electricity age has thoroughly pervaded the region and, indeed, has swept the Levant and the Gulf as much as it has western Europe and North America. Nearly inexhaustible supplies of energy in the Gulf deliver to virtually every urban household the electricity to operate air-conditioning, refrigerators, and a full range of household appliances. With plentiful electricity, main city streets—and even intercity highways—are well lighted, such as the 100-mi/161-km motorway between Abu Dhabi and al-Ayn. Electricity is not so cheaply generated in those countries without ample hydrocarbon resources; in the early 2010s, the discovery of offshore natural gas in the eastern Mediterranean has frequently been hailed in the littoral countries in terms of how the gas will be transformed into electricity.

Preservation or Modernization. Settlement morphology in the Middle East since the 1950s has evolved under unique conditions. Explosive development accompanying the oil boom has had profound effects on settlements in the region, especially in the Gulf area. There the impact of Western technological influence on traditional cities created a certain dichotomy of urban planning and execution: a major dilemma has been how to modernize and provide the desired conveniences without destroying or detracting from the charm and

historical values of a Jerusalem, Cairo, Istanbul, or Damascus. Charm and tradition have too often yielded to technology, economic demands, and the urge to modernize; historic structures and quarters have been razed for modular high-rise office and apartment blocks of little architectural value.

Hardly a city has escaped overuse of the bulldozer blade, leveling old buildings and quarters in Jiddah, Kuwait, Baghdad, Tehran, Beirut, and Jerusalem in seeming haphazard fashion sometimes. Sharp debate has accompanied such changes, particularly in Jerusalem, a city sacred to three great world religions. Plans to rebuild the war-damaged core of Beirut were fiercely disputed in the early 1990s before the design for the area was adopted. Reconstruction was virtually completed by 2005, although many outlying neighborhoods still had damaged structures when, during the "Summer War" of 2006 between Israel and Hizballah, some were hit with renewed aerial bombardment by the Israeli Air Force—a circumstance against which even the most careful planner is helpless. Similarly, parts of Kuwait City required rebuilding after the 1990–1991 Gulf War. In Iraq, enormous reconstruction programs are required to restore thousands of structures, transportation facilities, factories, utilities, and similar resources that were destroyed or damaged in 2003 and afterward.

The dilemma for urban planners in the Middle East had no simple solution: Central Business Districts (CBDs) had to be either modernized or overwhelmed with automobile traffic. Vigorous efforts of conservationists have rather successfully preserved most of the picturesque charm of the old cores of Sana, Istanbul, Esfahan, and Damascus. The entire town of Shibam, in the Wadi Hadramawt of eastern Yemen, as well as Sana's Old City have been declared world historic sites by the United Nations Educational, Scientific, and Cultural Organization (UNESCO) (see Chap. 6).

PATTERNS: CLIMATE CHANGE

Climate has been one of the major factors that historically has determined how the Middle East has been settled and how its societies and economies have developed. Within relatively recent times, changes in climate have had dramatic effects on settlement patterns, as archaeological evidence increasingly shows. For example, before about the eighth millennium BCE, what is now the Sahara was a grassland, where nomadic peoples wandered with their flocks. Marvelous petroglyphs in numerous caves[56] in western Egypt and northwestern Sudan depict lakes, boats, fish, and even swimmers. As the climate became warmer and drier, the grasses withered, and over time the nomads gravitated to the nearby Nile Valley.

In the twenty-first century, the Middle East, along with the rest of the world, faces the prospect of rapid changes in climate induced by human activity—specifically, increasing temperatures due to rising levels of gases like carbon dioxide in the atmosphere. Ironically, much of this is due to profligate use of fossil fuels, like the petroleum and natural gas that form so much of the basis of the Middle East's modern economy. Although this is not the place to discuss at length such a complex subject or to engage in speculation about exactly how, where, and when the region will be affected by climate change,[57] there are two different kinds of effects it may experience in the coming decades that we can at least consider at this time.

Contrary Impacts.   First, the Middle East, like other parts of the planet, will be directly impacted by any changes in temperature, rainfall, humidity, wind patterns, and sea levels. Second, if the prospect of unfavorable climate shifts actually results in serious reductions in the use of hydrocarbon fuels, the economies of many of the region's states (and not just the petro-exporters) will encounter major challenges to the continuation of living standards that have depended on the sale of these fuels.

Seven or eight millennia ago, hotter and drier conditions shifted the desert northward until in places it reached the Mediterranean. One scenario for the future envisages Saharan aridity spreading to the Levant, Turkey, and southern Europe, with possibly increased rainfall to the east along the slopes of the Zagros, resulting in a wetter Mesopotamia.[58] Whether the drought conditions in the eastern Mediterranean over the past two decades are harbingers of such a shift is still unclear. What is obvious, however, is that this area is already short of the water it needs to support its population and the still important agricultural sector upon which many depend for their livelihoods.[59] Similarly, an unfavorable shift in the extent of the summer monsoon in the Ethiopian highlands could severely reduce the water that the Nile brings to Egyptian farmers. It is not difficult to see how such changed circumstances would exacerbate the region's political conflicts. Rising sea levels would negatively affect low-lying productive areas like the Nile Delta and southern Iraq. In other parts of the region, the extensive and expensive coastal infrastructure for petroexports would be affected, and along all the littorals, seawater would increasingly impinge on freshwater aquifers.

Oil States' Different Futures?   On the other hand, if global sentiment supports a serious reduction in the use of fossil fuels, then within one or two decades the lifeblood of several of the region's economies would begin to be constricted. The smaller Gulf states have for some time been amassing revenues in excess of their current needs, and by the time oil demand might slacken noticeably, they might all be able to provide their citizens with a continued high standard of living from their foreign investment earnings. That would not be the case, however, for the "Big Three" in terms of both population and oil reserves—Saudi Arabia, Iran, and Iraq. To the extent they have engaged in long-range planning for the time when their reserves are exhausted, they have thought in terms of having several decades to prepare for a post-petroeconomy.

Perhaps the actions of Saudi Arabia in the late 2000s best illustrate the confused state of thinking on climate change in the region. On the one hand, the kingdom actually has a history of making alternative-energy investments—not surprisingly, solar-power development has been high on its agenda. Additionally, it has been pursuing ways of burying greenhouse gases in near-depleted oil fields. But in 2009, its representatives put forward its claim for compensation from consuming states in the event of a decline in demand for its hydrocarbon exports. At the UN Climate Summit in Copenhagen that year, its delegation actually went so far as to deny the existence of any link between human activity and climate change. To outside observers, both these actions seemed designed to prevent any meaningful agreement to reduce greenhouse gases from emerging from these negotiations.

Meanwhile, at the same summit, the UAE issued a strong joint statement with five other small countries, calling on the developed nations to make deep cuts in greenhouse gases and focus on the worldwide problem of insufficient fresh water. Breaking with the general tendency of major oil exporters to downplay the issue, the UAE, with its colleagues, pledged to increase its domestic efforts to promote clean-energy approaches. The joint statement succinctly described the specific situation that the Middle East may soon be facing: "Scientific evidence clearly shows that anthropogenic greenhouse gas emissions contribute significantly to global warming. The potential risks of unmitigated climate change are enormous. . . . The prospects are grim. Rising temperatures will cause major crop declines . . . and significant changes in the availability of water resources. . . . Storms, droughts, forest fires and floods will cause irreversible environmental degradation and desertification, affecting the food supply of millions and causing massive migration flows."[60]

NOTES

1. A recent study of how differing population estimates can seriously affect government policy decisions was summarized in *Orient Planet,* Jan. 4, 2010, www.orientplanet.com/Press_Release_Jan4.htm.

2. With Sudan's population adjusted for the independence in 2011 of South Sudan, a non-Arab League member.

3. Country estimated populations are for 2012 and taken from CIA *World Factbook 2012,* and the source for Muslim populations is the Pew Forum on Religion and Public Life 2009, the most comprehensive recent survey of the Muslim world, and used here despite its slightly earlier data.

4. Because across our group of countries the latest available estimates are for different dates and because countries define "city" in different ways, these numbers are approximate.

5. Yemen, with an estimated crude birth rate of 32.6 per 1,000 population in 2012, and Afghanistan are the only countries outside sub-Saharan Africa with rates higher than 30.0.

6. Of several useful studies of peoples, religions, and languages of the Middle East, a particularly helpful one is Weekes 1984, which includes a bibliography for each people. Non-Muslims are included in D. Bates and Rassam 1983; Eickelman 1981; Gulick 1983; and Bengio and Ben-Dor 1999. Minorities are discussed in Nisan 2002. Relatively up-to-date statistics of peoples within individual countries are given in the CIA *World Factbook.* For languages especially, see the excellent Grimes et al. 1996; and www.ethnologue.org.

7. Arabic is also the second official language in Israel; Arabic has some status regionally in Iran but none in Turkey. All three countries have substantial Arabic-speaking minority populations.

8. Although most scholars agree that the New Testament was composed in Greek, it contains many transliterations of Aramaic words: aside from place and personal names, examples include *abba* (father), *raka* (fool), *rabbuni* (master), and one of Jesus's utterances from the cross, *"Eli, Eli, lema sabachthani?"* ("My God, my God, why have you forsaken me?").

9. The two major dialects are Kurmanji (spoken in Turkey, Syria, and some parts of Iraq and Iran) and Sorani (spoken by the rest of Iranian and Iraqi Kurds).

Around Kermanshah in Iran, a version variously classified as a distinct dialect or as a subdialect of Sorani is spoken.

10. Of the scores of studies of Islam, useful ones include the classic W. Smith 1957; B. Lewis 1973; Esposito 1995; and Fuller 2003. Many books on Islam appeared after the 1991 Gulf War, and still more followed 9/11 and the 2003 war in Iraq.

11. A good and readable biography is Armstrong 1992.

12. As a result of this difference, 100 years CE are about equal to 103 years AH.

13. A good study of the Shia is Fuller and Francke 2001.

14. The commonly understood meaning of fundamentalism (especially in the United States) derives from its use to describe (mostly conservative) Protestants who hew to a literal interpretation of the entire Bible. Devout Muslims across the political spectrum accept the Quran in its entirety as conveying the exact words of God, yet Salafis are only a minority among devout Muslims.

15. The Pew Forum on Religion and Public Life 2009.

16. Among thousands of references on Christianity, two handy studies are McManners 1990 and D. Barrett et al. 2001. Comparative treatment is given in H. Smith 1991.

17. Technically, Orthodox communities are those in full communion with the Ecumenical Patriarchate (Greek) in Istanbul/Constantinople. Copts, Armenians, Nestorians, and the Jacobites of Syria are not; thus, they are sometimes termed "Oriental" or "Oriental Orthodox" communities. To simplify matters here, the term "Orthodox" is used for all these groups to distinguish them from Catholics (that is, those in communion with Rome).

18. The largest numbers of Christian expatriate workers come from the Philippines, India, Ethiopia, other parts of Africa, and Western countries. One knowledgeable source recently estimated that there are 1.5 million Roman Catholics in Saudi Arabia alone, 1.2 million of them Filipinos. *National Catholic Reporter,* Nov. 26, 2012.

19. As with Christianity, thousands of studies examine Judaism and its ramifications. In addition to H. Smith 1991, see Blau 1966 and Wigoder et al. 2002.

20. In 2012, the Israeli government for the first time agreed to pay the salaries of a small number of non-Orthodox rabbis. See *Haaretz,* May 29, 2102. Since the Orthodox rabbi who was minister of religious affairs threatened to resign rather than pay anything to non-Orthodox rabbis, the government resolved that their salaries would come from a different part of the budget.

21. The second-largest Karaite community—about 4,000—is in the United States.

22. Radio Free Europe/Radio Liberty, Mar. 9, 2010, www.rferl.org/content/Bahai_faith_iran_persecution /1077789.html.

23. In addition to the general references given in note 6 above, the studies of Middle East peoples include Gonen 1993 and National Geographic Society 2001.

24. Of scores of studies of Arabs, useful are the classic Hourani 1991; Baker 2003; Khashan 2000; Hoyland 2001; and Rogan 2009.

25. Most ethnic Copts are Orthodox in religious affiliation, but some are Catholic or Protestant.

26. Unlike other Christian sects, Maronites are not divided into Orthodox and Catholic groups—all are affiliated with Rome.

27. Betts 1988 is a concise and useful study of the Druze. For more details, see Nisan 2002, Chap. 5.

28. Nisan 2002, Chap. 6.

29. Ibid., Chap. 9.

30. See *Turkey* Country Study 1995; B. Lewis 1968; and D. Howard 2001.

31. An intensive study of the Qashqai is Beck 1986.

32. The Persians are examined in W. Fisher 1968; *Iran* Country Study 1989; and Hunter 1990.

33. Hinnels 2005, 6.

34. *Christian Science Monitor,* Jan. 16, 1998; www .the-samaritans.com.

35. This relationship is being studied by geneticists— for example, P. Shen et al. 2004.

36. The Armenian diaspora is more than twice the size of the population of Armenia itself.

37. For example, see Jamestown Foundation, *Eurasia Daily Monitor,* Feb. 8, 2012; Feb. 20, 2012; and Mar. 30, 2012.

38. Stiglitz, Sen, and Fitoussi 2009.

39. UNDP, *Human Development Report,* 1990–2011. For the Legatum Institute, see www.li.com, and for the index, see www.prosperity.com.

40. Data in this section are drawn from various sources, including the CIA *World Factbook 2012.*

41. IFPRI's partners in this endeavor are Welt Hunger Hilfe and Concern Worldwide. For the index, see www.ifpri.org/publication/2012-global-hunger -index. Cyprus, Israel, and the United Arab Emirates are not included in the study, nor is Palestine. Data from Qatar on underweight children were not available over the period in question, and other data limitations for Bahrain, Iraq, and Oman precluded estimating the GHI for them as well.

42. Iraq's continuing water problems were clearly related to the sanctions of the 1990s and the war damage and destruction from 2003 on. Yemen's situation, however, is much more difficult to ameliorate.

43. Immunization rates are from the World Health Organization, www.who.int/immunization _monitoring/data/data_subject/en/index.html.

44. *Lancet,* Sept. 3, 2011.

45. World Economic Forum 2012–2013.

46. Several works on Middle East cities have appeared since the mid-1960s, most of which have been collections of papers given at conferences and symposia. See, for example, Serjeant 1980, with especially stimulating and authoritative perspectives on the Islamic city at a UNESCO colloquium; Saqqaf 1987, which focuses on the ancient-modern confrontation; and Blake and Lawless 1980. Bonine 1977 contemplates the Islamic urban experience. Antoniou 1981 is another UNESCO look at the Islamic city from the aspect of conservation. English 1966, Bonine 1979, and Kheirabadi 1991 focus on Iranian urban development; Grill 1984 looks at Arabian Peninsula urbanization; and Altorki and Cole 1989 analyze the special case of Unayzah. Abu-Lughod 1971, Rodenbeck 1998, Ghannam 2002, and Raymond 2000 examine Cairo. Ragette 1983 considers the reconstruction of Beirut, as does Gavin and Maluf 1996. Al Sayyad 1991 looks at the genesis of Arab Muslim urbanism. MacAdam 2002 studies Roman settlement patterns.

47. Walter Christaller's classical theory of central places (1966), the most widely applied model for the study of the hierarchy of settlements, is of limited applicability in much of the Middle East.

48. The higher median value reflects the greater urbanization in the regional countries with the smallest populations.

49. For example, see Reuters, Jan. 12, 2011; and *Washington Post,* Sept, 11, 2011.

50. See Soffer and Minghi 1986.

51. The vulnerability of these vital plants was emphasized in August 2009 when a technical failure at a Kuwaiti sewage treatment plant resulted in the release of untreated wastewater into the Gulf close to an intake for a desalination facility. Sabotage, of course, is another danger.

52. B. Bates et al. 2008.

53. Jaganathan, Mohammed, and Kremer 2009.

54. Author Cummings remembers from personal experience in the 1960s when Baghdad's tap water was quite potable.

55. Sources include Oxfam, Save the Children, and EWASH. See *Jerusalem Post,* Aug. 7, 2012; and Reuters, Aug. 27, 2012.

56. The most famous of which is the Cave of the Swimmers in Egypt's Gilf al-Kabir region. Featured in the film *The English Patient,* its fame has unfortunately attracted many visitors despite the region's remoteness, and some have vandalized the petroglyphs. On a visit to the region in 2004, author Cummings saw several examples of such vandalism.

57. For a balanced discussion of the relative uncertainties of the science of climate change and the need to be cognizant of the consequences of inaction, see "The Clouds of Unknowing," *Economist,* Mar. 20, 2010.

58. As postulated in a study conducted at the University of New South Wales Climate Change Research Center, and reported in *Science Daily,* Aug. 13, 2008, www.sciencedaily.com.

59. The danger of recurring "water wars" on a local basis was, for example, reported for Lebanon in "Climate Change and Politics" 2009. See also Reuters, Mar. 22, 2012, for a US intelligence assessment of the danger of future water wars in the region.

60. The statement was signed also by Cape Verde, Costa Rica, Iceland, Singapore, and Slovenia. "Joint Statement of the Foreign Ministers" 2009.

5

The Desert and the Sown

Land Use

KEY POINTS: Although nearly two-thirds desert, the region has large segments of cultivation in areas in more northerly latitudes (Turkey and Iran), in lands with west-facing highlands that intercept moist westerly winds (western Syria, Lebanon, northern Israel, Yemen), and in irrigated areas. Traditional crops—dates, olives, grapes in many areas, scattered items like figs, pomegranates, citrus. More widespread are wheat and barley and other crops that thrive in sectors with limited precipitation. Industrial crops (cotton, tobacco) increasingly produced. Animal raising—sheep, goats, camels, water buffalo—a practice since Neolithic times of Agricultural Revolution, is still basic. Fishing practiced even longer and remains of great significance, with seas interpenetrating the Middle East lands. Irrigation is spreading, but water supply is limited even with extensive desalination.

INTRODUCTION

Agricultural conditions, systems, and products differ strikingly across the Middle East. Landscapes vary from irrigated plots in the Nile Valley to Mediterranean croplands and fruit orchards in the Levant and from extensive wheat fields in interior Anatolia to desert rangelands of Arabia's wandering herdsmen. Anatolian and Iranian mountain slopes and valleys are reminiscent of the European Alps. In contrast, vast arid expanses of interior Arabia and Iran appear barren. Although some areas, such as the Rub al-Khali, have little to offer agriculturally, other large desert stretches are used effectively by nomadic herders. The same generalizations apply to North Africa

and Central Asia, with much of the Trans-Caucasus region better watered and more similar to northern Turkey and northern Iran.

Agricultural lands in the region fall into three broad types—not all mutually exclusive—according to the availability of moisture: (1) subhumid and humid areas suitable for rainfed crops, from wheat and barley on the drier margin to maize and tea with more rainfall; (2) irrigated areas located primarily in deserts and semideserts but also increasingly as enclaves in the more humid areas; and (3) arid and semiarid lands traditionally used by pastoralists for grazing their animals. This chapter surveys these patterns of land use (Table 5.1), forestry and fishing, and land tenure and reform from a regional perspective.

TABLE 5.1 Land Use: General

	1	2	3	4	5	6	7
	TOTAL AREA	AREA UNDER IRRIGATION		PERCENTAGE OF TOTAL AREA UNDER:			
	Arable and		% of Cult.	Arable	Perm Mdw	Forest,	Waste,
Country	*Perm Crops*	Total	Area	Land	& Pasture	Woodland	Other
Bahrain	4	4	100	2	5	<1	89
Cyprus	121	46	38	9	<1	19	68
Egypt	3,689	3,650	99	3	—	<1	96
Iran	18,991	9,133	48	11	18	7	63
Iraq	4,750	3,525	74	10	9	2	78
Israel	383	225	59	14	6	7	69
Jordan	283	95	34	2	8	1	87
Kuwait	15	11	73	<1	8	<1	91
Lebanon	288	90	31	14	39	13	19
Oman	136	59	42	<1	5	<1	94
Qatar	15	13	87	1	5	—	94
Saudi Arabia	3,435	1,731	50	1	79	<1	19
Syria	5,664	1,238	22	25	45	3	22
Turkey	24,294	5,215	21	28	19	15	35
UAE	264	230	87	<1	4	4	89
Yemen	1,452	680	47	2	42	1	55
Gaza	—	—	—	—	—	—	—
West Bank	—	—	—	—	—	—	—
TOTAL/AVG.	63,784	25,945	41	—	—	—	—

Data in Columns 1 and 2 are in thousands of hectares (2009). Percentages in Columns 3–7 calculated from FAO data. (*Source:* UN Food and Agriculture Org., www.fao.org/corp/statistics)

AGRICULTURE

Before the oil boom began in the mid-1950s, the Middle East was by every criterion overwhelmingly an agricultural and fishing area. The manufacturing and services sectors were at best only minimally developed. Though agricultural yields were modest, the region was a net exporter of food. By the 1990s, however, these sixteen states were importing more than 50 percent of their food requirements; this percentage continues to rise as the population grows, acquires more purchasing power, and shifts from agricultural employment to more varied economic activity.

The decline in agricultural employment has been especially marked in the petroleum-producing areas, most significantly in the areas around the Gulf. There is still some fishing in the city-states that once relied heavily on this activity, but its economic contribution is now negligible, as is the percentage of the workforce employed in fishing. (The percentage of workers in the major sectors is seen in Table 7.1, which also shows the relative importance of agriculture in each country.)

Labor Productivity. Even in those countries with a relatively high percentage of the economically active population still engaged in agriculture, its percentage of GDP may be notably smaller. For example, in Egypt, 25 percent of the workforce is in agriculture and fishing, but only about 14.5 percent of GDP comes from these sources. In Iran, the 21 percent of the workforce engaged in agriculture and fishing contributes 10.5 percent to GDP, while from the 18 percent engaged in manufacturing and mining comes 38 percent. Labor

Figure 5.1 Agricultural development in the Syrian Jazirah, east of the Euphrates River: harvesting a bumper wheat crop by hand (note sickle in the woman's right hand).

productivity is notably higher in the modern economic sectors than in traditional agriculture. Moreover, manufacturing now surpasses agriculture as the leading employer in some formerly agricultural countries, as in Jordan.

The relative decline of agriculture may obscure government efforts to develop the sector's potential. Agriculture is such a vital element that all regional states are conducting systematic, wide-ranging development programs. Oil income may taper off in a few years, but meanwhile some of that capital can be invested in irrigation and high-tech projects that will yield long-term returns.

Some General Aspects

By its very nature, agriculture is so highly interactive with ecological factors and cultural traditions that it differs from one area to another as well as within an area. For example, the mixed farming practiced in the United States and western Europe is not often found in the Middle East; it would not be very suitable for a farmer to grow what he then feeds to his animals in an environment with more grazing land than grain surpluses. Livestock income—including dairy, eggs, meat, and meat by-products—accounts for less than one-third of the agricultural income in the region. Nevertheless, animals play a significant role in the cycle, providing income between harvests. Traditional livestock herding by nomadic pastoralists, however, is steadily declining not only in the deserts of the oil states but also in the mountains of Iran, Turkey, and Central Asia.

Wheat is found throughout the region, leading all crops in area sown (Fig. 5.1; Table 5.2). Specialized crops are produced in scattered areas: coffee and the mildly narcotic *qat* in Yemen, frankincense in southern Oman and Yemen, tea in northeastern Turkey and

Figure 5.2 Extensive date groves inland from Suhar, Oman, seen from a tower of the old fort.

northwestern Iran, dates around the Gulf (Fig. 5.2), licorice in southern Iraq, and pine nuts in Lebanon.

Food crops occupy most of the cultivated area, but industrial crops (cotton, tobacco, sugarcane, sugar beets, linseed, sesame) have also been locally important for more than a century. Cotton and flax have been major crops in Egypt since Pharaonic times. Where ecological conditions are favorable, industrial crops have been promoted by governments since the 1950s—for example, sugar beets in Syria and Turkey and cotton in Israel and Turkey.

Increasing Yields.   Except for intensively irrigated lands (like in Egypt), parts of Israel, and a few other scattered areas, low crop yields still typify agriculture, although there have been notable increases since the 1950s. For example, high-yield wheats have markedly raised output; wheat is usually grown on lands with

highly variable precipitation. Until the 1960s, mechanization was uncommon, but cooperative programs have increased machine use, especially tractors (see Table 5.2, Col. 7). Farming in Israel is especially highly mechanized, and it is becoming progressively more so in Turkey, Iran, and Syria, as is seen by the large number of tractors.

Small farms (often tenant operated) characterize the region—one reason for limited mechanization. Along with efforts to improve yields, farmers and governments have made systematic attempts to improve crop quality (and of the produce that reaches the consumer), conservation, efficiency, and other agricultural practices. Such programs produce a regionwide dynamic of change, with uneven but sometimes excellent results.

Physical Factors

1. Climate.   Moisture supply is the main factor in much of the region, and except in parts

TABLE 5.2 Land Use: Major Ground Crops and Number of Tractors

| | 1 | 2 | 3 | 4 | 5 | 6 | 7 |
| | Wheat | Wheat | All | | Seed | | |
Country	Area	Prod.	Vegetables	Tomatoes	Cotton	Grapes	Tractors
Bahrain	—	—	5	4	—	—	13
Cyprus	7	15	7	27	—	28	1,170
Egypt	1,288	7,169	575	8,545	193	1,360	99,300
Iran	7,035	15,029	1,857	5,256	110	2,256	265,000
Iraq	1,383	2,749	96	1,013	29	213	72,800
Israel	64	112	139	447	11	95	24,500
Jordan	21	22	86	737	—	30	—
Kuwait	—	—	45	56	—	—	105
Lebanon	46	138	20	278	—	122	8,300
Oman	—	2	143	81	—	—	215
Qatar	—	—	15	11	—	—	60
Saudi Arabia	200	1,300	505	490	—	162	9,930
Syria	1,599	3,083	231	1,156	382	326	107,946
Turkey	8,054	19,660	265	10,052	750	4,255	1,037,383
UAE	—	—	25	165	—	—	380
Yemen	149	265	35	262	17	166	6,500
Gaza	—	—	—	—	—	—	—
West Bank	—	—	—	—	—	—	—
TOTAL	19,846	49,544	4,049	28,580	1,492	9,013	1,633,602

Wheat area, Column 1, is in thousands of hectares. Crop production, Columns 2–6, is in thousands of metric tons. Data for 2010. Tractors are in units. Data for 2007. (*Source:* UN Food and Agriculture Org., www.fao.org/corp/statistics)

of Turkey and in some mountain areas it is inadequate, seasonally concentrated, and unreliable. Where climate is marginal, drought years are frequent and severe, and such areas experience wide swings in grain production. For example, in the dry year of 1984, Jordan produced only 15,000 mt (metric tons) of wheat; in unusually wet 1980, the crop was 134,000 mt—793 percent greater.

Only 7 percent of the region can regularly support rainfed agriculture (note isohyets on Map 2.5 and see Table 2.1). Approximate precipitation parameters for agriculture are the 5-in/125-mm isohyet as the minimum for grains and the 12-in/300-mm isohyet as the lower limit for other crops. Irrigation can extend the cultivated area, but only to a limited extent, and it must be developed at great expense and effort for the most intensive and effective methods of water use. Available water is finite, and irrigable land is limited. Despite

the problem of aridity, crops benefit from the long growing season, prevailingly clear skies, and favorable light for plant growth.

2. Soils. Because naturally productive soils are limited, higher yields need good farm management, including intensive fertilization, good drainage, improved fallowing, and wise crop rotation. Salinity buildup is an ever-present problem in drier areas, notably in southern Iraq.

3. Relief. Mountainous areas and rough terrain reduce the amount of land naturally suitable for cultivation. Although valuable for their cooler climate and as major sources of runoff for irrigation water, mountains have only limited agricultural potential (see Fig. 2.6). However, in places, laborious terracing and other techniques have made production of specialty crops possible. Nevertheless, population pressure on the land long ago induced cultivators to plow highland slopes; the resulting loss of shrubs and trees that slowed runoff and protected the soil seriously escalated soil erosion. For their part, the low-lying plains and plateaus, which are appropriate for cultivation, are often areas of inadequate moisture and less productive soils.

Traditions, Techniques, and Technology

Improvements have been hindered by persistent traditional practices inimical to better farming and marketing. Until recently, farm input costs (fertilizer, pesticides, machinery) were only 25 percent of the gross output value, in contrast to 70 percent in the United States. Thus, value added per agricultural worker has been generally low, but the situation is improving markedly. The rapidly expanding production of horticultural crops in plastic greenhouses impresses even the casual observer, not only in the Fertile Crescent but also in Egypt, Saudi Arabia, and the Gulf amirates. Although more costly, greenhouse production of tomatoes, beans, peppers, eggplant, strawberries, and similar crops permits earlier marketing, much higher yields, more attractive produce, and higher revenues.

Ironically, the countries that have the resources needed for capital-intensive agriculture have, with some exceptions, the lowest agricultural potential: Oman, Saudi Arabia, and the Gulf states. Iraq and Iran have both oil income and agricultural potential but have squandered much of their wealth on weaponry. However, every Middle Eastern government has an active, if not uniformly effective, national program for upgrading agriculture, and oil-producing states with a limited agricultural potential have given financial assistance to their less wealthy Arab neighbors who have greater crop possibilities. Such aid is mutually beneficial, as it produces a multiplier effect, and regional agricultural progress has been appreciably stimulated.

Mechanization. Perceptible mechanization has come late and slowly, and because it needs a systems approach that has been neglected, the mere adoption of machines does not optimize benefits. Even the greatly increased use of internal-combustion engines, common even in remote areas for irrigation, can be a mixed blessing because of overpumping. Tractors have become steadily more common; regionally, their number grew by more than 750 percent between 1970 and 2007, led by a tenfold increase in the number in Turkey, which has more than 66 percent of the region's total. Iran is second, with 17 percent (see Table 5.2). More sophisticated and expensive machines—cotton pickers, maize pickers, wheat combines—are still relatively unusual. Milking machines were rare until the 1990s, except in Israel, but by 2008 Turkey had almost 184,000 compared to an estimate of only 150 in 1970.

With major financial aid from the United States and international Jewish agencies, Israel devotes even higher capital inputs per unit area to land reclamation and improvement than do the Gulf states with oil income but desert environments. In proportion to its size, Israel has executed the most intensive programs in the region; one of its major reclamation projects, the drainage and cultivation of the Huleh Marshes in extreme northern Israel, was undertaken as early as the 1950s. It should be noted that by the 1990s, it was realized that this project had damaging ecological side effects, and parts of the marsh were reflooded. Whereas "making the desert bloom" has actually been accomplished only in limited "oasis" areas in the dry Negev, scores of projects have improved cropland or rangeland, irrigated cultivated areas, drained marshes, and installed systems for drip irrigation.

Some areas, especially in Turkey, have good rainfed yields on average, but in most of the region irrigation is either essential, as in Egypt, or highly beneficial, as on the Levant coastal plains. Since water is usually the critical input, governments have prioritized projects harnessing more of their water, distributing it to improved cultivable areas, and utilizing more efficient techniques. Some of the world's major irrigation projects, with construction of world-class dams, have been undertaken in the region: the Southeast Anatolia Project (GAP) in Turkey, the Jazirah Project in Syria, and the Aswan High Dam in Egypt. Political problems ensuing from these projects are examined in Chapter 8, "Regional Conflicts."

Feeding the People

In the Middle East, where the climate is often less than favorable and water is increasingly scarce—and where climate-change projections indicate agricultural circumstances may worsen—it is not surprising that imports supply an increasing share of edible consumables. But that is not to say that agriculture in the region has not achieved advances with improved technology and better husbandry. For example, food production per capita indexes reveal impressive gains in some of the countries where agriculture is significant. Over more than four decades from the early 1960s to the late 2000s, per capita food output grew by 121 percent in Iran, 88.1 percent in Egypt, 56 percent in Lebanon, 24.8 percent in Syria, 22 percent in Jordan, and 20.8 percent in Cyprus. More modest but still positive growth was realized in Israel (9.4 percent) and Turkey (6 percent). On the other hand, per capita output in Yemen fell by 12.5 percent—perhaps illustrating the lure of *qat* cultivation over food crops in allocating scarce water resources; in war-ravaged Iraq, the index declined by 36.8 percent. (By way of comparison, food output per capita in the United States over the same period rose by 35.9 percent.)[1]

This per capita increase does not imply, of course, anything like self-sufficiency, and the region's trade figures show increasing food imports across the board. For the six mostly desert countries of the peninsula, producing even a modest proportion of their food needs domestically is out of the question—thus, here there has been a significant movement toward investment in agriculture in countries with more favorable growing conditions. For example, in 2008, the UAE announced its interest in projects in Kazakhstan and the Sudan, as well as in purchasing farmland in Southeast Asia and Latin America. A Saudi Arabian firm was planning in 2009 to develop as much as 1.24 mn ac (acres)/500,000 ha (hectares) in Ethiopia. Also in 2009, several Gulf states announced an increase of $2 billion in the capital of the Arab Authority for Agricultural Investment and Development (AAAID), founded in 1977 with the intention primarily of investing in the Sudan. The political instability of that country and other factors had kept the organization's activities quite modest until this renewal of interest.[2]

LANDHOLDINGS AND LAND REFORM

Land Tenure

Land tenure is an essential socioeconomic aspect of agricultural patterns and is extraordinarily complex in the Middle East—partly because each country has its own system and partly from the various legal systems of earlier rulers. The prevailing system developed in an Islamic context after the seventh century, modified over four centuries under the Ottoman Empire (excluding Iran). Islamic law deals with land-related issues extensively, and so they are often intimately connected to religion. Additionally, although the League of Nations mandate periods were brief, elements of law from Britain and France were introduced in those lands under their rule.

Traditional Categories. In simplified terms, landholdings everywhere, except in Cyprus and parts of Israel, fall into three major categories: (1) state-owned land, the most common type, with strong usufruct rights vested in the occupant (*miri* lands, called *khaliseh* in

Iran); (2) freehold or privately owned land (*mulk*); and (3) land in a religious trust (*waqf*), a unique Islamic trusteeship for the endowment of some religious or other social purpose, such as a mosque or school. The amount of *waqf* land is steadily decreasing; the trusts are discouraged by modern governments because they are difficult to control or tax. Despite reverence for the institution, *waqf* land has been widely expropriated in land-reform programs.

Two subcategories of land tenure play important roles in agriculture. The nomadic tribal grazing range (*dirah*) is based on the concept of land as territory rather than land as property. In its *dirah,* a major tribe considers that it has priority rights to the communal range and to access to water sources. Hundreds of thousands of square miles are nomadic tribal ranges in the region as a whole. A second subcategory, the communal village—*musha* in Syria and Palestine—permits villagers in marginal areas to shift between sedentarism and nomadism as circumstances dictate.[3]

Mandatory Changes.   Large state landholdings often passed quietly into private control during the post–World War I period; when the mandatory powers took over from the Ottomans, they often applied European concepts of private landownership. Taking advantage of the situation, trustees under the old system took title to tracts of *miri* land under their own names; tribal leaders especially were registered as "owners" of extensive communal areas by the mandatories. This later caused considerable problems, particularly in Iraq (see below, "Holdings and Reform").

In Palestine, traditional systems changed sharply between the world wars; the Jewish National Fund (JNF) acquired land from Arab titleholders, often absentees, evicted the usufruct tenants, and turned it over to Zionist immigrants. The new arrangement suggested aspects of the Islamic *miri* and *waqf* systems— the JNF, as trustee, took title "in the name of

the Jewish people" and leased it for nominal sums to the colonists. More significantly, in the course of the fighting in 1948 and 1949, Israel confiscated about 1,112,000 ac/450,000 ha of cultivated land from Palestinian Arab owners who had become refugees. Absorbed by the state or the quasi-official JNF, it was then leased to Jewish settlers. After 1967, as the occupying power, Israel expropriated major swaths of land in the West Bank (much of which was *miri* land under the previous Jordanian regime) and Gaza, to establish Jewish settlements, build strategic roads, and set up military outposts, all very controversial.

Holdings and Reform

Landholding size is another significant aspect of land tenure and agricultural patterns; it has had a major impact on the social and political stability of several countries in the region. Since World War II, reform-minded governments have pursued land-reform programs, breaking up holdings considered to be excessively large and lessening the influence of powerful landlords.

Even before land reform, smallholdings were typical in the Middle East, especially in irrigated areas where land is scarce, highly desirable, and expensive, and this is still the case. In Egypt, for example, where all cultivated land must be irrigated, farms of less than 2.5 ac/1 ha make up 96 percent of all agricultural land. Such smallholdings occupy only 15 percent of the nonirrigated areas in Syria.

Before reform programs began in the mid-1950s, small numbers of wealthy landlords possessed huge holdings in Egypt, Syria, Iraq, and Iran. In Iraq, for example, a study by the UN Food and Agriculture Organization (FAO) revealed that 2 percent of the landowners held 66 percent of the land in the mid-1950s; in Iran, large owners and tribal leaders controlled 50 percent of the land. Following the model of revolutionary republican Egypt under Gamal Abd al-Nasser, Syria and Iraq initiated reform programs during the

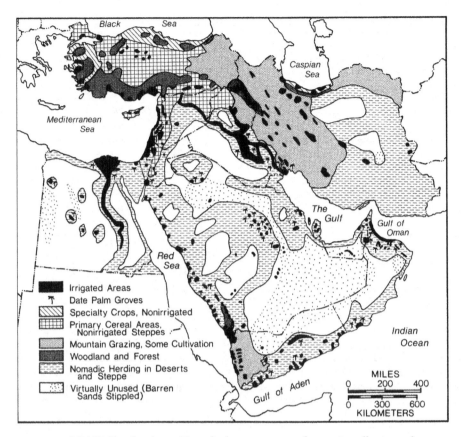

Map 5.1 Middle East land use. Note the large amount of area virtually unused or useful only for nomadic herding.

late 1950s and early 1960s. One result of redistribution: the number of great landlords in the Middle East declined sharply. The same reforms changed landowning patterns: individual ownership replaced many of the tribal rights to planting and pasture, and consolidation programs reduced fragmented, scattered holdings.

RAINFED CROP FARMING

Extensive Grain Farming

As the mean annual rainfall increases to about 5 in/125 mm along the inner margin of the Fertile Crescent, desert and semiarid grasslands give way to subhumid cropland (Map 5.1). Cereal grains in this subhumid belt—wheat, barley, and millet—are in fact

highly bred grasses. Here, though poor rain years are frequent, grains grown without irrigation yield moderately good crops in wet years and at least minimum crops in drought years. Wheat yields might range between 2.5 and 15 bu (bushels) per ac/165 and 1,000 kg per ha; barley does as well or better. Yields have increased significantly since the new dwarf wheats were introduced.

Crop failures in marginal lands are frequent. With a comprehensive range-management program, it could be better if the more drought-prone areas grew high-quality forage grasses to increase meat production, but changing might be difficult, since some nomadic groups on the margins of grain-farming areas operate as both wandering herdsmen and part-time grain farmers. In a wet cycle,

TABLE 5.3 Land Use: Tree Crops, Timber (Roundwood), and Fish

Country	1 All Fruits	2 Oranges	3 Tree Nuts	4 Olives	5 Dates	6 Timber	7 Fish
Bahrain	22	—	—	—	14	—	13.5
Cyprus	186	42	1	16	—	5	5.5
Egypt	9,581	2,401	26	612	1,353	268	1,304.8
Iran	12,126	1,503	901	37	1,023	697	663.7
Iraq	1,094	98	4	15	567	59	46.0
Israel	1,279	135	10	74	22	25	22.2
Jordan	280	43	3	172	11	4	1.0
Kuwait	18	—	—	—	17	—	4.4
Lebanon	976	241	33	98	—	7	4.6
Oman	352	—	—	—	276	—	164.1
Qatar	24	—	—	—	24	—	13.8
Saudi Arabia	1,736	—	—	—	1,078	—	91.5
Syria	2,174	669	143	960	2	40	15.2
Turkey	13,946	1,711	1,023	1,415	26	15,695	653.7
UAE	818	—	1	—	775	—	79.6
Yemen	1,031	122	—	—	58	—	191.1
Gaza	—	—	—	—	—	—	—
West Bank	—	—	—	—	—	—	—
TOTALS	46,643	6,965	2,145	3,399	5,246	16,800	3,274.7

All data are for 2010. Crops and fish are in thousands of metric tons. Timber is in thousands of cubic meters of industrial roundwood. Column 1 excludes melons. (*Source:* UN Food and Agriculture Org., www.fao.org/corp/statistics)

they settle down, shifting back to nomadic herding in a dry cycle, as in the *musha* village. In each cycle, a few more families tend to remain sedentary, so nomad numbers gradually diminish.

Whether grown on the dry margins or in the more humid areas, it is all winter wheat, planted in autumn to get the cool-season rainfall, then harvested in the early days of the warm, dry summer.

Mediterranean Agriculture

Wheat and Other Cereals. In the rainfed agriculture of the more humid Mediterranean climate areas, wheat is still the dominant crop, but there is considerable variety, including specialized arboriculture (tree crops), viticulture (grape cultivation), and a great range of irrigated crops. Wheat is more intensively cultivated in this wetter area where yields are higher and more reliable than in the steppes

(14–17 bu per ac/940–1,145 kg per ha is typical). Millet and barley are also common.

Vegetables and Fruits. Mediterranean-type agricultural conditions are ecologically suitable, particularly with supplementary irrigation, for a variety of vegetables and fruits, many of which evolved in the area. Coastal plains from western Turkey to southern Israel and in Cyprus are veritable vegetable gardens and fruit orchards. Irrigation supports citrus groves, especially oranges, in segments all along the coastal belt; bananas are grown in southern Turkey, Cyprus, Lebanon, and Israel. Oranges in Lebanon, Israel (the Jaffa orange), and Gaza are prime products, although Iran, Egypt, and Turkey greatly exceed the Levant in production (Table 5.3 and Fig. 5.3). Soft fruits—peaches, apricots, plums, pears, and cherries—and vines are grown higher up, at cooler and more humid elevations. Two espe-

Figure 5.3 Sorting oranges and tangerines in a grove in the Egyptian Delta north of Cairo.

cially important perennials, olives and grapes, occupy 40 percent of the region's fruit area. Less favorable lower hillsides are clothed with olive groves well into the interior, even east of the Bekaa–Jordan Rift. On dry, stony slopes in much of the eastern Mediterranean and on the Zagros in Iran, nut trees such as almonds, walnuts, and pistachios thrive, despite the dry, hot summers. Figs appear where irrigation permits; Smyrna (Izmir) figs, rich and purple and large as lemons, are world renowned.

Fruits, vegetables, and nuts are also specialties in favorable areas well away from the coasts and far into the interior of Anatolia, Syria, and Iran. The Bekaa-Galilee-Jordan trench shelters fruit orchards, including bananas. The Damascus oasis, the Ghutah, is a fabled garden, and well-tended groves flourish in protected basins and valleys in Turkey and Iran, where harvested fruits are spread on rooftops and roadsides to dry under the sum-

mer sun. Dried apricots and a variety of pistachios from Iran are widely marketed. Oilseeds, including sunflower, sesame, and safflower, are commonly grown in large fields in the all-season rain areas of northwestern Turkey.

The Olive: A Special Note. The most widespread tree crop is, as it has been for thousands of years, the olive—hallmark of true Mediterranean conditions (Fig. 5.4). With a very long taproot, as deep as 30 ft/9 m, and a small, waxy leaf, the evergreen tree is well adapted to cool, wet winters and warm, rainless summers. Adapted to soil characteristics, it requires no irrigation and only modest attention to live for more than fifteen hundred years and to produce plentiful crops for centuries. The tree bears an average 90 lbs/40 kg in alternate years, with yield varying with soil moisture. Peoples of the Mediterranean Basin, including North Africa, have for millennia

Figure 5.4 New olive groves on west-facing slopes of Jabal al-Zawiyah, near the northern end of the Ghab Depression in northwestern Syria. Syria has been conducting a major campaign of increasing olive production in its agricultural development.

depended upon the olive for both food and oil: the basic oil for cooking, soap, cosmetics, food preservation, and even for greasing wagon wheels. Olive branches long ago became a symbol of peace,[4] but in recent years, olive trees have taken on further political significance, as Israeli settler vandals have taken to destroying ancient Palestinian olive groves as part of their campaign of opposition to peace negotiations; these and other settler actions in their "price-tag" campaign were classified as terrorism by the US State Department in 2012.[5]

Industrial Crops.   To compensate for the dry conditions in summer, farmers in Mediterranean climate areas use supplementary irrigation where feasible to produce industrial crops—cotton, tobacco, sugar beet, sugarcane (more common in warmer Upper Egypt), linseed, and hemp. Egyptian long-staple cotton, an improved variety of a crop cultivated for

thousands of years, is in wide demand globally. Cotton has been greatly expanded in Turkey, Syria, and Israel, as has the sugar beet in Turkey and Syria.

Carob, or "locust," trees grow on dry, uncultivated hillsides. A major crop in southern Cyprus, carob beans are exported for use as cattle feed, varnish base, and a health-food substitute for chocolate. The trees also grow along the southern coast of Turkey and in the Levant.

Agriculture in Year-Round Rain Areas

Compared with the steppe and Mediterranean areas, a different crop ecology characterizes northern Turkey and northwestern Iran, where appreciable amounts of summer rain complement that of winter. The landscape exhibits fields of maize in Turkey (see Fig. 1.2), tea plantations in both Turkey (on the southeastern Black Sea coast) and Iran (south of the Caspian), rice (sometimes with

Figure 5.5 Typical terraced agriculture on steep slopes west of Sana, Yemen. The main crop is *qat* (discussed in Chap. 18), although some coffee is also grown here. Agricultural villages are perched on narrow mountain ridges.

supplementary irrigation) in the same areas, and the world's greatest hazelnut (filbert) groves on the seaward-facing slopes around Trabzon in Turkey. The famous Turkish tobacco predominates farther west along the Black Sea, and still farther west are extensive fields of sunflowers.

The High Yemen also gets summer precipitation, as does the Asir north of Yemen. Utilizing the monsoonal rains to grow grain sorghum (milo maize), a summer crop, Yemen is the region's leading producer. The highlands also produce small amounts of Yemen's famous coffee, which, however, is yielding to *qat,* another specialty crop of the remarkable steep terraces (Fig. 5.5). Two other specialty crops of the Middle East are narcotic—opium poppies in western Turkey and Iran, grown under government control, and hashish grown illegally in Lebanon and Iran. In Af-

ghanistan, unregulated poppy growing gives it the invidious distinction of being the world's leading producer.

WATER IN THE DESERT: IRRIGATION

As it has for more than eight thousand years, irrigation plays a vital role in the life of the Middle East, as well as in the extended areas to the east and west, where more than three-fourths of the area is arid or semiarid. It helps remedy the deficiency, seasonality, and variability of rainfall to maximize the benefits of a long, frost-free growing season. Much of it is supplementary, rather than the only source of water, and rainfed and irrigated cultivation intermingle in many areas. If irrigation is possible year-round in an area with a long growing season, two and even three crops a year are grown, as in Egypt.

Sources of Water

Life from the Rivers.   Most irrigation water
comes from rivers (see Chap. 2). The Nile, Tigris, and Euphrates are the three main sources,
but scores of smaller rivers and hundreds of
streamlets also supply water. Fed by runoff
from rains and snows on highlands adjacent
to the desert valleys, their flow depends on the
timing of the rainfall and snowmelt. Some
rivers are tapped indirectly—from dammed
reservoirs, shallow wells in alluvium adjacent
to riverbanks, underground tunnels, or diversion canals—but the river remains the primary source.

Groundwater.   Second most important for
irrigation source are aquifers tapped primarily
with wells. Many are only a few feet deep, but
some ancient hand-dug wells reach 300–400
ft/90–120 m; modern drilling reaches 2,000–
3,000 ft/610–915 m. In many instances, water
has been found when exploring for oil, as in
the great Wasia aquifer in central Arabia. Elsewhere, modern hydrogeological technology
has found moderately productive aquifers in
areas long considered hopelessly waterless—
Egypt's Western Desert, western and eastern
Arabia, Inner Oman, and landward from the
UAE coast.

Springs.   Naturally flowing springs are a
third source. They usually occur where the
water table intersects the ground surface,
often in a series along a stratum outcrop or
fault line. Nearly every state in the region has
at least some springs, thousands of which are
used to irrigate plots ranging in size from a
few square feet to a score or more acres. Some
issue from horizontal solution channels, as in
Mount Lebanon, others from vertical solution shafts in limestone karst regions, as in
eastern Arabia. Artesian springs bring water
from appreciable depths to support several
extensive oases. Saudi Arabia's three largest
oases—Hofuf, Qatif, and al-Kharj—are irri-

gated in this way, as are oases in Bahrain and
Egypt.

Irrigation Methods.   Both the type of water
source and the available technology determine
the irrigation methods used. Since World War
II, huge dams, elevated concrete water chutes
(Fig. 5.6), drilled wells, and mechanical pumps
have rapidly replaced traditional techniques,
yet the old methods survive in many areas.
Gravity-flow canals, hand-bucket transfer of
water, counterpoised buckets (Egypt's *sha-
dufs*), Archimedes' screws, and water wheels
(the picturesque *noriahs* of Hamah, on the
Orontes in Syria) are still to be seen.

A more complicated traditional method
for transporting irrigation water under certain conditions is the *qanat* system (see Fig.
21.3), which taps water at an upslope source
and conducts it downslope through an underground tunnel. The ideal environment is a
large alluvial fan, the cone of gravel deposited
by a stream emerging from a constricted valley onto a piedmont. Originating in Persia
millennia ago, the concept spread eastward to
Central Asia and westward through Arabia
to Morocco—and, indeed, eventually was applied by Spanish colonists on a small scale in
the Western Hemisphere. It has other names
in different places—*karez, falaj, foggara*.

Excavation of a *qanat* involves both horizontal and vertical digging to construct a
carefully controlled, gently sloping tunnel to
carry the water, as well as regularly spaced
vertical shafts down to the tunnel. On the
surface, a telltale alignment of holes, each
surrounded by a circular spoil ridge, reveals
a *qanat*. Scores of thousands tunnel through
alluvial fans at the foot of mountains in Iran
and surrounding countries, especially Oman.
Although many still supply water to towns,
villages, and fields, increasing numbers are
abandoned each year for cheaper and more
easily maintained pipelines.

Another method of irrigation from the
Middle East (*as-saqiya*—the water conduit)

Figure 5.6 Elevated precast concrete irrigation channel in a recently irrigated area, part of the major Syrian Jazirah development scheme.

has been more widely applied in the southwestern United States as the acequia system—a network of ditches through which water is gravity drawn from a source to the field. Arabs brought this technology to Spain, and Spanish missionaries took it to the New World.

Irrigation Technology. Modern technology has introduced efficient methods of applying water directly to crops, including overhead sprinkler systems and drip (trickle) irrigation. The latter sends moisture—sometimes mixed with fertilizer—to each individual plant via spaced openings. Although expensive initially, it makes very efficient use of water, fertilizer, and labor, and it is being utilized on an increasing scale. Overhead sprinklers, although more efficient than basin and furrow methods, lose some water to evaporation both in the air and on the surface. They also require sizable investment, but both movable impulse sprinklers and self-propelled center-pivot circular sprinklers are nevertheless

widely found; the latter were used on a grand scale in the wheat fields of central Saudi Arabia. Greenhouse horticulture, which traps evaporated water for reuse and greatly increases crop yields, has become widely used in the region from Cyprus to the UAE.

Irrigated Lands

A Quantitative View. In 1980, irrigated cropland covered 55,360 mi²/143,380 km², which was 1.9 percent of all the land and 20 percent of the agricultural land in the sixteen states. By 2009, the total was 100,170 mi²/259,450 km²—about 4 percent of the total area and 41 percent of the cropland—a 73 percent increase over nearly three decades. This clearly indicates regionwide efforts to intensify agriculture. The value of crops raised by artificial watering constitutes a disproportionate percentage of the value of total production, perhaps as much as three-fourths. One explanation is that all cultivated land is irrigated in Egypt (Fig. 5.7), which ranks as the second

Figure 5.7 Aerial view of irrigated agriculture in the Nile Valley, central Egypt. The dividing line between verdant irrigated crops and barren desert is knife sharp. The photograph illustrates Rudyard Kipling's comment on the Nile as "that little damp trickle of life."

most agriculturally productive country in the Middle East (Turkey is first). From one-quarter to one-half of the cultivated land in most other major agricultural countries in the region is irrigated (see Table 5.1); in Turkey, with 21 percent so watered, and Syria, with 22 percent, irrigated crops are more than 38 and 60 percent of production, respectively.

Obstacles.   Although expanding irrigation is obvious for increasing production, this encounters four serious obstacles: decreasing availability of water, increasing expense in terms of cost-effectiveness, competition for land availability, and conflicts over riparian rights. Although high expenditures per unit area in Israel, Saudi Arabia, and some of the Gulf states have produced excellent returns, such expenditure levels are of questionable cost-effectiveness, and they are not practica-

ble in most parts of the region. In southern Iraq, expanding irrigation presents its own problems, including salination. Drainage, both surface and underground tile, may offer more benefit than irrigation in some areas. In several of the country chapters in Part Two, the point is made that policy makers need to make some hard decisions about such questions as cutting agricultural use of water in favor of other economic sectors and, within the agricultural sector, which modifications to current crop patterns must be made to maximize returns from water inputs.

Dates: A Special Note.   Dates play an even more crucial role in traditional desert agriculture than do olives along the Mediterranean. The date palm (*Phoenix dactylifera*) is the most familiar and historically important plant of the entire North African–Middle

Eastern–South Asian desert region. Throughout this zone, from Morocco to the Indian subcontinent, it provides a staple food, construction material (see Fig. 17.4, top), and fiber for weaving baskets and mats. It is so fundamental in the Middle East that it appears on stamps, currency, coins, and Saudi Arabia's royal flag. It has been a basic food in desert areas for millennia; the tree survives searing heat and lasts for generations, thriving on minimal water in large groves in oases (see Fig. 5.2). Its fruit can be preserved for months, with high nutritional value and a range of vitamins. Its essential role has diminished as modern transportation and trade have brought both unlimited amounts of food and also refrigeration to even once remote desert areas.[6]

ROLE OF ANIMALS

Livestock raising, dating to 8000 BCE, is common in all three types of land, differing from one area to another. Nomadic herding in the desert or in the Zagros Mountains is quite different from raising animals on farms, especially on irrigated farms. Available statistics do not distinguish between farm animals and those herded by nomads, so the following cited data pertain to all types of livestock.

Commercial animal husbandry is most intensive in specialized agricultural settlements in Israel. In addition, commercial raising of small animals has made rapid strides elsewhere since 1950. Chicken farming, for example, surged sharply during the 1970s and has expanded in every country, especially in Iran, Turkey, Saudi Arabia, and Egypt. With no religious or social-consumption taboos, their production has increased in Turkey, for example, from 59 million in 1988 to 230 million by the late 2000s. Although no figures are available, pigeons are raised in large numbers in towns and villages as well as by farmers in many areas, especially in Egypt. Fish farming is an important aspect of land use in Israel and Egypt and has begun in Saudi Arabia and other Gulf countries.

Wide Variety. Meat animals are produced in large numbers (Table 5.4). Poultry, sheep, goats, and cattle (*Bos taurus*) are the most numerous (Fig. 5.8). Hogs are raised in Cyprus, Israel, Egypt, Lebanon, and Turkey, although pork cannot be marketed in conservative Muslim or Jewish areas. Sheep have been numerous for millennia and are an important source, not only of meat, wool, and skins but also of milk and cheese. Iran, Turkey, and Syria together have almost 75 percent of the region's sheep.

Goats are about half as numerous as sheep. Despite their reputation for destroying vegetation, if properly managed goats are hardly more damaging than sheep or cows and are uniquely valuable in their grazing of the poorer types of forage. Vegetation can best be protected by excluding them from designated areas, and goat-exclusion laws have been very successful in Cyprus, Israel, and Turkey. Angora goats in Turkey are especially valuable for their unique hair, used in making mohair.

Cattle numbers increased steadily with population and the standard of living from the early 1960s to the mid-1980s when farmers in Turkey and Egypt turned to raising crops and concentrating on smaller animals. Numbers stabilized during the 1990s, and the quality of cattle improved as farmers turned to better breeds. With dairy cattle, this has greatly improved milk yield. A growing awareness of the nutritional benefits of milk has encouraged dairying in many areas; Ras al-Khaymah now produces cow's milk for the UAE's urban areas. Israel has imported and bred some of the best dairy cattle in the world, and it leads the region in milk output per animal by a wide margin. Egyptian farms, with plenty of water in which buffalo can submerge themselves, have three-fourths of the region's stock (*Bubalus bubalis*, or water

TABLE 5.4 Domestic Animals (Thousands of Head)

Country	1 Camels	2 Cattle	3 Sheep	4 Hogs	5 Chickens	6 Goats	7 Buffaloes
Bahrain	1	10	40	—	530	19	—
Cyprus	—	56	227	464	2,960	209	—
Egypt	111	4,530	5,650	12	100,000	4,200	4,000
Iran	152	8,500	54,000	—	507,000	25,700	650
Iraq	59	1,600	7,800	—	29,000	1,500	275
Israel	5	430	445	224	42,599	100	—
Jordan	13	65	2,176	—	25,000	752	—
Kuwait	6	32	900	—	33,800	145	—
Lebanon	<1	77	335	10	37,500	450	—
Oman	130	333	389	—	4,200	1,719	—
Qatar	34	8	150	—	4,900	145	—
Saudi Arabia	230	421	5,900	—	146,000	4,500	—
Syria	50	1,010	15,511	—	25,401	2,057	7
Turkey	1	10,724	21,795	2	229,969	5,128	87
UAE	412	69	1,300	—	18,000	1,850	—
Yemen	403	1,605	9,206	—	60,000	9,016	—
Gaza	—	—	—	—	—	—	—
West Bank	—	—	—	—	—	—	—
TOTAL	1,607	29,470	125,824	712	1,266,859	57,490	5,019

Data for 2010. Animal raising has always been a major economic-cultural activity in the region, and numbers have increased appreciably during the past two decades. Chickens have tripled in numbers. (*Source:* UN Food and Agriculture Org., www.fao.org/corp/statistics)

Figure 5.8 Anatolian shepherd with sheep and goats on steppe lands east of Ankara. Some of the goats are of the famous Angora (Ankara) breed.

buffalo, quite different from the American bison). They were common in the marshes of southern Iraq until these were drained by Saddam Husayn after 1991; they seem to be slowly returning in the 2000s.

Horse populations have declined sharply in every state, with the exceptions of Saudi Arabia and Qatar, as the workhorse has been displaced by the tractor and the truck. Fine Arabian show horses constitute only a small percentage of the equine population; after becoming rare in the region by the mid-twentieth century, they are again being bred by a few wealthy Saudis and other Arabs.

The number of camels (see below) was slowly declining, from more than 1 million in 1969–1971 to 763,000 in 1985; however, it had risen to 1.6 million by 2010 as interest in camels revived—for the sport of camel racing, for example. The traditional significance of the camel, including its use for feasts, suggests that it will continue to play an important, if diminished, role well into the twenty-first century.

Nomadic Pastoralism

Nomadic pastoralism is an essential aspect of the Middle East in the popular perception and also in fact. Animal herding by nomads involves a wide range of periodic migrations by tribal groups and their animals in search of grass and water. These periodic movements, both across country and vertically to higher or lower elevations, resulted in the interrelated triad of nonsedentary herding—nomadism, pastoralism, and tribalism. Nomadic pastoralism extends over a larger area than any other type of agricultural activity—more, in fact, than all other types combined. It dominates dry areas not only in the core Middle East, from Egypt's Western Desert across the Arabian Peninsula to Iranian Baluchistan, but also in North Africa and Central Asia.

Major nomadic pastoral groups include the Arab Bedouin of the deserts and steppes (see Fig. 4.2), Qashqai and Bakhtiari of the High Zagros, Turkmans of the Kopet ranges, Baluch of southeastern Iran, and in the extended eastern area Turkmans, Uzbek, and Kazakh in Central Asia and the Berber in North Africa. Although the numbers engaged in nomadic herding are steadily decreasing, it remains a significant aspect of tradition, culture, and economic life, especially in the Arabian Peninsula and Syrian Desert in the core region and in vast areas of the peripheral countries.

Using marginal resources and very basic technology, Bedouin are well suited to their environment, primarily through a symbiotic relationship with their animals. Alone on the open desert in summer, a Bedouin family could survive only a day or two, as there would be no water, food, or shelter. But the family's camels, which feed on salty shrubs, supply milk consumed as liquid, yogurt, or cheese; hair for weaving; hides and leather; dung for fuel; in an emergency, meat; and, of course, transportation.

Most contemporary Bedouin also herd sheep and goats for wool, milk, hides, and meat. Their essential characteristic is their geographically cyclic movements to sustain their herds and flocks. Other nomads follow cycles that may vary in frequency, types of animals, and other details.

The Remarkable Camel

The domesticated camel appeared about 2000 BCE. Although the two-humped Bactrian camel (*Camelus bactrianus*) is common in parts of Anatolia and Iran and dominant in Central Asia, the Arabian camel, or dromedary (*C. dromedarius*), with one hump, has long been herded in the Arabian Peninsula, North Africa, and adjacent lands. In the Syrian Desert, Mesopotamia, Anatolia, and Iran, sheep and goats are common, whereas camels are less so—indeed, there are none at all in mountainous areas.

The camel adapts especially well to desert life with its remarkable ability to conserve

Figure 5.9 Camels watering at a water tank installed and maintained by Aramco (now Saudi Aramco), Rub al-Khali (Empty Quarter), Saudi Arabia.

water in hot weather and its low water requirements in winter (Fig. 5.9). Its long neck allows it to graze both surface vegetation and tree leaves. Its soft padded feet operate like snowshoes and enable it to walk over drift sand without sinking and over hot surfaces without pain.

Traversing terrain that other beasts cannot, the "ship of the desert" can carry heavier loads through greater heat and aridity for a longer working life than oxen, horses, or donkeys. Using camel caravans, Arabs monopolized ancient trade routes and laid the bases for mercantile cities over a wide area. The camel actually delayed the development of desert roads in the region, since wagons and carts drawn by oxen or horses were less efficient than camels. However, after the mid-twentieth century, motor vehicles, aircraft, and railroads displaced the camel as transport, certainly for long distances, and mod-

ern Bedouin even transport their camels and other animals by the omnipresent Toyota pickup.[7]

FOREST PRODUCTS

Forestry plays a minor role in the region, as is suggested by the sparse forest vegetation (see Map 2.8). Only Turkey and Iran have noteworthy industries, and extensive systematic timber exploitation is found only in Turkey. Production in the high Pontus in the north, the high Taurus in the south, and the highlands between Istanbul and Ankara yielded 555 mn ft^3/15.7 mn m^3 of roundwood in 2010 (see Table 5.3). Iran's 2010 output was less than an one-eighth of its 1995 figure. The still smaller production noted for Egypt consists of fast-growing trees planted largely along canal banks and then harvested for use in the construction of small buildings.

Figure 5.10 Daily fish auction in the small port of Khasab, Oman, near the Strait of Hormuz. Note prows of tour dhows to the left. See also smugglers' boats in Khasab in Figure 17.5.

FISHING

Surrounded and deeply penetrated by seas, and with a total coastline exceeding 14,585 mi/23,470 km, Middle East countries have an appreciable potential for a fisheries industry (Fig. 5.10). However, other factors inhibit progress toward reaching that potential, including overfishing and pollution.

Facing three seas and with vigorous maritime activity, Turkey had long led the sixteen countries in fish landed. However, Egypt has overtaken Turkey, partly by increasing its freshwater catch. Iran ranks second, and after Turkey come Yemen and Oman (see Table 5.3). Iran exploits its long coastline on the Gulf, as well as on the Gulf of Oman and the Caspian Sea. It takes nearly 665,000 mt annually, and it reaps a notably valuable—but decreasing—harvest of caviar (fish roe) from the Caspian. Access to rich fisheries associated with the upwelling waters along the southern coast of the Arabian Peninsula provides Yemen and neighboring Oman with their considerable catches. All the leading fishing states have increased their landings in the new century.

NOTES

1. Production indexes are drawn from the UN Food and Agriculture Organization *Production Yearbook,* published annually.

2. See www.aaaid.org/ for further information.

3. J. Held 1979. Studies of Middle East land use that are more general include Askari and Cummings 1976 and Beaumont and McLachlan 1985. The crucial role of water is studied in Rogers and Lydon 1994; Ventner 1998; Biswas et al. 1997; Soffer 1999; and Fox 2003. The UN's FAO *Production Yearbook,* published annually, is indispensable for production data, more promptly available on the excellent FAO website, www.faostat.fao.org.

4. For example, in the first century BCE, Virgil used the olive branch this way in the *Aeneid,* book 8.

5. *Haaretz,* Aug. 18, 2012. For the US State Department annual report on terrorist activities, see

www.state.gov/j/ct/rls/crt/2011/195544.htm; see also *Haaretz,* Nov. 7, 2012; and the *Times of Israel,* Nov. 27, 2012.

6. Dates continue to have a religious significance for Muslims, as the fruit is the food with which the Ramadan fast is commonly broken at sundown, based on a tradition that this was the practice of the Prophet Muhammad.

7. For interesting discussions of Bedouin and camels, see Dickson 1949; Hills 1966; Bulliet 1975; Jabbur 1995; *Saudi Aramco and Its World* 1995; and Mandaville 2011 (especially recommended).

6

Riches Beneath the Earth

KEY POINTS: Middle East wealth in petroleum and natural gas resource—half the world's oil reserves and huge natural gas reserves—has attracted worldwide attention since 1930s. Saudi Arabia leads area and world in reserves, vies with Russia as leading producer. Table gives data on oil and gas reserves and production for all states of region. Tankers carry oil through Strait of Hormuz to South and East Asia and to Europe and America. Qatar and Iran share mid-Gulf gas field, world's largest. Several regional states are members of OPEC, worldwide marketing organization. Region not rich in solid minerals, but considerable concentration in northern tectonic belt of Anatolian and Iranian Plateaus. Sedimentary rocks of heart of region yielding world-rank amounts of phosphates for fertilizers.

A PERSPECTIVE

With its enormous hydrocarbon wealth, the Middle East is without equal and perforce has a unique global role.[1] Moreover, the region's share of the world's oil and gas reserves and production has generally been portrayed as likely to increase, since the conventional petro-reserves elsewhere have been more rapidly depleted by intensive exploitation. However, the still uncertain future of shale oil and gas technology makes it difficult to assess to what degree this prognosis will need modification over the long term.[2]

At the outset, natural gas must be given special attention, because recent discoveries mean that the Gulf province has surpassed Russia as having the world's largest gas re-

sources and because production can be easily exported as LNG (liquefied natural gas) to meet rapidly mounting world demand. In economic terms, never before in history has a region achieved such explosive large-scale development so quickly as this area did during the decades following World War II.

Western cognizance of the vital importance of Middle East oil was manifest in 1990 when US and European forces responded immediately to the imperilment of Kuwaiti and Saudi oil fields. By the mid-1990s, these more dramatic aspects of the Gulf "oil boom" had subsided, and immense production came to be routine. The region and its huge energy output were taken for granted, and some Western powers—especially the United States—refocused their main attention on the emerging (and reemerging) Caspian oil province, partly to offset the supremacy of the Middle East.

More than Just Oil.   Notwithstanding the importance of energy reserves, emphasis on oil should not obscure the region's other important characteristics. The Middle East also has historical, geopolitical, political, geographical, human, and nonenergy economic significance. The gravity of these other aspects is often overlooked or is subordinated to petroleum and more limited regional interests. This chapter focuses on oil, but the book as a whole aims to weigh the region's variety and achieve a more balanced perspective.

Petroleum, natural gas, and petro-products are virtually the sole items produced and exported on any scale by some Middle East countries. At the three-year average production rate in the early 2010s, regional petroleum resources will last for about ninety years if there are no further discoveries. Unlikely as this may be, these countries are well aware of the singularity on which their wealth is based and of its eventual depletion. They also know that external forces influence the production, transportation, and marketing of their most important product. In view of the relatively rapid exhaustibility of this unique resource, and with the lessons of other boom-and-bust situations to guide them, they have sought to control their own destinies—through the Organization of Petroleum Exporting Countries (OPEC), for example. In pursuit of long-term economic viability, they are undertaking intensive diversification programs, including agricultural development, as discussed in Chapter 5.

Other Resources.   With a few exceptions, the overall percentage of the world's supply of underground resources other than petroleum in the region is relatively modest. Nevertheless, nonenergy minerals are major items in several countries with limited oil output.

Non-oil minerals are or have been of historic importance in Turkey, Iran, and Cyprus; now this is also true for Jordan, Egypt, Syria, Israel, and Saudi Arabia. (The region's other most important natural resource—water—is discussed elsewhere in the book.)

PETROLEUM: HISTORICAL DEVELOPMENT

From Ancient Times.   Asphalt, gas, and oil seeps from underground hydrocarbon deposits have been known for millennia at numerous sites in the Middle East—in northern Mesopotamia, near Hit on the Euphrates, on both sides of the head of the Persian/Arabian Gulf, under the Dead Sea, at the northern end of the Gulf of Suez, and in a dozen other places. Bitumen (asphalt, pitch, tar) is mentioned several times in the Old Testament: Noah used pitch in constructing the ark, and Moses's mother used bitumen and pitch to line the basket in which she floated her baby on the Nile. Bitumen was used as mortar in the construction of brick walls, ziggurats, and other buildings in Sumerian and Babylonian times and can still be identified in many ruins in Iraq and western Iran.

The biblical "fiery furnace" of Shadrach, Meshach, and Abednego may refer to the still-burning gas seepage known as the "eternal fires" near Kirkuk in northern Iraq. Gas flares were the focal points of fire-reverencing religions of ancient Persia, and fire temples were numerous. Oil from seeps and oozes was collected for lamps, and it was used in warfare long before the Christian era. Thus, twentieth-century oil explorers had historical indicators for siting their early wildcat wells. Politically, subsurface oil and gas fields are indifferent to human (and mutable) surface authority and boundaries, and reservoirs may extend under two or more nations.

Beginnings of an Industry.   Financed by a British syndicate, William Knox D'Arcy, a

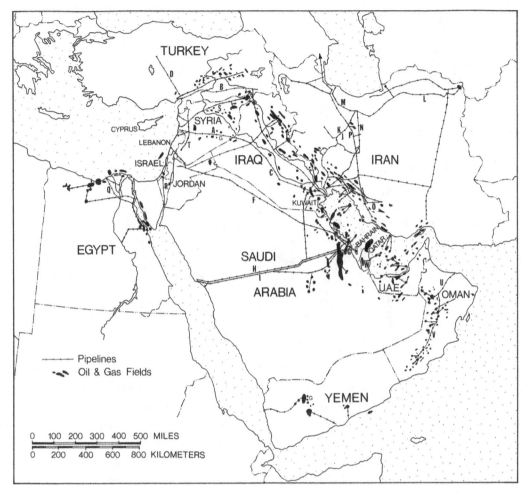

Map 6.1 Major petroleum and natural gas fields and pipelines in the Middle East, 2012. Gulf fields are detailed on Map 6.2. (Adapted from several sources)

British subject, obtained a concession in 1901 to drill in western Iran; his crew made the Middle East's first major strike in 1908. The initial discovery was in the Masjed-e Soleyman field, the first of many fabulous reservoirs (Map 6.1). The next year, the D'Arcy group formed the Anglo-Persian Oil Company (APOC), which became the Anglo-Iranian Oil Company (AIOC) in 1935 and British Petroleum (BP) in 1951. APOC made the first shipment of oil in 1912 from Abadan on the Shatt al-Arab, today still a major oil center. World War I proved the superiority of

oil over coal for fueling naval and commercial vessels and accelerated development of the industry. Demand for oil spiraled upward and is still mounting.

The United States Arrives. Other European entrepreneurs sought exploration rights across the border in Mesopotamia after the find in Iran. The Turkish Petroleum Company (TPC), formed before World War I by British, German, and Dutch interests, found oil in 1927 by drilling a few hundred meters from the "eternal fires." This discovery near Kirkuk

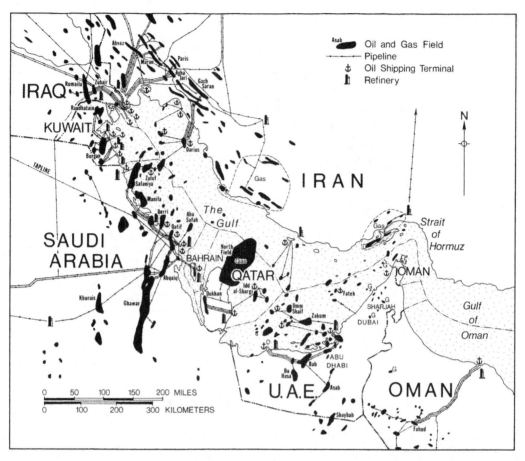

Map 6.2 Petroleum and natural gas fields, pipelines, oil-export terminals, and refineries, Gulf region. Ghawar in Saudi Arabia is the world's richest known oil field. (Adapted from several sources)

opened what remains one of the world's major oil fields. In 1928, the United States made its first entry into the region's oil race when the Near East Development Corporation (NEDC) obtained an equity interest in TPC, renamed Iraq Petroleum Company (IPC) in 1929. NEDC originally comprised five companies but later was equally divided between Standard of New Jersey (later Exxon) and Socony Vacuum (later Mobil, which merged with Exxon in 1999, becoming ExxonMobil).

A Red Line. From the early years of exploration, agreements among companies divided up operating areas. One accord was the Red Line Agreement, reached in 1928, which cov-

ered former Ottoman possessions, excluding Kuwait and Egypt. It provided that any oil deals involving areas within the Red Line must be unanimously approved by all companies operating there. Although later rescinded, this agreement regulated concession patterns in much of the region over a critical period.

Neither the worldwide depression nor discoveries of other large supplies of oil, like the East Texas field, slowed intensive exploration in the 1930s. By World War II, exploration had revealed the presence of huge quantities of oil beyond southern Iraq in the Mesopotamian-Gulf trough (Map 6.2).

The modest but historically important Bahrain field, found in 1932, was the first dis-

Figure 6.1 Large crude carriers (oil tankers) taking on crude oil at Saudi Aramco loading pier in the Gulf. With exports sometimes of more than 10 mn barrels per day (bpd), Saudi loading facilities must be extensive. (B. H. Moody, *Saudi Aramco World*, SAWDIA)

covered in the Gulf area proper, outside Iran and Iraq. It was also the scene of the region's first all-US oil venture. A subsidiary of Standard Oil of California (Socal—later in partnership with Texaco), the Bahrain Petroleum Company (Bapco) was chartered in Canada in order to meet the requirement that concessions in British territories be granted to "British companies." From the hills on the upturned strata of Bahrain's structural dome, US geologists using binoculars studied Dammam Dome on the mainland 20 mi/32 km away, becoming convinced that a likely oil reservoir lay under it.

A Desert Bonanza. Urged by these geologists, Socal obtained a concession in 1933 for the eastern part of the newly united Kingdom of Saudi Arabia; it then operated there as California Arabian Standard Oil Company (Casoc) and found oil in 1938 in Dammam Dome as predicted. A new and more appropriate name—Arabian American Oil Company (familiarly known as Aramco)—was adopted in 1944. Even after it became a national company—officially, the Saudi Arabian Oil Company—in 1988, it retained the well-known acronym as "Saudi Aramco" (Fig. 6.1). In the 1930s, the Kuwait Oil Company—formed by APOC (BP) and Gulf (later merged with Chevron)—discovered the rich Burgan reservoir in the amirate.

Growing realization of the oil potential accelerated exploration in the lower Gulf, and after World War II more than a score of new enterprises were exploring on land and offshore. British, Dutch, French, and US "majors" had dominated the industry for forty years; now they were joined by firms from Italy, Germany, Spain, Japan, Brazil, India, and elsewhere. Still later, producing countries formed their own companies and gradually took over most or all the operations within their borders.

Down Along the Gulf.   The Dukhan field in western Qatar was discovered in 1940 by an IPC subsidiary that later became the Qatar Petroleum Company, but production was delayed until 1949. Companies with multiple and international ownerships were given concessions in offshore areas of Abu Dhabi; others received onshore concessions. These huge oil and gas resources are now generally under the Abu Dhabi National Oil Company (ADNOC). The offshore Umm Shaif field, in Abu Dhabi territorial waters, was the first of many major offshore discoveries to complement the onshore fields in the lower Gulf. This field was found in 1958, but it did not produce until 1962 because of difficulties producing, transporting, and storing offshore oil. The large onshore Bab field opened in 1963, and production began in other amirates several years later, primarily by smaller companies. In Oman, after successive concession companies had disappointing results, Petroleum Development (Oman), or PDO, hit oil in 1963 and 1964, and production began in 1967. PDO is now 60 percent government owned, with Shell holding 34 percent, and is responsible for more than 90 percent of the sultanate's output. Several other companies operate on a limited scale in Oman, and production is from about 120 mostly small fields.

Mediterranean Producers.   In the western part of the region, exploration—which began early in Egypt—has shown that resources are comparatively modest. Oil seepages near the mouth of the Gulf of Suez, known from Roman times, attracted attention soon after the opening of the petroleum age, and, indeed, the first well drilled in Egypt (1886) was the earliest in the Middle East. However, commercial production did not begin until 1913, a year after the first Iranian oil shipment, and major output levels were not reached until the 1960s. Major natural gas fields offshore from the Nile Delta now dominate the Egyptian energy scene. In addition to the public-sector Egyptian General Petroleum Company, more than a score of international companies operate in Egypt, including BP, Shell, Agip, and British Gas. As in Oman, production in Egypt is from many small fields.

Syria finally made a small find in 1956 and began commercial production in 1959 in the far northeast (in segments of the Fold Belt in which the Kirkuk field had been found in Iraq), but production was delayed until pipelines could be laid. After new discoveries in the mid-1980s, Syria undertook an intensive and successful search for new fields, especially around Dayr al-Zawr.

To the south, drilling in Jordan in the mid-1950s, when the kingdom controlled the West Bank, found nothing on either side of the river, and more efforts in the 1980s resulted in only negligible production. With further exploration, modest gas deposits have been found near the Iraqi border. Jordan also has sizable deposits of oil- and gas-bearing shale (see Chapter 12), and it signed an agreement in 2011 with a Canadian company to conduct feasibility studies with a view to future production. Current shale technologies are generally water intensive, and Jordan is the most water-short country in its immediate Levantine neighborhood.

Yemen.   Discoveries were made in the two Yemens in the 1980s before their merger in 1990. Earlier tests in the west of the then Yemen Arab Republic (YAR) had been negative, but a US company (Hunt) made a major oil strike in 1984 in the Marib Basin area in the east. Production and export began in late 1987. The Marib success encouraged the People's Democratic Republic of Yemen

(PDRY) to drill in an extension of the structure south of the border, and tests found oil in appreciable quantities that by the early 1990s far exceeded the reserves found in the original strikes to the north. Total discovered reserves are modest but domestically important.

Levant Basin: Prelude.   In Lebanon, a test well in the 1940s showed no likely prospects; no further onshore development has been undertaken. Similarly, onshore test wells drilled in Cyprus in the 1950s and 1960s failed to indicate any commercially viable prospects, but there were hints of possible offshore deposits. In Israel, hydrocarbon indications in and around the Dead Sea attracted surveys, but only minor resources have been found. Turkey found oil in 1940, and development there achieved a steady pace in the 1960s and is continuing. Results have been limited, since the extreme folding and faulting typical of this area fragment the reservoirs and cause the individual fields to be small and scattered, as in Oman. Simply put, these four countries bordering on the eastern Mediterranean until recently were seen as the region's orphans as far as petro-reserves were concerned.

Levant Basin: Discovery.   Egypt's successes north of the Nile Delta encouraged exploration farther north beyond its territorial waters into what is known as the Levant Basin. From a modest beginning in 2003 when gas from a field offshore Gaza and Israel began to feed a gas-fired generating plant in Ashdod, Israel, came further studies of the region. The United States Geological Survey (USGS) released a report in 2010 that estimated that there were 1.7 bn bbl (billion barrels) of oil and 122 tn ft^3 (trillion cubic feet) of natural gas offshore Gaza, Israel, Lebanon, and Syria alone (the maritime areas belonging to Cyprus and Turkey are in different basins, and there are as of yet no estimates of what may lie beneath their offshore waters).[3] Before exploitation of these resources can proceed too

far, there is the question of settling maritime borders (see Chapter 8, "Boundary and Territorial Disputes"), and in some cases this means negotiations between countries already hostile to each other (Israel and Palestine, Israel and Lebanon, and Cyprus and Turkey). The implications for each country of its newly discovered petro-assets are discussed in Part Two, in Chapters 10, 11, 13, and 20.

PATTERNS OF RESERVES

As of 2012, 806.9 bn bbl of oil—about 49.3 percent of the world's proved reserves—lay under the Middle East, most of it around and under the Gulf and to the northwest along the Tigris and Euphrates (Map 6.3; see also Map 6.1). Exploration in recent decades continues to be intensive: new discoveries during just the years 1987–1991 augmented reserves by nearly 40 percent. In the new century, reserves increased by only about 11 percent, but the new discoveries totaled about 78 bn bbl, or an amount equivalent to about 375 percent of US reserves.

Around the Gulf Trough.   By far the largest in both the Middle East and second largest in the world after Venezuela,[4] Saudi reserves (including half those of the Divided Zone) of 267.9 bn bbl are almost equal to the total outside the Middle East in Africa, Asia, and Europe. After Saudi Arabia, the second through fifth regional rankings go to Iran, Iraq, Kuwait, and the UAE (Table 6.1 and Graph 6.1). These four shift in rank among themselves periodically; Iran claimed a large increase in 2002–2003 that put it in second place. Globally, after Venezuela (297.6 bn bbl) and Saudi Arabia come Canada (173.1 bn), Iran, Iraq, Kuwait, the UAE, Russia (80.0 bn), Libya (48.0 bn), and Nigeria (37.2 bn). The latest estimate for US reserves is 20.7 bn bbl.[5]

Eastern Saudi Arabia has about a third of the region's reserves, distributed over fifty fields, onshore and offshore, extending from

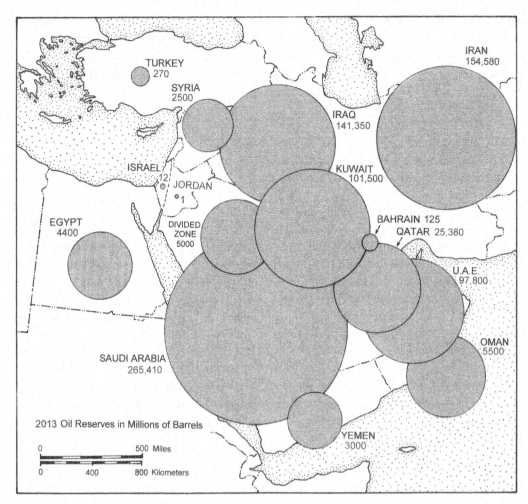

Map 6.3 Proved petroleum reserves in the Middle East, by country. Proportional circles show amount of proved reserves in millions of barrels as of 2013. (From data in *Oil and Gas Journal,* Dec. 3, 2012; and US Department of Energy, Energy Information Administration (EIA), *Country Analysis Briefs,* 2012, www.eia.doe.gov/emeu/cabs/cabsme.html)

Kuwait south to the Abu Dhabi border (Map 6.2). Prominent is the large, linear Ghawar field, the world's greatest single oil reservoir. The gently folded and domed structures of northeastern Arabia continue northward into Kuwait, with which Saudi Arabia shares the world's biggest offshore field, Safaniya-Khafji. The Arabian-Kuwait structures then extend into Iraq, joining the northwest-southeast trend of the Zagros fold reservoirs in southern Iraq. One particular field, the Rumaila, straddles the border and was signifi-

cant in the lead-up to the invasion of Kuwait in 1990 and in boundary revisions in 1992. In Iraq, with 134.1 bn bbl of reserves, oil reservoirs have been found in subsurface folds from Ain Zalah in the far north through the Kirkuk and Baghdad reservoirs to Rumaila and Zubair in the extreme south. After decades of only desultory exploration activity, Iraq in the 2010s may now be undertaking this task much more seriously.

In the southern Gulf (Fig. 6.2), most of the major fields lie in Abu Dhabi, largest and

TABLE 6.1 Petroleum: Reserves, Recent Production, Wells, and Fields

Country	1 Oil Resrvs 2010 1,000s Bbl	2 Gas Resrvs 2010 Bills Ft.³	3 Oil Prod. 2012 1,000s Bpd	4 Gas Prod. 2012 Bills Ft³/d	5 No. Prod. Oil Wells 2011	6 Number of Fields 2004
Bahrain	124,560	3,250	41.0	307.4	496	1
Cyprus	0	0	0.0	0.0	0	0
(Divided Zone)[a]	5,000,000	1,000	615.7	[a]	761	5
Egypt	4,400,000	77,200	673.0	1,069.0	1,482	134
Iran	154,580,000	1,187,000	3,053.0	4,725.0	2,074	41
Iraq	141,350,000	111,520	2,880.0	260.0	1,526	20
Israel	11,500	9,482	0.6	0.0[b]	4	6
Jordan	1,000	213	0.0	0.0	4	1
Kuwait	101,500,000	63,000	2,753.0	387.0[a]	1,286	8
Lebanon	0	0	0.0	0.0[b]	0	0
Oman	5,500,000	30,000	908.1	894.0	4,918	106
Qatar	25,380,000	890,000	749.5	3,525.0	513	8
Saudi Arabia	265,410,000	287,844	9,960.0	2,465.0[a]	2,895	50
Syria	2,500,000	8,500	170.0	150.0	146	17
Turkey	270,433	218	43.8	1.9	915	79
UAE	97,800,000	215,035	2,649.9	1,630.0	1,458	24
Yemen	3,000,000	16,900	172.5	0.0	2,578	27
TOTAL	806,827,493	2,901,162	24,670.1	15,414.3[c]	21,056	527
Abu Dhabi	92,200,000	200,000	2,500.0	[d]	1,200	14
Dubai	4,000,000	3,785	100.9	[d]	200	5
Ras al-Khaymah	100,000	1,140	0.8	[d]	7	1
Sharjah	1,500,000	10,110	48.2	[d]	51	4

The question of oil reserves has become a matter of vigorous debate in recent years. [a]Divided Zone production is normally divided between Kuwait and Saudi Arabia; undivided gas production is not available. [b]Israel is beginning to be a moderate offshore gas producer, with additional discoveries, and Lebanon has new adjoining offshore finds. [c]This total does not include 78.3 bcf/d distributed among Israel, Jordan, and Yemen. [d]Gas production data not available. Note units used in Columns 1-4. The last four rows give petroleum data on the four amirates of the UAE that produce petroleum. (*Sources: Oil and Gas Journal,* Dec. 3, 2012 [Columns 1, 2, and 5], and Jan. 14, 2013 [Column 4]; Energy Information Administration, www.eia.doe.gov [Column 3]; *International Petroleum Encyclopedia 2003* [Column 6])

westernmost of the seven component shaykhdoms of the UAE. In 2012, it had nearly five times the reserves of the United States. Onshore in the north, Kuwait has the fabulous Burgan field, with more oil per unit of surface area than any other field known. With Saudi Arabia and Kuwait holding half shares in the oil of the Divided Zone (the former Neutral Zone), Kuwait's 104.0 bn bbl accord it fourth rank in reserves in the Middle East and sixth in the world.

Iran now claims second place regionally and fourth globally, with 154.6 bn bbl, even

after producing some 70 bn bbl over the century since oil was discovered in 1908. Virtually all of the country's fields follow the trend of folds in the Zagros Mountains in western Iran, from Kermanshah in the northwest to Bandar-e Abbas in the southeast at the Strait of Hormuz. Lying in the southeastern part of the sedimentary basin, opposite the Qatar Peninsula and east toward the Strait of Hormuz, are more than a dozen rich gas fields. Like Saudi Arabia and Kuwait, Iran also possesses offshore fields with impressive reserves and production. Both recent production and,

MIDDLE EAST PETROLEUM RESERVES, 2012

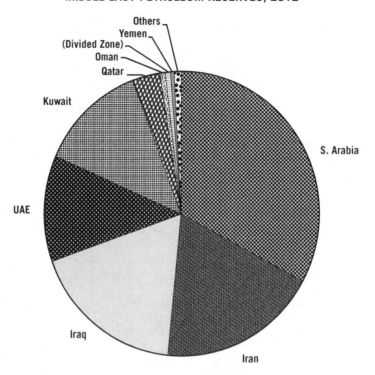

WORLD REGIONS PETROLEUM RESERVES, 2012

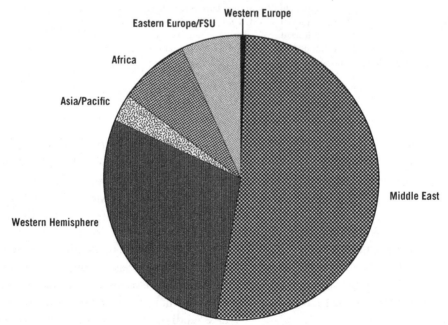

Graph 6.1 Petroleum reserves of Middle East countries (*top*) and of world regions (*bottom*). (From data in *Oil and Gas Journal,* Dec. 3, 2012; and US Department of Energy, Energy Information Administration (EIA), *Country Analysis Briefs,* 2011–2012, www.eia.doe.gov/emeu/cabs/)

Figure 6.2 Some of the surface facilities of Dubai's offshore Fateh field, 56 mi/90 km from the coast. Resting on the seabed are huge bell-shaped tanks that store oil from surrounding wells until it can be loaded onto tankers such as the one shown.

probably more important, new investment in the hydrocarbon sector have been seriously affected by international economic sanctions leveled against the country.

Qatar's reserves in its onshore Dukhan field and three offshore fields were, until 2000, about equal to those of Egypt and Yemen, but then new discoveries raised the total to 25.4 bn bbl. But its relatively modest oil reserves are richly supplemented by the supergiant gas reservoir in its part of North Field,[6] the world's largest, which alone gives it the world's third-greatest gas reserves after Russia and Iran (see Table 6.1). Development of this field and of the systems to distribute its production were some of the region's most active energy projects in the 2000s.

Oman was the last of the Gulf area states to achieve significant levels of petroleum production. The original discoveries in 1963 and 1964 were followed by more than 100 other scattered modest discoveries by the 2000s. Although none are as rich as the fields in less complex structures farther northwest up the Gulf trough, Oman is now credited with 5.5 bn bbl of proved reserves.

Bahrain, although the earliest of the actual Gulf producers, has the smallest reserves. During deep-test drilling for oil in 1949, Bapco was first to find gas in the Khuff formation (Permian Age), which is now known to have enormous gas reserves. Commercial development of Bahrain's Khuff deep gas began in 1969. Most of Bahrain's oil comes from Abu Safa, an offshore field primarily in Saudi Arabian waters west of the island. Its output of 140,000 barrels per day has been donated to Bahrain by the field's Saudi operators, and production doubled in 2002–2004, although only half of the new output will be donated.

In the Levant

Although reserves on the western side of the region are only a minor part of the regional total, sizable fields have been found and yielded roughly 1.1 mn bpd (million barrels per day) in 2011. Production is primarily from Egypt, Yemen, and Syria, with limited output from Turkey.[7]

Egypt ranks eighth in reserves (4.4 bn bbl), just after Oman and ahead of Yemen, in the region. Petroleum and gas are found in more than 135 fields in and on both sides of the Gulf of Suez, in many small fields in the Western Desert, and, particularly yielding non-associated gas, in recently discovered fields in the northern Nile Delta and offshore. With increasingly large gas finds, Egypt's reserves are becoming significant on the western side of the region. These reservoirs are in completely separate basins from those of the Gulf. Yemen's reserves are modest at 3.0 bn bbl, placing it between Egypt and Syria; this poorest corner of the Middle East desperately needs oil income.

Syria's older fields lie in the extreme northeastern corner of the country, just west of the Tigris River, and are an integral part of the structures containing the Batman fields of southeastern Turkey and the fields of northern Iraq. A significant discovery in late 1984 near Dayr al-Zawr initiated a modest boom in eastern Syria that spread to the center of the country, opening some small new fields, for a country total of 17. Lacking new discoveries (possibly offshore), Syria's reserves have been steadily diminishing (2012 estimate: 2.5 bn bbl). Recent production, of course, has felt the brunt of the country's civil war.

Jordan's recently found Hamzah field, near al-Azraq, has shown only limited potential. There is promising potential for shale oil production, depending on water-saving technological advances (see Chap. 12).

Turkey's small fields lie at the upper end of structures reaching northwestward from Oman up the Gulf trough and through the Mesopotamian depression. About 80 minor fields have been found on the upper Tigris and, more recently, on the upper Euphrates; total reserves are only 270 mn bbl. Turkey also has hopes of offshore discoveries.

PETROLEUM PRODUCTION

Some Influences on Production

Whereas reserves reveal the production potential of individual fields and countries, the trend of actual production and marketing is volatile and reflects a combination of complex factors. Production may move upward as new reserves are exploited, as in Saudi Arabia for thirty-five virtually unbroken years after World War II. Conversely, production may drop steadily as reserves are depleted, as in Bahrain after 1970. In Kuwait, daily production was deliberately reduced by government fiat in 1972 to extend the life of the reserves. Production may drop in a country because of labor unrest, political tensions, natural disasters, or wartime conditions, as in Iran and Iraq in the 1980s and in Iraq and Kuwait in the early 1990s. Iraqi output dropped to a fraction of its normal level in 1991–1992 because of UN-imposed sanctions, and it continued to produce below its 1989 "normal" level until it collapsed in 2003. By the end of the decade, Iraq had seen some recovery, but a combination of factors—pipeline sabotage, obsolete facilities, insecure working conditions—has kept output below 3 mn bpd until mid-2012, when it also became OPEC's second-largest producer, surpassing an Iran now subject to sanctions on its sales.

Technology. Global production was transformed by advances in offshore drilling techniques, which allowed operations in ever-deeper and rougher waters. Greatly upgraded exploration techniques and data interpretation have led to new discoveries. Output has increasingly been affected by less dramatic innovation and technology to raise production in mature fields: enhanced oil recovery (EOR) methods, such as horizontal drilling, waterflooding, gas injection, fracture stimulation, and improved output transportation. Investments in new techniques and procedures have been encouraged, as even slight improvements in discovery efforts and small increases in output translate into much higher returns with rising prices. Old wells, producing only 2–3 bpd, that had been shut in are reopened as strip wells when prices exceed operating costs.

Demand. However, along with these factors, market demand is obviously a crucial influence on production levels. (See "Markets and Marketing" later in this chapter.) After more than twenty-five years of steadily and even dramatically increasing production as unparalleled industrial development occurred in much of the world, Middle East output curves became erratic in the early 1970s. Noteworthy was the impact of the 1973 Arab-Israeli war and the subsequent Arab oil boycott (which was aimed at the United States after it began resupplying armaments to Israel during the war);[8] the sharp rise in oil prices as OPEC and other producers increasingly took control of the output and marketing of their own resources; the growing realization among oil-consuming nations that they must both conserve and substitute for petroleum and natural gas; the market entry of new producing areas in the North Sea, Alaska, and the Soviet Union; and the OPEC decision to vary production to support prices.

The impact of market demand was dramatically demonstrated in the price spike of 2004–2005 and even more so in 2008, when soaring demand in China and India (and likely intense speculative activity) drove spot prices to record levels, close to $150 a barrel, before collapsing in the face of global reces-

sion (and the apparent withdrawal of speculators from the market). Producer cuts in output did little to stem the decline as demand shrank, and it is not clear whether high prices contributed to the global recession. With a sluggish world economy over the following year, demand pressure slackened, but price patterns proved erratic after that, reacting to exogenous factors both easy to identify (the oil spill off the US Gulf Coast, the Libyan civil war, sanction on Iran, threats of regional war) and those less clearly discerned (speculator activity, Chinese economic prospects).[9] Increasing attention also needs to be paid to growing domestic demand in the producing countries; this cuts into exports and, to the extent domestic consumption is subsidized, into government revenues as well.

On the technical level, it should be noted that an oil or gas field has an optimal production level that theoretically permits maximum production over a maximum time period. In the Middle East, this can be more readily determined and followed than in the United States—in virtually all Middle East fields, exploration and production are controlled by one operator, whereas US fields are typically developed by many different companies competing for oil underlying a checkerboard of leases. A statistical comparison shows the consequence: in the Middle East, 24.7 mn bpd came from 21,056 wells in 2012, an average of 1,173 bpd per well, while in the United States production of 6.33 mn bpd was obtained from 413,116 wells, an average of 15.3 bpd per well. US production costs are thus appreciably higher, and oil-recovery percentages are lower without expensive secondary recovery procedures.

Natural Gas

Natural gas reserves include both "associated" and "nonassociated" gas. The former is found with petroleum and reaches the surface along with the oil in which it is dissolved. Nonassociated gas occurs separately in underground reservoirs that produce only gas. The distinction is significant in several ways, including the availability to consumers of one kind of gas or the other. In the processing of natural gas, it is "scrubbed" of natural gas liquids (NGLs) to produce pipeline-quality dry natural gas. NGLs are also hydrocarbons with a wide range of downstream uses as fuels and petrochemical feedstock (and should not be confused with liquefied natural gas—LNG).

Associated gas must be separated from crude oil as soon as the mixture reaches the surface. In the early years of Middle East production, the demand was for oil; since associated gas had no market, it was separated and immediately burned off ("flared"; see "Gas Flaring" below). Gradually, as increased population and economic development created a major market demand for gas, flaring diminished, and it was piped to nearby markets. Rapidly increasing oil production made enormous amounts of associated gas available after separation. These seemingly inexhaustible supplies came to be taken for granted by local consumers—power companies, fertilizer companies, water desalination plants, aluminum smelters, and residential customers. Gas was utilized in more sophisticated ways—after being broken down into its major components of methane, ethane, propane, butane, and heavier hydrocarbons.

Nonassociated Gas Importance.   Thus, when oil production decreased sharply in the early 1980s, not only did the exporters suffer reduced oil income, but they also suddenly had insufficient supplies of the gas that had become a fringe benefit of high oil production levels. This impelled increased searches for and production of nonassociated gas, which could be exploited independently of the demand for oil.

After Bahrain found a major gas reservoir in the deep Khuff formation in 1949, its neighbors also drilled into the Khuff and likewise found enormous amounts of nonassociated gas. Qatar's huge North Field reservoir is in the same zone; all Gulf states have found large reserves both there and in other deep reservoirs. The fields discovered by Iran since the late 1970s, many in the Khuff zone (it shares the offshore North Field, the world's largest), raised its reserves to 1,187 tn (trillion) ft^3/33.6 tn m^3, by far the largest reserves outside Russia. Qatar, with the major share of the North Field, has about 890 tn ft^3/25.2 tn m^3, and is third in rank behind Iran. At the end of 2012, the region had about 43 percent of world reserves.[10] Thus, as in other places, gas is assuming an increasingly significant role in the region's energy pattern.

Exports and Domestic Markets.   Middle East gas, as much as its oil, may well power much of the world's industry in the twenty-first century and beyond; however, if new technologies satisfy environmental and cost concerns, extensive deposits of gas-bearing shale in both North America and Europe could make those markets self-sufficient for many years. Regionally, the historic tendency to emphasize identifying and evaluating oil deposits as opposed to those of nonassociated gas, has continued to the present in some countries still showing relatively low gas reserves relative to those of oil, like Iraq and Saudi Arabia. This allows for the possibility that more intense exploration may result in higher gas-reserve figures. If so, the region could come to rely much more on its own gas, as domestic energy consumption soars and cuts into oil exports.

Gas Flaring.   As mentioned above, associated natural gas must be removed from crude oil when it reaches the surface and before it can safely be piped elsewhere. In the early years of regional production, the only way to dispose of the gas was to "flare" or burn it at the wellhead. Over the years, most producing countries built extensive gas-gathering networks to bring the gas to where it can be used by industry and consumers.[11] However, not all associated gas in any major producing country has yet been put to such final uses. Much is still flared; in 2005, when flaring peaked at 172 bn m^3, this was the equivalent of about 6.5 percent of global gas production.

In 2002, the World Bank undertook an initiative to reduce flaring—the Global Gas Flaring Reduction Partnership (GGFRP)—bringing together governments and both privately and state-owned petro-companies.[12] GGFRP aims to share best practices and to implement country-specific programs, while cutting atmospheric pollution and reducing poverty through better utilization of a valuable resource.

Over the past decade, GGFRP has noted some successes. By 2011, flaring was down almost 20 percent globally from the 2005 peak, but an estimated 140 bn m^3 was still flared. Two Middle East countries—Iran and Iraq—are among the world's top five flarers; as a group, the countries in this study were responsible for about 21 percent of global flaring.

Production Comparisons

OPEC Producers. Map 6.4 presents a graphic comparison of petroleum production by Middle East countries in thousands of barrels per day in 2012. Saudi Arabia ranked second or third during the 1970s and 1980s, behind the Soviet Union and the United States, but it moved into first place in 1991 and has kept that position. It hit a new world record in 2003—an average of 9.8 mn bpd. The kingdom has a history of varying output in response to market conditions and has reached its goal of having a production capacity of 12.5 mn bpd; production in 2012 set a new record—an average of 9.96 mn bpd. Iran reached peaks of more than 6 mn bpd in 1974 and 5.9 mn bpd in 1976 before tumbling to 1.37 mn bpd in the war year of 1981. Under stable conditions, Iran, which hovered around 3.8 mn bpd into the early 2010s,

could probably sustain an average daily production of 5 mn bbl for many years. In 2012, however, it faced the prospect of curtailing production both because of sanctions cutting into exports and as a tactic against those same sanctions, and production saw a one-year drop in average production of almost 15 percent—to 3.05 mn bpd. Although Iranian officials disputed the figures, international sources indicated that by year's end, the daily average was down to close to 2.6 mn bpd.[13]

Iraq moved up to third from fourth in 1975, surpassing Kuwait; it exceeded 1 mn bpd from 1960 on, with a peak of 3.4 mn bpd in 1979 (its last "normal" production year for the next three decades). Output dropped periodically during the early 1970s, when confrontations with Syria interrupted pipeline throughput to the Mediterranean. This situation happened again in the early 1980s during the Iran-Iraq War; it averaged less than 1 mn bpd in 1981–1983. Output reached 3 mn bpd in mid-1990, when Iraq bitterly disputed quotas and overquota production with its OPEC comembers. These and other oil issues were part of its stated rationale for invading Kuwait. When the coalition went into action, Iraq suffered heavy bomb damage and was temporarily forced to shut down all exports. For the next six years, UN controls limited official production to 305,000–600,000 bpd, then after 1997 to 2 mn–2.4 mn bpd. Output collapsed following the 2003 invasion but recovered quickly to 2 mn bpd by year's end and continued at that level through 2007. The intermediate goal of 3 mn bpd was slow to be achieved, as continued insecurity and field-equipment obsolescence remained as hindrances, but that level was at last reached, as mentioned above, in mid-2012; by year's end, it was reported to have reached 3.4 bpd.[14] In 2009, the central government began aggressively seeking contractual arrangements with large international oil companies with a view to achieving its much higher medium and long-term goals; issues between Baghdad and

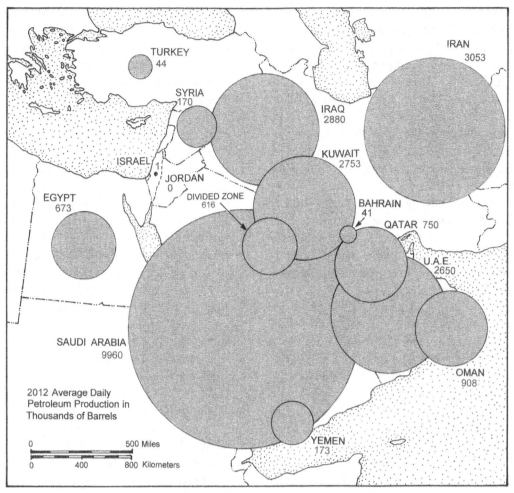

Map 6.4 Petroleum production in the Middle East, by country, in thousands of barrels per day, for 2012. (From data in *Oil and Gas Journal,* Dec. 3, 2012; and US Department of Energy, Energy Information Administration (EIA), www.eia.doe.gov/emeu/cabs/)

the Kurdish Regional Government have further complicated Iraq's production situation (see Chap. 14).

The next-largest producer in the Gulf and in the Middle East is the UAE, where production rose from a negligible amount in 1963 to 2 mn bpd in 1977 before joining the regional downward trend. Before UAE independence in 1971, oil was produced only in Abu Dhabi, still by far the federation's major producer. Dubai's offshore Fateh field contributed a growing share of the total until output fell

after 2001. UAE production in 2012 was an estimated 2.65 mn bpd.

Kuwait led Middle East production from 1954 to 1966; it peaked in 1972 at 3 mn bpd, and then, for conservation purposes, output was intentionally reduced (dropping it to fourth or fifth place), and fell to 675,000 bpd in 1982 because of the oil crisis, rebounding to more than 1.5 mn bpd in 1989. It was interrupted, of course, with the Iraqi invasion in 1990 (see Chap. 16) but recovered to average 1.9 mn bpd during the remainder of the

1990s. Output increased after 2003 to supplement the needs of the US-UK forces in Iraq and reached 3.06 mn bpd (including half of the Neutral Zone's production) in 2012.

Non-OPEC Producers.   Production in Oman, which is not a member of OPEC, quickly reached stride in the late 1960s; production ranged between 300,000 and 400,000 bpd before falling off. Then new discoveries and improved recovery techniques led to gains—from 283,000 bpd in 1980 to a peak of 933,000 bpd in 2000. Production declined gradually to about 720,000 bpd in 2007 before Oman's major investments in enhanced oil-recovery techniques resulted in increases in output that took average daily output back to about 910,000 bpd in 2012.

Egypt, also not constrained by OPEC quotas, varied between 800,000 and 900,000 bpd in most years through the 1980s and 1990s but lost ground in the 2000s; in 2012, the daily average was about 675,000 bpd. Sector earnings were boosted by growing gas production.

Syria's very heavy crude output varied from 160,000 to 175,000 bpd in the late 1970s and early 1980s. The discovery in eastern Syria of a light sweet crude oil in the mid-1980s more than tripled output by 2000, before the level dropped to 320,000 bpd in 2011.The onset of civil war cut this average by some 47 percent in 2012—to an estimated 170,000 bpd. The country had been exporting one-third of production, but growing domestic demand has been eating into exports.

Far to the south, Yemeni production peaked in 2005 at 413,000 bpd, but as in Syria output fell and by 2012 was about 172,500 bpd. Instability has been a major factor in the recent decline; however, prospects for a doubling (or even more) of average daily output are considered to be good if security, petroleum-ministry efficiency, and sector investment can be considerably improved. Israel's negligible present output vies with Jordan's as the smallest of all producers.

Over the Long Term.   In assessing the Middle East's long-range significance in the petroleum sector, two production ratios are important: the ratio of its annual production to its reserves and the ratio of its percentage of world production to its percentage of world reserves. Middle East production in 2012, for example, was 1.1 percent of its reserves, while in the United States it was 11.2 percent and in western Europe 10.2 percent. That same year, Middle East production amounted to 31.6 percent of the world total, from 49.0 percent of the world's petroleum reserves; the United States produced 8.3 percent of global output from 1.2 percent of reserves; western Europe was responsible for 4 percent of the global total output from 0.7 percent of the reserves; and corresponding figures for other petro-provinces showed the same high ratio of production to reserves. The vital lesson: more intensive exploitation of oil resources will exhaust conventional reserves more rapidly in areas outside the Middle East.

Thus, the world could be even more highly dependent on the Middle East for oil by the mid-twenty-first century than it is at present because of its remarkably high ratio of reserves to production; however, in the event that concerns about climate change result in a serious medium-term decline in consumption, then a very different consumer-supplier situation will evolve (see Chap. 4's "Patterns: Climate Change"). It should be noted that in 2009, the International Energy Agency, the members of which are the major consuming countries, seems to have determined that the time horizon for so-called peak oil may be as soon as 2020—which suggests that in a decade or so, the global output of conventional oil will begin to decline, assuming that demand continues to grow as it has in recent years.[15] The key word in the previous sentence is "conventional"—as indicated above, the recent reclassification of tar-sands oil reserves as conventional in the authoritative data sources boosted those figures by more than a fifth; additionally, these same sources generally do not yet incorporate allowances for the potential from shale deposits.

MAJOR OIL FACILITIES

Raising petroleum and gas to the wellhead is only the beginning of a complex handling and processing procedure. The crude oil must be gathered from the field; associated gas must be separated and either flared in the field or piped to a consuming or processing facility. The degassed crude may then require "sweetening" before it is transported to an export terminal or a nearby refinery. Refining "cracks" the crude into a series of hydrocarbons, from the lightest fractions at one end (naphtha and gasoline), through the middle distillates (kerosene and aviation jet fuel), to heavy fractions like fuel oil and asphalt. Each product requires separate handling and has its own market. A salient development in the regional petroleum industry during the past two decades was the marked expansion of the petrochemical sector, especially in the major producing countries. Saudi Arabia, Iran, the UAE, and—because of its huge gas resources—Qatar have been constructing large plants and expanding existing plants. Petrochemical facilities utilize a plentiful raw material, add greatly to its value, and supply a profitable export. Moreover, oil production processed in these plants is not included in a country's OPEC quota (discussed in the section "OPEC: Pricing and Participation" later in this chapter).

In the early years, most of the Middle East's degassed crude petroleum was directly exported by tanker ships to overseas consumers. Much production is still exported in the same way. However, over the years, increasing amounts have been refined in the region, and the products either consumed locally by the larger and more affluent populations or else exported in a more valuable refined form. Refineries were built in Iran, Bahrain, and Saudi Arabia soon after production began in each country, and refining is now a significant industry in every state.

A fairly high correlation exists between the patterns of producing fields and of handling and processing facilities—particularly with regard to pipelines and export terminals, but not necessarily refineries and petrochemical industries. Crude feedstock can be transported hundreds of miles by pipeline to refineries far distant from an oil field; more frequently, it is transported by tanker ship to coastal refineries in more heavily populated industrial states. Major pipelines, export terminals, and refineries are shown on Maps 6.1 and 6.2.

Pipelines

Pipelines are the arteries of the petroleum industry. Indeed, they are a unique transportation system from the time the oil approaches the surface of the ground until it arrives at the interconnected refinery or shipping terminal. Since oil is of little value until it is moved from the well to an export or processing facility, pipelines are integral and vital links in the industry.

Numerous factors greatly influence the routes and costs of long-distance pipelines, such as topography, surface rock, population density, and environmental sensitivities (Fig. 6.3). Increasingly important is the security of the pipelines and of the oil passing through them, the attitude of authorities concerned, and the political stability of the areas traversed. International pipelines have been particularly susceptible to shutdowns because of disputes among states along the routes and, more seriously, because of sabotage by dissident groups. (Specific pipelines are also discussed in detail in some country chapters.)

More than 10,000 mi/16,093 km of large-diameter pipelines transport crude petroleum from major fields to regional shipping terminals and refineries. Three systems merit attention because of the leading roles they

Figure 6.3 Constructing a pipeline through the mountains of the Hijaz in western Saudi Arabia. (Michael J. Isaac, Saudi Aramco)

play or have played and because they exemplify the problems that can affect pipelines and other oil facilities as a result of the regional crosscurrents.

Pipelines and Politics: Iraq. Iraq's pipeline systems illustrate the problems of an interior location and the importance of good relations with neighboring states. For more than forty years, Iraq exported through Iraq Petroleum Company (IPC) lines from Kirkuk across Syria to the Mediterranean, the oldest long-distance network in the region. Opening in 1934, they ran parallel from Kirkuk to Hadithah on the Euphrates, where they divided, with one line crossing the then Transjordan to Haifa, in the British mandate of Palestine, and the other, via Syria, terminating in Tripoli, in the French mandate of Lebanon. By 1950, new political circumstances decreed abandoning Haifa as a destination, and the IPC laid pipe to Baniyas in Syria. Heightened "family quarrels" between the Baathi regimes in Iraq and Syria led to the latter's closing all IPC lines crossing its territory in 1982, but not before Iraq had undertaken alternatives lessening its dependence on the Syrian connections.

In the 1970s, Iraq built two new networks. In 1975, it finished an entirely internal line to terminals at the head of the Gulf, where the export facilities were highly concentrated on its narrow strip of coast. This arrangement was soon disrupted when the terminals were destroyed in 1980–1981, early in the war with Iran. Fortunately, Iraq had supplemented its Gulf outlet with a new 603-mi/970-km, 40-in/102-cm line from Kirkuk through Turkey to Yumurtalık on the Mediterranean near Iskanderun, which opened in 1977. Its capacity was increased in 1984, and a parallel 46-in/117-cm line was opened in 1987, giving the system through Turkey a capacity of 1.6 mn bpd, although throughput was about 500,000 bpd in 2012 when the line was not interrupted by sabotage.

Still concerned about depending on only one neighboring country, Iraq discussed with Jordan and Saudi Arabia possible routes through their territories to Aqabah and Yanbu, respectively. Aqabah was rejected as a terminus as it is just across the border from Elat in Israel and therefore an easy target for Israeli artillery or air strikes. Instead, construction went ahead on a 500,000-bpd 48-in/122-cm line (IPSA-I) to connect with Petroline, the huge Saudi crude oil line. Balked at exporting through Syria and through its own terminals on the Gulf, Iraq could then send crude through Turkey and Saudi Arabia for the remaining years of its war with Iran. Later, a separate 48-in/122-cm line, IPSA-II, parallel to the Saudi lines across the peninsula to a separate Red Sea export terminal, Muajjil, 30 mi/48 km south of Yanbu, opened in January 1990, with a capacity of 1.65 mn bpd.

No Friends—No Pipelines.   Thus, in 1990 Iraq had an export capacity of 3.15 mn bpd through Turkey and Saudi Arabia and 800,000 bpd through its own Gulf terminals when they were in operation, plus at least the potential for 1.25 mn bpd across Syria through the old IPC lines. However, its dependence on the goodwill of its neighbors for its exports became dramatically evident once again later that year when Saddam inexplicably disdained all favorable neighborly ties and invaded Kuwait. Complying with UN sanctions against Iraq, both Turkey and Saudi Arabia closed the lines crossing their territories, vowing to keep them shut in as long as UN sanctions required it. Thus, as the invasion had quickly led to a coalition blockade of its own terminals, Iraq soon had no export outlets—the price of being virtually

landlocked and of not maintaining friendly relations with at least some of its neighbors.

By the mid-1990s, UN sanctions were modified to allow oil to flow through the Turkish lines, but Saudi Arabia never relented on its closure of IPSA. In fact, in 2012, it began using part of the line as a means of exporting its own crude without traversing the Strait of Hormuz as tensions built over the issue of Iran's nuclear policies. Exports were interrupted again in March 2003; when pumping through Turkey was resumed after formal hostilities ceased, sabotage frequently interfered.

Tapline.   The second international petroleum pipeline of major significance was the Trans-Arabian Pipe Line (Tapline), which extended 1,068 mi/1,718 km from eastern Saudi Arabia to the Mediterranean in southern Lebanon. Although the line was shut in by the early 1980s, Tapline played a noteworthy role in Middle East oil developments over three decades, and it provides an excellent case study in geographic petroleum economics.

Plans were considered during World War II and completed by 1946 for a Gulf-to-Mediterranean route—a shortcut avoiding the long, slow voyage around the Arabian Peninsula and through the Suez Canal. Compared with the route of the original IPC lines across the Syrian Desert, the proposed route was much longer and its environment much more barren, virtually uninhabited except for small numbers of Bedouin, across almost unknown terrain. Tapline's diameter of 30–31 in/76–79 cm was also much larger than that of its predecessors.

Opened in December 1950, it crossed Saudi Arabia, Jordan, Syria, and Lebanon (see F, Map 6.1). Five large pump stations were needed to move the eventual capacity of 500,000 bpd, and a given barrel of oil required eleven days to transit the line to the Zahrani loading terminal near Sidon. Most of the oil was exported, but feedstock was also supplied to refineries in Zarqa in Jordan and

Figure 6.4 One of the world's largest tank farms, on a sand spit at Saudi Aramco's Ras Tanura export terminal on the Gulf coast. The terminal is one of the world's largest. (Shaikh M. Amin, Saudi Aramco)

Sidon in Lebanon. Tapline was a signal success for many years, but its situation became awkward after June 1967, when control over part of it passed to Israel, which had occupied the Golan Heights. Problems ranging from sabotage to disputes over royalties were exacerbated after the 1973 Arab-Israeli war.

Supertankers. Another difficulty was that closure of the Suez Canal after the 1967 war stimulated the construction and use of increasingly larger oil tankers. Very Large Crude Carriers (VLCCs) could transport crude from the Gulf around southern Africa to western Europe and North America even more cheaply than could the smaller tankers that had formerly followed either the Red Sea–Suez Canal–Mediterranean route or, more important for Tapline, lifted crude from the Zahrani terminal. With mounting operational problems and expenses, after February 1975 the fabled line was no longer used for exports—oil lifted at Ras Tanura (Fig. 6.4) could be landed at English Channel ports by VLCCs at a rate more than $2 per barrel cheaper than oil lifted from Zahrani.

Obsolescence. Thus, technology, economics, politics, and geography combined to render Tapline obsolete after twenty-five years of operation. Using only a small fraction of its capacity, it did continue to move less than 100,000 bpd to supply the refinery at Zarqa to maintain Saudi Arabian goodwill toward Jordan. These shipments gradually lessened, partly because of nonpayment, and they stopped entirely in August 1990 when Jordan hesitated in support of UN actions against Iraq (see Chap. 12), and Tapline fell into disuse. By the early 2000s, its physical condition had deteriorated, and a possible reopening to Jordan was estimated to require an investment of as much as $400 million.

Saudi Internal Network. A third noteworthy line began as an internal facility but gained international connections. In 1981, Saudi Arabia opened the largest-diameter long-distance crude oil line in the region, the 48-in/122-cm Petroline from the Eastern Province to the Red Sea at Yanbu, with a new export facility, refinery, and petrochemical complex. The original capacity of 1.85 mn bpd was raised to 3.3 mn bpd with the opening of a 56-in/142-cm parallel interconnected (looped) line in 1987. This East-West system was further upgraded during the early 1990s to a capacity of 4.8 mn bpd to ensure a protected outlet during crisis periods in the Gulf. Normally, it carries only a fraction of its capacity but is sufficient to supply Yanbu's facilities and small amounts for export. During crises, it can deliver about half the kingdom's output to the Red Sea for export via tanker, either northward through the Suez Canal or to Egypt's "Sumed" lines or southward through the Bab el-Mandeb. Together with the confiscated IPSA, as mentioned earlier, these lines mean Saudi Arabia now has major alternatives to transit through the Strait of Hormuz in the event of hostilities involving Iran.

Pipelines for Newcomer Exporters.   In the late 1990s, after the oil-producing former Soviet republics became independent, questions arose as to how to bring output from the Caspian petro-province to export terminals; controversies slowed determining the routing of new pipelines. A partial and temporary solution was the limited 115,000-bpd line that opened in 1999 connecting the Baku fields with Supsa in Georgia on the Black Sea. From there, tankers deliver oil to other Black Sea ports or transit the Turkish Straits to the Mediterranean. This line could have been paralleled by a large-capacity line, but Turkey strongly objected for two reasons: first, the growing environmental threat from already heavy tanker traffic through the narrow Bosporus, and, second, Turkey's desire—supported by others—for a new line to transit its own territory. Proposed was a route

from Baku to Tbilisi, Georgia, and then through Erzurum in eastern Anatolia to a port near Ceyhan on the Gulf of Iskanderun.

The United States gave top priority to the Baku-Tbilisi-Ceyhan (BTC) route to decrease reliance on Middle East oil and to have a route crossing friendly countries, avoiding Iran and Russia (see Map 6.1). It therefore put determined pressure on the countries and companies concerned. With its growing friendship with Turkey, Israel was a key supporter for the Ceyhan outlet, which would be close to its import facilities. The project was finally approved, and BTC construction began through very difficult terrain. The 1,040-mi/1,674-km line with a capacity of 1 mn bpd became operational in 2005. In the 2010s, plans are proceeding to further expand pipeline capacity across Turkey as increased production comes on line from Azerbaijan and Central Asian producers (see Chap. 20 for more details).

Gas Pipelines.   Another important aspect of the pipeline network is the large—and steadily growing—number of natural gas lines in the region. Most are internal, but several major gas pipelines are being laid across international borders. Notably, Turkey increased its gas imports in 2002 through new lines from Iran and Russia: a large line from Tabriz into eastern Turkey and the dual "Blue Stream" line from Russia under the Black Sea to Samsun. Turkey is now so well supplied with gas that a planned line from Baku to Erzurum, paralleling the BTC, is being held in abeyance. However, Turkey and the European Union (EU) agreed in 2009 to build the Nabucco gas pipeline designed to carry gas 2,000 mi/3,220 km from the Caspian region to Austria. Gas from Qatar's supergiant North Field will inevitably be exported in great quantities, and the necessary infrastructure is already under construction. Europe, Turkey, the Levant, the UAE, Oman, Pakistan, and India have been suggested as potential markets. A UAE group has evolved the Dolphin

TABLE 6.2 Petroleum: Refineries and Refining Activity

Country	1 Number of Refineries	2 Total Refinery Capacity (Bpd)	3 Largest Refinery in Respective Country	4 Main Refinery Capacity (Bpd)
Bahrain	1	254,000	Sitra	263,000
Cyprus	0	—	—	—
(Divided Zone)	0	—	—	—
Egypt	9	726,000	Suez	146,300
Iran	9	1,451,000	Abadan	350,000
Iraq	11	638,000	Baiji	310,000
Israel	2	220,000	Haifa	180,000
Jordan	1	90,000	Zarqa	90,400
Kuwait	4	936,000	Mina al-Ahmadi	466,000
Lebanon	0	—	—	—
Oman	2	222,000	Sohar	116,000
Qatar	2	339,000	Umm Said	200,000
Saudi Arabia	7	2,080,000	Ras Tanura	550,000
Syria	2	240,000	Baniyas	133,000
Turkey	6	714,000	Izmit	251,600
UAE	5	773,000	Ruways	400,000
Yemen	2	140,000	Little Aden	130,000
TOTAL	63	8,823,000	—	3,586,300

Data as of 2012. (*Source:* Energy Information Administration, www.eia.doe.gov)

initiative for an $8–$10 billion project for piping Qatar gas to Abu Dhabi, Dubai, Suhar (Oman), and later on to Pakistan. The export of Egyptian gas began in 2003 through a pipeline under the Gulf of Aqabah to Jordan; this has now been extended north to Syria and Lebanon, but exports have encountered increasing difficulties, as sabotage on the Sinai portion of the line has become more common and domestic demand for gas in Egypt presses against the supply available for sales abroad.

Other Pipelines, Terminals, and Refineries

In addition to the major long lines just described, several internal pipelines are of noteworthy regional importance and have a significant impact on international movements of Middle East petroleum. Both Egypt and Israel provide shortcuts that permit oil to move from the Red Sea to the Mediterranean, serving tankers that are too large for the Suez Canal or that prefer to avoid the canal. Egypt's Suez-Mediterranean system (Sumed) consists of twin parallel 42-in/107-cm lines that run to a terminal just west of Alexandria. Israel's 42-in/107-cm Trans-Israel Pipeline (Tipline) runs 158 mi/254 km from Elat to a terminal at Ashqelon. It opened in 1968 in a deal with Iran under the monarchy to supply Israel secretly with petroleum, but became largely moribund after the Islamic Revolution. Since 2004, however, the flow has been in the opposite direction, competing with the Suez Canal—Russian oil bound for Asian markets. There had been reports of plans to expand its capacity of 400,000 bpd to 1.1 mn bpd, tying it to a direct marine pipeline connection from Ceyhan in Turkey to Ashqelon;[16] since Israeli-Turkish relations have varied, the prospects for this have become doubtful. Details on the more important oil-export terminals and refineries are given in the individual country chapters. However, Table 6.2 gives comparative data on refineries.

MARKETS AND MARKETING

Early developers of Middle East petroleum fields—all from western Europe and North America—envisaged exploiting the resources for export to their respective home countries or for fueling naval ships. Local consumption was limited. However, as the pace of regional development increased, demand for the petro-products mounted in the Middle East as elsewhere, and governments in oil-exporting countries gained control over the exploitation and marketing of their highly valuable and sometimes sole resource and then contracted for local basic processing facilities.

Seven Sisters.   Marketing large amounts of petroleum has traditionally been through long-term contracts. Concessionary companies operating in a producing country were often the direct sellers, disposing of their product within a stable if highly complex global system. For decades, the system was essentially controlled by a few major companies—the "Seven Sisters": Jersey Standard (Exxon), British Petroleum, Royal Dutch/Shell, Standard of California (Chevron), Texaco (which has merged with Chevron), Socony-Vacuum (Mobil, now merged with Exxon), and Gulf (which has also merged with Chevron). Italian, Spanish, Brazilian, and Japanese companies later joined in, thereby gaining international marketing influence.

Until 1970, the main importers of Middle East crude were industrial countries that required supplies beyond their own production capacity, including those countries that held major concessions in the region. Some importers had only limited or even no known petroleum resources of their own. Virtually every major oil exporter in the Middle East in the 1960s and 1970s counted the same half-dozen purchasers among its top ten customers: Britain, France, West Germany, Japan, the Netherlands, and the United States. Secondary buyers included Italy, Spain, Canada, and Brazil; Australia, India, Sweden, and Switzerland were also regular customers.

New Producers.   After 1970, steadily increasing production from new offshore fields on the continental shelves of Britain and other North Sea littoral countries afforded northwestern Europe a large supply of local oil and gas. As one result, the demand for Middle East crude by these countries dropped by more than 3 mn bpd as both Britain and Norway became net exporters, completely redirecting the world oil industry. Another significant development in the 1990s was the opening of the Caspian petro-province—with particular impetus from the United States—to commercial exploration and exploitation. From the early 1970s on, the trend of oil exports from the Middle East from year to year has been markedly more variable than that during the previous decades. The import pattern of the United States also changed and varies considerably: in 1977, the United States imported 46 percent of its oil, about 18 percent from the Middle East; in 1983, it imported only 28 percent of its oil requirements, just 4 percent from the Middle East; by1988, they had soared to about 41 percent, about 11 percent from the Middle East; in 1999, they were 55 percent, about 20 percent from the Middle East; in 2008, imports were 57 percent, and 18 percent were from the Middle East; but by 2011, increased domestic production cut imports to 45 percent, with the region responsible for about 10 percent.

In addition to increased local use of petroleum, natural gas consumption in the Middle East has also grown dramatically. Whereas in 1972 more than two-thirds of the gas produced in association with oil was either flared or reinjected (pumped back into the oil reservoir), by 1982 only half of the gas was being flared, and utilization had increased by 38 percent. Flaring dropped below 10 percent by the mid-2000s. As mentioned above, two regional countries were still in 2011 among the world's top five gas-flaring countries—Iran and Iraq.[17]

OPEC: PRICING AND PARTICIPATION

In the 1940s and 1950s, companies operating concessions in the Middle East generally determined output and prices, taking into account production costs and world demand. With little input from the countries involved, they periodically set and publicly stated posted prices as the "list" prices at which various grades of crude would be sold at Gulf terminals. Highly complex arrangements, royalties, taxes, deductions, and discounts affected government revenues and company profits.

OPEC and OAPEC. When posted prices fell in 1960, governments of major producing countries became disgruntled, and in an effort to gain greater control over pricing they met in Baghdad in September 1960 and created the Organization of Petroleum Exporting Countries (based in Vienna). Charter OPEC members were Saudi Arabia, Iran, Iraq, Kuwait, and Venezuela; other members would be Algeria (joining in 1969), Angola (2007), Ecuador (1973, inactive from 1992 to 2007), Gabon (1975, withdrew 1995), Indonesia (1962, withdrew 2008), Libya (1962), Nigeria (1971), Qatar (1961), and the UAE (joined as Abu Dhabi in 1967). Of the twelve current members, six are in the region considered in this work, and five of these are Arab countries. In the aftermath of the 1967 Arab-Israeli War, three Arab exporters—Kuwait, Libya, and Saudi Arabia—formed a parallel group, the Organization of Arab Petroleum Exporting Countries (OAPEC, headquartered in Kuwait), which now includes all Arab members of OPEC plus Bahrain, Egypt, Syria, and Tunisia (membership suspended in 1988). OAPEC has not played a consistently significant role in the regional oil industry. Oman and Yemen have never joined either group.

Prices of virtually all other commodities rose steadily from the late 1940s, but petroleum was increasingly underpriced into the early 1970s. Not until late in 1973 was the free-on-board price of the benchmark Arabian light crude at Ras Tanura to surge decisively above $3 per barrel. (All prices and sales were, and still are, in US dollars, although whenever the dollar weakens there is nervous speculation about substituting the euro.) Mounting determination by OPEC members to strengthen their hold on the pricing and handling of their petroleum was sharpened by the 1973 Arab-Israeli war, and OAPEC members embargoed oil shipments to the United States and the Netherlands in retaliation for actions or policies considered supportive of Israel.

The End of Posted Prices. Late 1973 was the turning point in company-government relations, as company-set "posted prices" were abandoned in favor of OPEC-announced prices. The posted price had increased from the long-set $1.80/bbl in 1970 to $2.18 in 1971, then three times in six months—to $2.90 in mid-1973, $5.12 in October, and in one historic jump $11.65 in December. OPEC had arrived. The price then rose gradually to $13.34 at the beginning of 1979, doubled in one year to $26.00, and peaked at $34.00 in October 1981 with Iran-Iraq War jitters. Unified pricing, however, was often disregarded by sellers—increasingly so into the mid- and late 1980s, until the price fell to about $13.00 a barrel.

The 1973–1974 price escalation (which proceeded independently of the OAPEC embargo) broke the previously steady and often rapid growth of global petroleum consumption since 1945. Shaken by a tenfold price increase from late 1973 to early 1981, major consuming countries tried to minimize the shock not only by promoting conservation and more efficient use of oil but also by using alternative forms of energy. In addition, increased prices stimulated development of resources and higher production in non-OPEC countries, depressing demand for OPEC oil. The changing balance dropped OPEC's share of world production from 56 percent in 1973 to 29 percent in 1985. However, it rebounded and averaged about 40 percent in the mid-1990s. The seemingly insatiable demand for oil into the late 1970s, despite escalating prices, had created surplus productive capacity, which in turn exerted downward pressure on market prices and caused financial stress in several OPEC states.

Quota Problems.   In the early 1990s, OPEC continued to struggle with the difficult problem of apportioning quotas among cartel members and hence with price maintenance. As in any such arrangement, members try to maximize revenues but are often unwilling to adhere to assigned quotas—the sine qua non for cartel success. OPEC had mixed results during the 1990s, and prices fell with the crash of Asian economies until they were less than $10/bbl in early 1999, an all-time low in adjusted real prices. However, at a meeting in March 1999, OPEC managed to get both members and nonmembers to lower output to realistic levels, and average prices rose considerably over the following years, averaging about $25/bbl over 2000 to 2003. Then the average annual price rose steadily to a high of nearly $100/bbl in 2008, before collapsing after the bursting of a speculative bubble and the onset of global recession. Relatively modest production cuts, led by Saudi Arabia, restored price levels in 2009 and 2010, but uncertainties over the Arab Spring and its consequences pushed prices up again in 2011. Since then, the interaction of various events—the Libyan civil war, the ongoing Eurozone crisis, fear of regional war over Iran's nuclear policies, slower growth in China, increased US domestic production—

has contributed to considerable short-term price volatility.

During the late 1990s, market forces made clear the dilemma faced by both companies and producing countries. If controls are meaningful, artificially reduced production has a push-pull effect: it extends field life and supports higher prices, but it also reduces consumption (especially in poorer countries), drives conservation, encourages the search for alternative sources of energy, and lowers the threshold for exploiting unconventional oil resources like heavy oil, tar sands, and shale. Moreover, standard cartel theory holds as inevitable that there will be greater centrifugal forces and cheating on quotas; this induces a breakdown in the production and pricing structure, and the cycle starts all over again.

When the price falls below a certain optimum (not just a certain minimum), the income squeeze on producing countries and oil companies seriously impacts the entire world economy. Similarly, an excessively high price depletes the budgets of the poorer nonproducing states and creates resistance from main consumers. Most consumer states now have some flexibility in switching among various fuels for such major requirements as generating electricity guided by relative cost considerations.

Restructuring the Industry.   One repercussion of an excessively low price during the late 1990s was a startling series of mergers of major Western oil companies in an effort to stay economically healthy. Some of the mergers involved exchanges of stock worth tens of billions of dollars. In addition to the mergers mentioned above, British Petroleum acquired Amoco in late 1998 to become BP Amoco, absorbing in 1999 Arco (which had acquired Union a year earlier), and is now just plain BP; ExxonMobil was formed in 1999 in a megamerger of two corporate giants; Total (French) and Fina (Belgian) merged and added Elf Aquitaine in 1999 to become the world's fourth-largest oil company; Chevron (which had already acquired Gulf) and Texaco combined in 2001 and picked up Unocal in 2005; Conoco and Phillips merged in 2002 to form the third-largest US oil company and acquired Burlington Resources in 2006. All of these companies have long been very much involved in the Middle East.

While Middle East producers were pooling the marketing prices of their output in OPEC in the 1960s and 1970s, each individual government steadily increased its "participation" in the private companies holding concessions in its country. By 1980, most OPEC countries had complete ownership of local producing operations through national oil companies. Since then, these companies have increased their downstream operations (refining, distributing, retailing) both domestically and in customer countries, thus expanding interdependence between producers and consumers.

OTHER MINERALS

The production and utilization of petroleum and natural gas have been the focal point of economic mineral activity in the Middle East for decades. However, several areas are highly mineralized, have produced limited to modest quantities of ores for many centuries, and are now the focus of intensified mineral exploration activities (Map 6.5). The oil-producing countries have joined their neighbors in intensively searching for commercially useful deposits.

Even limited production can bring significant benefit to a local area, especially one lacking petroleum; conversely, processing ores in areas like western Iran and northern Oman can be relatively economical because of the availability of large amounts of local gas. Additionally, many minerals industries are more labor intensive than the petro-sector and therefore can create many jobs. Income from mining and quarrying indus-

tries is expected to increase appreciably in the near future.

Turkey and Iran, which lie across the mineralized Fold Belt, have long produced large amounts of a wide variety of solid minerals. Cyprus is part of the belt and has been a considerable mineral producer historically, although it faces approaching depletion of its once appreciable resources of copper, iron pyrites, and chromite. Jordan, Syria, Israel, Egypt, and Iraq produce phosphate rock in significant quantities, and Israel and Jordan also have noteworthy potash output from the Dead Sea. Both Saudi Arabia and Egypt hope to revive and expand mining in the crystalline shield areas in their territories.[18]

Solid Fuels

Coal. Although sparse coal resources retarded Middle East industrial development in the nineteenth century, the problem has diminished since World War II. Only Turkey, Iran, and Egypt have noteworthy coal reserves, and only Turkey's production has been significant, with Iran's now gradually increasing.

Turkey compensates for its small petroleum output by intensively exploiting its considerable coal (1.4 bn mt) and lignite (8 bn mt) resources. Solid fuels production in 2010 was 78 mn mt, 95 percent of which was lignite. Although Iran's coal reserves are in some of the same structures that contain coal beds in Turkey, production has lagged—about 2.3 mn mt in 2010—because of its enormous hydrocarbon reserves; however, it has plans to double output by 2014. Egypt's more modest coal production (300,000 mt in 2010) is useful locally, and production is increasing in newly opened mines in northern Sinai.[19]

Metals

Most (although not all) metallic ores occur in mineralized igneous and crystalline rocks. They cannot, therefore, be normally expected in the extensive sedimentary areas of the

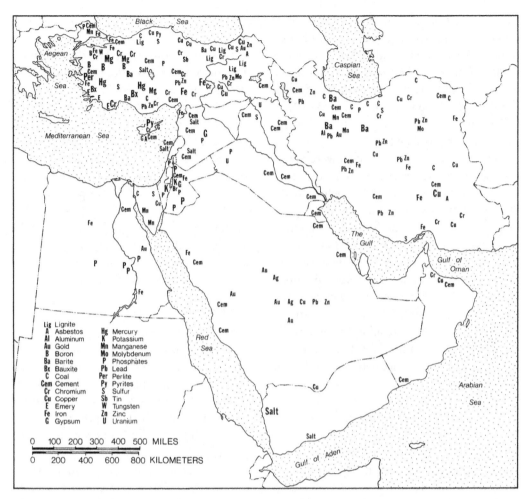

Map 6.5 Distribution of more important deposits of solid minerals in the Middle East. Note the richness of mineral occurrences in the zones of tectonic plate contacts in Turkey, Iran, and Cyprus. (Adapted from several maps in US Geological Survey, *Minerals Information,* 2002 and 2003, and from maps and reports of 2010 in http://minerals.usgs.gov/minerals/pubs/country)

Fertile Crescent countries or the Arabian Peninsula. Certain metals may be found in either class of rocks, and, indeed, some limited deposits of iron, lead, and zinc are found in the sedimentary strata just mentioned. Concentrated mineralization is found primarily in three specific areas of the region—the complex rocks of the Anatolian and Iranian plateaus, the shield blocks on either side of the Red Sea, and the unusual Oman Mountains—and it is mainly these areas that have been exploited for their metals.

As is the case for solid minerals in general, Turkey possesses by far the greatest variety and quantity of metal ores, and Iran is second. Several ores in Turkey are minable by large-scale methods: bauxite, chromite, copper, zinc, gold, iron, and silver. Only its chromite production ranks on a world scale—a comfortable second. More significant, however, are a number of industrial minerals; it is one of the world's leading producers for several of these: barite, boron, kaolin and other clays, magnesite, pumice, and strontium. Its minerals exports, including cement, now exceed $2.5 billion annually. Iran, emphasizing hydrocarbons, has not given commensurate effort to solid mineral production. However, it has developed some major deposits and is a significant producer of copper, chromium, iron ore, lead, zinc, and molybdenum. Iran, Turkey, and Egypt, leaders in iron-ore resources, also share leadership in the production of pig iron and steel. The Hittites exploited Anatolian iron before 1800 BCE; they had a near monopoly on ironworking for centuries. Iran's iron reserves are twice those of Turkey and Egypt combined, but its production is appreciably less than Turkey's.

Nonferrous metals regularly produced in noteworthy quantities in the region include especially copper, but also lead, zinc, mercury, and bauxite (aluminum ore). Historically, Turkey, Cyprus, and Iran have been the region's leading copper producers; since the early 1980s, Iran has taken first place after more than a decade of developing its resources. Oman appeared as a copper producer for the first time in 1983 and ranks third, after Turkey, in output, although its quite limited reserves are nearly exhausted. Production from Cyprus's ancient mines varies and in some years ceases to be commercially worthwhile. Some of the motivation behind Saudi Arabia's recent interest in railroad construction is to open remote areas where bauxite (as well as phosphates and other minerals) is found to commercial exploitation.

Iran normally leads in the output of lead and zinc, with Turkey in second place. Turkey is the region's only producer of bauxite and mercury worth noting, and it has significant reserves of uranium, unexploited at the present time. Israel, however, produces small amounts of uranium from its Negev phosphate deposits for supplementary use in the reactor at nearby Dimona, the center of its nuclear weaponry program. Jordan signed an agreement in 2010 with a French firm to begin uranium mining; in 2012, the reserves were estimated to be up to twenty-five thousand tons, but the deal with the company nevertheless was canceled later that year.[20]

Nonmetals

Certain nonmetallic minerals may be found in several different rock environments, others are found only in sedimentary rocks, and still others occur only in igneous rocks. Thus, the Middle East's nonmetallic ores are more widely distributed over the region than are its metallic resources and may even be processed from sea- or lake water.

The most widely produced solid mineral is salt, produced in virtually every country in the region but in especially large quantities in Turkey, Egypt, and Iran. Lebanon, Yemen, Egypt, and Iraq produce salt by evaporating seawater in small ponds or evaporation pans along the shore. Others evaporate surface or underground brines, and Iran and Yemen mine rock salt from underground salt plugs that have pushed their way toward the surface from deep subsurface strata.

Phosphates. Regional output of phosphate rock, valuable for making chemical fertilizers, is of considerable significance on the global scale, as demand for phosphate rock has mounted sharply with the growing need for soil fertilizers to increase productivity. Middle East resources have therefore been vigorously exploited, with production steadily growing through the late 1970s and 1980s. The region's leading producer is Jordan, which in 2010 also ranked seventh in the world, with output of 6.5 mn mt. Three neighboring states are significant producers from similar rock strata: in order, Syria (Fig. 6.5), Israel, and Egypt.

Other nonmetallic minerals of the region may be noted, especially with regard to the unusual aspects of several of them. For example, meerschaum is found in significant commercial quantities only in Turkey. Despite its name ("sea foam" in German), it is a

Figure 6.5 Facility for open-pit mining of phosphates near Palmyra in central Syria. Phosphate-rich beds extend through much of the area of Syria, Jordan, Iraq, and Israel.

hydrous magnesium silicate—a fine white clayey mineral—used to make special kinds of smoking-pipe bowls, many of which are elaborately carved and highly prized. Potash is produced in large amounts from Dead Sea water by both Israel and Jordan, with the newer Jordanian plant having world rank. Among other minerals Israel produces from the Dead Sea is bromine; output is about one-third of the world total. Asbestos has long been a major product of the metamorphic rocks of Cyprus and is produced from related structures in Turkey and Egypt. However, output has decreased sharply because of health dangers arising from its use.

NOTES

1. Hundreds of sources cover various aspects of Middle East oil, both in general and for respective producing countries. For detailed early development of the Gulf oil industry, see Marlowe 1962. Peterson 1983 discusses the politics of oil. An excellent source for current data on petroleum, natural gas, and coal is US Department of Energy, Energy Information Administration, at www.eia.doe.gov/emeu/cabs/. PennWell's weekly *Oil and Gas Journal* is almost indispensable, and PennWell's annual *International Petroleum Encyclopedia* (*IPE*) has also been very useful, but publication ceased in 2011. *Saudi Aramco and Its World* 1995 and earlier editions are authoritative and available. The BP annual statistical report, found at www.bp.com, is useful. For solid minerals, refer especially to the US Geological Survey *Minerals Yearbook*, which also includes some petroleum information. It is published every year or two, and some of the latest editions may also be found at http://minerals.usgs.gov/minerals. For a readable best-seller account of the oil industry, see Yergin 1991; an opinion piece by the same author, "It's Still the One," *Foreign Policy Special Report*; Aug. 24, 2009, www.foreignpolicy.com/articles/2009/08/17/its_still_the_one; and Yergin 2011. Aspects of US dependence on oil are covered in Roberts 2004 and Klare 2004.

2. In the past few years, global oil reserve figures have been increased considerably in authoritative sources by the inclusion of Canadian and Venezuelan tar-sands deposits that have become more commercially exploitable through a combination of high oil prices, technological advances, and supply security considerations (i.e., Canadian oil piped directly from

Alberta to US markets). Estimates of shale-related reserves are still too tentative to have been included in global oil and gas reserve figures so far.

3. As important as future Levant Basin oil and gas production may be to the currently energy-importing countries that will benefit from it, it is useful to put the estimated discoveries up to the present into a regional perspective. The 1.7 bn barrels of oil are more than the reserves of Sharjah but less than those (onshore) of Syria, and the 122 tn ft³ of natural gas are more than the reserves of Iraq, but less than those of Abu Dhabi and about one-eighth those of Iran.

4. Venezuela is now listed in first place and Canada in third by virtue of their huge deposits of oil-bearing tar sands.

5. US oil and gas reserve figures do not include shale deposits at this time.

6. The field is located astride the Iran-Qatar border.

7. With severe civil strife during 2011 in both Syria and Yemen, production was down in both countries; the three-year average, 2008–2010, for this group of producers was close to 1.6 bbd.

8. The boycott was eventually extended to the Netherlands, Portugal, South Africa, and Rhodesia: the last three were targeted as a gesture against lingering colonialism in Africa.

9. Generally speaking, factors having an essentially short-term nature affect oil prices, in both current and futures markets, whereas those with longer-term characteristics (such as more fuel efficiency in transport or current US government policies regarding drilling permits) affect share prices in energy-sector companies.

10. Conventional reserves; no global estimates of the full extent of shale gas reserves are currently available.

11. Alternatively, the excess gas can be reinjected in the well to maintain pressure.

12. For more information on GGFRP, see http://web.worldbank.org/WBSITE/EXTERNAL/TOPICS/EXTOGMC/EXTGGFR/0,,contentMDK:21022944~menuPK:828161~pagePK:64168445~piPK:64168309~theSitePK:578069,00.htm.

13. Several countries heavily dependent on Iranian oil have been exempted from the sanctions. See Reuters, Oct. 23, 2012; and Energy Information Agency, Dec. 11, 2012.

14. *Zawya*, Dec. 10, 2012.

15. "A Sticky Situation," *Economist* Dec. 10, 2009.

16. *Journal of Energy Security*, Feb. 19, 2009, www.ensec.org.

17. According to the World Bank, Iran and Iraq ranked third and fourth after Russia and Kazakhstan. Unfortunately, unlike the latter two countries, Iran and Iraq had actually increased flaring since 2007. See note 16.

18. The best source for solid minerals information is the USGS, formerly in various editions of the *Minerals Yearbook*, mentioned in note 1, but now at http://minerals.usgs.gov/minerals/pubs/country/index.html#pubs.

19. USGS *Minerals Yearbook*.

20. *Jordan Times*, May 24, 2012, and Oct. 23, 2012.

7

Manufacturing and Transportation

KEY POINTS: Both sectors limited prior to beginning oil production, were mainly in Turkey, Egypt, Iran. Most manufacturing was of traditional "oriental wares" in copper and brass, inlaid woods, carpets, textiles. With inflow of billions of petrodollars after 1960s, manufacturing developed explosively, again primarily in the three early leaders. Few skilled workers in most countries, which were forced to import labor. Vigorous manufacturing and processing now well developed in early leaders, as well as Iraq, Israel, Saudi Arabia. Airlines preceded railways and major highways in petroleum areas except Iran. Virtually no railways south of Turkey/Iraq/Iran except in Egypt, but rail systems now under development. Shipping well developed since early sailing days.

PRELIMINARY VIEW

The Stimulus of Oil

The unparalleled petroleum development surveyed in the previous chapter naturally stimulated growth in other economic sectors. Although the entire region benefited from the ripple effect on a grand scale, the expansion was most remarkable along the Gulf. Along the coast, tiny fishing villages like Abu Dhabi and Doha became within a few years capitals of nations with some of the world's highest per capita incomes. Farther inland, caravan trails and rutted tracks became motorways threading across rolling deserts. By the early 1990s, the Gulf states and Saudi Arabia had achieved remarkable material progress that was striking to local inhabitant and outside specialist alike. By the 2000s, the splendor and

even opulence of public buildings, hotels, airport terminals, shopping centers, and universities were matched by the number and complexity of technologically advanced gas-oil separating facilities, shipping terminals, oil refineries, petrochemical plants, dry docks, aluminum smelters, and similar installations that seemed to have sprung out of the desert.[1]

Several states have built modest to appreciable industrial foundations and have developed impressively diversified producing sectors. Even so, none of the major oil exporters is a true "industrial" state, in the Western sense, although prerevolutionary Iran as well as Iraq aspired to high levels of industrialization. Modern manufacturing started earlier in the eastern Mediterranean, especially in Egypt, where it began in the early 1800s under Muhammad Ali, and in Turkey, where it originated in the nineteenth century Ottoman New Order. Economic evolution during the regional oil boom and the emergence of Israel contributed to the pattern of manufacturing discussed later in this chapter, which reveals the importance of manufacturing in the older areas of Turkey, Iran, and Egypt as well as more recently in Syria, Israel, and Iraq, and on a smaller scale in Cyprus and Lebanon.

Statistical Problems.   Quantification of the industrialization of states in the region is difficult because of a shortage of meaningful and comparable statistics. Determining the values of the usual criteria used to analyze the degree of industrialization—percentage of GDP derived from manufacturing and other industrial output, percentage of the workforce employed in manufacturing and other industries, and per capita energy consumption, steel output, and other indicators—is thus problematic. For example, the region is unique in that its high consumption of electric energy is not closely linked to industrial activity. Additionally, much of the industry is capital intensive, highly automated, and labor extensive: a refinery is a huge facility with high output, but it employs few workers.

The Role of Capital.   Since the overwhelming emphasis is on petroleum exploitation, the Gulf's recently evolved economic patterns and activities differ from those of neighboring non-oil areas. There are considerable gaps in the per capita income between the Gulf and the eastern Mediterranean—except Israel—but the ripple effect of oil income in part of the region has been noteworthy in other parts. In Cyprus, Jordan, and—before 1975—Lebanon, the ripple effect has been impressive. Israel's dramatic development has been independent of the regional oil boom; it has been heavily financed by capital transfers—grants, especially from the United States and Germany—and by other favored

treatment by the United States. Capital availability from oil revenues has set the pace throughout the region, even though development has been uneven among the states and sectors of their economies. In any given year over the past thirty years, Saudi Arabia expended $250–$275 billion (in 2009 dollars) for development in a large area with a relatively small population, whereas Egypt had only one-tenth that amount for a small inhabited area with a population three to four times that of the kingdom.

The Role of Labor.   Rapidly developing Gulf states soaked up surplus labor not only from Yemen, Egypt, Lebanon, Jordan, and Syria but also from India, Pakistan, the Philippines, and other Asian countries. At the same time, a reverse flow of cash in grants, loans, and worker remittances transferred a share of oil profits to nonproducing areas or to smaller producers. From Baghdad to Beirut, Kuwait to Cairo, Dubai to Damascus, capital and development fever became the common denominators. Contractors, artisans, and consultants came by the thousands and laborers by the millions to take advantage of the boom.

Historical Perspective

Islamic Period.   During the golden age of Islam in the ninth and tenth centuries, the Middle East boasted the world's best-developed economy and a flourishing international trade. High-quality textiles were a specialty—linens from Egypt, damask from Damascus, silks from Kufah, brocades from Shiraz, and muslin from Mosul, as well as carpets from Iran, Bukhara, and elsewhere. Colored glass from Syria, decorated tiles from many places, pottery, porcelain, inlaid and decorated wood, embossed and inlaid brass and copper (damascene), engraved gold and silver jewelry, leather wares, and fine soaps and perfumes were produced in the small workshops of the *suqs*, or bazaars. Within the realm of Islam, products moved between

Spain on the west and Samarkand on the east, and beyond it they moved as far as Scandinavia and China.

Some goods moved by sea, with Basrah a preeminent port. However, more of the traffic was overland, and great dromedary caravans plodded eastward from Baghdad to Samarkand, where loads were transferred to the Bactrian camels of the Mongols and Chinese (see Map 4.5). Towns favorably located as trade centers thrived; some of them have kept their fame and prosperity to the present.

Europe Arrives. However, with the age of discovery, ships flying the flags of Portugal, Holland, and Britain sailed around Africa, gaining control of trade routes to southern and eastern Asia. Middle East arts and crafts declined and, their markets lost, continued only at a survival level. By the eighteenth century, the great caravans along the Silk Road between the Islamic world and China were only a memory.

Renewed European interest in the Middle East and its products in the nineteenth century revived some aspects of the region's economic activity—carpet making, metalworking, and woodworking. Steamships carried far-greater loads than had the earlier small sailing vessels, and European investors built railways from ports into interiors under concessionary terms.

COOPERATION AND AID

Arab Economic Coordination

The ideal of Arab unity has always had an economic component, but economic coordination after World War II has been inhibited by recurrent political tensions and conflict. Numerous successive economic agreements have been negotiated, only to become ineffective in reality. As early as 1953, the Arab League sponsored the signing of the Arab Joint Defense and Economic Cooperation Agreement, but the agreement quietly expired after three or four years. The Arab Economic Unity Agreement of 1956 sought the economic union of Egypt, Iraq, Jordan, Kuwait, and Syria. It, too, failed. The same countries, minus Kuwait, motivated by desire for pan-Arab cooperation, formed the Arab Common Market in 1964, but with no new members the effort was officially abandoned in 1971. The fate of these examples is typical of that of other efforts that did not succeed because members were unwilling to subsume national interests to regional ones.[2] Similar friction has hindered regionwide cooperation, and Israel, Iran, and Turkey are excluded from Arab groupings.

One subregional effort has achieved some success: the Cooperation Council of the Arab States of the Gulf, better known as the Gulf Cooperation Council (GCC), created in 1981. The GCC is more than an economic agency, although it has an effective economic component (see Chap. 8, "Regional Linkages"). The Greater Arab Free Trade Area, launched in 1998, is the latest Arab League effort to promote trade and economic unity (also see Chap. 8, "Regional Linkages"). A broader business-oriented grouping intended to link all Middle East states, including Israel, with other countries, the Middle East/North Africa Economic Conference was initiated in 1994 under the auspices of the World Economic Forum, but it has languished in tandem with the peace process.

Economic Aid

A further influence on Middle East economic patterns is that of direct transfers of capital into and within the region. Huge amounts of petrodollars flowed to the exporters after 1972 and were used for development projects by them, as well as for aid to non-oil states.

International Donors. Going back sixty years, industrialized states have made large grants and loans to many governments in the Middle East. The United States has been the biggest source, primarily to Israel, Turkey, Egypt, Jordan, and, since 2003, Iraq; however, virtually every country in the region—other than the Gulf amirates—received US aid at some point since the 1940s, including Iran and Saudi Arabia (see individual chapters in Part Two for more details). Israel received—and continues to receive—by far the greatest amounts, up to one-third of all US foreign aid at times, along with generous indirect grants and loans of many types. Most western European countries—especially Britain, Germany, and France, but also some of the smaller states—have also granted and loaned large amounts to regional countries. The Soviet Union gave its client states massive assistance, primarily military but also economic—for example, for major dams in Egypt and Syria. Japan is the leading Asian donor; the People's Republic of China has been active in recent decades.

In addition to bilateral assistance, technical and development aid has also been given to most states through the UN and its specialized agencies, including the World Bank Group; the UN Relief and Works Agency has funneled large amounts to Palestinian refugees from 1949 to the present. Technical assistance has also gone to the oil states on a reimbursable basis.[3]

Regional Donors.   Aid from regional donors starting in the 1960s began a wealth-sharing process; at first, the beneficiaries were poorer Arab states, but within a few years the efforts became global in scope. In 1961, the Kuwait Fund for Arab Economic Development was founded; it had disbursed some $16.2 billion in loans and grants for 798 development projects in 107 countries across the Third World through 2011. Similar bilateral funds were created by other oil states—the Abu Dhabi Fund for Arab Economic Development, the Iraqi Fund for External Development, and the Saudi Fund for Development. Large grants are regularly made by oil states

to non-oil states outside the channels of the funds, especially on an emergency basis. Aid to countries assisting the defense of Gulf producers is especially substantial. "Frontline states"—Egypt, Syria, Lebanon, and Jordan—have received billions from the oil producers in the wake of Arab-Israeli conflicts, and Egypt and Syria were rewarded for their participation in the coalition to liberate Kuwait in 2001. Many of the oil-rich rulers, like the late Shaykh Zayid of Abu Dhabi, the sultan of Oman, the amirs of Kuwait and Qatar, and members of the Saudi royal family have donated billions to educational, medical, religious, and developmental institutions in Egypt, Pakistan, Indonesia, and other friendly countries. Multilateral entities from the Islamic Development Bank and the World Bank to the OPEC Fund for International Development, UN-affiliated agencies, and nongovernmental charities have also been major recipients.

Kuwait, Saudi Arabia, Qatar, and the UAE paid more than $55 billion of Iraq's wartime expenses during its war with Iran. Kuwait, Saudi Arabia, and the UAE helped defray costs incurred by coalition members (including the United States) in their rollback of the Iraqis in 1991; reimbursements totaled $84 billion, and material support was another $51 billion. They also contributed billions for losses to Turkey, Jordan, and Egypt because of the UN sanctions and coalition actions.

REGIONAL DEVELOPMENT PROBLEMS

Remarkable though it has been, regional development has been hindered by several fundamental problems in addition to the lack of effective coordination and the originally inadequate infrastructure. Shortages of skilled labor required importation of millions of technicians and ordinary workers, and then required time to train indigenous workers and managers to replace expatriates. The original dependence of the Gulf oil states on northwestern Europeans and Americans for oil exploration and development evolved into a relationship involving oil supplies, dollar payments, technological needs, and petrodollar recycling. Nearly everywhere, the shortage of water—and in places an actual lack of water—has had a serious negative impact on the pattern of economic development.

Therefore, despite its energy resources, the Middle East faced serious problems in the first quarter century of moving toward economic development, yet achieved admirable results. Nevertheless, it still faces difficulties in achieving comprehensive economic development. Progress in certain sectors has been dramatic, but gaining long-term self-sufficiency in balanced economies is more challenging.

Labor and Skills

An insufficient pool of skilled labor initially was the most serious single development deterrent in much of the Middle East, especially in the Gulf states, and the steps taken to meet labor demands have had profound spatial implications. For much of the last half of the twentieth century, there was a sharp contrast in labor availability between the northwestern and southeastern parts of the region. The northwest had a labor surplus and a modest supply of technical and managerial people. By contrast, the Gulf area possessed a sparse and primarily pastoral and fishing population, inadequate in number and unequipped with the skills necessary to meet the needs of a booming oil economy.

Labor requirements in the Gulf states were both qualitative and quantitative. Unskilled workers from nearby areas were available in almost unlimited numbers, but engineers, technicians, managers, and similar professionals were in short supply. As the pace of development increased during the 1960s and 1970s, workers at all levels came from Jordan, Egypt, and Lebanon to Saudi Arabia and the smaller Gulf states. Yemenis filled thousands of unskilled jobs in Saudi

Arabia, and Indians, Pakistanis, and Baluch poured into the lower Gulf. By the 2000s, about 11 million migrant workers in Saudi Arabia and the Gulf amirates constituted from one- to two-thirds of the labor force.

Cultural affiliations were important, since Arabic speakers and Muslims tended to adapt most easily in the Gulf. Initially, Pakistanis and Indian Muslims often adjusted more readily than cosmopolitan Lebanese. In addition, technical and managerial positions generally required fluency in English, the lingua franca of the oil industry. As a consequence, the workforce was transformed in size and composition throughout the Gulf within a few years, with a higher percentage of the expatriate workers being Filipinos, Thais, Sri Lankans, and South Koreans. With its almost insatiable demand for additional labor, Saudi Arabia in 2012 still had an estimated 5.6 million expatriate workers.

Palestinians. The situation of Palestinian workers in the Gulf is a special one. The demand for skilled workers and professionals was rapidly escalating in Kuwait some six decades ago just when the Palestinian Arabs had been forced to leave their homeland. Many moved to Kuwait, and by 1986 the number of Palestinians/Jordanians there had climbed to more than 400,000. In Kuwait, as was true to even a greater extent in Jordan, the Palestinians helped create the economy that absorbed them. However, Kuwait later became concerned about the growing political power of the Palestinians and discouraged further Palestinian immigration. During the Iraqi occupation of Kuwait from August 1990 to February 1991, many Palestinians, among others, evacuated their homes and went elsewhere for the duration of the conflict. When Palestinian leaders either approved Saddam Husayn's invasion or refused to condemn it, Kuwait was deeply offended, and many of the Palestinians (and other expatriate evacuees) were neither invited back nor permitted to return; indeed, some of the Palestinians who had stayed were accused of collaboration with the enemy. By the late 2000s, the Palestinian population of Kuwait was, although not accurately known, estimated to be about 40,000 (and perhaps the same number with Jordanian citizenship), less than 10 percent of the number before August 1990. More South Asians were brought in to replace departed Arabs.

Home Countries.   The migration of hundreds of thousands of people to the Gulf area exerted a profound effect on the workforce in both the supplying and the receiving countries. For example, more than 20 percent of the population of North Yemen was working in Saudi Arabia during the 1970s and early 1980s. Then some 800,000 were expelled during the Gulf crisis of 1990–1991 because of Saudi anger over Yemen having taken an anticoalition stance. Their lost remittances plunged Yemen into even deeper poverty.

Working Conditions.   The working and living conditions of foreign workers have varied from semiluxury for European and American bankers and PhDs[4] to penury and close to semislavery in some cases for unskilled Somalis or Bangladeshis. The latter are often victimized both by the migration or employment agencies that place them in jobs and by unscrupulous employers who confiscate their passports and cheat them of their earnings. Conditions are worse in some countries than in others, but even in more open societies like Jordan, Lebanon, and Israel exploitative treatment is not uncommon. Israel became dependent on "guest workers" from the mid-1990s, to replace Palestinians especially after the onset of the First Intifadah. As many as 300,000—half of them illegal—have been in the country at various times, working in agriculture and construction and as servants and caregivers, and coming from countries ranging from Bolivia to Bulgaria to the Philippines. Cases of abuse have been better documented there because of the presence of human rights nongovernmental organizations and investigative journalists.[5]

Remittances

One measure of the magnitude of the labor migration to the Gulf oil states is the amount of money the migrant workers sent back to their home countries. For example, in 1981, Jordanians working outside their own country sent back more than $1.23 billion, which was equal to 28 percent of the kingdom's GDP, 39 percent of its imports, and 168 percent of its exports. Similarly, in 1982, Egyptians remitted $1.87 billion, which nearly doubled by 1997 to $3.4 billion. Illustrative of the increase in Pakistani workers in the Gulf is the fact that remittances to Pakistan totaled $339 million in 1974–1975 and $2 billion in 1980–1981, a sixfold increase in six years. Remittances to North Yemen also exceeded $2 billion annually in the early 1980s.

When recession hit the oil states in the mid-1980s, many expatriates lost their jobs and returned home; others who remained had lower incomes and sent smaller remittances home. This reduction in income inevitably created economic difficulties for the labor-supplying countries. Even after the partial recovery in the late 1980s, the demand for labor in the Gulf did not return to its earlier levels, since the peak of the construction boom had passed. Since the late 1980s, the service sector has provided many expatriate jobs—for example, for filling the large number of hotel and restaurant positions.

Even more serious than the recession were the economic blows that struck many expatriates as direct and indirect results of the Iraqi invasion of Kuwait. Hundreds of thousands of workers and professionals found themselves without jobs and no longer welcome in their adopted lands, and they were forced to return to depressed economic conditions in their home countries—Jordan, Lebanon, Egypt, and Yemen. Many also lost savings and other assets they had held in Kuwait. By the late 1990s, the Gulf labor market had recovered, and many expatriates were again at work. In the 2000s, the situation was much the same—despite many countries replacing expatriates with indigenous workers. However, when Dubai's economy crashed in 2008, the impact on foreign workers was considerable.

Remittances have become the largest source of capital flows for many regional countries.[6] Jordanian expatriates sent home $3.6 billion officially (and perhaps another $3 billion unofficially) in 2010, with the official remittances equivalent to about an eighth of Jordan's GDP. A similar degree of remittance benefit was realized by Egypt and Pakistan— $14.2 billion and $12.2 billion and equivalent to about 3 and 5 percent of GDP, respectively, in 2010;[7] Yemen, however, was less fortunate, at least as far as officially reported remittances were concerned—only $1.5 billion in 2011[8]—reflecting continuing problems with Saudi Arabia, previously the major employers of unskilled Yemeni workers.[9] The largest source of remittance outflows in 2010 was Saudi Arabia, with some $27.1 billion (about 6 percent of GDP) going to countries all over the world.

PATTERNS OF INDUSTRY

Factors of Industrial Location

The region's patterns of manufacturing are determined by the classic geographical factors of raw materials, labor supply, transportation, market, and power (energy), along with such intangibles as financial incentives, momentum, tradition, and technology. Concentrations of the greatest number of factors attract the largest ensembles of manufacturing.

Distribution of Centers

Despite the remarkable economic development since 1950, most of the region's industrial complexes other than petroleum

processing still tend to be relatively modest on a world scale. Originally serving domestic requirements, some manufacturing centers now include plants that export most of their output. Many more textile mills (in Turkey, Egypt, and Israel), clothing factories (not only in the Levant but even in the UAE), wineries (in the Levant and Cyprus), and similar operations cater to foreign markets. Israel is especially export oriented, from diamond cutting and armaments to high-tech electronics and software. Similarly, petrochemical plants in the oil states market output globally.

Although data reporting lags behind development, some comparisons are useful: in absolute terms—ignoring per capita output— Turkey in the 2010s is by far the leading Middle East country in terms of total value added by manufacturing, followed by Israel, Iran, Saudi Arabia, the UAE, and Egypt. Iraq was formerly a ranking industrial state but, after losing many of its factories and much of its industrial organization in three wars, is now struggling to regain its footing.

Turkey had the largest industrial workforce (3.85 million) in 2007, followed by Iran (2.82 million) and Egypt (2.31 million)—in each case, from 12 to 18 percent of the workforce (Table 7.1). Turkey and Iran have the largest number of producing enterprises, many of them small. Manufacturing contributed 32 percent of GDP in Egypt, 18 percent in Turkey, 13 percent in Israel, and 11 percent in Iran.

Certain industries—including such basic production as processed foods and beverages, construction materials, and clothing—are widespread and are found in every country and in many parts of the larger countries. Less widespread but nevertheless found virtually everywhere are textiles, leather, wood products, cement, printing, cigarettes, metalworking, ceramics, and jewelry. Less common are glass, plastics, chemicals, tools, small appliances, and irrigation pipe and sprinklers. States with significant oil and gas production

TABLE 7.1 Economically Active Population: Total and Sector Distribution

	1	2	3	4	5	6	7	8
	ECONOMICALLY ACTIVE POPULATION		PERCENTAGE OF ECONOMICALLY ACTIVE POPULATION IN SELECTED SECTORS					
Country and Year of Data	Total No. in 1,000s	% Total Population	Ag, For, Fishing	Mfg, Mng, Qg	Construc-tion	Trnsp, Comm	Trade, Htl, Rt	Servs, Other
Bahrain 2005	350	48.3	1.5	16.2	8.6	4.5	15.5	19.9
Cyprus[a] 2006	341	49.6	5.0	11.7	10.2	5.1	25.8	23.5
Egypt 2006	19,253	30.0	24.8	12.0	6.7	5.7	13.5	24.7
Iran 2006	16,027	26.7	20.9	17.6	10.3	6.1	12.0	21.1
Iraq 2006	4,757	24.8	11.6	10.6	11.2	6.4	6.8	52.3
Israel 2006	2,610	39.0	1.6	15.2	4.9	5.8	15.6	37.6
Jordan 2006	1,293	23.6	3.0	13.1	5.5	8.5	17.3	33.9
Kuwait 2006	1,364	56.4	1.6	7.3	7.9	3.2	16.1	59.5
Lebanon 2005	1,362	34.0	19.1	18.9	6.2	7.0	16.5	28.8
Oman 2007	737	31.5	7.9	11.4	16.0	3.8	14.8	20.6
Qatar 2006	280	53.7	2.2	18.3	18.4	3.1	13.2	28.2
S. Arabia 2007	7,437	32.8	7.8	11.6	14.6	4.1	14.3	30.2
Syria 2006	5,460	31.9	26.8	12.1	11.6	4.9	13.3	30.3
Turkey 2007	23,641	33.2	30.3	16.3	4.1	4.3	17.1	19.8
UAE 2006	2,191	54.2	7.7	16.6	16.5	6.1	24.1	13.6
Yemen 2006	4,091	24.2	48.0	4.0	5.8	3.0	10.7	19.1
Gaza —	254	19.0	11.7	6.2	7.0	3.5	11.4	60.2
W. Bank —	555	23.6	11.6	9.5	9.8	4.3	14.9	39.2
TOTAL/AVG.	91,961	35.3	13.5	12.8	9.7	5.0	15.2	31.6
U.K. 2003	29,595	49.7	1.4	12.8	7.0	6.0	23.2	30.5
Venezuela 2002	11,674	46.4	8.2	10.8	6.7	6.1	22.4	41.5

Sectors include agriculture, forestry, fishing (3); manufacturing, mining, quarrying (4); construction (5); transportation, communications (6); trade, hotels, restaurants (7); and services and other (8). Data among countries are difficult to compare because of varying dates of data. [a]Cyprus data for Republic of Cyprus (Southern Cyprus) only. Corresponding data for United Kingdom and Venezuela given for comparison. (*Source: Britannica World Data 2012* [used with permission])

have evolved an ensemble of industries using hydrocarbons as feedstock or fuel—oil refineries, water distillation plants, electricity generation, petrochemical plants, fertilizer factories, and, in two Gulf states, such energy-dependent operations as aluminum smelters. Leading natural gas producers are expanding gas-processing facilities to meet growing world demand for LNG.

Complex Industries.   Only in the most industrialized countries are there industries making or assembling motor vehicles, ships, machine tools, major appliances, electronic items, and armaments. Only Israel, Egypt, and Turkey produce aircraft, and Israel alone

has diamond cutting. Few countries engage in basic research and development to any noteworthy extent, and Israel, which ranks on the world scale, is far in the lead in information technology, developing and producing world-class computer chips and electronic components. During the mid-1990s, UN inspection teams found that Iraq had developed research programs beyond anything that had been expected; however, its industrial complex was brought to a virtual standstill in 2003, except for basic oil processing; recovery has been slow. Turkey, Egypt, Iran, Saudi Arabia, and others are steadily increasing research efforts. In an unusual cooperative effort, several regional (and otherwise mutually hostile) gov-

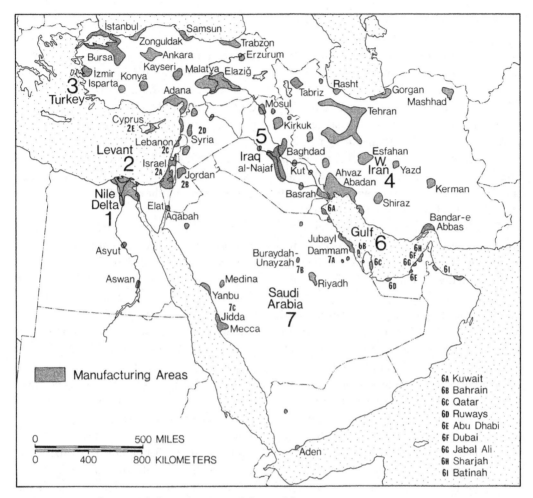

Map 7.1 Manufacturing belts and centers of the Middle East.

ernments and their scientists are collaborating in financing the Sesame Project to build a synchroton particle accelerator in Jordan: with the encouragement of the EU and UNESCO, joint scientific experiments could begin in 2015.[10]

Seven economic zones may be geographically differentiated within the area (Map 7.1; see also Table 7.1). They form a rough arc following the trend of the Fertile Crescent but extending beyond and below it, and each area is separately examined in the country chapters.

1. Nile Delta. Egypt's manufacturing sector is one of the two earliest and most diversi-

fied in the region and comprises the area bounded by Alexandria-Cairo-Suez–Port Said–Alexandria. Greater Cairo and Alexandria are the most important locales, along with the textile towns in the delta. Served by a thick road and railway net and with one of the world's highest population densities, the area calls upon creative traditions of the ancient, medieval, and modern ages. Moving beyond prized handcrafted items, products range from processed foods and textiles to aluminum, iron and steel, metal products, motor vehicles, fertilizers, refined petroleum products, furniture, light armaments, and helicopter assembly.

2. Levant.   Northeast of the first zone is a grouping of five neighboring but unconnected manufacturing concentrations in the four Levant states and Cyprus.

2A. Israel.   The dense concentration in Israel makes up the most nationally balanced and systematized range of manufacturing facilities in the region. One reason for this variety is that Israel was until the 1990s basically isolated, with few materials moving into or out of it on the landward side, which encouraged autarky. Moreover, Israel has many inventive and technologically advanced people, like technically trained immigrants from the FSU, Europe, and the United States. With considerable support from the United States, Israel has developed leading research laboratories and built a sophisticated military establishment that stimulates and feeds a large high-tech industrial complex. This, in turn, supports a dense population at a high standard of living. Most types of manufacturing are found in Israel, from food processing to one of the world's largest armaments industries (including a controversial nuclear facility at Dimona). Software development was stressed during the 1990s, and now software production has rocketed to a leading position in manufacturing and exports. The coastal conurbation of Greater Tel Aviv and Haifa (Fig. 7.1) comprises the main industrial concentrations, but manufacturing is widely dispersed for both development and security reasons. Many specialty factories—electronics plants, for example—operate in kibbutzim and other smaller settlements.

2B. Jordan.   The industrial area of Jordan has only a modest range of light manufacturing facilities concentrated primarily in the Amman-Zarqa-Irbid triangle in the northwestern part of the country. Aqabah, the only port, is expanding chemical production. Growth rates have been high since 1960, but Jordan started from a very low industrial

base. As one benefit Jordan received as a "peace dividend" for signing a treaty with Israel in 1994, several modest Qualifying Industrial Zones (QIZs) have been set up in northwestern Jordan. Some plants in the QIZs are partly Israeli financed, and their products include Israeli-made content that "qualify" them for duty-free entry into the United States, to which Jordanian exports have grown a hundredfold from $15 million in 1997 to $1.5 billion in 2011.

2C. Lebanon.   Traditionally, Lebanese manufacturing has been consumer oriented, often related to the retail trade, with most activity concentrated in Beirut, Tripoli, and Sidon. As in Egypt and Syria, handcrafted articles are produced in great variety, from inlaid wood furniture to jewelry. Manufactured products include textiles, clothing, leather items, paints, chemicals, cement, glassware (a tradition dating to Phoenician times), cigarettes (a state monopoly), and raw steel and other metal products. Lebanon's open economy attracted huge amounts of investment capital before 1975, but industrial production dropped sharply with the outbreak of conflict and then limped along. Recovery has been slow, but by the late 2000s there were many encouraging signs.

2D. Syria.   Damascus has been famous for more than twelve hundred years for its handcrafted metals (damascene), textiles (damask), inlaid woods, and glass. Since the 1960s, more factory-made goods have been produced on a modest scale: machine-made textiles, clothing, appliances, machinery, cement, chemicals, cigarettes, and similar items. The ancient trade center of Aleppo has modern industry. Expanding petroleum production stimulated industrial growth during the 1980s and 1990s. Homs and Hamah, on the Damascus-Aleppo axis; the coastal centers of Latakia, Baniyas, and Tartus; and the developing centers of Raqqah and Dayr al-Zawr in the Eu-

Figure 7.1 Main Haifa industrial area, just north of the city of Haifa, Israel, seen from Mount Carmel. The area specializes in petroleum refining and chemical production but makes a broad spectrum of products.

phrates Valley are also worth noting. A period of more than four decades of Baathi rule favored large-scale state enterprises over the private sector, but private-sector growth was notable in the first decade of the new century. Industrial activity, like most aspects of Syrian society, has been considerably disrupted since the onset of civil war in 2011.

2E. Cyprus. The main producing areas are around Nicosia and on the south coast in Limassol and Larnaca. Despite the loss of northern Cyprus after 1974, the republic's vitality encouraged the emergence or expansion of plants producing cigarettes, processed foodstuffs, wine, paper products, clothing, shoes, textiles, and cement. The manufacturing sector, like the rest of the economy of the island, has faced the problem of uncertainty in both the south and north, but especially in the north. Cyprus is a member of the EU,

giving it access to a market of more than 500 million consumers, and since 2008 it has used the euro, the common currency of seventeen EU members.

3. Turkey. Endowed with many elements conducive to industrial development, Turkey's reported total value added by manufacturing equals those of all the other of this study's countries combined, Israel excepted. Food processing is by far the most important activity and is on a much greater scale than elsewhere in the region. Textiles, leather goods, tobacco products, wood and paper products, ceramics, appliances, chemicals, petroleum products, electronic items, pharmaceuticals, heavy and light machinery, assembled automobiles, railway equipment, farm tractors, small ships, and handmade and machinemade rugs are among its products. Manufacturing is widespread, and most larger cities have several factories. Major centers are Istanbul, Izmir, Zonguldak, Ankara, Kırıkkale, Divrici, Mersin, Adana, and Erzurum, plus the others shown on Map 7.1. Turkey and the EU are in a customs union, considerably enlarging the market available to its manufacturers.

4. Western Iran. Like Turkey, Iran has a large population, workforce, and domestic market, as well as numerous raw materials and other advantages for manufacturing. Unlike Turkey, Iran also has huge oil resources. The two lead the region in numbers of industrial workers and manufacturing plants. With a creative, inventive, and energetic core population, Iran has a long and distinguished history of manufacturing, traditionally producing rugs, textiles, handcrafted metalwares, jewelry, ceramics (especially tiles), and similar items. Its highly diversified modern industrial products—many made in small five- to ten-employee shops—include fabricated metals (utilitarian wrought iron as well as traditional copper and brass, as shown in Fig. 21.5), jewelry, a wide range of food products, plain and art textiles and leather goods, hand-knotted rugs, and petroleum products and chemicals.

Major areas include Tehran, the Ahvaz-Abadan–Bandar-e Khomeini triangle at the head of the Gulf, Kharg Island, Shiraz, Sar Cheshmeh, Arak, Esfahan, Tabriz, and Gorgan. By the time of the revolution in 1979, Iran had clearly ranked with the moderately large industrial producers. However, the Iran-Iraq War damaged many of its plants, and the Islamist regime's policies retarded broader industrial development and subjected it to international sanctions. Its advanced and controversial nuclear program was of great international concern in the early 2010s (see Chap. 21).

5. Iraq. The amount and variety of manufacturing in Iraq increased steadily after a modest start in the mid-1950s and by the late 1980s had made impressive advances. However,

much effort was devoted to the military—indeed, more so than was realized at the time. As one result, coalition bombing targeted and heavily damaged much of its industrial complex in 1991, and the complex was closely inspected by UN technicians for several years after. Many of Iraq's remaining factories—excluding most of the petroleum-related plants—were destroyed or damaged during the American preinvasion bombings in March 2003 or during the ground operations after the invasion. A major rationale given for the attack was that Saddam Husayn's industries produced weapons of mass destruction (WMD), although neither the plants nor the weapons were subsequently found. Like much of the rest of the economy, post-2003 industrial recovery has been uneven, with some signs of progress by the end of the decade.

The pattern of its industrial operations and potential persists: Baghdad is the center of a sprawling modern industrial zone, which proved much more developed and sophisticated than expected when UN inspectors checked it in 1991. Government planning had spread facilities to Mosul (Fig. 7.2) and Kirkuk in the north and to Basrah and al-Zubayr in the south. Southern areas were the most heavily damaged in 1980–1988 and 1991, and reconstruction there had proceeded only slowly by 2003. Petrochemicals and other petroleum-related products normally make up a considerable share of the country's industrial output, but Baathi military ambitions also mandated a large and varied armaments industry, now mostly in ruins. Many smaller establishments produce processed foods and beverages, cigarettes, textiles (muslin from Mosul), clothing, shoes, furniture, and metal goods. Traditional handcrafts include silver-smithing, copper- and brasswares, textiles, and rug making.

6. Gulf. The Gulf industrial zone, including Oman—but excluding Saudi Arabia, Iraq, and Iran—might be divided into subzones based

Figure 7.2 Interior view of one of the several large textile mills in Iraq. The city of Mosul long produced lightweight cotton textiles that became known as muslin. (Nik Wheeler, *Saudi Aramco World*/SAWDIA)

partly on national boundaries, as was the case with the Levant. Facilities have a substantial degree of similarity and have developed almost entirely since the 1960s, with petro-development stimulating dramatic growth. The core economic activity in every subcenter of the zone is petroleum production and processing, and the main satellite facilities produce related products—petrochemicals, fertilizers, liquefied natural gas derivatives, secondary sulfur, plastics, and a range of refinery products.

However, there is an impressive array of manufacturing in parts of the area; further diversification is under way, with an emphasis on ready-made clothing (see Chap. 17). Because construction has been prominent in the economy since the mid-1950s, construction materials are a major industry. It includes cement, cement blocks, bricks, steel

reinforcing rods, and metal frames for windows and doors. Dhow building is still carried on in traditional centers: Kuwait, Bahrain, Ajman, and Ras al-Khaymah. Most larger new industries are capital intensive as well as large energy users.

Major subcenters are as follows:

(6A) the Kuwait Bay and Gulf coast area, with refineries and petrochemical plants

(6B) northeastern Bahrain, with locational advantages and the earliest industrial development, including the Sitra refinery

(6C) east-central Qatar, with a booming concentration of petro-processing, around Musayid and Doha

(6D–6H) five UAE industrial developments of (6D) al-Ruways near the Jabal Dhanna terminal, (6E) Abu Dhabi Island with light production, (6F) Dubai City with a wide range of small plants producing consumer

Figure 7.3 Rusayl Industrial Area on the Batinah Coast of Oman, west of Muscat. The success of this project prompted Oman to develop similar industrial areas in other locations.

goods, (6G) Jabal Ali—a major and still expanding and diversifying heavy industrial center south of Dubai, and (6H) Sharjah with modest manufacturing establishments

(6I) the Batinah coast of Oman, which produced only a few handcrafted articles until the mid-1960s but now includes copper-related plants near Suhar and an impressive industrial estate at Rusayl, west of Muscat (Fig. 7.3); an additional industrial park is in operation in Salalah, where an expanding port is a manufacturing core.

7. Saudi Triad: al-Hasa, Najd, Hijaz. From a pre-1935 manufacturing production level below that of any other major country in the Middle East, Saudi Arabia by the 1990s had developed a vigorous and diversified range of production. Latest available data on value added by manufacturing show Saudi Arabia ranking fourth in the region, after Turkey, Is-

rael, and Iran. Initially, development focused almost entirely on oil in the Eastern Province, but there are now diversified industries not only in the east but also in both mid-Arabia and the west. Developments include an industrial city and port on each side of the peninsula—Jubayl on the Gulf and Yanbu on the Red Sea. Thus, it now has three main producing centers:

(7A) on the Gulf coast along the Jubayl-Dammam-al-Khobar axis, with outliers in the Hofuf-Abqaiq area

(7B) the two centers of Qasim and Riyadh in Najd

(7C) the Jiddah-Mecca area in the Hijaz, with an outlier in Yanbu.

TRANSPORTATION

Roads were of limited significance before World War I because of centuries of preference for maritime trade whenever possible and transport via camel caravans when land movement was necessary. In 1859–1863, a French company built a 69-mi/111-km road from the Beirut port to Damascus, and an additional 258 mi/415 km of roads had been built in Lebanon by 1900. At the onset of the twentieth century, the French, British, Germans, and—in Iran—Russians were involved in building roads, railroads, and ports in and around the region, mostly under concessionary terms. The Dutch, Portuguese, and British successively controlled the main sea-lanes after the sixteenth century, and British steamships played a major role in the Gulf until World War II.

Consequently, the mandates and recently independent states of the region had a basic transportation net by the late 1920s that was appreciably improved by the end of World War II. However, it was soon apparent that the net was inadequate for modern development; within the peninsula, there was no semblance of sufficiency. Fortunately, the huge petrodollar influx permitted transformation of the regional communications network—roads, seaports, airports, pipelines, and, more recently, railways.

Linking "Island" Cores. Two aspects of regional communications patterns are worth noting. First, the region has "islands," or cores of development, separated by uninhabited or sparsely populated deserts, mountain masses, or seas. Before the mid-nineteenth century, these were linked by land caravans or by small vessels, with flexible schedules and capacities and minimum costs. Railway and road nets were not required, nor would they have been profitable, since there was little cargo traffic between the centers. Even today, the two main rail nets, in Turkey and Iran, and two secondary ones, in Egypt and Iraq, are primarily internal, with limited international movement of freight or passengers; by 2012, a number of significant changes in this regard were under

way. However, the three most extensive road nets, in Turkey, Saudi Arabia, and Iran, have become increasingly linked with the outside, and both cargo and passengers cross frontiers along roads in steadily growing numbers. In peaceful periods, the main highway border crossings, especially on weekends and holidays, are crowded—between Lebanon and Syria, Syria and Jordan, Turkey and Bulgaria, Turkey and Iran, Kuwait and Iraq, and Saudi Arabia and Bahrain.

Second, airways in parts of the Middle East developed to a significant level while railroads lagged, and airlines serve the "island" pattern of the region's urban centers very well. Aircraft overfly and thereby ignore both the physical-environmental hazards and the political perils—the expanses of desert, sea, and mountains when flying Istanbul–Dubai, Beirut–Tehran, or Cairo–Sana, and the political obstacles of a sanctioned Iraq during the 1990s. Where airlines are locally unavailable or inadequate, the road net serves most purposes. Railways have been of less regional importance than other available means of transportation (Map 7.2), although this is in the process of changing in the coming decade (see "Railways" below).

Highways

Cross-Border Links. Prior to midcentury, most of the road systems in the Middle East were scattered webs around capitals or other primary cities in the Fertile Crescent or in Egypt, Turkey, and Iran. Only a few miles of surfaced roads existed anywhere in the Arabian Peninsula. By the early 2010s, the region had 628,980 mi/1,012,244 km of roads, of which more than three-fourths were paved highways (Fig. 7.4). Barring unexpected frontier closures, a motorist can now drive on paved roads—mostly first-class highways—from Istanbul over the Bosporus bridges to the Pakistan border via Erzurum, Tabriz, Tehran, and Yazd; or from Istanbul to Aden via Adana, Damascus, Amman, and Jiddah;

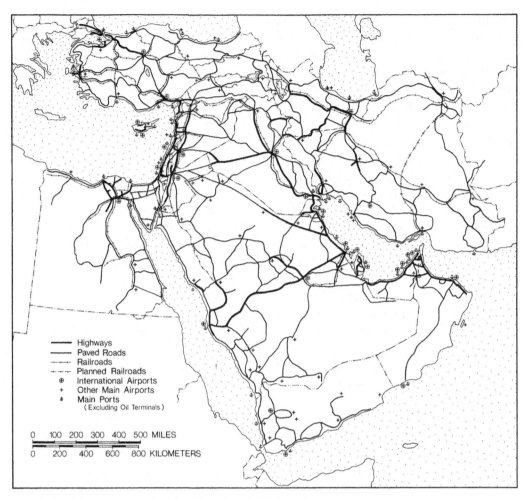

Map 7.2   Major transportation facilities of the Middle East.

or turn east at Jiddah and reach Abu Dhabi and Muscat via Riyadh and Dammam.[11] Even Bahrain can now be reached by highway via a causeway opened in 1986 (Fig. 7.5); planning for a second one linking it to Qatar was under way in 2012. Another proposed causeway and bridge across the Strait of Tiran would tie Egyptian roads to Saudi Arabia and the intraregional net.

The regional network is also linked to the Trans-European Motorway (TEM) through Turkey. When completed, this special integrated, high-grade motorway will run north and south through eastern Europe, from Gdansk on Poland's Baltic coast to Istanbul,

then east to Ankara and the Iranian border, about 6,215 mi/10,000 km. Spur roads in Anatolia will extend the main TEM to the borders of Syria and Iraq; 2,235 m/3,600 km of the TEM will be in Turkey.

Israel's extraordinarily dense network of roads is very heavily traveled and has been regularly upgraded, although it is somewhat isolated. Before 1967, there were no connections with the country's neighbors open to the public, although UN and diplomatic personnel could cross in several places, like the famous Mandelbaum Gate in Jerusalem. By 2000, there were moderately traveled cross-border connections with Egypt and Jordan.

Figure 7.4 Highways old and new. In 1964 in remote areas of the Trucial States in the northern Oman Mountains (*top photo*), the already rugged track (maximum speed, 10 mph/16 kph) degenerated into a rocky streambed in one narrow pass (maximum speed, about 3 mph/5 kph). By 1979 in the same area, a first class, well-built highway had been built (*bottom photo*)—one of the many blessings of the oil boom in the UAE.

Figure 7.5 One of the major highway links in the Middle East: a stretch of open causeway connecting Saudi Arabia and Bahrain, a 15.5-mi/25-km facility opened in 1986 at a cost of more than $1 billion.

Virtually 100 percent of Israeli roads are paved.

Cyprus, where driving on the left side of the road is a British legacy, also has a dense road net and an administration that has been divided between north and south since 1974. It has the second-highest ratio of road length to area in the region, behind only the other island state, Bahrain (Table 7.2). Both parts of Cyprus are tied to the Levant's road system by frequent car ferry; the north is also linked the same way directly to the Turkish network. Other ferries transport private cars and trucks, connecting eastern Mediterranean ports like Istanbul, Izmir, and Mersin in Turkey; Latakia in Syria; Beirut and Juniyah in Lebanon; and Alexandria in Egypt. A special truck ferry from Volos in Greece to Tartus in Syria enabled truckers to avoid the long, winding drive through Anato-

lia, but as with so many economic activities the Syrian civil war has interrupted this routing.

Predictably, the most densely inhabited areas, if reasonably prosperous, have the densest highway networks, as can be seen in Table 7.2 and Map 7.2. Bahrain, Cyprus, and Israel have the region's densest nets, but these countries are small and absolute road length is limited. Turkey, Saudi Arabia, Egypt, Iran, and Syria, in that order, have the greatest total extent of roads.

Engineering and Scenic Marvels.   Some segments of the road net are noteworthy both for their engineering and for their scenic impact. The paved 62-mi/100-km highway from Hudaydah, on Yemen's Red Sea coast, up the steep, rugged escarpment to the capital, Sana, affords magnificent vistas as it winds past ter-

TABLE 7.2 Transportation: Roads, Railroads, and Merchant Marine

Country	1 Roads: Length in Km	2 % of Roads Paved	3 Km of Roads per Km²	4 Number of Vehicles (all types)	5 Persons per Vehicle	6 RR Track: in Km	7 Airports w/Sched. Flights	8 Merchant Marine 1,000s DWT
Bahrain	3,942	81	5.20	369,583	3.6	—	1	192.5
Cyprus	12,321	65	2.09	568,698	1.4	—	2	36,198.1
Egypt	99,672	81	0.10	3,914,273	21.1	5,500	11	1,685.2
Iran	72,611	92	0.04	1,104,765	68.1	8,702	19	8,345.3
Iraq	45,550	84	0.10	2,242,268	14.6	2,272[a]	—	1,578.8
Israel	18,470	100	0.85	2,381,027	3.1	975[a]	7	723.4
Jordan	7,768	100	0.09	784,723	7.9	506	2	113.6
Kuwait	6,342	85	0.36	1,323,725	2.8	—	1	3,188.5
Lebanon	6,970	85	0.67	1,384,640	2.5	401[b]	1	438.2
Oman	58,554	48	0.19	593,090	4.7	—	6	11.7
Qatar	7,790	90	0.67	605,699	2.7	—	1	744.0
Saudi Arabia	183,925	29	0.09	4,446,973	6.4	1,423[a]	28	1,278.0
Syria	64,983	91	0.35	1,159,709	17.9	2,833[a]	5	210.4
Turkey	352,046	89	0.45	10,611,303	7.0	8,699	26	7,114.3
UAE	4,080	100	0.01	1,327,303	5.9	—	6	1,491.7
Yemen	71,300	9	0.14	1,029,203	24.1	—	12	13.7
Gaza	—	—	—	45,166	23.0	—	—	—
West Bank	—	—	—	112,380	18.0	—	—	—
TOTAL/AG.	1,012,244	76	—	34,004,528	13.0	25,679	128	63,336.4
U.K.	420,009	100	1.73	32,609,700	1.9	16,454	57	4,355.0
Venezuela	96,200	34	0.10	4,044,012	7.3	806[a]	20	1,355.4

[a]Route length (other railway lengths are for total track length). [b]Little of Lebanon's network is usable. Column 3 is the ratio between the length of roads and the area of each country. Number of vehicles in Column 4 includes automobiles, buses, and trucks. Column 8 is the total of merchant marine ships in thousands of deadweight tons. (*Sources: Britannica World Data 2012* [Columns 1-6], *BWD 2008* [Column 3], *BWD 2007* [Columns 7 and 8] [used with permission])

raced fields and picturesque villages to reach the plateau, 9,000 ft/2,743 m above sea level. Similarly, the highway from Jiddah to Taif offers spectacular views, leaving the heat of the coastal plain and ascending to the cooler height of the Saudi summer capital. The highway from Beirut over the mountains and across the Bekaa toward Damascus is famed for its vistas. Less dramatic with lower elevations, but still interesting, is the drive from Tel Aviv and Jaffa on the Mediterranean to Jerusalem (2,500 ft/762 m) and down the eastern slopes to the Jordan (1,200 ft/365 m below sea level).

The drive along the coast of southern Turkey offers a scenic beauty similar to that of the French and Italian Rivieras, as well as sites of major archaeological interest. Another dramatic mountain drive begins in Tehran and proceeds over the Elburz Mountains, at 9,000 ft/2,745 m, to Chalus on the Caspian Sea shore, 80 ft/24 m below sea level. Spectacular scenery also characterizes two roads into northeastern Iraq, the ones climbing into the Ruwanduz Gorge from Irbil and into the Sulaymaniyah area from Kirkuk (see Fig. 14.3). With almost no change in elevation, the drive between Cairo and Alexandria on the Delta Road, through the villages and green landscape of the irrigated delta, provides an interesting contrast to the other Cairo–Alexandria link, the Desert Road.

A Mature Network.   The region's road net is rapidly achieving maturity. All major cities and towns are now connected, and the need in the twenty-first century is to integrate more of the villages, to construct shorter routes between some major cities, to make dual highways of standard roads in some high-traffic areas, and to continue to densify the net. In Table 7.2, data on all types of vehicles (Col. 4) and persons per vehicle (Col. 5) are revealing in several ways: they may be indicative of a country's standard of living according to income per capita; however, because they include all types of vehicles, they may also suggest the usage level of mass transportation (number of buses) and the degree of automotive transport (number of trucks). The entire population of nine countries could be transported by available vehicles at one time. Kuwait has the smallest number of persons per vehicle (2.3), and Cyprus, Lebanon, Qatar, Bahrain, and Israel have fewer than 4. These six have smaller areas and populations, but they are either oil states (like Kuwait) or have more advanced industrialized economies (like Israel). Syria and Yemen have appreciably more trucks and buses than passenger cars, and Saudi Arabia has equal numbers of cars and heavy vehicles. With the oil industry's requirements and the kingdom's vast expanse, large numbers of heavy trucks are needed.

Railways

Economics did not justify the construction of extensive rail nets in the region during the heyday of railway building elsewhere, and development from the 1960s onward employed the greater flexibility of highways and airways. As in many other areas with numerous long-distance travelers, passenger traffic has been mostly by air, and since most cargo could be shipped by truck, cargo aircraft, ships, or—in the case of petroleum and petroleum products—pipelines, any appreciable expansion of rail nets seemed unlikely and, indeed,

unnecessary. However, with the explosive development of the petroleum-exporting Arabian Peninsula states after the 1970s, planning turned toward railway transportation.

In 2009, the total length of railway lines in the Middle East was 16,454 mi/26,480 km, only about 2.6 percent of the total mileage of paved roads. The region's average 0.0046 km of rail line per square kilometer of area compares with Australia's ratio and roughly the same amount of territory. By contrast, Britain, somewhat smaller than Oman, has 10,563 mi/17,000 km of rails, about three-fifths of the total Middle East rail length, with 0.07 km of railway per square kilometer of area.

Map 7.2 shows that the densest net is in Turkey, with nearly one-third of the region's total. Under the Bosporus, the Marmaray tunnel project links Turkey's European and Anatolian lines. The nets of Egypt and Iran are less extensive, but they are nevertheless heavily traveled (Fig. 7.6) and reasonably adequate in length, particularly in view of their extensive, virtually uninhabited desert areas.

A Railway Construction Golden Age?   In 2009, the entire Arabian Peninsula, with more than 1.30 mn mi^2/3.17 mn km^2, had only 884 mi/1,423 km of railway, all connecting Riyadh with the Dammam economic complex in eastern Saudi Arabia. But in the early 2010s, an advanced plan was under way for a Gulf Cooperation Council $25 billion integrated railway network: it calls for the GCC states to be linked with a 1,315-mi/2,117-km rail net starting in Kuwait and Saudi Arabia, extending on to Bahrain, Qatar, the UAE, and Oman. The target date for initial operations is 2017.[12] The possibility of extending this line south of Muscat to Salalah and on into Yemen was also under discussion, as was a proposal to rebuild the old Hejaz railway from Jordan south to Medina. Saudi Arabia has already begun work on a major rail link connecting Riyadh to the Jordan border (and on to Europe), which will provide transport for the

Figure 7.6 Railway station in Tanta, Egypt, in the Nile Delta. Railways are heavily utilized in Egypt, especially by passengers.

output of phosphate and bauxite mines along the route; this will tie into two lines also in various stages of implementation, one crossing the peninsula—the Landbridge—from the Red Sea to Riyadh (with a spur linking Mecca to Medina to facilitate pilgrim traffic) and the other tying into the GCC net and running north from Dammam to the Kuwait border.

Elsewhere in the region, Israel is proceeding with the construction of a technically challenging high-speed link between Tel Aviv and Jerusalem; it is due to be finished in 2017. Other plans include an Iraq-Jordan link announced in 2012 that will tie Baghdad to the port of Aqabah. A new line from Dayr al-Zawr in Syria to the Iraq internal network al-Bukamal was under construction and, although it was due to open in 2012 or 2013, it has been delayed by civil strife in Syria. Iraq and Iran were cooperating on a line between

Basrah and Khorramshahr, and the Iranian portion was completed in 2011. Iraq and Jordan are cooperating on tying their domestic networks so as to link Baghdad with Aqabah port.

Urban Rapid Transit. Urban rail systems are also part of recent activity: Dubai's state-of-the-art system opened in 2009 and Mecca's in 2010. Networks for Kuwait City, Doha, Riyadh, Jiddah, and Baghdad are planned; Cairo, Istanbul, Ankara, Bursa, Izmir, and Tehran already have metros. A controversial and long-delayed light rail system began operating in Jerusalem in 2011, and construction of another system for Tel Aviv was to get under way in 2012. Abu Dhabi also began building its light rail net in 2012. Amman's plans for a similar network were reported in 2012 to be temporarily in abeyance because of financing difficulties.

Historic Lines.   Certain rail lines in the Middle East are renowned historically: the Orient Express from France, which technically terminated in Istanbul but actually continued to Konya and Aleppo on a reduced scale (in another change with the times, the famed rail service was officially discontinued in 2009); the Alexandria-Cairo-Luxor-Aswan line, part of the never-completed Cape-to-Cairo railway; the line built in Palestine in 1892 to transport pilgrims from Jaffa to Jerusalem (being replaced in the 2010s by a new high-speed intercity line); the Hijaz Railway from Damascus to Medina, which was built by the Ottomans at the beginning of the twentieth century for Muslim pilgrims traveling to Mecca but was destroyed south of Maan by the Arab Revolt in 1916–1917;[13] and the route through the scenic Dez River gorge through the Zagros Mountains in southwestern Iran.

Airways and Airfields

The Middle East's location, astride the land, sea, and air routes crossing the tricontinental hub, led to the establishment of a few transit airports prior to World War II. Rapid petroleum development stimulated demand for air service and airports from the early 1950s, and by the early 1990s the Middle East possessed an excellent pattern of airports (see Map 7.2), including not only the world's largest but some of the world's technologically best equipped. By 2012, Dubai's airport was the tenth busiest in the world in terms of passenger traffic. Others, like Jiddah, Istanbul, Cairo, Tehran, and Lod (Tel Aviv), are regularly in the top fifty airports outside the United States in passenger numbers.[14]

After normal air traffic resumed following the attacks of 9/11, explosive growth took place in the region, and it became the world's hottest air transport market. Especially in the Gulf region, carriers and airports underwent billion-dollar expansions. Dubai's sumptuous new airport terminal served 51 million passengers in 2011, and it has received top ratings for passenger satisfaction. Istanbul, Antalya, Jeddah, and Cairo were also among the hundred airports serving the most passengers globally. Among several other openings, Tehran inaugurated a new airport in 2004, and Qatar is building a facility at Doha that will increase passenger capacity from 4.6 million annually to 60 million by 2020. Israel opened an impressive and efficient new terminal at Ben Gurion (Lod) International Airport in 2004.

National Airlines.   Every Middle East country has its own national airline, and some states also have private carriers. Half of the fleets have thirty-five or more jet aircraft each, and Emirates Airlines (Dubai), Saudia (Saudi Arabian Airlines), and THY (Turkish Airlines) rank between twentieth and thirtieth among world airlines in available seat-kilometers (ASK, a key index of airline capacity).

Turkey's THY, EgyptAir, and IranAir are large, long-established airlines carrying both domestic and international passengers. El Al, the Israeli national airline, though small, is an important link with international destinations, especially the United States. Gulf Air was an early joint carrier for Bahrain, Qatar, the UAE, and Oman; however, after the 1970s, the last three owners sold their stakes and started their own fleets—Oman Air (the region's smallest), Emirates (Dubai) and Etihad (Abu Dhabi), and Qatar Airways. Gulf Air continues to thrive as Bahrain's state airline. Iraqi Airways collapsed after the 1991 sanctions, but it resumed limited operations in 2004. Most of the region's large international airports have regular flights to Asian, European, and North American destinations, and increasing numbers of them—in Turkey especially—are flying to Central Asia.

Competing World-Class Airlines.   Petrodollars and aggressive marketing have combined to advance airlines in the Gulf region to world status. Emirates Airlines, inaugurated in Dubai in 1985, now has the largest fleet in the region—173 planes with another 202 reportedly on order in 2012. Qatar Airways began only in 1994 and by 2011 had 113 jets on order to add to the 111 it already operates; not to be outdone, Abu Dhabi started Etihad Airways in 2003 as the UAE national carrier—with a fleet of 67 planes with orders for 205 more placed in 2010. The Trade magazine *Air Transport World* in 2011 awarded Emirates Airlines the title of Airline of the Year. Then, in 2012, for the second year in a row, Qatar Airways was named the World's Best Airline in the Skytrax World Airline Awards, while Etihad the same year was named World's Leading Airline for the third consecutive year by the World Travel Awards.

Water Transportation

The people of the Middle East have long made use of the region's interpenetrating seas, another effect of the influence of land-water relationships on human patterns. Only the heart of the Arabian Peninsula, more than 200 mi/322 km from a seacoast, has been until recently too far from a body of water for easy access. The seas of the region have been sailed for at least five thousand years, and numerous ruins of ports from earlier days are found in the Gulf and eastern Mediterranean. Sailing reached a golden age during the Abbasid Empire, notably during the eighth to twelfth centuries.[15] The basic seagoing craft has long been some version of the ship popularly known as the dhow (from Swahili, *daw*), which is locally called by specific terms designating type of hull—*bum* (boom), *sanbuq, ganja*, and others. As they have been for more than two thousand years, dhows are still equipped with the lateen sail, a triangular fore-and-aft sail hung from a very long yard. This rigging permits the ship to keep very close to the wind. However, more and more of the vessels are equipped with engines, either auxiliary or primary; many no longer have sails.

The Dhows of the Gulf. Following tradition, many dhows still sail around the shores of the Gulf, along the coasts of Oman and Yemen, down the east African coast, or on the age-old routes to the mouths of the Indus, the Malabar Coast, and Sri Lanka. Small modern ships are increasingly replacing the picturesque dhows; nevertheless, the latter serve a unique function and are still to be seen by the score anchored in "the Creek" in Dubai and in other Gulf ports. They are still built in small numbers in the traditional way in Kuwait, Bahrain, most of the coastal towns of the UAE, and Oman.

Despite construction of the Suez Canal in the 1860s, the Middle East did not enter the mainstream of modern shipping until the mid-twentieth century. Turkey was most active in sailing, having regained its maritime lead after its World War I defeat, and as oil production mounted in the Gulf the leading petroleum states entered the tanker market in order to ship their own exports. Iran and Kuwait developed sizable national fleets, and Egypt, Iraq, the UAE, and Saudi Arabia have a modest tonnage in tankers (see Table 7.2). Offering both a neutral flag of convenience and a long shipping tradition, Cyprus ranks first in the Middle East and tenth in the world in registered fleet tonnage, with Iran, Turkey, and Kuwait following in that order.

River Traffic. With the notable exceptions of the Nile, Tigris, and Euphrates, inland waterways—and therefore inland water transportation—are negligible in the region. The Nile was the main way to move people and goods up and down Egypt's linear axis for more than five thousand years. Construction of modern rail lines and highways has scarcely diminished either the number of picturesque but practical *faluqas,* the typical Nile sailboat, or the tonnage they transport, and the river carries a fair amount of barge traffic as well. More than three hundred modern ships can transport thousands of tourist passengers up and down the river daily, enjoying a holiday between Aswan and Luxor or a sojourn on Lake Nasser.

Shallower and more irregular than the Nile, the Tigris and the Euphrates are little used today for navigation since they can accommodate only small boats with very limited draft. Picturesque circular rafts (*balams*), which were waterproofed with bitumen and used to float small loads downstream on the Tigris, have long given way to modern land transportation. By contrast, on the Shatt al-Arab, below the confluence of the Tigris and Euphrates, and on the Karun, which joins the Shatt al-Arab at Khorramshahr, there is normally a fair number of medium-large ships of considerable draft. Basrah, Khorramshahr, and Abadan, all fronting on the Shatt al-Arab, are three of the major river ports, not only of the Gulf but also of the Middle East. Though it was Iraq's only port for decades, Basrah had become inadequate by the 1970s.

Ports

Many modern Middle East coastal cities have been ports for hundreds or even thousands of years—Istanbul (Byzantium or Constantinople), Beirut (Berytus), Jaffa, Alexandria, Aden, Muscat, Basrah, and several others along the Gulf. Some famed in antiquity now lack sufficient harborage or depth for modern shipping, such as Sidon and Tyre; other ports have silted up and now lie well inland, as is true of Miletus, Ephesus, and Ur, for example.

Oil and General Cargo Ports. By virtue of the tonnage represented by the millions of barrels of oil pumped through an export terminal, large oil-shipping ports exceed even the most major dry-cargo ports in tonnage. (An average barrel of petroleum weighs about 300 lb/136 kg, so that only 7.35 bbl weigh 1 mt.) By the early 1980s, petroleum shipments pushed Saudi Arabia to first place and Iran to third place in rankings of export

tonnage among all countries of the world. Distinctions should be made depending on the type of cargo handled, and so the relative ranking of general-cargo ports in the region differs from that of ports that include oil handling. Leading oil-export terminals are Mina al-Ahmadi and Mina Abdullah, Kuwait; Juaymah and Ras Tanura in eastern Saudi Arabia and Yanbu on the Red Sea; Kharg Island (Darius) and Bandar-e Khomeyni, Iran; Musayid (Umm Said), Qatar; Jabal Dhanna, Abu Dhabi; and Mina al-Fahal, Oman. Export terminals in Yemen, Egypt, and Syria handle smaller tonnages. At the Mediterranean end of several pipelines in Turkey is Yumurtalık, near Ceyhan.

Although the container and roll-on/roll-off (Ro-Ro) revolutions in maritime shipping forced older ports to make costly modifications, the advanced technology was accommodated in the planning and construction of the more recent Gulf ports. Also, in the Gulf there was space for the huge storage yards needed for containerization and Ro-Ro operations, whereas such space was at a premium in Istanbul, Beirut, and Alexandria, for example. In addition, several Gulf ports have included dry docks in their port facilities—at Dammam, Bahrain, and Dubai, for example; such repair facilities are also in Jiddah on the Red Sea and Alexandria on the Mediterranean.

By the early 1990s, major modern ports were well distributed among the Middle East states, and in the late 2000s several dry-cargo ports handled well over 5 million tons annually: Shuwaykh, Kuwait; Dubai and Khor Fakkan, UAE (Khor Fakkan is on the Indian Ocean), both important for transshipment; Jiddah, the main Saudi Red Sea port; Alexandria and its auxiliary ports, Dikhaylah and Damietta, and Port Said, Egypt; and Haifa, Israel. (See port symbols on Map 7.2.) Ports that lead in the handling of general cargo include Dammam, the main general-cargo port for the sprawling oil industry and cities of the Eastern Province of Saudi Arabia; Abu Dhabi,

Figure 7.7 Aerial view of burgeoning container port in Dubai, UAE. Goods arrive in Dubai in bulk and are broken down for smaller onward shipments.

UAE; Muscat/Matrah, Oman; Aqabah, Jordan's only port; Ashdod, Israel; Beirut, Lebanon; and Iskanderun in the northeast Mediterranean, Izmir on the Aegean, and Istanbul, Turkey.

Maritime economics and risk insurance have impacted the port geography on the two sides of the Horn of Arabia. As Dubai augmented its role as an entrepôt (Fig. 7.7) and free port in the Gulf, Oman expanded its southern port, Salalah, on the Indian Ocean. Using it saves time and reduces risk, as ships do not have to enter the Gulf (see Chaps. 15, 16, and 17). Piracy in the western Indian Ocean became a serious problem in the 2000s, with vessels ranging from fishing boats to supertankers falling prey to Somalia-based pirates. The greater risks of traversing this area translate into higher insurance fees and long detours, increasing shipping costs (see **www.middleeastpatterns.com**, "Piracy").

TRADE

The external trade of Middle East states has expanded exponentially since the 1960s, particularly under the impetus of petroleum; revenue from its sales created a large market for imports of capital and consumer goods (Table 7.3). Intraregional trade has also expanded greatly; non-oil producers import petroleum from their oil-exporting neighbors, and some exchange food products in return. However, quantitatively, only the oil-short industrialized countries can absorb the enormous exports of the Gulf states, and they turn to their industrialized-country customers for the advanced technology items that constitute the bulk of their nonfood imports (Table 7.4). Thus, intraregional trade is constrained by the fact that neighboring states often produce similar crops, consumer items, or energy products.

TABLE 7.3 Foreign Trade: Exports and Imports (Values and Selected Products)

		1	2	3	4	5	6	7	8	9	10
		TOTAL VALUE		RAW MATERIALS (%)				MANUFACTURED GOODS (%)			
Country and		Millions $US		Agric, Etc.		Fuel/Enr		Total		%Mach/TE	
Year of Data		Exports	Imports	Exp	Imp	Exp	Imp	Exp	Imp	Exp	Imp
Cyprus	2008	1,717.0	10,849.0	30.5	13.8	8.1	10.9	59.4	75.0	27.3	29.6
Egypt	2008	26,224.0	52,752.0	2.9	18.1	39.2	4.8	55.5	74.4	1.7	24.1
Iran	2005–2006	100,571.0	40,969.0	4.1	11.7	86.5	2.7	9.1	84.8	0.7	47.9
Iraq	2008	63,726.0	35,496.0	0.8	31.5	96.8	0.4	2.1	68.1	0.2	30.3
Israel	2008	61,337.0	65,170.0	5.4	7.0	0.4	9.4	58.5	61.4	28.7	31.5
Jordan	2008	7,782.0	16,872.0	14.4	19.3	0.2	16.5	73.5	63.6	10.7	23.0
Kuwait	2007	17,811.0	6,069.0	0.5	17.8	90.6	0.6	8.6	80.6	1.3	39.7
Lebanon[a]	2008	3,478.0	16,137.0	23.7	18.7	0.2	17.7	71.5	62.0	13.9	23.6
Oman	2008	14,503.0	8,814.5	6.2	22.9	80.5	2.8	13.1	72.6	7.7	39.6
Qatar	2008	54,912.0	27,900.0	0.2	12.7	87.1	0.7	12.6	85.1	1.8	46.9
Saudi Arabia	2008	1,175,354.0	431,753.0	1.0	17.0	86.0	0.2	12.8	82.3	1.6	43.6
Syria	2007	11,546.0	14,655.0	16.5	20.1	72.2	3.0	10.5	76.4	0.4	24.1
Turkey	2008	132,002.0	201,961.0	11.1	7.6	2.0	16.6	85.7	72.5	26.6	31.1
UAE	2008	210,000.0	175,486.0	7.3	33.6	64.2	0.9	28.5	65.4	8.8	28.5
Yemen	2008	7,065.9	9,711.0	2.5	37.2	96.5	12.0	0.9	50.7	0.3	20.8
TOTAL/AVG.		808,482.0	587,100.5	8.0	18.9	54.8	8.5	33.2	69.9	8.3	31.5
U.K.	2008	455,596.0	631,804.0	6.3	10.4	8.0	4.6	82.3	82.5	44.4	43.6
Venezuela	2008	83,288.0	45,128.0	1.9	14.0	81.4	2.6	15.8	82.9	2.3	43.1

Columns 3 and 4 include animal and vegetable foods, beverages, and industrial agricultural products (tobacco, cotton, etc.). Columns 5 and 6 (fuels and energy materials) include mineral fuels (petroleum, natural gas, coal, lignite), lubricants, and related products. Manufactured goods include all classes of manufactured products, including machinery. "% Mach/TE" indicates the percentage of machinery and transportation equipment included in the percentage total of manufactures. [a]Data for Lebanon in Columns 5 and 6 include minerals. Spread of data over several years makes comparisons difficult and risky. (*Source: Britannica World Data 2011* [Columns 1 and 2] and *BWD 2007* [Columns 3–10] [used with permission])

Intraregional Trade. Most of the states in the region would not include even one other Middle East country as one of their three leading customers according to percentage of value of commodities traded. But four of Lebanon's top five customers in 2011 were Middle East states, as were three of Jordan's top five. Isolated as it has been from its neighbors, Israel had no overt trade with its neighbors until the 1978 Camp David accords, which provided that Israel could purchase petroleum from Egypt. That arrangement languished, but other Israel-Egypt trade increased gradually after the peace treaty between the two countries took effect. In the late 2000s, Egypt began sizable sales of natural gas to Israel, but these have fallen victim

to pipeline sabotage in the Sinai and political factors (see Chap. 19).[16]

It should be noted that even though they are relatively limited, exports from the non-oil states to their neighbors normally form a considerable percentage of their total exports. For example, Jordan may produce only modest amounts of vegetables, pharmaceuticals, and clothing, but its export markets are significant. Since the 1994 Israel-Jordan peace accord, Israel has been among those markets under reciprocal arrangements. Iraq was particularly important in Jordan's foreign trade, since it was Jordan's main customer before August 1990 (and is again in the 2010s) and its main oil supplier after 1990 until the 2003 conflict. The 1990–1991

TABLE 7.4 Directions of Foreign Trade (Export and Import Percentages)

		1	2	3	4	5		6	7	8	9	10
Country and			*Percentage of Exports to*					*Percentage of Imports from*				
Year of Data		EU	USA	Japan	China	Other		EU	USA	Japan	China	Other
Bahrain	2007	—	8.1	—	—	91.8		10.9	2.0	2.0	2.0	74.0
Cyprus	2006	64.3	—	—	—	19.9		44.2	—	—	—	8.0
Egypt	2008	21.7	4.9	—	—	37.8		16.2	10.8	—	8.4	5.9
Iran	2005–2009[a]	—	—	14.0	15.0	21.0		9.0	—	—	13.0	26.0
Iraq	2006	10.0	36.0	—	—	7.0		—	11.0	—	6.0	52.0
Israel	2008	10.8	32.6	—	6.8	3.8		18.6	12.3	—	6.5	17.0
Jordan	2008	—	13.5	—	—	53.2		6.0	4.6	—	10.4	25.9
Kuwait	2007	—	9.0	19.0	—	36.0		8.0	12.0	9.0	8.0	7.0
Lebanon	2008	9.5	—	—	—	26.0		21.6	11.5	—	8.6	4.3
Oman	2008	—	—	10.6	29.3	27.3		—	5.7	15.6	4.6	31.7
Qatar	2008	—	—	34.3	—	42.4		15.8	9.0	9.6	7.2	6.6
S. Arabia	2008	—	16.3	15.2	8.9	15.9		7.4	13.7	8.2	11.0	4.5
Syria	2007	35.2	—	—	—	21.4		27.5	—	—	8.0	5.7
Turkey	2008	31.8	—	—	—	6.0		34.8	5.9	—	7.8	—
UAE	2008	—	—	27.0	—	36.0		6.0	9.0	6.0	13.0	12.0
Yemen	2008	—	—	—	22.5	47.6		—	—	—	7.0	45.9

EU = member states of the European Union. USA = United States. Other = mainly neighboring Middle East states, but also India, Taiwan, and Vietnam. Many of the figures are estimates based on data from trading partners. (*Source: Britannica World Data 2012* [used with permission])

Gulf crisis adversely affected Jordan's trade with Iraq and Saudi Arabia, and Jordan later worked eagerly to restore trade relations with both. Natural gas exports by Egypt, Saudi Arabia, Qatar, and Iran will reorient some trade patterns over time. Many of the exports from Lebanon, Bahrain, and the UAE are, in fact, reexports. Such trade has particularly made Dubai and Sharjah lively commercial centers. Turkish exporters have found considerable success in post-2003 Iraq, especially (and somewhat ironically) in Kurdistan.

Exports. Not surprisingly, petroleum is by far the dominant feature of Middle East trade. It is the main export of the area to the rest of the world; indeed, petroleum and petroleum products constitute at least 85 percent of the primary exports of all the major oil producers and normally 90–95 percent of the exports of Iraq, Kuwait, Yemen, and the UAE. Hydrocarbons even constitute more than one-third of the exports of Egypt and

more than two-thirds of those of Syria (see Table 7.3).

Among the top two or three non-oil exports are, by percentage, fruits, vegetables, and nuts (Cyprus, Turkey, Lebanon, Iran, Jordan, Syria, Palestine), chemicals and fertilizers (Israel, Saudi Arabia, Iran, Qatar, Turkey, Jordan, Lebanon), textiles (Turkey, Syria, Egypt), and clothing (Cyprus, Turkey, Jordan, Israel). A few of the region's specialty exports include aluminum (Bahrain, UAE), footwear (Cyprus), and phosphates (Jordan, Israel, Syria, Egypt, Iraq). A unique export from the region is cut and rough diamonds from Israel, with the gems forming 12 percent of the state's exports in 2011, second to burgeoning software sales. Armaments from Israel are a large but not completely known percentage of its exports—another unusual export item from the regional perspective.[17]

Imports. As they are around the world, oil and petroleum products are high on the import lists of the region's non-oil states (see Table 7.3). They constitute about a sixth of Turkey's and Jordan's imports but only a tenth of Israel's. Although crude petroleum, transported through a direct underwater pipeline from Saudi Arabia, accounts for more than 37 percent of Bahrain's imports, the crude is refined in the island's Sitra refinery and then reexported.

Food ranks among the three leading imports into virtually all Middle East countries, with the notable exception of Turkey. Of Egypt's imports, 10 percent are foodstuffs, a major shift from the early 1960s. Again with the exception of Turkey, Israel's food-import percentage is the lowest in the region. Excluding food, the four leading imports by percentage are usually machinery, motor vehicles, chemicals, and iron and steel. Until the worst years of Lebanon's civil war, that country's second-leading import was gold bullion. In Israel, a leading import (14 percent by value) is cut and rough diamonds; Israel is no longer a major center for cutting and polishing diamonds, having lost out to lower-cost locales like India, but it remains a major participant in all stages (except mining) of the global diamond trade.

NOTES

1. The material covered in this chapter has been the subject of scores of studies since the late 1960s. For a historical perspective, see Issawi 1982. The latest data on production, transportation, and trade are in the US Department of State's annual *Country Commercial Guides;* the Encyclopaedia Britannica's yearbook, *Britannica World Data;* Central Intelligence Agency, *World Factbook;* US Department of Energy, Energy Information Administration, *Country Analysis Briefs; Middle East and North Africa;* UN annuals; *Middle East Economic Digest;* and *Middle East Economic Survey.*

2. See Owen 1999 and Shafik 1999, both found in M. Hudson 1999. Much of the following section is based on these two studies.

3. For example, the US–Saudi Arabian Joint Commission on Economic Cooperation brought several hundred American specialists from US government agencies and private institutions to work on more than forty projects in the kingdom from the mid-1970s to the mid-1990s, with Saudi Arabia paying all the expenses.

4. As author Cummings can personally affirm.

5. See, for example, International Federation for Human Rights 2003 and Sasser 2004.

6. Shafik 1999.

7. Lebanon is by far the region's biggest beneficiary of remittances, which come from Lebanese all over the world, not just in the Middle East. In 2010, it received $7.6 billion in inflows, equivalent to almost 20 percent of GDP.

8. World Bank, *World Development Indicators Database,* Apr. 2009.

9. Some Yemeni workers are present illegally in Saudi Arabia, so this official figure for remittances may not be representative of the actual situation.

10. Among the member countries of the project are Bahrain, Egypt, Palestine, Israel, Turkey, Iran, and Cyrus.

11. The Syrian civil war has sharply reduced transit traffic through that country; many Turkish truckers have resumed traveling through Iraq despite the fact that this is still occasionally dangerous.

12. See www.english.globalarabnetwork.com, Jan. 3, 2010.

13. Discussions of a joint Saudi Arabian–Turkish project to rebuild the line were announced in 2009 (see Chap. 15).

14. See Airport Operators Council International periodic reports, www.airports.org/; and UN International Civil Aviation Organization annual reports, www.icao.int/. These sources are also used in the following analysis.

15. See Hourani 1963.

16. It is difficult to estimate the extent of Israeli trade with the Palestinian Territories. Palestinian statistics indicate that in the early 2010s, more than 80 percent of imports came from Israel, but this obviously includes goods in transit through Israel. Israel and the Palestinian Territories form a customs union.

17. In 2010, Israeli military exports amounted to $7.2 billion and consisted of some 80 to 85 percent of the country's armaments industry's output. *UPI,* June 17, 2011.

8

The Earth and the State
Geopolitics

KEY POINTS: Political-geographical (geopolitical) patterns of crucial importance in analysis of tricontinental hub polities. Must also consider aspects of the Broader Middle East. Early imperial political systems sophisticated and well developed. Evolution of sixteen current states as independent units a highly varied process and mainly influenced by post–World War I territorial settlements. Colonial subterfuge in Arab Revolt, Sykes-Picot Agreement, and Balfour Declaration. Promises to Arabs slighted but others to Zionists observed. Political-geographical analyses of regional polities include consideration of state location, size, shape, population, and institutions. Raison d'être also of basic significance. Major regional linkages include OIC, Arab League, OPEC, GCC, others. Efforts at union have failed (e.g., UAR), as have most alliances (Baghdad Pact, CENTO). Regional tensions and conflicts have varied bases. Long-running boundary disputes have been settled. Access to water supplies a major political problem (hydropolitics), certain to become more serious (Euphrates, Jordan, Nile). Aspects of recent Arab Spring (Arab Reawakening) in several countries of global interest and concern, especially Syrian civil war, unrest in Egypt and Yemen.

The Middle East has served as a tricontinental hub for millennia. Peoples, armies, merchants, and ideas have flowed to, from, and across the region. Political ideology and processes in the flow were sometimes adapted and sometimes rejected but often influenced the internal evolution of these sixteen states. Externally, the spatial patterns discussed in the five previous chapters profoundly influenced the relationships established among the states, with neighboring areas, and with more distant lands. The interaction between these patterns and political behavior—geopolitics—is the theme of this chapter.

In this book, geopolitics concerns the interface between geographical area and political phenomena. Geopolitics is conceptually equivalent to political geography; the terms will be used interchangeably. This chapter focuses on the state as a political-geographic phenomenon. It will examine a number of topics of a more general global, regional, and/or historical nature after first putting the region into the broader context of the Heartland of the Tricontinental Hub discussed in Chapter 1, providing a brief statistical sketch of the countries immediately surrounding our sixteen-nation core (Map 8.1; see also

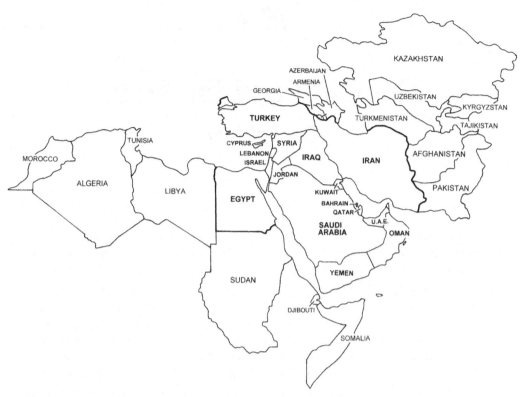

Map 8.1 The core Middle East, shown inside heavy borders, with related states of North Africa, virtually all Arab and Muslim; adjacent republics of the Trans-Caucasus, none Arab and only one Muslim; the five "stans" of Central Asia, none Arab but all Muslim; plus Afghanistan and Pakistan, both Muslim. The entire area is sometimes referred to as the "Broader Middle East," although that term may apply only to the core Middle East and North Africa.

Tables 8.1 and 8.2). Chapter 9 will treat some of the major events and issues that have arisen in our core region during the past several decades but have then developed into matters of global concern.

HUB AND HEARTLAND

Early geopolitical concepts of "Heartland" and "World-Island" appeared in Sir Halford J. Mackinder's paper of 1904[1] with his conceptual modifications in 1919 and 1943. Mackinder defined the Heartland bastion basically as Siberia, which he conceived of as ringed by an Inner Crescent extending from northwestern Europe through southern Asia to north-

eastern Asia. Beyond the Inner Crescent, he viewed an Outer Crescent—the Americas, southern Africa, and Australia. He labeled tricontinental Europe, Asia, and Africa the "World-Island" and proposed in 1919 that:

Who rules East Europe commands the Heartland;
Who rules the Heartland commands the World-Island;
Who rules the World-Island commands the World.

Although the Mackinder dictum has received its just share of criticism, the idea of a World-Island emphasizes the links among the three "inner continents." Emphasizing those links, it coincidentally spotlights the pivotal location of the Middle East in the World-Island.

Mackinder's Heartland concept was challenged by Professor Nicholas John Spykman during World War II. To Spykman, controlling the Heartland is only a strong defensive position; it is control of western and southern Europe, the Middle East, southern and southeastern Asia, China, and Japan that is crucial. For Spykman, thus, it was Mackinder's Inner Crescent that was key, calling it "Rimland." He further theorized that, on the one hand, domination of both the Heartland and the Rimland by one superpower or power group would create an unmatched power base. On the other hand, control of the Rimland, or most of it, by one power would offset domination of the Heartland by another. Viewed from such global geopolitical perspectives, the Middle East's location confers enormous strategic importance. Its geostrategic value thus enhances its oil wealth, human resources, and commercial role.

In World War I, Ottomans, Germans, Russians, British, French, and even Greeks and Italians contended for Middle East territory. The British and French emerged dominant and became the main imperialist powers in the region between the wars. France controlled Syria and Lebanon with a foothold on the Horn of Africa; Britain had control over not only the three mandates of Palestine, Transjordan, and (until 1932) Iraq but also Cyprus, the Sudan, the Gulf shaykhdoms, and Aden with its hinterland (and bases as well in Egypt).

In World War II, Germany sought but ultimately failed to gain the Suez Canal and other regional lines of communications on the route to Middle East oil fields. Control of the region by the Western allies was also vital to keep supplies of war matériel moving into the Soviet Union in support of its efforts to hold down the eastern front.

THE STATE IN THE MIDDLE EAST

A Recent Political Mosaic

Of our core Middle East states, only seven were independent before 1943—Egypt, Turkey, Iraq, Iran, Saudi Arabia, Oman, and Yemen—and Britain still limited the sovereignty of Oman, Iraq, and even Egypt. The area has, therefore, ancient cultures in new states—old wine in new bottles.

Much of the region's recent history reflects the political inexperience and insecurity of newly independent states. Although Kuwait gained its independence in 1961, middle and lower Gulf states achieved sovereignty only in 1971 after decades under British "protection." Following a period of uncertainty, the crown colony of Aden and the adjoining hinterland protectorates merged into an independent entity, the People's Democratic Republic of Yemen (PDRY), in 1967; a united Yemen, with the PDRY merging with the Yemen Arab Republic (YAR), materialized in 1990. Cyprus, another former British Crown colony, gained independence in 1960, only to face invasion by Turkey in 1974 and the creation of a de facto Turkish republic in the north of the island. The four Levant states achieved independence from mandate status between 1943 and 1948; the fifth mandate (Iraq) had already realized nominal sovereignty in 1932. Saudi Arabia did not become a unified kingdom with that name until 1932, and while Egypt ended formal British protectorate status in 1922, colonial vestiges remained until 1956. Both Turkey and Iran are centuries-old sovereign countries; they declared themselves republics, following long histories of monarchical rule, only in 1923 and 1979, respectively (Iran endured partial occupation by Britain and the Soviet Union during World War II). Egypt, Iraq, and North Yemen (YAR) also replaced monarchies with republics between the early 1950s and early 1960s.

Thus, the political character of the Middle East is a complex of ambiguities, contradictions, and efforts at differentiation. Muslim

TABLE 8.1 Peripheral States: Selected Representative Data

Country	1 Area in Sq. Miles	2 Pop. in 1,000s	3 Pop. per Sq. Mile	4 Literacy (Latest)	5 GNP/Cap (2010)	6 Persons Per Veh.	7 Oil Resrvs (1,000s Bbl)	8 Oil Prod. Bpd, 2010
Algeria	919,595	36,649	39.9	76.3	4,460	18	12,200,000	1,250,000
Libya	679,362	6,423	9.9	88.1	12,020	5	47,100,000	1,550,000
Morocco	268,117	32,476	121.1	56.0	2,850	20	684	200
Sudan	967,499	36,787	51.6	69.3	1,270	778	5,000,000	475,000
Tunisia	63,170	10,594	177.6	77.6	4,070	15	425,000	77,700
Sub-Total	*2,897,743*	*122,929*	—	—	—	—	*64,725,684*	*3,352,900*
Armenia	11,484	3,100	270.0	99.5	5,450	—	—	—
Azerbaijan	33,409	9,150	273.9	99.4	5,180	12	7,000,000	985,000
Georgia	27,086	4,474	202.7	100.0	2,700	10	35,000	1,000
Sub-Total	*71,979*	*16,724*	—	—	—	—	*7,035,000*	*986,000*
Kazakhstan	1,052,090	16,560	15.7	99.7	7,440	8	30,000,000	1,590,000
Kyrgyzstan	77,182	5,168	66.9	100.0	880	—	40,000	2,000
Tajikistan	55,300	7,681	138.9	99.7	780	—	12,000	—
Turkmenistan	188,500	4,998	26.4	99.5	3,700	22	600,000	216,000
Uzbekistan	172,700	28,129	164.0	99.2	1,280	—	594,000	87,000
Sub-Total	*1,545,772*	*62,536*	—	—	—	—	*31,246,000*	*1,895,000*
Afghanistan	249,347	28,266	113.4	28.1	319	88	—	—
Pakistan	307,374	187,343	550.2	60.0	1,050	118	280,647	65,500
Sub-Total	*559,446*	*213,785*	—	—	—	—	*280,647*	*65,500*
TOTALS/AVG.	5,074,940	415,974	—	—	—	—	102,837,331	6,299,400

Population in Column 2 is estimate for midyear 2011. Literacy in Column 4 is in percentage over age fifteen and is latest available, although data vary from 2005 to 2010. Oil reserves as of 2013. BPD in Column 8 = production in average number of barrels per day. Sudan includes South Sudan. (*Sources:* Data in Columns 1–6 from *Britannica World Data 2011* [used with permission]; data in Columns 7 and 8 from *Oil and Gas Journal,* Dec. 3, 2012)

and especially Arab states have made conceptual efforts toward solidarity, but practical obstacles repeatedly intervene. Because of varied imperial or colonial influences, most have nonindigenous, artificial structures that did not evolve out of their own socioeconomic-political context or culture.[2] Most acquired their institutions and political-geographical boundaries from British-French delineations. Only a handful of initial alignments in the entire region were negotiated entirely by indigenous states on both sides of the border. Boundaries set by outsiders often ignored local, tribal, or traditional considerations, creating resentment against imperialist dictates. Iraqi bitterness over Britain's defining the boundary between it and the then British protectorate of Kuwait repeatedly manifested itself—culminating in the invasion of Kuwait in 1990. But in other cases, imposition of borders by outside powers settled territorial disputes of long standing.

World War I Territorial Agreements

Among several such accords, three contradictory agreements from World War I and others in its aftermath profoundly influenced future developments, contemporary political-geographical boundaries and current patterns, crises, and conflicts in the Middle East.

Britain concluded two conflicting pacts in 1915 and 1916 disposing of Ottoman territories after the war (Fig. 8.1). The 1915 accord was an exchange of official correspondence between Sir Henry McMahon, British high commissioner in Cairo, and Sharif Husayn of

TABLE 8.2 Peripheral States: Land Use and Irrigated Land

Country	1 Arable & Perm Crops	2 Area Under Irrigation	3 % of Crops Irrigated	4 Forests	5 2007 Percentage of Area Under: Mdw & Past	6 Agr & PC	7 Other
Algeria	8,435	570	6.8	0.6	13.8	17.3	82.0
Libya	2,050	470	22.9	0.1	7.7	8.8	91.0
Morocco	9,055	1,458	16.1	11.5	47.1	67.3	21.2
Sudan	20,391	1,863	9.1	29.5	49.0	57.5	13.0
Tunisia	4,936	445	9.0	6.0	31.2	63.0	30.0
Sub-Total	*44,867*	*4,806*	—	—	—	—	—
Armenia	511	274	53.6	9.3	43.6	61.6	29.0
Azerbaijan	2,101	1,433	68.2	11.3	32.1	57.6	31.1
Georgia	568	433	76.2	39.5	27.9	36.1	24.4
Sub-Total	*3,180*	*2,140*	—	—	—	—	—
Kazakhstan	23,480	3,556	15.1	1.2	68.5	77.2	21.5
Kyrgyzstan	1,351	1,018	75.4	4.9	48.3	55.3	39.8
Tajikistan	875	719	82.2	2.9	27.7	33.9	63.1
Turkmenistan	1,910	1,800	94.2	8.8	65.3	69.4	21.8
Uzbekistan	4,651	4,223	90.8	7.7	51.7	62.6	29.6
Sub-Total	*32,267*	*11,316*	—	—	—	—	—
Afghanistan	7,910	3,199	40.4	2.1	46.0	58.1	39.8
Pakistan	21,280	20,200	94.9	2.2	6.5	34.0	63.7
Sub-Total	*29,190*	*22,399*	—	—	—	—	—
TOTALS	109,504	40,661	—	—	—	—	—

Data in Columns 1 and 2 are in thousands of hectares (2009). Macro land-use patterns tend to change slowly. Column 1 is area in cultivated crops (e.g., grains and cotton) and permanent crops (e.g., olives and vineyards). Columns 4–7 calculated from FAO data. Column 5 is Meadow and Pasture. Column 6 is equivalent to Column 1, Agriculture and Permanent Crops. Data for Sudan are combined figures for both Sudans, before the South split as independent in 2011. (*Source:* UN Food and Agriculture Org., www.fao.org/corp/statistics)

Mecca, Ottoman governor of the Hijaz. They agreed that the sharif's Arab followers would revolt against the Turks in Arabia and Syria and that Britain, in return, would support the creation of an independent Arab state in former Ottoman lands after the war. Despite this pledge of independence for most of the Fertile Crescent, Britain then proceeded to sign the secret Sykes-Picot Agreement with France with czarist Russia's knowledge and assent in May 1916, by which this region was to be divided between British and French control and influence (Map 8.2).[3] Basically, the same territory was to be treated in two vastly different ways.

The third contradiction was incorporated into the Balfour Declaration of November 1917, in which Britain unilaterally promised support for a Jewish homeland in Palestine (see "The Arab-Israeli Problem" in Chap. 9). Thus, an undefined part of the Fertile Crescent was to be disposed of in a way conflicting with both previous agreements.

The Arab Revolt

In accordance with the Husayn-McMahon correspondence, and with British support, the Arab Revolt against the Ottomans began in June 1916. Coordinating the Arab attacks with British operations in Palestine was the legendary Colonel T. E. Lawrence, the storied "Lawrence of Arabia" who chronicled the fighting from the Hijaz to Damascus in *Seven*

Figure 8.1 Topkapı Saray, palace complex of the Ottoman sultans and heart of the Ottoman Empire (Map 8.3) for more than 550 years. The sultan's private quarters were to the right, harem in the center of the figure, and huge kitchens in the lower wing. The complex is now a world-class museum, with unique collections of porcelain, timepieces, jewels, and tiles.

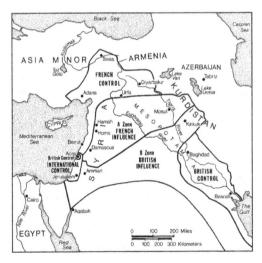

Map 8.2 Sykes-Picot Agreement territorial allotments that, although later disavowed, became the basis for the post–World War I mandate system.

Pillars of Wisdom.[4] The principal Arab leader in the field was Amir Faysal, third son of Sharif Husayn.

The Arabs, having met their obligations under the Husayn-McMahon letters, were dismayed to learn of the Sykes-Picot Agreement and the Balfour Declaration, both of which contradicted Britain's promises to Arab leaders. They had been further encouraged by US president Woodrow Wilson's Fourteen Points, the twelfth of which supported self-determination for peoples formerly under Ottoman control. The Arabs came to mistrust Britain, France, and, later, the United States after the Allies reneged on promises to them. In contrast, Jewish groups gained support for their proposed homeland in the Middle East.

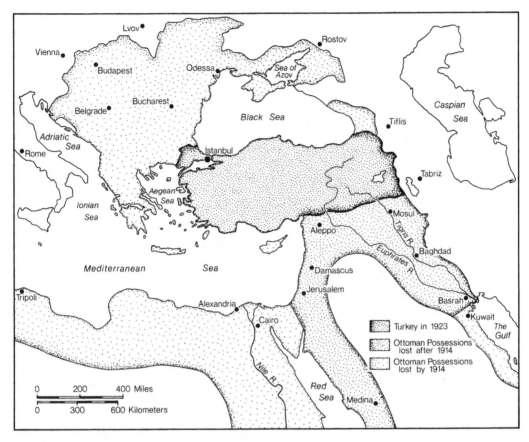

Map 8.3 Ottoman Empire at its maximum extent, showing territorial losses by 1914 and after World War I. Losses after 1914 are of special interest in this book.

PEACE TREATIES AND MANDATES

In the several postwar peace conferences, Britain and France dominated the decisions on the disposal of the erstwhile Ottoman territories (Map 8.3).[5] Unable to reconcile the overlapping promises they had made in 1915–1917, the two powers held generally to the Sykes-Picot Agreement and specifically to the Balfour Declaration. For Britain, the aim above all was as it long had been: protect the route to India;[6] for France, there was the opportunity to solidify its centuries of connections to the Levant; for both, there was the promise of economic gain from control over the region's already known endowment of increasingly vital petro-resources. The United

States did insist on an official inquiry into Arab opinion, and the King-Crane Commission went to the Levant in 1919. But the US efforts were undermined by its two wartime allies, and its report—citing the risks of French control in Syria and Zionist goals in Palestine—was disregarded; it was not even published for more than three years.[7]

Middle East mandates under the new League of Nations took shape at the San Remo Conference in April 1920.[8] Territorially, the outlines of the Sykes-Picot Agreement (see Map 8.2) were followed. Historical Greater Syria was divided so that the north (future Syria and Lebanon) passed to France and the south (future Palestine and Jordan) to Britain—which also received the mandate for Mesopotamia (Iraq). Other mandates covered African and western Pacific territories of defeated Germany.

The mandates were to be temporary, emphasizing the importance of the principles of self-determination and calling for early independence for the mandated areas. Uniquely, the provisions for the Palestine mandate were incompatible with the stated purposes of the overall mandate system. It included the essential points of the Balfour Declaration, supported a Jewish homeland in Palestine (a victory for the Zionists), and passed over the goal of self-determination by the majority of the population—the 90 percent who were indigenous Palestinian Arabs.

Following complex territorial trades and further divisions of the areas in question, the mandates became official and de jure in 1923. By that time, Transjordan had been excluded from the Palestine mandate, and Greater Lebanon ("Grand Liban"—see Chaps. 10 and 11 for details and consequences) had been constituted as a separate French mandate.

PRESENT BASIC PATTERNS

The State and Its Location

In political geography, a state's location is the most important single factor in its evolution. Other fundamental state geopolitical factors considered below include population and its composition, state institutions, and raison d'être.

Whether the location is a matter of latitude, coastal versus landlocked, island versus mainland, bordering on few or many neighbors, or lying astride a mountain range as opposed to being in an intermontane basin, each aspect influences the state's geopolitical development. Lebanon's à cheval position (lit., "on horseback") astride a linear mountain range, for example, imposes the challenge of how to unite people and link communications on opposite sides of the mountains. Egypt's extension up the Nile Valley to just beyond the first

cataract, and its union of the valley and the delta, is a classic case of a riverine state maintaining linear unity, although the entire Nile Basin has never been united. Iraq, as modern heir to the Tigris-Euphrates Basin, is another classic example of a riverine state. Turkey and Iran illustrate mountain bastions holding long-lasting, independent polities.

Every Middle East state possesses some seacoast, although only Oman, the UAE, and Yemen directly face open ocean (the Indian Ocean). Deep maritime indentations facilitate access, and most states are well endowed with coastlines. Jordan and Iraq are exceptions: Jordan has only 16 mi/26 km on the Red Sea for its Aqabah port; Iraq—with a narrow 36-mi/58-km opening at the marshy head of the Gulf—lacks adequate natural port facilities. Critical during the Iran-Iraq War, Iraq cited the problem in its several attempts to seize part or all of Kuwait. Saudi Arabia, Israel, Egypt, and Iran have two-sea locations (Iran also fronts the inland Caspian Sea for 460 mi/740 km). Turkey has by far the longest seacoast in the region, opening onto the Mediterranean, Aegean, Marmara, and Black Seas.

In the region, every state's location has a strategic aspect. Bahrain's situation midway in the Gulf has historically been an asset; it still affords the advantages of an entrepôt and meeting point—now enhanced by the causeway link to the mainland. Similarly, the island of Cyprus benefits from its situation—it can serve as neutral ground for Arabs and Israelis, Middle Easterners and Europeans, Lebanese factions during 1975–1991, and, in better times, Greeks and Turks. On land, Turkey's "bridge" location has brought advantages and disadvantages from Hittite times to the present. Syria's central location has provided commercial advantages, reduced lately by tensions along all its borders.

The State and Its Population

Both demographically and geopolitically, a state's population is significant in terms of number, distribution, density, and composition (see Maps 4.1 and 4.2; Tables 4.1 and 4.3). Each major ethnic group has strong sentiments of nationalism.

Every Middle East state has minorities, and some countries have as many as ten or twelve sizable ethnic groups. A minority's geopolitical significance increases with the extent of its antinational sentiment or separatism. Militant minorities in Lebanon and Cyprus have fractured the basic integrity of those states. Israel considers its Arab minority, a nine-to-one majority in 1920, a threat. In Iraq, Turkey, and Iran, the central governments have periodically faced rebellions by sizable Kurdish minorities. Others have experienced ethnic conflict—Egypt with Copts, Saudi Arabia with Shii (some of whom are Iranian descended), and Iran with Azeris, Arabs, Baluch, and a dozen other groups.

The State and Its Institutions

Nine Middle East states are republics, six are monarchies, and one—the UAE—is a unique hybrid. Most of the polities entered the second half of the twentieth century as traditional societies and monarchies. However, those societies faced technological, economic, and political influences arising after World War II. Egypt, Iraq, and Yemen opted for modernization (theoretically) and republican structures. The Iranian monarchy, by contrast, was overthrown in a reaction against modernization and for the restoration of religious traditionalism.

Leftist pressures have declined since the 1970s, when *anciens régimes* came under internal and external revolutionary pressures; since the 1990s, existing governments have faced mounting threats from extreme religious fundamentalist movements. Egypt fought back—successfully at first, but too violently, according to many observers. In the end, with the Arab Spring and its aftermath, Egypt saw the electoral triumph of Islamist parties, and extreme Sunni religious elements became increasingly prominent in the Syrian insurgency. Turkey both resisted and accommodated its Islamists with apparent success, while Oman adapted through incremental change and Jordan attempted to follow the same course. The Saudis have faced the dilemma of simultaneous extremist fundamentalist attacks and liberal pressures—along with external coercion—and have responded with small but often significant changes. Individual rulers of Kuwait, Bahrain, Qatar, and the constituents of the UAE have practiced economic liberalism while maintaining much political traditionalism. Popular impatience with the slow pace of reform provoked widespread resistance to the Bahraini and Kuwait regimes in the wake of the Arab Spring.

After 9/11, international attention focused on the region, with the Bush administration claiming that increased democracy would both promote political stability in the Middle East and combat terrorism worldwide. But citizen participation levels in the region's republics were highly variable, with democratic processes observed in Israel, Cyprus, and Turkey (and in Jordan to a lesser extent), excluding certain minorities as well as the Israeli-occupied territories. These were the only states that conduct open elections with freedom for most opposition parties.

Lebanon's basically sound electoral system had long been marred by Syrian influence. Party activities were limited in other republics so that elections more often than not lacked legitimacy. Egypt had a history of political restrictions, but in the 2000s the role of the fairly independent judiciary in monitoring elections increased, and oppositionists gained. Yemeni elections had seemed to become successively more open, according to international observers of the presidential elections of 1999 and 2006 and the parliamentary voting of 2003. But then the legislative poll scheduled for 2009 was abruptly postponed, to the dismay of the US State

Department. Iraq, of course, held a widely publicized series of elections beginning in January 2005 (see Chap. 14 for details). Iran had held elections with relatively open voting since 1979, but candidates were prescreened for their Islamic reliability by a panel of conservative clerics. As opposition to the authoritarian clerical rule mounted in Iran, the Council of Guardians nullified the eligibility of more than two thousand reformist candidates for parliament in both the 2004 and the 2008 elections. The 2009 presidential election was seriously compromised, with rioters protesting the results in many cities, and, in consequence, there was a clear loss in the regime's legitimacy.

Among the monarchies, Jordan had held several parliamentary elections under its 1952 constitution.[9] But the legislature elected in 2007 was dismissed by King Abdallah in 2009, and the elections held in 2010 were boycotted by the opposition. Gulf monarchies had slowly relaxed the rigidity of their governance of four and five decades ago, noting warning signs of dethronements in Egypt and Iraq in the 1950s and in Yemen in 1962. Kuwait and Bahrain theoretically became constitutional states and elected parliaments in 1963 and 1973, respectively. Kuwait held regular elections for its National Assembly;[10] that of 2009 was pronounced generally free and fair, and women had the vote beginning in 2005. The amir of Bahrain suppressed the parliament in 1975, but the new ruler, who was elevated to king, allowed a resumption of parliamentary elections in 2002, the first in nearly three decades. Another round was held in 2006, with one woman among the successful candidates, and in the 2010 polling Shii oppositionists made slight gains.

No national elections have ever been conducted in Saudi Arabia, although one-half of the municipal council members were chosen in stages in early 2005 by an all-male electorate; the reprise scheduled for 2009 was postponed to allow for settling the issue of

female suffrage. Qatar held a third round of municipal elections in 2007, with women voting under the 2004 constitution, but those for the Consultative Council were again postponed in 2010. Oman's sultan declared universal suffrage for the 2003 elections to that country's Consultative Council; a second election was held in 2007. In the UAE, a limited electoral college, including women, chose half the members of the Federal National Council in 2006: the government promised to expand the electorate considerably for future elections.

The Palestinian Authority (PA) conducted elections for president and assembly, the latest in December 2004; when the Islamist bloc led by Hamas won a plurality, the Bush administration's professed enthusiasm for free elections in the region faded noticeably. Elections scheduled for January 2010 were postponed indefinitely because of the split between the West Bank and Gaza.

On the eve of the onset of the Arab Spring in December 2010, electoral change was under way in most regional states, although it would be clearly seen in the new decade that the pace to that point had been too slow to satisfy the desires of people in country after country (see discussion below in this chapter, "Arab Spring—Arab Awakening").

Raison d'Être

The state idea, or its raison d'être (reason for being), is its basic centripetal force—the unique, distinctive idea seen in the emergence of a particular piece of territory and segment of humanity in a specific unit. As developed by Richard Hartshorne,[11] the raison d'être reflects the dominance of unifying factors over divisive factors—of centripetal over centrifugal forces. The impact of an abstract idea on state evolution was further examined by Stephen B. Jones,[12] who traced the motivating political idea through four subsequent links: decision, movement, field, and political area. Both the raison d'être and the links in Jones's unified-field idea aid us in understanding Middle East state patterns.

Some regional states were created by outside powers in contradiction to British assurances and to pre-1919 Arab expectations. Their evolutions have been hampered by the lack of an indigenous initial idea or a consensus regarding their raison d'être. As defined by international treaties, the mandates of Iraq, Lebanon, Palestine, Syria, and Transjordan all had artificial boundaries, and after 1920 many among their populations were frustrated by developments. Eventual independence did not bring with it consensus on a state idea.

Historically independent areas, in contrast, had a traditional raison d'être that could be adapted and followed. Turkey, under Kemal Atatürk, was clearly motivated by "Turkey for the Turks, and the Turks for Turkey!" Iran under Reza Shah had centuries of Persian culture as a core state concept. Egypt had an extremely long history as a culture and polity. In the south of the region, although ruled by unenlightened monarchs, Oman and Yemen also had a sense of polity going back centuries. To their north, after 1932, the tribal leader in the Arabian Peninsula, Abd al-Aziz Al Saud (Ibn Saud), developed a raison d'être for Saudi Arabia as a Muslim desert monarchy.

The regional state with the most explicit reason for being is the only settler state, Israel, which extended "a national home for the Jewish people" in the Palestine mandate into an independent Jewish state. By contrast, Cyprus has not found a commonality of purpose and modality between its Greek-Cypriot majority and its Turkish-Cypriot minority. The island now consists of two de facto Cypruses as polities, although the northern Turkish entity has not gained international recognition. The remarkable UAE, a federal republican union of monarchies, would appear to have no real raison d'être; nevertheless, it has so far effectively succeeded as a state.

REGIONAL LINKAGES

Bases for Links

Large and diverse, the Middle East faces several centrifugal forces; however, it also possesses some regional centripetal forces, with Islam being the strongest unifying link. Only Israel and South Cyprus lie outside the Islamic realm (*Dar al-Islam*), with Lebanon divided between Muslims and Christians. In times past, Islam has unified all of the area—and more—in one empire (see Map 3.5). Nevertheless, as in times past, localism, ethnic separatism, nationalism, religious zealotry and militancy, and ambitious local leaders disrupt unity. Turkey and Iran sharply distinguish themselves ethnically and linguistically from other states; these in turn counterbalance regional unity with local concerns. Israel does not participate in regional political institutions—indeed, it excludes itself and is excluded from them. Arab unity often yields to national interests and competition among leaders.

Regional and Subregional Organizations

Regional cooperation persists despite differences. Seven agencies exemplify both the benefits and the obstacles to regional cooperation. Five multilateral development funds represent cooperative efforts.

Agencies

1. Organization of Islamic Cooperation. The organization that embraces the largest number of Middle East states—fourteen of the sixteen, excluding only Israel and Cyprus[13] but including Palestine—is the Organization of Islamic Cooperation (OIC, formerly the Organization of the Islamic Conference), headquartered in Jiddah since 1969. It promotes Islamic solidarity and has fifty-seven members, from Suriname in South America to Brunei on Borneo. It thus embraces all of the

North African and Central Asian countries in our peripheral extension shown in Map 8.1.

2. Arab League. The twelve Arab states (plus Palestine) of the region are the core of the twenty-two members of the League of Arab States, better known as the Arab League. It includes nine additional African states—Mauritania, Morocco, Algeria, Tunisia, Libya, Sudan, Comoros, Somalia, and Djibouti. Six Middle East states founded the league in 1945, locating its headquarters in Cairo. It has never achieved its intended integrative role, but even so it is the most unifying of the organs of which most of the region's countries are members. Frequent contradictory national interests have obstructed league unity, as was apparent during the Gulf crisis in 1990 and during the US-led invasion of Iraq in 2003. The league makes statements on the Arab-Israeli problem and other Arab concerns, but conspicuous differences weaken their impact. However, the group has been more active recently. It suspended Libya from membership in February 2011 and called for NATO action to overthrow the notorious Qadhafi regime, and it sent monitors to Syria in December 2011 after suspending Syria's membership the previous month.

3 and 4. OPEC and OAPEC. Of the organizations dealing with specific aspects of inter-Arab coordination and involving Arab participation in wider groupings, two of the best known are the Organization of Petroleum Exporting Countries (OPEC, of which Iran is also a member) and the Organization of Arab Petroleum Exporting Countries (OAPEC), both discussed in Chapter 6. OPEC plays a particularly important role in the regional economy, although only six Middle East countries are members—Iraq, Iran, Kuwait, Saudi Arabia, Qatar, and the UAE. OAPEC, which also includes Bahrain, Egypt, and Syria, has been less influential.

5. Gulf Cooperation Council. Created in 1981, the Cooperation Council of the Arab States of the Gulf—the Gulf Cooperation Council (GCC)—aims to coordinate economic, cultural, military, and political affairs among its members, Saudi Arabia, Kuwait, Bahrain, Qatar, the UAE, and Oman, with focus on oil policy, development, social problems (including expatriate labor), Gulf trade, resolution of border disputes, and, especially, security. Seeking security for their regimes and preservation of their national sovereignty and territorial integrity, they have cooperated in the antiterrorist efforts of the United States, and four members—Kuwait, Qatar, Bahrain, and Oman—supported US operations against Iraq.

Both the GCC's revolutionary republican neighbors, Iran and Iraq—at war when it was formed—have at times had hegemonic pretensions over the Gulf. Forming a unified front motivated the GCC's creation, and the members maintain a regional military force. Among their economic goals, the members agreed in 2001 to form a customs union and a single market and adopt a common currency in the following decade, but efforts have lagged. Some members have been dissatisfied with the slowness of the internal and external trade negotiations and have proceeded unilaterally with their own arrangements—for example, Bahrain in 2006 and Oman in 2009 entered into free trade agreements (FTAs) with the United States. A planned currency union to be launched in 2010 has had some difficulties; Oman never joined, the UAE held back in 2009, while Kuwait occasionally voiced some hesitation. The smaller GCC members will have to come to terms with the reality of Saudi Arabian dominance if such a union is to be achieved.

In 2012, the members announced their intention to evolve into a confederation, partly as a reaction to the Arab Spring, partly as a further defense against perceived threats from Iran. Jordan and Morocco submitted membership applications in 2011; preliminary discussions on possible membership are also under way between Yemen and the GCC, but Yemen seems to be more enthusiastic about that prospect than are the six GCC members.

6. Economic Cooperation Organization. In 1964, Turkey, Iran, and Pakistan—members of the pre-1979 Central Treaty Organization (CENTO)—formed the Regional Cooperation for Development (RCD) as CENTO's economic arm. Initial financial underwriting came primarily from ambitious and oil-wealthy Iran, and it addressed transportation links as well as tourism, postal services, frontier formalities, and other areas of potential coordination. Its efforts were phased down after the 1979 Iranian Revolution and the dissolution of CENTO, but it was revived in 1985 as the Economic Cooperation Organization (ECO) with expanded goals. In 1992, six new Muslim ex-Soviet republics—Azerbaijan, Kazakhstan, Kyrgyzstan, Tajikistan, Turkmenistan, and Uzbekistan—were admitted, along with Afghanistan; the Turkish Republic of North Cyprus has observer status. Its members have significant natural resources and potential, but have not progressed much toward implementation of a common market among them scheduled for 2015.[14]

7. Greater Arab Free Trade Area. In keeping with the Arab League's aim of promoting economic unity, there have been several attempts to institutionalize this goal; until recently, none has had much success. The Greater Arab Free Trade Area (GAFTA) is the latest and most ambitious—and perhaps is more likely to advance. It began in 1998, but adherence has been gradual, with Algeria, the last of its eighteen members, joining in 2009. Some members have already begun to reduce tariffs on trade among themselves. What makes this attempt at unity different is the concurrent involvement of the European Union with all the members; in one way or another, the EU is negotiating free trade agreements bilaterally with each—through the Euro-Mediterranean Partnership, discussions with the GCC, and separate talks with Iraq and Yemen. Most GAFTA states are anxious to affiliate with the EU—which has promoted a GAFTA-like institution as a highly desirable adjunct.

The EU's long-term goal is a fully operative FTA encompassing all of both Europe and the Middle East by sometime in the 2020s.[15] To promote this goal, the EU funds programs as part of its European Neighborhood Policy under which the countries studied here benefit; for example, for the 2010–2012 period, €5.7 billion ($7.4 billion) was appropriated. The events of the Arab Spring have heightened EU efforts among its southern and eastern neighbors, and it has made an additional €670 million ($866 million) available to support reform efforts.[16]

Multilateral Development Funds

1. Islamic Development Bank. In its origin an offshoot of the OIC, the Islamic Development Bank (IDB) began operations in 1975, providing development finance to OIC members that was Islamically acceptable: in short, free of any taint of *riba*—usury or interest. Fourteen of the countries in this study, plus Palestine, are IDB members; collectively, they have subscribed more than 68 percent of the bank's capital of more than $25 billion. Through 2011, the IDB had extended 7,260 loans amounting to more than $78 billion to its fifty-six member countries. The institutional success of the IDB has contributed to the growth among private-sector institutions of the use of Islamically acceptable financial instruments.

2. Arab Fund for Economic and Social Development. Authorized by the Arab League, the Arab Fund for Economic and Social Development (AFESD) commenced operations in 1974. All twenty-two members of the Arab

League have contributed to the fund's resources; the twelve countries plus Palestine in
this study are the sources of more than 76
percent of the paid-in capital. Through 2011,
the AFESD had committed about $26 billion
in loans and grants to 580 projects in seventeen Arab countries.

3. Arab Monetary Fund.   Also originating
with the Arab League, the Arab Monetary
Fund (AMF) became active in 1978. As with
the AFESD, all twenty-two Arab League members have subscribed to the AMF's capital—
about $2.8 billion at the end of 2011; of this,
more than 73 percent had been subscribed by
the countries in this study. The AMF is a regional version of the International Monetary
Fund and assists members with balance-of-
payments deficits, structural adjustments, and
the reforms needed to offset these problems.
Through 2011, it had extended some $6.6 bil-
lion in 153 loans to fifteen member countries.
The biggest beneficiaries have been Egypt,
Morocco, Iraq, and Yemen.

4. OPEC Fund for International Development.
The OPEC Fund (OFID) was founded in
1976 with capital from the then thirteen
members of OPEC; six are included in this
study, and they have contributed about 66
percent of OFID's paid-in capital. Through
2011, some 3,040 loans and grants to 131 developing countries and numerous official and
private institutions have amounted to $14.2
billion.

*5. International Fund for Agricultural Devel-
opment.*   With much of Africa facing famine,
the UN convened the World Food Conference
in 1973. OPEC spearheaded negotiations with
the Organization of Economic Cooperation
and Development (OECD), leading to the
foundation of the International Fund for
Agricultural Development (IFAD) that began
operations in 1978 dedicated to alleviating
rural poverty. Saudi Arabia has been IFAD's

second-largest subscriber of capital, and
twelve OPEC members have provided 27 percent of the fund's resources. Through 2011,
IFAD had loaned about $12.9 billion for more
than 890 projects in 108 countries.

Most other agencies are economic (many
under the aegis of the Council of Arab Economic Unity) and deal with everything from
olives to tourism, but some agencies are
at the people-to-people level—for example,
Arab historians, jurists, or athletes.

Unions: Attempts and Failures

Despite the continuing influence of Britain
and France and inter-Arab rivalry, Arab states
attempted several subregional political mergers between the 1950s and 1980. Notably, the
United Arab Republic (UAR) joined Syria
and Egypt in 1958, but Syria withdrew in
1961, its elites chafed by Egyptian domination. Yemen nominally federated with the
UAR in 1958 to form the short-lived United
Arab States, but this alliance also collapsed
in 1961.

Jordan and Iraq, ruled at the time by
Hashimite monarch cousins, became the
Arab Federation in 1958 to counterbalance
the UAR, but this soon dissolved after the
overthrow of the Iraqi king the same year.
The new Iraqi leader proposed a union of
Iraq, Syria, and Jordan, but this never materialized. Other efforts at political unity faded
quickly: a resurrection of the United Arab Republic with Egypt, Syria, and Iraq in 1963;
plans for a Federation of Arab Republics with
Egypt, Syria, and Libya in 1971; and a merger
of Egypt and Libya in 1972. Prompted by
Egyptian president Anwar Sadat's dramatic
visit to Jerusalem in 1977 and ensuing
Egyptian-Israeli détente, Syria and Iraq talked
seriously in 1978–1979 about unity, but again
the plans came to naught.

Princely Federations.   Before its "East of
Suez" withdrawal, Britain set up the Federation of Arab Amirates of the South in 1959 in

the Aden Protectorate, which then expanded to became the Federation of South Arabia. It fell to the Marxist People's Democratic Republic of Yemen, which in turn merged with North Yemen in 1990 to form the Republic of Yemen. Despite a bloody but short civil war in 1994, the union survived, although by the early 2010s, it was apparent that southern separatism had regained considerable support (see Chap. 18).

A different type of union took place two decades earlier on the other side of the Arabian Peninsula. In 1968, before Britain's withdrawal from the Gulf, the seven Trucial States proposed to form a Federation of Arab Amirates with Bahrain and Qatar. The latter two eventually opted for separate independence, but the other seven federated in the United Arab Emirates, in which the principalities maintain semisovereignty but voluntarily join in certain common political, economic, cultural, and security structures. The federation—instead of full union—has seen cooperation and stability (see Chap. 17).

The Gulf Cooperation Council (GCC, mentioned earlier) was initiated more than thirty years ago with security its principal motivation. These concerns continue to be paramount, but the six GCC states have added limited economic unification efforts to their agendas. The Greater Arab Free Trade Area (GAFTA, also discussed above) may offer a more practicable way to further Arab unity by forgoing the political aspects and concentrating on the benefits to be gained on the economic side, particularly within the framework of promoting free trade with the EU.

Alliances and the Baghdad Pact

Regional military alliances—sometimes merely placement of military forces under one command—have formed during emergencies. The impetus for such pacts has usually been a crisis between the Arab frontline states and Israel, and temporary alliances preceded the four major Arab-Israeli wars. The 1990–1991 coalition against Iraq, which mixed Arab and non-Arab states, created tensions between participating and rejectionist states. Similar tensions arose over the degree of support or opposition to the US-led invasion of Iraq in 2003. More recently, the civil wars in Libya and Syria have led to de facto alliances of some Arab states with non-Arab powers like NATO in the case of Libya and Turkey in the case of Syria.

The Baghdad Pact, a long-range pact involving the Middle East, originated in 1955, with US and British encouragement, as a cordon sanitaire against Soviet expansionism. Formally termed the Middle East Treaty Organization, it initially included only Turkey and Iraq, but Britain, Pakistan, and Iran later joined. The pact was vigorously opposed by Nasserist Egypt and its allies. Following the monarchy's overthrow in 1958, Iraq withdrew. Renamed the Central Treaty Organization, it was headquartered in Ankara for two decades until it disintegrated in 1979, when revolutionary Iran, and then Pakistan, withdrew. The ECO (see above) is in some respects (economic but not military) a successor organization.

REGIONAL CONFLICTS

Once several polities in the region were independent, the Middle East experienced conflicts over such matters as borders, access to scarce resources, competing ideologies, leadership, and self-determination. Geographically, the conflicts may cross frontiers or may be subregional, regional, or between the region and outside forces.

Not all major clashes have arisen between sovereign governments. Some conflicts have been and are between nonstate organizations and states, between paramilitary forces of subnational groups, between religious and secular groups, or between individual leaders. Lebanon was fragmented for more than fifteen years by fighting between the PLO and

Kataib,[17] the PLO and Shii, Druze and Kataib, and other intergroup conflicts (see Chap. 11). The PLO also fought Jordanian forces in 1970 and later periodically battled Israeli troops and conducted guerrilla raids into Israel. The 2006 "Summer War" involved Hizballah and Israel, and the latter's target in Gaza in 2008–2009 and again in 2012 was Hamas. Various spin-offs from or affiliates of al-Qaida have targeted regimes in Iraq, Saudi Arabia, Syria, and Yemen.

Zealots: Religious and Secular.   Militant extremist groups, claiming to be acting for Islam or representing Islamist organizations, have posed threats to nearly every government in the region. From 1991 to 1997, antigovernment forces mounted a virtual insurgency in Egypt—some seeking political power, some opposed to Egyptian-Israeli détente, some demanding adherence to their version of Islam. The Muslim Brotherhood, originally an Egyptian opposition group, revived and became active not only in Egypt but also in Jordan and Syria; in 2011, one of its members became the first freely elected president of Egypt. Some organizations have created internal and transnational movements, discussed later. The Baath (Arab Renaissance) Party has been influential in the Fertile Crescent states, but opposing factions governed in Syria and Iraq until the fall of Saddam Husayn, and the Syrian regime came under increasing attack starting in 2011. The 1964–1975 Dhufar Rebellion in southern Oman pitted an isolated marginalized group—joined by Marxists from South Yemen—against an authoritarian sultan (see Map 17.2). After 9/11, a new era in regional conflicts brought more widespread and intensified terrorism, discussed in Chapter 9. Yemen in the early 2010s was experiencing zealotry on multiple fronts: tribal (the Huthi rebels), geographic (southern secessionists), and ideological (AQAP—al-Qaida in the Arabian Peninsula). Even in Israel, settlers on the West Bank have lately spawned groups that have taken to terrorist activities—the so-called price-tag operations—attacking not just Palestinians but also Israeli military outposts and non-Jewish religious sites.[18]

Boundary and Territorial Disputes

Most Middle East countries have at one time or another engaged in disputes with neighbors over the location or demarcation of their boundaries. These disputes have usually been limited to diplomatic exchanges or skirmishes, but three have provoked devastating wars (discussed in greater detail in Chap. 9). Most of the long-standing disputes had been resolved or were otherwise inactive by the early 2010s. However, irredentist and nationalist claims retain the potential for conflict and may reassert themselves in the future, and in several cases maritime borders remain unsettled, leading to potential economically motivated conflicts.

Early Disputes.   Three preindependence territorial disputes in the Fertile Crescent involved the following: (1) inclusion of the Mosul area in the British mandate of Iraq, (2) delineation of the southern Transjordan–Saudi Arabia border, and (3) status of Alexandretta (Turkish: Iskanderun) in northwestern Syria. The first two were soon resolved, but the third dispute echoed for several years. A 1921 accord provided for the Sanjak (subprovince) of Alexandretta—with a large Turkish minority and port facilities desired by both Turkey and Syria—a special regime within the Syrian mandate. The League of Nations created the separate Republic of Hatay in 1938, but in 1939 France ceded it to Turkey, violating mandate provisions. Syria has still not entirely accepted the loss, and many Syrian-made maps show both the 1936 and the 1939 boundaries; both are indicated in Chapter 10 (Map 10.1). In 2012, some of the sizable Alawi minority in the region actively opposed Turkey's role in supporting the insurgents in the Syrian civil war.

Figure 8.2 Internation interaction: an unusual international border crossing, on an artificial island at the median line between Saudi Arabia (*foreground*) and Bahrain on the causeway connecting Bahrain island to the peninsular mainland (see Fig. 7.5).

Saudi Northern Boundaries. Saudi Arabia, with the largest number of immediate land neighbors in the region (seven), sought to rationalize most of its boundaries through quiet negotiations during the 1960s and 1970s, although border tensions continued with Yemen.[19] A bilateral agreement in 1965 gave Jordan an additional 10 mi/16 km of coastline for the expansion of its port of Aqabah in exchange for an inland desert tract. A settlement with Kuwait in 1969 divided the Saudi Arabia–Kuwait Neutral Zone, and another in 1981, with Iraq, divided the other neutral zone and straightened the boundary extending westward.

Saudi Eastern Boundaries. An agreement with Qatar in 1965, revised in 1992, defined this boundary, and a 1974 accord defined a long-disputed boundary with the UAE involving the Buraymi Oasis. A Saudi agreement with Oman in 1982 deferred territorial questions, but in March 1991 the two governments ratified the delimitation of their common border of more than 400 mi/645 km through the eastern part of the barren Rub al-Khali. This has now been demarcated and is de jure. Final ratification of Saudi boundaries with Iraq, Qatar, and the UAE was delayed for several years, although the delineations were generally accepted and shown as de facto on the official maps of all four countries. The several boundaries were registered with the UN by Saudi Arabia in 1995, and later agreements led to designation of the borders with Iraq, Qatar, and the UAE as de jure.

Saudi Yemeni Boundary.   The border between Saudi Arabia and Yemen has been particularly difficult to settle because of frequent antagonism between the two governments. The 1934 Treaty of Taif resulted in demarcation of a short segment of the boundary between Yemen and the Asir region of the Saudi kingdom, but dispute continued over the remaining part of the border until a boundary treaty was signed in 2000 covering the entire line from the coast to Oman. Demarcation of the new segment was to be undertaken "in an amicable way." General relations between Saudi Arabia and Yemen concurrently improved with the resolution of the boundary problem; beginning in the late 2000s, the Houthi rebellion in northern Yemen recalled the still-troubled nature of this region.

Elsewhere on the Peninsula.   Of four other significant Arabian Peninsula boundary disputes, two were readily resolved. In the south, the frontier between Oman and the former South Yemen saw fighting in the 1970s, but in 1992 united Yemen readily agreed to a definitive settlement, ratified in 1998. Similarly, in 1993 Oman and the UAE delineated their long-disputed border. In the north, Iraq and Jordan agreed in 1984 to a slight modification of their boundary to permit an exchange of small parcels of territory;[20] this de jure delineation is shown in several maps in this book. Another long-standing boundary problem—between the two former Yemens—disappeared with their unification in 1990. A lengthy dispute between Bahrain and Qatar involved Gulf islands (and potentially valuable maritime territory). Citing its historic ties to western Qatar, Bahrain claimed the Hawar islands and the Dibal and Jarada shoals off the western coast of the peninsula. In 1996, Qatar took its case to the International Court of Justice, which decided in 2001 that the islands should go to Bahrain but denied all its claims to mainland territory. Both sides accepted the verdict amicably. Jordan and Saudi Arabia agreed to demarcate their maritime border in 2007.

Iraq-Kuwait Boundary.   Another long-disputed boundary, between Iraq and Kuwait, included Iraq's maximalist claim to the whole of Kuwait (see below). A border defined (but not demarcated) by an agreement between Iraq and Kuwait in 1963 was confirmed and demarcated by a special UN Iraq-Kuwait Boundary Demarcation Commission after Iraq was forced to withdraw from Kuwait in 1991. The commission's work and report were accepted by the UN Security Council (UNSC) in Resolution 833 in 1993. Iraq at first refused to accept the line but agreed to it in November 1994, refused it again briefly in 1999, then accepted it in an apparently final stance.[21] In 2012, the two countries requested UN assistance in physically demarking the border; one problem remaining relates to Iraqi concerns that port development on Kuwait's Bubiyan island will obstruct access to the Gulf for its own port of Umm Qasr. Thus, at long last, after decades of disputes and negotiations, nearly all political boundaries on the Arabian Peninsula have been formally settled and are internationally accepted as de jure.

Four disputes involving irredentist territories on the Arabian Peninsula and in offshore areas became seriously acute during the 1961–1991 period:

1. Iraq-Kuwait.   Iraq denounced British delineations and territorial allotments at the head of the Gulf in 1923, arguing that its access to the Gulf was too narrow for its size and needs. It had received most of the former Ottoman province of Basrah and claimed the remainder, which had been given to Kuwait. Since in other cases former Ottoman administrative units were divided in creating mandates, Iraq's claim was declared invalid by international-law specialists. Although it accepted the status quo in 1932 upon independence, it reasserted its claims during the late 1930s, including threats of military action. With Kuwaiti independence in 1961 and the end of British protection, Iraq moved to annex Kuwait by force, but after a stiff warning by both Britain and the Arab League, it again accepted the status quo. But in 1973–1974, Iraq claimed once again part of Kuwait—the islands of Warba and Bubiyan—to expand its Gulf outlet; once again, it dropped its claims and withdrew its forces.[22] With this history, Saddam Husayn's threat to Kuwait in 1990 initially just appeared to be more posturing (see "The Gulf Crisis, 1990–1991," in Chap. 9).

2. Iran-Bahrain. In 1968, as Britain prepared to withdraw from the lower Gulf, Iran moved to fill the impending vacuum and affirm its dominance by reasserting old claims to Bahrain as Iran's "fourteenth province," as well as to several small islands in the southern Gulf. However, in 1970 the shah accepted the UN finding that Bahrainis preferred independence and renounced further claims to Bahrain. With the onset of the Arab Spring, when mostly Shii Bahrainis began generally peaceful protests calling for reforms, the Sunni Bahraini government accused Iran of fomenting the disturbances and acted forcefully to suppress the outbreaks. Iran, on the other hand, has criticized what it termed persecution of its Shii coreligionists (see Chap. 16).

3. Iran-UAE. However, Iran's claims in the south continued. On November 30, 1971, the day before Britain withdrew, it occupied three islands in the lower Gulf that had long been understood to belong to Sharjah and Ras al-Khaymah, asserting its need to protect the Strait of Hormuz. Accord was reached re-

garding Abu Musa—located well away from the strait and closer to Sharjah than to Iran; this included dividing any oil revenue from or around the island between the two parties. In 1992, Iran restricted access to the island, and it periodically reasserts its control, followed by UAE protests. The other two islands, Greater Tunb and Lesser Tunb, nearer the Strait, had been under Ras al-Khaymah sovereignty before 1970, but Iran occupied them prior to the UAE's independence.[23]

4. Iran-Iraq. Finally, the median line (*thalweg*) river boundary down the Shatt al-Arab between Iraq and Iran involved the two riparian states in disputes and then warfare (discussed in "The Iran-Iraq War, 1980–1988," in Chap. 9).

Gulf Maritime Boundaries and Oil. For the Gulf, there are problems of maritime boundaries in this semienclosed sea. As offshore oil discoveries reached mid-Gulf from both sides, delineation became essential. Law of the Sea agreements elsewhere provided precedents for establishing median lines in the central Gulf, as opposed to the north and south, and the lines were surveyed in the late 1950s and the 1960s. In the north, complexities regarding the lines among Iran, Iraq, Kuwait, and the former Neutral Zone have delayed final agreement, and similar problems arose with the UAE's component amirates and Iran in the south. Despite the potential for confrontation over huge offshore oil and gas resources, agreements have been reached relatively promptly, and nonagreed-upon lines have so far caused few difficulties (see Fig. 8.2).[24]

Aegean Boundaries. Another continental-shelf dispute concerns determining a median line in the Aegean Sea between Turkey and Greece. Since its territory includes several large islands just off the western and southern coasts of Asia Minor, Greece favors a median line between the islands and the Turkish mainland. However, that would extend its Exclusive Economic Zone rights over practically the entire Aegean Sea, including all potential offshore petroleum resources—a solution Turkey has declared it will not accept.

The conflict over partitioning the Aegean is heightened by the situation in Cyprus. Since both Turkey and Greece are members of the North Atlantic Treaty Organization (NATO), and since Turkey has sought to join Greece (and Cyprus) as a member of the EU, the international community closely monitors any possibility of military action over the Aegean or Cyprus. The Cyprus dispute received intensive attention in 2003 and 2004, culminating in the accession of southern (Greek) Cyprus to the EU and the continued isolation of northern (Turkish) Cyprus. (See Chap. 11.)

Levant Basin.   If one of the long-standing factors in settling Aegean boundaries is the *potential* discovery of petrocarbons on its continental shelf, a more recently arisen problem is in an area where petrocarbon deposits *actually* have been discovered—in the Levant Basin, which stretches northward from Egyptian maritime territory off the Nile Delta along the coasts of Palestine (Gaza), Israel, Lebanon, and Syria. The first three of these countries were until the early 2000s thought to be without any significant oil and natural gas resources, but offshore exploration was prompted by the knowledge of Egypt's adjacent discoveries. In 2010, the United States Geological Survey issued a report indicating the probable presence of 1.7 bn bbl of oil and 122 tn ft^3 of natural gas (or even more). But until recently, there was little urgency in negotiating offshore boundaries in the region despite the fact that these countries are embroiled in considerable onshore conflict.

It is not just these four countries that are involved in the future exploitation of this regional bonanza. Beyond the limits of the geologically defined Levant Basin are the offshore areas of Cyprus (South and North) and Turkey, and expectations of profitable discoveries here as well are not unreasonable. In 2011, Israel and Cyprus agreed on their mutual border, but a dispute has arisen in demarcating the Israel-Lebanon boundary, and of course Palestine's offshore claims are subject to the wider question of a Palestine-Israel territorial settlement. Additionally, Turkey disputes the right of the Greek Cypriot government to negotiate about the areas offshore from the breakaway Turkish Republic of North Cyprus. This topic is discussed in more detail in Chapter 6 and in the relevant country chapters in Part Two.

What's in a Name?   Territorially, there is another problem relative to the Gulf: what it is to be called, not only by the states surrounding or near it, but by other countries, businesses, and individuals (including writers of books about the Middle East). Iran insists that it is the "Persian" Gulf, and cites long historical usage to back up its claim. The littoral Arab states prefer "Arabian" (or "Arab") Gulf, but have accepted use of just "the Gulf."[25] That this is not a minor matter can be seen from two incidents in early 2010. The second Islamic Solidarity Games (ISG), originally scheduled for October 2009, were to be held at several Iranian venues. When Iran included "Persian Gulf" in the ISG logo and related materials, the Arab states, led by Saudi Arabia, objected; when negotiations failed to yield a solution, the games were finally canceled in January 2010. Then Iran threatened in February 2010 to deny the use of its airspace to any airline that referred to the waterway by any name other than "Persian Gulf." The warning was particularly aimed at airlines based in Gulf Arab countries that have numerous flights to Iranian destinations. Iranians across the political spectrum expressed their outrage in 2012 that Google Maps had left the Gulf unlabeled on its sites; Google was condemned for "spreading lies," and Iran's police chief accused it of being a "spying tool."[26]

Hydrogeopolitics

The availability, management, and sharing of the natural resource of water increasingly rival the influence of petroleum in the political geography of the area. Whereas petroleum is a valuable economic resource, water is essential to life itself.

Population increases in many countries have overwhelmed water resources. Rivers, because of their transnational character, automatically become subjects of international concern. Egypt has seen the amount of water in the Nile—rising in other countries to the south—decrease in recent decades by the time the river reaches Lake Nasser. Use of Tigris and Euphrates water by the three riparian states—Turkey, Syria, and Iraq—has dramatically increased since the 1960s. Notable is Turkey's Southeast Anatolia Project (GAP), with the Atatürk Dam on the Euphrates generating electric power and irrigating millions of acres (see Chap. 20) and diminishing downstream flow in Syria and Iraq. Syria's Jazirah Project, with its core facility the Tabaqah Dam on the Euphrates, involves irrigating hundreds of thousands of acres, further decreasing the flow to Iraq. In Iraq, the wars of 1991 and 2003 and cross-border Kurdish-related tensions have stalled meaningful progress in water negotiations. Saudi Arabia overused its groundwater in an ill-advised effort to be self-sufficient in wheat, with the water table dropping by 7 or 8 ft/2.1 or 2.4 m before the program was reduced in the late 1980s.

In part, the effort to gain access to the Jordan, Yarmuk, and Litani Rivers and to underground aquifers prompted Israel to seize the Golan Heights in 1967 and southern Lebanon in the 1980s and to plant settlements in the West Bank. Palestinian-Israeli peace talks have periodically addressed water sharing without making significant progress.

Nile Basin Initiative. The nine states[27] of the Nile Basin discussed regional cooperation in Cairo in June 1990, and the UN Economic Commission for Africa and the UN Development Programme are promoting group water projects. With resources from the World Bank and the African Development Bank, the Nile Basin Initiative was launched in 1999 with the goal of promoting sustainable development through agreed-upon and equitable utilization of Nile water resources. Thus, initial steps have been taken toward water-sharing protocols, but the real problems have yet to be addressed. According to the 1966 Helsinki Rules and a 1972 UN convention, water rights depend on population and need, keeping historical allocations in mind. On the other hand, international law acknowledges the absolute sovereignty of a state over its own resources. This dichotomy illustrates the basic division between Egypt and the Sudan, on the one hand, and the upriver states, on the other hand. Without regional and international agreements, national development plans and the growing thirst of increasing populations will lead to more conflicts over water use in the Middle East.[28]

Religious and Ideological Conflicts

The Role of Religion. Religious movements have strongly impacted the Middle East, and they are of crucial importance in the regional geopolitical equation today. The Islamic state was a theocracy, and religion and politics— "church and state"—are congenitally linked in Muslim concepts. Extreme politicization of Islam divides Muslims and creates some of the region's sharpest cleavages. As with other religious conflicts, the real dissension often arises from national political hostilities, economic competition, ethnolinguistic and cultural dissensions, territorial disputes, and outside interference.

Religious contentions also merge with others in many struggles between religious groups in the Middle East. A closer look at the conflict "between Jews and Muslims" reveals underlying territorial, political, and cultural bases for hostility. The fifteen-year civil war in Lebanon "between Christians and Muslims" reflected dominant-group economic-cultural discrimination and competition as much as religion. Revolutionary activities of the Shia in Lebanon and elsewhere reflect not only religion but also historic economic disadvantages and Iranian and Iraqi nationalism. The Syrian Civil War has increasingly brought religious differences to the fore, especially between the Sunni Arab majority and the long-ruling and heterodox Alawi minority, with other minority communities—Christian and Druze—caught in the middle.

Modernization since the 1950s has revealed inadequacies in modern industrialized culture, leading to a strong resurgence of an Islamic religious-political framework. Older groups like the Muslim Brotherhood (*Ikhwan al-Muslimun*), founded in Egypt in 1929, received new impetus (and in the aftermath of the Egyptian revolution ousting the Mubarak regime, a member of the *Ikhwan* became the country's first freely elected president in 2012). Many newer "fraternities" (*jamaats*) have arisen in Egypt and the Fertile Crescent, advocating revolutionary and antigovernment positions, rejection of modern trends, and a return to traditional Islam. Among the better-known groups are al-Qaida, Hamas, and Hizballah (see "Terrorism" in Chap. 9).

Arabism in the Region.   Partly an outgrowth of the regional identification of Arabism with Islam and partly a product of anticolonial nationalism, Arab ideologies may display slightly different emphases; they are categorized with such terms as "Arabism," "Arab nationalism," "Arab solidarity," "Arab unity," and "Arab socialism." Under some circumstances, Arab identity transcends state nationalism, prompting coordinated political and economic stands,[29] though differing interpretations of identity periodically create conflict

among states. Although Arabs value consensus, political crises led to dissension during 1990–1991 and again with the 2003 invasion of Iraq.

Non-Arab Aspects.   From outside the "Arab system," Iranian Shii fundamentalism has had less impact since the mid-1990s, but it still has an influence. In the late 2000s, Saudi Arabia, the Gulf states, and Jordan, for example, were increasingly concerned at what was called the "Shii Crescent," stretching from Iran through Shii-majority Iraq and Alawi-dominated Syria into Lebanon with the strong presence of Hizballah in government. Also externally, Turkey has seen ideological conflicts between secular and Islamic ideologies, with one overt indication being the more prevalent wearing of headscarves by women. Nationalism, ideological and political clashes, and religious divisions have also caused internal conflict in Israel.

GREAT-POWER RIVALRY

The Great Game.   Britain and Russia long vied for spheres of influence from the Balkans to the Himalayas. Britain's protective umbrella over Cyprus, the Suez Canal, Aden, and the Gulf defended its lifeline, first, to India and, later, to oil. Russian pressure on the "Northern Tier" diminished during the 1920s and 1930s, but the Soviet Union resumed the historic push into southwestern Asia after World War II. With Britain no longer able to counter the pressure, the United States increasingly took over as protector of the Northern Tier—Turkey and Iran—against Russian expansion into an area of increasingly vital concern. Rivalry between the United States and the USSR in the region became a major dynamic in the global Cold War and in the region's relations and geopolitics for forty-five years. Much of this "Great Game in the Middle East" seemed to have ended with the Soviet collapse and the subsequent cooperation between the United States and some former Soviet republics. However, highlights of the rivalry are worth a brief review.

US Doctrines, from Truman to Reagan. The policy of "containment" first advocated in a watershed article by "X" (Ambassador George Kennan)[30] was formalized in the Truman Doctrine in March 1947. The declaration signaled a US commitment to maintain the balance of power in the Middle East while Britain withdrew in phases from Greece, India, and the Palestine mandate. Later, Britain lost its influence in Iran, gave up Suez in 1956, and left the Gulf and the periphery of the Arabian Peninsula in 1971–1972. However, it continues to have vital interests in the region and generally coordinates political and military operations with the United States, as it did on a major scale during the 1990–1991 Gulf crisis and its aftermath—including the no-fly zones—and even more prominently in the invasion of Iraq in 2003.

The Eisenhower administration sought to unify regional resistance to Soviet pressure. With US and British encouragement, the Baghdad Pact was formed in 1955, eventually including Turkey, Iraq, Iran, Pakistan, and Britain. The United States was a full member of the economic committee and the major source of pact funding. Consequent to the Suez imbroglio of 1956—the joint Israeli-British-French invasion of Egypt—the Eisenhower Doctrine, announced in January 1957, committed the United States to countering Communist moves in the Middle East. Not always applied consistently, it nonetheless was pursued by succeeding administrations. But while the United States tried to minimize Soviet regional influence, it also adopted policies antagonizing key Arab countries, easing the way for the Soviets.

The Nixon Doctrine encouraged the region's states to be responsible for their own defense, focusing on Iran and, secondarily, Saudi Arabia, to counter the Soviets. In the eastern Mediterranean, Turkey and Greece were NATO's southeastern flank, with the British providing support in Cyprus. In the Fertile Crescent, Israel's so-called special relationship with the United States was strengthened.

The Carter Doctrine, promulgated in 1980 following the Iranian Revolution, collapse of the Central Treaty Organization (the former Baghdad Pact), and the Soviet invasion of Afghanistan in December 1979, emphasized US interests in the Gulf. It laid the groundwork for a Rapid Deployment Force—later the Central Command. The Reagan administration continued to finance anti-Soviet forces in Afghanistan and sent US naval forces to the Gulf in 1987 and 1988. The dispatch of US troops to Saudi Arabia in 1990–1991 by the first Bush administration was based on the Carter Doctrine and was an extension of Reagan's support of Kuwait.

War on Terror. The next projection of US policy into the broader region was a major part of the "War on Terror"—the dispatch of coalition troops to Afghanistan in October 2001 after the 9/11 terrorist attacks (see "Nonstate Threats," in Chap. 9). A stiffening of US policy toward Iraq also emerged during 2002 based on allegations of Iraqi links to al-Qaida and Iraqi stockpiles of so-called weapons of mass destruction, climaxing with invasion in 2003. Amid criticism of the actions toward Iraq, President George W. Bush announced a complex policy that, refined and enlarged, became the Broader Middle East and North Africa Initiative. A White House fact sheet in June 2004[31] gave as the initiative's aims to "advance freedom, democracy, and prosperity" and to "support political, economic, and social reform" in the states of the region. The invasion and subsequent occupation of Iraq were cast as integral parts of furthering the goals of fighting terrorism, suppressing weapons of mass destruction, and promoting freedom and democracy.[32] Viewed with hindsight, the question must be asked as to what extent any of these goals have been realized through US actions in either Afghanistan or Iraq.

In the twenty-first century, there are numerous signs that the "Great Game" may still be being played, perhaps with more players and somewhat different objectives and rules. There has been extensive maneuvering, for example, over the routing of pipelines designed to bring the petro-resources of the Caucasus and Central Asia to European markets (for more details, see Chaps. 6 and 20) or to the India-Pakistan subcontinent (see Chap. 21). In 2012, the United States was alleged to have objected to a multibillion-dollar arms deal that it may have felt would have given Russia a foothold in Iraq.[33] The resources of the Middle East and the adjoining areas in Central Asia are vital to the prosperity of a world in which the old imperial powers are no longer alone in their ability to participate in regional affairs.

ARAB SPRING—ARAB AWAKENING[34]

On December 17, 2010, a young Tunisian street vendor named Mohamed Bouazizi set himself ablaze, despondent after police had confiscated his wares and his livelihood and municipal officials had humiliated him when he reported his loss. Before his death less than three weeks later, protests erupted across Tunisia that culminated in mid-January with the overthrow of the long-entrenched Ben Ali dictatorship, and consequently set off what has most commonly been termed the "Arab Spring"—though perhaps "Arab Awakening" would be a more appropriate term for a series of events that has lasted much longer than a single season.

But it was events in Cairo a month later that focused the attention of first the region and then the world on the broader implications of Bouazizi's sacrifice. Crowds gathered by the thousands in the city's central Tahrir Square from January 25 on, their numbers swelling as they made it clear they would stay there until their demands received satisfactory answers. Unlike what had transpired in Tunisia, developments in Egypt were telecast live and around the clock by the al-Jazeera television network. When the high command of the Egyptian Army made the critical decision that it would keep order but not suppress the demonstrations, it gradually became clear that the days of the Mubarak regime were numbered and that "people power" worked, at least in Egypt.

In short order, city streets were filled with protesters in Jordan, Yemen, Syria, Iraq, Bahrain, Kuwait, and Saudi Arabia's Eastern Province.[35] Regime resistance in all these places mounted, as the overriding significance of the successful depositions of the Tunisian and Egyptian autocrats was confronted by rulers long accustomed to deference from their people. Still, by the end of February, incipient civil wars were well under way in Yemen, Syria, Libya, and Bahrain; by year's end, two more dictators would be overthrown and a third would be increasingly besieged. In other countries, regimes moved quickly to heighten security and cobble together hastily constructed programs that promised political reforms and much-increased spending on programs and projects that seemed likely to deflate some of the most glaring inequities in their societies.

In the chapters below in Part Two, Arab Spring–related events in individual countries are discussed in some detail. But here it would be useful to consider at least briefly not just the underlying causes that led to these events, but also why the Arab Spring occurred when it did and how and why it spread so rapidly across the region. Additionally, although there are similarities in these societies, there are also differences, and the latter help to explain why events have not transpired in the same way in each country.

Early observers of the Arab Spring tended to stress the heavy participation of younger

Arabs in the demonstrations. Although the extensive television coverage of the Tahrir Square events revealed the presence of a wider cross-section of ages, there is nonetheless a degree of truth to these initial generalizations. Younger people (roughly the under-thirty-five generation) have been particularly frustrated by their situations in many countries of the region. Two reasons for this stand out: first, a shortage of decent employment possibilities for new entrants into the job market, and second, a widely perceived lack of respect for them on the part of government officials, from the top down to the lowliest clerk in a ministry office.

While countries like Tunisia, Egypt, Syria, and Jordan had through 2011 enjoyed a decade or more of reasonable economic growth, partly as a result of neoliberal reforms undertaken from the 1980s onward, job growth in most cases had lagged well behind that of the labor force. Additionally, many younger people, males and females, had not been well prepared to meet the demands of the more modern sectors of the economies by the existing mediocre educational systems they had encountered. Entry into employment (with the prospect of eventually being able to marry and begin a family) often seemed to depend more on personal contacts and kinship rather than on individual talent and merit.

In retrospect, conditions on the side of the governments also opened the way to the events that began in 2011. A generation or so earlier, they almost fully controlled the sources of information—the press, radio, television, cinema—available to their people. But beginning in the 1980s, satellite television came to the region, and its presence was quickly felt even in countries that tried to regulate or even forbid the use of individual satellite receivers. Al-Jazeera arrived in 1996, providing in Arabic reasonably balanced programming previously available only in foreign languages. Then in the new century came the Internet, with its myriad of poten-

tial links, along with the growing number of social media networks. In short, largely without fully realizing it, governments lost control over what their citizens knew and when they knew it—and younger Arabs were as plugged into the wider world as their European and American contemporaries.

What this meant, among other things, was that the sins and shortcomings of governments were more widely known than ever before—the blatant corruption at high levels, the economic gains accruing to elites closely linked to presidents and ministers, and the maneuvers of the existing leaderships to perpetuate their control of senior government positions and industrial enterprises. The details of the extravagant shopping trips of the Tunisian first lady, of the economic boons realized by Assad family members, of the putative succession of Mubarak's son to the Egyptian presidency, and of many more such topics not only were known and discussed but resented.

The role that the social media have played has received considerable attention as well. However, it needs to be stressed that their importance has been as facilitators of the events that transpired, whereas the news and other information media played a more formative role over a longer period. It certainly did prove to be important that many younger Arabs knew how to make best use of the social media, while their gerontocratic government leaders were frequently almost totally unaware of the developments that were unfolding.

Amazing to many observers was the speed with which the Arab Spring spread—as pointed out above, within little more than a month of Bouazizi's self-immolation, protesters filled the streets of nearly a dozen countries. The demonstration effect of al-Jazeera telecasts was very important, but many Arabs had closely followed the reactions in Iran to the disputed presidential election in 2009, and that event did not inspire them to take to the streets themselves. The case can be made that the Arab Spring has shown that Pan-Arabism still exists in the region—a sort of twenty-first-century counterpart to the Nasserism that swept the Arab world in the 1950s.

In several of the country chapters in Part Two, the Arab Spring is discussed in greater detail, and both similarities and differences across the region are pointed out. So far, the most definitive results have occurred in the less wealthy countries that are at most minor oil producers. The regimes with abundant resources have reacted to the regional revolution by announcing massive new spending programs and promising future political reforms (accompanied by sharp crackdowns on dissidents). For the most part, they have been successful so far in maintaining their own existences.

NOTES

1. Mackinder 1904, which has been reprinted in several political geography studies. Sir Halford expanded and revised his thoughts in Mackinder 1919 and again in a 1943 *Foreign Affairs* article. An underrated challenge to Mackinder came in Spykman 1944. The Rimland challenge is discussed below.

2. Ayubi 1995 comprehensively examines Arab states and gives realistic insights. See also note 8 below.

3. Russia was to receive Constantinople (Istanbul), the Turkish Straits, and those Anatolian provinces that had been inhabited by Armenians. The Russian revolution voided this part of the agreement, and the Bolshevist government released the secret agreement in 1917 to the great embarrassment of Britain and France.

4. T. E. Lawrence's personal account appeared in his classic *Seven Pillars of Wisdom: A Triumph,* which appeared in several versions and many editions. He and his saga were much celebrated during the 1920s and had a renaissance in the 1970s and 1980s. In the extensive literature about him, an excellent authorized biography is J. Wilson 1990, which places Lawrence in the context of the momentous events of the period.

5. Fromkin 2000 is a comprehensive treatment of how the contemporary Middle East emerged from the dealings of Britain and France with each other and with third parties during and after World War I.

6. Busch 1971 is an excellent study of the interaction between Britain's Indian and Middle East policies during World War I and its aftermath.

7. See H. Howard 1963.

8. The League of Nations mandates were divided into three categories, depending basically on the degree of political development in each territory. All Middle East mandates fell into Class A, former Ottoman territories deemed to have "reached a stage of development where their existence as independent nations can be provisionally recognized subject to the rendering of administrative advice and assistance by a Mandatory until such time as they are able to stand alone. *The wishes of these communities must be a principal consideration* in the selection of the Mandatory" (emphasis added).

9. With a hiatus of about twenty years following the June 1967 war.

10. Though it was twice suspended by the amir—in 1976 and 1986.

11. Hartshorne 1950.

12. S. Jones 1954.

13. North Cyprus has observer status with the OIC.

14. At the ECO Summit Meeting of October 2012, Pakistani president Zadari was particularly critical of this lack of progress on trade and several other issues. *Express Tribune* (Karachi), Oct. 17, 2012.

15. See http://ec.europa.eu/external_relations/euro med/index_en.htm for further information.

16. *Global Arab Network,* Mar. 2, 2010. See also "Delivering on a New European Neighbourhood Policy," European Commission, May 2012, at http://ec .europa.eu/world/enp/docs/2012 . . . /delivering _new_enp_en.pdf.

17. The Kataib is better known in English as the Phalange, a political party and its supporting militia that draws its strength from the Maronites.

18. *Haaretz,* Sept. 7, 2011; *Jerusalem Post,* Dec. 13, 2011.

19. Several boundaries mentioned in this paragraph are depicted and briefly accounted for in successive issues of the US Department of State's *Geographic Notes.* A general map of the Arabian Peninsula lines as of 1991 is in Bradford Thomas, "Gulf Boundaries," no. 13 (1991): 1–5. The Saudi-Iraq boundary is shown on pp. 2–3 of the same issue and is covered again in vol. 2, no. 2 (1992): 11–12. Saudi-Qatar and Saudi-UAE are covered in vol. 2, no. 4 (1992–1993): 1–2, and in vol. 3, no. 4 (1993–1994): 12–13. Saudi-Oman is in vol. 3, no. 1 (1993): 2–3. All Middle East boundaries are discussed in A. Day 1982, 178–233. A concise review of Arabian Peninsula borders is given in Schofield 1996. Boundaries on Middle East maps in National Geographic Society 2004 are correct.

20. The Oman-Yemen boundary is shown in *Geographic Notes* vol. 3, no. 1 (1993): 3–5; the Jordan-Iraq line in no. 13 (1991): 2; again in vol. 2, no. 4 (1992–

1993): 2–3; and again in vol. 3, no. 4 (1993–1994): 9–10. See also Schofield 1996, which mentions the Oman-UAE boundary.

21. *Geographic Notes* vol. 3, no. 2 (1993): 1–2, with more details in vol. 4, no. 2 (1994): 23–29. For exhaustive studies, see Schofield 1993 and H. Rahman 1997. For concise coverage, see Cordesman and Hashim 1997, 184–189. A useful Kuwaiti summary is at www.kuwait-info.org/borders.html.

22. The Iraq-Kuwait territorial dispute is discussed in Kelly 1980; Crystal 1990; Finnie 1992; and H. Rahman 1997.

23. Details are given in Taryam 1987, which includes a useful bibliographical essay covering good sources on the islands and on the UAE.

24. The Gulf maritime boundaries are succinctly examined in *Geographic Notes*, no. 14 (1991): 11–12. See also Blake 1987.

25. In the early days of Iran's Islamic Revolution, there was a suggestion, alleged to have the support of Ayatollah Khomeini, to use the neutral appellation "Islamic Gulf," but this term never gained much currency.

26. *Daily Telegraph,* Jan. 17, 2010; *Daily Star* (Beirut), Feb. 23, 2010; *Guardian,* May 12, 2012.

27. In addition to Egypt, these are Sudan, Ethiopia, Uganda, Kenya, Tanzania, Rwanda, Burundi, and the Democratic Republic of the Congo. Since South Sudan's independence in 2011, there are now ten riparian states, and South Sudan was admitted to membership in 2012. Eritrea has observer status in Nile Basin Initiative activities.

28. Many recent studies examine various aspects of Middle East hydrogeopolitics. See, especially, *Water for the Future* 1999; Biswas et al. 1997; Elmusa 1997; Wolf 1995; Rogers and Lydon 1994; Berkoff 1994; Rowley 1999, 2008; and Fox 2003.

29. The subject is examined from different viewpoints in dozens of studies: for example, Curtis 1981; Salamé 1987; Esman and Rabinovich 1988; Andersen, Seibert, and Wagner 1990; Ajami 1993; M. Hudson 1999; Khashan 2000; Dawisha 2003; and Rubin 2003.

30. Kennan 1987 is a reprint of the widely read 1947 article and is accompanied by comments and a retrospective by that author, who died at age 101 in March 2005.

31. This can be accessed at www.presidency.ucsb .edu/ws/index.php?pid=81021.

32. See *New York Times*, May 13 and June 6, 2004. For a broader view, see Murden 2002, especially Chap. 3, "The Pax Americana in the Middle East."

33. *RIANovosti*, Nov. 13, 2012.

34. The onset of the Arab Spring quickly spawned a mini publishing industry among the members of international punditry circles. A selection of some of the more insightful articles, listed more or less chronologically, would include: al-Amrani 2011; Ignatius 2011; Hamid 2011; Dervis 2011; Gausse 2011; Saletan 2011; Freeman 2011; Sorenson 2011; Agha and Malley 2011; Ross 2011; Lynch 2011; Freedom House 2012; Fukuyama 2012; Ajami 2012; Fam and Shahine 2012; Miller 2012; Mabrouk 2012; Ibish 2012; Ramadan 2012; S. G. Jones 2013; and Berman 2013.

35. Beginning in the summer of 2011, even Cyprus and Israel saw homegrown versions of street protests echoing those in the neighboring countries (see Chaps. 11 and 13).

9

The Earth and the State

Conflicts on the Ground

KEY POINTS: Continued political-geographical analysis of region leads to examination of factors in major regional conflicts, of which by far the most significant is Arab-Israel conflict. Origins include Zionism, Balfour Declaration, other actions in post–World War I settlements. In wars of 1948–1949, 1956, 1967, 1973, and, to some extent, 1978 and 1982, Israel established supremacy, expanded territory, lays basis for future claim of all of Palestine by establishing "facts on the ground"—illegal and internationally condemned settlements. Persistent refugee problem a matter of subdued but critical significance. "Peace process"—efforts at general settlement of dispute—continues futilely, seems intractable, with Israel steadily gaining advantages. In 2012, UNGA recognized Palestine as a nonmember state. Other wars elsewhere in region include Iran-Iraq War (1980–1988), Gulf Crisis (1990–1991), and US invasion of Iraq (2003). Many strategic maritime straits in Mideast: Bosporus-Dardanelles, Suez, Iran, Bab el-Mandeb, and especially Hormuz. Terrorism a very critical problem, with Middle East–Afghanistan both source and venue.

Over nearly a century, since the beginning of World War I, the region we have been considering has gone from basically being a political backwater—at most, of secondary concern to the world's major powers—to an area that dominates global headlines; tops the agendas of foreign, defense, finance, trade, and energy ministries in scores of the world's countries; and injects itself into election campaigns on every continent. In the previous chapter, we discussed the demise of the Ottoman Empire that had comprised much of the region for half a millennium and then, after defeat in 1918, splintered into a mélange of successor

states. The two leading imperial powers among the World War I allies, Britain and France, sought, through the newly fashioned mandate system, to add to their domains Middle East polities, the artificial borders of which they themselves had drawn up.

The numerous peace conferences that followed "the war to end all wars" neither ended wars globally nor brought much peace—certainly not to the Middle East. Conflicts mostly confined within the borders of individual post-Ottoman states—such as Greeks against Turks in Cyprus, Sunnis versus Shiis and Arabs versus Kurds in Iraq, southerners opposed to northerners in Yemen, intercommunal strife in Lebanon—are treated in the country chapters of Part Two. In this chapter, we will consider several of the wars—hot and cold—and conflicts that have transgressed national borders, even involving countries far from the region.

THE ARAB-ISRAELI PROBLEM

Among geopolitical problems since World War II, the emotionally charged conflict between Arabs and Israelis is unique in its regional impact, global ramifications, Great Power involvement, intractability, and impact on the US role in international affairs. It has many facets: ethnic confrontation, conflicting historical-territorial claims, religious implications, ethical dilemmas, and political and geopolitical repercussions. The problem also has many perspectives, with Arab and Israeli viewpoints fragmented into many subperspectives.[1] From any one of these, the conflict has caused tragic amounts of casualties, suffering, and physical destruction, and it has retarded regional development and wasted human and other resources. This study emphasizes the essentially geographical basis of the conflict, with "geographical" including the human factor (Map 9.1).

Two Nationalisms.   The modern conflict began with embryonic nationalism among Jews in Europe and Arabs in the Middle East. Jewish nationalism arose in the 1880s, taking shape as Zionism, the aspiration to establish a Jewish polity in "Zion"—a hill in Jerusalem, but by extension all of Palestine. Its influence and activity expanded until, with support from several sources, it achieved a Jewish state in Palestine in 1948. By contrast, Arab nationalisms developed in isolation, based on local situations—of which Palestine was only one—and were weakened and fragmented by imperial and colonial powers that frustrated their aims.

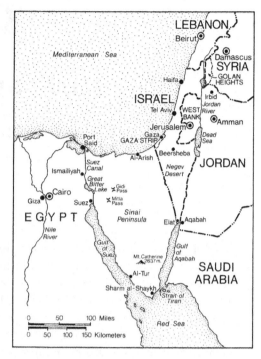

Map 9.1 Political-geographical setting of the Arab-Israeli problem, showing the territories directly involved in the conflict.

Jews in late-nineteenth-century Europe sought a national identity similar to that of the Germans or French, joining in common efforts to achieve self-determination and group liberation, all according to Enlightenment concepts. Jewish nationalism combined with secularism to direct attention to the Land of Israel (Eretz Yisrael) as the territory of a revived Jewish nation, stressing links between Jews in the Diaspora and the Land of Israel and focusing on Jews as a minority people "in exile," not just a religious group. It encouraged the revival of Hebrew, for centuries strictly a liturgical language, as the literary and linguistically unifying medium of Jewish-Hebrew nationalism.

Evolution of Zionism

Beginning in the 1880s, eastern European pogroms against Jews engendered some migration to Palestine.[2] It was institutionalized by Theodor Herzl, a Hungarian journalist, who came to believe that Jews must achieve self-determination territorially. In 1896, in his book *Der Judenstaat* (The Jews' State), he called for an independent state for Jews; in 1897, he organized the First Zionist Congress, founding the World Zionist Organization (WZO), still a preeminent organization supporting the state of Israel.

The WZO and subsidiary organizations attracted Jewish settlers to Ottoman Palestine, enlisting the support of world Jewry. Following Jones's "Unified Field Theory," mentioned above, Zionism is the idea that led through decision and movement over a world field to Palestine. One proponent ironically encouraged immigration for "a people without a land for a land without people" in 1901— when more than 400,000 Palestinian Arabs lived in that land: Palestine.[3] The settler effort proceeded, sometimes with Ottoman and British mandatory opposition. Colonists came for many reasons, but the predominant goal was a modern, secular, socialist state to serve as a territorial base for Jews as a people more than as a religious group.

The Balfour Declaration

Foreseeing the end of Ottoman rule, British Zionists pressed Britain early in World War I to officially support the establishment of a Jewish state in Palestine, originally arguing this would motivate Jews in the United States to urge that country to join the Allies against Germany. The result was Britain's one-sentence Balfour Declaration in 1917:

His Majesty's Government view with favour the establishment in Palestine of a national home for the Jewish people, and will use their best endeavours to facilitate the achievement of this object, it being clearly understood that nothing shall be done which may prejudice the civil and religious rights of existing non-Jewish communities in Palestine, or the rights and

political status enjoyed by Jews in any other country.[4]

This sentence, with its two conflicting parts, was as internally contradictory and cynically expedient as some of Britain's other wartime pronouncements, but it has had far more serious and long-lasting implications. For better or worse, it set the course of history for the modern Middle East.[5]

World War I Through World War II

Clarifying the Balfour Declaration in 1922, Britain stated that, although the declaration was a basic factor in establishing the Palestine mandate (Map 9.2A), this did not mean that all of Palestine was to become a strictly Jewish polity or that it intended the "disappearance or subordination" of the indigenous Arab population or its culture. But in fact, Palestine was excluded from what the Allies had promised would become an independent unified Arab state, according to Woodrow Wilson's Fourteen Points under a League of Nations mandate, and only the first half of the Balfour Declaration became operative. Arab violence followed from 1919 on, as Palestinians tried to forestall further Jewish colonization.

Attacks and counterattacks marked the 1920s and 1930s, with the Jewish efforts highly organized and those of the Palestinians fragmented. This set the pattern that has continued into the twenty-first century.

Land Purchases. The amply funded Jewish National Fund undertook the systematic purchase of prime agricultural land, frequently from absentee landlords, then dispossessing Palestinian tenants while immigration increased, especially in the 1930s with the onset of Nazi persecution. An Arab general strike in 1936 turned into an uprising against British rulers and the colonists, sparking British consideration of partitioning Palestine.

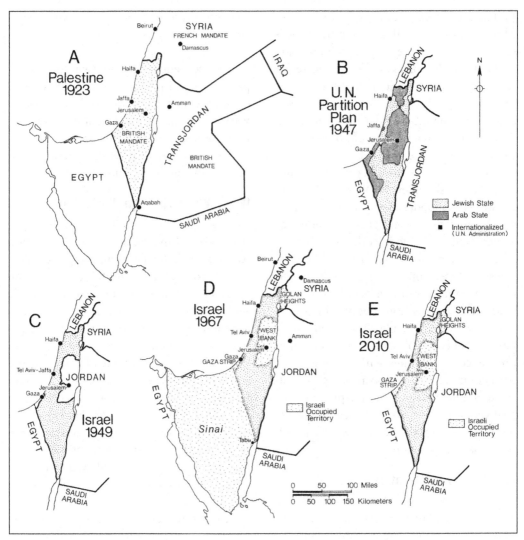

Map 9.2 The territorial evolution of Israel, from Palestinian mandate to contemporary state, with Occupied Territories. See also Map 9.4.

During World War II, Jewish extremists struck several times at British mandatory authorities in an attempt to seize Palestine. At the end of the war, Zionist recruiters in Europe enabled surviving Jewish refugees to go to Palestine as both fighters and settlers. British efforts to control immigration were unsuccessful and led to more attacks—notably on British mandatory offices in Jerusalem's King David Hotel in July 1946. Conducted by the Jewish terrorist group Irgun Zvai Leumi,

led by Menachem Begin (Israeli prime minister, 1977–1983), the blast killed ninety-one Britons, Jews, and Arabs. Many observers consider this attack the first case of classic terrorism in Palestine.

The Emergence of Israel

Tired of the dilemma they had created with the Balfour Declaration, a war-weary Britain announced in 1947 that it intended to relinquish the mandate and leave the future of

Figure 9.1 The Dome of the Rock, the celebrated 1,300-year-old shrine in the center of the Haram al-Sharif, or Temple Mount, in the Old City of Jerusalem. Its setting is shown in Figure 13.2. The blue tiles on the upper walls are some of the most magnificent in the world. (*Source:* Nik Wheeler, Saudi Aramco World/SAWDIA)

Palestine to the UN. Zionist pressure came from many directions, especially the United States, with President Harry S. Truman demanding that 100,000 Jews be admitted immediately to Palestine. Arabs argued that the British adhere to their obligations to the indigenous Palestinians.

Partition.   To replace the mandate, the UN Special Committee on Palestine drew up a Partition Plan for Palestine. The UN General Assembly (UNGA) voted for the plan on November 29, 1947, under US pressure.[6] Although it was never implemented, its provisions still have a certain juridical force and serve as a geopolitical point of reference. It called for three entities: a Jewish state with 56 percent of mandate Palestine; an Arab state,

43 percent; and a small enclave comprising Jerusalem to become a UN-administered international zone (Map 9.2B)—a *corpus separatum* (separate entity), accessible to all faiths and peoples but belonging to neither Arabs nor Jews (Fig. 9.1).

Theoretically based on ethnic distribution, the proposed political-geographical jigsaw reflected the difficulty of equitable partition. Zionists wanted all of Palestine for the Jewish state, in keeping with their interpretation of the Balfour Declaration. Other critics of the plan pointed to its partiality for the Jewish state, which received 56 percent of Palestine, although Jews still made up only one-third of the population and owned only about 7 percent of the land. The proposed boundaries would have included 407,000

Arabs in the Jewish state and 10,000 Jews in the Arab state, as well as 142,000 Jews and 68,000 Arabs in international Jerusalem.

The Arabs, relying on the principle that a mandate territory could not be legally alienated from the indigenous population, rejected the proposed surrender of more than half their homeland to comparatively recent settlers. But the Zionists accepted the proposal, which granted UN legitimacy to their sovereignty over half of Palestine. Jews and Arabs engaged in preliminary fighting, sometimes battling British forces, with the more organized Jewish paramilitary units securing control over their allotted territory as well as areas outside this territory where Jewish settlements were concentrated.

Israel Independent.   Israel's declaration of independence on May 14, 1948, made no mention of boundaries. Military units from contiguous Arab states entered the former mandate at the same time to aid Palestinians. Only the British-trained Jordanians and Iraqis held their ground in the highlands. Fighting alternated with cease-fires, but the other Arab forces were defeated by better-armed and -organized Jewish fighters.

In the end, Israel controlled not only the area allotted the Jewish state but also half the territory of the Arab state. The Jordan Arab Legion, with Iraqi troops on its right flank, held the highlands to the north, south, and east of Jerusalem, and Egyptians held a narrow tract northeast of the Sinai—the Gaza Strip. Jerusalem was split between Jordan and Israel—Jordan with the Old City and most of the holy sites, along with the rest of the West Bank.

Territorial Phases

Theoretically, Israel became an independent state within the borders of the Partition Plan—what could be called the first "territorial phase." However, a second territorial phase was based on the situation at the end of the

fighting—the cease-fire lines negotiated by a UN mediator.[7] These expanded Israel's original area by 50 percent and became (and still are) Israel's internationally recognized boundaries (Map 9.2C). Although Jordan held the eastern part of Jerusalem, including the Old City, Israel unilaterally declared Jerusalem as its national capital in 1950. This was pronounced invalid by the UN because the original Partition Plan had designated Jerusalem as a *corpus separatum* under UN administration. A short-lived third territorial phase came when Israel occupied Sinai during the Israeli-British-French collaborative assault on Suez in 1956. It later pulled out under international pressure, especially from US president Dwight Eisenhower.

June 1967.   The fourth phase of Israel's territorial evolution began after the Six-Day (or June) War in 1967, in which Israel seized Sinai, Gaza, the West Bank, and the southwestern corner of Syria, the Golan Heights (Map 9.2D). This reunited Jerusalem, a major Israeli goal; the boundaries of East Jerusalem were then extended, and the entire area was unilaterally annexed—an act that has gained no international recognition. No foreign embassies are currently located in Jerusalem;[8] the city does have an extensive consular corps stationed there in recognition of its status as a *corpus separatum*.[9]

This phase lasted until Israel's withdrawal from Sinai under agreements mediated by US secretary of state Henry Kissinger after the Egyptian-Syrian attacks on Israeli positions in Sinai and Golan in 1973—the Yom Kippur/Ramadan War—and accords reached at Camp David in 1978 and the Egyptian-Israeli peace treaty of 1979.

In the North.   Israel's annexation of the Golan in 1981 could be termed a fifth phase—an action also never recognized by any country. A sixth phase can be seen in Israel's invasions of Lebanon in 1978 and 1982. Although most of its forces were withdrawn by 1984, Israel maintained control of a heavily fortified 440-mi^2/ 1,140-km^2 "security zone" in Lebanon, ostensibly to deter rocket attacks on and infiltration into northern Israel. After twenty-two years and more than 900 casualties, mounting domestic and international criticism, and resistance from Hizballah and other guerrillas, Israel unilaterally withdrew in May 2000.

First called by Israelis "occupied territories," then "administered territories," then simply "territories," four areas—the West Bank, the Gaza Strip, the Golan Heights, and Sinai— were under military government from 1967 until the Sinai was evacuated and the Golan Heights was annexed. The West Bank and East Jerusalem remain the territorial core—but not the only territorial aspect—of the Arab-Israeli conflict, globally as well as locally. As Israel has continued to build and expand illegal settlements in these areas, Palestinians are determined to remain in their homes and to keep their farmlands (see Fig. 9.2).

First Intifadah. A widespread citizens' rebellion—the First Intifadah (literally, "shaking off")—broke out in Gaza in 1987 and soon spread to the West Bank as a full-scale insurgency. Armed Israeli soldiers confronted rock-throwing youths protesting the continuing occupation and settlement expansion. Open resistance increased Palestinian confidence, but as more extreme groups (like Hamas) emerged, the struggle became more intense. The 1990–1991 Gulf Crisis (see below in this chapter) led the coalition partners to initiate the formal peace process, and the intifadah subsided with the first Israeli-Palestinian accord in September 1993.

Second Intifadah. After the assassination of Israeli prime minister Yitzhak Rabin by a Jewish extremist in 1995 and the succession of Benjamin Netanyahu to his first term as head of government, the peace process stalled (see below in this chapter and Chap. 13 for more details), and frustration again built among Palestinians. The Second Intifadah broke out in September 2000 with a violent clash occasioned by a visit to the Haram al-Sharif/Temple Mount by Ariel Sharon, then campaigning for election as prime minister and accompanied by a thousand-strong armed retinue. What came to be known as the "al-Aqsa Intifadah" was characterized by greater militancy and suicide bombings on the Palestinian side and, on the Israeli side, by heavy-handed responses, including targeted assassinations, bulldozing of homes and olive groves, and destruction of Palestinian government buildings in Ramallah. The cycles of violence ebbed after 2004 with the death of Palestinian president Yasser Arafat and Sharon's announcement of the evacuation of troops from Gaza, a decision Sharon made and justified as being to Israel's benefit from both a security and a fiscal point of view. Construction of the so-called West Bank barrier or wall, partly along the pre-1967 border, partly deviating well into the West Bank, began in earnest during the height of the Second Intifadah.

The Palestinians

Although most Palestinians are refugees, they may be grouped geographically in seven categories: those who stayed in areas designated by the UN as the Jewish state; those who remained in the Arab areas taken over by Israel in 1948–1949 (mostly the Galilee); those who lived in the areas held by the Arab armies (the West Bank and Gaza); those who fled the areas incorporated into Israel in 1948–1949, becoming refugees in adjoining districts (West Bank and Gaza, later occupied by Israel); those who fled to the East Bank between 1947 and the present (and were granted Jordanian citizenship); those who fled into adjoining countries and have remained there; and those who emigrated to other countries (see discussions under Palestine in Chap. 13 and Jordan in Chap. 12 for more details).

Figure 9.2 Armed Jewish settlers in the West Bank, in the heart of Hebron, which has theoretically been turned over to the Palestinian Authority (*top*), and a new settlement in 1997 near Hebron in the process of being developed (*bottom*). First come the mobile homes (shown here), then the permanent houses. Both are illegal under the Fourth Geneva Convention, which Israel rejects.

Even before the outbreak of full-scale fighting in May 1948, Palestinians had lost the initiative to Zionist forces, and thousands fled from areas in which Arabs and Jews were contending for land and military advantage. They had been especially terrified by the massacre of 254 Palestinian villagers in Deir Yassin, near Jerusalem, by Jewish terrorists in April 1948, which was then widely reported in order to cause panic among the Arabs. Beginning in May, the thousands of refugees became hundreds of thousands, as Israeli military units gained the advantage.

Al-Nakbah.   By the time fighting subsided in 1949, some 800,000 Palestinians had fled or been expelled from their homes and lands by Israeli forces.[10] Arabs refer to these watershed events as *al-nakbah,* "the catastrophe." After studying newly declassified documentation in the mid-1980s, a group of Israeli scholars, who became known as the "New Historians," wrote that *inter alia* the expulsion of the Palestinians, and the effort to cause panic among them, was more deliberate and common than previously admitted, conclusions now widely accepted.[11]

UN Relief and Works Agency.   The hill country of central Palestine, Transjordan, Gaza, Lebanon, and Syria became the principal places of refuge, while about 160,000 Arabs, mostly in Galilee, refused to leave their lands and homes and stayed in what became the Jewish state.[12] The refugees expected to return home when the fighting ceased. When it became clear that Israel would not allow this, the UN created the UN Relief and Works Agency (UNRWA) to provide emergency refugee aid, setting up camps where the refugees were concentrated, as mentioned above (see Map 9.3).[13] Not all the refugees have called the camps home; those with professional skills or sufficient funds generally did not register with UNRWA. Many refugees have steadfastly rejected integration into their host countries,

deliberately maintaining refugee status as a symbol of determination to return to their homeland and regain their patrimony.

With Israel's 1967 conquests (Map 9.4), an estimated 116,000 original refugees were again uprooted, mostly from the West Bank, and crossed to the East Bank; 99,000 Syrians took flight from Golan; and 35,000 Bedouin and villagers in the Sinai fled across the Suez Canal. Thousands more abandoned camps and villages with Israeli incursions into southern Lebanon, especially after the invasion of 1982.

Unskilled refugees could at best find only menial jobs outside the camps, but many educated Palestinians (often schooled in UNRWA institutions) prospered in their host countries; they were significant in developing the Gulf states. Beirut was a center of Palestinian intellectual activity, Amman a demographic center, and Kuwait a center of commercial activity. However, their role in Beirut diminished with the fighting in Lebanon in the 1980s, and they have never regained their role in Kuwait after being expelled because of Arafat's support of Iraq in 1991.

Refugee Categories.   Palestinians categorized in the seven geographical groups mentioned earlier may also be divided into four categories according to their status as refugees: (1) all Palestinians, (2) registered refugees from the 1948–1949 fighting (under specific UNRWA criteria), (3) "displaced persons" who first fled the West Bank in the 1967 war, and (4) those living in the camps—about one-fourth of registered refugees. With these various ways of classifying them, differences in enumeration inevitably arise.

Palestinian Population.   By 2012, there were about 4.3 million Palestinians residing in the West Bank, East Jerusalem, and Gaza and about 1.6 million in Israel proper, 3.2 million in Jordan, 0.5 million in Syria, 0.4 million in Lebanon, from 0.4 to 0.5 million in other Middle

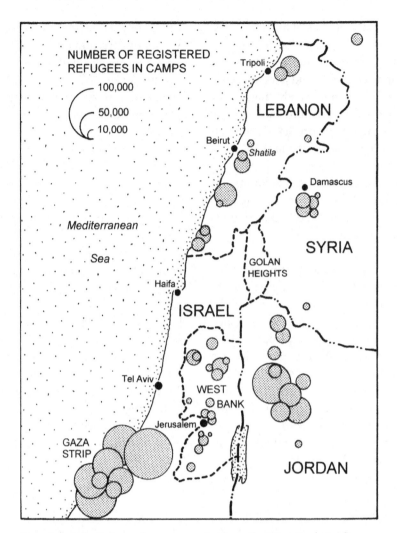

Map 9.3 Palestinian refugee camps in Gaza, the West Bank, Jordan, Syria, and Lebanon, operated by the United Nations Relief and Works Agency. As of 2013, these fifty-eight camps had a population of 1.5 million, a significant portion of the 4.9 million refugees registered with UNRWA.

East countries, and 0.3 million or more elsewhere—for a total of close to 11 million.

Fatah and the Palestine Liberation Organization.   Facing international inaction after 1949, the Palestinians slowly began to organize. Fatah (the reverse acronym for Harakat al-Tahrir al-Filastiniyah, Palestinian Liberation Movement) was founded in 1958 and conducted guerrilla raids by *fedayeen* (literally, "sacrificers") into Israel from neighboring countries. It later became the leading element within the coalition forming the Palestine Liberation Organization (PLO). With Arafat as its chairman beginning in 1969, it gradually gained a leading if highly controversial role in Palestinian and Middle East affairs and evolved into a complex institution that expanded beyond paramilitary activities, with several welfare agencies serving refugees.

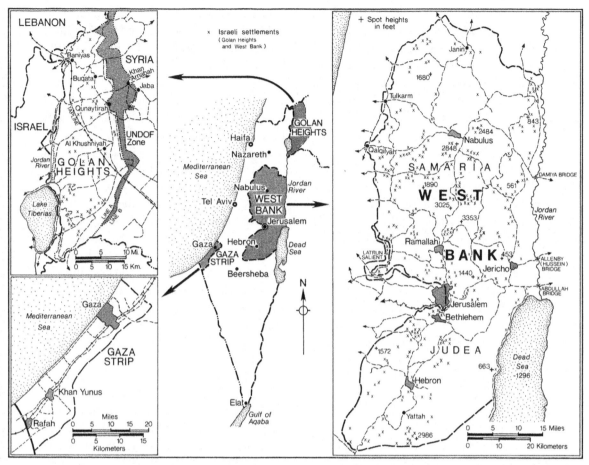

Map 9.4 Territories occupied by Israel in 1967 and, except for Gaza, still occupied in 2013. Israel announced a unilateral withdrawal from Gaza by the end of 2005 but invaded it briefly in December 2008 and has traded rockets other times, especially in late 2012. Israel considers Golan as part of Israel, but the claim is not recognized by any other government.

Jordan was its initial base, and it became a "state within a state," provoking opposition from King Husayn, who defeated it in 1970 in a short but bloody war—"Black September." It then moved to Lebanon, which was too disunited to resist. In 1974, Arab governments recognized the PLO as the sole official representative of the Palestinians. It remained in Lebanon through the onset of that country's civil war until 1982, when it was forced, under Israeli military and Western diplomatic pressure, to withdraw to Tunis. With the onset of the peace process, it moved to Gaza in 1994 as

the Palestinian Authority and then to Ramallah in the West Bank, where it has remained through an Israeli siege in 2002 as the widely recognized quasi government of the Palestinians (though Hamas has controlled Gaza since 2007).

The Peace Process

A confluence of events in the early 1990s led to what was soon called the peace process that, by fits and starts, has continued to today. The First Intifadah had led some Israeli leaders (including Yitzhak Rabin) to conclude that the PLO could no longer be ignored; the Iraqi invasion of Kuwait had cobbled together a broad coalition led by the United States that shared a consensus, after Iraq had been defeated, that outside powers could no longer stay aloof from the Israeli-Palestinian problem; in addition, the fall of the Soviet Union left in its place a Russian government willing to work with its former foes to secure a more stable Middle East. The Madrid Conference of October 1991 brought all these elements together, and it was followed by secret bilateral talks between Israel and the PLO in Oslo. The famous White House handshake between Rabin and Arafat marked the formal signing of an agreement in September 1993.

Positive Factors.   Some important practical advances resulted: for the first time, the two parties recognized each other as negotiating partners; there was mutual acknowledgment that a settlement could come only through negotiation; Israel evacuated enough of the Occupied Territories to allow the PLO (and Arafat) to return to Palestine and be transformed into the Palestine Authority (PA), heading a quasi state; the United States stopped treating all Palestinians as terrorists; and Jordan and Israel signed a peace treaty.

And Negative Ones Too.   But there were negative factors as well, and these kept the early promise of peace and Palestinian statehood from being fulfilled. Extremists on both sides condemned the rapprochement. On the Palestinian side, Hamas set out to sabotage the PA as a negotiator and achieved some success in its efforts: for the Israelis, a Jewish fanatic assassinated Rabin, paving the way for the election of a right-wing government headed by Benjamin Netanyahu and notably less interested in pursuing peace with the Palestinians. Meanwhile, suicide bombings persisted, and settlement building and expansion on the West Bank continued apace; Netanyahu, citing the PA's inability to control

violence, reneged on implementing the provisions of the Oslo accords and the Wye River Memorandum brokered by President Bill Clinton in 1998.

Close—but No Peace.   Ehud Barak replaced Netanyahu as prime minister in May 1999. Dialogue resumed with some successes, encouraging Clinton to bring Barak and Arafat together at Camp David in July 2000. Controversy surrounds why this summit and its follow-up failed to solidify the progress that had been made and to move on to other issues; each side has blamed the other. But other observers have noted that the final US-Israeli offer was subtly inadequate, while the Palestinians missed the opportunity to make a timely counteroffer.[14] Meanwhile, the Second Intifadah had broken out, followed by Barak's defeat in the February 2001 election by right-wing leader Ariel Sharon.

Into the New Century.   The new century saw a mixture of events, some of which favored the peace process, but probably more that militated against it. Saudi Arabia offered a comprehensive peace plan in 2002 and secured Arab League endorsement for it; the UN, the United States, the EU, and Russia, constituting the Quartet, developed a "road map" to achieve an overall settlement in stages; Prime Minister Sharon pulled out of the Gaza Strip and broke with his right-wing Likud Party; his successor, Ehud Olmert, won reelection in 2006, promising to pursue disengagement; and the Second Intifadah drew to a close. On the other hand, settlement building on the West Bank continued and even sped up, with a concomitant increase in the number of settlers; the West Bank wall project moved forward (Fig. 9.3), slicing the region into dozens of pieces and de facto annexing as much as 15 percent of its area to Israel proper; the so-called Summer War of 2006 pitted the Israeli armed forces against the irregulars of Hizballah in Lebanon, and the result—essentially a

Figure 9.3 One segment of the Israeli "Separation Fence," which Israel claims is essential for its security. A wall in certain stretches, the barrier is actually built almost entirely on Palestinian lands and here divides a village. It has been a matter of continuing controversy.

standoff—demoralized the Israeli people; the American invasion of Iraq in 2003 and the consequent insurgency against the occupation dominated Middle East politics for many years afterward; the Bush administration faltered in the role of honest broker; the Palestinians carried out their second free election in 2006, but the rejectionist Hamas list won a plurality; while Fatah ruled on the West Bank, Hamas took control of Gaza; Operation Cast Lead in 2008–2009 saw Israel reinvade Gaza and inflict heavy casualties on the population and some $2 billion in property damage; and, finally, Netanyahu returned as prime minister in 2009 in partnership with the far-right party supported by Russian immigrants (facing the 2013 election, he engineered a semimerger of his Likud Party with the Russian party to present voters with a single list).

Obama Succeeds Bush. Two months before Netanyahu took office, Barack Obama was inaugurated in the United States, and it seemed that American involvement in the peace process might be rejuvenated after the eight years of the neoconservative (neocon) Bush administration. Obama set out to repair the badly damaged American relationship with the Arab and wider Muslim world while maintaining the high level of military and financial support traditionally given to Israel. But more than two decades after the heady days of Madrid and Oslo, peace remains elusive. Netanyahu was unable or unwilling to call a meaningful freeze on settlement building and expansion and thus antagonize an important element in his coalition. The PA is weak and divided; hard-pressed by Hamas, it is unable to seem too conciliatory. Disagreements over tactics in dealing with the Iran nuclear crisis contributed to distancing the United States and Israel. Finally, Israel's growing isolation in the world (as illustrated in the overwhelming UN General Assembly vote in November 2012 recognizing Palestine as a nonmember state) makes its government all the more defensive and nationalistic.

No Peace, No Process? With no peace in sight, the question must be asked as to whether there is any real process remaining. President Obama tried to regain the position of the United States as the honest broker between the two sides, but even an optimistic assessment would conclude that he has had only limited success through 2013 (see Chap. 13 for more discussion of the peace process).

THE IRAN-IRAQ WAR, 1980–1988

Historic Divide Revisited. Ancient enmities flared into open conflict along the Zagros piedmont between "Mesopotamians" to the west and "Iranians" to the east with the overthrow of the shah in 1979. For centuries, the Sunni Ottomans were to the west, while the Shii Persians held the Zagros and the Iranian Plateau. Post–World War I Iraq and Iran periodically clashed along the ridges and the Shatt al-Arab. The new Islamic Republic's aggressiveness and apparent instability led Saddam Husayn, newly self-elevated to Iraq's presidency, to try forcing Iran to accede to several long-standing demands by invading across the Shatt in September 1980. It soon held several positions inside Iran and called for the return of Gulf islands that Iran had occupied since 1971. Thus began the Iran-Iraq War, which Iraq expected to last a few weeks but dragged on for eight years. At the war's outset, Iraq expected support from the Arab population of the oil-rich Iranian province of Khuzestan that it invaded; as it continued, Iran tried to rally Iraqi Shii to its side. For the most part, both failed in these efforts.

War Aims. Iraq aimed to reinstate the pre-1975 boundary along the Shatt and thus regain complete control of the outlet to the sea of a major port, Basrah. Difficult to delineate equitably, the modern boundary was first drawn in 1847 and slightly modified in 1913–1914. In 1937, it was changed to follow the *thalweg* (deepest channel) near Abadan but the low-water mark on the east (Iranian) bank (Map 9.5A), in accordance with the 1913–1914 agreement. In 1969, the shah renounced this treaty, and by 1975 a powerful Iran forced Iraq to accept a boundary that followed the *thalweg* along the entire Shatt (Map 9.8B) in return for ceasing to assist the rebellion of Iraq's Kurds.

War Results. War operations damaged or destroyed many major facilities in the northern Gulf, including Iraq's ports and much of the city of Basrah. Air raids and missile attacks struck major cities on both sides, and oil production decreased sharply in both countries: physical infrastructure in both countries suffered damage to the tune of uncountable billions. Casualties were tragically high, especially among young Iranians, and combined fatalities were reliably reported to exceed 500,000.[15]

Regional Implications. Because of the war, all the Gulf states were affected economically—losses estimated at $200 billion directly and more than $1 trillion indirectly. Oil tankers calling at export terminals were attacked—the "tanker war," which intensified in 1987. The Gulf amirates and Saudi Arabia gave Iraq about $50 billion in aid, and the latter allowed Iraq to build a pipeline connecting to the Saudi East-West line, thus accessing Red Sea export facilities. The United States committed to keeping the Gulf accessible by providing naval escorts to US-registered tankers—actually mostly reflagged Kuwaiti vessels. In the confusion of the Gulf's confined area, mistakes led to the USS *Star*'s being hit by an

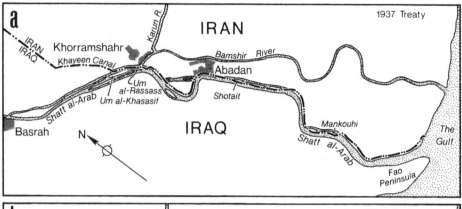

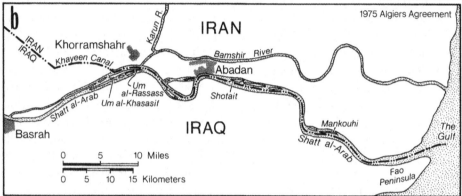

Map 9.5 Iran-Iraq boundary along the Shatt al-Arab. The boundary shift from the east bank of the river to the deepest part of the channel (the *thalweg*) in 1975 was one reason for the Iran-Iraq War, 1980–1988. (Redrawn from Tareq Y. Ismael, *Iraq and Iran: Roots of Conflict* [Syracuse, NY: Syracuse University Press, 1982], 23. Names as on original. Used with permission.)

Iraqi Exocet missile in May 1987, killing 37 of its crew, and to the USS *Vincennes*'s shooting down an Iranian civilian aircraft with a missile in July 1988, with a loss of all 290 people aboard. Both Iraq and the United States agreed to pay damages for their errors.

Stalemate.   With both countries exhausted, Iran surprisingly accepted a UN Security Council resolution calling for an immediate cease-fire, possibly because of fears of Iraqi chemical attacks. In March 1988, Iraq had used poison gas against the Kurdish village of Halabja, killing several thousand, in reprisal for some Kurds having joined Iran in a prior attack. A UN-sponsored armistice took effect in August 1988.

Ironies and Aftermath.   The war engendered some curious transnational relationships. Syria, although Arab and Baathi ruled like Iraq, refused to allow Iraq the use of pipelines across its territory; the Syrian-Iranian alliance, born in the 1980s, has persisted through the early 2010s when both regimes were under attack. Despite the Islamic Republic's vociferous condemnations of Israel, the Jewish state followed its principle of aiding an enemy of the Arabs by supplying Iran with spare parts and arms in collaboration with the United States, as was revealed by the Iran-Contra scandal. But by 2012, Israel was in the forefront, urging military action against Iran and the nuclear policies its regime had followed, partly in reaction to the vulnerability Iran felt as a result of the Iraqi attack. Two of radical republican Iraq's biggest financial and logistical supporters, conservative and monarchical Kuwait and Saudi Arabia, became its victims in turn in 1990. After the US-led coalition overthrew the Saddam regime (with Iran's tacit approval) in 2003, the long-oppressed Shii majority gradually solidified its control in Iraq. Iran, with outstanding claims against Iraq of billions of dollars in war reparations still unresolved after two decades, put these claims aside at least temporarily as it sought, with some success, to build a close relationship with the new Shii-dominated government in Baghdad.

THE GULF CRISIS, 1990–1991

Despite the huge losses from the 1980–1988 fighting, Iraq launched a second Gulf war less than two years later. Saddam Husayn resurrected his country's long-standing claim to Kuwait, demanding that Kuwait forgive the billions in loans it had made to Iraq during the 1980s and cede to Iraq its part of the rich Rumaila oil field; Kuwait rejected these demands. While giving assurances that he would not attack an Arab country, on August 2, 1990, he ordered the 100,000 troops massed on the border—supposedly only for maneuvers—to advance into Kuwait.

Regional and world reaction varied in kind, degree, and speed. Iraq sought support from the more oppressed and militant Arabs, claiming to champion Arabism, Islam, the Palestinians, the overthrow of wealthy monarchies, anti-imperialism, and other popular causes. One Iraqi proposal linked withdrawal from Kuwait with Israeli withdrawal from the Occupied Territories and Syrian withdrawal

from Lebanon. Some frustrated Palestinians cheered these declarations, and the PLO leadership expressed support, as did Yemen, Sudan, Libya, Algeria, and Tunisia. Jordan, with close economic ties to Iraq, equivocated. Iraq gained Iran's neutrality by hastily accepting the harsh terms Iran had put forward in 1988 for a treaty ending their war.

Coalition Response

Acting under the Carter Doctrine, the United States sought and received prompt Saudi permission to dispatch troops to northeastern Saudi Arabia within days of the invasion. Most Western reaction to the invasion was channeled through the UN Security Council (UNSC). Under its resolutions, thirty-six states joined the US/UK-led coalition and cooperated in Kuwait's liberation. Germany and Japan sent no troops but contributed large funds; the Soviet Union, long an ally of Iraq but close to its own collapse, at first tried to broker negotiations. Frustrated by Saddam's unwillingness to compromise, it generally concurred in carrying out the UNSC resolutions against Iraq.

Although Iraq claimed Kuwait as its "rightful nineteenth province," its occupation forces committed many atrocities—executions, widespread mistreatment of hundreds of Kuwaitis, hostage taking, and large-scale looting, including museum collections and $3–4 billion in gold bullion as well as cash in the banks (UN resolutions eventually secured the return of most of the museum collections and gold bullion). The invasion also set in motion a human tide of more than 3 million refugees of many nationalities, and hundreds of Europeans and Americans were held hostage in Baghdad.

The UNSC gave Iraq a deadline of January 15, 1991, to leave Kuwait or face a full-scale military attack in both Kuwait and Iraq. When Iraq did not withdraw, intensive target-specific air strikes were directed at Baghdad and other major cities in Iraq. Saddam refused to capitulate, and the coalition ground attack began on February 24, 1991, overwhelming Iraqi forces in Kuwait in a few days.

Destruction and Ecoterrorism

Scuds and Oil Spills.   Details of the military operations are well covered elsewhere. However, two Iraqi wartime actions are noteworthy. First, thirty-two ground-to-ground Scud missiles were launched at targets in Saudi Arabia and thirty-nine at Israel. Some were destroyed by Patriot antimissile batteries, but others damaged buildings in both countries; one caused twenty-seven US military fatalities in Dammam, Saudi Arabia. Second, after the beginning of hostilities, Iraq employed a new and highly destructive tactic, appropriately labeled "environmental terrorism," or "ecoterrorism"—dumping and setting fire to oil, thus making a weapon of the one commodity available in abundance. To deter expected coalition offensive operations along the coast, the Iraqis opened the valves of storage facilities in the export terminals and on tankers in the area, deliberately creating the greatest oil spill in history, perhaps as much as 6 million barrels (in comparison, the 2010 BP spill in the Gulf of Mexico was about 4.4 million barrels), which worked its way down the Gulf coast, destroying enormous quantities of plant and animal life.

As the Iraqis pulled back in defeat, they escalated the ecoterrorism by blowing up and setting fire to most of the amirate's oil wells. Some 651 wells were set ablaze, and another 60 spewed crude oil under high pressure. By the early summer of 1991, about 5.5 million barrels of oil and enormous quantities of natural gas were lost each day—approximately twice the normal average daily production of Kuwait. Upon the liberation of Kuwait, the best oil-well firefighting teams in the world arrived to extinguish the blazes and cap the flowing wells, a task that, despite dangers and difficulties, they accomplished by early November.

Renewed Focus on the Palestinian Problem. One positive outcome of the war was that it focused the attention of the Western powers on the Palestinian-Israeli conflict and the possibility of initiating a peace process. The Madrid Conference convened in October 1991 for this purpose. On the negative side was the failure of Iraq and the UN coalition—primarily the United States—to resolve the impasse over weapons inspections and other provisions of the sanctions. There was also the later criticism that "the United States didn't finish the job" and that it should have pushed on to Baghdad to overthrow the Baathi once and for all. Although this idea might have appealed to its hawkish proponents, such action would have violated the very specifically worded UNSC mandate and betrayed the terms of the coalition, instantly transforming partners into enemies. It was, however, a factor in formulating the neoconservative policies of the United States a decade later that led to full-scale invasion of Iraq. (See Chap. 14 for details of events following the 1991 cease-fire.)

OPERATION IRAQI FREEDOM

Following the 9/11 attacks and US president George W. Bush's declaration of a "War on Terror," three developments led up to the invasion of Iraq: the US incursion into Afghanistan in search of Osama bin Laden and other al-Qaida leaders, several months of well-publicized US planning—including presentations to the UN—and revelations of intentions regarding Iraq, and many weeks of inspections by UN teams for the suspected weapons of mass destruction (WMDs) in Iraq. With a modest coalition—Britain the main partner—of forces in place in Kuwait and the lower Gulf,[16] and with hot weather approaching, the US-led invasion of Iraq began on March 20, 2003, with the code name "Operation Iraqi Freedom."

Invasion Rationale.   Reasons given by the US administration and the British prime minister for the preemptive attack included the threat posed to the United States and Britain from the alleged WMDs, the supposed links between Iraq and al-Qaida, and the oppression of the Iraqi people by the Saddam Husayn regime. President Bush's letter to Congress justifying the attack stated that its aims were to "protect the national security of the United States, as well as the security of other countries," against the threat of the Iraqi WMDs and to obtain Iraqi compliance with relevant UN resolutions.

The claims and actions surrounding the invasion and the subsequent occupation provoked a vigorous negative international response, with the United States receiving more condemnation than it had in many years. Domestic reaction was bitterly divided, with opinions particularly strong regarding the influence of a small but influential group of prowar neocons centered in the Department of Defense and the Office of the Vice President.

The operations in late March 2003 achieved their military objectives relatively promptly, and the United States announced the formal end of hostilities in mid-April. Coalition casualties were light in the invasion but increased considerably during the subsequent occupation. (Developments in postinvasion Iraq are discussed in Chap. 14.) In concluding this section, it should be pointed out that in Operation Iraqi Freedom, no WMDs were ever discovered; as to the presence of al-Qaida, there was none until after the invasion, when the insurgency brought that group and others like it into Iraq (from where they later spread over into Syria).

Enormous US Costs.   By the time of the US withdrawal from Iraq in December 2011, the war had cost the country some 4,460 military fatalities, more than 32,200 physically wounded, and possibly as many as 500,000 troops with severe psychological problems.[17] US taxpayers had by then been burdened with more than $1.7 trillion in direct war-related

outlays—deficit spending covered by borrowing from foreign lenders (especially China). This is roughly thirty-five times what the Bush administration estimated costs would be at the outset, and future US budgets will see as much as $6 trillion in long-term expenses (veterans' care and compensation, military equipment replacement, debt service, and other costs).[18]

The tenth anniversary of the invasion was the occasion for a plethora of published articles and reports summarizing all aspects of the war from widely different viewpoints. But it would not be inaccurate to say that there has been wide agreement that the human and financial costs have been enormous, that much waste and corruption were involved, that US foreign policy suffered serious setbacks because of the invasion and occupation, and that it is not clear whether lasting democracy has really been planted in Iraq.[19]

Inestimable Iraqi Costs.   On the Iraqi side, it is impossible to pinpoint the losses reliably; the number of civilian and military deaths has been variously estimated at from more than 100,000 to as many as 1.3 million. By the late 2000s, population displacements had soared to levels rarely seen previously in localized warfare. At the peak, some 2.5 million Iraqis had fled to safer havens in neighboring countries and farther afield; the number of internally displaced persons in Iraq reached at least 1.8 million.[20] Nearly one in six Iraqis was forced to leave their home; the economic costs to the country are truly incalculable. A 2012 study of global terrorism by the Institute for Economics and Peace (see "Terrorism" in this chapter for more details) found that of the 100 worst terrorist incidents in the decade following 9/11, no fewer than 49 of them occurred in Iraq.[21]

STRATEGIC STRAITS

Five sea passages, four major and one minor, in the region are of geostrategic significance:

the Suez Canal, the Turkish Straits (Bosporus and Dardanelles), the Strait of Hormuz, Bab el-Mandeb, and the Strait of Tiran. Some are familiar historically; all have made news in recent decades. The US Department of Energy identifies six major chokepoints for global oil trade; four are in the Middle East (all of those mentioned above except Tiran).[22]

Waterways and War. Control of the Turkish Straits was an issue during World War I and its immediate aftermath, the Suez Canal was twice blocked by military action between 1956 and 1975, closure of the Strait of Tiran was a factor in the buildup to the June 1967 war between Israel and its immediate Arab neighbors, and the ability of Iran to hamper, even partially, vital oil shipments through the Strait of Hormuz is of major concern as the dispute over Iran's nuclear ambitions has developed.

Suez Canal

Egypt's Suez Canal was excavated between 1859 and 1869 through the Isthmus of Suez, which linked Africa and Asia. Entirely at sea level with no locks, it is approximately 110 mi/177 km long. It has been enlarged numerous times to a navigational width of 650 ft/198 m and a depth of 62 ft/18.9 m. A long-term project to both widen and deepen the canal had by 2010 achieved its intermediate depth goal of 66 ft/20.1 m, allowing passage of about 67 percent of the global tanker fleet and 100 percent of container ships and other freighters. A combination of global recession and fears of piracy south of the Red Sea led to a decrease in traffic in 2008–2009, but in 2011, revenues hit a record high of $5.2 billion, with an average of slightly fewer than forty-nine ships transiting daily.

Its opening shortened the sea trip between Britain and India by 5,000 mi/8,000 km, so that after the 1870s most world shipping shifted from the route around Africa to the Mediterranean–Suez–Red Sea route. Suez Canal closures, for six months in 1956 and for eight years prior to June 1975, diverted traffic—including increasing numbers of VLCCs (very large crude carriers)—to other routes, and some shipping never returned to Suez. The canal also faces competition from Egypt's own Sumed pipeline, which carries crude oil from the Red Sea to the Mediterranean, thus bypassing the canal. In 2011, the Sumed pipeline (see Chap. 6) and the canal together carried 3.8 mn bpd. An underwater extension across the Red Sea to link Sumed directly to Saudi Arabia's East-West pipeline at Yanbu is being discussed.

Straits

Turkish Straits. These straits, the Dardanelles to the southwest and the Bosporus to the northeast, are linked by the Sea of Marmara (Map 9.6) and have been of crucial importance since the Bronze Age. The legend of the Trojan War tells of fighting over the beautiful Helen, a romanticization of the struggle during the twelfth century BCE for control of the entrance to the Black Sea and its rich coastlands. The World War I Gallipoli campaign in 1915 is the most recent clash over control of the straits; possession of the straits was a major war goal of czarist Russia before the revolution of 1917. International access to the straits was spelled out in the Lausanne Convention of 1923 and again in the Montreux Convention of 1936, which still governs international use of the waterways.

The Bosporus (Greek for "ox-ford"; Turkish: Karadeniz Boğazı) is shorter, narrower, and shallower than the Dardanelles—about 17 mi/28 km long, 2,500 ft/762 m wide at its narrowest, and 100 ft/30 m at its minimum midstream depth. Since the Sea of Marmara is as deep as, and much wider than, the two straits, any ship afloat can make the passage between the Aegean and the Black Seas. Although the three bodies of water separate Europe from Asia Minor, the Bosporus was bridged in 1973

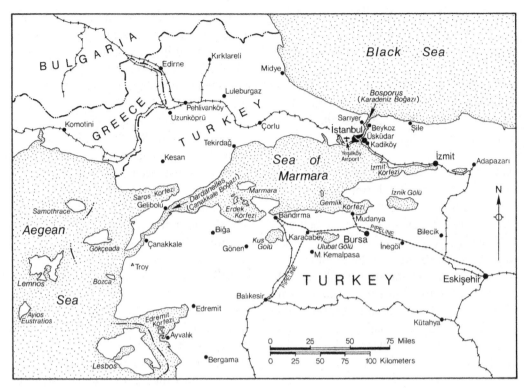

Map 9.6 The Turkish straits (Bosporus and Dardanelles) and their geographic setting—a major world maritime connection and "chokepoint." The disastrous earthquake of August 17, 1999, was centered just south of Izmit.

and again in 1988. The Marmaray project, including a rail tunnel billed as earthquake proof under the strait, is to serve both Istanbul's metro system and through trains; construction difficulties have been encountered, but completion is still scheduled for late 2013. Plans for a third bridge at the northern end of the Bosporus have also been delayed, but the launch of the project was announced in May 2012.

The Dardanelles (Turkish: Çanakkale Boğazı), the ancient Hellespont, connects the Aegean Sea and the Sea of Marmara and lies between the Gallipoli Peninsula on the northwest and Asia Minor to the south. It is about 36 mi/57 km long, 4,000 ft/1,200 m wide at its narrowest, 4 mi/6.4 km at its widest, and 150–300 ft/45–90 m deep.

Maritime Traffic Jam.   Transits through the straits have increased markedly since World War I—international traffic by more than ten times. In the early 2010s, daily traffic was about 135 ships transiting—more than 175 percent above Suez Canal levels. Half the larger ships are tankers, and nearly half of all vessels fly the flags of Russia and other successor states of the FSU, especially Ukraine and Georgia. Straits traffic is expected to increase still more with the further development of Caspian oil fields and the growth of the Danube–Main Rivers waterway. The increase will begin to stretch the capacity of the straits to accommodate tanker traffic. In 2010, 2.9 mn bpd of crude—twice the amount of the late 1990s—transited the straits daily, raising serious concerns about environmental

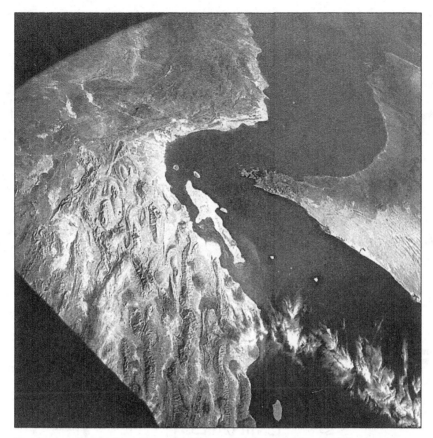

Figure 9.4 Image from space, looking southeast, of the Strait of Hormuz, one of the world's most important economic chokepoints, with Iran to the left and Oman and the UAE to the right. The dark oval areas are salt domes, which often indicate petroleum and gas reservoirs. Compare with Map 9.7. (Photograph courtesy of National Aeronautics and Space Administration)

safety; the possibility of terrorist sabotage in the Bosporus is also a consideration. The Turkish government issued new regulations governing nighttime passage in 2011. Various Anatolian pipeline proposals were under consideration in the early 2010s (see Chaps. 6 and 20 for relevant discussions), and in 2011 the government revealed that it was studying the possibility of constructing a bypass canal specifically designed to carry the largest tankers at a cost of at least $12 billion.

Strait of Hormuz. Connecting the Gulf and the Indian Ocean, the Strait of Hormuz squeezes between Iran to the north and an ex-clave of Oman on the Musandam Peninsula to the south (Fig. 9.4 and Map 9.7). It is by far the world's most vital oil chokepoint, and although no longer do 90 percent of the region's petroleum exports pass through it, as was true before the various Gulf wars, it still carried some 17 mn bpd in 2011. Some of its previous traffic is now piped to the Red Sea and the Mediterranean (and a new bypass pipeline to Fujayrah on the UAE's Indian Ocean coast opened in 2012), but general cargo is growing. Traffic varies with the world petroleum market, the political climate in the Gulf, and tanker size. Increasing shiploads of natural gas liquids (NGL) and product transit each day.

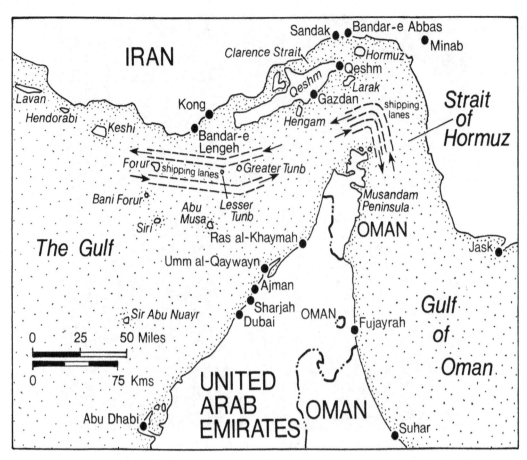

Map 9.7 The Strait of Hormuz, showing countries involved, strategic islands, and shipping lanes. Compare Figure 9.4.

With a depth of 290 ft/88 m and widths of 28–59 mi/45–95 km, Hormuz is the widest of the significant straits in the Middle East. Nevertheless, it is vulnerable to sabotage and some kinds of weaponry, and its defense is vital to both petroleum exporters and petroleum consumers. Thus, the security of the Gulf and the strait is a major aim of the Western powers and their regional allies. As the crisis over Iran's nuclear policies heightened and the sanctions imposed on Iran became more constricting in 2012, the possibility that open conflict might close the strait at least partially became a regular topic in world headlines.

Bab el-Mandeb. At the opposite corner of the Arabian Peninsula, the Bab el-Mandeb (Gate of Lamentation) connects the Red Sea and the Gulf of Aden. The strait is divided into two channels by the small but strategically located Yemeni island Perim. Two other states, Eritrea and Djibouti, share the territorial waters in the straits. The main channel, with a width of 10 mi/16 km and a depth of 1,056 ft/322 m, is to the west of Perim on the African side, next to Djibouti.

Bab el-Mandeb's importance grew significantly when the Suez Canal opened, since virtually all shipping transiting the canal also passes through it. Canal traffic developed more ports along the Red Sea, and so, even with the canal closed, the strait was busy in order to serve Jiddah, Yanbu, and others. Aden, lying a few miles east of the Bab el-Mandeb, owes much of its modern importance to the rise in Suez use. About eighty ships a day transit the strait, with tankers carrying 3.4 mn bpd in 2011. Increased piracy in the seas to the south raised the risks along this route. The hijacking of the Saudi-flagged *Sirius Star* in November 2008 accelerated the trend of tankers to opt for the longer trip around Africa.

Strait of Tiran.   Connecting the Red Sea and the Gulf of Aqabah at the southeastern tip of the Sinai Peninsula, with Egypt on the west and Saudi Arabia on the east, the Strait of Tiran is of relatively minor importance in comparison with the Suez Canal and the straits already described. Nevertheless, its closure was cited as a major justification for the Israeli preemptive attack on Egypt in June 1967. The debate over the precise international principles relating to Tiran has not yet resolved the exact status of the strait. In 2012, an agreement to build the long-discussed 31-mi/50-km causeway-bridge system between Egypt and Saudi Arabia was reportedly reached by the two governments; the project would face both environmental and political controversies.

NONSTATE THREATS

Especially with the beginning of the new century, regional nonstate actors increasingly threatened both the citizens and the economies of countries far from the Middle East, sometimes with the compliance of rogue states like Taliban Afghanistan and ungoverned Somalia, but often acting on their own. Neither of their methods—terrorism and piracy—was new, but changes in international politics and technology have made them manifest in a number of new ways that have challenged the effectiveness of conventional political and military responses.

TERRORISM

In recent decades, violence has been wreaked against civilians to spread fear and terror in many parts of the world; a cult of terrorism has been linked to the Muslim world in general and the Palestinian-Israeli problem in particular. Terrorism—both in concept and in practice—is not new and can be traced to centuries past: for example, the Ismaili Assassins of the eleventh and twelfth centuries and the "Reign of Terror" of the eighteenth-century French Revolution. Modern terrorists are truly global, not only Islamist and Jewish extremists in the Middle East but also the Shining Path in Peru, Red Brigades in Italy, offshoots of the Irish Republican Army, Basque separatists in Spain, Chechen rebels, Tamil Tigers, Aum Shinrikyo in Japan, and right-wing bombers in Oklahoma.

How to Define Terrorism.   The definition of terrorism is crucial, since it can imply responsibility; terrorism is often violence against a favored group by a disfavored group, and there is no single widely accepted definition. In US State Department terms, it is premeditated, politically motivated violence perpetrated against noncombatant targets by subnational groups or clandestine agents, usually intended to influence an audience. The Federal Bureau of Investigation defines it as the unlawful use of force and violence against persons or property to intimidate or coerce a government, the civilian population, or any segment thereof, in furtherance of political or social objectives. The *Encyclopaedia Britannica* and other sources recognize that it can also be a government tool.

Similarly, the application of the very terms "terrorism" or "terrorist" in specific instances can be biased, as some newspapers have stated in their guidelines for reporters, and although useful, the terms are labels and, if employed, should not be tendentious. An act labeled "terrorism" by one side is not necessarily terrorism in an objective sense and may at least more properly be referred to as "alleged terrorism." Distinctions are also drawn between brutal acts committed during open warfare or against military targets and heinous acts committed against innocent civilians in full peacetime. Similar distinctions may sometimes be drawn between acts of unquestionable terrorism and legitimate acts of resistance against an oppressive government or foreign occupation.

Focus on Root Causes.   In the Middle East, Israel and (generally) the West have declared that there is no room for excuses, denying that one side's "terrorist" is another's "freedom fighter." Yet all sides agree that an entire people or religious group must not be incriminated because of the violent actions of a few. No one factor can be identified as the cause of terrorism, and it is difficult to specify one that is even broadly comprehensive. After 9/11, scholarship on the subject suffered as public shock and military action overwhelmed research into its root causes and effective antiterrorism strategies. Rational calls have been made for the "War on Terror" to counter terrorist actions with a focus on the conditions that produced them, emphasizing that terrorists will continue to emerge from environments of ignored or mounting grievances. Increasingly, policy makers are focusing on the geographical and geopolitical dynamics discussed in this chapter.

Following World War II, Zionist determination to achieve an independent Jewish state gave rise to some of the region's seminal acts of terrorism. Two notable examples were cited above: the bombing of the King David Hotel in 1946 by the Irgun Zvai Leumi to intimidate British mandate authorities and the well-planned Irgun-Lehi-Haganah massacre of more than 250 Arab villagers in Deir Yassin

in April 1948—then widely publicized to panic Palestinians into fleeing.[23] Decades of conflict between Jews and Arab Muslim and Christian populations followed, with cycles of violence sometimes erupting into open warfare before reverting to individual attacks that often killed innocent women and children.

Spread Beyond the Region.   Terrorist practices by Middle East groups spread to Europe (notably the 1972 seizure in Munich of Israeli Olympic athletes, who were killed during a rescue attempt) and Africa (hijacking of airliners in 1976 and bombings at American embassies in Kenya and Tanzania in 1998). After the most devastating attack of its type in history on September 11, 2001, President Bush announced the "War on Terror," focusing on terrorism by Muslim militant fundamentalists, and in particular on al-Qaida. Britain, Spain, and Russia have concentrated on domestic terrorism as well. US policy has been widely extended, targeting individuals, businesses, organizations, and polities that may be seen to aid, finance, or harbor terrorism, and it has led to debates regarding infringement of civil liberties and cultural biases against Arabs and Muslims. Actual warfare was initiated by US and allied forces on al-Qaida's presence in Afghanistan in 2001 and (allegedly) Iraq in 2003.

Basic Asymmetry.   Israelis claim their strikes against Arabs have been to preserve the safety and security of their citizens and state and thus have been based on existential needs; Palestinians argue that suicide bombings and similar attacks have been relatively small-scale desperation measures in response to Israeli actions, to call world attention to their grievances, or to press their rights to lands or resources taken by Israelis. The basic asymmetry between the capabilities of the two sides has been noted by Israelis, Arabs, and foreign observers. The cycles of violence have involved control over allotted lands, holy places, arable land, freedom of access, and water resources in contested areas; cataloging the sequence of terrorist attacks is difficult. By the end of 2005, relative quiet (after the Second Intifadah) had returned, but sporadic incidents continued. An Israeli source estimates that from the start of the First Intifadah in December 1987 through April 2013, 1,511 Israelis and 8,378 Palestinians had been killed; there are disputes over the relative numbers of combatant and civilian deaths on both sides, but indications are that civilian casualties were in a large majority among both Israelis and Palestinians.[24]

Al-Qaida. Names of some Middle East militant groups have been incorporated into the daily vocabulary of the 2000s, none more so than al-Qaida (or al-Qaeda, "the Camp"), led for many years by the late Osama bin Laden, who is considered to have coordinated the 9/11 attacks.[25] Ironically, in still another example of blowback, the United States and other countries that al-Qaida now targets originally supported it against the Soviet Union in Afghanistan. After the Taliban regime, which had hosted bin Laden, was ousted from Kabul, the coalition forces failed to follow up in the countryside, and slowly insurgents associated with both the Taliban and al-Qaida reclaimed much of Afghanistan. Groups claiming an al-Qaida affiliation have since shown up in many places across the region, especially in Iraq, Saudi Arabia, Libya, Yemen, and Syria, finding support among ultrafundamentalist Sunnis, especially those who are identified as Salafis.

Other groups include the Palestinian groups Hamas, Islamic Jihad, and the al-Aqsa Martyrs Brigades, which have claimed primary responsibility for the most lethal suicide bombings and other attacks in the Israel-Palestine area; Hizballah (or Hezbollah), a Shii group that arose in opposition to Israel's occupation of Lebanon—it has been supported by Iran with Syrian cooperation, and it has become an important political force in

Lebanon—and engaged Israel in the "Summer War" of 2006 with some success; Jamaat al-Islamiyya (Islamic Fraternity), an Egyptian Islamic organization implicated in the assassination of Anwar Sadat in 1981; and Israeli extremist groups like Kach and Kahane Chai that were part of a movement leading to the assassination of Prime Minister Rabin. In 2012, for the first time, the United States designated Israeli West Bank settler acts (the so-called price-tag attacks) against Israeli peace activists and Palestinian individuals, property, and Muslim and Christian places of worship as "terrorist incidents."[26]

Anti-Iranian Groups. That the question of "terrorist or freedom fighter" is not always clear can be seen in the case of two Iranian groups long opposed to the clerical regime. One, the Mujahideen-e Khalq (Strugglers of the People), participated in the revolution against the monarchy but was leftist and relatively secular in politics, blending this with Shii theology. Persecuted by the Islamic Republic, many of its members fled to Iraq, from which they opposed Tehran during the Iran-Iraq War. It was branded a terrorist organization by Iran; the United States and Canada agreed and gave it the same designation. But in 2009, after it secured considerable support from Europeans who see it as a group seeking Iran's liberation, the EU dropped it from this status; in September 2012, the United States followed suit.[27] The other group, Jundullah (Soldiers of God), is Sunni and Baluch nationalist in its makeup. It has undertaken numerous bombings and assassinations aimed at Shii Persians. To Tehran, it naturally is a terrorist group, but there is some evidence it received encouragement and assistance from the United States during the Bush administration;[28] in 2010, the United States designated it as a "foreign terrorist organization."

Kurds and the Kurdistan Workers' Party. The Kurds, some 31 to 35 million strong, have historically inhabited a region that spreads across parts of modern Turkey, Iraq, Iran, and Syria. Frustrated when the post–World War I Treaty of Sèvres, which promised them an independent homeland from part of erstwhile Ottoman territory, was never ratified, they became known as the world's largest generally cohesive ethnic group with no country of their own. The Kurdistan Workers' Party (PKK) has an armed wing that has fought the Turkish government off and on since 1984 in pursuit of an autonomous Kurdish state in southeastern Turkey. It has carried out numerous attacks on military and civilian targets within the country as well as some on Turkish diplomatic missions abroad (see Chap. 20 for more details). The EU (except for Greece) and the United States declared the PKK to be a terrorist organization in 2004. Turkey recently accused Iran of helping the group with logistical support in order to discourage Turkey from helping the insurgency in Syria.[29] On the other hand, Iran has accused the United States of assisting the PKK's Iranian offshoot—the Party of Free Life of Kurdistan—in its moves against the theocratic government in Tehran.[30]

Motivation. Although numerous groups commit many kinds of terrorism, specific motivations vary. In the Israeli-Palestinian context, for example, some terrorist attacks have been intended primarily to call attention to a given cause or movement, to terrorize an opposing population into leaving a given piece of territory, to bargain for the release of prisoners held by the targeted group, or to avenge the assassination or execution of members, especially leaders, of the acting group.

Motivations likewise differ on a broader scale: terrorists carrying out attacks in Saudi Arabia in the early 2000s sought regime change and hoped to intimidate foreign technicians; daily attacks against civilians in Iraq from 2003 on were designed partly to coerce emerging domestic authorities, partly to ter-

rorize other religious groups and weaken them politically, and partly to further "ethnic cleansing"; regular terrorist attacks in Egypt during the 1990s were attempts to forge a dominant role for Islamists in government; and, as mentioned above, conflict and terrorism in southeastern Turkey from 1984 on by the PKK were waged in pursuit of an independent or autonomous Kurdish state. But in much of the militancy of the Muslim world, from the Maghrib to Indonesia, the intra-Islamic search for identity, revival, and dominance is an important underlying theme.

Cyberterrorism. Defined as the premeditated use of disruptive activities against computers or networks or both to further ideological religious or political objectives, cyberterrorism has manifested itself in the region on several occasions since the late 2000s. However, it is not clear that any of the reported attacks have been carried out by terrorist-type groups. Rather, some of the major examples might better fall under what is called "state-sponsored" terrorism, with Israel, the United States, and Iran being the chief suspects. One target has been Iran's nuclear program with the so-called Stuxnet virus, discovered in 2010; Israel or the United States or both may have been the originators of the virus. The dangers of using cyber techniques in this way were exposed when this virus spread worldwide; it was estimated that only 60 percent of the infected computers were actually in Iran. More recently, the oil giant Saudi Aramco was the target of an attack in August 2102 on its internal communications network by a virus named Shamoon that wiped clean the memories of thousands of computers;[31] a similar attack hit RasGas, the production company for Qatari natural gas, at about the same time. In September and again in October 2102, a technique called "denial of service" hit some of the biggest banks in the United States, possibly by a group that claimed to be Islamic, taking vengeance for a controversial film made in the United States about the Prophet Muhammad and circulated via the Internet.[32]

Observers who label the complex patterns of mutual violence as a clash of civilizations or as some similar Islamic onslaught on the West fail to comprehend the fundamental dynamics of this crucial encounter. It is essential that all factions understand the wellsprings of the others' actions. For the more powerful West, this would mean confronting the complex dimensions of the resentment directed against it; for the extremists, it would mean recognizing the counterproductivity of terrorism.

Global Terrorism Index. In 2012, the Institute for Economics and Peace published a comprehensive study of global terrorism during the decade following the 9/11 attacks; included in the study was the Global Terrorism Index (GTI), which ranked 158 countries according to the degree they had been affected by terrorist activities in 2011, considering the number of incidents and casualties, as well as the level of property damage. The GTI is based on data from the Global Terrorism Database, which has been constructed by the National Consortium for the Study of Terrorism and Responses to Terrorism by codifying some 104,000 incidents and uses a definition of terrorism similar to those of the State Department and FBI indicated above, omitting acts carried out by states.[33] The study found that the impact of terrorism reached its peak in 2007, with most of the increase through that year attributable to events in Iraq; since 2007, the impact level has plateaued.

Leading the list of affected countries, not surprisingly, is Iraq. Other countries from our region ranking among those with the fifty highest GTI values in 2011 are Yemen (fifth), Syria (fourteenth), Iran (seventeenth), Turkey (nineteenth), Israel (twentieth), Egypt (twenty-seventh), Lebanon (thirty-first), Saudi Arabia (forty-eighth), and Qatar (forty-ninth).[34] By way of comparison, the United Kingdom

ranked twenty-eighth and the United States forty-first.

For information on the problem of piracy off the coasts of Yemen and Somalia in the Indian Ocean and on possible links between piracy and terrorism, see the website associated with this book: www.middleeast patterns.com.

NOTES

1. Literally thousands of books and articles examine the Palestine-Israel problem from every conceivable perspective. Some are very good even when supporting one viewpoint. Others subtly screen their bias, and many are merely polemic. Students and readers must select sources with a critical eye; many polemics focus on peripheral issues (for example, religious ambiguities) by way of pursuing an agenda. On the overall conflict, a well-regarded and balanced study is C. Smith 2013. A suggested balance of other studies includes Gerner 1994; Tessler 1994; Morris 1989; Pappé 1999, 2004; Newman 1999; Quandt 2001; Laqueur and Rubin 2001; Rogan and Shlaim 2001; Gilbert 2002; Chomsky 2003; N. Finkelstein 2003; Gazit 2003; and Sand 2009. It is worth noting that some of the severest critics of some Israeli actions are Israelis. See also the introductory note to the Bibliography and the Bibliography itself.

2. It should be kept in mind that far more Jewish migrants sought other destinations as havens, such as North America and western Europe. For example, from 1880 to 1924, an estimated 2 million Jewish immigrants arrived in the United States, and more than 120 thousand came to Canada during approximately the same period.

3. Credited to Zangwill 1901; in fact, this oft-cited phrase seems to be a slight rearrangement of Zangwill's actual words: "Palestine is a country without a people; the Jews are a people without a country."

4. It is contained in a brief letter from Foreign Secretary A. J. Balfour to Lord Rothschild dated November 2, 1917. An image of the original letter can be seen at http://blog.balder.org/billeder-blog/Balfour-Declaration .jpg.

5. The Balfour Declaration has been analyzed in many books and articles. The massive and authoritative Stein 1983 (a reprint of the 1961 edition), by a man associated with the World Zionist Organization, is the most detailed.

6. On the same date sixty-five years later, in 2012, the UN General Assembly voted overwhelmingly to

recognize the State of Palestine and to give it the UN status of nonmember state.

7. American diplomat Dr. Ralph Bunche, who assumed the task after the assassination of his predecessor, Folke Bernadotte, by Israeli terrorists. Bunche received the Nobel Peace Prize for his efforts.

8. As of 2013, all embassies are in Tel Aviv or its immediate environs except that of Paraguay, which is located in a western suburb of Jerusalem.

9. The United States has a consulate general in Jerusalem that also deals with West Bank Palestinians. The US Congress, urged by the Israeli lobby, has legislated a move of the embassy to Jerusalem; however, successive presidents of both parties have held this is an unconstitutional infringement on their right to conduct foreign policy and have resisted any change.

10. Estimates run from 720,000 to 960,000.

11. Regarding Deir Yassin, Begin 1977 includes an account by that author and later Israeli prime minister, who then was commander of Irgun Zvai Leumi, the terrorist group that, along with the Stern Gang, conducted the massacre. For a quite different version, see the report by the local Red Cross representative, Jacques de Reynier, in W. Khalidi 1971, 761–766. Deir Yassin is discussed in any good account of events of the period. See, for example, the sources given in note 1 of this chapter, as well as McGowan and Ellis 1998. Some Israeli sources contest the number of villagers killed, claiming it to be nearer 150, while not minimizing the enormity of the massacre. The birth of the Palestinian refugee problem is addressed by a then leading New Historian in Morris 1989, which is vigorously rebutted in Karsh 1997, then rerebutted in Morris 1998, and finally "revisited" in Morris 2004. See also Pappé 1999.

12. They and their descendants—Israeli Arabs—now constitute about 21 percent of Israel's population.

13. In 2012, some 1.4 million Palestinians, out of a total population of some 11 million worldwide, remain in fifty-eight UNRWA camps—nineteen in the West Bank, eight in Gaza, twelve in Lebanon, nine in Syria, and ten in Jordan.

14. See Ross 2004 for an insider interpretation of the US side in much of the peace process, including the 2000 Camp David talks. See Hanieh 2001 for a detailed Palestinian version of the Camp David talks by a participant. In Agha and Malley 2001, a Palestinian and an American, who each participated, give their joint view. For an intensive scholarly study of the negotiations, see Swisher 2004.

15. Among many studies of the origins and ramifications of the Iran-Iraq War, see Chubin and Tripp 1988; Khadduri 1988; Karsh 1990; and Gause 2002.

16. The exact size of what the US administration called the "Coalition of the Willing" is not easy to pin down. At different times, the official list in 2003 included forty-six countries, then forty-nine, followed by forty-eight. At least two countries, Costa Rica and the Solomon Islands, claimed their inclusion on the lists was without their consent. Of actual participants in the invasion, a bit less than 76 percent of the forces were Americans, a bit more than 23 percent were British, 1 percent were Australians, and 0.1 percent were Poles. In 2006, different US sources listed twenty-seven, thirty-four, or thirty-seven countries as contributing forces on the ground; see www.global security.org/military/ops/iraq_orbat_coalition.htm.

17. In 2012, more active-duty US military personnel committed suicide than died in combat.

18. Estimates from the Watson Institute, Brown University, Cost of War Project. See http://costsofwar .org/.

19. For example, in addition to the source cited in note 18, see the final report of the US Special Inspector General for Iraq Reconstruction, "Learning from Iraq," March 2013, www.sigir.mil/learningfromiraq/index .html. See also "Iraq Ten Years On," Chatham House, May 3013, www.chathamhouse.org/publications/papers /view/191107; and Council for Foreign Relations, March 2013, www.cfr.org/iraq/iraq-invasion-ten-years -later-wrong-war/p30204.

20. Internal Displacement Monitoring Centre, "Challenges of Forced Displacement Within Iraq," Dec. 29, 2008, www.internal-displacement.org.

21. Institute for Economics and Peace, *Global Terrorism Index 2012,* http://economicsandpeace.org /research/iep-indices-data/global-terrorism-index; see also note 33 below.

22. See the concise and useful EIA *Country Analysis Briefs: World Oil Transit Chokepoints,* Jan. 2008, at www.eia.doe.gov/cabs/World_Oil_Transit_Choke points/Full.html.

23. An overview of Jewish terrorism from mandate days into the twenty-first century is found in Pedahzur and Perliger 2009; see also Begin 1977.

24. B'Tselem; this source breaks down casualties during this period among Israelis as follows: civilians (1,027) and military (484). See www.btselem.org /statistics.

25. In 2009, a US Senate report was released that argued that bin Laden was allowed to escape from US military forces in December 2001 by a decision of then secretary of defense Rumsfeld. See *New York Times,* Nov. 29, 2009; and "Tora Bora Revisited: How We Failed to Get bin Laden and Why It Matters Today," Report to the Committee on Foreign Relations, United States Senate, Nov. 30, 2009, at http:// foreign.senate.gov/imo/media/doc/Tora_Bora_ Report.pdf.

26. *Guardian*, Aug. 19, 2012. See US Department of State, *Country Reports on Terrorism, 2011,* www.state .gov/j/ct/rls/crt/2011/.

27. See www.state.gov/r/pa/prs/ps/2012/09/198443 .htm.

28. *BBC News*, Oct. 19, 2009.

29. *Al-Monitor*, Dec. 30, 2012.

30. S. Hersh, "The Next Act," *New Yorker*, Nov. 20, 2006.

31. *New York Times*, Oct. 23, 2012.

32. *Wall Street Journal*, Oct. 17, 2012.

33. "A terrorist attack is 'the threatened or actual use of force and violence by a non-state actor to attain a political, economic, religious, or social goal through fear, coercion, or intimidation.'" Institute for Economics and Peace; see note 21 above for reference and URL.

34. Other countries ranked as follows: Bahrain, 85th; Jordan, 86th; Kuwait, 99th; UAE, 105th; and Cyprus, 112th. Oman experienced no terrorist events in 2011.

PART TWO

REGIONAL GEOGRAPHY

10

Syria

Middle East Heartland

KEY POINTS: Keystone location from Mediterranean coast to Tigris River, shares Mesopotamia and ancient cultures. Open steppe and desert lands long used for transit, trade, and spread of cultural and political influences. Base for Omayyad Caliphate 661–750. Modern state formed in stages by French mandatory in 1920s, suffered instability in governance until 1970s. Enjoyed ethnic and secular social harmony until 2011. Tenaciously opposed Israel, which seized Golan in 1967 war. Unable to achieve potential economic development because of economic and political policies. Opposition to the Assads, father and son, finally became rebellion during regional unrest beginning 2011, and regime reacted brutally and persistently.

REGIONAL KEYSTONE

Ancient Role, Modern Role

Historical-geographical Syria, lying between the Mediterranean and the middle Euphrates, has often functioned as the geographical keystone of the Middle East. Not only is its situation central, but its location near the regional heart is also enhanced by patterns of landforms, climates, and travel routes. Damascus and Aleppo have played outstanding roles as commercial and cultural centers for thirty-five hundred years, and Syria's cereal belt has served as a granary for empires over many centuries. Three major corridors cross the Syrian realm: the main one south of the Turkish mountain wall and north of the desert, a second one through the Palmyra Oasis, and a north-south one through western Syria that

long served as a segment of the long north-south land route between Yemen and Asia Minor. The routes were for thousands of years—indeed, until after World War I—the major passageways through the region for the movement of people and goods.

Migrating peoples, marching armies, and multiple political influences have flowed and ebbed through this geographical location for millennia. Indigenous Syrians have at various times absorbed several of these ethnic and cultural groups and have sustained challenges to their own capacity for unity and even survival. Periodically during its long history, the Syrian realm has served as a major power base, reaching its apogee during the Damascus-centered Umayyad Empire (661–750). Later, it was a focus of Islamic-Arab aspirations and potentially a modern political-spiritual center of the

Arab world. Contemporary Syria, with only moderate size and population, and with limited resources, has a prominent role in the region regardless of the serious problems it faces and despite its shifting relationships with its neighbors and with major world powers. We can trace some of its economic difficulties during the past several decades to its policy planning and foreign relations. Other more general problems arose from the country's ideologically self-imposed isolation, anachronistic restrictions, and illiberal political agenda. Still others stemmed partly from a mutual failure by Syria and the West to establish meaningful rapport. Many of these problems became only too obvious as Syria was thrust into world headlines in 2011 with the onset of a brutal civil war. This chapter will examine Syria's capabilities and role.[1]

The Three Syrias

"Syria" as used in this chapter will usually refer to the Syrian Arab Republic, so named in 1961. The republic is coextensive, except for the Alexandretta (Iskanderun) area, with the French League of Nations mandate (1923–1946). However, "historic Syria" (or "*bilad al-sham*") existed for more than two thousand years and comprised the general area that is now Syria, Lebanon, Jordan, western Iraq, Israel, the Israeli-occupied parts of Palestine, and parts of Turkey. References to "Syria" in some writings refer to "Greater Syria."

THE IMPRINT OF TIME

Ancient Patterns

In the western and northern parts of Syria, many of the earliest known settlements date well back into the ninth millennium BCE (see Chap. 3). Some of the earliest pottery ever found was discovered on the banks of the Euphrates, and Damascus claims the title of the world's oldest continuously inhabited capital city. Ugarit just north of Latakia on the coast, Ebla 30 mi/50 km southwest of Aleppo,

and Mari on the middle Euphrates are among the most important ancient sites in the region; they were thriving city-states or imperial capitals early in the second millennium BCE (see Map 3.1). The oldest known alphabet—twenty-nine characters in cuneiform script, dating from the fifteenth century BCE—was found during the excavation of Ugarit.[2] Late in the second millennium, the Syrian region became and continued to be for almost a thousand years a marchland, contested among successive great empires, including the Amorite and the Aramaean (the biblical Aram), which were rooted in Syria itself.

Alexander the Great's conquest of the Persians in 334–326 BCE led to Syria's inclusion in the Seleucid Empire for more than two hundred years. After Rome supplanted the Seleucids and made Syria a Roman province in 64 BCE, the Greco-Roman culture prevailed, and later became infused with Christianity. The new sect gained its first major foothold in Antioch, flourishing under the eastern Roman and Byzantine Empires. Ruins of churches and of entire towns from this period—Syria's several "dead cities"—continue to inspire visitors in the northwest and south. Impressive Greco-Roman tourist sites are Palmyra (Fig. 10.1), Apamaea, Bosra, and Dura Europos. From 540 CE, Byzantines and Sassanians fought for a century and inflicted severe destruction on the countryside and cities. Ghassanians—Christian Arabs mainly in southern Syria—provided many powerful families in the sixth and seventh centuries CE.

Arab Invasions and After

When the Arab Muslims arrived, Byzantines, weakened by conflict with the Sassanians, were unable to defend their possessions, and in 636 CE historic Syria was the first area to fall to the Muslims after their eruption from the Hijaz. Just twenty-five years later, Syria entered its ninety-year Golden Age when the Islamic Umayyad Empire, with Damascus

SYRIA

Long-form official name, anglicized: Syrian Arab Republic

Official name, transliterated: al-Jumhuriyah al-Arabiyah as-Suriyah

Form of government: unitary multiparty republic with one legislative house (People's Assembly) (current civil war may result in different form of government)

Area: 71,498 mi²/185,180 km² (including 500 mi²/1,295 km² of Israeli-occupied Golan)

Population, 2011: 20,766,000; Literacy (latest): 79.6%

Ethnic composition (%): Arab 86.2, of which Syrian 74.9, Bedouin 7.4, Palestinian 3.9; Kurd 7.3; Armenian 2.7; other (including Circassian, Turkmans, Assyrian) 3.8

Religions (%): Muslim 85, of which Sunni 74, Alawi 11; Christian 10; other (including Druze) 5

Demography: Life expectancy—72.53 yr (M), 77.45 yr (F); Birthrate (per 1,000)—23.52; Fertility rate—2.85

GDP, 2011: $64.7 billion; purchasing power parity: $107.6 billion; per capita: $5,100

Currency: Syrian Pound (SYP), US$1 = 68.93 pounds; 1 SYP = $0.0141 (mid-May 2013)

Energy reserves: oil—2.5 bn bbl; natural gas—8,500 bn ft³; coal—nil

Main exports (% of total value, 2007): $11.55 billion (of which crude petroleum 34.5; food 17.3; apparel 7.9; yarns and fabrics 7; refined petroleum 6.5; machinery and apparatus 4.9)

Main imports (% of total value, 2007): $14.7 billion (of which refined petroleum 29.5; iron and steel 10.5; food 10.1; machinery and apparatus 9.5; road vehicles 6.6; plastics 5.9)

Capital city, 2009: Damascus (al-Dimashq, often al-Sham) 2,597,000; other cities: Aleppo (Halab) 3,087,000; Homs (Hims) 1,328,000; Hamah 897,000; Latakia (al-Ladhiqiyah, 2004) 424,392

Note: Some data in these tables may vary slightly from other references in the book; in the case of Syria, the ongoing civil war has radically impacted many data.

---

the capital, was established. The new official language, Arabic, gradually displaced Aramaic and Greek, and Islam became increasingly dominant over Christianity, although the native Christians remained a small but continuing social elements. As it had before and did later, Syria showed its ability to fuse cultures and evolve into something "Syrian."

When the Abbasids supplanted the Umayyads in 750 and the power center shifted to Baghdad, Syria became a contested land for the next eight hundred years. Abbasids, Egyptians, Seljuks, Crusaders, and Mongols vied for control. Each held Syria, or parts of it, for varying lengths of time, leaving signs of their control in aqueducts, forts, and caravansaries. Ruins of spectacular Crusader castles in western Syria attract both tourists and serious students of medieval architecture (Fig. 10.2). The Ottomans then conquered Syria in 1516, controlling it for four hundred years until their empire broke up after 1918.

Figure 10.1 Ruins of the colonnade of Palmyra (modern Tadmur) in central Syria, prosperous oasis trade center under Queen Zenobia in the late third century, as a key caravan station, and briefly a military power.

This long and complex history, under such a variety of cultures and rulers, endowed modern Syria with an almost uncountable number of sites and edifices with considerable potential to support a major tourism industry. In the 1990s and 2000s, this sector was becoming an increasingly important contributor to the national economy. Unfortunately, not only has the civil war had the short-term effect of shutting down the sector, but it has also meant that the sites themselves are seriously at risk—from destruction in the fighting and from looting as protective systems break down.[3]

Mandate to Independence

When France took the League of Nations mandate of Syria in the early 1920s, demarcation of the borders signaled the first time in history that a separate, quasi-independent polity of "Syria" had been formally defined. After Lebanon was officially made a separate entity and internal pieces were shifted to suit France, the mandate became the direct precursor of the contemporary state (see "The State in the Middle East," in Chap. 8).

To inhibit unity and anticolonial nationalism, France divided the territory into statelets: Aleppo, Damascus, and Alawite (called Latakia after 1930) in 1920; Jabal al-Druze in 1921; and an autonomous Sanjak (subprovince) of Alexandretta (Turkish: Iskenderun) in 1923. In 1925, Damascus and Aleppo were united, and Alawite and Jabal al-Druze were added in 1936; they were separated again in 1939 and finally reunited in 1942. Revolts and instability typified the mandate, but after World War II Syria became formally and officially an independent state on April 17, 1946. Except for a revised

Figure 10.2 Krak des Chevaliers, Castle of the Knights (Arabic: Qalat al-Husn), an especially well-preserved Crusader castle in the Homs Gap west of Homs in west-central Syria. It was built in the eleventh century. (Liam Cummings)

boundary around Alexandretta-Antioch (Iskenderun-Antakya, in a province called Hatay by Turkey) (see "Regional Conflicts," in Chap. 8), postindependence Syria embraces virtually the same territory as the mandate after Lebanon's separation (see Map 10.1).

The United Arab Republic

Independent Syria, along with Lebanon and Jordan, experienced insecurity and instability after World War II, the sudden assumption of independence, and with the trauma of the emergence of an increasingly powerful Israel on a portion of historic "Greater Syria." The Baath (Arab Renaissance) Party was founded in 1947 by Christian, Sunni, and Alawi Syrians, explicitly based on a secular state where common Arab identity preserved the equality of adherents of all religions. On several occasions, Syria expressed interest in unions—perhaps manifesting the Greater Syria syndrome—with one or another of its Arab neighbors. Only once did an actual merger transpire—between 1958 and 1961 it linked with Egypt in the United Arab Republic (see

"Regional Linkages," in Chap. 8). Although the union served its original purpose, forestalling a feared pro-Communist coup in Syria, Egyptian domination deeply offended Syrians, who saw themselves as the standard-bearers of Arab nationalism. After three years of this unequal partnership, a military coup in Damascus dissolved the union, and Syria once again was independent.

A Troubled Polity

The instability of coups and attempted coups, civilian cabinets, and military interventions that had marked the 1950s resumed, with a Baath[4] Party–dominated cabinet taking power in March 1963. The civilian party leadership was in turn ousted by Baath military elements in February 1966, with General Hafez al-Assad[5] assuming a central position of power as minister of defense. In June 1967, Syria went to war with Israel after Egypt was attacked. Its forces were quickly pushed back, and its air force was largely destroyed, with Israel seizing the Golan Heights, thus beginning an occupation that has continued to the

Map 10.1 General map of Syria with major towns and physical features. Circled numbers indicate geographical regions of the country.

present. Despite this major setback, the Syrian military regime survived. Within the regime, internal struggles continued until Assad overthrew the leadership and assumed the presidency in 1970.

Assad *Pere*

Confirmed in his new position by an unopposed plebiscite, Assad continued the basic policies, domestic and international, that had guided Baath regimes since 1963— that is, socialist in economic policy and neutralist (leaning toward the Soviet bloc) in

international affairs. The other mainstays of Baath philosophy—Arab nationalism and secularism—were also followed, but over time another, more parochial, characteristic emerged under his regime. The Assads were Alawis, professing the heterodox Shii-origin creed and originally concentrated in the western mountains of Syria. Under the Mandate, the French authorities began the practice of recruiting heavily among the Alawis for military service, and so President Assad had substantial support among his former colleagues in the armed forces. He promoted these allies to positions of power throughout the government, and this Alawi domination was increasingly resented by the Damascene elite and the more devout Sunnis. Religiously inspired unrest quickened in the early 1980s, with the Muslim Brotherhood playing a leading role. Open revolt broke out in Hamah in February 1982; it was brutally suppressed by the military, with artillery leveling large sections of the city and a reported twenty-five thousand civilians killed in the three weeks of fighting or executed afterward.

Lebanon. On another front, Syria never fully reconciled itself to the French separation of Lebanon from their Syrian mandate. The two independent states of Syria and Lebanon found themselves in an anomalous situation, despite their cooperation against the French, with Lebanon maintaining its separateness but acknowledging a close link to Damascus, and Syria not considering Lebanon truly discrete. The two states did not maintain normal diplomatic relations despite—or perhaps due to—their closeness.[6] Always maintaining links with Lebanese factions, Syria reacted to the outbreak of the Lebanese Civil War (see Chap. 11) by intervening in 1976 to maintain the status quo—that is, to keep the Maronite Christians in power and to stifle any attempt of the Palestinians to change Lebanon's internal politics. Thus began almost thirty years of Syrian military presence in Lebanon, during which Syrian political alliances shifted among various Lebanese sects and factions. While Syria dominated the Lebanese scene, the Israelis invaded Lebanon in 1982 and stayed for almost twenty years, leading to Syrian and Israeli forces clashing on several occasions. Forces from the United States, France, and Italy came and withdrew with little accomplished. When Syria was forced to leave in 2005, it was difficult to see that it had gained anything from its long, expensive venture; indeed, it had intensified Lebanese resentment of Syrian actions.

Within Syria, Assad gradually initiated shifts on several fronts beginning in the 1980s. The majority sect of Islam was emphasized with the presidential presence in Sunni mosques prominently featured in the press. Although Syria had made some economic gains in the 1970s, it had generally lagged the region. In the 1980s, oil revenues faltered, and the assistance Syria had long received from Eastern-bloc countries began to dry up. With the fall of the Soviet Union in 1990, the first stirrings of economic reform appeared. Syria joined the coalition assembled to oust the invading Iraqi forces from Kuwait and also participated in the Madrid Peace Conference in 1991, initiating discussions with Israel about the Golan Heights. Hafez al-Assad called his younger son Bashar home from London in 1994 after the eldest son and presumed heir, Basel, was killed in a car accident. The president's brother Rifaat was "relieved of his post" as vice president and sent into exile in 1998. In June 2000, Hafez died of a heart attack, setting the stage for Bashar's succession.

Assad *Fils*

Before Bashar al-Assad could succeed to the presidency, the Syrian constitution had to be quickly amended—at thirty-four, he was six years too young for the office. There was considerable speculation that the technology-oriented younger man who had studied for two years in England would possibly accelerate the cautious reforms that had begun in the 1990s. In many ways, this turned out to be true, at least on the surface. For example, the massive stories-high portraits of the leader that had graced the facades of Damascus buildings on special occasions disappeared. More substantially, the heavy hand of the state on the economy was lightened; private banks were licensed, foreign exchange was loosened, import controls were lessened, and the stock exchange opened. On the international front, results were mixed. Relations with the European Union improved, and an

Association Agreement was initialed in 2009. But American neoconservatives considered Syria almost a member of the Axis of Evil;[7] Syria was charged with developing chemical weapons and actively aiding Iraqi insurgents. In Lebanon, Syrian intelligence operatives were clearly deeply involved in the assassination of Prime Minister Rafiq Hariri in 2005.

The pace of change was slow and uneven after the first years of reform under the new presidency. There was very little tangible change on the political side—the regime preserved their Baathi/Alawi monopoly and suppressed political discourse. As for the economy, the benefits of growth, though considerable, were distributed very unequally, heavily favoring the cities and the urban elites. Many among the minorities—Alawites, Christians, and Druze (but not the Kurds)— and the traditional Sunni business classes benefited from the increased economic openness, but most Syrians were disappointed that Bashar al-Assad did nothing substantial to change the political and security status quo. Still, a decade into Bashar's presidency, stability and economic progress seemed enough to maintain the regime.[8]

POLITICAL GEOGRAPHY

Before briefly assessing Arab Spring developments in Syria and the ensuing descent into civil war, we will review key aspects of the political geography on which these events are unfolding.

Irredentism

As mentioned earlier, historic or "Greater" Syria was much larger than the current republic, and it continued to exist theoretically in some form through the fall of the Ottoman Empire in 1918. With the League of Nations mandates, it was truncated in several ways. The southern portion—Palestine and Transjordan—was assigned to Britain as the mandatory power, while the rest was entrusted

to France. In 1920, this mandatory power proclaimed the "State of Greater Lebanon"— with today's boundaries—separate from the rest of the mandate. In 1938, France assented to actions that separated the Sanjak of Alexandretta from Syria and eventually united it with Turkey. In none of these actions were the Syrians consulted, and when independence finally came it was to a state much smaller than Ottoman Syria. The most recent territorial challenge resulted from the 1967 war with Israel when Israeli forces occupied the Golan Heights, an area of about 445 mi^2/1,150 km^2. All of these losses of territory have, since independence, to some extent influenced Syria's external policies and have been used to justify policies of internal repression. Influence over Lebanon and the recovery of Golan have loomed particularly large in the minds of regime leaders.

Centrifugal Forces

Not until the early 1970s did Syria stabilize enough politically to achieve national unity and a rational government structure. Prior to that time, it experienced more coups d'état than any other regional state. But stabilization came at a steep price—under a government based on a double-minority power structure. Ideologically, the Baath Party regime first achieved power in a 1963 coup, and it has never been confirmed in office through a free and competitive election. Socially, the party apparatus itself—and therefore the government—was dominated for more than forty years by father-and-son presidents (plus assorted relatives) drawn from the relatively small Alawi minority.

Major social competitions acting centrifugally have been the periodically acute conflicts between liberal and conservative Islam and the opposition of both groups to the official secularism of the Baathi-Alawi alliance. The best organized of the fundamentalist groups, the Muslim Brotherhood, seriously challenged the Assad regime twice before

2011, killing more than sixty Alawi military cadets in Aleppo in 1979, and then, as the Islamic Front, seizing Hamah in February 1982. In both cases, the regime brutally suppressed the perpetrators and those unfortunate enough to be caught in the middle. Unlike the situations in Jordan and Lebanon, the presence in Syria of a large number of Palestinian refugees—approximately 487,000 in nine camps and many cities—has been mitigated by granting them greater inclusion and legal rights, while their political action was kept under strict control. Through this period, the Christian, Druze, and, to a lesser extent, Kurdish minorities steered clear of political involvement.

Centripetal Forces

Considering these potent divisive forces, it is noteworthy that two related movements, Syrian nationalism and Arab nationalism, have been effective in offsetting centrifugal forces and bringing Syrians together into a viable national group. The regularity of coups d'état was broken after the reemergence of Syria from Egyptian domination in the United Arab Republic. The external threat from Israel, coupled with its occupation of Syrian Golan, solidified the regime's hold on the population, as to some extent did the political criticism and insistent opposition from the United States and other Western countries. But it became clear after early 2011 that, in the face of popular opposition, probably the primary source of support for the regime has been a fragile coalition of minorities—Alawi, Christians, and Druze, together with an important portion of the Sunni population—notably of the commercial, business, and intellectual communities. For all of these groups, stability was, until 2011, far more important than political freedom—and for some, the fear of change and instability that have been seen nearby in Lebanon and, more recently, in Iraq has continued to bind them to the increasingly desperate Assad family.

THE ARAB SPRING

Al-Jazeera's coverage of the unfolding events in Cairo's Tahrir Square beginning in January 2011 kept Syrians from all classes and in all parts of the country glued to their televisions. Scattered demonstrations followed in Damascus and elsewhere, mostly in support of the antiregime movements in Egypt and later Libya, with some calls for reforms in Syria. Almost all such gatherings were broken up by the authorities, often violently, although in the early weeks there was little overt criticism of Bashar al-Assad himself. On February 17, a spontaneous protest arose in the ancient Suq al-Hamadiah in Damascus's Old City when police beat one of the shop owners; videos of the protest were soon posted on YouTube for a wider audience in Syria and abroad to see.

More than any other single event, it was the arrest and beating of several young boys (and later their parents) for posting pro–Arab Spring graffiti in the southern border town of Dara in early February that sparked a continuing series of demonstrations that grew larger, spread across the country, and eventually led to outright civil war. The protests in Dara also brought to the fore the issue of high-level corruption within the regime; the protesters targeted and burned Baath Party headquarters and the offices of Syriatel, which operates more than half of the country's mobile telecommunications network and belongs to the president's unpopular cousin Rami Makhlouf.

As overt opposition spread, the regime found support in counterdemonstrations, especially in Damascus and Aleppo, not all of which were staged and officially sponsored. The split in the population between Assad supporters and opponents widened, but not clearly along ethnic or religious lines. On both sides, though not in equal proportions, were to be found Sunni Arabs, Kurds, Christians, Druze, and even Alawi. Even well into

2011, not all opponents called for a total overthrow of the Baath Party or even of the Assad presidency; the regime would alternate suppressive tactics with promises to pursue political reform "within the system," including an end to the emergency law in place since 1963.

The precise moment when Syria's version of the Arab Spring became Syria's civil war is hard to identify, but after nationwide protests set in during March, the army was deployed in April with units authorized to fire directly on the demonstrators. After that, by fits and starts, the opposition began to coalesce into an increasingly organized resistance, its ranks enhanced by deserters from the official forces and its stock of weapons enlarged through local capture and, increasingly, by external suppliers. The Syrian National Council (SNC) was inaugurated in June, and the formation of the Free Syrian Army (FSA) was announced in July. Large numbers of refugees began crossing into Turkey, Lebanon, and Jordan as the government's military moves against the population became harsher.

From the earliest months of the uprising, the regime claimed that it had near-unanimous support of the people (who, it allowed, might have some legitimate grievances that the government was eager to address), but that its opponents consisted of criminals, mercenaries hired by foreign enemies, fundamentalist Islamists known as *Salafis,* and Islamist terrorists. Ironically, as Assad's tactics become more openly oppressive, foreign involvement in Syria did increase, as eventually did the presence of Sunni extremist fighters, many from other countries, like the members of al-Qaida Iraq.

Saudi Arabia, Egypt, the Gulf states, Iraq, and Jordan all condemned Assad's use of deadly force against his own people, which culminated in the Arab League suspending Syria's membership in November. Canada, France, Germany, the United Kingdom, Turkey and the United States called for Assad to

relinquish power, about the time the EU placed sanctions on the sale of Syrian oil, cutting deeply into the government's main source of revenue and foreign exchange. Although Russia and China blocked the UN Security Council from adopting broader sanctions, the UN did become increasingly involved in humanitarian efforts for Syrians both within the country and in the growing refugee camps in surrounding countries. Later in 2012, even Russia and China seemed to be distancing themselves from the regime, which, as it became more isolated, also became more dependent on its one last ally—Iran.

As the civil war's second year moved along in 2012, the number of Sunni extremist fighters grew, especially close to the country's borders, as a result of spreading chaos within the country as the government lost control of large swaths of territory. This facilitated the infiltration of foreign Salafi elements, especially across the long and porous Iraqi border. Some of these groups readily took advantage of the poor organization and increasing accusations of corruption among the indigenous insurgents and their organizations, the SNC and the FSA. The Salafis also gained from the growing resentment among Syrian Sunni Arabs, the largest group in the country, against the continued rule of the heterodox Alawi Assad family.

In mid-2013, after two years of the struggle that had become the most tragic aspect of the Arab Spring, Syria had, according to the UN, suffered at least 70,000 casualties, up from 5,000 a year earlier; other estimates were even higher.[9] More than 1.5 million Syrians had by then fled the country to Lebanon, Jordan, Turkey, Egypt, and Iraq, with 2,000 crossing the border each month; in addition the number of internally displaced persons (IDPs) had passed an estimated 4 million. Perhaps 90 percent of these people had left their homes in 2012, and the rate of increase continued to grow in 2013. As the war moved into its third year, incidents of savagery, carried out by both sides and often widely publicized via social media, became more common.[10]

The conflict between the regime and the insurgents showed no sign of imminent resolution, although a rapid collapse as happened in Libya in 2011 was not an impossible outcome. However, the core of Assad's support is the sizable Alawi minority (about 10 percent of the population) who quite reasonably fear for their continued existence in the event of a victorious insurgency that might be dominated by Salafis, even al-Qaida forces.[11] Whether a large group of Alawi could retreat and hold a redoubt in the western mountains, the sect's traditional home, is not clear, but it seems likely that in such an eventuality, the conflict could at the least continue for a considerable time. Beginning in 2012, there were signs that Alawi civilians and militia were concentrating in Syria's northwestern corner.[12]

The possible futures for the other minorities in a post-Assad Syria contrast sharply. The Druze have a traditional homeland south of Damascus. The Christians, concentrated in Damascus, Aleppo, and numerous villages scattered throughout the country, have no redoubt to fall back on. They were thought to be disproportionately found among the refugees and IDPs in early 2013. Many of them fear that their future will repeat that which befell Iraq's Christians in the years following the US invasion—persecution, displacement, and exile.

For the Syrian Kurds, on the other hand, the insurgency has represented an opportunity for them to seize the autonomy that some of them have long wanted. There is even the possibility of unity with Kurds in other countries, especially Iraq. Many Kurds have associated themselves with the SNC and the FSA, but others have sided with Asad or stayed aloof from both contending parties. Any future degree of Syrian Kurdish autonomy would concern Turkey, as the development of the Kurdish Regional Government in Iraq has already.

THE PHYSICAL CHALLENGE

Regions of Syria

Syria has six well-differentiated natural regions, indicated on Map 10.1 by encircled numbers. [1] A plain extends the length of the coast, widest in the north behind Latakia and in the south near Lebanon. It is agriculturally productive and the base for the main port of Latakia, the oil-export port of Baniyas (less active now that Iraqi pipelines are no longer operational),[13] and the developing port and oil terminal of Tartus. [2] A succession of mountains lies to the east: in the north is the continuous north-south Jabal al-Sahiliyah ("Coastal Mountains"—the official toponym, formerly Jabal al-Nusayriyah or Jabal al-Ansariyah), in the center are the southwest-northeast Anti-Lebanon Mountains dividing Syria and Lebanon, and in the south is the complex mass of Mount Hermon. The uplifted Jurassic and Cretaceous limestone Jabal al-Sahiliyah is bounded on the east by an impressive fault with both vertical displacement and a strike slip of more than 12 mi/20 km, which is also the west side of the Ghab graben, the northern end of the Levant Rift System. East of the mountains is a large plateau divided by [3] a southwest-northeast zone of complex folding and faulting associated with the Palmyra Folds. There are several local names for sections of the splayed ridges, including Jabal al-Ruwaq northeast of Damascus, Jabal Abu Rajmayn in the center, and Jabal Bishri toward the Euphrates.

North of the Palmyra Folds and west of the Euphrates, the level to rolling steppe land [4] supports a north-south zone of extensive grain cultivation, coextensive with a constellation of settlements, including the cities of Homs (Hims), Hamah, and Aleppo. South of the Palmyra Folds, the plateau has a quite different character. Toward the west are [5] extensive basaltic lava flows of several ages, accompanied by numerous cinder cones.

Figure 10.3 View over Salkhad, looking generally west over the agricultural Hawran from a volcanic neck in the Jabal al-Druze (now Jabal al-Arab), southwestern Syria.

Jabal al-Druze (officially, Jabal al-Arab) is a huge lava dome that reaches 3,300 ft/1,000 m above the plain and is flanked on the northeast by the wide basalt plain of al-Safa and on the northwest by the thin, scabby, blistered lava flow of al-Laja. The plains to the west of the Jabal are the well-cultivated Hawran (Fig. 10.3), its western edge a lava plateau that forms the Golan overlooking the Sea of Galilee. (It is here in the border city of Dara that the first Arab Spring protests in Syria occurred.) East of the lava belt, the Syrian Desert extends into Iraq, Jordan, and Saudi Arabia, offering little except sparse grasses and bushes for the grazing animals of the Bedouin. In northeastern Syria is [6] the Jazirah, which lies east of the entrenched Euphrates River and continues the level to rolling landscape that lies west of the river. It became a focus of major economic development after 1970 following increased exploi-

tation of the oil fields located there and completion of the Euphrates Dam and its associated installations.

The Agricultural Base

On one hand, Syria's share of the Fertile Crescent's climate, soil, landforms, and other beneficial characteristics gives it large areas of relatively productive agricultural land. Making up about one-quarter of the country, this land supplies the sustained economic base for the country, as it has for twenty-five hundred years. On the other hand, problems of aridity and rough relief in the other three-quarters present a major physical challenge. This challenge and the responses to it are part of the saga of contemporary Syria.

By its very nature, the Fertile Crescent's inner boundary is a zone of marginal precipitation. Cyclical oscillation of the 12-in/300-mm isohyet (see Map 2.5) between wet and dry periods is a tensional element in Syrian agriculture. Consequently, it affects many aspects of economic and social life, including shifts between sedentarism and nomadism along the frontier. In seasonal distribution, rainfall in this typical dry summer Mediterranean climate (Koeppen Csa) is concentrated in the cool months. Annual precipitation ranges from 30 in/750 mm along the coast to 55 in/1,400 mm on the upper west-facing slopes of the Jabal al-Sahiliyah/Jabal al-Nusayriyah, then decreases sharply to the east, in the rain shadow of the mountains, to 22 in/550 mm in the Ghab Depression.

East of the mountains, the north-south subhumid agricultural belt with its steppe soils extends southward from Aleppo well into Jordan, and rainfall typically averages 12–20 in/300–500 mm along this southwestern horn of the Fertile Crescent. Eastward from Aleppo, averages are 10–12 in/250–300 mm, with double those amounts in the extreme northeast. Away from the more humid Crescent, the southeastern two-thirds of the country averages less than 8 in/200 mm, with the driest area, abutting the Jordan panhandle, receiving less than 4 in/100 mm. Here and along the Euphrates in the extreme southeast, mean July temperatures exceed 90°F/32°C. There the Syrian Desert is in full sway.

THE SYRIAN MIXTURE

Patterns of Population

With 22.5 million inhabitants, Syria ranks seventh among the Middle East states. Population doubled between 1963 and 1987, but Syria's earlier high growth rate, 3.5–4 percent annually, fell to 1.8 percent by 2011 (the estimated rate for 2012 was actually negative because of refugees fleeing the fighting). Rapid population growth has contributed to such socioeconomic problems as high unemployment, stagnant per capita income, and housing shortages. The surplus population has even begun repopulating the historically important

"dead cities," economically important tourist destinations in normal times. As in other regional countries, the raw population density figure is misleading, since the population is markedly concentrated in the more humid western area (see Map 4.2 and Table 4.1).

Syria has, from early times, had scattered cities of appreciable size and fame along the Euphrates and especially in the more humid west of the country. Damascus (Fig. 10.4) and Aleppo have long alternated leadership in population, but recently Greater Damascus surpassed Greater Aleppo.

The historical population concentration axis along the humid steppe belt, Damascus-Homs-Hamah-Aleppo, now includes Latakia, the main port. With development of the Euphrates Valley and the Jazirah to the east, cities in those areas have expanded rapidly, especially Dayr al-Zawr, Raqqah, Qamishli, and Hasakah. In addition, scores of villages—many with populations of 10,000–20,000—are found in the broad, flat-floored river valley and adjacent plateaus consequent to development projects in the area. Suwayda, in the Jabal al-Arab, and Dara, on the Jordan border, are the largest centers in the south. Major universities are located in each of the largest cities.

Human Diversity

Arab Majority.   Although Syria has less religious and ethnic diversity than its neighbors Lebanon and Iraq, the variety that does exist is both noteworthy and influential in the state function. Among the several ethnolinguistic groups, Syrian Arabs, 82 percent of the population, professing Islam, Christianity, and other faiths have formed the principal group for more than one thousand years. Included in this majority are the Bedouin, steadily less nomadic, now less than 8 percent of the total. As in most Arab societies, identity is a double categorization: linguistic (e.g., Arabic) and religious (e.g., Islam), as Chapter 4 indicates. Syria has several religious and social minorities distinct from the primary group. In addition to

Figure 10.4 The "new" downtown Damascus, telephoto view looking east from the top of Mount Qassiun. The multistory buildings date from the 1980s, the uniform-height buildings in the foreground from the French mandate prior to World War II. The Old City of Damascus is slightly above center, surrounding the Umayyad Mosque, whose minarets are plainly visible. The rich, irrigated Ghutah is in the distance but is being encroached upon by the urban sprawl of Damascus. Fighting through 2013 did not involve downtown Damascus.

Arabs, the national mixture comprises Kurds, Armenians, Circassians, Turkmans, and Assyrians, plus small groups of Azeris, Gypsies, and Jews. After Sunni Muslims, religious minorities include a few heterodox Islamic sects and a dozen Christian denominations.

From the 1960s through 2011, with one or two notable exceptions, ethnoreligious social groups exhibited a high degree of intergroup tolerance. Partly because continued domination by a minority sect required that religious identities be secondary, but also due to tight domestic political controls, limited economic potential that did not engender fierce competition for advantage, and external pressures on the nation, Syrians benefited from intercommunal concord. Expressed differently, the government, under rather rigid one-party and one-sect control, tended to leave its citizens

alone if they stayed out of politics. Religious minorities—especially Christians—enjoyed far greater stability and security under the Baath regime than their counterparts in most other states in the region. Although these groups remain deeply uncertain of their future as the civil war proceeds, many adherents have joined the opposition in response to the regime's brutality.

Kurds.   After the Arabs, the largest ethnolinguistic group in Syria is the Kurds—about 7 percent of the population. With their own non-Semitic language, Kurds are mostly distributed across the north, with concentrations in the mountains of the northwest and in the northeast along the Turkish and Iraqi borders and next to their ethnic compatriots in the broader area sometimes called "Kurdistan."

Many of them, along with Armenians, fled from Turkey in the 1920s and early 1930s following a failed insurrection against Turkish authorities in eastern Anatolia. In addition to the main Kurdish belt in the north, several thousand Kurds live in the cities, especially in the Damascus Kurdish Quarter. Although most are Sunni Muslims, some are Shii, Christian, or Yazidi. While Syrian Kurds were not immune from the long-standing nationalistic yearnings of their kin in Turkey, Iraq, and Iran, Kurdish stands on the Syrian revolution were divided. With the outbreak of civil war, the prospect of autonomy or even secession came to the fore, and opposition alliances are engaged in dialogue about the balance between Syria's traditionally Arab identity and its heterogeneous population.

Armenians. The second-largest ethnolinguistic minority is the Armenians, about 3 percent of the population, and the least-assimilated group. Entirely Christian, they fled Turkish Armenia in the 1920s and 1930s and settled in Aleppo, where nearly 75 percent of them live, as well as in Damascus. Educated and skilled, they work in trade, crafts (many jewelry artisans in Damascus are Armenians), small industry, and the professions. Many emigrated to other countries in the 1990s in search of better socioeconomic conditions.

Other Minorities. Smaller groups include Turkmans, Circassians, and Jews. Nearly all speak Arabic, but the Turkmans and Circassians, like Kurds and Armenians, often also use their own languages. The roughly 110,000 Turkmans, who are Sunnis and Turkic speakers, are mostly seminomadic herdsmen in the Jazirah, but some are settled agriculturalists in the Aleppo area. In addition to their urban Damascus population, the particularly distinct Circassians inhabit the Hawran in the south, with Druze east and west of them. Only half as numerous as Turkmans, they have played a more significant role in the economy and society. With the onset of the civil war, some Circassians and Armenians have begun considering returning to their Caucasian homelands.[14]

Jews numbered more than 30,000 before World War II and, like Armenians, lived mostly in Aleppo and Damascus. Israeli-Syrian hostility after 1948 put them in an ambivalent position; their status periodically led to acute friction between Syria and Israel (and the United States), when Israel asserted, and Syria denied, that they were mistreated. In April 1992, under US pressure, the government declared that any of the 4,000 remaining who wished to emigrate could do so. Only about 400 chose to stay at that time. By 2012, in the midst of the insurgency against the Assad regime, probably less than 25 elderly Jews remained.

Sunni and Shia. About 90 percent of the Syrian Arabs are Muslims or members of Muslim-derived sects, reflecting the high correlation in Syria of Arab and Muslim identities. Of these, four-fifths are Sunni. The Shii Imamis (or *Ithna Asharis–Twelvers*) are a tiny group in Syria, although the largest within Shii Islam as a whole; with Iran's close links to the Assad regime, their faith has achieved some prominence, and two traditional Shii shrines near Damascus became major destinations for Iranian pilgrims from the 1980s on. Shii Ismailis (or *Seveners*), perhaps numbering a quarter million, are mostly in the area of Salamiyah east of Hamah and in the mountains west of Hamah, where the Ismaili Assassins were important during the Crusades.[15] Adherents of two heterodox sects with Shii origins—the Alawi and the Druze—have had historical impacts in Syria disproportionate to their size.

Alawi. The largest and, since the 1960s, most important minority sect is that of the Alawi, about 11 percent of the population and more than two-thirds of the inhabitants around the Jabal al-Sahiliyah in the northwest. Prior to the 1960s, they were primarily agriculturalists, but from the mandate period onward, they served in the army in numbers beyond their percentage of the population. The Baath coup in 1963 enhanced their role, especially in the military, and when an Alawi, Hafez al-Assad, became president in 1971, their position improved decisively. Before he died in 2000, he ensured that his son Bashar al-Assad would succeed him, preserving Alawi control. This fact, of course, has become a central issue in the civil war.

Druze.   Also prominent in the military since the mandate have been the Druze. The Jabal al-Druze was one of the statelets created by France, and periodic Druze revolts were a serious problem for the French mandate, but the 700,000 or so Druze (about 3 percent of the population) gradually became more subdued. They are still concentrated in the rough lava dome of the Jabal al-Arab/Jabal al-Druze and in the Mount Hermon area in the south, where they are more than 80 percent of the inhabitants.

Christians.   As many as 10 percent of Syrians are Christians, and except for the Armenians—a separate group ethnolinguistically—nearly all are Arabs. Syrian Christian groups trace their tradition to the oldest Christian communities, recalling Paul's conversion near Damascus and the early role of Antioch; their spiritual ancestors predated Islam in Syria by more than five hundred years. They congregate in western Syria's larger cities and are splintered into a dozen sects, the largest of which are the Greek Orthodox (nearly 5 percent of the population), Armenian Orthodox (Gregorians), Syrian Orthodox (Jacobites), and Catholic Uniates, including Maronites. Greek, Arabic, Syriac (Aramaic), and Latin are liturgical languages; it is worth noting that one Aramaic variant remains as the spoken language for several thousand Greek Catholics

and Orthodox in the mountains north of Damascus, including the villages of Malula and Saydnaya (Fig. 10.5). Nestorian Assyrians are some of the most recent arrivals in Syria. Fleeing Iraq in 1933, they were settled in a score of villages on the upper Khabur River, west of Hasakah; many more Assyrians, both Nestorians and Chaldeans, were among the hundreds of thousands of refugees who fled to Syria from Iraq during the 2000s. Historically, Syrian Christians have been prominent in Arab nationalist movements, yet they have also felt an affinity with the West, having been a favored group during the Crusader and mandate periods.

EVOLVING ECONOMIC PATTERNS

Mandate Syria developed modestly during two decades of French economic dominance. Like most of the area, it faced constraints as a new state trying to enter the modern industrial world. Conflict with Israel during and after 1948 substantially slowed development, and it was not until well into the 1960s that Syria saw significant growth and development. Even so, continued confrontation with Israel (and consequently with the United States) has cost it dearly in its efforts to achieve its long-range economic potential. Such constraints were especially acute after the US invasion of Iraq in 2003 when US congressional and UN actions imposed sanctions in 2003–2004, accusing Syria of sheltering fleeing Iraqi officials and then of aiding the insurgency. Demonstrations by a growing opposition movement in 2011, leading to open civil war in 2012, has brought economic development to a halt; continued economic activity will have to focus strongly on reconstruction when Syria returns to normality.

For several Middle East states in recent decades, growth in the productive sectors postindependence was slowed by internal and regional instability, experimentation with political-economic ideologies, and over-

Figure 10.5
The Greek Orthodox convent of Saydnaya, located 12 mi/20 km north of Damascus at the foot of the Anti-Lebanon Mountains in western Syria. The shrine of the Virgin in the convent was at one time a major attraction for pilgrims and still brings scores of visitors each day, both Muslim and Christian.

concentration on military buildup. Additionally in Syria, government controls until 2000 dictated prices, wages, and what could be produced, imported, and sold. As long as the economy was propped up by foreign funding, much of it from the Soviet bloc, socialist management worked to a degree, although the inefficient centralized bureaucracy constrained development and access to the world market and a range of goods was highly limited until economic reforms after 2000.

Shifting Economic Policies

From 1961 to the onset of the civil war, Syria's economy can be described in terms of five stages, each lasting about a decade:

1. *1960s*: marked by growth increasing from 2 to 3 percent annually to 6 to 7 percent;

land redistribution and reform; nationalization of private enterprises, natural resources, and transport facilities, with some resultant capital flight (Map 10.2)

2. *1973–1982*: continued rapid growth, stimulated by large-scale foreign funding; completion of the Tabaqah Dam on the Euphrates; expanded irrigation and land reclamation; diversification of manufacturing

3. *1982–1990*: a marked downturn as oil prices and external economic assistance fell off; inflation as high as 100 percent annually; a 90 percent loss in the currency's value; constraints on imports of both consumer and capital goods; heavy monetary and international political cost of continued involvement in Lebanon; with the fall of the Soviet Union, some accommodation with the West began[16]

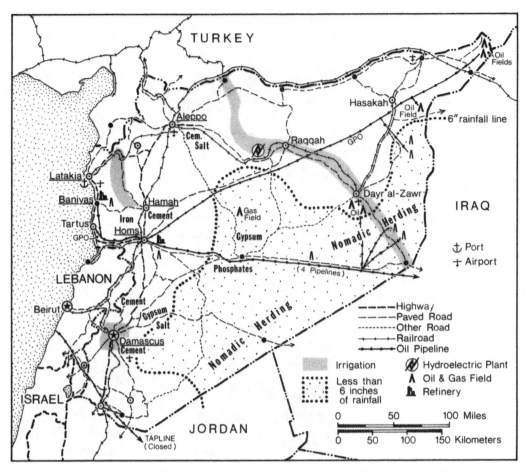

Map 10.2—Economic map of Syria. Manufacturing centers are underlined. Aleppo, Homs, and Hamah have been damaged in the fighting of 2012–2013.

4. *1990s*: economic fluctuations followed by more stability; improved relations with the West and Arab neighbors brought increases in economic assistance; some reforms initiated, but the heavy hand of Baathi bureaucracy lessened their possible effects; heavy military expenditures and involvement in Lebanon continued

5. *2000–2010*: initial hopes for accelerated reform were in part realized for the economy but much less on the political side; major changes due to growth apparent in the major urban areas, but high-level corruption also obvious; withdrawal from Lebanon following Hariri assassination; worsening relations with

the United States led to sanctions; at the end of the decade, impatience with slow implementation of reforms with blame placed mostly on Baathi power structure rather than the president.

Considerable Reform, Slow Progress

The European Union was heavily engaged in development assistance with the Syrian government in the 2000s, offering Syria the prospect of an Association Agreement that would have opened many opportunities for expanding Syrian exports to the world's largest economy. But in a 2007 EU report, a diplomatically phrased explanation for why an apparent barrage of economic reforms had brought only modest result was as follows: "The political and economic reforms announced at the beginning of [President al-Assad's] term are materializing slower than expected, causing frustration among some parts of the population."[17] The problems seem to have had a double cause: insufficient follow-through on many economic changes and strong political resistance to loosening statist controls needed to make reform a success. Still, Syria seemed at the time to weather both increased US-imposed sanctions and the global crisis of 2008 with few discernible effects and seemed to be attracting the interest of foreign investors again in 2009, as both France and, to a lesser extent, the United States moved to increase engagement. Economic growth lagged population growth, not only forestalling improvements in the standard of living but also preventing job creation from keeping pace with the entry of young Syrians into the job market. Officially, in 2010, the government estimated the unemployment rate at about 10 percent; observers of the economy put it much higher—perhaps 20 percent even in urban areas and higher in the countryside—and increasing.

Emigrant Remittances

Emigration from Syria for economic reasons has long been a historic trend, and high domestic unemployment continues to encourage this population movement. As many as 1 million Syrian workers, mostly unskilled, have sought jobs in Lebanon for at least part of most recent years; the latest available World Bank figures for emigrant remittances ($1.65 billion in 2010) probably missed much of the flow from Lebanon, thus considerably understating the importance of emigrant wages in the economy. Of course, with Syrian refugees seeking havens in Lebanon, Turkey, and Jordan, the direction of the flow of remittances has been sharply altered.

Living Standards on the Eve of Civil War

Economic changes in Syria benefited some groups far more than others, and it is difficult to determine whether the living standards of the average Syrian have tangibly improved. Using the Human Development Index (HDI) of the United Nations Development Programme (UNDP), which has components representing health, education, and per capita income, some improvement is apparent. In 2013, Syria ranked 116th of 186 countries worldwide and 15th of the 17 countries (Palestine included) in this book. The 2013 HDI was 29 percent above 1980, mostly due to health and education gains (however, the 2013 figure was calculated using data prior to the outbreak of the civil war—future values of the index are likely to decline. The index climbed by about the same amount in the 2000s as it had in each of the two previous decades. The more broadly based Prosperity Index of the Legatum Institute had placed Syria in 81st place of 110 countries globally and 7th regionally in 2011, but the most recent listing saw Syria fall to 113th place of 142 countries globally and 11th regionally, ahead only of Iraq,[18]

An Aside: Iraqi Refugees

An unanticipated economic problem arose after the US-led invasion of Iraq—the flood of refugees entering Syria to escape the chaos following the fall of Saddam Husayn. As many as 1 million Iraqis sought refuge in Syria, mostly in Damascus and a few other large cities. Many arrivals came from the middle class and arrived able to support themselves, but with the passage of time more and more fell into penury. External assistance to the aid efforts of Syria—basically a poor country—was slow in materializing. The UN High Commission for Refugees (UNHCR) registered the sizable fraction who were looking for settlement outside the region; its statistics showed that minorities—Christians, Mandaeans, and Yazidis—were represented among the refugees by more than their proportions in Iraq's population. As political opposition to the Assad regime grew among Syrians, exploding into civil war, many Iraqi refugees saw Iraq as a safer alternative and returned home.

AGRICULTURE

Traditionally a major element in the economy, agriculture in the late 2000s still engaged about 27 percent (together with small numbers in forestry and fishing) of the labor force and accounted for about 17 percent of GDP and 15 percent of exports. A large share of the development investment after the late 1960s went into land reclamation and improvements, irrigation schemes, and agricultural programs. Agriculture and the oil industry have been the government's top economic priorities. Syria sought to maximize food self-sufficiency in order to free limited foreign exchange for essential uses, although this strategic decision caused overuse of other scarce resources, including water. After 1996, Syria became a net exporter of wheat and flour, thus not only saving hard currency but also earning it. Syrian cotton, all handpicked, is high quality; some 235,000 mt of cotton lint was produced in 2008–2009; 40,000 mt was exported. The textile industry relied heavily on locally produced cotton. Agricultural production and distribution, both domestic and export, have been deeply impacted by civil war and nonfunctioning infrastructure.

Water.   Cyclic variations in rainfall totals and seasonal distribution are a crucial factor in the western Fertile Crescent because they create enormous swings in grain production. Between 1947 and 1960, about every third year was dry; for example, the wheat crop in the dry year of 1973 was only one-fourth that in the very wet year of 1972. The advantages of and need for expanded irrigation are obvious, and despite financial, technical, and geographical problems Syria has worked toward that goal. The area under irrigation doubled between 1975 and 1993 and has continued to increase steadily, but the expansion of irrigation has not been enough to liberate the far northeastern region from the need for reliable rainfall. Drought conditions have persisted in this poorest part of the country since 2006, and by 2009 there was large-scale hunger and extensive migration from rural areas toward Syria's better-watered west in 2009–2011.[19]

Crops.   As is true for the region as a whole, wheat and barley are the dominant crops, claiming nearly three-fourths of cultivation. The more humid agricultural lands produce cotton and sugar beets, and cotton leads in the expanding irrigated areas of the Jazirah. Tomatoes and lentils grow widely, as do more than a score of seasonal vegetables. Permanent tree and vine crops grow both in irrigated areas and on rainfed slopes: citrus on the coastal plain and in the Ghutah (the extensive oasis around Damascus), and olives, figs, and grapes on many slopes in the west, where they are well adapted to the Mediterranean regime. As part of its agricultural development program, Syria is vigorously expanding olive production (Fig. 5.4), doubling output in the past twenty years. By 2011, Syria vied with Turkey, the longtime leader, as the region's leading olive producer (see Table 5.3). Rice is increasingly grown in the Ghab and in the Jazirah. Overall, from the early 1960s through the late-2000s, food production per capita rose by about 25 percent.[20]

Major Developments

Ghab Project.   The Ghab Project involved drainage, hydroelectric production, and irrigation and was completed in 1965. It reclaimed 61,780 ac/25,000 ha of former marshland in the Ghab Depression, east of and parallel to

Figure 10.6 Euphrates Dam in northern Syria, key element in the Syrian plan to develop the Jazirah (area east of the Euphrates), including the broad Euphrates Valley itself. Lake Assad is to the left. Note the eastern valley wall in the distance.

the Jabal al-Sahiliyah in northwestern Syria. Roughly 31 mi/50 km long by 9 mi/15 km wide, this northern end of the Levant Rift System was formerly flooded by the lower Orontes River, and new agricultural lands were made available when the basalt lava flow that dammed the Orontes at the Ghab's northern outlet was cut through. In addition to the land reclaimed, twice as much already arable land was improved in the project, and the area now yields cotton, rice, sugar beets, wheat, and barley.

Euphrates Dam. The most important development project in modern Syria is the Euphrates Dam (sometimes Tabaqah Dam), involving not only the huge dam but also a hydroelectric installation, a long-line electrical distribution net, the lake behind the dam, an extensive irrigation system, a new town, and agricultural development in the Jazirah. Like Egypt's Aswan High Dam, the project was facilitated by Soviet financial and technical assistance. Initiated in 1961 and dedicated

in 1973, it is 197 ft/60 m high and 3 mi/4.5 km long (Fig. 10.6). When full, the reservoir, Lake Assad, extends 50 mi/80 km upstream, covers 247 mi²/640 km², storing 12 bn m³ of water. The power station, opened in 1978, has eight 100,000-kilowatt turbines and at first generated more than 90 percent of Syria's electricity; this share dropped sharply as demand grew rapidly and as new thermal power plants came on line. By the late 2000s, these plants contributed about 80 percent to installed capacity. Gas was gaining on oil as the leading fuel in use, but oil was still slightly in the lead.[21]

A major goal of the project has been to irrigate 1.58 mn ac/640,000 ha along the Euphrates and its tributaries. It has virtually achieved its original goals—by the mid-2000s, irrigation had nearly tripled in extent. Tabaqah, the village at the original dam site, rapidly expanded and was renamed Madinat al-Thawrah (Revolution City), now with more than a hundred thousand inhabitants. More than a dozen new villages were built to accommodate the scores of thousands at-tracted to the Jazirah.

Riparian Conflict. Nevertheless, several problems have affected the project. The Eu-phrates enters Syria from Turkey and leaves it for Iraq, so the three states involved have con-tended sharply over complex water rights (see Chap. 8). After the dam's completion, Syria and Iraq disputed the division of water, bring-ing them to the verge of war in 1975 before Saudi Arabia mediated resolution. Then Tur-key largely ignored Syria by undertaking a triple damming of the river, thus upsetting the Syrian timetable for Jazirah irrigation projects. More immediately serious was the revelation that large sections of the intended irrigation areas are underlain by easily soluble gypsum. Since dissolution of the gypsum would both reduce soil quality and result in water loss, elevated concrete-trough channels must be used to carry water, and plans to irrigate some areas had to be canceled. The 77,170 ac/31,230 ha of irrigated land (and 18,532 ac/7,500 ha of other land) drowned by Lake Assad (its wa-ters displaced nearly sixty villages) must be counted against the projected benefits.

ICARDA

Syria's climate and its agricultural experience under prevailing climatic conditions led to its being chosen by the Consultative Group on International Agricultural Research (CGIAR)—a major international sponsor of efforts to improve living standards in devel-oping countries—as the site for studying water-scarce agriculture. The International Center for Agricultural Research in Dry Areas (ICARDA) had been located near Aleppo since 1976; it is internationally renowned and operates a dozen specialized laboratories in fields ranging from biotechnology to virology and soil physics. In addition to concentrating on improving crops traditionally grown in dry areas, its particular concerns include

water-use efficiency, rangeland management, and environmental preservation. After July 2012, ICARDA was forced to close its re-search facilities due to raids from armed gangs and to transfer its staff to ICARDA re-gional units in other countries.

GROWTH OF INDUSTRY

Minerals.   A dearth of mineral resources hindered economic progress in Syria for centuries. Only recently has modern technol-ogy facilitated identification of two moder-ately large and important mineral resources: petroleum and phosphates. In the late 2000s, the sector, primarily petroleum, accounted for more than 40 percent of export earnings for the government—in 2007, 27 percent of GDP.

Petroleum.   Intensive exploration led to dis-covery in 1956 of oil in the extreme northeast-ern corner of Syria, where several small, closely spaced fields align with adjacent fields in Iraq and in Turkey farther north. Following Qarat-shuk (Karatshuk), Syria's discovery field, Suwaydiyah was found in 1959. All of these fields unfortunately produce heavy, sour (high-sulfur) crude. Major output began only in 1968 after a 404-mi/650-km pipeline opened to the Homs refinery and Tartus terminal.

Until 1986, the heavy crude had to be blended with lighter ones, originally tapped at the Homs refinery from IPC pipelines from Iraq. Following Syria's shutdown of those lines in the early 1980s (see Chap. 6), it blended light crude brought by tanker from Iran to Tartus with its own heavy oil. Syria discovered very light sweet crude at the Tayyim field and some small fields around Dayr al-Zawr after 1984, and production from this cluster was pumped to refineries and export terminals through the appropriated IPC pipelines, enabling Syria to meet its own blending requirements.

Average daily production rose from 27,000 bpd in 1968 to a high of 605,000 bpd in 1995, vying with Qatar's daily average before falling back in the following years. Production continued to average 560,000 bpd in the late 1990s but declined steadily to 320,000 bpd by 2011, when oil reserves were 2.5 bn bbl (see Table 6.1); with sanctions and civil war, production fell to an estimated average of 170,000 bpd in 2012. Syria's first refinery, in Homs, originally used feedstock from IPC pipelines. Its throughput of 107,000 bpd is exceeded by the 135,000 bpd capacity of the later Baniyas refinery, built on the coast in 1980. Both blend Syrian heavy and light crudes. Multilateral international sanctions on Syrian petroleum exports following the regime's violent response to domestic opposition caused an abrupt drop in oil production and exports after 2011. By early 2013, it was reported that most of the locales of the country's petro-resources were at least intermittently in the hands of rebel forces, especially Kurdish militias.

Gas. A half-dozen small gas fields south of Lake Assad and others near Palmyra supply power plants and industry. A large field discovered in 1997 in the Abi Rabah area is tied by pipeline to power plants near Aleppo and in Damascus and Homs. A major gas plant near Palmyra began operations in 2010, producing 95.3 mn ft3/2.7 mn3 annually, although international sanctions in 2012 limited expansion. In addition to increasing its own power-generating capacity, Syria agreed in 1996 to integrate its grid into a regional network with Egypt and Jordan (and eventually Iraq); it was completed for the first three countries in 2001 when Lebanon also became a participant. The Arab Gas Pipeline, built to carry gas from Egypt via Jordan to Syria, began operations in 2008. Settling transit fees with Egypt in 2009 allowed deliveries to Tripoli in Lebanon as well (which began in 2009) and eventually to Turkey. However, in the wake of the Egyptian revolution, pipeline facilities crossing the Sinai were damaged on numerous occasions in 2011 and 2012, interrupting the flow of gas.

In the early 2010s, Syria's neighbors in the eastern Mediterranean from Turkey to Gaza were all eagerly undertaking exploration of very promising offshore deposits of gas and possibly petroleum. Bids on offshore blocks were invited in 2011, but the response was weak in light of the heightening conflict in the country and increasingly harsh international sanctions on the oil sector. It seems unlikely that much serious exploration will be done in the Syrian section of the offshore basin as long as the civil war continues.

Phosphates. Rock strata comparable to those giving Israel, Jordan, and Iraq enormous reserves of phosphate rock were traced into central Syria in the early 1970s, and production rose from 600,000 mt in 1974 to 3.8 mn mt by 2010, ranking ninth in the world. Reserves near Palmyra totaling 2 bn mt, although of lower quality than in neighboring states, are sufficient for many years of production and merited building a railroad to the mines in the late 1970s (see Map 10.2). Increased exports were planned to help compensate for declining oil revenues and may provide an additional source of income as Syria rebuilds. In 2010, Syria and India signed an agreement by which Indian fertilizer companies would upgrade facilities, aiming for 10 mn mt of phosphate rock output. Production of other minerals—salt, gypsum, sulfur from petroleum processing, cement (from two large mills at Tartus and Hamah), and steel from a plant near Hamah—is for domestic use only. All mineral resources were nationalized in 1964, but the reforms of the 2000s contained promises to open the sector to private investment, and the Indian deal seemed an important step in that direction.

MANUFACTURING

For many centuries, Damascus and other Syrian cities enjoyed fame for their damascene metalwork, damask fabrics, muslins, linens, silk brocades, tapestries, carpets, tooled leather, carved and inlaid furniture, glassware, pottery, jewelry, mosaics, and similar craft work. Fortunately for Syria and the world, these crafts have survived to the present and produce prized handmade creations; however, they are an inadequate basis for a manufacturing complex in the modern technological world.

Syrian industrial development suffered institutional limitations that became apparent in the late 1940s. Management lacked expertise, and labor lacked technical skills. The merchant families were unable or unwilling to invest the amounts needed for expansion, and domestic instability discouraged outside investors. When the Baath government nationalized major industries, privately held money was moved outside the country and investment capital for certain industries became available only through government channels. However, in general, all of Syria's political-economic deficiencies converged to inhibit rational industrial development.

Planning and development during the 1970s gave early emphasis to infrastructure and basic industries: highways, railroads, the Euphrates Dam, cement plants, iron and steel mills, and similar industries. Little consideration was given to precision goods or high-technology items. Well into the mid-1990s, heavy industry, sugar production and other food processing, cement, chemicals, textiles, and other enterprises continued as parastatals, as did banking and oil. But with the easing of government restrictions—especially through the 1991 Investment Law No. 10—private investment moved into food processing, pharmaceuticals, textiles, ready-made clothing, and transportation.

By the late 1990s, industry was moving forward more than in the past, but Syria was not gaining on its neighbors. Virtually every city benefited from industrial expansion: Aleppo gained tractor, agricultural machinery, appliance, food-processing, and cement plants;

Hamah, iron and steel, textile, and cement operations; Homs, fertilizer plants, using phosphates from near Palmyra; Tartus, the largest cement plant; Baniyas, a refinery bigger than the older Homs facility; and smaller factories in Latakia, Dayr al-Zawr, Hasakah, and Raqqah. Still hampered by regulations and endemic corruption, entrepreneurs hoped to gain under the new regime. To some extent, this has proved true in the 2000s with the economic reforms mentioned above, plus increased emphasis on the private sector and changes in the laws on corporate governance. But even before civil conflict began to interfere with the day-to-day operations of the manufacturing sector, the burden of state control and arbitrary enforcement of regulations remained heavy. Having the appropriate political connections brought some manufacturers high profits, while others languished in a system rife with high-level corruption. The increasing disparity between rich and poor contributed to public anger with the regime, which welled up into the streets in 2011.

TRANSPORTATION

As a keystone in the Fertile Crescent, Syria has been the focus of route junctions and crossings for millennia, and in part it still fulfills that function. From the late Neolithic onward, the Damascus-Aleppo axis served routes from the south—the Via Maris (Sea Route) from Egypt and the King's Highway from Arabia; the east—from Persia and Mesopotamia; and the north—through the Cilician Gates from Anatolia. With today's technologically advanced transportation systems, intraregional highway and air routes cross Syria both north-south and east-west.

Syria's road and rail network (see Table 7.2) is adequate for current needs. The more thickly settled areas naturally have the densest network of roads, and only through routes cross the sparsely inhabited deserts. Modern paved highways now connect all major cities;

a four-lane divided throughway extends from Jordan to Turkey through Damascus, Homs, Hamah, and Aleppo. New rail lines facilitate development of the Jazirah and the center of the country. The line from Latakia through Aleppo, Madinat al-Thawrah, Raqqah, Dayr al-Zawr, and Hasakah to Qamishli has been a major factor both in developing northeastern agriculture and Latakia port and in stimulating all the cities it passes. The massive investments in new rail lines that the Gulf States and Saudi Arabia have announced (see Chaps. 15, 16, and 17) are aimed not only at linking major points in these countries, but also at tying their new networks to Turkey and Europe. At least one proposed line—a reconstruction of the Ottoman era rail line through Syria and Jordan to Medina in Saudi Arabia—will obviously involve upgrading the existing Syrian section. In the late 2000s, plans for the first phase of a metro system in Damascus were under discussion, but political upheaval stopped most major planning in 2011, and post–civil war reconstruction may well have other priorities.

By the late 1940s, with no adequate general-cargo ports of its own after losing access to Iskenderun in 1939 and Haifa in 1948, Syria relied on the Lebanese port of Beirut. The government began a long-range development program for Latakia and, later, Tartus. Baniyas had long been the terminus for Iraq pipelines. Latakia is now a major general-port facility, and Tartus has undergone significant expansion since the 1980s.

RELATIONS

Regional Relations

Damascus's leading role in Arab nationalism was widely accepted in the Fertile Crescent at the end of World War I. The Arab leadership that backed the Arab Revolt of 1916–1917 had been centered there, and a short-lived kingdom was established under Faysal ibn Husayn in 1920. In taking the mandate,

France forced Faysal to abdicate, but Syria never forgot its moment of glory. However, its attempts to assert regional leadership have consistently met resolute resistance from its neighbors.

Observing the mistakes of Nasserist Egypt, Syria balanced backing for Arab socialism and Arab nationalism—already an overcrowded arena—with a focus on Syrian nationalism and domestic development. Showing its support for Palestine in three wars with Israel, it has taken in thousands of Palestinian refugees and allowed them greater rights than other countries did (except for Jordan). It was a charter member of the Arab League and has played an active role in that organization. Although Syria considers itself part of the Islamic world and has participated in the Organization of the Islamic Cooperation, under the Alawi-Baathi regime it has advocated and practiced a greater degree of secularism than that found in more conservative Muslim states.

Syria's relations with virtually all of its neighbors since 1950 have been marked by frictions and, in the case of Israel, by successive hostilities. Relations with Lebanon are of special significance, and this dynamic has already been discussed above in Chapter 8, in the section "The State in the Middle East," and will be further examined in Chapter 11.

Iraq. Syria and Iraq pursued mutual economic interests until the mid-1960s. For many years, Iraq's only petroleum outlets were its pipelines across Syria, with terminals in Baniyas and in Tripoli, Lebanon. These were vital to Iraq and earned Syria annual royalties of more than $120 million, plus discounts of similar magnitude on Iraqi crude for the Homs refinery. Ironically, it was after both countries came under the control of Baathi regimes in the 1960s that more serious and persistent disputes arose, largely on the basis of ideology, though disagreements over oil royalties also played a role. As mentioned above, Syria supported Iran during the Iran-Iraq War, despite its long and vigorous advocacy of Arab unity. Then, defying domestic opposition, the government had little hesitation in 1990 about joining, along with Egypt, the coalition that forced Iraq to withdraw from Kuwait. Renewed détente between Syria and Iraq led to their signing a free trade agreement in 2001. Syria was elected a non-permanent member of the UN Security Council that year and in 2002 supported the resolution requiring Iraq to readmit weapons inspectors. However, in the lead-up to the US-UK invasion in 2003, it was part of the large majority on the council that refused to sanction preemptive military action. After Iraq regained the ability to act independently of the occupying powers, the two countries resumed full diplomatic relations in 2006, ending a quarter-century hiatus. At the end of the decade, however, Iraq was accusing Syria of sheltering hostile Baathis and of facilitating terror attacks in Iraq. In November 2011, Iraq joined with many other member countries in voting for the suspension of Syria's membership in the Arab League; Iraq's close relationship with Iran, however, has allowed some support to reach Assad across Iraqi territory. Iraq began receiving both returning Iraqi refugees and Syrians seeking refuge in 2012, an ironic reversal of the flow of Iraqi refugees into Syria after 2003.

Jordan.   Relations with Jordan on the south have ranged from close to several border closures and even to at least two brief abortive Syrian invasions of northwestern Jordan. The governments differed on Iraq's invasion of Kuwait, and Syria condemned the Jordanian-Israeli peace treaty of 1994. With the ascension of King Abdullah to Jordan's throne in 1999 and the ascension of Bashar al-Assad to Syria's presidency in 2000, they achieved their closest relations in decades despite the personal distance between the two leaders. However, in November 2011, Jordan voted to suspend Syria's Arab League membership, and King Abdullah urged Assad to step down from the presidency. In 2012, Jordan—like Iraq, Turkey, and Lebanon—became host to growing thousands of Syrian refugees.

Saudi Arabia.   Baathi, secular, Alawi-led Syria has had an ambiguous, mostly rocky relationship with conservative, religious, Sunni Saudi Arabia, despite the fact that, as a "front-line state," Syria has been the beneficiary of considerable Saudi financial assistance. On the one hand, its alliance with revolutionary Iran stretching over three decades alarms the kingdom; on the other, Syria was an active participant in the coalition against Iraq when the latter was threatening Saudi territory. In the late 2000s, Saudi King Abdullah seemed to have achieved some rapport with Assad, perhaps to offer some counterbalance to Iran and assuage his country's fears of a "Shii Crescent" extending from Iran to Lebanon. King Abdullah pressed Assad to work with him on resolving communal tensions in Lebanon in the summer of 2010. With the outbreak of civil war in Syria following Assad's increasingly anti-Sunni campaign, the kingdom became one of principal financial supporters of the insurgents.

Turkey.   Syria's decades-long dispute with Turkey over Alexandretta (Iskenderun, in the province Turks call Hatay) lost cogency many years ago, although as late as the mid-2000s official Syrian maps showed a double border with the area as Syrian. In the 1970s and 1980s, relations were exacerbated by Euphrates water problems, but they remained correct until 1998. Triggering tensions then was Syria's support of Kurdish rebels, especially the Kurdistan Workers Party (PKK), fighting Turkish troops in southeastern Turkey. The Syrian government revived Alexandretta irredentism, denounced interference with the Euphrates, and condemned Turkey for its increasing collaboration with Israel.

But following Turkish threats of military action and regional mediation, Syria reduced its support of the PKK (see also Chap. 20). Turkey tried in 2008 to revive negotiations between Syria and Israel. This effort faded out after Netanyahu resumed the prime ministership and was rejected entirely as Turkey fell out with Israel following the Gaza flotilla incident in 2010. Turkey, in spite of strong trade and diplomatic relations with the government of Bashar al-Assad in the 2000s, became a prominent supporter of the insurgents since 2011. At the end of 2012, the Turkish government had entered NATO talks about protecting Turkish soil but had hesitated to become directly involved in the fighting despite Syria's downing of a Turkish fighter jet and several incidents of shell landings in Turkish territory. Like Iraq, Jordan, and Lebanon, Turkey is now hosting tens of thousands of Syrian refugees.

Iran. With non-Arab revolutionary Iran, Syria forged a strategic alliance rooted from the early 1980s in their mutual antipathy toward the Saddam Husayn regime in Iraq (and perhaps maintained after 2003 by the Bush administration's attempts to isolate both from the global arena). On a practical level, Shii shrines in or near Damascus have drawn hundreds of thousands of Iranian pilgrims to Syria. Of particular importance is the mausoleum of Sayyida Zainab, daughter of Ali, the first Shii imam, and sister of Hassan and Husayn, the second and third imams. In the Old City of Damascus, the tomb of Husayn's daughter Sayyida Ruqayahis is another destination for most pilgrims. Increasingly in the 2000s, this alliance came to concern Syria's Arab neighbors, and countering it was a factor in the Obama administration's early moves to engage Syria in dialogue. The spreading civil war clearly shocked Tehran, which had harshly but less brutally put down its own internal rebellion in 2009, and it has provided military support for the failing regime in the form of arms and military "advisers." Iran has tried to promote itself, unsuccessfully, as a mediator between Assad and the insurgents. In fact, Iran emerged as the Syrian regime's only significant foreign ally, but its ability to assist in any substantial fashion was limited, not only by distance, but also by its increasing preoccupation with sanctions and the threat of external attack as a result of its controversial nuclear policies.

Israel. The cold relations between Syria and Israel are covered in more detail in Chapter 13. In the context of Syria's civil war, Israel's attacks in mid-2013 on possible advanced weapons systems they claimed were to be transferred to Hizballah forces in Lebanon were the first external action against the Assad regime. As of this writing, reactions and repercussions are unclear but may complicate coordinated action in support of the Syrian opposition. Syria had since 2011 been accusing the opposition of being in league with Israel.

Global Relations

France. Syria developed special relations with France during the latter's administration of the mandate. Despite its resentment of that country, it inevitably adopted aspects of French culture: French-language private schools are popular in the cities, and French is still used by some elite groups. Franco-Syrian relations after 1946 gradually diminished to ordinary commercial exchange. However, France was active in pressuring Syria to withdraw from Lebanon, and following the Hariri assassination in 2005 it pushed for an international investigation into possible Syrian involvement. Citing Syria's constructive role in settling the crisis in Lebanon over the presidential succession in 2008, French president Nicolas Sarkozy and Assad exchanged visits later that year. France was an early advocate for political reforms in 2011, and after the regime continued its violent crackdown on the opposition, France began, in 2012, to supply nonlethal equipment to the Free Syrian Army.

Soviet Bloc.   As was true with Egypt and Iraq, 1950s Syria found its channels with the West highly constricted because of Western— especially US—support of Israel, Syria's main adversary. It turned to the USSR and Eastern Europe for arms, economic aid, and technical assistance, including funding for such projects as the Euphrates Dam. Soviet military advisers and liaison personnel served in Syria for more than three decades, and Russian military advisers continue to play a role. However, it kept communism at home firmly under control and, like Egypt, did not become a Soviet satellite. Disintegration of the USSR in 1991 suddenly deprived Syria of its politico-economic mainstay and compelled President Hafez al-Assad to pursue accommodation with the West. Inter alia, he sought greater concord with the EU and with individual European states. Russia, which has had a warm-water naval supply base at Tartus since 1971, has blocked anti-Syrian resolutions in the UN Security Council.

United States.   Syria's relations with the United States were friendly in the early years of the twentieth century. In 1919, the King-Crane Commission found a reservoir of goodwill toward the United States, partly because of the work of the Syrian Protestant College (later the American University of Beirut) and partly because of the widely heralded ideals of President Wilson's Fourteen Points. US recognition of Syrian independence and the initiation of diplomatic relations came in 1944. Relations cooled after US endorsement of the Balfour Declaration and support for Zionist colonization in Palestine.

Following the 1948–1949 Arab-Israeli war, and especially after Syria accepted help from the USSR in the mid-1950s, US-Syrian relations ranged from fair to strained until

1990. Indeed, diplomatic relations were actually broken after the 1967 war and resumed only in 1974. The United States and other Western countries criticized Syria's decision to send thousands of troops into Lebanon in 1976, and brief skirmishes erupted between US and Syrian forces in Lebanon during the ensuing confused period.

A pragmatic détente followed Syria's internal political moderation in the late 1980s, which coincided with its participation in the 1990–1991 coalition against Iraq and, concurrently, the phasing out of Soviet aid. The United States also welcomed its cooperation in the active peace process of the early 1990s, but when these efforts foundered the United States joined Israel in accusing Syria of harboring those it considered terrorist leaders. The US State Department kept Syria on its annual list of states sponsoring terrorism, although Syrian officials had not been proven to have engaged in terrorist acts since 1986.

Washington-Damascus relations worsened when the Bush administration alleged that Syria was facilitating militiamen crossing into Iraq and joining the insurgency that in some cases attacked Americans. In 2003 the US Congress passed the Syrian Accountability and Lebanon Sovereignty Restoration Act, which coupled a demand for withdrawal from Lebanon and rejection of terrorism with diplomatic and economic sanctions. The United States was the principal sponsor of a UN Security Council resolution also demanding an end to Syrian presence in Lebanon.

The assassination of former Lebanese prime minister Rafiq Hariri in February 2005 (as well as twenty-two others, including a number of other prominent anti-Syrian individuals) strongly indicated the involvement of at least elements of the Damascus regime. The United States and France spearheaded another UN resolution setting up a commission to investigate the attack on Hariri, and its preliminary findings were that it was unlikely that it could have been carried out without the knowledge of Syrian intelligence. The Special Tribunal for Lebanon, established in 2009, has identified four members of Syrian-supported Hizballah as responsible for the attack. Completion of the investigation and trial is due in 2015, but the process has been fraught with political and security complications.

In 2009, the new Obama administration moved to reduce Syrian opposition to peace talks with Israel. High-level officials visited Damascus and conferred with Assad, and in 2010 the administration nominated an ambassador to Syria after a gap of five years when the embassy was headed by a chargé d'affaires. However, with the civil war raging, the United States withdrew all its American Embassy personnel in December 2011, but did not break relations. In 2012, the United States began to extend nonmilitary aid directly to the rebel forces.

For information on the business environment in Syria, see the website attached to this book: www.middleeastpatterns.com.

NOTES

1. P. Khoury 1987 is an excellent account of Syria as mandate. Hopwood 1988 examines independent Syria's political and cultural evolution. *Syria* Country Study 1988 is an excellent general study in an authoritative series. Pipes 1990 is a critical study. Theroux 1996 is a recent useful illustrated *National Geographic* report. *Economist*, Dec. 31, 2004, has a summary update.

2. In 2010, a report was published suggesting miners in northern Sinai may have been responsible for the first alphabet in the nineteenth century BCE. Goldwasser 2010.

3. *BBC News*, Mar. 10, 2013.

4. The Arab Socialist Baath Party is an international organization that dominated politics for more than a generation in both Syria and Iraq and has branches in several other countries in the region. Baath can be translated as "renaissance" or "resurrection."

5. A better transliteration would be Hafiz al-Asad, but we have opted for the more common English spelling of his name. Similarly, we have included the article "al-" only when the complete name or title of office is cited.

6. They did not agree to exchange ambassadors until 2008.

7. Then–Undersecretary of State John Bolton so designated Syria in a speech entitled "Beyond the Axis of Evil" on May 6, 2002.

8. For a discussion of Syria's political economy, see B. Haddad 2011.

9. The Syrian Observatory for Human Rights issued an estimate of at least 94,000 and possibly as high as 120,000, with 41,000 deaths among the Alawi community. *Reuters*, May 14, 2013.

10. See, for example, *Reuters*, Jan. 29 and May 14, 2013; *New York Times*, Jan. 30, 2013; and *Time*, May 12, 2013.

11. The long-standing Alevi-Sunni rivalry is discussed in Fildis 2012.

12. See, for example, *Independent*, Jan. 7, 2013; *Observer* (London), May 4, 2013; *Arab News* and *Times of Israel*, May 5, 2013; and *Ha'aretz*, May 14, 2013.

13. The pipeline from Kirkuk was put out of action during the invasion of Iraq in 2003. After a false start to rehabilitate the old pipeline, Syria and Iraq agreed in 2010 to build a new one—a project now in abeyance since the start of the Syrian civil war.

14. For example, see Jamestown Foundation, *Eurasia Daily Monitor*, July 30, 2012, and Aug. 8, 2012.

15. See Bengio and Ben-Dor 1999, Chap. 7.

16. See Perthes 1992.

17. European Commission 2007.

18. United Nations Development Programme 2013. Each report is based on data that lag by about two years. Also *Legatum Prosperity Index 2012*, www .prosperity.com/.

19. *Daily Star* (Beirut), Mar. 7, 2010.

20. UN Food and Agricultural Organization (FAO), *Production Yearbook* (Rome), various issues. See also http://faostat.fao.org. For Syria and the countries in the following chapters, changes in per capita food production were calculated using a three-year average in the base period and the average in the late 2000s.

21. International Energy Agency (IEA), "2006 Energy Balance for Syria," www.iea.org/country/index.asp.

The reader is advised to consult this book's associated website (**www.middleeastpatterns.com**) for additional information on **Syria**, such as a historical time line and a chronology of recent events, as well as essays on selected topics and various international economic, social, and political indicators.

Lebanon and Cyprus

A Mountain and an Island

Lebanon

KEY POINTS: Base for rich ancient Phoenician culture and commerce, with flourishing Mediterranean coastal plain and small ports. Western slopes of Mount Lebanon well watered, originally forested with highly prized cedars. Mountains a refuge for Druze, Shii, Christian groups. Chiefly Arab, modern Lebanon polity detached from Syria in early 1920s by French mandatory, but Syria never reconciled to loss. Eighteen sects rarely cooperate to permit Lebanon to achieve its high potential in tourism and trade.

THE CHARACTER OF LEBANON

Lebanon differs strikingly both physically and culturally from the rest of the Middle East. Dominated by the rugged and well-watered range of Mount Lebanon, its green and rainfed western slopes face the blue Mediterranean, and its brown steppes and deserts face east toward Syria. It is small enough to be traversed by car in a few hours even on its long axis, yet it displays almost as much landscape diversity as does Turkey, seventy-six times its size. Culturally, it is one of the most genuinely cosmopolitan countries in the Middle East, with an open entrepreneurial economy and society that benefits greatly from Lebanon's liberal, literate, educated, and modern citizenry. Under normal circumstances, Lebanese engage in enjoying the good life and sharing it with more than 2 million visitors in a regionally calm year—a pleasant environment, an array of excellent cuisines, and a varied nightlife.

Lebanon is also the region's most multisectarian state, and interconfessional tensions—even within its several religions—have frequently flared into open conflict. Between 1975 and 1991, the political and territorial competitions of these religious identities intensified and exploded into externally fueled warfare. With traditionally inadequate military and police forces, and weakened by internal factionalism, Lebanon became the confused battleground for its own militias and its neighbors' armies. Sinking steadily into anarchy, it eventually became the area's most devastated and endangered country. Once called the Switzerland of the Middle East, in the 1980s it was fragmented, a nation in jeopardy, in the process of collapse. Not

LEBANON

Long-form official name, anglicized: Republic of Lebanon

Official name, transliterated: al-Jumhuriyah al-Lubnaniyah

Form of government: unitary multiparty republic with one legislative house (National Assembly)

Area: 4,036 mi²/10,452 km²

Population, 2012 (est.): 4,143,000; Literacy: 87.4%

Ethnic composition (%): Arab 84.5, of which Lebanese 71.2, Palestinian 12.1; Armenian 6.8; Kurd 6.1; other 2.6 (many Christians consider themselves descendants of ancient Phoenicians, not Arabs)

Religions (%): Muslim 56, with Shia somewhat more than Sunni; Maronite 22; Greek Orthodox 8; Druze 5; Greek Catholic 4; other 5 (eighteen religious sects recognized)

Demography: Life expectancy—73.67 yr (M), 76.88 yr (F); Birthrate (per 1,000)—14.92; Fertility rate—1.76

GDP, 2011: $38.41 billion; purchasing power parity: $61.44 billion; per capita: $15,500

Currency: Lebanese Pound (LBP), US$1 = 1,484 pounds, 1 LBP = $0.00065 (mid-May 2013)

Energy: oil and natural gas—nil (however, promising gas discoveries, and possible oil finds, have been made since 2011 offshore in Lebanon's territorial waters); coal—nil

Main exports (% of total value, 2008): $3,478,000,000 (of which precious metal, jewelry, and stones 16.5; electrical equipment 15.4; base and fabricated metals 15.2; chemicals and chemical products 12.5)

Main imports (% of total value, 2008): $16,137,000,000 (of which mineral products 26.5; food and live animals 13.2; transportation equipment 10.6; electrical equipment 10.5)

Capital city, 2007: Beirut (agglomeration) 1,846,000; other major cities: Tripoli (Tarabulus) 212,900; Sidon (Sayda) 149,000; Tyre (Sur) 117,100; Nabatiyah 89,400

---

until 1991 did internecine killing finally cease under determined pressure from other Arab states. Through 2000, however, it remained an arena in the Arab-Israeli conflict until, after twenty-two years, Israel unilaterally withdrew from the south. For fifteen years after 1991, Lebanon made slow but steady progress toward recovery, before losing many of its gains in 2006 when the "Summer War" between Israel and Lebanese Shii militias exploded briefly but intensely on its soil. Lebanon's economy has recovered much of its lost ground, but in late 2012 Syrian domestic conflicts were mirrored in cities along the Mediterranean coast and threatened to generate another surge of instability—even hints of a return to civil war.

RICH PAST, COMPLEX EVOLUTION

Human Development. The advantages and resources of Lebanon attracted humanoids more than eight hundred thousand years ago during the Mindel glaciation, as artifacts found near Sidon and in the high intermontane Bekaa valley reveal. Byblos and many other sites show evidence of occupancy before and during the Neolithic period, from the ninth to the fourth millennium BCE. The important export of textiles dyed "royal purple" with secretions from the murex shellfish found in abundance at Sidon and Tyre probably gave rise to the name Phoenicia—the Greek translation of "Canaan," or land of purple-red—after 1200 BCE. The coastal city-states of Tyre, Sidon, Beirut, and Byblos used the famous Cedars of Lebanon for shipbuilding and for export to timber-starved Egypt before 2400 BCE. By the thirteenth century BCE, the Phoenicians had also developed, probably for use in their active maritime trade, an alphabet that was gradually adopted, adapted, and diffused throughout the ancient world; it is the direct forerunner of the modern Latin alphabet. Despite repeated invasions and later control by the Seleucids, Romans, and Byzantines, the area thrived, as monuments and ruins in every part of modern Lebanon attest.

Christianity developed in strength during the Roman-Byzantine centuries and has shaped modern Lebanon. After the Muslim conquest, the confessional balance and, later, the linguistic pattern slowly changed, but Christian dominance in Mount Lebanon persisted through thirteen centuries under the Umayyads, Abbasids, Crusaders, Mamluks, and Ottomans. Under the latter's *millet* system, the region enjoyed considerable autonomy and slowed the spread of Islam in the mountainous north; after fighting between Christians and Druze in 1860, it gained a special status that continued through World War I.

Mandate and Independence. Lebanon emerged as a separate entity as a French-controlled League of Nations mandate. As the

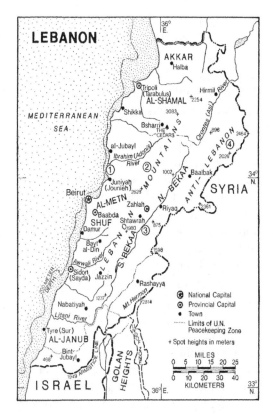

Map 11.1 General map of Lebanon. Circled numbers identify regions discussed in the text.

previous chapter explained, its territory was detached from the original mandate of Syria and was enlarged to create *Grand Liban*, "Greater Lebanon." This included not only the coastal plain and Mount Lebanon, but also, to the east, the Bekaa, paralleling Mount Lebanon, and the separate Anti-Lebanon mountain ridges (Map 11.1). After two decades under French auspices, it was declared independent by the Free French in November 1941; independence was reaffirmed on November 22, 1943, now the official independence day. As in Syria, the last French forces did not evacuate the country until 1946.

LEBANON'S DIVERSITY

Lebanon is synonymous with cultural diversity; virtually every major ethnic and religious group in the Fertile Crescent is represented.

However, the underlying diversity is sectarian rather than ethnolinguistic. Emphasis on antagonisms between Christians and Muslims neglects the tensions within these religions, among more than a dozen Christian and a half-dozen Muslim subgroups. Intercommunal tensions are so complicated that many sects have opposed a census since that of 1932, which showed a Christian majority and, under the system arranged by the French, gave dominant government and military power to the Christians. This arrangement was not changed until 1990, although there had been an obvious Muslim majority for decades. With no new census data since 1932, Lebanon's present demographic details can only be estimated.

The 2012 estimated population of about 4.15 million is a modest increase from the estimated 3 million in 1975, the lowest population growth in the region over that period. This is traceable partly to family choice in a relatively educated society and partly to emigration; during the worst years of fighting, including the 1982 Israeli invasion, as many as 900,000 Lebanese may have left.[1] When the 1989 accord seemed to be holding, many returned, although voluntary emigration has long been a feature of Lebanese history—and of the economy. Remittances from emigrants were $8.4 billion, about 22 percent of GDP, in 2011; this was the equivalent of about $2,000 per Lebanese resident.

Ethnolinguistic Groups

Lebanese Arabs.   Ethnolinguistically, about 85 percent of the Lebanese are Arabs in that their mother tongue is Arabic. However, the cultural variations among Arabs seen elsewhere in the region are especially wide and critical here. Some Maronite Christians, for example, deny Arab ancestry, claiming descent from Phoenicians or Byzantines. Yet other Lebanese Christians resolutely consider themselves Arab, advocating religious tolerance. DNA studies show that the Lebanese— Christians and Muslims—share the genes of Phoenicians and Canaanites, as well of those groups (like Arabs) who arrived later in the region.[2] By contrast, Palestinian refugees in Lebanon find their identity, in addition to being Palestinian, in their Arabism and in Islam, or as Palestinian Christians.

Ethnic Minorities.   The largest non-Arab minority are the Armenians, some 7 percent of the population. Kurds are the second-largest minority, about 6 percent, followed by small numbers of Circassians, Assyrians, Turks, and Jews. There were more than 20,000 Jews a century ago and more than 7,000 in the 1950s; there were fewer than 100 by 2012.

Refugees—Palestinians.   Although not a separate ethnolinguistic group in Lebanon, the large Palestinian refugee minority (most are Sunni, with a small Christian minority) has been a focus of contention since their arrival in 1948. Of the 800,000 who were displaced from Palestine during 1947–1949, about 150,000 crossed into southern Lebanon, most expecting to return home within a short time. More came during the 1967 Arab-Israeli war and after the 1970 fighting in Jordan. They crowded into twelve refugee camps built by the UN Relief and Works Agency (UNRWA) near Tyre, Sidon, Tripoli, Beirut, and Baalbak (see Map 9.3). In 2012, some 436,000 were registered with UNRWA; they comprise about 12 percent of the country's population.

A few Palestinians, especially professionals, have obtained citizenship, but most are poor, stateless camp dwellers. The government and a majority of the Lebanese have always rejected settlement or assimilation of the Palestinians, largely because of the sociopolitical threat it would pose to the country's delicate power balance and to the already stressed social fabric.[3] In 2002, parliament banned landownership by Palestinians, but in 2005 the Labor Ministry increased the number of professions open to them.

Iraqis and Syrians. More recent additions to the refugee population were approximately 50,000 Iraqis fleeing the post-2003 chaos of their homeland. Their presence in Lebanon was much smaller than in Syria or Jordan, and only about 10,000 were registered with the Beirut office of the United Nations High Commission for Refugees at the end of 2008. Perhaps 70 percent of the Iraqis were in the country illegally and thus could be imprisoned, deported, or both. By 2012, many had returned home, only to be replaced that year by thousands of Syrians fleeing across the nearby border from the chaos enveloping their country. In March 2013, Lebanese president Michel Sleiman said his country could not accommodate more than the 1 million Syrian refugees he said were already there, but the government was already projecting that, by the end of the year, the number would exceed 1.2 million.[4]

Other Foreigners. Also present has been a kind of "hidden minority" amounting to as many as 1 million foreign workers, many of whom have been Syrian Arabs or Kurds, mostly unskilled laborers seeking day labor in construction or agriculture. As conflict in Syria echoes among parallel populations in Lebanon, it is not clear what effect events in Syria will have on these workers. More recently, a sizable number of Asians have found employment here, as they have elsewhere in the region. A European–North American colony has reemerged since the 1990s, despite the brief evacuation in 2006, but its relative size is much smaller than before the 1975–1990 war.

Confessional Groups

Religious affiliation may well be the most decisive determinant in social intercourse within Lebanon's complex societal matrix. Crucial among the country's multidimensional and interactive factors, it is the basis for political organization and state structure, with seats in parliament allocated on a confessional

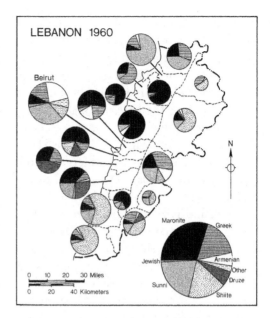

Map 11.2 Patterns of religions in Lebanon for 1960, the latest year with reliable data. Circles are in proportion to the populations involved, and pie graphs indicate percentages of adherents to the various sects. Figures have, of course, changed over the past fifty years, as discussed in the text, but the graphs still reflect the complexity of communal structure in this small country.

basis. Even personal identification cards must indicate an individual's religious affiliation.

Christians and Druze enjoyed special status under the Ottomans, and Maronite Christians were the core around which France created mandate Lebanon. Distinct from the Sunni Muslim lands around it, Lebanon—as a mandate and an independent state—evolved under a carefully fabricated balance of confessional elements: the Christian "majority" held key positions, but power sharing and the distribution of offices were designed to produce stability and effectiveness. The system can be better understood by reviewing the religious groupings. Map 11.2 shows the distribution of the major groups before civil war began in 1975; although the demography has changed, it is instructive in understanding the causes of this pivotal event.

Muslims. Mainstream Muslims make up at least 56 percent of the population in the early 2010s, and the Sunni and Shii sects are more evenly divided in Lebanon than elsewhere in the region. Probably more than half are Shia who, excluding the heterodox Druze and Alawi, make up the largest single sect. Once referred to as Mutawalis, Shia have also been the most oppressed group. Emerging from passivity in the 1970s, they matched others with their own militias—first, Amal (Hope), in 1974, and Hizballah (Party of God), in 1980. They are concentrated in the south, Beirut's southern slums, and the northern Bekaa. Although most Shia are *Imamis* (or Twelvers), there are also a few thousand *Ismailis,* who follow a different line of imams.

Sunnis, perhaps as much as 28 or so percent of the population and formerly the largest and most influential Muslim group, are widely distributed, with concentrations in Beirut, Tripoli and the Akkar, the southern Bekaa, and the Shuf (see Map 11.2). More than any other sect, the Sunnis resented the separation of mandate Lebanon from Greater Syria. Still, the quiet sympathies of this conservative, mostly middle-class group today often lie more with moderate Christians than with militant Muslims. Indeed, the deep divide between the politically and economically influential Sunni Hariri family and the Syrian Assad dynasty (itself of the minority Alawi sect) demonstrates how diverse Sunni Lebanese views have become about Syria.

Druze and Alawi. Two offshoots of Shiism, also part of the Lebanese mosaic, are so distinct in their beliefs and practices that they deserve mention apart from mainstream Muslims. The Druze, despite being only about 5 percent of the population, have loomed large in the area's sociopolitical dynamics for centuries. Concentrated in the mountains southeast of Beirut ("Druzistan") and especially in the Shuf, they played a key role in the fighting of both 1958 and 1975–1991, and

they remain very much a substantial factor in everyday political life. The Alawi have spilled over from their home grounds in northwest Syria and number around 60,000, mostly in Tripoli, where growing Syrian tensions between supporters of the Alawi Assad dynasty and opposition groups have been reflected in Lebanese clashes beginning in 2012.[5]

Christians. Among all the sects, Maronites were once the largest and most influential, but owing to emigration and a lower birth rate, they are now not much more than 20 percent in the 2010s. Considering themselves the creators and developers of the state, they assumed the role of guardians of its sovereignty and Christian character. In both mandate and independent Lebanon, they fashioned a Christian haven, and they dominated the unique polity that evolved into the early 1970s. Seeking to shape Lebanon's integrity during 1975–1991, Maronite Phalangists (the *Kataib*), with Israeli support, formed the core of the militias opposing Palestinian and Muslim groups. Under the Taif Accords that ended the civil war, they have shared power fairly equally with Sunnis and Shia.

In addition to Maronites, another dozen Christian sects have separate identity and roles in the political structure. Most of them appear in Table 4.2. The Greek Orthodox (about 6 percent—some would prefer to be called Arab Orthodox) are survivors from the Byzantines; they are widely distributed and urge accommodation with other groups. None of the other groups has played a major role in politics, but in the late 2000s the non-Arab Armenians seem to have become a rising factor in the new politics of coalitions.[6]

A SUBREGIONAL PERSPECTIVE

Looking down at Lebanon, an air passenger flying eastward from Beirut can clearly see the four distinct parallel regions that extend south-southwest to north-northeast: [1] a narrow coastal plain, [2] the Lebanon Mountains core area, [3] the linear flat-floored depression of the Bekaa, and [4] the complex Anti-Lebanon Mountains on the border with Syria (see circled numbers on Map 11.1).

Coastal Plain

Extending the full length of the 140-mi/225-km Mediterranean shore, a narrow plain is partly wave-cut rock platform and partly alluvial fan deposits of streams debouching from deep mountain valleys. Interrupted in five places by mountains reaching the sea, in some places it is wide enough only for the highway and parallel little-used railway. Between Tyre and Sidon, it is carpeted by citrus groves for more than 1 mi/1.6 km back from shore; in the extreme north, it widens to 20 mi/32 km in the Plain of Akkar.

Beirut. Urban sprawl up and down the plain is rapidly supplanting the orchards and market gardens that long characterized the area. Greater Beirut extends more than 20 mi/32 km from Juniyah in the north to Damur in the south. Scenically located on a separate low structural peninsular plateau, one of the few significant protrusions from the eastern Mediterranean coast, the site of Beirut has been occupied since the Neolithic period. A minor Phoenician port and city-state, it achieved greater stature as a Roman city with its famous law school; it was destroyed in an earthquake and tidal wave in 551 CE.

As Lebanon's primate city, Beirut developed rapidly after 1950 when the population was estimated to be 335,000. Luxury apartment buildings and hotels (Fig. 11.1) contrasted with slums and Palestinian camps at the onset of civil war in 1975, when the population had passed the 1 million mark. Slum areas mushroomed with the displacement of poor Shia and others by conflicts on the southern border, especially during the Israeli occupation. In 1991, after sixteen years of division between Christian East and Muslim West, the city lost some of the old "Beirut élan," but it has revived to some extent in the past two decades.

The virtually destroyed city center was almost completely rebuilt, not without controversy. Construction excavations confirmed that for five thousand years Beirut was indeed the nucleus of successive Canaanite/Phoenician, Roman, Byzantine, and Ottoman cities. Significant remains of each city level are preserved in a fascinating below-street-level "Archaeology Trail."

North and South. Toward the north end of the coastal plain lies Lebanon's second city and second port, Tripoli (Arabic: Tarabulus), a Sunni Muslim stronghold. Its basalt and limestone twelfth-century Crusader castle faces fourteenth- and fifteenth-century Mamluk castles, all impressive reminders of its tapestried history. On the southern plain is the Phoenician port of Tyre (Arabic: Sur), overlying and adjoining extensive Greco-Roman ruins. The ruins and Old Tyre are a UNESCO World Heritage Site. The Phoenician port of Sidon (Arabic: Sayda) lies north of Tyre, with a picturesque Crusader castle offshore. Also worth noting is the small northern port of Jubayl (better known as Byblos), with its renowned excavations showing civilizations from Neolithic times on (see Fig. 3.1).

Mount Lebanon

The country's traditional core is Mount Lebanon (Arabic: Jabal Lubnan), technically called Jabal al-Gharbi (Western Mountains). The range divides the coastal plain and western slopes from the eastern slopes and the Bekaa, making Lebanon a state that is geopolitically *à cheval*. Like rugged mountains in many humid areas, it provided isolation and security to several groups, notably Maronites and Druze. Mount Lebanon has thus played a profound role in the area's historical-cultural development.

Lying west of the great Yammunah Fault (see Chap. 2), the range's sedimentary strata

Figure 11.1 High-rise apartment buildings in mainly Muslim southern Beirut along Ramlat al-Bayda beach (*top*), and in Juniyah, a Christian area north of Beirut (*bottom*). Juniyah was a village before 1975 that developed very rapidly during the fighting in 1975–1990. The vineyard in the foreground is a remnant of former extensive agricultural exploitation of this west-facing slope.

Figure 11.2 Typical western slope of Mount Lebanon, showing scattered villages, terraced agriculture, low pine woodlands, and interspersed maquis and garigue flora. The main village shown is Baqlin, located in the Druze area west of Bayt ed-Din.

were arched up by relatively gentle east-west compressional forces during the Miocene-Pliocene epochs. The resulting arch is a rather open anticlinal structure aligned southwest-northeast and extending from the low Homs Gap at its northern end to the complex tectonic junction in southern Lebanon. The range is affected by several faults along its axis and by many cross faults. Highest elevations are toward the north, reaching 10,129 ft/3,088 m at Qurnat al-Sawda, east-southeast of Tripoli; elevations around 6,500 ft/2,000 m continue southward along the ridgeline to east of Sidon.

A significant hydrogeological feature of Mount Lebanon is the outcropping of extensive aquifers, bringing groundwater to the surface in lines of springs along the outcrops. Some of these springs are exceptionally large, feeding short, swift rivers that have eroded and dissolved spectacular canyons in the western slopes, adding to the rugged relief.

The springs irrigate the terraces and the more gentle slopes, as well as supply drinking water, some of which is bottled for consumption in Beirut and for export.

Cedars of Lebanon. The western slopes were originally heavily forested with oak, pine, fir, cedar, and juniper, with the famous Cedars of Lebanon (*Cedrus libani*—the national symbol) forming a belt at elevations between 4,600 and 7,200 ft/1,400 and 2,200 m. Some four thousand years of exploitation has degraded the vegetation to maquis, although a few small stands of cedars are preserved. The main group is in central Lebanon on Jabal Baruk, but the most famous is in the north, near the ski resort of Bsharri. Plantations of stone pine (*Pinus pinea*) and Aleppo pine (*P. halepensis*) give small areas a wooded aspect (Fig. 11.2), and stone pine yields the edible piñon nut (Arabic: *snubar*).

Maronites and Druze intensified and diversified agriculture on the western slopes, building thousands of terraces. Villages developed on spectacular sites, some formerly Phoenician and Roman settlements, whose ruins often survive. After World War II, many towns in the 2,000–4,500-ft/600–1,475-m zone became summer resorts. At upper levels, around 6,500 ft/2,000 m, ski resorts such as the Cedars and Laqluq thrive between mid-December and late March (see also Fig. 2.9).

The Bekaa

The Bekaa (Arabic: al-Biqa, "basin" or "depression") is a young tectonic intermontane trough, a segment of the Levant Rift System paralleling Mount Lebanon. Along the western side of the Bekaa, the Yammunah fracture slices off Mount Lebanon on its eastern side and creates a vertical displacement of several thousand meters and a left-lateral horizontal displacement of about 4.4 mi/7 km. It is the most seismically active of the many fractures in the Levant. Perceptible earthquakes result from displacement along one or another of Lebanon's fault planes every few years. Severe tremors strike once every 100–150 years, with the most recent being in 1956, when seven thousand buildings were destroyed east of Sidon by slippage along the Roum Fault.

The main drainage of the Bekaa, the Litani River, flows southward from near Baalbak, with a flow of 700–900 mn m³ a year at Qirawn (Qaraoun). It has been dammed to create a reservoir, and water is diverted to produce electricity and to supply water for limited irrigation. It is a completely Lebanese river from its source to its mouth in the Mediterranean; it should be noted, however, that early Zionist planners sought it as a water source from 1919 for the future Jewish state.

Water and Cultivation. A low, barely perceptible divide near Baalbak separates the watersheds of the Litani and the Orontes (Asi) River flowing to the north. The Orontes follows the Bekaa into Syria past Homs and Hamah and through the Ghab Depression. Both rivers are fed by springs that attracted Paleolithic wanderers on both sides of the Bekaa; the tells of at least thirty Neolithic villages are prominent features in the area.

Although the northern Bekaa lies in the rain shadow of the highest segment of Mount Lebanon and receives only 9 in/230 mm of rain a year, the central area around Shtawrah gets 24 in/610 mm, the south even more. The valley was an important granary from Roman times well into the last century, but wheat and barley production has declined as more area is irrigated for fruit trees, sugar beets, and market gardening. Seen from adjacent heights in spring, it is colorful with fruit blossoms, cultivated flowers, green fields, and, when law enforcement is lax, bright-red opium poppies. It is said that marijuana finds the valley a hospitable location, climatically and politically.

Anti-Lebanon

Properly the Jabal al-Sharqi (Eastern Mountains), the Anti-Lebanon Mountains are folded linear highlands east of the Bekaa and along the frontier with Syria; indeed, only the western ridges lie within Lebanon. An anticlinal structure similar to Mount Lebanon, these eastern highlands have several ridges exceeding 6,500 ft/2,000 m, and the summit of volcanic Mount Hermon (Jabal al-Shaykh), a southerly extension of the eastern highlands, reaches 9,230 ft/2,813 m. The Anti-Lebanon Mountains are the least-exploited part of Lebanon and in the north are virtually uninhabited.

ECONOMIC PATTERNS

From Phoenician times, Lebanon's major economic activities have taken advantage of locational and physiographic assets: (1) its central location on the coast, positioning it for trade between the hinterland to the east and Mediterranean lands to the west; (2) its central location in the Middle East, making it an intraregional and interregional crossroad; (3) its well-watered coastal plain and somewhat indented coastline, facilitating port development; (4) its also well-watered mountains, through which passes lead inland; and (5) its original forest cover and agricultural (horticultural) development.

A Long Tradition of Trading

Despite the foregoing advantages, mandate Lebanon had a small population and area and limited agricultural and virtually no mineral resources; the enterprising residents therefore revived their Levantine skills as traders. Further expanding the service economy after 1950, they developed financial and medical services, educational facilities, a modern port and airport, consultative expertise, recreation areas—services then inadequate in most of the region. Foreign embassies and businesses based representatives in "the Paris of the East." When the UN sought a site for its Middle East regional offices in 1963, it chose Beirut and returned after a fifteen-year hiatus in 1997.[7]

Beirut functioned for decades as an efficient and thriving port and service center for the emerging oil areas of the Gulf. But when fighting erupted in this nerve center in 1975, Lebanon lost its economic role, while rapid development was taking place in the wealthy oil states. By the time relative peace and stability returned in the early 1990s, it had much less to offer its former patrons, who in turn had less need for Lebanese goods and services.

Problems and Potentialities

By the early 2010s, more than two decades after the fighting ended, the economy presented a mixed picture, with much accomplished and much yet to do. One problem has been the persistence of the business methods of the war years and the immediate aftermath. Most regional states have followed world trends and rationalized procedures and relationships, but Lebanon—once the leader in such trends—has been slow to catch up. For example, inadequate regulatory procedures led to scandal in 2009 when a prominent Shii businessman was arrested for promoting a Ponzi-like scheme that reportedly bilked local investors out of more than $1 billion; when population differences are considered, this was about the equivalent for Lebanon of the $65 billion Madoff fraud in the United States.[8]

Living Standards. Notable economic improvements have been offset by serious problems: high unemployment, a bloated bureaucracy, and static wages accompanied by rising prices. Fifteen percent of the population holds 45 percent of the wealth; a third of the population lives in poverty. On the other hand, peace does seem to have had a broad positive effect on living standards. Using the Human Development Index (HDI) computed by the UNDP, Lebanon ranked 72nd out of 186 countries globally and 8th of the 17 in the region in 2013. More important, Lebanon's HDI has risen dramatically since 1990, when internal warfare was drawing to a close, promoting it into the "high human development" category. A similar but more comprehensive measure is provided by the Legatum Institute—the Prosperity Index, which includes, like the HDI, considerations of health and education, but several other factors as well. In 2012, Lebanon ranked 74th internationally of 142 countries and 6th in the region.[9] The EU and Lebanon signed an Association Agreement that entered into force in 2006, opening the way for the country to be fully incorporated into the European Neighbourhood Policy.[10]

Higher Education and Health Services

The service sector drives the modern economy, accounting in 2011 for about 75 percent of GDP. Before 1975, Lebanon offered a full range—from tourism and banking operations to personal services and aircraft engine maintenance. It had (and still has) excellent educational and medical facilities: in addition to the second-oldest university in the Arab world and one of the best—the American University of Beirut—there was the French Jesuit Université St. Joseph, Beirut University College (formerly Beirut College for Women, now Lebanese American University), Beirut Arab University, Lebanese University, and the Armenian Hagazian College. Medical facilities, especially the American University Hospital and the Hôtel Dieu de France Hospital, both connected to good medical schools, served patients from Lebanon and much of the region. These facilities still offer high-quality medical care, but the Gulf states now enjoy larger, better-financed, and more highly technological facilities.

Finance and Banking

Lebanon's reputation as the "Switzerland of the Middle East" before 1975 also applied to the extensive banking system, which is being revived, complete with banking secrecy and unrestricted capital movement. Not only were deposits and trusts attracted from Saudi Arabia and the Gulf oil states, but so was capital from less stable economies like Syria, Egypt, Iraq, and Jordan. This helped fuel remarkable development between 1955 and 1975, and renewed flows aided reconstruction efforts. But as with other parts of its service sector, after years of warfare Lebanese banking never quite recovered its former dominant level—in the late 2000s, only two of the region's thirty largest banks were headquartered in Beirut, as opposed to fourteen in the four Gulf states. On the other hand, the country's banks apparently had a justifiably healthy suspicion of the dubious financial instruments that rose to global importance in the 1990s and 2000s; when the crisis struck internationally in 2008, they weathered the storm, with sharp increases posted in assets,

deposits, and profits. Responding to international concern about transnational criminal and terrorist financial flows, the Lebanese Central Bank has instituted improved monitoring procedures. The Lebanese lira (or pound), 90 percent gold backed and freely convertible, was one of the world's most stable currencies before 1975; however, during the fighting it dropped from 3.2 to the US dollar to as low as a disastrous 3,000 to the dollar in late 1992. Pegged to the US currency in September 1999, it was stable at an average of 1,485 to the dollar over the first quarter of 2010 through August 2013. From the end of 2007, the reserves of Banque du Liban, the central bank, rose from $9.8 billion to $24.1 billion in less than two years, despite the global financial crisis. At the end of 2012, its official gold reserves (286.8 mt) were the nineteenth largest in the world and the third highest in the region after Turkey and Saudi Arabia (375.7 and 322.9 mt, respectively).[11]

Tourism

Before 1975, tourism was a major industry, as Gulf Arabs enjoyed moderate temperatures in the mountains and Europeans sought the sunny coasts. While the war raged, wealthy Arabs went elsewhere, vacationing and shopping in the United States and western Europe. After 9/11, however, they began to return to Lebanon, partly to avoid profiling and security delays in the West. As before, Arab visitors felt welcomed and comfortable in the cultural milieu: tourism has recovered to prewar levels—growing through 2010, peaking that year at 2.35 million arrivals, despite the global recession; its health helped Lebanon weather this economic crisis. The conflict across the border has driven both wealthy and destitute Syrians to the shelter of Lebanon, putting upward pressure on property prices in the cities at both the high and low ends of the housing spectrum. At the same time, tourism itself was sharply and negatively impacted by the problems in Syria, and in 2012 visitors and earnings were reported to be off by as much 50 percent.

Lebanese entrepreneurs ensure that inducements are plentiful: hundreds of modern hotels (including numerous luxury five-star facilities), spacious marinas near coastal hotels, many excellent restaurants, attractive beach resorts, beautiful scenery, both summer and winter mountain resorts, shopping opportunities that still compare well to the megamalls sprouting along the Gulf, relaxed social mores, nonstop nightlife in Beirut, several World Heritage Sites, cultural festivals—in general, a palpable joie de vivre—along with easy access by land, sea, or air. Tourism put Lebanon in 22nd place globally in 2011 as regards both its contribution to GDP (9.8 percent) and to employment (9.4 percent). However, because investment in the sector has been lagging (114th globally), long-term growth prospects relative to both GDP and total employment are less positive.

Map 11.3 Economic map of Lebanon.

Transportation

Beirut's seaport and airport were ideally situated to serve as gateways to the Levant and beyond during the early years of regional economic development. The port, sixteenth busiest in the world in the early 1970s, was often inoperative during the 1975–1990 fighting. It has been rebuilt, expanded, and modernized, but in the changed regional commercial dynamics of the new millennium it now plays a more modest role. A smaller sister port for central Lebanon is Juniyah (see Map 11.3 for all ports), which developed primarily for importing war matériel for the Maronites during the civil war. At that time, the ancient port of Sidon also expanded to serve the south, but by the mid-2000s it was unloading only one-fourth as many ships as during the 1980s. In the north is Tripoli, Lebanon's second port, formerly the terminus of one of the IPC pipelines from Iraq.

For air transportation, Beirut International Airport once served as the Middle East's avi-

ation hub for both passengers and cargo. Although squeezed into a narrow strip between mountains and coastline, it was the region's busiest civil airport during the 1960s. Often nonoperational during the 1980s, it embarked on a $500 million modernization and expansion, including a new runway built on a remarkable ramp reclaimed from the Mediterranean. A new terminal opened in 1998, with a capacity of 6 million passengers annually. Renamed after Rafiq Hariri in 2005, the facility in 2012 was still awaiting the return of direct flights to the United States, suspended since 1985. Whether this delay is due to airlines' decisions or to American political considerations is hard to say.

Middle East Airlines, rescued by the Central Bank in 1996 from closure, slashed one-fourth of its workforce and showed an operating profit in 2004 for the first time in twenty-five years. In 2012, it joined the SkyTeam airline alliance that also includes Delta Airlines; its fleet consists of seventeen jets, with eighteen more on order. Gradual reprivatization has been planned for several years, but no concrete steps in that direction have yet been taken. Trans-Mediterranean Airlines, a cargo carrier based in Beirut, relaunched service in 2010 after a six-year hiatus.

Lebanese rail lines are antiquated and essentially inoperative due to damage suffered during the civil war. As interest in rail lines has blossomed recently throughout the Middle East, there has been some talk of renovating the lines in Lebanon. However, little priority has yet been given to this sector, a situation unlikely to change as long as Syria is mired in chaos; for the indefinite future, goods and passengers will continue to move by road. The road net is relatively dense (see Map 11.3), considering the rugged terrain. Many mountain roads are narrow and steep, but most are well surfaced to withstand winter rains and, at higher elevations, deep snows. The Beirut-Damascus highway and the coast road are famously scenic routes, and both have recently been upgraded to accommodate the heavy traffic in this automobile-minded country. Lebanon has a very low ratio of 2.5 persons per vehicle.

Manufacturing

Lebanon's modest production of specialized craft items and textiles diversified after 1950 until manufacturing surpassed agriculture in importance. Little heavy industry evolved, however; cement factories and oil refineries constitute this sector. Manufacturing was severely disrupted by warfare but gradually recovered during the 1990s. Although it has not yet attained its earlier level, it is about 20 percent of GDP. Most establishments, like most shops and service institutions, are small—85 percent employ fewer than twenty-five people. Light industries cluster around Beirut, producing clothing, textiles, processed foods, jewelry, oriental handicrafts, printed materials, cigarettes, paints, and furniture. Three cement plants and two steel plants operate near Tripoli.

The Tripoli and Sidon oil refineries were originally fed by Iraqi and Saudi Arabian pipelines, respectively: when these closed, tanker deliveries took over in the early 1980s. Both refineries were heavily damaged in the civil war, but the Tripoli plant is operational again, using as feedstock Syrian crude delivered through part of the old IPC line. Lebanon relies on imported oil for the generation of about 92 percent of its electricity.[12] In addition to furniture and metal products, Tripoli produces soap from olive oil. The Bekaa has several food-processing plants, including beet-sugar mills and wineries. The cement plants operated at close to full capacity, supplying the needs of reconstruction after Israeli bombing raids during the Summer War of 2006.

Agriculture

Lebanon's physical assets allow high-grade varied horticulture. Generations of farmers have harvested fruits, nuts, and vegetables that are scarce in the Middle East. Though precipitation is concentrated in the cool season, hydrogeological conditions permit direct collection of runoff, directly or indirectly through springs, for irrigation well into the summer. Meltwater from heavy snows is particularly useful. Elaborate terracing protects the slopes from erosion from heavy rainfall (50–60 in/1,270–1,525 mm) at this elevation and spreads water from runoff, irrigating crops in the terraces.

Mount Lebanon's upslope offers ecological conditions for subtropical crops along the coast and progressively cooler-environment crops at increasing elevations—vertical zonation on the principle that "altitude equals latitude." In alluvial soils along the coast are irrigated groves of bananas, lemons, oranges, and grapefruit. Hothouses proliferated during the 1990s; their vegetables are in high demand during the winter and early spring in the Gulf states (Fig. 11.3). Slightly higher and on rocky soils are extensive olive and smaller almond groves that need little or no irriga-

Figure 11.3 Agriculture on the coastal plain of southern Lebanon, north of Sidon. This fertile strip has been cultivated for millennia (note foreground) and now has hundreds of plastic hothouses to aid early yields of horticultural crops.

tion. Still higher—2,000 to 5,000 ft/610 to 1,525 m—is a vertical succession of irrigated orchards of peaches, apricots, pears, plums, and cherries; vineyards are at several levels. At still higher elevations are apple orchards.

Vineyards have thrived in the Bekaa since Phoenician times, and the three well-known wineries in the Ksara and Zahlah area, on the lower and drier eastern slopes, had by the mid-2000s increased to fifteen. They produce up to 7 million bottles annually, a third for export. Otherwise, crops here are normally of three types: nonirrigated wheat and barley; semi-irrigated sugar beets, onions, potatoes, and melons; and irrigated fruits, tomatoes, and a wide range of other vegetables, especially in the Shtawrah (Chtoura) "oasis." The Bekaa also includes a lively food-processing industry, producing sugar, fruit juices, canned fruits and vegetables, and wine. In 2011, agri-culture accounted for only about 5 percent of Lebanon's GDP but 10 percent of its exports. From the early 1960s through the mid-2000s, per capita food production increased by more than 55 percent.[13] On the other hand, the country's dependence on imports for much of its food is shown in the fact that, for agricultural items, imports are about six times the value of exports.

Water

Lebanon is the best-watered country in the Middle East, as its two mountain ranges coax precipitation from eastward-bound clouds coming off the Mediterranean. Nonetheless, persistent shortages plague many villages and larger urbanized areas because of mismanagement, the poor state of many parts of the distribution network, and the low quality of drinkable water. Altogether, the country's per capita available renewable resources do not exceed the water poverty level—1,000 m³ annually. Probably 60 percent of water use still is in the agriculture sector, which contributes only about 5 percent to GDP. Greater water efficiency is certainly possible, but farms are small and fragmented. The most recent agricultural census (1999) found that of the some 195,000 holdings, 87 percent were less than 2 ha/4.94 ac in size.

The Litani is Lebanon's largest river (see Chap. 2), which rises in and then waters the fertile Bekaa valley. There are concerns over the long-term future flow of the river if climate change in the eastern Mediterranean makes the lower precipitation levels that have prevailed since the mid-2000s permanent. In January 2012, Lebanon launched the $330 million first phase of a major project to harness more of the Litani's resources, not only to add to the nation's water supplies but also to safeguard the river against the express aspiration of many Israeli politicians since before World War I to divert Litani water ("otherwise 'wasted' by flowing into the Mediterranean") to the farms of Upper Galilee.

Energy

It is at least slightly ironic that the four countries long customarily labeled as petrocarbon-poor—Cyprus, Israel, Lebanon, and Turkey (plus two other polities, the Palestinian Authority and North Cyprus)—have in the past few years become some of the hottest new prospects for expanding the global supply of natural gas (and to a lesser extent oil) as claimants to parts of the Levant Basin and adjacent subsea regions. Egypt has seen oil and gas production from beneath the waters of its portion of the adjoining Nile Delta Basin Province for more than twenty years, but only recently has exploration extended northeastward. Modest gas discoveries in the early 2000s off the Israeli/Gaza coast have since been extended by much larger finds west of Haifa. Assessments of the reserves in the Lev-

ant Basin by the US Geological Survey are quite sizable,[14] but maritime boundaries, particularly as they affect Lebanon, have yet to be clearly delineated (see "Regional Conflicts," in Chap. 8). It is obviously to Lebanon's advantage for prompt action on the part of the government to establish its energy exploration policies and arrive at a settlement of boundary issues with all its neighbors. The United States became actively engaged in seeking a diplomatic solution to the Lebanon-Israel boundary dispute in late 2012.[15] After a slow start, caused to some degree by the usual intercommunal considerations, the government seemed in 2013 to be coming to grips with the steps needed to realize the potential of the offshore reserves.[16]

FACTIONS AND TERRITORIES

Grand Liban. In separating Mount Lebanon from Greater Syria in 1920, the French intended to create a mandate around the Maronites, the area's dominant sect. But to make it economically viable, they had to add the coastal plain, the Bekaa, and part of the Anti-Lebanon—along with Sunni and Shii Muslims, Druze, non-Maronite Christians, and increased political vulnerability— plus long-lasting Syrian irredentism.

The groups in Lebanon did evolve, with some French prodding, a unique political structure of pragmatic representative government, based on pluralism, power sharing, and compromise. The informal National Pact of 1943 enshrined the system, basing it on the 1932 census that showed the three largest sects to be the Maronites, the Sunnis, and the Shia. So the president of the independent republic would be a Maronite, the prime minister a Sunni, and the president of the parliament (speaker) a Shii, with other groups represented in lesser offices (but, importantly, a Maronite heading the armed forces).

The events in Lebanon beginning in the mid-1970s are far too complex to treat in detail here, and many excellent accounts exist elsewhere. But at least a brief outline is required in order to understand the current situation in the country.

Falling Apart. The system began unraveling in the late 1950s and accelerated in the late 1960s and early 1970s, as economic progress more obviously favored some (Maronites and some Sunnis) over others (most Shia). Meanwhile, the demographic balance shifted drastically against the Christians, as the numbers of "outsiders" in the form of Palestinian refugees became substantial. In addition, the situation prevailing in the 1940s neglected the territorial aspects of the groups, each of which more or less predominated in a fairly well-defined territory of "turf," which led over time to a mosaic of ministates, each with its own *zaim* (group leader). In 1975, open fighting between Maronite and Palestinian protomilitias in Beirut finally sparked full-scale civil war that would devastate the country and the society for more than sixteen years.

The elected government became essentially powerless, as more than a dozen factions fielded heavily armed militias, some of which split into even more groups over time, forming coalitions that often shifted and showed no clear ideological or even religious consistency. Making things even murkier and also antagonizing already brutal conditions were the interference and physical presence of outside forces.

Outsider Interference. The Palestinians have already been mentioned, and strikes by their guerrillas against northern Galilee brought in the Israelis in 1978; then, in a massive invasion in 1982, the Israelis established themselves in southern Lebanon until unilaterally withdrawing in 2000. Syria arrived first as an ally and "protector" of the Maronites in 1976 but remained with shifting alliances and enemies until it was finally forced out in 2005.

The Multi-National Force (MNF), composed of American, French, Italian, and British troops, came in 1982 to oversee the withdrawal of the Palestine Liberation Organization (PLO) and its forces. The MNF faced hostile anti-Western and anti-Israeli militants who employed suicide bomb attacks that killed hundreds of American and French troops in their barracks.

Lebanon and all of its peoples suffered egregiously. Hundreds of Westerners and Lebanese alike were kidnapped and either murdered or held captive for years, and two presidents were assassinated. By 1991, probably 140,000 had been killed and at least as many more wounded. One incident in particular indicates the savagery of the fighting: after the PLO had left and the MNF finally withdrew, the Israeli-backed Maronite Phalange (*Kataib*) militia massacred more than 800 Palestinian civilians in the Sabra-Shatila refugee camps in Beirut in September 1982.[17] Much of the country's infrastructure and thousands of buildings were destroyed, and hundreds of thousands of residents sought refuge abroad, many never to return to Lebanon. Total damage in monetary terms was almost incalculable; one estimate exceeded $50 billion, spread across the country from the largest cities to small mountain villages.

Taif Agreement. Finally, in October 1989, under the aegis of the Arab League, plus strong Syrian pressure, and with all Lebanese weary of death and destruction, most of the surviving members of the 1972 parliament met in Taif, Saudi Arabia, and agreed on a Document of National Understanding. The militias agreed to disarm (at least in theory), and the political structure was altered. The powers of the president, prime minister, and speaker were rebalanced, and parliamentary seats were divided equally between Christians and Muslims. Confessionalism remained, but on a more realistic basis and with some hope for its future diminution.

New Power for the Shia.   Perhaps the biggest change in post-Taif Lebanon was the much improved political position of the Shia, the largest and poorest of the major groups. Not only were the sect's larger numbers recognized in the government settlement, but its two largest militias, Amal and especially Hizballah, became parliamentary powers as well through their political party subsidiaries. Hizballah became the state-within-the-state that many Lebanese feared the PLO would become in the 1970s; its new status was amply demonstrated in the "Summer War" when its sustained rocket attacks in July 2006 developed into full-fledged warfare between it and the much stronger Israeli Defense Forces (IDF). Thousands of rockets fell as far south as Haifa and beyond, leading to widespread panic rarely seen in Israel before. The IDF eventually prevailed, with massive air bombardments of Beirut and elsewhere, but Hizballah emerged having proven its ability to wreak serious damage on Israel and designated as the agent of "national resistance."

Rafik Hariri.   With the Taif agreement in place, a religiously balanced parliament was elected in 1992, and widely admired Sunni reformer and businessman Rafik Hariri became prime minister; he retained the position until 1998 and then returned to it in 2000. Israel unilaterally evacuated most of what it held in Lebanon in May 2002, but Syrian occupation continued. Hariri resigned in protest in October 2004, and he was assassinated four months later, almost certainly with some involvement of Syrian forces and allies, including Hizballah. Although a full investigation of the Hariri assassination would continue to be blocked by pro-Syrian political forces, Syria was forced to withdraw the last of its forces in 2005.

Since then, two rival political blocs have dominated national politics, one headed by Hariri's son Saad and the other by Hizballah. The former was reelected in 2009 with a ma-

jority of the seats (but not of the votes) and, after several months of negotiations, formed a national union government including Hizballah. This collapsed in January 2011 and was replaced eventually by a coalition including Hizballah that Hariri refused to join. Although the government actually included more Maronites than Shia, the United States has largely treated it as Hizballah dominated.

Hizballah, Syria, and Iran.   Hizballah's major foreign supporters, the Assad regime in Syria and the Islamic Republic of Iran, were by late 2012 both sorely troubled and somewhat distracted. But its domestic base in the poor Shii neighborhoods of southern Beirut and the villages near the Israeli border remains strong. The chaos in Syria began to spill over into Lebanon in 2012, leading, among other things, to open conflict between Shii and Sunni populations in Beirut and northern Lebanon. The assassination of the Sunni (and anti-Syrian) chief of intelligence, General Wissam al-Hassan, in October 2012, further polarized the intra-Muslim relationship. Border incidents became more frequent, as opposing Syrian forces sometimes crossed into Lebanon. As mentioned earlier, tensions rose between Lebanese communities, especially in the north, as they took sides with Syrian factions. More ominously, perhaps, jihadist groups (including reportedly al-Qaida) were infiltrating into Lebanon.[18]

RELATIONS

At least at the government level, Lebanon has been the Middle East's quintessential neutral. It avoided taking sides in the intra-Arab conflicts beginning in the 1950s between revolutionary republics and the traditional monarchies, and it stayed aloof for the most part in the Cold War rivalry of East and West. At the level of ethnic/religious groups, however, neutrality was not characteristic. The Maronites had traditional links to France and the Vatican, and more broadly to western Europe. The Greek (or Arab) Orthodox favored Russia. Most Sunnis favored Syria from which many of them felt they had been unjustly severed by the mandate powers; other Sunnis had strong family ties to Saudi Arabia. After the overthrow of the shah in 1979, the Shia increasingly looked to the Islamic Republic. Official neutrality was disrupted during the civil war, and the allegiances of the major groups became dominant. Since the Taif Agreement took hold, the government has returned to a semblance of neutrality in its international relations.

United States. US diplomatic relations with Lebanon date to 1942, and full relations came in 1944 with Lebanese independence; as indicated earlier, close unofficial ties began with the founding in 1866 of what became the American University of Beirut. A small program of economic assistance began in the late 1940s that increased with the passage of the US Foreign Assistance Act. By 2010, development grants and loans totaled $1.81 billion, and military grants and loans came to about $400 million. The 2010 program of the US Agency for International Development ($109 million) focused on a variety of areas, including water, education, and promotion of the rule of law.[19]

Europe. As mentioned above, Lebanon has an Association Agreement with the European Union as part of the latter's European Neighbourhood Policy, and the EU, through its various agencies, is the largest donor of economic assistance to Lebanon. The Association Agreement includes some aspects of a free trade agreement, and the EU is Lebanon's largest trading partner. France continues to be closely involved in the country and not just with the Christian population: visiting Beirut in November 2012, French president François Hollande pledged to protect Lebanon against threats of destabilization from Syrian fallout.

Inter-Arab Relations. With regard to relations to other Arab countries, Lebanon has throughout its independent existence had a highly ambiguous and clearly subordinate relationship with Syria. Formal diplomatic relations—in effect, Syria's recognition of Lebanon's sovereignty—were established only in 2008, and the first embassies were exchanged in 2010. Lebanon has tried to stay out of the fighting that has engulfed Syria since 2011, despite Lebanese Hizballah's overt support for the Assad regime, and it is difficult to project how these dynamic Syrian events will affect future relations between the two countries. Lebanon has had generally cordial relations with the oil-exporting states and has benefited from the largesse of several Arab aid agencies. Additionally, thousands of Lebanese, especially those with advanced skills, have spent much of their careers in the Gulf region.

Israel. Lebanon has technically been in a state of war with Israel since 1948, and as indicated above it has been invaded, occupied, bombed, and shelled by Israeli forces more than have any of the latter's other neighbors with the exception of the Palestinians. Somewhat of a canard is the statement that Lebanon will be the last Arab state to sign a peace treaty with Israel,[20] which reflects Lebanon's weak position relative both to its Arab neighbors (particularly Syria) and to Israel.

For information on the business environment in Lebanon, see the website attached to this book: www.middleeastpatterns.com.

Cyprus

KEY POINTS: Central island location in eastern Mediterranean brought ancient settlers and encourages modern trade and tourism. Copper resources (*Cyprus* = copper) and other minerals added importance. Historical changes in sovereignty produced mainly Greek and minority Turkish population and orientation. Invasion by Turkish military in 1974 led to division of island into Greek south (Republic of Cyprus, part of EU) and Turkish north (Turkish Republic of North Cyprus, recognized only by Turkey). Reunification efforts repeatedly stalled, but continue. Serious economic crisis began 2012.

HISTORICAL GEOGRAPHY

Two geographical facts—that Cyprus is an island and that it is located in the eastern Mediterranean—are the most important aspects of its existence. About the size of Puerto Rico, it is the third-largest Mediterranean island after Sicily and Sardinia. Its mountains are clearly visible across the 43 mi/69 km of water that separate it from Asia Minor, and it lies 65 mi/105 km from Syria and 475 mi/765 km from mainland Greece. Its coastline has several semiprotected bays that have sheltered ships for millennia. Occupied during the Neolithic period, about 9000 BCE, it has been fought for and used as a base for more than thirty-five hundred years, with its original mineral wealth—especially copper—and agricultural resources valuable bonuses.[21] The island was formed during the Tertiary mountain-building period along the arcuate boundary between the African and Eurasian Plates (see Map 2.2). Seismic repercussions from continuing plate convergence produce periodic earthquakes, some of them catastrophic.

A third basic geographical fact is the island's division since 1974 between two antagonistic ethnic groups, Greek and Turkish. The imposed separation installed a Turkish regime of ambiguous standing in the island's northern third, while the internationally rec-ognized and overwhelmingly Greek Republic of Cyprus ruled the south.

Developments Before Independence

Crossroads of Empires.   Six crucial events in the island's long history are fundamental to the contemporary situation. First, timber for shipbuilding and copper brought Bronze Age Minoans (from Crete) and Mycenaeans (from Greece), a connection emphasized by Greek Cypriots. Successive masters—Assyrians, Egyptians, Persians—ruled Cyprus until the Greco-Roman period, when the second important event occurred: the New Testament tells of Paul and Barnabas preaching Christianity on the island (45 CE), and the religion was reinforced during eight hundred years of Byzantine rule from 364. Brief Crusader and Frankish episodes preceded its cession in 1489 to Venice, which built the magnificent walls of Old Nicosia.

The third main event was the Ottoman conquest in 1570 and the migration of thousands of Muslims to the island over the next three hundred years. These three events set the stage for the modern conflict between Greeks and Turks. The fourth crucial event was the arrival in 1878 of Britain; the island with around 180,000 residents then was to be a base for protecting the new Suez Canal and the route to India; for well or ill, Britain then affected Cypriot fortunes for most of a criti-

CYPRUS

Long-form official name, anglicized: Republic of Cyprus (ROC in the South); (Turkish Republic of North Cyprus [TRNC] in the North, recognized only by Turkey)

Official name, transliterated: Kipriaki Dhimokratia (Greek) in south; Kibris Cumhuriyeti (Turkish) in north

Form of government: unitary multiparty republic with a unicameral legislature (House of Representatives)

Area: 3,572 mi²/9,251 km² (entire island)

Population, 2011: 1,118,000 (entire island); Literacy: 97.6% (entire island)

Ethnic composition (entire island %, latest): Greek Cypriot 67; Turkish Cypriot/Turk 26.1; Armenian 2.4; Arab 2.1, of which Lebanese 1.8; British 1; other 1.4

Religions (entire island %, latest): Greek Orthodox 69.2; Sunni Muslim 26.6; Roman Catholic 1.5, of which Maronite 0.4; Anglican 0.7; other 2

Demography: Life expectancy (entire island)—75.21 yr (M), 80.92 yr (F); Birthrate (entire island, per 1,000)—11.44; Fertility rate (entire island)—1.45

GDP (ROC), 2012: $22.45 billion; purchasing power parity (entire island): $23.57 billion; per capita (entire island): $26,900

Currency: Euro, US$1 = €0.782; 1 euro = $1.312; (TRNC): Turkish Lira, US$1 = 1.791 liras; 1 TRL = $0.558 (mid-May 2013)

Energy: oil and natural gas—nil (promising offshore finds in process of evaluation 2013); coal—nil

Main exports (ROC % of total value, 2008): $1.72 billion (of which refined petroleum 19.8; food 16.9; medicine 9.2; prostheses/body implants 6.1; photosensitive semiconductor devices 5.2; tobacco products 4.6)

Main imports (ROC % of total value, 2008): $10.85 billion (of which refined petroleum 18.7; machinery and apparatus 14.6; road vehicles 12.2; food 9.9)

Capital city, 2008: Nicosia (Lefkoşa) (agglomeration) 281,037; other cities: Limassol 183,000; Larnaca 81,700

---

cal century, and the British imprint on the island remains obvious to the present.

Independence and Its Problems

Uneasy Independence. Formally annexed by Britain in 1914,[22] Cyprus demanded an end to colonial status after World War II; in the 1950s, Greek Cypriots revolted. Behind the sometimes savage attacks of the EOKA (National Organization of Cypriot Fighters) guerrillas (deemed terrorists by the British) with support from Greece, the majority of the population wanted union with Greece (*enosis*), not independence. But after five years of conflict, Britain, Greek and Turkish Cypriots, and the Greek and Turkish governments signed the Zurich-London Agreements, creating the independent Republic of Cyprus (ROC) in August 1960—the fifth crucial event. Britain retains two strategically valuable Sovereign Base Areas (SBAs) on the south coast after more than fifty years (Map 11.4); they remain

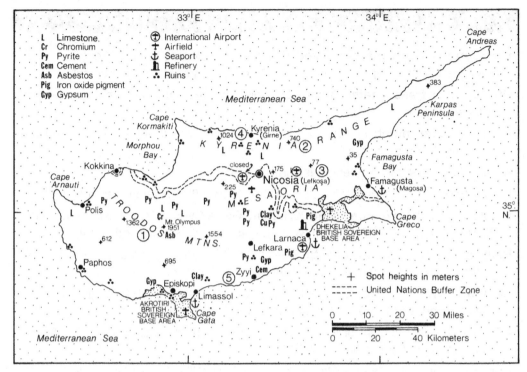

Map 11.4 General and economic map of Cyprus, showing dividing line between North Cyprus and South Cyprus. Circled numbers indicate the regions discussed in the text.

British overseas territories and constitute about 2.7 percent of the island's area.

The ROC faced predictable dilemmas. Of a total population of 550,000, 79 percent were Greek speaking and Greek Orthodox in religion, and most strongly desired enosis; about 18 percent were Turkish speaking and Sunni Muslims and sought autonomy under either confederation or partition (*taksim*); 3 percent were descendants of Armenian and Maronite refugees, all Christians, and there were a few thousand British and other expatriates. All lived intermingled on the island; though most villages tended to be either Greek or Turkish, some villages and the larger towns were mixed.

Unsuccessful Power Sharing. Upon independence, a power-sharing agreement prorated political positions seven Greeks to three Turks (six to four in the proposed army), al-

though the demographic ratio was about eight to two; it was not successful. By the end of 1963, intense frictions led many Turkish Cypriots to withdraw "behind the barricades," and tension heightened between Greece and Turkey. This prompted the UN Security Council to establish the UN Peacekeeping Force in Cyprus in 1964. It has regularly demonstrated its value and has served its purpose now for almost fifty years. Through the 1960s and into the 1970s, Greek Cypriots operated the government virtually alone, with conflicts between those wanting enosis and those content with an independent republic. After further intercommunal violence in 1967–1968, Turkish Cypriots formed a provisional administration of their own.

Invasion

The ideological struggle among Greek Cypriots culminated in July 1974 in a foolhardy attempted coup by pro-enosis hard-liners—supported by the military junta in Athens—against the all-Greek Cyprus government. It quickly failed when the president, Archbishop Makarios, escaped assassination. Nevertheless, Turkey responded quickly, invading under the terms of the 1960 Treaty of Guarantee to protect the Turkish population. Backed by this strong military presence, the Cypriot Turks posthaste divided the island, with the Turkish north ending up with 36 percent of the land, 18 percent of the population, and half of Nicosia. Consequently, some 200,000 Greeks fled south, 45,000 Turks northward, and 6,000–8,000 died—all within a few weeks. This division into a Turkish-Cypriot north, backed by 40,000 Turkish troops, and a Greek-Cypriot south, protected by 6,000 Greek troops, is the sixth and most climactic crucial event affecting today's Cyprus. (Both the consequences of the island's division and economic factors have resulted in there being a sizable Cypriot diaspora—both Greek and Turkish; conservative estimates start at 500,000.)

Divided Island—and Frustration

With the two sides separated by a UN buffer zone, the ROC in the south is the internationally recognized legitimate government. Despite losing much of its productive capacity, it energetically pursued revitalization. It quickly gained more tourists, industrial output, and income from services than the pre-1974 state had islandwide. Through its own efforts and with external assistance, it generated remarkable political and economic development, culminating in its admission to the EU in 2004.

By contrast, North Cyprus has suffered more political ambiguity and has seen less economic development. Under Turkish tutelage, the de facto autonomous administration was recast in February 1975 as a unilaterally declared Turkish Federated State of Cyprus, implying for the future the kind of federation

Turkish Cypriots had demanded twenty years earlier. When there was no movement toward a solution, it renamed itself the Turkish Republic of Northern Cyprus in 1983. Internationally isolated, the TRNC has received no recognition by any country other than Turkey. To enhance the north's Turkishness, the Ankara government had settled about 55,000 mainland Turks in the TRNC by the mid-2000s.

Elusive Settlement. Despite the early violence and bitterness, the two communities have shown remarkable physical restraint under complex measures either negotiated between them or externally imposed. Attempts to devise institutional arrangements for reunification acceptable to both groups and also to Greece and Turkey have been continuous and were especially vigorous after violence broke out at the dividing line in 1996. In all these negotiations, success has been elusive, with four basic sticking points: (1) the constitutional character of a reunified government, (2) the territorial extent of each entity, (3) the right of return of refugees to their pre-1974 homes, and (4) troop strength in each territory.

With fits and starts, the UN got the two sides to negotiate, led by their "community leaders," thus avoiding the political overtones of "presidents," and when this failed to achieve a mutually agreed solution, the UN secretary-general proposed his own—the so-called Annan Plan: a united republic of two states in confederation, limited right of return for refugees with some border adjustments, and a continued presence of Greek and Turkish military; the plan was to be voted on separately by the two communities. In the meantime, the ROC was one of a group of nine countries, mostly ex-communist, ready for EU membership in 2004. The EU was eager to admit the Eastern European states promptly and knew that Greece would delay this unless the ROC was guaranteed admission regardless of whether a settlement for the island was reached before admission. So it capitulated to Greece—thus losing whatever leverage it might have had to forward the Annan Plan. The Annan Plan went down to defeat—accepted by two-thirds of Turkish Cypriots but only a fourth of the Greeks.

An Open Border—and Continued Frustration

In 2003, to offset his earlier inflexibility, Turkish Cypriot leader Rauf Denktash suddenly opened the border between north and south to crossings in both directions for all islanders, and within a year more than 3 million crossings were recorded, markedly improving the intercommunal atmosphere. But when the time came to vote on the plan in April 2004, the improved attitude was to no avail, despite backing from the United States, the EU, Greece, and Turkey. The Turks (eager for inclusion in the EU) accepted it by 65 percent, as mentioned above, but the Greeks, urged on by a hard-line president, rejected it by 75 percent, knowing full well that the ROC would enter the EU in any case a few days after the vote. In consolation, the EU promised the TRNC about $311 million in development aid, and the ROC was roundly criticized internationally for rejecting the proposals.

In 2008, Greek Cypriots chose a new, more conciliatory president, Demetris Christofias, who campaigned promising to restart negotiations. He quickly met with his Turkish counterpart in the first of many sessions between them, and there were even more meetings between joint working groups; in the first year, more than twenty confidence-building measures were agreed upon. Intraisland trade rose from zero in 2003 to $12.4 million in 2008, and personal shopping by Cypriots visiting the "other side" was easily several times higher. At the end of the 2000s, prospects for forward movement were much brighter; after a late-2009 election, the new government in Athens was headed by a prime minister who espoused a federal solution for Cyprus. Inten-

sified intercommunal negotiations took place through 2010, but for all the activity and the quite real confidence building initiatives, by 2011 it was becoming clearer that real progress on the core issues remained elusive. The major sticking points in negotiations have remained the details of the form a unified government would take for both sides, security for the Turks, and the status of property ownership for the Greeks.[23]

By 2012, Christofias was so discouraged by the lack of progress in the many rounds of talks and by considerable erosion of his previous support within the Greek community that he announced he would not run for re-election in 2013. His prospects for remaining in office had been sharply diminished by an explosion in 2011 that destroyed the island's biggest power plant, and an official inquiry placed the blame on government negligence.

The prospects of discovering natural gas off the coast of the island have only complicated negotiations and the relations between Turkey and both Cypriot communities. In some ways, the Cyprus problem seemed to be even more intractable than the Israeli/Palestinian conflict. With no solution in sight, all parties stand to lose. For the Greeks, any hope of compensation for lost property is forlorn, and there is the long-term prospect of facing a large and powerful Turkish military force across the demarcation line. For the Turks, the likelihood of further isolation from Europe is strong, as is the further dilution of the character of the Turkish Cypriot community through continued migration from the mainland. For the EU, a festering Cyprus problem further complicates its already complex relations with Turkey. For a younger generation of Cypriots with no history of contact with each other, eventually recognizing the island's division as permanent may increasingly become an option.

A Cypriot Spring?   Admittedly inspired by both the Arab Spring and the worldwide Occupy Movement, in October 2011 a group of Greek and Turkish Cypriot activists began a weekly occupation of the Ledra Street checkpoint between the two sectors of Nicosia. Frustrated by the lack of progress in the negotiations between the political leaders of both communities, they announced a twofold aim; first, to bring about reunification, and, second, to raise awareness that the Cyprus problem is a symptom of the unhealthy global system. They expanded to camping in the buffer zone to the chagrin of both the two governments and the UN Peacekeeping Force. In April 2012, Greek Cypriot police evicted the activists with considerable force.

TWO MOUNTAINS, THREE PLAINS

With a remarkably varied landscape for such a small area, the island has five distinct regions: two east-west mountain ranges in the north and south, a broad basin in between, and narrow plains along north and south coasts (see Map 11.4). In the southwest are [1] the Troodos Mountains, the oval geomorphic nucleus of the island and a true massif, with an intruded highly mineralized granite core exposed by erosion. Mount Olympus, the island's highest elevation, reaches 6,400 ft/1,951 m. Extensive mineralization accompanied the intrusions, and breakdown of the Troodos rocks produced fertile soils. Stretching the length of the northern edge of the island is [2] the Kyrenia Range, a narrow, steep mountain ridge primarily of Cretaceous limestone that attains 3,360 ft/1,024 m. Some igneous patches occur, and metamorphism has produced marble in places. Much of the range is porous because of solution cavities and is a source of springwater. Its ridges are rough and craggy, appropriately wild for the Crusader castle ruins that cling to its pinnacles.

Nestled between the Kyrenia Range and the Troodos is [3] the Mesaoria, the island's breadbasket, an alluvial plain with fertile soils with a platform of upturned sedimentaries between the Kyrenia ridge and the lower basin. Open at both east and west ends, the Mesaoria slopes primarily eastward, from about 700 ft/215 m to sea level on the coast. Nicosia, the divided primate city of the island and capital of both the ROC and the TRNC, nestles in the center. North of the Kyrenia Range, [4] a narrow coastal plain separates the steep northern slopes from the shore, with citrus groves in irrigated areas and rainfed crops elsewhere. [5] The coastal plain south of the Troodos is generally wider but more irregular. It is also more densely populated and more industrially developed, with three centers, Limassol, Larnaca, and Paphos, plus the two British SBAs—Akrotiri and Dhekelia.

MEDITERRANEAN CLIMATE, MEDITERRANEAN CROPS

Cyprus has a typical Mediterranean climate, with hot, dry summers and mild, moist winters. It receives 75 percent of possible sunshine in an average year, attracting tourists with its warmth, scenic sites, and well-developed resorts; tourism is the primary economic sector, with 2.4 million arrivals in 2008. With only 13 in/340 mm of rainfall at Nicosia on the Mesaoria (see data for Nicosia in Table 2.1), crops other than the dominant grains must be irrigated. The upper Troodos slopes exert the typical orographic effect and wring up to 45 in/1,145 mm of moisture from winter's westerly winds, much of it as snow, allowing a modest skiing season most years. Much of the runoff from the impermeable igneous rocks is captured in reservoirs or aquifers to be used for irrigation during the summer. With cool temperatures and appreciable moisture, the slopes are forested with pine, cedar, cypress, and poplar (Fig. 11.4). These woodlands contrast sharply with the typical low, open maquis and garigue typical of Mediterranean lowlands in much of Cyprus. Resorts do double duty in summer and winter.

Figure 11.4 Typical landscape on south-facing slopes of the Troodos, western Cyprus. A well-varied area, with olive groves (*right foreground*), vineyards (*left foreground*), terraced cultivation (*middle distance*), and scrub oak and pine forest (*slopes in the distance*).

With assets of climate, relief, and soils, the island has had a favorable agricultural base for centuries. However, during the past thirty-five years, agriculture has fallen to less than 3 percent of GDP and 8 percent of the labor force. Produce includes several tree crops—olives, carobs (it leads the region in carob-bean exports), almonds, citrus, and other fruits—and especially grapes. Its wine, although not of premium quality, is quite good, and extensive vineyards occupy the Troodos southern midslopes. Table grapes, raisins, and wines are major products and exports, as are citrus fruits of all types. Potatoes rank with citrus and grapes in tonnage and are also a major export. More than half of farms have some irrigation, mostly from shallow wells; 35 percent of cultivated land is irrigated.

WATER

Water supply and pollution are increasingly serious problems, not only for agriculture (which claims about 70 percent of the island's available water), but also crucially for the vital tourist economy and for households; it is not altogether an exaggeration to state that by 2012, the water deficit of the entire island was close to replacing its political division as its most serious problem. A prolonged drought during the 1990s gravely upset the island's water balance, reducing the level in the artificial reservoirs to less than 15 percent of normal in 1997–1999. Heavy rainfall in 2001–2003 broke the ten-year drought and refilled most of the reservoirs, but a return of dry years led to water rationing in

2007. Both Greek and Turkish sides have been seeking drastic new solutions to the problem, ranging from building offshore desalinization facilities to importing water by ship and pipeline from Greece and Turkey. By 2010, Cyprus was on many lists of the world's most water-distressed countries.

NONAGRICULTURAL ECONOMY

Mineralization in the Troodos during the igneous intrusions and the accompanying metamorphism gave the island major resources of copper, iron pyrites, chrome, asbestos, and iron-oxide pigments as well as lesser amounts of gold, silver, and zinc. Deposits of copper, the main metal in bronze, were exploited as early as the third millennium BCE and became a major source of the metal for the eastern Mediterranean during the Bronze Age. Indeed, the Greek and Latin words for copper are related to the island's name. In modern times, mining was second only to agriculture during the 1950s and 1960s, but the major older deposits of copper and chrome had been virtually exhausted by the late 1970s. Feasibility studies on exploiting other possible deposits, especially of copper and gold, were undertaken in the late 2000s, by which time the island produced only modest tonnages of pyrite, iron-oxide pigments (for paints), bentonite clays, celestite, and gypsum. After long exploitation of large asbestos reserves in the Troodos, the Amiantos mine closed in 1989 because of decreased world demand. Thus, the island's once-considerable income from mineral exports is now negligible, although asbestos, bentonite, celestite, chromite, copper, gypsum, iron-oxide pigments, pyrite, and salt resources are still noteworthy.[24]

ENERGY

Cyprus and Lebanon have been the only countries in the region with no known petroleum or natural gas resources, and all of the island's electricity is still generated in plants fired with imported oil. However, as was mentioned earlier regarding Lebanon, this is a situation likely to change drastically in the next few years. The US Geological Survey has estimated that there are some 122 tn ft^3/3.45 m^3 of natural gas and 1.7 bn bbl of oil in the Levant Basin that adjoins Cyprus's offshore territory to the east.[25] Serious exploration is under way off the coasts of all countries bordering the eastern Mediterranean. Maritime borders are either already negotiated (for Cyprus, with Egypt, Israel, and Lebanon) or under dispute (Cyprus and Turkey), and border issues, along with the need for considerable financing, will determine the pace at which discovered resources are exploited, along with the construction of a proposed natural gas liquification plant on the island's southern coast. Likewise, the parlous state of the Cypriot economy in the wake of the financial crisis of 2012–2013 will be a major factor in determining progress in the energy sector. The government is eager to proceed rapidly in hopes of promoting recovery from the sharp economic downturn following from the crisis.

INDICATORS IN THE ECONOMY

The republic has had a thriving open, free-market, service-based economy until 2012, with manufactured products (foods, clothing, textiles, chemicals) constituting 54 percent of the exports in 2007. Taking advantage of an educated and English-speaking population, good airline and maritime connections, and exceptional telecommunications, it makes a "bridge" of its geography. Contributing 78 percent to GDP is the service sector, including tourism, employing 71 percent of the labor force. Tourism was hit fairly hard by the global recession—2009 earnings were down more than 15 percent; these recovered somewhat, and in 2011 they were estimated to be about $1.02 billion, or equivalent to about 5.7 percent of GDP.

Euro Difficulties: Financial Disaster.   Cyprus had become an international business hub—more stable than Beirut, attracting regional offices, banks, and investments; adopting the euro as its currency in 2008, it became well integrated into the EU. However, the heavy and unwise exposure of Cyprus banks to the sorely troubled Greek economy and Greek sovereign debt led the country's financial sector to near total collapse in 2012. Forced to seek a bailout from the EU, it was faced with terms more onerous than had been previously imposed on any other troubled Eurozone economy. The rating agency Moody's had reduced the Cyprus government's credit rating to essentially junk-bond status in June 2012; in August, a team of economists headed by the International Monetary Fund informed the government that its problems went beyond the island's banking system and that serious fiscal imbalances must be addressed with dispatch. Coupled with massive employment disruptions in the financial sector, government cutbacks sent the unemployment rate soaring into double digits.

Other EU countries (particularly Germany) felt that the outsized Cypriot banking sector was the result of lax regulation that had led to the island's becoming a center for money laundering, especially from Russian sources—a charge denied by the Cypriot government.[26] The bailout terms imposed what was essentially a confiscation of more than half of all bank deposits exceeding 100,000 euros and the termination of the island's second largest bank. The "bailout tax" was particularly criticized by international financial observers.[27] The total cost of the bailout was estimated to have come to 23 billion euros.[28]

Living Standards.   The ROC's per capita GDP in 2011 was one of the highest in the region. In 2013, it ranked 31st of 186 countries globally (and 2nd in the region) according to the UNDP's Human Development Index, placing it among the very high human devel-opment countries, although little more than a generation ago it was considered a third-world developing country. It registered a gain of about 19 percent in the value of its HDI since 1980. An alternative but similar measure, the Legatum Institute's Prosperity Index, put Cyprus 30th among 142 countries globally in 2012 and 2nd regionally after only the United Arab Emirates.[29] However, the financial crisis portended a considerable shrinkage of the economy in 2013, accompanied, as mentioned earlier, by significant increases in unemployment.

South-North Differences.   The economic disparity between north and south is obvious. Although the TRNC also has a free-market economy, political and economic uncertainty has discouraged investment. The mid-2000s did see several years of strong growth led by construction. Compared to that in the south, tourism in the north is relatively modest, concentrated around the beautiful port of Kyrenia (Fig. 11.5); most visitors are British or Turkish. The TRNC's economy relies on agriculture and government services, which together employ more than half the workforce. Lack of skilled labor and inflation have hurt the economy, which is closely tied to that of Turkey. Since the sectoral border opened in 2003, several thousand northerners have found employment in the south. Per capita GDP is about half that in the ROC, and the TRNC is heavily dependent on its patron for most of its trade and financial assistance—$400 million annually in the late 2000s. Although it is de jure part of the European Union, it is not a member of the seventeen-nation Eurozone. However, the currency is widely used there.

RELATIONS

Though of little international influence politically or economically, the ROC has surprisingly complex relations, particularly as a result of the intraisland discord. Traditionally

Figure 11.5 Pleasant outdoor café on Kyrenia harbor, North Cyprus's premier resort area.

nonaligned in foreign policy, it has consistently identified with the West culturally. It has long had close associations with Greece and Britain (though the SBAs are an irritant); as an EU member, it is moving more toward broader European concerns. In July 2012, it assumed the EU presidency for the following six months. The recent discovery of gas in the Levant Basin and the resulting additional conflict with Turkey seemed in 2012 to be moving the republic to a closer relationship with Israel.

The United States established formal diplomatic relations with Cyprus at the time of the island's independence in 1960. The US Agency for International Development extended economic assistance in the aftermath of the 1973 invasion, and through 2010 this amounted to $540 million. More recently, USAID has supported intercommunal activities; from 2008 to 2010, this came to about $42 million. The TRNC is recognized diplomatically only by Turkey and remains fairly isolated, but assistance from EU states after the ROC became a member has increased contacts in that direction. It has observer status but not membership in the Organization of the Islamic Cooperation.

For information on the business environment in Cyprus, see the website attached to this book: www.middleeastpatterns.com.

Our focus now returns to the Levant mainland for a contrasting view of the Kingdom of Jordan.

NOTES

1. Estimates of the Lebanese diaspora vary widely. A conservative figure would be in the range of 4 to 5 million, but much larger numbers are claimed elsewhere—for example, 12.4 million in September 2009 in http://identitychef.wordpress.com/2009/09/06/lebanese-diaspora-worldwide-geographical-distribution/.

2. Gore 2004.

3. See S. Haddad 2003, Pt. 1.

4. *Zawya*, Mar. 14 and Apr. 19, 2013.

5. Another group with roots in Islam are the Bahai with a small but long-established presence in Lebanon. They are not among the recognized sects but are free to practice their faith.

6. Gambill 2009. See also Sanjan 2009.

7. Beirut is now the permanent home of the UN Economic and Social Commission for Western Asia.

8. *New York Times*, Sept. 16, 2009.

9. United Nations Development Programme 2013; *Legatum Prosperity Index 2012*, www.prosperity.com/.

10. For further details on the relationship, see "EU-Lebanon Action Plan," http://ec.europa.eu/world/enp/pdf/lebanon_enp_ap_final_en.pdf; and European Commission, "Lebanese Republic: Country Strategy Paper, 2007–2013."

11. World Gold Council. By way of comparison, US gold holdings were 8,133.5 mt.

12. IEA, "2006 Energy Balance for Lebanon," www.iea.org/country/index.asp.

13. FAO, *Production Yearbook,* various editions.

14. US Geological Survey, "Assessment of Undiscovered Oil and Gas Resources of the Levant Basin Province, Eastern Mediterranean," http://pubs.usgs.gov/fs/2010/3014/pdf/FS10–3014.pdf.

15. *Daily Star* (Beirut), Dec. 20, 2012.

16. The minister of energy announced that preliminary surveys indicated reserves of 660 mn bbl of oil and 30 tn ft^3 of natural gas; *Zawya*, May 10, 2013.

17. See the Israeli government's Kahan Commission 1983; its official report charged Gen. Ariel Sharon with "personal responsibility" and recommended his removal from office. In January 2002, Elie Hobeika, a onetime minister in the Lebanese government and the leader of a pro-Israeli Christian militia implicated in the massacre, was assassinated after he claimed that he had proof of his innocence and was willing to testify in legal proceedings seeking an indictment of Sharon, by then Israeli prime minister.

18. *Al-Monitor,* Feb. 3, 2013; *Daily Star* (Beirut), Mar. 6, 2013.

19. See www.usaid.gov/lb/programs/index.html.

20. A variant is that Lebanon will be right after Syria in signing a treaty.

21. Hundreds of antiquities from 9500 BCE to the late Roman period, along with ruins from medieval times, are scattered over the island and are among the most important attractions of Cyprus. Especially famous are the Greco-Roman mosaic floors in Paphos, in southwest Cyprus, and the Greco-Roman city of Salamis on the east coast.

22. In some ways, a harbinger of British wartime Middle East policies designed to protect the route to India; see Busch 1971.

23. *Economist,* Dec. 2, 2009.

24. US Geological Survey, "The Mineral Industry of Cyprus," in *Minerals Yearbook* 2011.

25. See note 13 above.

26. *Reuters,* Jan. 15, 2013; *EU Observer,* Jan. 11, 2013; *EurActiv,* Jan. 14, 2013.

27. For example, see *BBC News,* Mar. 19, 2013.

28. *BBC News,* Apr. 11, 2013.

29. United Nations Development Programme 2013; *Legatum Prosperity Index 2012,* www.prosperity.com/.

The reader is advised to consult this book's associated website (**www.middleeastpatterns.com**) for additional information on **Lebanon and Cyprus,** such as historical time lines and chronologies of recent events, as well as essays on selected topics and various international economic, social, and political indicators.

12

Jordan

The Land Beyond and Between

KEY POINTS: Artificial creation as British mandate (Trans-Jordan), early 1920s. Continues serving as buffer state. Highland Western belt just beyond Jordan River Valley a relatively humid strip, long the most developed and populated part of polity, with desert eastward. Independent 1946 as kingdom, attached remainder of Palestine ("West Bank") 1948, relinquished it officially 1988. Hundreds of thousands of Palestinian refugees fled to Jordan in 1948, many more in 1967, outnumbering native East Bankers. Of Jordan's Hashimite kings, Husayn bin Talal reigned 47 years. He signed peace treaty with Israel 1994, following Egypt. Modest economic development. Maintained fair stability during unrest in Arab world 2011 and later.

THE NAME'S THE THING

During its long history, the area of the modern Kingdom of Jordan has undergone many changes in economic level, political status, and even name. Confusion over Jordan's political geography—specifically its territorial base—was especially common in the twentieth century, not least because "Jordan" has been used since ancient times for both the famed river and its valley and as the name of the country.

The autonomous polity of Transjordan was created in the early 1920s as a British mandate under the League of Nations in lands taken from the Turks during World War I, following the Arab uprising against the Ottoman Empire. The Amirate of Transjordan—in other words, the principality across the Jordan River (from a Eurocentric cartographic perspective)—as it was known for twenty-five years, became independent in May 1946. Attachment of the West Bank, part of the former Palestine mandate, to the kingdom in 1948 (officially in 1950) made "Transjordan" a misnomer and led to the adoption of the Hashimite Kingdom of Jordan as its official designation. Israel's occupation of the West Bank in 1967 led to more ambiguity until Jordan announced its disengagement from the West Bank in 1988.

For the sake of clarity, we will use terms for this area in this way: The expression "trans-Jordan" basically indicates direction, "beyond the Jordan River," as opposed to "cis-Jordan," "this side of the river"—from the European perspective. The term "Transjordan" refers to the polity occupying a specific area east of the

JORDAN

Long-form official name, anglicized: Hashimite Kingdom of Jordan

Official name, transliterated: Al-Mamlakah al-Urdunniyah al-Hashimiyah

Form of government: constitutional monarchy with two legislative houses (Senate, House of Representatives)

Area: 34,277 mi²/88,778 km²

Population, 2011: 6,180,000; Literacy: 92.6%

Ethnic composition (%): Arab 97.8, of which Jordanian 32.4, Palestinian 32.2, Iraqi 14, Bedouin 12.8; Circassian 1.2; other (including Armenian) 1

Religions (%): Sunni Muslim 93; Christian 5 (mainly Greek Orthodox, but several other Christian sects); other (including Shii Muslim and Druze) 2

Demography: Life expectancy—78.82 yr (M), 81.61 yr (F); Birthrate (per 1,000)—26.52; Fertility rate—3.36

GDP, 2011: $28.42 billion; purchasing power parity: $36.94 billion; per capita: $5,900

Currency: Jordanian Dinar (JD), US$1 = 0.705 dinars; 1 JD = $1.408 (mid-May 2013)

Energy: oil—1 million bbl; natural gas—213 bn ft³ (shale gas may be worth exploiting in near future); coal—nil

Main exports (% of total value, 2008): $7.8 billion (of which fertilizers 24.3; apparel/ accessories 13.4; food products 10.8; machinery and apparatus 10.7; medicines 6.6; inorganic chemicals 5.8)

Main imports (% of total value, 2008): $16.9 billion (of which crude petroleum 16.1; machinery and apparatus 16; food 14.2; chemicals and chemical products 9.5; road vehicles and parts 6.8; iron and steel 5.1)

Capital city, 2009: Amman 1,088,000; other major cities: Zarqa 396,227; Irbid 250,645; Rusayfah 227,735; Quwaysimah 135,500; Wadi as-Sir 122,032

---

river between 1923 and 1948–1950 as a mandate and then as a kingdom. With no political implications, trans-Jordania revives an old regional name. It could be said that Transjordan was a trans-Jordan polity in trans-Jordania.

The Genesis of Jordan

Four general aspects of the polity's spatial relations are noteworthy. First, whatever its name or status, its location "beyond the Jordan" has been a significant factor in its geography and history. The physical barriers of the deep Jordan Trench to the west and the desert expanses to the east were serious obstacles to the movement of peoples and goods, although caravans had some useful routes. Second, the narrow, better-watered, and most densely populated highland zone squeezed between trench and desert was a north-south transit route, the eastern counterpart of the Trunk Road or Via Maris (Way of the Sea) extending from Egypt through Gaza and Megiddo to Damascus. Caravans followed either of two routes in trans-Jordania: the King's Highway past Petra, Karak, and Amman to Damascus, or the generally level Desert Road, about 18.5 mi/30 km farther to the east out on the plateau (Map 12.1).

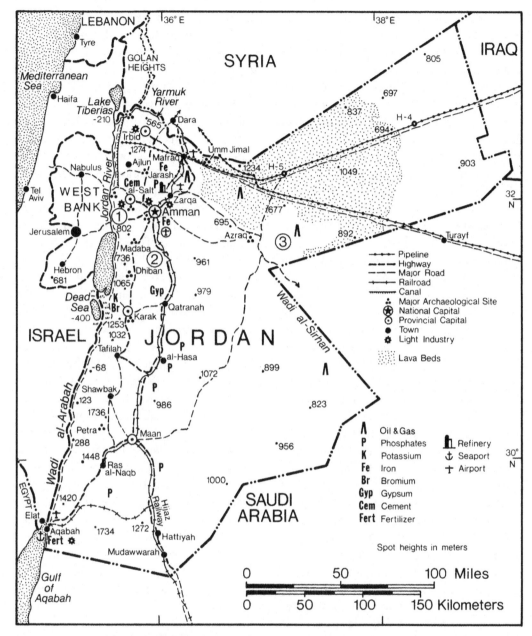

Map 12.1 General and economic map of Jordan. Circled numbers indicate regions discussed in text. Note concentration of settlement and development in the uplands of western Jordan.

The "Land Between." Third, the area's transitional character is another very basic geographical aspect. It has been the "land between"—never a significant power center or a major part of one. Conflict between "the desert and the sown," between nomads and settlements, inhibited development east of the Jordan Valley. It embraced petty kingdoms such as Rabboth-Ammon and Moab three thousand years ago, and places like Gilead had regional identity, but the area lacked specific regional unity until after World War I.

The *raison de création* of mandate Transjordan, beyond the purely political goals mentioned below, destined it to be a buffer state. To keep French control north of the Yarmuk, to hold back expansionist Saudis from the Jordan Valley, and to focus Iraqis on Mesopotamia, the mandate was designed, delineated, and operated by Britain as a buffer. With Israel's creation in 1948, independent Transjordan—a bit smaller than the US state of Indiana—became the archetypal buffer among its neighbors, its fate inextricably linked to the vagaries of conflict between Israel and the Palestinians and other Arabs. Jordan not only has the longest border with Israel of all the Arab states, but it has also long been targeted by Israeli extremists who see it as the future home for all the Arabs remaining in Israel and the Occupied Territories. Indeed, the western and better-watered part of trans-Jordania has been envisioned by some Zionists as part of Greater Israel.

The fourth aspect concerns Jordan's territorial stability and integrity. During the mandate and its first independent years, it lay entirely east of the river—its Arabic name then was Sharq al-Urdunn (East of the Jordan). In 1950, incorporation of the central Palestine hill country (the West Bank) expanded its territorial base by a very important 2,270 mi^2/5,880 km^2, but this was lost to Israeli conquest and occupation in the June War of 1967. After twenty-one years of uncertainty, it renounced claims to the West Bank; therefore, description, data, and analysis of Jordan here pertain only to the East Bank—in effect, to virtually the same territory as the 1923–1946 mandate.[1]

HISTORICAL EVOLUTION

From Early Times to the Muslim Conquest

Vestiges of the early history of the area are sharply etched into the landscape of the western fourth of contemporary Jordan. In this settled part of the country, one is rarely out of sight of some reminder of the past—a dolmen, tell, ruined building, Roman milestone, or the excavated ruins of an entire city, such as Jarash, Umm al-Jimal, or Petra.

Trans-Jordania's golden age began with the Seleucids of Syria, continued through the Roman era, and extended into the Byzantine period (about 200 BCE–600 CE), when it benefited from thriving caravan routes and trade centers. Prominent traders were the Semitic Nabataeans, who operated from their extraordinary capital of Petra. Modern Amman was Rabboth Ammon of the Old Testament and then Greco-Roman Philadelphia. It and Jarash (see Fig. 3.5) were two major members of the Decapolis, a league of ten autonomous cities formed to resist nomadic attacks that flourished under Roman overlordship from the first century BCE to the second century CE. Mosaic floors from Byzantine Christian churches and other buildings of the fifth and sixth centuries are found in many sites. Especially remarkable are those in the small highland town of Madaba, southwest of Amman; one preserves the famous Madaba Map, which shows in intricate detail Palestine and adjacent areas, including a recognizable plan of Jerusalem. Still largely unvisited is Umm ar-Rasas, a World Heritage Site since 2004 that features several large geographic mosaics, including those of the extensive Church of St. Stephen, with large depictions of fifteen cities with Christian sites, pride of place nearest the altar again given to Jerusalem.

From Muslim Conquest to Mandate Amirate

This golden age waned with Byzantium's ejection by invading Arabs in 634–636. Traditional routes lost stability and security; the profitable land trade dwindled and virtually disappeared by the ninth century—especially undermined as maritime traders linked the Indian Ocean and the Mediterranean. Cities declined, villages vanished, and Bedouin overwhelmed settled areas. Not until the Ottoman Hijaz Railway reused the corridor in the early 1900s was the area economically reawakened even marginally. Then World War I action and, a few years later, the memoirs of T. E. Lawrence (*Seven Pillars of Wisdom*) reintroduced trans-Jordania to the West. This vague undefined area east of the Jordan Trench sprawled beyond its highland backbone out into its desert realms, merging into the barren wildernesses of the future Syria on the north, the future Iraq on the east, and, to the south, what would become the Kingdom of Saudi Arabia.

Britain, as League of Nations mandatory for both sides of the Jordan Valley, initially oversaw the area through the fledgling Palestinian mandate administration, but it promised self-government to East Bank notables at al-Salt in August 1920. British experts meeting with Colonial Secretary Winston Churchill in Cairo in March 1921 agreed that the inchoate region would become a separate mandate, ruled by Amir Abdullah. The decision had two aims: (1) to be a token fulfillment of British promises to the Arabs in the Husayn-McMahon correspondence of 1915–1916 (see "The State in the Middle East," in Chap. 8) and (2) to placate the Hashimite family—direct descendants of the Prophet Muhammad—in the person of Amir Abdullah ibn Husayn, son of the sharif of Mecca and brother of Amir Faysal, who simultaneously became king of Iraq. Churchill met Abdullah in Jerusalem to inform him of the plan, regularized with the official launch of the Middle East mandates in September 1923. The penurious amirate gained independence in 1946 with Abdullah as king.

Independent Kingdom

The political-geographical, demographic, economic, and social character of the kingdom altered dramatically and permanently after the advent of Israel on May 14, 1948: scores of thousands of Palestinian refugees crossed over the Jordan River to Transjordan, Abdullah provisionally annexed the West Bank, and Jordan was pulled into the vortex that has characterized Arab-Israeli relations into the new millennium. Partly because of his confidential dealings with the Israelis—an ill-kept secret—he was assassinated in Jerusalem in 1951.[2] His son Talal succeeded him briefly, but in 1952 his then only sixteen-year-old grandson, Husayn, ascended the throne.[3]

From Boy King to World Figure. King Husayn (or Hussein) deftly balanced the many conflicting forces impinging on his vulnerable realm, having learned well from his grandfather how to walk a geopolitical tightrope. He usually chose the moderate and often mediating role, seeking consensus, sometimes at great risk. However, he made the first of two costly strategic mistakes when he joined Egypt and Syria against Israel in the 1967 June War. Jordan suffered heavy military and territorial losses in the debacle, losing all areas west of the Jordan to conquest, more than a third of the kingdom's most educated population, much of its arable land, and its Holy Land sites. Territorially, it returned to its trans-Jordan status of pre-1948, a status confirmed by Husayn when he renounced all legal ties with the West Bank in 1988.

Cyclic turbulence has characterized Jordan's situation from independence to the present: the 1948–1949 war with Israel, the 1967 disaster, periodic border clashes, internal engagements between army and insurgents, many coup attempts, terrorist attacks, and persistent socioeconomic turmoil in its efforts to balance transnational interests with its relations with Palestinians on both sides of the Jordan Valley. In the name of stability, martial law was imposed from 1967 to 1989. The most serious internal conflict was the showdown between the government and Palestinian *fedayeen* in September 1970 ("Black September" to Palestinians); an estimated thirty-three hundred were killed on both sides. In this civil war, the army gained control, forcing the *fedayeen* to withdraw, mostly to Lebanon (see Chap. 11). Husayn later reconciled with PLO leader Yasser Arafat, but relations remained strained.

The king moved toward a limited democracy, balancing the interests of his "guest" Palestinian constituents and his still somewhat tribalized native East Bank subjects. In parliamentary elections in 1989 and 1993, he expanded political limits but still controlled the process. The year 1990 brought a grave dilemma when Iraq invaded Kuwait. In a classic no-win situation, Jordan would be isolated politically and economically from the international community if he failed to censure Saddam, but he would risk his throne if he denounced Iraq and joined the coalition. In making his second costly strategic mistake, he opted for neutrality and was, indeed, immediately isolated, losing all aid from the Gulf states, the United States, and Europe; thousands of Jordanian/Palestinian expatriate workers in the Gulf were expelled, returning home to a shattered economy. But domestically the king's popularity was affirmed and the national consensus solidified—even under the stresses his choice had imposed.

Peace with Israel.   After skillfully managing the 1993 parliamentary elections, Husayn again took a chance—signing a peace treaty with Israel, then under moderate prime minister Yitzhak Rabin, in 1994. The measure refurbished relations with the United States, bringing some economic rewards. The treaty also promised "peace dividends"; in practice, short-term returns were disappointing. The deteriorating economy provoked riots in 1996 and led to the suspension of parliament. Both for economic and for political reasons, popular opposition to rapprochement with Israel mounted, especially when Rabin's successor, Binyamin Netanyahu, stalled on implementation.[4] As an antinormalization movement gained momentum, Husayn died in February

1999, ending a reign of forty-seven years. He was succeeded by his son Abdullah II, who reaffirmed his father's stance for peace and moderation, ties to the West, and links to Arab neighbors.

Passing the Baton

The new king was tested by repeated crises during the following years. Focusing on both political stability and economic reform, he pushed for a "Jordan First" program and further privatization of state enterprises. An increasingly assertive parliament was dissolved by Abdullah in 2001. From his point of view, two years later, the first elections since 1997 went well, as gerrymandering favored rural constituencies favorable to the king. The 2007 elections further reduced the Islamist presence in the 110-seat parliament but added seven women to the body. Widespread criticism of inactivity in the face of the global economic crisis allowed the king to dissolve this parliament in November 2009 and to hold new elections one year later that were boycotted by opposition Islamic groups. The king's actions continued the drift of Jordan from democracy.

Throughout the first decade of the new century, Jordan faced crises that followed from the events of 9/11. At first cooperating in the ensuing fight against terrorism, the king faced a dilemma with the invasion of Iraq. Emphasizing Jordan's need for security, the king maneuvered adroitly, expressing personal opposition to the invasion but opening Jordanian airspace for coalition military overflights, providing rest and recreational opportunities for coalition troops, and opening Aqabah port for their use.

In the invasion's aftermath, Jordan's economy benefited from both massive transit trade and as a supplier of goods to Iraq. Security conditions on the Iraq highway were often terrible, but the route was too important not to use. Amman quickly became the headquarters for scores of official delegations, international institutions, nonprofit organizations, and businesses that had interests in Iraq but found the city a far more agreeable location than Baghdad. On the other hand, the country soon found itself hosting hundreds of thousands of Iraqis fleeing the chaotic situations they encountered at home. Their numbers sorely taxed Jordan's fragile infrastructure—from housing to schools and hospitals (more on this below).

A Jordanian Spring?

The events in Tunisia and especially those in Cairo, widely covered throughout the region by television and through the social media, quickly spilled over in 2011 into Jordan. A stagnant economy and a youthful population hard-pressed to find gainful employment combined with widespread dissatisfaction with the perception of corruption at high levels of government and the slow pace of economic and political change under Abdullah to bring crowds into the streets of Amman and other cities. The king acted quickly, dismissing the cabinet and appointing a new prime minister. In March 2011, he established a National Dialogue Committee charged with writing legislation governing parties and elections and in April another committee to consider constitutional amendments. Constitutional amendments intended to strengthen the judiciary and the rule of law were passed in October.

The pace of protest then slowed, but the royal initiatives did not produce the quick results that the public wanted and expected from the changes they saw in nearby Egypt. Two more changes of prime ministers followed in October and then in April 2012. Parliament eventually produced a new electoral law in August intended to set the stage for new elections in 2013. Sharply reduced subsidies on fuel, as urged on the government by the International Monetary Fund, led to violence and rioting in November, which the government then attempted to calm by cut-

ting taxes on tobacco. All of this was taking place as neighboring Syria was deteriorating into civil war and thousands of Syrians started to seek refuge in Jordan, replacing the Iraqis who had gradually been returning home. The elections in January 2013 seemed to have given the government some breathing space to implement the announced reforms.[5]

PEOPLES: ARABS, MINORITIES, AND REFUGEES

Arabs

During the millennium prior to World War I, the inhabitants of trans-Jordania were, as now, overwhelmingly Arab ethnolinguistically and predominantly Sunni Muslim in religion. The mandate population of the 1920s was entirely made up of villagers and Bedouin, but the nomads gradually became sedentarized. Jordan is now more than 80 percent urbanized, and villagers enjoy most modern amenities, often commuting to work in nearby towns.

More than half of urbanized Jordanians live on one or another of the several *jabals* (hills) of Amman, the capital and primate city (Fig. 12.1). These residents, many of whom are Palestinians, flourished along with the rapid growth and development of the economy. Many have been educated abroad and speak English as a second language, and an appreciable number of them are Christian. Rusayfah and Zarqa to the east of Amman are actually large suburbs of the capital. Irbid is the population node in the northwest, and Aqabah in the southwest is the kingdom's thriving single port.

Before 1900, tribal Bedouin constituted most of the population, but like Bedouin in neighboring countries, they gradually shifted away from nomadism. Nevertheless, a sense of tribal identity and heritage remains significant in both society and political culture. Bedouin in the army repeatedly showed traditional loyalty during crises to their paramount

Figure 12.1 Amman, capital of Jordan. The amphitheater was the heart of Roman Philadelphia. Beyond the theater is a modern residential area on Jabal al-Jawfa; to the right is Jabal al-Ashrafiyah. This older area of Amman is yielding to the post-1980 urban development farther west.

chieftain, the king, thereby maintaining the political structure. The tribal element in Jordan's society persists and periodically asserts itself.

Minorities

Ethnic.   Both ethnic and religious minorities play noteworthy but amicable roles in the Jordanian political and social systems. About 50,000 Circassians (see Chap. 4) live in villages around Amman and in the capital itself. As many as 18,000 Chechens (sometimes called Shishanis) preserve their language and culture, brought with them a century ago. Several hundred Armenians sought refuge in Jordan between the 1880s and 1920s; perhaps 48,000 of their descendants remain mostly unassimilated in the population. The expatriate community, small and almost en-

tirely British before World War II, has grown steadily, is much broader in composition, and numbers in the tens of thousands.

Religious.   Jordan's social fabric has not been torn by intersectarian conflict, like Lebanon's; relations between the Sunni Muslims (more than 93 percent of the population) and the Christians (about 5 percent) have always been good. Christians are mostly Greek Orthodox but also include Armenian Orthodox, Greek and Roman Catholics, Syrian Orthodox, and Copts. They constitute a community that dates back to the earliest spread of Christianity in the second century. Some towns are Christian centers—Karak, Madaba, and al-Salt—and Amman also has a high percentage of Christians. Small numbers of Druze and Shia live mostly in the north near the Syrian border. The Bahai community counts a few hundred members as well.

East and West.   Ethnic and religious distinctions aside, it is the division between native "East Bankers" and "Jordanian Palestinians" that is the crucial dynamic in Jordan's sociopolitical system. Both East Bankers and Palestinians are Arab, speak Arabic, are mostly Sunni Muslim, and have other characteristics in common. But the essential difference is that the Palestinians are refugees, having been dispossessed of their homeland, property, and national identity, and therefore have profoundly different national sentiments and aspirations from those of indigenous Jordanians.

Refugees

Palestinians.   The 300,000 population of the Transjordan mandate in 1921 had grown to 433,000 by 1946 and independence. However, this figure increased dramatically in 1948–1949 with the influx of about 132,000 Palestinian refugees to the East Bank. Another 365,000 took refuge among the 400,000 permanent inhabitants of the West Bank, defended against Israel by Jordan's Arab Legion. In a matter of weeks, the East Bank population rose by nearly one-third; the subsequent annexation of the West Bank increased the country by another 765,000. Overall, the original Transjordan inhabitants found themselves outnumbered two to one by Palestinians displaced by Israeli conquest from their lands and livelihood. On the West Bank, both the refugees and the natives resented the Jordanian annexation.

Israel's conquest of the West Bank in 1967 altered radically Jordan's demographic and territorial extent. The kingdom lost tourist attractions and arable lands, along with half its population. More than 125,000 from the West Bank and 45,000 from Gaza—"old refugees"—fled the invasion to the East Bank.

They were followed by 100,000 West Bank residents—"new refugees." Thus, 270,000 additional Palestinians augmented those from the late 1940s, their children, and others who had arrived between 1949 and 1967. Of Jordan's 6.5 million people in 2012, about two-thirds were Palestinians; almost 2 million were officially registered refugees, one-sixth living in ten UNRWA camps. Most Palestinians have taken Jordanian citizenship; Jordan is the only Arab country to have granted such status to nearly all its refugee population.

Iraqis, Then Syrians.   A new and in some ways even more pressing refugee problem followed the invasion of Iraq in 2003. During the Saddam Husayn regime, Jordan already had an Iraqi exile population. But as the failure of the United States to provide domestic security became increasingly obvious, the trickle of Iraqis arriving in Amman became a flood in 2004 and 2005. By 2007, at least 700,000 were believed to be in Jordan; most were Sunnis fleeing the battle zones of Baghdad or western Iraq, but a large percentage were from minorities—of those registered with the UNHCR, 16 percent were Christians and 6 percent were Mandaeans. Although many were from the middle class, able at first to support themselves, as their exile lengthened their situations became more straitened. Jordan, despite its extensive experience in dealing with large population displacements, is still a relatively poor country, and not until almost five years after the invasion did its problems in this regard (and similar ones in Syria) receive much official attention abroad. As the situation in many parts of Iraq gradually improved, many refugees returned home; by 2012, however, Jordan was faced by a new deluge of desperate people—Syrians fleeing that country's increasingly violent civil war. By mid-2013, unofficial estimates were that close to 500,000 Syrian refugees had already crossed into Jordan.[6]

PHYSICAL RESOURCE BASE

Regions of Jordan

Jordan has exhibited remarkable flexibility during the changes in its territory and population, particularly in view of its limited physical resource base. A brief survey of this and the state's exploitation of its resources will aid in understanding the challenges to this buffer kingdom.

An east-west cross-section shows a three-fold physical division (see circled numbers on Map 12.1): [1] Along the western edge is the Jordan Valley and its continuation southward in the Wadi Arabah, a major part of the Levant Rift System, with the lowest continental elevations on earth along the Dead Sea. [2] Immediately east of the valley is a north-south belt of highlands—4,100 ft/1,250 m in the north and the highest elevations in the Palestine-Jordan area, 5,575 ft/1,700 m in the south. [3] Extending eastward at a level of 2,625–2,950 ft/800–900 m is the Eastern Desert, occupying 85 percent of Jordan with a surface that is variously flat, rolling, or exhibiting erosional remnants.

[1] Jordan Valley.   The Jordan Valley (Arabic *al-Ghor*), 65 mi/104 km long, may be subdivided into four narrow parallel belts.

(1) The river itself (see Fig. 2.5), winding in tight meanders in a narrow bed, receives the Yarmuk River just south of the Sea of Galilee and falls to the Dead Sea, 1,385 ft/422 m below sea level at the end of the 2000s (recently, the sea's level appeared to be falling even faster than what had been an annual average of 3.3 ft/1 m). (2) The floodplain (Arabic *al-Zor*), with a mantle of rank vegetation called "thicket of the Jordan" in biblical passages, has a level surface that is just a few meters above the river level. (3) The upper terrace level, the *Ghor,* is several hundred meters wide and is divided from the *Zor* by a narrow, eroded slope. The King Abdullah Canal (originally East Ghor Canal) was constructed on the gently sloping upper-terrace level (see "Water: The Vital Resource" below), enabling development of the most productive farmland in Jordan. The East Ghor is an archaeologist's paradise, with 224 ancient sites identified. (4) A high, ruggedly eroded escarpment—with a total rise of more than 4,265 ft/1,300 m within 1.2 mi/2 km—forms the eastern wall of the great trench that extends from the Sea of Galilee to and beyond the Gulf of Aqabah (see Chap. 2 and Fig. 2.2).

[2] Highland Belt.   Extending from the Yarmuk in the north to the Gulf of Aqabah in the south, the highland belt receives the country's most precipitation and therefore has always served as the core of settlement, development, and culture east of the valley. It varies markedly in width and relief, and there are fundamental differences in rocks and structure among its northern, central, and southern thirds. Because of their basic significance and clear differentiation, the five principal subregions of the highland belt require examination in some detail.

(1) With an annual average of 24–30 in/600–750 mm of precipitation, moderate slopes, productive soils, and a remarkable number of flowing springs, the Ajlun Highland is the best-watered and most naturally productive part of Jordan. It extends from the Yarmuk southward to the deep, broad valley of the Wadi Zarqa, the biblical River Jabbock, which cuts through a long sequence of geological strata. It supports the densest population in the greatest number of villages outside the Amman metropolitan area. Along with cultivated crops, natural woodland has been legendary since ancient times, when resin of trees on these hills yielded the celebrated "balm in Gilead" (Fig. 12.2).

On the plateau north of the Ajlun Dome lies Irbid (ancient Arbela), Jordan's third-largest city. East of Irbid is Ramtha (ancient Ramoth or Ramoth Gilead), an old caravan station. Until relatively recently, it was the

Figure 12.2 The humid northwest of Jordan: contemporary scrub oak and pine woodland in the formerly forested, moist Ajlun Highland, biblical Gilead.

main border crossing between Syria and Jordan; this is now on the north-south motorway to the east. Along the eastern flank is the ancient city of Jarash, with a well-preserved gate, colonnaded main street, forum, theaters, and temples spanning Hellenistic, Roman, and Byzantine times (see Fig. 3.5). Rising near Amman, the Zarqa joins the Jordan after a descent of 3,580 ft/1,090 m. The King Talal Dam, Jordan's largest, was built on the lower Zarqa in 1977; its reservoir supplies Amman.

(2) South of the Wadi Zarqa is the Northern Balqa Highland, sometimes called the Amman Highland. On its western slope is al-Salt, the main center of trans-Jordania before the mandate. On its southeastern edge is Amman, the capital and administrative, economic, communications, industrial, and cultural center of Jordan. With buildings of limestone and chalk dimension stone covering the steep slopes of the several *jabals,* the

city's morphology is dramatic (see Fig. 12.1). With some 6,000 people in the 1920s, Greater Amman reached 2.9 million by the early 2010s.

(3) The Southern Balqa lies south of the Northern Balqa/Amman Highland on the partly dissected Karak Plateau, an area of grain cultivation and seminomadic pastoralism. This is the biblical Land of Moab and the classical Peraea ("on the other side"). It is bounded on the south by a spectacular gash, the Wadi Mujib, the biblical River Arnon (Fig. 12.3). Winding across the plateau is the scenic descendant of the historic King's Highway, connecting the cities of Hisban (ancient Heshbon), Madaba, Dhiban (ancient Dibon), and Karak (ancient Kir Hareseth, chief Moabite city)—all mentioned in biblical accounts and all with archaeological remains dating to that period. Northwest of Madaba is Mount Nebo, from which the biblical narrative relates that

Figure 12.3 Modern highway winding its way down into the Wadi Mujib, the biblical River Arnon, in the semidesert near Karak, southern Jordan.

Moses viewed the Promised Land; to the southwest is Machaerus, Herod's mountain-top fortress/palace where John the Baptist was beheaded.

(4) The most rugged part of Jordan, the Shara Mountains (from *seir* = rock) traverse the ancient land of Edom (red). The King's Highway continues southward along the crest of the Shara to the Hisma, passing fewer villages as aridity increases. The village of Wadi Musa adjoins and services the fabulous archaeological site of Petra, referred to by a British poet as the "rose-red city, half as old as time," hidden in the colorful mesas of Nubian sandstone on the Shara's western edge (Fig. 12.4). Petra is justifiably Jordan's most frequented tourist site, with nearly 1 million visitors in 2010.

(5) The Hisma landscape includes the Hisma Depression itself, with broad sand corridors winding their way among vertical-sided mesas and buttes of red Nubian sandstone—the dramatic, silent land of the Wadi Ram (or Rum). From here, a rugged highway and railway corridor reaches the Red Sea at Aqabah. The town has grown from a fishing village of fewer than 2,000 people in 1945 to an estimated 107,000 by 2011. Although, like the adjacent Israeli port of Elat, it is off the main sea-lanes, it has expanded into a bustling modern port, chemical-processing center, and resort city, serving as the anchor for Jordan's short coastline, 16 mi/26 km. It is the terminus of a planned railway connector to Iraq.

[3] Eastern Desert. Stretching eastward from the highland belt is the Eastern Desert, the Badia, traditional realm of the Bedouin. A dry tableland at the northwest of the Syro-Arabian Desert, it is, except in one or two depressions, everywhere more than 2,000 ft/610 m. Even so, it lies nearly 1,000 ft/305 m below the general level of the highland belt. Thus, it

Figure 12.4
Its original name and purpose unknown, this famous monument in Petra was carved out of a vertical red sandstone cliff about two thousand years ago. It is fancifully referred to in modern times as al-Khaznah ("the Treasury").

is in the rain shadow and receives only 2–8 in/50–200 mm of precipitation annually. Its western margin is Jordan's world-ranking phosphate belt; a small oil field and a natural gas field are farther east. One former notable feature of economic importance is the Hijaz Railway,[7] built by the Ottomans in the early 1900s along the line between the sown region on the west and the desert on the east.

Of the Eastern Desert's several subdivisions, two have served historic roles: the broad, shallow depression of Wadi al-Sirhan extending southeastward along the Jordan–Saudi Arabia boundary was a traditional route for caravans for centuries and is still used for Bedouin migrations, and Azraq

Oasis—shallow pools and marshes forming the only permanent body of water in the Jordan desert—provides sanctuary for enormous flocks of migrating birds during the spring and fall along the great Levant flyway. Much of the north-central desert is a barren lava plain (see Map 12.1), a *hamadah;* angular lava boulders constitute the surface. (See Fig. 2.3 for a related *hamadah* in Syria.)

WATER: THE VITAL RESOURCE

As in other Middle East countries, Jordan's water balance is increasingly a high-priority national issue, not just in agriculture but also for human survival. It is entirely dependent on limited and variable winter rainfall, with no major rivers to dam or draw from (but see section on Yarmuk below) and no aquifers to bring artesian water from well-watered areas. The two perennial streams worth noting flow along a sensitive border—the Jordan on the west and the Yarmuk on the north. With average annual precipitation generally less than 5 in/125 mm, Jordan's average annual water resources are about 875 mn m^3, ranking it tenth among the world's water-poor states. Daily per capita consumption has averaged eighty-five liters per day recently and is declining—compared with three hundred in Israel and six hundred in Europe and America. Severe droughts, like the one that began in 2005, cause not only crop failures but also industrial emergencies and domestic water interruptions during the summer season. A 2011 report identified Jordan as the country third most at risk of water security.

Disy Aquifer Project.   Government projects and other various efforts to increase water supply and to conserve what is available involve controversial remedies and offer few long-term solutions. The major project now under way to convey water from the Disy aquifer in the south to Amman has caused considerable apprehension because the water seems to be quite radioactive and because the aquifer straddles the border with Saudi Arabia. The $1 billion project is due to begin delivering water to the capital region in 2013. In 2012, the Ministry of Water announced the beginning of a renovation of Amman's water distribution network, from which an estimated one-third is lost in leakage.

Limitations

There has been one benefit: because irrigation is the biggest consumer, farmers are required to use more efficient systems, particularly drip irrigation. Still, since nearly 60 percent of the national water supply goes to an economic sector that contributes less than 3 percent of

GDP, serious questions arise, especially regarding the cultivation of such water-intensive crops as tomatoes and bananas.

Since Jordan's dependency ratio—the percentage of renewable water received from or shared with other countries (primarily Syria and Israel)—is about 23 percent, water-allocation agreements among the neighboring riparian states are critical. The Israeli-Jordanian peace treaty gives Jordan a specific allotment from the Sea of Galilee, designed to encourage cooperative efforts to develop, conserve, and expand water resources for both countries. The high variability of precipitation and stream flow, likely to increase with climate change, highlights the lack of a clear mechanism for sharing shortages and points to potential conflicts. Improved Syrian-Jordanian relations led to completion of the Unity Dam on the Yarmuk in 2006 after delays due to Israeli challenges and disputes between Jordan and Syria over allocations. Although the dam increases storage capacity and electricity generation, it has been criticized for further decreasing inflow into the Jordan River.

East Ghor.   Drawing water from the Yarmuk, the King Abdullah Canal—usually called the East Ghor Canal—supplies about three-fourths of Jordan's irrigated area. Begun in 1959 and opened in stages between the 1960s and 1980s, it diverts Yarmuk water into a canal along the level *Ghor* between the floodplain and the eastern wall of the valley. This takes advantage of the greater hydraulic head at its elevation and uses Yarmuk water before it mixes with the much saltier and diminishing Jordan River water. By the mid-1980s, the canal had been extended, in three stages, to reach a length of 72 mi/116 km to the Dead Sea, and the irrigated area was steadily increasing (see next section).

Red Sea–Dead Sea Link?   A potentially very controversial project is the Red Sea–Dead Sea Water Conveyance, a partnership of Jordan with Israel and Palestine to bring seawater north some 112 mi/180 km to stabilize or raise the falling level of the Dead Sea and to provide through desalination and hydroelectric facilities additions to the region's water and power supplies. Technical studies conducted under the auspices of the World Bank were released in 2013 indicating that the project is feasible, but environmental concerns seem likely to slow implementation of the project.[8]

ECONOMIC GEOGRAPHY

Independent Transjordan in 1946, soon to be overwhelmed with thousands of destitute refugees, faced bleak prospects. It had limited agricultural potential, minimal water supplies, virtually no developed resources, no industry, a very poor population, and a penniless government. But with moderate inflows of aid, vigorous effort from its inhabitants, and the stimulus from annexing the West Bank, the renamed Jordan developed into a politically and economically viable polity. It has achieved remarkable economic progress but still struggles with some of the same constraints. It exploits major phosphate and potash resources (see below), has an expanding manufacturing sector, promotes tourism, confronts high population growth, and participates in world organizations, international trade agreements, and regional schemes to share electric power. In the late 2000s, it struggled with inflation and persistent budget deficits; as a result, it agreed with the International Monetary Fund to end subsidies on petroleum and several consumer goods, adding to the cost of living for most residents and possibly heightening the appeal of radical Islamic political groups.

Human Resources

Well-Being. The Human Development Index (HDI)—calculated by the UNDP to allow comparisons of living standards on a global basis using measures of life expectancy, educational levels, and per capita income—in 2013 ranked Jordan 100th of 186 countries and 12th of those included in this book. The HDI showed a significant increase—a gain of more than 28 percent since 1980, based on notable improvements in all three components of the index. Jordan used the UNDP method on a national basis to compute variation across governorates; urban Amman, Aqabah, and Irbid had the highest HDIs and rural Tafila, Mafraq, and Maan the lowest, but the spread between the highest and lowest was only 7.2 percent. The Legatum Institute's Prosperity Index, which overlaps the HDI but includes more parameters, placed Jordan 77th of 142 countries worldwide and 6th regionally in 2011.[9]

Agriculture

Less than 5 percent of Jordan is arable; three-fourths of this area is rainfed, producing relatively low-yield crops of wheat and barley. By far most food—and 90 percent of exported food—comes from irrigated lands, mostly in the valley. The exceptional climate there permits intensive production of such crops as citrus and bananas; specialty crops are grown in hothouses (Fig. 12.5). Although agriculture accounts for only about 4.5 percent of GDP (2011) and employs only 2.7 percent of the labor force, it is still a significant sector of the economy—high-value horticultural products provide 6 percent of exports. Wheat imports, with the United States the biggest supplier, average 660,000 mt, since domestic production at best meets only one month of demand. The prolonged drought that has gripped the region beginning in 2005 has hit hard at non-irrigated production; it has also emphasized the urgent need for determining which crops offer the greatest return per unit of water required. From about 1970 to 2010, food production per capita rose by about 22 percent despite the environmental handicaps under which the sector operates.[10]

Figure 12.5 Irrigated citrus groves south of Karamah on East Ghor, Jordan Valley. The white structures in the distance are hothouses for producing early vegetables.

Minerals and Energy

The mining industry constituted only 2.8 percent of Jordan's GDP in 2010, but it is of increasing importance, as widening searches potentially lead to exploitation of oil shale, additional phosphate deposits, and uranium ore.

Phosphates underlie extensive areas of Jordan, generally along the axis of the Hijaz Railway, and total more than 1.41 billion tons of high-grade phosphate rock. Since mining began in 1934, exports have steadily increased in response to growing world demand and higher prices. Jordan is now among the world's six leading producers, exporting about 4.3 million tons annually to thirty countries, especially India. Production from the largest deposit—at al-Shidiyya, northeast of Aqabah—is being expanded to 7.5 mn mt per year and more if demand continues to be strong. On the Dead Sea, Jordan operates a major processing complex to recover chemicals from brines. The plant is one of the world's largest, with output of 2 million tons of potash plus 300,000 tons of associated bromine in 2010. Mineral products constitute a major share of Jordan's exports.[11]

Hydrocarbons.   Despite fifty years of hydrocarbon exploration, findings have been scant. The small Hamzah oil field, near Azraq, produces only 40 bpd, about one-tenth of its peak output in the mid-1980s. However, the government is actively promoting investment in the country's huge deposits of oil-bearing shale rock (possibly the eighth largest globally); a power plant fueled with oil shale at Attarat Um Ghudran is due to be on line by 2016.[12] Modest natural gas resources have been developed in the Rishah area, near the Iraq border, where output powers one nearby power plant. British Petroleum was exploring further for gas near Rishah in 2009. In 2003,

Jordan began importing natural gas from Egypt's increasingly abundant production by underwater pipeline to Aqabah. This source became increasingly unreliable by 2012, however, because of frequent attacks on the pipeline in Sinai, and in October of that year Egypt cut its exports, citing increased domestic needs. The cut was short-lived, but it reminded Jordanians once again of their fragile energy position. In 2011, Jordan and Qatar began discussions about building an offshore terminal at Aqabah to allow the importation and distribution of liquefied gas.

In recent years, Jordan's oil needs have been met by imports mostly from Saudi Arabia and Iraq. Since the shutting down of the Tapline (which is now inoperable) in 1990, all imports have had to come by tanker or else by truck overland from Iraq. In Zarqa is Jordan's only refinery, with a current capacity of 90,000 bpd. In 2012, Jordan and Iraq signed an agreement to build oil and gas pipelines linking Iraq's domestic network with both Zarqa and Aqabah; this would serve the dual purpose of supplying Jordan's needs and giving Iraq an alternative export venue. Jordan expects to save as much as $300 million annually in petro-transport costs, and in 2013 Egypt had entered discussions with Jordan and Iraq with the aim of extending the pipeline from Aqabah to Sinai.[13]

With continued high oil prices likely, processing shale for oil could become a practical alternative to ever-increasing imports; in late 2012, two shale-exploration blocks were awarded to a British company. However, the high water-intensity of shale oil production is problematic in water-short Jordan, and it may have to await the development of less water-dependent technologies.

Alternatives.   In 2001, Egypt, Syria, and Jordan linked their national electric grids, and later ties to the Lebanese and Turkish grids were added. Natural gas generates about 70 percent of Jordan's electricity, with oil powering nearly all the rest.[14] Uranium deposits are extensive, and considerable uranium can also be extracted from phosphate processing. Not only is there export potential, but the government has plans for a network of eight nuclear power plants, and the yellowcake would be the critical input into this system. In 2010, Jordan signed an agreement with a French firm to begin uranium mining (this deal was suspended in 2012) and began discussions with France about building nuclear power plants. (These plans have recently run into some domestic opposition based on security and environmental concerns.) In 2011, the government set a goal of 10 percent for the contribution of renewable sources to the nation's energy needs. Both solar and wind projects are under consideration.

Manufacturing

Better to accommodate the vast number of refugees, to emerge from a preindustrial agricultural economy after the 1950s, and to change from a rentier to at least a semirentier situation, Jordan sought diversification and the opening of appropriate manufacturing plants. Small and simple early enterprises produced processed foods, detergents, paper products, batteries, and similar items; they clustered around the Amman-Zarqa area, which soon added cement plants and the oil refinery. By the 1980s and 1990s, several larger and more complex plants opened in Irbid (diversified industries) and Aqabah (fertilizers, other chemicals) as well as in Greater Amman. Along with the Israel-Jordan peace treaty in 1994, followed by the 1995 Amman Economic Summit, the United States brokered formal economic relations between the two signatories in an effort to afford Jordan a tangible "peace dividend."

Transportation

Jordan's highway system has satisfactorily served the kingdom's needs. Along the basic routes earlier established, roads were significantly extended and upgraded during the

1980s and 1990s. The main north-south route is a well-engineered four-lane divided motorway that runs from Syria to Aqabah. Another highway extends northward from Aqabah through the Wadi Arabah and along the eastern shore of the Dead Sea; there is also a connector tying the main Baghdad highway to Azraq, Maan, and Aqabah.

Railroads. The historic Hijaz Railway (or Pilgrim Railway), inherited from the Ottomans and made famous by the Lawrence of Arabia legend, has been upgraded, and passenger express rail service was opened between Amman and Damascus in 1999. It is mostly used for freight and consists of narrow-gauge trackage. A similar link connects phosphate mines near Maan with Aqabah, where territorial exchanges with Saudi Arabia permitted extension of Jordan's coastline and expansion of the port. With extensive facilities for the export of phosphate rock and potash, Aqabah has expanded its capacity for handling general cargo and is a major link in Iraq's trade as well. In the late 2000s, Jordan announced plans for a major expansion of its rail network, turning the country into a regional rail hub, and began seeking some $6 billion in finance for the 671-mi/1,080-km effort. The north-south phase, scheduled to begin in 2010, will connect the Syrian system through Amman and Maan to Aqabah. Obviously, the outbreak of civil war in Syria has ramifications for Jordanian plans to link with its neighbor's network. An east-west line will run from Amman to the Saudi Arabian border, where it will link with that country's ongoing rail expansion program (see Chap. 15); a branch of this same line will also reach the Iraqi border and from there connect to Baghdad. Additionally, the proposed rebuilding of the Hijaz Railway would tie to Saudi Arabia's link between Mecca and Medina, already under way. A light-rail metro system for the Amman-Zarqa area is also part of the plan, but the world economic crisis has hampered financing efforts.[15]

The kingdom's national air carrier, Royal Jordanian Airlines (RJA), is headquartered at Queen Alia International Airport, south of Amman, and operates about forty jets with worldwide routes. RJA plays a major role in the growing tourism sector, built around the country's archaeological treasures, such as Petra, Jarash, Umm Qais, Karak, and Ajloun; resorts on the Gulf of Aqabah and the Dead Sea; and religious destinations like Mount Nebo, Madaba, Machaerus, and the Jordan River baptismal site. Tourist arrivals peaked in 2010 at 6.6 million before falling off by about 20 percent as a result of regional disturbances in 2011; a strong recovery in the sector was under way in 2012, with earnings running 20 percent above those of 2011. In recent years, Amman built a regional reputation as a medical center staffed by well-trained multilingual personnel; "medical tourism" attracted an estimated 240,000 foreigners to private Jordanian hospitals in 2011.

FINANCES AND AID

During the mandate years, domestic finances were woefully inadequate. For decades, Jordan survived only as a rentier polity: Britain provided basic budgetary support through 1957; the United States then became its main supporter. Saudi Arabia, Kuwait, and other Arab states rewarded the kingdom's role in the 1967 war with hundreds of millions of dollars in aid that promoted development during the 1970s and early 1980s. This support ceased when King Husayn tilted toward Iraq, losing Jordan billions in remittances, trade, and services. With soaring unemployment, he acceded to US pressure, signing a peace treaty with Israel in 1994. The "peace dividends" were limited but brought eventual improvement, as was explained earlier, but Jordan's graduation from semirentier status will take time. The economic reform program prompted by the reaction of Jordanian citizens to the events of the Arab Spring has received support from several donors, especially its immediate neighbors—for example, in August 2012, Qatar pledged $1.25 billion over the next five years.

Remittances from Jordanians working abroad have always been a major source of national income. In 2003, they were equal to 765 percent of export revenues and 337 percent of tourism receipts. By 2011, both export and tourist receipts had grown considerably, but remittances were still about equal to an eighth of GDP at an estimated $3.65 billion.

RELATIONS

Global

Britain. Jordan has primarily followed a pro-Western foreign policy—sometimes to its disadvantage and with inevitable ups and downs. Close ties between mandate Transjordan and Britain continued after the polity's independence, and they continue still. Britain has regularly supplied aid, and in 1958 it sent paratroopers to the kingdom after the coup in Iraq.

United States. Beginning in the 1950s, the United States gradually became Jordan's main benefactor. US support helped preserve the kingdom when government forces and Palestinian *fedayeen* were battling in 1970–1971. Rapport slowed in the late 1970s when the perception was that the United States was buying Jordan's pliability in the Arab-Israel problem with minimum support, compared with tenfold greater aid to Israel. Improvements in the 1980s cooled in 1990 when King Husayn waffled on Iraq's Kuwait misadventure, but warmed after the mid-1990s when he formalized ties to Israel, devoting his last days to the peace process. Relations have been warm with Abdullah, who, however, had reservations about the invasion of Iraq. In late 2012, it was announced that a small American military force had gone to Jordan to help the government cope with the crisis caused by the Syrian civil war.

The United States and Jordan established diplomatic relations in 1949, and American development assistance dates to 1951. The US Agency for International Development (USAID) still has an active program that in the past has ranged from fighting malaria to building water-treatment plants to supporting restoration at major tourist sites like Petra and Umm Qais. In the new century, considerable attention has gone to one of the most persistent problems—high unemployment; for example, to help create jobs, more than 175,000 microfinance loans have gone to small entrepreneurs, while others with slightly larger businesses have been trained in how to take advantage of the US free trade agreement (FTA) and find export markets for their products.[16] Jordan has received more than $8.2 billion in economic assistance grants and loans from the United States; another $4.8 billion has been allotted to a military assistance program that began in 1957. Since 1997, there has been a small Peace Corps presence in Jordan, and some three hundred volunteers have served in the country.

Jordan has good relations with several European countries that have also given appreciable aid. As mentioned above, Jordan has an Association Agreement with the EU, and a Jordan–United States FTA is being implemented.[17] The kingdom also has FTAs with Canada, Turkey, Singapore, and the European Free Trade Association (EFTA).

Regional

Jordan is not a prime mover in the Arab world, but it has periodically mediated and moderated frictions in the region. It is a founding member of the Arab League and is interlinked with its neighbors in economic, political, and cultural associations. Relations with Syria should be very close under geopolitical logic, but they have been bewilderingly uneven. In November 2011, King Abdallah called on Bashar al-Assad to step down from Syria's presidency, and after that

Jordan made no secret of its sympathies and support for the insurgents.

GCC. Saudi Arabia and Hashimite Jordan viewed each other with suspicion for several decades; however, the Saudis aided Jordan magnanimously during the 1970s and 1980s not only with monetary grants and crude oil through Tapline but also with small military forces. The break in 1990 over Saddam Husayn's aggression was mended after Abdullah's accession. Relations with Kuwait had also been very close, with Kuwait aiding Jordan with hundreds of millions of dollars and employing 250,000 expatriate Jordanians/Palestinians, but this ceased and the Jordanian expatriates (most in professional or semiprofessional capacities) were no longer welcome after Iraq's defeat. However, Kuwait reopened its embassy in Amman in 1999, signaling a return to normalcy. In 2011, at the apparent instigation of Saudi Arabia and in light of the Arab Spring, the Gulf Cooperation Council (GCC) began to discuss admitting Jordan (and possibly Morocco). As mentioned earlier, the GCC states are also extending aid in support of economic reforms.

Iraq. From the inception of the Transjordan and Iraq mandates in the early 1920s, relations between the two were special because Hashimite brothers occupied both thrones. Successor Hashimite cousins briefly united the kingdoms in the Arab Federation in 1958, but this quickly collapsed when King Faysal II of Iraq was assassinated in a violent coup. Encouraged by the West and by its neighbors, Jordan established a symbiotic economic relationship with Iraq during the Iran-Iraq War and prospered from the transit of Iraqi imports and exports. This was one reason for Husayn's reluctance to judge Iraq in 1990; during the Gulf War he straddled the fence by giving humanitarian aid to Iraq and quiet moral support to the coalition. When Abdullah faced much the same quandary in 2003, he avoided

conflict with Iraq but cooperated with the coalition and quickly resumed economic links with Iraq by mid-2003. In August 2003, Jordan's embassy in Baghdad was bombed, leaving eleven dead. Nevertheless, the kingdom continued to assist reconstruction efforts—for example, by facilitating the training of more than 50,000 police cadets and corrections officers in Jordan. In 2008, a Jordanian ambassador returned to Baghdad, and in the same year King Abdullah became the first Arab leader to visit Iraq since 2003. At the same time, Abdullah has been one of the clearest voices expressing concern about the rise of a "Shii Crescent," stretching from Iran through Iraq and Syria to Lebanon and threatening the Sunni-dominated monarchies.

Israel. Having had a close association with mandate Palestine, Jordan has believed it must maintain a relationship with Israel. Husayn pragmatically and realistically conducted clandestine contacts,[18] and talks continued more openly after the 1994 peace treaty. Recent history has shown that Jordan—the buffer, the "land between" and "land beyond"—is in a geopolitical quandary: this Arab state in an Arab world must maintain multiple associations with that world while relating to its powerful neighbor Israel and to the West, and all parties must make the best of it. Mentioned earlier is the environmentally and technically controversial proposal to build a canal or pipeline from the Red Sea to the rapidly shrinking Dead Sea in partnership with Israel and the World Bank.[19] Jordan's relations with Israel turned cold with the latter's invasion of Gaza in 2008, and King Abdullah has been increasingly vocal about his lack of confidence that the Netanyahu government has any real interest in pursuing the peace process.

Palestine. Finally, a major political consideration remains just as it was sixty years ago—the government's ability to balance its obligations to its Palestinian population, its indigenous East Bankers, West Bank Palestinians and the Palestinian Authority, the Palestinian diaspora, and other Arabs, as well as the United States and Israel. The earlier and once not unreasonable idea of a confederation between Jordan (the "East Bank") and the Palestinian Authority (the "West Bank") has now been overtaken by events. The fairly sophisticated electorate in Jordan, especially among the younger age cohorts, has had its hopes raised by the events in Tunisia and Egypt and are demonstrating less tolerance of the king's promises (and slow pace) of economic and political reforms. Adding still more complexity has been the revolt in Syria against the Assad regime, of which Abdullah has become one of the severest critics. Jordan can only hope that extremist elements in Israel will not increase their presence in that country's government and try to force it to accommodate, either gradually or in another catastrophe, the some 4.3 million Palestinians from west of the Jordan River. Meanwhile, the kingdom continues to seek the equilibrium essential to its survival and prosperity.

For information on the business environment in Jordan, see the website attached to this book: www.middleeastpatterns.com.

NOTES

1. In addition to relying on extensive field research by author Held, *Jordan* Country Study 1991; Naval Intelligence Division 1943; Fathi 1994; Baly 1957; Orni and Efrat 1980; and Salibi 1998 (with a strong geographical approach) have been employed. See also www.nic.gov.jo/.

2. These connections are the main subject of Shlaim 1990.

3. Talal bin Abdullah (1909–1972) abdicated for health reasons (probably schizophrenia) after a reign of only thirteen months. Queen Zein, his wife and mother of Husayn, was very influential during his reign and the early years of her son's.

4. A detailed study with a longer perspective is Lucas 2004.

5. "The Jordanian State buys itself Time," *MERIP,* Feb. 12, 2013, www.merip.org/mer/mero021213.

6. Al-Jazeera, Feb. 27, 2013; *Nation,* May 13, 2013.

7. And possibly of future importance: Turkey and Saudi Arabia have recently indicated an interest in rebuilding the line with standard-gauge tracks to link up with Saudi plans to connect Jiddah, Riyadh, and Medinah by rail (*Arab News* [Riyadh], Feb. 5, 2009; see also Chap. 15).

8. *Bloomberg,* Jan. 18, 2013; *National Geographic News Watch,* Mar. 4, 2013, http://newswatch.national-geographic.com/2013/03/04/desalinating-holy-waters-with-the-red-sea-dead-sea-conveyance/.

9. United Nations Development Programme 2013; Ministry of Planning and International Cooperation, *Jordan Human Development Report, 2004: Building Sustainable Livelihoods* (Amman, Jordan); *Legatum Prosperity Index 2012,* www.prosperity.com/.

10. FAO, various issues. For Jordan, unlike the other countries in this study, the base years for this calculation were 1969 to 1971, after Jordan lost much of its agricultural land to Israeli occupation in 1967.

11. US Geological Survey, "The Mineral Industry of Jordan," in *Minerals Yearbook* 2010. Jordan is the world's third-largest bromine producer.

12. *Zawya,* Dec. 23, 2012.

13. *Zawya,* Mar. 5 and Apr. 24, 2013.

14. IEA, "2006 Energy Balance for Jordan," www.iea.org/country/index.asp.

15. See http://amman-metro.com/press/ for details.

16. USAID Mission/Jordan: http://jordan.usaid.gov/.

17. See EU, European Commission, External Relations Directorate, *Jordan Strategy Paper, 2007–2013* and *National Indicative Programme, 2007–2010,* http://ec.europa.eu/world/enp/pdf/country/2011_enpi_nip_jordan_en.pdf and www.ustr.gov/trade-agreements/free-trade-agreements/jordan-fta. Duties on nearly all traded products were to be eliminated by 2010.

18. The not-so-secret contacts are treated at length in Shlaim 1990.

19. *Jerusalem Post,* June 28, 2009.

The reader is advised to consult this book's associated website (**www.middleeastpatterns.com**) for additional information on **Jordan**, such as a historical time line and a chronology of recent events, as well as essays on selected topics and various international economic, social, and political indicators.

13

Israel and Palestine
One Land, Two Polities

INTRODUCTORY NOTE

In this chapter, we will examine an ancient land—historic Palestine—and the two modern polities that in the twenty-first century constitute it: the still-young State of Israel and the emerging State of Palestine. We will first consider a few topics common to the land itself—such as landforms, climate, soil and vegetation, and natural resources—and then turn our attention to the two polities individually, following the general structure used in the other country chapters in Part Two of this book.

The long history of Palestine[1] is of special significance to nearly half the world's population: the adherents, at many levels of fervor, of the three Abrahamic religions—Judaism, Christianity, and Islam—because of the innumerable biblical and Quranic associations with the land. Much more recent history underlies the often-conflicting claims of Muslims and Christians. Historic Palestine's complex history of human habitation stretches back many millennia, long before the antecedents of these modern faiths emerged. In Chapter 8 (in the section "The State in the Middle East") we saw how the defeat in World War I of the Ottoman Empire, the penultimate in a long series of foreign and local suzerains of historic Palestine, led to the international League of Nations mandate over the geographic region discussed in this chapter.

FROM THE PALEOLITHIC TO THE MANDATE

Land Bridge. Geographically, what would become historic Palestine was, with the Sinai Peninsula, the land bridge between Africa and Asia that remained when the Red Sea opened fully in the Oligocene 23 to 34 million years ago. When, much later, the first modern humans migrated from Africa into the Eurasian landmass, this bridge offered an obvious route. Their use of it is demonstrated by the remains of modern humans found at Es Skhul, on the slopes of Mount Carmel about 12.7 mi/20 km south of Haifa and 1.9 mi/3 km from the Mediterranean, and at Qafzeh in Galilee, about 21.7 mi/35 km inland from the sea, dating respectively to about 100,000 and 92,000 years ago. In the Jordan valley, Jericho, the lowest city on the planet at 846 ft/258 m below sea level, can lay claim to being one of the oldest continuously settled cities. Archaeological evidence indicates that it was inhabited as long ago as 9600 BCE. The famous archaeologist Kathleen Kenyon uncovered Jericho's fabled walls in the 1950s, and her painstaking research showed that, at different times, there were several walls constructed, some of which fell millennia before the period indicated in the biblical account.

Rulers of the Land. Migrations, not always peaceful, have marked the history of the region ever since the first humans arrived. At one time or another, conquerors have come from Africa, Asia, and Europe, many leaving their stamp on the landscape and the people. In ancient and classical times, historic Palestine was at various times part of the empires of the Egyptians, Assyrians, Persians, Macedonians, Seleucid Greeks, and Romans. At other times, it was fragmented into a number of local ministates of Canaanites, Philistines, Hebrews, Moabites, Edomites, Phoenicians, and Aramaeans, among others. With Christianity came the Byzantines, and with Islam still more external rulers—Arabians, Umayyads, Abbasids, Fatimids, Mamluks, Ottomans, and Alids.

Rarely, and then only briefly, was the territory that more or less made up historic Palestine unified and ruled locally—possibly by the biblical King Solomon, more definitively under the Jewish Hasmoneans in the second and first centuries BCE. For a few brief years in the twelfth century CE, European Crusaders established themselves as kings of Jerusalem, but not until the twentieth century, with the League of Nations mandate granted to the British, was Palestine once again whole, distinct, and governed locally (more or less).

British forces long established in Egypt, after repulsing an Ottoman attack in 1915 on the Suez Canal, solidified their control over the Sinai and eventually entered historic Palestine in 1917, capturing Jerusalem in December of that year. At first, the area was governed as an occupied enemy (Ottoman) territory. A civilian administration took over in 1920, and the mandate was formalized in 1923. (See "The Arab-Israeli Problem" in Chap. 9 for developments during the mandate period up to its end in May 1948.)

PEOPLES OF PALESTINE

Genetic Mixtures. The genetic complexity of historic Palestine's inhabitants over the past few millennia is clear from this brief historic sketch. Generally, new arrivals in ancient times did not replace those already there but eventually blended in with them. Conquests certainly often involved casualties, but rarely mass killings and displacements. With the fall of the Judean Kingdom in 586 BCE, the Babylonians forced thousands of the elite and others into exile, but many remained behind. Similarly, when the Romans razed Jerusalem in 70 CE and when the Crusaders unleashed their shameful massacre after they captured Jerusalem in 1099, these disasters did not extend throughout the land. The final failure of the Samaritan revolts against the Byzantines in the fifth and sixth centuries led to the near extinction of Samaritanism as a religion and of the Samaritans as a distinct ethnic group, but most of their descendants survived as adherents of other faiths. The ordinary people of Palestine—essentially the peasants and village dwellers—simply endured and outlasted these successive waves of conquerors.

A Land of Peoples. The contentious phrase "A land without a people for a people without a land" was first used in the mid-nineteenth century by European Christian Restorationists who sought to hasten the Second Coming of Christ by reestablishing a Jewish state in Palestine. Several decades later, when it was taken up by early Jewish Zionists, it not only inflamed political developments over the following century but was also highly inaccurate from its first use—historic Palestine was never a land without a people—or, more appropriately, peoples, despite once widely circulated accounts now seen as fraudulent polemics.[2] No complete census figures prior to the mandate period exist, but indications are that for centuries the large majority of the population were peasants living on the land

and in small villages, exactly as their ancestors had for millennia past, as various conquerors came and went.[3] Toward the end of the nineteenth century, before the onset of organized Zionist immigration from Europe, about 80 percent of the population of about 530,000 was Muslim, a bit more than 10 percent was Christian, a bit less than 10 percent was Jewish, and there was a small Druze population.[4] The Muslims, the Druze, nearly all the Christians, and most likely a good majority of the Jews were native Arabic speakers. Although there are no reliable figures relative to the components of the nineteenth-century Jewish population, it is likely that only a small number were of Ashkenazi or European origin. Probably the majority were Mizrahim or Oriental Jews, descended from Jews who had always (or at least for a long time) lived in the Middle East (including Palestine), and most of the rest were Sephardim, descended from those expelled from Iberia in the fifteenth and sixteenth centuries and then resettled in various Mediterranean locations in North Africa, the Levant, and Europe.

The British conducted two censuses during the mandate period, the first in 1922 and the second in 1932; there is reasonable criticism of the completeness of both. Between the two censuses, total reported population increased by almost 38 percent: all groups grew in absolute size, but the Jewish proportion increased from 11 to 17 percent, a relative gain with regard to both Muslims and Christians.[5] A 1945 study estimated the Jewish proportion had grown to 31 percent, almost all at the relative expense of the Muslims, who by then were still estimated at 60 percent of the total.

VARIED LANDSCAPES

Regions

Long latitudinally and narrow longitudinally, the whole of historic Palestine is 265 mi/425 km long and 47 mi/76 km wide (Map 13.1).[6] Although the territory is small, it straddles

Map 13.1 General map of Israel, with main transportation routes. Circled numbers indicate regions mentioned in text.

several climate zones, and with its contrasting landforms, it embraces a wide range of environments relative to its size.

Palestine exhibits a simple regional pattern, with three parallel linear belts extending along a north-south axis in the northern and central sections, and a southern section, the desertic Negev (circled numbers on Map 13.1): [1] a moderately broad Mediterranean plain that runs northward from Gaza and continues on in similar fashion beyond the border of Lebanon; [2] a wider belt of limestone hills down the center, arched up by relatively gentle Miocene-Pliocene compressional forces, a lower southern continuation of the arch of Mount Lebanon; [3] the deep and unique Jordan–Dead Sea–Arabah trench on the east, which contains the lowest points on the surface of the earth and is part of the northern segment of the great African–Red Sea–Jordan rift system; and [4] the southern desertic Negev, a complex area of cross-folds and basins, with a maximum elevation of 3,390 ft/ 1,035 m, stretching south to the Gulf of Aqabah and bordered on the west by the Sinai.

In the north, the hills rise to 3,963 ft/1,208 m in Upper Galilee (the highest summit in all of historic Palestine); Jerusalem in the central hills is at an altitude 2,500 ft/762 m. Eastern slopes descend to the Jordan Trench, with the Sea of Galilee at 692 ft/211 m below sea level and the Dead Sea at 1,388 ft/423 m below sea level. Joined by the fabled Jordan River, the water surface levels in both bodies vary.[7] The Dead Sea has been falling by more than 3.3 ft/1 m annually in recent years, as both upstream use and diversion have escalated.

Soils

The patterns of soils and vegetation are, because of the area's varied environments, also notably complex.[8] Characteristic *terra rossa* soils developed on most of the hard carbonates (limestone and dolomite) in the hills, but many soils have long ago been eroded away. Similarly, Rendzinas that formed on the softer carbonate outcrops (marls and chalks) east and west of the main *terra rossas* have also been seriously eroded. These losses have exposed bare rock, often exhibiting *lapies* (fluting and grooving by solution processes), the common hill landscape of the Holy Land.

Alluvial soils dominate the Huleh and Jezreel valleys and much of the coastal plain, with *hamra* (red) clayey-sandy soils alternating with alluvials on the plain. Many basins in the uplands, especially in the Galilee and Samarian hills, contain alluvial soils derived from *terra rossas* and Rendzinas eroded from the slopes above. Productive loessal soils (loess is fine windblown material) occupy the Beer Sheva Basin and adjoin a belt of moderately fertile but dry steppe soil; however, the rest of the Negev has mostly sandy or stony desert soils, including *hamadahs*. Dark soils on basaltic lava occupy small areas north and southwest of the Sea of Galilee. Partly owing to twentieth-century reclamation work, the best agricultural areas are in the coastal plain and other plains areas, including the northern Negev, the plains and valleys of Jezreel and the Huleh, and the major basins.

Vegetation

The maquis, garigue, and *batha* vegetation (see Chap. 2) of the hills is the Mediterranean landscape most familiar to visitors. However, in Palestine three major phytogeographical zones meet—Mediterranean in more humid areas, desertic Saharo-Sindian in the southern Negev and the southern rift valley, and transitional Irano-Turanian in between—and display an exceptional variety of plants. About twenty-five hundred plant species are known in the land, compared with, for example, only seventeen hundred in much larger Britain. The vegetative landscape has been greatly modified over the past century by the active Israeli planting of pine trees in the humid north and center and of eucalyptus trees on the lower slopes and plains, including the northern Negev. However, true desert areas remain quite barren, with widely scattered bean caper bushes, broom, and, where more moisture is available at depth, acacia trees.

Climate

The latitude and climate are similar to those of Southern California, with a Mediterranean climate (Koeppen Csa) phasing southward into low-latitude steppe (BSh) and desert (BWh). Although summers are hot and dry, with almost no rainfall, Gaza, Tel Aviv, and Haifa on the Mediterranean coast are uncomfortably humid in August. Higher elevations are hot during the cloudless summer days, with low humidity, but are cool at night. January is comfortable in the lowlands but can be raw in the hills. Snow falls most years around Jerusalem and in Upper Galilee, occasionally heavily, and heavy rains may flood lower elevations. The coastal plain has a long crop season, and frosts are rare.

As in Syria and Lebanon, rainfall decreases from north to south and from the coast inland: Acre receives an average of 26 in/650 mm, Tel Aviv 20.8 in/529 mm, Gaza 10.5 in/263 mm, and Elat on the Red Sea only 1 in/26 mm. A site halfway up the western slopes of the Samarian Hills receives twice as much as one at the same elevation and latitude but located in the rain shadow on the eastern slopes. Agriculture in coastal areas has the bonus of 200 dew nights, which contribute an additional 1.2 in/30 mm of moisture. Much of the arable land has moderate to appreciable rainfall, with only the southern Negev and the southern Jordan Valley having actual desert climate.

NATURAL RESOURCES

Over the eons, natural forces have endowed historic Palestine and its adjacent offshore waters with a variety of natural resources. We will outline these briefly here and discuss their modern exploitation later in the chapter.

Nonmetallic Minerals. Historic Palestine's major subsurface mineral is phosphorite (phosphate-bearing rock), part of a great regional belt of late Cretaceous phosphates. High-grade ore is concentrated in the northern Negev, near Oren (see Map 13.4). A more unusual locale for several important minerals

is found in the waters of the Dead Sea. This lake with no outlet has been fed for countless millennia by the Jordan and its tributaries, carrying dissolved minerals from their mountainous origins to the north. The resulting brine of the lake is rich in potash, bromine, magnesium, lithium, sodium chloride, and aluminum chloride.

Hydrocarbons. The presence of hydrocarbons in the territory of historic Palestine has only recently been fully realized, but of course these resources have been present since before the dawn of the region's human history. Two quite different forms and locales of exploitable hydrocarbon deposits are present. In the northern Negev, there is oil shale (see discussions of this type of resource in Chaps. 6 and 12), and offshore is the Levant Basin with sizable deposits of natural gas and probably of petroleum as well. (See further discussion of the recent discoveries in this basin in Chaps. 6, 8, 11, and 20.)

Water: Supply. Official estimates indicate that for historic Palestine as a whole, total annual renewable resources of 92.5 bn ft^3/2.62 bn m^3, an adequate amount for a Levantine country;[9] this is almost three times what is available to Jordan and seven times Cyprus's allotment but only about 55 percent of Lebanon's resources. The critical nature of limited water supplies was grasped when the League of Nations was determining the mandate's boundaries. Early Zionist leaders lobbied Britain to extend the boundaries of mandate Palestine northward to include not only all the headwaters of the Jordan River, but also the lower Litani River (see Chap. 11). However, some of the Jordan headwaters and all of the Litani went to other mandates—Syria and Transjordan in the first case, Lebanon in the second (see Map 13.2).

Water: Demand. Despite the relative abundance of water resources, by regional standards,

Map 13.2 Water situation in Israel, the Occupied Territories, and adjacent areas. (Adapted from map in *Geographic Notes*, no. 13, US Department of State)

the potential for shortages is always present, especially now that the possibility of major changes in climate could impact considerably and unfavorably on the region. Agriculture has long been the sector most dependent on, and the largest user of, water resources. Modern agriculture, despite impressive advances in the efficient use of this input, now encounters the problem as to whether its demands can continue to be met or whether economies need to

divert more of the available water to more cost-effective end uses.

INFRASTRUCTURE

Modern economic infrastructure in historic Palestine had its beginnings in the last decades of Ottoman rule. The first railway connected the port of Jaffa with Jerusalem in the hills: built by a French company, it began service in 1892, and it was widened from narrow to standard gauge by the British military in 1920. A coastal line was opened from Sinai to Haifa at about the same time and was extended to Tripoli, Lebanon, in 1942; this became a vital supply route to the Allied forces in World War II. A narrow-gauge line through the Jezreel Valley connected Haifa in 1905 to the main line of the Hijaz Railway at Dara in contemporary Syria. All three international connections were terminated with the changed political situation in 1948.

The Palestine Electric Company was founded in the early days of the mandate, in 1923, and a grid was gradually constructed to serve the entirety of historic Palestine. The first generating plant was hydroelectric and was built at the juncture of the Jordan and Yarmouk Rivers.[10] Mandate Palestine was integrated into the global petroleum market in a small but important way with the inauguration of the Iraq Petroleum Company's Kirkuk to Haifa pipeline in 1935 (see Chaps. 6 and 14 for more details). The delivered crude was processed at the Haifa refinery, which provided supplies that were vital to Allied World War II efforts in the Middle East. Like the international rail linkages, the Haifa connection was terminated with the changed political situation after 1948.[11]

Israel

KEY POINTS: Evolved from 1920s British Palestine mandate. Gained sovereignty to half of mandate designated as "Jewish State" by 1948 UN special commission. Fought and won several wars with Arab neighbors and has expanded into "Arab State" territory designated by UN. Later built controversial wall to separate West Bank Palestinians from much of Israeli territory. Has had very rapid development with inpouring millions of Jewish emigrants and billions of dollars. Strongest military power in region. Is "creating facts on the ground" by building Jewish settlements in much of remaining Palestinian territory. With US financial, security, and diplomatic support, now the most highly developed state in region, with superior scientific technology. Leading tourism industry.

INTRODUCTORY NOTE

Among the 127 states that have gained independence since 1943, 10 of them in the Middle East, Israel has generated an unprecedented level of international involvement both in support and in opposition. In Chapter 9 (in the section "The Arab-Israeli Problem"), we discussed the long-standing Arab-Israeli conflict and the geopolitics of the Jewish state and of the territories it has occupied since 1967 in some detail. Now it is time to discuss the State of Israel itself.

One of Israel's leaders once commented that Israel is in, but not of, the Middle East. It is, indeed, distinct by virtually every criterion—political, ethnographic, geographic, economic, military. The circumstances of its founding and early evolution kept it isolated, relating to its neighbors only in hostile military operations for decades. Regionally perceived as a surviving outpost of European colonialism in a decolonizing era, the Jewish state was long a pariah to its Arab neighbors. Yet Israel has, with strong US support, signed peace treaties with Egypt and Jordan, and off and on has had working relationships with other Arab countries. However, despite overt negotiations stretching back two decades, the underlying conflict with the Palestinians remains unresolved.

POPULATION

Immigration

Zionism's biggest challenge, once the mandate was in place, was to take advantage of the Balfour Declaration's promises by mandatory Britain to bring about a Jewish majority in Palestine before the mandate concluded. By that time, several waves of immigration—or *Aliyah* ("ascent")—dating back to the 1890s, had added thousands of *olim* ("ascenders"). They culminated in the Fifth Aliyah of the 1930s with the arrival of more than 250,000 Jews as anti-Semitism grew in Europe. Unrestricted immigration was essential to the Zionist program, but the British faced the dilemma of being equally obligated under the Balfour Declaration to protect the rights of the native Arab population, still a majority. For the Palestinians, any sizable immigration meant displacement.

"Ingathering" After Independence. Once the mandate was concluded and independence was declared by Israel in 1948, all restrictions on Jewish immigration were lifted. Given the

ISRAEL

Long-form official name, anglicized: State of Israel

Official name, transliterated: Medinat Yisrael (Hebrew); Israil (Arabic)

Form of government: multiparty republic with one legislative house (Knesset)

Area: 7,886 mi²/20,770 km² (de jure Israel; excludes West Bank and Gaza Strip)

Population, 2012: 7,590,758 (including Golan Heights and East Jerusalem but excluding Israelis residing in the West Bank); Literacy: 97.1%

Ethnic composition (%): Jewish 75.4; Arab 20.5; other 4.1

Religions (%): Jewish 75.4; Muslim 17.2; Christian 2; Druze 1.7; other 3.7

Demography: Life expectancy—78.88 yr (M), 83.36 yr (F); Birthrate (per 1,000)—18.97; Fertility rate—2.67

GDP, 2011: $237 billion; purchasing power parity: $239.8 billion; per capita: $31,500

Currency: Israeli Shekels (ILS), US$1 = 3.550 shekels; 1 ILS = $0.281 (mid-May 2013)

Energy: oil—11.5 mn bbl; natural gas—9,482 bn ft³ (new offshore finds off northern Israel may increase these reserves considerably); coal—nil

Main exports (% of total value, 2008): $61.3 billion (of which polished diamonds 25.3; chemicals and chemical products 25.2; machinery and apparatus 19.5; rough diamonds 6.3)

Main imports (% of total value, 2008): $65.2 billion (of which machinery and apparatus 19.7; crude petroleum 16.7; diamonds 14.3; chemicals and chemical products 10.9; road vehicles 6.4; food 5.4)

Capital city, 2011: Jerusalem (seat of government) 788,100; other major cities: Tel Aviv (agglomeration) 3,350,400; Haifa (agglomeration) 1,048,000; Beersheba (agglomeration) 558,500; Rishon LeZiyyon 231,000

---

events of World War II, the resulting influx had long been anticipated, and exceptional organization permitted the flood of 686,748 arrivals by the end of 1951 to be processed, housed, and fed. Special air flights brought in virtually entire communities—more than 121,000 of the 130,000 Jews in Iraq, descended from an ancient community dating to the Babylonian Captivity, and 44,000 of the 45,000 Yemeni Jews. Another 810,000 came between 1952 and 1972. Until the mid-1970s, Jewish immigrants constituted more than half of the population, but this proportion decreased during the 1980s.

Fall of the Soviet Union. With the collapse of the USSR, the pent-up demand by Jews within its former borders to leave was expressed in massive emigration, and some 350,000 Former Soviet Union (FSU) citizens poured into Israel in less than three years. Monthly arrivals, which had peaked at 35,000 in December 1992, abated gradually, but emigration continued throughout the decade until some 900,000 altogether had come. Early on, Israel's absorptive capacity was so challenged that it turned to the United States for a $10 billion loan guarantee. In return, the new Labor government promised to reverse the policy of expanding Jewish settlements on the West Bank. The reversal was short-lived, and settlement building resumed, continuing to the present despite growing opposition both domestically and internationally.

Emigration. During the 1970s, a new phenomenon—emigration of Jews out of Israel, including Sabras (native-born Israelis)—set in to a notable extent. Emigration is difficult to quantify, as few declare that as their intention when they leave. Many Israelis have second passports from their own or their ancestors' native countries, and they simply return to those countries. Others join the thousands entering the United States, formally or informally. Emigrants have become so numerous that they are no longer stigmatized as *yordim* (those who "go down," the opposite of *olim*). In recent years there has been considerable discussion of emigration, the motives of emigrants, and what can be done to stem what is seen to be a brain drain of the young and highly intelligent. Although there has been some debate about the extent of emigration, with estimates from 750,000 to well over 1 million, most agree that it has greatly increased in the past fifteen years. Reasons vary by individuals, of course, but high on the list are greater opportunities abroad, relief of stress from the regional situation, rising cost of living in Israel, and notably dislike of the increasing religiosity in Israeli life. About 60 percent of the emigrants are believed to move to North America,[12] and most of the rest to western Europe or back to Russia. A 2008 report indicated that half of official emigrants were FSU Jews.[13]

MULTICULTURED PEOPLE

Immigration has created a unique multiethnic, multicultural, multilingual, and multireligious society, with a rich and complex structure and vigorous, if not always amicable, sociopolitical relationships within Israel.

The greatest numbers of immigrants have come from the FSU, Morocco, Romania, Poland, Iraq, and Iran. Many languages persist in Israel, reflecting both the immigrants' national origins and the perseverance of mother tongues: Russian (and other Slavic languages), Romanian, Western and Eastern Arabic, German, French, Spanish, Ladino (the language of Sephardic Jews), Amharic, English, and Yiddish—hence, the great variety of periodicals seen on newsstands. In addition to language and sometimes costume, the wide range of physical characteristics—the Ethiopian features of Falashas, the southern Arabian appearance of Yemenis, and the blond, blue-eyed Germans—attests to the varied origins of Israelis. Israel's people on the whole have achieved a high standard of living—in 2013, the UN Development Programme (UNDP) rated the country first in the region and 16th of 186 countries globally with a Human Development Index value of 0.900, an increase of 16.4 percent since 1980. According to the more broadly based Prosperity Index of the Legatum Institute, Israel placed 40th globally of 142 countries and 4th regionally in 2012.[14]

Who Is a Jew?

In 1950, the Knesset passed the Law of Return, granting immediate citizenship to any Jew settling in Israel. However, the law's vagueness led to questions about the criteria for citizenship, and debate on the so-called "Who is a Jew?" question has never ceased, despite numerous landmark court cases. A 1970 amendment opened citizenship to non-Jewish children, grandchildren, and spouses of Jews. Under the law, a Jew must have a Jewish mother or a mother converted to Judaism in accordance with traditional Jewish law (*Halakhah*) or must convert in an approved way. Those converted abroad by non-Orthodox rabbis have faced growing barriers from the state-paid Orthodox religious authorities, as do some groups (e.g., Ethiopians) whose historic links with Judaism are questioned especially by Orthodox Ashkenazi (European) Jews.

Citizenship Versus Religion

Orthodox religious practice is not required for citizenship,[15] and as many as half of Israeli Jews are "nonobservant" or secular. However, ethnic Jews who have converted to another religion are not eligible for citizenship under the Law of Return. It is significant that family descent has become the standard, reinforcing the ethnicity of Jewishness. The influx of FSU *olim* brought, for the first time, thousands of non-Jews—Russians who envisioned greater promise in a more affluent society. Many of them were spouses, children, or grandchildren of acknowledged Jews. Some 25 percent of all FSU immigrants as of 1999 were not Jewish by *Halakhah* standards; by the late 1990s, more than half of the newer arrivals were non-Jews, creating additional tensions. In the early 2010s, the Russians remain a highly distinct group; many never learn Hebrew and vote only for Russian-dominated political parties.[16]

Intergroup Conflicts

No Longer European Only.   Imbued with European nationalism, secularism, and socialism, European Jews—the Ashkenazim (from the Hebrew for "Germany")—established a Zionist state defined in terms of European principles. With large-scale immigration, however, groups from other regions and cultures brought new and often very different political, social, and religious concepts with them and tenaciously maintained them. The melting-pot idea dissipated. The unified monocultural society of the early Ashkenazi Zionists gradually became multidimensionally varied, transformed into a factionalized body politic, on the one hand, and, conversely, a vigorous, stimulating society, on the other.

The cleavages—sometimes abstruse—were ethnic: Ashkenazi/Sephardi/Mizrahi/Russian/ Ethiopian/Arab; political: left/right/center; religious: ultra-Orthodox/Orthodox/Conservative/Reform/Kabbalist/secular; economic: rich/middle class/poor; philosophical: Western/Eastern and modern/traditional; and residential location: inside pre-1967 Israel/West Bank settlements. Cutting across all the above categories are hawkish/moderate/dovish orientations toward the peace process. All polarizations become more acute in election periods, when more than a score of parties contest for Knesset seats. Although these cleavages should not be overemphasized, neither should they be underestimated. The Ashkenazi/Mizrahi, Jewish/Arab, and Orthodox/secular dichotomies are particularly important, and the tensions between communities both inside pre-1967 Israel and with regard to the West Bank settlements have increasingly come to the fore since 2000.

Orientalizing Israel?   As immigration increased, Jews from North Africa, the Middle East, and southern Asia came to outnumber the Ashkenazim. Now more accurately called the Mizrahim (Orientals or Easterners), for more than thirty years these Jews were integrated poorly into political and economic life; many were first sent to populate remote frontier settlements. By the late 1980s, they were 54 percent of the population but a far smaller proportion in upper employment and education ranks. They often saw themselves as "Jews in the form of Arabs," "imported" to outnumber Palestinian Arabs and as cheap labor for the elite Ashkenazim. Their protests increasingly took the form of voting against the historic liberal Ashkenazi establishment (Labor Party) and for existing right-wing parties and new parties tailored specifically to their own interests. This shift has solidified in the new century.

Many Ashkenazis, on the other hand, have long openly worried that higher Mizrahi birthrates, together with even higher Arab birthrates,[17] would relegate the largely secular

European/North American Jews to an increasingly minor role. Another serious challenge comes from the Haredim or ultra-Orthodox, adherents of sects that originated in eastern Europe and who have Israel's highest birthrates. In the past, service in the Israel Defense Forces (IDF) promoted the integration of diverse groups, but through 2013 the Haredim have largely remained exempt from military obligations (as, of course, have most Israeli Arabs).

Israeli Arabs or Palestinians in Israel?

In the first part of this chapter, we pointed out that over several millennia, when one conqueror after another overran historic Palestine, the mass of the population remained in place, with the conquerors usually blending in genetically with that population for the most part. That was not the case in 1948–1949 when Israeli forces prevailed against local and foreign Arab resistance (see "The Arab-Israeli Problem," in Chap. 9). For years afterward, the official Zionist position held that about two-thirds of the Arabs living in the United Nations–designated Jewish part of Palestine, and in those Arab areas conquered by Jewish forces, had left voluntarily or at the urging of foreign Arab radio broadcasts. In the late 1980s, the "New History" debate that emerged among Israeli intellectuals, led by young historians who examined official documents from the 1940s and 1950s that had been declassified in the 1980s,[18] found that these documents revealed a policy of "ethnic cleansing" that was clearly part of the Jewish leadership's strategy in the early years of the state.

In any case, in 1949, about 160,000 Arabs—Muslims, Christians, and Druze—remained within Israel's pre-1967 borders, with large concentrations in the Galilee. With a high average (though recently declining) birthrate, Arabs within Israel numbered more than 1.64 million in 2012, about 21 percent of the population.

Conflict. Broad historical, religious, and cultural differences underline the interethnic conflict between the majority Jews and the minority Palestinians.[19] Distrust and resentment, sometimes in addition to mutual preference for segregation, characterize contemporary Jewish-Arab attitudes, with some notable exceptions on both sides. Most Arab population centers are surrounded or surmounted by "mirror" government-planned Jewish housing. Budget allocations (five times higher per capita for Jewish communities than for Arab ones) and government grants to municipalities (three times higher for Jewish municipalities) have led to inequities in housing, economic development, education, employment, welfare, water, and general services.[20] Arab university graduates have difficulty finding suitable employment. Even so, entrepreneurial Arabs have developed small industries in Arab areas, and some have become reasonably successful (see Map 13.3).[21] The common belief that Israeli Arabs have lower incomes on average than Jews is difficult to show statistically, but they are demonstrably at a disadvantage as regards health care: in 2011, average life expectancy for Arab men was 3.7 years less than for Jewish men, and for Arab women it was 3.8 years less than their Jewish counterparts.[22]

Many Israeli Jews call for equal treatment of Israeli Arabs and for mutual tolerance. But there are also many Jewish extremists, such as the Kach Party's founder, the late US rabbi Meyer Kahane, who openly expressed determination to "cleanse" Israel of all Arabs.[23] Radical rabbis associated with West Bank settlements have more recently expressed even more extreme views—for example, that it is allowable under *Halakhah* to kill non-Jews, even children.[24] The Russian-oriented rightwing Yisrael Beytenu (Israel Is Our Home) Party, a major partner in the 2009–2013 governing coalition, advocates a vaguely defined "population transfer"; in the January 2013 election, it ran on a joint list with Netanyahu's Likud Party.

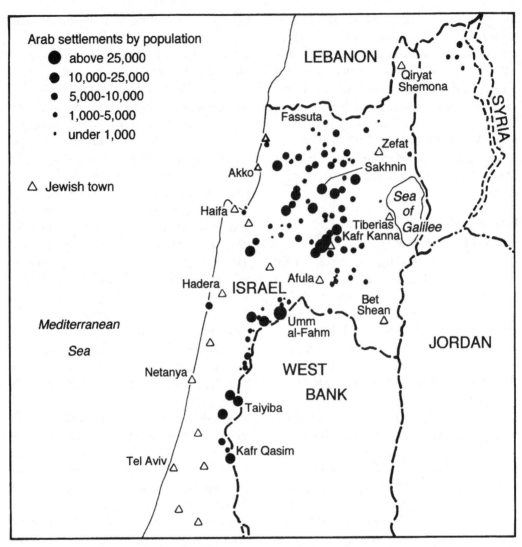

Map 13.3 Areas of continued Palestinian Arab settlement in Israel, indicating centers of Arab manufacturing enterprises. (Adapted from Izhak Schnell, Itzhak Benenson, and Michael Sofer, "The Spatial Pattern of Arab Industrial Markets in Israel," *Annals* [Association of American Geographers] 89, no. 2 [1999]: 312–337. Used with permission.)

RELIGIOUS DIVERSITY

Religious Frictions. In 2012, 75 percent of the population of about 7.9 million were Jews, 17 percent were Muslims (mostly Sunni), a bit over 2 percent Christian Arabs, and a bit under 2 percent Druze.[25] Frictions between Jews and Muslims (and Christians) are grave enough, but frictions among Jewish groups

are often more serious and sensitive. Somewhat as in Lebanon, religious communities, sects, and subsects are critical considerations per se and determine governmental structure, as elections repeatedly demonstrate.

Debate between religious conservatives and liberals, seen throughout the Middle East, is particularly intense in Israel. The rift between Israeli Orthodox rabbis and Conservative and Reform Jews—the great majority in the United States—is particularly noteworthy, in view of the crucial support given Israel by American Jews. The Orthodox authorities reject conversions, weddings, and other rites performed by non-Orthodox rabbis. Since 2009, a group of Israeli Conservative women have been harassed several times by the police for reading from a Torah scroll at the Western Wall, thereby breaking rules imposed there by the Orthodox authorities.[26] Similarly, the imposition of gender segregation by Haredim in and around their Jerusalem neighborhoods has led to several demonstrations by secular women since 2010.

Haredim Versus Seculars.   Public confrontations between Haredim and secular Israelis have seemed to occur with increased frequency in the 2000s. Haredim seek to impose religious law on all phases of life, while secular citizens demand freedom of choice. Secular groups also oppose rising amounts of government subsidies to ultra-Orthodox sects. Another divisive issue has been the military exemptions long granted to Haredi men who claim to be entirely engaged in religious studies.[27] The Israeli Supreme Court struck down the law allowing this in 2012, but the government was unable to craft a replacement that satisfies both secular Israelis and the rabbinical authorities.

In the 2013 election campaign, two major issues concerned this social divide: the military exemptions and the high subsidies given to religious schools that offer their students little in the way of modern subject matter. The result was the emergence of two parties that took strong stands against the Haredim, and, when they became equal partners with the Netanyahu list in the new government, they insisted on the exclusion of the religious parties from the new coalition.[28] Major changes in both military service and the educational sector are other conditions of their continued participation in the government.[29]

Other Jewish Sects.   Adherents of two ancient sects outside mainstream Judaism also live in the state. Karaites, as many as 25,000 mostly around Ramla, Ashdod, and Beer Sheva, reject the Oral Law of rabbinic Judaism, holding only to what is written in the Torah. Some sources trace their origin to the Saducees, the opponents of the Pharisees, the progenitors of rabbinic Judaism. Most Orthodox consider Karaites to be Jews according to the *Halakhah*, but controversies remain, partly because they are patrilineal in defining Jewishness, unlike matrilineal descent in the mainstream. A much smaller and more ancient group is the Samaritans, whose break with historic Judaism dates to King David's decree that all temple worship must be in Jerusalem. Claiming a direct link to those Israelites not taken into exile in Babylon and maintaining their own sacred site on Mount Gerizim near Nablus, they have dwindled to fewer than 725, divided between the Tel Aviv suburb of Holon and a village on Mount Gerizim.

Religions of Non-Jews.   Of the non-Jews in Israel, most are Arabs, of whom four-fifths are Sunni Muslims. Recognized as a separate group since 1957, the 120,000 or so Druze stand out because many remained through the hostilities in both 1948 (in Galilee) and 1967 (in the Golan); many serve in the Israeli Defense Forces. A few thousand Shia who came from Lebanon several decades ago dwell in the north, along with a few hundred Alawi. About 3,000 Circassians, non-Semitic Sunni Muslims with their own language, live primarily in two Galilee villages, Kafr Kama and Rihaniya, and also serve in the IDF. The eclectic Bahai, with origins in Shiism and a highly inclusive religious orientation, have their impressive world center on Mount Carmel (voted in a 2012 poll the most beautiful public building in Israel) overlooking Haifa, but have only a few hundred adherents of varied ethnic backgrounds within Israel.

Christian Sects.   Because of the close ties between Christianity and the Holy Land, at least thirty different Christian sects, representing many nationalities in addition to the original Palestinian Christians, are found in Israel. They congregate in Jerusalem and the Galilee, maintaining centuries-old churches, monasteries, hostelries, and schools. The approximately 140,000 Christians in official figures are mostly Arabs; there are also perhaps 25,000 Europeans and Americans, many connected with ecclesiastical or charitable institutions. Harder to classify are as many as 300,000 aliens, some with work permits but many illegal; they are largely from Asia, the Balkans, Africa, and Latin America and include Christians, Hindus, and Buddhists. As many as one-third of the FSU emigrants (or another 300,000) are not Jewish by religion, ethnicity, or tradition; unless they undergo conversion according to *Halakhah*, their personal status is ambiguous. In recent years, Israel-based evangelical Christian groups have targeted these Russians in their proselytizing efforts with some success.

Nearly three-fourths of indigenous Christians are Greek Orthodox and Greek Catholics. Roman Catholics, third in number, have a patriarch in Jerusalem and supervise many of the Christian holy sites. A bewildering variety of other Christian denominations maintain at least small congregations in the Holy Land. Anglicans and Lutherans have had a longtime presence. The Knesset is considering drafting laws to make proselytizing among Jews by Christian groups illegal, and so-called Messianic Jews face great difficulties and discrimination on a daily basis. A 2011 US State Department report was critical of the status of religious freedom in Israel, citing, inter alia, the situation of non-Orthodox religious Jews, non-Jewish FSU emigrants, and Christians, as well as the lack of protection accorded by the state to sacred sites of Christians and Muslims (all officially recognized such sites are Jewish).[30] There have been reports of an upswing in the harassment of Christian clergy, especially in Jerusalem, and many years of vandalism and desecration of Christian sites, including attacks by militant settlers, increased considerably in 2012 and 2013.[31] The heads of thirteen Christian groups strongly protested an incident in May 2013 in which a Coptic bishop was beaten by Israeli security forces at an Easter mass in Jerusalem's Church of the Holy Sepulchre.[32]

SETTLEMENT PATTERNS

Settlement patterns are particularly relevant because of Zionist ideology's focus on the quintessential role of settlement of the land. They are also significant in the landscape's rapid transformation and because of the unique aspects of settlement preplanning, design, functions, and interrelations with inhabitants. The societal organization foreseen by early planners called for collective and cooperative rural settlements. *Olim* of similar cultural background were assigned to the same settlement to maximize group effort, and the land, owned by the Jewish National Fund (JNF), would be leased to the group, not individuals.

Three Rural Types

Kibbutzim.   Three rural settlement types evolved: the kibbutz, moshav, and moshav *shittufi* (collective moshav). The kibbutz, the first of which was established in 1921, is a commune based on agriculture but with the potential to become an industrial collective. Eventually numbering more than 300 (down by 2011 to 256 with a population of 106,000), kibbutzim became one of the two main forms of Jewish rural settlement; they remained primarily Ashkenazi and secular institutions. Originally communes in every respect— holding land and other property in common, with a common mess hall and child-care center—the kibbutz was a great attraction. But as society evolved, kibbutzim became

Figure 13.1 Margaliyot, 1958 and 1990. A moshav founded in 1954 on a dramatic site on the Galilee Heights overlooking the Huleh Valley, Margaliyot replaced the old Arab village of Hunin, ruins of which are seen in the background (*top*). By 1990, the moshav had been largely rebuilt two or three times, and Hunin had virtually disappeared (*bottom*). It was even more changed in 1997, but bad weather prevented photography.

less communalized, and few now dine or care for children in common. Some are still agricultural, but many now earn income in other ways—polishing diamonds, producing electronic goods, maintaining tourist facilities, or serving as commuter towns near major cities.

Moshavim.   There are several subcategories of moshavim. The moshav ovdim is a smallholders' cooperative settlement, on JNF or government land, in which each family has an individual home and a plot of ground to work (Fig. 13.1). Marketing of produce, however, is done cooperatively. Moshavim became the main rural settlement type and in the early 2010s numbered about 440 with a total population close to 210,000. The moshav *shittufi* combine features of the moshav and the kibbutz: members have individual homesteads but conduct agriculture and economy as a collective unit. In a moshava, all land is individually owned. Moshavim proved more attractive to non-Ashkenazi Jews. A new form of rural settlement is the *yeshuv kehilati;* they are characterized by their selective membership policies. Members live independent economic lives, usually working outside the community. Many West Bank settlements fall into this category. Both kibbutzim and moshavim became increasingly reliant on outside labor, both Arab and foreign, since the 1970s.

Urban Planning

Of more than 650 Arab villages in historic Palestine before and during the mandate years, nearly 400 were destroyed by the victorious Israelis in the late 1940s; within Israel's pre-1967 boundaries, only a modest number remained. Many had few residents after the expulsion and flight of Palestinian refugees in 1947–1949; many still-occupied villages were sequestered by Israeli military authorities after independence. Since these sites usually had locational assets—water supply, good soil, defensibility, transportation—new Jewish settlements were usually built adjacent to or atop them (Fig. 13.1).

Urban Versus Rural.   Despite the early Zionist emphasis on rural settlement, the flow of immigrants to towns made urban planning also necessary. New separate quarters for Jews had been established outside the older sections of existing towns as far back as the late 1800s, and in 1909 the new town of Tel Aviv, the planned modern hub of the state, was founded just north of Jaffa town. New extensions of Haifa and Jerusalem were designed. Major institutions and monuments were planned for hilltop sites in Jerusalem: Hebrew University, the Knesset, other government buildings, memorials, and similar structures. The government built high-rise apartments in strategic locations around East Jerusalem after Israel took the West Bank in 1967 and in a controversial move extended the municipal boundaries of the city.

The Jewish Quarter inside the Old City of Jerusalem was largely cleared of centuries-old houses and rebuilt after 1967; one large block was bulldozed for the Wailing Wall plaza. As in many historical cities worldwide, construction has often occurred at the expense of traditional architecture and communities. In Haifa, several sites on Mount Carmel became Jewish residential areas, resorts, and institutions, including two universities. As nearly 1 million *olim* poured into an already densely populated Israel during the 1990s, urban housing was in short supply and consequently became more expensive. New apartment buildings were built taller, while in West Bank settlements individual houses were erected by the thousands to attract residents; various subsidies made these settlements attractive to many who might otherwise have preferred the greater certainty of towns inside Israel proper.

ECONOMIC PATTERNS

A General Perspective

Israel's economic distinctiveness is as marked as its political and religious differentiations. Initial planning, including economic planning, predated the immigration that began at the end of the nineteenth century. The base institution was the World Zionist Organization (WZO), founded in 1897 at the First Zionist Congress. The Jewish National Fund was founded in 1901 to obtain and manage land for Zionist colonies. The Keren Hayesod was founded in 1920 as the main Zionist international fund-raising agency; the United Jewish Appeal serves this function in the United States. The Jewish Agency, founded in 1919, served as an informal government under the mandate, and it continues, along with WZO, to work hand in hand with the government.

Economic Success. Specialized planning and research agencies coordinated virtually every phase of the economy before the major socioeconomic changes of the 1990s. Similar approaches addressed defense, science, education, and the arts. All this rested on interlocking national institutions (government, JNF, Jewish Agency) and the central labor organization (Histadrut), which until its status declined in the mid-1990s controlled not only labor activities but also industries and economic institutions. Lacking petroleum resources, this diverse base led to a society that, with the advantage of billions of dollars yearly in aid, achieved the most advanced and balanced economic development and the highest general standard of living in the region. Israel concluded advantageous free trade agreements with both the European Union and the United States, and its transformation into a developed economy is seen in its accession to membership in the Organization for Economic Cooperation and Development (OECD—the "rich countries' club") in 2010.

More economic stimulus came from the FSU immigrants—highly trained producers and eager consumers. Peace treaties with Egypt and Jordan, and apparent progress on agreements with the Palestinians and Syria, converged to produce a boom during the 1990s. Israel's regional isolation eased, and aid from the United States, Jewish organizations, and individual donors continued in large amounts. These resources maintained not only its high per capita GDP but also its military-industrial complex, ambitious technological research, and development more characteristic of a world power (information technology, nuclear weapons and energy, space technology, missiles and antimissile weapons, and biological and chemical technologies), a wide-ranging intelligence and diplomatic agenda, massive welfare programs, and an extensive bureaucracy. The economy largely recovered from a slowdown following the Second Intifadah (beginning in 2000). Growth was robust—about 5 percent annually—until 2008, when the global recession hit hard at diamond and high-technology exports and negatively impacted the important tourism sector.

Cost of the Settlements. Although usually seen as a political problem, settlements in the Occupied Territories have strong economic implications as well. Building and maintenance costs of the settlements have been dispersed among a plethora of budget categories, and putting an exact figure on how much their support costs the state is consequently difficult. One study estimated that through 2003, the nonmilitary total ran to $10 billion; another has put the annual figure in the 2000s at some $550 million, with additional military expenditures of $350 to $500 million yearly. Settlers are subsidized with low-cost housing, utilities, and transport—as well as, until recently, with tax breaks—and any government that seeks to change four and a half decades of settlement policies faces the vested interests of some 500,000 organized, highly vocal, and increasingly militant settler constituents whose numbers grow year by year. On the other hand, many in the rest of the country are becoming impatient with paying for these subsidies, when the Israeli Central Bureau of Statistics points out that settlers enjoy family incomes 10 percent above the national average and have an unemployment rate 1.5 percent below the average.[33] As Israel prepared for an election in January 2013, the finance minister claimed that the Netanyahu government had quietly doubled the proportion of the national budget going to the settlements since 2009.

An Israeli Spring?   Although an Arab Spring spillover into Israel might at first seem unlikely, sizable demonstrations spread through Tel Aviv, Jerusalem, Haifa, and Beer Sheva in the summer of 2011. At their peak, hundreds of thousands of people, not all young, were protesting increases in the cost of living and other social issues, settling around the clock in hundreds of tents erected in downtown areas. These protests were most frequently called the social justice protests, having their roots in opposition to the right-wing economic and social policies of the Netanyahu government. Of particular concern to many were the escalating costs of housing, and the shortage of affordable housing for the young and the elderly, while obviously luxurious apartments were being built in abundance as vacation homes for wealthy foreign Jews. Grim pictures of a wave of protest-related self-immolations, causing several deaths, shocked the nation. The government responded, as did several Arab regimes that fell in the face of popular revolt—with promises of reform and an accelerated program of housing construction. The protests continued into October 2012.

In retrospect, the protests were credited in part with the sharp decline in the fortunes of the two main parties in the ruling coalition and the concomitant rise to prominence of one new and one vitalized political party in the January 2013 Knesset elections.[34] When the new coalition's finance minister announced further cuts in social services and tax hikes, the protest movement revived.[35]

Agriculture

Significance Beyond Economics.   In the original Zionist plan for Palestine, agriculture was not merely standard economic activity or simply necessary for immigrant employment and food, but represented an ideological bonding of the Jewish people to the land of Israel. Nevertheless, the practical side of farming has been very much emphasized, with stress on research, experimentation, and efficiency. Thus, Israeli agriculture has become the region's most scientifically planned, organized, systematized, modernized, and mechanized, ranking it among the most productive in the world.

Maximizing Returns.   The range of crops, however, differs little from other Mediterranean lands. As in Lebanon, citrus is prominent: along with grapefruit, the famous Jaffa oranges grown for centuries on the coastal plain are one of Israel's most recognized exports. Market-oriented horticulture is especially highly developed, systematized by area, growing techniques, and exact dates so that specialty crops can be rushed to European markets earlier than those from other areas. In the relentless quest for maximum yield from each unit of land, agricultural researchers have promoted new varieties of plants, use of best patterns of planting (such as growing tender crops on gentle slopes for cold air drainage), and, above all, maximizing water efficiency (including use of slightly saline water or purified effluents) and drip irrigation—which was pioneered by Israelis—to apply water and liquid fertilizers. As has been mentioned above, tightening water constraints are the biggest threat to agriculture; even the most optimistic projections for efficiency gains indicate that the state will have to rethink and radically revise historic agricultural policies. Many crops now grown are too water intensive and will become unsustainable. From the early 1960s to the late 2000s, per capita food production increased by about 9.5 percent, a relatively small gain compared to others in the region but reflecting the generally high level of agricultural technology already employed in the 1960s base period.[36]

As with crops, the dairying, fishing, and forestry sectors are also scientifically planned and conducted. For example, the milk yield of dairy cows is the highest in the world. In forestry, more than 115 million trees have been planted in forests and woodlands as well as along roads, in windbreaks, and along frontiers and in other security areas.

The Arab Sector. Whereas virtually all Jewish agriculture is institutionalized and cooperative, Arab farms, located primarily in Galilee, are generally individual and traditional. Lacking the technological assistance and funding given the Zionist rural communities and without access to Jewish marketing cooperatives, they remain less mechanized, more conservative, less prosperous, and more subject to water problems. Outside of traditional agriculture, there were still about 200,000 Bedouin in the Negev in 2010. Although in the past they resisted settlement in an effort to preserve their traditional way of life, due to government demands about 60 percent are now sedentarized in legally recognized villages. In 2012, the government announced plans to resettle most of the rest in order to make room for a series of Jewish settlements inside Israel proper but close to the border with the West Bank.

Water

Water is crucial throughout the region. In Israel, planning and development rely on a high level of water consumption, so water supply is of particular significance, involving not only major technical challenges but also significant social, political, territorial, and military controversies.[37]

With the conquest of the Golan and occupation of the West Bank in 1967, Israel gained much it had sought from the British in extending the mandate boundaries northward, as discussed earlier. While Israel has justified holding these areas in the name of national security, control of the related water resources is clearly a major factor. Control of water contributed to foundation of Jewish settlements in the occupied areas, slowly at first in the late 1960s and 1970s, then at an increasingly faster pace under Israeli governments of all political orientations. Despite its powerful military position, Israel remains dependent on surface water and groundwater more than half of which originates outside its internationally recognized boundaries. Its own per capita consumption is increasing, even as per capita resources decline in all the upstream countries supplying its water.[38]

Water Under Palestinian Lands. Coastal plain aquifers are extensions of strata underlying the West Bank highlands, where they receive most of their water charge. Allocation of underground water in the hill country is therefore an issue of major contention between Jewish settlers and West Bank Arabs. The settlers use substantially more water per capita than do the indigenous Arabs, provoking the Palestinian claim that they are systematically deprived of their rightful share of water—or of any water at all.[39]

The Israel Water Commission has since 1967 added all surface water and groundwater in the West Bank to its existing control over all water sources inside Israel proper. Jewish settlements were linked to the National Water Carrier, limiting Palestinian rights to water resources, including the Jordan River. Water use in the West Bank settlements is similar to, or even higher than, that within Israel proper, and of the approximately 75 mn m³ supplied to the settlements annually, about 60 percent comes from wells under Israeli control within the West Bank.

A Water Megafacility.   The biggest project in Israeli history was the National Water Carrier. Partly a canal, mostly a massive underground pipeline 8.86 ft/2.7 m in diameter, it runs from Tabagha on the Sea of Galilee to the Negev (see Map 13.2). Opened in 1964, the project spans 140 mi/225 km and can deliver nearly 400 mn m³ per year, most of it during the summer months, from the water-surplus north to the water-deficient south. Drought years may reduce delivery to only 160 mn m³. A prolonged dry period extended through the 2000s; by 2009, the level was so critical that pumping was occasionally suspended. The relatively wet winter of 2009–2010 and the two following years restored the lake level above the lowest level of acceptability but still left it short by 11.5 ft/3.5 m of the optimal level.

On the coastal plain, groundwater is pumped from shallow aquifers fed by moderate rainfall and runoff from the slopes to the east (see Map 13.2). It augments water from Tiberias and the rehabilitated Yarqon River for urban consumption and intensive irrigation. Decades of overpumping have steadily depleted aquifers, despite increasingly efficient irrigation and consistent recycling of urban wastewater back into the aquifers. With record dry conditions in the 2000s, warnings of the consequences of overuse became increasingly dire. As an Israeli water expert said, "The water crisis is entirely of our own doing. . . . The government allocated funds for desalination plants but failed to allocate the resources for conservation."[40]

Possible Solutions?   Some planners urge a serious de-emphasis of agriculture, which claims almost 60 percent of total water

withdrawal. Industry—using just under 6 percent—has a much higher economic return per unit of water. However, agriculture is embedded in the mystique of Zionism, and, more practically, the farm lobby is very powerful; governments have so far considered it to be political suicide to decrease support of agriculture. However, water tariffs have been raised, and rationing has been imposed during critical shortages. To maximize efficiency, Israel has concentrated research on agriculture, as mentioned earlier, and has extended availability with processed effluents, saline water, and seawater. Three desalination plants are operating, and two more are to go on line in 2013. The heavy energy costs of desalination may be partially mitigated by the newly exploited offshore gas deposits.

Manufacturing

Even more than agriculture, manufacturing differentiates Israel from its neighbors in organization, scope, technical level, and marketing. In spite of a limited resource base and dependence until now on imported energy, its industrial development is by far the most diversified and technologically advanced in the region. Expertise brought by European and FSU immigrants, along with imported technology and research and engineering advances in Israel, yielded rapid development. Early industries produced basic items: processed food and beverages, textiles, clothing, and similar light articles. Diamond cutting began in the mandate period with immigrants from the Netherlands; polished diamonds have been a major export ever since.

Research Orientation.   Steady immigration, with its notable "brain gain" and transfers of both capital and technology, led to far more complex production than Israel's age as a state and its population, size, geographical area, and resource base would otherwise suggest. Research in universities and elsewhere—

especially at Technion, the Weizmann Institute, the Soreq and Dimona nuclear facilities, the Nes Ziyyona Israel Institute for Biological Research, and several military research facilities—has carried scientific and industrial technology well beyond that learned from immigrant researchers and outside sources. With a diversified, technologically advanced economy, Israel specializes in high-technology electronic and biomedical equipment, optical and other precision goods, safety and security items, and military equipment. Its computer software and hardware industry has boomed since the 1980s. Six Israelis have been awarded Nobel Prizes since 2000—four for chemistry and two for economics—and the country is among the top five globally in patents granted per capita.

Military-Industrial Exports. In the global arms trade, Israel ranks fourth in the world. Israel Aircraft Industries (IAI) produces combat and civil aircraft as well as armored cars, missiles, patrol boats, and similar military items. Specific armaments exports include the Uzi submachine gun, missiles, artillery shells, armored vehicles, and naval craft. IAI, partly using invested funds from US military sources, produced a Lavi-type aircraft; when it reportedly sold its avionics system to China, the United States objected, as it did again when IAI contracted for sophisticated radar systems with China.

Israel's most famous weapons plant is the Dimona nuclear facility, built secretly in the mid-1950s with French assistance. The uranium found in the nearby phosphorite rocks is supplemented with ore imported from South Africa. Indeed, Israel collaborated with South Africa on nuclear weapons development; the partners seem to have tested a weapon in 1979.[41] Israel's nuclear capability and possession of a sizable number of nuclear devices were revealed in 1986 when Mordechai Vanunu, an Israeli former technician at Dimona, gave photographs and details of

the underground operations to a London newspaper.[42] As a member of the exclusive nuclear club—although refusing to sign the Nuclear Nonproliferation Treaty—the State of Israel is far more technically advanced and militarily powerful than any of its neighbors or many industrialized states.[43] Despite having a nuclear arsenal estimated at 120 to 200 weapons, Israel has strongly advocated military action to protect its regional monopoly against an Iranian nuclear breakthrough.

Dispersed Locations. The main concentration of industry is along the coast from Haifa to Ashdod; outliers are Ashqelon and the Negev centers of Beer Sheva, Dimona, Arad, Sedom, and Elat. Haifa has the greatest single concentration, including oil refining, chemicals, fertilizers, shipbuilding, and more (see Fig. 7.1). Tel Aviv has a variety of lighter industries, and IAI, the state's largest employer, operates near Ben Gurion Airport.

Most domestic production comes from large enterprises, many either state-owned or owned jointly by government and quasi-government agencies, though some privatization has occurred. A growing proportion comes from small establishments; many develop in kibbutzim turning from agriculture to light industry. Manufacturing is increasingly dispersed, both for security and for local employment reasons, into and around small settlements literally from Dan to Beer Sheva.

Nonmetallic Minerals

As mentioned in the first part of this chapter, commercially viable mineral resources in modern times have had two major foci of activity: phosphates mining and Dead Sea water evaporation.

The major subsurface mineral resource in Israel is phosphorite (phosphate-bearing rock). Extensive open-pit mining of high-grade ore is concentrated in the northern Negev, where Oron is the main center (see Map 13.4). Phosphate production of a bit

Map 13.4 General and economic map of Israel, without transportation routes, which are shown on Map 13.1.

more than 3.1 mn mt in 2010, fourth in the region after Jordan, Egypt, and Syria, was shipped by rail to Ashdod for export. Some 183,000 mt of phosphatic fertilizers were also produced.

Evaporation of Dead Sea water in extensive ponds at Sedom at the lake's southern end yields large quantities of bromine, potash, and

magnesium chloride, plus smaller amounts of other chemicals. The Israeli portion of the Dead Sea is now the world's largest producer of bromine and bromine compounds and fifth-largest producer of potash.[44] Continued evaporation, combined with curtailed inflow of the Jordan River, is drying up the southern third of the Dead Sea (Map 13.4): one-third of the lake's previous surface area has been lost since 1960, as the water level has dropped drastically by more than 75 ft/22.9 m; water loss has intensified during the long regional drought that began in the early 2000s.

Energy

As we have seen earlier, with the discovery in the early 2000s of the northward extension of the Nile Delta gas reserves into the Levant Basin, the energy situation in the eastern Mediterranean region became considerably brighter. The full extent of these finds is yet to be determined, but all indications point to sizable levels. In 2010, the US Geological Survey estimated that, in the Levant Basin as a whole, there are 122 tn ft^3 of natural gas and 1.7 bn barrels of recoverable oil. (The Levant Basin includes the offshore areas of the Gaza Strip, Israel, Lebanon, and Syria only; offshore Cyprus—south and north—and Turkey are in separate geological basins.)

Since 2003, a pipeline from the Mari-B offshore field has fed a gas-fired power plant in Ashdod. More promising finds were made in 2009 and 2010—the Tamar and Leviathan fields, about 60 mi/97 km off west of Haifa, were reported in 2009. Awaiting the results of more complete evaluation, it is nevertheless obvious that Israel's natural gas (and perhaps oil) needs can be satisfied for many years to come from these sources. Gas from Tamar began to come ashore in March 2013; recently, there has been considerable debate whether, as further deposits are tapped, Israel should adopt policies favoring rapid development with a view to becoming an exporter to the expanding markets around the Mediterranean or move more slowly, aiming for a longer period of energy self-sufficiency.[45]

However, the final delineation of maritime boundaries (see "Regional Conflicts," in Chap. 8) in this region, until recently not a major economic concern, remains unsettled; when the difference of only 1 mi/1.61 km or so in the location of a boundary may involve hundreds of millions of dollars worth of gas or oil, settling the location becomes both more urgent and more controversial.

Onshore oil resources are negligible, but as mentioned earlier, there are extensive oil-shale deposits awaiting less water-intensive recovery techniques for profitable exploitation. Meanwhile, almost all oil has been imported—increasingly from Russia and the Caspian Basin. After resolving several problems, not all political, Israel and Egypt built a gas pipeline from al-Arish in Sinai to Ashqelon; deliveries started in 2008 and were expected to reach more than 60 bcf (billion cubic feet)/1.7 bcm (billion cubic meters) per year. However, a combination of payment disputes and repeated sabotage of the Sinai portion of the pipeline after the fall of Mubarak has effectively halted these deliveries.

Alternative Energy. As a heavy energy consumer, Israel exploits a range of sources. It is a world leader in solar technology, and 80 percent of homes have solar panels on their roofs to heat water. Coal-fired plant fuel requirements peaked in 2007 at 15 mn mt, about half imported from South Africa; these plants have added to local pollution, but as indicated earlier, cleaner-burning natural gas is reducing dependence on coal. Israel was studying the possibility of building a nuclear power plant in the Negev in 2009, but after the Japanese nuclear disaster in 2011, these plans were reportedly put on hold.

Transportation

Historic Palestine had long been a land bridge; by contrast, independent Israel was largely isolated within its boundaries until the border with Egypt opened in the 1980s and that with Jordan after 1994. Traffic flow with both neighbors is still limited. In any case, Israel recognized that its isolation after 1948 underscored the necessity for good air and sea connections with the outside world, and it has vigorously maintained them. It also developed in its limited territory an effective integrated domestic transportation system. The Negev corridor to the head of the Gulf of Aqabah gives it an outlet to the Red Sea and on to the Indian Ocean, and it serves as a land link between the Red Sea and the Mediterranean (Map 13.1). Conversely, the Negev triangle, with its apex at the head of the Gulf of Aqabah, divides the Arab states of the Fertile Crescent from those of North Africa, a matter of immense economic and strategic significance.[46]

Highways. North of Beer Sheva, Israel maintains an extraordinarily dense road net that is entirely paved, and heavily traveled sections east and north of Tel Aviv are divided throughways (Map 13.1). The main north-south trunk route extends southward from the Ladder of Tyre, north of Akko (Acre) in the northwest, along the coastal plain through Haifa, Tel Aviv, and Ashqelon to Gaza, cutting southeastward across the Negev to Elat. A parallel north-south route 30 mi/48 km to the east runs from Metullah at Israel's northern tip down the west side of the Jordan rift to Elat. Similarly, a main-crest road runs the length of the occupied West Bank hill country; other hill country roads are also integrated into the highway net of Israel. In the early 2000s, an ambitious plan for a 190-mi/300-km trans-Israel multilane toll highway down the coastal plain was adopted, and much of it is now in service. Excellent though the present highway system is, the great density of population and the high standard of living has overcrowded the roads with almost 2.7 million vehicles by 2011.

Railways.   Rail lines have been used primarily for transporting heavy bulk freight—such as phosphates and other minerals, grains, fuel, and citrus. However, they are increasingly carrying passengers in the central metropolitan area. Building on the modest rail net of the British mandate mentioned earlier, new standard-gauge lines have been constructed—from Hadera (south of Haifa) to Tel Aviv in 1953, to Beer Sheva in 1956 (with a branch line to Ashdod), on to Dimona in 1965, then to Oron and the phosphate pits in the Har Zin area. A final extension to Elat remains in the planning stage; its expense makes it unlikely that it will be approved in the medium-term future.[47] A new Tel Aviv–Ben Gurion Airport high-speed intercity line, opened in 2004, joins the main north-south line (Tel Aviv–Haifa-Nahariyya) at Tel Aviv; this is part of a project to connect Tel Aviv with Jerusalem, cutting travel time to thirty minutes. Begun in 2001, it has proven to be a difficult endeavor and is now scheduled for completion in 2017. In 2011, work commenced on a line between Haifa and Beit Shean along the Jezreel Valley; it is scheduled for completion in 2016. The first line of a projected multiline light-rail system in Jerusalem began operation in 2011. As far back as the 1960s, a subway system was projected for Tel Aviv, but this was changed to a light-rail network in 2002. After many delays, construction on the first line was to begin in 2011, aiming for completion in 2016, but in 2012 financing problems put a hold on the project, and a delay of at least two years is anticipated.[48]

Ports and Shipping. Supplanting Jaffa (Yafo), a major harbor since the Bronze Age, Haifa became the dominant port after 1900 and has become one of the busiest general-cargo ports in the Middle East. Ashdod, 20 mi/32 km south of Tel Aviv and formerly of negligible importance, has developed as a second major Mediterranean deepwater port to handle exports of phosphates and Dead Sea

chemicals and imports for south-central Israel. Ashqelon, south of Ashdod, is primarily a specialty port for handling imported coal and petroleum. Elat, the country's fourth major port, serves the Indian Ocean trade and handles the petroleum once again moving through Tipline.

Airlines.   As was mentioned earlier, full and effective air service was for several decades of particular importance for Israel because of its isolation from its land-side neighbors. Continuing to be important for strategic reasons, it early became the channel for the immense flow of tourists.

A commercial airport built in 1936 at Lydda (Lod) on the coastal plain southeast of Tel Aviv became Lod Airport after 1948 and later Ben Gurion International Airport; it handles virtually all of Israel's international air traffic. As mentioned above, it is now connected by high-speed train to Tel Aviv and the rest of the country's rail network. Small airports are located at Elat, Haifa, Rosh Pina in the north, and Sde Dov near Tel Aviv. A new international airport at Elat is to commence operations in 2014. El Al is Israel's international airline, and Arkia is a primarily internal airline.

Commerce and Services

Israel is one of the most trade-dependent countries in the world and was a founding member of the World Trade Organization. It has FTAs with the United States and the EU, its main trading partners, and many other countries. Much of its merchandise trade is with the EU—$37.5 billion in 2007—but the United States is its largest individual partner. Exports and imports are listed in the country summary box earlier in this chapter, and other data are given in Tables 7.3 and 7.4. The unique role of diamonds is noteworthy: in 2011, cut and polished diamonds remained a major item in Israeli trade, with gross exports accounting for more than 30 percent of total

Figure 13.2 Jerusalem, looking west from the Mount of Olives. The view shows the eastern wall of the Old City at bottom, the Dome of the Rock and other buildings of the Old City in the middle ground, and the ever-increasing new high-rise buildings of the burgeoning West Jerusalem in the distance (2005).

exports, despite much increased competition from lower-cost cutting centers in Asia. Domestic trade is significant: small businesses still thrive, but larger stores are gaining ground, and many large Western-style shopping malls have appeared since the mid-1980s.

A full range of services has developed, with banking and tourism as major segments after public services. The state's banking system has worldwide connections, and two banks are among the world's top one hundred institutions, with branches in the United States and Europe. The highly regulated banking sector, formerly state owned, is easing restrictions somewhat, and a controlling stake in the largest bank, Bank Hapoalim, has been privatized.

With some of the world's most important religious, historical, and scientific sites (Figs. 13.2 and 13.3), Israel has a vigorous tourist sector that the government intensively exploits. From 4,000 in 1948, tourist numbers rose to 2 million annually during the late 1990s, contributing $3 billion to the economy. However, the convergence of the Second Intifadah, the impact of 9/11, and a soft economy cut tourism by 60 percent in the early 2000s. Recovery was gradual, only to be hit again by the slump of 2008–2009. By 2011, arrivals had climbed to 2.8 million. Although the sector is relatively small—about 3 percent—relative to GDP, its high foreign-currency added value makes it the added-value leader among export industries.

Reflecting historic Jewish emphasis on education and medical care, Israel has built major universities and hospitals. Supported both by the government and by contributions from abroad, there are seven universities in Israel (excluding the Occupied Territories), the

Figure 13.3 View looking northeast over the Huleh Valley (upper Jordan Valley), with reclaimed land and artificial fish ponds in foreground and snow-covered towering mass of Mount Hermon in distance.

largest in Tel Aviv and Jerusalem. Hebrew University is best known and is one of the finest in the Middle East. The Israel Institute of Technology (Technion) in Haifa was founded in 1924, a year before Hebrew University. Hadassah Hospital, on a hilltop in West Jerusalem, is a world-class medical facility.

RELATIONS

Regional Relations

Because of hostilities between Israel and its neighbors over the circumstances of its establishment and expansion, as well as the impact of the Palestinian refugee populations, relations between the Jewish state and most of the region have generally been antagonistic since the 1940s. Details of the several wars and of relations between Israel and Egypt, Jordan, Syria, and Lebanon are given in Chapter 9 (in

the section "The Arab-Israeli Problem") and in the respective country chapters. Only after the US-mediated Israeli-Egyptian peace treaty in 1979 did Israel have diplomatic relations with any adjacent state. When the peace process was set in motion in 1991, the level of regional tensions did decrease, and the 1994 peace treaty with Jordan opened Israel's longest border. However, following Operation Cast Lead against Gaza in 2008 and with little progress apparent especially since Netanyahu's return to the prime ministership in 2009, intraregional relations have stagnated or even declined.

Egypt.   Before 1979, Egypt was Israel's most persistent and powerful military enemy, but after the peace treaty the Mubarak regime often cooperated with Israel in various peace efforts and other regional initiatives. Tens of thousands of Israelis visited the relatively in-expensive resorts in the Sinai every year, but the security situation there deteriorated after 2011 with a negative impact on cross-border tourism. The election in 2012 of the Muslim Brotherhood candidate to the Egyptian pres-idency cast serious doubt on the future of the relationship with Egypt.

Jordan. Israel and Jordan had a half cen-tury of covert contacts; after two wars and with US mediation, the 1994 treaty led to the most nearly normal relations Israel enjoys with any neighbor. In 2009, the two an-nounced that they would move ahead with planning an expensive and highly controver-sial canal between the Red and Dead Seas, designed to slow the recession of the latter, generate electric power, and desalinate some of the incoming water. There are numerous objections to the plan—economic, technical, and environmental—and despite the appar-ent interest of the World Bank in the pro-posal its execution is far from certain. Jordan valley water-quality and -quantity issues con-tinue to occupy the time of negotiators from both countries. In both Jordan and Egypt are Qualified Industrial Zones from which prod-ucts can be exported tariff free to the United States if they contain a certain percentage of Israeli inputs.

Syria. Israel and Syria have not only fought three wars but also shown the most persis-tent hostility in their day-to-day affairs, with control of the Golan Heights an issue of con-stant dispute. Curiously, in 2012, it was re-vealed that Netanyahu may have been close to signing a deal with the Assad regime over the Golan in February 2011, just before the outbreak of the violence that turned into the Syrian civil war and ended the discussions.[49]

For information on the Israeli-occupied Golan Heights, see the website attached to this book: www.middleeastpatterns.com.

Lebanon. Curiously, it has been with vul-nerable Lebanon, which has numerous inter-nal factions and little real control over its own domain, that Israel has had some of the most volatile relations (see Chap. 11 for more detail). Détente with Lebanon after Israeli troops withdrew in May 2000 after twenty-two years of occupation proved impossible, as Syrian influence remained. In the 2006 "Summer War," Israel considered Hizballah to be a Syrian proxy. Hizballah's successes in launching rockets into population centers like Haifa and Tiberias severely embarrassed the government. Despite heavy damage and loss of life from Israeli retaliation against Lebanese sites, Hizballah claimed victory be-cause it had "stood up" to Israel's advanced technology. By 2012, with civil war raging in Syria, the links between the Shia of Hizballah and Iran were a major concern to Israel.

Iraq. Israel's hostile relations with Iraq date back to Iraq's fighting alongside the Jordan Arab Legion in 1948–1949. The subsequent war of words was heightened by overt actions, like Israel's bombing of Iraq's Osirak nuclear reactor in 1981 and Iraq's launching of Scud missiles against Israel in 1991. Pro-Israel US groups (which had links with some promi-nent Iraqi exiles)[50] were leading advocates for invading Iraq in 2003. The then soon-to-be Israeli foreign minister Netanyahu even testi-fied before a US congressional committee in 2002, asserting the "certainty" of Iraq's alleged weapons of mass destruction.[51] Postinvasion Iraq showed little interest in détente with Is-rael without a settlement of the Palestinian problem, despite pressure exerted by the Bush administration.

Iran. Israeli-Iranian relations were more than cordial under the shah's regime, when the two countries' security establishments—Mossad and SAVAK—collaborated closely. Although Israel surreptitiously supported Iran during the Iran-Iraq War, it pushed afterward for a US policy of "dual containment" of Iraq and Iran. As far back as 1992, Israeli leaders were claiming that an Iranian "nuclear breakthrough" was immanent.[52] With the Bush-Cheney administration's hostility to Iran, the United States and Israel acted together in arguing that Iran's nuclear policies were extremely dangerous. The Obama administration has preferred to act with the EU, Russia, and China on the diplomatic front and has employed steadily increasing economic sanctions to bring pressure on Iran, while Israel has held out for military action, regardless of the consequences across the region. Hostility toward Iran has led Israel to increasingly warm links with Azerbaijan, which has an uneasy relationship with the Islamic Republic, where a majority of Azeris live.

Turkey.   Israel's closest rapport in the region has been with Turkey—Muslim and non-Arab—with which it has a long history of diplomatic, economic, and military relations, dating to Turkish recognition of the state in 1949. They exchanged ambassadors in 1991, signed a free trade agreement in 1996, and increasingly engaged in military collaboration, technical exchanges, and cooperation on water and oil projects (see Chap. 20). However, from 2009 on, the relationship was soured by a series of circumstances: Turkey's moderate Islamic government increased sympathy for Islamic causes, including Palestine; Israel's invasion of Gaza in 2008; the killing of nine Turkish civilians by the Israeli military during a raid on the Gaza Flotilla in 2010; and Israel's subsequent refusal to apologize. The future of Israeli-Turkish relations had become very clouded by the end of 2012. However, quiet negotiations between the two countries culminated in a very public telephone call between Prime Ministers Netanyahu and Erdoğan in the presence of President Obama in March 2013 in which Netanyah apologized and the two leaders agreed to further discussions.[53] Erdoğan paid a well-publicized visit to Gaza in May 2013, partly to counterbalance the new talks with Israel.

Palestine.   For many years, dealing with the Palestine Liberation Organization (PLO) was a criminal offense under Israeli law. From the 1970s on, in order to undermine the secular PLO, Israel encouraged Islamists in the occupied areas. Ironically, these same elements, in a classic case of "blowback" or the "law of unintended consequences," coalesced into such groups as Hamas and Islamic Jihad—and Hamas in the 2006 election defeated Fatah, the biggest secular party in the PLO, seizing power in the Gaza Strip the next year.

The law was repealed in 1993 in the context of the ongoing peace talks, which later that year led to mutual recognition and the transition of the PLO into a Palestinian authority. But twenty years later, the Palestinians feel that they have little to show from the so-called peace process. Certainly, the relations between Israel and the Palestinians have been and will be the critical external issue in Israeli politics for the foreseeable future, as is further discussed below under "Palestine."

Global Relations

Although isolated from its neighbors in the 1960s and 1970s, Israel steadily developed relations with more distant states and had diplomatic relations with 157 countries in 2011.

Great Britain.   In Europe, Britain was the most involved with early Zionist agencies and independent Israel. It issued the Balfour Declaration in 1917 (see "The State in the Middle East," in Chap. 8) and controlled the mandate in Palestine until 1948. In 1956, it acted with France and Israel in the Suez invasion. It has been active in the peace process, and after his resignation as prime minister in 2007 Tony Blair became the official envoy of the Quartet on the Middle

East—the UN, the United States, the EU, and Russia.

Germany. The enormous loss of life by Jews at the hands of the Nazis remains an overwhelming political, ethnic, and religious event in Israeli life. Postwar West German authorities not only expressed remorse but also paid more than $4 billion in reparations to Israel, in development loans and as restitution to individuals who suffered under the Nazis. United Germany continued to make amends. Germany opposed the preemptive war against Iraq in 2003, taking a more balanced stance on the Middle East in keeping with the EU as whole.

France. The French Jewish banking family of Rothschild was the first major supporter of Jewish colonization in Palestine in the early 1880s. In the 1950s, France helped Israel build the Dimona nuclear facility and sold it fighter aircraft and other military equipment. More recent French-Israeli relations have been occasionally thorny; Israel criticized France for opposing the invasion of Iraq.

Other Europeans. The Netherlands is often bracketed with the United States as Israel's strongest supporter globally. However, the 1992 crash in Amsterdam, with large loss of life and many injuries on the ground, of an El Al cargo plane apparently carrying the makings of sarin gas negatively affected relations for many years when Israel refused to supply details about the plane's cargo. Belgium has strong links based on the diamond industry.

In 2013, there was growing sentiment among EU members that Israeli goods produced on the West Bank be clearly labeled as to their origin;[54] in 2010, the European Court of Justice ruled that such goods are not covered by the EU-Israel free trade agreement. If labeling is adopted, it could negatively impact as much as a third of Israeli exports to the EU. A report prepared in 2013 by the consuls general of the EU countries' diplomatic missions in Jerusalem called for economic sanctions against Israel because of the continued construction of settlements on the West Bank, thus undermining the possibility of an independent Palestinian state.[55] The decline in Europe-Israel relations was clearly seen in the vote in the UN General Assembly on granting Palestine the status of nonmember state in November 2012: only one EU member (the Czech Republic) supported Israel and voted no, while fourteen members approved the new status and the rest abstained.

South Africa. Diamonds also link Israel and South Africa. However, relations were much stronger with the apartheid regime when the two shared military interests, including developing nuclear weapons, as mentioned above. Postapartheid South Africa renounced all nuclear weapons pursuits; as a result of the closeness of Israel and the previous regime, relations between the two countries have notably cooled except on the economic front. In 2012, the government decided that all imports originating in Israeli settlements must be labeled as coming from occupied Palestine.

Russia and China. Longtime antagonists Russia and China now have good relations with Israel, which sends and receives sophisticated arms to and from both. With nearly 1 million former Soviet citizens—mostly Russians—in Israel, and with Russia now supplying much of Israel's oil imports, Israel-Russia relations are increasingly close. These ties are particularly ironic, given the Soviet Union's long military support of Israel's most hostile neighbors.

Whereas Israel was one of the first countries to recognize the Communist Chinese regime, Beijing did not reciprocate, and due to its sympathy for the Palestinian cause normal diplomatic relations were not established until 1992. Since then, common economic interests have rapidly increased ties between the two countries, although, as pointed out above, Israeli attempts to extend these links to military weapons led to serious problems with the United States. Both Prime Minister Olmert and Prime Minister Netanyahu made high-profile visits to China, in 2007 and 2013, respectively.[56]

Holy See.   A centuries-long conflict between Jews and Roman Catholics continues to influence relations between Israel and the Vatican. The Vatican Council proclaimed an end to anti-Semitic phraseology in church rites and mandated placing Catholic relations with Jews and Judaism on a positive level. Vatican-Israeli diplomatic relations were established in 1993. However, questions regarding the status of church property that the Vatican believed would be settled promptly after the opening of relations remained still unresolved in the early 2010s. Three popes—Paul VI, John Paul II, and Benedict XVI—have made pilgrimages to Israel since 1964. However, in recent years, a series of vandalistic desecrations committed against Catholic sites prompted strong criticism in September 2012 from the church official responsible for Catholic holy sites for what he called Israeli government tolerance of attacks against Christians and their places of worship.

United States.   The independence of Israel was recognized by President Harry Truman eleven minutes after its proclamation in Tel Aviv in May 1948. Diplomatic relations were initiated the following year. From then until 2010, the United States extended grants and loans as economic assistance amounting to $34.1 billion and as military assistance $73 billion, for a total of $107.1 billion—far more than to any other country, despite Israel's high per capita income. Unlike assistance granted to all other countries, economic aid has been given with few or no strings at-

tached, and Israel is free to use much of the military assistance to support weapons programs and acquisitions within its own borders.

There is no formal alliance between the United States and Israel, but their so-called special relationship has been much closer than ties with almost any other country. When differences have arisen between the two countries, they are almost invariably discussed quietly, so as not to disturb the special relationship. The rather open dispute between Netanyahu and the Obama administration over Iran in 2012 has been unusual and represents the culmination of disagreements over Israel's continued building of West Bank settlements, perceived Israeli lack of interest in the peace process, and the ongoing assessment of Iran's nuclear policies. Netanyahu's barely disguised preference for Mitt Romney in 2012 and his close alliance with Jewish American Republican billionaire Sheldon Adelson left Israelis somewhat bewildered about the future course of the relationship with the United States after Obama's reelection. Differences between the two countries on some but not all the issues were somewhat narrowed during the Obama visit to Israel in March 2013.

The settlements issue and its intrinsic relationship to the peace process have become increasingly intractable, as the Netanyahu/Likud governments have been coalitions dependent on parties opposed to any concessions on territory. No Palestinian administration can seriously negotiate with a partner that seems unable to make the hard decisions that would lead to a geographically coherent and independent (if demilitarized) Palestinian state. In 2010, Israeli officials announced that fifty thousand new housing units for Jewish occupancy in East Jerusalem and nearby areas were in various stages of preparation and approval. Further complicating the issue have been the doubts expressed by the IDF about its ability to carry out any sizable settlement closures because of the growing influence of irredentist rabbis on ordinary troops. Since 2010, settler groups have been engaging in what they call the "price tag," physical reprisals against people (Palestinians and Jewish peace advocates) and property (West Bank mosques, orchards, and property, and, as mentioned earlier, Christian holy sites) in response to any perceived Israeli government action against the settlements. In 2012, for the first time, these actions were termed terrorism by the US government.[57] The United States has not recognized the unilateral Israeli declaration of Jerusalem as its undivided capital or its annexations of the Golan Heights and in the Jerusalem area.

For information on the business environment in Israel, see the website attached to this book: www.middleeastpatterns.com.

Palestine

KEY POINTS: (Ancient name of area [from Philistine], adopted 1920s for name of British mandate, current confusion regarding use.) To many, now equivalent to West Bank and Gaza. Remnant of "Arab State" designated by 1948 UN special commission, with remainder seized by Israel in 1948–1949. Much of West Bank being illegally settled by Israelis. Greatly restricted economy, so development limited and poverty widespread. Opposing political groups make administrations unstable between and within West Bank and Gaza and communications and economic relations difficult.

HISTORICAL NOTE

As was shown in Chapter 9 (in the section "The Arab-Israeli Problem"), Israel captured four pieces of land, at least one from each of its foes, in the 1967 war: Sinai and the Gaza Strip from Egypt, the West Bank from Jordan, and the Golan from Syria. Neither Sinai nor the Golan had been part of mandate Palestine; hence, they were not covered by the 1947 UN partition. However, both the West Bank and Gaza had been integral parts of mandate Palestine, and both were included in the part of the mandate allotted to the proposed Arab state in 1947. In keeping with "exchanging a piece of land for a land of peace," as urged from several sides, Israel withdrew from the Sinai—which is two-thirds larger than Israel itself—pursuant to the peace treaty with Egypt in 1979.

However, Israel still exercises ultimate control over the three remaining areas. Not until the Gulf crisis in 1990–1991 galvanized the peace process did the status of the West Bank and Gaza begin to change—with the signing of the first Oslo Agreement in 1992. Solidly Arab, they became a microcosm of the Arab-Israeli problem. It was in Gaza that the First Intifadah, the Palestinian uprising, escalated during 1987–1992, and it was in the West Bank that the Second Intifadah spread. The two regions became the geographical and human symbols of the struggle for the land itself. Israeli extremists claimed both as part of Eretz Israel; asserting what they believe is their right to settle there, they insisted on "creating facts on the ground"—so that by creeping annexation through building settlements, Israel would achieve permanent control without having to declare outright annexation. It

PALESTINE

Long-form official name, anglicized: State of Palestine (West Bank and Gaza Strip) (tentative; term the result of UN General Assembly vote in 2012)

Official name, transliterated: Dawlat Filastin (al-Daffah al-Gharbiyah and Qita' Ghazzah)

Form of government: West Bank: Palestinian Authority with one legislative house (Palestine Legislative Council); Gaza Strip: interim government led by Hamas

Area: 2,402 mi^2/6,220 km^2

Population, 2012: 4,332,801; Literacy: 92.4%

Ethnic composition: Palestinian Arab; Jewish

Religions (%): Muslim (mostly Sunni) 84.6; Jewish 10.3; Christian and other 5.1

Demography: Life expectancy—72.9 yr (M), 76.84 yr (F); Birthrate (per 1,000)—28.19; Fertility rate—3.61

GDP, 2008: $6.64 billion; purchasing power parity, 2009: $12.79 billion; per capita, 2008: $2,900

Currency: Israeli Shekels (ILS), US$1 = 3.550 shekels; 1 ILS = $0.281 (mid-May 2013)

Energy: oil and natural gas—offshore gas finds now under evaluation; coal—nil

Exports, 2010: $666.1 million (significantly agricultural products, stone, aggregates)

Imports, 2010: $4.3 billion (significantly food, consumer goods, construction materials, petroleum, chemicals)

Capital city, 2009: Ramallah (seat of government) 69,000; other cities, 2007: Hebron (al-Khalil) 156,147; Nablus 123,377

---

rejects the applicability of the Fourth Geneva Convention of 1949—which forbids the transfer of an occupying power's population into occupied territory—but the international community, including the United States, holds to the convention's relevance.

TOWARD STATEHOOD

From the Mandate to 1967

The emerging State of Palestine is based on two distinct areas separated by about 25 mi/40 km of pre-1967 Israel territory. As can be seen from Map 9.2B, the United Nations Partition Plan of 1947 envisioned somewhat larger versions of the two areas actually

touching geographically in one location, but after the Israeli conquests of 1948–1949 they were separated and over the next eighteen years had two different political histories.

West Bank. Much of the largest (totaling 2,262 mi^2/5,860 km^2) of the three pieces of the former mandate allotted by the UN to the Palestinian Arabs was held during the 1948–1949 fighting by Jordan's Arab Legion, as was the Old City of Jerusalem. At first, King Abdallah I of what was then Transjordan proclaimed that the West Bank was to be held in trust for the Palestinians, but what was a de facto annexation was made explicit in 1950. Transjordan's name was changed to Jordan, and most residents of the region were granted Jordanian citizenship, with the right to live anywhere in the enlarged kingdom (see Chap. 12 for more details).

Gaza Strip. A southern area (141 mi²/365 km²) much reduced from what was allotted by the United Nations to the putative Arab state was held by the Egyptian Army, comprising Gaza City and a strip of land extending to the Sinai border. Military control continued after the Egypt-Israel Armistice, but officially the civil authority was the All-Palestine Government, sponsored by the Arab League. It was dissolved by Egypt in 1959, and thereafter Gaza was ruled by an Egyptian military governor. Residents had no automatic right to enter Egypt proper and were considered Palestinian, not Egyptian, citizens.

People. Both regions saw considerable inflows of Arab refugees from both the area of the mandate allotted to the Jewish State and that lost by the Arabs to Jewish forces. In 1948, the estimated populations of the West Bank and Gaza were 462,000 and 82,500, respectively; by 1950, the numbers had swollen to 765,000 and 240,000, increases of about 66 percent and 191 percent, respectively. An Israeli census conducted shortly after the end of the June 1967 war counted 594,000 people on the West Bank and 352,000 in Gaza; that war had prompted more refugees to flee to Jordan's East Bank, so it is difficult to say how many people the two areas held just before the outbreak of war (see Chap. 12).[58] About 12.8 percent of the population of the West Bank (including Jerusalem) was Christian in the mid-1940s, but twenty years later their proportion had fallen to about 5.7 percent; nearly all the population of Gaza during this period were Sunni Muslims.[59]

After 1967

In retrospect, it is somewhat ironic that, on the one hand, the Israeli conquest of the West

Bank and Gaza had the effect of unifying the Palestinians under a single ruler, albeit an occupier, for the first time since the end of the mandate, and that, on the other hand, by persisting in the occupation into its fifth decade and by introducing hundreds of thousands of settlers into the conquered territories, Israel raised the issue of Palestinian sovereignty and independence to the level of primary concern to the world's major powers. Prior to 1967, there was no effective Palestinian voice in the international arena, and although many years would pass before the world's images of the Palestine Liberation Organization changed from that of airplane hijackers to recognized partner in regional negotiations, it is worth considering whether a similar transition would have occurred for the Palestinians had Israel quickly returned the territories to Jordanian and Egyptian rule.

Territorial Divisions. As events have evolved, the two areas became the constituent parts of a fragmented Palestinian Authority (PA), a state-in-becoming. In 2012, the lands of West Bank fell into three categories as defined under the 1995 Oslo Accords (see Map 13.6);

Area A: full PA civil and security control (although over the years this has often been overridden by Israeli forces in the name of security needs); under the accords, this was to cover about 18 percent of the West Bank (essentially the urban population centers) and contain about 55 percent of the Palestinian population

Area B: full PA civil and joint PA-Israeli security control, comprising about 21 percent of the land (including the main rural population centers) with about 41 percent of the population

Area C: full Israeli civil and security control, about 60 percent of the land and 4 percent of the population (and nearly all the Jewish settlers)

Included are the area of East Jerusalem and its environs unilaterally annexed by Israel, as

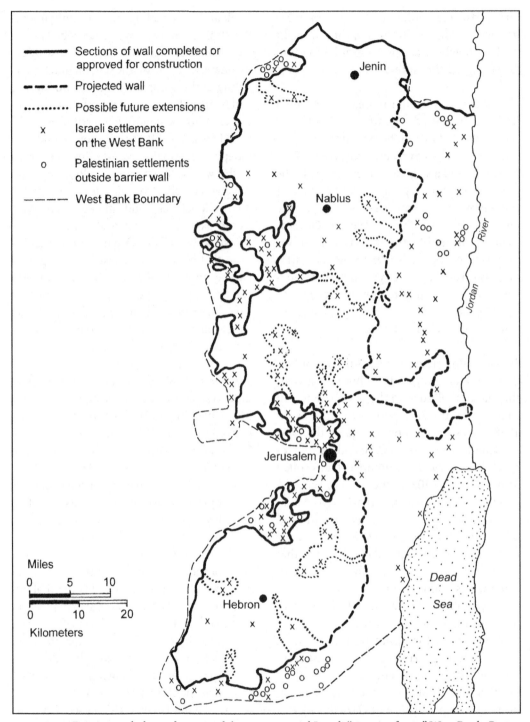

Map 13.5 Existing and planned extent of the controversial Israeli "security fence," West Bank. Part of the alignment was judged illegal in 2004 by the International Court of Justice in The Hague. Only selected Jewish settlements are shown.

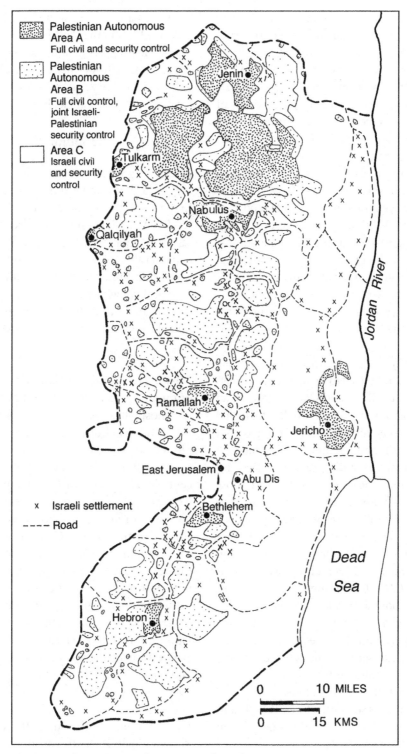

Map 13.6 Areas A, B, and C, West Bank, with Jewish settlements and strategic roads. Rapid developments around East Jerusalem have changed the earlier situation shown here.

well as those lands enclosed on the Israeli side of the barrier wall still under construction in 2012.

Areas A and B constitute more than 225 separate pieces of territory, all totally surrounded by Area C, including the routes of roadways reserved exclusively for Jewish settlers (see Map 13.6).[60] The accords envisioned a gradual transfer of Area C to the PA. Very little of this ever occurred, and since the beginning of the Second Intifadah in 2000, there have been no transfers. A UN report estimated in 2007 that about 40 percent of the total land area was taken up by Israeli infrastructure. Settler groups in 2012 were calling for the unilateral annexation of all of Area C to Israel, and settler encroachment on parts of both Area A and Area B have been reported in the Israeli press.[61]

Demography. As mentioned above, after the June 1967 war had led to further refugee flows from the West Bank and Gaza to Jordan, an Israeli census found a total of about 946,000 Palestinians remaining in the two regions. A 1997 census found a total of 1.87 million on the West Bank, excluding Jewish settlers, and 1.02 million in the Gaza Strip; by 2012, those numbers had risen to an estimated 2.62 million and 1.71 million, respectively.[62]

The settler population has surged since Netanyahu returned to the prime ministership in 2009, and by 2012 it had reached approximately 550,000 (including East Jerusalem); there are about 150 official settlements plus another 100 or so "outposts," many of which are illegal even under Israeli law. The settlements are strategically and meticulously patterned to consolidate Israeli holdings and, together with their access roads, to fragment Palestinian lands still further. The Palestinians live in about 450 towns and villages; about 72 percent live in urbanized areas in the combined West Bank/Gaza area. About a third of the 1.89 million refugees registered with UNRWA live in the nineteen official camps on

the West Bank and eight in Gaza. The largest urban entities in the West Bank are East Jerusalem, Hebron, Rafah and Nablus; others include Ramallah, Bethlehem, Jericho, Janin, and Tulkarm. Gaza urban centers are Gaza City, Khan Yunis, and Jabaliya.

RESOURCES

Palestine's greatest resource truly is its people. Well educated for several generations now, first under the mandate and then in the UNRWA school system, hundreds of thousands of expatriate Palestinians have gained considerable experience in a wide range of professions and occupations both in the region and elsewhere in the world. Along with the Lebanese and the Armenians, they are notable for their business and entrepreneurial skills.

Nonmetal Minerals. Palestine's endowment of mineral resources is rather limited. There are phosphates south of Jericho not far from the Dead Sea, but these have not been exploited so far. More important is the limestone that is found throughout the hilly central region. Ten Israeli companies in 2012 were quarrying stone on the West Bank; the Israeli Supreme Court in December 2010 ruled that the Geneva Convention limiting an occupying power's ability to profit from the natural resources of an occupied area did not apply to their activities, even though the royalties the companies pay go to the military government and most of the output is sold in Israel proper. A report published by the PA in 2011 estimated the potential value of mining and quarrying on the West Bank to be about $900 million annually.[63]

Hydrocarbons. Although there are no known onshore hydrocarbon deposits in Palestinian territory, the Gaza Strip's short Mediterranean coastline (25 mi/41 lm) is enough to claim offshore territory in the Lev-

Figure 13.4 Barbs of discord: Jewish settlement impinging on an indigenous Palestinian neighbor-hood in Hebron. Kiryat Arba, across the road in the distance, is one of the most controversial of all Jewish settlements in the occupied areas and is expanding into an area to the right in the foreground. Israeli soldier to the left.

ant Basin. One significant discovery has been made in this small sector, the Gaza Marine gas field, where British Gas has done exploratory drilling, estimating resources at 1 tn ft^3/28.3 mn m^3. Exploitation has been delayed, partly because Israel has disputed the Palestinian claim to the area, especially since Hamas took over the Gaza Strip, but by September 2012 it seemed that the Israelis were relenting in their opposition in new discussions with the PA.

Arable Land. The Gaza Strip is part of the Sinai-Palestine coastal plain, with high sand dunes along the shore backed by areas with good soils of sandy clay, silt, and loess; about a third of its area is arable land. To support the densely populated area, agriculture is intensely irrigated but very productive. Citrus

is a primary crop; other tree products include dates, almonds, and olives, plus grapes, vegetables, and field crops. Agriculture remains a major sector of the economy but employs only about 5 percent of the labor force. The West Bank is mostly rugged upland; about a quarter of the area is arable land, with seasonal crops planted on slightly more of the land than is used for pasture. Major crops include olives, vegetables, wheat, and barley. Agriculture provides a livelihood to about a sixth of the region's labor force.

In Gaza, since the 2005 unilateral evacuation of Israeli settlers, land resources are mostly pressed by the urbanization process in this densely populated entity,[64] but on the West Bank, the problem faced by Palestinians is the continuing encroachment of Israeli settlements. Much of the arable land is in Area C, which is under complete Israeli authority, or, if in Areas A or B, is close to Israeli settlements in Area C. Settlements have taken over land in various ways: (1) many are on land that was state owned under Jordan before 1967, then, after 1967, classified as security areas or nature reserves; (2) other land is requisitioned on the grounds that some Palestinian farmers have no legal proof of their long ownership (past governments—Ottoman, British, and Jordanian failed to establish complete and accurate cadastres); or (3) still other land is owned by farmers who are cut off from adequate water supplies and burdened with regulations enforced by a military government that gives preference to settlers, and some of them sell their land to Israeli agents. In the past decade, there has been a considerable increase in settler vandalism—uprooted olive and fruit trees, arson of field crops—against Palestinian farmers.[65]

A former Israeli official in the West Bank wrote, "Redemption of the land (*geulat ha-qarqa*) is a fundamental Zionist concept. . . . The history of the Zionist enterprise is an account of physical *faits accomplis* through land acquisitions and settlement, created to achieve national, political, and military objectives. . . . The Palestinians, attaching the same macro-national and symbolic value to the land, resist Israeli land acquisition efforts with whatever means they can muster. The unequal strength of the conflicting parties, however, dictates the results."[66] The Israeli Civil Administration was recently required to submit an accounting of its disposition of state lands on the West Bank to the High Court of Justice; this showed that although 38 percent of the land had been allocated to settlements, only 0.7 percent had been allocated to Palestinians.[67]

Water.   In addition to land itself, water is the basis for many conflicts between Israelis and Palestinians, at both the official and the individual levels. Disputes arise not only in the allocation of daily supplies but also in the

exercise of control over aquifers that supply both the West Bank and the densely populated Israeli coastal plain. Runoff from the considerable winter rainfall accumulates in these aquifers, some yielding water in springs, others feeding wells. Possessing the hydrogeological information, the technology, and official authority, Israel and Israeli settlers increasingly dominate water resources as well, leaving many Arab farmers with little or no water for farming or domestic use. Estimates are that the settlers use more water than the West Bank Palestinians who are about five times more numerous.[68]

In Gaza, marginal annual rainfall of 12 in/ 300 mm is supplemented by wells tapping the appreciable groundwater supplies. Intense irrigation has led to aquifers being overused, endangering both the amount and the quality of groundwater. The water table has been lowered near the seacoast, reducing aquifer resistance to seawater intrusion and raising the salinity level. A 2012 UN report argued, among other things, that Gaza's aquifer may be unusable for human consumption by 2016. A major increase in desalination is necessary, as is a halt to the pumping of three-fourths of the strip's wastewater untreated into the Mediterranean.[69]

ECONOMY

Limited Resources.   Before 1967, neither the West Bank nor Gaza received much in the way of funding that would promote development, either from the limited resources of the Jordanian and Egyptian governments or from international donors. UNRWA had been very active from 1949 on, but the agency concentrated on providing basic services—housing, health care, and education—to its hundreds of thousands of refugee charges.

From 1967 on until the 1990s, the basic situation regarding development resources remained the same. Considerable funding flowed especially into the West Bank from Israel, but nearly all of this went to subsidize the growing number of settlements and the military and civil infrastructure needed to support and protect the settlers. UNRWA continued to be the mainstay for the growing population in the camps. Jordan continued to pay the salaries of West Bank civil servants until its government renounced its claims to the area in 1988. Only with the Oslo Accords did multilateral and bilateral development agencies begin to be involved in the task of promoting Palestinian development.

Jobs Abroad, Unemployment at Home. In the private sector, the booming oil economies of Saudi Arabia, Iraq, and the Gulf states offered reasonably well-paid employment to tens of thousands of UNRWA-educated expatriate Palestinians. A large portion of their earnings was sent to families at home for basic support, but these remittances also provided for investment in housing and education and often for village improvements as well. However, the labor situations in the West Bank and Gaza were much more limited; for those unable or unqualified for employment abroad, there was often only menial labor in the settlements or nearby Israeli towns. Unemployment rates have been chronically high, especially in Gaza and among younger people in both regions—an estimated 24 percent in the West Bank and 40 percent in Gaza in the early 2010s.[70] With the onset of the First Intifadah in 1987, the movement of Palestinians within the West Bank and in and out of Israel proper became much more restricted, cutting deeply into employment opportunities. Israel filled the gap by importing cheap unskilled labor from Asia and Africa.

Since the 1990s. The Oslo Accords and the formation of the Palestinian Authority gave the Palestinians for the first time some limited control over economic development. But under the military government, dominating the Palestinian economy are the priorities of the Jewish settlements (in Gaza until 2005 and the West Bank up to the present) and the continued Israeli control over the flow of labor, capital, and goods within the regions and between the regions and Israel proper, Jordan, and Egypt.

As George W. Bush, no great friend of the Palestinians, famously put it in criticizing Israeli policies on the West Bank, "Swiss cheese isn't going to work when it comes to the territory of a state"; he might just as accurately have substituted "economy" for "territory."[71] Less colorful but equally cogent was the World Bank's assessment in 2011 that, despite considerable progress in Palestinian institution building, sustainable economic growth remains out of reach. For this, the bank said, a vibrant private sector was necessary, but this was unlikely to emerge "while Israeli restrictions on access to natural resources and markets remain in place and as long as investors are deterred by the increased cost of business associated with the closure regime."[72]

In the early 2010s, the proportion of the population of the West Bank living below the poverty line was 18 percent, and in the Gaza Strip it was 38 percent. In 2013, the UN Development Programme's annual report calculated a Human Development Index of 0.670, 110th of 186 countries globally and 13th regionally, ahead of Egypt, Syria, Iraq, and Yemen. Palestine's HDI was equivalent to 74 percent of Israel's.[73]

POLITICAL DEVELOPMENT

For more than a quarter century, from June 1967 until Israel and the PLO exchanged recognitions with the first Oslo Accords (1993) and the consequent Cairo Agreement (1994), all authority throughout both the West Bank and the Gaza Strip rested with the Israeli military government. The PLO was recognized by the Arab League as the sole legitimate representative of the Palestinian people in 1974, and that same year Yasser

Arafat addressed the UN General Assembly (UNGA), offering the alternatives of the olive branch or the freedom fighter's gun. In 1975, the PLO was granted observer status at the UNGA, and there followed diplomatic recognition of the PLO, first by neutral and Eastern-bloc countries but eventually by Western countries as well (see below, "Relations"). Israel tried to counter what influence the PLO had within Palestine by encouraging Islamist rivals to the secular PLO, as mentioned above. But all of this had little effect on the ground in the daily lives of West Bank and Gaza Palestinians.

Two events—the First Intifadah, beginning in December 1987 and the success of the US-led coalition in driving Iraq out of Kuwait—laid the groundwork for change in the 1990s. The intifadah's spontaneous origin and spread and its continuation over several years, despite the deaths of more than 1,000 Palestinians and the arrest of 120,000 more, made a growing number of Israelis realize that the status quo of military government was unsustainable. On the American side, its massive military involvement on the ground brought President George H. W. Bush to the conclusion that the United States had to become actively involved in searching for a reasonable solution to the Israeli-Palestinian conflict.

A Palestinian Statelet. With the agreements reached by Israel and the PLO in Oslo and Cairo, preliminary steps toward self-rule in the West Bank and Gaza began in May 1994. The Palestinian Authority became a virtual government of a quasi state at first composed of Gaza (excluding Jewish settlements) and the Jericho area. Oslo II in September 1995 began troop withdrawals from part of the West Bank areas, extending full PA control to six cities and scattered rural areas (Area A, Map 13.6). The Israeli Defense Forces and PA shared jurisdiction over a few more noncontiguous locations (Area B): the IDF had complete control of most of the region (Area C),

but the understanding was that this area would gradually be turned over to the PA. The first Palestinian elections in January 1996 made PLO chairman Arafat president of the PA and chose the Palestine Legislative Council (PLC). At this time, there were about 138,000 settlers on the West Bank and in Gaza, with another 157,000 in East Jerusalem.

Following the assassination of Prime Minister Yitzhak Rabin in 1995, right-wing forces triumphed in the 1996 election, and Binyamin Netanyahu became Israeli prime minister for the first time. Over the next three years, he pursued his long-declared views—including noncooperation with Palestinians—while signing several agreements under US pressure, but then equivocating on implementation. Ehud Barak defeated him in the 1999 elections, by which time the total number of settlers had grown to about 330,000. Movement toward a comprehensive settlement resumed, but it remained elusive at Camp David in July and December 2000. Frustration on the part of Palestinians contributed to the outbreak (in September 2000) and consequent spread of the Second Intifadah. In February 2001, the Israeli Right returned to power with Ariel Sharon as prime minister; he refused to continue the peace negotiations. In August 2005, arguing that he acted in Israel's best security and fiscal interests, he unilaterally withdrew about 8,000 settlers (and the full division of troops that protected them) from Gaza, while maintaining control over Gaza's land and sea borders, as well as its airspace. By this time, there were about 430,000 settlers on the West Bank, including East Jerusalem.

Establishing a Polity. In the 1990s, the PA encountered the complexities of establishing a political entity. Revolutionaries had to adjust to the realities of governance, including balancing authority with democratic processes. Graft and corruption were all too common, but some of the institutions of statehood gradually appeared. Private efforts to promote the economy helped in the short term. In 1997, the PA and the EU signed an interim Association Agreement that provided duty-free access to the EU for Palestinian exports. To save taxes and delays at Israel's Ashqelon port, the PA opened a modest but highly symbolic seaport in Gaza, and in 1998 President Bill Clinton dedicated a new Gaza international airport built with foreign economic assistance. With financial and political support from the United States[74] and Europe, and mutual accommodation between Israel and the PA, full statehood appeared to be achievable.

However, the PA's status regressed sharply with the Second Intifadah and the election of Sharon's coalition in 2001. Sharon declared Arafat to be "irrelevant," and the IDF destroyed the new Gaza airport and retook most of Areas A and B, laying siege to the PA compound in Ramallah, rendering the already crippled administration helpless. Arafat died in late 2004, and Mahmoud Abbas was elected to be his successor. Sharon suffered a stroke in January 2006, leaving him in a permanent vegetative state; he was succeeded by his deputy, Ehud Olmert.

The PA Splits.   The perception of rampant corruption and PA ineffectiveness gave a mostly Islamist list headed by Hamas a narrow plurality but a clear majority of legislative seats in the 2006 election.[75] Despite previous calls for free elections, the Bush administration and Israel pronounced a Hamas-led government unacceptable because of its nonrecognition of Israel. Abbas's attempts to form a Hamas-Fatah coalition failed, and the PA lost the financial support of some foreign donors, including the United States. When Hamas militants seized control in Gaza in June 2007, Abbas appointed a cabinet excluding Hamas to govern the West Bank, effectively splitting the PA territory in two. Attempts to reconcile the regimes have proven fruitless so far, despite a reconcilia-

tion agreement brokered by Egypt in 2011. The PLC has been unable to meet since the split between Hamas and Fatah, and new elections have been indefinitely postponed,

West Bank.   From 2007 to 2013, the West Bank government was headed by American-educated economist Salam Fayyad, who argued that neither negotiations nor violence has done much to advance the cause of Palestinian independence. He concentrated on advancing the economy, improving the standards of governance, and maintaining security cooperation with the United States (and, indirectly, Israel). His aim was to establish firmly the institutions of statehood, and he was praised for his successes on this front. However, as was pointed out earlier, the World Bank has maintained that the Palestinian economy cannot become self-sustaining and less dependent on external financial support as long as occupation continues in its current form. Beset by internal PA squabbles and discouraged by Palestine's continued financial straits and the failure of his efforts in the economic and administrative areas to advance the prospects for peace, Fayyad resigned in April 2013.[76]

Gaza.   The situation in Gaza has been decidedly less favorable. Foreign economic assistance has dwindled (Iran is said to have aided the regime through 2011), but humanitarian aid and UNRWA support for refugee institutions continued. Israeli control over Gaza's land borders tightened, considerably cutting the amount of goods legally entering the region. Operation Cast Lead in 2008–2009 resulted in as many as 1,400 Palestinian deaths, property damage amounting to an estimated $2 billion, as many as 50,000 Gazans made homeless, and damage to water systems that may have left half of the agricultural land no longer arable. A follow-up UN investigation led to war-crimes allegations levied against both sides.

Under the Mubarak regime, Egypt's border with Gaza was almost as tightly controlled (except for the smugglers' tunnels) as was Israel's, but in the summer of 2012 there were indications that that situation may be undergoing significant changes. It became much easier for people to pass through the Rafah crossing, although security remained high because of terrorist attacks in the Sinai and the Negev in later months. In February 2012, Hamas broke with the Assad regime and endorsed the insurgents in the Syrian civil war, setting the stage for a possible reconciliation of the Hamas regime with Arab donor states. In October 2012, the Qatari amir made a highly publicized visit to Gaza to open a representative office with responsibility for overseeing the hundreds of millions of dollars he has promised for projects in the region. But a month later, rockets from Gaza fired at Israeli targets prompted a response that quickly escalated, with Israel striking at more than fifteen hundred sites in Gaza. Mediation by Egypt's new Islamist president resulted in a truce between Hamas and Israel after seven days—without a full-scale invasion, as happened with Operation Cast Lead; nevertheless, 158 Palestinian and 6 Israeli deaths were reported. On the other hand, the truce agreements led Israel for the first time to deal openly with Hamas, agreeing to a loosening of restrictions on construction materials entering the strip.

A Palestinian Arab Spring?   Until the summer of 2012, there were few signs that the regional uprisings and demonstrations had had much effect on Palestine. On the East Bank, in Jordan, Palestinians have been prominent among those calling for reform; however, it has been suggested that in Palestine itself, people are so occupied with the "Israel question" that they have no time for other concerns. Rising prices of food and fuel nevertheless hurt nearly everyone, and these seem to have been a major factor in demon-strations in both regions in September. Self-immolations—one successful in Gaza, two aborted on the West Bank—were only part of the protest, as taxi drivers and trade unionists called a general strike. At the heart of the problem is the fact that because of the de facto customs union between the PA and Israel, Palestinians pay Israeli prices for many goods but have only a fifth of the income. Another factor is, once again, the lack of discernible progress toward independence. Demonstrators have called for abrogating the customs union and the replacement of both current PA regimes.

Dealing with Israel.   In 2008, discussions between Olmert and Abbas led to the former's offering a land swap—in return for settlement blocs on the West Bank, Israel would compensate the Palestinians with areas adjacent to Gaza and the southern part of the West Bank. The two sides were scheduled to come together in Washington in January 2009, but Israel's military campaign in Gaza intervened. With Netanyahu back in power from March 2009, heading a right-wing coalition with limited enthusiasm at best for the peace process, further progress stalled on the question of settlement expansion, with the Palestinians insisting on an indefinite suspension. Netanyahu did finally say he would recognize a Palestinian state, encouraging the United States to cajole the two sides into direct talks in 2010, but again the expansion of settlements derailed any progress. By this time, the number of settlers had reached 520,000. The two sides resumed informal discussions in 2012, but it seemed clear that both an American and an Israeli election would have to have passed before much real movement might occur.

RELATIONS

By 2013, Palestine had established some form of diplomatic relations with some 145 countries, as well as with the European Union. The United States initiated formal and overt diplomatic contacts with Palestine in connection with the signing of the Oslo Accords in 1993. Relations are carried on through the US consulate general in Jerusalem and the Palestine Mission to the United States in Washington. The US Agency for International Development (USAID) has been active in the West Bank and Gaza since 1994, and by 2010 a total of $4.34 billion in grants had been extended for budgetary support and to support programs focused on democracy and governance, water resources, education, and health. In 2008, Palestinians emphatically welcomed the election of Barack Obama to the presidency, but there was considerably less enthusiasm for his reelection in 2012.

The European Union, with a history of extending assistance to Palestinians dating to 1971, has included Palestine under the European Neighbourhood Policy as a full member. The EU has been the single biggest provider of assistance to Palestine, with a focus on budgetary support and institution building for a future democratic, viable, and independent state.

International Organizations. Palestine has full membership in several international organizations, including UNESCO, gained in 2011, despite strong opposition from the United States. It also has observer status at several UN-affiliated organizations. In 1974, it gained nonstate observer status with the United Nations General Assembly. In 2011, it began a campaign—Palestine 194—to gain full membership in the UNGA, which effectively would mean collective recognition of its independence and extend protection to the viability of the two-state solution; again, this move has been vigorously opposed by the United States. Membership would require the approval of the UN Security Council, where the United States has a veto, and so seems highly unlikely at this time. As mentioned

above, the UNGA voted in November 2012 to upgrade Palestine's existing status as a nonstate observer to that of nonmember observer, implicitly recognizing that Palestine is a state.[77] It also allows Palestine to participate in General Assembly debates, sign treaties, and join additional UN-affiliated specialized agencies. Only nine countries, including the United States, voted against the change.[78]

For further information on the negotiations between Israel and Palestine and on the debate in Israel over being either a democratic or a Jewish state (or both), see the website attached to this book: www.middleeast patterns.com.

NOTES

1. "Palestine" is universally used, even by Israeli writers, to apply historically to the general area between the Mediterranean Sea and the Jordan River and from Metullah at the northern tip of Israel to Elat at the head of the Gulf of Aqabah. The term includes contemporary Israel and all Occupied Territories except Golan.

2. Specifically, J. Peters, *From Time Immemorial.*

3. Lewis estimated that in the mid-sixteenth century, perhaps only a fifth of the population lived in the six towns of any size. B. Lewis 1954.

4. DellaPergola, IUSSP XXIVth General Population Conference in Salvador de Bahia, Brazil, Aug. 18–24, 2001.

5. Both censuses showed 1 percent in the "Other" category; this would have included the Druze.

6. The irregular shape of contemporary Israel proper gives the narrowest corridor north of Tel Aviv a width of less than 10 mi/17 km.

7. Approximate water levels, May 2013.

8. The best coverage of this topic is found in Zohary 1962.

9. The FAO AQUASTAT cites 1.78 bn m³ for Israel proper and 0.84 bn m³ for Palestine.

10. With a name change to the Israel Electric Corporation in 1961, it continues to serve the entire territory up to the present. As the company expanded, plants were built at coastal locations to facilitate the transport of imported fossil fuel from ship to plant.

11. Officially, shipment of oil through the pipeline ended with the outbreak of war in 1948, but unofficially it continued to be used for several more years.

12. One study reported that 13 percent of the Jews in Canada were Israeli emigrants. *Ynetnews,* Dec. 3, 2009.

13. Philippov 2008.

14. United Nations Development Programme, *Human Development Report 2013; Legatum Prosperity Index 2012,* www.prosperity.com/.

15. However, the religious authorities in recent years have increasingly (and controversially) demanded proof that prospective converts are practicing Orthodox Judaism; those individuals seeking citizenship through conversion are thus held to much stricter standards than other Jews.

16. The resentment of some Israelis toward the Russians, especially those who remain Christian, is obvious on virulent blogs like http://samsonblinded .org/blog/the-russians-have-come.htm and http:// jewishisrael.ning.com/profiles/blogs/tbn-christian -missionary. There may be as many as 250,000 Russians of nominal Christian background and unaccounted for in official statistics. See Sandro Magister, "The Invisible Christians of the Holy Land," http:// chiesa.espresso.repubblica.it/articolo/26006?eng=y.

17. Recent data have indicated that the gap between Ashkenazi, Mizrahi, and Palestinian birthrates has narrowed notably. For example, in 2012, the Jewish population grew by an estimated 1.8 percent and the Palestinian by 2.4 percent. The Haredim remain the fastest-growing group, as Haredi women still have total fertility rates more than three times higher than those of other Jews.

18. An early revelation by the New Historians was Morris 1989 (first published in 1987). Morris followed with several other critical writings, including "Falsifying the Record" in a 1995 issue of the *Journal of Palestine Studies.* Efraim Karsh led the attack on the New Historians in Karsh 1997 and 1999. For more by a New Historian, see Pappé 1999, 2004. Morris backtracks somewhat in Morris 2004. See also Morris 2008, 2009; and Thomas 2007. On the related issue of a growing critical reassessment of Zionism, see Pappé 1997 and Wurmser's 1999 defense of traditional Zionism. See also Sternhell 1998. For a lengthy analysis, see "The Battle over History," *Jerusalem Post* (North American edition), Nov. 5, 1999.

19. See Lustick 1980; Hazony 2000; Bisharah 2002; Efron 2003; Ghanem 2001; Goldscheider 2002; and M. Ellis 2002.

20. A recent attempt to measure the extent of social, economic, health, and educational gaps between Jewish and Arab Israelis was reported in *Jerusalem Post,* Nov. 19, 2009. The study, which is based on official statistics and indicates the gaps are growing, was carried out by Sikkuy, the Association for the Advancement of Civic Equality, and is available at www.sikkuy .org.il/english/en2007/sikkuy2007.pdf.

21. See Falah 1992 regarding "mirror housing" and other discrimination. For discrimination in employment, see the *Jerusalem Post,* Nov. 23, 1991. For Arab industries, see Schnell, Benenson, and Sofer 1999.

22. *Jerusalem Post,* Sept. 22, 2011.

23. Kahane 1981 voices a radical view but articulates demands by many Israeli extremists that all Arabs must be expelled from Eretz Yisrael. Kahane, who was formerly leader of the US extremist Jewish Defense League, was assassinated in New York in 1991.

24. *Ha'aretz,* Nov. 9, 2009; also see the website www.youtube.com/watch?v=UhFvfW3Pai0). The rabbi who wrote the book under discussion in this video, Yitzhak Shapiro, was hailed as a "Torah giant" on his recent death by Prime Minister Netanyahu. *Ha'aretz,* Apr. 23, 2013.

25. The estimate include Jews and Arabs in East Jerusalem; about 310,000 people were classified as "others," many of whom are immigrants from the former Soviet Union that do not religiously qualify to be considered Jewish.

26. *Ha'aretz,* Nov. 18, 2009. The group of women returned to pray at the wall the following month without incident and without the scroll (*New York Times,* Dec. 22, 2009; for example, see also *Forward,* Jan. 1, 2010), *Ha'aretz,* Oct. 19 and Dec. 15, 2012; *New York Times,* Feb 11, 2013; *Jerusalem Post,* April 11, 2013; *Guardian,* Apr. 25, 2013; and the website http:// womenofthewall.org.il/.

27. In 2011, it was estimated that a record high percentage of eligible males were exempted from military duties because of religious studies—13.8 percent. *Ha'aretz,* Oct. 31, 2012. Altogether, some sixty thousand men were enrolled in yeshivas.

28. *Yesh Atid* (There Is a Future) and *HaBayit HaYehudi* (The Jewish Home), respectively; together, they gained as many seats as *Likud-Yisrael Beiteinu,* the combined list headed by Prime Minister Netanyahu. *Ha'aretz,* Mar. 11 and 14, 2013.

29. A ministerial committee of the new government was reported to be preparing legislation that would cut exemptions to eighteen hundred annually by 2017 and to provide for jail sentences for religious draft dodgers. *Times of Israel,* May 11, 2013.

30. US Department of State 2009 and 2013.

31. For example, see *Asia News,* Dec. 16, 2009; *Jerusalem Post,* Nov. 27, 2009, and Mar. 9 and May 2, 2013; *Guardian,* Aug. 19, 2012; *al-Monitor,* Mar. 4, 2013; and *Ha'aretz,* Feb. 14, April 29, May 3, May 8, and May 14, 2013. In the past, the problem has been mostly with Haredi youth, but since 2011 West Bank settlers engaged in "price-tag" retribution attacks have

apparently been responsible. The authorities rarely seem able to identify and arrest any suspects.

32. The statement was signed, with unusual unanimity, by the patriarchs and bishops of all major Catholic, Orthodox, and Protestant sects. *Ecumenical News,* May 12, 2013, www.ecumenicalnews.com /article/holy-land-church-heads-denounce-easter -fracas-demand-full-access-22187; see also *Times of Israel,* May 9 and May 14, 2013.

33. *Ha'aretz,* Dec. 22, 2009.

34. See note 26. See also *Ha'aretz,* Jan. 23, 2013.

35. *Times of Israel,* May 9, 2013.

36. FAO, various issues. Still, the highly developed agricultural sector in the United States saw a 36 percent gain in per capita food output over the same period.

37. Israel's water problems are treated in many studies, but see Dillman 1989; Rogers and Lydon 1994; Hof 1997; Rouyer 2000; *Water for the Future* 1999; Soffer 1999; *Near East Report,* Sept. 6, 1999; Amery and Wolf 2000; Rowley 1999 and especially 2008; and Dolatyar and Gray 2000.

38. FAO AQUASTAT *Water Report,* no. 34, 2009, www.fao.org/nr/water/aquastat/water_res/index.stm.

39. *Ha'aretz,* Oct. 27, 2009; *BBC News,* Oct. 27, 2009, reporting on a study from Amnesty International (2009), which blames the Oslo Accords for institutionalizing Israeli control over Palestinian water resources.

40. Peretz Dar, quoted in *Ha'aretz,* Nov. 3, 2008.

41. See *Ha'aretz,* Aug. 2, 2009. South Africa later acknowledged that it had produced several nuclear weapons but that it had dismantled them at the time the apartheid regime ended; it then signed the Nuclear Nonproliferation Treaty. Several studies of Israel's role in South Africa's program are available: among them are Farr 1999 and McCreal 2006a, 2006b.

42. The revelations were widely covered in news media at the time. See Hersh 1991; Black and Morris 1991, 437–443; *Israel* Country Study 1990, 317–318; *Jerusalem Post* (North American edition), Dec. 3, 1999; and A. Cohen 1998. Imprisoned for eighteen years, Vanunu was released in April 2004 and called for the destruction of the Dimona reactor. Since his release, he has been refused permission to leave Israel or to have any contact with foreigners, although author Held had several long interviews with him and his brother in Jerusalem in 1997. See Y. Cohen 2003; *New York Times,* Apr. 20 and July 5, 2004; and *Telegraph* (London), Dec. 29, 2009.

43. For further details on Israel's arsenal, see www.nti.org/db/disarmament/country_israel.html.

44. Since Jordan ranks third in the world for bromine production and sixth in potash—from its Dead Sea facility—the chemical importance of this unique location is obvious.

45. *Ha'aretz,* Mar. 13, 2013; *Globes* [online], Mar. 10, 2013.

46. Egyptian–Saudi Arabian plans for a causeway and bridge spanning the Strait of Tiran would remedy this situation somewhat; as plans progressed, Israel expressed its concern in terms of the security of shipping to Elat (*Times* [London], May 4, 2007).

47. Opposition to the proposed route by environmental groups concerned that a rail line would damage the fragile ecology of the Negev may further delay any extension. *Ha'aretz,* Feb. 12, 2013.

48. *Ha'aretz,* Jan. 15, 2013.

49. *Ha'aretz,* Oct. 13, 2012.

50. Particularly with the Iraq National Congress and its founder, Ahmad Chalabi. See Chapter 14.

51. Former UK prime minister Tony Blair revealed in testimony he gave to a parliamentary inquiry in 2010 that when he and President George W. Bush were in the early planning stages in 2002 for the invasion, Israel was a major consideration and that "there may have been conversations that we had even with Israelis, the two of us, whilst we were there," as quoted in *Foreign Policy,* Feb. 8, 2010, www.foreignpolicy.com /posts/2010/02/08/I_dont_mean_to_say_I_told_you _so_ but.

52. Netanyahu in 1992 claimed Iran was three to five years from being able to produce a weapon, while then–foreign minister Shimon Peres predicted an Iranian weapon by 1999. *Salon,* Sept. 17, 2012, www.salon .com/2012/09/17/bibis_20_year_iran_warnings/.

53. *Bloomberg,* Mar. 22, 2013; *Daily Beast,* Mar 23, 2013.

54. *Ha'aretz,* July 9, 2012, and Apr. 20, 2013; *Jerusalem Post,* Apr. 25, 2013.

55. *EU Observer,* Feb. 27, 2013; *Ha'aretz,* Feb. 27, 2013.

56. For an interesting treatment advising Netanyahu on how to conduct relations with China, see the *Jerusalem Post,* May 6, 2013.

57. *Country Reports on Terrorism 2011,* US Department of State.

58. An estimated 225,000 West Bankers and 45,000 thousand Gazans arrived on the East Bank in the early months after the war.

59. D. Tsimhoni, "Demographic Trends of the Christian Population in Jerusalem and the West Bank, 1948–1978," *Middle East Journal* (Winter 1983).

60. The isolation of the geographic units in Area A was illustrated with the 2013 running of the first Palestinian Marathon: it was not possible to lay out a continuous 26.2-mi/42.2-km course for the race, so the runners did two circuits around the city of Bethlehem.

Guardian, Apr. 21, 2013; *Christian Science Monitor,* Apr. 21, 2013.

61. "The Humanitarian Impact on Palestinians of Israeli Settlements and Other Infrastructure in the West Bank." UN Office for the Coordination of Humanitarian Affairs–Occupied Palestinian Territory, www.ochaopt.org/documents/TheHumanitarianImpactOfIsraeliInfrastructureTheWestBank_full.pdf; *ynetnews.com,* Feb. 23, 2012; *Ha'aretz,* Feb. 18, 2012.

62. CIA *World Factbook 2012.*

63. *Ha'aretz,* Dec. 28, 2011; *Guardian,* Jan. 3, 2012.

64. Before the Israeli government withdrew the twenty-one settlements, about eighty-five hundred settlers, and the three thousand troops needed to protect them in 2005, some 30 percent of the Gaza Strip's area (and a similar share of its water) supported this tiny fraction of the region's population.

65. See, for example, *Guardian,* Oct. 15, 2012.

66. Benvenisti 1984, 19.

67. *Ha'aretz,* Mar. 28, 2013. Slightly more than half of these lands were still in the possession of the Civil Authority, and about 12 percent had been allocated to public utilities and local governments.

68. Nakhleh 1988; *Christian Science Monitor,* Sept. 14, 1992; *Water for the Future* 1999; Rouyer 2000; Soffer 1999; Ventner 1998; Frederiksen 2003; more recently, World Bank 2009; Amnesty International 2009; *Ha'aretz,* Jan. 17, 2012.

69. *Guardian,* Aug. 30, 2012

70. In 2011, UNRWA estimated that the reported rates understate the unemployment problem and stated that recent economic growth, though real, was insufficient to keep up with population growth. See "Labour Market Briefing: West Bank/Second Half 2010" and "Labour Market Briefing: Gaza Strip/Second Half 2010," Apr. 2011.

71. As quoted in many places—for example, *Jerusalem Post,* Jan. 11, 2008.

72. World Bank, "Building the Palestinian State: Sustaining Growth, Institutions, and Service Delivery," Apr. 2011. See also World Bank, "Stagnation or Revival: Palestinian Economic Prospects," Mar. 2012; and "Towards Economic Sustainability of a Future Palestinian State: Promoting Private Sector-Led Growth," Apr. 2012.

73. United Nations Development Programme, *Human Development Report 2013.*

74. USAID funds programs on the West Bank and Gaza. Since 1993, some $1.7 billion has gone to the economic growth, education, health, and water sectors. See www.usaid.gov/wbg/Programs.html.

75. Hamas and allies received 44.4 percent, Fatah 41.4 percent. Hamas won seventy-four seats, Fatah forty-five. Voting was on two levels—for party lists and for individual candidates. Hamas prevailed because, of the individual seats, it gained an overwhelming majority—forty-five to Fatah's seventeen.

76. *Guardian,* Apr. 13, 2013.

77. Nonmember observer status had been held only by the Holy See; it was also held by Switzerland before it opted for full membership in 2002.

78. Voting in favor were 138 countries, while 46 abstained or were absent. Only the Czech Republic, among the EU's members, opposed admission.

The reader is advised to consult this book's associated website (**www.middleeastpatterns.com**) for additional information on **Israel and Palestine**, such as historical time lines and chronologies of recent events, as well as essays on selected topics and various international economic, social, and political indicators.

14

Iraq

Modern Mesopotamia

KEY POINTS: Occupies core of ancient Mesopotamia, with "Iraq" a new name. Created 1920s as British mandate, soon became independent kingdom. Several groups combined in new state not compatible, especially Kurds and Sunni and Shii Arabs. Tigris and Euphrates Valleys long supported exceptional irrigation agriculture, and large oil resources discovered in 1926 and exploited to make Iraq major producer. Weak governments reduced achievement of high potential, then dictatorships, especially under Saddam Husayn, squandered wealth and manpower. Occupied by UN forces, especially US, 2003–2011. Now recovering, using oil wealth, but dissension among three main groups inhibits cooperative development to full potential.

IRAQ AND ITS ANTECEDENTS

Modern Iraq emerged as an independent kingdom in 1932, its boundaries and major institutions defined while it was a League of Nations mandate under British tutelage. In accordance with the 1920 San Remo talks and the 1923 Treaty of Lausanne, mandate Iraq incorporated three former Ottoman *vilayets* (provinces)—Mosul, Baghdad, and (partially) Basrah. With the exception of the western desert and the northeastern mountains, it was coextensive with the traditional geographical region of Mesopotamia (lit., "between the rivers"). The Arabic name *al-Iraq* had been applied geographically to lower Mesopotamia; for the first time, it designated a state occupying the basin.

The Two Rivers. Whether traditional Mesopotamia or modern state, Iraq is the land of two rivers, the Tigris and Euphrates, two of the three great rivers in the Middle East. The earliest known civilizations were born in this eastern limb of the Fertile Crescent as far back as the middle of the eighth millennium BCE. It served as the cultural hearth from which the first ideas of sedentary agriculture, domestication of animals, the wheel, writing, and urban development diffused westward to the Nile Valley and eastward to the Indus Valley. Evidence of the Neolithic Agricultural Revolution is scattered along the Zagros piedmont east of the lower Tigris, and ruins of the world's first cities have been uncovered between the two rivers south of Baghdad (see Chap. 3). Sumer, Akkad, Babylonia, and Assyria are part of

IRAQ

Long-form official name, anglicized: Republic of Iraq

Official name, transliterated: al-Jumhuriyah al-Iraqiyah

Form of government: multiparty republic with one legislative house (Council of Representatives)

Area: 167,618 mi^2/434,128 km^2

Population, 2011: 32,665,000; Literacy: 78.2%

Ethnic composition (%): Arab 70; Kurd 23; Turkmans/Azerbaijani 4; other 3

Religions (%): Muslim 96, of which Shia 62, Sunni 34; Christian (primarily Chaldean rite and Syrian-rite Catholic, and Nestorian) 3.2; other 0.8

Demography: Life expectancy—69.41 yr (M), 72.35 yr (F); Birthrate (per 1,000)—28.19; Fertility rate—3.58

GDP, 2011: $112.4 billion; purchasing power parity: $138.8 billion; per capita: $4,200

Currency: Iraqi Dinar (IQD), US$1 = 1,143 dinars; 1 IQD = $0.00085 (mid-May 2013)

Energy: oil—141.4 bn bbl; natural gas—111,520 bn ft^3 (new discoveries will increase oil and gas reserves appreciably); coal—nil

Main exports (% of total value, 2008): $63.7 billion (of which crude petroleum 97.1; refined petroleum 2.4; remainder 0.5)

Main imports (% of total value, 2008): $35.5 billion (of which machinery and transport equipment 38.5; assorted manufactured goods 27.2; mineral fuels and lubricants 9.8; oils and fats 6.4)

Capital city, 2009: Baghdad 5,751,000; other cities: Mosul 1,447,000; Irbil 1,009,000; Basra 923,000; Sulaymaniyah 836,000

Iraq's historical and cultural heritage, and their remains are a major element in the landscape, attracting modern scientists and tourists alike in peacetime.

Mesopotamia has been one of the major political and military power bases of the region (see "Power Cores," in Chap. 3). For two thousand years beginning with Cyrus the Great (ca. 540 BCE), it was usually linked with the adjacent plateau to the east, and the basin—rather than the plateau—was the core of the combined areas from the Persian Achaemenids to the Arab Muslims (who took all of Iraq by 638 CE). Twice in the half century after the death of Muhammad in 632, the Euphrates Valley saw conflict over succession

to the Islamic caliphate (see Chap. 4), resulting in the martyrdoms of Ali (d. 661) and his son Husayn (d. 680), whose tombs in al-Najaf and Karbala, respectively, are major Shii shrines.

Imperial Core. Only a province of the Damascus-based Umayyad Empire after 661, Mesopotamia supplanted Syria as the Muslim imperial heartland in 750. With the Abbasid Empire, it was the nucleus of cultural efflorescence under Caliph Harun al-Rashid (r. 786–809) of *Arabian Nights* fame. Decline followed this golden age; Baghdad was sacked by Mongols—first by Helagu, grandson of Genghis Khan, in 1258, then in 1393 by Tamerlane, who killed or enslaved the intellectual cadre of savants, artisans, writers, and engineers. Both conquerors destroyed the basin's extensive irrigation systems, built over millennia, as well as cities, craft shops, and trade routes. Ottomans and Persians later contended for the ravaged basin, with the Ottomans finally triumphing in 1638. Shifting political weight toward the west ended the long politico-economic symbiosis between the Mesopotamian Basin and the Iranian Plateau.

A Modern State. Since then, the Zagros piedmont has been the fault line of tension between Arab and Iranian culture and territorial aspiration. Ottoman rule continued until World War I, when British and Indian forces drove the Turks back into Anatolia, and Britain received the mandate over the newly created Iraq in the early 1920s.[1] In a complex and carefully crafted scheme for British hegemony over most of the Middle East, Colonial Secretary Winston Churchill and his team of regional specialists put Hashimite prince Faysal bin Husayn on the throne of the new kingdom. A plebiscite seemed to legitimize his accession, but resistance to Britain increased, with a bloody insurgency lasting several months. After a decade of tension, Iraq was the first mandate to gain independence, becoming a sovereign state (with British-imposed limitations) in 1932.

Before proceeding with the evolution of independent Iraq, we will first examine the land and the people that are the foundation of the contemporary state and on which post-2003 Iraq must rebuild.

REGIONAL PATTERNS

Cradled in the land segment of the great tectonic trough downfolded between the Arabian Platform to the southwest and the Zagros ridges to the northeast, Iraq has four distinct natural regions, with identifiable roles in Mesopotamian political and economic life: [1] western and southwestern desert plateau, [2] Jazirah or northern Mesopotamian upland, [3] southern Mesopotamian alluvial plain, and [4] northeastern uplands and Zagros Mountains (see circled numbers on Map 14.1).

[1] Western and Southwestern Deserts

Desert Battleground. This extension of the Syrian and Arabian Deserts west of the Euphrates Valley is the barren western third of Iraq—mostly the province of al-Anbar. The few thousand remaining Bedouin live in this least-populated and least-developed part of the country. It is a continuation of the Jordanian desert platform and the Arabian area of al-Widyan, furrowed with numerous east-west wadis and traversed by an express motorway from Baghdad to Amman, Aqabah, and Damascus. Rutbah developed from a dusty way station in the 1950s into a bustling highway junction, trading center, and military checkpoint. The highway was a vital link to Aqabah during the Iran-Iraq War and the aftermath of the 1991 Gulf War; it again became especially crowded as the ground link between Baghdad and Amman after 2003. Al-Anbar was constantly in world headlines in the mid-2000s, as it was a major focus of the mostly Sunni insurgency against the occupation.

Scuds and Insurgents. Farther east is al-Hajarah, a limestone platform strewn with flint and chert, crossed by the centuries-old caravan trail of the Darb Zubaydah for pilgrims to Mecca. Farther southeast is the sandy, gravelly plain of Dibdibah, cut by the prominent Wadi al-Batin, forming Kuwait's western boundary. The open desert to the west was used by US and coalition forces moving north from Saudi Arabia in February 1991 to outflank and encircle Iraqi forces in Kuwait. The far west gained a place in history when it was used to launch nearly eighty Scud missiles into Saudi Arabia and Israel in 1991; it saw intense conflict from 2003 until tribal leaders were able to establish social control by 2008.

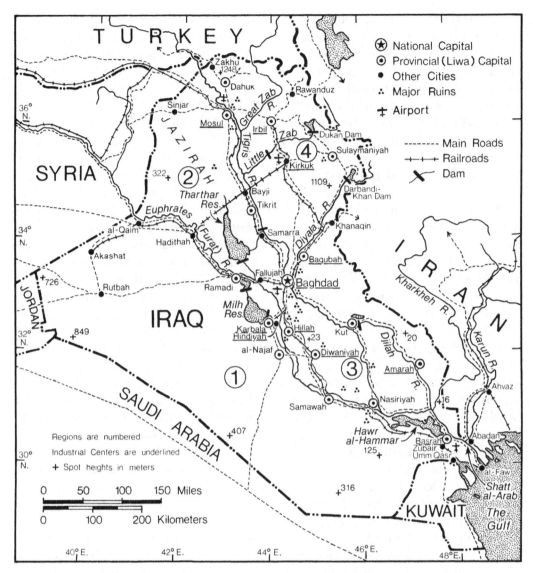

Map 14.1 General map of Iraq, with main cities, transportation, and antiquity sites. Circled numbers designate regions. The 33rd and 36th parallels marked UN "no-fly zones" after the 1990–1991 Gulf War, but the zones were irrelevant after March 2003.

[2] Jazirah: Northern Mesopotamian Upland

Most of the Jazirah upland, extending from Syria into central Iraq, is a desert plateau descending from 1,475 ft/450 m in the northeast to 260 ft/79 m at Baghdad. Except for the floodplains and the area northwest of Mosul, population in this broad interfluve is sparse.

In the extreme north, a prominent outlying ridge of the Zagros–Anti-Taurus folds, the Jabal Sinjar, extends westward from Mosul.

Potentials to Be Realized. The region is drained from north to south by the steep-banked Wadi Tharthar, emptying into the Tharthar Depression between the Tigris and

Euphrates. In the 1950s, an artificial lake was developed to hold Tigris floodwaters diverted by the Samara Barrage; any overflow moves southward into the Euphrates. North of Jabal Sinjar, the undulating plateau has rainfed cultivation of wheat and barley; modern Iraq's granary, it was vital to ancient empires. The plateau is bisected by the rail line to Baghdad. Jazirah development plans include significant irrigation like that in the Syrian part of the region. Mosul, on the site of Nineveh in the heart of ancient Assyria, has grown steadily over the past sixty years. Iraq's second-largest city, it lies on the Jazirah's northeast periphery but serves as the thriving main center for the northern third of the country; its heterogeneous religious and ethnic makeup is key to post-2003 political stability, but conflict among these groups remains a problem a decade after the invasion.

[3] Southern Mesopotamian Alluvial Plain

Essential Iraq. Southeastward from Ramadi on the Euphrates and south of Samarra on the Tigris is essential Iraq, a flat alluvial plain that in recent geological time grew Gulfward from silt dropped in the coalesced deltas of four rivers: primarily the Tigris and Euphrates, but also the Karkheh and Karun. The original shoreline is marked by a sinuous cliff that extends from Ramadi to near Samarra. Along and between the lower courses of the two rivers, ancient empires thrived, and ruins of the world's most ancient cities still stand; here is the cultural and economic core of modern Iraq. On the western edge lie the two most sacred Shii shrines, the tombs of the martyred Husayn in Karbala and of Ali—Husayn's father, the fourth caliph and first Shii imam—in al-Najaf.

Ancient and Modern Core. The northern end of the alluvial plain, where the rivers come closest, is one of the historically most strategic sites in the region. Its importance is shown in many ways: a major trade route has transited the narrow interfluve since Neolithic times; successive primate cities were here—Akkad (its exact site is uncertain), Babylon, Seleucia, Ctesiphon, and Baghdad; it has developed irrigation agriculture for centuries; and, of greatest current significance, its advantages and attractions for modern industry are many. Temperatures during the dry summers average 95°F/35°C in July, soaring in daytime to more than 122°F/50°C. Winter rainfall averages only 5.5 in/140 mm. Elevations and relief are low, heights ranging from 80 ft/25 m in the north to sea level in the south. Some areas beyond the natural levees are actually below sea level upstream from the still-growing deltas of the Karkheh and Karun Rivers debouching from Iran into the Shatt al-Arab. The long rivers have fed and formed this region for millennia; with modern agriculture, it also receives a concentration of fertilizers and other chemical runoff.

Baghdad. Modern Baghdad, heir to famed empires of the past, was founded in 754 as the Abbasid capital. Legendary in the *Arabian Nights* (see Chap. 3), it thrived for five hundred years before being sacked by the Mongols in 1258 and again in 1401, then sinking into five hundred years of obscurity. Resurgent as the capital of the new Iraqi state, contemporary Baghdad was, until 1991, and even until 2003, a vibrant, multifaceted city (Fig. 14.1). Major universities drew students from around the region, and Baghdad had one of the world's finest antiquities museums. Its unique collection was deplorably looted in April 2003 in the chaos following the US capture of the city, and it may never recover all its treasures.[2] Pre-2003 emphasis on militarism is seen in the capital's martial monuments. After US occupation, years of battles between foreign military and urban guerrillas and between competing Iraqi communal groups dramatically changed the city's character. Civil society has been slow to recover, and

Figure 14.1 Liberation Monument, Baghdad, by Iraqi artist Jawad Salim, erected following the 1958 revolution.

basic infrastructure is still inadequate for the urban population.

Marsh Country.   Southeast of Baghdad, the central interfluve was for centuries mostly wasteland or saline marshes because of the high water table and inadequate drainage. To punish the Madan—the Marsh Arabs—for sheltering dissidents, Saddam drained the marshes that sustained them. To reclaim the arable land and redistribute it to others, the government built the 350-mi/563-km Main Outfall Drain (MOD) in 1992 along the interfluve's axis (Map 14.2). Sometimes called the Third River, the MOD drained the central marshes and destroyed the Madan home-land.[3] On the same axis is a north-south ex-press motorway.

Traces of abandoned channels of the Tigris and Euphrates indicate radical course changes by the rivers, as do the sites of ancient cities— Kish, Nippur, Uruk, Ur, and others—no longer on riverbanks along which they originally lay. Both settlement and cultivation exhibit a rib-bon pattern, concentrated along the rivers and canals, strikingly green against the desert tan. Cultivation is due both to the proximity of water and, more important, to the better drainage on the low, broad natural levees built up on the banks during regular overflow. Where the stream has bifurcated, naturally or artificially, as the Euphrates has in several places below Hit, agriculture and settlement have been especially intensive.

Between Nasiriyah and the confluence of the Euphrates with the Tigris at Qurnah lies an area once unique—the marshes of the Madan, the Marsh Arabs, with their own unique culture. For thousands of years, they used reeds (*qasab*) growing there to build

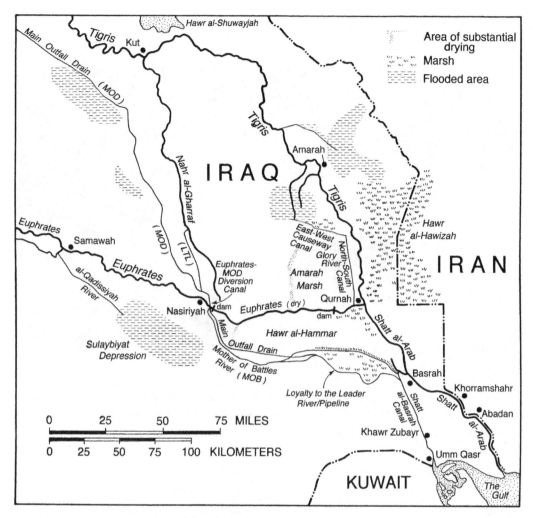

Map 14.2 Drainage schemes, southern Iraq, early 1990s. Some of the drainage was altered after March 2003, when some Marsh Arabs returned to their traditional homeland.

homes on artificial islands (Fig. 14.2A) and to construct their council houses (*mudhifs*) (Fig. 14.2B). They caught the plentiful fish; raised water buffalo for milk, yogurt, and hides; and moved between houses and villages in the high-prowed *mashhuf* (shown in Fig. 14.2A), poling through the shallows.[4] Shii fugitives took refuge in the marshes in 1991–1992, accelerating Saddam's determination to drain the marshes and corral the Madan. Their environment destroyed, thousands fled their homes, many to Iran; the remainder were forced into collective villages,

as were Kurds in the late 1980s. This remarkable group's millennia-old unique way of life disappeared for a decade, but some displaced Madan chose to return to their familiar but much degraded environs after 2003 when the levees holding back the water were cut, allowing some of the area to be reflooded. Although there has been significant progress in restoring the ecosystem, full recovery may not be possible, and it should be recalled that, for the Madan themselves, the marshes never offered more than the barest subsistence level of survival.[5] Efforts to extend education and

Figure 14.2 An all-reed village (*top*) and a typical *mudhif*, or all-reed council house (*bottom*), in the lower Euphrates marshes east of Nasiriyah, in 1979. The boat is a typical *mashuf.* Government drainage of the marshes in the early 1990s transformed the ecology of the area and displaced the marsh-dwelling Arabs (al-Madan) from their unique homes of many centuries. However, they began returning and restoring their ecology after mid-2003.

other services to the marshes have begun to rejuvenate cultural as well as ecological life.

East of the marshes and the Hawr al-Hammar, the confluence of the two rivers creates the Shatt al-Arab, which flows 100 mi/160 km to the Gulf. For much of the Shatt's length, a broad belt of date-palm groves paralleled both riverbanks, naturally irrigated by fresh water in an intricate canal network subject to the daily tides. Most of this productive landscape was obliterated during the Iran-Iraq War, leaving shattered stumps in place of great groves. Some replanting was undertaken in the 2000s.

Oilfields and Ports.   Midway up the Shatt on its west bank lies Basrah, Iraq's main port. This historic trade center is a Shii stronghold, and its older quarters attest to the longtime influence of India. Heavily damaged during the Iran-Iraq War, it was devastated again in 1991, with still further destruction during the Shii insurrection in 1991 and 1992, and yet more beginning in 2003. The government pointedly neglected it after 1991, leaving the once thriving port city shabby and intensifying animosity between southern Shia and central Sunni. Under the post-2004 Shii-majority government, Basrah has received more attention, damage has been repaired, and the airport and seaport have been refurbished.

However, tensions and disputes with both Iran and Kuwait over land, sea, and river boundaries that rub shoulders at the narrow head of the Gulf are still sticking points in bilateral relationships and development. Iraq argues that Kuwaiti plans for building the Mubarak Port Facility on Bubiyan Island will curtail the access of its Umm Qasr port to the open waters of the Gulf. In a tit-for-tat restriction of water, small dams have been built on both sides of the Iraq-Iran border, and disagreements of exact boundary lines have come close to conflict over oil wells (with Iran) and fishing and sea transit (with Kuwait).

Two of Iraq's main oil fields—Zubair and Rumaila—lie in the desert west of the Shatt.

Rumaila was the center of acrimonious dispute between Iraq and Kuwait in the 1980s. West of the Shatt's mouth is Iraq's narrow window on the Gulf, 36 mi/58 km of coastline at the lower end of the Iraq "funnel."

Borders as Problems.   In this strategic outlet to the sea is an increasing concentration of oil activity, heavier industries, and multiple port developments (discussed later in this chapter). It is also the focus of Iraq's historic grievance against Britain's delineation of boundaries in the early 1920s, and it is thus the basis of its territorial complaints and claims against Iran and Kuwait. From here it lashed out in 1980 and 1990. The details of its claims regarding the Shatt and the Kuwait boundaries are in Chapter 9 (in "The Iran-Iraq War" and "The Gulf Crisis"; also see also Map 9.5).

The physical geography of the extreme southeast is as much influenced by the southwestward-building deltas of the Karun and Karkheh Rivers as by the southeastward-building deltas of the Tigris and Euphrates and their common outlet, the Shatt al-Arab. The spread of these deltas has had three geomorphic effects: it has aided in filling in the head of the Gulf, it has forced the Tigris and Euphrates together into the Shatt, and it has simultaneously blocked some of the combined drainage and thus contributed to the formation of extensive and invaluable wetlands of lakes, intermittent lakes, and marshes—some below sea level—that sprawl over much of the deltas of the four rivers.[6] Some of these marshes were among those fully or partly drained during the 1990s.

[4] Northeastern Uplands and Zagros Mountains

Oilfields and Ethnic Divides.   Uplands, piedmont, and rugged mountains rising northeastward from the upper Tigris contrast sharply with most of the country. Except for a few prominent ridges near the Tigris, the highlands lie northeast of a line connecting Zakhu, Mosul, Irbil, Kirkuk, and Khanaqin. Elevations rise from 655 ft/200 m on the lower piedmont just east of the Tigris to 3,000 ft/915 m in the foothills, then reach 5,900 ft/1,800 m on the ridgetops and 11,808 ft/3,600 m on the Iranian border east of Ruwanduz. Lying at 36° N Lat, only 6° farther north than Iraq's torrid Gulf coast, the heights are blanketed with snow half the year and can be cool on summer nights. At lower elevations, Irbil and Kirkuk are hot in summer, but they get 15 in/385 mm of winter precipitation compared to Basrah's 6.5 in/164 mm. In the foothills and on the piedmont are Iraq's third- and sixth-largest cities: respectively, Irbil (sometimes Erbil or Arbil) with just over 1 million people, and Kirkuk, still a great oil center after eighty-seven years of production, with 750,000.

Both because of oil beneath it and because of its mixed ethnicity, Kirkuk has long been a center of contention, where dominant Sunni Arabs oppressed Sunni Kurds and Sunni and Shii Turkmans during the Baath regime and where tensions flared following resurgence of Kurdish influence after 2003. Kirkuk's resource wealth, combined with Kurdish anger over Saddam Hussein's expulsion and killing of Kurds throughout the region gave intensity to their demands to control the city. Sunni and Shii Arabs and Turkmans, and Christian Assyrians, largely consider the city part of Arab Iraq. Rights over oil resources and contracts continue to cause conflicts between the Kurdish regional government based in Irbil and the national government in Baghdad.

Well up into the mountains is Sulaymaniyah, competing with Irbil as a Kurdish political center, its population of 825,000 ranking fifth in Iraq.

Highlands. Ridges in the far north extend east-west, following the trend of folding in the Taurus and Anti-Taurus Mountains, whereas tectonic trends south of Ruwanduz turn south-east and thence combine with the dominant Zagros folds. The same forces that created the ridges and linear foothills also produced the subsurface structures in which petroleum and gas accumulated. Several streams follow deep gorges parallel to the folds in their upper courses and then cross the grain of the ridges to join the Tigris: the Khabur, Great Zab, Little Zab, Udhaym, and Diyala. The highest ridges contain Iraq's only forests, some quite extensive, preserved by the area's isolation and ruggedness. Most of the slopes permit only grazing, lower and gentler slopes support fruit and nut trees, and the broad valley bottoms are intensively cultivated. Access to the heights is limited, and passes through the Zagros into Iran are few. Most famous of these routes is the Ruwanduz River Gorge (Fig. 14.3), with the spectacular Spilak Pass and Ali Beg Gorge west of Ruwanduz and the Shinak Pass near the border.

Some of Iraq's earliest and largest hydraulic projects were developed in the 1950s in these well-watered, rugged mountain areas, where deep gorges and solid rock offered ideal sites for construction. The Dukan Dam and its large reservoir were built on the upper Little Zab, the Darbandikhan Dam and reservoir on the upper Diyala, and, later, the Dibs Dam on the Little Zab. The Great Zab's potential was finally harnessed in the late 1980s with the construction of a large dam in its upper course.

Kurdistan Region. Apart from its landforms, the northeast is also noteworthy for its non-Arab populations, for its underground reservoir of hydrocarbons, and as a political-cultural buffer and frontier. It is the Iraqi segment of Greater Kurdistan, the much larger area through which Kurdish tribesmen normally move freely across Iraq, Iran, Turkey, and Syria. With their main centers in Sulaymaniyah and Irbil, Iraqi Kurds are overwhelmingly the dominant group in the area (see Chap. 4). They have used the ruggedness

Figure 14.3 Western entrance to the dramatic and strategic Ruwanduz (sometimes Rawanduz or Rawandoz) River Gorge, northeastern Iraq. The gorge carries the main road from Irbil to Iran—the only route linking the two countries through the rugged northern Zagros Mountains.

and isolation of the elevated Zagros as their fortress and refuge in their successive wars for autonomy—including in 1991–1992. Under the Iraqi constitution of 2005, the Kurdistan Regional Government (KRG) controls the provinces of Irbil, Dahuk, and Sulaymaniyah. In the lower hills are many Turkmans and smaller numbers of Assyrians, Sarliyyas, Yazidis, and others.

POPULATION AND PEOPLES

Population Patterns

Iraq's estimated population of 31.1 million in 2012 was more than six times what it was in 1950. Maps 4.2 and 14.3 and Figure 4.1 show that population is found in linear patterns along the banks of rivers and canals on the plains but is more generally distributed in the

villages and towns of the northeastern uplands and mountains.

The greatest single concentration of population, about half the total, begins north and west of Baghdad, sprawls westward and southward across the mid-Iraq interfluve—encompassing the well-publicized "Sunni Triangle"—and then follows the Euphrates and its branches along the west side of the alluvial plain to Samawah. A highly mixed mélange of ethnic and religious groups, Greater Baghdad has almost one-fifth of Iraq's population; the metropolitan area is still home to a variety of ethnic and religious groups, but many of the city's once mixed neighborhoods have fallen victim to "ethnic cleansing," as the long chaos forced scores of thousands to seek safety and security with their own groups. West of Baghdad is Fallujah, a major center of

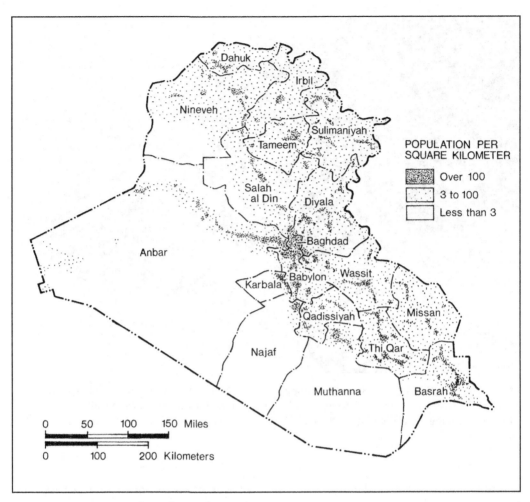

Map 14.3 Provinces and population density, Iraq.

Sunni insurgency and the site of a brutal weeklong offensive against insurgents in November 2004. Farther south are the Shii shrine cities of al-Najaf and Karbala, each with about a half-million people; Hillah, one of the main date-producing centers in Iraq; Diwaniyah; and, farthest south, Nasiriyah.

Secondary concentrations are found (1) in the south, where population in Basrah, the marshes between Basrah and Nasiriyah, and Amarah fluctuated wildly during the three wars of 1980–1988, 1990–1991, and 2003 and afterward; (2) around Mosul in the north; and (3) in the northeastern piedmont, with its twin nodes of Irbil and Kirkuk, and the outlying city of Sulaymaniyah.

Ethnolinguistic Groups

Some groups within Iraq's borders have maintained their separateness for many centuries, to the extent that group identities compete with Iraqi nationalism. The complexity of the country's ethnic and religious mosaic, along with the crucial significance of that complexity, has been emphasized by political geographers and other regional specialists for decades. The true relevance of the intricacy became abundantly clear after

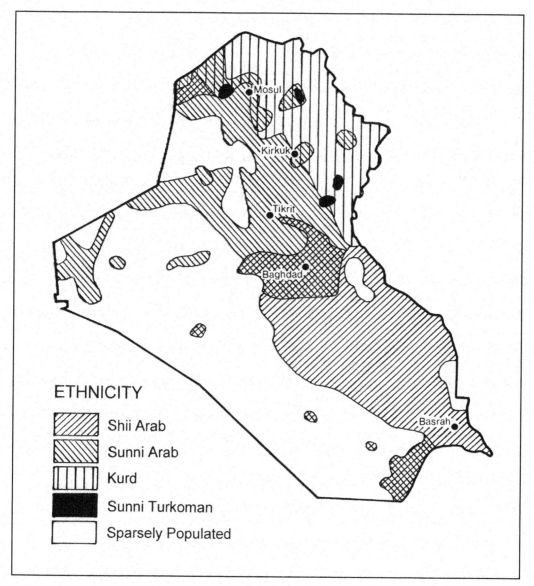

ETHNICITY

- Shii Arab
- Sunni Arab
- Kurd
- Sunni Turkoman
- Sparsely Populated

Map 14.4 Pattern of major ethnic groupings, Iraq.

2003. Although the primary ethnic conflict has been between Arab and Kurd, now more significant is the religious rift between Sunni and Shii, discussed below. Smaller ethnic minorities—Turkman, Assyrian, Armenian, Yazidi, Lur and smaller Persian-speaking groups, Mandaean, and others—remain distinctive but, except for the Assyrians between the world wars and some of the Persians in the 1980s, have not been actively separatist or antinational.

The geographic pattern of the three large adversarial groups in Iraq has always constituted an issue crucial to the country's internal and external policies (Map 14.4). With the highly nationalistic Kurds concentrated in the north and the restive Shia in the south, the minority Sunni elite in between kept control of the government and economy. This three-cornered conflict governed coalition actions against Iraq for the decade following 1991. Indeed, the brutal Sunni suppression of the Shia in the south and of the Kurds in the north in the early 1990s prompted the establishment of the southern and northern no-fly zones (see "Kurds" below). Intercommunal tensions became the single greatest problem facing the US-led occupation after April 2003 and the succession of independent Iraqi governments.

Arabs

Composing about 70 percent of the population, Arabs have been the largest ethnic group numerically for a thousand years. During most of that period, they have considered themselves the eastern bulwark against non-Arab influences. Iraqi Arabs actually represent a biological mixture of many peoples over thousands of years.

Although perhaps only about a fourth of the Arabs are Sunni, they dominated politics and the economy for centuries. Since Shia have long been associated with Iran and Iranians, Sunnis have considered themselves the "loyalists," with strong ties to other (and mostly Sunni) Arab countries. Over the centuries when Sunni Ottomans were in control, Shia became alienated, isolated through endogamy, and deprived through decreased cultural and economic opportunities. The majority of the Kurds are also Sunni, so that the combined Sunni groups make up a bit more than a third of the total population.

Shiism, based on Ali's faction, emerged in southern Iraq during the seventh century. Growing among the tribes especially since the eighteenth century, its strength there has continued up to the present time; Iraqi Shia are of the Imami or Twelver branch, like those in Iran. The Shia are some 60 percent of the population, mainly in the south and around the Baghdad area (Shii Turkmans are centered in Kirkuk). The political roles of Shii

Arabs, Sunni Arabs, and Sunni Kurds after 2003 are examined below.

Kurds

The Kurds, mostly Sunni and over a fifth of the population, live primarily in the northeast uplands and Zagros Mountains—Iraqi Kurdistan (see Chap. 4); they are also well represented in Baghdad. After 1927, petroleum development around Kirkuk, on the Kurdish periphery, prompted a new interaction between plain and mountain. The government and the Kurds never reached accommodation, leading to a seemingly unending cycle of internecine conflicts from the mandate period onward—in 1919–1930, 1943–1946, 1961–1970, 1974–1975, during the Iran-Iraq War, the late 1980s, and then the fateful months in 1991–1992 after the Gulf War, when more than 1 million Kurds fled military attacks before the no-fly rules were imposed.

The last two cycles were unique. The first was a climax to bitter fighting along the Iranian border in early 1988, when local Kurdish *peshmerga* guerrillas supported an Iranian attack inside Iraq. As Iraqi forces had on previous occasions when they were seriously threatened, they used poison gas both in the battle and against civilians in the Kurdish town of Halabjah, where several thousand died.[7]

From Repression to Autonomy. The government then razed Kurdish villages, expelling thousands of Kurds into the northern region, resettling others in cement-block collective settlements, and "disappearing" thousands whose bodies were exhumed from mass graves after 2003, expecting this to solve the Kurdish problem definitively.[8] During Iraq's venture into Kuwait, Kurds took advantage of the situation and sought control of their "homeland." Iraqi forces using helicopter gunships and bombers responded ferociously after withdrawing from Kuwait, driving more than 1 million to seek safety in Turkey and Iran. Through UN resolutions, the United

States and Britain declared an air exclusion, or no-fly zone, for fixed-wing aircraft north of the 36th parallel and enforced it until the 2003 invasion.

Protected by the zone, Kurds held elections in 1992, setting the stage for autonomy. In a power struggle between the two major groups, the Barzani faction allied at one point with Saddam against the Talibani faction, supported by Iran. This internecine conflict left two entities, one centered in Sulaymaniyah, the other in Irbil; their common enemy in Baghdad drew them back together. After establishing an autonomous area in the 1990s, even issuing their own currency, the Kurds were in a strong position when the Baathi regime collapsed. They assisted US forces during the fighting, working cautiously with them during the occupation and, in some cases, taking revenge against their erstwhile Sunni Arab oppressors.

Postinvasion.   By 2003, the Kurdish region was the fief of a coalition of two tribe-based parties—the Kurdish Democratic Party (KDP—Barzanis) and the Patriotic Union of Kurdistan (PUK—Talabanis). The Iraqi constitution, ratified in 2005, was federal in nature; the Kurdistan Regional Government (KRG— recognized ad interim under the Coalition Provisional Authority [CPA]) then reconstituted itself as a federal region within the republic, officially composed of three provinces.[9] Also in 2005, elections gave the coalition and its allies 104 of the 111 seats in the Kurdish National Assembly (KNA) and chose its candidate, Massoud Barzani, as president. Since then, the KRG has sometimes acted as a state in federal Iraq and sometimes as an almost independent entity. Controversial contracts were signed with foreign oil companies with little regard for Baghdad's theoretical authority, the KRG agenda of annexing parts of Kirkuk and three other provinces outside its official boundaries was forwarded, and elements of the Kurdistan Workers Party (the PKK of

Turkey—see Chap. 20) were given de facto asylum. Some PKK militants conducted cross-border raids into Turkey, embroiling the central government in a seriously inflammatory situation with its powerful northern neighbor. Turkish bombing of PKK sites in KRG territory, though condemned by Barzani, did not hinder the development of direct trade between Turkey and the KRG.[10] Recently, the civil war in Syria has stirred the Kurds in that country to seek autonomy, and they have established links with the KRG in their efforts.

Although these policies and others of similarly nationalistic derivation were undoubtedly popular among most Kurdish voters, the KDP-PUK coalition's growing reputation for cronyism and corruption was less so: in 2009, elections for the KNA saw an impressive showing by a newcomer party, Goran—the Movement for Change List—which garnered 23 percent of the vote to the disadvantage particularly of the PUK. The presence of a more vocal opposition in the KNA did mean that when young Kurds demonstrated against the KRG in February 2011 in the wake of the Arab Spring, they found support in Goran against KDP-PUK charges that they were seditionists and anarchists. Goran and two independent Islamic parties also criticized the coalition government for postponing elections in the KRG's three constituent provinces.

While the Iraqi Kurdistan Region has had greater security and economic growth than other Iraqi regions, it fares worse than the rest of the country in measures of democracy, press freedom, and transparency. Local frustration with limited political participation continues to increase support for alternative parties like Goran and also Islamist parties. In 2013, a report published by an international NGO, Human Rights Watch, demanded an end to the KRG repression of opposition figures and journalists.[11]

The minority Fayli Kurds (perhaps a tenth of the Kurdish population) are not associated with the KRG but vote primarily for their own Shii parties. Living mostly in Diyala province along the Iraq-Iran border and in Baghdad, they have been persecuted by both countries and often denied citizenship by each. In the 1970s, Saddam Husayn expelled more than one hundred thousand of them to Iran. Despite their Kurdish ethnicity and because their struggle with the Baathi regime was outside the KDP-PUK context, they have benefited little from the increased status of the KRG.

Turkmans

Making up at least 2 percent of the Iraqi population, Turkmans (sometimes Turkmens or Turkomen) live in the piedmont and foothills of the northeast. Settled between the Arabs of Mesopotamia and the Kurds of the Zagros, they are numerous in both Kirkuk and Irbil as well as in piedmont villages. They are both Sunni and Shia, live in agricultural villages, and are middle class, as well as constituting part of the urban population. Their ethnicity gives them an influential external protector that shares their serious concerns about Kurdish dominance—Turkey.[12]

Other Ethnic Minorities

Smaller minorities include Persian-speaking Shia with strong ties to Iran, many of whom were expelled to Iran in the early 1980s when they voiced pro-Iranian sentiments. Their strongholds were the shrine cities and neighborhoods of Karbala, al-Najaf, and al-Kazimiyah (near Baghdad), as well as Basrah. Another Persian-speaking group, the Lur, are concentrated in tribal villages near the Iranian frontier.

Jews numbered 118,000 in the 1947 census but were probably more numerous, since in 1951 about 121,000 emigrated to Israel and several thousand went to Iran. They generally had lived in urban areas, often as merchants, professionals, and government officials in Baghdad. A few thousand remained in Iraq in the mid-1980s, but most of them emigrated

later. After 2003, a few Iraqi Jews went to Israel from Iraq, while small numbers of Israelis and other Jews filtered into Iraq, especially in the north and in Baghdad.

The small group of Mandaeans—also called Sabians or (inaccurately) John the Baptist Christians—are an interesting ancient people of uncertain origin who are differentiated primarily by their Gnostic religion but also are physically distinct (see Chap. 4). The heterodox Yazidis, kin to groups in Syria and Turkey, live in villages along the Jabal Sinjar west of Mosul; they are generally considered to be ethnic Kurds, but many of them stress their separate identity. Their situation has become precarious because of their (erroneous) reputation as devil worshipers: in 2007, two Yazidi villages were attacked by Islamist militants.[13] The less numerous Shabak community has been slightly less threatened than the Yazidis, but nonetheless has been targeted by militants. The small Bahai community, the members of which were of various ethnicities, was much persecuted under the Baath regime; after 1975, they were forcibly registered as Muslims.

Christian Minorities. Christians have had a strong presence from early in the Christian era. The earliest and largest of the Christian groups are the Assyrians, numbering more than a half-million, distributed from the Syrian border to Irbil and Kirkuk, as well as in Baghdad; religiously, they are divided into Nestorian and Chaldean (Catholic) sects. Armenians number about twenty thousand and are usually urban dwellers. Christians have come under siege for their general liberalism (their shops sell alcohol, for example), beginning with the months of insecurity following the invasion, and Christian emigration has been very high since 2003. The kidnapping and murder of the Chaldean archbishop of Mosul in February 2008 and the seizure of a Baghdad church by militants in October 2010 leading to the deaths of more than forty parishioners, plus incidents almost too numerous to be counted, have intensified the fears of remaining Christians. Still, Christian leaders have called for constitutional protections for minorities, rather than the formation of special police or military forces charged with providing security.[14] Some Christians have relocated to the more stable Kurdish-controlled area, while thousands of others have fled the country. Since 2003, Iraq's Christian community has been far more than decimated, losing perhaps half its members by the early 2010s.

MONARCHY, REPUBLIC, DESPOTRY, AND BEYOND

Monarchy Established, Overthrown

Under British tutelage and a Hashemite dynasty, mandate Iraq developed only slowly, partly because of constraints imposed on oil exploration and production. Even after independence in 1932, British officials continued in key positions.[15] The first king, Faisal I, died in 1933, and succession went to his twenty-one-year-old son, Ghazi, who in turn died in a motor accident in 1937.[16] His only son, a three-year-old, then took the throne as Faisal II, under the regency of his uncle Prince Abd al-Ilah. A pro-German coup by Iraqi military officers in 1941 initially deposed the regent, but was put down by a returning British force, which remained in the country until 1947. During the 1950s, a degree of economic progress was achieved with the formation of the Development Board to direct the investment of oil revenues that had increased after a new agreement in 1952 between the government and the Iraq Petroleum Company. The autocratic pro-Western prime minister, Nuri al-Said, linked Iraq with the West and led his country into the Baghdad Pact (see "Regional Linkages," in Chap. 8) as the only Arab member. At the time, Nasserist Arabism was sweeping the Middle East and inspiring Iraqi nationalists to resist Western ties, and the

Baghdad Pact was a move squarely against Nasser's view of Arab unity. Consequently, a military coup d'état violently overthrew the Iraqi monarchy in July 1958, and the young and still inexperienced king, along with most of his family and closest advisers (including Nuri al-Said), was murdered (in October 2012, the governor of Baghdad called on the government to apologize for the massacre).[17] The coup leader, General. Abd al-Karim Qasim (Kassem), established a republic that, born in brutality, has since experienced more than six decades of intermittent violence.

Unstable Republic

The often-chaotic Qasim regime fell, in turn, to a coup in 1963 that first brought power to the Baath (Arab Renaissance) Party; it was ousted within months by nationalist army officers. Coup attempts in 1965 and 1966 failed before the party decisively regained power in July 1968. It remained dominant, with strongman Saddam Husayn increasingly in control until he seized the presidency in 1979, holding the office until April 2003. (Baath control in Syria also began in 1963; after 1966, the party split into two feuding factions—Syrian and Iraqi.)

From the moment of the mandate's imposition, Iraqis had felt marginalized and deprived of their proper place in the Arab sun. Resisting mandate status, they clamored for independence and afterward continued to object to British influence until the monarchy was overthrown in 1958 when, however unstable the government, they finally felt they had achieved real independence. They possessed a rich culture and often embraced political and cultural pluralism, regardless of the uncertain political situation in their country. Over the past eighty years, Iraqis have pursued many avenues to demonstrate political potency and to offset perceived external denigration. As Chapter 9 (in the section "The Gulf Crisis") explained, Iraq had long asserted its claim to Kuwait and a larger share of the

Gulf coast. For forty years, the government accused oil companies of acting against Iraqi interests—not a groundless charge—and later led the successful organization of OPEC. When Britain withdrew from the Gulf in 1971, Iraq promptly asserted its claim to be the new hegemon. However, when challenged by Iran, it prudently yielded to its more powerful neighbor, then under the shah and supported by the United States. But these claims served notice of the ambitions that led to war against Iran and the invasion of Kuwait.

Saddam Husayn

During the 1970s, prevailing high oil prices benefited Iraq, and the country achieved marked progress. When the Baath formally selected Saddam Husayn as president in 1979, Iraq was personified in the most ambitious and aggressive leader since its creation. Within a year, it was at war with Iran—the first of his several major miscalculations; by 1988, it had suffered not only hundreds of thousands of casualties but also the destruction of much of its new infrastructure. During the war, it received billions of dollars in aid from Gulf oil states, as well as assistance and encouragement from the United States; some sectors of the economy actually advanced during the 1980s. After the cease-fire, Iraq rebuilt and rearmed, borrowing tens of billions of dollars, with future oil production as collateral.

In August 1990, Saddam once again miscalculated and invaded Kuwait. When he refused to withdraw and coalition aircraft attacked Iraqi targets, the damage inflicted on Iraq's main cities and infrastructure during just a few weeks exceeded that dealt by Iran over eight years. In a decadelong stalemate with the UN—and specifically with the United States—over conditions for lifting sanctions, Iraq fell to its lowest standard of living since the 1920s. It appeared that, by choice, the leadership preferred pride and penury over perceived submission and prosperity. The cat-and-mouse game that the regime played with the UN Special Commission (UNSCOM) was later revealed to be mainly a device to keep Iran and Israel guessing as to its actual military capabilities, which in fact were largely imaginary. UNSCOM inspections were authorized by UN Resolution 687 of April 1991, setting the terms for the cease-fire between Iraq and the coalition. Nevertheless, when UN inspectors returned in 2002 after a four-year hiatus, Iraq's responses over several months were declared to be inadequate by the UN. The US administration under George W. Bush had decided that the putative weapons of mass destruction (WMD) were a casus belli. A US ultimatum was predictably rejected, and coalition attacks began on March 20, 2003 (see "Operation Iraqi Freedom," in Chap. 9).[18]

Invasion, Liberation, Occupation

Beginning with the coalition's formal declaration of the end of major combat activity seven weeks later on May 1, Iraq entered the most crucial period of its existence as an independent state under an occupation authority that was largely unprepared for whatever followed military victory. Iraqis toppled dozens of self-aggrandizing monuments to Saddam, and thousands of his life-size portraits were torn from their mountings; hundreds of his palaces, government buildings, and party offices had been reduced to bombed-out hulks. While occupation troops stood by, rioters and looters seemed to rule the day in Baghdad and other cities. The Coalition Provisional Authority (CPA) was established to exercise power with US/coalition military backing, the Iraqi army was disbanded, and thousands of government employees and teachers were dismissed for their pro forma Baath Party memberships. These decisions have since been identified as critical errors. The CPA appointed twenty-five Iraqis to a temporary Governing Council (GC), including many exiles with close ties to the invading forces but little local support.

With the old regime ousted, many Iraqis who had lost family members sought help in finding remains in the mass burials known to exist. Tens of thousands of bodies were discovered, and human rights groups estimated that as many as three hundred thousand missing Iraqis had been executed by the Mukhabarat, the Baathist intelligence service.

Insurgency.   A growing insurgency used increasingly destructive devices, from AK-47s, mortars, and rocket-propelled grenades to suicide bombers and car and truck bombs; these deadly vehicles destroyed the Jordanian Embassy and the UN headquarters in Baghdad in August 2003 and killed hundreds in al-Najaf, Karbala, and Baghdad. Improvised explosive devices (IEDs) caused hundreds of roadside blasts, unnerving military and civilian drivers alike. In December, Saddam was found in a small underground hiding place near his clan stronghold of Tikrit. After a dramatic trial, he was executed in late 2006.

With the gradual restoration of political and economic structures interrupted and sometimes offset by sabotage and attacks, Iraq moved haltingly toward revival. Despite its low level of credibility, the GC drew up a Transitional Administrative Law, and the CPA surrendered state sovereignty to the appointed Iraqi Interim Government (IIG), replacing the GC on June 28, 2004. The UN had already authorized ending the formal occupation. The IIG displayed some signs of exercising sovereignty, although it was obviously dependent on the coalition for security and solvency.

Regaining Autonomy

Elections.   The caretaker IIG scheduled national and local elections for January 2005, the first of several political events in a momentous year. Despite multiple daily insurgent attacks on Iraqi and coalition forces, preparations for the first free elections in Iraq in fifty years were not disrupted. Even a quadrupled level of

assaults on election day did not prevent fairly successful polling, as 8.45 million voters—59 percent of those eligible—cast their ballots. As expected, the Shii list won the largest number of seats (140 with 47 percent of the vote) in the 275-member Iraqi National Assembly (INA) and the Kurds the next largest (75 with 25 percent). With many Sunnis boycotting the polling, the Iraqi List—hoping to draw on Sunni voters—won only 40 seats and 14 percent.

Constitution.   The new parliament was charged with drafting a permanent constitution to replace the transitional law by August 15, arranging for a national vote on the constitution on October 15, and—if it was approved—conducting elections for a full-term government on December 15. It was also to choose an interim president and two vice presidents, who would decide on a prime minister. These offices were split among Kurds (president), Sunni Arabs (one vice president plus parliament speaker), and Shia (one vice president and prime minister). Overwhelming Kurdish and Shii support gave 79 percent approval to the constitution; it provided for (but did not require) a federal structure, thus institutionalizing the KRG. The proposal to divide the rest of Iraq into two more states—in the south a predominantly Shii entity and in the center one with a Sunni majority—remains unrealized, with strong Sunni opposition and less than united support from the Shia.

Nuri al-Maliki.   The December 2005 election for the Iraqi Council of Representatives saw notably more Sunni voters—more than 70 percent of eligible voters took part; the Shii and Kurdish lists lost seats (securing 128 and 53, respectively), a new Sunni coalition emerged (59 seats), and the more secular cross-community Iraqi List declined (25 seats). Losing their majority, the Shii parties allied with the Kurds and eventually selected

Nuri al-Maliki as prime minister; his cabinet also included some members of Sunni parties.[19] But for the March 2010 elections, al-Maliki broke his link with the main Shii bloc and campaigned at the head of a coalition, State of Law, that included Shii, Kurdish, Christian, and secular elements. Heading another coalition, Iraqiya, was former prime minister Ayad Allawi.

These two factions each won an almost identical number of parliamentary seats, and between them they constituted a majority. The process of forming a government, however, took almost nine months, and the resulting cabinet included both leading parties, along with Kurdish and more exclusively Shii groups. While this coalition was inclusive, al-Maliki forged strong links with the other Shia (and with Iranian supporters), and within a year the Sunni groups began to boycott both the government and parliament. In December 2011, the government issued an arrest warrant for the Sunni vice president, Tareq al-Hashemi, accusing him of instigating terror attacks against non-Sunnis. He fled to the Kurdish-controlled north and eventually left the country. In 2012, it became increasingly clear that the hoped-for inclusiveness in a broad-based government was impossible under al-Maliki; instead, he was negotiating with smaller parties and individual members of larger parties to form a government backed by a simple majority. The reaction among his opponents, especially among Sunni Arabs, might have been predicted: a resumption of civil disturbances in those areas where they are most numerous. Local elections in twelve of the eighteen governorates (the Kurdish region, predominantly Sunni areas, and Kirkuk polls were to be held at some later date) in 2013, the first since the US withdrawal, produced mixed results. Al-Maliki's list came in first but gained fewer seats than in the last round; the Shii vote was split among three major parties, and the Allawi list came in a distant fifth.[20]

The multitude of elections since 2004 has sometimes seemed confusing to both Iraqis and foreigners; they have not been totally devoid of controversy, but they have generally been free of the electoral fraud that was so apparent in the 2009 pollings in Afghanistan and Iran.

The Cost of War.   On the military side, the situation gradually improved in the late 2000s, but uncertainty about internal security remained after the US withdrawal. What the Bush administration in 2003 thought would be a short campaign followed by the emergence of a stable, democratic Iraq supported by oil exports turned into the United States' third-longest war (after Vietnam and Afghanistan), which by withdrawal in December 2011 had cost nearly 4,500 American lives and about $1 trillion in direct outlays (and trillions more in future budget obligations). For Iraq, the loss was far worse, though much harder to quantify with precision: quite likely the toll has been more deaths than the estimated 500,000 suffered in the war with Iran and more than the hundreds of billions of dollars in economic damage than was inflicted between 1980 and 2003. The rise in terrorist activity against both foreign troops and, even more, against Iraqi civilians and security forces was devastating. In surveying terrorism worldwide in the decade following 9/11, the Institute for Economics and Peace calculated a new measure in 2012—the Global Terrorism Index—to rank the countries most affected by terrorist activities; not surprisingly, Iraq topped the list of 158 states.[21]

Uprooted Iraqis.   Nine years after the invasion, as many as 4 million Iraqis remained dislocated from their former homes: some 2.5 million were internally displaced persons (IDPs), and at least 1.5 million had left the country as refugees.[22] The IDP problem has intensified ethic/sectarian conflicts—for example, in Kirkuk and in many Baghdad and

Mosul neighborhoods—and the government ministry tasked with mitigating the situation has been perennially underfunded. The refugees increasingly become a burden in those countries that offered sanctuary to the largest numbers of them—Syria and Jordan (see Chaps. 10 and 12), and the situation of Iraqis in Syria became increasingly precarious as that country struggled in civil war.

The Surge. "The New Way Forward" (commonly referred to as "the Surge") undertaken in the spring of 2007 was essentially a counterinsurgency campaign with limited objectives; on the whole, it seemed to accomplish these objectives, especially in Baghdad and in areas where units related to al-Qaida had been strong.[23] However, some high-ranking military observers have given more credit to the fact that al-Qaida brutality finally had led to the Sunni leadership in al-Anbar province breaking with them and then cooperating with the counterinsurgency program.[24]

In February 2009, the Obama administration decided that the situation allowed a phased drawdown of US troops with Iraqi forces taking charge of urban areas by mid-year, a US transition from combat and counterinsurgency to training and support by August 2010, and a redeployment of all US forces by the end of 2011.

The Arab Spring

Two years after the onset of what came to be called the Arab Spring in Tunisia, it might seem that somehow Iraq has been bypassed by the events that occurred throughout the region. This is not entirely true: in February and March 2011, crowds of young Iraqis demonstrated in Baghdad's own Tahrir Square, protesting against government corruption, unemployment, and the continued lack of basic services. Similar protests, with even larger turnouts, took place in the Kurdish north. In both cases, the protesters were met with repression from security forces and, as happened

also in Syria, government-sponsored mobs; strictly enforced curfews were imposed. Both the federal and the Kurdish governments dismissed the demonstrators as mere rioters and anarchists, claiming that Iraq already had a democratically elected government. This may have reduced any international support for the protests, but there was no groundswell of support within the country, either.[25] Still, al-Maliki's government slowly weakened as the non-Shii elements in the population became increasingly disenchanted, and in late 2012 Sunni demonstrators increasingly took to the streets.

As the tenth anniversary of the invasion approached, the threat of sectarian civil war was renewed. Partly due to a spillover effect from the deteriorating situation in Syria, a larger factor was growing Sunni dissatisfaction with the al-Maliki regime.[26] Growing violence revived the worst-case scenario of increased bloodshed, leading to outright civil war and/or division of the country along sectarian and ethnic lines.[27] In the same month marking the fall of Baghdad's tenth anniversary, some 460 people—the majority innocent civilians—died violently in Iraq.[28]

ECONOMIC PATTERNS AND PROBLEMS

Economic Interrelations

Mandate Iraq was, like its Arab neighbors, overwhelmingly agricultural. Despite its enviable agricultural potential, its actual land development and production were limited. Manufacturing was confined to handicrafts such as metalworking, weaving, and food processing.

Emerging from centuries of Ottoman colonial control, the new Iraq, with British help, steadily evolved a more diversified economy. The discovery of oil in 1927 brought a preeminent dimension to the economy; Iraq possessed superior economic potential—with plentiful water and arable land on the one hand, and enormous energy resources on the other, and a growing supply of productive labor to exploit them. Independent Iraq gradually took its place in the region's emerging political pattern and steadily developed its infrastructure: roads, railways, ports, dams, schools, and related structures. After the 1958 coup, major industries were transferred to the public sector, and nationalization of the petroleum industry began in 1972. By the late 1970s, Iraq had achieved considerable development but was squandering huge sums on military armaments and weapons industries. As we saw earlier, the 1980–1988 Iran-Iraq War and the invasion of Kuwait in 1990–1991 consumed capital and labor, diverted national energies, and destroyed much of the new infrastructure and industry.

Iraq's geographical vulnerability was exposed in the late 1970s as relations with neighbors deteriorated. First, intra-Baathi disputes led Syria to shut down Iraq's export oil pipelines to the Mediterranean, and, although Iraq gained a Turkish outlet in 1977, it still needed the export terminals on the Gulf. Then war with Iran destroyed those facilities. Before the country could catch its breath after the Iran-Iraq War, Saddam Husayn turned on Kuwait. With every chance to withdraw, he defied the UN coalition, and Iraq paid heavily for this third major blunder, as the new pipeline outlet opened across Saudi Arabia in 1985 was lost consequent to this invasion. (In 2012, Saudi Arabia announced that a portion of this pipeline, after rehabilitation, was again being used to convey crude oil from its own fields to the Red Sea for export, bypassing the Strait of Hormuz.) It seemed that every prospect for economic takeoff was blocked by some costly political or military miscalculation.

Agriculture

Although it was the country's major economic activity in the 1920s, agriculture contributed only an estimated 9.7 percent in 2011, providing livelihoods to about 22 per-

cent of the labor force. A new village revitalization program now in place hopes to advance the sector. Of the country's total area, about 13 percent is arable. A surprising 53 percent of the arable land is rainfed, nearly all of it in the mainly Kurdish north and northeast, although most of the actual production is from the intensively cultivated areas of the irrigated plains.

Major crops are grown on both the irrigated plains and the rainfed northern uplands—barley, wheat, cotton, potatoes, tobacco, millet, and sorghum. Wheat and barley are winter crops, utilizing the rains of the Mediterranean climate, whereas the other plants are summer grown, with some irrigation in the north. Other crops, especially rice and dates, are found in the southern irrigated areas along the rivers and canals, with citrus flourishing in the shade of date palms—thousands of which were destroyed by warfare. A complete range of temperate and subtropical fruits and vegetables is also grown.

From Exporter to Importer.   By the 1970s, Iraq had shifted from net food exporter to food importer, a shift prompted by several factors: population increase, a rising standard of living, increased industrialization, migration of farmworkers to the cities and to military service, punitive destruction of villages, and a loss of soil productivity in poorly drained, irrigated areas of the south. Ambitious land-reclamation projects were accelerated after 1988, especially in the Jazirah along the East Euphrates channel and in the Third River Project in the southern interfluve. Irrigated area was thus greatly increased in the late 1980s, and agricultural efficiency improved as collectivized farms were privatized. Iraq is dependent on external upstream sources for just over half of its renewable water resources, primarily Turkey and, to a lesser extent, Syria and Iran. Turkey's increasing preemption of Euphrates and Tigris water (see "Regional Conflicts," in Chap. 8, and

Chap. 20) has created significant tensions between the two countries, at a time when other stresses (Kurdish ambitions, oil pipelines, regional relationships) require immediate attention. The reduced flow has challenged Iraqi inventiveness and has caused serious problems for irrigated agriculture. Iraq must balance concerns about water with its need for the oil pipeline through Turkey to the Mediterranean. With improved internal security, the sector's future can be enhanced by the adoption of less water-intensive practices. Iraq's agriculture is currently in a state of crisis, with a sharp drop in productivity since 2003, as the rural labor force has drifted to the cities, government subsidies have dried up, and the region has experienced a severe and prolonged drought.[29]

Water Resources

Iraq, like Egypt, is formed by its rivers; however, water is of the greatest value when it comes in the right amounts and at the right time. Agriculture accounts for the vast majority of water consumption—in the early 2010s, more than 90 percent. The steady flow of the Tigris and Euphrates has historically provided for both irrigation and domestic needs, but as is mentioned in Chapters 10 and 20, upstream withdrawals in Syria and Turkey have depleted the riverine supply that reaches Iraq. Recent drought conditions have exacerbated the situation, and the prospect of climate change threatens a further worsening in overall availability.

Drinking Water.   Furthermore, since 1991 the deterioration of infrastructure has led to a decline in the access to safe water and sanitation in both urban and rural areas. Additionally, many Iraqis had taken refuge from the insurgency outside the existing service areas. Rural facilities suffered even more, from both physical damage and deterioration, with dependable service dropping from 75 to 43 percent over the same period.[30] Before

1991, 95 percent of urban dwellers had clean drinking water, and by 2007 this had fallen to 73 percent; by 2011, nationwide only about 42 percent had access to reasonably reliable water as a result of war, sabotage, and lack of maintenance.[31] Damage to distribution systems results in the loss of half the water before reaching its intended destinations. Sanitation has also been hard hit—outside of the KRG's domain, less than 10 percent of wastewater gets any sort of treatment. The rest flows directly into rivers and aquifers, contaminating drinking and irrigation water. Since the necessary large-scale infrastructure projects are expensive and have been slow to construct, stopgap measures have been used with mixed results.

Petroleum

The first well drilled in Iraq, by the Turkish Petroleum Company (TPC, later the Iraq Petroleum Company, or IPC—a British-dominated consortium with Dutch, American, and French partners), struck a major reservoir at Baba Gur, north of Kirkuk, in 1927. However, exports were delayed for seven years pending completion of pipelines. The government believed—correctly, as records later showed—that IPC slowed development in Britain's political-economic interests, and relations with IPC were discordant until Iraq finally nationalized the company in 1975. Iraq was a founding member of OPEC in 1960; it passed Law 80 in 1961, reclaiming all concession areas not in production, and created the Iraq National Oil Company. These frictions in the country's oil operations continued even after nationalization of IPC, to the detriment of national development.

Long ranked with Saudi Arabia, Iran, and Kuwait as the region's big four in reserves, Iraq is conservatively credited with at least 141.3 bn bbl of proved conventional crude resources, placing it third in the region and in the world after Saudi Arabia and Iran (see Table 6.1). Many geologists believe that further exploration will give Iraq an additional

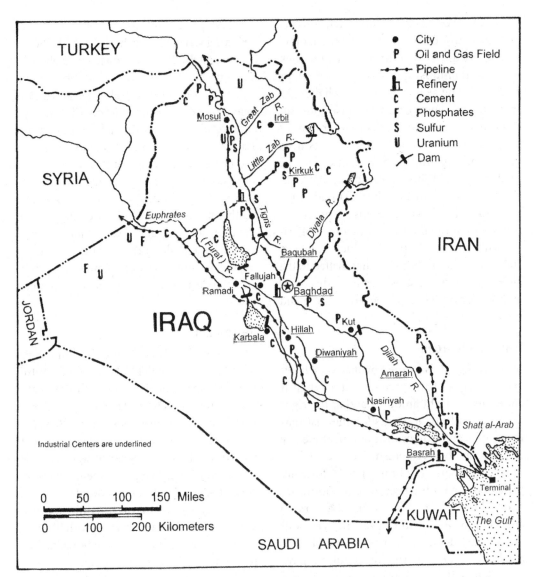

Map 14.5 Economic map of Iraq, with major pipelines, oil fields, mineral deposits, ports, and airports.

45–100 bn bbl.[32] Iraq's Ministry of Oil has announced plans to invest $130 billion in developing petro-resources over the 2013–2017 period.[33]

Known gas reserves, primarily associated gas, are 112 tn ft³/3.1 tn m³. Fields are scattered from the northern border to the Shatt al-Arab (Map 14.5; see also Map 6.1). However, only seventeen of the fields are developed, prima-

rily the multibillion-barrel reservoirs: 2012 production was from only 1,526 wells.

Chronic Underproduction. Iraqi production has never been commensurate with its known reserves. Output peaked at 3.4 mn bpd in 1979 but has since fluctuated greatly, mostly as a result of Saddam Husayn's military misadventures. After sharp drops during the war with Iran, production approached 3 mn bpd in 1989, only to drop to 283,000 bpd in 1991, its lowest level in forty years. Under international sanctions, Iraq was not able until the UN Security Council Resolution 986 set up the "Oil for Food" program to legally export oil in 1997. Receipts paid for humanitarian imports (later extended to critical machinery and equipment), compensation to Gulf War victims, UN teams, transit fees for pipelines through Turkey, and similar costs. It was later revealed that the program was often circumvented by corruption.[34]

As with other parts of the economy, oil faced enormous difficulties after April 2003. The fighting had not seriously damaged the infrastructure; however, twenty-three years of war and neglect had left the system crippled. Coalition repair teams dispatched to Iraq encountered daunting challenges. Insurgents systematically conducted sabotage, impeding production and exports, targeting pipelines especially. In May 2003, the UN lifted the sanctions and then ended the Oil for Food program. Limited production and export of crude resumed almost immediately after the formal end of hostilities and climbed to an average of 2 mn bpd in 2004, despite sabotage, faulty and obsolete equipment, and danger to personnel. With improved security, by the end of 2012 production was approximately at the same peak level last seen in the late 1970s.

Refineries. Iraq's refining capacity of 638,000 bpd throughput is distributed among eight installations, geographically distributed between Kirkuk and Basrah. The two largest are in the center: Bayji with 310,000 bpd north of Baghdad and Dawrah with 210,000 bpd in Greater Baghdad. The Basrah refinery, with 150,000 bpd normal capacity, serves the south. All refineries were operating well below capacity, were sorely in need of repair and upgrading, and were frequently attacked by insurgents. Through the 2000s, gasoline, kerosene, and other refined products were

constantly in short supply. At the end of the decade, the country was still importing about a quarter of its needs of some products.

Pipelines. Details of the several pipeline complexes are given in the "Pipelines" section of Chapter 6. It is worth noting that, although the old IPC multiple lines to the Mediterranean were shut in by Syria in 1982, it reopened them to illicitly import Iraqi oil between 2001 and March 2003. The 600-mi/965-km dual lines from Kirkuk across southeastern Turkey to Yumurtalık, opened in 1977 and 1987, have a fully operational capacity of 1.1 mn bpd and saved Iraq's economy during the Iran-Iraq War; they were shut in after 1990 at UN demand. Reopened under UN Resolution 986, they served as the main export facility until March 2003. Pumping resumed after April 2003 but was repeatedly interrupted by sabotage, so that for several years only occasionally could effective use be made of the facility. Even when operating fully as security improved, it is clear that the existing lines must be rehabilitated and new capacity installed to handle the potential exports from the northern fields. The large IPSA line through Saudi Arabia was also a major "backdoor" outlet, but as was mentioned earlier this was shut in with the Iraqi attack on Kuwait; it was expropriated by Saudi Arabia in 2001 (and as of 2012 was in part being used to export Saudi oil directly through the Red Sea). Two large trestle-tanker export terminals off the Shatt al-Arab were damaged in the 1980s fighting but were back in partial operation by the late 1990s; they were immediately pressed into service after April 2003. With the lines through Turkey subject to insurgent sabotage, the Gulf terminals were the sole reliable export outlet. The al-Basrah terminal has four 400,000 bpd berths for Very Large Crude Carriers; Khawr al-Amaya's handling capacity is 1.2 mn bpd.

Prospects. Soon after the formal end of hostilities in 2003, the coalition declared that oil income would restore the economy and social structure. Into the early 2010s, the sector had yet to realize its potential. But despite frequent interruptions of exports due to sabotage or the failure of aging petro-infrastructure, output rose through the late 2000s, and with high prices Iraq in 2008 had its highest petro-earnings ever—$61 billion. However, with the onset of the global recession, oil demand slackened, and earnings fell in 2009 to $39 billion, recovering a bit the next year to $49 billion. In 2011, output and prices were both on the upswing, and Iraq set a new earnings record of $71 billion.

Oil Strategy.   Iraq's ten-year strategy (2008–2017) has called for 4 mn bpd by 2012 and 6 mn bpd by 2017. As mentioned above, by the end of 2012 production at last arrived at pre–Iran-Iraq War levels, but was still short of the strategy's goal for the year. However, by late 2012, with sanctions biting in Iran, Iraq did, by default and increased daily output of 3.2 bbd, become OPEC's second-largest producer (after Saudi Arabia). In December 2009, the minister of petroleum had claimed Iraq could eventually produce 12 mn bpd,[35] but there was skepticism that so much expansion could occur by the 2017 target date, given regulatory, administrative, and political constraints.[36] Hoping to accelerate increases, in late 2009 Iraq signed several service contracts with foreign oil firms for developments in the rich southern fields of Rumaila and Zubair; ironically, one of the partners in the first deal was British Petroleum (BP), an original shareholder in IPC. Then ExxonMobil and Royal Dutch Shell, also ex-IPC shareholders, signed similar contracts; they agreed to be paid a set fee for each barrel they produce. The veterans have been joined by new players, like Russia's Lukoil, a partner in opening Iraq's vast and untapped West Qurna field, which alone could produce 1.8 mn bpd. Even Angola's state oil company, Sonangol, signed on to develop two fields. The major internationals have clearly

been looking to the future in Iraq; they see this in the south, and they want to be in on the ground floor. With its eye on greatly increased output in the not too distant future, Iraq indicated it would not discuss its place in the OPEC quota system until after 2012.[37]

Kurdish Oil.   But trouble for Iraq's prospects for significant output expansion is on the horizon. In 2012, conflict between the federal government and the KRG over oil contracts in the Kurdish-controlled north seemed to steadily heighten. Baghdad had steadfastly maintained that only the federal government had the authority to award contracts to international companies, while the KRG was pursuing a not very secret series of negotiations on its own. The federal government went so far as to threaten any company dealing directly with the KRG with being blackballed in the rest of the country and reportedly sought the assistance of the US government in dealing with American firms. The KRG retaliated by cutting back on exports from the northern fields, claiming that it had not been receiving its proper share of oil revenues. In view of the maturity of the northern fields and of the better prospects for large-scale new discoveries and production in the south, international firms must evaluate their risk of being excluded from involvement in the development of new southern fields by becoming closely tied to the KRG.[38] On the other hand, there is also the potential for new fields in the north, and that is attractive to some companies. The intensity of the confrontation between Baghdad and the KRG lessened somewhat toward the end of 2012, but the underlying issues remained unsettled.[39] Stoking the uncertainty was the KRG's announcement in 2013 of its intention to move forward with plans to build its own export pipeline to Turkey.[40]

Other Minerals

The nonfuel mineral resources of Iraq have so far proved to be relatively limited compared with those of Turkey and Iran; only sulfur and phosphates are noteworthy. In addition to by-product sulfur from its refineries, one of the world's biggest deposits of mineral sulfur—130 million metric tons—is at Mishraq south of Mosul, and nearby plants produce a range of acids and other products. Phosphate mining at Akashat on the Euphrates near the Syrian border was expanded several times after the late 1970s, and a large plant at al-Qaim processes some of the phosphates for acids and fertilizers. Mining operation levels in the early 2010s were still only at a small fraction of capacity. The US Geological Survey has estimated that Iraq's reserves of phosphate rock are equivalent to about 9 percent of global reserves, which would put Iraq second in the world regarding reserves, behind only Morocco.

Manufacturing

Most industrial development has occurred since 1960 and is concentrated around Baghdad, with its large market and labor supply but also with advantages in transportation and energy, and, in the south, around Basrah, with its import-export advantages and proximity to the oil and gas sector. Increased hydrocarbon production in the north stimulated industrial growth in the Mosul-Irbil-Kirkuk triangle, giving Iraq its third manufacturing region (see Map 7.1). The more important manufacturing centers are underlined on Map 14.1, although many smaller towns pursue various crafts.

Textiles have been a traditional product for centuries, with Mosul—which gave its name to muslin—still a center. Food and beverage processing have been major activities for decades. Increased oil production in the 1950s generated many enterprises exploiting energy or using hydrocarbons as raw materials. Concentration in the center intensified as additional plants produced a wide range of items—pharmaceuticals, paper and plastic products, household appliances, clothing, assembled automobiles and trucks, and, before 1991, large

amounts of military weaponry and support systems.

The mid-Iraq interfluve continues to be the country's industrial heartland. Before bombing by Iran during the 1980s and by the coalition in 1990–1991 and again in 2003, the strategic southern corridor was a center for petrochemicals and heavy industry—iron and steel, steel fabrication products, oil pipe, salt, and fertilizers and other chemicals. Oil revenues financed generous subsidies to socialized industries, giving rise to several large (and very often inefficient, overstaffed, and undermaintained) state-owned enterprises (SOEs). Postinvasion Iraq saw attempts to privatize some SOEs, but with little success. Foreign investment has been sought by the government, but aside from the oil sector and opportunities in the KRG, there has not been much interest; potential investors cite both security concerns and a pervading atmosphere of corruption.

Military-Industrial Complex. Increasing emphasis on military prowess in the 1970s and 1980s (with Soviet cooperation) spurred development of a sophisticated weapons industry. For most of the 1990s, the nature, location, capacity, and level of readiness of this industry were issues central to a grim cat-and-mouse game between Iraqi authorities and weapons inspectors from the UNSCOM team. The UN resolution that set the terms for the 1991 cease-fire between Iraq and the coalition provided for Iraqi disarmament and prohibited the possession or production of chemical, biological, and nuclear weapons. Following a serious confrontation in December 1998, Iraq refused to cooperate further with UNSCOM. In November 2002, inspectors returned to Iraq, this time as the United Nations Monitoring, Verification, and Inspection Commission (UNMOVIC), under UN Resolution 1441, to search for weapons of mass destruction or the facilities producing them. UNMOVIC had found no evidence of either by the time the US-led invasion was launched in March 2003; neither, of course, did the intensive search by the United States after the invasion ever turn up any trace of the alleged WMDs.

Transportation

Roads. Iraq's physical geography and early development—mostly along the two northwest-southeast axes of the Tigris and Euphrates—imposed a pattern on road and railroad development. Major roads generally parallel both rivers. The main north-south motorway from Mosul to Baghdad goes along the Tigris, but then takes the interfluve directly to Basrah and Kuwait (see Map 14.1). In addition to this motorway, three highways converge on Baghdad from the north and west: from Sulaymaniyah, from Irbil through Kirkuk, and from the Jordan border. The latter is an express motorway joined by the Euphrates highway from Syria. Highways also follow both rivers south of Baghdad.

The links to north, west, and south brought in essential food and military matériel during the Iran-Iraq War, especially from Jordan's Aqabah port through Rutbah and Ramadi to Baghdad. Dozens of bridges and road junctions destroyed or damaged in 1991 and again in 2003 were gradually repaired or replaced after the invasion; sabotage of these facilities was frequent through the mid-2000s. The highway system was heavily utilized for the US-led invasion and then by resupply and reconstruction trucks afterward. So regular were the supply runs that convoys were frequently attacked, especially by remotely controlled IEDs set by insurgents. The IEDs became such dangers to convoy personnel that ordinary trucks and vans had to be armored; nonetheless, there were many casualties among Iraqi civilians and Iraqi and Coalition security forces.

Railways. The Berlin-to-Baghdad railway was a pre–World War I German goal during the heyday of railroad building; it enters Iraq northwest of Mosul, parallels the Tigris to Baghdad, and then follows the Euphrates to Basrah and the Gulf. It was the country's only railway until development of phosphate deposits near al-Qaim prompted construction of a 318-mi/512-km link, completed in 1984, down the Euphrates and across to Baghdad. Another line, 156 mi/252 km long, finished in 1987, parallels the major pipelines from Kirkuk to Hadithah on the Euphrates, where it joins the line from al-Qaim to Baghdad. A third line into Baghdad links Irbil and Kirkuk with the capital. During the 1990s, the main lines were repaired, upgraded, and double-tracked between Baghdad and Basrah. Like those in Egypt, Iraqi railways normally carry a heavy passenger load. In 2008, the popular Baghdad–Basrah route was back in operation. In the early 2010s, the government was pursuing plans for a Baghdad metro system with two lines.

New Rail Connections. As Kuwait is planning a rail line from its border with Iraq to that with Saudi Arabia as part of the massive GCC rail expansion program (see Chaps. 15, 16, and 17), an extension of the Iraqi system to tie in with this will be needed. In 2011, agreement was reached between Jordan and Iraq for building a rail line that would give Iraqi exports direct access to the port of Aqabah. Similarly, in 2012, linkages to the Iranian system running between Khorramshahr and Basra and between Kermanshahr and Baghdad were in various stages of implementation. Trying to bolster the Assad regime in Syria, Iran has proposed building a rail line between Tabriz and Dayr al-Zawr that would cross northern Iraq. Obviously, realization of this scheme, if any, must await political developments.

Airlines. Although Iraqi Airways (IA), founded in 1946, evolved into a modestly successful operation, with twenty-three aircraft in the 1970s, it was virtually dormant after 1990. It ambitiously resumed flights to Amman and Damascus with one plane in October 2004. However, flights into Baghdad were such potential targets for insurgents that IA had little business during the early postinvasion period, but as the decade progressed a more normal schedule became possible. Basrah Airport, built in the 1980s by Saddam Husayn, went largely unused because of the sanctions after 1991 until civilian traffic resumed in 2005; the British military departed in 2009 and returned it to Iraqi control. Beginning in the late 2000s, IA began to look more like an operating airline, and by 2012 it was ready to receive newly ordered aircraft from the Boeing Company. Also in 2012, a dispute with Kuwait that hindered IA flying to many foreign destinations was settled, with Iraq agreeing to compensate Kuwait for aircraft looted by Saddam's forces in 1991. IA flights to Kuwait resumed in February 2013, and flights to major European locations as well as Irbil and Sulaymaniyah resumed during the spring. Kurdistan Airlines was launched in 2005 but became inactive in 2010; the KRG opened Sulaymaniyah International Airport the same year, and Irbil's Hawler International Airport was expanded to accommodate the largest passenger jets. Several foreign airlines have initiated direct service to the Kurdistan region. Al-Najaf's airport does a thriving business in religious tourism with links to locales with large Shii populations.

Ports. The narrowness of Iraq's Gulf window—only 36 mi/58 km—restricts potential port sites; only the exploitation of indentations (drowned estuaries, called *khawrs* or *khors*) has enabled useful port development. Although several ports are needed because of the scale and variety of imports and exports, Basrah served for centuries as the only major port, but its location on the relatively shallow Shatt al-Arab limited growth and led to congestion. Oil development and economic expansion after the 1950s demanded additional facilities, including (1) an oil terminal at al-Faw, down the Shatt al-Arab from Basrah; (2) two general-cargo ports, Khawr al-Zubair and Umm Qasr, on a drowned estuary near the Kuwait border, with Umm Qasr also serving as a naval base; and (3) two oil-export terminals—Mina al-Bakr (now called al-Basrah) and Khawr al-Amayah—on trestle causeways into the deeper water at the head of the Gulf. Even before the war with Iran, the ports were overloaded, and Iraq imported through Aqabah, Kuwait, and other Gulf ports. Iran destroyed the domestic complexes in the early 1980s, necessitating Iraq's greater reliance on Kuwait and especially Aqabah, both of which were denied to Iraq during the 1990–1991 war. Restored in the 1990s, the domestic ports suffered only limited damage in 2003; Umm Qasr was quickly made usable, and the trestles were soon put into limited operation. As mentioned above, Iraq has expressed serious concerns that Kuwaiti plans for the Mubarak port facilities on Bubiyan Island will hinder access to and from Umm Qasr. Over the longer term, development of Iraq's rail links to neighboring countries will give it better access to the ports of those countries as alternative import-export venues.

DEBTS AND REPARATIONS

War Debts. Any discussion of Iraq's current economy and its prospects would be incomplete without taking note of an enormous problem the current government has inherited from more than three decades of Baathi despotism and specifically from the regime of Saddam Husayn. To finance the military framework he deemed necessary to further his ambitions, he incurred huge debts, against future oil revenues, with obligations owed to foreign governments and armament suppliers from all parts of the political spectrum. Then using what he acquired in two disastrously undertaken aggressions against Iran and

Kuwait that ended in defeat, he obligated Iraq to make massive reparations for the havoc wreaked on his opponents and to others who could claim collateral damages. Within a few months of Saddam's toppling, Iraqi officials were aware of the enormity of the problem they were facing, although its exact size was difficult to identify—estimates ran as high as more than $350 billion if all potential reparations claims were considered. A 2005 report to the US Congress estimated the debt to be about $120 billion.[41]

Possibly because the United States was eager for Iraq's oil revenues to be used as soon as possible for reconstruction, it began to call for debt forgiveness very soon after the fall of Baghdad through the Club of Paris, an informal group of the largest creditor countries. In 2004, a compromise resulted in the forgiveness of 80 percent of Iraq's debt to club members. Some creditors forgave more—for example, the United States forgave all of its $4.1 billion and Russia 93 percent of about $13 billion. The members tied forgiveness to a package of reforms to be undertaken by Iraq, as did the International Monetary Fund when it extended a series of Stand-By Arrangements beginning in 2005—the third of which was for $5.5 billion in 2009. During the Iran-Iraq War, Iraq borrowed very heavily from Gulf Cooperation Council (GCC) states, and by the early 2010s progress was mixed on this front. The UAE announced the cancellation of $7 billion in 2008 and of another $5.8 billion in 2012. There were reports that Iraq's debt to Saudi Arabia amounted to some $30 billion and that the kingdom was unwilling to negotiate with the Maliki government about any adjustment.[42] From Kuwait, the Saddam regime borrowed about $16 billion during the 1980s. In 2009, Iraq asked China to forgive $8.5 billion, and the following year China wrote off 80 percent of this amount.

Reparations: Kuwait and Iran.   Reparations are separate from debt: in 1991, Iraq was re-quired by the UN to put aside 5 percent of all future oil revenues to pay more than $50 billion to Kuwait for damages during the occupation. By the end of 2011, Iraq said it had already paid more than $34.3 billion and owed about $18 billion more; it proposed negotiations with Kuwait, with the goal of putting future payments into a Kuwaiti investment fund for Iraq.

Iran has considerable claims as well; although these do not have official backing, the UN did estimate in 1991 that about $100 billion could be due to Iran. In the early 2010s, it seemed that Iran had not given up the possibility of pursuing its claims, but that it had given priority to establishing and maintaining strong links with a Shii-dominated regime in Baghdad and in settling long-standing issues like demarcating their long mutual border, as was originally agreed under the Algiers Accord in 1975 (see "Regional Conflicts," in Chap. 8).[43]

RELATIONS

Modern Iraq's earliest relations were perforce with Britain, the mandatory that also controlled the Iraq Petroleum Company, and links remained close—if not always friendly—until 1958. Relations were distant after the 1958 coup, and British forces guarded newly independent Kuwait against Iraqi threats in 1961. Britain was a leading member of both coalitions in 1990 and 2003, was a partner in air patrols of the no-fly zones, and shared the role of occupying power with the United States after the 2003 military action.

Iraq has had significant relations with many states, both neighbors and distant countries. With all its immediate neighbors, these have been unusually dynamic relations. Indeed, it has been at war with all of them except Jordan and has directly fought Iran and Kuwait, while Syrian, Saudi, and Turkish forces joined the 1990–1991 coalition (but not that of 2003). With all neighbors, relations have

Figure 14.4 Spiral minaret (al-Mawiyah), Samarra, Iraq, built in the ninth century while Samarra was the capital of the Abbasid Empire. Figures at base give scale of this unusual minaret, 171 ft/52 m high, which served the Friday Mosque, glimpsed at lower left.

swung from friendly to antagonistic and sometimes back again in a single decade.

Pan-Arabism, Pan-Islamism. Between 1958 and 1990, Iraq's primary foreign policy concern was to affirm and strengthen its Arab credentials and to assert leadership in the region. It supplied troops in the 1948–1949 war between Arab countries and Israel, and it

did so again in 1967. It consistently supported the Palestinian cause, winning appreciation among Palestinians and other Arabs on the street, especially in Jordan and Yemen.

Especially after the 1958 revolution, Iraq emphasized its role in Islamic history (Fig. 14.4), despite the dominance of the secularist Baath; it considers itself the eastern anchor of the Arab world and the natural eastern flank of the Mashriq, the Arab Middle East, with Egypt the western flank. As a member of the Arab League, it was regularly militant, a "rejectionist" state, under Saddam Husayn and its earlier leaders, often advocating more aggressive stands than the majority of members.

Its direct relations with Egypt have blown hot and cold since 1958. Other Arab states of the Mashriq have been ambivalent toward Iraq: they condemned the aggression against Kuwait and its firing Scud missiles into Saudi Arabia, but they still recognized its support of Arabism, its stand against Iran, its defiance of the vestiges of imperialism, and its opposition to Israel.

Syria.   Because of rifts between the Baath factions in Damascus and Baghdad, relations with Syria actually deteriorated when the Baath came to power in Iraq—especially as Syria supported Iran in the 1980s and joined the 1990–1991 coalition. However, both countries found closer relations to be expedient later in the 1990s. The United States repeatedly accused Syria of aiding Saddam up to 2003 and insurgent groups afterward. Iraq also voiced concerns that Syria-based terrorists had carried out several major bombing attacks; although hard evidence was not readily available, relations between the two countries were further damaged. With the deterioration of the situation in Syria beginning in 2011, numerous Syrian refugees began crossing the Iraqi border, a reversal of the human tide of the mid-2000s when as many as 1 million Iraqis sought refuge in Syria. Iraq voted to expel Syria from the Arab League and after some delay called for the end of the Assad regime. On the other hand, Iraq seemed to acquiesce, by allowing overflights through its airspace in Iran's delivery of weapons to Syria well into 2012. Reversing the movement of the previous decade, thousands of Syrian refugees sought haven in Iraq. Just as Iraq's own conflicts overflowed into the neighboring countries, there is now

considerable apprehension in Iraq in 2013 that events in Syria could exacerbate Iraq's fragile intercommunal tensions.[44]

Jordan.   Iraq's relations with Jordan between 1923 and 1958 rested on the kinship of the Hashimite kings of the two countries. Although meaningful implementation of the proposed Arab Federation between the two kingdoms was prevented by the 1958 revolution, mutual interests restored relations. The link proved to be critical to Iraq in the 1990–1991 crisis and through the following decade, as well as being economically beneficial to Jordan, as was shown in Chapter 11 and earlier in this chapter. Jordan's embassy in Baghdad was struck by insurgents in 2003, leaving eleven dead. Full relations between the two neighbors were restored in 2008 with the visit of King Abdullah, the first Arab head of state to visit since 2003. On the other hand, Abdullah has voiced his serious concern about a Shii Crescent led by Iran and stretching across Iraq and Syria to the Mediterranean.

GCC States.   Relations with its Arab neighbors of the Gulf are the most critical and sometimes ambiguous. When the Gulf states and Saudi Arabia organized the GCC, they excluded Iraq. Yet after invading Iran and proclaiming itself the bastion of Arabism against Persian designs, Iraq desperately required assistance, and all the GCC states came to its aid with billions in financial and material support. Kuwait and Saudi Arabia were especially helpful. In addition, they made proxy shipments of oil on Iraq's OPEC quota and account, and Saudi Arabia agreed to construct the IPSA pipeline to the Red Sea across its territory. Iraq's about-face invasion of Kuwait and its attacks on Saudi Arabia during the Gulf War thus seemed all the more inexplicable, and these actions contradicted its vociferous claims to be a leading supporter of Arab unity. Both Kuwait and Saudi Arabia supported US and UK air patrols of the no-fly zones, and Kuwait was a key factor, beginning in 2003, in operations connected with the invasion and occupation. But, along with other Arab states, even Kuwait was skeptical about the motivation of the United States regarding its role in the Gulf and the wider Middle East. As Iraq regained its sovereignty, relations with its southern neighbors improved, but there has been a strong undercurrent among them of dismay at the militant Shiism manifesting itself in Iraq, as well as concern about the perceived close ties between the al-Maliki government and Iran. Here again is the idea that a Shii Crescent threatens the Sunni-dominated status quo in the region—a resurgent theme in the 2010s.

Israel. As implacable opponents and genuine threats to each other's security, Iraq and Israel have viewed each other as major foes. Israel bombed Iraq's Osirak nuclear reactor in 1981, and Iraq struck back against the Jewish state in 1991 when it fired thirty-nine Scud missiles into Israel during the coalition's response to the invasion of Kuwait. Israel gave military assistance to Iran during the Iran-Iraq War, waged an effective war of words against Iraq, and was active through its supporters in the United States in urging and prioritizing the 2003 invasion. In 2002, Binyamin Netanyahu (at that time about to become Israeli foreign minister) testified before a US congressional committee that Iraq was unquestionably pursuing the development of weapons of mass destruction, including nuclear weapons.[45] Ahmed Chalabi, founder of the exile group the Iraq National Congress and putative candidate of the neocons in the Bush administration to head post-invasion Iraq, was believed by them to favor signing a peace treaty with Israel once he was in power.[46] Iraqi Kurds began pursuing their own contacts with Israel in the 1990s.

Turkey. Relations with Turkey were quiet for decades, but they were reinvigorated in

the 1970s by the agreement on the pipeline from Kirkuk to Yumurtalık. They were further improved by later arrangements to double the line, with Turkey receiving its oil supplies through the lines. However, this rapport collapsed in August 1990 when Turkey shut in the lines in accordance with UN sanctions against Iraq. Relations between Turkey and Iraq were on a roller coaster in the early 1990s, especially regarding the Kurds, and the Kurdish issue became a very serious problem in the period before and after March 2003.[47] Underneath the relations regarding oil and Kurds, running tension also persists over Turkey's reduction of Euphrates water to downstream riparians, as well as over Turkey's increasing support of Turkmans who are scattered among Iraqi Kurds. Ironically, Turkey has benefited considerably from a great increase in its exports to Iraq, especially to the Kurdish region. It is in Turkey's interest to promote Iraqi unity, and Turkey's growing economic influence in Iraqi Kurdistan is a potential advantage to Baghdad.

Iran. The historical antagonism between the people of the Mesopotamian Basin and those of the Iranian Plateau intensified after the 1979 Iranian Revolution and broke into open warfare between Iran and Iraq in September 1980 (see "The Iran-Iraq War," in Chap. 9). After eight years of combat and two years of bickering, Iraq made an uneasy peace with Iran in 1990 in order to ensure Iran's neutrality and to avert the danger of having to fight on two fronts. After the early 1990s, Iranian-Iraqi relations remained uneasily quiescent, and after 2003 Iranian Shii pilgrims flooded into al-Najaf and Karbala for the first time in nearly twenty-five years. Official relations have been cordial, but even the Shia-led government has been concerned by the links between certain factions in Iran and some Shii militias/political parties in Iraq. Despite the religious commonality, there is a transcending ambiguity based on historic Arab-Persian

antagonisms. As sanctions have been ratch-
eted upward on Iran, there have been accusations leveled at Iraq of helping its neighbor to
evade some of its problems; needless to say,
if this were true, it would be extremely em-
barrassing to the United States, as was Iraq's
agreement in 2013 to allow a proposed Iranian
gas pipeline to connect Iran and Syria.[48]

Russia.   Alienated from the West after 1958,
Iraq turned to the USSR, receiving military
supplies denied by the West, while keeping
domestic communists under strict control. It
intermittently resisted other relations with
the Soviets and, over time, attempted to balance its East-West relations, positioning itself
to receive assistance from the West as the Soviet Union disintegrated. Russia supported
the coalition in 1990–1991 but was sympa-
thetic to Iraq's plight under sanctions and the
US and UK air attacks. It opposed the US-led
invasion, perhaps hoping to better position
Russian companies bidding for oil and other
contracts. Russia canceled 93 percent of Iraqi
debt owed it in 2008. In November 2012, Iraq
suspended a $4.2 billion deal to purchase
Russian armaments, possibly because of US
pressure but ostensibly because of suspicions
of graft involved in securing the purchase.
These concerns seem to have been cleared
up, as the parties announced in early 2013
that the deal was on again.[49]

United States.   Crucial as Iraq's links were
with its neighbors, its relations with the
United States have proved to be the most decisive. The US presence in what is now Iraq
dates to 1888, when the first American consul
in Baghdad was appointed. Diplomatic relations were initiated in 1931 when Iraq became independent. But US-Iraqi relations
following the 1958 revolution were little more
than "correct," and along with several other
Arab governments Iraq broke relations after
the 1967 Arab-Israeli war on the grounds that
the United States had assisted Israel during

that conflict. Quiet negotiations based on
anti-Iran concerns finally led to a resumption
of full diplomatic relations in December
1984. During this period, despite opposition
in both countries, détente persisted based on
common opposition to Iran. Saddam's invasion of Kuwait led to relations once again
being severed, and following the coalition's
expulsion of Iraq from Kuwait relations became, if anything, even worse over the following years. International sanctions were placed
on Iraq, largely at US insistence, as were the
imposition of the so-called no-fly zones in the
northern and southern thirds of the country.

By 1998, the United States had virtually co-
opted the UN role in responding to Iraqi actions, despite increasing criticism from other
Security Council members. With the expulsion of UNSCOM inspectors in late 1998, the
almost daily bombing by US planes became a
war of attrition; Iraq gained appreciable, if
grudging, sympathy from its Arab neighbors
and other countries. The United States demanded full compliance with UN relations
before lifting sanctions, implying that only
"regime change" could meet these requirements; these hard-line policies characterized
the Clinton years.

At the same time, covert advance work by
American neoconservative policy planners
was brought into play with the onset of the
George W. Bush administration and the almost
immediate preparations for an early invasion.
These became overt after September 11, 2001,
with allegations of Iraqi links to al-Qaida and
claims that Saddam had secret caches of
"weapons of mass destruction" taken as established facts. The unlikelihood that secular
Baathis could be close allies of Islamic ultra-
fundamentalists was ignored, and the fact that
the recently returned UNMOVIC inspectors
found no evidence of WMDs was dismissed, as
were their pleas for additional time.[50]

The events following the invasion of 2003
have been described above in more detail (see
"Operation Iraqi Freedom," in Chap. 9, and

"Monarchy, Republic, Despotry, and Beyond," in this chapter). Only in 2006 did real diminution of US civil authority over the country begin to take hold, and in 2007 Iraq and the United States agreed to negotiate the framework for a long-term relationship.[51] In 2008, the two reached a Security Agreement, basically covering the conditions under which the US military would stay in the country during a phased drawdown. Additionally, a Security Framework Agreement was reached governing civil relations—on issues of an economic, cultural, scientific, technological, health, and trade nature. Shortly after his inauguration, President Obama announced that most American troops would be withdrawn by the end of August 2011; the last combat brigade was withdrawn on schedule, and the troop pullout was completed in September 2011. Left behind in the Green Zone, now guarded by Iraqi security forces, remains the largest official mission that the United States currently has anywhere in the world.

The foregoing analysis of Iraq should make clear that, despite the country's complex situation in the early 2010s, it is a land with many enduring physical and human assets. Although it has been tragically misguided and misgoverned, it should have the right to seize—and should seize—its opportunities to develop its great national potential.

For information on the business environment in Iraq, see the website attached to this book: www.middleeastpatterns.com.

NOTES

1. The creation of Iraq is recounted in several studies. A detailed account is Catherwood 2004. More background is given in Klieman 1970, Chap. 7. Busch 1971 discusses the military campaign and its aftermath in the framework of the sometimes competing interests of London and British India. The accounts of the crises of the early 1920s were revived in 2003–2004, when the resistance seemed to be replicated against the coalition.

2. Although government officials announced in 2011 that the museum would shortly reopen, almost two years later it was clear that a general opening was still some distance in the future. Associated Press, Apr. 11, 2013.

3. See Malinowski 2004; for the most intensive studies, made from an environmental viewpoint, see United Nations Environment Programme (UNEP) 2001, 2003.

4. The fascinating story of the former ecological symbiosis between marsh and Madan is recounted in the classic account Thesiger 1964. It has been republished and reprinted several times. For an excellent detailed recent study, see UNEP 2001.

5. See *Washington Post*, July 23, 2009, for a marvelous photo montage: www.washingtonpost.com /wp-dyn/content/gallery/2009/07/23/GA2009072 303612.html.

6. Discussed in Lees and Falcon 1952.

7. Though in the run-up to the 2003 invasion, the Bush administration used the Halabjah gassing as proof of the Saddam regime's perfidy, in 1988 the Reagan administration echoed Iraqi claims and tried to shift the blame to Iran (*New York Times*, Jan. 17, 2003). See also Silverstein 2007 at www.harpers.org/archive /2007/07/hbc-90000448, for an interview with Joost Hilterman, author of *A Poisonous Affair: America, Iraq, and the Gassing of Halabja* (2007).

8. Journalistic reports on the Kurds appeared daily during the spring and summer of 1991 and resumed in 2003. A spate of books on the Kurds has also appeared during the past twenty-five years. A good study by a veteran journalist is Randal 1998. More scholarly studies include Ghareeb 1981; Entessar 1992; Gunter 1999; McDowall 2000; and O'Shea 2003. During field observations in Kurdistan in mid-1990, author Held visited the ruins of scores of the razed Kurdish villages and observed several of the new settlements. The sight left no doubt as to the scale of the project or the government's determination to subdue the Kurds through reversing the geographical advantage. With some protection under the no-fly operations, the Kurds returned to their villages after the mid-1990s.

9. Dohuk, Irbil, and Sulaymaniyah. The KRG claims and has de facto control over parts of Nineveh, Tamim, and Diyala as well; this would give the KRG the cities of Kirkuk and Mosul.

10. The 2013 cease-fire agreement between the PKK and the Turkish government involves a withdrawal of PKK guerrillas, apparently into KRG territory; the Iraqi central government protested that, though it as willing to offer refuge to individuals, it did not agree that armed groups would be welcome. *Gulf Today* (Dubai), May 10, 2013.

11. "Iraqi Kurdistan Free Speech under Attack," Human Rights Watch, Feb. 2013; *al-Monitor,* Feb. 18, 2013.

12. For the Turkmans, the biggest source of contention with the Kurds is Kirkuk, where many of the former live and which the latter claim as the "Kurdish Jerusalem."

13. See http://chiesa.espresso.repubblica.it/articolo /162781?eng=y.

14. *Al-Monitor,* Oct. 16, 2012, translated from *al-Hayat,* Oct. 15, 2012.

15. Among several good histories of Iraq, see Helms 1984; Farouk-Sluglett and Sluglett 2001; Tripp 2002; and the especially good Marr 2004. *Iraq* Country Study 1990, like all volumes in that series, gives excellent broad coverage. Cordesman and Hashim 1997 studies the post-1991 situation.

16. Because of Ghazi's anti-British opinions and the mysterious nature of the fatal accident, many Iraqis (and others) suspected that he was actually assassinated.

17. *Christian Science Monitor,* Nov. 22, 2012. The Iraqi Post Office issued a set of three stamps depicting the country's kings in 2012.

18. There are almost innumerable treatments already available on these and consequent events; a sampling in alphabetic order: Ajami 2006; Allawi 2007; Bacevich 2008; Bremer 2006; Chandrasekaran 2006; Diamond 2005; Galbraith 2007; Goldberg 2008a; Haas 2009, Packer 2005; Phillips 2005; Pollack 2002; Ricks 2007; Shadid 2005; and Zinni 2006. See also Terrill 2009, a review article.

19. A useful brief biography of al-Maliki is "Notes from the Underground: The Rise of Nouri al-Malaki' by Parker and Salman, World Policy Institute, Mar. 11, 2013, www.worldpolicy.org/journal/spring2013/maliki.

20. *Iraq and Gulf Analysis,* May 4 and May 7, 2013, http://gulfanalysis.wordpress.com/category/iraq-local -elections-2013/; *Fikra Forum,* May 1, 2013, http:// fikraforum.org/?p=3259.

21. Institute for Economics and Peace; see www .visionofhumanity.org/globalterrorismindex/.

22. Internal Displacement Monitoring Centre. See www.internal-displacement.org/countries/iraq.

23. See Ricks 2009.

24. See, for example, the references to US Army colonel Sean McFarland and lieutenant colonel Daniel Davis and to Marine Corps major general John Kelley in "Hagel Was Right About the Iraq Surge," *Business Insider,* Jan. 13, 2013.

25. One observer suggested that sectarianism has become so enshrined in Iraqi politics that even though many Iraqis realize that the al-Maliki government has become dysfunctional, they believe that at least it can maintain a sectarian balance. See "2011: Why Did Iraq Miss the Arab Spring?," http://english.ahram.org.eg /News/30638.aspx.

26. *Arab News* (Jiddah), Apr. 26, 2013.

27. *BBC News,* May 2, 2013.

28. *Saudi Gazette* (Jiddah), May 7, 2013.

29. *Al-Monitor,* Jan. 29, 2013.

30. World Bank 2009.

31. UN Inter-Agency Information and Analysis Unit, "Water in Iraq Factsheet," 2011.

32. In 2013, the Ministry of Oil raised the figure for proven reserves to 150 bn bbl. *Arab News* (Jiddah), Apr. 12, 2013.

33. *Zawya,* Mar. 16, 2013.

34. The Independent Inquiry Committee was appointed to investigate charges of corruption; its report is available at www.iic-offp.org/documents/IIC%20 Final%20Report%2027Oct2005.pdf.

35. *BBC News,* Dec. 12, 2009.

36. Expressed by the International Energy Agency as reported by Reuters, July 1, 2009, in *Iraq Directory,* www.iraqdirectory.com/.

37. *Business Week,* Mar. 16, 2010.

38. Proven reserves outside the Kurdish-controlled areas are about three times those available to the KRG. See "Iraq's Rise to No. 2 Producer in OPEC Is Bad News for the World," *Forbes,* Aug. 13, 2012, www.forbes .com/sites/matthewhulbert/2012/08/13/opecs-new -heavyweight-iraq.

39. For a discussion of the interplay between politics and Kurdish oil, see D. Natali 2012.

40. *Zawya,* Feb. 7, 2013.

41. Congressional Research Service, *Iraq: Debt Relief,* Mar. 2005.

42. *Financial Times,* Dec. 12, 2011.

43. A spokesman for the Iranian Foreign Ministry reiterated Iran's claims and said they are on the agenda of discussions between the two countries, but that pursuit of the issue depended upon the "degree of the Iraqi government's control of the country's affairs." *Tehran Times,* July 31, 2011.

44. "Iraq, Syria, and the Twelfth Imam," *Small Wars Journal,* Sept. 25, 2012; *Reuters,* Sept. 5, 2012.

45. *Ha'artez,* Oct. 4, 2012

46. Dizard 2004.

47. See de Bellaigue 2007.

48. Given the chaotic situation in Syria and Iran's straitened financial circumstance due to international sanctions, it is not likely that this project will move ahead very quickly, if at all. *Peninsula* (Doha), Feb. 20, 2013.

49. *Khaleej Times* (Dubai), Feb. 22, 2013.

50. See Hiro 2004.

51. See Brumley and Campbell 2007.

15

Saudi Arabia

Development in the Desert

KEY POINTS: Long the realm of desert Bedouin, became cradle of Islam in seventh century. Mecca remains Islamic world center for prayer and pilgrimages. Little influenced by colonial powers after World War I. Unified by and still ruled by Al Saud family, hence name. Formerly a poor land with small population, it became enormously wealthy after world's largest oil reserves found by American companies beginning late 1930s. Small native population joined by millions of expatriates for exploiting oil and rapidly developing incredible infrastructure after 1970s. Now world's second-largest oil producer and largest oil exporter. Major influence in Islamic and Arab movements and agencies, including GCC; retains traditional conservatism in religion and society.

The Arabian Peninsula (Arabic: Jazirat al-Arab, "Island of the Arabs"), although lacking the massive monuments that have drawn travelers to Egypt or Jordan, has played a significant role through seven thousand years of Middle East history. Three especially important points need emphasis. One, it was the source area for Semitic peoples who migrated into the Fertile Crescent as Akkadians, Amorites, Assyrians, Aramaeans, and Chaldeans; as smaller groups that included Canaanites, Hebrews, Edomites, and Nabataeans; and, of particular interest, as Arabs in the seventh century. Two, it is the cradle of Islam, the religion of more than 1.5 billion people, and the destination of some 3 million pilgrims for the Hajj every year, while hundreds of millions of Muslims face Mecca for prayer five times daily. Three, under its eastern margin alone lie more than 30 percent of the world's known petroleum reserves. Seven states occupy the peninsula: Saudi Arabia, the four Gulf states, Oman, and Yemen (see Chaps. 16, 17, and 18).

A PREVIEW

Saudi Arabia's geography and economy place it prominently in international rankings. It is the largest of the countries in the core region treated here[1] and is the twelfth largest in the world. It possesses the world's largest oil reserves, the largest single oil reservoir, the largest-capacity oil-export terminal, the largest oil-storage tanks, the longest natural gas liquids pipeline, the largest-capacity seawater desalination plant, and the largest airport. Its Red Sea coast is longest of all the littoral states; its Gulf coast is second after

SAUDI ARABIA

Long-form official name, anglicized: Kingdom of Saudi Arabia

Official name, transliterated: al-Mamlakah al-Arabiyah as-Saudiyah

Form of government: monarchy

Area: 830,000 mi^2/2,149,690 km^2

Population, 2011: 28,572,000; Literacy: 86.6%

Ethnic composition (%, 2005): Saudi Arab 74; expatriates 26, of which Indian 5, Bangladeshi 3.5, Filipino 3.5, Egyptian 3, Palestinian 1; other 7

Religions (%, 2000): Muslim 94, of which Sunni 84, Shia 10; Christian 3.5, of which Catholic 3; Hindu 1; other 1.5

Demography: Life expectancy—72.37 yr (M), 76.42 yr (F); Birthrate (per 1,000)—19.19; Fertility rate—2.26

GDP, 2011: $587.5 billion; purchasing power parity: $687.7 billion; per capita: $24,400

Currency: Saudi Riyal (SR), US$1 = 3.75 riyals; 1 SR = $0.267 (mid-May 2013)

Energy: oil—267.9 bn bbl (largest liquid oil reserves in world); natural gas—288,344 bn ft^3; coal—nil

Main exports (% of total value, 2008): SR 1,175.4 billion (of which crude petroleum 78.8; refined petroleum 10.8; other mineral fuels 5.3)

Main imports (% of total value, 2008): SR 431.7 billion (of which machinery and apparatus 27.2; transport equipment 18; base and fabricated metals 15.3; food and live animals 14.4; chemicals and chemical products 12.3)

Capital city, 2010: Riyadh 5,188,286; other major cities: Jiddah 3,430,697; Mecca 1,534,731; Medina 1,100,093; Dammam 903,312

Iran's. It abuts every state on the peninsula, as well as Jordan and Iraq. Although Saudi Arabia normally keeps a low profile politically and militarily, it plays a quiet role as a regional balancing factor and maintains a modest defense capability.

Whereas Saudi Arabia is most known for oil and Islam, these are not its only significant characteristics. Politically and religiously conservative, and internationally oriented toward the West, its economic power reinforces its independence and the development of its distinctive assets. Funded with petrodollars, it progressed rapidly after 1960, employing millions of foreign consultants, managers, and laborers while striving zealously to preserve its deeply religious and traditional character. Nevertheless, its people demonstrated socioeconomic resilience in their adaptation both to decades of affluence and to years of recession, as well as to periods of nearby warfare. Nine five-year economic plans have focused on "Saudiization," the development of human services and resources—planners, managers, and workers—to replace expatriates with a new generation of educated Saudis trained in the skills needed by the nation.

Saudi Arabia is a young nation, founded in 1932 on a core area dating from earlier in the century. It was born of a special combination of circumstances and has adhered to many of the traditions that were an integral part of its raison d'être. Such conservatism has mixed consequences: it strengthens the social fabric but both inhibits social evolution and invites foreign and domestic criticism. Its contrasts received global attention when it hosted several hundred thousand foreign troops and media personnel from thirty-three countries during the 1990–1991 Gulf crisis. Saudis realized that the forces were there as protectors, but they were apprehensive about the social mores and values being introduced.

HISTORICAL-POLITICAL GEOGRAPHY

Earliest Days

Limited archaeological exploration had earlier found evidence of widespread ancient occupation, settlement sites, and burial mounds. Dramatic discoveries in the mid-1980s confirmed that bands of *Homo erectus* had brought their Developed Oldowan tool culture from the Olduvai Gorge area in East Africa to western Arabia more than 1 million years ago (see Chap. 3). Late Paleolithic and Neolithic tools found in the now-barren Rub al-Khali were left by hunters or settlers along old lakeshores more than seventeen thousand years ago and again ten to five thousand years ago. Finds along the northeastern coast and on Tarut Island reveal ties with Mesopotamian civilizations of 2500 BCE and earlier (see Map 3.1).

A retracing of old trade routes has shown that many towns depended economically on serving one or more caravan tracks. The major ancient route from Aden led northward through Asir and the Hijaz, to the caravansary and watering point of Mecca, before continuing northward. Traffic along this route in the early seventh century influenced the emergence of Islam.

When Islam's focus of power passed from Mecca and Medina to Damascus in the seventh century and later to Baghdad, the role of the Hijaz diminished for centuries. Most of

Arabia was a frontier zone, isolated and tribally fragmented. In 1258, Mamluk Egyptian control of the holy places replaced Abbasid suzerainty; this passed to the Ottomans who conquered Egypt in 1517. The interior evolved separately, leading to the emergence in the eighteenth century of the influential Al Saud grouping. Battling other clans, they gained a leading role in Najd, the peninsula's core and still the nucleus of Saudi power.

The Al Sauds

In the mid-eighteenth century, the Al Saud leader Muhammad ibn Saud led his family into alliance with a religious reformer, Muhammad ibn Abd al-Wahhab, linking Saudi political-military power and Muslim puritanism. The bond still persists as a strong symbiosis, a hallmark of the kingdom's political-religious identity. The religious element is sometimes called "unitarian" (less appropriately, Wahhabi). From their center in al-Diriyah near Riyadh, the alliance controlled most of the peninsula by the early 1800s. The wary Ottomans ordered Muhammad Ali of Egypt to overthrow the Al Sauds and to reestablish imperial authority over the holy places. Al-Diriyah was captured in 1818, and although Al Saud dominance was interrupted it was not eradicated. This invasion of the heartland, one of very few such successful penetrations into the deep interior in history, was only briefly effective. A few years later, the Sauds regained their lost territories other than the Hijaz and established a new capital in Riyadh, where it has remained.

When Saudi leadership was later weakened by family disputes, the Ottomans occupied al-Hasa in the east, enabling the rival Rashid clan to gain control over much of Najd. The Sauds fled to Kuwait, from which a charismatic young member of the family, Abd al-Aziz ibn Abd al-Rahman, reconquered Riyadh and Najd in 1902. He organized Bedouin into groups of *ikhwan* (brethren) and gradually reclaimed most of the peninsula, annexing the last major area in 1925 when his warriors conquered the Hijaz—the western highlands and coast of the peninsula, which had been the domain of the Hashimite family of Sharif Husayn, of Arab Revolt fame. With control of the holy cities of Mecca and Medina, Abd al-Aziz became "Custodian of the Two Holy Mosques." Each royal successor has used this official title, comparable to the British monarch's designation as "Defender of the Faith."

The Contemporary Kingdom

In January 1927, Abd al-Aziz was officially proclaimed "King of the Hijaz and Najd and Its Dependencies," with Mecca and Riyadh as his capitals. In the Treaty of Jiddah (1927), Britain recognized the status quo in Arabia. In September 1932, Abd al-Aziz, who became known in the West as Ibn Saud, renamed the unified country the Kingdom of Saudi Arabia.[2]

Uneducated but pragmatic, he accepted modernization and skillfully persuaded conservative religious leaders to accept new technologies: automobiles, radios, telephones, and aircraft. After fifty years of adroit rule, guiding his kingdom in unprecedented transformation, he died in 1953 and has been succeeded by five sons—Saud ibn Abd al-Aziz (1953–1964), Faysal ibn Abd al-Aziz (1964–1975), Khalid ibn Abd al-Aziz (1975–1982), Fahd ibn Abd al-Aziz (1982–2005), and, since 2005, Abdullah ibn Abd al-Aziz (regent from 1997 following Fahd's incapacitation from a stroke).

Al Saud–Ulama Alliance. Details of governance are unusually important in Saudi Arabia and deserve some attention. Reflecting the joint power structure, it is controlled by the Al Sauds, in the person of the king, and by the religious leaders, the ulama (sometimes ulema). They intervene if the king departs from conservative Islam. In 1953, Abd al-Aziz appointed the first cabinet; the Council of Ministers—about 30 by the 2000s—is the basic organ of state. In 1993, Fahd responded to pressure for liberalization, reviving the Consultative Council (Majlis al-Shura) originated by his father, with 150 members since 2005. Similar provincial bodies were also formed. Although formation of such groups represents a limited step forward, it is a significant one, as has been demonstrated in the council's frequent meetings and relations with the king and his ministers.

The Basic Law of 1992 codified the monarchy and its powers, declared the Holy Quran to be the country's constitution, and stated that government must observe Islamic law (Sharia). In 2006, Abdullah established the Allegiance Commission made up of senior family members to select the crown prince in the future. The king faces many constraints on his policies and actions, including those concerning modernization. As a consequence, the pace of reform has been slow, and it has been widely criticized, especially since 9/11, both by less conservative Saudis and by Western media.

Conservative Evolution. The steps taken to broaden political institutions have not only been cautious but also carefully consistent with the Saudi preference for evolution rather than revolution. There are no political parties, and the king leads as a shaykh of shaykhs in a male-dominated, largely tribal society. Tradition—not Islamic law—demands that women be severely limited socially, with some exceptions for foreigners: they may not dine alone in a gender-mixed restaurant, drive an automobile, or work in an open public office, and they must be segregated in schools and completely covered in public. Under the kingdom's raison d'être, there is no separation of religion and state. The religious police (*mutawwiin*) enforce adherence to Islamic norms by monitoring public behavior; however, a new head of the police was appointed in 2012, and he has taken steps to rein in some of their activities. According to a US Department of State summary, "Saudi law severely limits freedom of speech and press. Authorities do not countenance criticism of Islam, the ruling family, or the Government."[3]

Small Steps. Saudi Arabia took a small but important step forward in 2005 when it held its first nationwide elections. In three stages, half the members of 178 municipal councils were elected, the other half to be appointed by the king. Women (and members of the military) were not allowed to run for the council or to vote, and the same rules applied for the 2011 elections. Turnout among eligible males was rather low, showing perhaps that the councils have yet to be seen as very influential. Government spokesmen explained that steps toward wider elections had to be taken slowly so that the conservative society could adapt to the procedure: official identification cards, necessary for voting and obtaining government services, will become mandatory for Saudi women. In 2011 King Abdullah decreed that women will be allowed to vote in the next local elections in 2015; in February 2013, a new session of the Majlis al-Shura opened with the swearing in of 30 recently appointed women members.[4] The Ministry of Justice announced in October 2012 that women lawyers will now be allowed to plead before the nation's courts. Time will tell whether sociopolitical changes in the kingdom can be made quantitatively and qualitatively at the pace the Al Sauds believe is demanded by the country's special circumstances.

A Saudi Spring?

Whatever similarities may exist across Arab countries, we must stress that there are also considerable differences, and as a result they will experience the influence of events in Tunisia and Egypt—the initial Arab Spring—in very different ways. Saudi Arabia, a country with no civil society activism to speak of and few significant institutions separate from those of the government, could be seen as ripe for more rapid change. Saudi society is largely prosperous (although significant pockets of poverty exist, driven by high population and unemployment rates), and residents have wide access to traditional and social media, so Saudis were fully aware of what transpired in neighboring countries.

In the early months of 2011, the beginnings of protest appeared, especially in the same social media that had been so prominent in Egypt. This discontent derived from several factors present in the kingdom—discontent among the young about their employment prospects, dissatisfaction about the glacial pace of long-promised reforms, and the resentments within the sizable Shii minority in Saudi Arabia's Eastern Province. Yet through late 2012, despite the spread of revolt to three neighboring states—Bahrain, Yemen, and Syria—Saudi Arabia has remained apparently calm. But among the Shia, frustrated by decades of discrimination and incensed over the Saudi role in Bahrain's suppression of the Shii revolt, the embers of protest have smoldered and occasionally blazed up.

Demonstrations and mass arrests were also reported in early 2013 in Burayda, deep in the Sunni core of the royal family's home territory. Young Saudis have been increasingly vocal on the various social media that are widely available. Their concerns range from lack of employment opportunities and housing shortages to perceived official corruption and favoritism benefiting those with connections to the royal regime.[5]

Factors at Play. At the risk of oversimplification, this situation can be explained by these factors: (1) the prompt and severe actions of the kingdom's security forces against the initial signs of protest and the continued use of these forces against the Shia, (2) the mobilization of the Wahhabi religious establishment to condemn loudly and often any hint of protest as disloyalty to Islam, (3) the exploitation among the Sunni majority of their strong anti-Shia sentiments, and (4) the announcement of what eventually came to an estimated $135 billion in new spending on housing, job creation, subsidies, and other state activities, afforded by currently high world oil prices. Additionally, the government plainly demonstrated its resolve by its strong military support of the beleaguered Sunni regime in Shii-majority Bahrain.

However, it is certainly too soon to conclude that the Saudi regime has been successful in its counterrevolutionary efforts. An octogenarian king who has demonstrated understanding of the need for real reform, but also an inability often to carry through with his promises, may not offer Saudis the prospect of the decisive long-term leadership needed to preserve the regime in the midst of currents of change. A combination of force and money has provided a respite, with more than $130 billion in spending announced. But in August 2012, the International Monetary Fund warned the Saudi government, almost totally reliant on oil revenues, that even with current high oil prices it was spending at levels well beyond sustainability if it wished to provide for future generations. Counting on continued high revenues from oil sales could be a strategic mistake. In the 1980s, when oil prices crashed, the government was unable to curtail spending, and large reserves quickly melted away and were replaced by sizable debts. A replay of that scenario could jeopardize the Saudi approach to maintaining support and mitigating frustrations.

Even among the regime's traditional supporters, concern about the need for change has been publicly voiced. For example, an open letter was posted online in March 2013 by one of the country's most prominent and popular clerics warning that the government must be seen to be serious about instituting reforms, reining in corruption at all levels, and allowing more political discussion.[6]

PHYSICAL PATTERNS

Diversity in the Desert

Despite the preponderance of sand deserts, Saudi Arabia's landforms exhibit great diversity, even in the sizes, shapes, and colors of dunes.[7] Although there are some northern and eastern areas of vast seeming sameness, subtle differences exist and are of great significance to the Bedouin who roam these realms—although in steadily decreasing numbers. The relatively green mountains of Asir in the southwest are especially differentiated from the rest of the country. Scarped sedimentary Najd in the center, crystalline shield Najd farther west, lava-covered areas in the north and the west, and immense sand seas in north, south, and east contrast with one another in both geomorphology and cultural character.

The gross geomorphological characteristics of the peninsula are influenced by its formation as a separate tectonic plate that split from northeastern Africa along the Red Sea rift during the Tertiary period (see Chap. 2). The west-central third of the peninsula is a massive crystalline block of Precambrian igneous and metamorphic rocks, overlain with extensive young basalts on the west. Eastward, sedimentary layers cover the rest of the peninsula, except in al-Hajar in Oman, with strata dipping generally eastward and with successively younger outcrops toward the Gulf. Sand seas and sand dunes blanket more than one-third of the peninsula, including the Nafud in the north, the vast Rub al-Khali in the south, and the arc of the Dahna dunes connecting the two.

Regions

[1] Tihamah. Starting on the west, the first natural region (see circled numbers on Map 15.1) consists of a sandy-gravelly coastal plain, Tihamah, which extends virtually the full

Map 15.1 Reference map of Saudi Arabia. Circled numbers refer to regions discussed in text. Petroleum, solid minerals, transportation, and other topics are shown on maps in relevant chapters (Maps 6.1, 6.2, 6.5, 7.2, and others).

length of the Red Sea coast down through Yemen in the south. Squeezed between the coastline and the rugged Hijaz range, it varies in width from a few meters at the Gulf of Aqabah to more than 25 mi/40 km near Jaizan in southern Saudi Arabia. The plain is referred to in the north as Tihamat al-Sham, in the center as Tihamat al-Hijaz, and in the south as Tihamat Asir. Although it is naturally barren and forbidding, almost waterless between infrequent rains, and lacks significant harbor

indentations, it has been a major route of passage for centuries. During that time, small ports—Wajh, Yanbu, Jiddah, Jaizan—somehow persevered, supported by fishing and limited trade. Jiddah has served as the port of entry for Mecca pilgrims since the seventh century and is now the kingdom's leading general port, and the once small fishing villages are huge industrial ports. A first-class highway now extends along the ancient caravan route from Jordan to Yemen.

Figure 15.1 An unusual landscape in overwhelmingly desertic Saudi Arabia: terraced agriculture in Asir, the best-watered region of the kingdom, just north of Yemen.

[2] Hijaz-Asir Mountains. East of the coastal plain rises a mountain belt ranging in width from 25 to 87 mi/40 to 140 km. It is generally low in the north but increases in elevation toward the south, with crest elevations reaching 6,987 ft/2,130 m northwest of Medina and 9,840 ft/3,000 m near Abha. A gap in the ridges near Mecca has carried a travel route for centuries. From this formidable uplifted crystalline mountain block comes the name for the western region—al-Hijaz (the barrier). The elevated southern segment is Asir, the best-watered part of the country, collecting 12–20 in/300–500 mm of rain annually, especially during the summer monsoon. Moderate slopes echoing the dramatic terraces farther south in Yemen (Fig. 15.1) have long supported warm-season crops. In addition to the Asir rainfall, the Hijaz crest line receives the most winter rain of any part of the kingdom.

Nestled in barren volcanic basins in the center are Islam's sacred cities, Mecca and Medina, as well as al-Taif, the traditional summer capital boasting more pleasant weather than Jiddah or Riyadh. In the unique and fascinating Asir are the rapidly expanding agricultural and resort area around Abha, the military area of Khamis Mushayt, and the pleasant Najran district. A national park attracts thousands of visitors, enjoying spectacular views down the great seaward-facing escarpment populated by hundreds of hamadryas baboons that scamper through the wooded uplands.

[3] Najd. Continuing eastward from the central segment of the uplifted highland and extending to the middle of the peninsula, we find the crystalline block of the Arabian Shield. It comprises granites, gabbros, gneisses, schists, marbles, and related rocks. Like most

shield areas, it has mineralized areas, with deposits of copper, gold, silver, lead, zinc, and other metals. Amounts of most of these minerals are limited, although numerous ancient gold and silver workings have been found through intensive searches by US, French, and Saudi geologists. Persistent exploration has found more than a score of deposits worth large-scale exploitation, and several major mines are now operating. A contract was awarded in 2007 to develop phosphate deposits; initial production was under way at Jalamid in 2011.

Along the shield's western edge are six major lava fields, 390–7,720 mi²/1,000–20,000 km² in extent, forming a graphic reminder of the peninsula's tectonicly active past. The fields are dotted with numerous lava cones and cinder cones in north-south alignments (see Fig. 2.4), and a relatively young basalt flow near Medina dates from as recent as 1250 CE. As Map 4.2 shows, extensive areas of the crystalline shield between the Hijaz Mountains and central Najd are virtually uninhabited.

East of the shield and in distinct contrast to its rugged forms is sedimentary Najd, part of the central plateau, with outcropping sedimentary rocks in a great curved belt around the eastern edge of the crystalline basement. Escarpments, ridges, and buttes, each with a resistant cap, are characteristic features around this Central Arabian Arch. One particular escarpment, an Upper Jurassic limestone cuesta extending along a 1,000-mi/1,600-km crescent, forms Jabal Tuwayq, the most prominent physiographic feature of central Arabia. All of these outcropping strata dip eastward and are found at depths several thousand feet below the surface in the eastern oil fields. The layers of sedimentary rocks in eastern Najd both serve as catchment rocks for aquifers that are tapped in the Eastern Province and also provide conditions for many local contact springs. These gave rise to numerous ancient and still-persisting Najd settlements, and their presence prompted the

drilling of ever-deeper water wells in modern times.

Groups of villages around several central places and coordination of agricultural activity have resulted in a subregional consciousness along Jabal Tuwayq. The main subregion in the north is al-Qasim, located west of the Tuwayq cuesta and centered on the large towns of Buraydah and Unayzah, southeast of Hayil. South-southeast of al-Qasim and west of Jabal Tuwayq is the Washm subregion, with several small towns and an expansive agricultural economy. East of al-Qasim, on the backslope of the Tuwayq escarpment, is the Sudayr, less populated than al-Qasim and centered on Majmaah (see Fig. 4.9). All three districts experienced remarkable development of irrigated agriculture during the 1980s, as well as road-net intensification, population increase, and urban development.

Southeast of Riyadh is the subregion of al-Kharj, with significant solution springs and one of the largest oases in the peninsula. For many years after 1990, one of the most important of several concentrations of US military personnel was based here, until all were withdrawn in 2003. Extending southward from al-Kharj along a secondary cuesta are two well-defined subregions: al-Hawtah, with the villages of al-Hillah and al-Hilway, and, farther south, al-Aflaj, centered on Layla. Al-Aflaj refers to the irrigation system that formerly supported extensive gardens around Layla. The Hawtah subregion was launched into a local oil boom in the period 1989–1991 with the discovery of completely new resources of superlight petroleum in fields extending 47 mi/75 km from the southern Hawtah to al-Dilam, south of al-Kharj.

[4] Dahna, Summan, and the Coastal Plain. Between Najd and the Gulf coast lie three belts that generally parallel the arcuate Jabal Tuwayq. All are generally considered to be in the Eastern Province, and they contain most of Saudi Arabia's oil fields: (1) the Dahna, a

great arc of rust-colored sand dunes 30 mi/48 km wide and extending 800 mi/1,290 km from the Nafud in the north to the Rub al-Khali in the south; (2) al-Summan plateau, with escarpments and buttes on its eastern margins; and (3) near the Gulf coast an irregular plain terminating in a ragged coastline of *sabkhahs* (see Fig. 2.12), sand spits, and offshore sandbars.

Under the plateau and coastal plain and offshore in shallow Gulf water, the world's greatest petroleum reservoirs are now well delineated and intensively exploited. Except for the Hofuf and Qatif Oases and a few small coastal villages, this vast area was the haunt of Bedouin and their herds prior to World War II. Now it throbs with hundreds of oil wells flowing under high-pressure, gas-oil separator plants, flow lines, pump stations, heavy road traffic, oil-related industries, sprawling cities, bustling ports, and an expanding economy. The nerve center of the vast operation is the oil company headquarters in Dhahran, a historical magnet for related developments like the King Fahd University of Petroleum and Minerals, the older international airport, and the huge new King Fahd International Airport. On the coast, the expanding cities of Dammam (the provincial capital) and al-Khobar are creating an agglomeration of varied population and economy. The great oil-export terminal and refinery of Ras Tanura lies north of Dammam (see Fig. 6.4), with the newer and equally large export terminal of Juaymah still farther north and the industrial city of Jubayl topping the Saudi Gulf coast's petroleum-based urban and industrial series.

[5] Rub al-Khali. Vast seas of sand in the north and south of the country constitute two of the most distinctive physical features on the peninsula. The largest single dune field in the world, the Rub al-Khali (Empty Quarter) covers more than 230,000 mi^2/600,000 km^2. Referred to simply as al-Rimal (the Sands) by

Bedouin, the Rub al-Khali comprises almost entirely loose, dry sand shaped into dunes that vary depending upon the wind. Three types predominate: numerous linear or longitudinal dunes (*uruq*; singular, *irq*), some of them 60 mi/100 km long, in the western half (see Fig. 1.1); barchans or crescent dunes in the northeast; and giant dunes, the remarkable Sand Mountains, along the eastern and southern margins. Formless "sand seas" fill other areas. A few areas exhibit some vegetation, but the loose sands are barren; because few wells exist in the area, even Bedouin generally avoid it. Al-Murrah and occasional other tribesmen move along the edges, infrequently crossing it.[8] The eastern area has been opened by development of the rich Shaybah oil field on the UAE border during the 1990s.

[6] The Nafud. The great desert to the northwest is called by the Bedouin simply al-Nafud, the northern term for "sandy desert." Characterized by complex dune forms including deep pits, the reddish sands cover 45,000 mi^2/116,550 km^2. The sediment source for the sand is an extensive area of poorly cemented Paleozoic sandstones that lie upwind from it. The area is sparsely inhabited but constitutes an important seasonal grazing area.

[7] Northern Regions. In the northern reaches of the country lies a sequence of varied landscapes, each with its own identification. In the extreme northwest, at the northern end of the Red Sea, the rugged area of Midyan (biblical Midian) drops eastward to the plain around the military cantonment town of Tabuk. Farther east, the mountain mass of al-Tubayq sinks northeastward to the Wadi al-Sirhan, the great northwest-southeast depression extending from al-Azraq in Jordan to the oasis of al-Jawf in Saudi Arabia. The depression is more than 200 mi/322 km long, about 25 mi/40 km wide, and 1,000 ft/305 m below the level of the plateau. To the northeast, we see the extensive lava fields and cinder

cones of al-Harrah, with the stony plains of al-Hamad, al-Widyan, and al-Hajarah extending to the southeast and traversed by the abandoned Trans-Arabian Pipe Line (Tapline). Southwest of Kuwait is the well-marked Wadi al-Batin and the gravel plain of the Dibdibah.

Most of this vast expanse was virtually uninhabited before 1950, when Tapline spanned the desert and gradually opened the sandy-gravelly plains to development. Towns grew up around the five pump stations, and truck drivers and other travelers followed the pipeline track, later blacktopped and then upgraded to a major highway. Each town now boasts more than 25,000 residents and functions as a service center for traffic along the long highway. The military cantonment of Hafar al-Batin built near Qaysumah was key to ground-force operations during the Gulf War in 1990–1991.

POPULATION AND PEOPLES

Census taking is both a complicated procedure and a sensitive matter. It is complicated because the population is widely scattered, Bedouin move frequently and try to avoid government attention, urban populations shift rapidly, and expatriates present special problems of enumeration: they change fairly frequently, both individually and in total number, and the kingdom has been reluctant to acknowledge its large foreign population. A 1963 sampling suggested a total population of about 3.3 million; a 1992 census showed 16,929,294, about 30 percent expatriate; and in 2012, an estimated 26.5 million included more than 5.5 million expatriates. Census taking is sensitive because rich Saudi Arabia is surrounded by poorer neighbors with considerable military capability. The once-high overall population growth rate has dropped and is now probably less than 2 percent annually. The total fertility rate—the number of children the average woman will have—has been declining quite rapidly, and

although it is still thought to be fourth highest in the region after Yemen, Iraq, and Jordan, it was estimated to have fallen to about 2.9 by 2012. However, decades of high rates of population growth now mean that far more young Saudis are entering the job market than there are new jobs available for them, contributing to the growth in pockets of poverty, as mentioned earlier.

Population Centers

Saudi Arabia has three principal population nuclei and several outliers, all separated by empty or sparsely settled desert. Most populous is Najd, the Saudi heartland, with its node in Greater Riyadh, which now has about 4.4 million inhabitants and remarkably contemporary institutions and buildings (Figs. 15.2 and 15.3). Relatively concentrated Najd settlements extend from Hayil and Buraydah in the north southeastward to al-Kharj, and there are a score of towns of small to medium size in the irrigated depressions on the plateau and along the escarpments.

In the west, the Hijaz-Asir nucleus is aligned on the Jiddah-Mecca-Taif axis. The extended area reaches from Yanbu and Medina in the north to Jaizan and Najran in the south and includes Abha and Khamis Mushayt in the rapidly developing Asir. Across the peninsula, the Eastern Province population centers on Dammam Municipality (which includes Qatif, Dammam, Dhahran, al-Khobar, and al-Thuqbah). The extended agglomeration extends from the new industrial port city of Jubayl on the north to Hofuf in al-Hasa Oasis on the south and includes Qatif Oasis, the oil terminals of Juaymah and Ras Tanura, and the oil-producing center of Abqaiq.

Outliers with sizable populations include Tabuk, in the northwestern corner of the kingdom, with more than 350,000 population; the Hayil Oasis, south of the Nafud, with about 150,000; al-Jawf Oasis, north of the Nafud; settlements along Tapline; and the smaller settlements of al-Khamasin and

Figure 15.2 Young students attending the Visitors' Center for Environmental Awareness in Riyadh, suggesting a great advance from the former Bedouin culture of the peninsula—although Bedouin were acutely aware of their desert environment! Note that only males are in this class group. (Abdullah Y. Al-Dobais, *Saud Aramco World*/SAWDIA)

Figure 15.3 Modern and unusual high-rise buildings in Riyadh are replacing virtually all of the traditional and often-charming structures of the pre-1950s capital.

al-Sulayyil toward the southern end of the Jabal Tuwayq.

People

Although the indigenous Saudi population is relatively uniform ethnically outside of the Hajj cities, it includes varied tribal affiliations. During the thirteen centuries of annual pilgrimages to Mecca, some pilgrims have remained, and they and their descendants have added to the Saudi mixture strains from Indonesia to Morocco, Central Asia to West Africa—evident especially in the Hijaz. In coastal Asir, some Saudis have African physical traits, combined with characteristics that are neither typically Arab nor typically African. In the Qatif and Hofuf Oases of the Eastern Province, there are descendants of Iranians who settled centuries ago, bringing Shii Islam to the predominantly Sunni peninsula. Expatriates come from all corners of the globe.

Clothing is traditional, and centuries-old styles are very much maintained despite modernization. Males wear the loose-fitting, ankle-length white *thawb* (sometimes *thobe*) (see Fig. 15.2). In cool weather and on more formal occasions, a cloak (*bisht* or *mishlah*) is worn over the *thawb*. The head covering both outdoors and indoors is the ubiquitous *ghutrah* (called a *kufiyah* in the Levant), a head cloth with a double ring of black cord (*igal*) to hold it in place. In the oil industry and industrial plants, workers commonly wear Western work clothing during the day, and increasing numbers of young men prefer Western styles. A female in public wears the loose, floor-length *abayah* over her head and body. It may cover a dress similar to the *thawb,* except that it is usually colorful, the latest Paris fashion, or blue jeans. Any of several types of veil or partial face covering may be added to the *abayah*.

Centuries ago, the marginal economy and lack of unity and security prompted many kinship groups to seek localized order in tribal social and power structures. Although modernization has weakened this tribalism, tribal identity is retained by many Saudis, especially Bedouin. Village organization and tribal affiliation remain basic social identity factors among both settled and nomadic populations.

Foreigners. Foreign workers were drawn to the oil fields and cities as early as the 1940s, arriving in large numbers in the 1970s. Uneasy that there are so many non-Muslims in the cradle of Islam, the government strictly controls who enters, for what reason, and for how long; each must have a responsible local person or institution as sponsor. Early expatriates developed petroleum resources; later arrivals were brought in to expand the infrastructure and to maintain going concerns that were unable to find qualified or willing Saudi employees. Rising standards of living created demand for millions of custodial and domestic workers, available in seemingly unlimited numbers from Asia. For many decades, a rewarding symbiosis existed between Saudi Arabia and the large Yemeni labor pool. Before they were expelled because of Yemen's stance on Iraq's invasion of Kuwait, more than a million Yemenis worked in the kingdom during the 1980s; they are still officially banned twenty years later. In late 2012, it was announced that the Majlis al-Shura would consider how to treat the growing problem of an estimated 5 million illegal expatriates—mostly low-skilled workers, many of whom overstay their pilgrimage visas.

Tourists. In the past decade, restrictions against casual visitors have been gradually eased to admit organized groups of tourists eager to see such rarely visited sites as Madain Salih in the northern Hejaz, which is second only to Petra as a monument constructed by Nabateans who dominated the trade route from Yemen to Syria two thousand years ago. In 2010 it was reported that the government planned to increase tourism receipts by more than 350 percent to $64 billion by 2019, and in 2012 the government approved two more sites to be nominated for the World Heritage status now held by Madain Salih and al-Diriyah.[9] A senior member of the ulama (the influential body of Islamic scholars), visiting Madain Salih in September 2012, published a statement calling for increased tourism at the site to create more jobs for young Saudis.

SETTLEMENTS

Although nomadic traditions are strong in the peninsula, sedentarism preceded nomadism. Until after World War II, the typical settlement pattern was widely scattered oasis villages and occasional towns in a symbiotic relationship with nomadic Bedouin living in their long, rectangular tents. Nor were the two lifestyles mutually exclusive: during severe droughts, Bedouin moved into villages; conversely, in less dry years, villagers—especially former nomads—sometimes moved into the desert. Before the petroleum age, an estimated 60 percent of the population was at least partly nomadic. Settling the Bedouin has been a deliberate state policy since Abd al-Aziz's time. Oil stimulated sedentarization, and by the 1990s Bedouin had decreased to less than 4 percent of the population. Permanently settled nomads consider themselves *hadar*—that is, no longer Bedouin.

Since World War II, urbanization has accelerated in Saudi Arabia, as elsewhere, increasing with petroleum development. By the 2000s, nearly 80 percent of the population was urban. No extensive preindustrial cities had evolved, and even the largest settlements—Mecca and Medina, for example—were moderate-size towns of thirty thousand each in the 1930s. But few of today's towns or cities are on completely new sites; even Jubayl and Yanbu are extensions of earlier villages. Transformation of the landscape, epitomized in the metamorphosis of the urban scene, has had minimal outside cognizance; such is one of the drawbacks to the Saudi policy of admitting few Western scholars and reporters. Those who visited Jiddah, Riyadh, and Dammam in the 1950s, when all three were small with few amenities, marvel at what unlimited funds and reasonably intelligent planning have accomplished. Many unique, charming, and historic structures—palaces, forts, walls, and houses—were unfortunately swept away in the rush to modernize; many buildings, especially in Riyadh, were of mud and could not be saved, although a few major sites have been preserved, most of them in Riyadh and Jiddah. Generally, there is more than enough space in the surrounding desert for urban expansion.

Traditional Islamic architectural themes are often employed in new urban centers, universities, and museums. A wide variety of contemporary designs have characterized major new structures that, with generous funding, need not employ monotonous modular techniques. Indeed, Saudi structures are a great architectural success when Islamic traditions are combined with other Arabian features in a contemporary mode. In the mountain villages of Asir, unique exterior house walls typically show alternating courses of mud and projecting rock, with the rock ledges deflecting rain to prevent erosion of the primarily mud walls. Building walls in Najd are topped by decorative battlements, vestiges of military architecture. In Najd, but also in other parts of the country, the wooden doors of many houses are decorated with elaborate geometric designs.

ECONOMIC PATTERNS

Economic patterns had been stable for centuries when discovery of petroleum in 1938 initiated a literally fabulous transformation. Before then, remote and poor Arabia survived on limited pastoralism and oasis agriculture, coastal fishing, pilgrimage earnings, and meager trade. With modest but increasing oil production during the 1950s and 1960s, the kingdom had a glimpse of things to come—the development explosion of the 1970s. National income from oil exceeded $300 million per day between 1977 and 1981, supplying billions of dollars for perhaps the most complete transformation in history of a large country on a grand scale and in a short time. With urban and systems planners, design engineers, architects, contractors, educators, and workers from western Europe, North America, the Middle East, and South Asia, Saudi Arabia virtually built an entire country, from infrastructure to complete universities and US-style fast-food shops. Private capital contributed retail centers, many of the smaller industries, and most of the agricultural expansion.

Development According to Plans

Much of the development has been guided by series of five-year plans, with a peak during the $195 billion second plan, 1975–1980; twenty-eight dams, four ports, 175,000 new homes, 15,000 mi/24,000 km of roads, and the Jiddah airport (the world's largest until Riyadh's opened) were completed. Water projects, industrial developments, petroleum operations, infrastructure, and the billion-dollar causeway to Bahrain were constructed or greatly expanded. The fourth plan, 1985–1990, was curtailed following the sharp drop in the oil market in 1982. Daily oil sales dropped from $364.8 million in 1980 to $36.3 million in 1985—and the value of the dollar was also shrinking. The fifth plan, 1990–1995, budgeted for $100 billion, focused especially on the needs of the country's defenses arising from the Gulf War. The sixth plan, 1995–2000, emphasized government efficiency, more training, a more diverse economy—especially in industry and agriculture—and greater Saudiization of the labor force. The seventh (2000–2005) and eighth plans (2005–2010) focused on diversification and the pri-

vate sector. The current ninth plan (2010–2015) provided originally for $385 billion in projects focusing on improving the standard of living, increasing employment and economic competitiveness, and balancing regional development; as mentioned earlier, the government reacted to the Arab Spring by announcing additional spending on housing and job-creation efforts. For example, to counteract the growing housing shortage that is particularly burdensome on young Saudis planning on starting a family (and coincidentally in the same age cohorts so prominent in Arab Spring demonstrations elsewhere), 1.25 million new homes will be built by 2014 and another 3.4 million by 2020; an estimated 30 percent of Saudis had inadequate housing in 2013.[10]

Each plan has sought to reduce dependence on crude petroleum, to increase self-sufficiency and reduce imports and, in the long run, to develop national viability for the inevitable end of petroleum-based prosperity when the wells run dry. A secondary goal is to ensure that the enviable and highly efficient infrastructure, systematically developed at the cost of many hundreds of billions of dollars, is properly maintained, repaired, and upgraded. Although in many ways it is obvious how much the living standards for Saudi citizens have improved, using the Human Development Index computed by the UNDP illustrates the manner in which this has happened. The kingdom's HDI rose by about 36 percent between 1980 and 2013 because of major increases in the life-expectancy and education components of the index. In 2013, it ranked 57th out of 186 countries globally and 7th regionally. The Legatum Institute's more broadly based Prosperity Index placed the kingdom in 52nd place of 142 countries globally and 5th regionally in 2012.[11]

Agriculture

Agriculture's share in the economy decreased sharply after 1960, falling to only 3 percent by the mid-1970s. It jumped to 13 percent a decade later when fuel subsidies pushed a rapid expansion of irrigated crop production, but it has gradually receded in relative terms and was estimated to account for about 2 percent of GDP in 2012. In 2008, the government reversed its policy of self-sufficiency in wheat, formulated in the tense 1970s, in recognition of the devastating effect massive irrigation projects have had on the rapidly dwindling supply of nonrenewable groundwater. Rainfed agriculture dominates in Asir, where highlands intercept summer monsoon rains and the water is efficiently utilized on terraced plots (see Fig. 15.1).

As a result of planning for agricultural self-sufficiency, with the government offering many times the world market price for wheat produced domestically, and with subsidies for well drilling and pump fuel, wheat acreage rocketed from an average of 175,400 ac/71,000 ha 1979–1981 to 2.02 mn ac/816,000 ha in 1989–1991, and production increased from 180,000 mt to 3.69 mn mt. The Najdi landscape was transformed in the 1980s with hundreds of startlingly green circles of wheat, watered by self-propelled center-pivot sprinkler systems, appearing against the tawny sands. Because domestic demand was only 800,000 mt, the excess was exported or donated—in effect, "virtual water" was being exported from the desert kingdom. As the aquifer water level plummeted from overuse, and cost accounting showed the real costs involved, the government decreased subsidies and reduced quotas. In 2006, the agricultural sector used 88 percent of domestic water resources; the proportion had been declining slowly with the changes in the incentive structure. Wheat production had fallen sharply, and by the late 2000s was about 2.6 mn mt, when the most important commodities by value were meat, fruits, milk, eggs, and vegetables.

Oases. Of the many oases in the kingdom, the two largest—both in the Eastern Province—are classic examples. Hofuf (al-Hasa),[12] the largest on the peninsula and the largest groundwater-fed oasis in the world, is watered by 159 springs, including 8 major artesian springs (*ayns*) that flow a total of more than 1,900 g (gallons)/7,190 l (liters) per second. The largest single spring has a flow of 475 gal/1,800 l per second. A major project in the early 1970s modernized and systematized the irrigation and drainage, replacing ditches with concrete conduits. The greater drawdown is lowering the water table alarmingly. Qatif, a few miles north of Dammam, received much of the same modernization. Both oases have been improved and upgraded in successive development projects. Large areas of former date-palm groves are now devoted to fruit trees and vegetable production in plastic greenhouses. The transformation is another instance of the steady disappearance of the traditional and fascinating before the march of modernization and the imperative for efficiency.

Although their numbers are decreasing, many Bedouin still pursue a nomadic lifestyle and continue to supply animals and animal products to the economy. Increasing numbers of families divide their time between nomadism and raising crops or other economic pursuits in villages on the perimeters of their tribal *dirahs*. As have nomads in other parts of the Middle East, many have electric generators, televisions, and refrigerators in their tents, parking their pickup trucks alongside.

Water

Water studies have yielded approximations of the water balance, permitting systematic efforts for more effective use of renewable resources. Hydrogeological studies reveal that much of the deep aquifer water in Najd is "fossil water," stored as long ago as forty thousand years, and that water in the relatively shallow aquifers of the Eastern Province is eighteen to twenty-eight thousand years old. Thus, using this water amounts to "mining" nonrenewable resources, and systematic efforts must be made to substitute renewable water for fossil water in irrigation—particularly in the production of subsidized wheat, for example. The Disi aquifer, spanning the Saudi-Jordan border, is being used by both countries in a "race to the bottom," with little apparent regard for conservation; generally, with aquifers, it is difficult to determine how much water there is and how much can be withdrawn (see Chap. 12 for a discussion of Jordan's use of this aquifer).

Fundamental to the agricultural program has been a series of water development projects that added more than 200 dams with a capacity of 29.5 bn ft^3/836 mn m^3, several hundred deep wells, and many miles of irrigation conduits. Most of the dams were constructed in Najd and particularly in Asir, where the Wadi Bishah Dam is one of the largest in the Middle East outside Turkey and Egypt.

Desalination. The domestic water supply also relies on desalination. Availability of huge amounts of fuel prompted the initiation in 1965 of a massive construction program of large-scale plants. In less than five decades and with $25 billion in investment, the kingdom had the world's greatest desalination complex and led the world in the production of potable water—now estimated to be 17 percent of total world output. In the early 2010s, thirty facilities pumped desalted water through 2,300 mi/3,700 km of pipelines to supply 70 percent of the kingdom's potable water. With more large plants recently completed, the country has a daily capacity of 800 mn gal/3 mn m^3. The Jubayl operation is the world's largest and pumps millions of gallons of distilled water daily to Riyadh; however, prodigal use often creates shortages in summer months. Potable water, like many commodities, is heavily subsidized, and it is often not metered; thus, it is frequently wasted. Per capita water consumption in the kingdom was estimated in 2012 to be 91 percent higher than the global average. More seriously for the future, eventually plentiful cheap energy will be depleted, the population will have certainly doubled or more, and the country will face a crucial threat to its survival. Until now, these plants have been fueled mostly with natural gas, but a new solar-powered plant near al-Khafji is under construction, and some $10.6 billion has been budgeted for new, more efficient facilities. A 2013 report from the kingdom's largest bank warned that a combination of having the region's lowest water tariffs and growing demand from industry and consumers threatens the country's long-term economic-growth prospects.[13]

Fishing

Important on both coasts for centuries, fishing since the 1950s has been especially developed on the east coast. Traditional methods have been replaced by modernized techniques and equipment. Ships operate primarily out of Dammam, and there are processing and freezing plants in Dammam and al-Khobar. Additional facilities were built in the new port of Jubayl. With all of the Gulf littoral states intensifying fishing efforts, overfishing has occurred, and the total Gulf catch peaked in 1967–1968. In 2012, the government initiated a $67 million effort in cooperation with the Food and Agricultural Organization to improve the catches of small and medium-size fishing enterprises.

PETROLEUM

Beneath the deserts of eastern Arabia, the world's largest petroleum reserves lay unrecognized until the 1930s.[14] King Abd al-Aziz had granted a concession to a British syndicate in 1923, but it did not pursue exploration and lost the concession. In 1933, he gave Standard Oil of California (Socal) the exclusive right to prospect for and produce oil in eastern Arabia, along with preferential rights in other parts of the kingdom, originally for a period of sixty years. California Arabian Standard Oil Company (Casoc), a new subsidiary, took up the concession in 1934. Socal (which later became Chevron) agreed to a fifty-fifty ownership deal in Casoc with the Texas Company (which merged with Chevron in 2001) in 1937. In 1944, Casoc was renamed the Arabian American Oil Company, with the now world-famous acronym Aramco, which is still used even for the Saudi-owned company. In 1948, the Standard Oil Company of New Jersey (later named Esso and then Exxon) and the Socony-Vacuum Oil Company (later named Mobil) joined in the Aramco ownership (they merged and become ExxonMobil in 1999). The four owner companies formed the all-US capital and technical force behind oil development in mainland Saudi Arabia until 1973.

Dammam Dome.   Socal started drilling in April 1935 in Dammam Dome near the Gulf coast; the first discovery came in March 1938. (The discovery well, Dammam Number 7, was finally shut down only in 1983 after producing 1,600 bpd for forty-five years.) Exports started in May 1939 at Ras Tanura, eventually one of the world's great oil-export terminals (see Fig. 6.4). Exploration—which still continues—soon showed that the Eastern Province contained the world's largest fields. The first segment of Ghawar, the largest of these, was found in 1948, and Safaniya, the largest offshore field in the world, was discovered in 1951. By 2004, eighty commercial oil and gas fields had been discovered (see Maps 6.1 and 6.2), including the remarkable Shaybah oil and gas structure along the UAE southern border in the remote Rub al-Khali. In full operation by 1998, it produces 500,000 bpd of especially valuable extra-light crude and huge amounts of nonassociated gas (see Fig. 15.4). A cumulative total of more than 130 bn bbl has been produced just by Aramco since 1938, yet reserves were 265.4 bn bbl in 2012 and were expected to increase; reserves

of natural gas exceeded 287.8 tn ft³/8.15 tn m³ (fourth largest in the world), and major projects were under way to upgrade scores of facilities all over the kingdom.

Saudi Aramco

In 1973, the government took a 25 percent ownership of Aramco, increasing it to 60 percent in 1974 and to 100 percent in 1980; the US partners were bought out. Designated the Saudi Arabian Oil Company (Saudi Aramco) in 1988, it continues to be known in the industry by its familiar acronym and is both operator for Saudi production and intermediate contractor for a range of engineering and construction projects. The company first served this function in 1949, overseeing construction of the Dammam-Riyadh railway, and more recently the implementation of the Master Gas Plan.

Aramco took its first major step into downstream operations in 1988 in a joint venture with Texaco for refining, distributing, and marketing in the eastern and Gulf coast regions of the United States. It has since purchased or joined enterprises in South Korea and other Asian countries. Its fundamental structure and function changed greatly during the 1990s consequent to a royal decree of July 1, 1993. Entirely government owned, it was charged with all government oil operations in the kingdom, upstream and downstream, from exploration to marketing. It took over Tapline (originally a separate company), Petroline (East-West Crude Oil Line), all government-owned refineries, and Petromin retail marketing outlets. Thus, it is no longer simply an upstream company producing oil and gas but a fully integrated, diversified company with refining and shipping interests and worldwide joint-venture marketing operations. Its reserves, production capacity, production facilities, transport lines, markets, and workforce size (fifty-eight thousand) make it one of the world's four-largest integrated oil companies.

Figure 15.4 A triumph of technology: the major crude-processing facility built in "the middle of nowhere"—at Shaybah in Sand Hills of the Empty Quarter. The relatively recently discovered field lies just south of the southern UAE border. (Abdullah Y. Al-Dobais, Saudi Aramco)

As explained in Chapter 8, the former Saudi Arabia–Kuwait Neutral Zone was partitioned between the two neighbors in 1965, demarcated in 1970, and divided approximately equally. To avoid confusion, the two governments agreed to share equally the zone's oil reserves and revenues. Although parastatal Aramco was the sole operator in the kingdom, US-owned Texaco (which merged with Chevron in 2001) had the concession for the zone (held by Getty Oil Company before 1984 when it was acquired by Texaco), and after 1957 the Japanese-owned Arabian Oil Company held offshore rights until it lost them in 2000 to Saudi Aramco. Proved reserves are 5 bn bbl; production in 2012 averaged 615,000 bpd.

As the sole operator in its concession area, Aramco drilled only the optimum number of wells, without having to be concerned about leases and offset drilling; even after sixty years, none of them requires pumping. Reservoir pressure is maintained by reinjecting natural gas and by a huge water-injection system—more than 10 mn bbl of nonpotable water is pumped daily into major reservoirs as oil is withdrawn. Much of the water is brought to the great Ghawar field by three large pipelines 60 mi/100 km from the Gulf. In 2012, about 2,895 flowing wells produced about 9.96 mn bpd, or about 3,440 bpd each, compared with an average 15.3 bpd from each of the 413,000 wells in the United States.

Downstream

Handling, transporting, and processing the petroleum require a complex of facilities all across eastern Arabia—strung together with more than 13,050 mi/21,000 km of pipelines. Each of more than seventy gas-oil separator plants serves several wells within a considerable radius via flow lines, each well showing its fiery flare—now reduced to conserve natural gas—against the sky. Stabilizers in Abqaiq and Juaymah "sweeten" sour crude, and natural gas liquids (NGL) plants produce propane, butane, and natural gasoline. There are numerous large petroleum-related industrial plants along the Gulf coast, especially in the industrial city of Jubayl. Huge oil-export terminals operate at Ras Tanura and Juaymah, with crude and product storage capacities of 30 mn bbl and 25 mn bbl, respectively, as well as at Yanbu on the Red Sea, with 12.5 mn bbl storage capacity—two and a half times the average daily production in the United States.

Refineries.   The kingdom has seven active refineries with a total throughput of 2.1 mn bpd. In the east, the largest are in Ras Tanura, 550,000 bpd, and Jubayl, 290,000; in the west, in Rabigh, 400,000, and in Yanbu, 400,000 and 235,000; and in Najd, Riyadh, 120,000. Three new refineries are under construction with a total of 1.2 million bpd; they are due to become operational by 2017. As Chapter 6 explained, the great 500,000 bpd Trans-Arabian Pipe Line (Tapline) that opened in 1951 was beset by political problems and became unprofitable during the 1970s. It ceased pumping to Sidon in 1983 and to the Zarqa refinery in Jordan in 1990; it is now unusable without major new investment.

New Pipelines.   However, the concept of an outlet to the west was strategically revived for insurance against potential dangers to shipping in the Gulf and at the Hormuz choke-point, leading in the 1980s to a billion-dollar project spanning the peninsula, from the eastern fields to Yanbu on the Red Sea, with three pipelines. The East-West NGL pipeline, 726 mi/1,170 km long and 26–30 in/66–76 cm in diameter, was commissioned in 1981. The first component of a dual East-West Crude Oil Pipeline, 48 in/122 cm in diameter, was commissioned the same year; a huge second one,

56 in/142 cm in diameter and a "loop" of the first line, opened in 1987. Both are 745 mi/1,200 km long. The addition of pumps and the expansion of facilities at each end of this system in 1991 raised capacity to nearly 5 mn bpd—ten times Tapline's capacity and half of Aramco's production capacity. The parallel NGL line carries 270,000 bpd of ethane and natural gas liquids. This gives the kingdom an entirely domestic secure route, reducing the cutoff threat, although exports from Yanbu are still subject to possible interdiction at either end of the Red Sea. After the invasion of Kuwait in 1990, the government closed the 2.35 mn bpd IPSA pipelines, an Iraqi-owned facility, from southern Iraq to the Red Sea after less than one year in service; it was seized by the Saudis in 2001 in recompense for unpaid debts (see Chap. 6). After that, it saw some use transporting natural gas to power plants in the western part of the country, but in 2012 it was quietly resurrected as a Saudi oil-delivery system bypassing the Strait of Hormuz.

Natural Gas

During the 1960s, Aramco realized that the kingdom's combined natural gas resources, associated and nonassociated, were an asset rivaling oil wealth. By 2012, total proven gas reserves (about 288 tn ft^3) ranked fourth in the world (after Russia, Iran, and Qatar—ahead of the United States, not counting shale gas). In the late 1970s, the kingdom undertook the ambitious Master Gas System. Formerly flared associated gas (about 57 percent of proven reserves) now supplies power-generating stations, water desalination plants, numerous factories, and domestic lines—or is reinjected to maintain oil-field pressure. Huge reservoirs of nonassociated gas—including deep Khuff gas under the great Ghawar oil field—are yielding gas for the industrial cities of Jubayl and Yanbu as fuel and feedstock for oil refineries, petrochemical and fertilizer plants, steel plants and rolling mills, and other industries. Serious attention is being given to the considerable potential for large-scale exports. Jubayl and Yanbu together account for 10 percent of the world's petrochemical production and are further expanding their output. Now collecting and processing more than 5.67 bn ft^3/161 mn m^3 of gas per day, the system can add the equivalent of more than 1.25 mn bbl of crude oil a day to the world's supply of energy. In the late 2000s, about half the kingdom's electricity was generated using gas, and this proportion was increasing.

Master Gas Plan. The increasing importance of natural gas in both the domestic and the world economies prompted Saudi Arabia to complement the Master Gas Plan of the 1980s with a $20 billion Saudi Gas Initiative (SGI). The SGI is opening new gas fields and constructing processing facilities, all with foreign investment participation—the first since nationalization in the 1970s. Both newcomers and old Middle East hands are among the firms that have sought and won exploration concessions in joint ventures with Saudi Aramco. Successful contenders include Royal Dutch/Shell, ENI of Italy in partnership with Repsol YPF of Spain, Lukoil of Russia, and Sinopec of China; much of their efforts are directed at the previously underexplored Rub al-Khali. Test drilling in areas known to contain deposits of shale-bearing gas was planned for 2013; one estimate is that technically recoverable shale gas may amount to twice the currently known conventional deposits.[15]

A Global Player

Saudi Arabia is a charter member of both OPEC and OAPEC (see Chap. 6) and has played a particularly major role in the former since its founding. As its production constituted an increasingly greater share of the OPEC and world totals, it played a "swing role" in influencing the world price of petroleum for several years by varying its output. As the world's leading producer, it was the only country with sufficient spare capacity to increase output significantly enough—1.5 to 2 mn bpd—to stabilize or bring down oil prices. Through the mid-2000s, along with pressing all OPEC members to adhere to their quotas, the kingdom's role as a market maker still held up—for example, during the 2003–2004 oil crisis. The Saudi increase in mid-2004 was, indeed, helpful in causing prices to retreat from the record highs up to that time. However, during the oil-price spike later that year, not even maximum output from all producers could force the price to return to the $30–$40 range from its sustained record high—up to that time—in the $50-plus-a-barrel bracket.

By the late 2000s, the world oil market seemed to have entered a new stage, with the result that prices hit all-time record highs close to $150 a barrel in the summer of 2008. Whether this was due to escalating demand in two of the largest consumers, China and India, or speculative manipulations in the market or a combination of both still is not clear. What was obvious was that neither increased Saudi output nor the Bush administration's all-purpose prescription for whatever happened in world oil markets—more drilling in the United States—could dampen this rapid escalation. Similarly, when prices fell even more precipitously in the fall of that year, whether due to the deepening global economic crisis or speculators retiring from the market with enormous profits, it was equally clear Saudi output variations were not a factor. Similarly, when fears of war closing the Starit of Hormuz beginning in 2011 again sent prices climbing, increased production was not enough to offset the upward pressure. The kingdom's oil revenues hit a record level of $311 billion in 2011 and seemed likely to surpass this level in 2012.

In the face of opposition from Venezuela and Iran, the Saudis have remained a strong supporter of continuing the practice of pricing oil in dollars, reiterating in 2010 that it would keep the riyal linked directly to the dollar.[16] A study based on data from the International Energy Agency showed that, along with the UAE, Saudi Arabia has hewn most closely to its assigned OPEC production quota; these two states were in compliance about 98 percent of the time, while the overall average compliance rate was only 56 percent.[17]

Looking beyond hydrocarbons, the kingdom has undertaken an extensive program to harness its abundant solar power, not only for domestic energy needs (thus saving oil and gas for sales abroad) but also for export by the 2020s.[18]

OTHER INDUSTRIES

In the 1950s, manufacturing expanded with four key developments: expansion and diversification of oil operations and the industry's workforce, a rapid increase in population and consumer demand, growth in available private and government capital, and an increase in foreign company joint ventures with Saudi partners—including the government. Succeeding decades saw a marked increase in the number, size, and diversity of producing establishments. At first they turned out processed foods, paper and plastic items, clothing, and basic furniture. From the 1970s, they added items such as paints, air conditioners, aluminum prefabricated buildings, steel rods, and a number of products using oil and gas as feedstocks and fuel. It is products like petrochemicals and other chemicals, fertilizers, and by-product sulfur that have become the multibillion-dollar core of the industrial-complex output. The development plans have devoted considerable resources to the development of nonfuel minerals mining and processing, including phosphates, bauxite, copper, zinc, iron, and gold. By the early 2010s, some of these projects were beginning to come to fruition, and the vastly expanded railroad network now under construction (see below in "Transportation") is geared to expanding mining operations. In a joint venture with Sudan, a Saudi-Canadian company is aiming to begin deepwater mining in the Red Sea for gold and copper in 2014.[19]

Unlike the Gulf states, Saudi Arabia has not tried to link its domestic financial services sector too closely to the international market for a number of reasons: a history of tight banking regulations, a long-held policy of keeping the riyal from being internationalized, the sensitivity of having an interest-based system in the cradle of Islam, and the ability to let the domestic system enjoy most of the benefits accruing from corporate ties to some of the world's biggest banks. Nevertheless, the need for a modern and efficient financial system has long been recognized, and the domestic sector is extensive and a major employer; seven of its twelve banks are among the fifteen largest in the Arab world. Altogether, the country's historic conservatism with regard to the financial sector stood it in good stead as the global economic crisis took hold in 2008.

Investing in the Future

With a shortage of indigenous technological experience and trained labor, the kingdom relied on foreigners for technology, equipment, and labor for construction and industrialization projects—often on a turnkey basis (see Chap. 7). For many major efforts, contracts were on a build-operate-maintain (BOM) basis. However, educational and vocational programs have provided more trained local workers, and Saudiization is raising the percentage of Saudis in the labor force. More important is the large-scale development of education, including technical training, under the five-year plans.

The King Fahd University of Petroleum and Minerals (Fig. 15.5) is an example of the major institutions established since the 1960s. In 2009, two major new universities were launched. On a Red Sea coast campus,

Figure 15.5 The University of Petroleum and Minerals in Dhahran, Eastern Province. Built in the 1960s on a stretch of sand and rock south of Aramco headquarters, it was the first of several new universities built in Saudi Arabia with some of the rising oil income and represents the plans for a modernized and technological segment in Saudi society.

the King Abdullah University of Science and Technology began with an enrollment of some eight hundred students from more than sixty countries, all on full scholarships; women will attend classes with men and need not be veiled.[20] The Princess Noura bint Abdulrahman University in a Riyadh suburb will eventually enroll forty thousand women students, offering courses that they would have difficulty studying at gender-segregated institutions; its extensive 800 ha/3.1 mi^2 will have its own automatic metro system. By the early 2010s, the kingdom had about sixty institutions of higher learning, located in every major city in the country.

Investing the high petrodollar income of the 1970s, Saudi Arabia built the two model industrial cities mentioned earlier, Jubayl on the Gulf and Yanbu on the Red Sea. Focusing on industries based on oil and gas, both have refineries and plants producing petrochemicals and other chemicals, fertilizers, plastics, steel, and plastic and metal goods. Facilities now include ports and airports, huge dual-purpose systems combining seawater desalination and power generation, and satellite industrial and consumer-goods plants. Integrated planning and construction included both service and residential sectors in contemporary architectural designs.

By the late 2000s, manufacturing was contributing more than 10 percent to GDP. Many incentives attracted both local capital and joint ventures by foreign companies. The government established the Saudi Arabian Basic Industries Corporation (now partially privatized) in 1976 to develop large petrochemical and steel plants. In 2008, it was reported that nearly four thousand factories were capitalized at $81.7 billion and that petrochemicals were the most rapidly expanding industry.

TRANSPORTATION

Highways. With sparse population and a preindustrial economy, Arabia before the mid-twentieth century had no road network to move people and goods over the deserts. Camels plodding along ancient caravan trails continued to be the common mode of transport, especially of goods, until after World War II. A few automobiles drove across the open deserts, following old caravan routes, but they often foundered in deep sand before the advent of four-wheel drive and sand tires.

Petroleum development called for establishment and expansion of a road net, and the first surfaced roads linked the main towns and oil facilities in the Eastern Province. Highway construction peaked in the early 1980s; by the late 1990s, highways extended to every town, and remote villages were tied into the network by branch rural roads (Map 15.2; see also Map 7.2). A four-lane divided highway connects the Red Sea and the Gulf (Jiddah-Mecca-Riyadh-Dammam), with a spur to Medina in the west and another to Unayzah and Buraydah in the northern Najd. At the Gulf end, the highway crosses the 15.5-mi/25-km King Fahd Causeway to Bahrain that opened in 1986 (see Fig. 7.5), carrying unbroken lines of cars on Thursdays and Fridays, the Saudi weekend. It has been so successful that in the early 2010s, serious planning was under way for a $3 billion 31.1-mi/50-km causeway and bridge project across the Strait of Tiran to connect Saudi Arabia and Egypt's Sinai Peninsula, with Tiran Island as the midway link. Several major north-south highways in the west, central, and eastern regions tie the population centers to all eight of the kingdom's neighboring countries.

Air Facilities. Population concentrations widely separated by barren deserts encour-aged the use of air transportation in preference to railways and roads in the early years of the country's development. Saudia, the national airline, founded in 1945, evolved originally under a management contract with the US airline TWA. It steadily expanded to become the largest airline in the Middle East, with more than 140 jet aircraft serving a worldwide traffic net; however, Dubai's Emirates Airline's fleet surpassed Saudia's in the mid-2000s. A ten-year airport-building program has supplied all cities and major towns in the country with modern airports, their runways accommodating at least medium-size jet aircraft. In the new century, more than two hundred airports, twenty-six with regular commercial service, served Saudi cities and towns.

In the early 1980s, the kingdom opened two new international airports—in Jiddah and in Riyadh—then the two largest in the world. Jiddah's covers 40 mi²/103km² and includes a separate award-winning facility for up to 2 million Muslims making the annual pilgrimage to nearby Mecca. Now named after King Abd al-Aziz, the airport is now undergoing a major expansion, as both regular and pilgrimage traffic have grown beyond the original capacity; a direct rail link to Jiddah and Mecca is part of the enlarged facility. Three times the size of that in Jiddah, the Riyadh King Khalid International Airport opened in 1984, and its four terminals were designed to handle 15 million passengers a year. After much delay, in 1999, an even larger facility (King Fahd International Airport) covering 300 mi²/780 km² opened in the Eastern Province, 22 mi/57 km northwest of Dammam, replacing the kingdom's first modern airport in Dhahran.

Railways. The Saudi Government Railroad, opened in 1951, links the port of Dammam with Riyadh via Hofuf, Harad, and al-Kharj. This 360-mi/580-km link was the sole operating rail line in the kingdom—and the entire

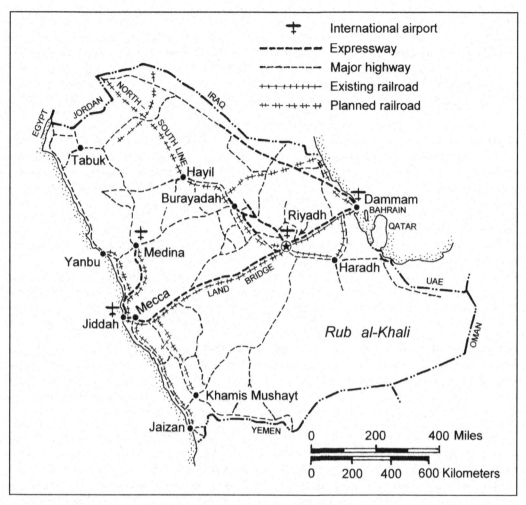

International airport
Expressway
Major highway
Existing railroad
Planned railroad

Map 15.2 Transportation and other economic aspects of Saudi Arabia. Roads are shown in greater detail than in Map 7.2, and planned rail lines are indicated.

peninsula—for thirty years. In 1985, the government's General Saudi Railways Organization opened a dual line that ran directly between Dammam and Riyadh, avoided the Harad loop, and shortened the trip by 20 percent. A major expansion of the Saudi rail net was either under way or in the advanced planning stages beginning in the early 2010s (see Map 15.2).[21] The north-south line from the Jordan border (and ongoing routes connecting to Europe) to Riyadh via Buraydah with a branch to Ras Azwar on the Gulf began limited operations in 2010. When completed, it will stretch 1,490 mi/2,400 km; the line is mainly for freight (including moving bauxite and phosphate from Saudi mines to processing plants), but plans provide for later passenger service.[22] The Saudi Landbridge will connect the Red Sea with the Gulf via a 590-mi/945-km line from Jiddah to Riyadh, together with an upgrade of the existing Riyadh-Dammam link and a 70-mi/115-km connector between Dammam and Jubayl. A link to the Kuwaiti system now being built is also planned as part of the Gulf Cooperation Council (GCC) plan to connect all the members by rail; this eastern line will extend farther south to reach the Qatari and United Arab Emirates borders. The Haramain (Two Sanctuaries) High Speed line will speed pilgrims some 273 mi/440 km from Jiddah's airport to Mecca and Medina at speeds up to 200 mi/320 km per hour; this line seems to be on target for an early-2014 completion.[23]

Connecting central Mecca with outlying pilgrimage sites since 2010 is an elevated urban line. Other intraurban projects currently at one stage or another are in Riyadh, Jiddah, and Mecca. The Riyadh network will include both monorail and conventional lines and will extend to the airport. In August 2012, the first phases of multiline networks for Jiddah and Mecca were approved.

The legendary Hijaz Railway—sometimes Pilgrim Railway—stopped operating after World War I, and much of its trackage no longer exists (see Chap. 7). However, again in 2009, during a visit of the Turkish president, the Saudis announced that the two countries would undertake a feasibility study for rebuilding the century-old line as a standard-gauge line linking Turkey's network with the new Saudi line to Medina. Any reconstruction would require considerable investment in Jordan and Syria as well; obviously, the current political situation in the latter country has put its own rail expansion plans on hold. Recognizing the historic regional significance of the railway, two museums, in Madain Salih and Medina, featuring old trains and other equipment, opened in 2006.[24]

Ports and Shipping. Beginning in the 1950s, the earliest infrastructural preparation for the enormous development ahead was the expansion of ports on both sides of the peninsula. Jiddah had for centuries served as the entry port for pilgrims to nearby Mecca as well as for the limited cargo to Hijaz. When dredging through coral reefs and the manifold expansions of docks, handling facilities, and storage areas were completed, Jiddah became one of the leading ports in the region for containerized and bulk cargo. A new pilgrim terminal, Jiddah Islamic Port, was added to its facilities. In the east, Dammam evolved into the Gulf coast equivalent of Jiddah. Large, newer specialized ports were built during 1975–1985 in the industrial cities of Jubayl on the Gulf and Yanbu on the Red Sea. As was noted earlier, two of the world's largest oil-export terminals were developed in Ras Tanura (an impressive 6 mn bpd capacity) and Juaymah, followed by Yanbu on the west.

RELATIONS

As a large, strategically located country with some of the world's most vitally valuable resources, Saudi Arabia inevitably has especially sensitive relations with its neighbors and with its global partners. Whatever its governmental structure and policies, this would be true, and all the more so given its unusually rigid conservatism. The monarchy has been heavily criticized for years, both cautiously within the country and vigorously on the world scene.

Emerged from isolation in the 1950s, it defined its national interests in relation to the Arab world, within the Islamic community, and among other oil-producing—and oil-consuming—countries. It was a charter member of the United Nations, and it has been active in many organizations, including the Arab League, Organization of the Islamic Cooperation, Gulf Cooperation Council (headquartered in Saudi Arabia), International Monetary Fund, World Bank, International Fund for Agricultural Development, African Development Bank, Islamic Development Bank, OPEC, and OAPEC. It is a member of the G-20, the principal economic and financial forum of the world's wealthiest economies.[25] In both absolute and percentage of GDP terms, it is one of the leading donor countries. Despite its natural dominance among its neighbors, it rarely plays a combative or hawkish role, preferring a more defensive posture as home of the Two Holy Mosques.

Arab Neighbors

The kingdom has generally maintained peaceful relations with its eight neighbors, with a few notable exceptions—most prominent were a short war with Yemen in 1934, a dispute with Abu Dhabi and Oman over the Buraymi Oasis during the 1940s and 1950s, support for the imam of Inner Oman against the sultan of Oman during the late 1950s and 1960s, and, of course, the 1990–1991 Gulf Crisis. In 1965, it concluded a border realignment agreement with Jordan that gave the latter a longer Red Sea coastline in return for some lands in the interior. It has also had off-and-on boundary disputes with Qatar, the UAE, Oman, and Yemen. These have all been smoothed over, and all of the kingdom's boundaries are now de jure (see "Regional Conflicts," in Chap. 8).

Yemen. Conflict in Yemen arose again in 1962–1969, when Saudi Arabia supported the royalists against Egypt-allied republicans, and in 1990, when it opposed Yemeni unification. Yemen's refusal to condemn Iraq's invasion of Kuwait (when Yemen was a member of the UN Security Council) angered the Kingdom, which then expelled 800,000 Yemeni workers; in 2013, a move to favor local labor resulted in expelling up to 300,000 Yemenis. Saudi military intervention against Huthi rebels in 2009 was a costly gamble. Saudi Arabia worked closely with the GCC to resolve the transfer of power in 2011 from Saleh to President Hadi and has pledged $3.25 billion to Yemen's recovery program.

Jordan. Also displaying an ambivalent stance regarding Iraq was Jordan, thus derailing the rapport between the two moderate monarchies. Financial support ceased along with major purchases, crude oil exports via Tapline stopped, and thousands of Jordanians lost their employment. With the visit of then Crown Prince Abdullah in 1996, bilateral relations with Jordan began to improve.

Iraq. Saudi support for Iraq in its war against Iran beginning in 1980 was both financial and political, including agreement to build the IPSA pipeline from southern Iraq to the Red Sea. Saudi Arabia turned bitterly against Saddam Husayn after he invaded Kuwait in 1990, and it closed the IPSA line, supplied bases for the coalition forces against Iraq, and joined the coalition. The kingdom incurred considerable financial costs during the war—an estimated $55 billion in direct payments to some of the coalition partners ($15 billion to the United States alone), foregone oil revenues, and donated supplies. During the 1990s, Saudi Arabia supported general enforcement of sanctions against Iraq but balked at the heavier attacks later in the decade. It was notably less involved in the 2003 Anglo-American invasion of Iraq, and later that year the United States finally pulled out the five thousand troops that had been stationed in the kingdom since 1990.

Kuwait, Bahrain. It has had good relations with Kuwait, sharing the Divided Zone and assisting Kuwait on a grand scale when it was invaded by Iraq in 1990. The history of cordial relations with Bahrain is evident from the modest amounts of crude oil that have been pumped to Bahrain for refining from the early years, and even more so in Saudi generosity in granting Bahrain most of the income from the offshore Abu Safah field near the two states' median line. Further evidence is the successful construction and operation of the causeway, financed by Saudi Arabia and completed in 1986, linking Bahrain to the mainland. This causeway allowed the kingdom's military to move quickly to the support of the island kingdom's Sunni regime in March 2011.

Palestinians. Financial support from Saudi Arabia and the other Gulf states was for many years the Palestine Liberation Organization's main source of income, although some of the PLO actions contrasted with Saudi Arabia's basically moderate stance. The PLO lost that support when its late chairman Yasser Arafat chose not to condemn Iraq's invasion of Kuwait. The post-Oslo Palestinian Authority continued to receive considerable financial assistance from the kingdom.

Developing Countries

Since the mid-1970s, the kingdom has extended considerable bilateral assistance to developing countries; part of this assistance has been channeled through the Saudi Fund for Development (SFD) that by 2011 had financed 492 projects and programs in eighty countries with total funding of $9.5 billion; most bilateral assistance went through other Saudi agencies.[26] It has also been a major source of capital for other multilateral development agencies, including the World Bank, African Development Bank, Islamic Development Bank, OPEC Fund, and Arab Fund for Economic and Social Development. Its capital subscriptions to the World Bank and the International Monetary Fund are high enough to earn it a permanent seat on these organizations' boards of executive directors.

United States

Political Relations. Saudi Arabia's close relations with the United States began with Aramco's exploration for petroleum in the 1930s. Diplomatic relations were established in 1933, and an American embassy opened in Jiddah in 1944, the same year that a consulate general opened in Dhahran to service the burgeoning American community in the oil industry. Although Riyadh had been the royal capital for decades, all foreign embassies were restricted to Jiddah until the mid-1980s, when a new specially designed diplomatic quarter opened on the outskirts of Riyadh.

When the US embassy moved to Riyadh, the consular section remained in Jiddah as a separate consulate general.

Technical and Economic Cooperation. As Aramco's operations expanded, thousands of US employees and their dependents came to the Eastern Province. They have lived in Aramco camps for decades, devoting their entire working lives to the ongoing project. Both Aramco and its four US corporate owners before 1973 maintained excellent relations with the provincial and central governments.

The United States and Saudi Arabia also cooperated in other technical areas during the heyday of their relations: the US Geological Survey conducted geological and mineral studies in the western shield area for many years and cooperated in the production of geographical and geological maps. In 1974, the US–Saudi Arabia Joint Commission for Economic Cooperation (JECOR) was established for research into issues of mutual interest and for technical assistance. Funded entirely by the kingdom, more than thirty development projects under the JECOR umbrella—ranging from establishing a national park in the Asir and bolstering the capabilities of Saudi Customs authorities to staffing an economic "think tank" in the Ministry of Finance and National Economy—were carried out by several hundred American consultants seconded to it by the US Department of the Treasury and other agencies.[27] As many as sixty-five thousand US citizens lived and worked in the kingdom in the early 1980s, but the number has steadily decreased, especially since 9/11.

Military Collaboration. In 1942, King Abd al-Aziz agreed to the construction of a US air base south of Dhahran, which was a combined military-civilian airfield until 1999, when the new King Fahd civil airport opened, and it became a Saudi military field. In 1953, the US Military Training Mission began training elements of the Saudi air force, army, and navy, and that program continues on a small scale. The United States has also been the kingdom's major supplier of military equipment and services—amounting to billions of dollars annually—and provides consultant and supervisory services by the US Army Corps of Engineers for military construction. As indicated above, the Saudi government compensated the allies for their costs during the 1990–1991 Gulf crisis, in addition to supplying airfields, facilities, and logistical support.

However, the continued US military presence after 1991 was highly unpopular both in the kingdom and around the region. Attacks killed twenty-six Americans in 1995–1996, and anti-American sentiment increased—as it did elsewhere in the region—after the beginning of the Second Intifadah in 2000. The resentment became mutual after 9/11, when it was revealed how many Saudi citizens were among those who hijacked the planes that targeted New York and Washington. Terrorists killed more than fifty people, including nine Americans, in Riyadh in 2003, and a full-scale assault on the US consulate general in Jiddah in December 2004 killed four non-American staff members. US-Saudi relations hit a low point in the mid-2000s, with both sides aware that these attacks were actually directed by al-Qaida and other groups against both countries. However, with the winding down of the American presence in Iraq under the Obama administration, the symbiotic linkages recovered somewhat. One sticking point remained, as it does throughout the region—the "special relationship" between the United States and Israel.

Other Relations

Britain. In the aftermath of World War I and Britain's close relationship with the Hashimites based in the Hijaz, UK relations with the Al Sauds were ambiguous. But with the passage of time, these improved, and overall, British-Saudi relations have remained good, with Britain filling multibillion-dollar arms contracts after US sales to the kingdom halted because of pressure by pro-Israeli groups in the United States. Increasing numbers of Britons are serving in a wide range of professional, managerial, and technical capacities, especially as more British military equipment is utilized in the kingdom. In addition, Saudi Arabia, through the GCC, is drawing closer to the EU in general.

Israel. The kingdom supports a peaceful resolution of the Arab-Israeli conflict but is firm in its support of justice for the Palestinians and in support of UN Resolution 242 calling for Israel's withdrawal from territories occupied in 1967. In 2002, then crown prince Abdullah put forward at an Arab League summit what has come to be known as the Arab Peace Initiative (API); to end the Arab-Israeli conflict, it proposes to normalize relations between all the Arab countries and Israel, in exchange for a complete Israeli withdrawal from the Occupied Territories (including East Jerusalem) and a "just settlement" of the Palestinian refugee problem. The API was reendorsed at another summit in 2007 and again, slightly revised, in 2013. As king, Abdullah has continued to promote the API, and when President Obama showed real interest in its possibilities, reports indicated that revisions to make it more palatable to Israel were possible: demilitarization of the future Palestinian state and a refugee settlement not involving a large-scale return to Israel proper. Although some Israeli political leaders during the ensuing decade since 2002 have indicated interest in pursuing the API, it has largely been rejected by the right wing, and especially by the Netanyahu-Lieberman government.

New Openings. Saudi Arabia's intentions to broaden its contacts in the world were demonstrated in the early 1990s, when the kingdom established diplomatic relations with long-shunned Russia and China; reestablished relations with Iran, which had been broken off in 1988; and indicated plans to exchange diplomats with East European countries. In addition, the Saudis have given numerous contracts to Russian and Chinese companies for major construction and natural gas exploration contracts.

In a move unprecedented in Saudi history, King Abdullah met with Pope Benedict XVI in 2007[28] and followed this with a call for dialogue among the three main monotheistic faiths—Judaism, Christianity, and Islam—and for mutual tolerance and cooperation. With the king's active support, 2008 saw the convening of three unusual conferences of religious leaders: the first was in June in Mecca with Muslim participants pledging to improve Sunni-Shii relations, the second was cosponsored by Spain in July with Jewish and Christian representatives, and the third was in November at the United Nations in New York, bringing political leaders together with attendees from the three faiths. King Abdullah addressed all three meetings, telling the third session, "Terrorism and criminality are the enemies of every religion and every civilization. They would not have emerged except for the absence of the principle of tolerance."[29] In November 2012, the King Abdullah bin Abdulaziz Centre for Interreligious and Intercultural Dialogue opened in Vienna—funded entirely by Saudi Arabia, cosponsored by Austria and Spain, with the Vatican participating as a "founding observer." Controversial both at home and in certain quarters abroad, the center announced an ambitious three-year "trial period" of conferences and research fellowships.[30]

For information on the business environment in Saudi Arabia, see the website attached to this book: www.middleeast patterns.com.

NOTES

1. Kazakhstan in Central Asia and Algeria in North Africa are larger.

2. The history of the interior of the Arabian Peninsula was little known until oil developments brought Arabia to world attention, and accurate, detailed history of the area is still limited. Useful, concise accounts are in *Saudi Arabia* Country Study 1995; *Saudi Aramco and Its World* 1995; and *A Land Transformed* 2006. For more details, see Holden and Johns 1982. More recent recommended studies are Barger 2000, an intimate presentation by a former president of Aramco; Vasiliev 2000 and al-Rasheed 2002, good histories; Champion 2003; and Lippman 2004. Some popular accounts are fanciful or spiteful.

3. US Department of State, *Country Commercial Guide: Saudi Arabia*, Aug. 2004.

4. Breaking with the tradition of avoiding public displays of disagreement with the government, a large group of traditionally minded clerics protested outside the Royal Court in Riyadh about the inclusion of women. On the other hand, several conservative women academics complained that the group of appointees comprised only women with more liberal outlooks. *Al-Monitor*, Jan. 23, 2013.

5. See, for example, *al-Monitor*, Jan. 7 and Feb. 4, 2013.

6. CNN, Mar. 12, 2013.

7. Coverage of Arabian regions and physical aspects is in Ministry of Agriculture and Water 1984; US Geological Survey 1966–1967, 1975, 1989; McKee 1979; Holm 1960; Brown and Coleman 1972; Brown 1972; Scoville 1979; *Saudi Aramco and Its World* 1995; and Farsi 1989.

8. The readable Thesiger 1959 on the Rub al-Khali realm has become a classic.

9. *Global Arab Network*, Feb. 7, 2010.

10. *Zawya*, Nov. 18, 2012; *Arab News* (Jiddah), Mar. 18, 2013.

11. United Nations Development Programme 2013; *Legatum Prosperity Index 2012*, www.prosperity.com/.

12. See the well-regarded Vidal 1955, although the oases have been greatly transformed since the study was made.

13. The report was prepared by the National Commercial Bank. *Zawya*, Mar. 7, 2013.

14. The history, development, and recent situation of the Saudi oil industry are authoritatively covered in *Saudi Aramco and Its World* 1995 and *A Land Transformed* 2006. Other sidelights are in Yergin 1991. For detailed current information see EIA, Aug. 2008.

15. *Arab News* (Jiddah), Mar. 19, 2013.

16. *Media Line,* Feb. 10, 2010.

17. *Media Line,* Mar 14, 2010.

18. *Zawya,* Dec. 7, 2012.

19. *Zawya,* Nov. 27, 2012.

20. For further information, see www.kaust.edu.sa/.

21. For further information on the new routes, see www.saudirailexpansion.com/saudirailexpansion /default.aspx and www.saudirailways.org/portal/page /portal/PRTS/root/Home/04_Expansion_Specification /02Expansion.

22. *Arab News* (Jiddah), Dec. 6, 2006. The considerable nonpetroleum resources in the kingdom have clearly been a prime motivation in the surge of interest in railway construction.

23. *Economist,* Apr. 23, 2009.

24. There is a third museum in Damascus, housed in the former northern terminus of the Hejaz railway.

25. Turkey is also a member of the G-20.

26. For further details, see the SFD website, www.sfd.gov.sa/english.

27. Harbison 1990.

28. Abdullah had met with Pope John Paul II in 1999 before he was king.

29. Remarks of King Abdullah at the Culture of Peace Conference at the United Nations, Nov. 12, 2008. For the full speech, see www.saudi-us-relations.org /articles/2008/ioi/081113p-un-speech.html.

30. *Zawya,* Nov. 24, 2012.

The reader is advised to consult this book's associated website (**www.middleeastpatterns.com**) for additional information on **Saudi Arabia**, such as a historical time line and chronology of recent events, as well as essays on selected topics and various international economic, social, and political indicators.

16

Three City States Along the Gulf

AN OVERVIEW

The body of water almost enclosed by the Arabian Peninsula and the Iranian coast is variously designated as the Persian Gulf, Arabian Gulf, Persian/Arabian Gulf, or, increasingly, simply the Gulf. By whatever name, it is now well known because of its oil resources and its place in news headlines during the wars of 1980–1988, 1990–1991, and 2003 onward—leaving no doubt about the explosive significance of Gulf geopolitics. Before the 1930s, the region was little known in the West other than by a few British officials and adventurers. Remote, isolated, and poverty ridden, the area was characterized by one British official in 1928 this way: "The amenities of life are few and far between. Nature is in her fiercest humour and man has done little to improve upon her handiwork."[1]

Rapid Change Without Precedent

Then between 1960 and 1985, the span of one generation, the eastern coast of the Arabian Peninsula underwent a dramatic transformation. Fishing villages mushroomed into cities with populations 50, 100, and 150 times those of 1928, including Kuwait, Dammam/al-Khobar, Manama, Doha, Abu Dhabi, Dubai, Sharjah, and Muscat-Matrah. Once impoverished indigenous peoples along that coast now have some of the highest per capita incomes in the world.

Although "nature is in her fiercest humour" even yet, "man" has done much recently to improve upon nature's handiwork. Billions of petrodollars built new cities and ports and, even more amazing, found (or "manufactured") water for urban domestic supplies and for irrigating parks and gardens. With enormous amounts of energy available, air-conditioning tamed the temperature. Although most commodities and much of the labor are imported, few of the conveniences and comforts of modern living are lacking along the Gulf. Oil has given these states a much improved standard of living, as can be seen from the gains in the Human Development Index, computed by the UNDP and embodying measures of health, education, and income. In 2013, the global rankings were 36th, 48th, and 54th out of 186 countries (and 3rd, 5th, and 6th regionally) for Qatar, Bahrain, and Kuwait, respectively. All have enjoyed the benefits of oil for more than a generation, but their HDI scores have continued to rise—by an average of about 17 percent since 1980, largely on gains in life expectancy and school enrollment. The more broadly based study conducted by the Legatum Institute has so far included, of this chapter's three countries, only Kuwait, which in 2012 was ranked 36th globally and 3rd regionally using the Prosperity Index.[2]

Earlier chapters covered several functional aspects of the Gulf: its physical characteristics, influence on climate, role in the petroleum industry, strategic aspects, organization in the Gulf Cooperation Council (GCC), and maritime function. Now it is time to examine the regional characteristics of the three smallest states—virtually city-states: Kuwait, Bahrain, and Qatar.

Glance at History

In addition to several Paleolithic (Old Stone Age) sites, a number of Neolithic sites have been found in various locations, and artifacts from rather intensive explorations can be seen in handsome museums in all the littoral states. The artifacts and other evidence testify to the vigor of the sea traffic through the Gulf and eastward to the Indus Valley from about 2300 BCE, with another peak during Babylonian times. With its gushing artesian springs, Bahrain was an important way station for ancient mariners sailing between the Indus Valley and Mesopotamia. Nearchus, Alexander the Great's military commander, transited this sea-lane while returning from Alexander's expedition to the Indus Valley in 325 BCE. The Romans mastered the art of sailing with the monsoons to and from India, but they went from the Red Sea rather than the Gulf.

Islamic civilization and its maritime trade reinvigorated the Gulf's economic role after the eighth century; the folktales of Sinbad the Sailor are woven around voyages from the Gulf. The basin's importance revived when the Portuguese arrived in 1514 after opening the sea route around Africa. Drawn by the wealth of Persia under Abbas the Great, the Dutch and British supplanted the Portuguese. Expanding Ottoman power coalesced with European bridgeheads in the Gulf, and Basrah, Bushehr (Bushire), Bahrain, Bandar-e Abbas, Hormuz, and other ports were thriving trade centers and entrepôts after the early 1600s. Two centuries later, Britain's economic, military, and political dominance extended along almost the entire littoral in consequence of its Indian interests.

By the end of the 1920s, southwestern Iran was a British "sphere of influence," Iraq was a British mandate, and Kuwait, Bahrain, Qatar, the Trucial States, and Muscat and Oman were all under some form of British control or influence. The British installed navigational aids (Persian Gulf Lighting Service) and undertook surveying, charting, and mapping of both the Gulf and its coasts and of the Tigris and Karun Rivers. The evolving British role, as well as the emergence of independent Gulf states, is discussed below.

A Note on Gulf Oil

In 2012, the eight petroleum producers facing the Gulf had reserves of 797 bn bbl, 49 percent of the world total, and their average daily output during 2012 was 23.6 mn bbl, 31 percent of world output. The three states discussed in this chapter had reserves of about 130 bn bbl (7.9 percent of world reserves) and an average production of 3.85 mn bpd (5.1 percent of world output). Natural gas reserves of the eight states totaled 79.0 bn m^3 and of the three totaled 27.1 bn m^3, about 41 percent and 14 percent of global reserves, respectively. The oil and gas fields in and around the Gulf are shown in Map 6.2; those that are completely or partially offshore are identified. Also indicated are the many oil terminals, several ranking among the world's largest: Ras Tanura, Juaymah, Mina al-Ahmadi, and Kharg Island. A general discussion of the Gulf's petroleum industry is in Chapter 6; additional details are found in Chapter 15 and below.

A Geopolitical Perspective

Intra-Gulf Relations. The Gulf has long been both an arena of contention and conflict and a theater of peaceful trade and regional intercourse. For most of the past 150 years, partly under the Pax Britannica, the littoral states have usually sought nonmilitary solutions. Most clashes that have taken place have occurred in the hinterland—over water sources, grazing rights, dynastic disputes, or territorial consolidation—rather than over the Gulf as such. Wells and springs in the desert have occasionally been contested, and Bahrain and Qatar contended for two centuries over dynastic and territorial questions.

Gulf states have periodically disputed control over offshore islands and pearl beds as well as freedom of navigation. Some oil fields straddle political boundaries, onshore and offshore, but differing claims over these boundaries have been settled surprisingly amicably. Britain sometimes served as arbiter, and the United States conducted a cross-Gulf survey in the mid-1960s, delineating a median line in the central Gulf. Bahrain and Qatar agreed in 2001 to a mediated split of islands and waters separating them. One unsettled offshore boundary is that of Kuwait, Iraq, and Iran at the head of the Gulf.

Recent Conflict. By far, three modern clashes have been the most serious: the protracted Iran-Iraq War in the 1980s, the Gulf crisis of 1990–1991 (both sparked by Iraqi aggression), and the controversial Iraq War beginning in March 2003 (all of these involved the three states considered in this chapter to a greater or lesser extent). The first continued

the historic conflict along the line of disjunction between the Zagros Mountain belt and the Mesopotamian Basin, two major regional power foci. The second was more complicated, but, inter alia, it manifested the resurgence of the Mesopotamian focus. The third has been, internationally, the most bitterly debated conflict since Vietnam.

Global Perspective. However, because the Gulf Basin countries possess 49 percent of the world's conventional petroleum resources and produce nearly one-third of the world's daily oil output, its geopolitical interactions extend to virtually every part of the world. This was clearly demonstrated when nearly forty countries contributed in some way to Kuwait's liberation in 1990–1991. The troubled waters of the Gulf are an unstable chessboard on which every energy-dependent country must try for checkmate—hence the intensity of the polemics over the US-led invasion and subsequent occupation of Iraq. This subject has been examined in Chapters 6 and 9 (the sections "The Gulf Crisis" and "Operation Iraqi Freedom," respectively) and will be touched on again in this chapter.

Kuwait

KEY POINTS: Formerly a small port and fishing town strategically located on a bay surrounded by desert, created as British protectorate 1899 partly because of suspected oil resources. Boundaries defined after World War I contended by new Iraq. Major petroleum fields developed after 1938, making Kuwait fabulously wealthy and supporting explosive development. Independent 1961. Became socially unbalanced with inpouring expatriates, who were restricted in political status and social benefits. Suffered severely during Iraq invasion in 1990, freed by mainly US Coalition Forces early 1991. Now thriving, but with social-political stresses.

Kuwait Fort and Port

Originally a small port and trade center, Kuwait ("little fort" from Arabic *kut,* "fort")

historically used its location on a small bay at the head of the Gulf for maritime activities and modest overland trade (Map 16.1). Landward,

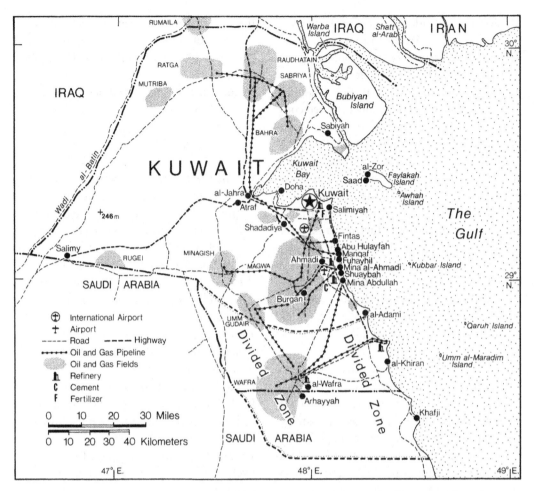

Map 16.1 General and economic map of Kuwait. The Divided Zone is the former Saudi Arabia–
Kuwait Neutral Zone, delineated with dashed line boundaries.

trade and pastoralism supported ten to fifteen
thousand townspeople and several thousand
Bedouin.[3] More important economically were
pearling, fishing, boat building, and trade with
India and Gulf coastal towns. Kuwait's greatest
asset was its excellent harbor, its greatest draw-
back a lack of fresh water. Considering this, its
population of fifty thousand after World War I
was surprisingly large.

The world depression of the 1930s and
competition from Japanese cultured pearls
undermined Kuwait's traditional livelihood.
Its economic future looked bleak as the 700
pearling dhows of 1921 dwindled to 125 by
1939.[4] Many of the dhows joined the fleet of

"booms" bringing fresh water from the Shatt
al-Arab, supplying up to 100,000 gal/378,500
l each day. But everything changed dramatically with the discovery of large petroleum
resources in 1938 and steadily increasing exports after World War II. Immense wealth
accrued, prompting rapid development in
little more than a decade.

Independence

With economic and political viability, Kuwait
gained independence in 1961 from Britain,
its protector since 1899. However, sovereignty for the amirate, including withdrawal
of British protection, brought problems. In-

KUWAIT

Long-form official name, anglicized: State of Kuwait

Official name, transliterated: Dawlat al-Kuwayt

Form of government: constitutional monarchy with one legislative body (National Assembly)

Area: 6,880 mi²/17,818 km²

Population, 2011: 3,650,000; Literacy: 93.3%

Ethnic composition (%, 2005): Arab 80, of which Kuwaiti 45, including Bedouin 4; South Asian 9; Iranian 4; other 7

Religions (%, 2005): Muslim 74, of which Sunni 59, Shia 15; Christian 13, of which Catholic 9; Hindu 10; Buddhist 3

Demography: Life expectancy—76.09 yr (M), 78.51 yr (F); Birthrate (per 1,000)— 20.96; Fertility rate—2.6

GDP, 2011: $158.4 billion; purchasing power parity: $153.5 billion; per capita: $41,700

Currency: Kuwaiti Dinar (KD), US$1 = 0.284 dinars; 1 KD = $3.508 (mid-May 2013)

Energy: oil—101.5 bn bbl; natural gas—63,500 bn ft³ ; coal—nil

Main exports (% of total value, 2007): KD 17.8 billion (of which crude petroleum 61.6; refined petroleum 29.8; liquefied propane and butane; polyethylene 1.7)

Main imports (% of total value, 2007): KD 6.1 billion (of which machinery and apparatus 26.6; road vehicles 15.1; food 11.5; iron and steel 9.3)

Capital city, 2007: Kuwait City (agglomeration) 2,063,000; other major cities, 2011: Qalib ash-Shuyukh 265,984; Salimiyah 238,577; Hawali 171,804

---

dependent Kuwait was extremely wealthy but also small and weak, and its long-covetous neighbor, Iraq, arguing from half-century old British-Ottoman agreements, immediately renewed its often-stated claim to its territory. Britain promptly offered support, which was then taken over by Arab League forces—and Iraq withdrew both threat and troops. But the claim was periodically renewed, right up to 1990.

Over three decades of independence, Kuwait saw almost unparalleled development. Billions of dollars allowed it to hire outside expertise and labor and to import goods and equipment. With the Iran-Iraq War beginning in 1980 came problems and fears for

Kuwait, but the amirate thought it could buy the security it needed.

Invasion

Then, on August 2, 1990, Kuwait's complacency was shattered when Iraq invaded. The formerly obscure amirate suddenly dominated world television screens, radio, and headlines. Although the 1990–1991 crisis is discussed in Chapter 8 (in the section "The Gulf Crisis"), the impact on Kuwait will be examined briefly here. Significantly, at the time of the invasion, as is true every summer, thousands of Kuwaiti residents were on vacation in cooler climes while many expatriates were in their homelands, making invasion easier for Iraq but vastly complicating the situation for residents unable to return home.

Destruction was extensive and often savagely senseless. Iraqis looted transportable items and sabotaged fixed facilities—an estimated $70–$100 billion loss. Some valuable items were later returned under UN cease-fire resolutions, but the sabotage of oil facilities was not so easily overcome. This caused not only direct financial and infrastructural losses but also environmental havoc. In an act variously called "environmental terrorism," "eco-terrorism," or "ecocide," Iraq blew up 749 of 935 wellheads, leaving more than 690 wells afire or blowing wild; millions of barrels flowed into the desert, while millions more burned.[5] In late January 1991, Iraq was dumping 150,000 bpd from storage tanks into the Gulf, a spill that eventually may have been close to 6 mn bbl. Stopping the destruction was the most prolonged firefighting exercise in history; the last fire was extinguished November 6, 1991.[6]

In 1976, when Kuwait decided to reduce oil production to extend the life of its main resource, it set up the Reserve Fund for Future Generations, to which 10 percent of ordinary revenues were allocated each year, as well as the General Reserve Fund. From the $100 billion the two funds had invested abroad by 1990, the government drew on about half during and right after the Iraqi occupation for operational and reconstruction expenses.

Marking the Border. To preclude future Iraqi boundary and territorial pretensions, the UN precisely demarcated the long-controversial line between Kuwait and Iraq in 1992–1993. The boundary generally confirmed the line described in two earlier documents exchanged between Kuwait and Iraq, in 1932 and 1963 (see "Regional Conflicts," in Chap. 8), and Iraq accepted this judgment in November 1994. However, the dispute lingered at a low level of intensity until 2012, when after the first visit of the amir of Kuwait to Baghdad in twenty-two years and the two

countries coming to agreements on several outstanding political and economic questions the two countries petitioned the United Nations to begin repairing the border markers.

Liberation Aftermath

Meanwhile, in response to pressures that built from the early days of the occupation, government and public attention was devoted to social and political reforms. Various levels of Kuwaiti reaction to the invasion and to the brutality of the occupation had revealed serious weaknesses and deficiencies in the body politic; the imperative for reform was patent, and pressures were exerted from within and without.

The Al Sabah have furnished the ruling shaykhs since the 1750s. Under the 1962 constitution, the ruler retained broad powers, including the final word on most policies, but a significant role was granted to the National Assembly—the first elected parliament in the Arab Gulf states. Although the amir suspended parliament in 1976–1981 and again in 1986–1992, legislatures elected after the national trauma of invasion—in 1992, 1996, 1999, 2003, 2006, 2008, 2009, and 2012—have grown stronger, and ideological representation has broadened. When the amir Shaykh Jabir died in 2006, the assembly exercised its prerogative and refused to acquiesce in the elevation of the then crown prince, who was in poor health, resulting instead in the accession of Shaykh Sabah.

Arab Spring

The assembly's increasing assertiveness led to frequent conflicts with the cabinet, still dominated by appointed royals, leading to dissolutions of the body in 2009 and 2011. In March 2011, Kuwait saw demonstrations by young people calling for major reforms. These did not arise to the level seen in neighboring Bahrain, although unrest continued through 2012. Still the government followed the same path as other GCC monarchies in promising considerable spending on new projects, especially in the health, education, and housing sectors.

In February 2012, a new assembly with an Islamist majority was elected, but in June the Constitutional Court ruled that the 2011 dissolution of the assembly chosen in 2009 was illegal, thus nullifying the results of the February election. By emergency decree, the amir promulgated a new law redrawing constituencies in advance of new elections, causing the opposition to claim this would benefit officially backed candidates. The court threw out the new law in September, the amir dissolved the reconstituted National Assembly in October, and new elections were held in December 2012. All the while, demonstrations continued, plunging the country into its greatest crisis since the Iraqi invasion. The wider implications of the continued unrest were emphasized when the international ratings agency Fitch warned in October 2012 that Kuwait's stellar credit rating might be threatened.

The elections, largely boycotted by opposition groups ranging from liberals to Islamists, predictably returned slates favorable to the amir, and the new parliament voted in January 2013 to ratify the provisions of the emergency decree modifying the constituencies. The constitutionality of the legislation was appealed to the courts where adjudication was scheduled by the end of 2013.

During this turbulent period, Human Rights Watch and other NGOs have claimed there has been a serious deterioration in human rights. Police used considerable force against demonstrators, there was a clampdown on online activists, oppositionists were arrested and charged with insulting the amir, and the cabinet approved a bill placing further restrictions on the press.[7]

ECONOMY

Oil: Discovery and Development

A surface showing of asphalt spurred interest in Kuwait's oil potential in 1911, and the first geological survey, in 1914, was encouraging. Without the promise of oil, Britain probably would not have retained Kuwait separately after World War I but more likely would have made it become part of the Iraqi mandate. The Anglo-Persian Oil Company and the Gulf Oil Corporation of the United States, in a jointly owned local subsidiary, the Kuwait Oil Company (KOC), obtained a concession in 1934. KOC struck a gusher in the Burgan Dome in 1938; with oil in several relatively shallow horizons, it was the world's biggest field up to that time. It is still the second-largest (after Saudi Arabia's Ghawar) and the world's richest field for its areal extent, with 70 bn bbl. Delayed by World War II, exports were first lifted in 1946. Exploration in the 1950s opened more fields—Ahmadi, Magwa (both in the Greater Burgan field), Raudhatain, Bahra, Sabriya, and Minagish. Into the 2000s, new discoveries continued, like Kara al-Marou in the west.

Concessions went to Aminoil (United States) for Kuwait's share in the Neutral Zone in 1945, extended in 1949 to include several offshore islands. It found the considerable Wafra field in 1953 and developed Umm Gudair after KOC found it in 1966. In 1958, Kuwait followed the lead of Saudi Arabia and awarded a concession for its half of the zone's offshore to the Japanese Arabian Oil Company (AOC), which discovered the Khafji field in 1960 and Hout in 1963. It also found the Lulu and Dorra fields in 1967; the unsettled maritime border with Iran has kept these shut in. Spanish exploration in northern Kuwait found both more oil and the amirate's only sweet groundwater in 1955.

Oil: Conservation and Nationalization

As production mounted, Kuwait became increasingly cognizant of its reliance on one depletable resource. Upon the advice of a group of young "technocrats," the government opted for conservation by reducing output. It also reined in wasteful flaring (because no economic market was then available) of gas separated from the crude prior to further handling. After having increased production each year to a peak of 3 mn bpd in 1972, Kuwait reduced output to less than 2 mn bpd during the late 1970s. By that time, Kuwait had amassed such enormous wealth for its small size and population and had been so intensively developed that conserving its oil was more logical than accumulating additional billions of dollars subject to the vagaries of global inflation.

Like other OPEC countries, Kuwait sought participation in its concessionary companies and by 1975 controlled KOC. It nationalized Aminoil and its operations in the Neutral Zone (by that time termed the Divided Zone) in 1977. In 1980, the Kuwait Petroleum Corporation (KPC) was created to serve as the umbrella for upstream and downstream operations as well as tanker transportation. Now a completely vertically integrated corporation, it competes with the multinationals, owning refineries in western Europe and North America and downstream operations in South Asia and the Pacific Rim. In Kuwait, three main refineries at Mina al-Ahmadi (the largest, with a capacity of 466,000 bpd), Mina Abdullah, and Shuaybah have a combined capacity of about 936,000 bpd throughput (see Table 6.2).

By 2012, Kuwait's 104 bn bbl of reserves (including half of Divided Zone reserves of 5 bn bbl) were the sixth largest in the world—6.3 percent of the world total—and an average of 2.75 mn bpd was produced from 1,286 wells. Project Kuwait is drilling a modest number of new wells in some fields, constructing new gathering centers to handle more output, increasing production capacity from 2.4 mn bpd to 4.0 mn bpd by 2020, relaxing policies on foreign company activities to gain outside expertise, and expanding the petrochemical industry. (Nationalists and Islamists oppose allowing foreign companies into the sector.) Overall, the sector accounts for half of GDP, 95 percent of export rev-

enues, and 80 percent of government income. High oil prices in 2011 meant record export earnings—$85 billion. The amirate's rapid recovery after the 1991 Gulf War was based on its huge resources, the intelligent use of outside expertise, and a resilient indigenous population.

Other Sectors

Industry. Development goals focus on capital- and energy-intensive industries (rather than labor-intensive manufacturing) like petroleum and by-products, construction materials, consumer goods, and electronics. Diversification and domestic production of traditionally imported basic commodities are deterred by the small size of the consuming population, despite high per capita GDP—$42,200 in 2011. The relatively few nonpetroleum industries include cement, pharmaceuticals, nonalcoholic beverages, processed foods, milled flour, plastics, paper products, and furniture.

With less than 4.5 in/114 mm of annual rainfall, no surface streams, and only small amounts of underground water, Kuwait once imported its water and "manufactures" it now. Plentiful energy desalinates water and simultaneously generates electric power; it produces close to 50 gigawatt hours (GWh) annually, while supplying more than 330 mn gals/1.25 mn m^3 of sweet water per day.[8] Per capita electricity consumption is among the highest in the world (and second only to Qatar in the region) at heavily subsidized prices. A 50 percent expansion in generating capacity is planned, along with a shift to using mostly natural gas as the fuel for the plants; in the late 2000s, oil was still being used for about 70 percent of its generating needs.[9] It will probably have to both import liquefied natural gas (LNG) and further develop its own deposits of nonassociated gas.

Finance. Indicating how globalized Middle Eastern economies have become, the Kuwaiti economy felt the impact of the world economic crisis of 2008 both quickly and emphatically. Over the course of the year, the Kuwait Stock Exchange—second largest regionally—saw a loss of close to 40 percent of market capitalization. Further, as the government had invested surplus oil revenues internationally, those very sizable investments were adversely affected, at least in the short term, by the downturn in global financial and real estate markets. In 2007, Kuwait ended its long-established practice of linking the dinar only to the dollar, switching to a basket of the currencies of its major trading partners—thus somewhat shielding its domestic economy from vagaries in the dollar's exchange rate. Record oil prices in 2008 gave it its tenth straight budget surplus; unfortunately, this lessened pressure on the government to take some needed economic and fiscal reforms. Revenues in 2009 fell by more than 40 percent to $47 billion from the previous year's high of $80 billion: 2011 saw a new record high of $87 billion.

Agriculture. From the beginnings of settlement in the Kuwait area, there has never been much agricultural activity; today, the amirate imports 95 percent of its food. The twelve to fifteen thousand Bedouin of a century ago supplied meat, but the few remaining ones contribute little to current food supply. Small date groves persist around brackish wells, and new dairy and chicken farms, along with limited hydroponic vegetable production, add to the fresh food supply. A negligible number of workers are in agriculture, while 50 percent are in public administration, 40 percent in services, and 9 percent in industry; 80 percent of the workforce is non-Kuwaiti.

Diversification. In an effort to further diversify the economy, the government announced in 2008 its intention to build the "City of Silk," a 97-mi^2/250-km^2 planned community at Subbiya near the Iraqi border across Kuwait Bay from the capital and to be linked to it by a 16-mi/26-km causeway. A major aim of the project is to provide facilities for financial and commercial services, securing for Kuwait some of the activities in these two sectors that have grown so rapidly in Dubai, Abu Dhabi, and Bahrain. By 2011, total project costs had grown to an estimated $132 billion, with completion scheduled for 2023. In 2010, the parliament approved a major $107 billion economic diversification program, about half of which will be spent in the expanding hydrocarbon production and downstream activities. Raising oil production by 10 percent by 2015 is intended to provide the additional funding for this program. Part of this program is proving to complicate relations with Iraq—the construction of Mubarak Port, close to the border that Iraq believes will block access to the new port facilities it is building on al-Faw peninsula.

Transport. At the early 2010s, Kuwait was coordinating with its neighbors in an overall GCC railroad-development program. Its section would be a 322-mi/518-km rail network that would tie in with that of Iraq and extend south to the Saudi Arabian border, linking to that country's national network now being expanded, and onward to the lower Gulf states. A 106-mi/171-km urban rapid-transit system for Kuwait City and its sprawling suburbs is part of the overall plan.

SOCIETY AND SETTLEMENTS

The town of Kuwait was settled in the early eighteenth century by Arabs from Najd, in central Arabia. Although the environment was niggardly, with its shortage of water, the benefits of the excellent harbor sustained a tenacious seafaring population. Gradually, other Arabs from Mesopotamia and the peninsula, as well as Iranians, joined the small settlement, ruled by Al Sabah shaykhs. In the early 1900s, the population was perhaps 35,000, doubling by 1946 when oil exports began. Increasing production and development attracted immigrants by the thousands, until the population reached 206,473 in the first census in 1957, and an estimated 2.65 million—about thirteen times that of the first census—in 2012.

Citizens and Others

By 1965, non-Kuwaitis, including both immigrants and expatriates, outnumbered native Kuwaitis, and an alarmed state-imposed criteria that restricted citizenship to residents prior to 1920 and their offspring. Conditions for naturalization effectively precluded it for immigrants, except for about 50 per year. In the late 2000s, only the citizen third of the population was entitled to the full range of social benefits.[10] Suffrage was gradually extended to all male citizens after 1996. Women were granted the vote by the amir in 1999, but exercising its constitutional right, the National Assembly refused to recognize this and other decrees. It eventually enfranchised women in 2005. Shortly thereafter, the first woman was appointed to the cabinet as planning and development minister; by the end of the 2000s, a second ministry went to a woman. Kuwaiti women voted for the first time in the 2006 elections; in 2009, three women won seats, and three were selected again in the December 2012 polling.

Kuwait for the Kuwaitis. After liberation in late February 1991, Kuwait denied many life-long resident expatriates reentry, and others who had remained during the Iraqi occupation were expelled. Seizing the opportunity for sociopolitical restructuring, the government embraced "Kuwait for the Kuwaitis," announcing a population goal of about 1.2 million. This proved unrealistic, however, severely hindering a return to national viability and prosperity, and the government later ad-

mitted or readmitted workers from countries that had supported Iraq. As a result, by 2011, there were an estimated 1.29 million expatriates, some 49 percent of the population.

Palestinians. Particularly numerous among the expatriate population before 1990 were Palestinians. As Arabs, mostly Muslims, educated, and motivated, they became available just as Kuwait had a critical need for their skills, and by the late 1980s they and their descendants in the state numbered nearly 400,000. A small number became politically active, raising government suspicions of the entire group. Perceived Palestinian support in Jordan and the Occupied Territories for Saddam Husayn caused considerable resentment and led to the expulsion of hundreds of thousands until fewer than 40,000 remained.[11] In the new century, restrictions on Palestinians have eased a bit, and by 2010 perhaps 80,000 (including those with Jordanian citizenship) were resident in the amirate. In October 2012, the Palestinian embassy in Kuwait reopened after being closed for twenty-two years.

Citizens have profited especially from the rapidly expanding political and economic systems of the state; however, expatriates have also enjoyed great benefits, though they are not entitled to certain privileges. Full benefits include virtually guaranteed employment, free medical service, housing subsidies, marriage bonuses, free education at all levels, and sizable pensions. Thousands of Kuwaitis, mostly men, have gone abroad for free university education, although most students now attend the impressive University of Kuwait, opened in 1967. In a sharp break with tradition, increasing numbers of Kuwaiti women both serve on the staff of and also attend the university, outnumbering men there since the early 1980s.

Stateless Bidoons. One group of often long-time residents has not been so fortunate—the so-called bidoons, or stateless people. Although the group is not homogeneous, most trace their origins to the days when formal frontiers did not exist in the Arabian Peninsula and nomadic tribes followed their flocks from water hole to water hole. In Kuwait, bidoons are people who cannot prove their families were citizens prior to 1920, and they are not eligible for most state services. Numbering as many as 100,000, in recent years they have won some recognition through the amirate's legal system. Their plight has increasingly won wider recognition, and, in 2012, Amnesty International and two other international human rights groups called on the government to end alleged abuses. In 2013, the parliament passed legislation allowing for a limited number of naturalizations, but local human rights groups have deemed it inadequate in relation to the number of stateless residents. It also seemed unlikely to be of much help to the largest group of bidoons—those who have Iraqi tribal roots.[12]

Shii Minority. The ruling family and the majority of Kuwaitis are Sunnis, but over a third are Shia. Some of those who were of Iranian origin were deported in the 1980s during the Iran-Iraq War, but after liberation treatment of the minority improved. In recent years, however, intercommunal tensions have emerged, and the Kuwaiti government subscribes to the fears common across the peninsula of the rising of a "Shii Crescent," stretching from Iran to Lebanon. In September 2012, the Iranian parliament indicated willingness to take unspecified steps to protect the minority.

Village to Metropolis

Once a small port, Kuwait City is now an elaborately planned metropolis with many ultramodern buildings echoing traditional Islamic architecture (Fig. 16.1). Each of its sectors suggests traditional urban quarters, with a mosque and shopping area reminiscent of the traditional *suq*. The city's symbol, the three Kuwait Towers on the tip of Ras Ajuzah, is a dominant feature of the urban landscape (Fig. 16.2). The southwest-northeast axis of the built-up area follows the coastline forming the city's northwestern boundary. Although the historic mud wall was dismantled with expansion of Kuwait City in the late 1950s, two old gates have been preserved. The Central Business District covers most of the old *madinah* (see Fig. 4.13). Three harbors retain features of the old Kuwait along the bay, and traditional dhows anchor inside the breakwaters. Concentric ring roads centered on the old town carry residential sectors southeastward and industrial sectors southwestward.

RELATIONS

The United States recognized Kuwait as a sovereign state even before independence, and the first US consulate was opened in 1951. Full diplomatic relations were initiated in 1961.

Like the shaking of a kaleidoscope, the disarray of the 1990–1991 crisis forced Kuwait into new patterns of regional and world relations. Bonds with such traditional friends as Saudi Arabia and other GCC neighbors, Britain, the United States, and Japan were greatly strengthened. Links to Iraq fell to a nadir after the invasion, improved little during the following decade, then fell further with Operation Iraqi Freedom in 2003. Relations with Jordan and Yemen were strained after their ambivalent reactions to Iraq's assault. Diplomatic relations with Jordan were restored in 1999, and those with Iran have improved from the low level of the 1980s. Ties to the United States have become extraordinarily close, building on the US Navy's convoying of Kuwaiti tankers in 1987–1988. After the coalition rescued it in 1991, Kuwait recognized that its security

Figure 16.1 Sawabar Residential Complex, Kuwait City, a modernistic adaptation of Islamic architectural themes.

Figure 16.2
Water towers, Kuwait. The capital's hallmark, the colorful towers serve an identifying function similar to that of the Eiffel Tower in Paris. The decorated spheres store municipal water, and the tower on the right includes a luxury rotating restaurant. Trees indicate scale.

ultimately depended on Western military power. It pragmatically acquiesced to cooperative security measures and was a major base for and supporter of US and British air operations against Iraq in the 1990s, hosting as well thousands of US ground troops. As noted earlier, it played a key role both before the invasion of Iraq in 2003 and during the ensuing occupation, serving as the ground base for coalition troops and provider of logistical support. Later, it made peace with the elected Iraqi government and renewed formal diplomatic relations in 2008, having supported Iraqi rebuilding efforts. In 2009, the foreign minister made the first Kuwait high-level visit to Iraq since 1990.

Globally, Kuwait has been very active in the developing world. The Kuwait Fund for Arab Economic Development, created in 1961, was the first Arab bilateral aid agency. Through 2011, it had financed some 798 projects in 102 countries ranging from Belize to the Solomon Islands and from Lithuania to Swaziland.[13] The government has also made huge grants to the "frontline states" of Egypt, Syria, and Jordan, as well as—ironically—loans of $4–$5 billion (never repaid) to Iraq during its war with Iran. Kuwait has also contributed to the resources of several multilateral agencies, such as the World Bank, Islamic Development Bank, African Development Bank, and International Fund for Agricultural Development.

For information on the business environment in Kuwait, see the website attached to this book: www.middleeastpatterns.com.

Bahrain

KEY POINTS: Smallest state in region. Island location in Gulf and major freshwater springs attracted prehistoric settlement, lured ethnically varied emigrants. Iranian interests overcome by British protectorate status in late 1700s. Site of first oil developments in Gulf, although modest reserves limited development. Location exploited for commerce, trade, and naval bases. Independent amirate in 1971, later a kingdom. Connected to Saudi Arabia by causeway in 1980, gained tourism. Persistent discord between Sunni rulers and Shii majority with protests continuing from 2011.

AN OVERVIEW

Bahrain (Arabic for "two seas") is the largest of a group of thirty-three low-lying islands that constitute the kingdom.[14] Smallest of the sixteen Middle East states, it is located 15 mi/24 km off the east coast of Saudi Arabia, to which it is connected by a causeway, and 18 mi/29 km from the Qatar Peninsula (Map 16.2). Only six islands are inhabited; the four main ones are linked by causeways. Of the archipelago's total area, Bahrain Island is 80 percent. Second most important is Muharraq, with the state's second-largest city (also

called Muharraq), an international airport, and a dry dock, connected to Bahrain with an expanded causeway. Other islands include Sitra, locus of the state's large refining and oil-export terminal, linked to Bahrain by a causeway; Nabih Salih, well watered by artesian springs; Umm Nasan, the ruler's private property; and Jiddah, with the state prison. Awarded to Bahrain in 2001, the Hawar Islands off the western coast of Qatar had long been disputed between the two states, poisoning relations for decades until Qatar took its claim to the World Court, which divided the contested territory. The award mostly

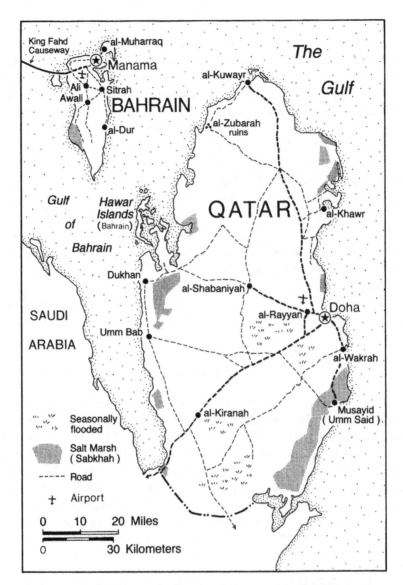

Map 16.2 General map of Bahrain and Qatar, an island and a peninsula in the middle Gulf.

favored Bahrain, and the islands are now a nature preserve with some ecotourism development. Most urban development is on the *sabkhahs* of northern Bahrain and southern Muharraq; these areas are surrounded by oases, which give way southward to rocky and gravelly barren desert.

Bahrain is very hot in the summer, with regular afternoon temperatures exceeding 106°F/41°C, with the heat made especially uncomfortable by consistently high humidity. November to March marks a milder season, when there is an average annual 3 in/ 76 mm of rainfall.

Oil and Water

The main island is fringed by a shallow rock platform and by extensive coral reefs. It is a

BAHRAIN

Long-form official name, anglicized: Kingdom of Bahrain

Official name, transliterated: Mamlakat al-Bahrayn

Form of Government: constitutional monarchy with a parliament comprising two bodies (Council of Representatives, Shura Council)

Area: 292 mi²/757 km²

Population, 2011: 1,325,000; Literacy: 94.6%

Ethnic composition (%, 2010): Arab 51.4, of which Bahraini 46; Asian 45.5; African 1.6; European 1; other 0.5

Religion (%, 2010): Muslim 70.2, of which Shia 46, Sunni 24; other (significantly Christian and Hindu) 29.8

Demography: Life expectancy—76.17 yr (M), 80.48 yr (F); Birthrate (per 1,000)–14.41; Fertility rate—1.86

GDP, 2011: $25.45 billion; purchasing power parity: $31.3 billion; per capita: $27,700

Currency: Bahraini Dinar (BHD), US$1 = 0.374 dinars; 1 BHD = $2.632 (mid-May 2013)

Energy: oil—124.6 mn bbl; natural gas—3,250 bn ft³; coal—nil

Main exports (% of total value, 2007): $13,7 billion (of which refined petroleum 79.1; aluminum 9; urea 2.4; iron-ore agglomerates 1.4; methanol 1.3)

Main imports (% of total value, 2007): $11.5 billion (of which crude petroleum 50.9; machinery and apparatus 10; road vehicles 7.9; aluminum oxide 5.8; food and live animals 4)

Capital city, 2009: Manama 163,000; other major cities, 2001: Muharraq 91,307; Rifa 79,550; Madinat Hamad 52,718; Ali 47,529; Madinat Isa 36,833

---

surface expression of a breached asymmetrical anticline with a north-south axis in which oil and gas are trapped at several depths. Erosional breaching of the anticline has produced a shallow basin in the center of the island surrounded by a low, oval-shaped inward-facing escarpment of resistant limestone. Several remnant hills that mark the former crest of the arch rise 100–200 ft/30–60 m above the inner basin. Most prominent is Jabal Dukhan, near the center of Bahrain's oil field, the highest elevation at 440 ft/134 m. Oil company headquarters are at Awali in the northern part of the basin.

Important as oil became after 1932, it was another liquid resource that attracted visitors and settlers as early as the Neolithic period and especially during the Bronze Age: the plentiful supply of sweet artesian water from numerous *ayns* in northern Bahrain Island and on adjacent islands. Other freshwater springs erupt from the floor of the Gulf between Bahrain and Saudi Arabia and have supplied mariners with drinking water for centuries. Its central location on the Gulf's long axis and, being the largest and best watered of the islands south of Kuwait, made it a transit point for Sumerians sailing between

Mesopotamia and the Indus Valley. The same basic advantages pertain today.

From Sumer to Independence

Excavations near the ruins of Bahrain Fort uncovered an ancient temple complex with artifacts linking it with Sumer and the Indus Valley. Archaeologists conclude that it is the Dilmun mentioned in Sumerian inscriptions and that it also had ancient cultural links with Faylakah Island in Kuwait Bay and with settlements in Abu Dhabi. Grave mounds, numbering more than one hundred thousand in a huge necropolis in the northwest, date from as early as 2400 BCE and from every period after that through the Sassanian. Such prominent landscape features have caught the attention of visitors for twenty-three hundred years. The National Museum, opened in 1988, has excellent displays tracing Bahrain's complex history. Unfortunately, thousands of the tumuli have been bulldozed for highways and new and expanding settlements.

Transit trade, dhow building, fishing, and pearling underpinned the island's economy for centuries as Bahrain was occupied or controlled by Sassanians, Umayyads, Abbasids, Hormuzis, Portuguese, Persians, mainland Najdis, and Ottomans. The leading shaykhs, the Sunni Al Khalifah—with tribal affiliations to the Al Sabah in Kuwait—were accepted as rulers in the eighteenth century, throwing off Iranian control in 1783, while the majority of the population remained adherents of the Shii sect, which had been imposed during the Iranian period. Soon after, they came under the British protective umbrella, which continued for 150 years. The decline of pearling during the 1930s coincided, fortuitously, with the discovery of oil. The Iranian parliament in 1957 passed legislation that claimed Bahrain as a province of Iran and allotted it two seats in that body. With Britain preparing to leave the Gulf in the 1960s, Iran demanded a plebiscite to determine Bahrain's future allegiance, but in 1971 accepted a UN report that concluded that the vast majority of Bahrainis wanted independence. Forty years after it became the first oil producer on the west side of the Gulf, independence came to Bahrain just in time for it to enjoy an economic boom as a sovereign state.

Strategic Location. With escalating oil prices and explosive development in the Gulf during the first decade of independence, Bahrain profited in many ways from its geographical location, relative stability, diplomatic finesse, and able workforce. As its economy expanded, its traditional strategic importance also increased. A balancing act during the Iran-Iraq War of the 1980s preserved its links with all sides, and during the Gulf War in 1990–1991 it was headquarters for the US Navy presence (which evolved into the reactivated Fifth Fleet in 1995) and a British-US air base. Bahraini pilots also flew strike missions in Iraq. Like Kuwait and Qatar, Bahrain also supported surveillance of Iraq during the 1990s, and it provided a base for US aircraft in 2003.

Khalifah Rulers. Descendants of the Khalifah family continue to rule the state. Shaykh Isa bin Sulman Al Khalifah led impressive economic development during the two Gulf crises in 1980–1988 and 1990–1991. A new constitution in 1973 allowed more political participation in an experimental National Assembly, but it was disbanded by the ruler in 1975, and afterward he gave no date for reintroduction of representative institutions. He did appoint a thirty-member Consultative Council in 1993 and made other overtures, but for much of the 1990s opposition Shii and liberal demands continued, with outbreaks of occasional violence indicating sustained defiance. In 1999, he died and was succeeded by his son Hamad bin Isa Al Khalifah.

A Tiny Kingdom and Reform

Soon afterward, the new ruler offered relatively democratic reforms and conciliation to the Shii majority. By a 2001 referendum, Bahrain changed from a hereditary amirate to a constitutional kingdom, and Hamad became king. He then set municipal and legislative elections for 2002, in which women cast more than half the votes. In 2006, another round of elections saw Shii parties emerge as the largest bloc, a woman elected for the first time, and a Shia named a deputy prime minister. Shii unrest remained a problem through the decade, partly because the powers of the elected Chamber of Deputies continued to be offset by the equal status of the still royally appointed upper house.

Arab Spring

Along with Yemen, Bahrain has been the Arabian Peninsula state most affected by the events that transpired in Tunisia and Egypt. In October 2010, parliamentary elections slightly increased Shii representation, and then, in February 2011, only days after the fall of the Mubarak regime in Egypt, full-scale demonstrations erupted on the streets of Manama and spread elsewhere around the kingdom. The government reacted strongly against the protests; in March, Saudi forces crossed the causeway as reinforcements. The level of resistance rose and fell through 2012, and half-hearted attempts on the part of the regime to effect a resolution of the conflict were interspersed with often-brutal police crackdowns. All eighteen parliament members from the main Shii party resigned their seats in the aftermath of the suppression of the demonstrations. Along with Bahrain's semidemocratic reputation, the kingdom's leading economic sectors—finance and tourism—were negatively impacted. Into 2013, no resolution was in sight; reforms promised after the demonstrations broke out remained unimplemented,

and both leaders of and participants in the demonstrations have been given lengthy jail sentences. Nevertheless, mass demonstrations remained frequent occurrences, including during the preparations for the latest Bahrain Grand Prix (Formula One auto racing) in April 2013.[15] Formal reconciliation talks began in February and continued to be held during the year.[16]

PEOPLE AND POPULATION

Shia, Sunni, Expatriates. In Bahrain's long history as a center for traders and seafarers, many ethnic groups settled there, producing a unique indigenous mixture. Iranian influence is seen in the 70 percent adherence of Bahrainis to Shii Islam, although the ruling family and most members of the power structure are Sunni, and governing dominance by a minority religious group has long caused tensions. The three main Shii groups are the Baharna, descended from the island's original inhabitants; the Hassawi, originally from oases in eastern Saudi Arabia; and the Ajami, who came from Iran more recently. The Hawala are Sunnis from Arabia who migrated to Iran and then to Bahrain. The ethnically complex population includes large numbers of Indians, Pakistanis, other Arabs, some Europeans, Americans, and East Asians, plus a few Jews and Africans; about one-fifth of the population is nonnational. Although not socioeconomically stratified, the groups tend to concentrate in certain areas of the island or city quarters.

Villages Become Cities. Bahrain's population has increased steadily since World War II. Rising from 90,000 in 1941 to about 1.25 million by 2012, it is still the smallest in the region, since Qatar's population has grown even more rapidly. The main concentration is around the capital Manama and its suburbs, with a secondary node on the island of Muharraq (see Fig. 4.12). Manama displays

Figure 16.3 Newer buildings in Manama, capital of the island kingdom of Bahrain. Compare with earlier view in Figure 4.12. (Photograph courtesy of the Bahraini Ministry of Information)

an interesting mixture of old and new, as its Indian-style bazaars are surrounded by new high-rise office buildings and luxury hotels (Fig. 16.3). A few miles southwest of Manama is Isa Town, begun in 1968 as a model town. Hamad Town, in western Bahrain, was added in 1982 and has expanded rapidly. In eastern Muharraq Island, the Shii city of al-Hidd is now developing as an industrial area. In central Bahrain, the amir's palace and its appurtenances have evolved into the desert town of al-Rifa. The oil company center Awali in the central basin has developed much like a small American suburban town.

ECONOMIC PATTERNS

The petroleum industry and related activities have dominated the economy since the 1930s, but such traditional activities as trade, shipping and servicing Gulf shipping (including entrepôt services), dhow building, fishing, and agriculture are still important. Only pearling—Bahrain led the world in the early 1900s—has virtually disappeared, although the pearl trade is still important in the Manama *suq*. In the 1950s, the government saw how limited oil reserves were, prompting diversification, especially by attracting activities not based on natural resources or a large labor supply. Planning was well conceived and by the 1980s was paying high dividends. Even so, oil and gas are still dominant, providing about 60 percent of government revenue, with surging prices in the new century a windfall. The sector is responsible for 11 percent of GDP and 60 percent of export earnings.

Oil.   The first oil well in Bahrain, and the first in the Gulf area outside Iran, was drilled by Bahrain Petroleum Company (Bapco) in 1931–1932 at Jabal Dukhan and produced 9,600 bpd from 2,008 ft/612 m. It is still producing. The refinery opened in 1936 and has grown to handle a throughput of 262,000 bpd, mostly Saudi crude received through undersea pipelines as feedstock to produce more than eighty products, most of them exported. Saudi oil constitutes 36 percent of Bahraini imports. A project to expand pipeline throughput to 450,000 bpd is due to be completed in 2015.

Holding at 30,000 bpd for many years, production rose steadily to a peak of 76,600 bpd in 1970 before declining to 40,000 bpd in the 1980s. Output statistically tripled in the 1990s, when Saudi Arabia assigned Bahrain all of the 140,000 bpd output from their joint offshore field of Abu Safah. Output there is being doubled, although it is likely that Bahrain's share will not be increased. Its onshore oil reserves are expected to be exhausted in ten to fifteen years; however, depending on production, nonassociated gas reserves in the deep (about 10,000 ft/3,048 m) Khuff formation should last for several decades, supplying new industries. With its Hawar Islands claim confirmed, Bahrain's maritime boundaries are now defined, and offshore exploration may expand production. Several licenses have been granted since 2008.

Bapco, which held the Bahrain concession for more than four decades, was incorporated in Canada but was originally a wholly owned subsidiary of Standard Oil of California (Socal), now Chevron. In 1936, Texaco bought 50 percent of Bapco and joined Socal in the California-Texas Oil Corporation, which became Caltex Petroleum Corporation in 1968 and owned Bapco as a subsidiary. The company was for many years the main employer in the islands. It enjoyed an amicable partnership with the government and played a vital role in the country's development. In 1975, Bahrain assumed 60 percent participation in Bapco, and it took over the other 40 percent

in 1980, administering control through Banoco (Bahrain National Oil Company), founded in 1976.[17] After some shuffling during the 1980s, the government bought out Caltex in 1997; in 1998, it merged all oil operations into a single company, renamed the Bahrain Petroleum Company BSC in 2002. In addition to the Sitra refinery, which has been extensively modernized and expanded, it operates a liquefaction plant and a sizable petrochemical plant. Bapco announced in 2011 plans for a larger liquefaction plant.

Aluminum, Ship Repair, and More. ALBA, a large aluminum complex 77 percent government owned, opened in 1971. It utilizes Bahraini gas and Australian alumina for a smelting operation with annual output that has steadily increased to more than 850,000 mt in the late 2000s. The complex includes several downstream facilities, including a rolling mill, an extrusion plant, a cable plant, and factories producing aluminum powder, wire-mesh screening, and automobile wheels. Plans to add up to 350,000 additional mt in production capacity require locating a dedicated source of gas beyond the country's current output.[18] Another large installation is the Arab Ship Repair Yard (ASRY), completed in 1977 on an artificial island linked to Muharraq. Owned jointly by Bahrain and six OAPEC states,[19] ASRY's huge facility services supertankers up to 500,000 deadweight tons. It was of great value during the tanker war of the 1980s, the 1990–1991 crisis, and Operation Iraqi Freedom. The large industrial area near Mina Salman has a score of smaller plants. The formal opening of Salman Industrial City saw the commitment of investments of $3.5 billion in plants and facilities. Electric power and desalination capacity is increasing, with a large installation in al-Hidd; about 95 percent of the electricity is generated using gas. Power and water production are the focus of privatization efforts: the al-Hidd plant was sold to an international consortium in 2006, and a second private power plant began operations the same year. Elsewhere are food-processing plants, clothing factories, potteries, and similar light industries. Dhows are still constructed for both commercial and recreational use.

Service Sectors. By the 1960s, Bahrain sought to supplement its modest petroleum industry with service-centered economic sectors, particularly entrepôt facilities, trade of various categories, financial services, education and training, and tourism. Coincidentally, regional dynamics directed billions of petrodollars toward Bahrain when Beirut was hit by domestic turmoil. The government and private capital built infrastructure for the expected commercial boom: state-of-the-art communications and information technology, a modern and efficient international airport, spacious modern office quarters, luxury hotels and upscale residential areas, a broad choice of restaurants, good roads and automotive maintenance facilities, and a hospitable administrative climate. Reasonable regulation has been complemented by a stable currency, no personal or corporate taxation, unrestricted capital flows, and a capable labor force. A cosmopolitan yet informal atmosphere prevailed in Manama's business district.

Finance. Bahrain grew into a major regional financial center, with more than 350 offshore banking units and representative offices in the late 2000s. Its financial sector is the largest contributor to GDP (30 percent); especially prominent is the presence of Islamic banking (in which it ranks with Malaysia globally) and insurance institutions. Three of the Arab world's twenty largest banks are Bahraini, and some sixty-five US companies established regional headquarters here. The international economic crisis hit Bahrain as it did other regional states, but the generally conservative approach to finance and development kept the kingdom from anything like what ensued in Dubai. On the other hand, maintaining a strong reputation as a global financial center requires political stability, a hard lesson that Lebanon learned in the late 1970s.

Tourism. Tourism has grown along with commercial development; most of Bahrain's millions of annual visitors arrive by the 15.5-mi/25-km causeway from Saudi Arabia. The more relaxed atmosphere and availability of alcohol and female companionship are attractive to mainlanders. Since Saudis are such a large share of visitors, the island was more insulated than Dubai when the 2008 economic crisis impacted world tourism. Tourist arrivals set a record in 2010 but fell sharply in 2011 and 2012 with the continued civil disturbances.

Transport. Like other parts of the Gulf region, Bahrain in the 2000s began to seriously consider rail-based transportation as a way to relieve growing urban traffic. In 2009, plans for a light-rail metro system were announced, with work to begin in 2011. There are also plans for high-speed rail lines connecting the kingdom by causeways to both Qatar and Saudi Arabia as part of the GCC-wide rail project. Progress on all these plans seems to have slowed with the political crisis in the kingdom. Also experiencing difficulties brought on by political uncertainty was Gulf Air, Bahrain owned and the oldest airline operating from the Gulf region. A smaller carrier, Bahrain Air, ceased operations in 2013.

ECONOMIC EFFECTS OF POLITICAL UNREST

Although it is clear that the unrest that has swept the kingdom since February 2011 has had a negative effect on the economy, it is still too early to determine whether the problems will linger or whether a restoration of calm and the undertaking of serious reforms on the part of the government will restore the reputation that Bahrain enjoyed before 2011. Two of the country's major sectors, both from a GDP and a jobs point of view—finance and tourism—are especially sensitive to political instability. As was mentioned earlier, in the 1980s, Bahrain gained from Beirut's problems. In the 2010s, there are several nearby locations that can easily provide these sectors with a more attractive atmosphere.

RELATIONS

Saudi Arabia.   Despite its small size and population, Bahrain has complex foreign relations. Its most intimate connections are with its neighbors through the GCC, complemented by its close relations with Britain and the United States. Most obviously, it has good rapport with Saudi Arabia. For many years, 75 percent of the feedstock for the Bapco refinery has come from the mainland. Saudi Arabian money paid for the causeway connecting the two kingdoms and fuels much of Bahrain's industrial development, banking operations, retail trade and entrepôt operations, tourism, and even its basic budget, since much of the revenue derives from Saudi-produced oil from the offshore Abu Safah field. Saudi troops moved into Bahrain in March 2011 ostensibly to protect government facilities from demonstrators. A semi-official proposal voiced a year later to effect some sort of Saudi-Bahraini union seemed to have been shelved by the end of 2012.

Iran.   With many of the families with Persian roots among its Shii population having ties to Iran, Bahrain has maintained correct relations with revolutionary Iran, hoping that it will continue to honor the late shah's repudiation of Iran's long-standing claim to the archipelago. In 2012, Iran protested the treatment of Shii activists, with the Bahrain government rejecting the protest.[20]

Other Neighbors.   The kingdom has a history of being cautious about involvement with Arab and Islamic issues and has maintained strict control over militant groups on the islands, whether pro-Palestinian, pro-Arab nationalist, or pro-Iranian. After the World Court settled the Bahrain-Qatar territorial dispute in 2001, relations between the two neighbors became quite amicable; in 2009, plans for a $3 billion 24.9-mi/40-km causeway connecting them were announced; it will be designed to carry both rail and road traffic.[21]

Bahrain assisted US and European convoys during the 1987–1988 tanker war, actively participated in the coalition against Iraq in 1990–1991, and supported the 2003 invasion. Afterward, it offered humanitarian assistance and provided technical training for reforming Iraq's banking sector.

United States.   Ties with the United States have been extensive, beginning with the American Mission Hospital, established more than a century ago. Diplomatic relations were established in 1971 with Bahraini independence. In 2008, Houda Nanoo, a Bahraini Jewish woman, became the kingdom's ambassador to the United States. Economic links date to the 1930s with Bapco, US owned though operating under British (Canadian) charter. Bahrain has been a base for US Navy activity in the Gulf since 1947; it now hosts the US Fifth Fleet (a relationship that has become increasingly complicated in US domestic politics for the navy as suppression of human rights became more visible) and receives modest military aid. While the United States quietly urged reforms and reconciliation on the government all through 2011 and most of 2012, the lack of results finally prompted the State Department to issue a statement of support in November 2012 for the opposition's commitment to nonviolence. The department's annual Human Rights Report for 2013 was quite critical of the situation in Bahrain, and the government reacted sharply, terming it as ignoring the attempts at reconciliation.[22] The Bahraini parliament went so far as to adopt a resolution urging the government to keep the US ambassador from meeting with the "instigators of sedition," the government term for the Shii opposition.[23]

In 2004, Bahrain raised some ripples with its neighbors, especially Saudi Arabia, when it signed a free trade agreement with the United States, part of the US initiative to create a Middle East Free Trade Area. It went into effect in August 2006, resulting in greater US commercial interest in the kingdom and a one-year increase of 60 percent in bilateral trade.

For information on the business environment in Bahrain, see the website attached to this book: www.middleeastpatterns.com.

Qatar

KEY POINTS: Pronounce similar to "cutter." Desert peninsula with limited water, few people, and meager economy until modest oil reserves developed 1940s. British protectorate until 1971 independence. Developed offshore oil and Qatari half of world's greatest gas field mid-Gulf. Now fabulously wealthy, explosively developed; relatively progressive socially and politically: hosts liberal TV channel al-Jazeera and US airbase as well as branches of several US universities. Influential beyond size and former role.

PENINSULA STATE

The State of Qatar lies on a mitten-shaped peninsula midway on the eastern Gulf coast (see Map 16.2). Formed by a broad, gentle anticlinal upfold, it is a generally flat, low-lying area of mostly barren Tertiary carbonate rocks (primarily Middle Eocene limestones, dolomites, and marls), with much of the surface overlain by aeolian sheet and dune sands and *hamadah* (gravel-like desert pavement). Elevations for the most part are less than 130 ft/40 m, with limestone ridges in the west and Miocene-Pliocene mesas in the south. The main western ridge is Jabal Dukhan, the surface expression of a tight north-south anticlinal fold that lies parallel to the main upwarp and to the similar Bahrain and Dammam folds to the northwest. The ridge also reflects the subsurface structure that contains Qatar's major Dukhan oil and gas field, the amirate's only onshore producer. Sterile sand dunes and *sabkhahs* characterize the base of the peninsula. The remarkable northwest-southeast lineation of aeolian sand ridges in all parts of the peninsula connotes the prevailing northwest wind, the *shamal*.[24]

Of the several islands included in the state, Halul, east of the peninsula, is of particular importance in oil operations. As mentioned above, the Hawar Islands off the west coast were awarded to Bahrain in 2001. The long-running dispute between Qatar and Saudi Arabia over their boundary at the base of the peninsula was finally resolved in 2008, and the border is finally de jure (see "Regional Conflicts," in Chap. 8).

The desert climate is reflected in the widely spaced and stunted flora, and temperature and precipitation are similar to Bahrain's. Qatar has no surface streams or springs, although in recent years modestly productive

QATAR

Long-form official name, anglicized: State of Qatar

Official name, transliterated: Dawlat Qatar

Form of government: constitutional amirate with one advisory body (Advisory Council)

Area: 4,468 mi^2/11,571 km^2

Population, 2011: 1,624,000; Literacy: 96.3%

Ethnic composition (%, 2008): Arab 40, of which Qatari 20; Indian 20; Nepali 13; Filipino 10; Pakistani 7; Sri Lankan 5; American 0.5; other 4.5

Religions (%, 2000): Muslim 83, of which Sunni 73, Shia 10; Christian 10, of which Roman Catholic 6; Hindu 3; Buddhist 2; nonreligious 2

Demography: Life expectancy—76.11 yr (M), 80.12 yr (F); Birthrate (per 1,000)— 10.23; Fertility rate—1.93

GDP, 2011: $170.7 billion; purchasing power parity: $174.9 billion; per capita: $98,900

Currency: Qatari Rial (QAR), US$1 = 3.638 rials; 1 QAR = $0.279 (mid-May 2013)

Energy: oil—25.4 bn bbl; natural gas—890,000 bn ft^3 (second largest in region after Iran and third in world after Russia and Iran); coal—nil

Main exports (% of total value, 2008): $54.9 billion (of which crude petroleum 46.9; liquefied natural gas 29.4; liquefied gaseous hydrocarbons 11.6; refined petroleum 3.3; polyethylene 2.5)

Main imports (% of total value, 2008): $27.9 billion (of which machinery and apparatus 37.2; iron and steel 12.7; road vehicles 12.2; manufactures of metal 5.9; chemicals and chemical products 5.6; food 5.1)

Capital city, 2010: Doha (al-Dawhah) 521,283; other major cities: Rayyan 392,428; al-Dhakirah 128,574; al-Khawr 80,220; Wakrah 79,457

---

underground aquifers have been found. Groundwater is pumped to scattered small agricultural plots that utilize generally circular surface depressions (*rawdahs;* often *rodas*) that are surface expressions of underground collapse of solution structures in limestone and evaporites. Irrigation of the *rawdahs* has led to dangerous overpumping, diminishing the capital's water supply and necessitating desalination of seawater.[25]

Gulf waters in the bay to the west are quite shallow; thus, maritime activities, including modern port and urban development, have always been on the east coast, despite the lo-cation of the Dukhan field just inland from the west coast. Land has also been reclaimed north and south of the capital city, Doha (al-Dawhah), which takes its name from the Arabic word for a small crescent bay.

FROM THE STONE AGE TO INDEPENDENCE

Several Neolithic sites have been found in northern Qatar, and pottery from the al-Ubaid culture (5,000 BCE) and burial mounds similar to those in nearby Bahrain have been found. But later occupation appears to have been limited, presumably because of increasing desiccation of the climate. Like several other places along the Arabian coast, the small peninsula had a short period of Portuguese occupation in the sixteenth century. By the eighteenth century, Qatar was controlled by the family of Al Khalifah in the west and the Al Thani clan, originally Bedouin from Najd, in the east. When the Al Khalifah moved to Bahrain, the Al Thani gradually assumed control over Qatar; it is still the ruling family there today. With a treaty in 1867, Britain promised protection against Bahrain and the Al Khalifah. The amir recognized the Ottoman sultan as his nominal suzerain but essentially maintained his independence from both Ottomans and the British. With World War I and the Ottoman Empire allied with Germany, Qatar formally became a British protectorate in 1916; it regained sovereignty in 1971, when the British withdrew from the Gulf.

ECONOMIC PATTERNS

Poverty to Prosperity.   Qatar was isolated, sparsely populated, and poor before the 1930s. Limited fishing and pearling with some irrigation agriculture supported fewer than twenty thousand people on the entire peninsula. Petroleum Development (Qatar), renamed the Qatar Petroleum Company (QPC) in 1963, an Iraq Petroleum Company subsidiary, received a concession in 1935, found oil in the Dukhan fold in 1940, and began exporting in 1949. Shell received the concession for the offshore areas in 1952 and discovered the Idd al-Shargi field in 1960. Deep drilling, especially in Dukhan, increased reserves from 3.7 bn bbl in 2000 to 25.4 bn bbl in the early 2010s in Dukhan and six offshore fields. In 1971, Shell exploring offshore 44 mi/ 70 km north of the peninsula drilled into the Khuff zone in water 165 ft/50 m deep and discovered the fabulous North Field gas reservoir. Its proven reserves have rapidly

mounted to between 600 and 750 tn ft^3/17 and 21.2 tn m^3, making it the largest-known single nonassociated gas reservoir in the world. Including all known reserves of gas, Qatar has 890 tn ft^3/25.2 tn m^3, third largest in the world after Russia and Iran.

Qatar assumed ownership of QPC in stages through 1976, added 100 percent of Shell operations in 1977, and consolidated both in the Qatar General Petroleum Company. It shares with Abu Dhabi production from the offshore Bunduq field, located astride the median line between the two amirates. Its oil output rose to a record 765,000 bpd by 2009 in response to unprecedented world demand (and prices); in 2012, average output was at the 750,000 bpd level. Thus, Qatar's small population enjoyed the world's highest per capita income—an estimated $104,300 in 2011.

Joining the Global Economy.   In modernizing and industrializing, Qatar faced shortages of almost everything except energy. To gain access to technical and managerial skills for industrial diversification, it arranged joint ventures with the Norwegians, Japanese, French, and others for a fertilizer plant, a direct-reduction iron and steel plant, and a petrochemical complex that is one of the largest in the Middle East. All were constructed in a heavy-industry park at Umm Said (Musayid), 25 mi/40 km south of Doha. This ever-expanding concentration has a sizable refinery, upgraded from 57,500 bpd throughput in the late 1990s to 200,000 bpd by 2008; two joint-venture natural gas liquids plants utilizing North Field gas that are among the world's largest; an extensive bulk-handling port; and several support activities.

LNG Giant.   After expanding processing capacity, Qatar accounted for one-third of the world's liquefied natural gas by 2010; it had become the world's leading exporter by 2007, supplying customers from Britain to South

Korea. It has invested heavily in delivery systems—a large fleet of state-of-the-art LNG ships—and in Europe's largest and most advanced LNG import terminal, opened in Wales in May 2009. Aberrations in gas deliveries to Europe from Russia, at least partly politically motivated, have made Qatar a more reliable potential future source for many countries. Further output growth was put on hold in 2010 while the world market's future for its LNG is reassessed. A major question in the new decade is whether technical, economic, and environmental obstacles to the development of major deposits of natural gas held in shale beds in the United States and Europe can be overcome in the medium-term future and, thus, possibly radically reshape the global gas market.

Financing its share of the North Field gas infrastructure in the 1980s made heavy demands on Qatar's capital resources just as oil prices dropped sharply and the Asian economic crisis occurred, but subsequent higher oil prices and production and the rapid growth of the natural gas sector have brought the amirate great wealth. Because of the supergiant scale of the North Field, numerous large-scale projects to exploit its resource have been undertaken. A mammoth venture ultimately to cost $10 billion—the Dolphin Project—was largely operational by the early 2010s. Gas is piped under the Gulf to Abu Dhabi, Dubai, and Fujayrah for use in gas-supply projects and large gas-based industries there and then to Suhar, Oman. In a related procedure, gas-to-liquids (GTL)—producing liquid fuels like low-sulfur diesel and naphtha from gas—progress has been slower; a GTL complex is jointly owned with Shell, but the first shipment of gasoil was delivered in June 2011. By 2012, the end of the ten-year construction boom associated with gas development had led to a definite slowing in Qatari economic growth.

Oil and gas account for more than 60 percent of GDP, 85 percent of export earnings,

and 70 percent of government revenues. Gas-fired plants now generate all of the country's electricity, and Qataris lead the region in annual per capita use of electric power, topping Americans by nearly 30 percent.

Beyond Petrocarbons. In 2007, construction of a 585,000 mt/yr aluminum smelter began; full production was reached in September 2011; Qatalum is the largest aluminum plant ever launched. The late 2000s saw concrete steps toward private-sector participation in the gas-powered electricity and desalination sectors. Despite its massive gas reserves, in 2010 Qatar initiated plans for building a $1 billion solar-power plant to cope with rapidly growing domestic energy demand and to preserve gas for export and other uses.[26] The interest in solar power extends to investing in the development of both the technology and the resulting products for domestic use and export markets.

Education. Qatar sees a first-class educational system as critical if it is to continue its economic progress and to become a major actor in world science and technology. As part of its efforts in this regard, it has built the Education City complex in the Doha area. The facility has attracted several major US and European institutions that now conduct graduate and undergraduate programs, including Cornell University's local degree-granting medical school and a branch of Georgetown's School of Foreign Service. In computing the Global Competitiveness Index for 2012, the World Economic Forum, for the education component of that index, rated Qatar as fourth worldwide in the quality of its educational system relative to the needs of its society (for comparison: the United States ranked twenty-sixth, Canada seventh). In 2012, about 4.1 percent of GDP and 18.6 percent of government spending went to education—in both cases, the highest levels in the region.[27]

Transport.   Remote in location, Qatar had no air connections until the early 1950s, when it first joined its neighbors in the Gulf Aviation (later Gulf Air) operation. It inaugurated its own Qatar Airways in 1994 and has financed its rapid expansion by 2012 to a fleet of 111 planes with another 250 on order. For the second year in a row, Qatar Air was voted the world's best airline at the World Airline Awards held at the 2012 Farnborough Air Show. A new international airport for Doha is due to open in 2013 despite reported delays due to security concerns.[28]

An active partner in GCC-wide planning for a regional rail network, Qatar envisions a land link to Saudi Arabia and to Bahrain via the combined road and rail causeway. Additionally, a four-line 300-kilometer metro system for metropolitan Doha is to be in place by 2019. In April and August 2012, several contracts for the initial steps were announced.

Tourism.   Only a few years ago, a well-known guidebook is supposed to have described Qatar as "possibly the most boring place on earth," and certainly at the time very few people would have visited the amirate for touristic reasons. But beginning in the mid-2000s, the number of visitor arrivals began to climb, and in recent years double-digit growth has been seen on a regular basis. Hotel construction, as well as that of other related facilities, has kept up a similar pace; world-class museums have been added to the amirate's attractions. In 2006, Qatar successfully hosted forty-five nations for the Asian Games, whetting its appetite for similar events. Although it failed in its bid for the 2020 Olympics, it will be the venue for the 2022 Football World Cup, probably the biggest international sporting event aside from the Olympics. Because the matches will be held in the scorching heat of a Gulf summer, Qatar is pioneering radically innovative cooling techniques to make the stadiums comfortable for both players and spectators.[29]

The new international airport and Doha's metro system are only part of the infrastructure to be put in place before the 2022 event; the additions will also strengthen the expected bid for the 2024 Olympics. On the other hand, Qatar's prominence in international sporting events has focused unwelcome attention on some of its restrictions on human rights.[30]

PEOPLE AND POLITICS

Population Explosion.   Qatar's small population has increased more than sixtyfold since the 1930s, rising to about 1.95 million by 2012 as it attracted thousands of Pakistanis, Indians, Filipinos, Iranians, and Baluch, as well as Arabs from Egypt, Jordan, Lebanon, and Yemen to swell its labor force.[31] (For the growing numbers of Christians among the expatriates, the amir has facilitated construction of several churches.) With these changes, Qatari citizens may now constitute no more than one-tenth of the population. The vast majority of the population lives in and around Doha, which was little more than a fishing village before World War II but, like Kuwait City, has become a modern capital with high-rise buildings of original design. The new palace of the ruler sits amid scores of handsome structures on the shore of Doha Bay. An older traditional palace now houses the national museum, and in 2008 a world-class Museum of Islamic Art opened its doors. The stunning museum complex, designed by I. M. Pei, would be worth visiting even if it did not contain its excellent collection (Fig. 16.4).

Modest Reforms.   The current amir, Amir Hamad bin Khalifah, deposed his father, Shaykh Khalifa bin Hamad, in 1995 in a bloodless coup amid accusations of diversion of too much national revenue to the latter's personal accounts. The more progressive new amir has encouraged democratic institutions, with a new constitution approved

Figure 16.4 The dramatic Doha Museum of Islamic Art, designed by I. M. Pei and opened in 2008. (Joanne Cummings)

in a 2003 referendum, coming into effect in 2005. The fourth round of municipal elections was held in 2011 in which one woman was elected to office. These polls were designated as precursors of elections to the still wholly appointed Advisory Council.[32] Compared to just about every other Arab country covered in this book, Qatar has seen surprisingly little direct domestic effect of the Arab Spring. Nevertheless, in 2011 the amir did finally announce a 2013 date for the first elections for the Advisory Council; on the other hand, in November 2012, a Qatari poet who wrote verses praising the Arab Spring was imprisoned for life for "insulting the Amir."[33]

Relative Openness

A more dramatic development has been al-Jazeera (formally al-Jazirah), the Qatar-based television network, which quickly attracted regional and world attention when it opened in 1996 under the amir's sponsorship. It introduced a unique medium without censorship and with liberal programming for Arab audiences; the network has often run afoul of regional governments (plus the United States) with its generally frank reporting, but it treads notably more carefully in reporting on Qatari events. The network has benefited from loans and grants from the Qatari government but demonstrates a considerable degree of independence in most of its programming, offering a platform that has run the gamut from Israeli politicians to Salafi preachers.[34] Since 2006, it has broadcast globally in English as well as Arabic.

Its early coverage of the Arab Spring, especially of the uprising in Egypt, is credited by many observers both with galvanizing the younger generation in the region to push for reforms in their own countries and with acquainting a global audience (even in the United States) with the changes erupting across the Middle East. Its reporters have been arrested, expelled, and even killed, and it has been claimed that in the aftermath of the invasion of Iraq, President Bush proposed to Prime Minister Blair in 2004 the possibility of bombing its Doha headquarters because of the network's alleged anti-American reporting.[35] On the other hand, in 2011 to the utter and complete dismay of neocons and Islamaphobes in the United States, Secretary of State Hillary Clinton praised its coverage of the Arab Spring as superior to what was available from American news outlets—which in fact had begun contracting with it to broadcast its news footage.[36]

RELATIONS

Having emerged from isolation with its oil resources, Qatar has recently found itself on the world stage economically with its gas reserves, politically with its role in the GCC, and socially with al-Jazeera. Long-standing boundary disputes with Bahrain and Saudi Arabia were settled amicably and have resulted in greatly improved relations with these neighbors. As mentioned above, a causeway linking Qatar to Bahrain by road and rail is being planned. Economic cooperation in the Dolphin Project with Oman and the UAE has strengthened its links with both states. Relations with Britain, the former protecting power, have remained cordial since independence. In the late 2000s, Qatari diplomats became quite active as mediators: in Lebanon between the government and Hizballah (and by breaking a deadlock in 2008, allowing the election of a new president [see Chap. 11]), in Sudan regarding Darfur, and in nearby trouble spots like Eritrea and Ethiopia.

Arab Spring Diplomacy.   However, it has been with the onset of the Arab Spring that Qatar's heightened diplomatic role came to greater international recognition. The amirate was very active in securing Arab League backing for the NATO role in the revolt against Qadhafi and in finalizing the eventual victory of the Libyan rebels. In January 2012, it called for Arab military intervention in the deepening Syrian civil war, and along with Saudi Arabia it became a major supplier of resources to the forces seeking Assad's overthrow. It tried for some time to mediate between the Saleh regime and its opponent in Yemen; though its direct efforts were frustrated, Saleh did finally capitulate in November 2011 (see Chap.18). But its role has not been entirely diplomatic during recent conflicts. In September 2012, it announced that it will invest $18 billion over five years in Egypt's troubled post-Mubarak economy; this came on the heels of a $2 billion emergency loan to the Egyptian government and a pledge of $1.25 billion to support Jordanian reforms. The assistance to Egypt and perceived Qatari links to that country's Muslim Brotherhood have reportedly caused considerable concern among Qatar's GCC partners.[37]

Qatar's successes in regional diplomacy have been based on what can be called its "soft power"—basically, its ability to offer financial assistance at critical times and the professed neutrality allowing it to act as a more or less honest broker in disputes. But more recently, perceptions of Qatar's neutrality have been shifting negatively—in Egypt and Syria particularly—illustrating that it may be overreaching the limits of that soft power.[38]

United States.   The United States and Qatar established diplomatic relations in 1972, a few months after the amirate's independence. Like his GCC neighbors, Amir Hamad has chosen to rely on US military protection and in supporting US military operations in the region. He has hosted a "United States–Islamic World Forum" annually since 2004, sponsored by the Brookings Institution's Saban Center; the 2012 forum returned to

Doha after being held for the first time in Washington the year before. More significantly, Qatar has permitted the United States to operate a large air force base at al-Udayd and hosts the US Central Command Forward Headquarters, which coordinated the Iraqi invasion. In a gesture of solidarity, Qatar established the Qatar Katrina Fund in 2005 to disburse $100 million to assist the victims of the disastrous storm that hit the US Gulf coast that year.[39]

Israel. The amir also cooperated with US efforts to smooth incorporation of Israel into the region's economic and political structure, allowing the Jewish state to open a trade office in Doha in 1996, followed by a visit from Israel's then prime minister, Shimon Peres. Qatar made further attempts to bridge the gap between Israel and the Arab states, but the onset of the Second Intifadah and, subsequently, Israeli actions in Lebanon and Gaza frustrated its efforts, and ties with Israel were severed in 2009 with the closing of the trade office after Operation Cast Lead (see Chap. 13). In 2010,[40] Qatar offered to restore relations if Israel would allow it to ship building materials and money to repair Gaza's infrastructure; Israel refused, claiming these could be used to build fortifications. In 2012, with Egypt opening its border with Gaza, Qatar announced plans for more than $250 million in project support, angering both Israel and the Palestinian Authority with a visit by the amir to Gaza in October.

For information on the business environment in Qatar, see the website attached to this book: www.middleeastpatterns.com.

NOTES

1. L. S. Amery, in his foreword to S. Wilson 1928, ix.

2. United Nations Development Programme, *Human Development Report 2013*; *Legatum Prosperity Index 2012*, www.prosperity.com/.

3. The classic work on the old Kuwait is the massive compendium Dickson 1949, followed by his *Kuwait and Her Neighbors* (1956).

4. Crystal 1990, 39.

5. Author Cummings, in Riyadh (500 km away) at the time, remembers smoke-darkened skies for weeks.

6. Among the many articles on the environmental catastrophe engendered by the oil spills and well fires in Kuwait, useful and easily available coverage, including ground photographs and space imagery, is given in R. Williams et al. 1991 and Earle 1992. An authoritative assessment with more perspective is given in *International Petroleum Encyclopedia* 1992, 222–229.

7. *Kuwait Times*, Feb. 10, Feb. 13, Apr. 1, and Apr. 11, 2013; al-Jazeera, Apr. 15, 2013.

8. Reliance on desalination plants does bring vulnerability, as happened when Iraq emptied crude oil into the waters surrounding Kuwait in 1991 and when a malfunctioning sewage plant leaked pollution, as reported in the *Kuwait Times*, Aug. 25, 2009.

9. IEA, "2006 Energy Balance for Kuwait."

10. A group called the *Bidoon jinsaya* (Arabic for "without nationality") or just *Bidoon* are longtime residents of Kuwait who for various reasons have been unable to claim citizenship; they are estimated by the government to number more than one hundred thousand. The antecedents of many but not all of them were nomadic tribesmen who roamed the Arabian Desert before modern political boundaries existed. They are subject to a fair amount of discrimination because of their indeterminate legal status.

11. The problem is examined in detail in A. Lesch 1991. See also Le Troquer and al-Oudat 1999.

12. *Al-Monitor*, Mar. 27, 2013.

13. Kuwait Fund for Arab Economic Development, *Annual Report, 2010–2011.*

14. The main island was called al-Awal in the past, hence the name Awali for the oil field and town. Believed to have been the ancient Dilmun, Bahrain was the classical Tylos, and, to add to the confusion, the name Bahrain was long applied to eastern Arabia as well as to the islands.

15. For a discussion of the somewhat surrealistic aspects of Bahraini politics in the run-up to the 2013 Grand Prix, see *al-Monitor*, May 5, 2013.

16. Al-Jazeera, Feb. 11, 2013.

17. A. Clarke 1990 covers the history and status of Bahrain oil in minute detail and includes very useful appendixes and a bibliography.

18. US Geological Survey, "The Mineral Industry of Bahrain," in *Minerals Yearbook* 2008.

19. Iraq, Kuwait, Libya, Qatar, Saudi Arabia, and the UAE.

20. See Mabon 2012 for a discussion of the rivalry between Iran and Saudi Arabia in Bahrain.

21. *National* (Abu Dhabi), Nov. 22, 2009.

22. *Khaleej Times* (Dubai), Apr. 25, 2013.

23. *Gulf Times* (Doha), May 6, 2013.

24. See the detailed Landsat images in Yehia 1983, which also includes sectional topographic and geologic maps of Qatar.

25. Batanouny 1981 gives good, concise coverage of the Qatar environment, as well as detailed scientific coverage of the flora. Yehia 1983 discusses and illustrates the *rawdahs* and coastal features.

26. *Media Line,* Jan. 8, 2010.

27. *Zawya,* Jan. 27, 2013.

28. *Zawya,* Apr. 1, 2013

29. *Zawya,* Apr. 19, 2013.

30. For example, see *BBC News,* Jan. 25, 2013.

31. The expatriates working in Qatar, as elsewhere in the region, are very important to their home economies. For example, it has been estimated that from Qatar alone, expatriate workers remitted home some $60 billion between 2006 and 2012. *Zawya,* May 2, 2013.

32. A less optimistic view of the evolution of Qatari political institutions is found in Kamrava 2009.

33. *Washington Post,* Nov. 29, 2012.

34. An interesting and thorough treatment of the network is found in El-Nawawy and Iskandar 2002.

35. *Guardian,* Nov. 23, 2005, and Jan. 9, 2006.

36. For example, see *Nation,* Jan. 31, 2011; *ABC News,* Mar. 2, 2011; *Huffington Post,* Mar. 3, 2012; and Kessler 2012.

37. *Al-Monitor,* Jan. 23, 2013.

38. For example, see *Zawya,* May 14, 2013.

39. Within fifteen months of its establishment, all of the funds had been committed to some eighteen projects in education, health care, and housing.

40. A comprehensive view of Qatar's relations with Israel is found in Rabi 2009; see *Ha'aretz,* Jan. 16, 2009, for details on the breaking of relations.

The reader is advised to consult this book's associated website (**www.middleeastpatterns.com**) for additional information on **Kuwait, Bahrain, and Qatar**, such as historical time lines and chronologies of recent events, as well as essays on selected topics and various international economic, social, and political indicators.

17

The Horn of Arabia

Stretching to the south and east from the city-states of Chapter 16 are littorals increasingly backed by rugged interiors as distance increases. Along the Gulf, the coastal regions remain as dry, hot, and humid as they are in those countries covered in the previous chapter. But past the Musandum Peninsula (the "Horn of Arabia" where the Gulf narrows to the 24 mi/39 km wide Strait of Hormuz) and into the Indian Ocean, the coastland gradually becomes less arid. Facing the open ocean, the highlands, if never exactly verdant, do catch monsoon rains

and, by the standards of most of the rest of the Arabian peninsula, are markedly more temperate in clime.

Straddling Hormuz—through which every day passes a fifth of the world's petroleum supply—are two states that are both much larger and more complex than the small city-states up the Gulf to the northwest. The United Arab Emirates and the Sultanate of Oman have some historical and economic similarities, but are quite different in many other ways. In this chapter, we will discuss both countries in greater detail.

United Arab Emirates

KEY POINTS: Federation of seven principalities, including Abu Dhabi, Dubai, Sharjah. Was British protectorate before independence 1971. Until 1950s, a series of poor fishing and pearling villages along southern Gulf. Development of huge oil resources onshore and offshore in Abu Dhabi and modest fields elsewhere enabled phenomenal development, with elaborate competition among main principalities. Dubai especially innovative, attracting huge investment: trade and tourism, offshore residential islands, world's tallest building, and so on. Expatriates majority of population. Abu Dhabi wealthiest and can afford experimental projects. Little unrest during Arab Spring.

A SURVEY

Most recent of the Middle East states to achieve independence, the United Arab Emi-

rates[1] (UAE) comprises seven component polities, including, on the Gulf, Abu Dhabi, Dubai, Sharjah, Ajman, Umm al-Qaywayn, and Ras al-Khaymah, and, on the Indian

509

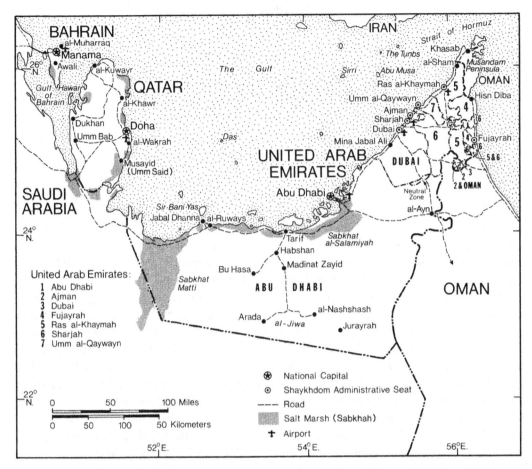

Map 17.1 General map of the seven United Arab Emirates, with neighboring Bahrain and Qatar. Numbers in the UAE identify the amirates and their respective exclaves. See maps in Chapter 6 for petroleum and gas fields. UAE boundaries are now de jure.

Ocean, Fujayrah (see Map 17.1). Thus, the UAE occupies coasts on both sides of the Musandam peninsula—an Omani exclave at the tip. Formerly an aggregation of British-protected tribal shaykhdoms known as the Trucial States, the amirates moved abruptly from isolation and poverty in the 1950s to oil wealth and dramatic development in the 1970s and 1980s and to world-famous spectacular development in the 1990s and 2000s.[2]

Ancient Beginnings to Coexisting Tribes

Several Neolithic sites have been found in the area, but recent excavations have also uncov-ered a Paleolithic presence in Sharjah many thousands of years older. The findings will in-fluence the "out of Africa" hypothesis that traces hominoid migrations out of Africa and across Arabia. Neolithic and Bronze Age set-tlements and tombs, found especially in Abu Dhabi, Dubai, and Ras al-Khaymah, reveal ties with the Dilmun, Harrapan, early Persian, and Sumerian cultures in Mesopotamia, the northern Gulf, and neighboring areas. The coastal area became familiar to Europeans—the Portuguese in the early 1500s and then the British in the 1700s—after the route around the Cape of Good Hope opened. A series of coastal islands and indentations,

UNITED ARAB EMIRATES

Long-form official name, anglicized: United Arab Emirates (UAE)

Official name, transliterated: al-Imarat al-Arabiyah al-Muttahidah

Form of government: federation of seven hereditary amirates with one advisory body (Federal National Council)

Area: 32,280 mi²/83,600 km²

Population, 2011: 7,891,000; Literacy: 77.9%

Ethnic composition (%, 2009): Asian Indian 29; Pakistani 21; UAE Arab 15; Bangladeshi 8; other Asian 17; other 10

Religions (%, 2005): Muslim 62 (mostly Sunni); Hindu 21; Christian 9; Buddhist 4; other 4

Demography: Life expectancy—74.12 yr (M), 79.42 yr (F); Birthrate (per 1,000)—15.76; Fertility rate—2.38

GDP, 2011: $336.5 billion; purchasing power parity: $256.5 billion; per capita: $47,700

Currency: Emirati Dirham (AED), US$1 = 3.672 dirhams; 1 AED = $0.272 (mid-May 2013)

Energy: oil—97.8 bn bbl; natural gas—215,035 bn ft³ (most of the oil and gas fields are in Abu Dhabi, onshore and offshore); coal—nil

Main exports (% of total value, 2008): $210.0 billion (of which crude petroleum 38.3; refined petroleum 10.9; gold 4.3; diamonds 3.2; road vehicles and parts 3; platinum 1.9; unspecified 26.6)

Main imports (% of total value, 2008): $175.5 billion (of which machinery and apparatus 18.7; base and fabricated metals 15.4; road vehicles 9.8; gold 8.4; food 5.1; diamonds 4.2)

Capital city, 2006: Abu Dhabi 630,000; other major cities: Dubai 1,354,980; Sharjah 685,000; al-Ayn 350,000; Ajman 202,244; Ras al-Khaymah 113,34

---

dotted with villages, offered shelter at that time to fishing and pearling dhows.

British Presence. Following several naval operations in the southern Gulf, the British imposed the first coastwide maritime truce in 1820 and followed it with other treaties and imposed agreements in 1835, 1839, and 1847.[3] The Treaty of Maritime Peace in Perpetuity (1853) gave the British navy supervision over maritime relations in the lower Gulf, leaving land relations to the shaykhdoms.[4] From this 1853 truce evolved the official designation of the coastal settlements as the Trucial States (sometimes Trucial Shaykhdoms, Trucial Coast, or even Trucial Oman), a designation that lasted for more than a century. Out of these "village states," which had shifting patterns of independence as ruling families altered relationships and domains, developed the post-1971 UAE.

In 1951, the British persuaded the rulers of the shaykhdoms to create a Council of Trucial State Rulers, and in the same year the

Trucial Oman Levies were organized to suppress slave traffic and maintain law and order. These forces later became the storybook Trucial Oman Scouts, who, under a handful of British officers seconded to them, were responsible for security in the area. Disbanded after independence, they supplied cadres to the new military units maintained separately at first in each of the amirates but later merged into a federal army.

Rapid Change, Confederation, Independence

The landscape along the coast has been dramatically transformed in one generation. Cross-country tracks and wadi bottoms served as roads until the mid-1960s (see Fig. 7.4A); a few small generators supplied electricity part-time in the towns. When pearling declined, the hardy inhabitants relied on a subsistence economy of fishing, herding, date culture, and a growing dhow trade. In the early 1960s, the oil boom began in Abu Dhabi, later in Dubai, and then in the other amirates. Within a few years of independence, the UAE achieved a level of economic development that could be described only as spectacular, its people enjoying one of the world's highest per capita incomes.

Before withdrawing from the Gulf, the British, for the first time, delineated shaykhdom boundaries, partly to inhibit later boundary conflicts and partly to prevent dissension over oil and gas exploration. With British warnings against political fragmentation, the Trucial States explored confederation with Bahrain and Qatar (which in the end remained separate), becoming independent under a provisional constitution in December 1971, with a reluctant Ras al-Khaymah joining up two months later.

British boundary efforts were not totally successful, but disputes did not destroy the initially very fragile unity. Dubai and Abu Dhabi resolved their problem by agreeing to a neutral zone, and Dubai and Sharjah reached a temporary settlement and finalized it in 1997. Although the seven amirs have been reluctant to surrender their traditional powers to the federation, the UAE has evolved into a vigorous, pragmatic, and prosperous polity. For the long term, the question remains about how much they will be willing to give up for the sake of unity. While Emiratis still identify first with their home amirate, a stronger sense of national identity—"Emiratization"—has emerged with the coming of age of the UAE's second generation in the new century and as urbanization has blurred some amirate boundaries.

To the relief of both neighbors and the British, centripetal forces have proved stronger than centrifugal ones. The UAE has emerged as a political-geographical oddity, a republic in which the federal units are monarchies.[5] With its seven constituents, it is the region's most complex polity. Yet, remarkably, over more than forty years a balance has been reached in the allocation of powers (and funds) between the principalities and federal institutions. Criteria for distributing offices proved acceptable, and in June 1996 the Federal National Council (FNC) approved a permanent constitution and designated Abu Dhabi the permanent capital. Executive power is exercised by the Federal Supreme Council, composed of the seven amirs, who elect the federation president from among their number (since independence, they have always selected the amir of Abu Dhabi for this role, with the amir of Dubai as vice president).

POPULATION

Development led population to grow from about 75,000 in 1950 to about 223,000 in 1970; then there was an explosive twenty-five-fold increase—to more than 5.3 million by 2012. Main concentrations are in the capital city of Abu Dhabi and in the conurbation of Dubai, Sharjah, and Ajman. Additional nodes of population mark the other amirate capitals and several oasis towns—especially the merging villages and towns of al-Ayn in the Buraymi Oasis that the UAE shares with Oman. The ethnic composition of the population is noteworthy, not only because it is the most complex of the varied population mixtures of the Gulf region but also because no more than 20 percent of the population is indigenous Emirati.

The sparse population of the early 1960s, although intelligent and energetic, could not possibly meet the demand for labor, either in numbers or in technical skills, of the early boom years; not only expertise and materials had to be imported, but also scores of thousands of workers. This created housing shortages, forcing many workers, some with families, into *barasti* (palm-frond) huts, tents, and other makeshift housing until the wealthier amirates erected extensive housing blocks. Like all the major Arab petroleum producers, the UAE is trying to reduce its need for outside personnel—still more than 90 percent of the workforce. Various regulations call for more "Emiratization" at managerial levels, but despite restrictions on further immigration, the pressing need for expatriates continues.

Living Standards. Prosperity has greatly improved living standards. The United Nations Development Programme's most recent Human Development Report places the UAE high among the group of countries with very high levels of human development. The report's index for 2013 placed it 4th in the region and 41st out of 186 countries globally. Since 1980, the UAE's Human Development Index has risen by 34.5 percent, as life expectancy and educational levels climbed dramatically. The broader-based Prosperity Index from the Legatum Institute ranked the UAE 29th of 142 countries globally and 1st regionally in 2012.[6]

ECONOMIC DEVELOPMENT

Petroleum and Diversification

Petro-industries dominate the economy of the UAE but not quite to the extent that they do in Qatar and Kuwait. Exports of crude and processed oil and gas supply 50 to 60 percent of export earnings, and 90 percent of government revenues are from oil. However, only 25 percent of GDP is from oil revenues, and economic diversification is being pursued aggressively. It is noteworthy that Abu Dhabi produces 82 percent of the UAE's oil and contributes three-fourths of the federal government's income. As in the other Gulf oil producers, especially Bahrain, the UAE has followed a vigorous program of industrialization along both energy-related and other lines. Although most of the plants are export oriented, some of them cater to the affluent population of the union and neighboring countries.

However, as important as the oil industry is, most related facilities are in remote areas and provide relatively little direct employment. Thus, the emphasis several amirates put on traditional economic activities—trade and transit trade, shipping, and modest but still important agriculture, horticulture, animal herding, and fishing—is significant. Diversification has cushioned low-oil-price recessions and has burgeoned dramatically during booms. Even more important has been the expanding role of administrative, financial, commercial, and personal services—government, banking, insurance, export-import, retailing, hotel and restaurant operation, and especially, since the 1980s, tourism.

Thus, a diversified and vigorous economy across a larger territory gives the UAE an outward and genuine air of energy and bustle. Different centers have developed specializations and characteristics: Abu Dhabi is an oil, financial, industrial, and administrative center (Fig. 17.1); Dubai is a lively recreational, trade, industrial, financial, and shipping

Figure 17.1 Row of high-rise office and apartment buildings along the Corniche on Abu Dhabi island, an awesome change from 1964, when the village of Abu Dhabi had fewer than a score of permanent buildings, none more than two stories high.

center, perhaps profligate in self-promotion; Sharjah focuses on cultural amenities with two universities and natural gas exports, complementing Dubai with commercial, transportation, and manufacturing activities; Fujayrah is a beach resort with an Indian Ocean port growing rapidly in importance; and al-Ayn is a productive agricultural oasis, as are Sharjah's Dhayd and Ras al-Khaymah's Diqdaqah (Digdagga) oases.

Petrocarbons

Ranking fifth in the Middle East and seventh in the world in proven petroleum reserves, the UAE has a known 97.8 bn bbl, about 6 percent of the world's resources. It is close behind Kuwait (see Table 6.1), with about five times the reserves of the United States, and it could produce 2 mn bpd for 135 years, al-

though it is expanding its average daily output to 3 mn bpd. In addition, as a result of the new discoveries in the 1980s, it has the seventh-largest gas reserves in the world.[7] Abu Dhabi alone has more than 94 percent of the federation's oil reserves and 93 percent of its gas. Each member of the federation retains full rights to its own oil and gas resources, sharing with other states only that income unanimously agreed upon. In practice, Abu Dhabi and Dubai help support the less wealthy amirates through the federal budget; Abu Dhabi importantly came to Dubai's aid in the credit crunch of 2009.

Abu Dhabi. Petroleum Development (Trucial States), an Iraq Petroleum Company subsidiary (now Abu Dhabi National Oil Company—ADNOC), conducted initial explorations in southwestern Abu Dhabi in 1939, found oil in 1958, but exported only in 1963. Produced in the great Bab field (originally Murban), the oil was lifted from a new terminal at Jabal Dhanna in extreme western Abu Dhabi. Meanwhile, oil had been found by Abu Dhabi Marine Areas (ADMA) in the offshore Umm Shaif field; production began in 1962. The Das Island terminal handles output from the offshore Zakum, Umm Shaif, and Bunduq fields. By the early 2010s, more than a score of fields had been found in Abu Dhabi waters (all are not yet on stream), along with ten major onshore fields. One crosses the Saudi border, an extension of the large Shaybah light-oil reservoir. ADNOC, operating mainly onshore, and ADMA, mainly offshore, are the principal operating and service companies.

Deep drilling for nonassociated gas in the Khuff zone, beneath already producing oil horizons, discovered immense reservoirs beneath Umm Shaif and Abu al-Dukhush offshore and Bab onshore. Khuff gas gave Abu Dhabi the huge reserves mentioned earlier, sufficient for 160 years at the present rate of production. Even so, Abu Dhabi and Dubai have pursued the Dolphin Project to bring Qatari gas to the UAE and Oman (discussed above in Chapter 16). Using Dolphin gas to generate power for several huge desalination plants and industries will permit the UAE to devote its own gas to the extraction of natural gas liquids and gas reinjection to maintain reservoir pressure.

Dubai. Petroleum Development (Trucial Coast) explored in Dubai in 1937 without success. Not until 1966 did Dubai Marine Areas (a consortium of US and European companies) find the moderately large field of Fateh, 56 mi/90 km offshore (see Fig. 6.2). With other later finds, total production rose to 469,000 bpd in 1990 before declining to 100,000 bpd by the late 2000s. A new offshore field was confirmed in 2010. Dubai also

imports gas from both Sharjah and Abu Dhabi to feed its industries.

Other Amirates. Sharjah and Ras al-Khaymah found oil still later. After onshore wells in Sharjah proved dry, a new concessionaire (Crescent Petroleum Company, with Buttes Gas and Oil of the United States as operator) found the small Mubarak field near Abu Musa Island, 45 mi/72 km offshore, in 1972; revenues were shared with Iran (which asserts claim to the island and its territorial waters). Production in 2012 was close to 50,000 bpd. Onshore, a deep gas condensate field found in 1980 at Saja, along with later condensate and dry gas discoveries, brings Sharjah significant revenues from sales to several neighbors. Ras al-Khaymah also produces small amounts of gas condensate from its offshore Saleh field, 26 mi/42 km into the Gulf. Exploration in Ajman, Umm al-Qaywayn, and Fujayrah has been commercially unsuccessful, but some gas has been found in Umm al-Qaywayn.

Downstream Facilities. The UAE operates five refineries and is steadily expanding other energy-related industries. The largest refinery, with a capacity of 400,000 bpd, operates in the western Abu Dhabi industrial zone of al-Ruways, near Jabal Dhanna, which also includes expanding petroleum-based plants for petrochemicals, fertilizers, and, increasingly, natural gas liquids. As the UAE steadily exploits its enormous gas reserves, gas-processing plants using 3 bn ft³/85 mn m³ per day are being developed offshore and onshore. The increasing condensate exports are not subject to OPEC quotas. Record prices in 2008 took oil export earnings to an all-time high of $90.9 billion, but with the drop in demand in 2009 revenues declined by more than 42 percent to about $52 billion.

Alternative Energy. In 2012, nearly all of the federation's electricity was being generated using gas,[8] but nuclear energy is in the offing. In July 2012, the federal government gave the go-ahead to the construction of two nuclear power plants by a Korean-US partnership for operation in 2017, and it has said it sees opportunities for as much as $100 billion in alternative energy investment in the coming decade. In its pursuit of alternate energy sources, it is building the first carbon-free city, Masdar City, in Abu Dhabi; that amirate saw the dedication in 2013 of the world's largest concentrated solar power plant.[9] In 2012, Dubai awarded a $3 billion contract for building a 13-megawatt solar-generating plant.

Other Industries

Al-Ruways also includes a steel mill producing iron bars for construction. In the mid-1970s, Dubai developed a man-made port, industrial area, and free-trade zone southwest of Dubai City at Jabal Ali that eclipses al-Ruways. Despite skepticism, an imaginative and enterprising ruler of Dubai, the late Shaykh Rashid bin Said Al Maktum, deep-dredged a channel and constructed a major port, put in a large power plant and desalination facility, invited dozens of industrial companies, and opened a free port area. Jabal Ali is now a multibillion-dollar regional economic node.

Like Bahrain and Qatar, the UAE has turned to aluminum smelting using the region's plentiful gas reserves as fuel. Current and future facilities in Dubai (in Jabal Ali) and Abu Dhabi will put total output at 2.3 mn mt/yr, close to half the total production of the GCC countries. The main power plant, regularly expanded, not only feeds the smelter but also desalinates tens of millions of gallons of water daily. The booming Jabal Ali zone includes other power and water plants; hundreds of factories, including refineries and gas-processing facilities, petrochemical plants, cement plants, steel fabrication plants, fertilizer and paint factories, food-processing establishments, grain silos, tank farms, and

metal fabricators; an ever-expanding free zone with comprehensive private rights of operation for twenty-four hundred companies from seventy-five countries; and the world's largest man-made port, a state-of-the-art facility that is the third busiest in the world in volume handled—after Singapore and Hong Kong. More modest industrial parks have also been developed in Sharjah and Ajman.

Transport

Ports. Each amirate has its own seaport. Large planned ports in Dubai, Abu Dhabi, and Sharjah contrast with their tiny predecessors, used now only by dhows for Gulf and Indian trade, fishing, and pearling. Port Rashid in Dubai is one of the largest ports in the Middle East—more than 500 ac/200 ha within its breakwater. East of Port Rashid, a large container port with efficient roll-on/roll-off facilities that have attracted additional cargo traffic has been built. Jabal Ali port in southern Dubai has steadily increased its cargo handling until it now has world rank. But the small-scale facilities in Dubai Creek (Khawr Dubai) still attract scores of dhows each day, besides being one of the city's major tourist attractions.

In a manner typical of the competitiveness among the amirates, Abu Dhabi expanded its Port Zayid, especially the container facilities. It is also installing a large free-zone facility on Saadiyat Island, adjacent to Abu Dhabi Island, to compete with Jabal Ali. With an investment of more than $7 billion, it launched Khalifa Port in September 2012. Sharjah has vigorously pushed its smaller Port Khalid in Sharjah town, its east coast container port of Khor Fakkan on the Indian Ocean, and a port at Hamriyah with a free trade zone. Khor Fakkan—an exclave of Sharjah—and Fujayrah have grown steadily in response to their locational asset: on the Gulf of Oman, outside the Straits of Hormuz. An international cargo ship can save up to twenty-four hours, and high insurance costs, by avoiding a trip through the straits. In July 2012, a pipeline that can carry 1.5 mn bpd began to deliver product to a new terminal in Fujayrah. Ajman and Ras al-Khaymah also promote their small ports on the Gulf.

Railways.   Like the other GCC countries, in the late 2000s the UAE embarked on railway development projects tying all six nations and the seven amirates together. Etihad Rail was established in 2010 to oversee the system. The initial phase will run from the Saudi Arabian border to Jabal Ali port near Dubai, and a $900 million contract for this phase was awarded in 2011. Altogether, the network is envisioned to stretch 684 mi/1100 km, terminating at Khor Fakkan on the Gulf of Oman, with a line between Abu Dhabi and al-Ayn linking to Oman. A spur will transport granular sulfur from desert gas fields to Ruways port. The first rail operations are scheduled for 2013.[10]

Airports.   Of the federation's four larger airports (Abu Dhabi, Dubai, Sharjah, and Ras al-Khaymah), the first three have vied for handling the most aircraft and passengers. They have spacious and impressive terminals with large duty-free shopping areas. By 2004, Dubai gained first rank with its extravagant terminal facilities and flight service. More recently, by early 2013, it moved into second place among the world's busiest airports for international travel; passenger arrivals in 2012 were estimated to top 55 million. At its current rate of growth, it could surpass London's Heathrow Airport as the world's busiest by the mid-2010s.[11] Some 8,000 flights use the facility weekly, connecting on 130 airlines to 220 destinations on six continents. It is surrounded by built-up areas that cramp long-term expansion, and this has led to the construction of al-Maktoum International Airport near Jabal Ali and 25mi/40 km southwest of Dubai airport. It opened to cargo traffic in 2010 and is scheduled to inaugurate passenger traffic in 2013. As mentioned earlier, Sharjah has specialized in shopping excursion flights, and Abu Dhabi receives governmental and business travelers. Again, competitiveness led Ras al-Khaymah and Fujayrah each to open its own airport.

The UAE is oversupplied with both seaports and airports, yet all of them are either crowded or reasonably utilized. Although the UAE was formerly a constituent owner of Gulf Air, three of its amirates have opened their own airlines: Dubai inaugurated Emirates Airline in 1985, and in a little more than twenty years it boasted the largest fleet in the region (see Chap. 7); in terms of international passengers carried, it has become the world's leading airline. Abu Dhabi is rapidly expanding its competing carrier, Etihad, started in 2003; and also in 2003, Sharjah began the budget airline Air Arabia, which in 2009 was named "Low-Cost Carrier of the Year."[12] Rotana Jet began operations in September 2012 as the UAE's first domestic airline, with flights from Abu Dhabi to Fujayrah and Ras al-Khaymah. All towns and villages of the UAE are integrated into the excellent and growing national highway network (see Fig. 7.4B).

Finance

As global financial markets moved to twenty-four-hour operations in the 1970s, the Gulf was uniquely positioned geographically between established centers in the Far East like Tokyo and Hong Kong and in Europe like London and Frankfurt. This largely explains the growing presence of international banks and financial institutions in the region—in Bahrain and Dubai particularly and Abu Dhabi to a lesser extent. Loose regulation in the UAE at first led to problems bordering on (or worse) the fraudulent—like the infamous Bank of Credit and Commerce International (BCCI) based in Abu Dhabi and once the world's seventh-largest bank. Financial fraud, on a scale never seen until then, finally forced it into liquidation in 1991. The bright side for the UAE was considerable tightening of oversight mechanisms and a healthier environment in which the sector continued to flourish. By 2012, some fifty-one foreign and domestic commercial banks were operating in the country. Seven of the Arab world's thirty largest banks are head-quartered in Abu Dhabi and Dubai. Considerable progress against money laundering has been made in recent years. However, in November 2012, the ratings agency Moody's repeated its negative-outlook warning for the banking system because of high provisioning requirements against possible losses due to continued uncertainty about past real-estate financing.

Crisis and Response

Of course, the 2008 global economic crisis first appeared in this sector, and the effects were quickly evident in the UAE. To avoid panic, the government injected $6.8 billion into local banks in 2008.[13] But the crisis snowballed, as Istithmar, Dubai's sovereign investment fund, suffered a steep decline in asset values; its short-term debt exceeded the value of its portfolio. Then Dubai World, also government related, had to ask creditors for an extension on its repayments.

While Dubai did eventually announce it would back restructuring efforts, the possible bankruptcy of not just these companies but the amirate itself and even the UAE loomed large, and panic was at least briefly evident on local and world markets. Facing this national threat, Abu Dhabi stepped in with funding to give Dubai some breathing space in settling what was a combination of the collapse of a domestic real-estate bubble and an international capital crunch. By 2012, Dubai was by no means out of the woods, although much of its economy was in reasonable shape. Prolonged negotiations with creditors continue, but in September 2012 three international banks seemed headed to the courts,

claiming a satisfactory deal seemed out of reach.[14]

Speculation was that the richer senior amirate might place conditions on Dubai that would permanently dampen the frenzied development in the previous decade.[15] At the very least, the symmetry in the power relations between the two amirates has changed, and in Dubai some observers felt that the nouveau riche entrepreneurs who gained so much from the real-estate boom had clearly lost ground to the old-line and more conservative trading families.

Tourism

As recently as twenty-five years ago, a Gulf state, with its notoriously hot, humid climate, aspiring to be a major year-round tourist destination would have seemed quite ridiculous. In the previous section, shopping tourism was mentioned, and this is where it all began. For many years, duty-free shops at Gulf airports (beginning with Bahrain) flourished as long-haul flights between Europe and the Far East discharged their passengers while they refueled. Airport installations led to new malls with more shops and hotels for the shoppers. With luxury resorts (including the world's only seven-star hotel, the Burj al-Arab and the massive Atlantis hotel and theme park on the tip of Palm Jumeirah), Dubai added attractions like world-class sporting events (golf, tennis, cricket, auto racing), top-name entertainers, amusement parks, and even an indoor ski slope. As with the financial sector, global tourism was hit hard by the 2008 economic turndown, but the concerns that Dubai had perhaps also overextended its investments in domestic tourism proved unfounded. The amirate registered an increase of more than 9.3 percent to about 10.2 million visitors in 2012.[16] In 2011, Dubai was rated the world's ninth most popular tourist destination, behind Frankfurt and ahead of Rome, according to MasterCard's Worldwide Index of Global Destination Cities.

Agriculture and Fishing

Although their relative contribution is now minor, fishing (including pearling) and agriculture (including nomadic herding) were, along with trade, the main bases of the economy prior to World War II. Agriculture in this desert environment was then confined to small oases and date-palm groves around the coastal villages, and the limited water resources were minimally developed. After the mid-1960s, the greatly increased availability of capital and the greater demand for fresh foods stimulated development of the few potentially productive agricultural areas.

Increased production has come from the three extensive oases of al-Ayn in eastern Abu Dhabi (see Map 17.1); Dhayd, east of Sharjah City; and Diqdaqah in Ras al-Khaymah. All three lie at the foot of the Oman Mountains and tap aquifers fed by runoff from the slopes. In use for at least four millennia, al-Ayn is exceptionally extensive and produces a variety of dates, fruits, and vegetables. Dhayd, somewhat farther away from the mountains, uses groundwater irrigation; it produces crops from strawberries to lemons. Diqdaqah, south of Ras al-Khaymah, has an agricultural experiment station established in 1956. Fruits and vegetables from the oases supply many of the needs of UAE cities. All three exemplify the marvels that can be wrought with huge inputs of capital and technology. Large dairy farms also operate in all the large oases, as do air-conditioned chicken farms marketing several million chickens each year. More than fifty date-palm groves extend along an arc of tiny oases in the isolated al-Jiwa (or al-Liwa) in southwestern Abu Dhabi.

Water

As in other energy-rich Gulf states, desalination is a major and expanding industry. Whereas, as indicated above, oasis agriculture makes use of groundwater, the needs of the UAE's growing population can be met only with desalination. In 2012, it was estimated that about 50 percent of the global production and consumption of desalinated water took place in the UAE and that the costs come to some $18 million a day. The federal government announced plans to spend about $18 billion on new capacity by 2016. Because conventional plants use considerable amounts of energy to produce fresh water, Abu Dhabi has embarked on a program to install some thirty smaller solar-power facilities around the amirate in remoter locations. Overuse of groundwater has caused aquifers to drop significantly, and many wells have run dry; encroaching seawater has caused other groundwater to become saline.

FEDERAL POLITICS, ARAB SPRING

The permanent constitution adopted for the federation provided for the Federal National Council (FNC) to be made up of 40 members representing all seven emirates. It was intended that at some point, half of the FNC would be elected, and in 2006 the first elections were held—with a very small electorate: some 6,689 citizens of whom 18 percent were women. The FNC could only recommend legislation for consideration by the amirs (who collectively sit as the Federal Supreme Council—FSC), and so had little real power. For the second election due in 2011, the government promised the electorate would be widened, but in the wake of the Arab Spring this widening proved much greater than expected—to 129,274, with 46 percent female and about a third younger than thirty. Despite the expansion, the powerlessness of the FNC seems to have inspired little interest in the election, and turnout among eligible electors was only 28 percent. One woman candidate was elected, and 7 more were among the 20 appointed members.

The regime has shown little tolerance of political dissent, whether from Islamists or more secular liberals. With the arrest of eight accused Islamists, reports indicated perhaps 60 dissidents had been detained, including several who signed a petition urging more power for the FNC. Some of those arrested were naturalized Emiratis and were stripped of their citizenship. In 2012, two international NGOs concerned with encouraging civil society—one American, the other German—were expelled from the country; also closed was the Abu Dhabi branch of the Gallup polling and research firm. Later in the year, the European Parliament adopted a resolution noting the deteriorating human rights situation. In December, a large group of alleged Islamists, including several Egyptians said to be members of the Muslim Brotherhood, were arrested, and opening in March 2013 was the trial of some ninety-four people charged with plotting with a "foreign group" to overthrow the UAE government.[17] Their defenders have claimed they are the victims of a sort of paranoia that has spread among the Gulf state regimes that see threats coming at them from several directions.[18]

What little dissent that is detected in the country seems to be confined to the Internet. However, perhaps to head off problems in the poorer northern and eastern emirates, the FSC announced in March 2011 a $1.6 billion infrastructure and jobs program.

RELATIONS

With some of the world's largest petroleum and gas reserves in a crucial location, yet with a small population and negligible military strength, the vulnerable UAE must walk a strategic tightrope. Locally, it places much of its diplomatic emphasis on the GCC (though in 2009 it opted out of the GCC common currency) and regionally and cautiously on the Arab League. It follows a pragmatic balancing act by maintaining, for example, mutually beneficial "correct" relations with Iran on one

side and Saudi Arabia on the other. Since its inception, the federation has disputed with Iran over ownership of three small Gulf islands (Abu Musa and the Greater Tunb and Lesser Tunb) just inside the Strait of Hormuz. The boundary with Saudi Arabia has been declared de jure, that with Oman was agreed to in 2004 and is now de jure, and there are no serious disputes on any land borders (see "Regional Conflicts," in Chap. 8). The UAE has applied the internationally adopted sanctions against the Assad regime in Syria, but has been less directly involved in aiding the rebels than fellow GCC members Saudi Arabia and Qatar. However, in September 2012, it did announce it would fund a camp in Jordan for Syrian refugees. Abu Dhabi, the richest of the amirates, has built strong links for the UAE with developing countries through the activities of the Abu Dhabi Fund for Development, which from its founding in 1971 up to 2011 extended $3.95 billion in assistance to fifty-six countries from Cape Verde to Tonga for 216 projects.[19]

Israel. Unlike Qatar and Oman, the UAE never initiated overt quasi-diplomatic links with Israel; however, with the onset of the Oslo peace process, ties on the commercial, touristic, and athletic levels grew quietly and steadily, especially with Abu Dhabi and Dubai. But in 2009, an incident involving the assassination of a Hamas official in a Dubai hotel, allegedly by the Israeli intelligence agency Mossad, brought these to a crashing halt. The clumsy actions of more than twenty-five agents using the pilfered identities and passports of dual nationals resident in Israel were repeatedly caught on surveillance cameras at various Dubai locales. Local authorities angrily claimed that Israel had violated the amirate's reputation as a neutral place to do business and had acted with arrogance and disdain, as though the amirate was an unsophisticated backwater.[20]

United States. Once a British protectorate, the UAE maintains numerous links with Britain. Since independence, it has built good relations with the United States—close private commercial ties and friendly government-to-government relations, including security assistance. Diplomatic relations were established in 1972, a few months after independence, and the United States has both an embassy in Abu Dhabi and a large consulate general in Dubai.

Ties became much closer after the Iraqi invasion of Kuwait, and the UAE contributed more than $4 billion, as well as a contingent of troops, to the 1990–1991 coalition. It opposed the US-led invasion of Iraq, but was discreetly supportive of Iraqi recovery, and large numbers of Iraqi refugees sought safe haven in Dubai and Sharjah. In 2008, it returned its ambassador to Baghdad and canceled all of Iraq's debt due from the Iran-Iraq War. Its military has also participated in peacekeeping missions, such as those in Somalia, Kosovo, and Lebanon. Like other members of the GCC with high oil income but incapable of mounting their own military defense, it has opted to place defense of its territory and resources with the United States. In 2004, the UAE signed a Trade and Investment Framework Agreement with the United States. It joined the World Trade Organization in 1996.

Relations with the United Kingdom remain close; some 120,000 British citizens resident in the UAE comprise the largest Western expatriate community.[21] In May 2009, France opened its first military facilities outside its own territories in fifty years in Abu Dhabi; three locations have been made available for army, navy, and air force use. The newest major intergovernmental entity—the International Renewable Energy Agency (IRENA)—designated Abu Dhabi as its interim headquarters in June 2009; by September 2012, IRENA had 159 signatories, including all 16 of the countries in this study.[22]

SKETCHES OF INDIVIDUAL AMIRATES

Abu Dhabi

The largest (86 percent of the total area) and by far the wealthiest of the seven amirates, with about 30 percent of total population, Abu Dhabi (or Abu Zaby) is the dominant member of the UAE. It is the southernmost and possesses the longest coastline. Located on a low near-shore island of *sabkhah* and sand, Abu Dhabi City, the population core and seat of the federal government, grew from a small village of *barasti* huts and a fort in the 1950s to a wealthy, bustling, planned city—now the second largest in the UAE. With high-rise office buildings, luxury hotels and palaces, divided boulevards, mosques and schools, housing estates, and irrigated plantings ornamenting the boulevards and traffic circles (see Fig. 17.1), it serves as the UAE capital.

Enhancing its international stature has been the construction of branches of the Louvre and Guggenheim Museums. As part of the UAE's railway plans, the Abu Dhabi Metro Project envisions as the first phase an 81-mi/131-km light-rail system to serve the city by 2016–2017; funding of about $700 million was approved in 2012.[23]

By 2010, the amirate had made several major investments that made clear its commitment to compete with Dubai in attracting the regional headquarters of media and entertainment companies. A secondary population core is the oasis of al-Ayn, seat of the UAE's first university and the federation's fourth-largest municipality; other clusters are in the al-Ruways–Jabal Dhanna oil and industrial area and in the arc of the al-Jiwa oases (see Map 17.1). In 2013, the amirate government announced the formation of a free zone specializing in providing locations and services for foreign financial firms; it is intended to rival a similar zone established nine years earlier in Dubai.[24]

Dubai

The next-largest polity in area, with perhaps 40 percent of the UAE's population, and adjoining Abu Dhabi to the north, is Dubai, with about 45 mi/72 km of sand and *sabkhah* coastline (Palm Jumeira, an artificial archipelago of islands that juts 3mi/5km into the Gulf, has more than doubled Dubai's effective coastline). Even before independence, its rulers were the most imaginative and aggressive of the ruling shaykhs, skillfully balancing the various cultural and economic factors affecting the development of the amirate and the area. The commercial and shipping center of the city developed on both sides of Dubai Creek, which affords an ideal harbor for dhows engaged in fishing, pearling, smuggling, and other maritime trade.

Dubai proper lies south of the creek and near the shore in the Batakia sector has a carefully preserved group of older structures topped by *badgirs*, Persian wind towers (see Fig. 2.10); Dayrah, with more of the original commercial and tourism functions, developed north of the inlet. The two are connected not only by four bridges and a tunnel but also by *abras*, picturesque small passenger ferries. With a laissez-faire commercial philosophy, Dubai is the largest city and the commercial center of the UAE, and with "hustle, imagination, and a willingness to indulge a degree of hedonism" it has opened superluxury theme malls, nightclubs, golf courses, racetracks, world-class hotels, an information-technology center, a diamond exchange, theme parks, a Media City (which includes the main studios of al-Arabiya, a television network competing with al-Jazeera), and other facilities utilizing the latest technology. The new century saw Dubai becoming renowned for innovative architecture and extravagant facilities, some of which were considered overly flamboyant. The extensive use of colored lighting illuminating the city's skyline has evoked comparisons (not always favorable) with Las Vegas.

Nevertheless, it has added to the city's touristic drawing power; in 2012, it was clear that Dubai's recovery from its economic challenges was being led by the tourism sector. Hatta, a Dubai exclave in the mountainous interior almost completely surrounded by Omani territory, has been undergoing modest development as a resort because of its cooler and drier climate and picturesque setting.

With the charming but cramped Dubai Creek business center constricting commercial and tourist facility growth, the audacious ruler founded a completely new Central Business District well to the south of the creek along Shaykh Zayed Road. Development exploded. In January 2010, Dubai opened the world's tallest building to that time at about 2,717 ft/828 m, with a surprise renaming of the tower to Burj Khalifa, in honor of the Abu Dhabi ruler and UAE president who had recently come to Dubai's aid financially (Fig. 17.2). September 2009 saw the inauguration of the Gulf's first metro system (Fig. 17.3); innovative as the world's longest driverless system, the first two lines cover 45 mi/73 km. The system marked its third anniversary in 2012 by transporting its 184 millionth passenger. Long-term plans include two additional lines farther inland in areas still mostly undeveloped and a high-speed link between Dubai's two airports.

Beginning in 2002, Dubai relaxed its rules on foreign property ownership and thus attracted many buyers for luxury villas and apartments, including those built on imaginative man-made islands that are in the pattern of palm trees, the first of which—Palm Jumeirah—housed its first tenants in 2009. Another off-shore residential project was designed to resemble a giant world map. The mid-2000s saw a housing boom take off in Dubai despite warnings that speculation was driving prices too high; the boom went bust in 2008, and within a year a well-known index of housing prices was down almost 50

Figure 17.2 Dwarfing the normal high-rise buildings surrounding it in Dubai, Burj Khalifa (Khalifa Tower) opened in early 2010 as the world's tallest structure. Its opening came at the height of the economic downturn, raising questions about the tower's viability. (Dr. John Fox, American University of Sharjah)

percent from the previous year. The collapse of the real-estate market preceded the crescendo of credit problems that built up in Dubai in 2009, and in the early 2010s that market's recovery was slow, with property experts urging caution. Although a breathing space has been gained, the amirate still faces the need to refinance some $48 billion in debt between 2014 and 2016.

Sharjah

The third-largest amirate, Sharjah (al-Shariqah), with a fifth of the UAE's people, is adjacent to and north of Dubai; the two have coalesced into one urban area now spreading on into Ajman. Despite this proximity, Shar-

jah, the federation's third-largest city, is distinctly more conservative than its neighbor.[25] Its 10-mi/16-km coastline included a small dhow harbor that developed into a modest modern port after 1970. Its territory is the most fragmented of the amirates (see Map 17.1). With three exclaves on the Batinah coast of the Gulf of Oman (Diba, Khor Fakkan, and Kalba), it thus has common borders with all six of the federation's polities, plus Oman. Khor Fakkan has a natural deep-water harbor and has been developed as a container port of growing economic importance; like neighboring Fujayrah, the port has the economic advantage of being on the ocean side of the Strait of Hormuz. Dhayd

Figure 17.3 Dubai's incredible southern Central Business District sprang from the almost empty desert in an explosive development along Shaykh Zayed Road, seen here in a view looking north. Note elevated metro system to lower right, as well as the variety of architecture in the high-rise buildings. (Dr. John Fox, American University of Sharjah)

Oasis and irrigation along the Batinah give it a plentiful supply of fruits and vegetables.

Sharjah has become the industrial heartland of the UAE, with more than sixteen hundred enterprises employing more then seventy-five thousand workers; the amirate accounts for about half of the industrial portion of the country's GDP. The Industrial City Development had already attracted more than $1.3 billion in infrastructural investment by early 2010 and offers some 2.7 mi²/7 km² for plant and facility expansion. Sharjah's traffic problems have worsened with growth, but as of 2013 there was no indication that any form of urban rapid transit is under consideration.[26]

With only limited hydrocarbon resources, Sharjah pursued a vigorous program of tourism tied to shopping (Fig. 17.4). As the fever of shopping by east European traders subsided, the present ruler, Shaykh Sultan bin Muhammad al-Qasimi, has encouraged cultural facilities, including two universities that opened in 1997. The impressive American University of Sharjah (AUS) is US accredited and has five thousand students; the University of Sharjah caters to evening and part-time students. Farther into the desert beyond AUS is the Desert Park and Natural History Museum, with world-class exhibits. The shaykh has also been restoring the *suqs,* houses with *badgirs,* and a mosque in the old city center, along with

Figure 17.4 Sharjah City's old *suq* (*top*, 1964) with palm-frond (*barasti*) roof for shade, and one of the city's newer *suqs* (*bottom*, 1979). In the background in the bottom photo, the high-rise buildings of the city's Central Business District can be seen. In the past decade, several "new new" *suqs* have opened in Sharjah and adjacent Dubai, some of them of world-class opulence.

the encircling wall. The historic area is mostly used for cultural events. Nearby are the Sharjah Art Museum with a collection of Orientalist and contemporary Arab art and the Islamic Arts Museum.

Two Gulf islands, Abu Musa and Sir Abu Nuayr, are claimed by Sharjah and Iran (which occupies them). They share revenues from the offshore Mubarak oil field in Abu Musa's territorial waters. Sharjah City was the site of the coast's first airfield; it also hosted a Royal Air Force unit and the headquarters of the Trucial Oman Scouts. Sharjah International Airport is heavily utilized for cargo transport and intraregional traffic, especially the flights of Sharjah-based budget airline Air Arabia.

Ajman

Next to the east up the coast is the amirate of Ajman, the smallest unit in the UAE: although it has only 5 percent of the UAE's population, it has grown rapidly in the new century as part of a conurbation with Sharjah and Dubai, with more than 3 million residents in 2013. It includes Ajman town, a strip of desert behind it, and two small interior exclaves, Masfout and al-Manama; it has a small but lively industrial park in its port area. A new interconnecting highway system has facilitated the merging of Ajman, Sharjah, and Dubai, but traffic problems abound. Observers have pointed out that solutions to common urban problems like transportation may take a federal initiative (and funding) to overcome the existing interamirate reluctances. It retains seafaring traditions with a large dhow-building yard and a fish-trap fabricating facility. In 2006, it followed Dubai in relaxing its rules on foreign property ownership. Mountainous Masfout exclave will be developed as a resort area like Dubai's Hatta region.

Umm al-Qaywayn

North of Ajman is the second smallest and the least populated (about 1.1 percent of the total) of the amirates, Umm al-Qaywayn. The town and amirate capital occupies the tip of a narrow peninsula, reached by a spur from the coastal highway; in many ways, it seems little changed since the federation's early days and is somewhat isolated from the rest of the country. With negligible energy resources, Umm al-Qaywayn has lagged well behind the other members of the federation in industrial growth. Adding to its traditional fishing, it has attracted clothing-manufacturing and printing establishments. As with Ajman, the expanding UAE highway network has promoted rapid population growth in the late 2000s.

Ras al-Khaymah

Northernmost of the polities and occupying a triangular area west of a mountain spur that reaches the sea, Ras al-Khaymah (with about 5 percent of the UAE's people) is quite diverse. The capital itself lies on a peninsula and has a long seafaring tradition. It has the Diqdaqah agricultural station and a half-dozen other towns and villages. In the mountains at the northern tip lives a small but interesting non-Arab ethnic group, the Shihuh (or Shikuh). Two offshore islands— Greater Tunb and Lesser Tunb—are claimed by Ras al-Khaymah but were seized by Iran in 1971. Its only known oil comes from its offshore field of Saleh, but it also has some modest gas reserves. Requisite raw materials for cement are near at hand, and three large plants operate between the mountains and the north-south highway. In the early 2010s, it was anticipating that an infrastructure boom throughout the GCC would be advantageous to its construction-materials sector. Like Dubai and Ajman, it now allows some foreign property ownership.

Fujayrah

The only UAE member located on the eastern, or Gulf of Oman, side of the peninsula, Fujayrah, with about 3 percent of the population, was isolated until federal highways made it easily accessible and encouraged beach-resort development. It had only a limited fishing economy and a few date palms until the 1960s; now, its successful resort facilities include stretches of clean, sandy, and still-uncrowded beaches, making it unrecognizable compared to the earlier period. The amirate has also developed its port to compete with Sharjah's nearby exclave, Khor Fakkan, and in 2012 a 1.5 mn bpd pipeline from Abu Dhabi inaugurated an oil terminal in the amirate beyond the potential chokepoint of the Strait of Hormuz. Also in 2012, the opening of a widened motorway through the mountains halved the travel time to Dubai. Huge chicken farms with air-conditioned henhouses and a major dairy have also been developed inland from the coast.

For information on the business environment in the United Arab Emirates, see the website attached to this book: www.middle eastpatterns.com.

Oman

KEY POINTS: Independent since the seventeenth century, had scattered pieces of small empire until after World War II. Only sultanate in region. Withdrawn and quite backward until current ruler, 1970. Qabus encouraged more openness and steady—not explosive—development utilizing modest wealth from moderate oil production. Mountain chain divides Inner Oman and Coastal Batinah, but interior and coast and north and south Oman now unified. Some security issues, especially since a small Omani exclave at tip of Musandam Peninsula (Horn of Arabia) occupies southern coast of strategic Strait of Hormuz.

AN INTRODUCTION

Termed "Muscat and Oman" prior to 1970, the Sultanate of Oman was sometimes confused with Trucial Oman, an alternate name for the Trucial States, now the UAE. Among other things, the several names reflect the regionalization of Oman into two basic parts: Inner Oman, west of the mountains, and the Batinah coast along the Gulf of Oman (Map 17.2).

The only sultanate in the Middle East, Oman has modernized in ways similar to those of the oil states of the Gulf, but with some unique characteristics while keeping much of its traditional culture. Caution and moderate conservatism have characterized its approach to development, and it has deliberately pursued modest growth rather than allowing the explosive expansion that has occurred in Kuwait, Qatar, Abu Dhabi, and Dubai.[27] For example, the population is estimated to have grown by about sixfold between 1950 and 2010, compared with more than twenty-five-fold in the UAE during the same period.

Most of Oman is south of the Tropic of Cancer; it is notably hot in summer and warm even in winter. It is a desert land except in a few higher elevations and in the uplands of southern Dhufar. Muscat, the capital, has an average annual temperature of 84°F/29°C, with less than 4 in/100 mm of rain. Highland Oman receives summer monsoon rain, particularly in the mountains around Salalah in the south, as well as orographically enhanced

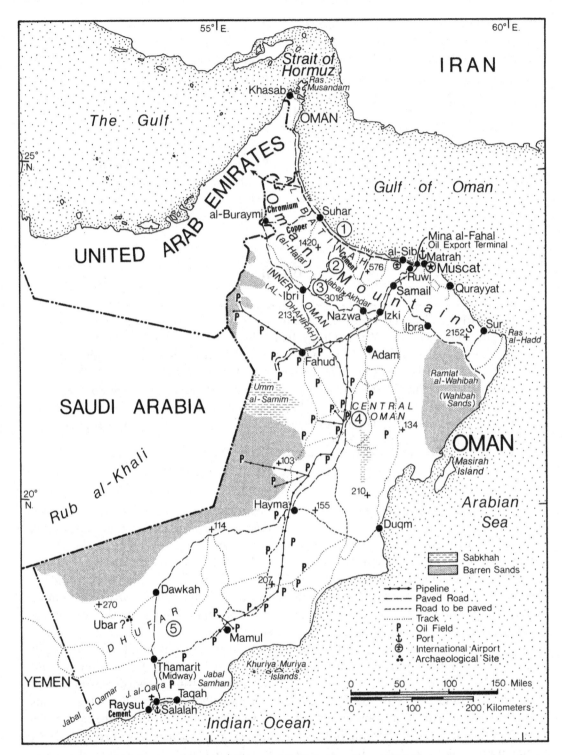

Map 17.2 General and economic map of Oman, with circled numbers indicating regions explained in text. Note the widespread distribution of petroleum fields, most of them small. Oman's boundaries with all three neighbors are now de jure, a historic achievement.

OMAN

Long-form official name, anglicized: Sultanate of Oman

Official name, transliterated: Sultanat Uman

Form of government: monarchy with two advisory bodies (State Council, Consultative Council)

Area: 119,500 mi²/309,500 km²

Population, 2011: 2,810,000; Literacy: 81.4%

Ethnic composition (%, 2000): Arab 55.3, of which Omani 48.1, other 7.2; Indo-Pakistani 31.7, of which Baluchi 15, Bengali 4.4, Tamil 2.5; Persian 2.8; Zanzibari 2.5; other 7.7

Religions (%, 2005): Muslim 89, of which Ibadhi 75, Sunni 8, Shia 6; Hindu 5; Christian 5; other 1

Demography: Life expectancy—72.61 yr (M), 76.43 yr (F); Birthrate (per 1,000)—24.33; Fertility rate—2.87

GDP, 2011: $71.52 billion; purchasing power parity: $85 billion; per capita: $27,600

Currency: Omani Rial (OMR), US$1 = 0.384 rials; 1 OMR = $2.59 (mid-May 2013)

Energy: oil—5.5 bn bbl; natural gas—30,000 bn ft³; coal—nil

Main exports (% of total value, 2008): OMR 14.5 billion (of which crude petroleum 58; LNG 11; refined petroleum 7.1; chemicals and chemical products 3.4)

Main imports (% of total value, 2008): OMR 8.8 billion (of which motor vehicles and parts 25.1; machinery and apparatus 22.4; food and live animals 9.3; iron and steel 9.2)

Capital city, 2009: Muscat (agglomeration) 634,000; other major cities, 2010: Sib 299,800; Bawshar 189,600; Matrah 150,124; Salalah 147,400; Suhar 128,500

---

winter cyclonic storm rain, exceeding 18 in/457 mm in its northern ranges. Runoff from such rains there supplies the irrigation water for crops along the Batinah coast and in interior oases.

PHYSICAL REGIONS

Oman comprises five distinct physical regions, each of which has its individual cultural character: [1] the Batinah coast; [2] al-Hajar (or Oman Mountains); [3] Inner Oman; [4] Central Oman; and [5] Dhufar. (See circled numbers on Map 17.2.)

[1] Batinah Coast. The Batinah is a coastal plain 6–18 mi/10–30 km wide extending 168 mi/270 km along the Gulf of Oman. The name implies "front" or "belly," as opposed to "al-Dhahirah" (Inner Oman), which suggests "back." Composed primarily of coalesced alluvial fan deltas of gravel, sand, and silt, the plain is squeezed between mountain chain and seashore and is Oman's primary agricultural area, cultivated for millennia. Crops are irrigated in a strip about 1.8 mi/3 km wide, using groundwater stored in the sandy gravels of the fans at the stream mouths. Date, citrus, and banana groves line the road, alternating

with "strip settlements" one house deep on each side of the road—the Omani version of the classic *strassendorf*. At the debouchment of the larger wadis, major fans support extensive agriculture and, usually, more populous settlements. Some towns are of considerable antiquity; Suhar, the largest, and many coastal settlements still engage in fishing. After the Capital Area, the Batinah is the sultanate's most densely populated region, with steadily developing commerce and industry. Sib International Airport is at the southern end of the plain; major industrial estates lie at each end, one at Rusayl, near Sib, the other a new one near Suhar in the north.

[2] Al-Hajar.   Often called the Oman Mountains, al-Hajar (literally, "the Rock") is a high rugged chain of mountains paralleling the Batinah in a 435-mi/700-km arc from the northern tip of the Musandam Peninsula (Horn of Arabia) to Ras al-Hadd. The mountains form the "backbone" between the Batinah "belly" and the "back" of Inner Oman. Much of the mountain chain exceeds 4,800 ft/1,463 m, with elevations of nearly 10,000 ft/3,048 m in the central block, the very rugged Jabal al-Akhdar (Green Mountain), a name sometimes mistakenly applied to the entire Hajar range.

The Oman Mountains are a virtually unique geomorphic feature, both scientifically and scenically. Two nappe complexes, one of ophiolite oceanic crust, have been thrust from former ocean deeps into stacked thrust sheets thousands of feet thick. Gigantic "windows" (*fenêtres*) carved into the nappes through erosion have exposed multiple overfolded strata of different ages, origins, and colors. Some almost vertical window walls are more than 6,500 ft/2,000 m high.[28] The one major pass through the chain is the Samail Gap, just east of Jabal al-Akhdar, traversed by the main route connecting Muscat with Inner Oman. Large oil and gas pipelines parallel the road, carrying the sultanate's entire produc-

tion to the export terminal west of Matrah. Created by erosion along a major tectonic fault, the trough divides the Hajar range into the larger scenically rugged Western Hajar (Hajar al-Gharbi) and the smaller Eastern Hajar (Hajar al-Sharqi).

Musandam.   In the north, the eroded mountains overlook the Strait of Hormuz from Ras Musandam, a striking desert fjord-type land that forms a maze of isthmuses and islands with coastal cliffs dropping sharply to sea-filled valleys (Fig. 17.5). Politically, it is an Omani exclave, separated from the rest of the sultanate's territory by UAE territory and recently connected to Muscat by high-speed ferry. Beginning in 2013, a challenging engineering project to connect Musandam by road to the rest of the country will be initiated; 40.5 mi/65 km long, 5.6 mi/9 km through tunnels, and rising in places to 8,200 ft/2,500 m, the road will connect Diba and Khasab. The peninsula may be considered a subregion of al-Hajar.

Capital Region.   The northern end of the Samail Gap intersects the southern end of the Batinah coastal plain, where al-Hajar pushes to the coast, embracing two harbors. Muscat, on the eastern bay, evolved as the main port and capital, but its small basin in the rugged ophiolites and pillow lavas curtailed development (Fig. 17.6). Matrah, in the next depression westward, has a larger basin and is now the main port. Urban development has leapfrogged over the lava ridges and has spread up the southern Batinah to Sib airport and beyond. Thus, the Greater Capital Area is a second subregion of al-Hajar.

[3] Inner Oman.   Inner Oman (al-Dhahirah—"the back") is an amorphous foreland area extending southwestward from al-Hajar to the sands of the Rub al-Khali. The pattern of picturesque, long-settled villages—Izki, Nazwa, Bahlah, Ibri, Dank, and the oasis town of

Figure 17.5 High-speed boats in Khasab harbor, Oman, at northern tip of the Musandam Peninsula ("Horn of Arabia"). Most of the boats engage in smuggling and take on loads of cigarettes, electronic goods, and other small high-demand items in Oman, then make a dash at night across the Strait of Hormuz to avoid Iranian customs. Note the steep sides to these inlets, often described as "fjords," although their origin is quite different.

Figure 17.6 Air view of Muscat, showing the capital crowded into the small pocket between rugged lava mountains and the sea, so that primarily only the older quaint houses remain. Growth has been in Matrah, Ruwi, Bawshar, and other developments beyond the mountains. The center building along the coast is the sultan's palace. (Tor Eigeland, *Saudi Aramco World*/SAWDIA)

Buraymi—along the internal piedmont and belt of alluvial fans resembles the string of settlements on the eastern side of al-Hajar. Watered by hundreds of small canals and *aflaj* (singular: *falaj*), extensive date-palm groves, deep green against the barren mountains, mark the several oasis towns and dozens of villages on the alluvial fans along the al-Hajar piedmont. However, the interior is less endowed with water and has traditionally been isolated, wedged between rugged mountains to the east and barren sands to the west. It has had ties with the Gulf shaykhdoms through the Buraymi Oasis and with the Batinah via the Samail Gap.

Subregional designations reflect variety in this seemingly uniform area. The northern extension of Inner Oman toward Buraymi is al-Jaw, with Ibri—the largest town in al-Dhahirah—as the center. The subregion of the Jabal Akhdar piedmont is the traditional heart of Inner Oman, al-Dakhiliyah, with the major oases of al-Hamra, Bahlah, Nazwa, and Izki. All have extensive date groves and are diversifying into fruits and cotton. Nazwa, with its well-preserved fort, is the major town, the political and cultural capital for centuries. East of the Samail Gap, the piedmont of the Eastern Hajar is usually referred to as al-Sharqiya (the East) with a string of oasis towns in Ibra, al-Mudayrib, al-Mintirib, and al-Kamil, as well as the ancient port of Sur and the eastern tip of Oman at Ras al-Hadd. Modern roads and excellent telecommunications now facilitate closer relations in both directions, integrate the interior economically, and strengthen political ties with the sultanate core around Muscat. Inner Oman is associated with a distinct Islamic sect, the Ibadhis, who enjoyed a militant autonomy under their own imam for several decades prior to 1959. It is also the location of Oman's main producing oil fields.

[4] Central Oman.   Central Oman, locally called al-Wusta (literally, "the middle"), extends from Inner Oman southward. A large

barren area, it has for centuries been the realm of fewer than a dozen small Bedouin tribes. In the east, wedged between the Arabian Sea and the eastern Oman Mountains, is an unusual dune field, the Wahibah Sands. It contains a range of dune formations, including fossil sand seas, of such interest that it was the object of an intensive multidisciplinary investigation by the Royal Geographical Society (London) and Omani counterparts in 1985–1987. Otherwise, Central Oman is a monotonous land of sand and gravel, much of it dissected by wadis in former pluvial periods, with little to offer until more than a score of oil fields were discovered beneath its surface (see Map 17.2). Continued exploration found another sixty small pocket fields, some of which are actually in Dhufar. A high-speed highway completed in 1986 traverses the region, connecting Muscat and Salalah. This formerly remote and isolated area has also been carefully mapped and is intensively crisscrossed by the tracks of oil-exploration and well-maintenance vehicles, although it is still devoid of significant settlements.

[5] Dhufar.   Dhufar (sometimes Dhofar) is an ill-defined area that merges with Central Oman to the northeast and Yemen to the west. A rough, barren, sparsely inhabited desert area inland, it has mountains just back of the coast with green slopes and monsoon woodlands, some producing frankincense, contrasting spectacularly with the inland desert. It was poorly known until exploration opened more than a dozen oil fields centered 100 mi/160 km northeast of Salalah, the provincial capital. It appeared in world headlines when it was contested between Dhufari rebels and Oman in the late 1960s and early 1970s (see next section). Mountain areas and some coastal villages are inhabited by a complex of ethnolinguistic groups, some believed to predate Arab presence in the area. In 1991, amateur archaeologists, guided by satellite imagery, discovered the ruins of an ancient city 93 mi/150 km

north-northeast of Salalah that is believed to be Ubar, famed center of frankincense trade from 2000 BCE to late Roman times.[29] Salalah is the southern anchor of administration, commerce, transportation, and, recently, tourism. Its unusual summer weather, unique in the sultanate, attracts thousands of Omanis to enjoy the cool, misty midsummer monsoons on the mountain slopes. The recently developed Port Salalah is one of the few ports between Europe and Singapore able to handle the largest container vessels. Lying offshore are the Khuriya Muriya Islands, officially named al-Hallaniyat.

HISTORICAL SKETCH

Prehistory to Maritime Empire

Although incompletely studied, the antiquity of human occupation has long been recognized in sites along the coast (perhaps as much as 100,000 years ago), in Inner Oman, and in Dhufar. Tombs in the village of Bat, near Ibri, contain artifacts similar to those found in Abu Dhabi, suggesting a relationship with Sumer from about 3000 BCE. In the extreme east, in the Ras al-Hadd area, Phoenician artifacts found in the port of Sur link it with the ancient Phoenician port of Sur (Tyre). Dhufar was a major source of frankincense, with significant trade for millennia.

Like the rest of the peninsula, Oman adopted Islam in the seventh century, but the theologically distinct Ibadhi sect, neither Sunni nor Shii, evolved here from the eighth century and remains dominant. Ibadhis are spiritual descendants of the Khariji (seceders), a group that first supported Ali in his claim to be caliph but then broke with him during his conflict with the Umayyads. Oman has the largest concentration of Ibadhis in the world, although there are small communities in Zanzibar and North Africa.

Even more than in the Gulf amirates, Portuguese control of key locations for more than 140 years left its mark in forts and towers still seen especially around Matrah and Muscat. Britain supplanted Portugal and Holland in regional control, and its influence remained strong for 300 years. The sultanate was technically independent after 1650, and Britain formally recognized its sovereignty in 1951. Isolated from fellow Arabs by mountains and formidable deserts, Omanis ventured into the Indian Ocean as able seafarers and colonists. They established political control over Zanzibar and the neighboring African coast as well as over the exclave of Gwadar on the Baluchi coast, near the present Iran-Pakistan border. Oman held Gwadar until 1958 and, indirectly, Zanzibar until 1964.

State Consolidation

The Al Bu Saids, an Ibadhi dynasty, have held the sultanate since 1744. Inner Oman and the coast have periodically been disunited, suffering a particularly sharp division in the nineteenth and early twentieth centuries, when the interior Ibadhis chose a theocracy ruled by the Ibadhi imam. The dispute subsided in 1920 when the Treaty of Sib granted the imam autonomy but recognized the sultan's nominal sovereignty. However, when Ghalib ibn Ali became imam in 1954, he rebelled against the sultan and was defeated and exiled, with British help, in 1959. The then sultan, Said bin Taimur Al Bu Said, was rather eccentric—prohibiting such diverse items as private vehicles, bicycles, and sunglasses; refusing to expand the small electricity and telephone net in the Capital Area; and maintaining a nighttime curfew in Muscat, with the city gates locked soon after dark. He isolated himself in Salalah, never returning to the capital after 1958. Oman at that time was the region's most backward and isolated area.

Change Sets In. Four developments have dominated Oman's history since 1960. First, petroleum was discovered (1964), eventually bringing annual income of billions of dollars. Second, Marxist rebels—the Dhufar Liberation

Front (DLF)—revolted in 1965. Third, the old sultan was forced to abdicate in favor of his son, the present ruler, Qabus (or Qaboos) ibn Said, in 1970. Fourth, the new sultan soon abolished many of his father's antiquated restrictions, urged educated Omanis to return home, oversaw the defeat of the Dhufar rebellion, united the country, and launched a major development program.

The Dhufar rebellion aimed at overthrowing not only the sultan but all conservative Gulf regimes. The original DLF later merged with the Marxist-dominated Popular Front for the Liberation of Oman and the Arab Gulf (PFLOAG), which proclaimed revolution against all traditional regimes in the Gulf region. In mid-1974, PFLOAG, renamed the Popular Front for the Liberation of Oman, was defeated and finally driven out of Dhufar by the combined efforts of Omanis, British officers, an Iranian task force, Jordanian military forces, and others, with logistical help from Abu Dhabi.

Modern Nation

Replacing his father's medieval practices, Qabus faced not only the Dhufar insurgency but also long-endemic diseases, illiteracy, and poverty. As the new sultan, he led Oman in an entirely new direction, both economically and politically: while retaining ultimate secular authority, he brought leaders of various segments of the complex society into the political process to balance tribal, regional, ethnic, and economic interests. In 1996, he approved Oman's first written constitution. In 1997, a limited electorate chose eighty-two members of the Majlis al-Shura; it has some powers to advise on legislation and question ministers. Then he appointed forty members, including four women, to the new Majlis al-Dawlah (with advisory powers only); it now has eighty-three members, fourteen of whom are women. He declared universal suffrage for the 2003 elections, and two women were elected to serve with eighty men. In 2007, no

women candidates were successful, and fewer than half the incumbents were reelected.

In general, Oman, with its stable, moderately conservative institutions, has had the region's lowest level of politico-economic tensions,[30] but in the late 2000s some problems emerged. Inroads by Saudi ultraconservative Wahhabi Islam brought a strong reaction from the Ibadhi Omani regime, which more militant Sunnis consider to be heterodox. As many as forty thousand Pakistani workers were deported in the mid-2000s, allegedly for illegal entry, but suspicions of religious extremism may have also played a part.

Arab Spring Reactions

Oman has a very young population, fairly well educated and definitely familiar with electronic links to the outside world; for several years, there were signs that the younger generation felt somewhat constrained by the sultan's paternalistic authoritarianism. With the onset of the Arab Spring, these young Omanis especially were stirred. In February 2011, there were demonstrations in Suhar, and although the protesters emphasized that they were not striking against the sultan, the outbreaks were put down with some fatalities and injuries. However, following the protests, the sultan reshuffled his cabinet, announced a job-creation program, and promised that the powers of the Majlis al-Shura would be broadened. The GCC pledged $10 billion to Oman to support programs aimed to deflect further protest. For the election already scheduled for October, there was a surge of registrations among eligible voters, and the rolls were almost quadrupled. One women was among the eighty-four members elected, as were at least two candidates who had been prominent activists during the previous months.

As the situation quieted down, the argument was made that Omanis, like their neighbors in similarly conservative states, were having second thoughts about the Arab Spring as a result of seeing the confusion in

Egypt and the violence in Bahrain, Syria, and Yemen. However, the summer of 2012 saw a resurgence of demonstrations followed by arrests; for the first time, open criticism of the sultan was voiced. Regime paternalism, corruption among the elite closest to the center of power, and uncertainty about the succession issue (Qabus has no sons) were among the issues being voiced. On the Internet, some Omanis continued to push the case for reform; in August 2012, eight individuals were given one-year jail sentences for "incitement against the government" in postings they had made.

On the other hand, in apparent response to one of the demonstrators' principal complaints, an obvious increase in anticorruption activity was noted during 2012.[31] Municipal elections for 192 local councils were held, more or less on schedule, in December 2012, with a reasonably heavy turnout resulting in the election of four female candidates.[32]

THE OMANIS

The 2003 census found nearly one-fourth of the population concentrated in the Muscat-Matrah-Ruwi core, the rest scattered mostly throughout a belt of Batinah towns and in the string of inner villages paralleling the southwestern piedmont of al-Hajar. Major population outliers include the area of Salalah-Raysut and surrounding villages on the southern Dhufar coast and Sur at the eastern corner of the country. The sultanate's first census, in 1993, and its successor a decade later statistically confirmed population distribution patterns that had been previously suspected. By 2012, probably more than 55 percent of the population lived in the Capital area and along the Batinah.

Mixed Ethnicities and Religions

Ethnic boundaries are generally defined by language or sect (or both) rather than by territory, occupation, or even class.[33] Because of the links with peoples on nearby coasts, ethnic groups are numerous, with at least a dozen languages spoken as mother tongues. Ethnic and especially tribal affiliation plays a role in employment and other social interactions. However, long accustomed to a complex society, Omanis have few intergroup tensions.

Arabs. Oman's basic Arab population differs perceptibly from that of neighboring Saudi Arabia and the UAE. The distinction arises partly because southern Asian and East African influences entered along the coast and partly because Arab influences from the interior diminished as they diffused into this easterly projection of the peninsula. Furthermore, fragmented by mountain ranges, highland masses, and desert belts, Oman has many different remnant ethnolinguistic and religious minorities, some still surviving from pre-Islamic centuries in isolated mountain refuges. Strong tribal affiliations further diversify the people.

Africans, Asians. Maritime connections with southern Asia and East Africa and Oman's control of Gwadar and Zanzibar attracted immigrants from those areas. Indians, Baluch, Iranians, Somalis, and other East Africans settled in Oman, with many of the Africans being brought as slaves. Baluch are especially numerous and are the largest non-Arab community. Omanis with an East African connection are called Zanzibari as returnees from Zanzibar and the adjoining mainland after the 1964 independence of those areas. Swahili-speaking East Africans, originally slaves, were freed by Sultan Qabus. Descendants of these groups are part of the Omani citizenry. To the above must be added the nearly six hundred thousand expatriates—close to a fifth of the population. As other Gulf states are doing, the aim is to reduce the expatriate presence with a program of "Omanization."

The Shii Khojas (Liwatiyya), a prominent minority, are a close-knit community of Hindu converts to Islam originally from India but resident in Oman as merchants for more than two centuries. They occupy a separate walled quarter in Matrah but also live in other Batinah towns. Other Shia include the Baharinah and the Ajam, of Persian background. Several minor groups, including some unassimilated pre-Arab peoples, occupy mountain areas in Dhufar.

Religious Distinctions.   Although Islam is the predominant religion, the sultanate's major sect, the Ibadhi, is quite distinct, historically and theologically, from other branches of Islam. Ibadhis first settled in the remoter parts of southeastern Arabia in the earliest centuries of Islam; Oman was established as an Ibadhi state and has evolved an Ibadhi particularity. Although Inner Oman has long been the main concentration and theological stronghold of the sect, the ruling dynasty is also Ibadhi. Conservative, fundamentalist, and simple in their principles without being extremist, Ibadhi norms have strongly shaped Omani culture, but there is a place for others in the national fabric. Sunnis are the largest non-Ibadhi sect—the Baluch are Sunni—and dominate in Salalah. Shia form the third-largest group and are concentrated in the Batinah, especially in Muscat-Matrah, with the Khojas.

Most Omanis of both sexes can be easily differentiated from their neighbors by their national dress. The standard male attire is the white calf-long *dishdashah,* comparable to the *thawb* in Saudi Arabia. Headgear is of two types: dominant is the *kumma,* a fitted, brimmed cap often colorfully and expensively embroidered and unique to Oman. More formal is the elaborate turban, the *amamma,* a square of light Kashmir wool artfully wound around the head. The well-dressed male traditionally wore a *khanjar,* a curved dagger with a highly decorated scabbard. Women also dress distinctively, echoing both Arabia and India. Under a colorful *dishdashah,* they wear ankle-length trousers, the *surawal,* and usually add one or more filmy decorated scarves or shawls.

ECONOMIC SECTORS

Traditional Pursuits.   Oman's preindustrial economy of seafaring, fishing, and irrigation agriculture rested on a broader base and supported a larger population than did the economies of the four Gulf shaykhdoms. For example, it has nearly twice the cropland of the four combined, with most of its agricultural area divided between the Batinah coast and the inner piedmont of the Hajar. Two-thirds of that area is in permanent crops, primarily dates, bananas, mangoes, and limes. Fishing remains significant, much of it still traditional, although increasingly it is being modernized to take advantage of the rich fisheries along the coast.

Petroleum.   Though last in the region to discover oil,[34] Oman's economy has also been revolutionized by its oil industry. The original concession holder, the Iraq Petroleum Company, had no success in the 1950s and abandoned its concession, later taken up by Petroleum Development (Oman) (PDO) with Shell as its major partner. The associates made initial strikes at Natih, Fahud, and Yibal, 140–185 mi/225–300 km southwest of Muscat in 1962–1964. A pipeline from the discovery area was laid through the Samail Gap to an export terminal at Mina al-Fahal, west of Matrah; all subsequent production has been linked to this same terminal, where Oman's single refinery is as well (see Table 6.2). Intensive exploration by PDO and a score of other companies has found more than 110 fields, but many are too small to tie into the system. Output is still mainly from the original area—Yibal, al-Khuwayr (Lekhwait), and Fahud fields—but it also comes from fields in Central Oman and Dhufar (see Maps 6.1 and 17.2).

The sultanate's very complex geology makes exploration, drilling, and production difficult and expensive. Reservoirs are scattered, small, less productive, and quickly exhausted, so production per well is much less than in the UAE and Saudi Arabia. As Table 6.1 shows, 70 percent more wells than in Saudi Arabia yield only 9 percent as much oil. Enhanced oil recovery (EOR) techniques—for example, horizontal and multiple drilling and water and gas injection—are increasingly used; some two thousand new wells are being drilled in the EOR program. By the end of the decade, successful results were apparent; output rose in both 2008 and 2009. Petroleum provides 70 percent of government revenue, 75 percent of exports, and about 48 percent of GDP. In the late 2000s, reserves have held steady at a moderate 5.5 bn bbl, sixth largest in the region and comparable to those of the Divided Zone. In 2012, production was about 910,000 bpd, close to what it was in 2001, the peak production year, and a modest increase to 940,000 bpd is planned for 2013.[35] Since Oman is not an OPEC (or OAPEC) member, it is not subject to quotas, but it coordinates closely with the group. In 2012, the planning began for building the world's largest tank farm with a capacity of as much as 200 mn bbl of oil safely located outside the Strait of Hormuz.

Natural Gas. Oman emphasizes the production, use, and export of the growing finds of natural gas. The Dolphin Project (see Chap. 16) links Oman with Qatar and the UAE with a natural gas pipeline. Qatar has very large gas deposits, and although both its partners have gas in more modest amounts, the project aims to distribute gas around the region to broadly diversify its uses; in Oman, imports began in October 2008 and initially are to be added feedstock in the EOR program. The sultanate tripled its production of natural gas in the first decade of the new century, but new discover-

ies from stepped-up exploration had slowed by 2010. It is used domestically as petrochemical feedstock, in the EOR program, and for generating electricity. Liquefied natural gas (LNG) is produced at three joint venture facilities. Most LNG exports went to the Far East, but the reduced pace of new discoveries has led observers to question whether Oman is overcommitting itself with long-term export obligations. The development of viable shale gas deposits was also under study.

Other Minerals. Few of the many minerals found in the complex rocks of al-Hajar have historically been of much worth commercially; however, ancient copper workings near Suhar, in the northern Batinah, have been re-opened and mined for several years, and new deposits found in 2001 should maintain copper output for several years. Also recently exploited are some small coal seams and deposits of chromite, manganese, asbestos, and marble. In the late 2000s, output of ores of chromium, copper, gold, and sulfur increased markedly, and in 2010 Oman opened its first chromite concentration plant close to a mine in Wadi Mahram.[36]

An intriguing future mineral possibility for Oman arises from geoengineering research related to global warming and aimed at literally scrubbing carbon dioxide from the atmosphere and selling it commercially. A study project under way proposes to build "artificial trees"—towers covered with filters containing ultramafic rock, which captures the CO_2 from moving air, then holds it until it is processed and stored.[37] It seems that Oman's mountains have one of the world's largest deposits of peridotite, a member of the family of this type of rock.

DEVELOPMENT POLICY AND PROGRAMS

After the 1970 coup, Sultan Qabus moved deliberately, with guidance from experienced consultants, toward systematic development of Oman. Following a series of five-year plans that began in 1976, he made basic infrastructure the first priority. Then came improved agriculture and fishing, educational and social programs, modern communications, and finally a modest import-substitution industrial program. Installed generating capacity was nearly 3 gigawatts electric, and gas supplied the plants with more than 80 percent of their fuel needs.[38]

As one major step in industrialization, an industrial estate was established in 1983 in Rusayl, near the airport at Sib (see Fig. 7.3). More than one hundred privately owned factories now produce a wide range of basic products for the local market, from car batteries to air-conditioning units. Industrial estates have opened at opposite ends of Oman: one in Suhar, in the northern Batinah, and one in Raysut, west of Salalah. Plans include others at Nazwa, Buraymi, Khasab, and Sur.

Ports and Airports. Because of the small size of Muscat's picturesque harbor, a modern and more spacious port—Mina Qabus—was constructed in Matrah, a few miles west, in the early 1970s. Development of the south included a new port at Raysut, near Salalah. Now called Port Salalah, it has been expanded to dominate container transit traffic on the Indian Ocean coast, competing with Khor Fakkan and Aden. In 1974, the Sib airport was opened west of Matrah; the only other airport with scheduled service had been Salalah's, but new ones to service tourism have opened recently. The sultanate participates in the regional Gulf Air but in 1993 inaugurated its own airline, Oman Air.

GCC Rail Network/Transport. At the end of 2009, it was announced that bids for carrying out the preliminary studies for a rail network would soon be sought as part of the GCC $60 billion megaproject to build an interconnecting rail network. In September 2012, it was announced that the first part to be built will connect al-Ayn in the UAE to Suhar—a distance of 109mi/176 km—and include a spur to Buraymi. The first phase will also connect Suhar northward to the border with Fujayrah—35mi/58 km—and southward to Muscat—another 150 mi/242 km—and will cost $5 billion. Later, the line will be extended to Salalah, which offers the possibility of connecting onward to the Yemeni border.

Due to open in 2013 is the first direct land link between Oman and Saudi Arabia. The 367-mi/592-km highway running through the Rub al-Khali desert—one of the most inhospitable places in the world for a major construction project—will cut the current route's distance by 40 percent and the cost of delivering goods by 23 percent per truckload.

Planning. Both the seventh and eighth five-year economic plans (2006–2010 and 2011–2015) have illustrated a determination to lessen dependence on petroleum. The goal is for petroleum to be no more than 20 percent of GDP in 2020, although the current plan's $78 billion in project and program spending does still have a large place for improving petro-infrastructure. Both plans have emphasized more resources going to natural gas–related activities, as mentioned above, as well as industrial and geographic diversification, job creation for Omanis (this has taken on particular importance in the wake of the Arab Spring demonstrations), and growth in the private sector. Also important is tourism—particularly significant when it is recalled that through the late 1980s, Oman did not even issue tourist visas. The Tourism Ministry has set an ambitious goal of 12 million visitors by 2020.[39]

Human Resources. The improvements brought to Omanis by oil revenues can be seen in the sultanate's Human Development Index as computed by the UNDP: in 2013, it ranked 84th among 186 countries and 10th

Figure 17.7 Ruins of the splendid old mud fort in Bahlah, in Inner Oman. The structure has been restored since this 1997 photo.

regionally. This rather modest index level puts Oman last among GCC members. Because the UNDP has recently changed its methods for computing the HDI and Omani data problems relative to the new method, it is not possible to make comparisons for the change in Oman's HDI value over the past two decades, as we have for most other countries in this work. However, Oman has seen considerable gains in the components that are used to compute the index.[40]

Respecting Tradition

While pushing modernization aggressively, Oman has taken remarkable care to preserve and restore important archaeological and cultural monuments. Although this has been done primarily for domestic reasons, it has resulted in further enhancing Oman's attractiveness as a tourist destination. Notable are the striking sixteenth-century Portuguese forts overlooking Muscat and Matrah, Muscat's fine old mansions, and the splendid forts of Rustaq (the old capital), Nazwa, and Bahlah (Fig. 17.7). Avoiding what has happened so often in the Middle East—sacrificing the older and historical urban areas to the modern developers—the Capital Area has instead been greatly expanded westward toward the airport. The commercial and banking center is in Greater Matrah-Ruwi, residential quarters are in Qurum and Madinat Qabus, and the ministries and embassies are in al-Khuwair. Many of the more affluent residents of the traditional houses in the old "inner cities" of Muscat and Matrah have moved to new upscale suburbs, leaving older sections to poorer families.

RELATIONS

While the sultanate was a British protectorate, most of its relations were handled by

Britain. With British withdrawal from the Gulf in 1971, Qabus expanded Oman's international presence. In the West, it retained its friendship with Britain but turned also to the United States, with which it has maintained fairly close ties. Relations with the United States actually date to a treaty of friendship and navigation signed in 1833; an American consulate was located in Muscat from 1880 to 1915. Full diplomatic relations were established in 1972; a free trade agreement (FTA) was negotiated and ratified by each in 2006. From 1980 to the mid 1990s, the US-Oman Joint Commission for Economic and Technical Cooperation operated through the US Agency for International Development; during this period, grants and loans for development projects were extended. There was a small Peace Corps program in Oman from 1973 to 1983 in which 160 volunteers served, mostly in the health and education sectors.

Oman joined the World Trade Organization in 2000. It has long supported efforts toward Israeli-Arab peace and was the only Arab country to support the Camp David Accords in 1978 and to maintain diplomatic relations with Egypt afterward. Like Qatar, it allowed Israel to open a trade office in the sultanate, but it was closed in 2000 after the outbreak of the Second Intifadah.

Facing Iran across the Strait of Hormuz, Oman pursues balance in the uneasy Gulf. It maintains a correct posture with Iran and in the late 2000s was particularly concerned by the growing confrontation between Iran, on the one hand, and the United States and Europe, on the other. It cooperated with the Gulf states, Britain, and the United States during the Iran-Iraq War and quietly but firmly supported the coalition against Iraq in 1990–1991, allowing Britain and the United States use of Masirah Island. It grounds much of its moderate foreign policy on its membership in the GCC; it belongs to the Arab League, Organization of the Islamic Conference, and Nonaligned Movement and

continues a centuries-long friendship with India. Long cordial relations with the UAE have become more so with the delineation of their mutual border in 2003. It has drawn increasingly close to Saudi Arabia and has negotiated de jure status of its long-uncertain boundaries with its larger neighbor and with Yemen as well.[41]

For information on the business environment in Oman, see the website attached to this book: www.middleeastpatterns.com.

NOTES

1. Although "amir" and "amirate" are the preferred transliterations and are generally used in this book, "Emirates" is part of the official English name for the UAE, and so it is, at the risk of some confusion, used in this specific application. As for the "most recent" Middle East state, unified Yemen might claim that distinction, since its two components combined in 1990, whereas the UAE became independent in 1971. However, each of the constituents of the new Yemen had previously been independent.

2. See Middle East Research Institute report on the UAE (1985); Peck 1986; Taryam 1987; Vine 1996; Zahlan 1998; Heard-Bey 1999; Al Sayegh 2004; Fox, Mourtada-Sabbah, and al-Mutawa 2006. Our thanks go to Dr. John W. Fox for his suggestions about this section on the UAE and for his photographs.

3. The traditional claim that the British assumed control of the Gulf to suppress Arab piracy is disputed in al-Qasimi 1988.

4. Britain's relations with the shaykhdoms, like those with Kuwait, Bahrain, Qatar, Oman, and Aden, were conducted from India, not London.

5. Malaysia has a similar political structure: nine of its thirteen states are hereditary monarchies, and the country's head of state is elected from among these rulers for a five-year term. It is also a parliamentary democracy.

6. United Nations Development Programme, *Human Development Report 2013*; *Legatum Prosperity Index 2012*, www.prosperity.com/.

7. After Russia, Iran, Qatar, Turkmenistan, Saudi Arabia, and the United States.

8. International Energy Agency (IEA), "2011 Energy Balance for United Arab Emirates."

9. *Gulfnews.com*, Mar. 27, 2013.

10. *Zawya*, Feb. 26, 2013.

11. As claimed by Willie Walsh, head of British Airways' parent corporation, in testimony before a parliamentary committee in London; see *Zawya*, Dec. 5, 2012.

12. *Khaleej Times* (Dubai), Dec. 8, 2009.

13. *New York Times*, Nov. 24, 2008.

14. Dubai's recovery and its remaining problems are discussed in the *Economist*, Jan. 5, 2013.

15. *New York Times*, Dec. 1, 2009.

16. *Zawya*, Mar. 7, 2013.

17. *Peninsula* (Doha), Jan. 3, 2013; *Khaleej Times* (Dubai), Mar. 5, 2013. Possibly to mollify the Egyptian government, the UAE announced that more than one hundred Egyptians already imprisoned on various nonpolitical charges had been pardoned. *Zawya*, Apr. 29, 2013.

18. *Huffington Post*, Apr. 8, 2013.

19. ADFD, *Annual Report, 2011/2012*, www.adfd.ae/.

20. For an outline of the events as they unfolded, see *BBC News*, Mar. 29, 2010.

21. *Khaleej Times* (Dubai), Apr. 29, 2013.

22. The Federal Government [of Germany], "Founding an International Renewable Energy Agency (IRENA)"; IRENA, "Report of the Conference on the Establishment of the International Renewable Energy Agency," Jan. 2009, www.irena.org/.

23. *Gulfnews.com*, Mar. 28, 2012.

24. *Zawya*, Apr. 25, 2013.

25. For example, it has and enforces a law against men wearing conspicuous jewelry. See *Gulf News* (Dubai), July 21, 2009, http://gulfnews.com/news /gulf/crime/.

26. Like extensions linking Sharjah to the Dubai Metro, Sharjah lacks the resources for such an effort and would need assistance from the federal government.

27. Sources for developing Oman include Townsend 1977; Allen 1987 (with good references for further reading); Anthony 1976; Zahlan 1998; Mandaville n.d.; O'Reilly 1998; Riphenburg 1998; *Persian Gulf States* Country Studies 1993; and US Department of State, *Country Commercial Guide: Oman*, 2005, and *Background Note: Oman*, Jan. 2012.

28. See details in Hanna 1995.

29. *New York Times*, Feb. 5, 1992; *Christian Science Monitor*, Feb. 19, 1992; Clapp 1998.

30. Al-Haj 1996; *Middle East Policy* 1995; Kechichian 1995.

31. *Al-Monitor*, Mar. 11, 2013.

32. *Financial Times*, Oct. 17, 2011; *Jadaliyya.com*, Nov. 18, 2012; *Chicago Tribune*, Dec. 22, 2012; *Gulf-news.com*, Jan. 8, 2013.

33. See the two excellent articles on "Oman's diverse society" by J. E. Peterson, both in 2004. Some of the following discussion is based on Peterson's detailed research.

34. For an authoritative study, see Al-Yousef 1995. See also the US Department of Energy, Energy Information Administration (EIA), *Country Analysis Briefs: Oman*, Aug. 2008. Latest details are on www .pdo.co.om/PDO/, the official website of Oman's main oil company.

35. *Arab News* (Jiddah), Mar. 4, 2013.

36. US Geological Survey, "The Mineral Industry of Oman," in *Minerals Yearbook* 2007; *Global Arab Network*, Feb. 24, 2011.

37. See *BBC News*, Aug. 27, 2009, for how this would work.

38. IEA, "2006 Energy Balance for Oman."

39. *Media Line*, Apr. 9, 2009, www.themedialine.org.

40. United Nations Development Programme 2013.

41. See Al Sayegh 2004, which is an intimate survey of UAE-Oman relations by a professor at the University of the UAE, al-Ayn.

The reader is advised to consult this book's associated website (**www.middleeastpatterns.com**) for additional information on **United Arab Emirates and Oman**, such as historical time lines and chronologies of recent events, as well as essays on selected topics and various international economic, social, and political indicators.

18

Yemen
Arabia Felix

KEY POINTS: High western escarpment and towering mountains of lava flows receive good rains spring and fall, water long utilized on extensive man-made terraces. Centuries ago was called Arabia Felix (Fortunate Arabia) for its well-watered highlands. Lower desert areas largely barren. Highly strategic position on Bab el-Mandeb opening to Red Sea. Relatively good food supply led to large population, then overpopulation and food insecurity. Physical and social divisions of country create disunity, have made governance difficult. Population a complex mixture: heavily populated Zaydi Shia north in tense relations with Sunni Shafii south, and eastern Wadi Hadramawt also somewhat divergent. Serious disunity during Arab Spring but limited civil warring. Yemen poorest country in region. *Qat* chewing adds to slow development and poverty. Isolation and disunity attracted radicals, including branch of al-Qaida, thus engaging security concerns of United States.

A NEW/OLD STATE

The Republic of Yemen (ROY), in an ancient and historic land, is the most recent state to appear in the Middle East, with the contemporary state emerging in 1990 with the fusion of the Yemen Arab Republic (YAR—North Yemen) and the People's Democratic Republic of Yemen (PDRY—South Yemen).[1] In 2011, the ROY experienced its part of the greater Arab revolution known as the Arab Spring, entering a transitional period extending through 2014. The ROY is second largest in area and population on the Arabian Peninsula. Indeed, its population exceeds the number of indigenous Arabs in Saudi Arabia,

although the foreign workers there—many of whom at times are Yemeni—swell the number of residents in the kingdom.

Yemen occupies the general area of classical Arabia Felix (Fortunate or Happy Arabia, blessed with greater rainfall than its peninsular neighbors), the southwest corner of the Arabian Peninsula. Like Oman, its highlands have been semi-isolated, with a tenuous, millennia-old link between the northwest of the country and both the coastal plain and the upper plateau. With its ancient connections to Africa from its Red Sea coast and with Indian Ocean rimlands from its south coast, it has evolved a distinctive and interesting culture, including a range of unique and remarkable architecture.

543

The Region's Poorest Relation

The PDRY was the poorest Middle East country and, as a radical client of the former Soviet Union, was virtually a pariah state in the region; the YAR to the north was the second-poorest country and was ambivalent in its East-West relations. Thus, united Yemen remains poorest in the region. Indeed, the process of unification left many problems unsolved and created new ones, including disruption of the PDRY's main accomplishment, a secular and well-functioning government. However, unification also had many benefits: it reduced many redundant expenses, numerous inter-Yemeni conflicts (such as control over Karaman Island and Perim Island), and other obstacles to economic and social development.

United Yemen started at a low level and still has a long way to go—with limited capital—to emerge from grinding poverty for the majority of its citizens. Petroleum discoveries raised cautious optimism, but actual development has been moderate. The challenges have been obvious: extraordinarily rugged topography; weak government control, insecurity, and even terrorist activity and training in some areas; poor integration among a half-dozen geopolitical cores; endemic tribal rivalry; alarmingly high population growth rate; limited internal communications; endemic corruption and economic distortion; and increasingly serious water shortages. In the UNDP's 2013 Human Development report, Yemen ranks last in the region and 160th out of 186 countries globally regarding human development. Although its HDI value is only 70.2 percent of the mean value for all Arab states, there has been considerable improvement from a low base—the index has increased about 60 percent since 1990.[2] According to the more broadly based Prosperity Index, Yemenis also lag all their neighbors—in 2012, their country ranked 134th of 142 worldwide and last in the region, lower even than Iraq.

Another measure, the Global Hunger Index (GHI, published annually by the International Food Policy Research Institute), illustrates Yemen's problems; it is a simple average of three key indicators: the percentage of the undernourished in the population, the percentage of underweight children under age five, and the mortality rate of under-five children. Any GHI above 10 indicates a serious problem; alone in the region above this level, Yemen's GHI in the 2011–2012 report was 25.4, improved somewhat from 30.4 in 1990, but still ranking 10th lowest among the 81 lower-income countries considered.[3] Over this period, there was virtually no change in the first component of the index—the prevalence of undernourishment in the general population—but some gains were noted in the other two components. The FAO has estimated that more than 30 percent of Yemenis—or more than 7.4 million people—are undernourished and that the average caloric intake per capita is only about 65 percent of what it is in the neighboring states.[4] Recent studies indicate increasing levels of food insecurity in many parts of the country, exacerbated by both internal unrest, which has generated thousands of displaced families, and a steady influx of refugees from the Horn of Africa.[5]

FIVE REGIONS

Yemen extends from the Omani border on the east along the southern peninsula coast, around the corner at the strategic Bab el-Mandeb, and northward along the Red Sea to Saudi Arabia. With greatly contrasting rocks and rock structures, as well as sharp variations in relief, its dramatically rugged volcanic landscapes (including craters of extinct volcanoes as in Aden) vary greatly from the flat-lying limestones of the Hadramawt Plateau. Most spectacular is the steep but highly dissected escarpment towering over

YEMEN

Long-form official name, anglicized: Republic of Yemen

Official name, transliterated: al-Jumhuriyah al-Yamaniyah

Form of government: multiparty republic with two legislative houses (Consultative Council and House of Representatives)

Area: 203,891 mi²/528,076 km²

Population, 2011: 24,800,000; Literacy: 63.9%

Ethnic composition (%, 2000): Arab 92.8; Somali 3.7; black African 1.1; Indo-Pakistani 1; other 1.4

Religions (%): Muslim 98, of which Shafii (Sunni) 57, Zaydi (Shia) 41; small numbers of Jewish, Christian, and Hindu

Demography: Life expectancy—62.05 yr (M), 66.27 yr (F); Birthrate (per 1,000)—32.57; Fertility rate—4.45

GDP, 2011: $33.22 billion; purchasing power parity: $57.97 billion; per capita: $2,300

Currency: Yemeni Rial (YER), US$1=214.6 rials; 1 YER=$0.0046 (mid-May 2013)

Energy: oil—3 bn bbl; natural gas—16,900 bn ft³; coal—nil

Main exports (% of total value, 2008): YER 1,519.2 billion (of which refined petroleum products 77.3; crude petroleum 9.9; food and live animals 5; transportation equipment 1.9; chemicals and chemical products 1.7)

Main imports (% of total value, 2008): YER 2,087.9 billion (of which crude and refined petroleum 29.1; food and live animals 22.3; transportation equipment 7; base and fabricated metals 6.5; chemicals and chemical products 6.4)

Capital city, 2009: Sanag 2,022,867; other major cities, 2004: Aden 588,938; Taizz 466,968; Hudaydah 409,994; Ibb 212,992

---

the Tihamah. Circled numbers on Map 18.1 show the five geographic regions.

[1] Tihamah. Tihamah, the Red Sea coastal plain, is part of the coastal fringe along the western edge of the peninsula. Averaging some 40 mi/65 km wide and sandy-gravelly for most of its length, it extends 325 mi/523 km from the Saudi border southward to the Bab el-Mandeb. Climatically a desert, the extremely hot and humid Tihamah is traversed by large wadis with heavy but brief runoff after spring and fall monsoon rains on the high escarpment. The broad wadi bottoms and alluvial fans are cultivated for cotton, melons, bananas, papayas, and similar crops; underground water in the wadi gravels is tapped for domestic use and irrigation. Smaller settlements are distinctly African in appearance, with round dwellings built of thatch and populations deriving from Ethiopia and Sudan across the Red Sea. Formerly isolated from the rest of Yemen, Tihamah is now connected by two highways to the Highlands. The centuries-old port of Mocha and the growing modern port and airport of

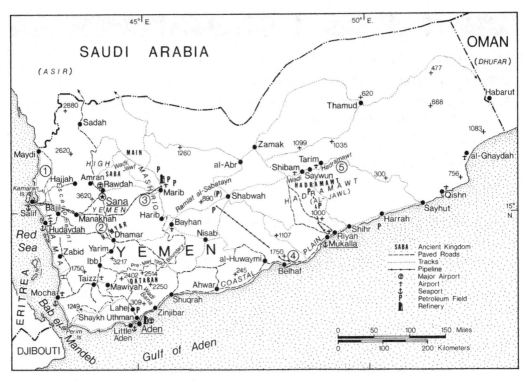

Map 18.1 General and economic map of the Republic of Yemen. Note the former boundary between North Yemen and South Yemen. Circled numbers indicate regions discussed in the text.

Hudaydah have given the coastal plain new vitality, as have the oil-export and new wheat-import facilities at Salif.

[2] Central Highlands. From Tihamah, a spectacular escarpment rises abruptly and steeply through block-faulted and ruggedly eroded topography to plateaus and shallow, flat-floored basins in the Central Highlands. Elevations commonly exceed 7,000 ft/2,135 m; southwest of Sana, a summit only 80 mi/130 km from the coast reaches 11,877 ft/3,620 m. The west-southwest-facing slopes intercept monsoon winds in April–May and August for 20–35 in/500–900 mm of orographically enhanced rainfall; more than 40 in/1,000 mm falls on the southern highlands around Ibb. The escarpment is almost vertical in places, but elsewhere slopes permit terraced agriculture (see Fig. 18.1), making this scenic subregion

Yemen's most productive, with a disproportionately high population.

The High Yemen varies in width from 40 to 75 mi/65 to 120 km. It is an extended plateau from the northern border to the former boundary of the two Yemens. Broken toward both ends, irregular mountain masses rise above it near Sana and in the south. The relatively dense population concentrates in and around Sana, capital and largest city of united Yemen. With the highest elevation of any Middle East capital—7,250 ft/2,210 m—it has moderate temperatures with a large diurnal range and cool nights year-round. More accessible and better known than the distinctive architecture of the Wadi Hadramawt (see [5] below), the building and ornamental style so well preserved in Sana's walled core forms a World Heritage Site (Fig. 18.2). Whitewashed surrounds of doors and stained-glass-topped

Figure 18.1 Typical village and terraced agriculture in the ruggedly dissected escarpment of western Yemen. Terracing is one effort to utilize steep slopes where rainfall is adequate for crops.

Figure 18.2 View of traditional buildings in the Old City of Sana, capital of Yemen, with their unique architectural styles. Note the painted surrounds of the windows.

windows give a unique character to multistory houses of basalt dimension stone or mud.

Noteworthy towns are population nodes along the backbone, all of them with the distinctive architectural styles and most with picturesque old walls, towers, forts, and mosques. From north to south, they include Sadah (center of Huthi rebel activity since 2004), with heavy road traffic to Saudi Arabia in normal times; Amran, with picturesque walls; Sana, anchoring the center; Dhamar, an old Himyaric city and agricultural center; Yarim, near a breathtaking pass; Ibb, an especially scenic old city, now a major development center; and Taizz, the former capital, clinging to a rugged volcanic slope. Indeed, evidence of volcanism is rarely out of sight anywhere on the plateau. Much of the highland itself is built up of successive lava flows, and a striking series of cinder cones extends northward from Sana. This is the southern end, in Arabia, of vulcanism related to the tectonic rifting that extends from East Africa up the Red Sea trough and Jordan Valley well into northwestern Syria (see Chap. 2).

From the plateau summit, the eastern escarpment descends to the interior less steeply and with much less relief than on the western escarpment. It steps down from more than 7,000 ft/2,135 m to the eastern desert at a general level of 3,300 ft/1,000 m. Lying in the rain shadow of the Central Highlands, its dry and sunny climate contrasts with the west. It also contrasts lithologically and primarily displays dissected Jurassic and Cretaceous sedimentary strata—mostly limestones—as opposed to the lava flows that predominate on the west. Like the vegetation, population is sparse.

[3] *Mashriq.* Toward the bottom of the escarpment, volcanic forms reappear, and then both the sedimentary layers and the lavas lose themselves under the sands of the Rub al-Khali; locally, the dune fields are known as the Ramlat al-Sabatayn. This region, the Mashriq ("the east"—not to be confused with the same

term used for the entire eastern Arab world), was well developed three thousand to fifteen hundred years ago, when Marib was on the Incense Trail during a more pluvial period and the Sabaeans maintained the famed Marib Dam system. It retained floodwaters in a large wadi, permitting intensive irrigation. Shifts in trade patterns, collapse of the main dam, and declining Sabaean vigor ended this civilization in the sixth century; the area was isolated and little known during the following millennium. Excavations in the 1950s revealed temples from Marib's heyday, but it was the discovery of substantial oil fields in the early 1980s that opened the Mashriq once again. A new Marib Dam now impounds floodwaters; extensive irrigation has created a green oasis in the otherwise barren landscape.

[4] *Indian Ocean Coastal Plain.* The coastal plain along the Indian Ocean is separated from Tihamah by volcanic masses at Aden and the right-angle intersection of two sets of ocean-spreading rifts (see Chap. 2, especially Map 2.2). It is a generally flat, sandy coastal strip varying from 5 to 10 mi/8 to 16 km in width. Reddish-black volcanic hills—some actual craters—and ragged, barren masses of lava frequently rise above and interrupt the plain, overlooking fishing villages that fringe the shore. Occasional wadis cross the plain, bringing runoff from the inland hills; along them are irrigated, cultivated plots. Up to the mid-twentieth century, the entire coast supported only scattered villages and a small port at Mukalla. Development since 1985 has stimulated growth along the coast, especially in Bir Ali, west of Mukalla and terminus of the pipeline from the Shabwah fields; Balhaf, west of Bir Ali, with a multibillion-dollar LNG plant; Riyan, east of Mukalla, the regional airport; Shihr, east of Riyan and terminus of the pipeline from the Masila fields; and Mukalla itself.

With its complex of harbors created by its location on one side of an old volcanic crater,

Aden has been a port and an entrepôt for centuries. The modern city's sections—Crater, Maala, Khormaksar, Steamer Point, Tawahi, and Little Aden with its refinery—play hide-and-seek with one another behind dark, barren, pockmarked volcanic masses. Nearly 300 mi/480 km to the east, Mukalla has been an important port for millennia, serving the population and trading families of Wadi Hadramawt, with which it is connected by a well-surfaced road up and over the intervening plateau. Facilities have been expanded and upgraded since the 1990s. The large island of Socotra, 215 mi/346 km off the coast (not included on Map 18.1, but see Map 2.1), is of particular interest: a separate fragment formed during the tectonic separation of Arabia from Africa, it displays a biological complex differentiated from the mainland since Tertiary times.[6]

[5] Hadramawt. Stretching over most of eastern Yemen inland from the coastal plain is the extensive Hadramawt, including several plateaus and the great flat-floored valley famed as the Wadi Hadramawt. Lying between the wadi and the coastal plain is the Jawl plateau, a broad tableland of flat-lying, reddish-brown limestones, dissected by wadis from a few feet to 200–500 ft/60–150 m deep. They were eroded mostly during earlier pluvial periods, seeming oversized for the water now being drained. The Jawl flats lie at 3,300 ft/1,000 m; on the south, they fall abruptly to the coastal plain 10–12 mi/16–20 km back from the shore, and on the north they drop vertically to the Wadi Hadramawt.

After the valley was initially eroded, silt, sand, and gravel partially filled the wadi bottom, giving it a flat floor that has been irrigated and cultivated along its course for thousands of years. Irrigation supports scores of small villages and several towns. Neighboring Shibam, Saywun (locally Sayoun), and Tarim are remarkable settlements with mud-brick architectural treasures con-

structed by local builders (see Saywun palace, Fig. 18.3, *top*). Centuries-old "skyscraper" mud-brick houses in Shibam were added to the UNESCO World Heritage list in 1982 (Fig. 18.3, *bottom*). Although they are rare, devastating floods can play havoc with the mud structures, as happened in 1989.

Wadi Hadramawt was little known even when it was theoretically accessible under the British; it was virtually a closed area under the PDRY. As a result, it has retained its special character, unique architecture, distinctive ethnic mix, and social and religious conservatism. Now opened to tourism, modernization seems inevitable. It customarily sent young men to Malaysia, Indonesia, East Africa, and later Saudi Arabia to work for and with fellow Hadramis established there. Most retired to the wadi, many of them wealthy, building mansions in a mixed Hadrami-Malay-Javanese style. Many such handsome homes contribute to the special character of the town of Tarim.

HISTORICAL SKETCH

During the first millennium BCE up until the sixth century CE, southwestern Arabia saw many kingdoms: Saba (Sheba), with the famous dam at its capital of Marib; Main (Minaea), farther north; Himyar, still flourishing into the sixth century, south of Saba; Qataban, southeast of Himyar; and Hadramawt, to the east. All (see Map 18.1) thrived on the prosperous and long-lived transit trade. Islam swept the region during the time of Muhammad, when Yemenis were among the earliest to contribute troops to Muslim armies moving across North Africa; in its various sects, it remains virtually the only religion practiced. Local rulers, Ethiopians, Persians, Muslim empires, Egyptians, Portuguese, and Ottoman Turks controlled part or all of the area before the British took Aden in 1839[7] and gradually extended control up the wadis and across the plateaus of the

Figure 18.3 Remarkable mud architecture in the Wadi Hadramawt, eastern Yemen: palace of the former sultan of Kathiri (*top*), in Saywun (Sayoun), built entirely of mud that has been painted white, and western facade of the all-mud city of Shibam (*bottom*). These unique mud "skyscrapers" earned Shibam inclusion on the UNESCO World Heritage list in 1982.

hinterland. Through 1990, the south and the High Yemen developed separately.

The South

Like the north, southern Yemen was mostly isolated from the cores of the various pan-Islamic empires, and so historically it developed largely autonomously. Unlike the Zaydi Shia–dominated north, however, the southern regions identified with Sunni Islam of the Shafii school. Both Aden and the island of Socotra saw brief periods of Portuguese rule in the sixteenth century, followed by similarly brief periods of Ottoman control. The ocean-facing south gave its people—especially those of the Hadramawt—an incentive to undertake maritime ventures like those pursued by the Omanis to the east. By the nineteenth century, traders from this region were established as far east as modern Indonesia and as far south as Kenya.[8]

Britain, always seeking bases to secure its links with its rich Indian Empire, captured the port of Aden in 1839. In the following years, it established relations with local rulers to the north and east of Aden, and, as with its Gulf interests, these were overseen from India, not directly from London. In 1904, Britain and the Ottomans concluded a treaty that effectively defined a border between the south and the Ottoman presence in the north. In the southern hinterland, a patchwork of as many as twenty-one shaykhdoms and sultanates composed the Western Aden Protectorate, with another six or so in the Eastern Aden Protectorate of Hadramawt. Aden and its environs became a Crown colony in 1937. This three-way pattern continued until the late 1950s, as Britain prepared to withdraw from the area.

Independence. The PDRY evolved through a complicated series of political and name changes. Preparatory to leaving the region, Britain cajoled the traditional leaders in the west into merging in a loose—and weak— Federation of Arab Amirates of the South in 1959, which morphed into the Federation of South Arabia, with Aden Colony added in 1963. Then Britain abandoned the shaykhs and negotiated independence with one of two rival radical groups, the National Liberation Front, and withdrew in 1967, leaving the amirates and the Hadramawt merged into a republic. The rivals contended for domination, fighting a costly civil war. The more radical Marxist wing prevailed, renaming the country the People's Democratic Republic of Yemen. As a one-party state, it was heavily influenced by the Soviet Union and China. Internally, it adopted regionally incongruous, radically centralized control over political and social structures. Partly reflecting the centuries-old mosaic of tribal loyalties tied to tiny quasi-independent polities, bitter enmities fueled a series of attempted coups. The PDRY pursued some progressive paths unique within the region, particularly on social issues, including women's rights and education, and institutional rather than organic government. Over the years, however, development was constrained by poverty and the gradual shrinkage of external assistance, and it increasingly became isolated from its neighbors.

Although tribalism was officially excluded from politics, recurrent conflicts reflected underlying tribal and regional competition. A short but bitter civil war in the PDRY in 1986, killing up to ten thousand in less than two weeks, led to victory by Ali Salim al-Bidh, an architect of the 1990 unification. By 2012, however—in exile, and with Iranian support—al-Bidh was a strong advocate of southern secession. The initiator of the 1986 conflict, Ali Naser Muhammad (then PDRY president), fled north with thousands of followers to make common cause with YAR president Salih. Struggles between leaders of these two southern groups, known as Zumra and Tughma, continue to shape the dialogue between northern and southern Yemen.

The North

The historical evolution of the north followed a quite different course over the past two millennia. Although both north and south grew wealthy from early trade between Aden and the Levant, particularly in frankincense and myrrh, the north had better climate and soil, and hence it had a more developed agriculture and a larger population.

Highland Yemenis embraced Islam in the mid-seventh century, serving in Muslim armies from North Africa to Central Asia. In 897, having been ruled from the Hijaz, Damascus, and Baghdad, the High Yemen came under the local rule of a descendant of Zayd, great-grandson of Ali. For most of the next eleven hundred years, until 1962, a Zaydi Shii[9] dynasty ruled all or part of the area as imams. At times in the Middle Ages, the region was fragmented into scores of petty shaykhdoms, sultanates, and kingdoms perched on mountainsides or peaks. Ottoman Turks exercised varying degrees of suzerainty, with full Turkish occupation only from 1872 to 1918; independence returned to the area with the Turkish defeat in World War I, but conflicts with Saudi Arabia over the following decade and a half lost the Zaydi regime considerable territory that it had ruled in the north. Elevated and protected contemporary villages, though picturesque and even spectacular in today's landscape, reflect long periods of disorder and insecurity (see Figs. 4.11 and 5.5). Tribal feuds and disputes over lands, water, and political influence have persisted and continue to challenge the latest Yemeni government.

Two very conservative Zaydi imams, Yahya (1904–1948) and Ahmad (1948–1962), were exceptionally isolated and resisted outside influence,[10] but Arab nationalism, especially of the Nasserist variety, increasingly appealed to many Yemenis. Trying to forestall this, Ahmad led the country into a loose and basically meaningless link to Egypt and Syria in 1958.

But when Ahmad died in 1962, Nasserist army officers opposed the succession of his son Badr and, with Egyptian support, declared the Yemen Arab Republic (YAR).

Revolutionary republican forces, mainly from the Shafii Sunni population south of Sana, were joined by thousands of Egyptian troops in a civil war against Badr's forces. Royalists led by Badr, primarily tribesmen and other Zaydi groups, were in turn aided by Saudi Arabia[11] and Jordan. More than two hundred thousand were killed as war dragged on until 1969, although Nasser withdrew his forces starting in 1967. Significantly, in the mid-1960s the republicans shifted the political capital from Taizz, in the southern plateau, to Sana, in the more neutral center, where the capital had been before 1948.

In 1971, the YAR's first nationwide elections marked reconciliation between republicans and royalists. During the following twenty years, it walked tightropes internally, externally, and with the "other Yemen." With moderately large capital transfers and technical assistance from many countries—including Saudi Arabia, the United States, China, Britain, the Soviet Union, and Kuwait—it built basic infrastructure, especially a highway net, that moved it beyond the level of the PDRY and stood it in good stead when development accelerated in the 1980s.

UNIFIED REPUBLIC

A Partnership of Opposites

Yemen to the north and Aden and the Hadramawt to the south and east have opposed and resisted control by the other for centuries. After the north declared itself a republic in 1962 and the British were expelled from an independent south in 1967, the two states outwardly professed the desire for unity, but in reality they sparred for dominance, with the north much more populous and the south much more radical politically and socially. They engaged in brief but savage bilateral warfare in 1972 and 1976, further wasting both human and financial resources already depleted by a decade of internal fighting in both states.

The PDRY's Marxist ideology promoted secularization, and its determined "progressivism"—especially in Greater Aden—had modernized the status of religion, social classes, women (less so in the Hadramawt), education, and, of course, government. The influence of the Soviet Union, China, and North Korea increased, including the formation of institutional government, as that of the West plummeted. In the YAR, while the 1962 revolution had brought sharp departures to the YAR from imamate days, many conservative customs remained, including restrictions on women's freedom. The YAR sought political nonalignment, and, unlike the PDRY, it accepted aid from all quarters.

Despite the obvious advantages of unity, practical and political obstacles remained between and within both north and south, especially merging dozens of disparate elements with their respective ambitions, ideologies, and traditions. After challenging discussions, preparation of a draft constitution, and votes in each parliament, the two united in May 1990 to create the Republic of Yemen.[12] Ali Abdallah Salih, who had been president of the YAR since 1978,[13] became the head of the newly unified state.

With a much larger population and owning the presidency, the northern part of the new union inevitably exerted unwelcome pressure on the south, despite the agreement to share government positions in Sana. Large numbers of southern public-sector employees were fired and replaced by those from, or affiliated with, the north. Salih, now with greater scope for his patronage network, distributed jobs and lands in the south to his family and cronies.

Unification presented several challenges to Yemen. Some obstacles were external: shortly after unification, the ROY decided not to condemn Iraq's invasion of Kuwait. Many donors withdrew support, and Saudi Arabia and other Gulf states expelled more than eight hundred thousand Yemeni guest workers; the expellees returned home to 40 percent unemployment, dealing the Yemeni economy a blow that still reverberates. Over time, there has been some recovery in regional labor flows, and now sizable numbers are again working abroad, many in Saudi Arabia. In 2012, annual remittances from about 1.1 million expatriates were estimated by the World Bank to be about $1.5 billion, or about 3 to 5 percent of GDP; these figures are likely to be understated, as emigrant workers often bring both funds and goods home on their visits. Recent moves in 2013 by Saudi Arabia to reduce the number of foreign workers may again deal a blow to Yemeni remittances.

Secession Defeated

With heightened friction and a sense that promised benefits had not appeared, the south tried to withdraw from the union, and civil war raged from May to July 1994. Tribes north of the previous border acted on apparent permission from Sana (through *takfir* [declaring someone to be an unbeliever]) to loot southern property, contributing to the ongoing frustration southerners felt with the effects of unification on them. Secessionists were defeated, the unified republic was restored—temporarily under greater control than before—and it gradually emerged from its near-pariah status. A series of generally free and fair elections with universal adult suffrage began with multiparty parliamentary polling in 1997 and the first direct presidential election in 1999. These were followed by further less reliable elections in 2003 (parliamentary) and 2006 (presidential). Parliamentary elections scheduled for 2009 were postponed under Salih until 2011 on the somewhat questionable grounds that a review of election procedures was necessary. Following Salih's resignation as part of the Gulf Cooperation

Council Initiative, resolving significant unrest after Yemen's uprising in 2011, both parliamentary and presidential elections were rescheduled to 2014 at the conclusion of the transitional period.

A Difficult Decade

Yemen's situation in the second decade of the twenty-first century was rather precarious. Weak central government control allowed dissident and even terrorist groups the opportunity to thrive in large parts of the countryside. Its long and mostly unpatrolled land border and coastline made penetration by outside forces fairly easy; the suicide bombing of the USS *Cole* in Aden harbor in 2000 was al-Qaida's first successful major operation in the Middle East, although 1992 hotel attacks in Aden narrowly missed killing US troops in transit to Somalia. Secessionist sentiment continued to grow in the former PDRY, as southerners increasingly complained of discrimination against them by the more numerous, tribal, and conservative northerners. Yemen maintained its open-door policy for Somali refugees, who fled Somalia across the narrow Bab el-Mandeb by the thousands during the chaos after 1991, although slowing in 2012, as a credible Somali government appeared to be reestablishing a degree of stability in the country. Offshore was the notorious hunting ground of Somali pirates and smugglers, continuing to defy the stepped-up policing efforts of naval forces from the United States, Europe, and the Far East; their presence, coupled with inadequate government security efforts, increased the cost of shipping through Yemeni ports. In September 2008, a car-bomb attack on the American Embassy compound in Sana killed nineteen people, and a mob angered by an anti-Muhammad film caused significant damage to embassy property in 2012. Post-2009 and increasingly as Yemen entered a transitional phase following Salih's ouster, the United States was increasing support for the ROY's domestic antiterrorist efforts under President Abd Rabbo Mansour Hadi.

There is a long history of friction between tribal/local elements and the government, but a dispute that began in 2004 in Sadah province in the northernmost part of Yemen had taken on international dimensions by the end of the decade. A revivalist Zaydi group, Shabab al-Mumineen (Believing Youth), led by Hussein al-Huthi, rebelled against perceived pro-Sunni and secularist tendencies of the ROY regime. Al-Huthi was killed by government forces in 2005, but the group continued its struggles and gained control over considerable territory straddling the major road link between Yemen and the Saudi Arabian province of Asir. The ROY (supported by the Saudis) accused Iran of supporting the Shii rebels and in October 2009 claimed to have intercepted a ship carrying Iranian weapons bound for the Huthis.[14] By the end of that year, as many as 175,000 civilians were estimated to have fled the area of the fighting, which involved intense aerial bombardment by Yemeni and Saudi troops. A fragile truce was declared in early 2010, although clashes on the ground with both government-supporting tribes and Saudi-supported Salafis continued. By 2012, US intelligence sources indicated that Iran was involved in Yemen to some extent with both the Huthis and the southern insurgents, known collectively as Hirak (the Southern Movement).[15] In January 2013, the Yemeni Coast Guard intercepted in the Arabian Sea a ship carrying forty tons of rockets and explosives; following this, the national security chief accused Iran of being the source of the cargo.[16]

In response to the freer political atmosphere that followed the fall of the Salih regime and more serious discussion of state structure, the Zaydi revivalist and the southern secessionist causes showed renewed vigor.[17] An ambitious National Dialogue Conference was convened in March 2013, with participants ranging from feminists to Salafis and from northern Huthis to southern secession sympathizers. The conference was charged with formulating a new constitution, restructuring the government, and preparing for the transition to follow the election now scheduled for 2014.[18]

Failed State, Terrorist Haven. The annual survey conducted by *Foreign Policy* and the Fund for Peace in 2012 placed Yemen high on its list of "failed states"—eighth, one place *ahead* of Iraq. In the region, no other state was rated in worse condition.[19] Every year in the new century has been marked by violent demonstrations, terrorist attacks, kidnappings of foreigners and Yemeni officials, and outright armed conflict. Particularly troubling was the potential for the continuing chaos in nearby Somalia—attempting to resolve two decades as a failed state—to bring al-Shabab into Yemen, where more than 150,000 Somalis were registered with UNHCR as refugees and even more were in the country illegally. The newly issued Global Terrorism Index rated Yemen fifth on the list of countries most affected by terrorism in 2011.[20] A major offensive by Yemeni government forces teamed with provincial Popular Committees in the spring of 2012 successfully drove al-Qaida out of its strongholds in some southern cities, but there have been continuing al-Qaida efforts to kill Yemeni, Saudi, and American officials.

ARAB SPRING

Yemen entered 2011 with a leader who had held power since 1978, three years longer than Husni Mubarak had been president of Egypt. Although Salih, unlike Mubarak, had faced a credible opponent who received 22 percent of the vote (Salih got 76 percent) in his most recent reelection, he had already been president for the lifetimes of two-thirds of Yemeni citizens. After the fall of Tunisia's Ben Ali and the first demonstrations in Sana,

Salih pledged not to run in the 2013 election (he had made a similar pledge a year before the 2006 election) or to promote a Syrian-style succession for his son. Nevertheless, a broad coalition of opposition groups, women, and youth grew more adamant in demands for reform and a transfer of power. Unlike in Egypt, however, Salih's security forces opened fire on the crowds, with many fatalities, causing many senior figures in his government and party to change sides. Despite this repudiation, Salih continued to maneuver for political survival. In June 2011, he was injured in a rocket attack on the presidential compound and was evacuated to Saudi Arabia for medical treatment. Opposing tribal and political groups within Sana fought over territory in the city, causing extensive property damage but relatively few deaths.

Beginning in April 2011, Salih attempted to manipulate domestic and international groups by vacillating between relinquishing power to his vice president and asserting his right to continue. He returned from Riyadh in September, still resisting his ouster. Finally, in November, Salih agreed to the handover spelled out in the GCC Initiative, and Abd Rahbo Mansour Hadi was elected unopposed in February 2012 for a two-year transitional term. Several of Salih's close kin were only removed from key government and military slots in 2013, in response to many who had demanded their ouster as part of a complete transition.

Shifting Alliances. In Yemen's complex society made up of interrelated religious, tribal, and regional groups, Salih had strong supporters as well as opponents. His continuing presence in the country, along with his persistent meddling in the political transition, has hampered the transition and caused further political tensions. Shifting tribal alliances, resistance among Huthi rebel groups, and the increased advocacy for secession in the South have made it difficult to assess the relative strength of the various political factions. It has also complicated Hadi's efforts to restore order and move Yemen back onto a track of economic progress. The previously ruling General People's Congress remains a large and influential party despite its leader's ouster from the presidency, and the previously opposition Joint Meetings Party is beginning to devolve into the dominant Islamist party Islah and other non-Islamist coalition partners.

Nobel Laureate.   Yemen's version of the Arab Spring drew the attention of the Nobel Peace Prize committee in Oslo: young anti-Salih activist Tawakkul Karman was honored with a Nobel Peace Prize in 2011 for her efforts—the youngest recipient to date, the first Arab woman in that august group. The international media have covered her outspoken comments on Yemeni and regional events.

Transition.   The Gulf Coordination Council (GCC) Initiative and Implementation Mechanism were finally agreed by all parties in 2011, after manifest irresolution from Salih. The initiative stipulated a transitional government, national dialogue, military restructuring, constitutional changes, and new parliamentary and presidential elections by 2015. Many fundamental issues—including degree of federalism, role of religion, level of centralization, and individual rights—must be addressed in this process. As of this writing, substantial progress has been made, but challenges remain.

During the two-year transitional phase, a technical preparatory committee laid the groundwork for a comprehensive national dialogue that began in March 2013. Southern leaders and politicians met in a long-delayed "south-south" conference and eventually agreed on some participation in the national dialogue. Hadi moved forward on the military restructuring as demanded by both the activists opposing Salih and the GCC Initia-

tive, removing key Salih-era commanders and consolidating military units in a unified command structure. Independent youth and women activists, key elements in Salih's ouster, began to develop stronger organization in order to maintain their voice, as political parties began to leverage the revolution for their own goals.

Many challenges to the success of the revolution remained. Yemen's security was still fragile, as both al-Qaida and Iran tried to maintain their footholds in the strategically located country. The multilevel and complex Yemeni allegiances and affiliations are based both on internal links to region, party, tribe, class, and sect and on external ties to other governments and groups. As political goals and benefits change, groups within Yemen tend toward diversification of alliances to guarantee that at least some members will be on the winning side. Complicating all this has been the previous regime's continuing attempts to manipulate the political scene, siding with one extreme and then the other, as well as the efforts of Huthis, Islahis, and Hirakis to reduce the power of the others.[21]

THE YEMENIS

The population was estimated in 2012 to be about 24.7 million, with 83 percent in the north and a high growth rate everywhere. With the region's highest total fertility rate—the number of children an average women will have is estimated to be 4.45[22]—the population is on track to double in fewer than twenty years. The Sana area has the most inhabitants, the Aden area the second largest, and Taizz and Hudaydah the third and fourth largest, respectively. Ethnic uniformity is high: Yemeni Arabs are the overwhelming majority, but biological differences and descent characteristics differ appreciably across regions. For example, an upper-class inhabitant of Sana is shorter with lighter skin than an upper-class Hadrami. Many Hadramis are descended from dark-skinned migrants from the subcontinent; others have Arab blood mixed with Malay-Indonesian and East African strains. Many villagers in Tihamah are of black African descent. Accents and dialects vary markedly, but the mother tongue of nearly all Yemenis is Arabic. Tribal affiliations are most dominant in the north and east, even among village and urban populations. The remaining Bedouin are found primarily in the Mashriq and the Jawl, and Bedouin tradition has even less influence than in the past.

Jews

A sizable minority of Jews once lived in the cities—especially Sana, Sadah, and Aden—some groups for more than twenty-five hundred years; in the late 1940s, they constituted more than 1 percent of the population of some 4.8 million. An integral part of Yemeni life, Jews are believed to have come in several waves. However, in 1949–1950, about 50,000 were airlifted to Israel on special flights, and only a few hundred remained in the country. In the late 2000s, regional events put stress on the community, and most moved to Sana. There is little overt anti-Semitism—although there is criticism of Israeli policy—and Yemeni Jews are considered full citizens; during the 2012 attack on the American Embassy, Jews in the adjoining neighborhood were not threatened. As a small community, however, Jews have little political leverage or access to political participation.

Tribal and Sectarian Differences

Relative ethnic uniformity is partly offset by persistent tribal distinctions and conflicts sometimes cast in economic or political terms; by sectarian division of the north into two main areas, dominated by Zaydi Shia in the northern two-thirds and Shafii[23] Sunni south of Dhamar; and among political groupings in the south. The greater power in the Highlands has traditionally been wielded by several tribes

of Zaydis, from whom came the ruling imams before 1962; but the Shafii Sunnis extending across the rest of the country have gained strength under the republican regimes. Always powerful, tribal leaders have periodically reasserted their prowess, sometimes in outright rebellion, to remind the government of their needs and aspirations. Tribes have kidnapped tourists or oil-company representatives, or conducted minor sabotage on pipelines, to reinforce demands for government funds and projects—roads, housing, irrigation, vehicles, and similar items. Victims were rarely harmed before the advent of al-Qaida in Yemen, but kidnappings and sabotage have become more deadly and direct conflict with security forces more common.[24]

Settlements

The western escarpment and the Central Highlands exhibit a surprisingly dense pattern of villages distributed over landscapes that would appear to limit settlement. Although only a small percentage of the Yemenis continue to be nomadic, less than one-quarter of the population is urban. The half-dozen cities are growing rapidly, as urban pull and greater security attract job seekers from the more impoverished rural areas. Another seventy towns have more than two thousand inhabitants each. Yemen as a country of villagers is seen in the detailed data for the former YAR, which are also generally applicable to the south and are still broadly relevant: eleven thousand villages had one to five hundred inhabitants, and an astonishing forty-one thousand hamlets had fewer than one hundred residents. This pattern of settlement is consistent with the topographic and climatic environments, which offer few sites for extensive settlement with adjacent cultivable area supporting agriculture. Further limiting settlement size was the traditional siting in medieval times of fortress-type villages on peaks and ridges for protection during the frequent local wars and

Figure 18.4
A Yemeni father and his two sons, all dressed in the traditional Yemeni calf-length robe and all three wearing the traditional Yemeni dagger, the *janbiyah*. (Joanne Cummings)

to avoid covering scarce arable land with dwellings (see Fig. 18.1).

Appearances

Like the landforms, historical evolution, and traditional architecture, Yemeni dress is distinctive. Unlike virtually all other Arabs, many males wear a calf-length, patterned wraparound skirt (*lungi* or *futah,* or, in the Wadi Hadramawt, where Malay-Indonesian influence is considerable, *sarong*); a colorful turban headdress similar to the Omanis' but wrapped differently; and, often, a folded shoulder shawl, especially in the higher elevations where temperatures can suddenly drop below comfort levels. More than anywhere else in Arabia, men also traditionally wear a *janbiyah* (Fig. 18.4), a sharply curved dagger in a decorated scabbard, like the Omani *khanjar*. Western wear is gradually

becoming more common, as it is in most of the Middle East, and Saudi *thobes* are increasingly seen among more conservative Sunnis. Female attire is similar to that in southwestern Saudi Arabia, with substantial regional variation. While a black *abaya* or *balta* is worn in public over other clothing, brightly patterned shawls are preferred for local shopping and visits. Some female activists in Sana have rejected face or hair coverings, as many women did in the more secular city of Aden, but this remains rare.

Qat

The daily pastime of chewing *qat* (*Catha edulis*), a leafy shrub containing cathinone, a natural chemical similar to amphetamine, is peculiar to Yemen and some parts of East Africa. About three-quarters of men—and one-quarter of women—of all social classes participate in this deeply rooted ritual that is a socially accepted and prevalent custom. Although previously a weekend tradition, *qat* "chews" have become a daily event for many Yemenis—a development some blame on the previous government's desire to redirect social energy away from opposition. Playing much the same role as meeting at a coffee shop or bar, men and women (separately) sit around a comfortable room called *mafraj* (from its viewing-platform location on top of traditional tall houses) or *diwan*. The consumer packs several leaves inside one cheek in early afternoon, sucking on the wad for two or six hours; relaxation and loquacity generally ensue.

Effects. Long-term effects are not clearly understood, although the World Health Organization considers *qat* only mildly psychologically habituating. There is evidence of increased mouth and throat cancer, similar to chewing tobacco. Whatever the health effects, the reduced productivity during the *qat*-chewing period slows economic progress. Leaves are picked fresh daily and rushed to the nearest *suq*, where they are quite expensive, and a daily supply can absorb one-third of a worker's earnings. Men begin shopping for *qat* shortly after noon, begin chewing about two o'clock, and continue the social gathering through the evening. Although *qat* chews, often used to discuss and sometimes resolve problems and political issues, have a significant role in social cohesion, the reduced focus and shortened work hours coupled with the plant's high water demand have drawn negative attention to daily *qat* use. The *qat*-chewing routine is receiving mounting criticism from national leaders and media personalities who denounce it as destructive of both soil and society. Two government ministries banned the use of *qat* in their facilities in 2012, and the movement to have a *qat*-free government environment appears to be gathering steam. The social prac-

tice, on the other hand, is likely to continue, and efforts focus on reducing the time, money, and water consumed by *qat* use rather than its abolition.

EMERGING ECONOMY

Rise and Fall of a Port

The more populous north has historically possessed the greater agricultural potential—recent findings indicate that irrigated farming in the Dhamar area dates from before 2500 BCE. In the south, Aden and its environs have been a major focus of economic activity for centuries. Aden's primary asset has been its excellent harbor and its location at the junction of land and sea routes to and from several directions. The port gained particular primacy after Britain took control in 1839 and made it the regional coaling station for the increasing number of steamships plying the Indian Ocean.

Aden's importance was greatly enhanced after the Suez Canal opened in 1869, when it became the midway port of call for ships sailing between the Mediterranean and India and points east. When oil replaced coal to fuel steamships, Aden served as a key oil-bunkering port. Increasing regional production of petroleum added to the importance of routes passing Aden; Britain constructed a major refinery in 1954 on the western arm of the harbor. By the late 1950s, it was one of the world's busiest ports, with as many as 250,000 transit passengers annually generating a booming trade in the duty-free shops, thus pioneering the merchandising taken to statispheric heights a generation later at Gulf airports. Ten years later, however, the port was languishing; the Suez Canal was closed, and civil conflict besieged the city. It served only local interests during the PDRY years and did not revive until unified Yemen designated Aden the "economic capital" of the ROY (Fig. 18.5). The hoped-for resurgence of economic activity in Aden was curtailed by piracy from Somalia, insecurity on

Figure 18.5 Port of Aden, "economic capital" of Yemen. The Aden harbor is nestled in a breached volcanic crater.

land, and a perplexing lack of support from Sana. The Aden Container Terminal (ACT) opened in 1999 and, combined with the Maalla Terminal, can process Ro-Ro ships, container ships, cargo ships, and tankers. Even before Yemen's political unrest in 2011, Aden Port was processing a steadily diminishing number of ships under a port-management contract that benefited the former president more than the country as a whole. Adenis are demanding that a post-Salih government refocus on port development and long-neglected economic growth in the south as a whole. A complicating issue are land confiscations carried out under the PDRY regime but never rectified after reunification;[25] during the transitional period of 2012–2014, committees began the long process of resolving southern grievances.

Economic Assistance and Remittances

More rural and isolated from European influence before 1970, northern Yemen desper-ately needed, and sought, large-scale aid abroad; as a result, it received substantial help from its neighbors and from both the West and the communist world. Foreign aid focused first on infrastructure, then on social services, public administration, and agriculture. With relations between Yemen and Saudi Arabia variable, official Saudi aid has varied greatly, but in 2012 the government pledged more than $3 billion of development assistance to the post–Arab Spring administration of Hadi. US assistance had been modest, although it built Yemen's first modern highway up the escarpment, but the combination of development, humanitarian, and security assistance reached more than $330 million in 2012. Chinese, British, Dutch, German, Swiss, Soviet, and especially UN technical assistance combined to endow northern Yemen with a badly needed basic network of paved highways, planned urban expansion, a number of small industries, and fair educational and health systems. China built a large cotton textile mill near Sana and, with Chinese labor, constructed the vital and scenic surfaced highway from Hudaydah up the escarpment to Sana, as well as roads in the south.

Much of the economic growth after 1975, especially in the north, was fueled by remittances from more than a million Yemenis working abroad, mainly in Saudi Arabia. Employment, salaries, and remittances of those workers rise and fall with oil prices. Several donors increased their assistance to support the 1990 union of north and south Yemen, but the newly unified republic's support for Saddam Husayn during the 1990–1991 Gulf crisis prompted renewed economic isolation. Compared to other countries of similarly low development criteria, Yemen was not a major recipient of either official development assistance or humanitarian aid from the late 1990s until 2009. Humanitarian and security issues in Yemen after 2009 generated higher levels of international support, largely through the international Friends of Yemen effort. Following Salih's ouster, a transitional government under Hadi, and the National Dialogue, pledges from a wide range of regional and international donors directed toward reconstruction, humanitarian assistance, counterterrorism, and institutional capacity building reached into the billions of dollars.

Important Sectors

Two sectors deserve special attention: agriculture, the traditional mainstay now challenged by water shortages, and oil and gas, lately the driving force but a limited resource.

Agriculture. Highland Yemen and Tihamah have been overwhelmingly agricultural. Agriculture engages almost 50 percent of the economically active population, by far the region's highest level (see Table 7.1). The contribution of agriculture to GDP dropped from almost 25 percent in 1992 to less than 8 per-

cent in 2011, partly due to declining production but also to relative growth in other sectors such as oil. Once self-sufficient in food, Yemen now imports large amounts of wheat, rice, and animal feed. Extensive rainfed agriculture is based on the centuries-long practice of terracing the slopes—thus conserving soil (virtually creating it in some ways) and maximizing use of seasonal rains (see Fig. 18.1). The degree of slope that has been terraced and the extent of the terraces are astonishing in parts of the escarpment. The terraces must be carefully maintained, especially after heavy rains, and the exodus of so many young men from the terraced farms is cause for concern. More efficient active irrigation is necessary in Tihamah, the south, and the extraordinary Wadi Hadramawt to increase agricultural yield. Irrigation efficiencies in Yemen are low, however, with a nationwide average of 40 percent.[26] Irrigation is responsible for 90 percent of total annual water consumption, and the introduction of tube-well and motor-pump technology in the late 1970s enabled agriculture to now consume more than 150 percent of the annually renewable water resources.

In addition to the expected crops of wheat, barley, maize, grapes, several fruits, and various vegetables, Yemen produces cotton and dates on the coastal plains and in the Wadi Hadramawt. It also produces three crops that are unusual among Middle East countries: sorghum (*durrah*), coffee, and *qat. Durrah* is especially well adapted to the double monsoon and formerly occupied up to three-fourths of the cropland. Yemen held a virtual world monopoly on coffee during the period 1500–1775, giving it appreciable local wealth. For many decades, most coffee was exported from the Red Sea port of Mocha—hence the popular name for coffee. It is estimated that a century ago, Yemen exported some 80,000 mt of premium Arabica coffee, but production has been declining for decades and now is little more than 10,000 mt—of which about 70 percent is consumed locally.[27] Although

Yemeni coffee commands a high price on the world market, negligible exports of less than 3,000 mt represent a decline of 75 percent between 2001 and 2011. With private-sector and government support, donors are encouraging coffee production as an alternative to *qat* to reverse the recent trend.

Qat, Coffee, Water, Food.   Unfortunately, coffee and *qat* have the same ecological demands; coffee trees have been uprooted on the high terraces of the western escarpment, replaced by *qat* bushes. Coffee plants require several years to reach optimum yield, and there is only one crop a year, although harvesting can be spread over a period of time. *Qat* bushes yield a high-value crop on a daily basis, averaging twenty times the annual income of coffee.[28] Thus, Yemen loses the value of an export while bearing the social and economic costs linked to *qat*. Food crops are also being replaced by *qat*, so Yemen is becoming less and less able to feed itself. The country's water problems are exacerbated by the *qat* cultivators—it has been estimated that their illegal wells use 40 percent of the available water in Sana's water basin.[29] However, since good statistics about *qat* production and price are lacking, the monetary value of the *qat* crop may be underrepresented. The market distortion introduced by *qat* cultivation is accompanied by high demand for water for the crop. The loss of land to *qat* also helps to explain why Yemen alone among the countries in the region showed a decline (about 12.5 percent) in food production per capita from the early 1960s to the mid-2000s.[30]

Water Resources.   Yemen's renewable water resources of 1 mi³/4.1 km³ per year are inadequate for the needs of its population, and, unlike the even more water-deficit Gulf states, it does not have the financial capacity to supplement supply with large-scale desalination. Per capita freshwater availability—4,767.5 ft³/135 m³ per year—is only one-tenth the average across this region characterized by aridity.[31] The portion of this amount that is renewable (i.e., not mined or fossil water) is even more dire—3,235 ft³/91.6 m³ in 2008.[32] No perennial streams enter or rise in Yemen, so the unsustainable rates of groundwater withdrawal—more than 150 percent of replacement—are rapidly depleting the country's endowment.

Spate irrigation—the capture of flash floods resulting from unpredictable precipitation—has traditionally supported complex systems of terracing and runoff management. Given the scarcity of the resource, social organization supported a communal framework of rules governing access and control of water. Changes in technology, such as deep wells, not only have led to greater privatization of water resources but also mean that fewer landholders, with less social accountability, have access rights. Politically motivated allocation of water rights has also increased regional frustrations. With increased demand for water by *qat* cultivators, as mentioned earlier, and rapid population growth, Yemen is seeing both growing shortages and more conflict over access. The market distortion introduced by *qat* cultivation is accompanied by high demand for water for the crop.

Although agriculture accounts for about 90 percent of freshwater withdrawals, its low contribution to GDP may be as high as 15 percent if the high cash value (but noting the probably higher social costs) of *qat* is taken into consideration. Water taken from the spate by upstream growers obviously does not reach downstream farmers; what is taken from aquifers is not available for other crops or urban consumers. The result has been increasing local and interregional disputes over available supplies. Conflict over agricultural water from the north being diverted to consumption in the capital, Sana, was a contributing factor to the six Huthi wars.

Water-distribution networks reach only 56 percent of city dwellers and 45 percent of rural residents, and sanitation provision is even lower—31 percent in urban areas, 21 percent in the countryside. Safe drinking water provision is low, and some attempts to improve the situation have led to other problems. For example, in the 1990s, the government tried to increase Sana's supply by transferring water from al-Haima wadi, an agricultural area—wells there then dried up, and crops failed. A similar attempt to provide Taizz with water diverted from Habir sparked armed conflict in the latter area. Plans to enhance storage with dams in al-Mahweet and Khawlan al-Tiyal intensified competition between potential beneficiaries. In some tribal areas, traditional leaders lost support when they expropriated the lion's share of water and its revenues.

Oil. Although Yemen is not a major player in oil and gas markets, revenues from this sector have been vital to the government. After peaking in the mid-1990s, oil production dropped due to both insecurity and inefficiency. Gas and oil exploration have identified new areas of potential, but international companies are hesitant to extend significant investment while Yemen continues to suffer from a range of issues in security and political instability. Currently, reserves are estimated to be 3 bn bbl, ninth in the region, ranking between Oman and Syria.

With Yemen's GDP under pressure due to reduced remittances and foreign aid, oil finds in the Mashriq and the adjacent Shabwah area of the south came at a particularly auspicious period. In the former YAR, the first strike came on July 4, 1984, in the Alif field in the Marib–al-Jawf Basin 37 mi/60 km east-northeast of the town of Marib in the Mashriq. The discovery was made by the Hunt Oil Company, a US firm, which later, as Yemen Hunt Oil Company and then Janna Hunt Oil, became the operator of a production-sharing agreement with participation by Exxon and a Korean consortium. During the same period, exploration near

Shabwah on the PDRY side of the border was under way by Soviet technicians, who were later joined by other companies and then replaced by an Arab group.

Marib production quickly reached 175,000 bpd, by which time a small 10,000 bpd refinery was in operation near the Alif field; meanwhile, a 24–26-in/61–64-cm pipeline with a capacity of 225,000 bpd was completed to Salif on the Red Sea, a total of 263 mi/423 km (see Map 18.1). Further exploration in the Mashriq led to the discovery of several new fields, some yielding significant amounts of nonassociated gas. Farther southeast, in the Ayad and Amal fields near Shabwah, early limited production increased after the completion in 1991 of a 20-in/51-cm pipeline to the small port of Bir Ali on the Gulf of Aden, 130 mi/210 km distant.

In the early 1990s, Canadian Occidental (Canoxy) discovered new fields in the Masila area. With completion of a 93-mi/150-km pipeline to Shihr in 1993, with a capacity of 300,000 bpd, the Masila fields became Yemen's most productive. A score of oil companies were exploring in the late 1990s under production-sharing agreements. Production curves suggest that Marib output peaked in 1995 and that overall production may well have peaked (at 420,000 bpd) in 2003 unless there are significant new finds. Output had dropped below 175,000 bpd by 2012. Yemen's two refineries, already mentioned, have capacities of 130,000 bpd (Aden) and 10,000 bpd (Marib). Damaged during the 1994 civil war, the aging Aden plant has been upgraded to restore its design capacity of 150,000 bpd throughput. A third refinery is tentatively planned for Ras Isa (Salif), north of Hudaydah, the terminus of the Marib-Salif pipeline.[33]

Hunt is planning to sell its Yemen subsidiary in Block 5, which it shares with Exxon-Mobil, Total, and others, to the Kuwaiti participant. In addition, Hunt is considering selling its LNG share, largely in response to continued security issues, but it and other companies are looking toward new exploration if political transition solidifies security gains.

Gas. Like its neighbors, Yemen is focusing its hydrocarbon hopes on nonassociated gas, which totals 16.9 tn ft^3/0.5 tn m^3 in the Marib Basin. A gas pipeline has been laid to a large joint-venture liquefied natural gas plant on the Gulf of Aden coast at Balhaf, and production began in 2009. Competing with plants in neighboring countries, the multibillion-dollar venture, exporting to the United States and Asia, is the largest single industrial project. Natural gas is also critical in plans to increase generation of electricity, available in the mid-2000s to only about 40 percent of the population and at that time entirely fueled by oil. The government admitted failure to keep up with increasing demand and embarked on a $2.9 billion system-expansion plan for 2009–2012 with incentives to attract private investment.[34] On a per capita basis, Yemenis use far less electricity annually than the citizens of any other regional country, and only about 1.5 percent of what Americans use, although personal consumption is increasing.

Other Sectors. Finally, fishing is important for food and income along both seacoasts; Hudaydah has good processing facilities. Air transportation has opened Yemen's links with the world more than anything else. International airports operate in Sana, Taizz, Hudaydah, and Aden, with five additional domestic airports; all require upgrading with adequate navigational aids. Much of the infrastructure also needs improvement to sustain development. Increased tourism, for example, would boost the economy considerably. Yemen has much to offer, especially to the more intrepid tourist, but political instability and security threats are major barriers to this sector reaching its potential.

After its neighbors began to implement plans in the late 2000s to build or expand rail-way networks, the ROY announced it would undertake a feasibility study for a 1,560-mi/2,000-km coastal line running from the Omani to the Saudi border, connecting with rail systems in those countries and passing through Aden.[35] After a break during the political transition, both government and private-sector investors are again working toward railway linkages with GCC countries. Foreign investment in nonhydrocarbon sectors continues to be deterred by excessive government red tape and by the reputation for corruption, although the government is actively working to improve in both areas.

Jobs and the Future

As is true throughout the Middle East, and especially in those countries that have seen uprisings since the onset of the Arab Spring, gainful employment opportunities are in short supply in Yemen. In 2011, the official unemployment rate was 15 percent, and among the fifteen-to-twenty-four-year-old age group, the government's estimate was 52 percent. International analysts placed it far higher, with current levels of unemployment following the 2011 sharp economic downturn constituting one of the transitional government's greatest challenges. Job creation and economic growth depend upon investment, whether domestic or from foreign sources. Unfortunately for Yemen, even if the country were not undergoing considerable political and social turmoil, even if *qat* did not impinge negatively on labor productivity, even if Yemen's most enterprising workers could be enticed from employment abroad, the environment in which investment decisions are made is less favorable than that in most neighboring countries.

RELATIONS

United States. US-Yemen (north) diplomatic relations date to 1946, but a resident mission was not established in the country until 1959; relations were severed in 1967 in the wake of the Arab-Israeli war but were renewed in 1972. When South Yemen became independent, relations were opened in 1967, but this situation quickly foundered, and they were broken in 1969. With unification, the United States and the Republic of Yemen have continued the links that had previously existed with the regime in the north. The presence of the US Agency for International Development in Yemen dates to 1959, and by 2010 a total of $1.24 billion in grants and loans had been extended to the Yemeni government. The current USAID program is based on a stabilization strategy emphasizing assistance to underserved communities that have provided fertile ground for both rebels and terrorists threatening the new government. Additionally, during this period, US military assistance amounted to $128 million. Since 2010, both types of assistance have been accelerated. From 1973 to 1994, the Peace Corps operated a program that involved some 564 volunteers during its duration.

In 2012, the United States pledged to the transitional government $346 million in security, humanitarian, and development assistance. Of this, more than half—$185 million—is aimed at political transition and much-needed humanitarian and development aid. With dedicated funds of $117 million, the United States is the largest single provider of humanitarian assistance to Yemen. International donors as a group pledged $6.4 billion in September 2012 to support the transition period, address urgent needs, and increase regional security.

Ongoing Security Issues. The United States and Yemen coordinated efforts in the search for the attackers of the USS *Cole* and worked even more closely after 9/11 and after the attack on the American Embassy in Sana in 2008. By 2013, the previously mentioned rebel activity in the north, the increasingly obvious activities throughout the country of

al-Qaida, and the disturbances that followed the onset of the Arab Spring and led to the ouster of the Salih regime worked together to place Yemen high on the list of the United States' international concerns. The greater use of armed drones against suspected terrorist havens has been, on the one hand, tactically successful, while at the same time potentially increasing resentment among some Yemenis of US actions in their country.[36]

American Embassy Attack, 2012. Following the release and broad distribution online of a short anti-Muslim polemic film, Muslims in many countries demonstrated at American embassies. In Sana, no Americans were injured but a small group of protesters used the demonstration to cause significant damage to embassy property. The ROY government overcame residual divisions within the armed forces and provided additional security to the embassy, preventing a recurrence.

Several aspects of insecurity remain, including both determined al-Qaida efforts to maintain a center of operations in Yemen and an unresolved conflict between Sana and the Huthis (now *Ansar Allah*) that Iran seeks to exploit. The National Dialogue process, scheduled to complete the conference in late 2013 and conclude with presidential and parliamentary elections in 2014, plans to address both political and security issues. The transitional government is engaged in restructuring the security forces, including reducing the influence of those closely associated with the Salih regime.

Donor Economic Assistance. Unification in 1990 eliminated the most persistent problems in foreign relations for both Yemens— those in relations with each other—and the collapse of communism provided a more salutary climate for the merger. Although some financial supporters of each state exacted unfortunate retribution after unification, since they had favored conflict between the two for their own reasons, most regional countries are providing funds to support Yemen's development and stability. The republic is in continual need of external capital transfers, particularly following the virtual collapse of the economy during the successful revolt against Salih. When oil prices are high, as they were in 2003–2004, 2008, and again in 2012, Yemen's income rises without obviating its reliance on generous external aid. In 2006, the ROY adopted a reform program to bolster the economy's non-oil sectors, and a donor conference in London brought in pledges of $4.7 billion for the 2007–2010 period. But by 2010, it was clear that only a small fraction of these pledges had actually been put to productive use, mostly due to the country's low absorptive capacity. This has been attributed to a number of causes: bureaucratic red tape, widescale corruption, difficulty in identifying priority projects, poor government control over many parts of the country, and the tendency of the former Salih regime to use the pretext of security concerns to divert aid resources to favored destinations.

In 2012, the new ROY government estimated that it needed $11 billion in external assistance to help it through the transition period under way. Donors recognized the immediacy of the country's needs but were also wary of moving too quickly and overwhelming Yemen's ability to process the funds and implement planned projects. A donor conference in Saudi Arabia in September of 2012 resulted in total pledges of $6.4 billion, with the prospects of additional funding provided conditions for allocation and disbursement are improved.

Ignoring the triple political threat facing the country—the Huthi rebellion, southern secessionism, and the al-Qaida presence—along with the economic realities of declining oil production and increasing water shortages would be disastrous.[37]

For information on the business environment in Yemen, see the website attached to this book: www.middleeastpatterns.com.

NOTES

1. The former North Yemen is covered in Steffen et al. 1978, which is highly geographical as well as demographic, and Daum 1987. *Yemen* Country Studies 1985 covers both former Yemens authoritatively; Dunbar 1992 examines the unification of the two Yemens. (Dunbar was US ambassador to Sana at the time of the merger.) See also Dresch 1989. The former PDRY is discussed in Stookey 1982. For more current coverage of unified Yemen, see US Department of State, *Background Note: Yemen*, Jan. 2010, and *Country Commercial Guide: Yemen* 2004. A good history is Dresch 2000.

2. United Nations Development Programme 2013; *Legatum Prosperity Index 2012*, www.prosperity.com/.

3. International Food Policy Research Institute 2009.

4. United Nations Food and Agriculture Organization 2009.

5. World Food Program, www.wfp.org/countries/yemen/overview.

6. See Mackintosh-Smith 1999.

7. Until 1937, Aden was ruled by the British from India, not London. Like Malta, Cyprus, the Suez Canal Zone, and the Gulf amirates, it was part of Britain's defense of the route to India. See Busch 1971.

8. Other Hadramawtis sought their fortunes closer by; for example, Mohammed bin Laden left home to find work as a porter in Jeddah, founding in 1930 his own construction company, which eventually secured enormous fortunes for him and his progeny.

9. The Zaydis (or Fivers) are one of the three main Shii sects (see Chap. 4).

10. Except, somewhat oddly in retrospect, Mussolini's Italy, which Yahya saw as a bulwark against the British and the Saudis, and with which he signed a treaty in 1925.

11. The very conservative Wahabbi Saudis disliked the secular and socialist Nasserists more than the Zaydi Shia.

12. See Dunbar 1992 and Dresch 2000.

13. Succeeding to the office after the assassinations of his two immediate predecessors eight months apart.

14. Former US ambassador to Yemen Edmund J. Hull warned against portraying Yemen's internal problems in Shia-versus-Sunni terms, as in Iraq. See *New York Times*, Jan. 12, 2010.

15. *New York Times,* Mar. 15, 2012; *Saudi Gazette,* Oct. 13, 2012.

16. *Khaleej Times* (Dubai), Feb. 10, 2013; see also *al-Monitor,* May 14, 2013.

17. *Daily Star* (Beirut), Oct. 12, 2012.

18. *Christian Science Monitor,* Mar. 20, 2013.

19. *Foreign Policy,* www.foreignpolicy/articles/2009/06/22the_2009_failed_states-index. With data drawn from 2011, Syria ranked twenty-fourth on the list. Most likely, later updates will reflect Syria's worsening situation in 2012.

20. Institute for Economics and Peace 2012.

21. For a discussion of the complex nature of the forces at play in Yemen, see Fattah 2011.

22. The CIA *World Factbook* has a slightly higher estimate—4.57—for the Gaza Strip, but since the estimate for the West Bank is 2.98, the combined estimate for Palestine would be about 3.6.

23. The Shafii school is one of four equally regarded Sunni schools of Islamic law (see Chap. 4, note 6).

24. US Department of State, *Country Commercial Guide: Yemen* 2004; *Daily Star* (Beirut), Apr. 9, 2005.

25. Al-Jazeera, Apr. 13, 2013.

26. World Bank, Report No: 31779-YEM 2005.

27. *Zawya,* June 14, 2010.

28. An interesting exploration of the economics of *qat* cultivation is found in Leonard Milich and Mohammed Al-Sabbry, "The 'Rational Peasant' vs. 'Sustainable Development': The Case of *Qat* in Yemen," available at http://ag.arizona.edu/~lmilich/yemen.html.

29. *Christian Science Monitor,* Nov. 5, 2009.

30. FAO, various issues. Iraq could not be included in this regard because of a lack of recent data.

31. World Bank 2009.

32. FAO AQUASTAT 2009.

33. See EIA, *Country Analysis Briefs: Yemen,* July 1999, July 2004, and Jan. 2010. Author Held is grateful to Yemen Hunt Oil Company for a briefing and for his visit to the offshore tanker at Salif in 1997.

34. Global Arab Network, Jan. 3, 2010, www.english.globalarabnetwork.com.

35. *Daily Star* (Beirut), Jan. 17, 2010.

36. See, for example, the testimony of Farea Al-Muslimi, a Yemeni writer, about an attack on his village, before a US congressional committee. *Reuters,* Apr. 23, 2013. See also *Media Line,* May 12, 2013.

37. For a comprehensive treatment of the Yemeni dilemma, see Boucek 2009. See also Dorsey 2010; more recent is Alley 2012.

The reader is advised to consult this book's associated website (**www.middleeastpatterns.com**) for additional information on **Yemen**, such as a historical time line and chronology of recent events, as well as essays on selected topics and various international economic, social, and political indicators.

19

Egypt

A River and a People

KEY POINTS: Classic riverine state, "the gift of the Nile." Rich ancient history and culture; wondrous monuments normally attracting millions of tourists. Only small percentage of area actually cultivated and populated—primarily the Nile flood plain with rich alluvial soil easily irrigated and cultivated. Largest population of all regional states, with about 10 percent Coptic Christian among mostly Sunnis. Possesses strategic Suez Canal. Richest of western Middle East states in energy resources, exports natural gas. First Arab state to make peace with Israel. One of three great regional power cores or power foci and long the cultural and political leader of the Arab world. However, instability from infighting during Arab Spring badly weakened Egypt; 2011–2013 relations with United States very important.

A VIEW OF EGYPT

"Egypt is the gift of the Nile," wrote Herodotus twenty-five hundred years ago. Kipling, in turn, described the Nile as "that little damp trickle of life." Both comments emphasize the role of a single river as the fundamental element in the existence of this ancient land.

In few countries are the basic geographical factors and their direct influences so plainly imprinted as in Egypt. The Nile Valley is unique in its singular symbiosis of people and environment and in its remarkable history and contemporary development. Flanked by desert ramparts, kingdoms have flourished in the valley for millennia, with only occasional major disruptions. Egypt's location on the nexus between Africa and Eurasia has long given it a pivotal position in the World-Island, whether in ancient, medieval, or modern times, right into the twenty-first century.

Ancient Riverine Polity

Inscriptions, carvings, bas-reliefs, statues, and monuments—all well preserved in the dry climate but now under serious stress from contemporary pollution—provide detailed documentation of everyday life and beliefs in Pharaonic and Ptolemaic Egypt. Both tourism and archaeological scholarship focus on such ancient works as the numerous pyramids, temples, tombs, and colossi, with their hieroglyphics and distinctive arts. History is an essential ingredient of everyday life in the country (see Figs. 3.2 and 19.1).

Figure 19.1 Abu Simbel monument in its repositioned setting. The monument was cut into segments and moved from its original cliff-side location, which is now under the water of Lake Nasser. The mound behind the monument is an empty shell of disguised concrete. Note cruise ship in lower right and tourist facilities in right distance.

Although the imperial domains of ancient Egypt were less extensive than those of Persia or Assyria, they often extended well into the Levant, and the Nile Valley persisted as one of the four power cores of the region (see Chap. 3). Ensconced behind its desert glacis (buffer zone) and well supplied with military resources, it saw fewer conquerors than Fertile Crescent states. Domestic stability and protected location contributed to a historical continuum that, although several times disturbed, was never devastated in the same way that the civilizations of the Hittites, Assyrians, and Israelites were. Similarly, growing along a riverine ribbon made it a linear geographical unity that, once integrated in about 3000 BCE, has rarely been seriously ruptured. The city-states that were so adapted to the environments of mainland Greece, western Asia Minor, and Phoenicia contrast with the integrated polities of the Nile Valley and

Delta. The productive agricultural economy along the river has always supported a relatively large population (see Table 4.1 and Graph 4.1).

Cultural Nexus

With the riches of the interior, the city of Alexandria (founded ca. 331 BCE) was a major intellectual and commercial center in the classical Mediterranean world, and then later in the early days of Christianity it provided the locale for debates at the core of philosophy and theology. Located near the center of the Islamic and Arab worlds, Egypt has long played an influential role in both realms, partly because of the influence of Cairo's al-Azhar University on religious affairs and partly because of the country's long intellectual tradition. Similarly, it has exercised a dominant influence in the Arab world, particularly since World War II, some-

EGYPT

Long-form official name, anglicized: Arab Republic of Egypt

Official name, transliterated: Jumhuriah Misr al-Arabiyah

Form of Government: Republic, elected president and parliament

Area: 386,874 mi²/1,002,000 km²

Population, 2011: 82,537,000; Literacy: 72%

Ethnic composition (%, 2000): Arab 93.6, of which Egyptian 84.1, Sudanese 5.5, Berber 2, Bedouin 2; Rom (Gypsy) 1.6; other 4.8

Religions (%, 2000): Muslim 89, mostly Sunni; Coptic Christian 10; other and nonreligious 1

Demography: Life expectancy—70.33 yr (M), 75.66 yr (F); Birthrate (per 1,000)—24.22; Fertility rate—2.94

GDP, 2011: $231.9 billion; purchasing power parity: $519 billion; per capita: $6,500

Currency: Egyptian Pound (EGP), US$1 = 6.922 pounds; 1 EGP = $0.143 (mid-May 2013)

Energy: oil—4.4 bn bbl; natural gas—77,200 bn ft³; coal—small reserves but some annual production for local use

Main exports (% of total value, 2008): $26.2 billion (of which refined petroleum 18.9; LNG 13.7; food products 9.6; crude petroleum 8.4; organic chemicals, fertilizers, and plastics 5.7)

Main imports (% of total value, 2008): $52.8 billion (of which machinery and apparatus 18.2; food products 12.3; chemicals and chemical products 12; mineral fuels 10.9; iron and steel 8.8; road vehicles 5.6)

Capital city, 2006: Cairo (agglomeration) 11,893,000; other major cities: Alexandria 4,085,000; al-Jizah (Giza) 2,891,000; Shubra al-Khaymah 1,026,000; Port Said 571,000; Suez 512,000

---

times contending with Syria and Iraq for leadership. Its cultural output—films, radio, television, publications—has long exceeded that of all other Arab countries combined. In 1988, an Egyptian novelist, Naguib Mahfouz, received the first Nobel Prize in Literature awarded to an Arab writer.

Egypt moved from power core to colonial possession to political leader of the Arab world, dropped to regional pariah status for several years after 1979, but regained a qualified political eminence in the 1990s. The dramatic events of January 2011, broadcast live from Tahrir Square in the heart of Cairo, established Egypt as the progenitor of the Arab Spring. In the wake of this political change, Egypt's future was again uncertain in the summer of 2013, as Islamists and liberals allied with the military vied for control. Domestic tensions and regional policies will play key roles in Egypt's economic future and its new internal and external patterns.[1]

A RICH HISTORY

Historical Continuity

Over the centuries, Egyptian civilization developed a stability that enabled it to survive, if not always to repel, foreign incursions. Although defeated occasionally, resilient Egypt not only preserved its population and sustained its culture but also absorbed newcomers, sometimes adapting their religious or political concepts, sometimes passing on Egyptian concepts to them—for example, to the Hebrews.

Valley and Delta Unification.   Once Lower Egypt (the Nile Delta) merged with Upper Egypt (the valley south of the delta) around 3000 BCE, the two physically different but interdependent parts remained integrated through five millennia. Reunification of the two after a 200-year cleavage preceding and during the Hyksos invasions in 1720–1580 BCE was celebrated by many new symbols, including the form of the royal crown, and in thousands of hieroglyphic inscriptions. Unity prevailed even when incompatibilities between valley and delta with their cultural and environmental differences could not be entirely overcome. The centripetal-centrifugal relationships between Upper and Lower Egypt remain meaningful, although modern communications and increased interregional dependence have reinforced the sense of unity.

The movement of royal capitals and religious centers between north and south in ancient times reflected shifts in the political center of gravity. Memphis, the first capital of the unified kingdom, was founded at an intermediate location near the apex of the delta, to which the capital returned periodically after shifts to Thebes (modern Luxor area) and other valley and delta cities (see Map 3.3). It is significant that Cairo, the political center for the past 1,350 years, is located—as was Memphis—at the junction of delta (Lower Egypt) and valley (Upper Egypt).

External Infusions.   Despite periodic incursions over the centuries—by Hyksos, Libyans, Nubians, Ethiopians, Assyrians, Persians—Egypt maintained a distinct national character. The Persian conquest in 525 BCE was the first by more distant powers: Greeks under Alexander the Great, 332–323 BCE; Greek Ptolemies, 330–304 BCE; Romans, 30 BCE–476 CE; and their Byzantine successors, 476–640 CE (see Chap. 3). A major modification of the ancient culture came during the Roman-Byzantine hegemony: Christianity became the dominant religion (see Chap. 4). It survives today among the minority Copts.

Arab-Islamic Transformation.   In 642 CE, the Muslim Arab conquest brought a momentous and permanent transformation of Egypt. The Arabs not only overwhelmed Egypt militarily but also immigrated into Egypt by the thousands, intermarrying with the indigenous population. Their intangible contributions included a proselytizing religion (Islam), a new language (Arabic), and a concept of strong ties between religion and government. Islam only gradually supplanted Christianity—and not for several centuries in the south—but by 706 Arabic had become the language of official transactions.

Once ingrained, Islam has never been challenged. Sunnism, however, gave way for two centuries to the Shii Fatimid state, 909–1171, which supplanted Abbasid control across North Africa. The Sunni Ayyubids reigned from 1171 to 1250; their dynasty included Salah al-Din (Saladin), a Kurd whose exploits against the Crusaders made him one of Arabdom's most honored heroes. The succeeding Mamluk (literally, "slave") sultans then ruled for more than 250 years, while Cairo gained architectural treasures, underwritten by the rich Red Sea–Mediterranean trade. Mamluk buildings, especially mosques with characteristic minarets and fluted domes, are some of the city's most distinctive monuments.[2] Portuguese merchantmen sailing around the

Cape of Good Hope after 1497 deprived the Mamluks of their main revenues, and Egypt fell to the Ottoman Turks in 1517.

Local Polity Restored.   Ottoman control was tenuous after the late 1700s, but technically it continued until 1914. From 1805, Egypt was locally ruled by the Muhammad Ali dynasty under nominal Ottoman suzerainty. British troops arrived in 1882, and the British presence continued in some form for more than 70 years. Egypt became an independent kingdom in 1922. The last country to join the League of Nations in 1937, it was a founding member of the United Nations in 1945.

CONTEMPORARY REPUBLIC

Gamal Abd al-Nasser.   Contemporary Egypt was born in a bloodless military coup on July 23, 1952, sending Faruq (Farouk), last king of the Alid line, into exile. A republic emerged, led by a revolutionary junta, and the following two decades saw a sequence of events in Egypt that shook the Middle East and sometimes the world. Many of these were orchestrated by Gamal Abd al-Nasser (al-Nasr), the charismatic coup leader who became president in 1954. Not for centuries had any other leader fired the imagination of his fellow Arabs as much as did this extraordinary army colonel, in word, image, or action.

Among his more memorable actions, he forced the withdrawal of Britain in 1954–1956, negotiated a Czech-Soviet arms deal in 1955, nationalized the Suez Canal in 1956, preached and promoted aggressive Arab nationalism, accepted Soviet aid (including for the Aswan High Dam), and promoted a far-reaching land-redistribution program. On the other hand, his merger of Egypt and Syria into the United Arab Republic failed after only three years, he embroiled Egypt in a disastrous eight-year military venture in Yemen, and he escalated regional tensions, leading to Israel's invasion of the Sinai in

June 1967. Trying to reconcile the Palestine Liberation Organization and the Jordanian government in September 1970 ("Black September"), he suffered a fatal heart attack.

Anwar Sadat.   Nasser's successor, the more pragmatic Anwar al-Sadat—also an army officer before going into politics—changed national policy directions. To counteract economic stagnation, he cut Nasserist socialism back with an economic "open-door" policy (*infitah*). Though Egypt signed a Friendship Treaty with the Soviet Union in 1971, he soon began downgrading mutual relations. After making peace feelers that were ignored by both Israel and the United States, he led a joint Egyptian-Syrian surprise attack on Israeli lines at the Suez Canal and in the Golan Heights in 1973.

The initial success of the campaign shocked Israel, though it eventually prevailed. Still, this brought the United States into what became known as "shuttle diplomacy," with American secretary of state Henry Kissinger initiating a process that culminated in both closer ties with the United States and serious negotiations between Egypt and Israel. Sadat made a dramatic visit to Jerusalem in November 1977 to address the Israeli Knesset. Then, with help from President Carter, he negotiated the Camp David Accords in September 1978 and the Egyptian-Israeli peace treaty in March 1979. Having championed resistance to Israel for thirty-five years, Egypt embittered its former allies by making a separate peace, and it was expelled from the Arab League. Domestically, the treaty was received with ambivalence, with some extremist opponents especially vocal. Although Sadat was praised in the West as a man of peace, receiving the Nobel Peace Prize (along with Israeli prime minister Begin) in 1978, he was assassinated by disaffected extremists in October 1981.

Husni Mubarak.   Sadat's successor, Husni Mubarak, an air force pilot and hero of the

1973 war, generally took a low-key approach, and by 2011 he had had the longest tenure among Egyptian leaders since Muhammad Ali. Pragmatic and politically shrewd, he skillfully maintained his power and the country's interests and security, engaging in a delicate balancing act. It would not be unreasonable to argue that he was reasonably popular domestically at least through his first three six-year terms. He was credited with further opening the economy and presided over a period of sustained and healthy growth. He had faced growing domestic terrorism in the 1990s, which threatened the vital tourism sector and, for the most part, had brought it under control. He showed considerable skill in conducting foreign policy, making Egypt a key player in international affairs, building on strong relations with other Arab countries, the United States, and the EU.

But problems gradually mounted for Egypt and the regime, growing more acute in the new century. It was increasingly clear that economic growth was mostly benefiting a small urban elite and was singularly unable to provide gainful employment for hundreds of thousands of young Egyptians. Whereas the 9/11 attacks elicited broad sympathy for the United States and support for moves against terrorism, the invasion and occupation of Iraq quickly dissipated these feelings—and the government's American ties plummeted in popularity. Finally, by the end of the 2000s, the prospect of a moribund octogenarian Mubarak seeking still another six-year term in 2011 (or perhaps worse, trying to manipulate a Syrian-style succession for his son Gamal) drained the regime of what support it still retained.

ARAB SPRING

Although it was in Tunisia where demonstrations starting in December 2010 culminated in the removal of the Ben Ali dictatorship that

what came to be known as the Arab Spring began, it was with the continuous occupation of Tahrir Square in central Cairo by hundreds of thousands of men and women, televised live to all corners of the globe by al-Jazeera, that the rest of the world came to realize that what they were seeing was no passing phenomenon.[3] Perhaps the critical turning point came with the decision of the armed-forces leadership only to maintain general order but to allow the demonstrations to proceed and grow. Within three weeks, the essential hollowness of the Mubarak regime was exposed, and the thirty-year president was placed under house arrest, yielding power to the Supreme Council of the Armed Forces (SCAF) that promised a quick transition to civilian and constitutional rule.

Democratic Succession. The following months were characterized by fits and starts, advances and setbacks—there was considerable skepticism about whether the SCAF would actually turn over the reins of government to an elected president and parliament. This is not the place to trace in detail the events of those months; such summaries are readily available elsewhere (for example, see the Arab Spring timeline found on this book's related website: **www.middleeast patterns.com**). In the months following Mubarak's ouster, on the positive side: a civilian prime minister was chosen; the national electorate approved a slate of constitutional reforms; the first free parliamentary elections were held, with the veteran Muslim Brotherhood party winning a plurality; and a two-round presidential election saw the narrow victory of Muhammad Mursi as Egypt's first civilian president. The SCAF allowed his inauguration, and he then took actions that trimmed some of the military's political power. On the negative side were: continued demonstrations, sometimes violent, showed popular dissatisfaction with the slow pace of the transition; attacks on Copts by security forces and Muslim mobs led to fatalities; the runner-up in the parliamentary election was a Salafi-dominated slate, well to the right of the Muslim Brotherhood; no fewer than three civilian prime ministers held office in the first eighteen months, with secular party representation eliminated; court rulings called the legitimacy of the elected parliament into doubt; and riots at the American Embassy imperiled Egypt's relationship with the United States.

Popular disappointment in Mursi increased in 2013 as he failed to deal with Egypt's most pressing problems. Liberals and even many former Mursi supporters by the millions joined in anti-regime protests in June 2013. Although both Salafis and the army had been seen as alternatives to Mursi, the demonstrations led the military alone to call on Mursi to step down and, when he did not, to remove him.[4] General Abdul Fattah al-Sisi installed an interim government under civilian Hazem el-Beblawi and promised early elections. Clashes between security forces and the Brotherhood that left hundreds dead and attacks on Christian churches and schools raised domestic and international tensions.

Answers to several questions could determine the course and success of Egypt's Arab Spring. First, could any Islamist-led government be fully inclusive of religious and political groups? Second, how would such a regime institutionalize human rights and equality in a broadly acceptable constitution? Third, can *any* government maintain reasonable order without repressive techniques? Fourth, faced with growing polarization and political unrest, can *any* government prevent a return of domestic terrorism?[5] Finally and most important, what form of government can implement economic policies that give real hope of gainful employment to the youth who have now twice filled Tahrir Square until they brought down the government?[6]

RIVER, DELTA, AND DESERTS

Egypt comprises five regions: [1] Nile River Valley; [2] Nile Delta; [3] Western Desert; [4] Eastern Desert; and [5] Sinai Peninsula (see circled numbers, Map 19.1). It is worth noting that although Egypt has generally been considered a seismically stable region, a 5.9 earthquake centered 20 mi/12 km southwest of Cairo occurred in 1992, causing more than four hundred deaths and three thousand injuries. Not built according to earthquake-resistant codes, many buildings collapsed; post-1950s structures especially showed damage and were condemned and sometimes razed. However, major ancient monuments seem to have escaped serious problems.[7]

[1] Nile River and the Aswan Project

Water Is Life. Egypt is the Nile, and the Nile is Egypt. The Nile–Lake Nasser system provides Egypt with its only significant renewable surface water. The river's headwaters are far to the south, fed by runoff from heavy summer rains in East Africa's lake district and Ethiopia's highlands. These form the White Nile and Blue Nile, which join at Khartoum in the Sudan, whence the single Nile enters Egypt through Lake Nubia/Lake Nasser. It then flows 938 mi/1,510 km up the entire length of the country, including Lake Nasser, before debouching into the Mediterranean.

Altogether, the complex of barrages, dams, canals, and water supply and wastewater treatment facilities is among the most extensive in the world. Because Egypt relies almost completely on water that passes through other countries—each of which has need for, and influence on, the waters of the two Niles—any change in the hydraulic infrastructure in upstream riparians affects water availability in Egypt and other downstream users. It has long held that its historic use of Nile waters, which dwarfs upstream withdrawals, has priority. As a downstream hegemon, it has claimed that negative changes in

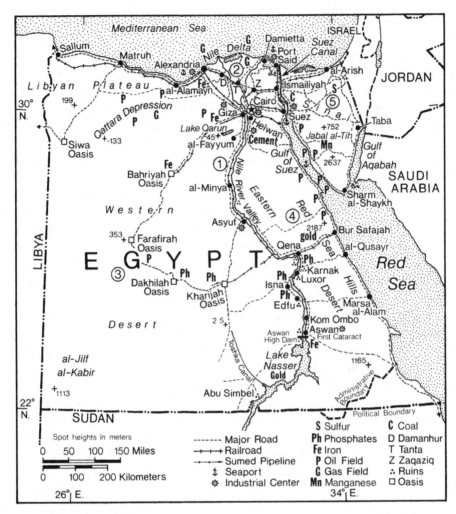

Map 19.1 General and economic map of Egypt. The five major geographical regions are identified by circled numbers. Note concentration of cities and main transportation lines along the Nile and in the Delta.

the quantities reaching it as a result of agricultural or other hydraulic development in upstream countries would be a casus belli.

Nile Basin. As the imperial power from the Mediterranean south through East Africa at the time, Britain secured Egypt's dominant position with the 1929 Nile Water Agreement with the then Anglo-Egyptian Sudan and in the 1959 Agreement for the Full Utilization of the Nile with the East African territories that were still British colonies. Essentially,

these pacts gave Egypt the right to veto any upstream work affecting the river and the use of about two-thirds of the river's annual flow (at least 55.5 bn m³), with the rest going to the Sudan. The East African states argue that, as colonies in 1959, they had no say in the agreement and therefore do not recognize its continued validity. Even more so, Ethiopia, the source of most of the river's water, was never involved in any discussions conducted by Britain and therefore does not acknowledge the current arrangement in any way. For

Egypt, maintaining the existing situation is a matter of national security—indeed, national survival—and any interference with the flow that it has not agreed to would be, as mentioned, a casus belli.

Water ministers of all the countries in the river's basin and watershed formed the Nile Basin Initiative in 1999,[8] aimed at creating a partnership among all nine riparians. With World Bank support, some $1 billion in grants and loans has been committed to projects dealing with watershed management, flood control, and other issues of mutual interest and benefit. However, more than a decade of negotiations failed to produce a Cooperative Framework Agreement (CFA) that satisfied both the Upper Basin states and Egyptian-Sudanese requirements. In 2010, the former group signed a CFA among themselves, saying they could wait no longer and felt that no agreement with Egypt and the Sudan was forthcoming. In 2011, Ethiopia announced it would proceed, without Egyptian permission, with construction of the Renaissance Dam on the Blue Nile—a project that, if and when completed, is to result in Africa's largest hydroelectric facility.

Preoccupied with domestic developments following the 2011 revolution, Egypt returned its attention to upstream diplomacy in 2013 with high-level official visits to the new state of South Sudan and the Horn of Africa. Cooperation among the Nile riparians south of the Sudan has proceeded apace without Egyptian participation in the past few years, a fact that must be a major concern for the government.[9]

Nile Valley: Upper Egypt. North of the first cataract at Aswan, the Nile enters a narrow, flat-floored valley, eroded as much as 1,000 ft/300 m below the flanking plateau near Qena (Qina). The valley continues flat, broadening downstream below the Qena bend, until it is 6–11 mi/10–18 km wide approaching Cairo. The valley walls drop to less than 165 ft/50 m high at Giza, then disappear entirely as the river moves out onto its delta. It is the lush ribbon of irrigated, cultivated fields on the flat floodplain along the valley that is the quintessence of traditional Egypt (see Fig. 5.7).

Just upstream of the delta, a prominent feature west of the valley is the Fayyum (Fayoum), a circular depression in the limestone plateau of the Western Desert. Nile waters formerly poured into it, at least during floods, through the Hawara channel, feeding the large Lake Moeris. However, later diversion of the river from the basin reduced it to a remnant (now called Lake Qarun), with a surface 147 ft/45 m below sea level. Most of the old lake bed is now intensively cultivated and supports a dense population in this significant subregion.

The evolution of the valley is extremely complex. Stream flow, valley erosion, and deposition of sediment both within the valley and in the delta have varied greatly, with alternating periods of pluvial and arid conditions in the watershed. On top of thousands of feet of earlier valley fill, an average of 30 ft/9 m of silt has been deposited since beneficial deposition began approximately ten thousand years ago.[10]

Ancient Sites. Although some major archaeological sites are found in the delta and in the desert, the vast majority are located along the valley (see Map 19.1). Few stretches of the river between Aswan and Cairo lack ruins of some period or other, and remarkable new finds have recently emerged in Luxor and on the Giza Plateau. Modern cities, some with large populations, have developed around some of the monuments, including Aswan, Luxor, Qena, Asyut, al-Mina, Helwan, and Giza. Tourist records were set in the new century (peaking at more than 14 million in 2010); although this is good for the economy, it does cause problems for the sites themselves. The tombs can be damaged by overvisiting, which raises the humidity within, leading to fungal growth that destroys wall paintings. The Supreme Council on Antiquities has made major improvements in ventilating the most popular sites, but it is necessary to limit the number of visitors to some of them and to periodically close others. Since 2011, the ancient and profitable pastime of tomb robbing has apparently been increasing as the government's political distractions have negatively impacted the security maintained at historic sites.[11]

Aswan High Dam. Inaugurated in 1971 after more than a decade of construction, the Aswan High Dam (Sadd al-Aali) has had the most momentous physical and symbolic impact of any modern project in Egypt. Transforming the country's vital resource—water—the dam impounded the world's largest reservoir, altered the river's equilibrium below Aswan, changed the rhythm of valley life, and had significant impact on crucial aspects of valley ecology. One example is the effect of the dam and lake on the Nile's silt load: now that the river empties into Lake Nubia (the Sudanese segment of Lake Nasser), the 50 mn mt of silt once spread annually along the valley and into the Mediterranean is forming a new delta spreading northward in the lake.

The constricted valley of the Nile at Aswan, where it crosses resistant granites and other basement rocks, had long been considered as an ideal site for a high dam. The original low Aswan Dam, constructed in 1902 and raised in 1912 and 1934, showed the benefits of river control and promoted plans for a higher structure. Work began on the multipurpose high dam in 1960, and specialists studied the potential environmental, historical, archaeological, and social effects of the project while it was under construction.[12]

The completed dam, power station, and reservoir are among the world's largest. A few statistics indicate the High Dam's impressive scale: it is 365 ft/111 m high, 2.36 mi/3.8 km long at the top, and 0.62 mi/1 km thick at the base; it contains seventeen times the volume of the Great Pyramid of Giza. The reservoir is 297 mi/478 km long, averaging 6 mi/10 km wide. The power station doubled Egypt's generating capacity in 1970; by the late 2000s, with numerous new thermal plants, mostly natural gas powered, the dam's 2.1 gigawatt capacity was about 14 percent of the national total (see Fig. 19.2).[13] With plans to expand nationwide electrical output to 32 gigawatts by 2013, its contribution will fall to 6.5 percent.

Pluses and Minuses. On the positive side, the dam permits flood control and, by regulating river flow for optimum benefit to downstream agriculture, allows perennial irrigation, multiple cropping, and greatly increased crop output. Water storage mitigates the effect of poor rainfall years in the areas where the Nile rises. As mentioned, it generates considerable amounts of electricity. The lake supports both commercial and sport fishing, and the lake and the dam are major tourist attractions.

Negative impacts, many of which were known from feasibility studies, are of serious concern. The water table under cultivated fields in the floodplain has risen, and poor drainage threatens salination of productive valley and delta soils; although underground drains can minimize these risks, they require major projects. Fields once naturally fertilized by the annual flood now need artificial supplements, changing the valley's chemical balance. The extent of reclamation from the project has, disappointingly, been a third less than was projected.

The now-clear river no longer feeds the delta with silt, and the Mediterranean coast has eroded as much as a mile. Erosion would become an even more serious problem if climate change raises the level of the sea. The loss of nutrient-rich materials to the sea has reduced fish life, especially sardines, up to 90

Figure 19.2 The Aswan High Dam, with large hydroelectric power station.

percent. In the exceptionally dry climate of southern Egypt, evaporation from the extensive lake surface is enormous—several hundred bn m³ each year. More manifest is the impact of periodically severe droughts in the Nile's upper catchment basin, reducing river flow. In 1988, the lake level dropped as much as 75 ft/23 m following the drought that caused widespread starvation in Ethiopia. By contrast, good rains in the late 1990s overfilled the lake. Such variations have, of course, beset the watershed throughout history. The dam mitigates but does not eliminate cyclical rainfall effects, but the balance is now so delicate that the potential scale of catastrophe is much greater.[14]

[2] Nile Delta: Lower Egypt

The Nile Delta encompasses about 8,495 mi²/22,000 km², the size of New Hampshire, and is more than half of Egypt's cultivated area (Fig. 19.3). A classic delta deposit, it was built up by continued sedimentation of silt in a former embayment on the African coast (the earlier coastline reached to present-day Cairo). Although distributaries of the river have varied in number and course over thousands of years, there are two main branches at present: the Rosetta on the west and the Damietta on the east.

Typical of deltas, the alluvial area is very flat, with a low gradient to the distributaries crossing the plain. The low mounds scattered over the surface are tells marking the sites of ancient settlements. The delta is one of the world's most intensively cultivated areas, with thousands of villages and several of Egypt's larger cities: Alexandria, an ancient city at the delta's northwest corner, Egypt's second-largest city and most important port; the large central-delta textile cities of Mahalla and Tanta; and others such as Zagazig, Rashid (Rosetta), and Damietta. Rural densities are thirty-five hundred to four thousand people per mi²/1,350–1,545 per km², among the highest in the world. Thousands of small settlements show as gray dots in the space photograph in Figure 19.3. Egypt made a

Figure 19.3 Image from space of the Nile Delta and the Sinai. The Suez Canal crosses the center of the photograph; sand-choked wadis crisscross the central Sinai. View looking southeast. Compare Fig. 2.2. (Photograph courtesy of the National Aeronautics and Space Administration)

major change in its own geographic environment with the completion of the High Dam—as mentioned above, the river no longer adds sediment to the delta with the annual flood, and the sea has already made extensive inroads along the coast. If climate change leads to higher sea levels, this low-lying area stands to be affected perhaps more than any other part of the Middle East: in

2012, about a third of the country's people lived in the governorates along the delta coast from Alexandria to Port Said.

[3] Western Desert

The huge Western Desert covers 263,000 mi^2/681,000 km^2, slightly less than Texas and more than two-thirds of Egypt's total area. Stretching west from the delta and valley, it is an extension of the Libyan Desert, itself part of the Sahara. Although the Western Desert is basically a low plateau with a cover of generally horizontal sedimentary rocks, landforms vary moderately from section to section depending on changes in rock types, wind erosion, and occasional faulting. Nubian sandstones prevail in the south but are overlain by Tertiary limestones to the north, with the extensive Great Sand Sea in the west blanketing nearly half of the region. Several strata of the Nubian Formation under much of the northern Sahara serve as aquifers, with large amounts of fossil water. Egypt plans to exploit these resources, as Libya does in its Kufrah Oasis, but budgetary constraints have limited progress.

Oases. Overlying the Nubian sandstone, the limestones form a barren plateau tableland extending eastward to the valley and sloping gently northward to the Mediterranean. Along their southern edges, they form prominent ragged escarpments 985–1,640 ft/300–500 m high. Embayments along the escarpments embrace several large semi-enclosed depressions watered by contact springs. Here lie five major oases: Siwa, al-Bahriyah, al-Farafirah, al-Dakhilah, and Kharijah (see Map 19.1). The last four inner oases lie along what is believed to be an ancient channel of the Nile and are currently being revitalized (see the "Agriculture and Water" section below). Geomorphically, the Fayyum Depression mentioned above may be included in the same category as these oases.[15]

Qattara. In the northwest is the largest of the depressions, the forbidding and uninhabited Qattara Depression, about the size of Massachusetts. With an irregular floor 436 ft/133 m below sea level in its lowest part, it has been considered for an ambitious but environmentally risky project to generate electricity. The plan, now in abeyance, proposes to pipe Mediterranean water to the depression's edge and then down through penstocks to drive turbines located halfway down the basin wall.

Mediterranean Coast. In addition to the Qattara Depression itself, towns along the northern coast became internationally known during World War II because of their roles in North African campaigns—Sallum, Sidi Barrani, Matruh, and al-Alamayn (el-Alamein). The stretch of shore west of Alexandria, toward al-Alamayn and beyond, developed in the 1990s as a mixed resort area with luxury summer villas. Such mansions were traditional in Alexandria in past decades, but these coastal estates permit extensive gardens and secluded swimming pools as well as inhibit the spread of planned resorts that might generate tourist revenues. Farther south, ongoing oil and gas exploration has opened several productive fields. In the far west and southwest is the vast emptiness of the Great Sand Sea, the Gilf Kabir, and the Uwaynat region, where stunning cave petroglyphs of boats and swimmers testify to the onetime much rainier and more peopled history of this part of the Sahara—probably as recently as ten thousand years ago.

[4] Eastern Desert

The two deserts divided by the Nile are markedly different in character. In contrast to the Western Desert just described, the Eastern Desert consists essentially of a backbone of elevated and mostly rugged mountains running parallel to and just inland from the Red Sea coast. These Red Sea Hills are an elevated and faulted edge of the Nubian Shield composed of igneous and metamorphic rocks of the basement complex (see Chap. 2). Overlapping the western and northern portions of the hills is a relatively low, maturely dissected, extensive Eocene limestone plateau. Farther to the south, the resistant crystalline hills reach 7,175 ft/2,187 m.[16]

More elevated and slightly better watered than the Western Desert, the Eastern Desert is less inhospitable and is traversed by several routes between the valley and the Red Sea. The crystalline rocks of the Red Sea Hills contain numerous mineral occurrences; gold mining is discussed below. The coast—fringed by long stretches of pristine white-sand beaches—has a number of small ports, some dating from ancient times. To promote tourism, Egypt has developed several lively resorts with such activities as swimming, diving, fishing, and seashell collecting. Farther north, the Gulf of Suez coast also has diving attractions, with mid-Gulf surrealistic off-shore oil-production platforms and flares visible from shore.

[5] Sinai

The large triangular Sinai Peninsula, 23,590 mi^2/61,100 km^2 in area, about the same size as West Virginia, belongs geomorphically to the Red Sea Hills but has been separated by sharp faulting along both sides of and beneath the Gulf of Suez (see Fig. 2.2). Such tectonics have in some stretches created structural conditions for petroleum. The southern extent of Sinai is composed of uptilted igneous and crystalline rocks that reach 8,650 ft/2,637 m in Jabal Katherina, the highest elevation in Egypt, and 7,495 ft/2,285 m in nearby Jabal Musa (Mount Sinai). Nestled in a dramatic site lies the famous Greek Orthodox Monastery of St. Katherine (Fig. 4.7), with its unique collection of ancient manuscripts. Some dating from the fifth and sixth centuries, they are now being painstakingly digitally reproduced. The monastery is an important tourist destination and in 2002 was added to the UNESCO list of World Heritage Sites.

Although the peninsula was long considered part of historic Egypt, in modern times it was formally attached to Egyptian control by the Ottoman authorities only in 1906. Once remote and isolated, Sinai has increasingly been opened since 1980. It has undergone rapid development by oil companies in the west of the peninsula and now has highly

successful resort operations—complete with airfields—on both coasts. Solid mineral mining operations are under way, and new roads have been constructed. New national parks and natural protectorates encourage international tourism, protect the unique environment, and help raise the Bedouin standard of living. Though the efforts have achieved some success, there have been problems of inadequate financing.

More recently, the vast and rugged nature of Sinai has attracted criminal and terrorist activity that police with limited resources have been unable to curtail. Large-scale smuggling into besieged Gaza, marijuana cultivation, and human trafficking and drug movements in both directions across the border with Israel have all proved profitable ventures. In August 2012, a jihadi attack on an Egyptian post on the Israeli border killed sixteen soldiers and prompted "Operation Sinai"—a month-long campaign that at least temporarily increased government control of the region. Sinai is intrinsically a difficult region to control because of its size, topography, and scattered population, and with the many security problems occupying the government since 2011 the resources needed to keep the region reasonably pacified are in short supply.

Sinai's landforms are seen in Figure 2.2: in the northern two-thirds of the peninsula, a great northward-draining limestone plateau rises from the Mediterranean coast and terminates southward in a high escarpment, Jabal al-Tih, on the northern flanks of the igneous core of Sinai. The backslope of the limestone is relatively open country that drains to the sea through numerous sand-choked tributaries, which merge into the Wadi al-Arish, the River of Egypt in the Old Testament. The northern reaches of the plateau have been crossed through the centuries by armies and migrating peoples, including Egyptian and Israeli armies in 1948–1949, 1956, 1967, and 1973. The peninsula is connected with Africa by the sandy Isthmus of

Figure 19.4 Suez Canal, with freighter in transit.

Suez, through which the Suez Canal was cut by 1869 (see Fig. 19.4 and discussion under "Waterways" below). Anchoring the northern end of the canal is Port Said on the Mediterranean, at the southern end is Suez, and midway is Ismailiyah.

EGYPTIANS AND THEIR SOCIETY

Population

With an estimated 2012 population of 83.7 million, Egypt adds 1 million people about every eight months. The population and rate of increase involve several significant geographical relationships. That so many people could mostly be supported (until recently) on such a limited amount of cultivable land is a tribute to the productivity of this great river and its people. However, increasing population is shrinking the amount of farmland per capita and, under foreseeable financial conditions, threatens to overwhelm the national capacity to supply basic services—even food and water. An increasing percentage of the food consumed is imported each year. A broad spectrum of projects to meet these daunting challenges, under way since the mid-1980s, is discussed below.

Peoples

Almost the entire population is made up of Egyptian Arabs, a mixture of the already mixed indigenous Egyptians and immigrant Arabs who entered the area during the seventh to ninth centuries. Egyptians long called the Bedouin "Arabs" and viewed the vast majority of the population as "real Egyptians." *Fellahin* (literally, "tillers of the soil") in many isolated valley villages have the features and many customs of ancient Egyptians, as seen in tomb paintings. By the late 1800s, Egypt had increasingly identified with the Arab world, inspiring some of the main currents of Arab nationalism; after the mid-1950s, Arabism's impact in turn defined Nasserist Egypt and its regional relationships.

Egypt does not show the complexity of the distinct ethnolinguistic groupings of Iraq or Iran. Most of the ethnic groups that entered Egypt in the past have long been absorbed into the population, although some small groups have emigrated en masse. Significant minorities, including Greeks and Jews going back millennia and Europeans more recently, were at home in Egypt for centuries, but many left during the Nasser period. Prominent among Egypt's growing social and economic elite, at least up until 2011, have been descendants of the former Turkish ruling class. About 90 percent of the population is Muslim—mostly Sunni with a small Shii minority (somewhat less than 1 million) that has endured some degree of discrimination. This minority seems to have become a particular target of some Salafis since 2011, partly for religious reasons, but also because of Sunni fears of increasing links between Egypt and Iran.[17] As many as 10 percent of Egypt's Muslims are affiliated with a Sufi order; the Sufi orders are similarly targeted by some Salafi elements. There is a small Bahai community; as in other regional countries, they have no legal status and now also feel threatened by the increased prominence of the Salafis.

Copts.   The largest subgroup—Copts—in the population is identified by nongenetic distinctions. By far the largest minority, they preserve an ancient Egyptian lineage, and some display physical differentiations. But their major distinction is religious, as the remnant of a Christian community that included most Egyptians prior to the Muslim conquest (see Chap. 4). The Coptic language, directly descended from Pharaonic Egyptian, is still used by the church. Firm numbers are hard to come by, but Copts probably constitute about 10 percent of the population; they are concentrated in Asyut and Minya provinces of Upper Egypt and in Cairo and Alexandria. They once

held many influential positions in the government, but, having been discriminated against since Nasserist days, they mostly are employed in the private sector now. Many have emigrated to escape the limitations on their opportunities and even periodic violence,[18] and of those who remain, many have turned inward, cutting the close day-to-day personal ties that have bound Muslims and Christians for centuries. After a hiatus of more than a decade, physical attacks against them began to rise in the late 2000s, and the pace has seemed to quicken since the overthrow of the Mubarak regime. Copts have been very vocal in the ongoing debate about the relationship between religion (i.e., Islam) and the state in the new republic.

Nubians.   The Nubians are the second-largest minority: they number possibly 200,000, now concentrated around Kom Ombo, north of Aswan. Formerly, they lived in villages stretching south from Aswan into the Sudan, but they were resettled in the early 1960s as their homes were submerged in Lake Nasser after completion of the High Dam. Although compensated for their lost property and given new lands and new homes, they have found the dislocation and loss of their homeland culturally disruptive.

Bedouin.   Egyptian Bedouin have been moving toward sedentarization for more than a century. The largest concentration of those who follow a more or less traditional lifestyle is found in the rugged Sinai;[19] they are often treated with suspicion by the government and the general Egyptian population as security risks and smugglers. The Jabaliyya and associated tribes in the southern Sinai have been closely involved in tourism and other forms of economic development in the St. Katherine area. A small Bedouin tribe, the Maaza, with probably 1,000 members, wanders the hills and wadis of the Eastern Desert.

Very much a long-neglected minority, the Bedouin have become much more active in pursuing their citizenship rights since the downfall of the Mubarak regime. While Sinai tourism has provided employment to some of them, it has also marginalized their traditional way of life. Criminal and jihadi activities and the consequent government police and military reactions have trapped them between the opposing sides. In 2012, there were some signs of recognition on the part of the newly elected government that the active cooperation of the Bedouin would be essential to regaining control over the Sinai and the borders with Gaza and Israel. The alternative could be a growing alliance between many Bedouin and jihadi groups.[20]

Jews. Although the Bible recounts that Hebrews lived in Egypt in serfdom as *Bnai Yisrael* (Children of Israel) in about the thirteenth century BCE, they are also portrayed as having left in the emigration described in the book of Exodus. A thousand years later, in Ptolemaic times, Jews settled in Alexandria, founding a community that expanded with the arrival of Spanish and central European Jews. Zionism, the later emergence of the state of Israel, and periodic wars between Israel and Egypt created a backlash against Egyptian Jews, most of whom gradually emigrated to Israel and elsewhere. Of about 80,000 Jews in 1947, no more than 100 remain in Egypt.

Others. Several thousand nomadic Beja people (non-Arabs) migrate into and out of southeastern Egypt from and into northeastern Sudan. A few other small groups are also elements in the mixture of peoples. Some 25,000 Berbers are found in the Western Desert, especially in the touristically significant Siwa Oasis in the northwest of the country, an area they have inhabited for many centuries. Berber activists have pressed for inclusion in the national dialogue under way since 2011.

The pluralistic coexistence in Egyptian society fractured during the revolutionary Nasser period, and the number of Westerners decreased at that time. However, the expatriate community was again expanding by the 1980s and by the early 2010s included thousands of oil and gas technicians, general contractors, aid personnel, diplomats, and consultants. Several thousand Armenians and a small number of Greeks live mostly in Cairo and Alexandria.

Fundamentalists, Jihadists, Terrorists

Egypt was further fragmented by increased Islamic fundamentalism beginning in the late 1960s. Sociopolitical readjustments under Sadat contributed to the growth of a number of militant opposition groups. The older Muslim Brotherhood (Ikhwan al-Muslimun), founded in 1928, originally agitated for an ultraorthodox society and government. The Brotherhood moderated its methods, but as it did more extreme and clandestine associations emerged. The most violent and secretive of the groups styled itself al-Jihad (literally, Arabic "struggle," often translated as "holy war"); it was this group that assassinated Sadat.

During the 1970s and 1980s, Copts were attacked by militants, evoking retaliation by Coptic students. The regime largely suppressed these outbreaks, but terrorist actions against the government, often in the form of attacks on tourists—with the aim of weakening the economy and therefore the government—became critical in the 1990s. Scores of incidents left more than 1,000 dead, including security personnel, terrorists, and foreigners; 20,000 accused were imprisoned and dozens executed. The culmination was a Jamaat al-Islamiyya atrocity in November 1997 at the Temple of Hatshepsut near Luxor (see Fig. 3.2); 58 European and Japanese tourists and 4 Egyptians were massacred before 6 perpetrators were shot. The vital tourist industry and the livelihoods of millions of Egyptians who rely upon it were devastated for nearly a year before greatly increased government security gradually restored confidence.

Refugees

Egypt is also the temporary home of a considerable number of refugees; the exact number is hard to pin down, but estimates ranged as high as 3 million in the new century. By far the largest contingent are Sudanese, many fleeing from long years of conflict in that country's southern and Darfur regions, but others are economically motivated migrants. There are also notable numbers of Palestinians, Ethiopians, Eritreans, and West Africans. At one point in the 2000s, as many as 100,000 Iraqis fleeing the chaos of their postinvasion homeland may have been in Egypt.[21] As the Syrian civil war intensified in 2012, refugees from the fighting arrived in increasing numbers; often, they have family ties to Egypt.

SETTLEMENTS

Villages. In its population distribution, Egypt has historically and traditionally been predominantly a land of small villages. Despite steadily increasing urbanization, thousands of these are still scattered the length of the valley and in the delta; many villages, however, are densely settled to minimize encroachment on agricultural land. Valley villages are often just beyond the edge of irrigation, in order to conserve irrigable land. Most of these villages are linear in morphology. Until recently, houses were constructed of mud from the clay-silt once in plentiful supply along the Nile or from nearby canals. Two or three villages can be seen from any given point, and there is a regular pattern of market towns that are service centers for surrounding villages. In turn, cities of 150,000–200,000 population have evolved every 40–50 mi/ 65–80 km as hierarchical central places.

Villages in the delta, in contrast, display a nucleated morphology and, in the absence of the stone available on the valley fringes, were even more likely to be constructed of mud brick. Obviously, as rapidly increasing population meant greater demand for housing, the use of mud from nearby fields turned once productive plots into barren pits. A farmer could earn more from the sale of the top 3.3 ft/1 m of his land for making mud bricks than he could earn from the sale of the land. So much arable land was being lost that in 1982, a law was passed prohibiting mud construction.

Cities.   The dominance of the village has been diminishing since the early 1950s, and the urban percentage has increased from less than one-third in 1950 to 45 percent by 2010. But despite the marked growth of several cities, especially Cairo, social structure retains village roots more than urban migration would indicate. Increasingly hundreds of thousands of landless and displaced *fellahin* have flooded into the cities since the 1950s, often grouping themselves by place of origin, thus preserving village identity. Indeed, this kind of urbanization, the virtual displacement of village to city, has been referred to as the "ruralization" of Cairo. Incoming migrants typically have little education, almost no money, and few relevant skills.[22]

Cairo has for many years been the largest city in the Middle East and, indeed, in all of Africa. During some recent years, it has added 1 million people annually; by 2012, the population of the Greater Cairo Region (GCR), plus fringe suburbs, was probably close to 19 million, about a quarter of Egypt's total. In contrast to the city's impressively modern front yard along the Nile in Garden City, Zamalak, and Qasr al-Nil (Fig. 19.5), seething squatter slums lie to the east and west. By some estimates, as many as 500,000 poor Cairenes live in the tombs of the City of

Figure 19.5 View down the Nile River at Cairo, with major bridges in foreground and buildings of Zamalak in center distance.

the Dead, the extensive cemeteries on Cairo's eastern outskirts.

Although unable to supply adequate municipal services, the government has made major efforts to clean up the slums and to reduce the serious pollution from automobiles, potteries, cement factories, and lead smelters. An especially notable transformation of the inner city opened 74 ac/30 ha of the diversified and attractive al-Azhar Park for public enjoyment in 2004. The $30 million project removed eighty thousand truckloads of debris from a centuries-old rubbish heap, uncovering in the process a section of the medieval wall. Traffic in the Central Business District was becoming virtually immobile until a new French-engineered subway system, opened in 1987 and considerably expanded during the following years, appreciably relieved surface circulation. Plans for an Alexandrian metro had not advanced much beyond the talking stage in 2012.

With nearly half of its population urbanized, Egypt has four cities with populations larger than 1 million, more than thirty-five exceeding 100,000, and more than twice as many with 50,000 to 100,000 inhabitants. Growth far outruns the census taker. With Cairo at the junction of valley and delta, relentless urban sprawl by it and other large cities mostly located in the delta consumes agricultural land at an alarming rate. As Cairo has grown historically, new urban quarters have expropriated more and more agricultural land to the south in the valley and to the north in the delta. As early as the 1960s, the government has had some success in steering urbanization along an east-west axis—that is, out into the deserts well away from Cairo and from farmland. At first, people were reluctant to relocate to these satellite cities, but as amenities, transport links to Cairo, and, more important perhaps, jobs became available in new localities like

Tenth of Ramadan City, Sixth of October City, and Sadat City, they became much more attractive alternatives to the crowded and more expensive established parts of Cairo.[23] Conversely, in areas where progress on developing infrastructure and services has been uneven, many migrants prefer living in a Cairo slum with old village friends and relatives to adopting an unfamiliar lifestyle in a strange environment.[24]

CHANGING ECONOMIC PATTERNS

An Economic Perspective

The historical riches of Egypt are proverbial—the productivity of the soil, the creativity of its artisans, the gold from Pharaonic and Ptolemaic tombs, and the transit trade between Red Sea entrepôts and Mediterranean coastal states. However, now an ever-increasing population presses on the maximum limits of even these fabled resources. Agricultural productivity is many times greater today than even a few generations ago, but demography demands even more. Once a net food exporter, then at least self-sufficient, Egypt now imports much of what it needs—well over half by 2012. The UNDP's Human Development Index (HDI), used to compare living standards globally, in 2013 ranked Egypt 112th out of 186 countries and 14th of the 17 countries (Palestine included) in this book. Though its relative placement regarding the index has remained low, the value of Egypt's HDI has increased by about 63 percent since 1980 on the strength of gains in the health and education components of the index. When the same calculations were done on a national basis, the urban governorates (Port Said, Suez, Alexandria, and Cairo) topped the list, while those in rural lower Egypt were at the bottom; the difference between the highest HDI (Port Said) and the lowest (Fayoum) was 12.6 percent. By the standards of the more broadly based Prosperity Index from the

Legatum Institute, Egypt ranked 106th of 142 countries globally and 10th regionally.[25]

Revolutionary Reforms. The political revolution of 1952 brought a correlative economic revolution. Junta efforts included land reform, controls over agriculture, nationalization of industries and institutions (notably of the Suez Canal in 1956), sequestration of foreign businesses and agencies, an inflow of bilateral and multilateral loans and grants, and construction of the Aswan High Dam. Progress toward these well-intentioned goals was impeded by administrative problems, bureaucratic inefficiency, and Egypt's military buildup and three wars with Israel. Nasser's insistence on state management repelled both foreign and domestic investment. Originally, the statist approach had popular appeal, since land reform, widespread nationalization, and tight control over the economy broke the power of large landowners, foreign capitalists, and wealthy Egyptians.

Nasser's revolution was, indeed, a watershed event in modern Egyptian history. Some reforms brought long-term benefits, but many apparent gains soon revealed serious flaws. For example, his "social contract" improved the lot of the average Egyptian, but only through price controls, heavy subsidies, and unselective guaranteed employment. Such broad paternalism and free university education, along with ensuring jobs to all graduates, seemed progressive. However, the bureaucracy and large public-sector enterprises were soon loaded with redundant employees, depressing the wage scale; the quality of education was degraded, and a downward economic spiral ensued.

Reforming the Reforms. Sadat reversed the trend, opening the economy's doors with his moderate *infitah* ("openness") policy of 1974, which reduced many restrictions. However, conditions in Egypt and in the Middle East as a whole countered many of his goals, resulting in deindustrialization and increased indebtedness. Falling incomes and government austerity measures led to riots in Aswan and Alexandria, intensifying the immediacy of his initiative to settle with Israel and request the contingent greater aid from the United States in order to realize a "peace dividend." After Sadat's assassination, Mubarak cautiously opened the economy further. During the 1990s, the macroeconomy enjoyed a significant turnaround and became increasingly globalized. Some state-owned enterprises were privatized, government spending was reined in, and the financial sector was slowly rationalized. Generally, the environment the private sector faced improved noticeably.

In the new century, some of these reforms—floating the pound, simplifying import-export procedures, reducing personal and corporate tax rates, privatizing state-owned enterprises, cutting subsidies, and making it easier and more attractive for foreign investment—started to pay off, at least on the level of national statistics. Annual growth surged to 7 percent or better on average through 2008, before falling back to 4.7 percent in 2009 with the global recession, as tourism and Suez Canal receipts slumped. With tourism sharply in decline and normal economic activity temporarily interrupted after the onset of political turmoil in 2011, GDP growth for the year fell to about 1.2 percent—well below the population growth rate. Some recovery came in 2012, but the government's goal of 4.5 percent was certainly not reachable.

By the late 1990s, tourism was the leading foreign-exchange earner, and although it plummeted after the Hatshepsut's Temple massacre, following 9/11, and again with the invasion of Iraq, it has recovered as a major component of GDP. Tourist arrivals peaked in 2010 at 14.7 million—second in the region after Turkey—but the demonstrations beginning in early 2011 dropped the sector sharply for the rest of the year, with arrivals off by 33 percent and earnings by 28 percent. There

was a definite rebound in 2012, but not yet back to the level of two years earlier. Remittances from the 2 million or more Egyptians working abroad, mostly in the Arabian Peninsula, peaked in 2008, fell in 2009 with the onset on the global economic downturn, but recovered in 2010 to an estimated $7.72 billion, equivalent to about 4 percent of GDP. Suez Canal revenues surged to an all-time high of $5.2 billion in 2011, an increase of 8.7 percent over the previous year, despite a slight decline in the number of vessels passing through the waterway.[26]

Agriculture and Water

The Nile Valley has supported flourishing agriculture for more than eighty-five hundred years, and much of the valley and delta was under cultivation soon after the union of Upper and Lower Egypt in about 3000 BCE. When cultivable area had been cleared of forest and brush, increasing portions of what is now cropland were farmed using the natural flood-irrigation system that was dominant until after 1800 CE.

The irrigation system so long practiced was basically simple. It utilized the runoff from the heavy summer rains in East African highlands, which poured down the Nile and raised the water level 20–25 ft/6–8 m, covering the entire floodplain with several feet of silt-laden floodwaters. When these receded after several weeks, the silt loam soils, built up by past floods, were water soaked and were also covered with fresh millimeters of nutrient-rich silt. Thus, valley soils naturally were watered, fertilized, and renewed annually without human intervention. Crops were planted to mature before the soil dried out months later. Carefully sited perennial tree and vine crops—somewhat lower than village locations—were also cultivated; only one crop per flood season could be harvested. In later centuries, water was retained in basins to prolong irrigation; still later, canals were installed by Pharaonic engineers. As experience passed down generations, the *fellahin* of the valley became expert hydraulic farmers, and their traditional culture was as immutable as the annual flood.

Beyond the Valley and Delta.   For centuries, virtually all production was restricted to the annual flood area. Not until application of modern technology in the mid-1800s was the irrigable area significantly increased— through construction of barrages at the head of the delta in 1860 and later at Asyut. Completion of the first Aswan Dam in 1902, and later additions to its height, extended perennial irrigation. The High Dam was the single most momentous element furthering irrigation and attendant year-round cropping virtually everywhere in the "old" settled area; despite bringing several major problems, the dam set the stage for the potential engineering of major "new" settlement areas.

The Tahrir (Liberation) Project west of the delta in the 1950s failed to meet expectations, but lessons learned offered hope for other schemes. Most ambitious is the New Valley Project (al-Wadi al-Jadid) for revitalizing the string of once productive and even wealthy oases of the Western Desert described earlier. Discovery of a Roman-era necropolis in Bahriyah revealed evidence of a thriving community two thousand years ago that prospered by making wine from dates and grapes.[27] After twenty years of planning and delay, agriculture has been vigorously expanded by using deep Nubian Formation groundwater; production focuses on high-value crops like dates, olives, fruits, and vegetables for Cairo and other urban markets. Complementary infrastructure has accompanied crop expansion, with roads, electricity, schools, and housing for new settlers, plus hotels for the growing number of tourists.

Toshka.   Designed to considerably enhance the New Valley was the grandiose Toshka (or Tushka) Canal Project begun in 1997 after

several years of planning. The basic premise of the project is to make better use of the waters stored behind the High Dam in Lake Nasser. A huge pumping station inaugurated in 2005 lifts water 175 ft/53 m from the lake to the canal, which is concrete lined and designed to extend 150 mi/240 km northward to Kharijah Oasis and eventually on to the other oases. An estimated $80 billion was needed for the project, including all the infrastructure needed to support a projected population of 3 million in the New Valley drawing their livelihoods from 3.5 mn ac/1.4 mn ha of reclaimed irrigated land; 2020 was set as the target date for project completion.

From its inception, the project was greeted with strongly expressed skepticism on the part of the donors that the government wanted to tap for funding the initial stages, hoping that grants and concessional loans would prompt private investors, especially from the Arab world, to participate in the endeavor. The skeptics (especially the US Agency for International Development, Egypt's biggest donor) argued that the government's expectations were highly optimistic and that Egypt was already close to using all its available Nile water, with little to spare for the New Valley. In 2012, the project was well behind schedule, and the canal had yet to reach its planned destination.

Considered to be a much more realistic scheme has been the North Sinai Agricultural Development Project, which takes water from the Nile before it empties into the Mediterranean and siphons it under the Suez Canal, delivering it on into Sinai using the Peace (al-Salam) Canal. Plans call for cultivated area of 415,000 ac/168,000 ha. In 2012, the project's supporting infrastructure was reported to be 95 percent complete.

Crops

Cropping patterns are complicated by two factors: cultivation of two or three crops a year on many plots and yield differences between "new lands" and "old lands." In terms of

Figure 19.6 Typical scene in the timeless Nile Valley in Upper Egypt: intensive cultivation in the fertile alluvial soils, date-palm grove and fruit trees, sugarcane, village under the shade of trees, and *fellahin* still hand-laboring as they have for centuries.

both area and weight, clover (*berseem,* cultivated for forage) is the leading crop; cereals—wheat, maize, and rice—claim 40 to 50 percent of cropped area. The new high-yield wheat varieties have increased yield nearly 50 percent since 1985. Cotton of all types is the leading nonfood crop, and sugarcane keeps its place as an important crop. Fruits such as citrus, dates, and grapes and a wide variety of winter and summer vegetables vie with rice in area, and all these crops are important exports. Figure 19.6 shows a typical mix of crops in the valley. From the early 1960s to the early 2010s, Egypt saw an increase of nearly 90 percent in food production per capita, despite already realizing fairly high crop yields during the base period.[28] The case has been made that there is still plenty of room for increasing crop yields in Egypt through greater efficiencies in the use of inputs (especially water) and that such gains directly and positively impact poverty reduction efforts.[29]

Cotton. Egyptian long-staple cotton has a long history as a premium product on world markets since its development by a French agronomist in the 1820s. Now grown in many other places, still a third of the world's crop originates in Egypt, where it is grown in the central delta. Government extension work and controls ensure quality and more realistic pricing, and production and marketing policies have encouraged farmers to plant more. In world markets, the long staple faces marketing challenges, partly because of subsidies given to the production of Pima grade—its most important competitor—in the United States. After a dip in planting in 2009 to the lowest level in decades, there has been a sharp recovery, despite the disturbances elsewhere in the national economy. Over the longer term, it makes more economic and commercial sense to divert the crop into the domestic manufacture of high-quality textiles and finished products, the export of which would capture for Egypt much more value added, while increasing jobs and family incomes.

Livestock

Livestock have been an integral element on virtually every Egyptian farm since ancient times. Tomb paintings depict the role of cattle and other animals in early agriculture, and the cow and the bull were venerated in the ancient pantheon. Sheep, goats, and ducks have also been of prime importance for more than forty-five hundred years, as has the donkey. Cattle, buffalo, and donkeys are still multipurpose farm animals, pulling plows and carts, carrying loads (the donkey serving also for individual transportation), supplying manure for fields and fuel, and furnishing milk. Camels came later and are still common. The Indian buffalo (*gamus* or *gamush*) was imported in the Middle Ages and is now the most numerous farm animal. It has adapted well along the river and canals, yielding milk, meat, manure, and hides and serving as a plow animal.

Fisheries

Fishery production in Egypt was 1.30 mn mt in 2010, well surpassing that of Turkey, formerly the regional leader. The fish catch more than doubled over the previous decade, with Lake Nasser replacing the Mediterranean as the main source, and it contributed about 20 percent of the country's consumption of animal protein. But in 2012, dead fish in aquaculture pens in the delta raised fears that toxicity in the river from agricultural and industrial runoff was rising.

Industry

Oil.   The first oil well in Egypt was drilled in 1886, although commercial production came only in 1913. After World War II, several companies, most of them American, conducted explorations, primarily under concession agreements. Operations in Egypt—which is not an OPEC member—expanded in the

1960s, and production peaked in 1995 at 992,000 bpd. Output has slowly but steadily dropped each year since then; in 2012, it was about 675,000 bpd. Sorely in need of economic stimulus and export products, the country benefited from increasing petroleum production during the 1980s, and the growing industry has had a major impact on the export sector. By 1981–1982, oil was the leading export, and, with some variations, petroleum and petroleum products have remained the most important exports into the 2010s.

The most important oil-field developments have been in and along the Gulf of Suez (see Map 19.1), which still supplies half of the country's production. Intensive exploration in the Western Desert has made new discoveries, especially of gas and condensates, some of world class. But in the late 2000s, rising domestic consumption caught up with production, and Egypt's days as a net oil exporter were clearly drawing to a close, barring major new discoveries or a reversal of consumption trends.

Natural Gas.   Whatever may result from continued intense exploration for oil, discoveries and output of nonassociated natural gas have increased dramatically—offering not only enhanced export earnings but also some reversal of oil-consumption patterns, with gas substituting for oil in some domestic sectors. Gas reserves in 1991 were 12.4 tn ft^3/0.35 m^3, up by 2012 to 77.2 tn ft^3/2.19 m^3. These are the largest reserves in the eastern Mediterranean, the third largest in Africa, and equivalent to about one-fourth those of the well-endowed United States. When major gas fields were found in three different Tertiary zones in the northern delta, offshore exploration opened several more major fields. Thus, the northern delta and adjacent offshore area, now a world-class gas province (indicating still greater reserves), possess more than two-thirds of Egypt's reserves.

By using gas for power plants, industry, and even for vehicles, the country can export more of its crude oil and product. With resources so plentiful, it also looked for markets for gas and liquefied natural gas (LNG) both among its neighbors and farther afield. An underwater pipeline to Aqabah, Jordan, began operation in 2003. The line now extends northward to Amman and Syria, where deliveries began in 2008 and to Lebanon in 2009. Turkey and Syria agreed in 2008 to tie the pipeline by 2011 into the existing Turkish network that is linked to European markets. With increased terrorist activity in the Sinai, the pipeline has been attacked and damaged on a regular basis. Another underwater line connects al-Arish to Ashkelon in Israel; exports to the Jewish state quickly became a politically sensitive subject. Despite increased opposition to the exports after Israel's campaign in Gaza in early 2009, by midyear the two parties announced agreement on a revised pricing schedule, and pumping at the rate of 60 bcf annually commenced. However, in April 2012, shipments were suspended, the culmination of a dispute with both political and commercial underpinnings. Two LNG export facilities on the Mediterranean coast were operative in the late 2000s, and exports, to Spain, began in 2004. A third installation was scheduled to come on line in 2011. In order to utilize the country's natural gas in additional ways, Shell has proposed building a gas-to-liquids processing plant, to be colocated with an LNG facility.

Egypt was credited in 2012 with having oil reserves of 4.4 bn bbl. About half of the oil production is from the Gulf of Suez, the oldest fields, and most of the remainder from the Western Desert. Exploration and production are carried out by more than thirty European and North American companies, particularly BP, British Gas, Agip (Italy), and Shell, under contract with the government, usually with the Egyptian General Petroleum Company.

Domestic supplies of petro-products have been experiencing periodic shortages since the late 2000s, leading to outbreaks of social unrest. The problems are related to infrastructural and institutional deficiencies from wellhead to retail outlets that require considerable amounts of investment funds—another problem now confronting the new regime.[30]

Downstream Facilities. Two Egyptian pipelines are noteworthy. The 200-mi/320-km Sumed (Suez-Mediterranean) line, from Ayn Sukhnah on the Gulf of Suez to Sidi Krir west of Alexandria, is a dual 42-in/107-cm line with an original capacity of 1.6 mn bpd, increased to 2.4 mn bpd in 1995 and 3.1 mn bpd by 2007. Egypt owns it jointly with Saudi Arabia, Kuwait, the UAE, and Qatar. It was opened in 1977 to bypass the Suez Canal, both because the largest tankers exceeded the capacity of the canal and because the canal had been shut down between 1967 and 1975 after the June War with Israel. As a competitor to the canal, the pipeline offers discounts to the largest class of tankers offloading and reloading at its terminals. The second line, opened in 1981, extends from Ras Shuqayr on the Gulf of Suez to refineries at Suez and Cairo. Ras Shuqayr is the export terminal for the adjacent offshore fields.

Of nine refineries processing a total of 726,250 bpd in 2009, the largest are at Mostorod near Cairo and at Suez, each with a throughput of more than 145,000 bpd. Noteworthy among refineries newly constructed is the MIDOR refinery in Alexandria, opened in 2001, with a throughput of 100,000 bpd. Originally an Egyptian-Israeli joint venture, it is now an all-Egyptian operation. Principal petrochemical plants are near Alexandria and Suez, and as gas production increases more such plants, as well as LNG trains, can be expected. Two large joint-venture LNG plants came on line in the early 2000s to produce export gas for the European market, one at Damietta on the eastern side of the delta in 2004 and a second at Idku on the western side in 2005. In the late 2000s, Egypt was exporting almost 30 percent of its gas output by pipeline or as LNG. Gas exports have been gradually squeezed by increased domestic demand, and in 2012 they were halted, not only to Israel, as mentioned earlier, but also to Jordan and Spain.

Other Minerals.   Contemporary commercial solid-mineral mining is extensive and involves a considerable range of minerals, but it is only a modest contributor to the national economy. Iron ore, manganese ore, and phosphate rock are the most important nonfuel minerals produced in Egypt. Iron ore from Aswan was used in the Helwan mill, south of Cairo, from 1958 until the mid-1970s; however, somewhat better and more plentiful sedimentary ore from al-Bahriyah Oasis now feeds the mill via a specially constructed railway. A recently discovered high-grade iron ore deposit 50 mi/80 km southeast of Aswan supplies a new Aswan Iron and Steel Company complex. Its products will include seamless tubing for export to the regional oil industry. By the late 2000s, a mini gold rush was in progress in the Eastern Desert inland from Marsa Alam. An Australian-Egyptian company, Centamin Egypt, after reopening Pharaonic workings, claimed that these had barely scratched the surface in antiquity and, in 2007, that it had discovered reserves estimated at more than 10 million troy ounces (31.1 mt). An underground mining contract was awarded in early 2009.

Phosphate rock is mined near Isna (south of Luxor), near Bur Safajah on the Red Sea, and near al-Kharijah Oasis. Production averaged 2.2 mn mt in the late 2000s, about 40 percent that of Jordan, the region's largest producer. Other nonmetallic minerals produced were of relatively low value and included large tonnages of gypsum, fire clay, kaolin, and salt, as well as many types of dimension stone, including Aswan granite. As is true elsewhere in the region, cement production is a major industry. Egypt's first coal mine

opened in 1995 at al-Maghara in the northern Sinai, and despite early prospects it and the national total production in the late 2000s was only 75,000 mt/yr.[31] The coal has been used to fire thermal power plants, but with the growing use of natural gas for this purpose in the 2000s, coal production decreased.

Other Manufacturing.   Egypt experienced modest early industrialization under Muhammad Ali in the nineteenth century but then stagnated for decades. Development was uneven after the 1952 revolution. Unskilled labor supply was adequate, and skilled labor was moderately available; however, capital was limited, as were planning and management skills. Petroleum development, the benefits of the High Dam, *infitah* policies, strong donor support, and realistic economic and political policies after 1991 finally stimulated significant and consistent growth of the sector.

However, the policies of industrial development under state socialism meant that virtually all large and medium-size establishments were in the public sector. The most important establishments were saddled with bloated employee rolls, bureaucratic mismanagement, and inefficient administration. Economic reform in the 1990s had as one major aim their privatization, and 193 out of 314 had been shifted into the private sector by the early 2000s. Another goal is geographical diversification. At present, nearly half of Egypt's manufacturing is centered in the Shubra al-Khaymah industrial area north of Cairo and in Helwan south of the capital (Fig. 19.7), leading to serious air and water pollution in the Greater Cairo Region. Major industrial areas outside the GCR are Nag Hammadi (west of Qena, processing imported bauxite to produce aluminum), Tanta and Muhallah al-Kubra (textiles) in the delta, Alexandria (refineries, petrochemicals, iron and steel, shipyards), Suez (fertilizers), and several mid-Nile cities. Medium-size armament industries, including the assembly of

Figure 19.7 Interior view of a steel mill in Helwan, south of Cairo, one of Egypt's many varied industrial facilities. (John Riddle, Saudi Aramco World/SAWDIA)

jeeps, tanks, helicopters, and other weaponry, are located in Lower Egypt. By 2012, industry supplied about 38 percent of GDP and employed 17 percent of the workforce.

Traditional private-sector establishments are small and often artisan in character. They are located primarily in and around Cairo, especially in the old *suqs* of the Muski and Khan al-Khalili, but also in other main cities and towns. They produce food products, specialty textiles, leather goods, jewelry, artistic glass objects, copper and brass ornamental and utilitarian items, and furniture and other wood products, including intricately inlaid boxes and other household items.

QIZs. Under a 2004 agreement with the United States, Egypt can designate within its territory "Qualifying Industrial Zones" (QIZs) that then enjoy duty-free status in exporting zone production to the United States. By 2011, about seven hundred factories with one hundred thousand workers were operating in numerous places in the Cairo, Alexandria, Delta, and Suez Canal regions, with exports approaching the $1 billion level. Egypt was reported to be negotiating with the United States in 2012 with a view toward increasing the Egyptian content in exported goods.[32]

Transportation

Roads. With settlement being intense in the Nile Valley and Delta, transportation by river, road, and railroad is equally concentrated (see Map 19.1). On paved highways extending the full length of the Nile Valley between Cairo and Aswan, donkey carts share space with buses and trucks, but there are only limited numbers of long-distance travelers in private automobiles. Major highways also extend from Cairo to Alexandria, other points in the northern delta, and now along the valley's desert fringe. At right angles to the valley-delta routes is the Mediterranean coastal highway between the Libyan border on the west and the Israeli border on the east. Successive military operations in Sinai, and increasing development of the area, have prompted the construction of transpeninsular and circumpeninsular roads there, opening an area isolated as late as the 1950s.

A north-south Red Sea coastal highway connects Suez and the Sudan border, accessing burgeoning beach resorts and secondary ports and relieving traffic on valley routes. The Suez Canal is paralleled on both sides by roads linked by the Ahmad Hamdi Tunnel under and a high bridge over the canal. The main north-south routes, in the valley and along the mainland and Sinai coasts, are connected by several east-west roads. In 2012, it was reported that a $3 billion 31.1-mi/50-km causeway tying Egypt and Saudi Arabia across the Strait of Tiran was progressing through planning stages.

Railroads.   Railways are heavily used by passengers, giving Egypt half the total passenger kilometers in the Middle East. Indicative of the pressure of the large, highly concentrated population on facilities, trains into and out of Cairo are often so overloaded that hundreds of passengers must either stand inside or cling precariously to the outside of trains. This hazard has been partially relieved by the new mass-transit system between al-Marg, a northern suburb of Cairo, and Helwan to the south. A second metro line connects Giza and downtown Cairo; a third line is partly in operation, and an extension to the airport is planned.

Some tourists travel between Cairo and Aswan one way by air, the other by rail in order to enjoy at close hand scenes of everyday village and city life along the length of the valley. Railways share transport of low-priority heavy freight with large cargo *faluqas* (feluccas) on the Nile. A major construction project opened a 620-mi/1,000-km rail line in 1996 between Safajah on the Red Sea and al-Kharijah Oasis; it carries phosphate rock

from Abu Tartu, just west of al-Kharijah, and bauxite for processing at Nag Hammadi. Double-tracking from Asyut to Aswan was completed in 2004.

Waterways.   In addition to the Suez Canal, Egypt has 2,175 mi/3,500 km of inland waterways, half along the river itself and half along several major canals, especially in the delta. Sailing the Nile was the only north-south method of travel until completion of the railway to Aswan and later construction of a drivable road. The river below Aswan to the Mediterranean is still used by hundreds of the typical Nile sailing boats, *faluqas,* which are a practical and inexpensive means of north-south shipment of heavy and nonperishable goods. On the picturesque stretch between Aswan and Luxor, rich in ancient monuments, more than 325 sizable cruise boats carry tourists on pleasant multiday trips.

Since its opening in 1869, the Suez Canal has been both a significant symbol and an integral economic element for Egypt (see Fig. 19.4). Operated by an Anglo-French company until dramatically nationalized by Nasser in 1956, the canal quickly became Egypt's leading foreign-exchange earner. When tanker traffic and revenues steadily declined for various reasons, the canal's earnings also declined, but they then rose to an all-time high of $5.1 billion in 2007–2008, when an average of 58 vessels transited it each day; with the onset of global recession and the threat from Somali pirates, revenues fell in 2008–2009 by 7.2 percent, and the decline continued through the end of 2009, when the average daily number of transits dropped to 47. It was closed by the 1967 Arab-Israeli war but was reopened in 1975, then dredged in 1980 to a draft of 52 ft/ 16 m to permit transit of larger tankers. By the end of 2009, dredging to a depth of 66 ft/ 20.1 m was completed, and to increase the pass-through rate, further widening is under consideration. (See additional details under "Strategic Straits," in Chap. 8.)

Ports. Alexandria, Egypt's most important port, was founded by Alexander the Great, and for much of twenty-three centuries it has functioned as one of the largest and busiest general-cargo ports in the eastern Mediterranean. It fills so many functions—port, resort, industrial center, commercial center—that traffic is increasingly being spun off to satellite facilities in Dikhaylah and Marsa Matruh to the west and in Damietta to the east. Port Said and Suez, at opposite ends of the Suez Canal, are thriving industrial centers as well as major ports; they enjoy free zones, as do Alexandria and Damietta. A new state-of-the-art port under private management opened at Ayn Sukhnah in 2003–2004 to handle much of the maritime trade with South and East Asia. Located 25 mi/40 km south of Port Suez on the mainland coast of the Gulf of Suez, it is also the head of the Sumed crude-oil pipeline. As mentioned above, Safajah on the Red Sea has export facilities for phosphates.

Air Transportation. The state-owned airline, Egypt Air, was founded in 1932 and operated for many years as Misr Air (Arabic *Misr* = Egypt). It flies an extensive network from the United States and western Europe to the Far East and Africa, operating more than fifty jet aircraft; by several criteria it ranks in the top six lines in the region. Along with its civilian fleet, Egypt has a large air force and maintains a large number of medium-size combined civilian and military airports. Cairo's airport is one of the four busiest in the Middle East, with many international connections as well as frequent flights to the main tourist centers in Upper Egypt and Sinai—Luxor, Aswan, and Sharm al-Shaykh.

RELATIONS

Egypt's relations, both with its neighbors and with the major powers, have been of crucial importance since the late 1940s.[33] Under Nasser, relations were confrontational and erratic. Under Sadat, they involved complete reversals in policies with Israel, the Soviet Union, and the United States. They then stabilized and followed a fairly consistent policy under Mubarak from the 1980s. With the new elected Islamist-led government, they are clearly again in a state of transition.

When President Sadat turned away from the Soviets in the early 1970s, established close ties with the United States, and signed a peace treaty with Israel in 1979, these were watershed events in Egyptian relations. His Israeli policy prompted most Arab countries to break diplomatic relations and precipitated Egypt's expulsion from the Arab League. Its regional role, however, was and continues to be too vital to be denied, and by 1989 it had been readmitted to the Arab League and reestablished relations with most league members. However, its Israeli ties continued to complicate its intra-Arab links.

Within the Region. In the regional reaction to Iraq's invasion of Kuwait in 1990, Egypt led the opposition to the incursion and vigorously supported the international coalition to liberate Kuwait. In addition to its critical political efforts, Egypt contributed thirty-five thousand men and a significant amount of equipment—making it the third-largest contributor after the United States and Saudi Arabia—to coalition forces. But, even with the regional tensions, Egypt's overall internal situation markedly improved with the financial support of the United States.

Arab States. Egypt's relations with its upstream neighbor, the Sudan, have been important since the dawn of history. But in recent decades, these have been troubled, even stormy at times—as when Sudan sided with Iraq after Saddam's invasion of Kuwait and when Egypt accused Khartoum of complicity in an assassination attempt on Mubarak in 1995. With its other immediate Arab neighbor, Libya, relations have been even more spasmodic, largely as a result of the quixotic nature of its former leader Qadhafi; both Egypt and Libya, of course, have experienced major regime changes since 2011. Under Nasser, Egypt often interfered in Iraq, with coup attempts by Nasserist elements against more nationalistic Iraqi regimes. Egypt did support Iraq in its war with Iran, but actively opposed its invasion of Kuwait. Egypt was quietly critical of the US-led invasion in 2003; afterward, it renewed diplomatic relations with the post-Saddam government.

Iran.   The Islamic Republic broke relations after Sadat offered refuge to the dying shah in 1980. Iran's activities since then have added to Egypt's uneasiness, and in recent years, like other predominantly Sunni Arab states, Egypt has been concerned about the possibility of the emergence of a "Shii Crescent" stretching from Iran through Iraq and Syria to Lebanon. There were signs of change with the onset of the Arab Spring, and President Mursi visited Iran in the context of attending of the Non-Aligned Movement summit in August 2012. In advance of the brief visit, Iranian media made much of a prospective improvement in mutual relations. But Mursi disappointed his hosts by denouncing Tehran's Syrian allies in his speech.[34]

Israel.   Egyptian-Israeli relations have been the mainspring of the post–World War II geopolitical evolution of the Levant and northeastern Africa. Egypt was the first Arab country to sign a peace treaty, and despite ostracism from other Arab states, it gained considerably from the peace dividend. Mubarak often took on the mediator's role among the various parties in both Palestinian-Israeli and broader Arab-Israeli disputes. Although his relations with Israel were never warm, there were periods when they were notably less frosty, as during the Rabin-Peres government in the first half of the 1990s. With the onset of the Second Intifadah, the rise to power in

Israel of Binyamin Netanyahu, and especially after Operation Cast Lead (2008–2009) directed at Gaza, political and diplomatic links became increasingly distant. However, on a business level, relations have been more "normal" (see above regarding QIZs). The fall of Mubarak and the election of an Islamist president have disturbed the Israeli government considerably, but the new regime has signaled its intention to honor the 1979 peace treaty. There was a degree of quiet cooperation between the two countries in Egypt's attempts to regain control over jihadi activities in the Sinai in August 2012, and a new Egyptian ambassador arrived in Tel Aviv in September. In the November flare-up of conflict between Israel and Hamas in Gaza, Egypt once again actively undertook the role of mediator, as the Mubarak regime had done in the past.

United States.   US–Egypt relations at the consular level date to 1882, and full diplomatic relations were established shortly after Egypt's independence in 1922. Broken after the 1967 Middle East war, they were reestablished in 1974, and have become central to Egypt's political-economic position. The United States sponsored the Camp David Accords and the Egyptian-Israeli peace treaty. From 1974, the United States first supplanted, then supplemented, Arab financial support, with military grants, credits, and training and economic and food aid. As part of the Camp David agreement, Egypt became the second-largest recipient (after Israel) of US funding: through 2010, a total of $30.51 billion in economic assistance grants and loans plus military assistance of $39.53 billion went to Egypt. Most recently, the US Agency for International Development program has focused on microfinance, health, education, and civil society at the level of about $400 million annually, providing more than $2 billion in military and economic assistance annually through the 2000s. President Barack Obama delivered a major reconciliatory speech to the

Islamic world at Cairo University in June 2009.[35] In 2012, the United States reopened its consulate in Alexandria and discussed debt reduction with the new Islamist-led government. US links with the previous regime and its military forces were strong, and engaging with the new government was not an easy task. However, diplomatic relations continued. Mursi's ouster by mass demonstrations and military demand, and violent dispersal of Muslim Brotherhood protesters, has challenged US military assistance and political relations with Egypt.

Europe. Despite having exercised imperialist control over Egypt after 1882 and having participated in the 1956 tripartite invasion of the Suez, Britain now has good relations with Egypt. France also had imperialist interests in the area and assumed an especially important role in the construction and operation of the Suez Canal. Both Britain and France were involved in the 1956 Suez affair, leading to Nasser's sequestration of British and French properties. European cultural influence carries over, however, and both English and French are second languages for many educated Egyptians. In addition, the EU is Egypt's leading trading partner. Egypt and the EU signed an Association Agreement in 2004 according free-trade status to much of the two-way movement of goods between them.

Former Soviet Union. Relations between the former Soviet Union and Egypt are primarily of historical interest, although the Aswan High Dam remains a long-term testament to what Egypt gained from seventeen years of close relations. The situation began to deteriorate with Sadat's accession to the presidency, and in 1972 he expelled thousands of Soviet advisers, eventually abrogating the 1971 friendship treaty. Since the breakup of the USSR, Egypt has pursued good relations not only with Russia but also with the new Muslim republics—Azerbaijan and the five Central Asian "stans."

With a democratically elected government for the first time in its millennia-long history, Egypt has necessarily been feeling its way gradually in reassessing its historical international relations. Through early 2013, signs of continuity generally prevailed; the country had certainly achieved positive recognition on the world stage as the result of the Tahrir Square events, and these events certainly had a major impact on similar developments throughout the region. All countries with which it has had close relations are now watching the post-Mursi developments.

For information on the business environment in Egypt, see the website attached to this book: www.middleeastpatterns.com.

NOTES

1. Egypt is one of the best-analyzed countries in the Middle East. Recommended studies of post-1952 Egypt include Waterbury 1983; Hopwood 1982; Makram-Ebeid 1989; Lorenz 1990; Goldschmidt and Davidson 2004; and *Egypt* Country Study 1991.

2. See Williams 2002.

3. See Lesch 2011 for a discussion of the underlying causes of the revolution of 2011.

4. See, for example, "Insight: Egyptian Opposition Can't Harvest Brotherhood Unpopularity," *Zawya,* May 5, 2013.

5. The Ministry of Interior claimed to have thwarted a suicide attack on an unnamed foreign embassy by a group linked to al-Qaida. *Zawya,* May 11, 2013.

6. *BBC News,* May 7, 2013.

7. Although technical in many aspects, R. Said 1962 is useful for the landforms of Egypt. Dr. Said was formerly director of the Geological Survey of Egypt.

8. For further information, see www.nilebasin.org/.

9. *Al-Monitor,* Apr. 23, 2013.

10. The evolution of the Nile is well covered in R. Said 1981, which is less technical than R. Said 1962. Even more readable is Collins 2002.

11. *BBC News,* Mar. 27, 2013.

12. A good account of all these efforts is in Keating 1975. Keating was with UNESCO and was deeply involved with that organization's Nubian Campaign.

13. IEA, "2006 Energy Balance for Egypt."

14. See Benedick 1979; Waterbury 1979; and the current and excellent Collins 2002. Nile water problems and some details of the Aswan High Dam are discussed in Elhance 1999 and Collins 2002. See also Haynes and Whittington 1981.

15. An excellent account of the Western Desert, its oases, landmarks, and people, is found in Vivian 2000.

16. The excellent Hobbs 1989 discusses the physical environment of the Eastern Desert and focuses on the Bedouin of the area.

17. *Al-Monitor*, Apr. 11, 2013.

18. See Nisan 2002, Chap. 7.

19. The total number of Bedouin is hard to pin down since it depends on how the term is defined. If all who claim membership in Bedouin tribes are counted, the number is in the several hundreds of thousands, but many of these people now live in or near cities like Port Said and Cairo. In the Sinai itself, they number perhaps one hundred thousand.

20. *Media Line*, May 5, 2013.

21. US Department of Defense, "Report to Congress: Measuring Stability and Security in Iraq," Nov. 2006.

22. Saqqaf 1987, 227, 234. Part 5 of Saqqaf analyzes urbanization in Egypt, especially Cairo. The readable Rodenbeck 1998 gives an intimate view of Cairo. See also Abu-Lughod 1971. Ghannam 2002 is a more recent examination of this unusual metropolis.

23. See Goell et al. 2009 for a discussion of Egypt's experiences with desert urbanization, at www.idec.eg /Upload/Documents/175/EN/Sustainable%20Cities% 20in%20Egypt.pdf.

24. Stewart 1996.

25. United Nations Development Programme, *Human Development Report 2013*; *Legatum Prosperity Index 2012*, www.prosperity.com/.

26. This section draws partly from three US Department of State publications: *Country Commercial Guide: Egypt*, 2003 and 2009; *Economic Policy and Trade Practices: Egypt*, 1998; and *Background Note: Egypt*, Aug. 2004 and Mar. 2010; and one from the U.S. Department of Agriculture: *Agricultural Situation Report: Egypt*, 1997.

27. Hawass 1999. The find is also reported in *New York Times*, Aug. 24, 1999.

28. FAO, various issues.

29. US Agency for International Development, pdf.usaid.gov/pdf_docs/PNACH598.pdf.

30. *Media Line*, Apr. 3, 2013.

31. US Geological Survey, "The Mineral Industry of Egypt," in *Minerals Yearbook* 2011.

32. To gain duty-free status, these products must include a specified degree of Israeli inputs. Currently, this amount is at least 10.5 percent, and Egypt would like to reduce it to 8 percent. The arrangement is particularly beneficial for exports of textiles and ready-made garments.

33. Lorenz 1990 gives an excellent discussion of the subject, including an introductory chapter titled "The Geographic and Historical Setting."

34. The Iranian media "accidentally" misreported his speech, making it seem that he had denounced the Bahraini, rather than the Syrian, regime.

35. See www.whitehouse.gov/the_press_office /Remarks-by-the-President-at-Cairo-University-6-04-09/ for the full text.

The reader is advised to consult this book's associated website (**www.middleeastpatterns.com**) for additional information on **Egypt**, such as a historical time line and chronology of recent events, as well as essays on selected topics and various international economic, social, and political indicators.

20

Turkey

Bridgeland in Anatolia

KEY POINTS: One of three regional power cores within its natural Anatolian Plateau stronghold. Extremely varied environments and geology, many earthquakes, highly diverse ethnic settlers, rich history, leaving wonderful monuments and decorated caves. Longtime base for Byzantine then Ottoman cultures and empires. Long coastline facing several seas, so naval interests and fishing economy. Founder and president of first republic Kemal Atatürk modernized Turkey and secularized government; some recent return by state to more conservative Islam but Turkey considered a model for moderation. Turkish language only regional language written in Latin alphabet. Moderately well watered, source of Tigris and Euphrates (from snowmelt). Well endowed with agricultural and mineral resources, including coal but little oil. Good transportation system, thriving varied economy, military power, member of NATO. Increasing influence in region.

The preceding country surveys reveal the pronounced variety of physical and cultural elements among those fourteen states. The analyses showed notable contrasts between Jordan and the UAE, Yemen and Egypt, Israel and Iraq. Yet twelve of the fourteen—the exceptions are two of the smallest, Israel and Cyprus—have been Arab states, members of the Arab League, their peoples mainly speaking Arabic. Except in Cyprus and Lebanon, the environments described have included or even been dominated by deserts, with all that implies. We now turn to two quite different, quite large countries, first Turkey and then Iran. Neither is Arab, and each differs from the other as greatly as it does from the other

fourteen. And although both are Muslim, each practices Islam differently from the other and in many respects differently from the Arab countries. Certainly, Turkey makes a startling contrast with the state just considered, Egypt.

BETWEEN EUROPE AND THE MIDDLE EAST

With its geopolitically strategic bridgeland location, Asia Minor has long been a transit land. Traversing that bridgeland millennia ago, Europeans moved down the valleys and over the passes of the Balkans into the Anatolian basins and beyond. Others from the

TURKEY

Long-form official name, anglicized: Republic of Turkey

Official name, transliterated: Türkiye Cumhuriyeti

Form of government: republican parliamentary democracy

Area: 303,224 mi^2/785,347 km^2

Population, 2011: 74,306,000; Literacy: 87.4%

Ethnic composition (%, 2008): Turk 71; Kurd 18; Crimean Tatar 5; Arab 2; Azerbaijani 1; Yoruk 1; other 2

Religions (%, 2005): Muslim 97.5, of which Sunni 82.5, Shia (mostly Alevi) 15; nonreligious 2; other (mostly Christian and Jewish) 0.5

Demography: Life expectancy—70.86 yr (M), 74.78 yr (F); Birthrate (per 1,000)—17.58; Fertility rate—2.13

GDP, 2011: $761.9 billion; purchasing power parity: $1.075 trillion; per capita: $14,400

Currency: Turkish Lira (TRL), US$1 = 1.791 liras; 1 TRL = $0.558 (mid-May 2013)

Energy: oil—270.4 mn bbl (offshore exploration is promising); natural gas—218 bn ft^3; coal—586 mn tons of hard coal and 2 bn tons of lignite

Main exports (% of total value, 2008): $132.0 billion (of which base and fabricated metals 18; machinery and apparatus 13.8; road vehicles 13.6; apparel 8.8; petroleum 5.4; agricultural products 4)

Main imports (% of total value, 2008): $202.0 billion (of which machinery and apparatus 18; petroleum 13.4; base and fabricated metals 11.3; road vehicles and parts 6.1)

Capital city, 2011: Ankara 4,223,398; other major cities: Istanbul 12,946,730; Izmir 2,774,103; Bursa 1,667,321; Adana 1,584,053; Gaziantep 1,324,520

Caucasus and the Iranian Plateau crossed the rugged mountains of eastern Anatolia, mingling with Europeans in the central basins. Later empires were centered in Constantinople and ruled lands from the Atlantic to the Arabian Peninsula coasts. Post–World War I republican Turkey retained its tenacious foothold in Europe and, now with bridges over the Bosporus, links Europe with Asia. Contemporary Turkey is also a Middle East Muslim state that has openly pursued Europeanization, uses a European (Roman) alphabet, and belongs to the North Atlantic Treaty Organization (NATO). Moreover, the European Union finally invited Turkey to accession talks in October 2005 on EU membership, although this may be slow in realization.

Geopolitical Characteristics

Turkey's geographical assets include not only its location in the geopolitically Anatolian power center but also its control of the strategic Bosporus and Dardanelles Straits. Facing imperial Russia, later the Soviet Union, and now the successor republics across the Black Sea and in the Caucasus, it has been in more wars with Russia over the past five hundred years than has any other nation. Its strategic position is evinced in its being the anchor on NATO's southeastern flank and simultaneously a key member of the Central Treaty Organization (CENTO) before the collapse of this group with the Iranian revolution. Soviet disintegration has somewhat diminished the importance of its NATO role, but its setting thrust it once again into a geopolitical vortex vis-à-vis the former Soviet satellites and successor republics in the Balkans, the Trans-Caucasus, and Central Asia. Moreover, Turkey is the only country that bordered both contestants in the 1980–1988 Iran-Iraq War. As one of Iraq's six immediate neighbors, it played an important part in the 1990–1991 Gulf crisis but, asserting its independence, limited its role in 2003. However, it has been active in postinvasion Iraq on several fronts, especially in Kurdistan.

Regional Leader. Fourth in size among Middle East states, Turkey has a much greater proportion of habitable productive environments than have the larger Saudi Arabia, Iran, and Egypt. It has by far the longest coastlines among all regional states. It leads the area in a wide range of agricultural products and, with the notable exception of petroleum, of both mineral resources and production. It ranks first in extent of roads and railroads, in vehicle numbers, in GDP, in total value added by manufacturing, and in many military categories. Development efforts have focused on human, agricultural, mineral, and industrial resources; after progressing slowly for decades, Turkey began realizing its national potential more rapidly in the mid-1980s. Serious problems remain, but it has made considerable advances toward modernization, democratization, and Westernization.[1]

Physical reminders of Asia Minor's rich history are found not only in Istanbul and other cities but also along the coastlands and in the remote valleys. Sites of the numerous successive civilizations in the richly diverse environments of the peninsula are becoming increasingly accessible and well known.

Geonomenclature

For clarity in nomenclature, "Turkey" refers to the Republic of Turkey, including the 3 percent of its territory in Europe (eastern Thrace). "Asia Minor" refers to the peninsula that lies between the Black Sea and the northeastern Mediterranean east of the Aegean. "Anatolia" (Turkish: Anadolu), frequently considered synonymous with Asia Minor, technically refers to the interior plateau excluding the three coastlands of Asia Minor. Both Asia Minor and Anatolia exclude Turkey-in-Europe—Anatolia implies Europe's antithesis. "Ottoman," of course, refers to the multinationality empire or aspects of that empire (dynasty, culture, territory) that centered in Constantinople before 1918, and that, at various times in the previous millennium and to a greater or lesser extent, exercised suzerainty over most of the region covered in this book, with the notable exceptions of Iran and Oman.

COMPLEX REGIONAL PATTERNS

A Physical Interlocation

The rugged and often picturesque landscapes of Turkey are the product of particularly complex and powerful earth forces that have shaped Anatolia for millions of years and still manifest themselves in frequent earthquakes and related seismic events (see Map 2.3). Like Iran, Asia Minor lay in the former Tethyan geosyncline, literally squeezed between the African and Eurasian tectonic plates (see Chap. 2). It is part of the huge belt of Alpine folding during the Tertiary period extending from the Atlantic to the eastern Himalayas. Anatolia and Iran are the two halves of the Mobile Belt Province (see Map 2.2); both exhibit exceedingly complex geomorphology that has a strong impact on other patterns.[2]

The massive tectonism that shaped Asia Minor created a virtually continuous belt of folded mountains across northern Anatolia and a similar one across the south. This pattern is replicated in Iran. In both countries, the diastrophism and volcanism accompanying plate convergence induced widespread mineralization (see Map 6.5). Compression enclosed resistant blocks in between, and accompanying forces raised and depressed masses in the east and west. In the west, the alternating raised blocks (horsts) and depressed basins (grabens) create the irregular coastline along the Aegean. In the east, the confused mountain mass comprises some of the most rugged topography in the region (see Fig. 2.6), including lofty volcanoes, such as the well-known Mount Ararat. Other volcanic cones rise high above the central Anatolian Plateau in symmetrical grandeur.

At least three geomorphic blocks in southern Turkey are allochthonous terrains—segments of the earth's crust rafted in from some considerable distance over millions of years and literally rammed into place as the African and Eurasian Plates compressed.[3] Thus, relatively recent folding, faulting, and volcanism combined with interrelated soils, vegetation, and climates to endow Turkey with a wide variety of environments. These, in turn, have been utilized and shaped by successive civilizations to produce the modern state.

A Mosaic of Regions

North

[1] Pontus and Black Sea Coast.   The northern fold belt comprises principally the Pontic (or North Anatolian) Mountains, which include a variety of sedimentary rocks, some igneous intrusions, and large areas of lava flows (see Map 20.1; circled numbers indicate regions). Topographically, the mountains comprise long, narrow chains and lengthy trough-like valleys and basins; rivers follow the structures for part of their courses toward the Black Sea. Some of the trenches mark the strike of the North Anatolian Transform Fault. Slippage along this very active fault zone caused several devastating earthquakes in the twentieth century between Erzincan in the east and the Marmara in the west. In addition to those mentioned below, the 7.4 magnitude quake in August 1999 on the Gulf of Izmit and its aftershocks, followed by another 7.2 quake at Düzce in November, were among Turkey's greatest natural disasters. More than seventeen thousand died, fifty thousand were injured, and five hundred thousand were made homeless in this densely populated area. As much as 16 ft/5 m of right-lateral strike-slip displacement occurred along a 75-mi/120-km zone of the North Anatolian Fault between Karamürsel and Golyaka.

Several ridges in the west and one toward the east form an almost unbroken wall between the Black Sea and the interior, with elevations of 5,000–6,000 ft/1,525–1,830 m in the west and higher ones in the east, 10,000–13,000 ft/3,050–3,960 m (see Fig. 1.2). The upper and steeper slopes, especially those facing northwest, support Turkey's densest forests, primarily hardwoods in the west and evergreen softwoods in the east.

Features with major historical, economic, strategic, and seismic significance include the down-faulted basins now flooded by the Sea of Marmara and its eastern extensions into the gulfs of Izmit and Gemlik. Qualifying as a separate geographic region by some authorities, the eastern Marmara area has the greatest concentration of population in the country, including the historic city of Istanbul (formerly Constantinople) and its suburbs. Especially in Thrace, the countryside has orchards and market gardens near the cities, with fields of sunflowers beyond. This foothold in Europe holds an especially important symbolic significance for Turks.

North of the Pontic Mountains, a narrow coastal plain extends the length of the Black Sea shore, with the Kızıl and Yeşil Rivers forming prominent deltas west and east of Samsun. Except where mountain shoulders

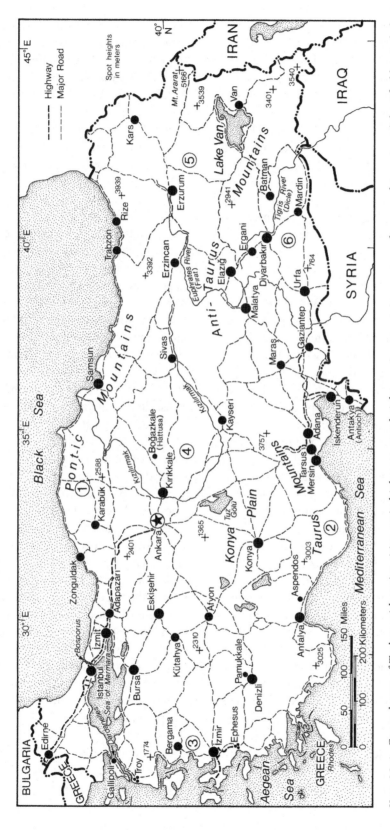

Map 20.1 General map of Turkey, with major cities, main highways, spot heights, main mountain ranges, and geographic regions (identified by circled numbers).

push against the shore, the plain is densely populated, with the major coal-mining and industrial town of Zonguldak to the west and one of Turkey's two tobacco areas to the east, around Samsun, which is the southern terminus of the underwater "Blue Stream" natural gas pipeline from Russia (see "Hydrocarbons," below). East of the tobacco belt lie citrus groves and, around the ancient city and port of Trabzon, the world's leading hazelnut area. Farthest east, beyond Rize, are extensive tea plantations; the southeastern Black Sea is Turkey's best fishery.

South

[2] Taurus, Anti-Taurus, Mediterranean Coast. Covering the southern third of Asia Minor, the Taurus Mountains (Toros Dağları) stretch from the southwestern corner of the peninsula east to the upper Seyhan River Basin north of Adana. From there, the Anti-Taurus extends to Lake Van. The complex Anti-Taurus also embraces extensive nappe structures, but it differs from the Taurus in having deep ocean crust masses (ophiolites, as in Oman), South Anatolian Suture structures, faulting along the South Anatolian Transform Fault, and thrust-faulted masses east of the transform fault. Mineralization in these complex structures enriches the area; around Ergani lies one of Turkey's most important mining and metallurgical areas. Around Elazığ and Malatya, the rugged topography, drained by the Euphrates and Tigris, is the focus of its most ambitious development scheme, the Southeast Anatolia Project (Turkish: Güneydoğu Anadolu Projesi—GAP). High atop the isolated peak of Nemrud Dağ stands the remarkable burial complex of a Commagene king from the middle of the first century BCE (Fig. 20.1). The eastern Anti-Taurus merges with the East Anatolian Accretionary Complex (see [5] below).

The upper elevations of the broad mountain belt of the Taurus vary from 7,000 to 9,000 ft/2,135 to 2,745 m. Primarily limestone, and including several nappes and fenêtres (see

Glossary) like those in the Swiss Alps, the maquis-clad highland separates the Mediterranean coast and the Anatolian interior. The few rivers that cut through the limestone mass follow almost vertically walled canyons, and only three or four major routes connect coast and interior. The most famous of them passes northwestward from Adana through the dramatic Cilician Gates (Gülek Boğazı), at 3,444 ft/1,050 m.

Along the southern coastal bulge from Alanya to Mersin, mountain shoulders drop steeply into the sea, separating eastern settlements from those to the west around Antalya. Impressive karst features are common—collapsed caverns, sinkholes, and dolines and poljes (larger solution basins). Several are spectacular tourist attractions. Many of the dolines and poljes are floored with alluvial soils; wheat, barley, grapes, and figs are grown. Where coastal plains exist, or on small deltas formed by rivers slicing through the Taurus, citrus, bananas, early vegetables, and other tender plants are cultivated.

At the eastern end of the coast is the flat Çukurova (Çukur Plain) on the extensive coalesced deltas of the Seyhan and Ceyhan Rivers. Sometimes called "smooth Cilicia," it is the best-developed agricultural area in Turkey, with large irrigated cotton fields. Cotton, cottonseed, textile mills, and clothing factories employ much of the plain's dense population. Adana is the fifth-largest city, and near it is the huge NATO air base of Incirlik (discussed in "Relations" below). The Gulf of Iskenderun, with a complex of ports for petroleum coming from three directions and agricultural products from the southeast, lies to the east of the Çukurova. Yumurtalık is the terminus for dual pipelines from Iraq and, perhaps more important, for the strategic Baku-Tbilisi-Ceyhan (BTC) pipeline from the Caspian, operational in 2005. Dörtyol is the export terminus for Turkey's Batman oil fields. Iskenderun (formerly Alexandretta) is the main import-export facility for the south-

20.1 Huge stone heads from a Commagene monument on remote Nemrud Dağ date from the second century BCE.

east, including the GAP, and has a major iron and steel mill.

West of the Çukurova lies Turkey's largest port—Mersin. Still farther west as far as Manavgat is the "rough Cilicia" coast, and farther, to Antalya, is the Pamphylian coastal plain. Between Mersin and Antalya, along this Turkish Riviera, the ruins of ancient settlements, most from Hellenistic and Roman times, attest to a dense, rich, and thriving seaward-facing population in classical times. Castles, theaters, and other vestiges attract archaeologists and tourists to Anamur, Alanya, Side, Aspendos, Perge, Termessos, and, especially, to Antalya, the western core of the coast that has been developed as a bustling tourist destination since the 1970s.[4]

West

[3] Aegean Area. Turkey's Aegean area resembles much of Greece in topography, climate, soils, and even the ruins of numerous classical cities along the coast. Until the early 1920s, much of its population was Greek. The upthrust horsts and down-dropped grabens follow the predominant east-west structure of Asia Minor, offering easy access to climatic and cultural influences. Grabens afford deep eastward penetration of valleys, some drowned by the sea, and horsts form extensions of the land westward as mountainous peninsulas. Rivers such as the Büyük Menderes drain the alluvium-filled grabens and have built deltas into the narrow bays. Some deltas advance several meters per year and in doing so have silted up ancient harbors, leaving classical ports like Ephesus and Miletus several miles inland.

These and other Greco-Roman cities combine with modern resorts and scenery to give Turkey some of its most outstanding tourist attractions. Major classical sites include Pergamum (modern Bergama, Fig. 3.4), Izmir (formerly Smyrna), Sardis, Colophon, Ephesus, Priene, Miletus, Didyma, and Halicarnassus (modern Bodrum).[5] The focal point of the region is Izmir, Turkey's third-largest city, with NATO's largest naval base in the eastern Mediterranean and the annual International Trade Fair. Among the coastal resorts, Kuşadası is one of the best developed. The alluvial-filled grabens are prime agricultural areas, planted in olive groves next to the coast, then fruit and nut trees (citrus toward the south and almonds toward the north), tobacco, and cotton. Aegean tobacco complements Black Sea tobacco, supplying one of Turkey's traditional exports. The broad grabens have long provided access between the Aegean and the productive interior.

Center

[4] Interior Anatolia.   Immured between the Pontic wall on the north and the Taurus barrier on the south is the inner Anatolian Plateau, technically the true Anatolia. Its surface, except in the heart of the region around Tuz Gölü, displays greater variety of relief than the term "plateau" might suggest.

Western Anatolia, which is hilly to mountainous, exhibits evidence of continuing tectonism, with numerous earthquakes, lava flows, and hot springs. Thermal springs indicate molten rock intrusions close to the surface. Hot springs near Denizli were a spa for classical Hieropolis, and dramatic calcium-carbonate travertine terraces at Pamukkale attract scientists and tourists. Still more volcanism is seen in the city of Afyon, which developed around a prominent mountain that peaks in a volcanic plug. Wheat and corn are widely grown, and uncommon specialty crops are produced in selected localities—for example, opium poppies around Afyon (Turkish *afyon* = opium), tobacco in several areas, and roses near Isparta, north of Antalya. An essential oil for rose water, used both in desserts and for fragrant hand washing on special occasions throughout the Middle East, is derived from roses.

The transitional area between the Aegean and central Anatolia was the major battleground for the Greek-Turkish war in the early 1920s. The same area received many of the Turkish immigrants from the Balkans in the population exchange with Greece and Bulgaria in the 1920s. Industry developed steadily in the area, bringing factories to Isparta, Kütahya, Eskişehir, and Afyon. A scenic lake district between Isparta and Konya includes twelve sizable lakes in grabens and solution basins, serving as local sumps. Most are saline without outlets.

Farther east, in the central and eastern parts of the interior, lies quintessential Anatolia with its vast flat-to-rolling treeless steppes and characteristic grain fields. Climatic stress typical of steppes brings poor rain years and sharp yield reductions, as in 1928 with harvests less than one-tenth the average. This semiarid core, with less than 12 in/300 mm of rainfall, grows wheat and barley; the more humid periphery has fruits, cotton, sugar beets, grapes, and tobacco.

Formerly poorly developed, central Anatolia was the focus of national attention when the Ottoman Empire broke up after World War I and the new republic's capital was shifted from Istanbul to Ankara. Then little more than an unprepossessing village in a hilly volcanic area, Ankara had a central, interior, protected location at a major route junction. Now Turkey's second-largest city, it is the central place for the Anatolian Plateau; it spread up the slopes of the original basin onto the surrounding plateau (Fig. 20.2). Economic growth brought infrastructure development like dams and highways. Hirfanlı Dam was built on the Kızılırmak northeast of the Tuz Gölü in the 1950s. Of special scholarly and touristic interest are Hattusa, the ancient Hittite capital east of Ankara; Göreme, with unique early Christian churches and homes hollowed out of volcanic tuff pinnacles west of Kayseri (Fig. 20.3); remarkable underground cities, excavated in the soft volcanic tuff and

Figure 20.2 View of Ankara, capital of Turkey, from the Hisar (ancient citadel), on a volcanic remnant in the center of the city. The view looks northeast along Etlik Caddesi to the northeastern suburbs of Ankara.

Figure 20.3 Hollowed-out tuff (solidified volcanic-ash) stacks in the Göreme Valley in Cappadochia were used as dwellings and churches by early Christians.

used by early Christians for refuge, at Derinkuyu and Kaymaklı; and Konya, the Seljuk capital. Tuz Gölü is a shallow salt lake at the bottom of the enclosed central Anatolian sump. With its surface near 3,000 ft/900 m, the lake's size varies greatly, depending on precipitation and runoff.

East

[5] Eastern Anatolia. The rugged eastern Anatolian Mountains at the eastern end of the Anti-Taurus show the complex folding and volcanism resulting from the junction of three tectonic units (see Map 2.2 and Fig. 2.6). Several extensive Tertiary lava flows and volcanic cones testify to vigorous volcanicity attending interplate compression, with Mount Ararat (Ağrı Dağı) towering to 16,948 ft/5,166 m. Several peaks reach 8,000–10,000 ft/2,440–3,050 m. Lake Van, largest of Turkey's lakes, has a surface elevation of 5,400 ft/1,646 m; it so completely blocks transit routes that the railway to Iran crosses it by ferry. Massive and frequent earthquakes here result from slippage along two fault systems (North and East Anatolian) intersecting west of the lake. Erzincan, near where they meet, has seen three disasters in the past seventy years—45,000 died in the 1939 quake, 1,330 in 1983, and 1,000 in 1992.

These rugged highlands have given refuge to several peoples, especially the Armenians (for whom the mountainous area of Armenia was named) and, to the south, the Kurds. Covered with heavy snow in the long winters, the mountains serve as a major hydrographic center, from which snowmelt and spring rains supply the headwaters of several rivers—the Tigris and Euphrates, flowing south to the Gulf; the Aras, flowing east to the Caspian; and several small streams emptying into the Black Sea or Lake Van.

Numerous villages lie in the valleys and on the steep slopes, but towns are widely separated. Erzurum has a large university and serves as a main station on the new BTC pipeline. To the northeast, Kars and Ardahan anchor territory often contested by Turks and Russians.

[6] The Southeast: The Arabian Platform. South of the Anti-Taurus and the Arabian Fold Belt is the Arabian Foreland, extending into Syria. The broad plateau surface exhibits gentle relief and elevations between 1,640 ft/500 m and 2,625 ft/800 m. The main center is Urfa (officially Şanlıurfa)—once the capital of the Crusader kingdom of Edessa. Gaziantep, one of Turkey's ten largest cities, serves as a center west of the Euphrates, as does Mardin to the east. Toward the northern edge of the platform, on the upper Tigris, is the ancient basalt-walled Kurdish city of Diyarbakır. Traditionally growing wheat and barley, the region saw only limited development until major new irrigation projects brought Euphrates water to the western section. The area is experiencing a boom in the transformation of the landscape through the GAP, the Southeast Anatolia Project. About six hundred thousand Arabs inhabit the area, along with Kurds who have moved from mountain villages in the north to the southeastern cities. The insurrection led by the Kurdish Workers Party (PKK) destabilized the region for fifteen years after 1984, but development accelerated after a qualified resolution of the conflict (discussed under "Relations" and in "Regional Conflicts," in Chap. 8).

HISTORICAL TAPESTRY

Like Egypt and Iran, Asia Minor reflects a long history of cultures and empires (see Chap. 3), and recent intensified field research has pushed back both the beginning dates and the scope of early Anatolian cultures. The increasingly rich physical evidence of this may be seen in the thousands of tells (*hüyüks* or *tepes*), tumuli, towers, tombs, and ruins. World-class museums in Istanbul and Ankara contain superb collections of prehistoric implements and later pottery, statuary, cuneiform tablets, and other artifacts.

Ancients, Byzantines, Ottomans

Caves near Antalya show evidence of Upper Paleolithic occupation. Hacılar, the earliest agricultural settlement in Asia Minor, dates to about 7040 BCE, and Çatal Hüyük, with its remarkable artworks, flourished in 6500–5650 BCE (see Map 3.1). The oldest man-made place of worship yet discovered is at Göbekli Tepe, where the earliest structures date as far back as 10,000 BCE.[6] Fabled Troy, guarding the entrance to the Dardanelles, has early layers predating 2500 BCE, although the legendary Trojan War was about 1200 BCE. The Hittites arose in central Anatolia and maintained a great capital at Hattusa, whose remarkable ruins are near Ankara. A score of other peoples waxed and waned in Anatolian fastnesses and along the rugged coastlines. Lydians in the west had Sardis as their capital and Croesus (fl. 550 BCE) their most famous king. Aeolian, Ionian, and Dorian Greeks ensconced themselves along the Aegean coast during classical times. Among the many peoples in the interior were the Galatians (Gauls), of European descent, to whom the apostle Paul addressed a New Testament epistle. Indeed, Asia Minor nurtured first-century Christianity, harboring the "Seven Churches of Asia" addressed in the book of Revelation—Pergamum, Smyrna, Ephesus, Sardis, Laodicea, Philadelphia, and Thyatira—and emerging as the area in which early Christianity then had its strongest foothold.

A watershed geopolitical event occurred in 330 CE, when Emperor Constantine transferred his capital from Rome to Byzantium, renaming it Constantinople. It was the capital of empires—Eastern Roman, Byzantine, and Ottoman—for nearly sixteen hundred years, putting its distinctive stamp on most of Asia Minor as well as on the Balkans and the Levant (see Chap. 3). With the empire's steady decline, Arab Muslims from one direction and Seljuk Turkish Muslims from another carved away at its territories. Crusader efforts to assist the Christian Byzantines delayed, but hardly prevented, Turkish inroads. In central Anatolia, Seljuks established the Sultanate of Rum (Rum = Rome, i.e., Europe), with other Turkish and Turkman principalities that rose and fell for two centuries. Finally, the Ottomans dominated and eventually gained control of Asia Minor and extensive areas beyond (see Chap. 3).[7] They seized Constantinople in 1453 and reached the peak of their power at the end of the sixteenth century with a realm that stretched from Algeria in the west to the Gulf in the east and from Hungary in the north to Yemen in the south. Decay was slow at first, increasing in the nineteenth century with the loss of most of the European lands. But the empire endured, with Constantinople as its capital, holding on to most of its Asian and African territory until it collapsed at the end of World War I.

Autocratic Reforming Republic

Contemporary republican Turkey arose from the ruins of the Ottoman Empire, the "sick man of Europe," defeated in war against the Allies.[8] Led by the charismatic Mustafa Kemal, later surnamed Atatürk (Father of the Turks), the young republic asserted itself in the early 1920s. It resisted partition of the Anatolian heartland, expelling British, French, and Greek forces, substituting the Treaty of Lausanne in 1923 for the onerous Treaty of Sèvres (1920). The aggressive Kemalist program called for republicanism, nationalism, populism, reformism, secularism, *etatisme* (state capitalism), and economic development.

This warrior-statesman insisted on Turkishness, the modernization of Turkey, and economic and cultural Europeanization. One fundamental and symbolic change, for example, was the abandonment of the Arabic alphabet and adoption of a modified Roman alphabet (1928). Also replaced were several items of traditional Turkish clothing, notably the fez (or tarbush) worn by men. Most adopted the visored cap, then common in America and Europe, headgear that still gives Turkish workingmen a characteristic appearance. The veil formerly worn by women was forbidden, angering conservative families, especially in inner Anatolia—an issue that was rekindled in the 1990s. The magnetic Atatürk served successive terms as president until his death in 1938. By then, Kemalism had been institutionalized into a quasi religion, countering some of Islam's conservatism. It continues to provide the state with an ideological base and is still the rationale for liberal policies.

Democratizing Republic

Turkey was neutral until the final days of World War II, when, by declaring war on Germany, it became a charter member of the United Nations. Soviet assertiveness immediately after the war prompted a mutuality of interests between Turkey and the United States. Under the Truman Doctrine (1947), military and economic aid was extended to Greece and Turkey, and Turkey joined NATO in 1952, abandoning Kemalist neutrality. In 1950, it held its first open election, which was won by the opposition Democratic Party.

Most Turkish concerns for the next forty years focused chiefly on Soviet intentions. Lacking Atatürk-like authority, government leaders repeatedly failed in economic matters, and domestic conflict—often violent—flared between Left and Right. The Kemalist-minded military staged three coups: in 1960, "by memorandum" in 1971, and in 1980. Thus, for decades Turkish democracy was regularly marred by episodes of instability and authoritarian rule.

Rebellious Kurds.   For fifteen years after 1984, the PKK (Partiya Karkeren Kurdistan—Kurdistan Workers' Party) insurrection in the southeast, the poorest and most neglected part of the country, became a quagmire for every administration. Capture of PKK leader Ab-

dullah Öcalan in February 1999 and his later death sentence provoked violent demonstrations. His request to his followers to cooperate with the state suppressed the level of domestic rebellion; pressure from the EU and other sources gained the commutation of his sentence to life in prison. The state of siege in the southeast was lifted in November 2002, and political and juridical reforms begun in preparation for EU acceptance somewhat smoothed Turkish-Kurdish tensions. In the aftermath of the invasion of Iraq and the consequent rise of autonomy in Iraqi Kurdistan, a new set of problems confronted Turkey, as PKK-related groups often sought refuge with their Iraqi kin (see Chap. 14). Turkey worries that Kurdish autonomy in Iraq is only the first step toward an independent Kurdish state cutting across current borders (and events in Syrian Kurdish areas—see Chap. 10—have added to these concerns). Additionally, Turks are concerned with the situation of their ethnic kin in Iraq, the Turkmans, who live mostly among Kurds in the autonomous area and in Kirkuk.

An End to Rebellion?   In March 2013, a potentially highly significant breakthrough in the long struggle of the Kurds against the central government came when Öcalan called for a cease-fire and for the PKK fighters to withdraw from Turkey. A few weeks later, the PKK military commander said the withdrawal would shortly commence. How this plays out on the ground remains to be seen. Öcalan's call was not unanimously accepted by his people, at least immediately, and the reactions among the Kurdish diaspora—an estimated 1.5 million in Europe alone—were not immediately apparent.[9] There was also opposition from Turkey's nationalist parties that see any sizable accommodation of Kurdish aspirations by Erdoğan as contrary to the republic's founding principles of Kemalism.[10]

Islamist Politics.   Meanwhile, beginning in the 1990s, basic shifts rapidly succeeded one another in Turkey's political orientation, structure, and electorate. Resurgent political Islamism dates to the 1960s and led to conflict with secularist elements, especially the ever-vigilant military. By fits and starts, a compromise was reached: Islamist politicians gained power by becoming increasingly moderate; from the mid-1980s, the military maintained watchfulness but mostly eschewed direct political involvement. Since 2002, the government has been in the hands of a temperate party, Justice and Development (AKP), with religious roots, headed by Prime Minister Recep Tayyip Erdoğan, a former reformist mayor of Istanbul. Making the qualifying for acceptance into the EU his top priority, he melded secularism and conservative Islam, coordinating an impressive overhaul of laws, policies, and procedures, even the constitution—modifying one-third of its provisions. He endeavored to maintain Turkey's longtime alliance with the United States in the face of his party's hostility when the invasion of Iraq was being prepared in 2003.

Reconnecting to the Middle East. Toward the end of the decade, the government seemed to be reemphasizing its connections with its Muslim neighbors for several reasons: partly as a result of the hostility of some European countries (France and Germany in particular) to Turkish EU membership; partly because of increased hostility toward Israel after the "Summer War" of 2006, the Gaza campaign of 2009, and especially the raid on the Turkish relief flotilla to Gaza in 2010; and partly because of Turkey's increased involvement with the petro-states to the east and south relative to transmission facilities. Whether this was to be at the expense of past links with Europe, the United States, and Israel was a subject receiving considerable attention at home and abroad. Domestically, between the devout and the secular, major issues remain, but through most of the period these were generally settled through compromise after periodic

confrontation. However, by 2012, hundreds of active and retired military officers (along with several journalists who reported on government actions in the matter) were under arrest in connection with the alleged Ergenekon plot of ultranationalists against the AKP; those detained included the former head of the armed forces, General Ilker Başbuğ. Some secularists feared the government was using the investigation to consolidate one-party Islamist rule,[11] and many observers argued that the influence of the military—the historic guardian of the Kemalist secular state—was waning.

On the other hand, with the rise of religiously linked parties in the wake of the Arab Spring revolts, the "Turkish Model" has been much discussed as a possible path for the Arab Islamist parties to follow. Continued concerns over questions like the Ergenekon affair, the treatment of minorities, a perceived decline in secularism, and deteriorating treatment of the press clouded Turkey's reputation as a democracy. In September 2012, the trial of forty-four journalists began, all of them charged with terrorism and "denigrating the state," mostly in connection with reporting on Kurdish developments. The US-based Committee to Protect Journalists reported in October 2012 that Turkey had more journalists in prison than any other country. The Economist Intelligence Unit in 2012 rated the country as 3rd in the region for its Democracy Index, but well down on the list globally—88th out of 167 countries—and classified it as ruled by a hybrid regime—partly democratic, partly authoritarian.[12] The press watchdog group Reporters Without Borders was even harsher, ranking Turkey 11th in the region and 154th out of 179 countries with regard to press freedom.[13]

THE TURKISH POPULATION

Turkey is among the three largest regional states in population, closely grouped with Iran and Egypt, and Turks are, after Arabs, the second-largest ethnolinguistic group in the region. Its population doubled from 1950 to 1975, exceeding growth in employment; thousands of jobless workers headed for labor-short Western Europe during the 1960s. Migration later ceased, but as many as 4 million Turkish citizens and their descendants, about one-quarter of them Kurds, remained there in the early 2010s.

Among the larger states of the region, Turkey has the most evenly distributed population geographically. Lacking deserts, it has low population densities only in the more rugged mountains and on the central steppe. Map 4.2 shows the highest densities are around Istanbul, along the Black Sea coast, along and inland from the Aegean coast, near Ankara, and on the highly developed Çukurova around Adana.

"Turkey for the Turks"

As a multiethnic empire, the Ottoman state followed a *millet* system that permitted ethnic groups autonomy. Inevitably, in more enlightened modern times, separatist sentiments evolved into anti-Turkish nationalism among some groups; and supported by European powers, many groups did gain independence. After the war, the republic sought greater homogeneity and renounced the multinational state; downplaying ethnic differences, it proclaimed "Turkey for the Turks and the Turks for Turkey." Having experienced centrifugal forces of separatism and foreign exploitation of minorities after World War I, the government has adamantly enforced "Turkishness," and recognition of minorities and of special minority rights contradicts the policy's most basic tenets. Kurds and Armenians are seen as specific examples of minorities fragmenting the republic, and changing this core belief is an alteration that Turkey will find difficult in preparing for EU membership.

Ethnic Turks are descendants of Central Asiatic nomadic tribes who intermarried with more than a score of identifiable groups over many centuries. In the Ottoman golden age, "Turk" was a term of disdain for Anatolian peasants as opposed to the cosmopolitan "Ottomans" of Constantinople. But republican leaders proclaim Turkishness with national pride and have systematically "purified" the language of many Arabic and Persian loanwords.

Non-Turkish Turks

Census reports minimize ethnolinguistic differences, grouping most citizens as Turks. As a result, the size of known minority groups can be only estimated. The obviously large Kurdish population is believed to be as much as 18 percent, and Arabs perhaps 2 percent. Smaller minorities include Armenians, Greeks, Assyrians, and Jews. Tatars, Turkmans, and Yoruk are grouped with Turks. Minorities from the Caucasus include Circassians and the related Abkhaz, with many living in the Adana area; Georgians, a group that actually comprises several different minorities; and the Laze, a small group in the southeastern Black Sea area, primarily fishermen.

Kurds.   By far the largest minority are the estimated 12–14 million Kurds, sometimes referred to as "mountain Turks"; they are firmly entrenched in the extension of their mountain homeland into southeastern Turkey. Kurds, Armenians, Turks, and Russians battled in eastern Anatolia in 1915, when Kurds and Armenians each sought independence from Turkey and Russia, sometimes fighting each other. Once Turkey had achieved stability in the mid-1920s, it specifically rejected Kurdish identity and checked any movement toward separatism, as it had earlier with Armenians. As Kurds in Iraq battled suppression under Saddam Husayn, the Marxist PKK initiated open rebellion in southeastern Anatolia in 1984. By the time of the trial of its leader, Öcalan, nearly thirty thousand rebels, military, police, and civilians had died during fifteen years of insurgency. The southeast was under martial law, and use of the Kurdish language in schools, courts, publications, and broadcasting was illegal. In the early 2000s, restrictions were slightly eased, and in 2008 a twenty-four-hour state-owned television channel even started broadcasting in Kurdish, Farsi, and Arabic.

The war against Kurdish separatism has been one of Turkey's two costliest ventures, with the GAP, also in the southeast, being the other. Turkey's human rights record, especially regarding the Kurds, evoked international censure and is a major issue in its preparation for EU membership. In late 2009, the government put forward a multifaceted peace initiative as the basis of negotiations with the Kurdish minority, including establishment of an independent human-rights oversight commission, ratification of the UN Convention Against Torture, legalization of the use of the Kurdish language in political campaigning, and restoring Kurdish names to places where Kurds are the majority. This bold move was soon complicated by a Constitutional Court ruling that outlawed the main Kurdish political party (then with twenty-one parliamentary seats), a move then strongly criticized by Prime Minister Erdoğan; within days, however, the government arrested eight mayors of Kurdish towns. Internally, the government's alternation between conciliation and oppression regarding the Kurdish question has done little to ameliorate the situation; casualties in 2011–2012 reached the highest levels since the late 1990s. Additionally, with the Assad regime's loss of control of Syria's northeastern region largely populated by Kurds, a new cross-border problem was added to Iraq for Turkey's conflict with Kurdish militants. As mentioned above, 2013 saw the launch of a possibly substantial accommodation by the government of Kurdish aspirations.

Yazidis, who may or may not be ethnic Kurds but definitely practice their own dis-tinctive syncretic religion, were reported in the late 2000s to have mostly emigrated to Germany.[14] Estimates for those remaining in Turkey range from 500 to a few thousand; a new Yazidi cultural center was reported to be in the works in Diyarbakir in 2012.

Greeks, Armenians, Assyrians. Greeks and Armenians are the major Christian groups in Turkey. Both are heavily concentrated in Istanbul; they are tiny remnants of much larger pre–World War I groups (see Chap. 4). Armenians were formerly dominant in eastern Anatolia but are now a small mostly urban minority numbering about 40,000. Details of the tragic deaths of perhaps as many as 1.5 million are given in Chapter 4. Armenian militants attacked Turkish diplomats in Europe during the 1970s and early 1980s, but with their own neighboring independent state since the collapse of the USSR, Armenians now present their case nonviolently in world media.[15] Fewer than 5,000 Greeks remain, clustered in Istanbul around the Phanar, the seat of the ecumenical patriarch, Bartholomew, the first among equals of the heads of the Eastern Orthodox communities and their 300 million believers. The historic patriarchate, dating to the fourth century, exists under a great deal of unofficial constraint, and some fear that it is in danger of either dying out or having to leave its traditional seat for exile.[16] After decades of harassment, remnants of Syrian Orthodox and Assyrian/Chaldean Christians who perhaps once numbered 200,000 remain in scattered locations in the southeast.

The Islamist government has made some tentative steps toward reconciliation with the religious minorities, particularly the Armenians and Assyrians; one cabinet minister has repeatedly called for the return of non-Muslims to the country. However, any returning numbers so far have been small, and much depends on the reception the returnees receive, not so much from the government, as from the residents of the areas to which they return.[17]

Jews.   Of an estimated 90,000 Jews in Turkey after World War II, fewer than 25,000 remain. About 30,000 went to Israel in the late 1940s, and more have left since then—not all to Israel. Most remaining are in business or the professions in Istanbul or Izmir. Nonhomogeneous, they include Sephardim, speaking Ladino; Ashkenazim, speaking Yiddish; and Karaites, speaking Greek and viewed by some other Jews as heretics. All speak Turkish as a second or equal language. Dönme (a somewhat opprobrious term like "turncoat") are the descendants of ethnic Jewish families who, as members of a seventeenth-century messianic sect, followed their leader, Sabbatai Zevi, when he converted to Islam. They have now merged with the general population, but are considered neither Jews nor Muslims by most of their compatriots.

Alevi and Alawi.   A noteworthy religious rather than ethnic minority based in the southeast are the Alevi, a somewhat heterodox offshoot from Shiism, somewhat akin to the Syrian Alawis (see Chap. 10) but much more numerous, numbering perhaps 15 million. Because adherents to the sometimes persecuted sect often disguise their affiliation, the Alevi are sometimes mistakenly equated with all Shia, although in actuality the Alevi are only one—though definitely the largest—of four Shii-related sects in Turkey. Alevi constitute a sizable percentage of the population and include ethnic Turks, Arabs, and Kurds. Although they were originally mostly in the southeast, many have migrated to urban areas in western Turkey and other parts of Anatolia. In recent years, they have become more politically outspoken, protesting the lack of official status for their institutions and places of worship. Around Iskenderun, in the area detached from France's Syrian mandate in the 1930s, are as many as 400,000 Alawi, almost all of whom are ethnic Arabs; this community has been active in protesting Turkey's espousal of the insurgent cause in the Syrian civil war. There is also a small legally unrecognized Bahai community.

VILLAGE AND CITY

Although Turkey is becoming more urbanized, it is still very much village oriented, with more than forty thousand villages well distributed over the country. The widespread pattern of humid climates and rainfed agriculture situates villages on upper slopes and hilltops, thus presenting landscapes more typical of the humid Levant or Europe. Widely differing house materials appear in different environments: wooden in forested areas, masonry on barren limestone slopes, and mud brick or with mud walls in river bottoms.

Mosque, public bathhouse, small fruit and vegetable market, and the teahouse (*halkevi*—literally, "people's house") form the village center. The *halkevi* is ubiquitous in both city and village, where the clientele is virtually all male. Increasing numbers of them offer Internet links. Village attitudes remain conservative regarding women. Except where they have become enclaves of expanding cities, villages are politically conservative, religious, and stable. Important in rural life is the weekly market, conducted in larger centrally located villages.

Urbanizing the Population.   Rapid rural population growth in the 1950s and 1960s sent millions of the landless to larger cities. Whereas the rural portion of the population was nearly 80 percent in the early 1950s, it was less than 30 percent by 2010. Migrants to Istanbul, Ankara, Izmir, and other cities found shelter in rapidly spreading *gecekondus* (literally, "built overnight"), squatter settlements enabled by a law prohibiting forced removal of habitations having completed roofs (see Chap. 4). The Muslim tradition of urban "quarters" for different groups carries over to the *gecekondus,* which cluster by ethnic and sectarian affiliation.[18]

The cities exhibit great variety, especially those that were once capitals of kingdoms or principalities. Istanbul, the imperial capital on a peninsula above Bosporus, Marmara, and Golden Horn waters, has a unique skyline of magnificent domes and minarets. Bursa, the Ottoman capital before Istanbul, preserves medieval monuments and is a major silk-producing center. The Seljuk capital of Konya, its ruins mixed with modern buildings rising from the Anatolian plain, preserves structures in the old Seljuk style. Turkey's modern capital Ankara has a core of contemporary government buildings and a picturesque old center clustered around the ancient *hisar* (fortress).

ECONOMIC DEVELOPMENT

Etatisme

Having lagged economically in the declining Ottoman years, Turkey made slow progress after World War I. To counter private capital shortages and forestall dominance by foreign capital, Atatürk adopted *etatisme* (state capitalism) as his basic economic philosophy. Government participation in industry had advantages for planning purposes at the price of bureaucratic constraints. Though domestic capital was usually in short supply, persistence brought the country to an appreciable level of development with a series of five-year plans under the State Planning Organization, created in 1961.

Reforms Take Hold

Reforms during the 1980s under Prime Minister and (later) President Turgut Özal, an economist, led to a development-oriented investment climate. The government gradually abandoned Atatürk's policies and steadily reformed and privatized state economic enterprises (SEEs). Turkey achieved an enviable level of prosperity: it averaged an annual 5 percent GDP growth for fifteen years, became the world's eighteenth-largest economy, was the fastest-growing member of the Organization for Economic Cooperation and Development, was the largest Middle East economy, was rated as one of the world's top tourist destinations, was designated by the United States as a "big emerging market," became— as a signatory to the General Agreement on Tariffs and Trade—a founding member of the World Trade Organization in 1995, and entered a customs union with the EU in 1996. The energy, telecommunications, transportation, and textile sectors of its economy were especially vigorous, and the labor-force share of manufacturing and services rose steadily.

On the economic downside in the 1990s, runaway inflation—averaging about 70 percent annually, peaking at more than 125 percent in 1995—resulted mostly from public-sector deficits. To illustrate the problem: the Turkish lira dropped from 9 to the dollar in 1957 to 2,618 in mid-1990, 624,000 in mid-2000, and a staggering 1,351,351 by the end of 2004. The situation demanded radical action, and a new lira dropping six zeros appeared on January 1, 2005, and the exchange rate has remained reasonably stable since then. These problems manifested the urgency for accelerating privatization, especially since it was obvious that the dynamic private sector was driving overall development. A 1998 accord with the International Monetary Fund obligated Turkey to speed up sale of SEEs, reduce subsidies and price supports, raise the retirement age (which, under three separate systems, averaged forty-three), and cut the budget deficit. Despite general infrastructural adequacy, Turkey needed to upgrade its ports, some airports, and railways. Its achievements were statistically impressive, as was noted earlier, and with the exception of its lack of petroleum, it was and is the most nearly balanced economy in the region.

Challenges and Potentialities

The Human Dimension. By the European criteria Turkey aims to fulfill, living standards for its citizens still lag. Using the Human Development Index (HDI) developed by the UNDP, Turkey's global rank was 90th of the 186 countries rated in 2013, 11th of the 17 Middle East countries (Palestine included), and below all the current and aspiring members of the European Union, even Albania, Macedonia, and Bosnia-Herzegovina. Still, its most recent HDI did show a gain of more than 52 percent over 1980, largely on the basis of rising life expectancy and per capita income. The more broadly based Prosperity Index from the Legatum Institute ranked Turkey 89th of 142 countries globally and 8th regionally in 2012.[19] Turks, in their self-evaluations reported by the Gallup organization in 2010, were rather pessimistic; according to the Global Wellbeing ranking, Turkey was 103rd of 155 countries—13th regionally ahead of only Iraq, Egypt, and Syria.[20]

The GAP

Hydroelectric Power. Turkey has the highest potential for hydroelectric power among all European countries except Norway and Sweden. Lacking petroleum resources, it turned to hydropower for energy.[21] Dams were constructed before 1970 in widely separated river basins—the Kızılırmak, Yeşil, upper Gediz, Sakarya, Seyhan—and smaller dams elsewhere. However, it was the ambitious program of constructing the giant Euphrates dams after 1965 that strongly established Turkey's impressive achievements in hydropower and large-scale irrigation. The keystone is the Southeast Anatolia Project (GAP), which took its basic form in the early 1980s.

Embracing thirteen interrelated subprojects distributed over 28,185 mi²/73,000 km², the GAP is one of the largest projects of its kind ever attempted and the most comprehensive ever implemented in Turkey. Included are twenty-two dams and nineteen hydroelectric installations—seven on the Euphrates and six on the Tigris. One goal is irrigating 4.2 mn ac/1.7 mn ha—equivalent to about half of Egypt's irrigated land. The Euphrates is dammed by three giant barrages, Keban (technically not part of the GAP), Karakaya, and Atatürk (shown on Map 20.2). It exploits the steep gradients of the rivers descending from the well-watered east Anatolian Mountains through deep canyons. The Euphrates profile permits high dams forming successive reservoirs in stair-step configuration, with a difference in elevation of 495 ft/151 m from one reservoir to the next.

Diverting the Flow. The first dam upstream is the Keban, 670 ft/204 m high and completed before the GAP in 1974 for power purposes only. Located 103 mi/166 km farther on is the Karakaya, completed in 1987—also for power generation only. Downstream 112 mi/180 km is the showpiece of the GAP, the Atatürk and its 2,400-megawatt power station (Fig. 20.4). This dam, near the southern margin of the Anti-Taurus, is to irrigate about 1.8 mn ac/730,000 ha of high-quality land in the Arabian Foreland north of Syria. Turkey's blocking the Euphrates flow and its increased consumption of water have greatly concerned the downstream riparian states, Syria and Iraq (see "Regional Conflicts," in Chap. 8). Six subprojects are on the Tigris between Diyarbakır and the border; although all are on smaller scales than those on the Euphrates, they nevertheless affect the river's flow. Both Syria and Iraq have argued that Turkey is violating international law by claiming its absolute territorial sovereignty with regard to water.

If completed, the GAP will generate 27 bn kilowatt hours annually, about 25 percent of the national total. Turkey has greatly increased its gas-fired thermal power capacity in an effort to maintain its pace of development; still, Turks consumed electricity on a

619

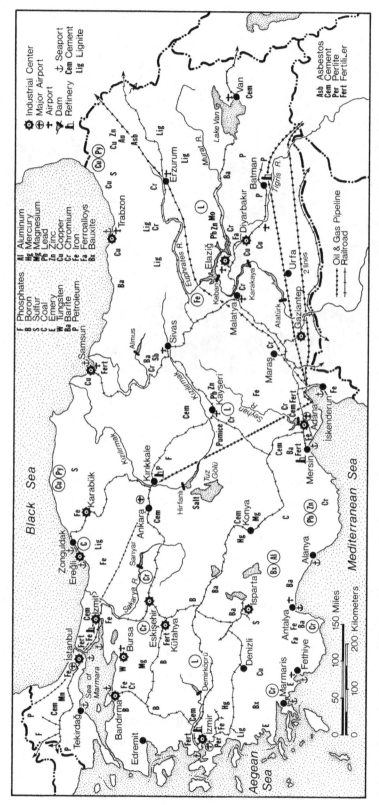

Map 20.2 Economic map of Turkey, showing railways, ports, airports, numerous solid-mineral mining areas, pipelines, and other economic features. Note Atatürk Dam on the Euphrates River west of Urfa (see also Fig. 20.4).

Figure 20.4 Atatürk Dam on the Euphrates River. Each of the eight giant penstocks of the power station (*center*) is 24 ft/7.25 m in diameter. The dam, completed in the early 1990s, is the centerpiece of Turkey's GAP. (Photograph courtesy of Turkish Government State Hydraulic Works [DSI])

per capita basis in 2006 far below the European average—only in Moldova and Albania was the rate lower. Gas-fired plants generated about 45 percent of the nation's electricity and coal about 25 percent.

Problems. The GAP ran into delays in the late 2000s because of budgetary, environmental, and lingering regional ethnic problems. European financing for the highly controversial Ilisu Dam on the Euphrates was canceled in 2009, but it was refinanced by Turkish banks and now is supposed to be on track for completion in 2014. Some observers have argued that so far, the poor southeastern provinces have yet to see the benefits claimed for the project and that the main beneficiaries have been electricity consumers in urbanized western Turkey; through 2008, the completion rate for the hydroelectric projects was about 85 percent, whereas that for irrigation projects was less than 25 percent.[22] The official rationale for the GAP has been to bring a measure of prosperity to the southeast (where so many of Turkey's restive Kurds live), but some critics have claimed that the enormous expenditure is primarily politically motivated, aimed at weakening and dividing the Kurdish minority. The original deadline for completion of the entire project has been extended several times, and a realistic estimate now points to 2017.

Agriculture

Varied climate and productive soils have sustained Anatolian agriculture for more than three thousand years. Farming, which had made little technical progress in centuries, was encouraged to modernize and diversify after World War II; Turkish agriculture is now a more productive sector. The most fruitful lands historically have been the Aegean and Marmara areas, but the irrigated Çukurova now vies with them. As more and more of the Arabian Foreland plains are irrigated in the GAP, they too will become prime areas. In the late 1990s, 123,550 ac/50,000 ha were devoted to irrigated crops, mostly cotton, in the Harran Plain (south of Urfa) alone. Overall, irrigated area has increased from 2.7 mn ac/1.1 mn ha in 1962 to 12.9 mn ac/5.2 mn ha by 2007.

Agricultural landholdings in the 4.5 million farms are generally small and fragmented, although wheat farms are medium size. Maintaining inherited land is traditional, and only Yemen in the region has a higher proportion of the workforce in agriculture. Mechanization, still-high rural birthrates, and urban attractions induce rural-to-urban and east-to-west migration.

Livestock. Animal husbandry has long been essential in Anatolia, both on farms and with nomadic pastoralists and their sheep, goats, and camels (see Fig. 5.8). As with crops, animal breeds, breeding practices, feeds, processing, and marketing are all being improved. Cattle receive particular attention, and dairying is important in the high pastures of the northern mountains. Grazing dominates the mountainous eastern fourth of the country. As elsewhere in the Middle East, poultry raising has expanded markedly; Turkey is second, after the United States, in mohair production, from the famous Angora (Ankara) goat.

Crops. With its great environmental variety, Turkey produces a great range of crops: bananas, dates, grapes, citrus, and cotton along the southern coast; olives, cotton, tobacco, citrus, grapes, soft fruits, and figs in the west; tobacco, tea, rice, and hazelnuts along the Black Sea; and wheat and barley in central Anatolia. Potatoes, sugar beets, pulses, melons, onions, and other crops are widely distributed. Sunflowers flourish in the open landscapes of Thrace. An unusual aspect of Turkish agriculture is the regulated cultivation of opium poppies in the west-central basins. Maize is well adapted to the more humid areas of Anatolia (see Fig. 1.2) and is increasingly produced for both food and feed. Turkey leads the Middle East in the production of a score of crops, producing from 40 to 70 percent of the regional total in many cases (see Tables 5.2, 5.3, and 5.4). In 2007, agriculture's contribution to GDP was 8.9 percent, while it continued to provide a livelihood to 36 percent of the labor force. From the early 1960s through the mid-2000s, food production per capita grew by a modest 6 percent, notably less than most of the other countries in the region.[23]

Forestry

Turkey and Iran are the only two countries in the Middle East with well-developed forest industries, and Turkey has the more extensive forests (45 million ac/18 million ha). Its production equals the roundwood output of the rest of the entire region. Forests cover the steeper slopes rimming the central Anatolian Plateau and basins, with particularly dense forests in the Pontic Mountains in the north. Sawnwood production fell off by more than a third in the 1990s, but by 2011, output had recovered to nearly double the levels that prevailed in the 1980s.

Fishing

Formerly the leading fishing country in the Middle East, Turkey is now second to Egypt. It increased its annual catch more than fivefold from 1975 to 2010, to 654,000 mt. Fish exports, mostly to western Europe, include such specialty items as shrimp, lobsters, snails, eels, sponges, tortoises, and frog legs. Half of the catch is taken in eastern Black Sea waters, but virtually every town and village along all three coasts engage in fishing. Aquaculture has grown from practically nothing as recently as 1990 and now accounts for about 25 percent of the total catch.

Industrial Development

An Overview.   As we have seen, Turkey leads the region with its range of industrial establishments and their total non-oil output. The variety and quantity of agricultural products support food processing and agribusiness, and the minerals industry—the most varied and highly developed in the region—further adds to manufacturing diversification. As they have from the early years of expansion, energy deficiencies (particularly petroleum and natural gas) challenge manufacturers to seek alternatives. Imported natural gas now supplies that energy at the cost of limited foreign exchange. However, Turkey's manufacturing sector has steadily increased its GDP share, reaching about 18 percent in value added terms by 2011.

As with agricultural production, mining operations, and population—all unusually uniformly spread over the country—industrial concentrations are likewise well distributed (see Map 20.2). The largest complexes, especially those producing consumer goods, are in the main population centers. As a consequence, the half-dozen largest cities are also the leading industrial centers: Istanbul (with more than half of all enterprises), Ankara, Izmir, Adana, Bursa, and Gaziantep. However, towns in specialty crop areas usually process foods, beverages, and industrial crops. Examples include Rize, tea packing; Trabzon, hazelnut shelling and packing; Tekirdağ, wine making; Afyon, opium processing; Bursa, silks; Isparta, rugs, using local wool; and Adana, cotton milling and textiles.

Mineral Industries.   The tectonic and structural conditions in the Mobile Belt, extending west-east across the Anatolian and Iranian Plateaus, give rise to several zones of extensive mineralization. Unfortunately, Turkey possesses a sizable number of small deposits but few large ones. Reserves of most metals are not large by world standards, although those for bauxite (aluminum ore), chromite, copper, lead, iron ore, gold, and silver are appreciable.[24] Most significant in reserves and production are such industrial minerals as barite, boron, emery, feldspar, magnesite, perlite, pumice, and dimension stone. Sharing the Mobile Belt mineralization, Turkey and Iran rank first or second in the region in output of a dozen minerals, including bauxite, copper, iron ore, and silver. They also rank second and third after Saudi Arabia in gold and lead ore.

The public-sector Etibank had long controlled minerals and mining, but during the 1990s it steadily sold off its holdings under the privatization program. Sectoral profitability has now notably increased, and solid minerals production contributes appreciably to GDP. Mineral utilization has a long tradition in Anatolia: ironworking—believed to have originated among the Hittites—was a profitable activity in their empire thirty-seven hundred years ago, the wealth of Croesus came from gold taken from the rivers of the Aegean region, and obsidian (volcanic glass) from the volcanic area of central Anatolia was traded in the Fertile Crescent during the Neolithic period.

Metallurgy.   Many processing plants and manufacturing establishments that use mineral raw materials are mine oriented; mining areas and mineral industry concentrations are locationally related (see Map 20.2). Steel mills are located in three widely separated areas: around Zonguldak, with large plants at Karabük and Ereğli; Iskenderun; and around the eastern part of the Sea of Marmara, where three small plants mostly use scrap metal. A small plant in Izmir also uses scrap. Aluminum ore is mined and processed in a large new complex at Seydişehir, southwest of Konya.

More important on the world scale is Turkish production of several ferroalloys, none of which is plentiful on the world market. These include chromite (from Kütahya, Ergani, and Muğla), antimony (northwest of Sivas), manganese (Thrace, Eskişehir, Ereğli, and Denizli), and tungsten (near Bursa). Also significant are such nonferrous metals as copper (from several sources but especially from Ergani and Murgul), lead, and zinc (around Kayseri and Elazığ). Turkey produces significant amounts of the world's emery, boron, magnesite, perlite, and barite. Near Eskişehir is the world's only commercial deposit of meerschaum, which is machined and carved in a cottage industry in and around the city for distinctive tobacco-pipe bowls.

Other Industries. In addition to the crop-related and mineral industries, Turkey has developed perhaps the widest range of manufactures in the region, although Iran may be comparable. With a large domestic market, it produces consumer goods from automobiles through household appliances and electronic items. For its farms, it makes tractors (it has more tractors than all other Middle East countries combined), milking machines, combines, and fertilizers. For its large military forces, it manufactures weapons and ammunition, tanks, military vehicles, aircraft, and naval vessels. It also produces a wide variety of electrical equipment, railway rolling stock and other equipment, cement, and automotive parts. It makes steel from its own pig iron, coming from its own iron ore, and exports a growing amount of its manufactures. Not to be overlooked are its well-regarded traditional crafts—ceramic tiles from Iznik and pottery from Kütahya, brass and copper items, leather products and traditional hand-knotted rugs, as well as machine-made carpets.

Tourism. It is not surprising that tourism is a major sector in a country that boasts historic and religious sites spanning millennia, spectacular scenery, Mediterranean beaches, and major shopping opportunities. In 2011, there were 31.5 million tourist arrivals, leading all the sixteen countries detailed in this book, and placing fourth in Europe after France, Spain, and Italy; sectoral earnings were estimated at $23 billion. Adding to the above attractions, the low cost of apartments and houses, together with the Eurozone crisis, increased Turkey's attractiveness to retirees from EU countries looking to preserve the buying power of their pensions in a more attractive winter climate.

Hydrocarbons

Fuel Reserves. Turkey's mineral fuels include coal, lignite, and small amounts of petroleum and natural gas. Although its coal and lignite production is more than 96 percent of the region's total, its oil output is by far the least of all Middle East producers and is less than one-fourth that of tiny Bahrain (see Table 6.1). Bituminous coal reserves, 1 bn mt, and lignite reserves, 8 bn mt, are sufficient for more than two hundred years at the present rate of production. By contrast, petroleum reserves of about 270 mn bbl indicate less than a ten-year supply, even at the low rate of production. Recent natural gas discoveries, primarily in Thrace, improve the energy outlook modestly, but Turkey must import more than 90 percent of its petroleum needs and 50 percent of its total energy requirements. A possible bright spot on the horizon has been the discovery of gas and probably exploitable oil reserves in the eastern Mediterranean off the coasts of Gaza, Israel, Lebanon, and Cyprus—not surprisingly, Turkey hopes that these deposits may extend northward into its waters. Additionally, preliminary seismic studies have been reported to indicate sizable shale-gas deposits in both the northwest and southeast of the country.

Coal and Lignite.   Whereas 45–60 mn mt of lignite is mined in most years in several areas, especially in east-central Anatolia, hard coal comes almost entirely from the Zonguldak area on the western Black Sea coast (3 mn mt of anthracite in an average year). Turkey has 4.6 bn mt of coal resources, only 7 percent of which is anthracite, but because the veins are thin and contorted extraction is increasingly costly, and coal is now imported for industrial use in the western and southern parts of the country.

Petroleum and Gas.   The first encouraging oil strikes, in the Batman area between Diyarbakır and Siirt in southeastern Anatolia, were not made until 1940. Royal Dutch Shell and ExxonMobil have been the most successful of several operating companies, but the public-sector petroleum company, TPAO, produces about 80 percent of the output. Despite widespread exploration, discoveries have been virtually limited to the Fold Belt; fields are small, scattered, often deep, and found in complex geological structures. Production by 2012 was less than 45,000 bpd. Output from the Batman fields moves by pipeline to Dörtyol on the Gulf of Iskenderun, but it satisfies less than 10 percent of Turkey's needs. Current production of natural gas supplies less than 5 percent of the country's demand; recently, however, not only have there been hopes for offshore discoveries, but there is also growing interest in the potential of shale-gas exploitation. In September 2010, Exxon was reported to be in serious discussions with the government about exploration licenses in the southeastern part of the country.

Offshore Developments.   Turkey has noted with considerable interest the identification of oil and gas reserves in the offshore Levant Basin that adjoins its southeastern Mediterranean coast. It has also explicitly warned the (Greek) Cypriot government against the lat-ter's plans to develop the petro-resources off the island's shores, stating that this cannot proceed unilaterally without the participation of the Turkish Cypriot regime. In 2013, Turkey launched its first domestically built ship designed for undertaking underwater exploration and put its neighbors on notice that the Turkish navy is ready to defend the nation's interests.[25]

Transmission.   Whatever may come of future developments regarding domestic discoveries, Turkey's true regional importance in the 2010s regarding hydrocarbons is in its geographic position—its "bridgeland" function as it lies between one of the world's leading hydrocarbon consuming regions (energy-intensive Europe) and the world's leading hydrocarbon producing regions (the Middle East and Central Asia).[26] From the new exporters in the latter area, Turkey has, inter alia, opposed increased tanker traffic across the Black Sea and through the narrow Bosporus to reach western markets. By 2010, that passage was near its capacity and could not safely accommodate many more ships. Hence, the attractiveness of land-based transmission facilities has dominated Turkey's preferences.

Since the opening of an oil pipeline from Iraq's Kirkuk fields to Ceyhan in 1977, the country has become the locale of a growing number of lines (and proposed lines). Turkey was deeply involved in the discussions over the controversial routing and financing of the Baku-Tbilisi-Ceyhan pipeline bringing Caspian oil to the Mediterranean, which began deliveries in 2005. An engineering triumph, at 1,038 mi/1,670 km in length through rough terrain in Azerbaijan, Georgia, and Turkey, it is about as long as Tapline with a larger diameter (42 in/107 cm) and twice the capacity (1 mn bpd). From 2002, gas has entered the Turkish market through a line from Tabriz in Iran and since 2003 through the submarine line across the Black Sea from Russia. The latter line—"Blue Stream"—is now linked to an export terminal at Ceyhan.

The gas-pricing dispute between Russia and the Ukraine in 2009 and the consequent interruption of deliveries through pipelines crossing Ukraine and on into western markets brought home to the EU the need for reliable alternative gas transmission routes—preferably outside Russian territory. That year, the EU and Turkey signed an $11 billion deal to build the 2,000-mi/3,220-km gas pipeline to cross Anatolia, stretching from the Caspian to Austria—the Nabucco or Trans-Anatolian pipeline. Since then, Nabucco has had an on-again, off-again history, and its eventual success depends upon finding enough gas from Caucasian Central Asian and Middle East suppliers to justify its high construction costs; by late 2012, solutions to this problem seemed to be on the horizon, with renewed EU interest in a trans-Caspian gas pipeline connecting Turkmenistan and Azerbaijan. Not surprisingly, Russia opposes Nabucco and has proposed as an alternative "South Stream"—a submarine line crossing the Black Sea from Russia to Bulgaria and costing even more than Nabucco.

Oil Processing. Of Turkey's seven refineries (see Map 20.2 and Table 6.2), with a total capacity of 714,000 bpd, the two largest are located at Izmit and Izmir and are supplied by imports by sea. The Kırıkkale refinery, opened in 1986, is fed by Iraqi crude brought by a dedicated pipeline from Yumurtalık; it has seen interrupted deliveries since 2003. Petrochemical production is limited, since feedstock has to be imported.

Transportation

Turkey's large size plus its well-distributed development and detailed planning have resulted in an impressive transportation network. Although several links require improvement, the basic nets are the largest and best balanced in the region. By rail and road, it is well connected with five of its land neighbors. With the former Soviet republics, there was some traffic even before 1990, and since then there have been many improvements. Shipping and airlines link it with its neighbors and more distant states.

Railways. A trans-Anatolian rail line served Turkey as early as 1918, and an additional 2,052 mi/3,302 km of rail lines were completed by the end of World War II. Since then, major additions have been made in the southeast and east, along the steadily developing Malatya-Elazığ-Diyarbakır-Siirt axis and on the line to Iran crossing Lake Van by ferry. All trackage is standard gauge (4.7 ft/1.435 m). Although the network has fallen behind schedule for completing a badly needed overhaul, two high-speed lines were operating in 2012—one from Ankara to Konya and the other a part of the Ankara-Istanbul line. Turkey's rail lines are especially adapted for shipping coal, other bulky minerals, and grain hundreds of miles to ports or internal markets. By the early 2010s, they made up one-third of the rail lines in the region. In 2009, Turkey and Saudi Arabia expressed an interest in rebuilding the old Hijaz railroad as a standard-gauge line to connect at Madinah with a Saudi line soon to be completed. Urban metro construction began in the 1990s, and by the end of the 2000s Istanbul, Ankara, Bursa, and Izmir all had operating systems.[27]

Roads. After World War II, Turkey had a very limited road network, mostly poorly surfaced. Some of the Truman Doctrine financial aid to Turkey was devoted to road building for economic and political purposes as well as for security reasons. By 2008, it had 41 percent of the total length of all roads in the Middle East (see Table 7.2); every town had been integrated into a well-designed, well-constructed, and serviceable network. Accelerated economic growth after 1985 overtaxed major routes, requiring construction of several four-lane divided motorways. About 2,175 mi/3,500 km of motorways has been completed, approximately one-third of what is planned. The Europe–Middle East route was first to be constructed: Edirne to Istanbul, across the second Bosporus bridge to Ankara, then to Adana and Gaziantep; sections around Izmir, Konya, and Ankara have also been completed. Turkey's goal is to build a net comparable to the German autobahns or the US Interstate Highway System.

The Trans-European Motorway (TEM) enters Turkey at Edirne, crosses the Bosporus by bridge, and extends eastward through Ankara to the Iranian border opposite Maku, a stretch of 1,120 mi/1,800 km. Branches reach south to Adana (and beyond to Syria, Iraq, and the peninsula countries) and north to the Black Sea at Trabzon—a total of 2,235 mi/3,600 km. Important for transiting traffic, especially tandem trailer trucks, between Europe and the Middle East, Turkey benefits appreciably from inclusion in the TEM network. Tourist facilities expect to attract larger numbers of Europeans from the northwest and Arabs from the southeast.

Linking Europe and Asia.   Despite an efficient and colorful ferry service across the Bosporus, heavy and rapidly increasing vehicular traffic by the late 1960s necessitated construction of a bridge across the strait. Spanning the narrowest part (about 0.6 mi/1 km) a few miles up the waterway from the old city and high above the water level, the suspension bridge linked Europe and Asia, enabling drivers to avoid long delays at ferry crossings. It was so successful at alleviating congestion that a wider second span was opened in 1988 to carry long-distance routes, leaving the first bridge for local traffic. Despite early fears, the structures detract little from the beauty of the Bosporus (Fig. 20.5). As intercontinental traffic over the bridges (and on the ferries) continued to mount, the Marmaray project—a rail tunnel under the Bosporus—was undertaken in 2004. Much

delayed, in part due to the discovery of a major archaeological site during the early excavations, the whole project is to be completed by 2015.[28] It will link the commuter systems on the European and Asian sides of the metropolis and will carry as well a high-speed rail link to Ankara and beyond. The tunnel is only a few miles from the very active North Anatolian Fault, thus requiring some innovative engineering approaches to its construction. The contract to build the somewhat controversial third bridge at the Bosporus's northern end was announced in May 2012.

Ports and Shipping.   With 4,474 mi/7,200 km of coastline—longest in the Middle East—and intimate interrelations between land and sea in the west and northwest, Turkey has a long maritime history. It has numerous ports, some active since ancient times, and a vigorous maritime trade. In addition to numerous small ports for coastal shipping, it has a half-dozen major and a score of secondary and minor ports for international trade. Although tonnage varies from year to year, leaders include Mersin and Iskenderun on the Mediterranean, Izmir on the Aegean, Samsun on the Black Sea, and Bandırma, Derince, and Hydarpaşa (opposite Istanbul) on the Sea of Marmara. All are served by railway. Secondary ports from Alanya around to Trabzon are indicated on Map 20.2.

The total tonnage of general international cargo, excluding petroleum, through all ports exceeds that of any other Middle East country. Free zones were established at the Mediterranean ports of Mersin and Antalya in the mid-1980s. Turkey operates the third-largest merchant marine fleet in the region, about 890 ships, but deadweight tonnage is less than that of Iran and only a fifth that of the fleet registered in Cyprus under that country's flag of convenience.

Airways.   Turkish Airways (Türk Hava Yolları—THY), with more than 120 jet aircraft,

Figure 20.5 The Bosporus Strait, looking north toward the Black Sea. Rumeli Hisar, built in 1453 by Ottoman sultan Mehmet the Conqueror to facilitate his seizure of Constantinople, is to the left. The second Bosporus Bridge, opened in 1988 and named after Sultan Mehmet, spans the strait in the distance.

ranks as one of the three or four largest in the Middle East. Turkey has more than forty airports with scheduled flights, and there are also several major military and NATO airfields, notably Incirlik (near Adana), Izmir, and Karamürsel (near Izmit). Istanbul's Atatürk International Airport opened a new international terminal in 2000; in 2010, it and Antalya's airport were the second and third busiest in the region (trailing only Dubai). Turkey also has a number of private airlines (scheduled, charter, and cargo) operating internationally.

RELATIONS

Turkey's location on the strategic bridgeland of Asia Minor with its geopolitical assets inevitably creates multidirectional reciprocal re-

lationships; these exist not only between the republic and its neighbors but also with more distant powers concerned about this critical area. Interactions with imperial Russia were a mainspring of Ottoman foreign policy for centuries; periodically, they turned to Britain or France—and, later, Germany—to counterbalance Russia. After Atatürk's revival of his defeated country and his preservation of its Anatolian territory, Turkey and Western European states reached an uneasy détente. Though neutral for most of World War II, Turkey eventually declared war on the Axis and became a charter UN member. As Soviet assertions after 1945 replaced historic Russian imperialism, Turkey allied with the West, especially with the United States, starting with the Truman Doctrine, against Soviet hegemonism.

United States. The United States established diplomatic relations with the Ottoman Empire in 1831. These were broken when the United States declared war on Germany in World War I (but not on the Ottomans) and were reestablished with republican Turkey in 1927. In addition to the embassy in Ankara, there is a consulate general in Istanbul and a consulate in Adana. Turkey sent an army brigade to Korea in 1950 to fight under the American-led UN forces there; at one point in the 2000s, Turkish forces constituted the third-largest contingent in the International Security Assistance Force in Afghanistan.[29] Economic assistance to Turkey began in the aftermath of World War II and continued with USAID playing a very active role; a total of some $5.5 billion in economic assistance grants and loans was extended, along with almost $13 billion in military assistance. There was a Peace Corps program in Turkey from 1962 to 1971, with some 1,460 volunteers serving there.

Through NATO, the two countries have been allies for more than sixty years, and the relationship on the whole has been close. Turkey gave the United States access to more than a dozen major facilities, including airfields, naval and communications bases, and intelligence-gathering installations. However, there have been a couple of periods of serious stress to the mutual ties—most notably, after Turkey's intervention in Cyprus in 1974, leading to a period of embargo regarding American arms deliveries, and in 2003 when Turkey's parliament rebuffed US desires to use Turkish bases in preparing to invade Iraq. On the other hand, in recent years, Turkey participated militarily in the US campaigns in Kosovo and allowed the use of air bases in the country to enforce the no-fly zones in Iraq from 1992 to 2003, as well as for US troop rotations after the 2003 invasion. In 2012, the two countries undertook close collaboration as the civil war in Syria drove thousands of refugees across the border into southeastern Turkey.

Western Countries. With the Turkish Straits a critical focus (see Map 9.6), Turkey as a significant segment of the Northern Tier and the Eurasian Rimland, played a major geopolitical role during the Cold War. It participated in NATO after 1952, the Baghdad Pact, and then CENTO (headquartered in Ankara from 1958 to 1979) as a regional military anchor. It joined the Council of Europe in 1949, was a founding member of the Organization for Economic Cooperation and Development in 1961, linked with the European Free Trade Association in 1991, and entered into a customs union in 1996 with the EU. After years of ambivalence, the EU agreed to consider Turkey for membership in 2005—the only Muslim state so far accepted for consideration. Along with Saudi Arabia, Turkey is a member of the so-called G-20, increasingly the principal economic and financial forum of the world's wealthiest economies; a nonregional contributing member of the Asian Development Bank; and a borrowing member of the European Bank for Reconstruction and Development.

European Union. Turkey has made qualifying for the EU a priority, especially since that would, inter alia, finally bestow on it the cachet of a genuine European entity—one of Atatürk's main goals. In early discussions, the EU identified problem areas that Turkey must correct or greatly improve: human-rights policies, military power in politics, treatment of minority ethnic and religious groups, and more open negotiation with Greece and Greek Cyprus. Turkey has made strides toward some of these aims but, as mentioned above, has had difficulty with others, and there is open hostility in some EU countries to its admission to full membership, regardless of how well Turkey handles these problem areas. In recent years, as mentioned above, Turkey has shown some ambivalence about joining, with popular support for joining falling from a reported 75 percent in 2004 to less than 50 percent by

2012. Additionally, the Turkish economy has actually performed better than those of most EU countries in the aftermath of the 2008 financial crash, while Turkey has been mostly immune from the effects of the Eurozone crisis (unlike Eurozone neighbors Cyprus and Greece). Concurrently, the country has turned more toward its Arab neighbors, Iran, and the newly independent states in the Caucasus and Central Asia.

Turkey's focus on the Soviet threat during the Cold War contrasted with the Arab focus on the threat posed by Israel. Its alliances with Western powers put it further at odds with its neighbors. During this time, it discreetly disengaged from its Middle East environment and avoided involvement in inter-Arab disputes and in the Arab-Israeli and other regional conflicts. Yet it attempted to maintain cordial, if not close, political and diplomatic ties with all Arab regimes and Iran—usually with the exception of Syria.[30] The Cold War's end profoundly affected Turkey because its role in the Western alliance was suddenly ambivalent; it then sought a more participatory role in its own neighborhood—the Balkans, the Caucasus, Central Asia, and the Middle East.[31] At that same time, the Iraqi invasion of Kuwait forced it to adopt a proactive policy in regional affairs, while seeking links with the newly independent ex-Soviet republics, especially the five with which it had ethnolinguistic links.

Muslim Neighbors. Relations with its three Muslim neighbors—Syria, Iraq, and Iran—have varied markedly. With Syria, they never have been warm, primarily because republican Turkey incorporated the Arabian Foreland plains inhabited by Arabs and because France unilaterally ceded it the disputed Hatay/Alexandretta area in 1938 (see "The State in the Middle East" and "Regional Conflicts," in Chap. 8). Two situations in the 1980s and 1990s heightened tensions dangerously: Syria's umbrage over Turkey's alleged overutilization of Euphrates water in the GAP and Turkish anger over Syrian support of Kurdish rebels, including harboring PKK leader Abdullah Öcalan during 1984–1999. Details of both disputes are given in other chapters.

When the Arab Spring came to Syria and the Assad regime met increasing demands for political reform with repressive actions, Turkey's policy in the new century of seeking peace with all its neighbors was sorely put to the test. By 2012, Turkey had called for regime change in Damascus, Syria had shot down a Turkish jet, Kurdish militants from Turkey were operating from Kurdish areas in Syria over which the regime had lost control, and tens of thousands of refugees from the fighting have continued to seek refuge in Turkey. Turkish support for the insurgent cause has not met with universal domestic support: secularists oppose close alignment with extremist Sunnis among the Syrian insurgents,[32] Alevis fear being tagged as supporters of the Assad regime, and Kurds identify with the aspirations of their Syrian kin.[33]

Relations between Turkey and Iraq are of signal importance to both parties on several matters: their Kurdish minorities, the Kirkuk-Yumurtalık pipeline, the shared Euphrates and Tigris basins, and communications and commercial relations. Cooperation between them during the Iran-Iraq War was of great mutual benefit, but after Iraq invaded Kuwait Turkey closed the pipeline from Kirkuk and joined the UN coalition. Both Iraq and Turkey benefited from the line's conditional reopening in 1997. They made tentative overtures for closer relations, but Turkey continued allowing US aircraft to operate from Incirlik. Turkey's stance before and during the US-led invasion attracted modest Arab approval. Since 2003, its interactions with and in Iraq have been complicated and ambivalent: on the one hand, it has been very wary of the autonomy enjoyed by the Kurdish provinces in northern Iraq and on several occasions has skirmished with Kurds based there and engaging in hostile activities within Turkey; on the other hand, Turkish entrepreneurs have been very active—and very profitably so—in supplying a wide range of goods to Iraq, especially to the Kurdish north. Exports to Iraq ran a close second only to those going to Germany in 2012, while Turkish firms received contracts for some $3.5 billion in projects.[34] Oil from fields under Kurdish control flows by pipeline to the Turkish port of Ceyhan, although the pipeline has been sabotaged several times, probably by Kurdish militants. Turkey has been actively supportive of Iraqi unity and of the government in Baghdad, which Prime Minister Erdoğan visited in 2008. It has also been increasingly vocal in backing the Turkman minority's rights in Kirkuk against Kurdish claims for the city.

Turkish-Iranian links were very close for twenty-five years under the Baghdad Pact/ CENTO, and even more so under the Regional Cooperation for Development (RCD), but ties loosened somewhat with Iran's Islamic Revolution.[35] Still, both are members of the RCD's successor, the Economic Cooperation Organization (ECO) founded in 1985 and expanded in 1992 to include Afghanistan and six former Soviet republics. ECO has a common market as its long-term goal. During the Iran-Iraq War, Turkey maintained links with both combatants; it still enjoys good, if not close, relations with the Islamic Republic and has tried to mediate between Iran and the West regarding Iran's nuclear program. Turkey has supported the NATO missile-shield program, which, among other things, is designed to protect Europe and Turkey from missiles originating to the east of Turkey. In 2012, Turkey was granted a waiver from compliance with the sanctions on Iran because of its heavy dependence on Iranian hydrocarbons. In return, Ankara agreed to gradually reduce its imports; in order to avoid restrictions on financial transactions with Iran, Turkey has been "selling" gold to Iran in return.[36]

Israel.   Along with the more crisis-driven developments in Turkey's redirected foreign relations during the 1990s, links with Israel quietly evolved until they became a major regional concern. Turkey as a Muslim state—albeit secular—had been cautious in its attitude toward the Arab-Israeli conflict, but it recognized Israel in 1949 and maintained low-key diplomatic and economic relations over the next forty years. But with the sea change in regional dynamics after 1990, it de-emphasized links with Arab states and, strongly encouraged by the United States, pursued closer ties with Israel. After exchanging ambassadors in 1991, Turkey and Israel reached a series of agreements, including one in 1996 permitting Israel to use Turkish airspace for training flights. Turkey also contracted with Israel for missiles and F-4 fighter jet upgrades. US, Turkish, and Israeli naval units conducted joint maneuvers in 1998 off the Israeli coast. The two countries entered into a free trade agreement in 2000. These moves, however, were not universally popular, and since the 2002 election installed a government with Islamic roots there has been some pullback. Turkey was positioned to mediate in the late 2000s, promoting Israeli-Syrian rapprochement, although it reacted very negatively to Israel's 2008–2009 "Cast Lead" campaign in Gaza and later that year refused Israeli participation in a joint air force exercise in Turkish airspace.

In May 2010, a flotilla carrying civilian goods and pro-Palestinian activists departed from Turkey, aiming to break through Israel's sea blockade of Gaza. While it was still in international waters, it was halted and boarded by Israeli naval forces. In the ensuing conflict, nine Turkish citizens were shot and killed, and many more were injured. Over the coming months, the acrimony between the two countries escalated, with Turkey demanding an apology and compensation and Israel refusing. In September 2011, Turkey broke diplomatic relations with Israel after previously having severed military and economic ties and closing Turkish airspace to some Israeli aircraft. Four high-ranking Israeli military officers were indicted in absentia, and a trial began in November 2012 with charges related to the flotilla deaths.

But in a much-publicized telephone call in March 2013, in the presence of President Obama, Prime Minister Netanyahu offered an apology to Prime Minister Erdoğan. Negotiations between the two countries had obviously prepared for the occasion and for the public reconciliation, prompted by mutual concerns about Syria and Iran and apparently promoted by elements in both countries, especially among the military, concerned that the rift had gone too far.

Former Soviet Union. Across the Black Sea, in the Caucasus, and in Central Asia, the independent ex-Soviet republics immediately attracted attention, and Turkey quickly reached out to them—especially to the five that are both Muslim and Turkic: Azerbaijan, Kazakhstan, Kyrgyzstan, Turkmenistan, and Uzbekistan.[37] In 1992, Turkey hosted eleven nations, including six former Soviet republics, to create the Black Sea Economic Cooperation project; in 1999, Turkey, Azerbaijan, and Georgia pledged to cooperate on Caspian pipelines, and in 2012 plans for the Trans-Anatolian pipeline were moving toward finalization (see above). Interestingly, in 2009, Turkey and Armenia announced that they would normalize relations after Turkish president Gul visited Yerevan after the brief war between Russia and Georgia in 2008; speculation was that Turkey wants to optimize its links with all the Caucasus states. Armenia reportedly was willing to postpone any discussion of the controversial events during World War I until diplomatic and trade relations were established. Rapprochement with Armenia, strongly promoted by the United States, complicated links with Azerbaijan, since part of its territory—Nagorno-Karabakh—is occupied by Armenia; Turkey has said full normalization will require settlement of this issue, and the normalization efforts have been suspended; by 2013, there appeared little incentive for either side to proceed toward normalizing relations.[38]

Greece and Cyprus. As important as the above relations may be, none are more critical than those with Greece and Cyprus. Dating from ancient times, antagonisms between Greece and Asia Minor revived more recently: the Greek war of independence from the Ottomans in the early 1800s, the Greek-Turkish war in the 1920s, conflict over Cyprus, and the dispute over the Aegean seabed (see Chap. 8). Among all the foreign-relations problems, Cyprus has been the most acute and the most difficult to resolve (see Chap. 11 for more detail on this situation). Turkey (along with the United States and the EU) supported the plan of Secretary-General Kofi Annan of the United Nations—a united republic of two states in confederation—and pressured Turkish Cypriots to vote in favor of it, which they did in 2004 by a 65 percent majority. Unfortunately, Greek Cypriots, with a hard-line president, rejected it by 75 percent. The year 2008 saw the hard-liners' defeat by a new president who pledged to restart negotiations. When the new Greek prime minister visited Turkey as his first overseas destination in 2009, the move was widely hailed in Greece. However, by 2012, extensive high-level discussions between the two Cypriot communities had broken down, and the Cyprus problem was starting to seem nearly as intractable as the Israeli-Palestinian problem. Further complicating the picture by 2012 were the prospects that the seabeds around Cyprus and those between the island and the Turkish mainland may contain considerable deposits of natural gas and oil.

Enjoying similarities and differences vis-à-vis Turkey and sharing the Mobile Belt with that bridgeland, Iran remains as the last—but far from the least—of the sixteen countries of the Middle East to be considered and now becomes the focus of our attention.

For information on the business environment in Turkey, see the website attached to this book: www.middleeastpatterns.com.

NOTES

1. Several good general studies of Turkey include *Turkey* Country Study 1995; B. Lewis 1968; Schick and Tonak 1987; Ahmad 1993; Mastney and Nation 1997; and Howe 2004.

2. A good, readable discussion is in Dewdney 1971, which also covers the general geography of Turkey. For technical geology, see Brinkmann 1976. For technical tectonics, see Dixon and Robertson 1984, which reveals the enormous complexity of Asia Minor's structure.

3. See Dixon and Robertson 1984, Sec. 3.

4. These and other sites are covered in Bean 1968 and Akurgal 1970.

5. For a detailed, scholarly, yet practical study of the many archaeological sites in Turkey, see Akurgal 1970.

6. *Archaeology* (Nov.–Dec. 2008).

7. See Pitcher 1972, a superb historical geography of the Ottoman Empire with excellent maps.

8. B. Lewis 1968 is a standard work on the evolution of modern Turkey. See also Ahmad 1993 and D. Howard 2001.

9. *BBC News,* Mar. 21, 2013; *al-Monitor,* Mar. 25, 2013; al-Jazeera, Apr. 11, 2013; and *Terrorism Monitor* 11, no. 8 (2013).

10. *Al-Monitor,* Jan. 29, Apr. 23, and Apr. 26, 2013.

11. For a comprehensive treatment of the affair and of interactions among secularists, nationalists, and Islamists, see Jenkins 2009.

12. The two countries that ranked higher, Israel (37th) and Cyprus (43rd), were classified as flawed democracies. Economist Intelligence Unit, "Democracy Index 2012."

13. Reporters Without Borders, "2013 World Press Freedom Index," http://en.rsf.org/press-freedom-index-2013,1054.html.

14. Maisel 2008.

15. For opposing viewpoints on Turkish treatment of the Armenians, see Jernazian 1990 and Gürün 1985.

See also *New York Times,* Mar. 6, 2004, regarding Turkish historians who advocate some Armenian claims. The success of rapprochement between Turkey and Armenia involved an understanding to put aside this dispute temporarily.

16. Following an interview aired on the US television program *60 Minutes* on Dec. 17, 2009, in which he expressed his fear that "the patriarchate is dying," he was interviewed by the Turkish press. See *Hurriyet: Daily News and Economic Review* (Istanbul), Dec. 24, 2009, www.hurriyetdailynews.com/; and *Today's Zaman* (Istanbul), Dec. 25, 2009, www.todayszaman/tz-web/. Political tensions between Greece and Turkey no doubt are at the root of the patriarchate's problems—in the mid-1980s, the Greek government rescinded the provision of the Treaty of Lausanne that allowed its Muslim minority to elect its own religious leadership and began appointing it instead. The continued Cyprus dispute is also a factor.

17. *Al-Monitor,* Jan. 17, Apr. 1, and Apr. 28, 2013.

18. For a detailed study of the Anatolian village, see Kolars 1968. For a study of the *gecekondu,* see Karpat 1976.

19. United Nations Development Programme, *Human Development Report 2013*; *Legatum Prosperity Index 2012*, www.prosperity.com/.

20. See Gallup Wellbeing Index at www.gallup.com/poll/wellbeing.aspx.

21. This section is partly based on briefings by officials of the Turkish State Hydraulic Works (DSI) at Atatürk Dam in 1990 and in DSI headquarters in Ankara in 1997, as well as on Kolars and Mitchell 1991.

22. *Christian Science Monitor,* May 27, 2008.

23. FAO, various issues.

24. US Geological Survey, "The Mineral Industry of Turkey," in *Minerals Yearbook* 2008.

25. *Al-Monitor,* Feb. 18, 2013.

26. For a discussion of Turkey as an energy hub, see Souleimanov and Kraus 2012.

27. For further information, see www.urbanrail.net/.

28. Istanbul municipal authorities are claiming an earlier completion date, but it is not clear whether they are referring to the entire project.

29. Turkish participation in ISAF was prompted by bombings in Istanbul in 2003 carried out by al-Qaida. It resisted Bush administration pressure to engage in combat operations, but committed its troops to providing security in Kabul and elsewhere.

30. See a good study in Sayari 1997.

31. Abramowitz and Barkey 2009 question whether Turkey is really the regional power its government claims it to be.

32. See *Al-Monitor,* Mar. 14, 2013, for the links between Turkey's largest opposition party and the Assad regime.

33. See "The Many Roles of Turkey in the Syrian Crisis," *Middle East Research and Information Project (MERIP),* Jan. 20, 2013; and *al-Monitor,* Mar. 19 and May 6, 2013.

34. *Reuters,* Mar. 14, 2013.

35. For further discussion of Turkish-Iranian relations, see Ayoub 2012 and Gürzel and Ersoy 2012.

36. *Today's Zaman* (Istanbul), Dec. 8, 2012.

37. Tajikstan's people are linguistically related to Iranians.

38. *Al-Monitor,* May 3, 2013.

The reader is advised to consult this book's associated website (**www.middleeastpatterns.com**) for additional information on **Turkey**, such as a historical time line and chronology of recent events, as well as essays on selected topics and various international economic, social, and political indicators.

21

Iran

Complex Republic on the Plateau

KEY POINTS: Greatly affected by tectonic forces, with Zagros chain in west and Elburz across north. Frequent earthquakes. One of three regional power cores. Moderately good precipitation in mountains, water channeled to irrigate crops. Rich history, base of powerful empires. Main base for Shiism and only dominantly Shii state in region, setting Iran somewhat apart in Middle East. Most varied large ethnic groupings among regional states, with Persians largest and Persian (Farsi) language dominant. Revolution in 1979 ended long history of monarchs (shahs), establishing absolute religious oligarchy led by ultraconservative ayatollahs. First oil discovery in region, has second-largest oil reserves in region. Well endowed with solid minerals, has flourishing and varied industry. Controls north side of Strait of Hormuz. Supports radical groups in region. Determined to regain traditional power, is developing nuclear power and, apparently, nuclear weaponry. Has poor relations with West and with neighbors.

YOUNG STATE, ANCIENT LAND

Iran-zamin. Iran's rankings serve as reminders of its importance: in the region, it is second in size, second in population, second in petroleum reserves, first in natural gas reserves, second in total area under cultivation, first in irrigated area, second in wheat production, first in copper output, and a major producer of other crops and minerals (see tables in Chaps. 4, 5, and 6). Gas reserves are second only to those of Russia, and those of petroleum fourth behind Venezuela, Canada, and Saudi Arabia, although it was one of the earliest producers with cumulative output of billions of barrels. Iran has been the core of Shii

Islam for centuries and the leader of militant Shiism and even of militant Islam since 1979. Ensconced in one of the region's strongest power foci (see Map 3.6), it has often shown resiliency, as in the Iran-Iraq War of the 1980s. Of special historical-geopolitical significance is its persistent concept of *Iran-zamin*, "the land of Iran." Somewhat comparable to the idea of Greater Syria, this broadly comprises the former Iranian imperial domain, implanted Iranian culture, and its historical influence through millennia—an ancient relationship between a people and their cultural homeland.[1] Although contemporary sentiment regarding *Iran-zamin* may not lead to emotional irredentism, its efforts to extend the

IRAN

Long-form official name, anglicized: Islamic Republic of Iran

Official name, transliterated: Jomhuri-ye Eslami-ye Iran

Form of government: unitary Islamic republic with one legislative house (Islamic Consultative Assembly)

Area: 636,374 mi²/1,648,200 km²

Population, 2011: 75,276,000; Literacy: 77%

Ethnic composition (%, 2000): Persian 34.9; Azerbaijani 15.9; Kurd 13; Luri 7.2; Gilaki 5.1; Mazandarani 5.1; Afghan 2.8; other 16

Religions (%, 2005): Muslim 98.2, of which Shia 86.1, Sunni 10.1, other 2; Bahai 0.5; Christian 0.4; Zoroastrian 0.1; other 0.8

Demography: Life expectancy—68.84 yr (M), 71.93 yr (F); Birthrate (per 1,000)—18.52; Fertility rate—1.87

GDP, 2011: $474.7 billion; purchasing power parity: $990.8 billion; per capita: $13,200

Currency: Iranian Rial (IRR), US$1 = 12,075 rials; 1 IRR = $0.00008 (mid-May 2013)

Energy: oil—154.6 billion bbl; natural gas—1,187,000 billion ft³; coal—limited reserves, from which small production

Main exports (% of total value, 2008–9): $100.6 billion (of which petroleum/natural gas 85.2; organic chemicals 3.1; plastics 1.4; pistachios 0.7; handwoven carpets 0.4)

Main imports (% of total value, 2005–6): $41.0 billion (of which nonelectrical machinery 23.5; base metals 13.8; road vehicles 13; chemical products 10.7)

Capital city, 2007: Tehran 7,873,000; other major cities: Mashhad 2,469,000; Esfahan 1,628,000; Karaj 1,423,000; Tabriz 1,413,000; Shiraz 1,240,000

Islamic Revolution to neighboring lands suggest that the idea is near the surface of its revolutionary consciousness.

Certain aspects of ethnicity and terminology also suggest Iran's individuality. One of the four states in the Middle East that is not Arab, it is the only major one in the region where the national language is neither Semitic nor Turkic. Migrating Aryans brought their Indo-European language to the plateau in the second millennium BCE, becoming ancestors of the Persians. The term "Iran" derives from "Aryan" and has always been preferred by the descendants of the Aryans as the name for the general area. Another toponym arose in the south-central part of the plateau—"Fars" became the root for both "Farsi," the designation for the main language, and "Persia," by way of Greek through a consonant shift. The area was best known in the West as Persia until Reza Shah in 1935 demanded that "Iran" be applied to the state and the oil company operating there. Thus, this official name is a reminder of the Aryans (literally, "nobles") who laid the foundations for the future state.

An Empire of Twenty-Five Centuries. Entrenched on its high plateau, Iran has been a significant imperial power for more than twenty-five hundred years. Since Cyrus the Great built his empire, it has kept a vigorous national base century after century, even when temporarily succumbing militarily and politically to Greeks, Arabs, or Mongols. Migrating peoples settled in less populated mountain basins and valleys, but, like China, it assimilated many of them; other groups were tolerated in isolated areas. Periodically absorbing powerful new influences that refreshed and reinvigorated it, the vibrant culture persevered and preserved its essence.

A Republic of One Generation. The Islamic revolution brought radical social change, none more radical than a shift in the ruling elite. Competing social groups have dynamized the body politic for decades: aristocracy, *bazaari* (merchants), clergy, tribal leaders, and army. Thought to be well under control, a highly politicized clergy asserted itself in the late 1970s, and the Iran of the 1980s reversed the sociopolitical trends of previous decades. People and environments once again interacted to search for identity and control.

Iran enjoyed many years of generally good relations with the rest of the world before 1979. Its status as a pariah afterward sometimes obscures its long cultural traditions, enduring geopolitical significance, petroleum wealth, economic potential, and human resources. As is true in any political-geographical evaluation of a state, the short-term conditions must be balanced with the enduring factors. This is difficult in Western estimates of Iran because of its direct and indirect involvement in hostage taking, terrorism, nuclear threat, and other abnormal behavior after the 1979 revolution. Nevertheless, Iran's abiding factors must be kept in focus, and those factors are emphasized in this chapter.

PLATEAU PALIMPSEST

Building a Persian State. The sequence of human occupancy over thousands of years is well preserved in the Iranian Plateau, and its antiquity is neither inconsequential nor academic. Evidence of ancient habitation is rarely out of sight in the more humid areas. More than a quarter-million archaeological sites include some from the Middle Paleolithic (Mousterian) period about forty thousand years ago, during the last glacial period. Thousands of tells covering successive Neolithic villages dot the valleys, piedmonts, and plains. Also called *tepes* or *chegas,* mound sites of later villages are equally numerous,[2] and excavations have yielded elaborate pottery and ornaments of bronze, silver, and gold. On the Marv Plain (Marvdasht) before Persepolis, more than a thousand tells have been identified, most from 6000–5500 BCE.

In the late seventh century BCE, the Medes, an Iranian people, threw off Assyrian rule and assembled a state comprising most of modern Iran, plus parts of Iraq, Turkey, and Afghanistan. In 550 BCE, the Medes were defeated by Cyrus the Great, who founded the Achaemenid dynasty that ruled the first Persian Empire; at its greatest extent, it stretched from the Aegean Sea and the Libyan Desert to the Indus Valley and north into Central Asia. The dominant (but not exclusive) religion of the Achaemenids was a form of an older Iranian religion, the beginnings of which are traced to Zarathustra (Zoroaster). Alexander the Great defeated Persia in 330 BCE, and following his death the eastern portion of his conquests fell to one of his generals, Seleucus, whose descendants ruled a Hellenistic state until supplanted by the Parthians, an Iranian people, in 140 BCE. They in turn were replaced in 224 CE by the Sassanids, who were the Roman Empire's primary eastern rivals for more than four centuries and who promoted Zoroastrianism throughout their domains.

Arrival of Islam. After this succession of powerful empires, the Arab Muslim invasion in the 630s led to momentous changes. The Sassanian collapse at the hands of desert warriors was at first staggering to the Persians, but a national revival demonstrated vitality once again. Borrowed and exploited by the Arabs, Persian expertise, vigor, experience, and cultural vibrancy strengthened the Umayyad Empire and then were major factors in the Abbasid ascendancy in Mesopotamia. The Persian language diffused throughout the region, exchanging hundreds of loanwords with Arabic and, later on, Turkish. Although Islam was cradled in Arabia and brought by Arabs to Iran, the Islamic civilization that evolved over the centuries was highly Persianized.

Iran suffered political fragmentation, cultural disruption, and physical destruction after the Abbasid collapse in 1258; Mongols and Tatars threatened its identity for three hundred years. But, as in the seventh century, it absorbed and integrated disparate ethnic and cultural influences, preserving "Persianality." Shii Islam became the state religion in the sixteenth century under the Safavids, one of whom gave Iran a golden age—Abbas the Great (1587–1629), whose lasting contributions to Persian culture are preserved in the splendid monuments of Esfahan. Safavid rule ended in 1736; the Zands followed until 1794, and then the Qajar mediocrities, with losses of both national vigor and territory.

Pahlavi Interlude.   Reza Khan seized the throne in 1925, founding the Pahlavi dynasty and embarking on modernization. Emulating Atatürk's authoritarianism in Turkey, his policies were less successful. Considered pro-German, he was forced by Britain and the USSR to abdicate in 1941. The reign of his son, Mohammad Reza, was threatened by nationalist prime minister Mohammad Mossadegh, who embroiled Iran in a prolonged dispute with Britain over the oil concession. With controversial US assistance, the shah regained power in 1953, ruling increasingly autocratically and with ever-increasing reliance on the savage tactics of SAVAK, his Israeli-trained secret police and intelligence service, until forced into exile in January 1979.[3]

A THEOCRATIC REPUBLIC

Ayatollah Khomeini.   Having sought political control in times past, Shii clerics joined laymen in the 1970s to fight foreign influence and widespread domestic corruption and repression. After the shah was ousted by Ayatollah Ruhollah Khomeini, however, many of his methods were no less harsh than those of the monarchy. Revolutionary courts condemned opponents on such a scale as to raise internal and external censure. As one Iranian scholar put it, "Iran's Islamic Republic is a religious oligarchy of intricately overlapping relationships among the leading clerics. . . . At the apex of the political pyramid is the Supreme Leader (*rahbar*) . . . the spiritual guide of the nation, the official head of state, the commander-in-chief of the armed forces and, as vali-e-faqih [Islamic jurist], the protector of the faith. . . . Since Islam is a polity ruled by God, disobedience toward God's surrogate rulers is seen as not only a sin against the Almighty but a crime against the state, leaving no room for criticism, disagreement or dissent."[4] Designating opponents as enemies of God[5] is only too common in the contemporary Middle East, from the Hizballah in Lebanon to Jewish extremists in Israel.

Institutionalizing the Republic.   The complicated constitution mixes the religious and the secular in the republic's leadership. The supreme leader (Ayatollah Ali Khamenei since Khomeini's death in 1989) is elected for life by the Assembly of Experts, and all clerics are popularly elected; theoretically, they could depose him. He has the final say on all policies, is the final arbiter on intragovernmental disputes, and appoints key officials. The popularly elected president has day-to-day executive responsibilities and commands the military; he can be removed by the supreme leader. The Majlis (parliament) is elected, but all candidates must be approved by the appointed Guardian Council made up of senior clerics and judges. The revolution thus replaced the monarchy with a complex theocracy.

With such a radical change, national cohesion became the republic's priority; separatist tendencies were repressed ruthlessly. The outbreak of the war with Iraq in September 1980 (see "The Iran-Iraq War, 1980–1988," in Chap. 9, and Chap. 14) helped the regime by unifying most of the population against the aggressor. But the war led to as many as 1 million Iranian casualties and tremendous destruction.

The regime completely reoriented its foreign relations, repudiating Western influences and especially those of the United States. The unprecedented seizure of the American Embassy and fifty-three diplomats violated international law and led to Iran's isolation globally, particularly problematic once the war with Iraq broke out. Despite its aggression, Iraq received more external aid, while only Syria and Libya in the region helped Iran.[6]

Post-Khomeini Transition. In the two years between the Iran-Iraq cease-fire and Iraq's invasion of Kuwait, the republic stabilized and made an unexpectedly smooth transition after Khomeini's death. The new leadership (Khamenei and President Hashemi-Rafsanjani) seemed more moderate and pragmatic and turned their focus toward mending the country's war-ravaged economy (see below, "Planning Under the Republic"), While the presence of the coalition forces led by the United States against Iraq presented the new leaders with the dilemma of the proximity of one enemy fighting another, it did force Iraq to conclude a peace on Iranian terms.

With the war past, the economy rather stagnant, and religious fervor weighing on society, the 1990s saw outbreaks of unrest. The election of 1997 brought in a new president, Muhammad Khatami, who promised both economic reform and social liberalization; his moves were frequently frustrated by powerful elements among the clergy who had added economic power to their religious authority. In 2005, he was defeated for reelection by Mahmud Ahmedinejad, a somewhat demagogic mayor of Tehran whose hard-line reputation won him the support of the more conservative elements of the clergy.

Ahmedinejad Presidency. Disputatious and regressive, Ahmedinejad was a populist both as mayor and president, given more to rhetoric than policy discussions. Domestically, his economic policies often verged on the reckless, with subsidies ballooning in advance of the 2009 election to some $90 billion, or about 30 percent of GDP, bringing on a state of crisis when the global recession was cutting oil demand and economic sanctions on Iran were an increasing problem. Strikes and demonstrations were common throughout his first term. Dissatisfaction among the republic's leaders led him into frequent conflict with the Majlis, despite his conservative religious orientation, but he kept the support of the supreme leader. Internationally, his rhetorical flourishes could fairly be said to be damaging to Iran's standing, as in, for example, his extreme and erratic statements about Israel and his often-confused and contradictory remarks about Iran's nuclear program (see below, "Relations: Nuclear Dispute").

In 2009, his most important election opponent was Mir-Hossein Mousavi, a former prime minister who ran as a reformer. When the results were announced that Ahmedinejad had been reelected with an unlikely 62 percent of the vote, protests from the defeated candidates and the general public brought hundreds of thousands into the streets. At first, the crowds questioned election irregularities, but despite the repression and arrests that followed they coalesced into the Green Movement, led by Mousavi. The regime said the election was fair and, blaming "foreign interests" for the protests, arrested several leaders for allegedly conspiring with those interests. The movement survived, and the opposition to Ahmedinejad grew to include the Islamic regime itself, but protests lessened during 2009 (with some resurgence as the Arab Spring blossomed in February 2011). During his turbulent second term, Ahmedinejad frequently appealed to Iranians' strong underlying patriotism, using the mounting effects of sanctions and the growing condemnation of Iran's nuclear activities as proof of foreign conspiracies. Ineligible for reelection, he was succeeded in 2013 by a relative moderate, Hassan Rouhani, who quickly indicated a significant change in rhetoric in dealing with both domestic and international matters.

Majlis Elections.   Parliamentary elections have highlighted the paradoxes of contemporary Iran. In the early years of the republic, the "mullahocracy" had evolved a genuine if quirky system of democratic elections. In the election of 2000, liberals and supporters of President Khatami took control, defeating the conservative clerical establishment for the first time. But as the next election approached, the Guardian Council used its authority to disqualify thousands of candidates believed to be reformers. The ensuing election returned the conservatives to legislative power, and the same process was seen again in the 2008 election. In 2012, the reformers boycotted the parliamentary poll altogether. Despite conservative dominance of the legislature, there were numerous conflicts between the Majlis and Ahmedinejad.

A Momentous Decade.   More than domestic political turmoil faced the regime in the new century. Although Iran condemned the 9/11

attacks as terrorism—and the extremism of Osama bin Laden's (Sunni) Islam as deviant to the religion—President George W. Bush included Iran along with Iraq and North Korea in his "Axis of Evil." Shortly thereafter, Iran and Russia concluded a deal under which Russian technicians began construction of the long-delayed Bushehr nuclear facility (part of which engendered the international outcries regarding the nature of Iran's nuclear plans). In 2003, the Nobel Peace Prize was awarded to Shirin Ebadi, a human-rights lawyer and activist, calling attention to the very difficult circumstances under which she had to work given the repressiveness of the regime. Her consequent targeting by the clerical establishment only called more attention to the regime's deplorable record regarding human rights.

Relations with the UN's International Atomic Energy Agency (IAEA) became increasingly confrontational as the regime, loudly proclaiming its right to purse nuclear development for peaceful purposes, would at times seem to be cooperating with the agency only to be caught in contradictory actions that strengthened international suspicions that it was hiding a military program. Among other consequences (and coupled with Iran's growing presence in Iraq and Syria), its actions have brought together its Sunni-dominated neighbors in opposition to what they see as a nuclear-armed "Shii Crescent" stretching from Iran to Lebanon. Iran has moved to the center of the world stage, but in ways not foreseen in the most megalomaniacal dreams of the late shah. In 2012, *Foreign Policy* placed Iran 34th of 177 countries on its failed-states list, a notable deterioration since the first such list was published in 2005, when it ranked 57th.[7]

A Decidedly Mixed Picture.   Inexplicable as the Islamic Republic often is, it has engendered political and social self-examination in all segments of society, which has engaged in tremendous intellectual ferment and dynamic debate over the Islamicization of politics, the role and status of women, pluralism, foreign relations, and the very essence and direction of the republic. The process has been very Iranian—sometimes painfully pronounced, sometimes subtly nuanced, always contradictory, oscillating between modernity and retrogression. With all its contradictions, Iran has seen some progress, often shrouded by abuses of human rights, rampant corruption, demagogic rhetoric, religious obscurantism, and challenges to norms of international behavior, especially regarding its nuclear program. There have been advances in rural development (electrification, water supply, road access, postal services), an almost doubled literacy rate, and the reconstruction of cities damaged in the Iran-Iraq War.

On women's rights, the presence of women at all levels of education and government increased—some 60 percent of university students in the early 2010s were female—while their role in society was suppressed and a strict dress code was (sometimes sporadically) enforced. But in 2012, it was announced without explanation that more than thirty universities were closing their doors to women in a variety of programs ranging from English language to engineering; conversely, other programs at some institutions were restricted to women only.

Living standards for the average Iranian, using the UNDP's Human Development Index as a guide, have improved, but remain relatively low—in 2013, Iran ranked 76th among 186 countries globally and 9th regionally. But compared to 1980, its index value had registered a gain of more than 67 percent, based largely on improvements in the health and education components. Using the more broadly based Prosperity Index from the Legatum Institute, Iran ranked 102nd of 142 counties globally and 9th regionally.[8]

A MOUNTAIN-RIMMED PLATEAU

Iranian Landscapes

Variety and Contrasts.   Even in a region of contrasts, the diversity among landscapes is greater than those in any other Middle East country. Turkey and Israel display great variety, but only Iran ranges from lush subtropical environments, like the mountain-backed Caspian coast, to totally barren, salt-encrusted deserts, like the huge *kavirs* of the interior basins. Its landforms, climates, vegetation, and people all spread across a wide spectrum.[9]

Landforms.   The Iranian Plateau is a region of intermontane plateaus and mountains, with high, rugged mountains providing walls on three sides (Map 21.1). It is shaped like a triangular bowl—the base runs from northwest to southeast, and the apex lies in the northeast near Mashhad. Coastlands and mountains framing the borders have historically served as ramparts.

Iran is the central segment of the Tethyan geosynclinal belt extending from Morocco to Indonesia. It is the eastern half of the Middle East's Mobile Belt, or Fold Belt (see Map 2.2), and was compressed between the Arabian Shield and the Russian Platform in the long period of intense folding from Triassic to Pliocene and Pleistocene times. The Zagros and Elburz-Kopet Mountains buckled upward with tectonic compression, embracing between them a relatively inflexible block, a denuded shield forming vast interior *kavirs*. Eastern Iran has one of the most remarkable geomorphic features in the region, a huge rafted tongue of exotic terrain clearly visible from space. Compression and thrust-faulting continue, with numerous seismic events on all sides; one hundred thousand people died in eleven major quakes during the past sixty years. The most disastrous hit Bam in December 2003, when forty-three thousand died.[10] Iran has so many mountains and high

Map 21.1 General map of Iran, with *ostan* (provincial) centers and other cities, highways, spot heights, and main mountain ranges. Regions are indicated by circled numbers.

plateaus that its average elevation is an unusual 4,920 ft/1,500 m.

Drainage. Reflecting Mediterranean-type precipitation, runoff peaks in late winter and early spring with seasonal rains and melting snow. In April, the Karun River, Iran's largest river, has ten times its October flow. Farther east, the Zayandeh Rud, the largest river in the Esfahan watershed, has a spring maximum discharge of 1,680 m³ per second, loaded with meltwater and fifty times more than in late fall—it actually dried up during

the severe drought of 2000–2001. Salty Lake Urmia, in a closed northwestern basin, covers one-third more area in May with snowmelt than in early October.

Several large dams impound seasonal runoff for use through the year, but many more are needed to increase irrigation and environmentally clean electricity. Scores of smaller streams carry runoff from upper slopes to piedmonts and alluvial fans on the inner sides of the many mountain chains and then dissipate in the sands, gravels, and saline crusts of interior basins. More than half of

Iran's drainage area lies in these basins, from the vast *kavirs* to pocket-size valleys in the Zagros. It is, nevertheless, these interior streams that are exploited by thousands of subterranean *qanat* systems for irrigation (Fig. 21.3). Table 2.1 shows the seasonality and yearly average of precipitation in Iran's four main climate areas.

Pattern of Regions

The pattern of regional physical and cultural features reveals especially significant contrasts, and some understanding of the regional design aids in appreciating Iran's general character and problems. For this reason, several representative central places that are notably differentiated both historically and regionally are included in the surveys below, considering first the mountainous and coastal margins and then the interior basins (the numbered regions are keyed to Map 21.1).[11]

[1] Zagros Mountains and Gulf Coast. Part of the southern arc of the great Alpine folding system, the Zagros Mountains extend northwest-southeast for 1,000 mi/1,600 km from Turkey to the Strait of Hormuz. Four parallel belts exhibit different lithology, structures, and landforms from west to east, and in the southeastern Zagros scores of salt domes pierce the folded sequence, forming prominent features in the desert climate (see Fig. 9.4). Many are domed-structure oil and gas reservoirs.

It is in the belts of the Zagros region that much of the population lives and most development has historically taken place. Winter precipitation intercepted by the considerable elevations irrigates in the succeeding season. Most oil fields are in the central-western folds (see Maps 6.1 and 6.2); many metallic minerals are found in the volcanic belt and thrust-faulting of the eastern Zagros, along the interplate zone of contact. Most of Iran's major and more famous cities are nestled in the valleys or along the piedmonts of the folds and along the Gulf coastal plain to the west (see Map 21.1).

In the northwest is Tabriz, the fifth-largest city, a former imperial capital and now capital of Azerbaijan Ostan (Farsi *ostan* = province). Its bustling old bazaar has the distinct atmosphere of a Turkic metropolis, but many ethnic groups jostle on its crowded streets. In the central Zagros valleys, basins, and eastern piedmont are several major centers, from Sanandaj and Qom in the north to Esfahan in the south. They include former capitals (Hamadan and Esfahan), noted carpet centers (Hamadan, Kermanshah, Qom, Kashan, Esfahan), and modern industrial concentrations. The important religious center of Qom was enhanced after the clergy gained power; Ayatollah Khomeini ruled like a sovereign from his home there. Esfahan preserves its former imperial status in its Safavid pavilions, picturesque main square or *maydan*, and blue-tiled royal mosque, Masjid-e Shah (now politically renamed Masjid-e Imam; Fig. 21.1). The third-largest city, it is credited with half the globe's beautiful sites in the proverb "Esfahan nesf-e Jahan" (literally, "Esfahan is half the world"). In the south, Shiraz is the main center—yet another city with the special aura of a former imperial capital. Climatic and soil conditions give it a particularly good ecology for growing roses, which crowd the hundreds of gardens adorning the city. Two of Iran's most famous poets, Hafez and Saadi, are memorialized in impressive tombs.

The Gulf coast of more than 800 mi/500 km once repelled human habitation and development, both by its topography and by its climate. Along most of the shore, Zagros ridges rise precipitously from the Gulf, leaving no room for settlement. Elsewhere, marshy flats dominate, and nowhere is fresh water plentiful. Nevertheless, Iran's extensive oil operations in the southwest require nearby export facilities, and imports need large-scale general-cargo ports. The main oil terminal is on Kharg (Khark) Island, 25 mi/40 km

Figure 21.1 Masjid-e Shah (Royal Mosque), Esfahan, from the reign of Shah Abbas the Great in the early 1600s, now officially called Masjid-e Imam. With its beautiful blue tiles, it is considered one of the world's most splendid mosques.

offshore, opposite Kuwait. Gulf cargo ports are Bandar-e Khomeini (originally Bandar-e Shahpur) in the north, Bandar-e Bushehr south of Kharg, and Bandar Abbas on the Strait of Hormuz (Farsi *bandar* = port). The coast is now more closely integrated with the rest of the country, especially as offshore oil and gas fields are developed (see "Ports" below). The small island of Kish has been transformed into a free port with a relatively liberal social atmosphere.

[2] Elburz Mountains and Northeast Chains. This region comprises not only the Elburz chain itself but also the eastern extension of the same compressional structures, plus the piedmonts or forelands that lie to the north and south. From the southwestern corner of the Caspian Sea to the far northeast beyond Mashhad, the range is part of the northern belt of Alpine folding, splaying from the Zagros structures west of Tehran. The eastern

extension comprises several parallel ridges, usually called the Kopet Mountains (*Kopet Dagh*—the name of the northernmost ridge along the Turkmenistan frontier).

Averaging about 60 mi/97 km in width, the range has many summits above 12,000 ft/3,658 m. It culminates in the symmetrical volcanic cone of Mount Damavand, 18,606 ft/5,671 m, highest in the Middle East. The steep northern slopes descend to the Caspian plain and shore, which lies 92 ft/28 m below sea level. On the opposite side, the southern slopes terminate at plateau level, 5,000 ft/1,525 m at Tehran, so that the total relief is much less than on the northern side. Several small glaciers emphasize the elevation of the peaks. Except for a few high passes, traversed by three spectacular highways, the chain is a major impediment to transportation and to the flow of moisture-laden winds from the northwest. The range is tectonically active, as indicated by frequent sharp earthquakes.

In the northeast, the folded Kopet ridges of northern Khorasan are appreciably lower than the Elburz proper and more comparable to the folded Zagros. Open valleys are devoted to cereal cultivation and support a moderately dense population. Mashhad is not only Iran's second city but, like Tabriz, also a center of ethnic complexity, with Persians, Turkmans, Baluch, Kurds, Hazaras, and others mingling in the bazaars and mosques. Like Qom, Mashhad has one of the holiest Shii shrines—the tomb of the eighth imam, Ali Reza. The opening of the border between Iran and Turkmenistan and the other new republics of ex-Soviet Central Asia (historically, a region long influenced by Persian culture) in 1991 has produced an appreciable influx of visitors from these long-isolated lands.

The large population of the Caspian coast is distributed in many small towns and villages rather than in a few metropolitan areas. Rasht, in the west, is noteworthy, along with the port of Bandar-e Anzali (once Bandar-e Pahlevi). In the east are Gorgan and Bandar-e Torkaman (formerly Bandar-e Shah). Several coastal towns are much-frequented resort centers, including Ramsar and Chalus.

The piedmont and foredeep south of the Elburz-Kopet belt support not only metropolitan Tehran but also Qazvin to the west, the ancient city of Rey south of Tehran, and a series of towns along the Tehran-Mashhad railway, following the old Silk Road. Suburbs and peripheral villages have coalesced to form Greater Tehran, sprawling along the alluvial fans south of the Elburz. About 20 percent of the population resides around the metropolis. Upper-class residences (now often those of favored officials and clergy) are concentrated in northern Tehran's higher slopes, especially in the suburb of Shemiran (Fig. 21.2). These neighborhoods had first use of the water from the *qanats* that formerly supplied the city; they both avoided lower Tehran's smog and were cooler because of their elevation.[12] The city has an impressive concentration of government buildings, embassies, banks, schools, and office buildings. The streets of the Central Business District have some of the most congested traffic in all the Middle East; in an effort to alleviate the escalating traffic problem, a road tunnel 10 km in length opened in 2013, allowing vehicles to pass from one side of the city to the other.[13] The bazaar, in the crowded southern sector, is one of the region's major shopping centers, especially noted for gold jewelry, carpets, and decorative brass- and copperwares.

[3] Eastern Highlands. Several separate complex ridges form the eastern rim of the Iranian "bowl." Runoff supports scattered villages, some of which include ruins of ancient settlements. South of Zahedan, at the southern end of the highlands, is the only recently active volcano, Kuh-e Taftan. The eastern reaches of Khorasan, the largest province, share a long porous border with Afghanistan, most of which was part of *Iran-zamin* for centuries. During the Soviet occupation in the 1980s and later fighting, as many as 2 million Afghans sought refuge here, and many still remained in 2012. After Pakistan, Iran has more refugees than any other country. The government gained control of the frontier zone only in the 1960s; now it is a battleground between drug smugglers and the army.

[4] Interior Basins. This east-central region is contained within the larger Iranian triangle. It includes several smaller basins, but its two major ones are Dasht-e Kavir in the north center and Dasht-e Lut in the southeast (Farsi *dasht* = desert or plain).[14] The lowest part of its watershed is the Great Kavir (*kavir* = playa or salt flat), an immense erosional surface with salt- and mud-filled depressions and extensive dune fields covering more than 20,000 mi²/ 51,800 km². Dasht-e Lut (*lut* = desert basin), the lowest sump in interior Iran at 672 ft/205 m above sea level, is somewhat smaller than the Great Kavir, separated from it by a low

Figure 21.2 Northern Tehran (Shemiran and Tajrish residential suburbs) nestled at the foot of the towering snow-covered Elburz Mountains.

divide and quite different from it. The weird surface is etched by wind into *yardangs*, alternating ridges and grooves, some as high as 195 ft/60 m, and wind-eroded material is piled into dunes to the south and east.

Neither the great salt expanse of the Dasht-e Kavir nor the rough Dasht-e Lut is inhabited, even by nomads. Neither soil nor meager precipitation permits perceptible vegetation, although desert bush survives on the higher parts of the basins and in the courses of seasonal streams. These barren interior basins are the least-useful parts of Iran.

PEOPLE: DEMOGRAPHY AND ETHNOGRAPHY

Population

With one of the three largest populations in the Middle East, Iran has about as many people as all six GCC states plus Iraq and Jordan. Moreover, it has the region's most complex ethnic structure, both in the number of major groups and in the concentrations of those groups. It has at least eight peoples numbering more than 1 million each and another half-dozen in the range of 100,000 to 1 million each (see Table 4.3 and Map 21.2).

The areas most favorable to habitation have long been densely populated: the Zagros valleys, Caspian coastlands, and inner piedmonts of the mountain frame. With socioeconomic change and a rising standard of living from the 1950s, faltering only in the late 1970s, Iran saw its net population increase to 4.6 percent annually, the highest in the region. Efforts initiated by the shah in the 1960s to slow the rate were showing modest success—2.9 percent by the mid-1970s—when the fundamentalists reversed course. It

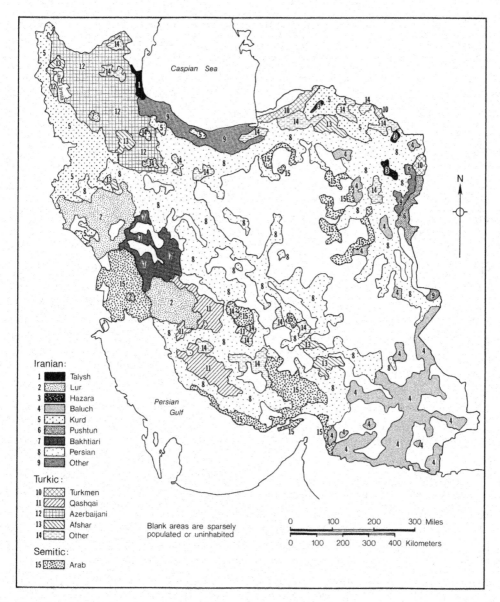

Map 21.2 Iran's complex patterns of ethnic groups.

jumped to 3.9 percent before the regime reacted and again encouraged birth control; the rate was down to about 1.2 percent by 2012. The estimated fertility rate had by then fallen below the replacement rate, leading Ayatollah Khamenei to reverse direction again, lamenting that family-planning policies had been a mistake and would prevent Iran from reaching its full potential.

Rapid Urbanization. As in other Middle East states and in most developing countries, the shift from rural to urban areas in Iran has been pronounced. Urban population, only 30 percent in the mid-1950s, reached 71 percent by 2010. With so many people (particularly young people) in cities like Tehran, the potential for urban unrest to shake governments has escalated, as can be seen from the riots that brought down the shah to the demonstrations of the Green Movement. But with all this movement of the population, millions of Iranians still reside in more than fifty-five thousand villages along the piedmonts and valleys of the countryside (see Fig. 4.8). Since they are concentrations of population, the pattern of village areal distribution correlates with patterns of available runoff and of higher rainfall. The Islamic city, as examined in Chapter 4, is clearly identifiable in Iran, where it also possesses its own "Persianality."[15]

Peoples of the Plateau

Ethnic Complexity.   Iran exhibits the most complex ethnic mosaic in the region. Indeed, its pattern of peoples is so motley that the central government has done well to maintain the state's national unity through the centuries; this section emphasizes this complexity. Although ethnic Persians (as distinct from Iranians) have played the most prominent role in Iran's development, events have also often been influenced by minority peoples. Both its location and its complex pattern of landforms have influenced the historical influx of various groups and the resultant ethnic pattern.[16]

Over the millennia, groups have invaded or migrated into the plateau from Asia Minor, the Caucasus, Central Asia, and the Indian subcontinent. Once they found themselves south of the barriers of the Black Sea, Caucasus Mountains, and Caspian Sea, migrants were forced through the mountain-ribbed Iranian "throat" between the Caspian and the Gulf. Some westward-moving peoples pushed into and across Mesopotamia; others elected to settle in the basins of the rugged Zagros Mountains.

Geographic Complexity.   Landform complexity—elaborate patterns of parallel and sometimes interconnected linear valleys and irregular basins—imposed difficulties

but also offered opportunities: for settlement, for survival where there was water, and for protection from neighbors as well as from central authority. Some migrants were partly or completely assimilated, but more than a score retain their identities in their own territories, like the Qashqai, Bakhtiari, and Lur. Several minorities have kept tribal organization, thus preserving their cultures. The preservation of minority languages provides a functional linguistic criterion to aid in distinguishing groups. In a few cases, religion becomes the main particularity.

Most of the peoples of Iran are discussed in Chapter 4 and are included in Table 4.3, hence only a few details need be added here to place them in more specific context. A few smaller groups are also mentioned. Map 21.2 shows the group patterns, and the identification numbers discussed below are keyed to that map.

Persians and Related Peoples.   Persian/Farsi is the principal language in a subfamily of languages that includes Kurdish, Luri, Baluchi, Gilaki, Mazandarani, and the tongues of several smaller groups. Although ethnic Persians [8] are the third-largest people in the Middle East and the largest single group in Iran, they are less than half the country's population. The most widely distributed of Iran's peoples, they are found especially in an almost unbroken, broad ring around the interior basins. They have constituted the great majority of managerial and government workers, the economic elite, and, under the republic, the ruling clerics.

Kurds [5] concentrate in the Iranian segment of Kurdistan, in the western Zagros along the Turkish and Iraqi borders. Like their kin in those countries, Iranian Kurds have opted for separatism, rebelling unsuccessfully in 1919, during World War II (the short-lived Mahabad Republic suppressed in 1947), and again in 1979. The semi-independence of Iraqi Kurdistan is as troubling to the rulers in

Tehran as it is to those in Ankara. The Kurds are mostly Sunnis—the largest group of Sunnis in the republic.

The Baluch [4], also mostly Sunni, dwell in the southeastern corner of Iran; still nomadic, they are the least-economically and least-socially integrated of the major minorities. Separatism has been a major issue in the 2000s; the government argues this is spearheaded by the Jundullah, which it terms a foreign-supported terrorist group (see "Terrorism," in Chap. 9). After the capture of the group's leader, Abdolmalek Rigi, in February 2010, Tehran claimed that he was about to travel to a US base in Central Asia.[17] Despite the arrest of many of Jundullah's leaders, Baluch radicals initiated a new series of bomb attacks on government facilities in October 2012.

Divided by the main concentration of the Bakhtiari [7], the Lur [2] have two clusters in the central Zagros. Khorramabad is the center of the northern area, Lorestan; the oil center of Gach Saran lies on the southern edge of the southern concentration. The Bakhtiari, mostly between the oil center of Masjid-e Soleyman and Shahr-e Kord, are perhaps the most powerful southern tribe. Both groups are mostly Shia.

Secluded in high mountain valleys and basins in Khorasan, a few tens of thousands speaking several Indo-European languages spill over from neighboring Afghanistan and Central Asia. Other groups live in scattered locations southwest and south of the Caspian. The numerous Shii Hazara, or "Berberi" [3], around Mashhad, have many kin in central Afghanistan where they have long been persecuted by that country's Sunni majority. The Aimaq, in the "Other" category on the map [9], include a score of groups, exemplifying the multiplicity in this rugged area of crisscrossing migrations.

Astride the northern part of the Iranian-Afghan border are many Pushtun [6], who have millions of kin farther east. West of the Caspian, on either side of the border, are several thousand Talysh [1]. Groups subsumed in the "Other" category [9] include a few tens of thousands of Tajik in the northern part of the Zabol salient. Along the Caspian coast are the Gilani (sometimes Gilaki) in the west, around Rasht, and the Mazandarani farther east; both peoples are predominantly Shia. The Gilani have shown separatism several times, most notably in a short-lived socialist republic after World War II.

Turkic Peoples. The Azeri, or Azerbaijani [12], Iran's largest ethnolinguistic minority, speak a Turkic language but are Shia and adhere to other Persian cultural traditions. Their center is Tabriz. While maintaining their identity and language, they join in Iranian nationalism, provided the government accepts their informal autonomy. Separatism emerged after World War II in a brief USSR-inspired republic. Thwarting this effort was one of the first effective acts of the UN. After the ex-Soviet republic of Azerbaijan became independent in 1991, Iranian Azeris—to the discomfit of the government—made tentative declarations of hope for union in an enlarged Azeri state.

The Qashqai [11] have perhaps the strongest nomadic tradition among the larger groups. In two large areas in Fars Province, to the north and south of Shiraz, and well organized in confederations, they have traditionally resisted government control. Like most Iranians, they are Shia.

Turkmans [10], mostly Sunni and tribally organized, are widely scattered in the northeast next to Turkmenistan. At one time a strong military cavalry cadre, now they are nomadic pastoralists and settled farmers, known for hand-knotted carpets named after various subgroups—Tekke, Yomut, Salor, and Saryk. Separatism, strong until the 1920s, reasserted itself after the 1979 revolution but was suppressed by the government. Afshars [13] inhabit several areas in the northwest. In the "Other" category [14] for Turkic groups, there are fifty or more Ilsavan (formerly Shahsavan) nomadic groups occupying a dozen scattered areas from the Aras River southeastward to the steppes south of Tehran. Qajars have an enclave among the Mazandarani on the southeastern corner of the Caspian. Other small tribal Turkic groups are scattered in the mountains of Khorasan and in the more rugged areas east of Shiraz, especially the Teymurtash and Qaragozlu.

Arabs.   More than 1 million Arabs [15] live primarily in Khuzistan, a plain at the head of the Gulf, which they refer to as Arabistan (land of the Arabs). They also live in the southern Zagros interior and in widely scattered areas northeast and east of the Dasht-e Kavir. Descendants of Arabs who invaded in the seventh century and of later settlers, they maintain their separateness and have not assimilated, although they are predominantly Shia.

Armenians and Assyrians.   Two quite different peoples constitute the largest Christian groups. The primarily Orthodox Armenians, whose sizable presence dates to the time of Shah Abbas, live in Tehran, Tabriz, and Esfahan. As in Lebanon and Syria, they maintain their separate language and schools and have achieved marked success in Tehran and in the Khuzistan oil fields. Numbering some 300,000 at the revolution's onset in 1979, the community has seen considerable emigration since then. Only a tenth as many as Armenians, Assyrians concentrate west of Lake Urmia, maintain their cohesion, preserve their Syriac vernacular, and are divided into Nestorian and Catholic Chaldean branches. They are the remnant of an ancient branch of Christianity that dominated the region (and much of Central Asia) in pre-Islamic times. Iran's legal system based on Sharia discriminates in some ways against non-Muslims, but overt persecution has been directed mostly against con-

verts from Islam to proselytizing evangelical sects. (The Bahai, whose faith has its roots in nineteenth-century Iran, are not a separate ethnic group. They have been severely persecuted under the republic because they are treated as apostates from Islam, though most were born into the faith. See Chap. 4.)

Jews.   Resident in Iran at least as early as the Babylonian Captivity, Jews numbered about 100,000 in the 1970s, when they prospered and were influential under the shah; along with Christians, they were respected as "people of the book." Much less favored after 1979, they maintain their identity in schools, synagogues, social institutions, and businesses. The government emphasizes that it draws a distinction between the Jewish state, Israel—which it reviles—and the Jewish faith. Even so, more than four-fifths of Iran's Jews have gradually chosen to emigrate, many to the United States, some to Israel. The present community, about 10,500, is the second largest in the Muslim world after Turkey.

In the Majlis elected in 2012, these last three ethnic-religious minorities (plus the Zoroasterian community) have a total of 14 reserved seats in the 290-member body.

ECONOMIC PATTERNS

Perspective

As in neighboring Gulf countries, development and modernization have escalated in oil-wealthy Iran since 1950. However, economic patterns exhibit comparatively greater complexity and subtlety of structure because of its long economic history, its early start in petroleum production, and its combination— unique in the Middle East—of having a large population, a large area, arable land, and huge petroleum resources.[18] Patterns are further complicated by revolutionary ramifications.

Before petroleum, the economy was based on a varied agriculture, trade, and widespread and artistic craftsmanship. Agriculture continues to be a major sector; in many regions, it is the only activity of significance. In 2011, it contributed 10.5 percent to GDP; for the labor force, it provided livelihoods to 25 percent; of exports, its products were about 4 percent. Fabled hand-knotted carpets, ordinary and specialized hand-printed textiles called *qalamkar,* copper and brass artifacts, decorated gold and silver items, enamel and inlaid work, and hand-painted miniatures attracted buyers worldwide. Although these traditional items now form only a modest percentage of exports, demand remains high—carpets lead non-oil exports—and for some tribal groups they provide much of their cash income. These products, rather than petroleum, symbolize the country's traditions and creativity.

Assured in the 1950s of a major place in the oil market, the shah pursued economic development almost frenetically. From 1960 to 1977, real annual growth averaged 9.6 percent—about double the average of developing countries. The stable currency was virtually convertible. Every sector received attention, especially physical infrastructure—roads, railroads, ports, airports, communications, industry, urban development. However, his quests for military superiority, becoming an industrial power, a modern welfare state, and a secular Westernized society overloaded the base. Pervasive authoritarianism and denial of basic freedoms set the stage for 1978–1979. By coincidence and design, the republic reversed much of his program, especially Westernization. Nevertheless, the new regime coasted on his accomplishments for several years, especially in the military sphere when Iraq invaded.

"Islamicizing" the Economy

The first decade of the republic was an economic disaster, partly due to the impact of the Iran-Iraq War, but even more so because of the new rulers' utter ignorance of economic complexities. Large and medium-size enterprises were taken from private owners and managers alleged to be monarchist supporters and placed in the hands of untutored clerics and their supporters. A massive brain drain of skilled professionals, considerable capital flight, plus declining oil prices, frozen Iranian assets abroad, and economic sanctions all dragged GDP down to pre-1973 levels by the late 1980s. Banking and finance were "Islamicized"—and rendered unprofitable.

Planning Under the Republic. The more moderate regime that succeeded Khomeini attempted to return to a degree of economic reality and undertook a series of five-year plans beginning in 1989. Some reprivatization began, and selected foreign investors were invited to enter the oil and manufacturing sectors. The return of peace helped somewhat, but the more conservative clerics hindered any hint of reform, and mismanagement and corruption were prevalent. Unemployment, especially among the young, was chronic; inflation was rampant; and population growth dwarfed economic advances. Per capita income fell by 57 percent between 1976 and 1994, while the gap between the poor and the new rich widened. The second plan focused on the financial and fiscal sectors, but ran into obstruction from the *bonyad,* independent monopolistic religious conglomerates that operated with few legal restraints, with little accountability, and with even less management expertise. Generous subsidies on basic items offered some relief to the poor but magnified the budget deficit.

With the new century, the third plan emphasized administrative reform, further privatization, increased investment, and human-resource development, and under the fourth plan, free-trade zones were established in hopes of increasing non-oil exports. The ambitious goal of the fifth plan (2010–2015) of diverting oil revenues into capital-development projects and away from funding the government's current expenses was derailed in 2012, as sanctions cut deeply into oil sales.

The petrosector by the 2000s badly needed investment and technical modernization; here the continued sanctions remained an obstacle. The Ahmedinejad administration pursued seemingly contradictory aims—regulating basic commodity markets and relieving the deficit by reining in subsidies on these same items. A bloated and corrupt bureaucracy remained in control, overseeing price controls, subsidies, and rationing. By 2012, Transparency International ranked Iran 133rd out of 174 countries and 13th regionally, ahead of only the even more troubled countries of Syria, Yemen, and Iraq in perceived corruption; even without sanctions, this was hardly a situation that encouraged private investment, domestic or foreign.

High oil prices in 2008 enabled the government to increase spending on temporary panaceas in advance of the 2009 presidential elections and to postpone implementing needed if unpleasant reforms. When the onset of the global economic crisis dampened demand for oil, Iran's revenues fell by more than a third, and the deficit soared accordingly. Revenues recovered in 2010 and hit a record level of $95 billion in 2011. However, as sanctions slowed exports, by the end of 2012 it was estimated that Iran was losing some $5 billion monthly in receipts.

If Iran has been, as is generally believed internationally, pursuing a nuclear weapons program, it would appear to be defeating its own developmental goals. If, however, it has actually been seeking peaceful nuclear power capability, as it has claimed, then greater transparency would certainly have resolved many of the tensions aroused by the program (discussed below in "Relations") and avoided the penalties its economy is paying under the current sanctions regime. As the sanctions tightened in 2012, protests escalated into riots, the rial collapsed, inflation soared, and some of the regime's strongest supporters in the past—the bazaar merchants—have few imported goods to sell. In October, the rial dropped by 40 percent against the dollar in one week alone.[19] While Khamenei and Ahmedinejad blamed foreigners and local money changers for the deteriorating situation, three grand ayatollahs posted an open letter on their websites that criticized the regime and the supreme leader for ignoring the plight of ordinary Iranians.

On the other hand, a 2013 poll conducted by an international firm found that while most Iranians (80 percent) felt that they had been hurt by the sanctions, almost half (47 percent) blamed the United States for their problems and only 10 percent felt their government was the most responsible.[20]

Agriculture

Land and Water. Although only a limited proportion of Iran is suitable for rainfed agriculture, human ingenuity exploiting the environment over thousands of years has created a broad agricultural base. Finding, conserving, and channeling water to cultivable areas in linear valleys and piedmonts were the essential challenge and the main accomplishment. Agricultural productivity, supplemented by imports, remained sufficient in the 1980s so that even under wartime conditions, there was no widespread hunger. Despite oil's dominance, 25 percent of the economically active population still depends on agriculture, which contributes 11 percent to GDP.

As in Syria and Iraq, large landowners and tribal leaders held huge areas before 1960; peasants worked the land as sharecroppers. Indeed, landowners controlled entire groups of villages along with the land and the inhabitants. Two major land-reform programs transformed the system. One was the shah's highly publicized "White Revolution" in 1963; the other was the revolutionary government's land reform in 1982. These curbed landowner power and reduced the size of their landholdings.

Extensive areas in the northwest and northeast support rainfed cultivation and ar-

Figure 21.3 *Qanats* on Iran's northwestern plateau. These underground tunnels with their surface chain of wells have been the standard Iranian irrigation method for millennia.

boriculture, as well as specialty horticulture in the distinctive ecology of the Caspian coast. However, typically, agriculture relies on water management. Several techniques are employed, but the ancient system of distributing water through the *qanat* network remains the most important (see Chap. 5). Ideally, these underground galleries, showing on the surface as a chain of wells, are constructed in alluvial fans that absorb runoff from adjacent watersheds on higher slopes receiving rain and snow. Scores of thousands of *qanats,* many constructed centuries ago and carefully maintained on northern and southwestern slopes, look like strings of beads on the long slopes of the fans from the air (Fig. 21.3). Although all irrigation requires local cooperation, *qanat*-watered basins demand an exceptionally high level of coordination and engender a complex and uniquely socioeconomic structure.

Crops. The four tables in Chapter 5 clearly show Iran's high rank in crop and livestock production. As noted earlier, in the region, it leads in irrigated area and in the production of oranges, combined fruits, dates, sheep, chickens, and goats and ranks second or third for many other crops. Nearly everywhere, except in the barren interior and southeast, the dominant crops are wheat and barley, grown in both rainfed and irrigated areas. Much wheat is rough milled to make the unusual Iranian bread: large, flat, and dimpled from being baked on hot pebbles in a large oven. Rice, the third major cereal, is grown in paddies on the alluvial plains along the Caspian coast. Much of the excellent rice is consumed in the favorite national dish, *chelo kebab*— grilled lamb kebabs on a bed of rice. Wheat and rice production fail to meet demand, necessitating substantial imports. Potatoes are grown in large quantities. Melons are grown everywhere, along with a wide range of vegetables. Also widely distributed are grapes, consumed as raisins, table grapes, and, in the past, wine. From the early 1960s through the mid-2000s, Iran saw a spectacular increase in per capita food production—more than 120 percent—well beyond the achievement of any other country in this study.[21]

Tree crops, common on the lower Zagros slopes, yield a wide range of fruits and nuts, with pistachios a particular specialty. Iran ranks first globally for pistachios (the United States is second but with less than half Iran's output), and nuts rank third in exports. Almonds and walnuts grow well in subhumid areas. Fruits, from citrus on the Gulf to apples in higher elevations, include all but humid tropical varieties. Tea grows along the Caspian in the same conditions that produce rice and other subtropical crops. It is the popular social beverage, far surpassing coffee, and imports are needed to meet demand.

On the Caspian coast and in favored locations in the southern Zagros, cotton and tobacco are major industrial crops. Both sugarcane and sugar beets have been expanded in acreage, and mills process these crops at refineries in the center and northeast. Opium poppies, once prohibited, are grown under government supervision, as in Turkey.

Livestock, Fishing, and Forestry.   Vast areas are well suited for grazing sheep and goats, and cattle are of increasing importance. Besides dairy products, cattle supply manure for fertilizer and domestic fuel (see Fig. 4.8). Fishing is important both off the southern coast and on the Caspian, where fisheries are especially famous for their superior caviar, the roe of large sturgeon. Already very limited and therefore expensive, caviar supplies are threatened by chemical pollution, the fluctuating water level of the Caspian, and overexploitation. Ranking third in amount of fish caught (see Table 5.3), Iran ranks second in the export value because of caviar. Forests in the Elburz are the only commercially productive ones in the region other than in Turkey.

Hydrocarbons: A Major Producer

Iran became the first major petroleum country in the Middle East in 1908 with the discovery of the great Masjid-e Soleyman field in the folds of the middle Zagros, southeast of Dezful (see Chap. 6). Oil has long played a dominant role in the economy and has undergirded the country's economic development for decades.

Reserves and Output.   By 2012, Iran's reserves had risen to 154.6 bn bbl with new finds in Khuzistan and elsewhere[22] to place it second in the Middle East, still ahead of Iraq, and fourth in the world. Even more impressive are its natural gas reserves of 1,187.0 tn ft^3/33.6 tn m^3, second globally after Russia. Like Egypt and neighboring countries, Iran is stressing gas, although it has vacillated about the details of allowing foreign investment. Oil output peaked in 1974 at more than 6 mn bpd before falling to a minimum of 1.37 mn bpd in 1981, early in the Iran-Iraq War. It returned to 3.6 mn bpd in the mid-1990s and then to about 3.7 mn bpd in 2009. With sanctions hitting exports severely as 2012 progressed, the average output for the year fell to 3.05 mn bpd; given the prevailing situation, it seemed to be headed to a much lower level for 2013.

Historical Note.   Early oil operations by Anglo-Persian (later Anglo-Iranian) Oil Company (AIOC) are traced in Chapter 6. After four decades of AIOC control, one of the first major crises in international oil history developed during the 1951–1953 dispute between the government, under Prime Minister Mohammad Mossadegh, and the company. It arose when he rejected a draft agreement between the AIOC and Iran and then nationalized the industry under the new National Iranian Oil Company (NIOC). During the ensuing dispute, oil sales fell to zero. In 1953, Mossadegh was ousted and the shah was restored, with covert US help, and under a completely new accord the former concession passed to a new consortium of British, Dutch, French, and, just coincidentally, US companies.

Under NIOC supervision, the consortium produced and refined most Iranian output for the next twenty-five years. However, NIOC partnered with several other US, Italian, and Canadian companies from the late 1950s for exploration and production outside the original concession area, including offshore. In the 1980s, it operated on its own in some areas and succeeded reasonably well under difficult wartime circumstances, finding giant nonassociated gas fields, especially offshore, the largest being South Pars, an extension of the supergiant North Field off Qatar (see Chaps. 6 and 15).

In the early 1990s, Iran acted to reinvigorate its hydrocarbon industry but faced two major obstacles: the deterioration of aging fields and facilities during the long spell of isolation and dramatic reductions in the availability of funding needed for implementation. Sanctions imposed by the United States exacerbated these obstacles, so the government actively sought foreign-company participation. Major projects included opening offshore gas fields (especially South Pars) and rejuvenating overexploited onshore oil fields using gas-injection techniques. Having neglected enhanced oil recovery (EOR) methods for two decades, NIOC initiated a vigorous program in several onshore fields. More than a dozen European companies showed interest in working in Iran, despite the US government's extraterritorial attempt to preclude foreign companies from operating there. For a different reason—Iran's nuclear program—sanctions have again become a factor since the late 2000s.

Oil and Gas Fields. Most oil fields are located in linear northwest-southeast reservoirs paralleling the Zagrosian fold structures in the orig-

inal discovery belt (Map 21.3; see also Map 6.2). After a century of exploration, there are twenty-five onshore fields extending from west of Khorramabad to Bandar-e Abbas, a distance of 600 mi/966 km, and seven offshore fields widely scattered the full length of the Gulf on Iran's side of the median line. Onshore gas fields are concentrated at the northwestern and southeastern ends of the oil belt (Map 6.2). Virtually no onshore reservoirs have been found outside the Zagros folds. As in Saudi Arabia, overall central control of operations permits drilling only the optimum number of wells, so that in 2012 Iran produced from just 2,074 wells, some of which still yielded thousands of barrels a day after ninety years.

Pipelines. Oil and gas pipelines form a dense network in the closely packed fields of Khuzistan and adjacent areas. Most lines feed the Kharg Island export terminal northwest of Bushehr, which is, with Ras Tanura and Juaymah in Saudi Arabia, one of the world's three largest terminals. Other lines carry feedstock to the refinery on Abadan Island on the east bank of the Shatt al-Arab, one of the largest in the Gulf, processing 350,000 bpd. Among the country's nine refineries, with a total capacity of 1.5 mn bpd, the three next largest after Abadan are in Esfahan, Bandar-e Abbas, and Tehran. This is not enough to satisfy domestic demand for partly subsidized petroproducts; considerable gasoline, for example, must be imported (at market prices), and in late 2009 the government reported that its budget for the last quarter of the year for these imports was short by $3 billion.[23]

Gas Development. With almost unlimited natural gas production potential, Iran is seeking export customers and widespread domestic use for its gas. Following installation of only a skeletal pipeline net, gas could completely replace oil in electricity generation (in the late 2000s, gas-fired plants produced about 75 percent of the national supply), supply a

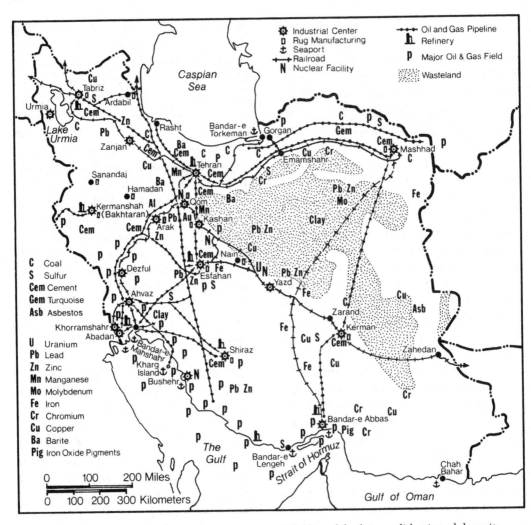

Map 21.3 Economic map of Iran, showing major oil fields and facilities, solid-mineral deposits, industrial centers, ports, and railways.

major new export, and permit widespread distribution of bottled liquefied petroleum gas (LPG) for domestic home and vehicle use; with more pipelines, gas could gradually be supplied to much of the country. Some of this potential has been realized: most power plants now use gas. By the late 1990s, more than three hundred cities were receiving piped gas, up from six before 1978. As one phase of the program to reduce serious pollution in the capital, many taxis run on LPG. Additionally, huge quantities of gas are reinjected into oil fields in EOR efforts. In 2010, a gas pipeline

linking Iran and Turkmenistan was inaugurated. Liquid petroleum gas sales, largely to South Korea and Europe, fell sharply in 2012 as a result of sanctions imposed by the EU.

As early as 1970, Iran opened a 40–42-in/102–107-cm pipeline, IGAT-1, from its southwestern fields into the Soviet Union. IGAT-2, from the Kangan gas field on the Gulf south of Shiraz to Astara, where the Azerbaijan border meets the Caspian Sea coast, opened in 1992. Its diameter is a huge 56 in/142 cm to Qazvin, northwest of Tehran, and 48 in/122 cm from Qazvin to Astara. IGAT-3, with the same diameter as IGAT-2, is under construction, and two more Iranian Gas Transport lines are in the planning stages. An export line to Turkey opened in 2002—the precursor of many others in various states of planning to supply Iranian gas across Turkey to Europe. In 2008, Iran and Pakistan agreed to proceed with a pipeline that could be extended to India at a later date. The United States has put considerable pressure, including a threat of imposing sanctions, on Pakistan to cancel the project, the Iranian portion of which was completed in 2011. After some hesitation, Pakistan announced in September 2012 that work on the pipeline would commence and be finished by 2014, although the Chinese bank that originally agreed to finance the project withdrew its participation in the face of international sanctions.[24]

Further to utilize its plentiful hydrocarbon wealth, Iran has an extensive program to construct ten new petrochemical plants, with Bandar-e Khomeini (sometimes Bandar-e Imam) as a special petrochemical economic zone. The National Petrochemical Company is offering inducements to foreign companies to join the program over the next several years. Utilizing petroleum and natural gas to produce petrochemicals has many advantages, including adding considerable value to raw materials and avoiding restrictions imposed by OPEC production quotas.[25]

Non-Oil Resources

Scattered mineral deposits, especially copper, were mined in ancient times on the Iranian Plateau. However, few commercially significant deposits were identified until modern technology, including space imagery, was applied to the exploration of the highly mineralized volcanic belt in Iran near the tectonic plate boundary along the inner Zagros. Geologists discovered one deposit after another—copper, iron, chrome, lead, zinc, bauxite, manganese, coal, barite—approximately along the axis of the railway from Qom to Kerman. Numerous finds are now being exploited,

some on a large scale. Thus, Iran possesses an array of mineral raw materials for domestic use and export (see Map 21.3).[26]

Metals. The most important discoveries were of copper along the entire length of the inner Zagros volcanic belt from the northwestern border to south of Bam in the southeast. Total reserves are more than 2.6 billion tons, with the largest deposits at Sar Cheshmeh, southwest of Kerman; some Western engineers claim these are the richest in the world. An integrated mining, smelting, and refining operation is based on the deposit; a new smelter has opened at Khatounabad, near Sar Cheshmeh. Mining at Ahar, north of Tabriz, has been expanded. Iran is aiming for an annual output of 250,000 mt of copper content a year, but it is having difficulty reaching this goal.

Iran is first or second regionally in production of several other ores, including iron, chrome, zinc, lead, manganese, and aluminum. A remarkable concentration exists near Bafq, southeast of Yazd, with major deposits of iron and lead-zinc ores not far from large coal resources. Iron is transported to the Esfahan steel works by rail from Bafq; still richer ore resources of 1.13 bn mt at Gol-e Gohar, south of Sirjan, feed both Esfahan and Ahvaz plants. By 2012, Iran had hoped to have total steel capacity of some 40 mn mt/yr, but it has fallen well short of that goal. Several major chrome deposits south and southeast of Kerman yield ores for export and for smelting near Bandar-e Abbas. The aluminum industry has burgeoned as bauxite production has increased, and in the late 2000s additional smelter capacity came on line at Arak, southwest of Hamadan, and at Bandar Abbas, bringing the total to more than 450,000 mt annually. Another 200,000-mt facility was being built by a Chinese company at Sarab.[27]

Nonmetals. Important nonmetallic minerals include coal; the largest deposits are northwest of Kerman, but more than a score

Figure 21.4 Hand-knotting an especially large and fine rug in an Esfahan workshop (1964). Three young girls are guided by two adult women. Handmade carpets are the second-ranking export of Iran.

of collieries extend across northern Iran from Lake Urmia to Mashhad. Fine turquoise from Neyshabur, west of Mashhad, is used in locally crafted jewelry, and some turquoise is exported. Inexhaustible supplies of salt occur in numerous plugs near Bandar Abbas; native sulfur from many of the same structures supply an important export item. Near Qom, local kaolin is used in the large ceramics industry for the decorative tiles used in walls, floors, and even house facades.

Industries

Industrialization during the 1960s proceeded on a scale that observers considered unrealistic, demanding too much, too fast—large-scale projects with inadequate infrastructure, provoking fundamentalist charges of "Westoxication" and anti-Islamic policies. Nevertheless, many different major industries were successfully established, from food processing to iron and steel production and automobile assembly. Joint ventures with foreign corporations brought technology transfers and training programs, even though few ventures achieved planned production levels. After the revolution, an unreliable labor supply and shortages of raw materials, spare parts, and other inputs meant few of these new enterprises could sustain production. The Iraq war turned the emphasis to military needs.

Industry is widely distributed in the western third of the country. Many plants are concentrated around Tehran; light industries and craft shops are found in dozens of towns and even villages. Major products include processed foods and beverages, cigarettes, home appliances, assembled automobiles, textiles, and machine tools. Iran is especially known for its excellent artisan work: hand-knotted rugs, jewelry, metalwares, inlay work, and decorated ceramic tiles (Fig. 21.4).

Figure 21.5 A one-man shop in the copper and brass bazaar of Esfahan. Traditional products such as these hand-hammered and hand-engraved trays are still major items of manufacture in several Iranian cities.

Greater Tehran dominates the manufacturing sector, with auto assembly, household appliance, and clothing plants. Esfahan, the second-largest industrial center, has the major iron and steel plant, cotton mills, and numerous small shops producing metal household items, including brass and copper trays (Fig. 21.5). Tabriz, with a major machine-tool plant, is the northwest's industrial focus. Arak, southwest of Qom, has one of Iran's aluminum smelters; about 60 percent of its output is exported. Still other cities with appreciable manufacturing are shown in Map 21.3, which illustrates the concentration in the western third, with Mashhad an outlier in the far northeast. Rug-making centers—Tabriz, Ardabil, Hamadan, Qom, Kashan, Esfahan, Nain,

Shiraz, Kerman, and Mashhad—are world renowned. Some sophisticated plants, especially nuclear processing facilities, are off-limits, but the government has allowed some visitors to see those in Natanz, Arak, and Bushehr. However, since the mid-2000s, the unmet requirements of the UN inspectors from the IAEA to make unrestricted and unannounced visits to all nuclear facilities has been at the heart of Iran's conflict both with the IAEA and the countries that have been most concerned with the republic's nuclear plans.

Transportation

Roads. Development after World War II was constrained by infrastructural limitations, and construction of a transportation network was both difficult and expensive. Terrain, climate, and distance combine to inhibit construction, even when financing and engineering skills are available. By the 1980s, however, all cities had been integrated into a well-engineered highway network constructed by foreign companies under contract. The net covers all parts of the country except the virtually uninhabited interior basins (see Map 21.1).

Railways.   The railway through the Zagros between Dezful and Qom was extended during World War II to Tabriz and the Soviet border to carry war matériel. In 2007, Iran, Azerbaijan, and Russia agreed to build a new line connecting the three countries. As part of the CENTO- and Regional Cooperation for Development (RCD)–sponsored railway from Istanbul to Karachi, a line was constructed to the Turkish border and from Qom through Kashan and Yazd to Kerman. An extension to Bam and on to Zahedan to finish the connection to Pakistan was at last inaugurated in July 2009. A major line ties Bafq (between Yazd and Kerman) through the mountains to the port of Bandar Abbas. An extension from Bafq to Mashhad got under way in the late 2000s, as were links to Basrah and Baghdad in Iraq (and thence to Syria) and to Herat in Afghanistan. In the far northeast, a short but strategic link in the late 1990s extended the Tehran-Mashhad line on to Sarakhs on the Turkmenistan border. From there, the Trans-Asian Railway follows along the old Silk Road to Mary, Bukhara, Samarkand, and Tashkent; in 2010, Iran and Turkmenistan signed an agreement to link Iran with Kazakhstan to the north by rail. Iran has thus positioned itself to link Central Asia to the Gulf, the subcontinent, and the Levant. In the northwest, Armenia and Iran agreed in 2009 to build a line, but like some other parts of Iran's expansion plans, this was on hold in 2012, due to Iran's budgetary strictures. In August 2012, it was reported that India, which is facing difficulties in paying for Iranian oil because of the sanctions

regime, has proposed building a rail link between Hajigak in Afghanistan (where India has extensive interests in minerals development) and the Iranian port of Chabahar. After construction, India would turn over the Iranian portion of the line to Iran Railways.

The Iranian network is standard gauge that connects directly to the neighboring lines to the east and on to Europe, but both Pakistan and the Former Soviet Union use different gauges, resulting in a break of gauge at all the new crossing points in those directions. The 2000s saw the opening of parts of a three-line metro system in Tehran, and the second phase was scheduled to be completed in 2013. Light-rail systems were under construction or in the planning stages in Ahvaz, Esfahan, Karadj, Mashhad, Shiraz, and Tabriz.[28]

Ports.   Along its coastline of 1,555 mi/2,500 km from the Shatt al-Arab to the Pakistan border, Iran has few good natural harbors. Since population and development centered near the head of the Gulf even in antiquity, most major ports lie in the arc from Khorramshahr to Bushehr, including the main oil-export terminal of Kharg Island. Bandar-e Khomeini (once Bandar-e Shahpur) was expanded during the 1990s to serve the burgeoning petrochemical center. Farther south, Bandar-e Bushehr is the site of Iran's nuclear reactor, mentioned earlier. Bandar Abbas was expanded during the war with Iraq and is now connected by rail to the main line through the country's center. It is a major general-cargo port, a passenger port for cross-Gulf traffic, and the main naval base, guarding the Strait of Hormuz. Chabahar (sometimes Bandar Beheshti) on the Indian Ocean was also developed during the war with Iraq (see Map 21.3). On the Caspian coast, Bandar-e Anzali is the leading port for fishing and trade with the littoral states.

Sanctions

The Iranian economy by 2012 was laboring on several distinct, but somewhat overlapping, international sanctions regimes. Briefly, these can be placed into two categories: first, sanctions applied as a result of Iran's being declared a state sponsor of terrorism, and, second, those imposed as a result of Iran's now long-standing conflict with the UN International Atomic Energy Agency over the exact nature of its nuclear program and its obligations as a signatory of the Non-Proliferation Treaty (NPT) to allow inspections of its nuclear-related facilities. Some regimes are bilateral in nature, while others are multilateral.

The first group of sanctions have mostly been imposed through bilateral US actions, and the earliest ones date to the taking of American diplomats as hostages in 1979. At that time, about $12 billion in Iranian assets were frozen by the United States. In the 1980s, sales of all military-related items were banned and imports from Iran were restricted, and in the 1990s dealings with Iran's oil industry were prohibited. The effects of American sanctions are thought to have been mixed. Iran's oil and aviation sectors were negatively impacted, as they found it difficult to buy key spare parts or to update relevant technologies, and Iranian banks encountered difficulties internationally because they were isolated from their American counterparts. On the other hand, US attempts to apply its laws to non-American companies aroused opposition from some of its closest allies in Europe and the Far East. It is not clear that American sanctions, acting alone, have had much effect on Iranian policies or behaviors.[29]

The second group of sanctions have involved the United Nations and several countries acting either together or separately. In 2005, the IAEA found Iran in violation of the NPT (see below, "Relations: Nuclear Dispute"), setting off a series of actions and reactions eventually involving not just Iran and the IAEA, but also the UN Security Council, the European Union, the United States, and more than a dozen other onetime Iranian trading partners. By 2012, sanctions had struck at Iran's Central Bank, through which its oil receipts had been processed; the EU had imposed a boycott of Iranian oil; and the United States was pressuring with some success other countries to follow the EU's example. Late that year, oil exports were down by about half over the past year, and, as mentioned above, the resultant cost to the Iranian economy was estimated to be $5 billion monthly. Major shipping lines canceled port calls in Iran, causing seaborne trade to fall by more than 50 percent. Importers of nonsanctioned goods, like foodstuffs, encountered considerable difficulties in obtaining the letters of credit needed to pay not only for goods, but also shipping bills. As inflation has ballooned and the demand for high-denomination banknotes has increased, the Central Bank has been notified by the security printing firms in Europe that have produced Iran's currency in the past that they have terminated their contracts for future deliveries.

However, by 2013, there were growing international calls for allowing some relief in the sanctions regime for a variety of reasons. These included giving government some maneuverability to make concessions on the nuclear issue and, because the sanctions, which were hurting the vast majority of ordinary Iranians, seemed to have united them in support of an otherwise unpopular government and its nuclear program.[30] The International Crisis Group pointed out that probably the major beneficiary of the sanctions was the Revolutionary Guard, which, because it was able to circumvent the sanctions, has as a result been able to reap large profits in the black market.[31] Even a bipartisan report issued in the United States called for allowing more people-to-people contacts and the resumption of some economic links.[32]

RELATIONS

Long before petroleum was found, the Iranian Plateau played an important geopolitical role both locally and internationally. On the contemporary scene, its geopolitical position, place in world oil and global finances and human resources, and aggressively idiosyncratic approach to internal and external relations converge to make Iran a vital partner or opponent in many global relationships. One scholar commented, "Iran is fortunate in its strategic situation. It has no historical enemies, no irredenta, no source of permanent tensions on its frontiers. It is well endowed with resources, material and human and well situated. . . . It has failed to capitalize on these assets due to an excessive cultivation of past grievances and . . . has thus squandered the country's potential."[33]

Regional

CENTO/ECO.   Although revolutionary Iran withdrew from the Central Treaty Organization in 1979 and thereby precipitated the bloc's collapse, it maintained its ties with Turkey and Pakistan and continued some participation in the RCD, later the Economic Cooperation Organization (see Chap. 8). ECO was expanded in 1992 to include Afghanistan and six former Soviet republics; membership potentially provides these states with more direct access to the sea than they had as members of the USSR. Most members signed the agreement on the Trans-Asian Railway mentioned above, and Iran is strongly attracted by the Silk Road concept.[34] The Caspian Basin states, resources, and problems are matters of priority in its grand strategy. For the Caspian Sea itself, recent years have seen increased militarization on the part of all the littoral states, with Iran adding a destroyer to its Caspian fleet in 2013.[35] Sunni and secular, Turkey contrasts with contemporary Iran, but Iran has been pleased by recent Turkish moves toward Islamism, even if they have been limited. They share the Kurdish problem but compete in independent Azerbaijan. Already well linked by rail and road, they have the gas pipeline mentioned earlier, but by 2012 the relationship was

foundering, partly because of the nuclear and sanctions issues and partly because of Iran's support for the Assad regime in Syria. Iran has maintained good relations with Pakistan, with which it has in common a domestic tug-of-war between conservatism and moderation. They also have a common minority problem on their border—the Baluch. Pakistan has continued its support for a pipeline linking the two countries, despite US opposition.

Iraq.   It is with its western neighbor Iraq that Iran has long had the most persistent conflict, a prolongation of the millennia-old cleavage between the Iranian Plateau and the Mesopotamian Basin; the bloody eight-year war of the 1980s was a return to earlier battles. Relations eased after Saddam's overthrow; however, Iran condemned the US-led invasion and occupation. Iranian Shii pilgrims flooded into Najaf and Karbala after April 2003, and Iranian religious influence has grown in the shrine cities. Its growing links with some Shii political parties are a major concern to the United States and to many Iraqis as well. Since 2006, the Iraqi president and prime minister have made numerous visits to Tehran, and in 2008 Ahmedinejad was the first president of the Islamic Republic to travel to Baghdad. Temporarily in abeyance, apparently, are Iran's claims for extensive reparations resulting from the Iran-Iraq War, with Tehran preferring to pursue policies that draw Iraq closer.

Gulf Cooperation Council.   The GCC members are states with whom Iran should logically maintain close relations; these, however, have been strained from the foundation of the GCC. It was no secret that perceived Iranian threats were (and continue to be) in large part the group's raison d'être. Incidents involving Iranian pilgrims in Mecca have periodically marred relations with Saudi Arabia. The UAE and Iran have contended over Abu Musa and the Tunb islands, discussed earlier; their traditional close trade ties have been hit hard by the growing strictness of international sanctions. In the new century, all GCC members have been increasingly alarmed at the prospect of a nuclear-armed Iran and the perceived "Shii Crescent" stretching across to Lebanon.[36]

Syria, Egypt. Iran's curious ties with Syria have a lengthy history of cordiality, and as the Assad regime became increasingly isolated in 2011 and 2012 its dependence on Iran has become stronger. At the same time, as sanctions have tightened, Iran has found itself more isolated, with Syria remaining as its last major ally. While Egypt has been concerned about Iran's nuclear program and its influence on Shia in other countries, its Islamist president, Mohammed Mursi, indicated he wanted to build a new relationship between the two countries. However, because of continued sensitivities in Egypt about Iran's Shii orientation, change will most likely be slow.

Israel. Israel, in contrast, is acrimoniously reviled in Iran, at least in public. This reverses the cordial relations that existed before 1979, when Israel sent technicians to Iran and Iran shipped petroleum to Elat, and their two intelligence services, Mossad and SAVAK, collaborated closely. During the 1990s, Israel battled Iranian-supported Hizballah guerrillas in their strip of occupation in south Lebanon. The "Summer War" of 2006, in which Israeli cities were attacked as they had not been since the 1940s, showed that Iran was still supplying Hizballah with sophisticated weaponry. As the crisis over Iran's nuclear program heightened, Binyamin Netanyahu returned to the prime ministership in 2009, and he has increasingly pushed for preemptive military action, disdaining the effects of diplomacy and sanctions and ignoring the contrary advice of a sizable segment of Israel's military, intelligence, and political communities.

Afghanistan. With close historic, cultural, and linguistic ties to Afghanistan, Iran moved to bolster relations with the post-Taliban regime (it played a supportive role in overthrowing the ultra-Sunni Taliban),[37] despite the US military presence. It is the largest regional donor to Afghanistan's recovery efforts, and the Kabul government has denied US claims that Iran has been backing insurgent elements. However, Iran's links with Afghanistan are still tenuous and are likely to remain uncertain while that country remains fragmented. Iran has had no affinity with the Taliban and has a special interest in the welfare of Afghanistan's Shii Hazara, a long-mistreated minority with kin in eastern Iran.

Former Soviet Union. When the Soviet Union collapsed, Iran quickly found itself with a group of newly independent neighbors—from Armenia in the northwest on into Central Asia. In the Caucasus, two very different situations arose: first, Muslim Azerbaijan's leaders soon betrayed their irredentist ambition to attract Iran's Azerbaijan Ostan into a reunited republic; second, Christian Armenia, before independence came, was at war with Azerbaijan over the Armenian exclave of Nagorno-Karabakh. Despite religious differences, Iran has essentially sided with Armenia, while Azerbaijan has built economic and military ties with Israel, leading to fears that the latter might use Azerbaijani facilities to attack Iran. A bargaining chip for Iran is the Azerbaijani exclave of Nakhchivan—it has borders only with Iran and Armenia, and Iran often seems to treat it as an independent entity.

Farther east, two new Central Asian states—Turkmenistan and Kazakhstan—share the Caspian littoral with Iran (and Russia and Azerbaijan). Given the Caspian Basin's emerging importance both for its petroresources and as a key locus for the transmission of those resources to world markets, it is vital to Iran to maintain good relations with these two states east of the Caspian. Its rival for their goodwill is independent Russia. There is a long history of Iranian ethnic, cultural, and linguistic influence throughout Central Asia, and Tajikistan's people speak a closely related tongue (as mentioned in Chap. 20, the other republics have languages related to Turkish). Iran's quest to move from observer status to full membership in the Shanghai Cooperation Organization (Russia, China, and four of the "stans") has been unsuccessful, since the group has held that no country under UN sanctions can join.

Global

United States.   Crucial as Iran's relations with Iraq and the GCC may be, those with the United States have been the most important for more than a half century and even earlier.[38] The two countries granted mutual recognition in 1850 and began full diplomatic relations in 1883. Before these were broken in 1980, the United States had made grants and loans totaling $817 million in economic aid and $1.412 million in military assistance. There was a sizable Peace Corps program between 1962 and 1976 involving about 1,750 volunteers.

The mutually hostile current attitudes stand in marked contrast to those of the twenty-five years following 1953, when the Central Intelligence Agency helped restore the shah to power. By the 1960s, Iran—an "island of stability" in the Middle East—became the United States' "chosen instrument," the eastern anchor of the US geopolitical position in the region, while critics complained of the United States ignoring glaring abuses of human rights.

As the shah's main supporter, the United States became the main target of the Islamic revolution. In this backlash, the United States became the "Great Satan." The seizure of the American Embassy, the US tilt toward Iraq during the Iran-Iraq War, and the downing of an Iranian civil aircraft in a tragic case of mistaken identity by the US Navy all deep-

ened the rift even further. In the 1990s, the United States coupled Iran with Iraq in the "dual-containment" policy, treating both as rogue supporters of terrorism and states seeking to develop weapons of mass destruction. There were attempts when Khatami and Clinton presided over their countries to broach détente, but one or another issue always revived mutual recriminations. When the Bush administration declared Iran to be part of the "Axis of Evil," an adversarial stance returned to the fore; sanctions and embargoes were regularly renewed. After the US invasions of Afghanistan and Iraq, Iran felt surrounded. Since long-term instability in either of its neighbors is not in its best interests, it actually assisted in many aspects of postinvasion reconstruction. However, as mentioned earlier, Tehran's close links to Shii political parties have been seen by the United States as frustrating its aims of forming an inclusive government in Baghdad. In 2009, the new American administration made a tentative offer to mute the stridency, but the disputed Iranian election and the repression that followed, coupled with the growing nuclear controversy (discussed below), have only deepened hostilities. There were indications at the end of 2012 that a new avenue of bilateral negotiation might be opening.

Other States.   Links with Russia have been generally cordial, although remnants of historic suspicion no doubt remain. Both czarist and Soviet Russia eyed Iranian territories covetously, and Iran was a key element in efforts to contain Soviet expansionism. To offset its enmity with the United States, revolutionary Iran cautiously established a military-economic link with Russia, which has supplied large amounts of heavy armaments and completed installation of the Bushehr nuclear reactor in 2011. Iran maintains similar ties with China, which supplies arms and also constructs major industrial plants, and China and India have been major customers for Iranian oil. Iran's long-standing, mutually beneficial relations with the EU as an entity seesawed during the 1990s, but in 2012 the EU embargoed further oil imports.

Nuclear Dispute

Ten Years of Controversy. In 2003, the International Atomic Energy Agency reported that Iran, a signatory of the Nuclear Non-Proliferation Treaty and a member of the IAEA, had contravened its obligations by concealing some of its nuclear activities since the 1980s. Responding to the agency's demand that it prove it was not pursuing a weapons program, Iran agreed to cooperate more fully and to suspend uranium enrichment. The IAEA concluded there was no evidence at that time of nonpeaceful activity, but within months it complained Iran was not keeping its promises. These were the opening salvos in a diplomatic cat-and-mouse game that has continued through 2013 without resolution.

International Involvement. Essentially, over the following years, various combinations of international players—the EU, Britain, France, Germany, the United States, Russia, China, the UN, and the IAEA—have alternatively cajoled and threatened Iran, seeking cessation of the enrichment efforts (but not of the parts of the nuclear program with nonmilitary ends) and full and transparent cooperation with IAEA inspectors. In return, various economic rewards (including nuclear assistance) and integration of Iran into global decision-making processes have been on offer, while ever-tighter sanctions—like those first imposed by the UN Security Council in 2006 and extended several times since—have been cited as the alternative. Meanwhile, Iran sometimes pursued further enrichment, sometimes suspended it; in 2008, it demonstrated its progress in weapons-delivery systems with successful medium-range missile tests. Toward the end of the decade, military preemption began being publicly indicated as a

possibility. As mentioned above, Prime Minister Netanyahu of Israel has led the charge, resolved to keep his country's long-standing regional monopoly of nuclear weapons. By 2012, he was openly challenging the United States to set "red lines," the crossing of which by Iran would lead to US attacks on key Iranian targets; to some extent, he crossed a red line himself by insinuating the Iran issue into the American presidential election, antagonizing the Obama administration.

Potential Repercussions. Even the Bush administration knew that Iran would retaliate for any attack on its facilities by moving against the United States in Iraq and Afghanistan and possibly block oil-tanker traffic in the Straits of Hormuz. The diplomatic approach thus prevailed through 2013, although the once-discredited neocons who led the United States into Iraq surfaced again as Netanyahu allies for military action. A wide political spectrum in the West and even in Israel recognized that even a successful air campaign against the nuclear facilities would at best only delay Iran, perhaps only for months. In fact, if Iran as late as 2013 remains undecided about whether to weaponize its nuclear efforts, an attack might only convince it of the need to proceed with weapons development. Furthermore, it would give a corrupt and weakened regime the opportunity to appeal, probably with some success, to its citizens' patriotism and sense of Persian identity. Whether the election of the new Iranian president, himself once a nuclear negotiator, will lead to a diplomatic solution remains to be seen.

While much of the world worries that the consequences of a preemptive attack could be a serious blow to the still shaky global economy if the flow of oil through the Strait of Hormuz (see Chap. 9) were blocked, such attack could also lead to a widespread outbreak of regional warfare. It is obvious that the actions and reactions of the two unpredictable antagonists—Iran and Israel—can easily trump any plans of the other parties. However this crisis plays out, it is obvious that the confrontation so far has interfered with Iran's developmental progress by diverting resources toward a military objective of doubtful strategic value and by subjecting the country to a rigid system of economic sanctions.[39]

For information on the business environment in Iran, see the website attached to this book: www.middleeastpatterns.com.

NOTES

1. See Limbert 1987, Chaps. 1 and 2.

2. For a focus on Fars, see Summers 1986. For general coverage of archaeological sites, see Matheson 1976.

3. Limbert 1987 covers these developments as well as Iran in general, including *Iran-zamin*. The well-documented role of the Central Intelligence Agency in the shah's restoration became and is still an issue of bitterness among Iranians, especially Khomeini revolutionaries.

4. Amuzegar 1995, 26, 22–23.

5. As a senior cleric did during the late 2009 riots when he called on the leaders of the opposition to repent or be declared enemies of God and face death. *Daily Star* (Beirut), Dec. 31, 2009.

6. Paradoxically, Iran did get help from and through Israel and the United States, as was disclosed in the Iran-Contra ("Irangate") congressional hearings in Washington in 1986–1987.

7. *Foreign Policy*, "Failed States Index 2012," www.foreignpolicy.com/failed_states_index_2012_interactive.

8. United Nations Development Programme 2013; *Legatum Prosperity Index 2012*, www.prosperity.com/.

9. An excellent, comprehensive coverage of Iran's geography is in W. Fisher 1968. A concise treatment is given in Limbert 1987, Chap. 1.

10. See the National Geographic Society map, *Middle East*, Oct. 2002. It was movement along the western edge of the rafted terrain that produced the Bam earthquake. The disaster is reported in *New York Times*, Dec. 28, 2003, and is reviewed in *Christian Science Monitor*, Feb. 17, 2004.

11. In addition to the standard US Department of Defense, Defense Mapping Agency 1985, see Adamec 1976–1988. Numerous place-names were changed by the revolutionary Iranian authorities (see "A Note on Transliteration" at the beginning of this book). Some names seem to have been changed back to the origi-

nals. Kermanshah (city) was renamed Bakhtaran, then rerenamed Kermanshah. Chah Bahar was renamed Bandar Beheshti but is now shown as Chabahar.

12. Montaigne 1999 discusses this topic and pictures northern Tehran.

13. *Zawya*, Feb. 17, 2013.

14. Detailed technical studies are in Krinsley 1970.

15. Useful studies regarding Iranian settlements are Bonine 1979; English 1966; and Kheirabadi 1991.

16. Concise discussion of peoples and their distribution is given in Limbert 1987 and *Iran* Country Study 1989.

17. *New York Times*, Feb. 24, 2010; *BBC News*, Feb. 25, 2010.

18. See Limbert 1987, Chaps. 1, 5, and 6; *Iran* Country Study 1989, esp. Chap. 3; and Hoogland 2002.

19. The rial's decline was taking a toll on Iranian's religious practices as well, as pilgrims in Mecca and Medina found that Saudi money changers were refusing to accept rials. *Zawya*, May 7, 2013.

20. The poll was conducted by the Gallup organization. *Al-Monitor*, Feb. 14, 2013.

21. FAO, various issues.

22. US Department of Energy, Energy Information Administration, *Country Analysis Briefs: Iran*, Aug. 2004 and Jan. 2010; *International Petroleum Encyclopedia*. Much of the following section is based on these sources, plus *Oil and Gas Journal* articles.

23. *Daily Star* (Beirut), Dec. 8, 2009.

24. Groundbreaking for the project took place in March 2013. *Oil and Gas Journal*, Mar. 14, 2013.

25. A detailed study is *Oil and Gas Journal*, Aug. 16 and Aug. 23, 1999.

26. US Geological Survey, "The Mineral Industry of Iran," in *Minerals Yearbook* 2011.

27. USGS 2008.

28. For further details, see www.tehranmetro.com /index.asp, www.subways.net/iran/, and www.shiraz metro.ir/english.html.

29. For a discussion of US sanctions, see, Kozhanov 2011.

30. See note 19 above and *al-Monitor*, Feb. 27, 2013.

31. *Zawya*, Feb. 27, 2013,

32. *Al-Monitor*, Apr. 4, 2013; *Christian Science Monitor*, Apr. 25, 2013.

33. Chubin 2000, 10. The statement perhaps overlooks the long-running enmity between Mesopotamia and the Iranian Plateau.

34. For further information, see www.ecosecretariat .org/.

35. Jamestown Foundation, *Eurasia Daily Monitor* 10, no. 61 (2013).

36. Iran's relations with the GCC states is discussed in Oktav 2011.

37. *USA Today,* June 9, 2009. Iran was close to open war with the Taliban after the murder of nine Iranian diplomats in Mazar-al-Sharif and a massacre of Afghan Shia in 1998.

38. For a penetrating study of these relations by a leading scholar, see Bill 1988 and Bill and Chavez 2002. *Middle East Policy* 1994 has a debate on "dual containment"

among four experts. For later developments, see Amuzegar 1998; Monshipouri 1998; Ramazani 1998, 2001; Sick 2001; Murden 2002, Chap. 3; and Pollack 2004. Relations with Israel are discussed in Sobhani 1999.

39. A thoughtful discussion of what the region's future with a nuclear-armed Iran might be like is found in Lindsay and Takeyh 2010.

The reader is advised to consult this book's associated website (**www.middleeastpatterns.com**) for additional information on **Iran**, such as a historical time line and chronology of recent events, as well as essays on selected topics and various international economic, social, and political indicators.

Glossary

See Index for the page numbers of the main discussion of most terms. For names of geological time periods (Pleistocene, Cretaceous, etc.), see the Geological Time Chart on page 680.

Abbasid: pertaining to the Muslim empire ruled by the Abbasid dynasty from Baghdad, 750–1258 CE.

Abrahamic faiths: religions tracing their origin to the Biblical/Quranic patriarch Abraham/Ibrahim—Judaism, Christianity, and Islam.

Acequia: Spanish from Arabic *as-saqiya,* gravity-driven irrigation system of ditches and sluices, brought by Arabs from the Middle East to Spain and then by missionaries to the southwest of the United States.

Age-gender cohort: in demography, a group between two specified ages.

AH: Latin *Anno Hijrae,* the chronological basis of the Islamic calendar (q.v.). Year 1 AH was 622 CE; 2013 CE = 1434/35 AH.

Ahl al-kitab: in Islam, "people of the book," i.e., Jews, Christians, and others who have their own revealed scriptures.

Ahmadiyya: nineteenth-century reformist Islamic movement originated in Pakistan; led to the formation of the Ahmadiyya Community, a group considered to be heretical by many Muslims and whose members are persecuted in some countries; there are a small number of adherents in Haifa, Israel.

Al, al- (el-): uppercase and not hyphenated, is derived from *Ahl* and connotes "family of, belonging to," as in Al Saud, Al Jabbar. Lowercase, represents definite article "the," as in al-Khalij, "the Gulf" (usually connected to the noun by a hyphen).

Alawi: a heterodox offshoot of Shii Islam, found primarily in Syria, with adherents who are mostly ethnic Arabs.

Alevi: a large somewhat secretive Shii sect found mostly in Turkey; adherents are of various ethnic backgrounds. Not to be confused with Alawi sect, with which they share some external resemblance.

Aliyah: literally, "ascent, going up," the immigration of Jews to Eretz Yisrael, the Land of Israel (*see also olim*).

Allah: Arabic for God; the word is used in the same way by Arabic speakers of non-Muslim religions as well.

Alluvial: pertaining to river-deposited materials, especially fine silt and silt-clay laid down on floodplains and deltas such as those of the Nile.

Amir (emir): commander, prince, ruler. May have, but need not have, territorial jurisdiction.

Amirate (emirate): realm of an amir. In lower Gulf, also called shaykhdom.

Aquaculture: also aquafarming; the farming of fish and other marine products under controlled conditions.

Arab League (League of Arab States): regional organization with membership open to all Arab countries; twenty-two members (including Palestine).

Arab Spring: sociopolitical movement perhaps more appropriately called the Arab Reawakening that swept the Middle East and North Africa from late 2010 onward.

Ashkenazim: Jews from central or eastern Europe, directly or by descent.

Assyrians: an ethnic and religious community following the Syriac branch of Christianity traditionally centered in eastern Turkey and northern Iraq; persecution and war have driven many into exile over the past century.

Axis of Evil: designation used first in 2002 by President George W. Bush in his State of the Union address to designate Iraq, Iran, and North Korea. Later, Syria seemed to be added as a junior member.

Ayatollah: "the sign of God." Title of respect for upper-ranking Shii clergyman. One title for the late Ruhollah Khomeini, former Iranian revolutionary leader, and for Ali Hosseini Khamenei, former president and current supreme leader of Iran.

Ayn: flowing spring, open-sinkhole water supply, or flowing artesian spring.

Baath (Ba'ath): Arab Renaissance (Revival) Party, separate branches of which controlled the governments of Iraq and Syria, until Baath in Iraq was ousted in April 2003.

Bahai (Baha'i): a relatively new universal religion with roots in nineteenth-century Iranian Shiism; adherents are found worldwide, but the largest community is still in Iran, where it has been subject to much persecution under the Islamic Republic.

Basalt: a common type of lava—dark, fine-grained, extrusive volcanic rock. In original molten state, flows readily from fissures; covers large areas of the Levant and western Arabia.

Basement (or basement complex): massive, very ancient igneous and metamorphic rocks, usually Precambrian, very complex and underlying sedimentary strata.

Bbl: barrel, barrels. Standard measure of oil, contains 42 US gallons (34.97 UK or imperial gallons).

Bedouin: pastoral Arab nomad of the desert; corruption of Arabic for "desert dweller."

Black September: open conflict in September 1970 between the Jordanian military and the PLO (q.v.) that resulted in the expulsion of the latter to Lebanon and the deaths of several thousand, mostly Palestinians.

Bpd: barrels per day (usually oil production).

Byzantine Empire: successor to the Eastern Roman Empire, centered in Byzantium (Constantinople); existing in slowly dwindling form for more than a thousand years, through 1453 CE.

C°: temperature in degrees Celsius or centigrade. Temperature in C° = Fahrenheit° minus 32 times 5/9. Temperature in F° = C° times 9/5 plus 32. Thus, 100°C = 212°F; 0°C = 32°F.

Caliph: from Arabic *khalifah,* "successor"—i.e., successor to Muhammad as head of the community of Islam, the *ummah* (q.v.).

Casus belli: Latin: "cause for war."

CE: Common Era (or, alternatively, Christian Era); also designated AD, *Anno Domini.* BCE = Before the Common Era.

Child mortality: *see* infant mortality.

Common Market: a group of countries with a common external tariff and no barriers to trade or to the movement of inputs to production—labor, capital, and resources—among them; for example, the European Union.

Copt: an adherent of Coptic (Egyptian) Christianity, the largest Christian community in the Middle East.

Cuesta: linear ridge with steep escarpment on foreslope and with gentle backslope. Asymmetry results from erosion of outcrop of gently dipping resistant stratum. Successive cuestas are prominent features of central Arabia.

Customs Union: two or more countries with a common external tariff and no tariff barriers to their own trade; for example, Turkey and the EU.

Dağ (dagh): Turkish for "mountain."

Desert: any area with scanty rainfall, little vegetation, and therefore limited agricultural use. May be plain, plateau, or mountains at any latitude. Area in Koeppen's BWh group (see Map 2.6).

DFLP: Democratic Front for the Liberation of Palestine, one of the earlier, more aggressive Palestinian guerrilla groups.

Dhow: general term for several types of traditional coastal sailing ships plying the waters around the Arabian Peninsula and parts of the Indian Ocean. The term is not widely used by Arabs, who employ specific names for different types of vessels: *boom, sambuq,* and others.

Diaspora: dispersion. Usually refers to the dispersion of Jews from Palestine after 70 CE. Also, Jews now outside Palestine constitute the diaspora. Palestinian refugees also apply the term to their dispersion and community outside Palestine. Used here for Lebanese, Cypriots, and Kurds as well.

Diastrophism: from Greek for "distortion, dislocation." Processes that have deformed the earth's crust, producing continents, ocean basins, mountains, folded strata, and other major features. Orogeny (q.v.) is one type of diastrophism.

Dirah: traditionally accepted tribal range of Bedouin tribe.

Diurnal: daily, occurring daily, or having a daily cycle; e.g., the range of high and low temperatures during a twenty-four-hour period.

Dolomite: light-colored stratified sedimentary rock similar to limestone but high in calcium magnesium carbonate rather than the calcium carbonate of limestone.

Druze: an eclectic faith and heterodox offshoot from Shii Islam; the endogamous community professing it is concentrated in Syria, Lebanon, and Israel.

Dunum: a unit of land-area measurement common in Palestine and Jordan. Equivalency varies between 900 m² and 1,000 m² but is most commonly 919 m² (0.23 acre, 0.0919 ha).

Economic Union: a common market that also has a common currency, central bank, and monetary policy; for example, the eurozone within the EU (q.v.). In 2013, seventeen members, including Cyprus.

EFTA: European Free Trade Area; in 2013, four members; has close trade and other economic ties to the EU.

Emir/Emirate: *see* amir/amirate.

Enosis: union of Cyprus with Greece.

Entrepôt: center—usually a city and often a port city—that receives goods in transit, warehouses them, and reships them.

Etatisme: economic system based on state capitalism; describes the system followed under the regime of Kemal Atatürk in Turkey.

Ethnolinguistic: pertaining to a distinct people (ethnic group) whose distinguishing characteristic is especially language, although other criteria may also make them distinctive (e.g., Armenians).

EU: European Union, successor to European Community; as of July 2013, twenty-eight members, including Cyprus. Turkey is an associate member and has been a candidate for full membership since 2005.

Expatriates: those who live (and may also work) in countries other than their own. Many Europeans, Americans, and South Asians work and live in several Middle East countries as expatriates (informally called "expats").

Extrusive: pertaining to pouring out of molten rock (lava) onto the earth's surface, where it solidifies; opposite is intrusive (e.g., granite). *See* basalt.

Falaj (**pl.** *aflaj*)**:** *see qanat.*

Faluqa (**felucca**)**:** traditional sailboat on the Nile and seas adjacent to Egypt; carries lateen sail.

Farsi: Persian, i.e., the language spoken by Persians; the official language of Iran.

al-Fatah (Fateh): reverse acronym for Harakat al-Tahrir al-Filastiniya (Palestinian Liberation Movement), a guerrilla group formed several years before the PLO. Power base for the late Yasser Arafat, one of Fatah's founders.

Fault: surface of fracture in rock involving vertical or horizontal (or both) displacement of rock on either side of the fault plane; result of tectonic strain in earth's crust. Faulting is a major cause of earthquakes (seismic crustal tremors). With horizontal shearing, a fault is left-lateral if displacement is to the left of an observer looking across the fault line. *See also* transform fault.

Fedayeen (*fidayyin*)**:** from Arabic for "sacrificers," usually applied to Palestinian guerrillas or to Shii fundamentalist fighters.

Feddan: a unit of land-area measurement used in Egypt, equal to 1.038 ac, 4,201 m², or 0.42 ha.

Feedstock: raw material for a processing plant, often applied to crude oil or natural gas for a refinery or petrochemical plant.

Fellah (**pl.** *fellahin*)**:** roughly equivalent to peasant, from Arabic for "tiller of the soil."

Fenêtre: French for "window." In geomorphology (q.v.), an opening or window caused by erosion in the upper limb of a nappe (q.v.) or overfolded strata. Comparable to a breach in an anticline (see Fig. 2.7), but a fenêtre floor has younger rocks than does the rim.

Fertile Crescent: modern term for arcuate area extending from Gaza northward and northeastward across northern Syria and then southeastward along Zagros piedmont (see Map 3.1), believed to be where Neolithic farming evolved.

Fertility rate: average number of children born to a woman over her lifetime.

Fourteen Points (for Peace): principles that constituted the World War I aims of the United States as enunciated by President Woodrow Wilson; prominent among them were self-determination of all people, no colonial acquisitions, and foundation of a League of Nations.

FTA: Free Trade Area (or Agreement); two or more countries retaining their own external tariffs but having no tariff barriers to their trade with each other; for example, Canada, the United States, and Mexico—NAFTA, and US separate FTAs with Bahrain, Israel, Jordan, and Oman.

GAFTA: Greater Arab Free Trade Area; open to all the members of the Arab League; in 2013, eighteen members.

GAP: Turkish, Güneydoğu Anadolu Projesi, Southeast Anatolia Project (see Chap. 20).

Garigue: stunted evergreen dry scrub vegetation on limestone in drier areas of Mediterranean climate in Asia Minor and the Levant (cf. maquis).

Gawr (gor, khawr, khor): river floodplain, narrow coastal indentation, or flat-bottomed valley.

GCC: Gulf Cooperation Council, short form of Cooperation Council for the Arab States of the Gulf, formed in 1981 and comprising Saudi Arabia, Kuwait, Bahrain, Qatar, the UAE, and Oman. Yemen is negotiating membership, and Jordan and Morocco have been invited to join.

GDP: gross domestic product, total value of goods and services produced by residents and nonresidents within a given country in a given year.

Gecekondu: Turkish for "built overnight," applied to spontaneous settlements built illegally on the peripheries of Turkish cities.

Geomorphology: "earth form," the earth science dealing with the origin and development of earth landforms; somewhat related to the older term "physiography."

Gneiss: coarse-grained crystalline rock usually with streaked or banded black-white-gray appearance. The product of dynamic metamorphism of granites and other igneous rocks. *See also* schist.

GNP: gross national product, total value of goods and services produced both from within a given country and from external (foreign) transactions in a given year.

Gondwana: a conjectured single landmass in Paleozoic times from which the southern continents are theorized to have been formed. *See* plate tectonics.

GOSP: gas-oil separator plant, an oil-field facility serving several producing wells to separate dissolved natural gas from the crude petroleum.

Graben: narrow, down-dropped block of the earth's surface bounded by parallel faults; related to rift valley. *See* rift.

Granite: intrusive igneous rock of various colors and grain size.

Hadith: a traditionally held statement or action of the Prophet Muhammad (or sometimes his companions); held by Muslims to be useful tools for understanding the Quran.

Hajj: the Muslim pilgrimage to Mecca, an obligation required in the Quran of those who can afford it and one of the five pillars of Islam.

Halakha: Jewish religious law.

Hamadah: a rock desert with barren, wind-scoured bedrock surface and little sand. There is an extensive *hamadah* where Arabia, Jordan, and Iraq meet.

Hamas: acronym for Harakat al-Muqawama al-Islamiyya (Islamic Resistance Movement), extremist group, one of several Palestinian resistance groups in West Bank and Gaza Strip. Active in both intifadahs; currently ruling the Gaza Strip.

Hammam: bath, bathing facilities, and/or toilet facilities.

Haredim: members of several distinct groups that adhere to the strictest form of Orthodox Judaism; outside of Israel, there are large communities in the United States.

Harem: quarters in a Muslim household set aside for women and children.

Hashimite (Hashemite): pertaining to descent from Hashim or the Hashimite clan, which included Muhammad's family and was part of the Quraysh tribe; commonly pertaining to dynasty in Jordan and, before 1958, in Iraq.

HDI: Human Development Index; measure of the quality of life allowing comparisons among countries, devised and calculated annually by the United Nations Development Programme.

Hectare: international unit of land-area measurement, 10,000 m^2 or 2.47 ac; 1 ac = 0.405 ha; abbr. = ha.

Hegira (hejira): from Arabic *hijrah,* "flight"; the flight of Muhammad and his followers from Mecca to Yathrib (renamed Medina) in 622 CE, which marked the beginning of the Islamic calendar (q.v.).

Hizb Allah **(Hizballah, from Arabic; Hezbollah, from Farsi):** Party of God, a group in Lebanon comprising Shii extremists who were involved in seizing hostages in the late 1980s and then conducted guerrilla warfare against Israelis and their proxy South Lebanon Army in the self-declared Israeli security zone, from which Israel withdrew in May 2000. Now an influential political party in Lebanon and recently involved in the Syrian civil war on the side of the Assad regime; listed as a terrorist organization by the US Department of State.

Horst: opposite of graben (q.v.); an uplifted block roughly paralleled by faults.

Horticulture: the cultivation of nonfield crops, such as fruits and vegetables.

Ibadhi: an Islamic sect distinct from both Sunni and Shii sects, dominant in Oman; descended from the Kharajites (q.v.).

IDB: Islamic Development Bank (see Chap. 6).

IDF: Israel Defense Forces.

IDP: internally displaced person; someone who, because of some disastrous situation, has had to leave home and seek refuge in some other part of his or her country. *See* refugee.

Igneous: pertaining to molten or formerly molten rock material, either extrusive (on the earth's surface) or intrusive (underground rock masses). Types include lava (extrusive) and granite (intrusive).

Ikhwan: Arabic for "brothers" or "brethren"; most common current use designates the Muslim Brotherhood of Egypt and its branches in other countries.

Imam: Shii religious or, sometimes, political leader; technically, one of the succession of Shii leaders who, beginning with Ali, are accepted by Shii sects as the legitimate successors of Muhammad; commonly, the leader of Muslim worship services.

IMF: International Monetary Fund.

Infant mortality: percentage of children who die in the first year after their birth; usually combined with child mortality to give the percentage of those who die before the age of five.

Infitah: Arabic for "opening," i.e., economic opening in post-Nasserist Egypt.

Interfluve: linear area lying between roughly parallel rivers, e.g., the location of Baghdad between the Tigris and Euphrates Rivers.

Intermontane: between mountains, usually a plateau between mountain ranges, e.g., the Anatolian and Iranian Plateaus.

Intifadah: Arabic for "shaking off" or "uprising"; the term applied to the two widespread Palestinian uprisings against Israeli occupation—1987 to 1993 and 2000 to 2005.

Iranian: pertaining to the country of Iran or to its citizens of whatever ethnic group (not equivalent to Persian).

Islam: "submission," the submission of the followers of Islam to the will of God (Allah).

Islamic calendar: the calendar used by Muslims mostly for religious purposes; it dates from 622 CE and is made up of 12 lunar months amounting to 354 or 355 days; 100 Common Era years is approximately 103 years according to the Islamic calendar.

Islamism: a complex ensemble of ideological extensions of Islam into political action, return to fundamentals ("Islamic fundamentalism"), resurgence or renaissance of Islamic ideals, revolutionary Islam, and others, sometimes through extremist and violent methods. A devotee is an Islamist.

Ismailis: the second-largest Shii sect, sometimes called the "Seveners"; ruled Fatimid Empire from Egypt, tenth to twelfth centuries.

Isobar: line on a map connecting points of equal barometric pressure.

Isohyet: line on a map connecting points of equal precipitation (see Map 2.5).

Isotherm: line on a map connecting points of equal temperature (see Map 2.4).

ITCZ: Intertropical Convergence Zone, the "monsoon trough."

Jabal (jebel): Arabic for "hill," "mountain."

Jamii (camii): Arabic for "mosque," often for the main or Friday mosque in a city. *See masjid.*

Jihad: Arabic for struggle on behalf of righteousness, especially within Islam; translation as "holy war" is rather ambiguous and focuses on only one aspect.

Jundullah: "Soldiers of God"; Baluch separatist/terrorist group operating in Iran and Pakistan.

Karaites: members of a Jewish sect that rejects the Orthodox Jewish position that Moses received oral law, as codified in the Talmud; most now live in Israel.

Karst: limestone or dolomite landscape subjected to carbonation solution and having underground drainage, caverns, sinkholes, and other typical surface features.

Kataib: Lebanese nationalistic political party associated with the Maronites; known better in English as the Phalange; its militia has been implicated in the massacres at the Sabra and Shatila Palestinian refugee camps in 1982.

Kavir: Persian for "salt flat," "salt waste," "playa." *Kavirs* are numerous and extensive in eastern interior Iran.

Khalifah: *see* caliph.

Kharajites: an Islamic group that originally supported Ali as caliph, like the Shia, but turned against him; the Ibadhis of Oman are the principal modern adherents of Kharajism.

Khawr (khor): *see gawr.*

Kibbutz: a Zionist collective and utopian community in Israel originally engaged in agriculture, now less collective, less utopian, and less agricultural.

Kilometer: international unit of distance measurement equaling 1,000 m, 0.6214 mi, 3,281 ft, 0.5399 nautical mi; 1 mi = 1.609 km; abbr. = km.

Knesset: Israeli parliament.

KRG: Kurdish Regional Government; officially comprises three northern provinces of Iraq that are a federal part of that country.

Kufiyah: common traditional male Arab headdress, a large square of cloth folded diagonally and worn with straight edge over the forehead. Usually white in Gulf area, red checkered or black and white in the Levant, but colors and patterns vary among localities. Called *ghutrah* in Saudi Arabia.

Lava: extrusive igneous rock that flows onto earth's surface while molten. *See* basalt.

League of Nations: intergovernmental organization founded in 1920 in consequence of the Paris Peace Conference; predecessor of the United Nations; at its peak had fifty-eight members; the United States never joined despite the fact that the league was a central feature of Woodrow Wilson's Fourteen Points (q.v.)

Levant: eastern Mediterranean coastal region, roughly the maximum area held by the Crusader states; comprises western Syria, Lebanon, Palestine, and western Jordan.

Lingua franca: a language or composite language spoken as a common tongue among several language groups in a given region.

Lithosphere: outermost shell of the earth's layers, 10–30 mi/16–48 km thick, comprising several rigid "plates" floating on the partly molten asthenosphere. *See* plate tectonics.

Littoral: of or pertaining to the shore (of seas or lakes), sometimes to banks of rivers.

LNG: liquefied natural gas—that is, natural gas cooled to approximately -260°F/-162°C, where it liquefies. It is then stored and shipped in special insulated containers. It is increasingly used in commercial transport. *See also* NGL.

Loess: fine, coherent, porous yellowish dust believed to have been picked up from barren areas by the wind and redeposited in amorphous layers nearby. Serves as parent material for fine-textured, deep, well-drained soils.

LPG: liquefied petroleum gas, primarily propane and butane, derived from NGL (q.v.).

Madan (Ma'dan): the Marsh Arabs; an ethnic group historically inhabiting the marsh country near the confluence of the Tigris and Euphrates Rivers; most were displaced when Saddam Husayn drained the marshes in the 1990s.

Madrasa (medrese): Muslim school, originally one attached to a mosque for religious training. Now used more generally.

Maghrib (Maghreb): Arabic for "west" and applied to the western Arab states in northwestern Africa: Morocco, Algeria, Tunisia, and sometimes Libya.

Majlis (mejlis): from general Arabic-Persian term for gathering, gathering place, reception; hence, an official reception room or audience of a ruler or tribal shaykh. In some countries, the consultative or legislative assembly, e.g., Iran, Kuwait.

Mamluk: literally "slave," but applied to Turkish and Circassian slave military oligarchy that ruled Egypt 1250–1517; also architecture and other aspects of the period.

Mandaeanism: an eclectic Gnostic and dualistic faith of ancient origin with a special reverence for John the Baptist; until recently the majority of its adherents lived in Iraq, but most have fled their traditional homes.

Mandate: in the Middle East, a commission awarded by the League of Nations to Britain or France to administer an assigned territory toward timely independence; also the polity so administered under this commission (Palestine, Transjordan, and Iraq by Britain; Syria and Lebanon by France).

Maquis: a low evergreen scrub vegetation typical of better Mediterranean climate areas of western and southern Asia Minor and the Levant; includes oleander, rosemary, myrtle, and similar plants and is a higher-order plant association than garigue (q.v.).

Maronite: autonomous Roman Catholic community based in Lebanon; its members constitute one of the three dominant groups in that country. Smaller groups in Israel, Syria, and Cyprus; large diaspora outside the Middle East.

Mashriq: Arabic for "east" and sometimes applied to the eastern Arab states in the Middle East as defined in this book. Less common term than Maghrib (q.v.).

Masjid: Arabic-Persian for "mosque." *See jamii.*

Massif: general term applied to a compact upland mass of complex rocks.

Maternal mortality ratio: the number of women who die during pregnancy, childbirth, or within six weeks of the end of pregnancy per 100,000 live births.

Mawali: "clients"; non-Arab converts to Islam during early period of the Muslim conquests; soon outnumbered Arab Muslims (*ummah,* q.v.).

Maydan: Arabic-Persian for an urban open area or city square, typical of the traditional Islamic city.

Median: a statistical measure of central tendency; it is the numeric value separating the upper and lower halves of a sample or population.

Mesolithic: Middle Stone Age, sometimes called Epipaleolithic; transitional between Paleolithic and Neolithic periods and dated roughly 12,000–8000 BCE.

Metamorphic: pertaining to rocks whose original structure has been altered by great earth pressures (dynamic metamorphism), heat (thermal metamorphism), or both, producing compact and resistant rock types (e.g., gneiss, schist, quartzite, marble).

Meter (metre): the basic international unit of measurement equaling 1,000 mm, 100 cm, or 3.28 ft.; 1 ft = 0.305 m; abbr. = m.

Metric ton (also tonne): 1,000 kg, or 2,204.6 lbs; abbr. = mt.

Millet: under the Ottomans, self-administered non-Muslim religious community (e.g., Armenians, Jews, Greek Orthodox), a logical extension of the early Muslim concept of "people of the book."

Mina: coastal inlet and, by derivation, port.

Minaret: tower associated with a mosque from which the call to prayer for the Muslim faithful is intoned at least five times daily by a *muazzin* (q.v.).

Mizrahim: Eastern or Oriental Jew, recently adopted term to distinguish Middle East and North African Jews in Israel from Ashkenazim (q.v.) and Sephardim (q.v.). Formerly grouped with Sephardim.

Monsoon: from Arabic word for "season"; the seasonal reversal of pressure and winds, especially across southern and eastern Asia; generally applied to rains typical of summer season in Asia and to winds in both summer and winter.

Muazzin (muadhdhin, muezzin): specially trained man who intones calls to prayer for the Muslim faithful from a minaret (q.v.) five times daily.

Muhammadan: loosely applied to follower of Muhammad, but correct term is Muslim (q.v.).

Mujahideen-e Khalq (MEK): Iranian militant group opposed to the Islamic government; listed as a terrorist organization by the United States until 2012.

Muslim: an adherent of Islam (q.v.), "one who submits" to the will of God.

Muslim Brotherhood: the largest Islamist movement in the Arab world; originating in Egypt, it has branches in several other countries: its candidate was elected president of Egypt in 2012.

Nakbah: Arabic for "catastrophe," the establishment in 1948 of the state of Israel in Palestinian areas and the displacement of Palestinian Arabs from their lands and homes.

Nappe: in geomorphology (q.v.), a tightly folded recumbent anticline thrust over other rock strata. Sometimes nappe over nappe (fold upon fold) structures occur. Nappes usually extend over many square miles.

Neocon: shortened form for neoconservative; most recently, political activists close to and/or holding high positions in the Bush-Cheney administration and responsible for formulating policies that led to the invasion of Iraq.

Neolithic: New Stone Age, beginning roughly 8000 BCE and ending 4,000–5,000 years later as copper and bronze came into use for implements.

NGL: natural gas liquids, derived from natural gas and yielding ethane, propane, butane, natural gasoline, and related substances. *See also* LNG and LPG.

Nomad: member of a social group that regularly migrates over a traditional realm in search of pasture for their flocks. Bedouin (q.v.) are the best-known true nomads of the Middle East.

OAPEC: Organization of Arab Petroleum Exporting Countries (see Chap. 6).

OIC: Organization of Islamic Cooperation—formerly the Organization of the Islamic Conference (see Chap. 6).

Olim (**sing.** *olah*): "ascenders," Jewish immigrants to the Land of Israel (*see aliyah*).

OPEC: Organization of Petroleum Exporting Countries (see Chap. 6).

Orogeny: a major tectonic process of fold-mountain building.

Orographic: pertaining to mountains; e.g., orographic rainfall is caused by the uplift, hence cooling, of humid wind blowing up a mountain slope—the process producing virtually all heavier rains in the Middle East.

Orthodox: from Greek "right belief"; in religion, applied to one of the main sects of Judaism—the most conservative—and to non-Protestant eastern Christian sects not in communion with the Church of Rome.

Ottoman: Turkish ruling dynasty founded by Osman around 1300 CE and lasting in power for more than 620 years; ruling from Constantinople, at its peak in the late sixteenth century, its realm extended from Hungary to Yemen and from Algeria to the Caspian.

PA: Palestinian Authority; title of the quasi-state apparatus headquartered in Ramallah.

Peshmerga: guerrilla fighters in the Kurdish quest for independence; currently the official military arm of the KRG (q.v.).

PFLP: Popular Front for the Liberation of Palestine, extremist Marxist Palestinian group known for earlier aircraft hijackings.

PKK: Kurdish Partiya Karkerên Kurdistan, Kurdistan Workers Party; Kurdish group leading struggle against Turkey; listed as a terrorist organization by the United States and the EU; now known as Kongra-Gel (Kurdistan People's Congress).

Plate tectonics: theory that the earth's crust (lithosphere) comprises about six main and several other minor rigid "plates" that broke away from one main mass and are now "drifting" slowly in respective directions (see Chap. 2).

PLO: Palestine Liberation Organization, formed in 1964, which became the umbrella organization for Palestinian aspirations; the late Yasser Arafat was replaced as chairman by Mahmoud Abbas upon Arafat's death in November 2004. Finally accepted by Israel as legitimate representatives of Palestinians for negotiations over the future of remaining Palestinian lands, first in Oslo and then for continuing peace process and for administration of Palestinian Authority.

Pluvial: rainy—pertaining to moister periods during the recent geological past, with such periods in the Middle East usually correlating with glacial advances and related climatic changes; opposed to alternating dry periods.

PNC: Palestine National Council, the Palestinian parliament.

Preferential Trade Agreement (PTA): agreement under which two or more countries abolish tariff barriers to mutual trade on a specified group of commodities; for example, separate PTAs between the EU and Egypt, Israel, Jordan, Lebanon, and the Palestinian Authority.

"Price tag": terrorist activities of Jewish militant settlers on the West Bank against IDF (q.v.) bases, Israeli peace proponents, Palestinian persons and property, and Muslim and Christian religious sites.

Primate city: a city much larger—even many times larger—than any other city in the country and with a much greater range of economic and social activities. Term suggested by Mark Jefferson, 1939. Cairo, Baghdad, and Tehran are examples.

Ptolemaic: Egyptian kingdom, successor to the realm of Alexander the Great under the Hellenized dynasty of the Ptolemies, 323–30 BCE.

Purchasing Power Parity (PPP): a method used by international institutions like the World Bank to allow more realistic comparisons of the cost of living in countries with different currencies. It equalizes the purchasing power of these currencies in their home countries for a given basket of goods and services; cross-national comparisons are then made using the United States and the dollar as the base.

al-Qaida (al-Qaeda): extremist Sunni group known for terrorist activities founded by Osama bin Laden; autonomous offshoots now exist in several countries, especially Iraq, Yemen, and Syria.

Qanat: an underground gallery water channel marked by a surface chain of wells; thousands of *qanats* are found on alluvial fans in Iran (see Fig. 21.3).

Qat: Catha edulis, a leafy shrub grown on terraced hillsides in northern Yemen. *Qat* leaves contain cathinone, an amphetamine-related chemical, and are chewed by Highland Yemeni men during afternoon hours for a mild euphoric effect.

QIZ: Qualifying Industrial Zone; industrial area from which goods produced there can enter the United States duty-free, if they have a certain percentage of Israeli inputs; these exist in Egypt and Jordan.

al-Quran (Koran): Arabic for "recitation"; Muslim holy scriptures, believed by Muslims to be the exact words of God revealed (or "recited") to the Prophet Muhammad through the angel Gabriel.

Ramadan: ninth month of the Islamic calendar, considered a holy month because Muhammad received the first revelations from Gabriel in Ramadan. During the entire month, Muslims are obligated to observe absolute fasting (*sawm*) between dawn and dusk. Such fasting is one of the five pillars of Islam.

Refugee: a person who, because of some disastrous situation, has had to leave home and seek refuge in a country other than his or her own; *see* IDP.

Remittances: economic term for a transfer of money by a foreign worker to his or her home country.

Rift: a narrow linear trough between parallel faults or along linear fissuring, e.g., the Levant Rift, a segment of the great rift from northern Syria to southern Africa.

Riparian: pertaining to riverbanks, especially rights of access to the river ("riparian rights") or occurring along rivers ("riparian powers"). As a noun, persons or polity along a river.

Sabkhah (subkha): a flat area of salty silt, whether a tidal flat, salt flat between dunes, or former tidal flat now cut off from the sea (see Fig. 2.12).

Sabra: from Hebrew for "prickly pear," term for a native-born Israeli Jew.

Salafis: Sunni Muslims who emphasize as their religious models the *salaf,* the earliest Muslims: some are violent and/or political, while others are nonviolent and/or apolitical.

Samaritans: ancient Jewish sect that traces its origins to those who refused to abandon their temple on Mount Gerizim for the Jerusalem temple decreed by King David and to the Israelites that remained in Palestine at the time of the Babylonian exile; they now compose a tiny remnant residing near Nablus and Tel Aviv.

Sanjak: provincial administrative district of the Ottoman Empire, administered by a sanjak bey, later by a mutassarif (e.g., Sanjak of Alexandretta).

Sassanian (Sassanid): pertaining to the Persian Empire or its ruling dynasty named after its founder, Sassan; 227–651 CE (see Map 3.4).

Saudi: concerning the central Arabian Peninsula dynastic family of Al Saud, the policies of that dynasty, or the country it rules—Saudi Arabia, Arabia of the Sauds—the kingdom founded and ruled by the Al Saud; its name and present extent date to 1932.

Schist: fine-grained, foliated crystalline metamorphic rock of varying color. *See also* gneiss.

Sedimentary: formed of sediments—materials laid down usually in seawater but also in lakes and rivers or by wind—and usually stratified (e.g., limestone, shale, sandstone).

Seismic: pertaining to earth tremors or earthquakes.

Seleucid Empire: successor to the realm of Alexander the Great under a Hellenized dynasty founded by Seleucus Nicator, centered in modern Iraq at Seleucia-Ctesiphon; at its peak (late third century BCE) stretched from the Mediterranean to the Indus Valley: last remnant (in Syria) fell to Roman forces in 63 BCE.

Semitic: of or pertaining to the subfamily of the Afro-Asiatic language family that includes Arabic, Hebrew, Aramaic, and several Ethiopian languages; also pertaining to certain aspects of speakers of these languages, excluding racial characteristics.

Sephardim: technically, Jews from Spain or descended from Spanish Jews; by extension, it formerly included "Oriental" Jews (from North Africa, Middle East, and southern and central Asia). However, this extended use is no longer favored; *see Mizrahim.*

Shah: Persian for "king"; title of royal rulers of Iran until 1979; Shahanshah—"king of kings" or "emperor."

Sharia: the right path; complex Muslim religious law and code of sociopolitical conduct and relations, derived primarily from the Quran and Sunna and secondarily from other traditions and opinions; four principal Sunni schools of law, one major Shii school.

Shaykh (sheikh): literally "elder," but specifically a term of respect and rank given to an Arab tribal leader; extended to the ruler of smaller states, which are then referred to as shaykhdoms (e.g., Qatar, also sometimes called amirates [q.v.]); further, by extension, a learned Muslim.

Shia: collective noun, Shii singular noun and adjective, from Arabic for "partisan," i.e., partisan of Ali, Muhammad's kinsman and son-in-law. The Shia believe Ali should have succeeded to leadership of the *ummah* (q.v.) upon Muhammad's death and that Ali and his several successors in his direct line (Shii imams) are the only true heads of the *ummah. See also* Sunni.

Shield: rigid mass of stable, ancient (Precambrian) rocks, usually greatly metamorphosed, forming the nucleus of a continent or subcontinent—e.g., the Nubian-Arabian Shield of the southwestern Middle East (see Chap. 2).

Shii Crescent: term frequently heard recently from Sunni sources as an expression of alarm regarding a potential alliance consisting of Shii or Shii-friendly governments in Iran, Iraq, Syria, and Lebanon.

Steppe: grassland, especially land of short grasses, thus indicating subhumid or semiarid climate (Koeppen BS); in the Middle East, transitional between desert and Mediterranean climate areas or other more humid areas.

Strait: a narrow, usually navigable channel of water connecting two larger bodies of water; for example, the Turkish Straits between the Black and Aegean Seas.

Sufism: mystical movement in both Sunni and Shii Islam, dating to tenth century CE; historically subjected to persecution by rulers professing each branch of Islam; in recent times, often targeted by Sunni Islamists.

Sultanate: realm of a sultan (e.g., Oman), a secular ruler equivalent to a king or other dynastic ruler.

Sunna: Arabic for "habitual practice"; sometimes used in place of Sunni (q.v.)

Sunni: Muslim who accepts the legitimacy of Muhammad's successors. So-called after *Sunna,* the admonitions and examples of Muhammad regarding proper Muslim belief and conduct. *See also* Shia.

Suq: Arabic for "marketplace," comparable to Persian *bazaar* and Turkish *çarşı.*

Taliban: Dari for "students," from Arabic *talab,* "student"; used first for the ultraorthodox government in Afghanistan through 2001 and now occasionally used to describe extreme Islamists in other countries.

Tectonism (tectonic, tectonics): internal earth forces that build up, form, or deform the earth's surface or subsurface. *See* plate tectonics.

Tell: Arabic for "hill" or "mound" (Turkish: *hüyük;* Persian: *tepe;* Egyptian *kom*), specifically a characteristic surface mound made up of accumulated layers of debris from successive human occupations of a settlement site over many centuries (see Chap. 3).

Transform fault: a fault zone involving mostly horizontal displacement along an edge of a tectonic plate, e.g., the San Andreas fault in California and the North Anatolian and East Anatolian transform faults; displacement along such faults periodically involves disastrous earthquakes.

Ulama **(*ulema*):** Arabic collective term for learned Muslim religious and legal scholars; theoretically, the ultimate repository of power in Saudi Arabia.

Umayyad (Omayyed): Arab Muslim dynasty of the Quraysh tribe and the empire it ruled from Damascus 661–750 CE; also the dynasties that continued to rule in Spain until 1030.

Ummah: Arabic for the community of Muslims, an especially important concept pertaining to Arab Muslims in the early decades of the Muslim conquests.

UNDP: United Nations Development Programme, compiler of the annual Human Development Index (HDI, q.v.).

Uniate church: autonomous Eastern Christian community in full communion with the Church of Rome.

UNRWA: United Nations Relief and Works Agency, which since 1949 has operated emergency housing and food distribution for hundreds of thousands of registered Palestinian Arab refugees, usually in UNRWA-operated camps (see Map 9.3).

USAID: United States Agency for International Development.

Vilayet: a province under the administrative pattern of the Ottoman Empire; term became crucial in post–World War I territorial settlements in the Levant.

Viticulture: cultivation of grapevines, almost a way of life in some specialized agricultural areas.

Volcanism (vulcanism): igneous activity processes in general, not just those associated with volcanoes; especially the processes by which molten materials and associated solids and gases are forced into the lithosphere or onto the earth's surface through craters or fissures. *See* basalt.

Wadi: widely used Arabic term for arid-area stream basin (and, by extension, the stream), including major valleys and broad, hardly perceptible linear depressions, whether stream flow is perennial or periodic. Arabic for a major river (Nile, Tigris) is *nahr.*

Wahhabi: often misused term pertaining to a reformist puritanical Muslim movement and group that evolved from the preachings of Muhammad ibn Abd al-Wahhab in the mid-1700s in central Arabia. Wahhabi puritanism is still strong in much of Arabia; teachings and practices associated with Wahhabism have recently been promoted throughout the Muslim world by Saudi funding.

Waqf (wakf): Arabic for Muslim religious endowment or trust involving land or other property (Turkish *vakf*); historically widespread in Islamic world but decreasing in more secular states such as Syria.

WMDs: weapons of mass destruction; their alleged presence in Iraq was cited by the Bush-Cheney administration as a *casus belli* (q.v.) in 2003.

Xerophytic: pertaining to specialized vegetation of arid lands. Special adaptations include deep or long roots, waxy leaves, and tough bark (see Chap. 2).

Yazidi (Yezidi): religious community of mostly Kurdish ethnicity; their faith is dualistic and syncretic, combining Kurdish, Zoroastrian, and Islamic strands; historically found in Turkey, Iraq, and Syria, many have fled their homeland for refuge in Europe. Sometimes inaccurately called "devil worshipers."

Zakat: obligatory annual almsgiving, one of the five pillars of Islam, based on a percentage of wealth.

Zaydis: Shii sect, sometimes called the "Fivers"; longtime rulers of Yemen.

Zionism: Jewish nationalism stressing unity of Jews and creation and maintenance of a Jewish state in Eretz Yisrael (Land of Israel) in greater Palestine as a territorial base for Jewry.

Zoroastrianism: ancient dualistic faith of Iran based on the teachings of its prophet Zoroaster (Zarathustra) and dating to about the sixth century BCE; contemporary adherents are concentrated in Iran and India.

Geological Time Chart

EON	PERIOD		EPOCH	AGE	MILLIONS OF YRS AGO
CENOZOIC	QUATERNARY		Holocene (Recent)		0.01
			Pleistocene		1.6
	TERTIARY	Neogene	Pliocene		11.2
			Miocene		23.7
		Paleogene	Oligocene		36.6
			Eocene		57.8
			Paleocene		66.4
MESOZOIC	CRETACEOUS		Late	Maastrichtian	74.5
				Campanian	84.0
				Santonian	87.5
				Coniacian	88.5
				Turonian	91.0
				Cenomanian	97.5
			Early		144
	JURASSIC		Late		163
			Middle		187
			Early		208
	TRIASSIC		Late		230
			Middle		240
			Early		245
PALEOZOIC	PERMIAN				286
	CARBONIFEROUS				360
	DEVONIAN				408
	SILURIAN				438
	ORDOVICIAN				505
	CAMBRIAN				570

PRECAMBRIAN

	ERA				
PROTEROZOIC	Late				900
	Middle				1600
	Early				2500
ARCHEOZOIC	Late				3000
	Middle				3400
	Early				3800

In this simplified geological time chart, *Ages* are shown only for the late Cretaceous, although *Age* subdivisions exist for all *Epochs* after the Middle Cambrian. The Middle East surface geology is dominantly Mesozoic and Cenozoic, although the Nubian-Arabian Shield is Precambrian. Western Gulf oil fields are mainly Jurassic and Cretaceous, whereas Iranian and Kirkuk fields are Paleogene.

Partial Bibliography

The following list of references includes only those sources that are available online and are of a general nature. The authors recommend that the reader consult those sources as may be appropriate for further information and for staying current with developments in this always volatile region.

The more extensive bibliography of published sources, including virtually all the works cited in the notes of the text that in previous editions was included with the text, may now be found in its entirety on the website associated with this book (**www.middleeastpatterns.com**). Also to be found there are numerous additional works in English that may be especially useful to a midlevel student or general reader. Most listings are reasonably available. More advanced sources and materials in languages other than English may be found in the bibliographies mentioned at the end of this section.

The simplest way to stay abreast of the explosion of new literature on the Middle East is to refer to the listings in the quarterly *Middle East Journal,* which includes reviews, short notices, listings of literature received, and a bibliography of periodical materials. The autumn issue has an annual index and lists the periodicals regularly surveyed for the bibliography. Besides *Middle East Journal,* useful and commonly available periodicals include *Middle East Policy* and *Journal of Palestine Studies.* These journal references may omit specialized geographical materials, most of which can be noted in one or another of the standard academic geographical journals (*Annals of the Association of American Geographers, Geographical Review, Professional Geographer, Geographical Journal, Arab World Geographer,* and others). References and articles in both the *International Journal of Middle East Studies* and the *Middle East Studies Association Bulletin* are also useful.

Reflecting the importance the Middle East has taken in global affairs, the journals *Foreign Affairs* and *Foreign Policy* rarely publish an issue without one or more articles concerned with our region of interest. Regarding the daily press, in the United States, the *New York Times* and the now weekly *Christian Science Monitor* report regularly on Middle East developments. Overseas, the Beirut *Daily Star* (URL below) is very useful, as are the Israeli *Ha'aretz, Jerusalem Post,* and the *Times of Israel.* Every issue of *Saudi Aramco World* magazine covers some aspect of the Middle East. Statistics may most easily be found in the CIA *World Factbook,* in the standard UN yearbooks, and the statistical volumes of UN specialized agencies (most are now available online).

Two US government data sources that are particularly invaluable are: Central Intelligence Agency, *World Factbook,* www.cia.gov/library/publications/the-world-factbook/index.html; and Department of Energy, Energy Information Agency (especially *Country Analysis Briefs*), www.eia.doe.gov/emeu/international /contents.html.

COUNTRY URLS

Bahrain: www.bahraingovernment.com
Cyprus: www.cyprus.gov.cy
Egypt: www.sis.gov.eg
Iran: www.mfa.gov.ir
Iraq: www.en.goi-s.com
Israel: www.mfa.gov.il/MFA
Jordan: www.jordanembassyus.org/new/index.shtml

Kuwait: www.e.gov.kw/sites/KGOEnglish/Portal/Pages/KGO.aspx
Lebanon: www.lebweb.com/dir/lebanese-government
Oman: www.omansultanate.com
Palestine: www.minfo.ps/English
Qatar Central Bank: http://english.mofa.gov.qa
Saudi Arabia: www.mofa.gov.sa/sites/mofaen/Pages.Default.aspx
Syria: www.moi-syriaonline.com/Categories/goverh.htm
Turkey: www.mfa.gov.tr/default.en.mfa
UAE: www.government.ae/gov/en/index.jsp
Yemen Central Bank: www.centralbank.gov.ye

DATA AND MAPS (SEE ALSO "UNITED STATES GOVERNMENT" BELOW)

British Petroleum: www.bp.com/home.do
Ethnologue, Languages of the World: www.ethnologue.com
National Geographic: www.nationalgeographic.com
Nation Stats: www.NationMaster.com
Perry-Castaneda Library Map Collection (University of Texas, Austin):
    www.lib.utexas.edu/maps/index.html
World Climate: www.worldclimate.com

JOURNALS AND OTHER PUBLICATIONS

Al-Ahram (Cairo): http://english.ahram.org.eg
Al-Monitor: www.al-monitor.com/pulse/home.html
Arab News (Jiddah): www.arabnews.com
Christian Science Monitor: www.csmonitor.com
Cyprus Mail (Nicosia): www.cyprus-mail.com
Daily Star (Beirut): www.dailystar.com.lb
Economist: www.economist.com
Foreign Affairs: www.foreignaffairs.org
Foreign Policy: www.foreignpolicy.com
Guardian (UK): www.guardiannews.com
Gulf News (Dubai): http://gulfnews.com
Ha'aretz (Tel Aviv): www.haaretz.com
Jerusalem Post: www.jpost.com
Jordan Times (Amman): www.jordantimes.com
Le Monde Diplomatique: http://mondediplo.com
Media Line: www.themedialine.org
National (Abu Dhabi): www.thenational.ae
New York Review of Books: www.nybooks.com
New York Times: http://global.nytimes.com
Oil and Gas Journal: www.ogj.com/index.htm
Times of Israel: www.timesofisrael.com
Washington Post: www.washingtonpost.com
Washington Report on Middle East Affairs: www.wrmea.com
Yemen Post: www.yemenpost.net
Zaman (Turkey): www.todayszaman.com
Zawya (Lebanon): www.zawya.com

INSTITUTES, THINK TANKS, AND OTHER DATA SOURCES

American Israel Public Affairs Committee: www.aipac.org
Americans for Middle East Understanding: www.ameu.org

The Brookings Institution: www.brookings.edu
B'tsalem: www.btselem.org/English/index.asp
Council on Foreign Relations: www.cfr.org
Encyclopedia of the Orient (Looklex Encyclopaedia): http://i-cias.com/e.o/index.htm
Foundation for Middle East Peace: www.fmep.org
Fraser Institute: www.fraserinstitute.org
Freedom House: www..freedomhouse.org/
Heritage Foundation: www..heritage.org
Human Rights Watch: www..hrw.org/
Institute for Research Middle Eastern Policy: www.irmep.org
Israeli Democracy Institute: http://en.idi.org.il
Jamestown Foundation: www.jamestown.org
Jewish Virtual Library: www.jewishvirtuallibrary.org/index.html
Legatum Institute: www..li.com/
Middle East Institute: www.mideasti.org
Palestine Center (The Jerusalem Fund): www.palestinecenter.org
Palestine Facts: www.palestinefacts.org
Pew Forum on Religion and Politics: http://pewforum.org/religion-politics
Political Islam Online: www.politicalislam.org
Reporters without Borders: http://en.rsf.org/
Transparency International: www.transparency.org
Washington Institute for Near East Policy: www.washingtoninstitute.org
World Economic Forum: www.weforum.org

SPACE PHOTOS

Digital Globe: www.digitalglobe.com
Earth from Space: http://earth.jsc.nasa.gov/sseop/efs
Earth Resources Observation System: http://eros.usgs.gov
Gateway to Astronaut Photography of Earth: http://eol.jsc.nasa.gov/sseop/clickmap

UNITED STATES GOVERNMENT

Central Intelligence Agency: www.cia.gov
Department of Energy, Energy Information Administration (EIA), *Country Analysis Briefs*:
    www.eia.gov/countries
Department of State: www.state.gov
Federal Research Division, Country Studies: http://lcweb2.loc.gov/frd/cs/cshome.html
Geographic Names: http://geonames.usgs
National Climatic Data Center Resources: www.ncdc.noaa.gov/oa/climate/ climateresourcesother.html
National Geospatial Intelligence Agency: www1.nga.mil/Pages/default.aspx
NSGS Earthquakes: http://eartquake.usgs.gov
US Agency for International Development: www.usaid.gov
US Energy Information Administration: www.eia.doe.gov/countries
US Geological Survey (USGS): www.usgs.gov
USGS Africa and the Middle East Mineral Information: http://minerals.usgs.gov/minerals/pubs
    /country/africa.html

UNITED NATIONS

International Atomic Energy Agency: www.iaea.org
International Fund for Agricultural Development: www.ifad.org
International Monetary Fund: www.imf.org/external/index.htm
UN Development Programme: www.undp.org/content/undp/en/home.html

UN Economic and Social Commission for Western Asia: www.escwa.un.org
UN Food and Agriculture Organization: www.fao.org/index_en.htm
UN High Commission for Refugees: www.unhcr.org/cgi-bin/texis/vtx/home
United Nations Homepage: www.un.org
UN Office for the Coordination of Humanitarian Affairs—Occupied Palestinian Territory:
    www..ochaopt.org/
UN Refugee and Works Agency: www.unrwa.org/
World Bank Group: www.worldbank.org
World Health Organization: www.who.int/en
World Trade Organization: www.wto.org

OTHER INTERNATIONAL ORGANIZATIONS

Abu Dhabi Fund for Development: www.adfd.ae
Arab Fund for Economic and Social Development: www.arabfund.org
Arab League: www.arableagueonline.org
European Union: http://europa.eu/
Gulf Cooperation Council: www..gcc-sg.org/eng/
International Energy Agency: www.iea.org
Islamic Development Bank: www.isdb.org
Kuwait Fund for Arab Economic Development: www.kuwait-fund.org
Nile Basin Initiative: www.nilebasin.org
Organization for Economic Cooperation and Development: www..oecd.org/
Organization of Petroleum Exporting Countries: www.opec.org/home
Organization of the Islamic Conference: www.oic-oci.org
Saudi Fund for Development: www.sfd.gov.sa
UK Foreign and Commonwealth Office: www.fco.gov.uk/en

Index